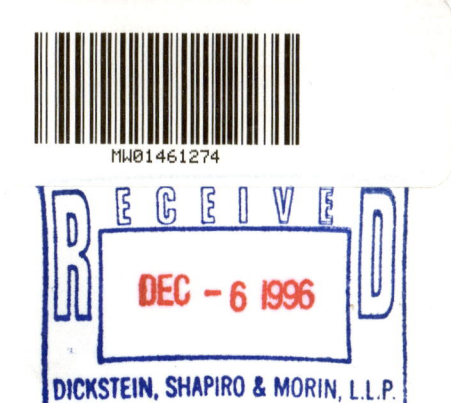

RECEIVED DEC - 6 1996
DICKSTEIN, SHAPIRO & MORIN, L.L.P.

ANALYTICAL INDEX

GUIDE TO GATT LAW AND PRACTICE

VOLUME 1
Articles I - XXI

Geneva, 1995

WTO
WORLD TRADE
ORGANIZATION

Copyright © World Trade Organization, 1995
All rights reserved

Applications for the right to reproduce this work or parts thereof in any form should be sent to the Director of the Information and Media Relations Division at the WTO Secretariat, 154 Rue de Lausanne, 1211 Geneva 21, Switzerland. Contracting parties to the GATT 1947, Members of the WTO and their governmental institutions may reproduce this work without application, but are requested to inform the WTO Secretariat of such reproduction.

Co-published by the World Trade Organization and Bernan Press 1995. Sixth Edition.
Printed in the United States of America on acid-free paper.

∞

96 95   4 3 2 1
Bernan Press
4611-F Assembly Drive
Lanham, MD 20706-4391
(800) 274-4447
Internet: query@kraus.com
ISBN 0-89059-054-0

PREFACE

This volume presents a guide to the legal interpretation and application of the General Agreement, and a repertoire of GATT practice and drafting history, including decisions, panel reports and discussions between contracting parties. It is updated to 1 January 1995, the date of entry into force of the Marrakesh Agreement Establishing the World Trade Organization.

This updated sixth edition of the Analytical Index was prepared and updated by Amelia Porges with contributions by Friedl Weiss and Petros C. Mavroidis. It is a redrafted, reorganized and updated version of the fifth edition of 1989 which was prepared by Ernst-Ulrich Petersmann. The size of the Index has tripled from the fifth to the present edition mainly due to the addition of further material from the drafting history and the years 1948-1989, excerpts from the large number of recent panel reports, a chapter on the institutional aspects of the GATT, material on the transition from the GATT to the WTO, additional tables, and a subject index.

Suggestions for improvements are welcome and should be addressed to the Legal Affairs Division of the Secretariat.

Frieder Roessler
Director, Legal Affairs Division
World Trade Organization

This volume may be cited as
GATT, Analytical Index: Guide to GATT Law and Practice, Updated 6th Edition (1995).

TABLE OF CONTENTS

VOLUME 1

Introduction 1

Preamble 21

PART I

Article I	General Most-Favoured-Nation Treatment	23
Article II	Schedules of Concessions	63

PART II

Article III	National Treatment on Internal Taxation and Regulation	121
Article IV	Special Provisions relating to Cinematograph Films	209
Article V	Freedom of Transit	213
Article VI	Anti-dumping and Countervailing Duties	219
Article VII	Valuation for Customs Purposes	257
Article VIII	Fees and Formalities connected with Importation and Exportation	267
Article IX	Marks of Origin	287
Article X	Publication and Administration of Trade Regulations	293
Article XI	General Elimination of Quantitative Restrictions	313
Article XII	Restrictions to Safeguard the Balance of Payments	355
Article XIII	Non-discriminatory Administration of Quantitative Restrictions	397
Article XIV	Exceptions to the Rule of Non-discrimination	417
Article XV	Exchange Arrangements	427
Article XVI	Subsidies	443
Article XVII	State Trading Enterprises	469
Article XVIII	Governmental Assistance to Economic Development	487
Article XIX	Emergency Action on Imports of Particular Products	515
Article XX	General Exceptions	561
Article XXI	Security Exceptions	599

Index i

VOLUME 2

PART II (Cont'd)

Article XXII	Consultation	611
Article XXIII	Nullification or Impairment	629

PART III

Article XXIV	Territorial Application – Frontier Traffic – Customs Unions and Free-trade Areas	789
Article XXV	Joint Action by the Contracting Parties	873
Article XXVI	Acceptance, Entry into Force and Registration	907
Article XXVII	Withholding or Withdrawal of Concessions	927
Article XXVIII	Modification of Schedules	933
Article XXVIII bis	Tariff Negotiations	985
Article XXIX	The Relation of this Agreement to the Havana Charter	995

Article XXX	Amendments	1001
Article XXXI	Withdrawal	1011
Article XXXII	Contracting Parties	1013
Article XXXIII	Accession	1017
Article XXXIV	Annexes	1029
Article XXXV	Non-application of the Agreement between Particular Contracting Parties	1031
PART IV	TRADE AND DEVELOPMENT	1039
Article XXXVI	Principles and Objectives	1053
Article XXXVII	Commitments	1059
Article XXXVIII	Joint Action	1069

PROVISIONAL APPLICATION OF THE GENERAL AGREEMENT ... 1071

INSTITUTIONS AND PROCEDURE ... 1085

APPENDIX ... 1135

INDEX ... i

Detailed tables of contents appear at the head of each chapter.

INTRODUCTION

I.	**INTRODUCTORY**	1
	A. SCOPE	1
	B. STRUCTURE	1
II.	**EDITORIAL CONVENTIONS AND GUIDE TO REFERENCES**	2
III.	**DRAFTING OF THE HAVANA CHARTER AND THE GENERAL AGREEMENT ON TARIFFS AND TRADE**	3
	A. APPLICATION AND AMENDMENT OF THE GENERAL AGREEMENT	6
	B. PUBLICATIONS COLLECTING THE PRACTICE OF THE CONTRACTING PARTIES	8
IV.	**DOCUMENT REFERENCES**	9
	A. DRAFTING OF THE GENERAL AGREEMENT AND THE HAVANA CHARTER	9
	B. INTERIM COMMISSION FOR THE ITO	11
	C. GATT DOCUMENTS	11
	1. CONTRACTING PARTIES	11
	2. GATT documents: active series	14
	3. Document series of the Preparatory Committee for the WTO	16
	4. Uruguay Round document series	17
	5. Documents of past negotiating rounds	18
	6. Lists and indexes of GATT documents	18
	7. Lists and indexes of documents of negotiating rounds	19
V.	**SOURCES FOR OBTAINING COPIES OF DOCUMENTS REFERRED TO IN THIS INDEX**	19

I. INTRODUCTORY

A. SCOPE

This book provides a guide to the interpretation and application of the General Agreement on Tariffs and Trade, drawn from official documentary sources of the GATT. The material is arranged in forty-three chapters covering the Preamble of the General Agreement, its thirty-nine Articles, Part IV, provisional application of the General Agreement, and the institutional and decision-making practice of the GATT, plus appendix tables and this introduction. Except where otherwise indicated, this edition has been updated to 1 January 1995, the date of entry into force of the Marrakesh Agreement Establishing the World Trade Organization. A new section in the chapter on Institutions and Procedure summarizes the decisions taken by the Preparatory Committee for the WTO and the CONTRACTING PARTIES to the GATT regarding the transition from the GATT to the WTO.

B. STRUCTURE

Each chapter is structured in four sections: the text of the relevant GATT provisions, the application and interpretation of those provisions, the drafting history, and relevant documents.

- Section I includes the text of the Article concerned, the Interpretative Notes relevant to that Article from Annex I of the General Agreement, the provisions of other Annexes to the General Agreement where appropriate, and the text of relevant Understandings incorporated in GATT 1994.

- Section II includes excerpts from documents bearing on the interpretation of the General Agreement and the Havana Charter, and the practice of the CONTRACTING PARTIES in applying the provisions of the General Agreement in question. The material in Section II is arranged systematically corresponding to the phrase or word of the General Agreement interpreted or other relevant categories. Some chapters also include tables or other descriptive material.

- Section III provides a general account of the relevant preparatory work of the Havana Charter and the General Agreement, and a discussion of any relevant amendments to the General Agreement. Additional material on drafting history also may appear in section II.

- Section IV provides a list of relevant documents from the preparatory work, the early years of the GATT, and the Review Session of 1954-55. The document references for Articles V through X appear at the end of the chapter on Article X. In the case of Part IV of the GATT, which is the sole amendment since the Review Session, a list of relevant negotiating documents appears at the end of the chapter on Part IV.

II. EDITORIAL CONVENTIONS AND GUIDE TO REFERENCES

The text of the General Agreement provisions quoted at the head of each chapter has been taken from the edition published by the Secretariat. The asterisks therein indicate the portions of the text which should be read in conjunction with the Notes and Supplementary Provisions in Annex I. These asterisks do not have any independent legal basis.

The names used to refer to contracting parties in descriptive material conform in principle to the most recent United Nations list of Member States. In historical references and in direct quotations, the names used at the time have been kept. References to the various European Communities (principally the European Economic Community) reflect those in the original documents referred to. The original spelling and punctuation have been kept in each quotation. Inconsistencies in these respects therefore reflect the variability of the original documents.

Because this work is both for general distribution and for use by contracting parties to the GATT, references are provided to some documents which are still subject to restriction. Verbatim quotations from unadopted panel reports that are still in a restricted status have generally been avoided except where the material has already appeared in derestricted GATT documents. The rules on document restriction and derestriction are discussed in the chapter on Institutions and Procedure.

As provided in Article XXV:1 of the General Agreement, wherever reference is made to the contracting parties acting jointly, they are designated as the "CONTRACTING PARTIES". An individual government which has accepted or provisionally applies the General Agreement is referred to as a "contracting party". Where a reference is prefaced by "it was agreed", it reflects an agreed interpretation by the body which drafted or approved the text of the Article in question, by the CONTRACTING PARTIES, or by the body otherwise cited. Where a reference is prefaced by "it was stated", this indicates that the statement was made by one or more delegates, but that the body in question did not pronounce itself on the validity or otherwise of the statement.

The indication that Reports of Panels and Working Parties were adopted on a certain date refers to adoption by the CONTRACTING PARTIES or from 1968 onwards, to the adoption by either the CONTRACTING PARTIES or the Council of Representatives (commonly referred to as the "GATT Council" or the "Council"). A reference to a panel report or working party report in relation to a particular year refers, unless indicated otherwise, to the year of adoption. In the case of reports which were not adopted or not subject to an adoption process, the year refers to the date of circulation of the report.

References to the Articles of the Havana Charter are given in Arabic numerals whereas the corresponding Articles in the General Agreement are given in Roman numerals. Whenever reference is made to an Article in the Charter, the corresponding Article of the General Agreement is often given within square brackets or otherwise indicated.

In this work, "General Agreement" has in general been used to refer to the agreement itself, and "GATT" to the institution or the institutional context, although the documents themselves are not always consistent in their usage. "WTO" refers to the World Trade Organization and "WTO Agreement" to the Agreement Establishing the World Trade Organization which was done at Marrakesh, Morocco on 15 April 1994 and entered into force on 1 January 1995. In conformity with Article II:4 of the WTO Agreement, "GATT 1947" refers to the General Agreement on Tariffs and Trade, annexed to the Final Act Adopted At the Conclusion of the Second Session of the Preparatory Committee of the Committee of the United Nations Conference on Trade and Emplyment, as subsequently rectified, amended or modified. "GATT 1994" is as defined in the text "General Agreement on Tariffs and Trade 1994" in Annex 1A of the WTO Agreement; see further in the chapter on Institutions and Procedure.

The material in this work has been taken from the preparatory work for the Havana Charter and the General Agreement; the decisions, panel reports, working party reports and legal instruments collected in the Basic Instruments and Selected Documents (BISD) series; the session records of the CONTRACTING PARTIES; the minutes of the Council of Representatives; and other GATT documents. A list of document series appears below.

Citations in footnotes generally include the original GATT document series symbol and number for the source document, a citation to its reprinted version in the BISD series, and the BISD page and paragraph number for the passage quoted. For instance, the citation "L/833, adopted on 23 October 1958, 7S/60, 63, para. 6" refers to paragraph 6 of a document which was originally issued as L/833, which was adopted by the CONTRACTING PARTIES on 23 October 1958 and which was then reprinted starting on page 60 of the Seventh Supplement of the Basic Instruments and Selected Documents series; the paragraph in question is to be found on page 63 of the Seventh Supplement. Repeated citations to the same material or the same document are indicated by the word "*Ibid.*" Where a document has been published twice and the texts diverge, the most widely available version (normally that printed in the BISD series) is used except where otherwise noted.

Information on how to obtain copies of the documents cited and other GATT documents appears at the end of this introduction.

III. DRAFTING OF THE HAVANA CHARTER AND THE GENERAL AGREEMENT ON TARIFFS AND TRADE

The General Agreement on Tariffs and Trade was agreed during negotiations which partially paralleled the negotiations for a larger agreement, the Havana Charter for an International Trade Organization. The negotiation of the Havana Charter took place during 1946-48, but the Charter never entered into force. The General Agreement was negotiated and agreed during 1946-47 and has been provisionally applied since 1 January 1948.

The idea of an International Trade Organization was developed in discussions during World War II on planning for reconstruction of the world trading system in the postwar period. The first public proposal was the 1945 document "Proposals for Consideration by an International Conference on Trade and Employment". The Proposals were developed by the United States and were published separately by the United Kingdom, which stated it was "in full agreement with all important points in these proposals". They proposed the establishment of an International Trade Organization of the United Nations, the members of which would agree to abide by the rules in the Charter of the Organization. The Proposals contained suggestions for rules to govern trade barriers, restrictive business practices, intergovernmental commodity arrangements, and the international aspects of domestic employment policies, and also proposed a structure for the Organization. Separate negotiations on reduction of tariff barriers were also to be conducted.

"Proposals for Consideration by an International Conference on Trade and Employment" in *Proposals for Expansion of World Trade and Employment*, US Department of State Publication 2411, Commercial Policy Series 79. Washington D.C. November 1945 (reprinted in Department of State Bulletin, Vol. XIII, Washington D.C., December 1945)

Proposals for Consideration by an International Conference on Trade and Employment, as transmitted by the US Secretary of State to H.M. Ambassador at Washington, 6th December 1945. HMSO. Cmd. 6709. London, 1945.

When it met for the first time in London in February 1946, the United Nations Economic and Social Council (ECOSOC) adopted a Resolution calling a United Nations Conference on Trade and Employment for the purpose of promoting the expansion of trade and production, exchange and consumption of goods. The Resolution established a Preparatory Committee of representatives of the governments of nineteen countries, to elaborate an annotated draft agenda, including a draft convention for consideration by the Conference, taking into consideration suggestions which might be submitted to it by ECOSOC or any Member of the United Nations.[1]

In September 1946, the US Government published a more detailed "Suggested Charter" consisting of seven chapters, of which Chapter IV (Articles 8-33) dealt with commercial policy. This "US Draft Charter" became the basis for discussions at the First Session of the Preparatory Committee.

Suggested Charter for an International Trade Organization of the United Nations, US Department of State Publication 2598, Commercial Policy Series 93. Washington D.C. 1946.[2]

The First Session of the Preparatory Committee was held in London at Church House, Westminster from 15 October 1946 to 26 November 1946. The First Session adopted a Report of its deliberations (the "London Report"), which included a narrative account of the treatment of various agenda items, the draft Charter text provisionally agreed as of the end of the First Session, and various other documents.

"London Report"

Report of the First Session of the London Preparatory Committee of the United Nations Conference on Trade and Employment (UN Document EPCT/33). London: dated October 1946. Includes the "London Draft" of the Charter, as well as the ECOSOC Resolution of January 1946, the US Draft Charter, the agenda and rules of procedures for the Preparatory Committee, various other resolutions, and (in Annexure 10 at page 51) "Report on Procedures for Giving Effect to Certain Provisions of the Charter for an International Trade Organization by Means of a General Agreement on Tariffs and Trade Among Members of the Preparatory Committee".

The "London draft" is also included in *Preliminary Proposals for an International Trade Organization*, US Department of State Publication No. 2456, Commercial Policy Series 99, Washington D.C., 1947.

At the First Session, chapters on commercial policy, employment, restrictive business practices and commodity agreements were worked out, and a new chapter on economic development was added. However, no agreement was reached on voting or other organizational provisions nor on state trading; the technical articles (corresponding to GATT Articles III-X) were left incomplete. Work on the commercial policy provisions of the Charter took place almost entirely in Committee II and in subgroups thereof such as the Working Party on Technical Articles (Articles III-X) and the Procedures Sub-Committee (the most-favoured-nation clause, tariff schedules and tariff negotiations).

The First Session decided to convene a Second Session the following April to do further work on the Charter, and agreed that the governments members of the Preparatory Committee should hold a round of trade and tariff negotiations at that time. The Procedures Sub-Committee drew up a "Resolution Regarding the Negotiation of a Multilateral Trade Agreement Embodying Tariff Concessions",[3] and "Procedures for Giving Effect to Certain Provisions of the Charter of the International Trade Organization by Means of a General

---

[1] The members of the Preparatory Committee appointed by the Resolution were the representatives of the following countries: Australia, Belgium-Luxembourg Economic Union, Brazil, Canada, Chile, China, Cuba, Czechoslovakia, France, India, Lebanon, Netherlands, New Zealand, Norway, South Africa, the Union of Soviet Socialist Republics, the United Kingdom and the United States. All of these countries except the USSR became contracting parties to the GATT under the Protocol of Provisional Application. See copy of the Resolution in Annexure 1, p. 42 of the London Report (EPCT/33). The Union of Soviet Socialist Republics "indicated that it did not feel able to participate in the work of the Preparatory Committee as it had not found it possible to devote sufficient preliminary study to the important questions which were the subject of the Committee's discussion". All other members of the Preparatory Committee participated in the First and Second Sessions and the Drafting Committee. In addition, Colombia, Denmark, Mexico, Peru and Poland sent observers to the First and Second Sessions; Colombia and Mexico to the Drafting Committee; and the following countries also sent observers to the Second Session: Afghanistan, Argentina, Ecuador, Egypt, Greece, Iran, Saudi Arabia, Sweden, Thailand, Turkey, Uruguay, Venezuela and Yugoslavia. In addition, representatives of the International Labour Organization, the Food and Agriculture Organization of the United Nations, the International Monetary Fund and the International Bank for Reconstruction and Development participated without vote on agenda matters within the scope of their respective activities. The arrangements agreed in ECOSOC for consultation with non-governmental organizations were applied in respect of consultation with certain organizations having Category A consultative status with ECOSOC (the American Federation of Labour, the International Chamber of Commerce, the International Co-operative Alliance and the World Federation of Trade Unions). Geneva Report, p. 6.

[2] The US Draft Charter also appears in the London Report, EPCT/33, as Annexure 11, pp. 52 *et seq.*.

[3] London Report, Annexure 7, p. 47-48.

Agreement on Tariffs and Trade Among the Members of the Preparatory Committee".[4] The Resolution, noting that the United States government had invited the members of the Preparatory Committee "to meet to negotiate concrete arrangements for the relaxation of tariffs and trade barriers of all kinds and the invitation has been accepted", recommended to the governments concerned "that the meeting envisaged by the invitations ... should be held under the sponsorship of the Preparatory Committee in connection with, and as a part of, the Second Session of the Committee".

The First Session also appointed a Drafting Committee of technical experts. The Drafting Committee met at Lake Success, New York from 20 January to 25 February 1947 and prepared a further draft of the Charter and a full draft of the General Agreement.[5]

"Drafting Committee Report" or "New York Report"

Report of the Drafting Committee of the Preparatory Committee of the United Nations Conference on Trade and Employment (UN Document EPCT/34). Lake Success, N.Y.: dated 5 March 1947. Includes the "New York Draft" of the Charter, and a draft General Agreement at page 65.

The Second Session of the Preparatory Committee was then held at the European Office of the United Nations in Geneva from 10 April 1947 through 30 October 1947. The Preparatory Committee at this session was organized in two plenary Commissions, of which Commission A considered commercial policy matters and Commission B considered other issues including the structure of the Organization. The Preparatory Committee completed work on 22 August 1947 on a draft Charter as a basis for discussion at the Havana Conference and submitted this draft to governments in their Report in early September. Meanwhile, the first round of GATT multilateral tariff negotiations was conducted between members of the Preparatory Committee.

"Geneva Report"

Report of the Second Session of the Preparatory Committee of the United Nations Conference on Trade and Employment (UN Document EPCT/186). 10 September 1947. Includes the "Geneva draft" of the Charter.

The tariff negotiations and the drafting of the General Agreement continued for two months afterward, principally in the Tariff Agreements Committee. Drafts of the General Agreement appear in the following Geneva documents: EPCT/135, EPCT/189, EPCT/196 and EPCT/214/Add.1/Rev.1. The results of the negotiations were embodied in the "Final Act Adopted at the Conclusion of the Second Session", signed at Geneva on 30 October 1947 by representatives of the twenty-five governments involved. The Final Act, including the 30 October 1947 text of the General Agreement, the Schedules of Tariff Concessions negotiated at Geneva in 1947 and the Protocol of Provisional Application, was published by the United Nations.

"Geneva Final Act"

Final Act Adopted at the Conclusion of the Second Session of the Preparatory Committee of the United Nations Conference on Trade and Employment UN Sales No. 1947.II/10. Four volumes including text of Final Act and General Agreement on Tariffs and Trade, Schedules I-XX and Protocol of Provisional Application; 55 UNTS 187.

The following publications of the United States and United Kingdom Governments are also relevant:

US Government	*Analysis of the General Agreement on Tariffs and Trade, signed at Geneva, 30 October 1947.* US Department of State Publications 2983, Commercial Policy Series 109. Washington, D.C. 1947
UK Government	*Report on the Geneva Tariff Negotiations, with text of the General Agreement on Tariffs and Trade, and supplementary agreements with the United States and Canada.* HMSO. Cmd. 7258. London. 1947

Provisional application, under the Protocol, of the 30 October 1947 text of the General Agreement began as of 1 January 1948.

---

[4] London Report, Annexure 10, p. 48-52. See also generally the verbatim records of the Sub-Committee on Procedures, EPCT/C.II/PRO/PV/5-15 and its summary records in the series EPCT/C.II/W/2-31.

[5] The same eighteen governments were represented in the Drafting Committee, with observers from the same intergovernmental organizations, Colombia, and Mexico.

The United Nations Conference on Trade and Employment was then held at Havana, Cuba, from 21 November 1947 to 24 March 1948. At the conclusion of the Havana Conference the "Final Act and Related Documents of the United Nations Conference on Trade and Employment", which included the text of the Havana Charter for an International Trade Organization, was published in English and French by the United Nations and in English, French and Spanish by the Interim Commission of the International Trade Organization. The text of the Havana Charter was also published in English by the United States and United Kingdom Governments. An authentic text of the Charter in Spanish was established in 1949 and appears in the Spanish-language ICITO edition of the Havana Final Act.

United Nations Conference on Trade and Employment held at Havana, Cuba, from 21 November 1947 to 24 March 1948: Final Act and Related Documents. UN Document E/Conf.2/78, dated April 1948. UN Sales No. 48.11.D.4. Includes the Havana Final Act, the Havana Charter and annexes, and Conference resolutions.

United Nations Conference on Trade and Employment held at Havana, Cuba, from 21 November 1947 to 24 March 1948: Final Act and Related Documents. Interim Commission for the International Trade Organization, Lake Success, New York (reprint of UN Document E/CONF.2/78), dated April 1948. Includes the Havana Final Act, the Havana Charter and annexes, and Conference resolutions.

Havana Charter for an International Trade Organization. US Department of State Publication No. 3117, Commercial Policy Series 113, Washington D.C. 1948: Also published with a commentary: *Havana Charter for an International Trade Organization, March 24, 1948, Including a Guide to the Study of the Charter*, by R.P. Terrill. US Department of State Publication 3206, Commercial Policy Series 114, Washington D.C. 1948.

United Nations Conference on Trade and Employment. November 21, 1947, to March 24, 1948. Final Act and the Havana Charter for an International Trade Organization, with related documents. HMSO. Cmd 7376. London 1948.

The Executive Committee of the Interim Commission for the International Trade Organization (ICITO), at its first meeting, directed the Executive Secretary to "publish the reports of the principal committees [of the Havana Conference], supplemented by such sub-committee reports and other documents or extracts as may be necessary for an understanding of such reports".[6] These were published by ICITO under the title *Reports of Committees and Principal Sub-Committees*: ICITO I/8, Geneva, September 1948 (reprinted by the GATT). In this Analytical Index, this publication is referred to as "Havana Reports".

The Havana Charter never entered into force. No acceptances of the Charter were received by the Secretary-General of the United Nations, its depositary. On 6 December 1950 the United States Department of State issued a statement of policy indicating that the Havana Charter would not be submitted again to the United States Congress. It subsequently became evident that the establishment of the ITO would be indefinitely postponed.[7]

A. APPLICATION AND AMENDMENT OF THE GENERAL AGREEMENT

Article XXVI:6, as revised in 1955, provides that the General Agreement will enter into force, as between governments which have accepted it, on the thirtieth day following the day on which instruments of acceptance have been deposited on behalf of governments named in Annex H, representing 85 percent of total external trade of the territories of such governments, computed in accordance with the percentages in Annex H. However, the General Agreement has been accepted definitively only by Liberia and Haiti, and therefore has never entered into force. Instead, the General Agreement has been applied provisionally by contracting parties under the Protocol of Provisional Application or subsequent Protocols of Accession to the General Agreement.

The Protocol of Provisional Application, attached to the Final Act of the Second Session of the Preparatory Committee, provided that the signatory governments would apply provisionally on and after 1 January 1948 Parts I and III of the General Agreement, as well as Part II of the General Agreement to the fullest extent not inconsistent with existing legislation. All accession protocols since the 1949 Annecy Protocol have provided that

---

[6] ICITO/EC.1/SR.1.
[7] Sec/36/53. The US announcement of its decision not to resubmit ITO to Congress appears in GATT/CP/86 dated 7 December 1950. See also under Article XXIX.

acceding governments would provisionally apply the General Agreement in the same manner. See the chapters of this Index on the provisional application of the General Agreement and on Article XXVI.

The text of the General Agreement, as agreed in 1947 and first provisionally applied beginning 1 January 1948, was based on the commercial policy provisions of the Geneva Draft Charter. It was envisioned that the general clauses in Part II might be further changed through negotiations at Havana; Article XXIX of the General Agreement therefore provided that when the Havana Charter entered into force, Part II of the General Agreement would be superseded by the corresponding provisions of the Charter. However, even after the Charter entered into force, Parts I and III of the General Agreement would remain in effect, and the ITO would coexist with the CONTRACTING PARTIES.

At the first three Sessions of the CONTRACTING PARTIES, amendments were agreed to bring the General Agreement text closer to the text of the Charter. The First Session of the CONTRACTING PARTIES, held during the Havana Conference, agreed to three protocols of amendment to enter into force before the Charter: two which replaced Articles XIV and XXIV respectively with provisions reflecting compromises reached at Havana[8], and a third which amended accession provisions (inserting Articles XXV:5(b) and (c) and XXXV and amending Articles XXXII and XXXIII).[9]

At the Second Session of the CONTRACTING PARTIES, held in August and September 1948, a Working Party on Modifications to the General Agreement considered further incorporation of the results of the Havana Conference and decided to "limit amendments to cases where the retention of the present provisions of Part II would create serious difficulties for contracting parties".[10] The Working Party decided on the replacement of Articles III, VI and XVIII by their Havana counterparts, rewording of Article XXIX and a few other minor amendments. Due to the different acceptance requirements applying to different provisions of the General Agreement under Article XXX, two protocols were prepared: the Protocol Modifying Part II and Article XXVI of the General Agreement on Tariffs and Trade[11] and the Protocol Modifying Part I and Article XXIX of the General Agreement on Tariffs and Trade[12].

The Third Session in 1949 agreed on amendments to the territorial application provisions of Article XXVI:4, effected through the Protocol Modifying Article XXVI of the General Agreement on Tariffs and Trade.[13] The Fifth Session in 1950 agreed to an amendment to Article XXVIII, done by a paragraph added to the Torquay Protocol.

In 1953 it was decided to convene a session of the CONTRACTING PARTIES in late 1954 to review the operation of the General Agreement and to examine possible amendments or supplements thereto, and possible modifications to arrangements for its administration. The Review Session of 28 October 1954 to 8 March 1955 resulted in agreement on a number of amendments to the text of the General Agreement, and on an Agreement on the Organization for Trade Cooperation (OTC). These amendments were incorporated in three instruments, only one of which - the Protocol Amending the Preamble and Parts II and III - entered into force.[14]

In 1965 the Protocol to Introduce a Part IV on Trade and Development was drawn up. It entered into force on 27 June 1966.

---

[8]Special Protocol Modifying Article XIV of the General Agreement on Tariffs and Trade, signed at Havana on 24 March 1948, entered into force 9 May 1949, 62 UNTS 40; Special Protocol Relating to Article XXIV of the General Agreement on Tariffs and Trade, signed at Havana 24 March 1948, entered into force 7 June 1948, 62 UNTS 56.

[9]Protocol Modifying Certain Provisions of the General Agreement on Tariffs and Trade, signed at Havana 24 March 1948, entered into force 24 March 1948, 62 UNTS 30. See further in section III under Articles XXV, XXXIII and XXXV.

[10]Report of the Working Party on "Modifications to the General Agreement", adopted 1 and 2 September 1948, GATT/CP.2/22/Rev.1, II/39, para. 3.

[11]Signed at Geneva 14 September 1948, entered into force 14 December 1948, 62 UNTS 80.

[12]Signed at Geneva 14 September 1948, entered into force 24 September 1952, 138 UNTS 334.

[13]Signed at Annecy 14 September 1948, entered into force 28 March 1950, 62 UNTS 113.

[14]As regards the other two instruments: the entry into force of the Protocol of Organizational Amendments was contingent upon the entry into force of the Agreement on the Organization for Trade Co-operation, done at Geneva on 10 March 1955, which never entered into force. The Protocol amending Part I and Articles XXIX and XXX failed to gain the required acceptance by all contracting parties. At their twenty-fourth session, the CONTRACTING PARTIES decided to abandon the Protocol if, by 31 December 1967, it had not entered into force. This condition having been fulfilled, the Protocol was abandoned; see 15S/65.

The text of the English language version of the General Agreement as it has been provisionally applied since entry into force of the Part IV Protocol can be found in *The Text of the General Agreement*, published by the Secretariat.[15]

On 1 January 1995 when the WTO Agreement entered into force, the GATT 1947 and the WTO entered a brief period of coexistence as separate organizations with overlapping membership. The length of this period of coexistence was determined on 8 December 1994, when the Preparatory Committee of the World Trade Organization, and the CONTRACTING PARTIES meeting in Special Session, each adopted a decision on "Transitional Co-existence of the GATT 1947 and the WTO Agreement". This decision provides, *inter alia*, that "The legal instruments through which the contracting parties apply the GATT 1947 are herewith terminated one year after the date of entry into force of the WTO Agreement. In the light of unforeseen circumstances, the CONTRACTING PARTIES may decide to postpone the date of termination by no more than one year".[16] With this termination, almost fifty years of provisional application of the General Agreement will come to an end.

B. PUBLICATIONS COLLECTING THE PRACTICE OF THE CONTRACTING PARTIES

The principal widely-available source for documents on the GATT is the Basic Instruments and Selected Documents (BISD) series published since 1952 by the Secretariat.[17] Volume I of the BISD includes the text of the General Agreement (incorporating the first six protocols of amendment) and other instruments and procedures[18] and Volume II includes decisions, declarations, resolutions, rulings and reports of the first six sessions of the CONTRACTING PARTIES. Volume I (revised) of the BISD, published in 1955, included the text of the General Agreement incorporating all of the Review Session amendments, and the text of the Agreement on the Organization for Trade Cooperation. Volume III of the BISD, published in 1958, included the text of the General Agreement as in force in 1958. After the addition of Part IV, the text of the General Agreement as in force in 1969 was published as Volume IV of the BISD.[19] Volume IV also includes the text of the Protocol of Provisional Application and, in an Appendix, a guide to the legal sources of all the GATT provisions and the titles, effective dates and UN Treaty Series (UNTS) references of all the Protocols of amendment. The text contained in Volume IV has been republished by the Secretariat in a separate volume entitled *The Text of the General Agreement*.

The BISD series contains the texts of legal instruments drawn up by the CONTRACTING PARTIES or under their auspices, as well as decisions, resolutions, recommendations, reports, texts of protocols of accession and other relevant material. Supplements to the BISD have been published approximately annually since 1952. Since the Fourteenth Supplement, each Supplement has included a cumulative index to all material in the Supplements and Volume II.

The periodically-updated loose-leaf publication *Status of Legal Instruments* lists the legal instruments drawn up by the CONTRACTING PARTIES or under their auspices under various titles (Protocol, Agreement, Declaration, Procès-Verbal, Memorandum, Certification, Arrangement), together with details of dates of signature, of entry into force and of termination (where applicable), registration with the United Nations, parties to each instrument, and publications containing the text of the instrument concerned.[20]

---

[15]Sales No. GATT/1986-4. The English language text of the General Agreement is identical to the English language text in Volume IV of the Basic Instruments and Selected Documents, and is identical to the text which, with various other texts, is incorporated into the General Agreement on Tariffs and Trade 1994 ("GATT 1994"). The French and Spanish language texts published in Volume IV differ from the respective texts incorporated into GATT 1994, as the GATT 1994 texts in these languages include certain corrections and rectifications. See further under Article XXVI.

[16]PC/13, L/7583, adopted 8 December 1994, para. 3.

[17]For the earliest sessions of the GATT, the Secretariat issued compendia of the decisions of the CONTRACTING PARTIES and indexes listing the business that had been transacted at Sessions, with relevant document references. A number of compendia were issued in the CP/ series of intersessional documents, starting with CP/1 which lists the decisions of the First Session in 1948.

[18]Sales No. GATT/1952-3 (out of print). Earlier consolidated texts of the General Agreement were issued in the CP/ series.

[19]Sales No. 1969-1 (in print). BISD Volumes I(revised) and III are out of print. Volume IV included for the first time asterisks inserted into the text by the Secretariat for the convenience of the reader, marking the portions of the text which should be read in conjunction with the Notes and Supplementary Provisions in Annex I to the General Agreement. The asterisks have no independent legal status.

[20]GATT/LEG/1.1971, with updating supplements (loose-leaf, English and French).

When Volumes I and II of the BISD were published in 1952, the first edition of the Analytical Index was compiled and published in 1953. Later editions were prepared in 1959, 1966, 1970 and 1985.

The Summary Records of the sessions of the CONTRACTING PARTIES, the Minutes of the Council of Representatives, and most other documents issued by the GATT secretariat are not reproduced in the BISD for reasons of space. Instead they are published on microfiche. For the various document series, see the key to document symbols below.

IV. DOCUMENT REFERENCES

A key to the document symbols or short titles employed in this Index and in other GATT documents is given below. For information on how to obtain microfiche copies of these documents, see page 20 below. The list of negotiating documents reflects the holdings of the GATT Library in Geneva.

A. DRAFTING OF THE GENERAL AGREEMENT AND THE HAVANA CHARTER

While Preparatory Committee documents have the United Nations symbol "E/PC/T", throughout the history of the GATT and in this Index these documents have been referred to as "EPCT".

1. **First Session of the Preparatory Committee of the United Nations Conference on Trade and Employment (London, October-November 1946)**

EPCT/1-33	Plenary documents including summary records and committee reports
EPCT/33	**Final Report of the First Session ("London Report")**
EPCT/INF/1-8	Information documents
EPCT/INF/9	Cumulative list of First Session documents
EPCT/PV/1-6	Plenary session verbatim reports
EPCT/DEL/1-17	Chairman's Committee (heads of delegations) papers and summary records
EPCT/EC/1-5, Corr.1	Executive Committee, summary records
EPCT/C.I/1-18	Committee I (Employment) papers and summary records
EPCT/C.I/PV/1-4	Committee I verbatim reports
EPCT/C.I&II/1-24	Joint session of Committees I & II (Industrial development)
EPCT/C.I&II/PV/1-4	Committees I and II, verbatim reports
EPCT/C.I&II/D/PV/7	Committees I and II, Drafting Sub-Committee, verbatim report
EPCT/C.II/1-66	Committee II (General commercial policy) papers and summary records
EPCT/C.II/PV/1-13	Committee II verbatim reports
EPCT/C.II/W/2-31	Committee II working papers including summary records of Technical Sub-Committee and Sub-Committee on Procedures
EPCT/C.II/PRO/PV/5-15	Committee II, Sub-Committee on Procedures, verbatim reports
EPCT/C.II/ST/PV/1-6	Committee II, Sub-Committee on State-Trading, verbatim reports
EPCT/C.II/QR/PV/1-6	Committee II, Sub-Committee on Quantitative Restrictions and Exchange Control, verbatim reports
EPCT/C.II&IV/PP/PV/1-2	Committees II and IV, Joint Drafting Sub-Committee on Subsidies on Primary Products, verbatim reports
EPCT/C.III/1-19	Committee III (Restrictive business practices) papers and summary records
EPCT/C.III/PV/1-9	Committee III verbatim reports
EPCT/C.IV/1-20	Committee IV (Commodity agreements) papers and summary records
EPCT/C.IV/PV/1-9	Committee IV verbatim reports
EPCT/C.V/1-35	Committee V (Administration and organization) papers and summary records
EPCT/C.V/PV/1-15	Committee V verbatim reports

2. **Drafting Committee of the Preparatory Committee of the United Nations Conference on Trade and Employment (New York, January-February 1947)**

EPCT/34	**Report of the Drafting Committee ("New York Report")**
EPCT/C.6/1-108	Committee documents and summary records of Plenary and Sub-Committees
EPCT/C.6/107	Cumulative list of documents
EPCT/C.6/108	Index of Drafting Committee documents
EPCT/C.6/W/1-87	Working papers

3. Second Session of the Preparatory Committee of the United Nations Conference on Trade and Employment (Geneva, April-October 1947)

EPCT/35-267	Plenary documents
EPCT/186	**Report of the Second Session ("Geneva Report")**
EPCT/INF/10-330	Information documents (periodic document lists in EPCT/INF/53, 92, 134, 193, 240, 285, 330)
EPCT/INF/331	Index of Second Session documents
EPCT/W/23-344	Plenary working papers
EPCT/EC/SR.2/1-22	Executive Committee, summary records
EPCT/EC/PV.2/1-21	Executive Committee, verbatim reports
EPCT/DEL/18-75	Chairman's Committee (heads of delegations) papers and summary records
EPCT/DEL/INF/1-6	Chairman's Committee document lists
EPCT/S/1-12	"Secret" documents relating to work plan and reports of Tariff Negotiations Working Party
EPCT/TRF/1-155	Tariff negotiation documents
EPCT/TAC/SR/1-18	Tariff Agreement Committee, summary records
EPCT/TAC/PV/1-28	Tariff Agreement Committee, verbatim reports
EPCT/A/SR/1-43	Commission A (chapters on employment, economic development, and general commercial policy except for Articles relating to subsidies), summary records
EPCT/A/PV/1-43	Commission A, verbatim reports
EPCT/B/SR/1-33	Commission B (chapters on purposes, organization, restrictive business practices, commodity agreements and Articles on subsidies), summary records
EPCT/B/PV/1-33	Commission B, verbatim reports
EPCT/WP.1/SR.1-11	Working Party on Technical Articles, summary records
EPCT/WP.1/AC/SR.1-3	Working Party on Technical Articles, Ad-Hoc Sub-Committee, summary records

4. United Nations Conference on Trade and Employment (Havana, November 1947 to March 1948)

Note: an asterisk* indicates the existence of other un-numbered informal conference "white papers" of the Sub-Committee concerned.

E/CONF.2/1-78	Plenary documents
E/CONF.2/78	Report of the Conference (Final Act and related documents; also published as ICITO/4)
E/CONF.2/SR/1-21	Plenary Summary Records
E/CONF.2/W/1-15	Plenary working papers
E/CONF.2/INF/37, 69, 89, 110, 131, 152, 172, 206	Periodic lists of documents
E/CONF.2/INF/1-206	Information documents
E/CONF.2/BUR/1-39	General Committee (conference management)
E/CONF.2/BUR/W/1	General Committee working paper
E/CONF.2/BUR/SR/1-12	General Committee summary records
E/CONF.2/CO/	Co-ordination Committee informal conference documents
E/CONF.2/C.1/1-26	**Committee I (Employment and economic activity), Chapter II**
E/CONF.2/C.1/SR/1-13	Committee I summary records
E/CONF.2/C.1/A/W/1*	Committee I, Sub-Committee A (Fair labour standards) report
E/CONF.2/C.1/B*	Committee I, Sub-Committee B (Other articles of Chapter II) informal documents
E/CONF.2/C.1/C/1-4	Committee I, Sub-Committee C (Resolution on employment)
E/CONF.2/C.1/C/W/1-11*	Committee I, Sub-Committee C working papers
E/CONF.2/C.2/1-50	**Committee II (Economic development), Chapter III**
E/CONF.2/C.2/A/1-3	Committee II, Sub-Committee A (Article 8)
E/CONF.2/C.2/B/1-6	Committee II, Sub-Committee B (Article 12)
E/CONF.2/C.2/B/W/1-14	Committee II, Sub-Committee B working papers
E/CONF.2/C.2/C/1-3	Committee II, Sub-Committee C (Articles 13 and 14)
E/CONF.2/C.2/C/W/1-16	Committee II, Sub-Committee C working papers
E/CONF.2/C.2/D/1-3	Committee II, Sub-Committee D (footnote to Chapter III on reconstruction)
E/CONF.2/C.2/D/W/1-3	Committee II, Sub-Committee D working papers
E/CONF.2/C.2&3/A/1-15	Joint Sub-Committee on Tariff Preferences
E/CONF.2/C.2&3/A/W/1-3	Joint Sub-Committee on Tariff Preferences working papers
E/CONF.2/C.2&6/A/1-24	Joint Sub-Committee on Articles 9, 10 and 11
E/CONF.2/C.2&6/A/W/1-33	Joint Sub-Committee on Articles 9, 10 and 11 working papers
E/CONF.2/C.3/1-88	**Committee III (Commercial policy), Chapter IV**
E/CONF.2/C.3/SR/1-48	Committee III summary records
E/CONF.2/C.3/A/	Committee III, Sub-Committee on Articles 16, 17, 18 and 19
E/CONF.2/C.3/A/W/1-55*	Committee III, Sub-Committee A working papers
E/CONF.2/C.3/B/	Committee III, Sub-Committee on proposed new Article 18A
E/CONF.2/C.3/B/W/1-7	Committee III, Sub-Committee B working papers
E/CONF.2/C.3/B/	Committee III, Sub-Committee on Articles 32-39
E/CONF.2/C.3/C/W/1-20*	Committee III, Sub-Committee C working papers
E/CONF.2/C.3/D/	Committee III, Sub-Committee D on Articles 40, 41 and 43

INTRODUCTION 11

E/CONF.2/C.3/D/W/1-13	Committee III, Sub-Committee D working papers
E/CONF/2/C.3/E/	Committee III, Sub-Committee E on Articles 20 and 22
E/CONF.2/C.3/E/W/1-23	Committee III, Sub-Committee E working papers
E/CONF.2/C.3/F/	Committee III, Sub-Committee F on Articles 21, 23 and 24
E/CONF.2/C.3/F/W/1-32	Committee III, Sub-Committee F working papers
E/CONF.2/C.3/G/	Committee III, Sub-Committee G on the Swiss Proposal
E/CONF.2/C.3/G/W/1-13	Committee III, Sub-Committee G working papers
E/CONF.2/C.3/H/	Committee III, Sub-Committee H on Articles 25-29
E/CONF.2/C.3/H/W/1-9	Committee III, Sub-Committee H working papers
E/CONF.2.C.3/J/	Committee III, Sub-Committee J on Articles 30 and 31
E/CONF.2/C.3/J/W/1-8*	Committee III, Sub-Committee J working papers
E/CONF.2/C.4/1-25	**Committee IV (Restrictive business practices), Chapter V**
E/CONF.2/C.4/SR/1-25	Committee IV summary records
E/CONF.2/C.4/A/1-21	Committee IV Sub-Committee on amendments to Chapter V
E/CONF.2/C.4/A/W/1-9*	Committee IV Sub-Committee working papers
E/CONF.2/C.5/1-19	**Committee V (Inter-governmental commodity agreements), Chapter VI**
E/CONF.2/C.5/SR/1-15	Committee V summary records
E/CONF.2/C.5/W/1-6	Committee V working papers
E/CONF.2/C.5/A/1-2	Committee V, Sub-Committee on amendments to Chapter VI
E/CONF.2/C.5&6	Joint Sub-Committee on national security exception for commodity agreements; informal conference documents only
E/CONF.2/C.6/1-112	**Committee VI (Organization), Chapters I, VII, VIII, IX**
E/CONF.2/C.6/SR/1-41	Committee VI summary records
E/CONF.2/C.6/W/1-126	Committee VI working papers
E/CONF.2/C.7/1-2	**Committee VII (Credentials)**
E/CONF.2/C.8/1-28	**Committee VIII (Central Drafting Committee)**

See also:

ICITO/I/8	**Reports of Committees and principal Sub-Committees ("Havana Reports")**

B. INTERIM COMMISSION FOR THE ITO
(meetings held in 1948, 1949, 1950, 1968, 1980, 1993 and 1994)

ICITO/I/1-39	Documents and summary records
ICITO/INF/8	Cumulative list of documents
ICITO/INF/1-8	Information papers
ICITO/I/SR.1	Summary Record of first meeting of ICITO
ICITO/1/W.1-4	Working papers
ICITO/EC.1/1-6	Executive Committee, First Session, documents
ICITO/EC.1/SR.1-2	Executive Committee, First Session, Summary Records
ICITO/EC.2/1-21	Executive Committee, Second Session, documents
ICITO/EC.2/SR.1-16	Executive Committee, Second Session, Summary Records
ICITO/EC.2/W.1-2	Executive Committee, Second Session, Working Papers
ICITO/EC.2/OD.1-18	Executive Committee, Second Session, Orders of the Day
ICITO/EC.2/SC.1/1-11	Executive Committee, Second Session, Sub-Committee on World Court
ICITO/EC.2/SC.2/1-2	Executive Committee, Second Session, Sub-Committee on Economic Development
ICITO/EC.2/SC.3/1-9	Executive Committee, Second Session, Sub-Committee on Administration

C. GATT DOCUMENTS

1. CONTRACTING PARTIES

Basic Instruments and Selected Documents

	Sessions	Dates	Symbol
Volume I: Text in force 1952, with text of other instruments and procedures			I/
Volume I revised: Text incorporating 1955 amendments, with text of Agreement on the Organization for Trade Cooperation			I (Rev.)
Volume II: Decisions, Declarations, Rulings and Reports	1-6	Feb. 1948 - Dec. 1951	II/

	Sessions	Dates	Symbol
Volume III: Text in force 1958			III/
Volume IV: Text in force 1969			IV/
First Supplement	7	Oct.-Nov. 1952	1S/
Second Supplement	8	Sept.-Oct. 1953	2S/
Third Supplement	9 (Review)	Oct. 1954-Mar. 1955	3S/
Fourth Supplement	10	Oct.-Dec. 1955	4S/
Fifth Supplement	11	Oct.-Nov. 1956	5S/
Sixth Supplement	12	Oct.-Nov. 1957	6S/
Seventh Supplement	13	Oct.-Nov. 1958	7S/
Eighth Supplement	14-15	May-Nov. 1959	8S/
Ninth Supplement	16-17	May-Nov. 1960	9S/
Tenth Supplement	18-19	May-Dec. 1961	10S/
Eleventh Supplement	20	Oct.-Nov. 1962	11S/
Twelfth Supplement	21	Feb.-Mar. 1964	12S/
Thirteenth Supplement	22, 2SS	Feb. 1964-Mar. 1965	13S/
Fourteenth Supplement	23	Apr. 1965-Apr. 1966	14S/
Fifteenth Supplement	24	May 1966-Nov. 1967	15S/
Sixteenth Supplement	25	Dec. 1967-Nov. 1968	16S/
Seventeenth Supplement	26	Dec. 1968-Feb. 1970	17S/
Eighteenth Supplement	27	Mar. 1970-Nov. 1971	18S/
Nineteenth Supplement	28	Nov. 1971-Nov. 1972	19S/
Twentieth Supplement	29	Nov. 1972-Nov. 1973	20S/
Twenty-first Supplement	30	Nov. 1973-Nov. 1974	21S/
Twenty-second Supplement	31	Nov. 1974-Nov. 1975	22S/
Twenty-third Supplement	32	Nov. 1975-Nov. 1976	23S/
Twenty-fourth Supplement	33	Nov. 1976-Nov. 1977	24S/
Twenty-fifth Supplement	34	Nov. 1977-Nov. 1978	25S/
Twenty-sixth Supplement	35	Nov. 1978-Nov. 1979	26S/
Twenty-seventh Supplement	36	Nov. 1979-Nov. 1980	27S/
Twenty-eighth Supplement	37	Nov. 1980-Nov. 1981	28S/
Twenty-ninth Supplement	38	Nov. 1981-Nov. 1982	29S/
Thirtieth Supplement	39	Nov. 1982-Nov. 1983	30S/
Thirty-first Supplement	40	Nov. 1983-Nov. 1984	31S/
Thirty-second Supplement	41	Nov. 1984-Nov. 1985	32S/
Thirty-third Supplement	42	Nov. 1985-Nov. 1986	33S/
Thirty-fourth Supplement	43	Nov. 1986-Dec. 1987	34S/
Thirty-fifth Supplement	44	Dec. 1987-Nov. 1988	35S/
Thirty-sixth Supplement	45	Nov. 1988-Dec. 1989	36S/
Supplement No. 37	46	Dec. 1989-Dec. 1990	37S/
Supplement No. 38	47	Dec. 1990-Dec. 1991	38S/
Supplement No. 39	48	Dec. 1991-Dec. 1992	39S/
Supplement No. 40	49	Dec. 1992-Jan. 1994	40S/

The summary records of the Sessions of the CONTRACTING PARTIES and most other documents have not been reproduced in the BISD and are referred to by their symbols.

Session documents and summary records

GATT/1/	First Session	Havana	28 Feb-23 March 1948
GATT/1/SR.1-14			

GATT/CP.2/ GATT/CP.2/SR.1-25	Second Session	Geneva	17 Aug-15 Sept. 1948
GATT/CP.3/ GATT/CP.3/SR.1-44	Third Session	Annecy	8 Apr.-12 Aug. 1949
GATT/CP.4/ GATT/CP.4/SR.1-21	Fourth Session	Geneva	23 Feb.-3 April 1950
GATT/CP.5/ GATT/CP.5/SR.1-26	Fifth Session	Torquay	2 Nov.-19 Dec. 1950
GATT/CPS/ GATT/CPS/SR.1-5	First Special Session	Torquay	29 Mar.-3 Apr. 1951
GATT/CP.6/ GATT/CP.6/SR.1-27	Sixth Session	Geneva	17 Sept.-27 Oct.1951
SR.7/1-17	Seventh Session	Geneva	2 Oct.-10 Nov. 1952
SR.8/1-21	Eighth Session	Geneva	17 Sept.-24 Oct.1953
SR.9/1-47	Ninth Session	Geneva	28 Oct. 1954-8 March 1955
SR.10/1-21	Tenth Session	Geneva	27 Oct.-3 Dec. 1955
SR.11/1-18	Eleventh Session	Geneva	11 Oct.-17 Nov. 1956
SR.12/1-22	Twelfth Session	Geneva	17 Oct.-30 Nov. 1957
SR.12/1-21	Thirteenth Session	Geneva	16 Oct.-22 Nov. 1958
SR.14/1-11	Fourteenth Session	Geneva	11-30 May 1959
SR.15/1-18	Fifteenth Session	Tokyo	26 Oct.-20 Nov. 1959
SR.16/1-11	Sixteenth Session	Geneva	16 May-4 June 1960
SR.17/1-12	Seventeenth Session	Geneva	31 Oct.-19 Nov. 1960
SR.18/1-6	Eighteenth Session	Geneva	15-19 May 1961
SR.19/1-12	Nineteenth Session	Geneva	12 Nov.-9 Dec. 1961
SR.20/1-12	Twentieth Session	Geneva	23 Oct.-16 Nov. 1962
SR.21/1-11	21st Session	Geneva	24 Feb.-20 Mar.1964
2SS/SR.l-5	2nd Special Session	Geneva	17 Nov.1964-8 Feb. 1965
SR.22/1-11	22nd Session	Geneva	2-25 Mar. 1965
SR.23/1-11	23rd Session	Geneva	24 Mar.-6 Apr. 1966
SR.24/1-19	24th Session	Geneva	9-24 Nov. 1967
SR.25/1-11	25th Session	Geneva	12-29 Nov. 1968
SR.26/1-9	26th Session	Geneva	16-27 Feb. 1970
SR:27/1-12	27th Session	Geneva	16-26 Nov. 1971
SR.28/1-12	28th Session	Geneva	1-14 Nov. 1972
SR.29/1-3	29th Session	Geneva	12-14 Nov. 1973
SR.30/1-5	30th Session	Geneva	19-21 Nov. 1974
SR.31/1-4	31st Session	Geneva	26-27 Nov. 1975
SR.32/1-3	32nd Session	Geneva	22-23 Nov. 1976
SR.33/1-3	33rd Session	Geneva	29-30 Nov. 1977
SR.34/1-3	34th Session	Geneva	27-28 Nov. 1978
SR.35/1-5	35th Session	Geneva	26-29 Nov. 1979
3SS/SR/1	3rd Special Session	Geneva	28 April 1980
SR.36/1-4	36th Session	Geneva	24-26 Nov. 1980
SR.37/1-5	37th Session	Geneva	23-25 Nov. 1981
SR.38/1-10	38th Session	Geneva	22-30 Nov. 1982
SR.39/1-4	39th Session	Geneva	21-23 Nov. 1983
SR.40/1-9	40th Session	Geneva	26-30 Nov. 1984
4SS/SR/	4th Special Session	Geneva	30 Sept.-3 Oct. 1985
SR.41/	41st Session	Geneva	25-29 Nov. 1985
MIN(86)/SR/	Special Session at Ministerial level (Uruguay Round)	Punta del Este	15-20 Sept. 1986
SR.42/	42nd Session	Geneva	24-27 Nov. 1986
SR.43/	43rd Session	Geneva	1-3 Dec. 1987

SR.44/	44th Session	Geneva	7-8 Nov. 1988
SR.45/	45th Session	Geneva	4-5 Dec. 1989
SR.46/	46th Session	Geneva	12-13 Dec. 1990
SR.47/	47th Session	Geneva	3-4 Dec. 1991
SR.48/	48th Session	Geneva	2-3 Dec. 1992
5SS/SR/1	5th Special Session	Geneva	9 June 1993
SR.49/	49th Session	Geneva	26-27 Jan. 1994
6SS/SR/1	6th Special Session	Geneva	8 Dec. 1994
SR.50/1-4	50th Session	Geneva	8-9 Dec. 1994, 8 Feb. 1995
7SS/SR/1	7th Special Session	Geneva	24 March 1995

Before the Seventh Session (1952), documents issued during a session of the CONTRACTING PARTIES or in connection with a session were issued under the session symbol, and intersessional documents were issued in the series CP/. As from the Seventh Session, inclusive summary records have been numbered SR.7/... etc. Except for summary records and working papers, the practice of issuing documents under a session symbol was discontinued after the Sixth Session. The following documents are issued for each session (taking as an example the 50th Session):

SR.50/	Summary records of Annual Sessions of the CONTRACTING PARTIES
SR.50/Index	Index of summary records for each Session
SR.50/ST/	Statements made at the Session
W.50/	Working papers, order of business, checklist of documents
FIFTY	Circular on administrative arrangements for the Session

2. GATT documents: active series

The list below indicates those document series for which the body issuing the document is in existence and documents have been issued recently. ../INF/ and ../W/ subseries also exist for documents issued by committees or negotiating groups, and msot often consist of delegate lists and working documents respectively. ../M/ subseries indicate minutes of the body issuing them. Since entry into force of the WTO Agreement on 1 January 1995, the bodies of the WTO have begun to issue documents in new series which are not listed here.

General

L/	General documents: Notifications, communications, membership (since 1952)
Let/	Letter series of notifications of acceptances, invitations for informal meetings
DS/	*Dispute settlement* (since 1989)
DS[number]/	Consultation requests and dispute-related notifications, numbered consecutively by dispute
DS[number]/R	Dispute settlement panel reports
GATT/	Press releases and annual report on international trade, 1948-1994
GATT/AIR/	Airgrams notifying meeting dates and agendas
INF/	List and Index of GATT Documents (monthly), notices concerning document derestriction, informational notes
Spec(..)	Special distribution series

Principal bodies of the GATT

C/	***Council of Representatives***
C/M/	Council minutes
C/M/Index	Index of the Council minutes
C/W/	Working papers, draft agenda, other relevant information
C/COM/	Communications; statements
COM.TD/	***Committee on Trade and Development***
COM.TD/INF/, COM.TD/W/	
COM.TD/LLDC/, ../W/, ../INF/	Sub-Committee on Trade of Least-Developed Countries
C/RM/	***Trade Policy Review Mechanism***
C/RM/M, C/RM/W/, C/RM/INF	Minutes, working papers, lists of representatives
C/RM/G/	Reports by governments
C/RM/S/	Reports by Secretariat
C/RM/OV/	Overview of developments in international trade and the trading system
C/RM/OV/M/	Same - Minutes of meeting

Other standing bodies

BOP/	***Committee on Balance-of-Payments Restrictions***
BOP/R/	Reports of the Committee
BOP/INF, BOP/W	
TAR/	***Committee on Tariff Concessions***
TAR/INF/, TAR/M/,	
TAR/Spec/	
TAR/W/	Working documents including acceptances of protocols
SECRET/	Notification and results of Article XXVIII negotiations
SECRET/HS, SECRET/C/HS	Harmonized System negotiations, notification of HS changes
NTM/W/	***Technical Group on Quantitative Restrictions and Other Non-Tariff Measures***
IDB/, IDB/INF, IDB/W,	***Integrated Data Base***: Information, progress reports, Secretariat notes,
IDB/Q, IDB/URM	outstanding questions, User Reference Manual

Committees established under certain arrangements

COM.TEX/	***Textiles Committee and Textiles Surveillance Body***
COM.TEX/INF/,	Information, reports, status of acceptances of MFA Protocols
COM.TEX/W/	Working papers, proposals, draft reports
COM.TEX/SB/	Textiles Surveillance Body notifications and reports
TEX.SB/	Bilateral agreements
TEX.SB/W/	Draft reports; draft agendas
CPC/	***Committee of Participating Countries***
CPC/W	

Committees and Councils established under the Tokyo Round agreements and arrangements

ADP/	***Committee on Anti-Dumping Practices***
ADP/INF/, ADP/M/,	
ADP/W/	
AIR/	***Committee on Trade in Civil Aircraft***
AIR/INF/, AIR/M/, AIR/W/	
AIR/TSC/W/	Technical Sub-Committee
GPR/	***Committee on Government Procurement***
GPR/INF/, GPR/M/,	

GPR/W/, GPR/Spec/
GPR.DS/   Dispute settlement under the Agreement on Government Procurement

LIC/
LIC/INF/, LIC/M/,   *Committee on Import Licensing*
LIC/W/, LIC/Spec/

SCM/
SCM/INF/, SCM/M/,   *Committee on Subsidies and Countervailing Measures*
SCM/W/, SCM/Spec/

TBT/
TBT/INF/, TBT/M/,   *Committee on Technical Barriers to Trade*
TBT/W, TBT/Spec/
TBT/Notif.   Notifications of technical regulations and certification systems

VAL/
VAL/INF/, VAL/M/,   *Committee on Customs Valuation*
VAL/W, VAL/Spec/

Recent inactive series

TRE/   *Group on Environmental Measures and International Trade*
TRE/M/, TRE/W/,   Documents 1991-1994
TRE/INF

DPG/   *Working Group on Export of Domestically*
DPG/W/, DPG/Notif.   *Prohibited Goods and other Hazardous Substances*

DPC/   *International Dairy Products Council* 1980-1994
DPC/INF/, DPC/W
DPC/PTL/, DPC/PTL/W   Committees of Protocols on Certain Cheeses, Milk Fat, Milk Powders
DPC/INV/   Inventory of information on domestic policies and trade measures
DPC/STAT/   Statistics

IMC/   International Meat Council 1980-1994
IMC/INF/, IMC/W
IMC/INV/   Inventory of domestic policies and trade measures
IMC/STAT/   Statistics

3. Document series of the Preparatory Committee for the WTO

PC/R   Report of the Preparatory Committee
PC/W, PC/M, PC/INF

PC/BFA, ../W/, ../M/, ../INF   Subcommittee on Budget, Finance and Administration
PC/IPL, ../W/, ../M/, ../INF/   Subcommittee on Institutional, Procedural and Legal Issues
PC/SCTE/, ../W/, ../M/, ../INF/   Subcommittee on Trade and Environment
PC/SCS   Subcommittee on Services
TS/NGBT   Negotiating Group on Basic Telecommunications Services
S/IGFS   Interim Group on Financial Services
S/NGNP   Negotiating Group on Movement of Natural Persons
S/NGMTS   Negotiating Group on Maritime Services

4. Uruguay Round document series

Legal instruments

	Final Act text signed at Marrakesh 15 April 1994
MTN/FA/Corr.1-7	Corrections to Final Act text tabled in legal drafting process Feb.-Mar. 1994
MTN/FA	Text of the Final Act as adopted by TNC on 15 December 1993
MTN.TNC/W/FA	Draft text of the Final Act as issued by the Secretariat 20 December 1991 ("Dunkel Draft")
MTN.TNC/W/35	Draft text of the Final Act as issued 26 November 1990 for the Ministerial Meeting held at Brussels in December 1990
MTN.TNC/MIN(90)/	Trade Negotiations Committee - Meeting at Ministerial Level, Brussels, 1990 - Documents
MTN.TNC/MIN(88)/	Trade Negotiations Committee - Meeting at Ministerial Level, Montreal, 1988
MIN.DEC	Ministerial Declaration on the Uruguay Round 1986 (reprinted at 33S/19)
MIN.DEC/Chair	Statement by Chairman, Adoption of Ministerial Declaration 1986

Principal document series

MTN.INF/	List & Index of Uruguay Round Documents, lists of representatives, information bulletins
MTN.TNC/ MTN.TNC/INF/, MTN.TNC/W/	Trade Negotiations Committee
MTN.GNG/, ../INF/, ../W/ MTN.GNS/, ../INF/, ../W/	Group of Negotiations on Goods Group of Negotiations on Services
MTN.SB/, ../INF/, ../W/ MTN.SB/RBN/ MTN.SB/SN/	Surveillance Body Rollback notifications Standstill notifications

Document series 1991-1994

MTN.GNG/MA/, ../W/	Negotiating Group on Market Access
MTN.GNG/AG/, ../W/	Negotiating Group on Agriculture
MTN.GNG/INST/	Negotiating Group on Institutions
MTN.GNG/RM/, ../W/	Negotiating Group on Rule Making and Trade-Related Investment Measures
MTN.GNG/TC/	Negotiating Group on Textiles and Clothing
MTN.GNG/TRIPS/, ../W/	Negotiating Group on Trade-Related Aspects of Intellectual Property Rights, including Trade in Counterfeit Goods
MTN.TNC/LD, ../W/	**Legal Drafting Group** 1992

Document series 1986-1990

(including INF/ and W/ documents in most cases)

MTN.GNG/NG1/	Negotiating Group on Tariffs
MTN.GNG/NG2/	Negotiating Group on Non-Tariff Measures
MTN.GNG/NG3/	Negotiating Group on Natural Resource-Based Products
MTN.GNG/NG4/	Negotiating Group on Textiles and Clothing

MTN.GNG/NG5/	Negotiating Group on Agriculture
MTN.GNG/NG6/	Negotiating Group on Tropical Products
MTN.GNG/NG7/	Negotiating Group on GATT Articles
MTN.GNG/NG8/	Negotiating Group on MTN Agreements and Arrangements
MTN.GNG/NG9/	Negotiating Group on Safeguards
MTN.GNG/NG10/	Negotiating Group on Subsidies and Countervailing Measures
MTN.GNG/NG11/	Negotiating Group on Trade-Related Aspects of Intellectual Property Rights, including Trade in Counterfeit Goods
MTN.GNG/NG12/	Negotiating Group on Trade-Related Investment Measures
MTN.GNG/NG13/	Negotiating Group on Dispute Settlement
MTN.GNG/NG14/	Negotiating Group on Functioning of the GATT System

5. Documents of past negotiating rounds

Tokyo Round: Tokyo Round documents were issued in the MTN/ series with a blue band across the top. See also the MIN(73) series for the proceedings of the Ministerial Conference of 1973 which led to the Tokyo Declaration launching the Round, and the COM.IND/ and COM.AG/ series for work done preliminary to the Round in the Committee on Trade in Industrial Products and the Committee on Trade in Agriculture.

Kennedy Round documents were issued in the TN.64/ series with a blue band; Dillon Round documents were issued in the TN.60/ series; documents from the 1956 trade round at Geneva were issued in the TN.56/ series; Torquay Round documents were issued as TN.2/; and Annecy Round documents were issued as TN.1/. Each of these series includes session records (/SR/) and documents of working groups.

6. Lists and indexes of GATT documents

GATT documents are systematically listed in the following document series:

(1) *"List & Index of GATT Documents"*: Annual in the INF/ series since 1981: list of documents, titles and dates, with attached cross-indexes by subject, country, articles of main legal instruments referred to, products referred to, body issuing the document, and other GATT instruments. Monthly updates are cumulated in the annual List & Index.

INF/210 (1981), INF/204 (1982), INF/206 (1983), INF/214 (1984), INF/222 (1985), INF/229 (1986), INF/236 (1987), INF/242 (1988), INF/252 (1989), INF/256 (1990), INF/260 (1991), INF/263 (1992)

(2) *"List of Documents Issued"*: Approximately annual in the INF/ series up to 1980:

GATT/CP/INF/2/Rev.1 (21/9/48-29/2/52), CP/INF/16 (4/1/52-30/11/52), INF/19 (1/12/52-31/10/53), INF/23 (1/11/53-31/12/54); INF/23/Add.1 (1/1/55-31/3/55), INF/68 (1958), INF/79 (1959), INF/86 (1960), INF/95 (1961), INF/99 (1962), INF/105 (1963), INF/110 (1964), INF/118 (1965), INF/123 (1966), INF/129 (1967), INF/135 (1968), INF/138 (1969), INF/141 (1970), INF/148 (1971), INF/151 (1972), INF/155 (1973), INF/159 (1974), INF/165 (1975), INF/169 (1976), INF/173 (1977), INF/179 (1978), INF/189 (1979), INF/198 (1980)

(3) *"Documents Index"*: Approximately annual in the INF/ series up to 1980:

GATT/CP/INF/3/Rev.1 (21/9/48-5/11/51), INF/3/Rev.1/Add.1 (6/11/51-31/11/52), INF/3/Rev.1/Add.2 (1/12/52-31/12/53), INF/3/Rev.2 (1/1/54-10/10/55), INF/27 (Documents related to the Review Session), INF/44 (1956), INF/54 (1957), INF/67 (1958), INF/81 (1959), INF/87 (1960), INF/98 (1961), INF/100 (1962), INF/106 (1963), INF/111 (1964), INF/117 (1965), INF/124 (1966), INF/130 (1967), INF/135 (1968), INF/139 (1969), INF/142 (1970), INF/149 (1971), INF/153 (1972), INF/157 (1973), INF/161 (1974), INF/167 (1975), INF/171 (1976), INF/177 (1977), INF/180 (1978), INF/191 (1979), INF/200 (1980)

(4) *C/M/Index/*: Cumulative index to minutes of the Council and its predecessor body, the Intersessional Committee, since 1952, updated and reissued annually; the most recent is C/M/Index/26 dated 11 May 1994, indexing minutes through December 1993.

(5) *Session Record Indexes* for Annual Sessions of the CONTRACTING PARTIES, issued separately for each session; not cumulated. Now issued as SR/--/Index; early Sessions were indexed within the periodic indexes in the INF/ series.

7. Lists and indexes of documents of negotiating rounds

Documents associated with negotiating rounds since 1948 have been listed in the following lists and index series:

(1) *"List & Index of Uruguay Round Documents"*: Annual since 1986 in the MTN/INF/ series: list of documents, titles and dates, with attached cross-indexes by subject (including service sectors), country, articles of main legal instruments referred to, products referred to, and body issuing the document.

MTN.INF/1 (1986), MTN.INF/2 (1987), MTN.INF/5 (1988), MTN.INF/9 (1989), MTN.INF/12 (1990), MTN.INF/14 (1991), MTN.INF/16 (1992)

(2) *Tokyo Round*: Indexes of Tokyo Round documents were issued periodically in the MTN/INF series:

INDEXES: MTN/INF/2 (1974), MTN/INF/3 (1975), MTN/INF/6 (1976), MTN/INF/9 (1977), MTN/INF/44 (1978), INF/190 (1979)
LISTS: MTN/INF/1 (1974), MTN/INF/4 (1975), MTN/INF/7 (1976), MTN/INF/10 (1977), MTN/INF/48 (1978)

A cumulative index of selected documents oriented toward topics of interest to developing countries was also compiled, the final revision of which, updated to 2 August 1979, was issued as TA/INF/1/Rev.8.

(3) *Kennedy Round and earlier rounds*: see lists and indexes of GATT documents for the relevant years.

V. SOURCES FOR OBTAINING COPIES OF DOCUMENTS REFERRED TO IN THIS INDEX

GATT publications: Copies of the Basic Instruments and Selected Documents series, the texts of GATT legal instruments, the Status of Legal Instruments, tariff protocols and schedules, this book, and other in-print GATT publications are available from the Publications Office of the WTO Secretariat and its sales agents. Price lists are available from:

Publications Office
WTO Secretariat
Centre William Rappard
CH-1211 Geneva 21
Switzerland

Telephone: (022) 739 52 08/739 53 08
Telefax: (022) 731 42 06
Telex: 412 324 GATT CH

Photo-offset reprints of certain out-of-print publications including the Havana Conference Final Act (including the Havana Charter) and the Havana Reports can be purchased from the WTO Publications Office directly. Copies of certain document series on computer diskette are also available from the same office.

In 1995/96 the Secretariat will publish a series of CD-ROM disks, including a collection of data from the Integrated Data Base (now available); the complete results of the Uruguay Round including full legal texts and market access schedules (available in fall 1995); and two CD-Roms to be available in 1996, including a collection of 18,000 GATT documents in electronic form including the texts of GATT legal instruments, the complete text of the BISD series, panel reports and other documents of legal interest, and a searchable document data base. For information contact the Publications Office.

Documents on microfiche: All of the negotiating documents for the General Agreement and the Havana Charter, as well as derestricted GATT documents since 1948, are available on microfiche directly from the WTO Secretariat, which is their sole distributor. A standing order may be placed for microfiche documents. As of May 1995, the cost of a complete set of the negotiating documents for the Havana Charter and the General Agreement was SF810 for English and SF645 for French; certain negotiating documents exist only in one language. All current GATT documents are available in English, French and Spanish; as of May 1995 the cost per year and per language for all current GATT documents was approximately SF750. Inquiries regarding current pricing and ordering information should be directed to the WTO Publications Office.

As of May 1995, GATT documents on microfiche were received at the following universities, public libraries and institutions:

EUROPE

Max Planck Institute for Comparative Public Law and International Law, Heidelberg, Germany
Institute of International Law, Graz, Austria
British Library of Political and Economic Science, London

NORTH AMERICA

University of California library (Berkeley);
Law libraries of: Boston University, Duke University, Georgetown University, University of Georgia, Harvard University, University of Miami, University of Michigan, University of Minnesota, New York University, University of Pennsylvania, University of Saskatchewan, University of Texas, University of Toronto

LATIN AMERICA

Economic Commission for Latin America, Santiago, Chile

ASIA

Fair Trade Center, Tokyo
Osaka City University

PREAMBLE

I.	TEXT OF THE PREAMBLE	21
II.	RELATIONSHIP WITH OTHER ARTICLES	21
III.	PREPARATORY WORK AND SUBSEQUENT MODIFICATIONS	21
IV.	RELEVANT DOCUMENTS	22

I. TEXT OF THE PREAMBLE

The Governments of the COMMONWEALTH OF AUSTRALIA, the KINGDOM OF BELGIUM, the UNITED STATES OF BRAZIL, BURMA, CANADA, CEYLON, the REPUBLIC OF CHILE, the REPUBLIC OF CHINA, the REPUBLIC OF CUBA, the CZECHOSLOVAK REPUBLIC, the FRENCH REPUBLIC, INDIA, LEBANON, the GRAND-DUCHY OF LUXEMBURG, the KINGDOM OF THE NETHERLANDS, NEW ZEALAND, the KINGDOM OF NORWAY, PAKISTAN, SOUTHERN RHODESIA, SYRIA, the UNION OF SOUTH AFRICA, the UNITED KINGDOM OF GREAT BRITAIN AND NORTHERN IRELAND, and the UNITED STATES OF AMERICA:

Recognizing that their relations in the field of trade and economic endeavour should be conducted with a view to raising standards of living, ensuring full employment and a large and steadily growing volume of real income and effective demand, developing the full use of the resources of the world and expanding the production and exchange of goods,

Being desirous of contributing to these objectives by entering into reciprocal and mutually advantageous arrangements directed to the substantial reduction of tariffs and other barriers to trade and to the elimination of discriminatory treatment in international commerce,

Have through their Representatives agreed as follows:

II. RELATIONSHIP WITH OTHER ARTICLES

References to "the objectives of this Agreement" appear in Articles XV:7(a), XVI:2, XVI:5, XVIII:1, XXIII:1, XXVIII*bis*:1, XXXVI:1, XXXVII:2(b)(iii), and the Notes Ad Articles XXIV:11 and XXXVI:1.

III. PREPARATORY WORK AND SUBSEQUENT MODIFICATIONS

The material in paragraphs 2 and 3 of the Preamble was inserted at Geneva, and reflects some of the objectives listed in Article 1 of the Geneva Draft Charter. The document references below pertain either to Article 1 of the Charter or to the Preamble of the General Agreement.

At the Review Session held in 1954-55, the CONTRACTING PARTIES agreed to incorporate the Preamble to the GATT, with some additions, in the text of Part I of the Agreement as a new Article I entitled "Objectives." However, this amendment was included in the Protocol Amending Part I and Articles XXIX and XXX of the General Agreement, which failed to gain the requisite unanimous approval and was abandoned on 31 December 1967.[1] The text of the new Article I would have been as follows:

"1. The contracting parties recognize that their relations in the field of trade and economic endeavour should be conducted with a view to raising standards of living, ensuring full employment and a large and steadily growing volume of real income and effective demand, developing the full use of the resources of

---

[1] 15S/65.

the world and expanding the production and exchange of goods, and promoting the progressive development of the economies of all the contracting parties.

"2.   The contracting parties desire to contribute to these objectives through this Agreement by entering into reciprocal and mutually advantageous arrangements directed to the substantial reduction of tariffs and other barriers to trade and to the elimination of discriminatory treatment in international commerce."

IV. RELEVANT DOCUMENTS

New York

Discussion:	EPCT/C.6/23, 90, 91
	EPCT/C.6/31, 57, 83
Reports:	EPCT/34
Other:	EPCT/C.6/78, 99+Corr.1
	EPCT/C.6/W/1, 2, 84

Review Session

Discussion:	SR.9/18, 19, 47
Reports:	W.9/164, 197, 198, 236
Other:	L/276, W.9/27

Geneva

Discussion:	EPCT/EC/PV.2/22
	EPCT/B/SR/20, 21, 29
	EPCT/TAC/PV/26
Reports:	EPCT/139+Corr.1, 159,
	180+Corr.1-9, 186+Corr.1
	EPCT/135, 189, 196, 211,
	214/Add.1/Rev.1
Other:	EPCT/W/123, 176, 234, 236, 238

PART I

ARTICLE I

GENERAL MOST-FAVOURED-NATION TREATMENT

I.	TEXT OF ARTICLE I, ANNEXES A THROUGH G OF THE GENERAL AGREEMENT, AND INTERPRETATIVE NOTE AD ARTICLE I			24
II.	INTERPRETATION AND APPLICATION OF ARTICLE I			28
	A.	SCOPE AND APPLICATION OF ARTICLE I		28
		1.	Interpretation and Application of Paragraph 1	28
			(1) "customs duties and charges of any kind imposed on or in connection with importation or exportation or the international transfer of payments for imports or exports"	28
			(a) Unbound tariffs	28
			(b) "charges of any kind"	28
			(c) Import surcharges	28
			(d) Variable levies	29
			(e) Trade conducted at most-favoured-nation duty rates	30
			(2) "the method of levying such duties and charges"	30
			(3) "all rules and formalities in connection with importation and exportation"	30
			(4) "matters referred to in paragraphs 2 and 4 of Article III"	30
			(5) "any advantage, favour, privilege or immunity granted by any contracting party ..."	31
			(a) Duty waiver conditional on certification by a particular government	31
			(b) Export price monitoring schemes	31
			(c) Exemption from charges	32
			(d) Actions with respect to countervailing duties	32
			(6) "originating in" and country of origin	32
			(7) "shall be accorded immediately and unconditionally"	33
			(a) Reciprocity clauses	33
			(b) Tax exemptions on condition of existence of a tax system of family allowances in the exporting country	33
			(c) Exemptions on condition of minimum import price guarantees	34
			(d) Reservation of import quotas for outward processing traffic	34
			(e) Tariff treatment conditional on the existence of a co-operation contract	34
			(f) Special treatment for diplomatic gifts, supplies and equipment accorded on the basis of reciprocity	35
			(g) Application to individual cases and "balancing"	35
			(8) "like product"	35
			(a) General	35
			(b) Examination of "like product" issues in particular cases	36
			(c) Price discrimination	39
		2.	Paragraphs 2 and 4: Historical preferences and margins of preference	40
			(1) Modification of margins of preference	40
			(a) Relationship between negotiated reductions in the most-favoured-nation duty rate and the margin of preference	40
			(b) Increase in margins of preference	42
			(c) Reinstatement of historical preferences	42
			(d) Change in historical preferences due to tariff reclassification	42
			(2) Base dates for purposes of paragraph 4 and Annex G, and modification thereof	43
			(3) "in respect of duties or charges"	43
		3.	Paragraph 3	44
	B.	RELATIONSHIP BETWEEN ARTICLE I AND OTHER PROVISIONS OF THE GENERAL AGREEMENT		44
		1.	Article III	44
		2.	Article VI	44
		3.	Article IX	45
		4.	Article XIII	45
	C.	RELATIONSHIP OF ARTICLE I TO OTHER INTERNATIONAL AGREEMENTS		45
		1.	Agreement on Implementation of Article VI	46
		2.	Agreement on Interpretation and Application of Articles VI, XVI and XXIII	46
		3.	Agreement on Government Procurement	46
	D.	EXCEPTIONS AND DEROGATIONS		47
		1.	"imports of products for immediate or ultimate consumption in governmental use"	47
		2.	Exceptions and derogations provided in other Articles of the General Agreement	47
			(1) Anti-dumping and countervailing duties	47

		(2)	*Frontier traffic and customs unions*	47
	3.	\multicolumn{2}{l}{**Exceptions and derogations authorized in Protocols of Accession and in Declarations on Provisional Accession** . . . .}	48
		(1)	*Protocol of Provisional Application*	48
		(2)	*Protocols of Accession*	48
			(a) General	48
			(b) Particular contracting parties	48
	4.	\multicolumn{2}{l}{**Waivers granted under the provisions of paragraph 5 of Article XXV** . . . .}	49
		(1)	*Decision on "Generalized System of Preferences" of 25 June 1971*	49
		(2)	*Decision on "Trade negotiations among developing countries" of 26 November 1971*	50
		(3)	*Waivers granted to individual contracting parties*	51
	5.	\multicolumn{2}{l}{**Preferential arrangements authorized by Decisions of the CONTRACTING PARTIES without reference to paragraph 5 of Article XXV** . . . .}	51
		(1)	*First Agreement on Trade Negotiations Among Developing Member Countries of the Economic and Social Commission for Asia and the Pacific (Bangkok Agreement)*	51
		(2)	*Agreement on the Association of South-East Asian Nations (ASEAN) Preferential Trading Arrangements*	52
		(3)	*Trade Expansion and Economic Co-operation Agreement*	52
	6.	\multicolumn{2}{l}{**Differential and More Favourable Treatment, Reciprocity and Fuller Participation of Developing Countries ("Enabling Clause")** . . . .}	53
		(1)	*Scope*	54
		(2)	*Preference schemes*	56
		(3)	*Preferential arrangements notified under the Enabling Clause*	56
		(4)	*"Graduation"*	58
	7.	\multicolumn{2}{l}{**Coexistence of the GATT 1947 and the WTO Agreement** . . . .}	59
III.	\multicolumn{3}{l}{**PREPARATORY WORK AND SUBSEQUENT MODIFICATIONS** . . . .}	59
IV.	\multicolumn{3}{l}{**RELEVANT DOCUMENTS** . . . .}	61

I. TEXT OF ARTICLE I, ANNEXES A THROUGH G OF THE GENERAL AGREEMENT, AND INTERPRETATIVE NOTE AD ARTICLE I

Article I

General Most-Favoured-Nation Treatment

1. With respect to customs duties and charges of any kind imposed on or in connection with importation or exportation or imposed on the international transfer of payments for imports or exports, and with respect to the method of levying such duties and charges, and with respect to all rules and formalities in connection with importation and exportation, and with respect to all matters referred to in paragraphs 2 and 4 of Article III,* any advantage, favour, privilege or immunity granted by any contracting party to any product originating in or destined for any other country shall be accorded immediately and unconditionally to the like product originating in or destined for the territories of all other contracting parties.

2. The provisions of paragraph 1 of this Article shall not require the elimination of any preferences in respect of import duties or charges which do not exceed the levels provided for in paragraph 4 of this Article and which fall within the following descriptions:

(a) Preferences in force exclusively between two or more of the territories listed in Annex A, subject to the conditions set forth therein;

(b) Preferences in force exclusively between two or more territories which on July 1, 1939, were connected by common sovereignty or relations of protection or suzerainty and which are listed in Annexes B, C and D, subject to the conditions set forth therein;

(c) Preferences in force exclusively between the United States of America and the Republic of Cuba;

(d) Preferences in force exclusively between neighbouring countries listed in Annexes E and F.

3. The provisions of paragraph 1 shall not apply to preferences between the countries formerly a part of the Ottoman Empire and detached from it on July 24, 1923, provided such preferences are approved under paragraph 5 of Article XXV, which shall be applied in this respect in the light of paragraph 1 of Article XXIX.

4. The margin of preference* on any product in respect of which a preference is permitted under paragraph 2 of this Article but is not specifically set forth as a maximum margin of preference in the appropriate Schedule annexed to this Agreement shall not exceed:

(a) in respect of duties or charges on any product described in such Schedule, the difference between the most-favoured-nation and preferential rates provided for therein; if no preferential rate is provided for, the preferential rate shall for the purposes of this paragraph be taken to be that in force on April 10, 1947, and, if no most-favoured-nation rate is provided for, the margin shall not exceed the difference between the most-favoured-nation and preferential rates existing on April 10, 1947;

(b) in respect of duties or charges on any product not described in the appropriate Schedule, the difference between the most-favoured-nation and preferential rates existing on April 10, 1947.

In the case of the contracting parties named in Annex G, the date of April 10, 1947, referred to in sub-paragraph (a) and (b) of this paragraph shall be replaced by the respective dates set forth in that Annex.

Interpretative Note *Ad* Article I from Annex I

Paragraph 1

The obligations incorporated in paragraph 1 of Article I by reference to paragraphs 2 and 4 of Article III and those incorporated in paragraph 2 (b) of Article II by reference to Article VI shall be considered as falling within Part II for the purposes of the Protocol of Provisional Application.

The cross-references, in the paragraph immediately above and in paragraph 1 of Article I, to paragraphs 2 and 4 of Article III shall only apply after Article III has been modified by the entry into force of the amendment provided for in the Protocol Modifying Part II and Article XXVI of the General Agreement on Tariffs and Trade, dated September 14, 1948.

Paragraph 4

The term "margin of preference" means the absolute difference between the most-favoured-nation rate of duty and the preferential rate of duty for the like product, and not the proportionate relation between those rates. As examples:

(1) If the most-favoured-nation rate were 36 per cent *ad valorem* and the preferential rate were 24 per cent *ad valorem*, the margin of preference would be 12 per cent *ad valorem*, and not one-third of the most-favoured-nation rate;

(2) If the most-favoured-nation rate were 36 per cent *ad valorem* and the preferential rate were expressed as two-thirds of the most-favoured-nation rate, the margin of preference would be 12 per cent *ad valorem*;

(3) If the most-favoured-nation rate were 2 francs per kilogramme and the preferential rate were 1.50 francs per kilogramme, the margin of preference would be 0.50 franc per kilogramme.

The following kinds of customs action, taken in accordance with established uniform procedures, would not be contrary to a general binding of margins of preference:

(i) The re-application to an imported product of a tariff classification or rate of duty, properly applicable to such product, in cases in which the application of such classification or rate to such product was temporarily suspended or inoperative on April 10, 1947; and

(ii) The classification of a particular product under a tariff item other than that under which importations of that product were classified on April 10, 1947, in cases in which the tariff law clearly contemplates that such product may be classified under more than one tariff item.

ANNEX A

LIST OF TERRITORIES REFERRED TO IN PARAGRAPH 2 (*a*) OF ARTICLE I

United Kingdom of Great Britain and Northern Ireland
Dependent territories of the United Kingdom of Great Britain and Northern Ireland
Canada
Commonwealth of Australia
Dependent territories of the Commonwealth of Australia
New Zealand
Dependent territories of New Zealand
Union of South Africa including South West Africa
Ireland
India (as on April 10, 1947)
Newfoundland
Southern Rhodesia
Burma
Ceylon

Certain of the territories listed above have two or more preferential rates in force for certain products. Any such territory may, by agreement with the other contracting parties which are principal suppliers of such products at the most-favoured-nation rate, substitute for such preferential rates a single preferential rate which shall not on the whole be less favourable to suppliers at the most-favoured-nation rate than the preferences in force prior to such substitution.

The imposition of an equivalent margin of tariff preference to replace a margin of preference in an internal tax existing on April 10, 1947 exclusively between two or more of the territories listed in this Annex or to replace the preferential quantitative arrangements described in the following paragraph, shall not be deemed to constitute an increase in a margin of tariff preference.

The preferential arrangements referred to in paragraph 5(*b*) of Article XIV are those existing in the United Kingdom on April 10, 1947, under contractual agreements with the Governments of Canada, Australia and New Zealand, in respect of chilled and frozen beef and veal, frozen mutton and lamb, chilled and frozen pork and bacon. It is the intention, without prejudice to any action taken under sub-paragraph (*h*) of Article XX, that these arrangements shall be eliminated or replaced by tariff preferences, and that negotiations to this end shall take place as soon as practicable among the countries substantially concerned or involved.

The film hire tax in force in New Zealand on April 10, 1947, shall, for the purposes of this Agreement, be treated as a customs duty under Article I. The renters' film quota in force in New Zealand on April 10, 1947, shall, for the purposes of this Agreement, be treated as a screen quota under Article IV.

The Dominions of India and Pakistan have not been mentioned separately in the above list since they had not come into existence as such on the base date of April 10, 1947.

ANNEX B

LIST OF TERRITORIES OF THE FRENCH UNION REFERRED TO IN PARAGRAPH 2 (*b*) OF ARTICLE I

France
French Equatorial Africa (Treaty Basin of the Congo[1] and other territories)
French West Africa
Cameroons under French Trusteeship[1]
French Somali Coast and Dependencies
French Establishments in Oceania
French Establishments in the Condominium of the New Hebrides[1]
Indo-China
Madagascar and Dependencies
Morocco (French zone)[1]
New Caledonia and Dependencies
Saint-Pierre and Miquelon
Togo under French Trusteeship[1]
Tunisia

[1] For imports into Metropolitan France and Territories of the French Union.

ARTICLE I - GENERAL MOST-FAVOURED-NATION TREATMENT

ANNEX C

LIST OF TERRITORIES REFERRED TO IN PARAGRAPH 2 (*b*) OF ARTICLE I
AS RESPECTS THE CUSTOMS UNION OF BELGIUM, LUXEMBURG
AND THE NETHERLANDS

The Economic Union of Belgium and Luxemburg
Belgian Congo
Ruanda Urundi
Netherlands
New Guinea
Surinam
Netherlands Antilles
Republic of Indonesia

For imports into the territories constituting the Customs Union only.

ANNEX D

LIST OF TERRITORIES REFERRED TO IN PARAGRAPH 2 (*b*)
OF ARTICLE I AS RESPECTS THE UNITED STATES OF AMERICA

United States of America (customs territory)
Dependent territories of the United States of America
Republic of the Philippines

The imposition of an equivalent margin of tariff preference to replace a margin of preference in an internal tax existing on April 10, 1947, exclusively between two or more of the territories listed in this Annex shall not be deemed to constitute an increase in a margin of tariff preference.

ANNEX E

LIST OF TERRITORIES COVERED BY PREFERENTIAL ARRANGEMENTS BETWEEN CHILE
AND NEIGHBOURING COUNTRIES REFERRED TO IN PARAGRAPH 2 (*d*) OF ARTICLE I

Preferences in force exclusively between Chile on the one hand, and

1. Argentina
2. Bolivia
3. Peru

on the other hand.

ANNEX F

LIST OF TERRITORIES COVERED BY PREFERENTIAL ARRANGEMENTS BETWEEN LEBANON
AND SYRIA AND NEIGHBOURING COUNTRIES REFERRED TO IN PARAGRAPH 2 (*d*) OF ARTICLE I

Preferences in force exclusively between the Lebano-Syrian Customs Union, on the one hand, and

1. Palestine
2. Transjordan

on the other hand.

ANNEX G

DATES ESTABLISHING MAXIMUM MARGINS OF PREFERENCE
REFERRED TO IN PARAGRAPH 4 OF ARTICLE I

Australia	October 15, 1946
Canada	July 1, 1939
France	January 1, 1939
Lebano-Syrian Customs Union	November 30, 1938
Union of South Africa	July 1, 1938
Southern Rhodesia	May 1, 1941

II. INTERPRETATION AND APPLICATION OF ARTICLE I

A. SCOPE AND APPLICATION OF ARTICLE I

1. Interpretation and Application of Paragraph 1

(1) "customs duties and charges of any kind imposed on or in connection with importation or exportation or the international transfer of payments for imports or exports"

(a) Unbound tariffs

The Panel Report on "Spain - Tariff Treatment of Unroasted Coffee" includes the following Panel finding: "Having noted that Spain had not bound under the GATT its tariff rate on unroasted coffee, the Panel pointed out that Article I:1 equally applied to bound and unbound tariff items".[1]

(b) "charges of any kind"

The Chairman of the CONTRACTING PARTIES ruled on 24 August 1948 that "consular taxes would be included in 'charges of any kind'; Article VIII merely dealt with the magnitude of such taxes in relation to the cost of services rendered, whereas Article I embodied the principle of non-discrimination". Consequently the application by Cuba of a 5 per cent consular tax to certain countries, but only of 2 per cent to others, was inconsistent with Article I.[2] The Panel on "United States Customs User Fee" found, in connection with an argument that exemptions from this fee were inconsistent with Article I:1, that "The Panel understood the argument that these exemptions were inconsistent with the obligations of Article I to be as follows: The merchandise processing fee was a charge imposed on or in connection with importation within the meaning of Article I:1. ... No answer in opposition to these legal claims was given, nor was the Panel aware of any that could be given".[3]

(c) Import surcharges

The Reports of the Working Parties on "United Kingdom Temporary Import Charges"[4] and "United States Temporary Import Surcharge"[5] each note the arguments of developing countries in favour of exempting from the surcharge products of developing countries or products of which developing countries were the principal supplier. These Reports also note the arguments in response that special exemption of imports by origin would produce trade diversion and, to the extent that it encouraged imports, delay removal of the surcharge.[6] The Report in 1971 of the Group of Three (constituted of the Chairmen of the CONTRACTING PARTIES, the Council and the Committee on Trade and Development) recommended that if the United States surcharge were maintained beyond 1 January 1972, "the United States Government should take steps to exempt imports from developing countries from the charge", and that the Danish temporary surcharge should exempt products covered by the Danish preference scheme for imports from developing countries.[7] The Working Party Report on the "Danish Temporary Import Surcharge" provides that "Without prejudice to the legal issues involved, the Working Party noted that as from the introduction of the Danish general preference scheme on 1 January 1972, products included in that scheme would be exempted from the surcharge when imported from members of the Group of Seventy-Seven. Several members of the Working Party welcomed this decision of the Danish Government noting that this had been one of the recommendations of the Group of Three. Other members expressed concern that the exemption did not extend to all developing countries. Some other members said that the discrimination created by these exemptions gave their delegations cause for concern".[8]

---

[1] L/5135, adopted on 11 June 1981, 28S/102,111, para. 4.3.
[2] II/12, CP.2/SR.11, pp. 7-8.
[3] L/6264, adopted on 2 February 1988, 35S/245, 289-290, paras. 122-123.
[4] L/2676, adopted on 17 November 1966, 15S/113, 115, para. 10.
[5] L/3573, adopted on 16 September 1971, 18S/212, 220-222, paras. 34-38.
[6] 15S/115-116, para. 10; 18S/218, para. 25.
[7] L/3610, 18S/70, 74, para. 17(ii) (US surcharge); 75, para. 20 (Danish surcharge).
[8] L/3648, adopted on 12 January 1972, 19S/120, 126, 129 (identical text in paras. 22 and 41).

Paragraph 2 of the 1979 Declaration on "Trade Measures Taken for Balance-of-Payments Purposes" provides that:

> "If, notwithstanding the principles of this Declaration, a developed contracting party is compelled to apply restrictive import measures for balance-of-payments purposes, it shall, in determining the incidence of its measures, take into account the export interests of the less-developed contracting parties and may exempt from its measures products of export interest to those contracting parties".[9]

A 1984 Statement by the Chairman of the Committee on Balance-of-Payments Restrictions to the Council, summarizing the result of discussions in 1982-83 concerning the work of the Committee and the role therein of balance-of-payments problems confronting heavily-indebted developing countries, notes *inter alia* that these discussions had endorsed the view that "any action taken in the balance-of-payments field should be consistent with the multilateral principles embodied in the General Agreement",[10] and adds:

> "In clear language this means that actions should be taken on a most-favoured-nation basis or, pursuant to the provisions of Part IV of the General Agreement (particularly Article XXXVII) and the 1979 Decision on Differential and More Favourable, Treatment, Reciprocity and Fuller Participation of Developing Countries, in a manner consistent with that decision, including special treatment for the least-developed among the developing countries. It was noted that Paragraph 2(c) of the Decision allows for the possibility of more favourable treatment to be accorded among developing contracting parties. ...

> "In view of the consensus to respect multilateral principles in responding to the needs of countries experiencing severe balance-of-payments difficulties, the possibility of focussing trade actions on such countries would depend on the choice of products for which a particular country is a principal or substantial supplier to a particular market, or on the choice of specific measures which would particularly benefit that country, it being understood that the implementation of each particular measure would be consistent with the multilateral principles referred to".[11]

(d) Variable levies

In 1961 Uruguay requested a ruling from the CONTRACTING PARTIES concerning whether the application of variable import duties was compatible with the General Agreement. A 1961 Note by the Executive Secretary on "Questions relating to Bilateral Agreements, Discrimination and Variable Taxes" states, *inter alia:*

> "... the question might arise as to whether a variable import duty is consistent with the provisions of Article I on most-favoured-nation treatment. This question can, however, hardly be discussed *a priori* without a knowledge of the exact nature of the measure in question or the manner in which it is operated".[12]

See also the discussion of this Note in summary records of the Nineteenth Session.[13] The 1962 Panel Report on the "Uruguayan Recourse to Article XXIII" notes as follows:

> "The Panel was faced with a particular difficulty in considering the status of variable import levies or charges. It noted the discussion which took place at the nineteenth session of the CONTRACTING PARTIES on this subject during which it was pointed out that such measures raised serious questions which had not been resolved. In these circumstances the Panel has not considered it appropriate to examine the consistency or otherwise of these measures under the General Agreement".[14]

---

[9]26S/206, 207; for background to this provision see Report of the Working Party on "United States Temporary Import Surcharge", L/3573, adopted 16 September 1971, 18S/212, 220-223, paras. 34-38, 40.
 [10]C/125, dated 13 March 1984, approved by the Council on 15/16 May 1984 (C/M/178, p. 26), 31S/56, 60, para. 13.
 [11]*Ibid.*, 31S/60-61, paras. 14, 16.
 [12]Note dated 21 November 1961, L/1636, para. 7.
 [13]SR.19/8, pp. 111-120.
 [14]L/1923, adopted 16 November 1962, 11S/95, 100, para. 17.

(e) Trade conducted at most-favoured-nation duty rates

A Note by the Director-General of 21 June 1972 on "Main Findings Concerning Trade at Most-favoured-nation and at Other Rates" presents data gathered by a working party, in response to a decision reached at the Twenty-seventh Session, from 34 governments concerning the share of trade at most-favoured-nation rates, at preferential rates, and at higher-than-most-favoured-nation rates for the years 1955, 1961, 1964 and 1970.[15]

(2) "the method of levying such duties and charges"

In November 1968, at the Twenty-fifth Session, the Director-General was asked for a ruling on whether parties to the Agreement on Implementation of Article VI of the General Agreement had a legal obligation under Article I of the General Agreement to apply the provisions of the Anti-Dumping Code in their trade with all GATT contracting parties. The Director-General replied that "In my judgment the words of Article I - 'the method of levying duties and charges (of any kind)' and 'all rules and formalities in connexion with importation' cover many of the matters dealt with in the Anti-Dumping Code, such as investigations to determine normal value or injury and the imposition of anti-dumping duties. ... Furthermore, for a contracting party to apply an improved set of rules for the interpretation and application of the GATT only in its trade with contracting parties which undertake to apply the same rules would introduce a conditional element into the most-favoured-nation obligations which, under Article I of GATT, are clearly unconditional".[16]

In 1980 a Panel was established to examine the complaint of India that "the United States action to levy countervailing duties on imports of dutiable products from India without applying injury criteria referred to in paragraph 6 of Article VI, while extending the benefit of such criteria to imports from some other contracting parties, is not consistent with the obligations of the United States under GATT, including the provisions of Article I thereof". However, the proceedings of the Panel were terminated in 1981 at the request of India, after resolution of the matter as a result of bilateral consultations between India and the United States.[17] See also references to this dispute at page 46 below.

In a discussion in 1985 of the application of "value-for-duty" legislation by Canada to garments imported from Hong Kong, it was stated that country-specific discriminatory mark-ups for customs valuation purposes were contrary to the provisions of Articles I and VII.[18]

(3) "all rules and formalities in connection with importation and exportation"

The Panel Report on "United States - Denial of Most-favoured-nation Treatment as to Non-rubber Footwear from Brazil" includes the following finding:

"The Panel considered that the rules and formalities applicable to countervailing duties, including those applicable to the revocation of countervailing duty orders, are rules and formalities imposed in connection with importation, within the meaning of Article I:1".[19]

(4) "matters referred to in paragraphs 2 and 4 of Article III"

This phrasing was inserted during the Geneva session of the Preparatory Committee in 1947, in order "to extend the grant of most-favoured-nation treatment to all matters dealt with in [these paragraphs] regardless of whether national treatment is provided for in respect of such matters".[20]

---

[15]Summing up by the Chairman at the Twenty-seventh Session, L/3641, 18S/37, 38, para. 4(d); Note by the Director-General, L/3708; see also discussion at C/M/78, C/M/79.
[16]L/3149, Note by the Director-General dated 29 November 1968.
[17]28S/113.
[18]C/M/165, p. 20; VAL/M/6, p. 9.
[19]DS18/R, adopted on 19 June 1992, 39S/128, 150, para. 6.8.
[20]US proposal at EPCT/W/146; annotated agenda, EPCT/W/150; EPCT/A/PV/7, p. 14.

In response to a request for an interpretation of paragraph 1 of Article I with respect to rebates of excise duties, the Chairman of the CONTRACTING PARTIES ruled on 24 August 1948 that "the most-favoured-nation treatment principle embodied in that paragraph would be applicable to any advantage, favour, privilege or immunity granted with respect to internal taxes".[21]

The 1952 Panel Report on "Belgian Family Allowances" discusses a Belgian system of tax exemptions for products imported from countries considered to have a system of family allowances similar to that of Belgium, in relation to Article I.[22] See below at page 33.

Under the Protocol Amending Part I and Articles XXIX and XXX of the General Agreement, which was agreed in the Review Session of 1954-55, the words "and with respect to the application of internal taxes to exported goods" would have been included in paragraph 1 to remove any uncertainty as to the application of Article I to discrimination in the exemption of exports from the levy of an excise tax.[23]

The Panel Report on "Japan - Trade in Semi-Conductors" examined, *inter alia*, measures by Japan to promote sales of foreign semi-conductors in Japan. The EEC claimed that Japan had thereby been granting preferential market access to US producers and exporters of semi-conductors and that, in the light of "the general tendency of the Agreement to address issues on a bilateral basis," this "could not but have discriminatory effects contrary to Article I of the General Agreement".[24] Japan denied that it granted preferential market access to the producers of the United States and claimed that its policy was to improve market access on a non-discriminatory basis.[25] The Panel considered these arguments but "found that the information submitted to it did not demonstrate that the Japanese measures to improve access to its market for semi-conductors favoured United States products inconsistently with Article I of the General Agreement".[26]

See also Interpretative Note *ad* Article I, paragraph 1.

(5) "any advantage, favour, privilege or immunity granted by any contracting party ..."

(a) Duty waiver conditional on certification by a particular government

The 1981 Panel Report on "European Economic Community - Imports of Beef from Canada" examined the compatibility with the General Agreement of EEC regulations implementing a levy-free tariff quota for high quality grain-fed beef; these regulations made suspension of the import levy for such beef conditional on production of a certificate of authenticity. The Panel found that "the only certifying agency authorized to certify the meat ... listed in Annex II of the Commission Regulation, was a United States agency mandated to certify only meat from the United States", and concluded "that Commission Regulation (EEC) No. 2972/79 ... had the effect of preventing access of 'like products' from other origin than the United States, thus being inconsistent with the most-favoured-nation principle in Article I of the General Agreement".[27]

(b) Export price monitoring schemes

The 1988 Panel Report on "Japan - Trade in Semi-Conductors" examined the argument of the EC that the system of third country market monitoring[28] instituted by the Japan-US Agreement on Trade in Semi-Conductors was inconsistent with Article I since it was only applied to Japanese exports to 16 countries, 14 of which were contracting parties. The system, the EEC claimed, violated Article I "to the extent that Japan granted immunity to all but the 14 contracting parties and that the Community did not benefit from the advantages granted to those

---

[21] II/12, CP.2/SR.11, CP.3/SR.19.
[22] G/32, adopted on 7 November 1952, 1S/59; GATT/CP.6/25 and Add.1.
[23] 3S/206, para. 3. This Protocol was abandoned as of 31 December 1967; see 15S/65.
[24] L/6309, adopted on 4 May 1988, 35S/116, 135-136, paras. 60- 61.
[25] *Ibid.*, 35S/136, para. 62.
[26] *Ibid.*, 35S/161, para. 127.
[27] L/5099, adopted on 10 March 1981, 28S/92, 98, paras. 4.2-4.3.
[28] This system, as described in a Japanese position paper, consisted essentially of two mechanisms: requests by the Government to producers and exporters that dumping should be avoided, and export approval and monitoring costs and export prices, cf. 35S/116, 120, paras. 19-20.

countries to which the system did not apply". The Panel found the Japanese measures to be inconsistent with Article XI:1 and "did not consider it necessary to make a finding on whether or not their administration was contrary to Article I:1 ... the Panel considered that, once a measure had been found to be inconsistent with the General Agreement whether or not it was applied discriminatorily, the question of its non-discriminatory administration was no longer legally relevant. The Panel noted that another Panel had also refrained from examining the alleged discriminatory aspects of a restriction after having found it to be inconsistent with Article XI".[29]

(c) Exemption from charges

In the panel proceeding on "United States - Customs User Fee",[30] Canada and the EEC requested the Panel to find the United States merchandise processing fee enacted by the Omnibus Budget and Reconciliation Act 1986 to be in breach of Articles II and VIII. India, an intervening party, "requested the Panel to consider whether the exemption contained in the merchandise processing fee legislation in favour of imports from least developed countries was consistent with the MFN obligations of Article I:1".[31] The issue was also raised by Australia and Singapore as intervening parties, but not by the two complainants which reserved their rights on the issue and did not object to the Panel dealing with it. The Panel refrained from a formal finding on the issue, in accordance with GATT practice, which it considered sound legal practice, to make findings only on those issues raised by the parties to the dispute. The Panel stated:

"The Panel understood the argument that these exemptions were inconsistent with the obligations of Article I to be as follows: The merchandise processing fee was a 'charge imposed on or in connection with importation' within the meaning of Article I:1. Exemptions from the fee fell within the category of 'advantage, favour, privilege or immunity' which Article I:1 required to be extended unconditionally to all other contracting parties. Such preferential exemptions therefore constituted a breach of the obligation of non-discrimination of Article I:1. The exemption from the fee granted to beneficiaries of the CBERA was not authorized by the waiver granting the US authority to extend duty-free treatment to these beneficiaries (31S/20). Nor was it authorized by the Enabling Clause of 28 November 1979 ... the relevant provisions of which authorized preferential tariff and non-tariff measures for the benefit of developing countries only if such measures conformed to the Generalized System of Preferences or to instruments multilaterally negotiated under GATT auspices. Nor, finally, did the Enabling Clause, cited above, authorize the preferential exemption from the merchandise processing fee for products from least developed developing countries. Under the Enabling Clause, special measures for least developed developing countries were permitted only if taken 'in the context of any general or specific measures in favour of developing countries'".[32]

(d) Actions with respect to countervailing duties

The Panel Report on "United States - Denial of Most-favoured-nation Treatment as to Non-rubber Footwear from Brazil" found that "... the automatic backdating of the effect of revocation of a preexisting countervailing duty order, without the necessity of the country subject to the order making a request for an injury review, is properly considered to be an advantage within the meaning of Article I:1".[33]

(6) "originating in" and country of origin

The wording "originating in" was deliberately chosen to exclude the concept of "provenance". As stated in the course of the discussion at the London session of the Preparatory Committee, "what you need ... to obtain the benefit of the minimum rates is to prove the origin and those rates would apply even if [the products] entered

---

[29]L/6309, adopted on 4 May 1988, 35S/116, 159, para. 122. The reference in the text is to the Panel Report on "Canada - Administration of the Foreign Investment Review Act", L/5504, adopted on 7 February 1984, 30S/140.
[30]L/6264, adopted 2 February 1988, 35S/245.
[31]*Ibid*, 35S/289, para. 121.
[32]*Ibid*., 35S/289-290, para. 122.
[33]DS18/R, adopted on 19 June 1992, 39S/128, 150, para. 6.9.

the importing country by way of a third country".[34] The Preparatory Committee did not consider it necessary to define these phrases and suggested that such a definition should be studied by the ITO.[35] A sub-committee of the Preparatory Committee at its Geneva session considered it "to be clear that it is within the province of each importing member country to determine in accordance with the provisions of its law for the purpose of applying the most-favoured-nation provision, whether goods had in fact originated in a particular country".[36]

The 1991 Panel Report on "United States - Restrictions on Imports of Tuna," which has not been adopted, examined, *inter alia*, the labelling provisions of the US Dolphin Protection Consumer Information Act (DPCIA), which provide that when a tuna product exported from or offered for sale in the United States bears the label "Dolphin Safe" or any similar label indicating it was fished in a manner not harmful to dolphins, this tuna product may not contain tuna harvested on the high seas by a vessel engaged in driftnet fishing, or harvested in the Eastern Tropical Pacific Ocean (ETP) by a vessel using a purse-seine net unless certain facts are certified under penalty of law. The use of such labels is not a requirement but is voluntary. The Panel examined Mexico's secondary argument that these provisions were inconsistent with Article I:1 because they discriminated against Mexico as a country whose exclusive economic zone was entirely in the ETP. The panel noted that the harvesting of tuna by intentionally encircling dolphins with purse-seine nets was practised only in the ETP because of the particular type of association between dolphins and tuna observed only in that area.

"By imposing the requirement to provide evidence that this fishing technique had not been used in respect of tuna caught in the ETP the United States therefore did not discriminate against countries fishing in this area. The Panel noted that, under United States customs law, the country of origin of fish was determined by the country of registry of the vessel that had caught the fish; the geographical area where the fish was caught was irrelevant for the determination of origin. The labelling regulations governing tuna caught in the ETP thus applied to all countries whose vessels fished in this geographical area and thus did not distinguish between products originating in Mexico and products originating in other countries.

"... The Panel found for these reasons that the tuna products labelling provisions of the DPCIA relating to tuna caught in the ETP were not inconsistent with the obligations of the United States under Article I:1 of the General Agreement."[37]

Concerning the work done in the GATT on rules of origin for goods, see under Article VIII. On marking of origin, see under Article IX.

(7) "shall be accorded immediately and unconditionally"

(a) Reciprocity clauses

The 1952 Report of the Working Party on the "International Convention to Facilitate the Importation of Commercial Samples and Advertising Material" notes concerning the draft text of the Convention: "A proposal to insert in the Convention a reciprocity clause was considered by the majority of the members of the Working Party to be inconsistent with Article I of the General Agreement".[38]

(b) Tax exemptions on condition of existence of a tax system of family allowances in the exporting country

The 1952 Panel Report on "Belgian Family Allowances" contains the following finding.

"According to the provisions of paragraph 1 of Article I of the General Agreement, any advantage, favour, privilege or immunity granted by Belgium to any product originating in the territory of any country with respect to all matters referred to in paragraph 2 of Article III shall be granted immediately and unconditionally to the like product originating in the territories of all contracting parties. Belgium has

---

[34] EPCT/C.II/PV/11, p. 9.
[35] London Report, p. 9; EPCT/C.II/PV/12, pp. 3-4.
[36] EPCT/174, p. 3.
[37] DS21/R (unadopted), dated 3 September 1991, 39S/155, 203-204, paras. 5.43-5.44.
[38] G/33, adopted on 7 November 1952, 1S/94, 98, para. 27.

granted exemption from the levy under consideration to products purchased by public bodies when they originate in Luxembourg and the Netherlands, as well as in France, Italy, Sweden and the United Kingdom. ... it is clear that that exemption would have to be granted unconditionally to all other contracting parties. The consistency or otherwise of the system of family allowances in force in the territory of a given contracting party with the requirements of the Belgian law would be irrelevant in this respect, and the Belgian legislation would have to be amended insofar as it introduced a discrimination between countries having a given system of family allowances and those which had a different system or no system at all, and made the granting of the exemption dependent on certain conditions."[39]

(c) Exemptions on condition of minimum import price guarantees

In the 1978 Panel Report on "EEC - Programme of Minimum Import Prices, Licences and Surety Deposits for Certain Processed Fruits and Vegetables"

"The Panel ... examined the provision for an exemption from the lodging of the additional security associated with the minimum import price for tomato concentrates in relation to the obligations of the Community under Article I:1. The Panel noted that Article 10 of Council Regulation (EEC) No. 516/77 stated that the 'lodging of such additional security shall not be required for products originating in non-member countries which undertake, and are in a position, to guarantee that the price on import into the Community shall be not less than the minimum price for the product in question, and that all deflection of trade will be avoided'. The Panel noted the argument by the representative of the United States that this provision amounted to conditional most-favoured-nation treatment inconsistent with Article I:1 of the General Agreement, since it removed one of the requirements for certain countries while leaving a burden on other countries. The Panel further noted the argument by the representative of the Community that this provision did not make any distinction based on the economic system or any other factor between third suppliers and that the possibility to guarantee that the minimum price would be respected was open to all unconditionally. The Panel considered that, regardless of whether a guarantee had to be provided by the importer or the government of the exporting country, so long as a guarantee was necessary for all imports from all potential third country suppliers, there would be no discrimination within the meaning of Article I:1. Therefore the Panel concluded that the provision for an exemption from the lodging of the additional security associated with the minimum import price for tomato concentrates was not inconsistent with the obligations of the Community under Article I:1".[40]

(d) Reservation of import quotas for outward processing traffic

During the discussions on proposals regarding the extension, modification or discontinuance of the Protocol Extending the Arrangement Regarding International Trade in Textiles in the ninth meeting of the Textiles Committee under the Arrangement as extended in 1977, several signatory states considered the proposed reservation of a portion of import quotas for outward processing traffic as being not consistent with either the Arrangement Regarding International Trade in Textiles or the provisions of GATT, in particular Article I.[41]

(e) Tariff treatment conditional on the existence of a co-operation contract

The 1973 Working Party Report on the "Accession of Hungary" notes the view of several delegations that the implementation of the regulations submitted by the Hungarian delegation with respect to co-operation contracts (countertrade), in particular as regards the question of tariff exemptions and reductions granted in this framework, would be inconsistent with Article I of the General Agreement. In response to a request for a legal opinion, "the GATT secretariat, while emphasizing that questions of interpretations of the General Agreement were matters for the CONTRACTING PARTIES and not for the secretariat, gave certain comments, *inter alia* that the prerequisite of having a co-operation contract in order to benefit from certain tariff treatment appeared to imply conditional most-favoured-nation treatment and would, therefore, not appear to be compatible with the General Agreement".[42]

---

[39] G/32, adopted on 7 November 1952, 1S/59, 60, para. 3.
[40] L/4687, adopted on 18 October 1978, 25S/68, 106, para. 4.19.
[41] COM.TEX/W/127.
[42] L/3889, adopted on 30 July 1973, 20S/34, 36, para. 12.

(f)   Special treatment for diplomatic gifts, supplies and equipment accorded on the basis of reciprocity

The Report of the Review Session Working Party on "Schedules and Customs Administration" records that:

> "Referring to the provisions for most-favoured-nation treatment, the representative of Germany informed the Working Party that German customs law requires that special treatment for gifts to heads of foreign states, equipment for diplomatic and consular offices and goods for the use of representatives of foreign governments may be granted only on a basis of reciprocity, thus not permitting observance of most-favoured-nation obligations for such imports. Many other countries follow the same practice. The Working Party took note of this situation and saw no reason why established practice in these cases should be disturbed".[43]

(g)   Application to individual cases and "balancing"

The Panel Report on "United States - Denial of Most-favoured-nation Treatment as to Non-rubber Footwear from Brazil" states with respect to Article I:1:

> "The Panel ... considered that Article I:1 does not permit balancing more favourable treatment under some procedure against a less favourable treatment under others. If such a balancing were accepted, it would entitle a contracting party to derogate from the most-favoured-nation obligation in one case, in respect of one contracting party, on the ground that it accords more favourable treatment in some other case in respect of another contracting party. In the view of the Panel, such an interpretation of the most-favoured-nation obligation of Article I:1 would defeat the very purpose underlying the unconditionality of that obligation".[44]

(8)   "like product"

(a)   General

During discussions at the London session of the Preparatory Committee, it was stated that "the expression had different meanings in different contexts of the Draft Charter".[45] The Preparatory Committee did not think it necessary to define this phrase and recommended that such definition be studied by the ITO.[46] Both at that time and later at the Havana Conference, it was suggested that the method of tariff classification could be used for determining whether products were "like products" or not.[47]

See also the discussion of "like product" in the context of Article III:2 and III:4. The term "like product" or "like domestic product" is used in several other GATT provisions as well, including Articles II:2(a); VI:1(a); VI:1(b); IX:1; XI:2(c); XIII:1; and XVI:4. Other terms such as "like commodity" (Article VI:7), "like merchandise" (Article VII:2), and "like or competitive products" (Article XIX:1) also occur. See also the classification problems arising under Articles II and XXIV:5 ("corresponding duties").

The Panel Report on "United States - Denial of Most-favoured-nation Treatment as to Non-rubber Footwear from Brazil" notes with reference to this concept:

> "The Panel noted that Article I would in principle permit a contracting party to have different countervailing duty laws and procedures for different categories of products, or even to exempt one category of products from countervailing duties altogether. The mere fact that one category of products is treated one way by the United States and another category of products is treated another is therefore in principle not inconsistent with the most-favoured-nation obligation of Article I:1. However, this provision clearly prohibits a

---

[43] L/329, adopted 26 February 1955, 3S/205, 206 para. 3.
[44] DS18/R, adopted on 19 June 1992, 39S/128, 151, para. 6.10.
[45] EPCT/C.II/65, p. 2.
[46] EPCT/C.II/PV/12, pp. 6-7; London Report, p. 9, para. A.1(c).
[47] EPCT/C.II/PV/12, p. 7-8; E/CONF.2/C.3/SR.5, p. 4.

contracting party from according an advantage to a product originating in another country while denying the same advantage to a *like product* originating in the territories of other contracting parties".[48]

(b) Examination of "like product" issues in particular cases

The 1950 Report of the Working Party on "The Australian Subsidy on Ammonium Sulphate" examined a claim by Chile regarding the following facts: the Australian government had formerly subsidized the distribution of both imported and domestic ammonium sulphate and imported sodium nitrate fertilizers, and had ceased to subsidize distribution of imported sodium nitrate; the subsidy on ammonium sulphate was maintained because its users were subject to price ceilings, while the agricultural producers who used most of the sodium nitrate were not.

"As regards the applicability of Article I to the Australian measure, the working party noted that the General Agreement made a distinction between 'like products' and 'directly competitive or substitutable products'. This distinction is clearly brought out in Article III, paragraph 2, read in conjunction with the interpretative note to that paragraph. The most-favoured-nation treatment clause in the General Agreement is limited to 'like products'. Without trying to give a definition of 'like products', and leaving aside the question of whether the two fertilizers are directly competitive, the working party reached the conclusion that they were not to be considered as 'like products' within the terms of Article I. In the Australian tariff the two products are listed as separate items and enjoy different treatment. ... In the tariffs of other countries the two products are listed separately. In certain cases the rate is the same, but in others the treatment is different. ..."[49]

The 1978 Panel Report on "EEC - Measures on Animal Feed Proteins" examined EEC measures requiring domestic producers or importers of oilseeds, cakes and meals, dehydrated fodder and compound feeds and importers of corn gluten feed to purchase and denature skimmed milk powder held by EEC intervention agencies, as a condition for the receipt of production subsidies (in the case of domestic producers) or as a condition on importation (in the case of importers). A security deposit could be substituted for proof of such purchase; the amount of the security varied depending on the type of feed. Examining *inter alia* a claim by the United States that, as proteins added to animal feeds should be considered to be like products, the requirement of different levels of security deposit for different vegetable proteins was inconsistent with Article I:1,

"The Panel began by examining whether all products used for the same purpose of adding protein to animal feeds should be considered to be 'like products' within the meaning of Articles I and III. Having noted that the General Agreement gave no definition of the concept of 'like product', the Panel reviewed how it had been applied by the CONTRACTING PARTIES in previous cases.[50]

"The Panel noted, in this case, such factors as the number of products and tariff items carrying different duty rates and tariff bindings, the varying protein contents and the different vegetable, animal and synthetic origins of the protein products before the Panel - not all of which were subject to the EEC measures. Therefore, the Panel concluded that these various protein products could not be considered as 'like products' within the meaning of Articles I and III".[51]

"The Panel noted that the general most-favoured-nation treatment provided for in Article I:1 applied to 'like products' regardless of territorial origin but did not mention 'directly competitive or substitutable products'. In this regard the Panel did not consider animal, marine and synthetic proteins to be products like those vegetable proteins covered by the measures. The Panel also noted that a significant proportion of EEC imports of 'like products', including soybeans, subject to the measures originated from contracting parties other than the United States".[52]

---

[48]DS18/R, adopted on 19 June 1992, 39S/128, 151, para. 6.11.
[49]GATT/CP.4/39, adopted on 3 April 1950, II/188, 191, para. 8.
[50]The footnote to this sentence provides: "For instance BISD II/188, BISD 1S/53, BISD II/181, 183".
[51]L/4599, adopted on 14 March 1978, 25S/49, 63, paras. 4.1-4.2.
[52]*Ibid.*, 25S/68, para. 4.20.

The 1981 Panel Report on "Spain - Tariff Treatment of Unroasted Coffee" examined a claim of Brazil under Article I:1 with respect to a Spanish Royal Decree which divided unroasted coffee into five tariff classifications: "Colombian mild," "other mild," "unwashed Arabica," "Robusta" and "other". The first two were duty-free and the latter three were subject to a duty of 7 per cent *ad valorem*; the tariff on raw coffee was unbound.

"The Panel found that there was no obligation under the GATT to follow any particular system for classifying goods, and that a contracting party had the right to introduce in its customs tariff new positions or sub-positions as appropriate.[53] The Panel considered, however, that whatever the classification adopted, Article I:1 required that the same tariff treatment be applied to 'like products'. The Panel therefore.. focused its examination on whether the various types of unroasted coffee listed in the Royal Decree 1764/79 should be regarded as 'like products' within the meaning of Article I:1. Having reviewed how the concept of 'like products' had been applied by the CONTRACTING PARTIES in previous cases involving, *inter alia*, a recourse to Article I:1,[54] the Panel noted that neither the General Agreement nor the settlement of previous cases gave any definition of such concept.

"The Panel examined all arguments that had been advanced during the proceedings for the justification of a different tariff treatment for various groups and types of unroasted coffee. It noted that these arguments mainly related to organoleptic differences resulting from geographical factors, cultivation methods, the processing of the beans, and the genetic factor. The Panel did not consider that such differences were sufficient reason to allow for a different tariff treatment. It pointed out that it was not unusual in the case of agricultural products that the taste and aroma of the end-product would differ because of one or several of the above-mentioned factors.

"The Panel furthermore found relevant to its examination of the matter that unroasted coffee was mainly, if not exclusively, sold in the form of blends, combining various types of coffee, and that coffee in its end-use, was universally regarded as a well-defined and single product intended for drinking.

"The Panel noted that no other contracting party applied its tariff régime in respect of unroasted, non-decaffeinated coffee in such a way that different types of coffee were subject to different tariff rates.

"In the light of the foregoing, the Panel *concluded* that unroasted, non-decaffeinated coffee beans listed in the Spanish Customs Tariff ... should be considered as 'like products' within the meaning of Article I:1.

"The Panel further noted that Brazil exported to Spain mainly 'unwashed Arabica' and also Robusta coffee which were both presently charged with higher duties than that applied to 'mild' coffee. Since these were considered to be 'like products', the Panel *concluded* that the tariff régime as presently applied by Spain was discriminatory vis-à-vis unroasted coffee originating in Brazil"[55] and "not in conformity with the provision of Article I:1".[56]

The 1989 Panel Report on "Canada/Japan: Tariff on Imports of Spruce, Pine, Fir (SPF) Dimension Lumber" examined Canada's claim that Japan's application of an 8 percent tariff on imports of SPF "dimension lumber" (surfaced softwood lumber designed for use as framing members in construction) was inconsistent with Article I:1 because SPF dimension lumber and dimension lumber of other types, which benefited from a zero duty rate, were "like products" within the meaning of Article I:1. Citing documents dealing with the drafting history and interpretation of the "like products" concept[57] Japan argued that these were different products, in practical terms, physical origins, characteristics, end-uses, consumer perception, etc. and so were not "like products" in the sense of Article I:1; Japan noted that concessions distinguished by species had been exchanged and upheld in successive GATT tariff negotiations.[58] Canada argued that past panels had considered the interpretation of the

---

[53]The footnote to this sentence provides: "Provided that a reclassification subsequent to the making of a concession under the GATT would not be a violation of the basic commitment regarding that concession (Article II:5)".
[54]The footnote to this sentence refers to BISD Vol. II/188; 1S/53; 25S/49; 27S/98.
[55]L/5135, adopted 11 June 1981, 28S/102, 111-112, paras. 4.4-4.10 *passim*.
[56]*Ibid.* 28S/112, para. 4.11.
[57]References given are to EPCT/C/II/65 p. 2; EPCT/C.II/PV.12 p. 7; EPCT/C.II/36 p. 8; E/CONF.2/C.III/SR.5 p. 4; GATT/CP/4/39 para. 8; IC/SR.9 p. 2; BISD 25S/49-53; and BISD 28S/92-98.
[58]L/6470, adopted on 19 July 1989, 36S/167, 180, paras. 3.19-3.20.

"like product concept" to be the same in both Articles I and III, and that because these were trade-creating obligations a narrow definition of like products would not be appropriate; Japan argued that they were not the same.[59]

"... In substance, Canada complains of the fact that Japan had arranged its tariff classification in such a way that a considerable part of Canadian exports of SPF dimension lumber to Japan was submitted to a customs duty of 8 per cent, whereas other comparable types of dimension lumber enjoy the advantage of a zero-tariff duty. The Panel considered it impossible to appreciate fully the Canadian complaint if it had not in a preliminary way clarified the bearing of some principles of the GATT-system in relation to tariff structure and tariff classification.

"The Panel noted in this respect that the General Agreement left wide discretion to the contracting parties in relation to the structure of national tariffs and the classification of goods in the framework of such structure ... The adoption of the Harmonized System, to which both Canada and Japan have adhered, had brought about a large measure of harmonization in the field of customs classification of goods, but this system did not entail any obligation as to the ultimate detail in the respective tariff classifications. Indeed, this nomenclature has been on purpose structured in such a way that it leaves room for further specifications.

"The Panel was of the opinion that, under these conditions, a tariff classification going beyond the Harmonized System's structure is a legitimate means of adapting the tariff scheme to each contracting party's trade policy interests, comprising both its protection needs and its requirements for the purposes of tariff- and trade negotiations. ...

"Tariff differentiation being basically a legitimate means of trade policy, a contracting party which claims to be prejudiced by such practice bears the burden of establishing that such tariff arrangement has been diverted from its normal purpose so as to become a means of discrimination in international trade. Such complaints have to be examined in considering simultaneously the internal protection interest involved in a given tariff specification, as well as its actual or potential influence on the pattern of imports from different extraneous sources ..."[60]

"... if a claim of likeness was raised by a contracting party in relation to the tariff treatment of its goods on importation by some other contracting party, such a claim should be based on the classification of the latter, i.e. the importing country's tariff.

"The Panel noted in this respect that 'dimension lumber' as defined by Canada was a concept extraneous to the Japanese Tariff ... nor did it belong to any internationally accepted customs classification. The Panel concluded therefore that reliance by Canada on the concept of dimension lumber was not an appropriate basis for establishing 'likeness' of products under Article I:1 of the General Agreement.

"At the same time, the Panel felt unable to examine the Canadian complaint in a broader context ... Canada did not contend that different lumber species *per se* should be considered like products, regardless of the product-form they might take ... Thus there appeared to be no basis for examining the issue raised by Canada in the general context of the Japanese tariff classification."[61]

In Council discussion when this panel report was adopted, Canada raised the concern that "this interpretation could lead to pre-eminence being given to the tariff classification of a contracting party when determining 'like products' under Article I ... this interpretation could well preclude a contracting party from exercising its rights under Article I:1 for equal treatment of like products if the products involved were not specifically identified in the tariff classification system of the importing contracting party. The Harmonized System of tariff classification was not designed with Article I:1 rights in mind ... Tariff classification systems cannot identify specifically each and every possible product which may be imported. In the tariff classification system of contracting parties it is regularly the case that an individual tariff line or description will cover a wide range of different products,

---

[59]*Ibid.*, 36S/186-187, paras. 3.37-3.39.
[60]*Ibid.*, 36S/197-198, paras. 5.7-5.10.
[61]*Ibid.*, 36S/199, paras. 5.13-5.15.

particularly in the example of lines which read 'other' or 'not elsewhere specified'. Additionally, there are new products continually entering the marketplace which are not identified in tariff schedules".[62]

The 1990 Panel Report on "European Economic Community - Regulation on Imports of Parts and Components" examined Japan's claim that the imposition of anti-dumping duties on certain products assembled inside the Community on the basis of an earlier anti-dumping order applicable to imports of finished products was not permissible under Articles VI or XX (d) and thus violated Articles I, II, III and VI. During the dispute, "Japan pointed out that Article 13:10 of Council Regulation (EEC) No. 2423/88 provided for the imposition of duties on products produced or assembled in the EEC on the basis of the proportion of parts imported from Japan used in the production or assembly of such products. As such, these duties could be seen as a special type of customs duties levied on parts imported from Japan ... If one considered the duties imposed under Article 13:10 as customs duties on imported parts, these duties violated Article I:1 of the General Agreement because they were imposed only on parts imported from Japan; thus, discrimination occurred between parts originating in Japan and like products of third countries".[63] The Panel made no finding with respect to this claim.

The 1992 Panel Report on "United States - Denial of Most-favoured-nation Treatment as to Non-rubber Footwear from Brazil" examined a claim relating to the automatic backdating of the effect of revocation of a countervailing duty order (see above at page 32).

"The Panel ... examined whether the products to which the United States had accorded the advantage of automatic backdating are like the products to which this advantage had been denied. The Panel noted that the products to which the procedures under Section 331 of the Trade Act of 1974 had actually been applied (industrial fasteners, industrial lime, automotive glass) are not like the product to which Section 104(b) of the Trade Agreements Act of 1979 had been applied in the case of Brazil (non-rubber footwear). However, the Panel also noted that Brazil not only claimed that the application of these two Acts in concrete cases was inconsistent with Article I:1 of the General Agreement but also that the United States' legislation itself was inconsistent with that provision. The Panel recalled that neither Section 331 of the 1974 Act nor Section 104(b) of the 1979 Act makes any distinction as to the particular products to which each applies, other than that the former applies to duty-free products originating in the territories of contracting parties and the latter applies to dutiable products originating in the territories of contracting parties signatories to the Subsidies Agreement. The products to which Section 331 of the 1974 Act accords the advantage of automatic backdating are therefore in principle the same products to which Section 104(b) of the 1979 Act denies the advantage of automatic backdating".[64]

(c) Price discrimination

The 1978 Note by the GATT Secretariat on "Modalities of Application of Article XIX" notes concerning actions notified as having been taken under Article XIX that

"A number of actions of a quantitative and tariff-type nature have been linked to the price of the products concerned. In practice, such measures, although applied on a global basis, may have been selective in their application to one or a limited number of countries. In the current ten-year period, ten such instances have been notified, compared to eight during the preceding twenty years. Some of these measures took the form of special customs valuation methods levied for imports at lower prices during a short agricultural or horticultural season. In addition to these measures, there were a few cases in the earlier years where specific duties or sur-taxes were replaced by ad valorem rates".[65]

In Council discussion of a 1977 Article XIX action by Finland imposing a surcharge on imports of pantyhose (tights) below a basic price, the representative of Singapore noted that Article XIX referred to "any product" and

---

[62] L/6528; see also C/M/232, p. 9-12; C/M/234, p. 44-49; C/M/235, p. 15-18.
[63] L/6657, adopted on 16 May 1990, 37S/132, 147, para. 3.32.
[64] DS18/R, adopted on 19 June 1992, 39S/128, 151-152, para. 6.12.
[65] L/4679, para. 45.

stated that this action was aimed at low-cost suppliers in developing countries. The representative of Finland stated that the measure was fully in accordance with Article XIX.[66]

During discussion in the Committee on Trade and Development in March 1983 of a Canadian Article XIX action on leather footwear, which exempted footwear above a certain value, it was stated that "This price discrimination was not only contrary to the letter and spirit of Article XIX, but also established a dangerous precedent, and had an adverse effect on the export interests of developing countries. The representative of Canada stated that in the view of his authorities, the Article XIX action referred to ... was consistent with the relevant provisions of the General Agreement, and the price discrimination element in the action did not constitute a new precedent under the GATT". Several other contracting parties expressed concern at the price-discriminatory use of Article XIX and stated that they regarded a discrimination between suppliers, either geographically or on the basis of prices, as an infringement of GATT rules.[67] Canada's Article XIX action on imports of footwear was discussed again in the GATT Council meeting in March 1985. Concern was expressed at "Canada's application of price breaks in the context of this Article XIX action. Such devices could produce such a narrow and selective definition of source that the action could no longer be said to be truly non-discriminatory. This would appear to conflict with the fundamental principles of the General Agreement".[68]

2. Paragraphs 2 and 4: Historical preferences and margins of preference

For a general discussion of the negotiating history of the provisions of Article I on historical preferences, see section III below.

The interpretative Note *ad* Article I:4 provides that the margin of preference is the absolute difference between the most-favoured-nation rate of duty and the preferential rate of duty for the like product and not the proportionate relation between those rates; this definition was decided on (during the Geneva negotiations on the General Agreement) because of the difficulty of calculating a percentage margin when the preferential rate is zero, and because it was determined that only the absolute size of the margin, and not the percentage difference, was economically meaningful.[69]

In discussions at the London session of the Preparatory Committee, it was agreed that the exemption to the most-favoured-nation clause for historical preferences refers only to preferences in the form of tariff margins and has "nothing to do with quotas or quantitative restrictions".[70]

The present form of Annex B (territories of the French Union) reflects the deletion in 1955 of certain territories, which had been raised to the status of French départements on 1 January 1948 and then formed part of the metropolitan customs territory.[71]

Many of the historical preferences referred to in paragraph 2 have been subsequently changed or terminated, although some still exist.

(1) Modification of margins of preference

(a) Relationship between negotiated reductions in the most-favoured-nation duty rate and the margin of preference

The rules for the tariff negotiations conducted in 1947 at the Geneva session of the Preparatory Committee, in connection with the conclusion of the General Agreement, referred to the provisions in Article 24 of the

---

[66]C/M/119 p. 21-22.
[67]COM.TD/114, p. 10, paras. 41-43.
[68]C/M/186, p. 5.
[69]EPCT/230; EPCT/TAC/PV/16, pp. 21-35. The method of calculation of margins of preference in paragraph 4 was utilized in the 1949 Report of the Working Party on "Brazilian Internal Taxes," GATT/CP.3/42, II/181, 183-184, paras. 11-12.
[70]EPCT/C.II/PV/4, p. 35; EPCT/C.II/PV/12, p. 9. See also Article XXIV:5(a).
[71]Fourth Protocol of Rectifications and Modifications to the Annexes and to the Texts of the Schedules of the General Agreement (done 7 March 1955, entered into force 23 January 1959); see also W.9/162. See also discussion of status of territories within French Union as of 1946 at EPCT/C.II/PV/4 p. 18-20.

London Draft Charter that "Prior international commitments shall not be permitted to stand in the way of negotiations with respect to tariff preferences, it being understood that action resulting from such negotiations shall not require the modification of existing international obligations except by agreement between the contracting parties or, failing that, by termination of such obligations in accordance with their terms. All negotiated reductions in most-favoured-nation tariffs shall operate automatically to reduce or eliminate margins of preference". These rules further stated that "all margins of preference remaining after negotiations would be bound against increase".[72]

Similarly, the procedures for the Annecy tariff conference of 1949 and the Torquay tariff conference of 1950 each provided that

"The negotiations will be conducted in accordance with the rules set forth in paragraph 2 of Article 17 of the Havana Charter, *i.e.*,

...

"(c) in negotiations relating to any specific product with respect to which a preference applies,

   (i) when a reduction is negotiated only in the most-favoured-nation rate, such reduction shall operate automatically to reduce or eliminate the margin of preference applicable to that product;
   (ii) when a reduction is negotiated only in the preferential rate, the most-favoured-nation rate shall automatically be reduced to the extent of such reduction;
   (iii) when it is agreed that reductions will be negotiated in both the most-favoured-nation rate and the preferential rate, the reduction in each shall be that agreed by the parties to the negotiations; and
   (iv) no margin of preference shall be increased. ...

"(e) Prior international obligations shall not be invoked to frustrate negotiations with respect to preferences, it being understood that agreements which result from such negotiations and which conflict with such obligations shall not require the modification or termination of existing international obligations except with the consent of the parties to such obligations, or in the absence of such consent by modification or termination of such obligations in accordance with their terms".[73]

The procedures for the 1956 tariff conference and for the Dillon Round in 1960-61 provided that "In so far as negotiations relate to preferences, the applicable provisions of the General Agreement shall be applied in accordance with the rules, as relevant, followed hitherto in negotiations sponsored by the CONTRACTING PARTIES".[74]

During the Third Session, held at Annecy in 1949, Cuba sought a ruling that the reduction of most-favoured-nation tariff rates by the United States in the tariff negotiations conducted at that time at Annecy would be inconsistent with the provisions of a bilateral trade agreement between Cuba and the United States predating the General Agreement, which guaranteed certain percentage margins of preference. On 9 August 1949 the CONTRACTING PARTIES adopted a Decision on "Margins of Preference" which provided *inter alia*, that "A margin of preference, on an item included in either or both parts of a schedule, is not bound against decrease by the provisions of the General Agreement. This decision does not preclude the possibility of resort to Article XXIII".[75]

---

[72]London Report, p. 49. See also the discussion of the effect of preferences on tariff negotiations, in the Sub-Committee on Procedures (which drafted the procedures for the Geneva 1947 negotiations): EPCT/C.II/PRO/PV/12.

[73]Procedures Adopted for Torquay Tariff Conference, I/104-105, para. 3; Memorandum on Tariff Negotiations to be held in Geneva commencing 11 April 1949, adopted 31 August 1948, GATT/CP.2/SR.15, p. 5, GATT/CP.2/26, para. III.1.

[74]"Rules and Procedures for the Tariff Conference commencing in Geneva on 18 January 1956", 4S/79, 81, para. 11(d); "Rules and Procedures for the Tariff Conference commencing in Geneva on 1 September 1960", 8S/114, 118, para. VII(d).

[75]Decision of 9 August 1949 on "Margins of Preference", II/11; see also draft decision and footnote in GATT/CP.3/71, statements of Cuba in GATT/CP.3/63 and GATT/CP.3/89, discussion at GATT/CP.3/SR.34-SR.38, and adoption of ruling and footnote by vote at GATT/CP.3/SR.38 p. 6-9. See also discussion of related Cuban legal claims and Article XXIII at II/152-153 paras. 22-25. See also reference to this Decision at pages 41, 45 below.

(b) Increase in margins of preference

It was stated during the negotiation of the General Agreement text in 1947 "that negotiations should not lead to the increase of margins of preference. This appears in Article 17 [of the Geneva Draft Charter], and is in fact our guiding thread to this Article".[76]

At the Review Session in 1954-1955, reference was made to the rigid "no-new-preference rule ... contained in Article I".[77] Proposals to amend Article I:4 or Article XXIV to permit increase in margins of preference, even by negotiation, were unsuccessful; the Review Working Party on Schedules and Customs Administration which examined these proposals considered that the objectives of these proposals could best be sought by an application for a suitable waiver.[78] In 1954, Italy brought a complaint against the imposition by France of a temporary compensation tax on certain imports, from which certain imports from the French Union were exempted. During the 1954-55 Review Session the CONTRACTING PARTIES adopted conclusions that "the tax has increased the incidence of customs charges in excess of maximum rates bound under Article II, and the application of this tax introduces, in respect of the products affected, an increase in the incidence of preferences in excess of the maximum margins permissible under Article I; and it follows that the action of the French Government justifies the invocation of the provisions of Article XXIII and that any contracting party whose trade is adversely affected has grounds to propose under paragraph 2 of that Article such compensatory action as it may think appropriate for authorization by the CONTRACTING PARTIES".[79]

For examples of examination of preferential margins in the light of the rules in Article I on margins of preference, see the 1971 Panel Report on "Jamaica - Margins of Preference"[80] and the 1969 Working Party Report on "Malawi Tariff Preferences - Preferential Margins".[81]

See also Article XXIV:9 and its interpretative note regarding the coexistence of margins of preference and customs unions or free-trade areas, and the adjustment of preferences by negotiation in conjunction with the formation of a customs union or free-trade area.

(c) Reinstatement of historical preferences

The wording "existing on 10 April 1947" in paragraph 4 was adopted in order to "include rates or margins which had legal existence on the base date but were not actually applied".[82] The Interpretative Note to paragraph 4 provides that the re-application to an imported product of a tariff classification or rate of duty, properly applicable to such product, in cases in which the application of such classification or rate to such product was temporarily suspended or inoperative on April 10, 1947, is not contrary to a general binding of margins of preference if taken in accordance with established uniform procedures.

(d) Change in historical preferences due to tariff reclassification

The Interpretative Note to paragraph 4 provides that the classification of a particular product under a tariff item other than that under which importations of that product were classified on April 10, 1947, in cases in which the tariff law clearly contemplates that such product may be classified under more than one tariff item, is not contrary to a general binding of margins of preference if taken in accordance with established uniform procedures. However, the preparatory work indicates that it was understood that the "general provisions relating to the binding

---

[76] EPCT/TAC/PV.9, p. 16.
[77] SR.9/17, p. 3.
[78] L/329, adopted 26 February 1955, 3S/205, 207-208 para. 6 (proposals by Australia, New Zealand, Chile). See also the waivers of Article I:4 granted to the United Kingdom in 1953 for increases in margins of preference for items admitted duty-free from the Commonwealth (2S/20, amended at 3S/25) and in 1955 for preferential treatment for imports from overseas territories for whose international relations it is responsible (3S/21).
[79] Decision of 17 January 1955 on "French Special Temporary Compensation Tax on Imports", 3S/26, 27; see discussion and adoption at SR.9/28, 29; see also reference to this decision at 6S/96 para. 20.
[80] L/3485, adopted on 2 February 1971, 18S/183.
[81] L/3194, adopted 15 April 1969, 17S/156.
[82] EPCT/174, p. 5.

of margins would not override specific undertakings in the tariff schedules to maintain particular products under a particular tariff classification".[83]

(2) Base dates for purposes of paragraph 4 and Annex G, and modification thereof

The date of 10 April 1947 referred to in paragraph 4 was the opening date of the Second Session (held in Geneva) of the Preparatory Committee for the Havana Conference;[84] for those countries listed in Annex G this date is replaced by the dates specified in Annex G, except as modified by the waiver decisions listed below.

The 1971 Panel Report on "Jamaica - Margins of Preference" examined the base date applicable to Jamaica under Article I:4 and its implications for increases in margins of preference after 10 April 1947 and before the date of succession to the rights and obligations of a contracting party under Article XXVI:5(c).

"The Panel held that since Jamaica had acceded to the General Agreement on Tariffs and Trade under the provisions of Article XXVI:5(c) it had acquired the rights and obligations which had previously been accepted by the United Kingdom in respect of the territory of Jamaica. This meant that Jamaica assumed the rights and obligations involved in the application to it of the General Agreement by the United Kingdom before Jamaica became independent. On 6 August 1962, the day Jamaica became independent, Article I:4 formed part of the General Agreement as it had been applied by the United Kingdom on behalf of the territory of Jamaica. The provision of Article I:4 establishing 10 April 1947 as the base date for permissible margins of preference was therefore applicable to Jamaica".[85]

However, on recommendation of this Panel, a waiver changing the base date was granted to Jamaica; see below.

The date "April 10, 1947" under Article I:4 is replaced by other dates in certain protocols of accession:

- Cambodia, by "1 September 1960", Protocol of Accession, 11S/13, para. 3; however, this Protocol has not been accepted by Cambodia; and

- Ireland, by "30 June 1967", Protocol of Accession, 15S/42, para. 2.

The date "April 10, 1947" and the respective dates set forth in Annex G to the General Agreement are replaced by other dates in certain waiver decisions of the CONTRACTING PARTIES under Article XXV:5:

- Australia ("in relation to products of the Federation of Rhodesia and Nyasaland"), by "20 November 1959", Decision of 19 November 1960, 9S/46;

- Rhodesia and Nyasaland (Malawi, Zambia and Zimbabwe), by "3 December 1955", Decision of 19 November 1960, 9S/46;

- Union of South Africa ("in relation to products of the Federation of Rhodesia and Nyasaland"), by "30 June 1960", Decision of 19 November 1960, 9S/46; and

- Jamaica, by "1 August 1962", Decision of 2 March 1971, 18S/33.

(3) "in respect of duties or charges"

These words in paragraph 4 of Article I were inserted to make it clear that the obligations therein applied not only to ordinary customs duties but also to other charges such as primage and surtaxes.[86]

---

[83]EPCT/174, 194; EPCT/TAC/SR.16; EPCT/TAC/PV/28, p. 14; EPCT/EC/PV/2/22, pp. 30-32.
[84]Concerning base dates for margins of preference, see also discussion in the Sub-Committee on Procedures at the London session of the Preparatory Committee, EPCT/C.II/PRO/PV/8 p. 25ff.
[85]L/3845, adopted 2 February 1971, 18S/183, 187, para. 13. The Panel suggested that the CONTRACTING PARTIES consider granting a waiver to Jamaica to change the base date to 1 August 1962, and prepared a draft waiver decision; see Decision at L/3503, 18S/33.
[86]EPCT/TAC/PV/26, pp. 11-12.

3. Paragraph 3

Paragraph 3 corresponds to Article 16, paragraph 3 of the Havana Charter; however, where the Charter paragraph referred to Charter Article 15 (for which no counterpart exists in the General Agreement), the General Agreement paragraph refers to the use of the waiver provisions of Article XXV in the light of Article XXIX.[87] This insertion was agreed by the Working Party on "Modifications to the General Agreement" which met during the Second Session of the CONTRACTING PARTIES in September 1948 to consider updating the General Agreement to reflect the results of the Havana Conference.[88] "The working party agreed to recommend the insertion of a new paragraph in Article I in order to provide for the special position of certain countries of the Near East. It was the view of the working party that, under the proposed new paragraph of Article I, the CONTRACTING PARTIES, in taking action pursuant to Article XXV with respect to preferences among countries formerly a part of the Ottoman Empire, would be required to make a decision in accordance with the principles and requirements of Article 15 of the Havana Charter".[89]

This preference exception was exercised on the occasion of the accession of the United Arab Republic in February 1970. The Report of the Working Party on "Provisional Accession of the United Arab Republic" notes:

"... the Working Party ... decided that the preferential arrangements under the Arab League Convention should be dealt with under paragraph 3 of Article I of the General Agreement. Although the United Arab Republic was detached from the Ottoman Empire prior to 24 July 1923, paragraph 3 of Article I could be considered as applying to the United Arab Republic by analogy. ... The Working Party considered that this matter could be appropriately dealt with in the instrument of accession of the United Arab Republic since the legal requirements of a two-thirds majority contained in Article XXV:5 would be covered by the requirements of a two-thirds majority for the vote on terms of accession. The Working Party recognized that any subsequent addition of new items to the number of those enjoying preferences on the base date could be dealt with when the question arose in accordance with paragraph 3 of Article I by a further Decision of the CONTRACTING PARTIES under Article XXV:5".[90]

Accordingly, the Protocol for the Accession of the United Arab Republic refers to Article I:3.[91]

B. RELATIONSHIP BETWEEN ARTICLE I AND OTHER PROVISIONS OF THE GENERAL AGREEMENT

In addition to Article I, the General Agreement contains a number of other most-favoured-nation or non-discrimination clauses, relating to internal quantitative regulations (Article III:7), cinematographic films (Article IV(b)), transit of goods (Article V:5, 6), marks of origin (Article IX:1), quantitative restrictions (Article XIII:1), state trading (Article XVII:1), governmental assistance to promote the establishment of a particular industry (Article XVIII:20), and measures essential to the acquisition or distribution of products in short supply (Article XX(j)).

1. Article III

See under Article III.

2. Article VI

See under Article VI.

---

[87] E/CONF.2/C.3/77/Rev.1 and SR.44. Article 15 of the Charter permitted authorization of new preferential agreements between two or more countries in the interest of economic development or reconstruction.
[88] GATT/CP.2/22/Rev.1, adopted on 1 and 2 September 1948, II/39, 40, para. 5.
[89] *Ibid.*, II/43-44, para. 25; see also Havana Reports p. 40.
[90] L/1876, adopted 13 November 1962, 11S/75, 76, para. 3.
[91] 17S/2, 3, paragraph 2(b).

3. **Article IX**

    See under Article IX.

4. **Article XIII**

    See under Article XIII.

C. RELATIONSHIP OF ARTICLE I TO OTHER INTERNATIONAL AGREEMENTS

During the Third Session, held at Annecy in 1949, Cuba sought a ruling that the reduction of most-favoured-nation tariff rates by the United States in the tariff negotiations conducted at that time at Annecy would be inconsistent with the provisions of a bilateral trade agreement between Cuba and the United States predating the General Agreement, which guaranteed certain percentage margins of preference. The CONTRACTING PARTIES adopted a Decision by vote on "Margins of Preference" which provided *inter alia*, that "the determination of rights and obligations between governments arising under a bilateral agreement is not a matter within the competence of the CONTRACTING PARTIES".[92] This Decision was subject to the following footnote.

> "¹This Decision by its terms clearly refers only to the determination of the rights and obligations as between the parties to the bilateral agreement and arising from the agreement. It is, however, within the competence of the CONTRACTING PARTIES to determine whether action under such a bilateral agreement would or would not conflict with the provisions of the General Agreement".

In a Decision of 28 November 1979 on "Action by the CONTRACTING PARTIES on the Multilateral Trade Negotiations," the CONTRACTING PARTIES reaffirmed "their intention to ensure the unity and consistency of the GATT system" and decided, with respect to the agreements reached in the Tokyo Round:

> "3. The CONTRACTING PARTIES also note that existing rights and benefits under the GATT of contracting parties not being parties to these Agreements, including those derived from Article I, are not affected by these Agreements".[93]

The Decision of the same date on "Differential and More Favourable Treatment, Reciprocity and Fuller Participation of Developing Countries" provides, *inter alia*, that

> "1. Notwithstanding the provisions of Article I of the General Agreement, contracting parties may accord differential and more favourable treatment to developing countries, without according such treatment to other contracting parties.
>
> "2.   The provisions of paragraph 1 apply to the following:
>
> ...
>
> "(b) Differential and more favourable treatment with respect to the provisions of the General Agreement concerning non-tariff measures governed by the provisions of instruments multilaterally negotiated under the auspices of the GATT; ...
>
> ...
>
> "(d) Special treatment of the least developed among the developing countries in the context of any general or specific measures in favour of developing countries."

---

[92]II/11; see also draft decision and footnote in GATT/CP.3/71, statements of Cuba in GATT/CP.3/63 and GATT/CP.3/89, discussion at GATT/CP.3/SR.34-SR.38, and adoption of ruling and footnote by vote at GATT/CP.3/SR.38 p. 6-9. See also discussion of related Cuban legal claims at II/152-153 paras. 22-25.
[93]26S/201.

See further at page 53 below concerning this Decision. See also a Secretariat Note of 1987 on "MTN Agreements and Arrangements: Special and Differential Treatment for Developing Countries", which lists provisions in the Tokyo Round agreements providing such special and differential treatment.[94]

1. **Agreement on Implementation of Article VI**

In November 1968, at the Twenty-fifth Session, the Director-General was asked for a ruling on whether parties to the Agreement on Implementation of Article VI of the General Agreement had a legal obligation under Article I of the General Agreement to apply the provisions of the Anti-Dumping Code in their trade with all GATT contracting parties. The Director-General replied in the affirmative; see page 30 above.[95] At the first meeting of the Committee on Anti-Dumping Practices on 15 November 1968 the representative of the European Communities stated that "the Communities maintained the position they had taken at the discussion of the same question in April 1967, i.e. that the parties were under no obligation to apply the provisions of the Code to non-signatories".[96]

2. **Agreement on Interpretation and Application of Articles VI, XVI and XXIII**

In 1980 the Council established a Panel to examine the complaint of India that "the United States action to levy countervailing duties on imports of dutiable products from India without applying injury criteria referred to in paragraph 6 of Article VI, while extending the benefit of such criteria to imports from some other contracting parties, is not consistent with the obligations of the United States under GATT, including the provisions of Article I thereof". In its panel request, India, referring to the Agreement on Interpretation and Application of Articles VI, XVI and XXIII of the General Agreement on Tariffs and Trade of 12 April 1979, maintained "that as the U.S. government has taken the obligation to apply the injury test to subsidised products imported by it, it has to apply the test unconditionally to all contracting parties of the GATT irrespective of whether the new Agreement applies between the USA and other contracting parties".[97] The proceedings of the Panel were terminated at the request of India after resolution of the matter as a result of bilateral consultations between India and the United States.[98] The matter was again raised by India in 1982 and referred to the Committee on Subsidies and Countervailing Measures for conciliation,[99] but was not pursued further.

The Report of the Panel on "United States - Definition of Industry Concerning Wine and Grape Products", established under the Agreement on Interpretation and Application of Articles VI, XVI and XXIII of the General Agreement to examine a dispute regarding a provision of the United States countervailing duty laws, notes that "the Panel held the view that Article VI of the GATT and the corresponding Code provision should, because they permitted action of a non-m.f.n. nature otherwise prohibited by Article I, be interpreted in a narrow way".[100]

3. **Agreement on Government Procurement**

Article II of the Agreement on Government Procurement provides:

"1. With respect to all laws, regulations, procedures and practices regarding government procurement covered by this Agreement, the Parties shall provide immediately and unconditionally to the products and suppliers of other Parties offering products originating within the customs territories (including free zones) of the Parties, treatment no less favourable than: ...

"(b) that accorded to products and suppliers of any other Party.

---

[94] MTN.GNG/NG8/W/2, dated 4 May 1987.
[95] L/3149.
[96] COM.AD/1.
[97] L/5062.
[98] 28S/113.
[99] SCM/20, SCM/M/11, SCM/M/Spec/7.
[100] SCM/71, adopted on 28 April 1992, 39S/436, 447, para. 4.5.

"2. The provisions of paragraph 1 shall not apply to customs duties and charges of any kind imposed on or in connexion with importation, the method of levying such duties and charges, and other import regulations or formalities".

However, Article III:11 of the same Agreement provides:

"… The Parties may also grant the benefits of this Agreement to suppliers in the least-developed countries which are not Parties, with respect to products originating in those countries".

D. EXCEPTIONS AND DEROGATIONS

1. "imports of products for immediate or ultimate consumption in governmental use"

Article 8 of the US Draft Charter (the most-favoured-nation clause) included within its scope "all matters relating to internal taxation or regulation referred to in Article 9" (the national treatment clause of the US Draft Charter, which included in turn "laws and regulations governing the procurement by governmental agencies of supplies for public use other than by or for the military establishment"). The last sentence of the proposed Article 8 provided: "The principle underlying this paragraph shall also extend to the awarding by Members of governmental contracts for public works, in respect of which each Member shall accord fair and equitable treatment to the commerce of other Members". At the London session of the Preparatory Committee it was agreed to remove governmental contracts from the scope of the most-favoured-nation and national-treatment clauses.[101] See the material in this Index on Article XVII:2 for a more detailed discussion of this question.

The scope of the exception for government procurement was discussed in the 1952 Panel Report on "Belgian Family Allowances", which concerned a charge levied on foreign goods purchased by public bodies; the panel found that the charge was an internal charge under Article III:2, and therefore subject to the most-favoured-nation clause of Article I. The Panel Report notes that "As regards the exception provided in paragraph 2 of Article XVII, it would appear that it referred only to the principle set forth in paragraph 1 of that Article, i.e., the obligation to make purchases in accordance with commercial considerations and did not extend to matters dealt with in Article III."[102]

See also the exceptions for government procurement provided for in Articles III:8(a) and XVII:2 of the General Agreement. See also Articles II and III:11 of the Agreement on Government Procurement.

2. Exceptions and derogations provided in other Articles of the General Agreement

(1) Anti-dumping and countervailing duties

See material under Article VI on the relationship between Article VI and Article I.

(2) Frontier traffic and customs unions

See under Article XXIV.

The Report of the Sub-Committee of the Havana Conference which examined Articles 16 and 42 of the Havana Charter (corresponding to Articles I and XXIV of the General Agreement) notes as follows: "The Sub-Committee discussed with the delegate of Italy the latter's proposal to except the special regime existing between the Republic of Italy and the Republic of San Marino and the State of the Vatican City from the provisions of paragraph 1 of Article 16. The Sub-Committee was of the opinion that the special arrangements existing between Italy and these two territories were not contrary to the Charter".[103]

---

[101]London Report, p. 9, Chapter III para. A.1((d)(i); see also EPCT/30.
[102]G/32, adopted on 7 November 1952, 1S/59, 60, para. 4.
[103]Havana Reports, p. 48, para. 11.

3. **Exceptions and derogations authorized in Protocols of Accession and in Declarations on Provisional Accession**

(1) Protocol of Provisional Application

The Interpretative Note to Article I paragraph 1 was based on a proposal by the United States the object of which was to reserve legislation regarding preferential internal taxes until definitive acceptance of the Agreement.[104]

(2) Protocols of Accession

(a) General

Protocols for the Accession to the General Agreement on Tariffs and Trade contain a standard provision according to which the acceding government

"... shall, upon entry into force of this Protocol pursuant to paragraph 6, become a contracting party to the General Agreement, as defined in Article XXXII thereof, and shall apply to contracting parties provisionally and subject to this Protocol:

"(a) Parts I, III and IV of the General Agreement, and
"(b) Part II of the General Agreement to the fullest extent not inconsistent with its legislation existing on the date of this Protocol.

"The obligations incorporated in paragraph 1 of Article I by reference to Article III ... of the General Agreement shall be considered as falling within Part II for the purpose of this paragraph".[105]

(b) Particular contracting parties

Argentina - Preferences accorded to Bolivia, Brazil, Chile, Paraguay, Peru, Uruguay (Declaration on Provisional Accession, para.1(d));[106] however, on acceding under Article XXXIII in 1967 the Government of Argentina advised that tariff preferences were no longer granted, the beneficiaries now being members of the Latin American Free Trade Area.[107]

Egypt - Preferences accorded to Jordan, Syria, Iraq, Lebanon, Libya, Saudi Arabia, and Yemen (Declaration on Provisional Accession and Protocol of Accession); however, see under Article I:3 above at page 44.[108]

Germany - Provision in Decision on Accession that "notwithstanding the provisions of Article I ... the accession of the Government of the Federal Republic of Germany will not require any modification in the present arrangements for, or status of, intra-German trade in goods originating within Germany".[109]

Hungary - Maintenance of existing trading relations with the countries enumerated in Annex A to its protocol of accession.[110] In a communication dated 5 May 1977, Hungary stated that, with effect from 1 July 1977, it would add the Republic of Cuba to the list of countries enumerated in Annex A, while respecting the obligations that it had entered into as set forth in the relevant paragraphs of the Protocol.[111]

---

[104] Proposal at EPCT/W/343; discussion at EPCT/TAC/PV/9, EPCT/TAC/PV/10, EPCT/TAC/PV/26, p. 9-11 (referring to preferential internal tax on processing of coconut oil from the Philippines, later notified as measure under the Protocol of Provisional Application; see L/309/Add.2).

[105] E.g. paragraphs 1 in the Protocols for the Accession of Bolivia (L/6562), Costa Rica (L/6626), El Salvador (L/6795), Tunisia (L/6656), Venezuela (L/6717), 37S/5, 7, 27, 41, 72.

[106] 9S/12.

[107] 15S/99, para. 18.

[108] 11S/47, 11S/76, 17S/2.

[109] II/34.

[110] 20S/3, para. 3.

[111] 24S/4.

Japan - Provision that "so long as the status of any island referred to in Article 3 of the Treaty of Peace with Japan, of 8 September 1951, remains provisional under the terms of that treaty, the provisions of the General Agreement shall neither apply to such island not require the modification of such treatment as is presently accorded by Japan to such island".[112]

Portugal - maintenance of preferential treatment between customs territories in respect of which Portugal applies the General Agreement, provided that duties and other restrictive regulations of commerce are eliminated on substantially all such trade.[113]

Spain - Maintenance of preferential treatment of trade between customs territories listed in Annex B of accession protocol, provided that such trade is duty-free.[114]

Uruguay - Preferences accorded to Paraguay (Annecy Protocol, para. 1(d));[115] These preferences terminated as of 31 December 1961 when the Uruguayan-Paraguay Treaty was terminated.[116]

4. Waivers granted under the provisions of paragraph 5 of Article XXV

A table under Article XXV lists all waiver decisions by the CONTRACTING PARTIES. See also the discussion under Article XXV:5 concerning procedures for waivers to Article I.

(1) Decision on "Generalized System of Preferences" of 25 June 1971

This Decision[117] waived the provisions of Article I for a period of ten years. Although it did not refer to paragraph 5 of Article XXV, this Decision was made on the basis of a Communication from the prospective preference-giving contracting parties (C/W/178) applying for a waiver in accordance with Article XXV:5. In the Council discussion regarding this Decision, it was pointed out that

(i) the waiver made possible the implementation of a system of generalized non-reciprocal and non-discriminatory preferences as agreed at the Second UNCTAD (1968);

(ii) the waiver did not specify the determination of the beneficiary countries and covered general guidelines for a decision on beneficiary countries presented by preference-giving countries in the UNCTAD, "according to which donor countries would in general base themselves on the principle of self-election";

(iii) the waiver is without prejudice to any Article of the General Agreement other than Article I; rights under Article XXIII are fully preserved;

(iv) an amendment proposed to add the word "developed" in operative paragraph (a) of the waiver so as to permit preferences to developing countries "without according such treatment to like products of other *developed* contracting parties ..." was not accepted.[118]

The 1971 waiver was not renewed in the light of the Decision of 28 November 1979 on "Differential and More Favourable Treatment, Reciprocity and Fuller Participation of Developing Countries" ("Enabling Clause"), which authorizes "preferential tariff treatment accorded by developed contracting parties to products originating in developing countries in accordance with the Generalized System of Preferences". See section II.D.6 below.

The 1972 Working Party Report on the "Danish Temporary Import Surcharge" provides that "Without prejudice to the legal issues involved, the Working Party noted that as from the introduction of the Danish general

---

[112] 4S/7, para. 1(d).
[113] 11S/20, 21, para. 3.
[114] 12S/27, 28, paras. 3-4.
[115] I/79.
[116] L/1845.
[117] L/3545, 18S/24.
[118] C/M/69.

preference scheme on 1 January 1972, products included in that scheme would be exempted from the surcharge when imported from members of the Group of Seventy-Seven. Several members of the Working Party welcomed this decision of the Danish Government noting that this had been one of the recommendations of the Group of Three. Other members expressed concern that the exemption did not extend to all developing countries. Some other members said that the discrimination created by these exemptions gave their delegations cause for concern".[119]

(2) *Decision on "Trade negotiations among developing countries" of 26 November 1971*

This Decision[120] waived Article I:1 to the extent necessary to permit each contracting party participating in the arrangements set out in the Protocol relating to Trade Negotiations among Developing Countries[121] to accord preferential treatment as provided in the Protocol with respect to products originating in other parties to the Protocol. While the Decision

GSP Schemes Notified to the GATT

Australia	L/3982+Adds., L/7205+Adds.
Canada	L/4027+Adds.
Hungary	L/4106+Adds.
Japan	L/3559; L/3691; L/3876; L/4397; L/4531+Adds.; L/7035
New Zealand	L/3693; L/4366+Adds.
Norway	L/3570; L/4242+Adds.; L/7042+Adds.
Switzerland	L/3667; L/4020+Adds.
United States	L/4299+Adds.; L/5153+Adds.; L/7072+Adds.
European Communities	L/3550; L/3671; L/3954; L/4000; L/4161; L/4282; L/4468; L/4624; L/4804+Adds.; L/5116+Adds.; L/7376

* GSP schemes that have been replaced by the EC's due to accession to the EC, or where the contracting party no longer exists (Czechoslovak Republic) do not appear. See earlier editions of this work for document references.

contains no reference to paragraph 5 of Article XXV, the Chairman of the CONTRACTING PARTIES noted that there was no formal request for a ballot and therefore concluded that the conditions for the grant of a waiver under paragraph 5 of Article XXV had been met and that the Decision had been adopted in accordance with the requirements of that paragraph.[122]

The Chairman of the Contact Group put on record a statement by the countries participating in the negotiations that the Protocol would be open for accession to all developing countries and that, according to the participating countries, paragraph 14 of the Protocol would enable them to give, on a case by case basis, sympathetic consideration to a request from a least developed among developing countries to accede to the Protocol without negotiations; and secondly, that the Committee of Participating Countries to be established under paragraph 4 of the Protocol would study, examine and consider, on a case by case basis, the question of accession of developing dependent territories as and when a request for accession was received from any developing dependent territory.[123]

In reply to a question, the Director-General explained that a waiver from the provisions of paragraph 1 of Article I related solely to the obligation to grant most-favoured-nation treatment in respect of the matters expressly referred to in that paragraph and in respect of which there was no obligation under other provisions of the General Agreement to grant non-discriminatory or most-favoured-nation treatment. It was clear from the text of paragraph (a) of the Decision that the stipulations contained in other provisions of the General Agreement were not affected.[124] The representative of India stated that the States which had participated in the negotiations had taken note of the statement by the Director-General and would consult with the CONTRACTING PARTIES if they needed any further legal coverage.

---

[119]L/3648, adopted on 12 January 1972, 19S/120, 126, 129 (identical text in paras. 22 and 41).
[120]18S/26.
[121]L/3643 and Add.1, 18S/11.
[122]SR.27/12.
[123]SR.27/6.
[124]SR.27/12.

The Protocol relating to Trade Negotiations among Developing Countries entered into force 11 February 1973.[125] As of June 1993, the Protocol had been ratified by fifteen developing countries: Bangladesh, Brazil, Chile, Egypt, India, Israel, Mexico, Pakistan, Peru, Republic of Korea, Romania, Tunisia, Turkey, Uruguay and Yugoslavia; Paraguay had signed the Protocol *ad referendum* and the Philippines had signed but not ratified the Protocol.[126] India withdrew from the Protocol effective 29 March 1993.[127]

Referring to the Decision on Differential and More Favourable Treatment, Reciprocity and Fuller Participation of Developing Countries ("Enabling Clause") referred to below, the Committee of Participating Countries stated in its Seventh Annual Report to the CONTRACTING PARTIES: "There is thus a standing legal basis resulting from the Tokyo Round for the Protocol Relating to Trade Negotiations Among Developing Countries".[128] The annual reports of the Committee have stated: "The Protocol is applied under the provisions of the Enabling Clause, and in particular under the terms of its paragraph 2(c)".[129] See also the references to preferential arrangements under the Enabling Clause, below at page 57.

(3) Waivers granted to individual contracting parties

See the table of waivers under Article XXV:5.

5. **Preferential arrangements authorized by Decisions of the CONTRACTING PARTIES without reference to paragraph 5 of Article XXV**

(1) First Agreement on Trade Negotiations Among Developing Member Countries of the Economic and Social Commission for Asia and the Pacific (Bangkok Agreement)

The Decision of 14 March 1978 on "First Agreement on Trade Negotiations Among Developing Member Countries of the Economic and Social Commission for Asia and the Pacific (Bangkok Agreement)"[130] was drafted by the Working Party which examined the provisions of this agreement, concluded between Bangladesh, India, Laos, Philippines, Republic of Korea, Sri Lanka and Thailand. The Report of the Working Party records that the spokesman for the parties to the Agreement stated

> "that Articles I, XXIV and XXXVII of the General Agreement all had equal force. In the Bangkok Agreement, the participating States were fulfilling the commitments and undertakings accepted by developing contracting parties in Part IV of the General Agreement in a manner which was consistent with their individual development, financial and trade needs ..."..

In the view of the participating States, a waiver of GATT obligations under Article XXV of the General Agreement was not necessary for the implementation of the Bangkok Agreement.[131] In the view of the other members of the Working Party

> "the Bangkok Agreement which was not aimed at the establishment of a customs union or a free-trade area in accordance with Article XXIV of the General Agreement, introduced an element of discrimination against traditional suppliers in a way which could affect their trade. As, in their view, the Bangkok Agreement was not covered by Article I of the General Agreement and Part IV did not override other Parts of the General Agreement, a waiver or other appropriate decision by the CONTRACTING PARTIES seemed called for in this case".[132]

---

[125] Status of Legal Instruments, p. 15-1.1.
[126] See also Decisions on Accession to the Protocol by Bangladesh, 23S/157 (entry into force: 29 March 1977); Paraguay, 23S/154 (not yet in force); Romania, 25S/174 (entry into force: 15 September 1978). See also annual reports of the Committee of Participating Countries at 21S/126, 22S/73, 23S/147, 24S/154, 25S/163, 26S/337, 27S/172, 28S/129, 29S/155, 30S/203, 31S/291, 32S/191, 33S/224, 34S/218, 35S/409, 36S/475, 37S/325, 38S/114.
[127] Let/1790, dated 15 October 1992.
[128] 27S/172.
[129] See, *e.g.*, L/7106, CPC/W/161.
[130] 25S/6.
[131] L/4635, adopted 14 March 1978, 25S/109, 111, para. 7.
[132] *Ibid.*, 25S/110-111, para. 5.

The US delegate "stated his delegation's understanding that the draft Decision was intended to meet the waiver requirements of Article XXV:5".[133]

The Report of the Working Party states: "It was understood that the Agreement would in no way be considered as affecting the legal rights of contracting parties under the General Agreement".[134]

The Standing Committee of the Bangkok Agreement has submitted biennial reports to the Committee on Trade and Development "having regard to paragraph 2(c) of the CONTRACTING PARTIES Decision of 28 November 1979 on Differential and More Favourable Treatment, Reciprocity and Fuller Participation of Developing Countries".[135] See also the references to preferential arrangements under the Enabling Clause, below at page 57.

(2) Agreement on the Association of South-East Asian Nations (ASEAN) Preferential Trading Arrangements

The Decision of 29 January 1979 on "Agreement on ASEAN Preferential Trading Arrangements"[136] was drafted by a Working Party which examined the provisions of this Agreement between Indonesia, Malaysia, the Philippines, Singapore and Thailand. The Report of the Working Party notes that the parties to the Agreement were not claiming that it constituted a free-trade area or an interim agreement leading to the formation of a free-trade area, and also provides:

"A number of members of the Working Party stated their belief that some form of GATT cover should be provided for the Agreement, since in their view it was not fully consistent with the provisions of the General Agreement. While some of these members believed that an Article XXV:5 waiver would be most appropriate, they were prepared to recommend a decision by the CONTRACTING PARTIES. The spokesman for the parties to the Agreement stated that in the view of the ASEAN countries, the Agreement followed the letter and spirit of the provisions of the General Agreement, especially those in Part IV. However, in the light of a previous developments in GATT with regard to the examination of economic groupings among developing countries, the ASEAN countries would be prepared to accept a decision".[137]

"The United States delegate stated his delegation's understanding that the Draft Decision was intended to meet the waiver requirements of Article XXV:5 ... It was also understood that the Agreement would in no way be considered as affecting the legal rights of contracting parties under the General Agreement".[138]

Reports on trade co-operation among ASEAN member states have been submitted and examined under the Enabling Clause; see also the references at page 57 below to preferential arrangements between developing countries under the Enabling Clause.[139] The ASEAN Common Effective Preferential Tariff Scheme (CEPT) and Framework Agreement on Enhancing ASEAN Economic Cooperation were notified under the Enabling Clause (see page 57).

(3) Trade Expansion and Economic Co-operation Agreement

A Decision of 14 November 1968 on the "Trade Arrangement between India, the United Arab Republic and Yugoslavia" provided that the three participating contracting parties may implement the Trade Expansion and Economic Co-operation Agreement between them notwithstanding the provisions of Article I:1, subject to certain

---

[133]*Ibid.* 25S/113, para. 18.
[134]Para. 21.
[135]L/5243 and COM.TD/112; report and review in 1990, L/6718 and L/6744. Report to the Committee on Trade and Development in 1982 and Committee review,
[136]L/4768, 26S/224.
[137]L/4735, 26S/321, 326, para. 19.
[138]*Ibid.*, paras. 21, 23.
[139]The most recent such report is L/7111.

conditions and procedures including a review at the Twenty-sixth Session.[140] This Decision was renewed successively through 1983.[141]

The Report of the Working Party in 1968 which examined this agreement and drafted the Decision notes that several representatives considered that "Part IV ... did not override the obligations of other parts of the General Agreement. In their view the Tripartite Agreement was inconsistent with the basic most-favoured-nation provision of Article I of GATT and accordingly some decision of the CONTRACTING PARTIES was required".[142] The US representative said "that in the view of his Government the draft decision ... was intended to meet the requirements of Article XXV:5 of the General Agreement".[143] "The representatives of the three countries reiterated that the Agreement was in pursuance of their obligations under Part IV and consistent with the spirit of the General Agreement".[144]

The different views on the compatibility of the Agreement with the General Agreement were maintained in the Working Party which carried out the review of this Decision[145] and in a 1973 Working Party reviewing the renewal Decision of 1970, in which several members stated that "in their view the Agreement was in full conformity with the provisions and spirit of the General Agreement, in particular Article XXXVII. ... The representative of the participating States ... could not agree that the Tripartite Agreement was inconsistent with the GATT even though it involved a departure from Article I".[146]

See also the references to preferential agreements under the "Enabling Clause" below at page 57.

6. **Differential and More Favourable Treatment, Reciprocity and Fuller Participation of Developing Countries ("Enabling Clause")**

The Decision of the CONTRACTING PARTIES of 28 November 1979[147], insofar as it provides for departures from Article I of the General Agreement, provides as follows.

"1. Notwithstanding the provisions of Article I of the General Agreement, contracting parties may accord differential and more favourable treatment to developing countries[1], without according such treatment to other contracting parties.

"2. The provisions of paragraph 1 apply to the following:[2]

"(a) Preferential tariff treatment accorded by developed contracting parties to products originating in developing countries in accordance with the Generalized System of Preferences,[3]

"(b) Differential and more favourable treatment with respect to the provisions of the General Agreement concerning non-tariff measures governed by the provisions of instruments multilaterally negotiated under the auspices of the GATT;

"(c) Regional or global arrangements entered into amongst less-developed contracting parties for the mutual reduction or elimination of tariffs and, in accordance with criteria or conditions which may be prescribed by the CONTRACTING PARTIES, for the mutual reduction or elimination of non-tariff measures, on products imported from one another;

"(d) Special treatment of the least developed among the developing countries in the context of any general or specific measures in favour of developing countries.

---

[140] 16S/17.
[141] Decision of 20 February 1970, 17S/21, expiry 31 March 1973; extended by Decision of 22 March 1973, 20S/23, until the 29th Session; Decision of 13 November 1973, 20S/23, expiry 31 March 1978; Decision of 14 March 1978, 25S/8, expiry 31 March 1983.
[142] L/3032, adopted on 14 November 1968, 16S/83, 87, para. 12.
[143] Ibid., 16S/88, para. 16.
[144] Ibid., 16S/87, para. 13.
[145] L/3341, adopted on 13 February 1970, 17S/138, 143, para. 14.
[146] L/3950, adopted on 7 November 1973, 20S/224, 227-228, paras. 12-13.
[147] 26S/203.

"3. Any differential and more favourable treatment provided under this clause:

"(a) shall be designed to facilitate and promote the trade of developing countries and not to raise barriers to or create undue difficulties for the trade of any other contracting parties;

"(b) shall not constitute an impediment to the reduction or elimination of tariffs and other restrictions to trade on a most-favoured-nation basis;

"(c) shall in the case of such treatment accorded by developed contracting parties to developing countries be designed and, if necessary, modified, to respond positively to the development, financial and trade needs of developing countries.

"4. Any contracting party taking action to introduce an arrangement pursuant to paragraphs 1, 2 and 3 above or subsequently taking action to introduce modification or withdrawal of the differential and more favourable treatment so provided shall:[4]

"(a) notify the CONTRACTING PARTIES and furnish them with all the information they may deem appropriate relating to such action;

"(b) afford adequate opportunity for prompt consultations at the request of any interested contracting party with respect to any difficulty or matter that may arise. The CONTRACTING PARTIES shall, if requested to do so by such contracting party, consult with all contracting parties concerned with respect to the matter with a view to reaching solutions satisfactory to all such contracting parties".

The footnotes 1 - 4 state:

"[1]The words 'developing countries' as used in this text are to be understood to refer also to developing territories.

"[2]It would remain open for the CONTRACTING PARTIES to consider on an *ad hoc* basis under the GATT provisions for joint action any proposals for differential and more favourable treatment not falling within the scope of this paragraph.

"[3]As described in the Decision of the CONTRACTING PARTIES of 25 June 1971, relating to the establishment of 'generalized non-reciprocal and non-discriminatory preferences beneficial to the developing countries' (BISD 18S/24).

"[4]Nothing in these provisions shall affect the rights of contracting parties under the General Agreement".

(1) Scope

The Report of the Working Party on "United States Caribbean Basin Economic Recovery Act (CBERA)" notes that at "the request of the Working Party, the representative of the secretariat described the secretariat's understanding of the meaning of footnote 2 of paragraph 2 of the Enabling Clause. In brief, the Enabling Clause provided authority or cover only for the kinds of preferential treatment described therein. Footnote 2 of paragraph 2 of the Enabling Clause recognized that there could be other situations involving preferential treatment not falling within the scope of paragraph 2 which the CONTRACTING PARTIES might wish to cover under the GATT provisions for joint action. The provisions in question could not be those of Part IV, including Article XXXVIII thereof, as these did not provide authority for preferential treatment. The joint action envisaged had to be in terms of paragraph 5 of Article XXV irrespective of whether this was specifically mentioned or not".[148]

---

[148]L/5708, adopted on 6-8 and 20 November 1984, 31S/180, 189-190, para. 31.

Regarding the application of the Enabling Clause to preferences extended to least-developed countries and not to less-developed countries generally, see the material from the Panel Report on "United States - Customs User Fee" above at page 32.

The 1990 Report of the Working Party on "Accession of Tunisia" records the request of a member, referring to Tunisia's preferential agreements, for "information on the meaning and method of implementation of the 'principle of priority supply', in the context of non-tariff import trade preferences ... The representative of Tunisia said that the principle of priority supply which appeared in certain trade agreements with the Maghreb and Arab countries was not a specific trade measure but rather a political and moral commitment to seek to increase their mutual trade. In his view, the principle of priority supply was in conformity with Part IV of the General Agreement and paragraph 2(c) of the Enabling Clause Decision of November 1979 which had authorized developing countries to exchange tariff and non-tariff measure preferences in the context of regional or global arrangements".[149]

The 1992 Panel Report on "United States - Denial of Most-favoured-nation Treatment as to Non-rubber Footwear from Brazil" examined arguments of Brazil concerning the scope of the exception to Article I under the Enabling Clause, and its application to Section 331 of the Tariff Act of 1930, which provided certain treatment in the case of revocation of countervailing duty orders:

"... the United States accords duty-free status under a variety of laws only to products of a particular origin, the most important being the law establishing the GSP. The GSP programme of the United States, both in its nature and in its design, accords duty-free status to only certain products originating in only certain developing countries. The Panel noted that, together with the grant of a tariff advantage to the designated beneficiary countries under this programme, Section 331 of the Trade Act of 1974 accords a *non-tariff advantage* to the same beneficiary countries in the form of the automatic backdating of countervailing duty revocation orders. The Panel considered that the grant of this non-tariff advantage under Section 331 of the 1974 Act to duty-free products originating in a country beneficiary of the GSP programme, which advantage is denied to dutiable products originating in the territory of a Subsidies Agreement signatory, is inconsistent with the most-favoured-nation provision of Article I:1 of the General Agreement.

"The Panel then examined whether the CONTRACTING PARTIES had taken any action which would permit the United States to accord the non-tariff advantage of Section 331 of the Trade Act of 1974 to duty-free products emanating from countries beneficiaries of the GSP programme, without unconditionally and immediately according this same advantage to dutiable products originating in the territories of signatories of the Subsidies Agreement. In this regard, the Panel noted that ... the 'Enabling Clause' permits, in paragraph 2(a) thereof, 'preferential tariff treatment accorded by developed contracting parties to products originating in developing countries in accordance with the Generalized System of Preferences ...', notwithstanding the provisions of Article I. It was clear that the Enabling Clause expressly limits the preferential treatment accorded by developed contracting parties in favour of developing contracting parties under the Generalized System of Preferences to tariff preferences only.

"The Panel referred in this context to a discussion of this issue by an earlier panel concerned with the customs user fee of the United States.[150] The panel in that case considered the claim that exemption from a merchandise processing fee granted to the beneficiaries of the Caribbean Basin Economic Recovery Act was not authorized by the waiver granting the United States authority to extend duty-free treatment to these beneficiaries, and that it was also not authorized by the Enabling Clause. That panel noted that no answer in opposition to this legal claim was given and that it was not aware of any that could be given. However, in view of the fact that this claim was raised by third parties and not by the parties to the dispute, this earlier panel did not consider it appropriate to make a formal finding on the issue.

"Accordingly, the Panel found that there is no decision of the CONTRACTING PARTIES justifying the given inconsistency with Article I:1 of the non-tariff advantage accorded to duty-free products originating

---

[149]L/6277, adopted on 12 December 1990, 37S/30, 39, para. 33.
[150]The footnote to this sentence refers to the Panel report on "United States - Customs User Fee," adopted on 2 February 1988, BISD 35S/245, 290.

in countries beneficiaries of the United States GSP programme in the backdating of the effect of the revocation of countervailing duty orders".[151]

(2) Preference schemes

The 1980 Report of the Committee on Trade and Development refers to a statement from a representative of a developing country that the preferential treatment of certain textile imports under the European Communities' GSP scheme for 1980 had not been extended to all beneficiaries of the Communities' GSP scheme and amounted to discrimination inconsistent with the spirit of the GSP. The representative of the European Communities replied that in view of the increasingly serious difficulties in the textiles sector, the Communities had to limit their zero duty treatment for textile imports under the GSP to countries which were either a signatory of the MFA or had entered into a commitment to abide by obligations similar to those under that Arrangement.[152]

The July 1992 session of the Committee on Trade and Development discussed the issue of extension of GSP treatment to East European countries and republics of the former USSR; however, no consensus has yet been reached on this issue.[153]

See also the section on "graduation" below.

Concerning the Lomé Convention, see Article XXIV.

(3) Preferential arrangements notified under the Enabling Clause

When an agreement is notified under the Enabling Clause, it is inscribed on the agenda of the Committee on Trade and Development (CTD). Subsequent actions of the CTD may include "noting" the agreement, requesting additional information, establishing a working party and adopting its reports, and reviewing reports made by members on developments under the agreement. The following trade arrangements had been notified under the Enabling Clause as of March 1994:

- 1971 Protocol relating to Trade Negotiations among Developing Countries[154]

- 1980 Montevideo Treaty establishing the Latin American Integration Association (ALADI)[155]

    - ALADI bilateral economic complementarity agreements[156]

    - Southern Common Market Agreement (MERCOSUR)[157]

- Association of South-East Asian Nations (ASEAN)

    - Asian Trade Expansion Programme (1975 Bangkok Agreement)[158]

---

[151]DS18/R, adopted on 19 June 1992, 39S/128, 152-153, paras. 6.14-6.17.
[152]L/5074, adopted 26 November 1980, 27S/48, 51, paras. 10-11.
[153]COM.TD/132, L/7124.
[154]See Seventh Report of the Committee at 27S/172; activities in framework of Protocol are annually reviewed by CTD. See further at page 51 above.
[155]Successor to the 1960 Montevideo Treaty for the establishment of LAFTA. Members: Argentina, Bolivia, Brazil, Chile, Colombia, Ecuador, Mexico, Paraguay, Peru, Uruguay and Venezuela. Notification in 1982 (L/5342, C/M/144) reviewed by CTD (COM.TD/112); reports in 1984 (L/5859) reviewed by CTD (COM.TD/118); 1985 (COM.TD/W/423) reviewed by CTD (COM.TD/120); 1987 (L/6158+Add.1) supplemented in 1988 (L/6158/Add.1, COM.TD/W/469) reviewed by CTD in 1987, 1988, 1989 (COM.TD/126, L/6241, L/6418, COM.TD/129); 1989 (L/6531, reviewed by CTD (L/6605); 1991 (L/6946).
[156]L/5689, L/6158+Add.1, COM.TD/W/469, L/6531, L/6946, discussed at COM.TD/127, COM.TD/128, L/6418 (35S/31, 34).
[157]Members: Argentina, Brazil, Paraguay and Uruguay. Notified 1992, L/6985+Add.1, L/7044; see also COM.TD/W/496, COM.TD/W/497. Working party established on 28 May 1993 under the Committee on Trade and Development: terms of reference at L/7373, circulation of text in L/7370 and L/7370/Add.1, notification of implementation of common external tariff from 1 January 1995 in L/7615, questions and replies in L/7540.
[158]Authorized initially through Decision of 14 March 1978; reports submitted under Enabling Clause in 1982 (L/5243) reviewed by CTD (COM.TD/112); 1990 (L/6718) reviewed by CTD (L/6744, 37S/76).

- 1978 Agreement on ASEAN Preferential Trading Arrangements[159]

- Common Effective Preferential Tariff Scheme (CEPT) for the ASEAN Free Trade Area and Framework Agreement on Enhancing ASEAN Economic Cooperation[160]

- 1980 South Pacific Regional Trade and Economic Cooperation Agreement (SPARTECA)[161]

- 1982 Unified Economic Agreement among member states of the Gulf Cooperation Council[162]

- 1987 Cartagena Agreement (Andean Group) on sub-regional trade liberalization and adoption of a common external tariff[163]

- 1989 Global System of Trade Preferences Among Developing Countries (GSTP)[164]

- 1991 Trade Agreement between Thailand and the Lao People's Democratic Republic[165]

- 1991 Additional Protocol on Preferential Tariffs negotiated among members of the Organization for Economic Cooperation[166]

In addition, as noted above, the Protocol relating to Trade Negotiations among Developing Countries and the 1967 Trade Expansion and Co-operation Agreement ("Tripartite Agreement") between Egypt, India and Yugoslavia, both of which predated the Enabling Clause, have since 1979 been treated as having a basis in the Enabling Clause.

The 1989 Report of the Committee on Trade and Development records that in response to a question in the Committee on Trade and Development regarding whether the CONTRACTING PARTIES were expected to approve the GSTP, which had been notified under the Enabling Clause,

"a representative of the Secretariat said that the Committee has not established detailed procedures for the examination of arrangements which were notified under the Enabling Clause. The Committee was given from the CONTRACTING PARTIES in 1980 the responsibility for supervising the operation of the Enabling Clause. Under this mandate the Committee had so far received a limited number of notifications on arrangements concluded in accordance with paragraph 2(c) of the Enabling Clause. The practice of the Committee so far had been to take note of these arrangements after having duly examined them and

---

[159] Authorized initially by Decision of 29 January 1979 (L/4768, 26S/224). Members of ASEAN: Indonesia, Malaysia, Philippines, Singapore and Thailand (Brunei Darussalam joined in 1984). Notification under Enabling Clause in 1982 (L/5243), reviewed by CTD (COM.TD/112); report (L/5455) reviewed by CTD (COM.TD/114); notification in 1989 (L/6569) reviewed by CTD (L/6605, 36S/49, 55); 1990 (L/6718) reviewed by CTD (L/6744, 37S/76).

[160] Members: Brunei Darussalam, Indonesia, Malaysia, Philippines, Singapore and Thailand. Notified in L/7111; supplements the 1978 Agreement on ASEAN Preferential Trading Arrangements.

[161] Members: Australia and New Zealand, and Cook Islands, Fiji, Kiribati, Niue, Papua New Guinea, Solomon Islands, Tonga, Tuvalu and Western Samoa; extension to Nauru and Vanuatu by New Zealand notified 1982.. Notified at L/5100, L/5488; Council decision 26 November 1971 to require submission of reports by Australia and New Zealand in accordance with procedure for the examination of biennial reports on regional agreements, C/M/148, p. 12.

[162] Members: Bahrain, Kuwait, Oman, Qatar, Saudi Arabia and United Arab Emirates. See L/5676, L/5735.

[163] Members: Bolivia, Colombia, Ecuador, Peru and Venezuela. The 1987 Cartagena Agreement superseded the 1969 Cartagena Agreement which established the Andean Group, concluded in the context of the 1960 Treaty of Montevideo establishing the Latin American Free Trade Association (LAFTA). In 1988, the Cartagena Agreement became independent as regards aspects relating to the Montevideo Treaty which had expired. The Andean Group originally was composed of Bolivia, Chile, Colombia, Ecuador and Peru. Chile withdrew from the Treaty in October 1976 and Venezuela acceded in 1973. Agreement notified 1990 (L/6737), noted by CTD (L/6744, 37S/76-77); further notification 1991 (L/6841) reviewed by CTD (COM.TD/131); notification 1992 (L/7088, L/7089).

[164] Notified 1989 (L/6564+Add.1); reviewed by CTD in 1989 (L/6605, 36S/55-58, paras. 22-28, 30) and 1990 (COM.TD/130).

[165] Notified under Enabling Clause, L/6947.

[166] Members: original: Iran, Pakistan and Turkey; subsequent: Azerbaijan, Kyrgzstan, Tajikistan, Turkmenistan and Uzbekistan. Notified 1992 (L/7047).

completed such examination. On that basis the Committee reported statements made in regard to such arrangements and any action taken in relation to them in its annual reports to the CONTRACTING PARTIES".[167]

During 1992, there were extensive discussions in the Council and the Committee on whether the MERCOSUR Agreement should be notified and examined under the Enabling Clause or under Article XXIV. This agreement was notified under the Enabling Clause and the Committee established a working party with the following terms of reference:

"To examine the Southern Common Market Agreement (MERCOSUR) in the light of the relevant provisions of the Enabling Clause and of the General Agreement, including Article XXIV and to transmit a report and recommendations to the Committee for submission to the CONTRACTING PARTIES, with a copy of the report transmitted as well to the Council. The examination in the Working Party will be based on a complete notification and on written questions and answers."[168]

(4) "Graduation"

The question of the compatibility of "graduation" with the Enabling Clause was discussed in 1981-82 in the Committee on Trade and Development and the Council.[169]

At the Fifty-eighth Session of the Committee on Trade and Development, one representative stated that in the view of her authorities "the Enabling Clause had provided a useful mechanism for permitting temporary departures from the most-favoured-nation principle, and this had been achieved with a minimum of damage to the integrity of the General Agreement. However, this would continue to be the case only if the use of preferential treatment was gradually phased out. Contracting parties should give high priority to ensuring a timely transition to fuller participation in the framework of rights and obligations under the General Agreement. The Enabling Clause provided the legal basis for GSP programmes and the GSP had offered an opportunity for developing countries to expand and diversify their exports to the developed countries. ... She said that the guidelines provided in paragraph 3 of the Enabling Clause were important, and particularly paragraph 3(c), which indicated that special and differential treatment should be provided on a dynamic basis, taking into account changes in development levels and the development, financial and trade needs of developing countries. ... She noted that paragraph 7 required differentiation between developing countries beyond that envisaged for the least-developed countries. In the light of the economic progress made by some countries there should be a greater degree of differentiation among developing countries in regard to access to preferential treatment and to the degree of reciprocity required in negotiations".[170] "In regard to the provisions of paragraph 7 of the Enabling Clause, some representatives said that this paragraph did not provide the basis for discrimination among developing countries. ... Another representative noted that the decision to participate more fully in the GATT system of obligations was an autonomous decision to be taken in terms of a country's own judgment of its development, trade and financial needs".[171]

During the review of the implementation of Part IV and of the operation of the Enabling Clause at the Sixty-third Session of the Committee on Trade and Development on 19 April 1988, the representative of Brazil stated that "although preferential concessions constituted a unilateral act of the donor country the exclusion of countries from GSP was *per se* a discrimination which was not based on the agreed principles .... some countries were clearly moving away from the observance of the basic principles set out in the Decision of the CONTRACTING PARTIES of 25 June 1971 and of 28 November 1979 concerning the granting of preferential treatment to products originating in developing countries. ... developed contracting parties acting individually had been authorized to grant such a preferential treatment provided that the corresponding schemes were of a generalized, non-discriminatory and non-reciprocal nature. The fact that such schemes were of a voluntary character and did not

---

[167]L/6605, adopted 4 December 1989, 36S/49, 57, para. 25.
[168]L/7029 (request); L/7373 (WP terms of reference) see Council discussion in C/M/202, C/M/223, C/M/226, C/M/247, C/M/249, C/M/254, C/M/255, C/M/258, C/M/259, C/M/260; see discussion in Committee on Trade and Development, COM.TD/132, L/7124; SR.48. See also documents listed under MERCOSUR above.
[169]C/M/152.
[170]L/5913, adopted 28 November 1985, 32S/21, 32-33, para. 34.
[171]*Ibid.*, 32S/33, para. 36.

constitute a binding obligation for the preference-giving countries did not in his view give them the right to ignore the legal framework under which they had been authorized to implement such schemes".[172]

See also above under "Preference schemes".

7. Coexistence of the GATT 1947 and the WTO Agreement

On 8 December 1994, the Preparatory Committee for the WTO, meeting on the occasion of the Implementation Conference, adopted a Decision on "Coexistence of the General Agreement on Tariffs and Trade 1947 and the World Trade Organization". The CONTRACTING PARTIES meeting in Special Session on the same date also adopted this decision, which provides *inter alia*:

"The CONTRACTING PARTIES to the General Agreement on Tariffs and Trade (hereinafter referred to as 'GATT 1947'),

"*Noting* that not all contracting parties to the GATT 1947 meeting the conditions for original membership in the World Trade Organization ... will be able to accept the Marrakesh Agreement Establishing the WTO ... as of its date of entry into force, and that the stability of multilateral trade relations would therefore be furthered if the GATT 1947 and the WTO Agreement were to co-exist for a limited period of time;

"*Considering* that, during that period of co-existence, a contracting party which has become a Member of the WTO should not be under a legal obligation to extend the benefits accruing solely under the WTO Agreement to contracting parties that have not yet become WTO Members and should have the right to act in accordance with the WTO Agreement notwithstanding its obligations under the GATT 1947; ...

"*Decide as follows:*

"1. The contracting parties that are Members of the WTO may, notwithstanding the provisions of the GATT 1947,

"(a) accord to products originating in or destined for a Member of the WTO the benefits to be accorded to such products solely as a result of concessions, commitments or other obligations assumed under the WTO Agreement without according such benefits to products originating in or destined for a contracting party that has not yet become a Member of the WTO; and

"(b) maintain or adopt any measure consistent with the provisions of the WTO Agreement."[173]

Concerning the transition to the WTO, see further in the chapter on institutions and procedure.

III. PREPARATORY WORK AND SUBSEQUENT MODIFICATIONS

Article I of the General Agreement corresponds to Article 16 of the Havana Charter, Article 8 of the US Draft, Article 14 in the London and New York Drafts, and Article 16 in the Geneva Draft Charter. Paragraph 1 is modelled on the standard League of Nations most-favoured-nation clause.[174] References to "international

---

[172]COM.TD/127, p. 5.
[173]PC/12, L/7583, preamble and para. 1.
[174]London Report, p. 9. See also EPCT/C.II/W/10 (Note by the Preparatory Committee Secretariat comparing the League of Nations clause with Article 8:1 of the US Draft Charter).

transfer of payments" and "internal taxes" were introduced into the standard clause by the United States in the US Draft.[175]

Article 8 of the US Draft Charter included both a general most-favoured-nation clause and an exemption therefrom of certain preferences in the rate of ordinary import customs duties. The margin of preference could not be increased above the level existing on 1 July 1946, and would be subject to negotiations for its elimination.[176] The London Draft Charter provided an m.f.n. exemption for (*1*) preferences in force exclusively between territories in respect of which there existed on 1 July 1939 common sovereignty or relations of protection or suzerainty; (*2*) Imperial preferences; (*3*) U.S.-Cuban preferences; and (*4*) preferences in force on 1 July 1946 exclusively between neighbouring countries. The margin of preference could not exceed the level remaining after negotiations which were to be conducted to reduce tariffs and preferences. All negotiated reductions in m.f.n. tariffs would operate automatically to reduce or eliminate margins of preference.[177] The Geneva Draft Charter limited the maximum margin of preference to the maximum margin permitted under the General Agreement, or, if not thus provided for, the margin existing on 10 April 1947 or any earlier base date established for GATT negotiations; it was at this point that the Annexes took the form that they have in the General Agreement.[178] At Havana, the Charter was amended to provide for additional groups of preferences; these proferences appear in the Havana Charter but were not as such taken into the General Agreement.[179]

Paragraph 4 is more precise than the corresponding Havana Charter paragraph (Article 16:4) as it had to cover all the cases resulting from the tariff negotiations.[180] Also, the word "margins" is used in paragraph 2 of the Charter Article instead of "levels;" the preferences between the United States and the Philippines are set out as a sub-paragraph of paragraph 2 in the Charter, and in the General Agreement are listed in Annex D; and the final paragraphs of Annexes A and D concerning certain preferential internal taxes are included in the Charter as paragraph 5.

Article I has been amended only once, in 1948, through the Protocol Amending Part I and Article XXIX; the amendments (insertion of paragraph 3) are discussed above at page 44. Amendment of Article I was again discussed in the Review Session of 1954-55. A number of amendments were proposed then regarding margins of preference and failed to gain acceptance; see above at page 42. One amendment of substance was agreed, the inclusion in paragraph 1 of a reference to internal taxes applied to exported goods; see page 31 above. In addition, it was agreed to group into one Annex all preferences between neighbouring countries under paragraph 2(d) and to include in it the preferences provided for between Uruguay and Paraguay in the Annecy Protocol of Accession, and to delete Annex F since Lebanon and Syria were no longer contracting parties.[181] These amendments were effected through the Protocol Amending Part I and Articles XXIX and XXX, which failed to gain the requisite unanimous acceptance and was abandoned at the end of 1967.[182]

---

[175] EPCT/C.II/25, p. 2.
[176] US Draft Charter, Art. 8(2).
[177] London Draft Charter Arts. 14(2), 24(1)(c). See also initial discussion of historical preferences in EPCT/C.II/PRO/PV/5.
[178] Geneva Draft Charter Article 16.
[179] Preferences between Portugal and Portugese territories; Colombia, Ecuador and Venezuela; republics of Central America; and Argentina and neighbouring countries. Havana Charter Annexes E, H, I, J.
[180] EPCT/TAC/PV/9, pp. 16-23.
[181] L/329, adopted 26 February 1955, 3S/205, 206-207, para. 5.
[182] 15S/65.

IV. RELEVANT DOCUMENTS

London

Discussion:	EPCT/C.II/7, 25, 27, 41, 65
	EPCT/C.II/PV/4, 11(a), 12
Reports:	EPCT/30

New York

Discussion:	EPCT/C.6/10, 106
Reports:	EPCT/C.6/97/Rev.1
Other:	EPCT/C.6/W.8, 25

Geneva

Discussion:	EPCT/EC/SR.2/6, 7, 8, 22
	EPCT/EC/PV.2/22
	EPCT/A/SR.7, 42, 43
	EPCT/TAC/SR.2, 7, 8, 9, 16
	EPCT/TAC/PV/16 (p. 20), 23, 24, 26 (p. 9-12), 28, 29
Reports:	EPCT/135, 158, 174, 178, 189, 192, 194, 196, 211, 215, 230
	EPCT/W/150, 164, 179, 183, 189, 242, 249
Other:	EPCT/105
	EPCT/W/27, 49, 64, 141, 146, 147, 149, 159, 162, 287, 312, 318, 321, 341, 343

Havana

Discussion:	E/CONF.2/C.3/SR.3, 4, 5, 6, 7, 39, 43, 44
	E/CONF.2/19, 23
Reports:	Havana Reports pp.40-41, 47-49, 53, 55
	E/CONF.2/C.3/59, 78, 79
	E/CONF.2/C.2 & 3/A/14
Other:	E/CONF.2/C.3/77/Rev.1
	E/CONF.2/C.3/A/15
	E/CONF.2/C.3/SR.29

Review Session

Discussion:	SR.9/17, 25, 36, 47
Reports:	W.9/193, 200, 212, L/329, 3S/205
Other:	GATT/184, 193
	L/189, 261/Add.1, 270, 272, 274, 282
	W.9/45, 53, 114, 124, 162, 217+Corr.1, 236
	Spec/3/55, 85/55, 94/55

ARTICLE II

SCHEDULES OF CONCESSIONS

I. TEXT OF ARTICLE II, INTERPRETATIVE NOTE AD ARTICLE II, AND UNDERSTANDING ON THE INTERPRETATION OF ARTICLE II:1(B) OF THE GATT 1994 64

II. INTERPRETATION AND APPLICATION OF ARTICLE II 67
   A. SCOPE AND APPLICATION OF ARTICLE II 67
      1. Paragraph 1(a): "treatment no less favourable than that provided for in the appropriate Part of the appropriate Schedule" 67
         (1) "Treatment" and interpretation of the scope of concessions in Schedules 67
            (a) Tariff escalation 68
            (b) Replacement of quantitative restrictions by tariffs 69
         (2) Maintenance of "treatment" versus modification of a concession 69
            (a) Alteration in tariff nomenclature 70
            (b) Alteration of the basis for levying duties 70
            (c) Conversion of rates to reflect change in customs valuation 71
            (d) Imposition of a variable import duty on bound items 72
            (e) Tariff reclassification 72
         (3) "Treatment": Schedule concessions other than duties on importation 73
            (a) Export duties 73
            (b) Schedule commitments by certain contracting parties 73
            (c) Other non-tariff concessions 74
         (4) Withholding or withdrawal of concessions 75
      2. Paragraphs 1(b) and (c) 75
         (1) "products of territories of other contracting parties" 75
            (a) Origin of goods for the purposes of most-favoured-nation treatment 75
            (b) Direct consignment requirements 75
         (2) "subject to the terms, conditions or qualifications set forth in that schedule" 75
         (3) "ordinary customs duties" 78
         (4) "other duties or charges of any kind" 78
            (a) Import surcharges 79
            (b) Deposit schemes 80
            (c) Revenue duties and import taxes 81
            (d) Charges on transfer of payments 81
            (e) Charges imposed by import monopolies 82
         (5) "imposed on or in connection with importation" 82
         (6) "date of this Agreement" (paragraphs 1(b), 1(c) and 6(a)) 83
         (7) "directly and mandatorily required to be imposed ... by legislation" 85
         (8) Paragraph 1(c): "preferential treatment" 85
      3. Paragraph 2 86
         (1) Paragraph 2(a): "a charge equivalent to an internal tax imposed consistently with the provisions of paragraph 2 of Article III" 86
         (2) Paragraph 2(b): "any anti-dumping or countervailing duty applied consistently with the provisions of Article VI" 86
         (3) Paragraph 2(c): "fees or other charges commensurate with the cost of services rendered" 87
      4. Paragraph 3: impairment of concessions by alteration in valuation or currency conversion 87
      5. Paragraph 4 88
         (1) "a monopoly of the importation of any product described in the appropriate Schedule" 88
         (2) "except as provided for in that Schedule or as otherwise agreed": concessions on the operations of import monopolies 89
         (3) "in the light of the provisions of Article 31 of the Havana Charter" 90
            (a) Application of the Interpretative Note 90
            (b) Article 31 91
            (c) Interpretative Note Ad Article II:4 92
         (4) "protection on the average in excess of the amount of protection provided for in that Schedule" 93
      6. Paragraph 5 96
      7. Paragraph 6 97
         (1) "currency at the par value accepted or provisionally recognized" 97
         (2) Adjustment of specific duties in accordance with paragraph 6(a) 98
         (3) "date of this Agreement" 98
         (4) Article II:6(b) 99
      8. Paragraph 7: "an integral part of Part I of this Agreement" 99
   B. RELATIONSHIP BETWEEN ARTICLE II AND OTHER GATT ARTICLES 99

			1.	Article III	99
			2.	Article VIII	99
			3.	Articles XI and XIII	100
			4.	Article XXIII	101
			5.	Article XXVIII	101
	C.	EXCEPTIONS AND DEROGATIONS			101
			1.	Article II:2	101
			2.	Protocol of Provisional Application	101
			3.	Other Protocols of accession	101
			4.	Waivers under Article XXV:5	102
			5.	Coexistence of the GATT 1947 and the WTO Agreement	103
	D.	TARIFF PROTOCOLS, SCHEDULES OF CONCESSIONS, AND NATIONAL TARIFF SCHEDULES			103
			1.	Schedules in general	103
			2.	Protocols of concessions	104
			3.	Consolidated Schedules	105
			4.	Loose-leaf Schedules	105
			5.	Implementation of the Harmonized System	106
				(1) Conversion of schedules to Harmonized System nomenclature	106
				(2) Implementation in GATT schedules of amendments to Harmonized System nomenclature	108
			6.	Concessions in schedules	110
				(1) Authentic texts of Schedules	110
				(2) Description of concessions	110
				(3) Legal basis for determining initial negotiating rights (INRs)	110
			7.	Application of concessions	111
				(1) National tariff schedules	111
				(2) Changes in tariff nomenclature	112
				(3) Provisional accession to the General Agreement	112
			8.	Modification of concessions	112
			9.	Modification and rectification of Schedules	112
				(1) Procedures for modification or rectification of Schedules	112
				(2) Certifications of rectifications and modifications	113
				(3) Legal effect of certification	114
				(4) Application of rectification procedures in other agreements	115
			10.	Withholding or withdrawal of concessions	115
			11.	Notification of national tariff schedules, the Tariff Study and the Integrated Data Base	115
III.	PREPARATORY WORK AND SUBSEQUENT MODIFICATIONS				116
IV.	RELEVANT DOCUMENTS				118
V.	SCHEDULES OF CONTRACTING PARTIES TO THE GATT 1947				119

I. TEXT OF ARTICLE II, INTERPRETATIVE NOTE AD ARTICLE II, AND UNDERSTANDING ON THE INTERPRETATION OF ARTICLE II:1(B) OF THE GATT 1994

Article II

Schedules of Concessions

1. (*a*) Each contracting party shall accord to the commerce of the other contracting parties treatment no less favourable than that provided for in the appropriate Part of the appropriate Schedule annexed to this Agreement.

(*b*) The products described in Part I of the Schedule relating to any contracting party, which are the products of territories of other contracting parties, shall, on their importation into the territory to which the Schedule relates, and subject to the terms, conditions or qualifications set forth in that Schedule, be exempt from ordinary customs duties in excess of those set forth and provided therein. Such products shall also be exempt from all other duties or charges of any kind imposed on or in connection with the importation in excess of those imposed on the date of this Agreement or those directly and mandatorily required to be imposed thereafter by legislation in force in the importing territory on that date.

(c) The products described in Part II of the Schedule relating to any contracting party which are the products of territories entitled under Article I to receive preferential treatment upon importation into the territory to which the Schedule relates shall, on their importation into such territory, and subject to the terms, conditions or qualifications set forth in that Schedule, be exempt from ordinary customs duties in excess of those set forth and provided for in Part II of that Schedule. Such products shall also be exempt from all other duties or charges of any kind imposed on or in connection with importation in excess of those imposed on the date of this Agreement or those directly or mandatorily required to be imposed thereafter by legislation in force in the importing territory on that date. Nothing in this Article shall prevent any contracting party from maintaining its requirements existing on the date of this Agreement as to the eligibility of goods for entry at preferential rates of duty.

2. Nothing in this Article shall prevent any contracting party from imposing at any time on the importation of any product:

(a) a charge equivalent to an internal tax imposed consistently with the provisions of paragraph 2 of Article III* in respect of the like domestic product or in respect of an article from which the imported product has been manufactured or produced in whole or in part;

(b) any anti-dumping or countervailing duty applied consistently with the provisions of Article VI;*

(c) fees or other charges commensurate with the cost of services rendered.

3. No contracting party shall alter its method of determining dutiable value or of converting currencies so as to impair the value of any of the concessions provided for in the appropriate Schedule annexed to this Agreement.

4. If any contracting party establishes, maintains or authorizes, formally or in effect, a monopoly of the importation of any product described in the appropriate Schedule annexed to this Agreement, such monopoly shall not, except as provided for in that Schedule or as otherwise agreed between the parties which initially negotiated the concession, operate so as to afford protection on the average in excess of the amount of protection provided for in that Schedule. The provisions of this paragraph shall not limit the use by contracting parties of any form of assistance to domestic producers permitted by other provisions of this Agreement.*

5. If any contracting party considers that a product is not receiving from another contracting party the treatment which the first contracting party believes to have been contemplated by a concession provided for in the appropriate Schedule annexed to this Agreement, it shall bring the matter directly to the attention of the other contracting party. If the latter agrees that the treatment contemplated was that claimed by the first contracting party, but declares that such treatment cannot be accorded because a court or other proper authority has ruled to the effect that the product involved cannot be classified under the tariff laws of such contracting party so as to permit the treatment contemplated in this Agreement, the two contracting parties, together with any other contracting parties substantially interested, shall enter promptly into further negotiations with a view to a compensatory adjustment of the matter.

6. (a) The specific duties and charges included in the Schedules relating to contracting parties members of the International Monetary Fund, and margins of preference in specific duties and charges maintained by such contracting parties, are expressed in the appropriate currency at the par value accepted or provisionally recognized by the Fund at the date of this Agreement. Accordingly, in case this par value is reduced consistently with the Articles of Agreement of the International Monetary Fund by more than twenty per centum, such specific duties and charges and margins of preference may be adjusted to take account of such reduction; *Provided* that the CONTRACTING PARTIES (*i.e.*, the contracting parties acting jointly as provided for in Article XXV) concur that such adjustments will not impair the value of the concessions provided for in the appropriate Schedule or elsewhere in this Agreement, due account being taken of all factors which may influence the need for, or urgency of, such adjustments.

(b) Similar provisions shall apply to any contracting party not a member of the Fund, as from the date on which such contracting party becomes a member of the Fund or enters into a special exchange agreement in pursuance of Article XV.

7. The Schedules annexed to this Agreement are hereby made an integral part of Part I of this Agreement.

Interpretative Note *Ad* Article II from Annex I

Paragraph 2 (a)

The cross-reference, in paragraph 2 (*a*) of Article II, to paragraph 2 of Article III shall only apply after Article III has been modified by the entry into force of the amendment provided for in the Protocol Modifying Part II and Article XXVI of the General Agreement on Tariffs and Trade, dated September 14, 1948.[1]

Paragraph 2 (b)

See the note relating to paragraph 1 of Article I.

Paragraph 4

Except where otherwise specifically agreed between the contracting parties which initially negotiated the concession, the provisions of this paragraph will be applied in the light of the provisions of Article 31 of the Havana Charter.

UNDERSTANDING ON THE INTERPRETATION OF ARTICLE II:1(b) OF THE GENERAL AGREEMENT ON TARIFFS AND TRADE 1994

Members hereby agree as follows:

1. In order to ensure transparency of the legal rights and obligations deriving from paragraph 1(b) of Article II, the nature and level of any "other duties or charges" levied on bound tariff items, as referred to in that provision, shall be recorded in the Schedules of concessions annexed to GATT 1994 against the tariff item to which they apply. It is understood that such recording does not change the legal character of "other duties or charges".

2. The date as of which "other duties or charges" are bound, for the purposes of Article II, shall be 15 April 1994. "Other duties or charges" shall therefore be recorded in the Schedules at the levels applying on this date. At each subsequent renegotiation of a concession or negotiation of a new concession the applicable date for the tariff item in question shall become the date of the incorporation of the new concession in the appropriate Schedule. However, the date of the instrument by which a concession on any particular tariff item was first incorporated into GATT 1947 or GATT 1994 shall also continue to be recorded in column 6 of the Loose-Leaf Schedules.

3. "Other duties or charges" shall be recorded in respect of all tariff bindings.

4. Where a tariff item has previously been the subject of a concession, the level of "other duties or charges" recorded in the appropriate Schedule shall not be higher than the level obtaining at the time of the first incorporation of the concession in that Schedule. It will be open to any Member to challenge the existence of an "other duty or charge", on the ground that no such "other duty or charge" existed at the time of the original binding of the item in question, as well as the consistency of the recorded level of any "other duty or charge" with the previously bound level, for a period of three years after the date of entry into force of the WTO Agreement or three years after the date of deposit with the Director-General of the WTO of the instrument incorporating the Schedule in question into GATT 1994, if that is a later date.

5. The recording of "other duties or charges" in the Schedules is without prejudice to their consistency with rights and obligations under GATT 1994 other than those affected by paragraph 4. All Members retain the right to challenge, at any time, the consistency of any "other duty or charge" with such obligations.

6. For the purposes of this Understanding, the provisions of Articles XXII and XXIII of GATT 1994 as elaborated and applied by the Dispute Settlement Understanding shall apply.

7. "Other duties or charges" omitted from a Schedule at the time of deposit of the instrument incorporating the Schedule in question into GATT 1994 with, until the date of entry into force of the WTO Agreement, the Director-General to the CONTRACTING PARTIES to GATT 1947 or, thereafter, with the Director-General of the WTO, shall not subsequently be added to it and any "other duty or charge" recorded at a level lower than that prevailing on the applicable date shall not be restored to that level unless such additions or changes are made within six months of the date of deposit of the instrument.

8. The decision in paragraph 2 regarding the date applicable to each concession for the purposes of paragraph 1(b) of Article II of GATT 1994 supersedes the decision regarding the applicable date taken on 26 March 1980 (BISD 27S/24).

II. INTERPRETATION AND APPLICATION OF ARTICLE II

A. SCOPE AND APPLICATION OF ARTICLE II

1. Paragraph 1(a): "treatment no less favourable than that provided for in the appropriate Part of the appropriate Schedule"

(1) "Treatment" and interpretation of the scope of concessions in Schedules

The 1981 Panel Report on "Spain - Tariff Treatment of Unroasted Coffee", which examined the tariff treatment of imports of unroasted coffee into Spain, states:

> "The Panel found that there was no obligation under the GATT to follow any particular system for classifying goods, and that a contracting party had the right to introduce in its customs tariff new positions or subpositions as appropriate".[1]

This finding was subject to the following footnote: "Provided that a re-classification subsequent to the making of a concession under the GATT would not be a violation of the basic commitment regarding that concession (Article II:5)".

The 1982 Report of the "Panel on Vitamins" (see below at page 71) provides, *inter alia*: "The Panel considers that the United States did not have an obligation to maintain the de facto tariff rate differentiation between feedgrade and pharmaceutical quality vitamins, provided that the method used for the conversion of the previous common bound rate was neutral and did not involve any arbitrary increase".[2]

At the special meeting of the Council in October 1988 to review developments in the trading system, the Director-General informed the Council that in April 1988, Canada and the EC had asked him, with reference to paragraph 8 of the 1979 Understanding, to render an advisory opinion on whether a tariff concession granted by Portugal to Canada in 1961 was applicable to wet salted cod. This issue had arisen in tariff negotiations between Canada and the EC under Article XXIV:6. He had agreed on 15 April to render such an opinion and on 15 July had made it available to the two parties concerned.[3]

The 1989 Panel Report on "Canada/Japan: Tariff on Imports of Spruce, Pine, Fir (SPF) Dimension Lumber" examined Canada's claim that Japan's application of an 8 per cent tariff on imports of SPF dimension lumber was inconsistent with Article I:1 because SPF dimension lumber and dimension lumber of other types, which benefited from a zero duty rate, were "like products" within the meaning of Article 1:1.

> "... The Panel considered it impossible to appreciate fully the Canadian complaint if it had not in a preliminary way clarified the meaning of some principles of the GATT system in relation to tariff structure and tariff classification.
>
> "The Panel noted in this respect that the General Agreement left wide discretion to the contracting parties in relation to the structure of national tariffs and the classification of goods in the framework of such structure (see the report of the Panel on Tariff Treatment of Unroasted Coffee, BISD 28S/102, at 111, paragraph 4.4). The adoption of the Harmonized System, to which both Canada and Japan have adhered, had brought about a large measure of harmonization in the field of customs classification of goods, but this system did not entail any obligation as to the ultimate detail in the respective tariff classifications. Indeed, this nomenclature has been on purpose structured in such a way that it leaves room for further specifications.
>
> "The Panel was of the opinion that, under these conditions, a tariff classification going beyond the Harmonized System's structure is a legitimate means of adapting the tariff scheme to each contracting

---

[1] L/5135, adopted on 11 June 1981, 28S/102, 111, para. 4.4.
[2] L/5331, adopted on 1 October 1982, 29S/110, 117, para. 22(e).
[3] C/M/225, p. 2.

party's trade policy interests, comprising both its protection needs and its requirements for the purposes of tariff- and trade negotiations. ...

"Tariff differentiation being basically a legitimate means of trade policy, a contracting party which claims to be prejudiced by such practice bears the burden of establishing that such tariff arrangement has been diverted from its normal purpose so as to become a means of discrimination in international trade. Such complaints have to be examined in considering simultaneously the internal protection interest involved in a given tariff specification, as well as its actual or potential influence on the pattern of imports from different extraneous sources ..."[4]

"The Panel considered that the tariffs referred to in the General Agreement are, quite evidently, those of the individual contracting parties. This was inherent in the system of the Agreement and appeared also in the current practice of tariff negotiations, the subject matter of which were the national tariffs of the contracting parties. It followed that, if a claim of likeness was raised by a contracting party in relation to the tariff treatment of its goods on importation by some other contracting party, such a claim should be based on the classification of the latter, i.e. the importing country's tariff."[5]

In Council discussion when this panel report was adopted, Canada raised the concern that "this interpretation could lead to pre-eminence being given to the tariff classification of a contracting party when determining 'like products' under Article I ... Tariff classification systems cannot identify specifically each and every possible product which may be imported. In the tariff classification system of contracting parties it is regularly the case that an individual tariff line or description will cover a wide range of different products, particularly in the example of lines which read 'other' or 'not elsewhere specified'. Additionally, there are new products continually entering the marketplace which are not identified in tariff schedules".[6]

See also the material on Greek reclassification of gramophone records below at page 96.

(a) Tariff escalation

The Ministerial Decision of 29 November 1982 on "Tariffs" provides, *inter alia*, that "prompt attention should be given to the problem of escalation in tariffs on products with increased processing with a view to effective action towards the elimination or reduction of such escalation where it inhibits international trade, taking into account the concerns relating to exports of developing countries".[7]

See also various Secretariat Notes from 1981-85 on the theory and practice of measurement of tariff escalation.[8] See also records of discussions in the Committee on Trade and Development and the Committee on Tariff Concessions, on the basis and methodological issues involved in studies on tariff escalation.[9]

---

[4]L/6470, adopted on 19 July 1989, 36S/167, 197-198, paras. 5.7-5.10.
[5]*Ibid.*, 36S/199, para. 5.13.
[6]L/6528; see also C/M/232, p. 9-12; C/M/234, p. 44-49; C/M/235, p. 15-18.
[7]L/5424, 29S/9, 18, para. 1.
[8]"Tariff Escalation", COM.TD/W/315, dated 4 July 1980; "Measurement of Tariff Escalation", TAR/W/18, dated 5 March 1981; "Study by the Secretariat on the Copper Producing and Copper Consuming Industries", Note dated 7 April 1982 issued as TAR/W/26 and COM.TD/W/361; "Tariff Escalation", Note dated 8 June 1982 issued as TAR/W/29 and COM.TD/W/369; and "Tariff Escalation", COM.TD/W/425, dated 22 March 1985. See also Report of Group of Governmental Experts on "Measures Affecting the World Market for Copper Ores and Concentrates", L/6167, adopted on 2 December 1987, 34S/168, and Note by the Director-General on "Measures Affecting the World Market for Copper Ores and Concentrates", L/6456, 36S/199.
[9]COM.TD/108; L/5253, 28S/53, 64-65, para. 36; L/5401, 29S/66, 73, para. 25; TAR/34, 28S/68, 70-71, para. 9; TAR/63, 29S/75, 76-77, para. 7. Tariff escalation affecting tropical products was also discussed in 1965-66 in the Expert Group on Trade and Aid Studies of the Committee on Trade and Development: see "Secretariat Note on the Effects of Differential Tariffs" (estimating effective protection of groundnuts and cocoa), Spec(65)144 dated 17 December 1965.

(b) Replacement of quantitative restrictions by tariffs

The Report of the Review Session Working Party on "Schedules and Customs Administration" notes as follows:

> "Some members of the Working Party proposed that it should be recognized that when quantitative restrictions imposed for balance-of-payments reasons are removed an increase of customs duties or other charges on imports, having the effect of impairing the benefits which might reasonably be expected from removal of the restrictions, could be referred to the CONTRACTING PARTIES by a contracting party having a substantial interest in the export of the products affected. They admitted that the CONTRACTING PARTIES when considering any such reference, should take account of all relevant considerations including the fiscal, developmental, strategic and other needs of the contracting party concerned, and also the relative progress of both parties in the reduction of tariffs and other obstacles to trade. This proposal was supported by some other members, but the majority of the Working Party opposed it mainly on the ground that it might result in an extension of control of the CONTRACTING PARTIES over unbound rates of duty. The majority decision, however, is without prejudice to the operation of Articles XXII and XXIII with respect to such cases as could appropriately be brought under those Articles".[10]

See also the unadopted panel report of 1994 on "EEC - Import Régime for Bananas".[11]

(2) Maintenance of "treatment" versus modification of a concession

The 1984 Report of the "Panel on Newsprint" examined the claim of Canada concerning the application of a tariff concession on newsprint established by the European Communities. The concession in the EC's Schedule LXXII provided for an annual tariff quota of 1.5 million tonnes duty-free, leaving the bound duty rate at 7 per cent for imports exceeding that quota. Under agreements between the EC and the EFTA countries, newsprint imports from EFTA countries became duty-free as from 1 January 1984, and the EC then opened a duty-free tariff quota for m.f.n. suppliers of 500,000 tonnes for newsprint for the year 1984.

> "The Panel could not share the argument advanced by the EC that their action did not constitute a change in their GATT tariff commitment. It noted that under longstanding GATT practice, even purely formal changes in the tariff schedule of a contracting party, which may not affect the GATT rights of other countries, such as the conversion of a specific to an ad valorem duty without an increase in the protective effect of the tariff rate in question, have been considered to require renegotiations. By the same token, the EC action would, in the Panel's view, have required the EC to conduct such negotiations. The Panel also noted that in granting the concession in 1973, the EC had not made it subject to any qualification or reservation in the sense of Article II:1(b) although at the time the concession was made, it was known that agreement had already been reached that the EFTA countries would obtain full duty-free access to the Community market for newsprint from 1 January 1984 onward. The Panel therefore found that although in the formal sense the EC had not modified its GATT concession, it had *in fact* changed its GATT commitment unilaterally, by limiting its duty-free tariff quota for m.f.n suppliers for 1984 to 500,000 tonnes. ...
>
> "Taking all factors mentioned above into account, the Panel concluded that the EC, in unilaterally establishing for 1984 a duty-free quota of 500,000 tonnes, had not acted in conformity with their obligations under Article II of the GATT. The Panel shared the view expressed before it relating to the fundamental importance of the security and predictability of GATT tariff bindings, a principle which constitutes a central obligation in the system of the General Agreement".[12]

---

[10] L/329, adopted 26 February 1955, 3S/205, 220 para. 40; for discussion and rejection of the proposed interpretation by majority vote, see SR.9/37 p. 7-9.

[11] DS38/R, dated 11 February 1994, para. 136.

[12] L/5680, adopted on 20 November 1984, 31S/114, 131-132, paras. 50, 52.

(a) Alteration in tariff nomenclature

The 1954 Report of the Ninth Session Working Party on Schedules, on "Transposition of Schedule XXXVII (Turkey)" notes that "The adoption of the Brussels nomenclature presents no basic problem so far as schedules to the General Agreement are concerned. At their Fifth Session, the CONTRACTING PARTIES agreed that a contracting party wishing to change the nomenclature of its schedule could resort to the normal rectification procedures. ... In the event of an objection being lodged concerning the change in nomenclature of any time, consultations should be held between Turkey and the governments concerned".[13]

The Decision of 12 July 1983 on "GATT Concessions under the Harmonized Commodity Description and Coding System" notes, *inter alia*:

"... The fact that one bound tariff line is divided up into a number of new lines, without changing the content of the original line, will not create any problem for the maintenance of the concession. Since, however, the introduction of the Harmonized System will result in a considerable number of cases where tariff lines with different bound rates are combined or bound rates combined with unbound rates, renegotiations under Article XXVIII will in many cases be necessary".[14]

(b) Alteration of the basis for levying duties

The 1953 Report of the Working Party at the Eighth Session on "Rectifications and Modifications of Schedules" notes:

"The Working Party also concerned itself with the proposal of the Greek Government to introduce a minimum *ad valorem* rate in certain specific rates and came to the conclusion that such changes could not be considered rectifications to be dealt with by the Working Party. It decided therefore to refer the question to the CONTRACTING PARTIES so that such changes could form the object of consultations and negotiations with the parties having an interest in those items. After the conclusion of the negotiations, the changes agreed upon could be embodied in a protocol of rectifications and modifications".[15]

In approving this report, the CONTRACTING PARTIES authorized the Government of Greece to enter into consultations and negotiations with the interested contracting parties.[16]

The 1955 Report of the Ninth Session Working Party on Schedules, on "Transposition of Schedule XXXVII (Turkey)" notes:

"... The Working Party considered the proposals [of Turkey] in relation to the provisions of the Agreement and to the practices of the CONTRACTING PARTIES which deal with the modification of schedules. It was found that there is no provision in the General Agreement which authorizes a contracting party to alter the structure of bound rates of duty from a specific to an ad valorem basis.

"The obligations of contracting parties are established by the rates of duty appearing in the schedules and any change in the rate such as a change from a specific to an ad valorem duty could in some circumstances adversely affect the value of the concessions to other contracting parties. Consequently, any conversion of specific into ad valorem rates of duty can be made only under some procedure for the modification of concessions".[17]

---

[13]L/294, adopted on 20 December 1954, 3S/127, 128, para. 2. For Fifth Session decision on modification of schedules consequent to adherence to the Brussels Convention for Tariff Nomenclature, see GATT/CP.5/7 (Secretariat proposal), GATT/CP.5/SR.3 p. 1-3 (discussion).
[14]L/5470/Rev.1, 30S/17, 18-19, para. 3.1.
[15]G/62, adopted on 24 October 1953, 2S/63, 2S/66, para. 8. See also similar decision at Fifth Session, GATT/CP.5/45, II/144, 145, section (3).
[16]SR.8/20, p. 5.
[17]L/294, adopted on 20 December 1954, 3S/127, 128, paras. 3-4; see also SR.9/4 p. 12.

The 1958 Working Party Report on "Conversion of Specific Duties in the Norwegian Schedule" cites this passage in discussing the proposal of Norway to establish simplified procedures for the conversion of specific to ad valorem duties, and observes that "It was obvious, therefore, that the relevant procedures were those of Article XXVIII which related to modifications of concessions in the Schedules".[18]

The 1954 Report of the Ninth Session Working Party on Schedules on the "Fourth Protocol of Rectifications and Modifications" discusses whether, even in the case where the existing (specific duty) concession reserved the right to convert specific duties into *ad valorem* rates, the retention of the former specific rate would constitute a modification of that concession:

"... Among the rectifications requested by the Austrian Government were those relating to Items 140 to 144 of the Austrian Tariff which were being made under the authority of the Note to these items included in the Austrian Schedule XXXII which granted the Austrian Government freedom to change the specific into ad valorem rates. The Austrian Government felt that it would not be impairing the value of the concessions if it retained beside the ad valorem duty the old specific rate as a minimum rate.

"The Working Party took the view that such changes would constitute modifications of Austria's obligations and that it could not recommend their acceptance as rectifications. Such modifications could only be inserted in a protocol of rectifications and modifications after negotiations authorized by the CONTRACTING PARTIES in accordance with the proper procedures ...".[19]

The 1978 Panel Report on "Canada - Withdrawal of Tariff Concessions", which examined a withdrawal resulting from negotiations concerning the EC's conversion to ad valorem duties of specific duties on unwrought lead and unwrought zinc, notes that:

"The Panel based its consideration of the case on Article XXVIII of the GATT which, as both parties agreed, was the applicable provision, *inter alia*, for negotiations which are undertaken with the aim of converting specific rates of duty into ad valorem rates".[20]

Concerning the application of Article II to a conversion from ad valorem rates to specific duty rates, see the unadopted panel report on "EEC - Import Régime for Bananas".[21]

See further under Article XXVIII.

(c) Conversion of rates to reflect change in customs valuation

The 1982 Report of the "Panel on Vitamins" examined the application of the Kennedy Round concession on feed-grade and pharmaceutical-grade Vitamin B12 by the United States. While the nominal bound duty rate for both qualities of Vitamin B12 was the same, this rate was subject to the "American selling price" ("ASP") method of tariff valuation applied by the United States under the Protocol of Provisional Application. Under the ASP method, the dutiable value imputed to feed-grade Vitamin B12 (and thus its effective duty rate) was lower than that on pharmaceutical-grade Vitamin B12. The granting of the concession had been subject to a general note reserving the ability of the US to adjust the duty rate in the event of elimination of ASP valuation. In the Tokyo Round, the US agreed to eliminate "ASP" valuation and to incorporate the extra duties charged as a result of this valuation method into the new base rate for Tokyo Round duty reductions. In the conversion, the effective rates of duty for both qualities of Vitamin B12 were converted together on the basis of a trade-weighted average, resulting in a single concession rate for Vitamin B12. The Panel Report provides, *inter alia*:

"The Panel considers that the United States did not have an obligation to maintain the de facto tariff rate differentiation between feedgrade and pharmaceutical quality vitamins, provided that the method used for the conversion of the previous common bound rate was neutral and did not involve any arbitrary increase.

---

[18]L/913, adopted on 14 November 1958, 7S/112, para. 3.
[19]L/335, adopted on 3 March 1955, excerpted at 3S/130, para. 1-2.
[20]L/4636, adopted on 17 May 1978, 25S/42, 47, para. 14.
[21]DS38/R, dated 11 February 1994, paras. 134-135.

The Panel believes the method used by the United States for the calculation of the level of the base rate - the weighted average of actual duties collected for feedgrade and pharmaceutical quality vitamins - to be in conformity with that proviso".[22]

In the Council discussion of this report, several contracting parties stated their view that the use of a trade-weighted average in conversion of tariffs should not constitute a precedent for future cases such as transposition of existing bound tariffs into the Harmonized Commodity Description and Coding System nomenclature, in view of the particular procedures outside Article XXVIII that had been adopted by the parties to the dispute.[23]

See also the discussion below of Schedules of Concessions.

(d) Imposition of a variable import duty on bound items

In 1961 Uruguay requested a ruling from the CONTRACTING PARTIES concerning whether the application of variable import duties was compatible with the GATT. A 1961 Note by the Executive Secretary on "Questions relating to Bilateral Agreements, Discrimination and Variable Taxes" states, *inter alia:*

"The General Agreement contains no provision on the use of 'variable import duties'. It is obvious that if any such duty or levy is imposed on a 'bound' item, the rate must not be raised in excess of what is permitted by Article II of the Agreement. ... It should be noted that if a variable levy system should be accompanied by the imposition of restrictions by specified volume, or a prohibition, of imports such measures would of course be subject to the examinations and considerations referred to in sections (a) and (b) above [relating to Articles XI, XIII, XII, XVIII:B and XIV]".[24]

See also the discussion of this Note in summary records of the Nineteenth Session.[25] The 1962 Panel Report on the "Uruguayan Recourse to Article XXIII" notes as follows:

"The Panel was faced with a particular difficulty in considering the status of variable import levies or charges. It noted the discussion which took place at the nineteenth session of the CONTRACTING PARTIES on this subject during which it was pointed out that such measures raised serious questions which had not been resolved. In these circumstances the Panel has not considered it appropriate to examine the consistency or otherwise of these measures under the General Agreement".[26]

In the Agriculture Committee in 1984, it was stated that where a variable levy was applicable to a product in respect of which the tariff duty rate was bound, the bound tariff rate constituted a maximum upper limit for the levy.[27]

(e) Tariff reclassification

Concerning tariff reclassification, see various notes by the Secretariat and the minutes of the Committee on Tariff Concessions[28] discussing the legal consequences of reclassification, and methods for maintaining GATT bindings in cases of tariff reclassification. In one discussion of this subject in the Committee on Tariff Concessions in 1980, it was noted by the representative of Austria that "The problem only arose directly in respect of [bound] items but it affected indirectly all items, since when transferring a GATT bound item from one heading to another with the same rate of duty, there might be a difference with respect to the so-called 'other charges'".[29]

---

[22] L/5331, adopted on 1 October 1982, 29S/110, 117, para. 22(e).
[23] C/M/160, 161.
[24] Note dated 21 November 1961, L/1636, paras. 7-8.
[25] SR.19/8, p. 111-120.
[26] L/1923, adopted 16 November 1962, 11S/95, 100, para. 17.
[27] AG/M/3, p. 63.
[28] TAR/W/14, TAR/W/19, TAR/M/3, TAR/M/4.
[29] TAR/M/3, p. 12, para. 5.3.

(3) "Treatment": Schedule concessions other than duties on importation

(a) Export duties

The United Kingdom Schedule XIX, Section D (Malayan Union) attached to the 30 October 1947 text of the General Agreement contained a concession on export duties on tin ore and tin concentrates, to the effect that "The products comprised in the above item shall be assessed for duty on the basis of their tin content; the rate to be levied on such tin content being the same as the rate chargeable on smelted tin, *Provided* that the rate of duty on this item may exceed the rate chargeable on smelted tin in the event that and so long as the United States of America subsidised directly or indirectly the smelting of tin in the United States".

(b) Schedule commitments by certain contracting parties

The US "Suggested Charter for an International Trade Organization" contained a separate Article 28 concerning expansion of trade by any Member establishing or maintaining a complete or substantially complete monopoly of its import trade. This Article envisaged the negotiation by each such Member of an arrangement providing for a minimum periodic value of imports from the other Members. This Article was kept with the same wording provisionally in the London and New York Draft Charters, and was deleted at Geneva. The Geneva Report states that the Preparatory Committee believed that the text of the revised Article 31 (requiring negotiations to limit or reduce protection afforded by import or export monopolies) would be sufficiently flexible to permit any appropriate negotiations with a Member which maintained a complete or substantially complete monopoly of its external trade, and that since no representative of such a country had attended the sessions of the Committee, the matter remained open for the Havana Conference.[30]

The Report of the Working Party on the "Accession of Poland" records that

> "The Working Party noted that the foreign trade of Poland was conducted mainly by State enterprises and that the Foreign Trade Plan rather than the customs tariff was the effective instrument of Poland's commercial policy. The present customs tariff was applicable only to a part of imports effected by private persons for their personal use and it was in the nature of a purchase tax rather than a customs tariff. The Working Party agreed that due consideration had to be given to these facts in drawing up the legal instruments relating to Poland's accession to the General Agreement. The representative of Poland stressed that, as a result of possible changes in the economic system of Poland, a different situation might arise enabling Poland to renegotiate its position towards the provisions of the General Agreement.

> "It was agreed that in view of the nature of the foreign trade system of Poland its main concession in the negotiations would be commitments relating to an annual increase in the value of its imports from contracting parties".[31]

Paragraph 1 of Poland's Schedule LXV, as set out in Annex B to the Protocol for the Accession of Poland, provides: "Subject to paragraph 2 below, Poland shall, with effect from the date of this Protocol, undertake to increase the total value of its imports from the territories of contracting parties by not less than 7 per cent per annum".[32] Schedule LXV and the Polish import commitment were modified on 5 February 1971.[33] In December 1989 Poland announced its intention to request renegotiation of its terms of accession in view of the entry into force 1 January 1990 of laws establishing a market economy for which the customs tariff would be the effective instrument of commercial policy.[34] At the February 1990 Council meeting a Working Party was established to

---

[30] London Report, p. 18, New York Report p. 29, Geneva Report p. 29. See also Secretariat Note of 1988 on this issue in MTN.GNG/NG7/W/15/Add.1 p. 1-3.

[31] L/2806, adopted on 26 June 1967, 15S/109, 110, paras. 7-8.

[32] 15S/52. Paragraph 2 provides, *inter alia*, that Poland may modify the commitment under paragraph 1 by negotiation and agreement, on 1 January 1971 and thereafter on the "open season" dates specified in Article XXVIII:1.

[33] L/3416 (notification by Poland of intent to renegotiate); C/M/64, p. 17-18; L/3475, "Third Review under the Protocol of Accession", adopted on 2 February 1971, 18S/188, section C, "Renegotiation of Schedule LXV - Poland", 18S/198-200 (noting adoption 5 February 1971 of modification of Schedule LXV by postal ballot).

[34] SR.45/ST/11, L/6634, C/M/238 p. 10-13.

examine the request of the Government of Poland to renegotiate the terms of accession of Poland.[35] This working party did not conclude its work before 1 January 1995.

The Working Party Report on "Accession of Romania" records that "It was agreed that because of the absence of a customs tariff in Romania the main concession to be incorporated in its Schedule would be a firm intention to increase imports from contracting parties at a rate not lower than the growth of total Romanian imports provided for in its Five-Year Plans".[36] Accordingly, paragraph 1 of Romania's Schedule LXIX provides that "Subject to paragraph 2 below, Romania, on the basis of mutual advantage which is inherent in the General Agreement, will develop and diversify its trade with the contracting parties as a whole, and firmly intends to increase its imports from the contracting parties as a whole at a rate not smaller than the growth of total Romanian imports provided for in its Five-Year Plans".[37] In 1974 a working party was established to examine the customs tariff introduced by Romania from 1 January 1974.[38] In 1991, Romania was granted a temporary waiver of its obligations under Article II in order to enable it to implement a new customs tariff in the context of measures for transition to a market economy, and pending renegotiation of its Schedule; Romania also requested renegotiation of its accession protocol in the light of, *inter alia*, the abolition of its former system of central planning.[39] At the February 1992 Council meeting a Working Party was established to examine the request of the Government of Romania to renegotiate the terms of accession of Romania.[40] This working party did not conclude its work before 1 January 1995.

(c)   Other non-tariff concessions

See material at page 89 on concessions made on monopoly markups and minimum importation by monopolies, and material under Article IV regarding screen quota concessions made during the period 1947-1950. Concessions have also been made with respect to mixing requirements.[41] In recent years certain governments acceding to the GATT have included in their Schedules, in addition to tariff concessions, such non-tariff commitments as minimum import quotas[42], or commitments for elimination of import permit requirements, import licensing schemes, or import prohibitions.[43]

The Review Working Party on "Other Barriers to Trade" which considered proposals for strengthening the provisions of the Agreement on subsidies and state trading, "also agreed that there was nothing to prevent contracting parties, when they negotiate for the binding or reduction of tariffs, from negotiating on matters, such as subsidies, which might affect the practical effects of tariff concessions, and from incorporating in the appropriate schedule annexed to the Agreement the results of such negotiations; provided that the results of such negotiations should not conflict with other provisions of the Agreement".[44] In this context the 1989 Panel Report on "United States - Restrictions on Imports of Sugar" found that "Article II permits contracting parties to incorporate into their Schedules acts yielding rights under the General Agreement, but not acts diminishing

---

[35]C/M/239, p. 5.
[36]L/3557, adopted on 6 October 1971, 18S/94, 95, para. 7.
[37]18S/10.
[38]L/3989 (notification of tariff by Romania); C/M/94. The working party did not make a report.
[39]L/6967, Decision of 4 December 1991, 38S/80.
[40]C/M/254 p. 5-6; see also L/6838 and Add.1, L/6981, SR.47/2 p. 15-16.
[41]Benelux Schedule II (1947), Items ex 68 and 75 (binding on mixing requirement for imported wheat and wheat flour).
[42]Schedule XXXII - Austria, Part III, non-tariff concessions (1979); Schedule XX - United States, note 2 to chapter 2, unit B.
[43]See Schedule LXXVII - Mexico (indication in Column 7 of items to be exempt from prior import permit requirement); Schedule LXXXVI - Venezuela (indication in Column 7 of items for which certain notes to Venezuelan tariff to cease to apply); Schedule LXXXVIII - Guatemala (indication in Column 7 of items to be exempt from prohibitions, licensing and restrictive permits, and other quantitative import restrictions); Schedule LXXXV - Costa Rica (indication in Column 7 of items to be exempt from licensing or quantitative restrictions or from duties and charges inconsistent with Articles III and VIII); Schedule LXXXVII - El Salvador (indication in Column 7 of items to be free from quantitative restrictions except to protect health or morals or national security, and free from charges and taxes inconsistent with Article III); Schedule LXXXIV - Bolivia (exemption from import licensing or quantitative restriction for items for which US has initial negotiating rights); Schedule LXXXIII - Tunisia (indication of exemption from import licensing or other quantitative restrictions for certain items).
[44]L/334, and Add., adopted on 3 March 1955, 3S/222, 225, para. 14.

obligations under that Agreement"[45] and that "Article II gives contracting parties the possibility to incorporate into the legal framework of the General Agreement commitments additional to those already contained in the General Agreement and to qualify such additional commitments, not however to reduce their commitments under other provisions of that Agreement".[46] See below at page 76.

Concerning negotiations on concessions other than on tariffs, see Article XXVIII *bis*.

(4) Withholding or withdrawal of concessions

See below at page 115 and see the material under Article XXVII.

2. **Paragraphs 1(b) and (c)**

The 1988 Panel Report on "United States - Customs User Fee" notes generally with respect to paragraph 1(b): "... Paragraph 1(b) of Article II establishes a general ceiling on the charges that can be levied on a product whose tariff is bound; it requires that the product be exempt from all tariffs in excess of the bound rate, and from all other charges in excess of those (i) in force on the date of the tariff concession, or (ii) directly and mandatorily required by legislation in force on that date".[47]

(1) "products of territories of other contracting parties"

(a) Origin of goods for the purposes of most-favoured-nation treatment

In discussions on the General Agreement at the Geneva session of the Preparatory Committee it was decided that it was unnecessary to add the words "originating in" to the phrase "products of territories of other contracting parties" (1(b) and (c)).[48] It was agreed that "it is within the province of each importing member country to determine, in accordance with the provisions of its law, for the purpose of applying the most-favoured-nation provisions whether goods do, in fact, originate in a particular country".[49]

Concerning work done in the GATT on rules of origin and origin of imported goods generally, see Article VIII; concerning rules of origin applied in the context of regional trade agreements see Article XXIV.

(b) Direct consignment requirements

The last sentence of paragraph 1(c) preserves the ability of a contracting party to maintain "its requirements existing on the date of this Agreement as to the eligibility of goods for entry at preferential rates of duty". (See also the reference in Article V:6 to "requirements of direct consignment existing on the date of this Agreement" as a condition for eligibility for entry at preferential rates.) However, in discussions on the draft text of the General Agreement during the Geneva session of the Preparatory Committee it was agreed that "direct shipping requirements would not be permitted" as a condition of granting the most-favoured-nation rate of duty.[50]

(2) "subject to the terms, conditions or qualifications set forth in that schedule"

The 1981 Panel Report on "European Economic Community - Imports of Beef from Canada" examined a 10,000-ton levy-free tariff quota for fresh, chilled or frozen high quality grain-fed beef included within a global tariff quota of 21,000 tons in the EEC schedule of concessions annexed to the Geneva (1979) Protocol. In a footnote to the concession it was provided that "Entry under this subheading is subject to conditions to be determined by the competent authorities". The concession was implemented through Commission Regulations which provided for a certificate of authenticity; Annex II of one of these Regulations listed the issuing authorities

---

[45] L/6514, adopted on 22 June 1989, 36S/331, 342, para. 5.2.
[46] *Ibid.*, para. 5.3.
[47] L/6264, adopted on 2 February 1988, 35S/245, 273, para. 70.
[48] EPCT/TAC/PV/23, p. 23.
[49] EPCT/TAC/PV/23, p. 31-33.
[50] EPCT/TAC/PV/23 p. 31.

for such certificates; and the sole such agency listed for high-quality grain-fed beef was the US Department of Agriculture.

"The Panel found that the European Economic Community had, by virtue of the footnote in the Schedule reserved its right to set conditions for the entry under the levy-free tariff quota in question. The Panel further found that the right to set conditions was presupposed in Article II:1(b) of the General Agreement. The Panel found, however, that the words 'terms, conditions or qualifications' in paragraph 1(b) of Article II could not be interpreted to mean that countries could explicitly or by the manner in which a concession was administered actually limit a given concession to the products of a particular country. The Panel further found that the fact that in Annex II there was only one certifying agency for the meat in question and that this agency only certified meat of United States origin in effect prevented access of high quality meat ... from other countries.

"Consequently, the Panel concluded that the manner in which the EEC concession on high quality beef was implemented accorded less favourable treatment to Canada than that provided for in the relevant EEC Schedule, thus being inconsistent with the provisions of paragraph 1 of Article II of the General Agreement".[51]

In the 1989 Panel Report on "United States - Restrictions on Imports of Sugar", the Panel examined quantitative restrictions by the US on the importation of raw and refined sugar. The United States claimed that the proviso "subject to the terms, conditions or qualifications set forth in that Schedule" in Article II:1(b) permitted contracting parties to include qualifications relating to quantitative restrictions in their Schedule; in a headnote to the tariff concession on raw and refined sugar in Schedule XX the United States had reserved the right to impose quota limitations on imports of sugar under certain circumstances.

"The Panel first examined the issue in the light of the wording of Article II. It noted that ... the words 'subject to the ... qualifications set forth in that Schedule' are used in conjunction with the words 'shall ... be exempt from ordinary customs duties in excess of those set forth in [the Schedule]'. This suggests that Article II:1(b) permits contracting parties to qualify the obligation to exempt products from customs duties in excess of the levels specified in the Schedule, not however to qualify their obligations under other Articles of the General Agreement. The Panel further noted that the title of Article II is 'Schedules of Concessions' and that the ordinary meaning of the word 'to concede' is 'to grant or yield.' This also suggests, in the view of the Panel, that Article II permits contracting parties to incorporate into their Schedules acts yielding rights under the General Agreement, but not acts diminishing obligations under that Agreement.

"The Panel then examined the issue in the light of the purpose of the General Agreement. It noted that one of the basic functions of the General Agreement is, according to its Preamble, to provide a legal framework enabling contracting parties to enter into 'reciprocal and mutually advantageous arrangements directed to the substantial reduction of tariffs and other barriers to trade.' Where the General Agreement mentions specific types of negotiations, it refers to negotiations aimed at the reduction of barriers to trade (Articles IV(d), XVII:3 and XXVIII bis). This supports in the view of the Panel the assumption that Article II gives contracting parties the possibility to incorporate into the legal framework of the General Agreement commitments additional to those already contained in the General Agreement and to qualify such additional commitments, not however to reduce their commitments under other provisions of that Agreement.

"The Panel then proceeded to examine the issue in the context of the provisions of the General Agreement related to Article II. It noted that negotiations on obstacles to trade created by the operation of state-trading enterprises may be conducted under Article XVII:3 and that a note to that provision provides that such negotiations

---

[51] L/5099, adopted on 10 March 1981, 28S/92, 99, paras. 4.5-4.6.

'may be directed towards the reduction of duties and other charges on imports and exports or towards the conclusion of *any other mutually satisfactory arrangement consistent with the provisions of this Agreement* (see paragraph 4 of Article II and the note to that paragraph).' (emphasis added).

"The negotiations foreseen in Article XVII:3 are thus not to result in arrangements inconsistent with the General Agreement, in particular not quantitative restrictions made effective through state-trading that are not justified by an exception to Article XI:1. The Panel saw no reason why a different principle should apply to quantitative restrictions made effective by other means.

"The Panel then examined the issue in the light of the practice of the CONTRACTING PARTIES. The Panel noted that the CONTRACTING PARTIES adopted in 1955 the Report of the Review Working Party on Other Barriers to Trade, which had concluded that:

'there was nothing to prevent contracting parties, when they negotiate for the binding or reduction of tariffs, from negotiating on matters, such as subsidies, which might affect the practical effects of tariff concessions, and from incorporating in the appropriate schedule annexed to the Agreement the results of such negotiations; *provided that the results of such negotiations should not conflict with other provisions of the Agreement.*' (emphasis added) (BISD 3S/225).

"Whether the proviso in this decision is regarded as a policy recommendation, as the United States argues, or as the confirmation of a legal requirement, as Australia claims, it does support, in the view of the Panel, the conclusion that the CONTRACTING PARTIES did not envisage that qualifications in Schedules established in accordance with Article II:1(b) could justify measures inconsistent with the other Articles of the General Agreement.

"The Panel finally examined the issue in the light of the drafting history. It noted that the reference to 'terms and qualifications' was included in a draft of the present Article II:1(b) during the Second Session of the Preparatory Committee of the United Nations Conference on Trade and Employment. The original draft had referred only to 'conditions'. This amendment was proposed and adopted 'in order to provide more generally for the sort of qualifications actually provided in the form of notes in the specimen Schedule. A number of these notes are, in effect, additional concessions rather than conditions governing the tariff bindings to which they relate' (E/PC/T/153 and E/PC/T/W/295). Schedule provisions qualifying obligations under the General Agreement were not included in the specimen Schedule nor was the possibility of such Schedule provisions mentioned by the drafters. The Panel therefore found that the drafting history did not support the interpretation advanced by the United States.

"For the reasons stated in the preceding paragraphs, the Panel found that Article II:1(b) does not permit contracting parties to qualify their obligations under other provisions of the General Agreement and that the provisions in the United States GATT Schedule of Concessions can consequently not justify the maintenance of quantitative restrictions on the importation of certain sugars inconsistent with the application of Article XI:1.[52]

The 1990 Panel Report on "United States - Restrictions on the Importation of Sugar and Sugar Containing Products Applied under the 1955 Waiver and under the Headnote to the Schedule of Tariff Concessions" examined the claim by the EEC that US import fees and import restrictions on sugar under Section 22 of the US Agricultural Adjustment Act were inconsistent with Articles II and XI interpreted in the light of the 1989 Panel Report on "United States - Restrictions on Imports of Sugar", and were not justified by the waiver accorded to the United States in 1955 for actions taken under Section 22.

"... As to the fees on refined sugar, the Panel noted that the United States made its concession for sugars, and covering refined sugar, subject to the existence of Title II of the Sugar Act of 1948 or substantially equivalent legislation. The United States considers that, given the lapse of the Sugar Act and the absence of substantially equivalent legislation, its tariff rates for sugars are presently not bound. In the

---

[52] L/6514, adopted on 22 June 1989, 36S/331, 342-343, paras. 5.2-5.7.

view of the United States, Article II:1(b), which allows contracting parties to make the tariff bindings in their Schedule of Concessions 'subject to ... terms, conditions or qualifications', allows contracting parties to make tariff concessions subject to the existence of domestic legislation. The EEC considers this qualification of the tariff concession to be inconsistent with the General Agreement and consequently not a valid limit of the concession.

"The Panel examined the EEC's claim in the light of Article II:1(b) and the above-mentioned report. The Panel noted that the report states that 'Article II gives contracting parties the possibility to incorporate into the legal framework of the General Agreement commitments additional to those already contained in the General Agreement and to qualify such additional commitments, not however to qualify their obligations under other articles of the General Agreement' (L/6514, page 13). The Panel found that the United States assumed in its Schedule of Concessions a commitment additional to the commitments already contained in the General Agreement, namely the avoidance of import duties beyond specified levels, and qualified this additional commitment by making it dependent on the existence of certain domestic legislation. This qualification does not constitute a qualification of a commitment of the United States under provisions of the General Agreement other than Article II; it merely qualifies the commitment under Article II not to impose import duties in excess of the rates set forth in the Schedule. Although the granting of concessions conditional upon the discretion of the concession-granting government may not be meaningful because of the obvious legal uncertainty thereby created, the General Agreement does not oblige contracting parties to make concessions and specifically allows them in Article II:1(b) to subject to conditions the concessions they decide to make. The fact that the United States subjected the effectiveness of the tariff rates for sugars to the existence of domestic legislation is for these reasons not inconsistent with the General Agreement. The Panel recognized that a concession cannot validly be subjected to a qualification that is inconsistent with the General Agreement. Such a qualification would be contrary to the principle recognized by the contracting parties that the results of negotiations included in a Schedule of Concessions must be consistent with the General Agreement (BISD 3S/225). The Panel however found that the evidence submitted to it by the parties did not permit it to conclude that legislation equivalent to Title II of the Sugar Act of 1948 would necessarily be inconsistent with the General Agreement, in particular Article XI:2. The Panel therefore concluded that, while sugars are subject to tariff concessions in the United States' Schedule of Concessions, the maximum rates for sugars set forth in that Schedule are, in the absence of legislation substantially equivalent to Title II of the expired Sugar Act of 1948, presently not effective. The imposition of the fees on refined sugar therefore does not entail the imposition of duties in excess of those set forth in the United States' Schedule of Concessions".[53]

(3) "ordinary customs duties"

The word "ordinary" was used to distinguish between the rates on regular tariffs shown in the columns of the schedules (in French: *"droits de douane proprement dit"*) and the various supplementary duties and charges [imposed on imports] such as primage duty.[54]

(4) "other duties or charges of any kind"

The Council Decision of 26 March 1980 on "Introduction of a Loose-Leaf System for the Schedules of Tariff Concessions" states with regard to the term "other duties or charges" that "such 'duties or charges' are in principle only those that discriminate against imports"[55] -- i.e., they do not include charges applied to imports and domestic goods alike. The Decision further states that "As can be seen from Article II:2 of the General Agreement, such 'other duties or charges' concern neither charges equivalent to internal taxes, nor anti-dumping or countervailing duties, nor fees or other charges commensurate with the cost of services rendered".[56]

In 1953, the United States brought a complaint that a French statistical tax of 0.4 per cent ad valorem of imports and exports was inconsistent with Article II:2(c) and thus with Article II:1(b). The French government

---

[53]L/6631, adopted on 7 November 1990, 37S/228, 255-256, paras. 5.7-5.8.
[54]EPCT/TAC/PV/23, p. 24-25.
[55]C/107/Rev. 1, adopted on 26 March 1980, 27S/22, 24, para. 9.
[56]*Ibid*.

"agreed that it did infringe the provisions of the General Agreement" and took steps to abolish the tax.[57] In 1955, the United States brought a complaint against the increase in the rate of stamp tax on customs duties in France, which was stated to be inconsistent with Article II and Article VIII as revised at the Review Session. "The CONTRACTING PARTIES took note of the undertaking of the French Government to cancel the measure ... which was inconsistent with the obligation of the French Government under the General Agreement".[58]

(a)   Import surcharges

In a Decision of 17 January 1955 on a "French Special Temporary Compensation Tax on Imports", which had been stated by the French Government to be a temporary and transitional device designed to facilitate the removal of quantitative restrictions on imports from OEEC member countries, and an alternative to action under Article XII, the CONTRACTING PARTIES ruled that "whatever may have been the reasons which motivated the French Government's decision ... the tax has increased the incidence of customs charges in excess of maximum rates bound under Article II ...".[59] Similarly, in a Decision of 21 November 1958 on "Peruvian Import Charges", the CONTRACTING PARTIES decided that Article XII could not be invoked to justify, as an alternative to the imposition of import restrictions, the imposition of surcharges on products described in schedules to the General Agreement.[60] The CONTRACTING PARTIES then granted a waiver to the Government of Peru covering the levying of such surcharges as an emergency measure designed to overcome a threat to Peru's monetary reserves and to ensure the success of its programme of monetary stabilization. The Decision on "Canadian Import Surcharges" adopted by the CONTRACTING PARTIES on 15 November 1962 states that the import surcharges are "inconsistent with Article II of the General Agreement".[61] The Report of the Working Party on the "United States Temporary Import Surcharge",[62] and the Report of the Working Party on the Danish Temporary Import Surcharge,[63] each "noted that the surcharge, to the extent that it raised the incidence of customs charges beyond the maximum rates bound under Article II, was not compatible with the provisions of the General Agreement".[64] The Declaration on "Trade Measures taken for Balance-of-Payments Purposes" adopted on 28 November 1979 provides in its paragraph 1 that "The procedures for examination stipulated in Articles XII and XVIII shall apply to all restrictive import measures taken for balance-of-payments purposes ..." but also provides that "The provisions of this paragraph are not intended to modify the substantive provisions of the General Agreement".[65]

The Understanding on the Balance-of-Payments Provisions of GATT 1994, which is incorporated into GATT 1994, provides in paragraph 2 with respect to "price-based measures" (defined as including "import surcharges, import deposit requirements or other equivalent trade measures with an impact on the price of imported goods") that

"... It is understood that, notwithstanding the provisions of Article II, price-based measures taken for balance-of-payments purposes may be applied by a Member in excess of the duties inscribed in the Schedule of that Member. Furthermore, that Member shall indicate the amount by which the price-based measure exceeds the bound duty clearly and separately under the notification procedures of this Understanding. "

In each of the three 1989 Panel Reports on "Republic of Korea - Restrictions on Imports of Beef" - Complaints by Australia, New Zealand and the United States[66], the Panel examined the "contention that Korea imposed surcharges on imported beef in violation of the provisions of paragraph 1(b) of Article II and noted that Korea claimed that it did not impose any surcharges in violation of Article II:1(b). The Panel was of the view that, in the absence of quantitative restrictions, any charges imposed by an import monopoly would normally be

---

[57] SR.8/7, p. 10; G/46/Add.4; L/64; SR.9/28.
[58] SR.10/5 p. 52; see also L/410, SR.9/28 p. 4, L/1412.
[59] 3S/27, Preamble para. 3.
[60] 7S/37.
[61] 11S/58.
[62] L/3573, adopted on 16 September 1971, 18S/212.
[63] L/3648, adopted on 12 January 1972, 19S/120, 129.
[64] 18S/223, para. 41; 19S/129, para. 37.
[65] L/4904, adopted on 28 November 1979, 26S/205.
[66] L/6503, L/6504, L/6505, adopted on 7 November 1989, 36S/202, 234, 268.

examined under Article II:4 since it was the more specific provision applicable to the restriction at issue ... It concluded, therefore, that it was not necessary to examine this issue under Article II:1(b)".[67]

(b) Deposit schemes

See also the discussion of import deposit schemes under Article XII. See also the reference directly above to the Understanding on the Balance-of-Payments Provisions of GATT 1994.

In 1978, an import deposit scheme was examined by the Panel on "EEC - Programme of Minimum Import Prices, Licences and Surety Deposits for Certain Processed Fruits and Vegetables". The EC Commission Regulation in dispute provided that importation of certain products would be conditional on production of a certificate; the issue of the certificate would be conditional on the lodging of a security to guarantee that the imports in question would be made, and an additional security to guarantee that the imports would be made at a minimum price. The United States argued that the minimum import price system operated as a charge on imports, and that charges in excess of bound duties were levied through lost interest, debt servicing, and clerical and administrative costs associated with the provision of security deposits, and through the forfeiture of security deposits if the importation did not occur within the 75-day validity of the licence or if the minimum import price was not respected.[68] The Report of the Panel notes:

> "The Panel ... examined the status of the interest charges and costs in connection with the lodging of the additional security associated with the minimum import price for tomato concentrates in relation to the obligations of the Community under Article II:1(b). The Panel noted the argument by the representative of the United States. ... The Panel further noted that the minimum import price and additional security system for tomato concentrates had not been found to be consistent with Article XI, nor had any justification been claimed by the Community under any other provision of the General Agreement. The Panel considered that these interest charges and costs were 'other duties or charges of any kind imposed on or in connection with importation' in excess of the bound rate within the meaning of Article II:1(b). Therefore, the Panel concluded that the interest charges and costs in connection with the lodging of the additional security associated with the minimum import price for tomato concentrates were inconsistent with the obligations of the Community under Article II:1(b)."[69]

With regard to the provision that all or part of the additional security associated with the minimum import price for tomato concentrates would be forfeited if the minimum import price were not respected, the Report notes that "The Panel considered that such a forfeiture should be considered as part of an enforcement mechanism and not as a charge 'imposed on or in connection with importation' within the purview of Article II:1(b) ...".[70] With regard to the provision that the security associated with the import certificate would be forfeited if the goods covered by a certificate were not imported during the certificate's period of validity, "The Panel considered that such a forfeiture could not logically be accepted as a charge 'imposed on or in connection with importation' within the meaning of Article II:1(b), since no importation had occurred, but only as a penalty to the importer for not fulfilling the obligations which he had undertaken when he applied for the certificate. The Panel further considered that such a penalty should be considered as part of an enforcement mechanism and not as a charge imposed on or in connection with importation within the purview of Article II:1(b) ...".[71]

The 1978 Panel Report on "EEC - Measures on Animal Feed Proteins" examined the complaint by the United States that an EEC regulation requiring domestic producers or importers of certain feed proteins to purchase and denature surplus skimmed milk powder from intervention stocks, and an associated certificate and security deposit requirement, constituted 'charges of any kind' in excess of the bound duty rates within the meaning of Article II:1(b). The Panel "concluded that the EEC measures should be examined as internal measures under Article III and not as border measures under Article II" in view of the Panel's findings "that (a) the EEC measures applied to both imported and domestically-produced vegetable proteins (except in the case of

---

[67]*Ibid.* at 36S/230, para. 107; 36S/267, para. 123; 36S/305, para. 129.
[68]L/4687, adopted on 18 October 1978, 25S/68, 87-88, para. 3.56.
[69]*Ibid.*, 25S/103, para. 4.15.
[70]*Ibid.*, 25S/104, para. 4.16.
[71]*Ibid*, 25S/98, para. 4.7.

corn gluten); (b) the EEC measures basically instituted an obligation to purchase a certain quantity of skimmed milk powder and, as an internal quantitative regulation fell under Article III:1; (c) the EEC security deposit and protein certificate were enforcement mechanisms for the purchase obligation".[72]

(c)   Revenue duties and import taxes

The Report of the Working Party on the "Accession of the Democratic Republic of the Congo" discusses Zaire's "Tariff of Import Duties" which was composed of two elements: the customs duty, and the revenue duty. It was pointed out that the rates bound in the schedule as proposed by the Congo would relate to the customs duty only, which would be bound at a higher level than the current applied rate. "After discussion of the nature and effect of the revenue duties, the Working Party considered that the revenue duties in the tariff of the Congo were not internal charges in the sense of Article III but should be considered as other duties or charges, in the sense of Article II:1(b). Following the discussion that ensued on the subject of the potential effect of shifts in the rates of revenue duties on the value of the bound customs duties, and taking into account the particular structure of the customs tariff, the representative of the Democratic Republic of the Congo agreed to make a Declaration of Intent ... concerning the level of the aggregate import duties ... [which] would be referred to by a Note in the Schedule".[73]

The Report of the Working Party on "Accession of Morocco" notes the existence of a special import tax, and notes the undertaking of Morocco that "Morocco will apply the special import tax system in full accordance with the relevant GATT provisions".[74] In February 1987 the Council agreed that the CONTRACTING PARTIES would carry out a review of this commitment in 1990. In November 1990 Morocco brought to the attention of the Council that this import tax, as well as the stamp tax, had been replaced by a single ad valorem levy on imports as part of a fiscal reform; Morocco had requested authorization under Article XXVIII:4 to renegotiate the four bound tariff headings affected by this levy.[75]

See also the reference to the accession of the United Arab Republic at page 101 below.

See also references to revenue duties in Working Party Reports on regional trade agreements, listed under Article XXIV:8.

(d)   Charges on transfer of payments

The Report of the Review Session Working Party on "Schedules and Customs Administration" notes that:

"The wording of sub-paragraphs 1(b) and (c) of the existing text is the same as that used in the most-favoured-nation clause in Article I, but it does not go on to include, as does Article I, 'charges ... imposed on the international transfer of payments for imports.' Thus sub-paragraphs (b) and (c) could be construed as meaning that the provision does not apply to charges on transfers. But clearly the value of tariff concessions would be impaired if contracting parties were free to introduce additional levies on imports in the form of transfer charges. It is considered that the language of this sentence is all-inclusive for it speaks of '... all other duties or charges of any kind imposed on or in connection with importation' and paragraph 2, which sets out the special charges which do not fall under paragraph 1, does not refer to charges on transfers. The insertion of the words 'including charges of any kind imposed on the international transfer of payments for imports' will remove any possibility of misunderstanding. It is the understanding of the Working Party that 'charges of any kind' do not include ordinary commercial charges for effecting the international transfer of payments for imports".[76]

---

[72]L/4599, adopted on 14 March 1978, 25S/49, para. 4.17.

[73]L/3541, adopted on 29 June 1971, 18S/89, discussion at 18S/90-92 paras. 8-10; passages cited at 18S/92-93 paras. 11-12; Declaration of Intent appears at 18S/93-94.

[74]L/5967, adopted on 22 May 1986, 33S/87, 91, para. 13.

[75]C/M/246, p. 26-27; L/6326.

[76]L/329, adopted on 26 February 1955, 3S/205, 209, para. 7.

An amendment to this effect was provided for in the Protocol Amending Part I and Articles XXIX and XXX which did not gain the requisite unanimous approval and was abandoned on 31 December 1967.

See the discussion of the difference between trade and exchange measures under Article XV.

(e)   Charges imposed by import monopolies

The three parallel Panel Reports in 1989 on the complaints of Australia, New Zealand and the United States regarding "Republic of Korea - Restrictions on Imports of Beef"[77] each dealt with a claim regarding alleged import charges by the Livestock Products Marketing Organization, an import monopoly in Korea:

"The Panel ... examined [Australia's/New Zealand's/the United States'] contention that Korea imposed surcharges on imported beef in violation of the provisions of paragraph 1(b) of Article II and noted that Korea claimed that it did not impose any surcharges in violation of Article II:1(b). The Panel was of the view that, in the absence of quantitative restrictions, any charges imposed by an import monopoly would normally be examined under Article II:4 since it was the more specific provision applicable to the restriction at issue. In this regard, the Panel recalled its findings [see these findings below at page 90] ... It concluded, therefore, that it was not necessary to examine this issue under Article II:1(b)".[78]

(5)   "imposed on or in connection with importation"

The 1990 Panel Report on "European Economic Community - Regulation on Imports of Parts and Components" examined the legal nature in relation to the GATT of Article 13:10 of the EEC anti-dumping regulations, which provided for levying of anti-dumping duties on products "introduced into the commerce of the Community after having been assembled or produced in the Community" under certain circumstances; the Panel referred to such duties as "anti-circumvention duties".

"... The Panel noted that Japan argued that the anti-circumvention duties could be considered to be *either* duties imposed on or in connection with importation within the meaning of Article II:1(b) *or* internal taxes within the meaning of Article III:2. The EEC considered that the duties do not fall under Article III:2. The Panel recalled that the distinction between import duties and internal charges is of fundamental importance because the General Agreement regulates ordinary customs duties, other import charges and internal taxes differently: the imposition of 'ordinary customs duties' for the purpose of protection is allowed unless they exceed tariff bindings; all other duties or charges of any kind imposed on or in connection with importation are in principle prohibited in respect of bound items (Article II:1(b)). By contrast, internal taxes that discriminate against imported products are prohibited, whether or not the items concerned are bound (Article III:2). The Panel therefore first examined whether the duties constitute customs or other duties imposed on or in connection with importation falling under Article II:1(b) or internal taxes falling under Article III:2.

"The Panel noted that the anti-circumvention duties are levied ... 'on products that are introduced into the commerce of the Community after having been assembled or produced in the Community'. The duties are thus imposed, as the EEC explained before the Panel, not on imported parts or materials but on the finished products assembled or produced in the EEC. They are not imposed conditional upon the importation of a product or at the time or point of importation. The EEC considers that the anti-circumvention duties should, nevertheless, be regarded as customs duties imposed 'in connection with importation' within the meaning of Article II:1(b). The main arguments the EEC advanced in support of this view were: firstly, that the purpose of these duties was to eliminate circumvention of anti-dumping duties on finished products and that their nature was identical to the nature of the anti-dumping duties they were intended to enforce; and secondly, that the duties were collected by the customs authorities under procedures identical to those applied for the collection of customs duties, formed part of the resources of

---

[77]L/6503, L/6504, L/6505, adopted on 7 November 1989, 36S/202, 234, 268.
[78]*Ibid.*, 36S/230, para. 107, 36S/267, para. 123, 36S/305, para. 129.

the EEC in the same way as customs duties and related to parts and materials which were not considered to be 'in free circulation, within the EEC.

"In the light of the above facts and arguments, the Panel first examined whether the *policy purpose of a charge* is relevant to determining the issue of whether the charge is imposed in 'connection with importation' within the meaning of Article II:1(b). The text of Articles I, II, III and the Note to Article III refers to charges 'imposed on importation', 'collected ... at the time or point of importation' and applied to an imported product and to the like domestic product'. The relevant fact, according to the text of these provisions, is not the policy purpose attributed to the charge but rather whether the charge is due on importation or at the time or point of importation or whether it is collected internally. This reading of Articles II and III is supported by their drafting history and by previous panel reports (e.g. BISD 1S/60; 25S/49, 67). A recent panel report which has examined the provisions of the General Agreement governing tax adjustments applied to goods entering into international trade (among them Articles II and III) stated that

'*the tax* adjustment *rules of the General Agreement* distinguish between taxes on products and taxes not directly levied on products; they *do not distinguish between taxes with different policy purposes*'. (BISD 34S/161, emphasis added).

The Panel further noted that the policy purpose of charges is frequently difficult to determine objectively. Many charges could be regarded as serving both internal purposes and purposes related to the importation of goods. Only at the expense of creating substantial legal uncertainty could the policy purpose of a charge be considered to be relevant in determining whether the charge falls under Article II:1(b) or Article III:2. The Panel therefore concluded that the policy purpose of the charge is not relevant to determining the issue of whether the charge is imposed in 'connection with importation' within the meaning of Article II:1(b).

"The Panel proceeded to examine whether the mere *description or categorization of a charge under the domestic law* of a contracting party is relevant to determining the issue of whether it is subject to requirements of Article II or those of Article III:2. The Panel noted that if the description or categorization of a charge under the domestic law of a contracting party were to provide the required 'connection with importation', contracting parties could determine themselves which of these provisions would apply to their charges. They could in particular impose charges on products after their importation simply by assigning the collection of these charges to their customs administration and allocating the revenue generated to their customs revenue. With such an interpretation the basic objective underlying Articles II and III, namely that discrimination against products from other contracting parties should only take the form of ordinary customs duties imposed on or in connection with importation and not the form of internal taxes, could not be achieved. The same reasoning applies to the *description or categorization of the product subject to a charge*. The fact that the EEC treats imported parts and materials subject to anti-circumvention duties as not being 'in free circulation' therefore cannot, in the view of the Panel, support the conclusion that the anti-circumvention duties are being levied 'in connection with importation' within the meaning of Article II:1(b).

"In the light of the above, the Panel found that the anti-circumvention duties are not levied 'on or in connection with importation' within the meaning of Article II:1(b), and consequently do not constitute customs duties within the meaning of that provision".[79]

(6) "date of this Agreement" (paragraphs 1(b), 1(c) and 6(a))

Article XXVI:1 provides that the "date of this Agreement" shall be 30 October 1947. For the purposes of Article II, the date of 30 October 1947 is still the applicable date for those concessions made in the round of tariff negotiations held in 1947.

When the modalities of accession to the General Agreement were considered for the first time at the Third Session in Annecy in 1949, the Working Party on this subject decided that in the Annecy Protocol of Terms of Accession, the "date of this Agreement" for the purposes of Article II would be changed "with the object of

---

[79]L/6657, adopted on 16 May 1990, 37S/132, 37S/191-3, paras. 5.4-5.8.

placing acceding governments in a comparable position to that in which the present contracting parties were at Geneva"[80]. The Annecy Protocol of Terms of Accession in October 1949 therefore provided that "In each case in which Article II of the General Agreement refers to the date of that Agreement, the applicable date in respect of the Schedules annexed to this Protocol shall be the date of this Protocol".[81] This approach has guided subsequent protocols of accession and tariff protocols. Provisions on Schedules in Protocols of Accession contain the following standard formula:

"(a) In each case in which paragraph 1 of Article II of the Agreement refers to the date of the Agreement, the application date in respect of each product which is the subject of a concession provided for in the Schedule annexed to this Protocol shall be the date of this Protocol.

"(b) For the purpose of the reference in paragraph 6(a) of Article II of the General Agreement to the date of that Agreement, the applicable date in respect of the Schedule annexed to this Protocol shall be the date of this Protocol".[82]

The 1958 Report of the Working Party on "Rectification and Modification of Schedules and Consolidation of Schedules" discussed the preparation of consolidated Schedules, and noted in this connection:

"A problem arises with respect to the date applicable to each concession for the purposes of Article II:1(b) of the Agreement: the most important purpose being the date as of which 'other duties and charges' are bound. Article II:1(b) specifies that this date shall be the date of the Agreement, and protocols of accession and of supplementary concessions have in each case specified that for the schedules annexed to each protocol, the date should be the date of that protocol. The Working Party *recommends* that the date applicable to any concession in a consolidated schedule should be, for the purposes of Article II, the date of the instrument by which the concession was first incorporated into the General Agreement".[83]

The Council Decision of 26 March 1980 on the introduction of a loose-leaf system for the schedules of tariff concessions provides that the instrument by which the concession was first incorporated into a GATT schedule (and thus its date) will be indicated in a special column of the loose-leaf schedules.[84]

The various tariff protocols to the General Agreement have provided that "In each case in which paragraph 1(b) and (c) of Article II of the General Agreement refers to the date of that Agreement, the applicable date in respect of each product which is the subject of a concession provided for in a schedule of tariff concessions annexed to this Protocol shall be the date of this Protocol, but without prejudice to any obligations in effect on that date".[85] The Geneva Protocols of 1990 and 1992 in connection with the introduction of the Harmonized System provide that the "date of this agreement" in respect of each product that is the subject of a concession "shall be the date of acceptance of that Protocol by the contracting parties concerned, but without prejudice to any obligations in effect on that date". These Protocols also provide that the applicable date for the purpose of the reference in paragraph 6(a) "shall be the date of acceptance of the Protocol by the contracting parties concerned".[86] A Secretariat Note of 1987 on "Harmonized System Negotiations Under Article XXVIII" notes that "The words ... 'but without prejudice to any obligations in effect on that date' make it clear that the relevant cut-off date beyond which additional duties or charges may not be imposed remains the date at which

---

[80]Report of the Working Party on "Accession at Annecy", GATT/CP.3/37, adopted 9 June 1949, II/148, 153-154, para. 26.
[81]Annecy Protocol, dated 10 October 1949, I/79, 81, para. 5(a).
[82]See, e.g., the Protocols for the Accession of Mexico (L/6036, 33S/3, para. 7(a) and 7(b)), Bolivia (L/6562, 37S/5, 6, para. 4(a) and 4(b)), Costa Rica (L/6626, 37S/7,8, para. 6(a) and 6(b)), El Salvador (L/6795, 37S/27, 28, para. 4(a) and 4(b)), Tunisia (L/6656, 37S/41, 42, para. 4(a) and 4(b)) and Venezuela (L/6717, 37S/72, 73, para. 4(a) and 4(b)).
[83]L/934, adopted on 22 November 1958, 7S/113, 116, para. 9.
[84]27S/22.
[85]See, e.g., Geneva (1967) Protocol to the General Agreement on Tariffs and Trade, 15S/5, 6, para. 4; Geneva (1979) Protocol to the General Agreement on Tariffs and Trade, L/4812, 26S/3, 4, para. 4; Para. 2 in each of the Geneva (1987), Geneva (1988), and Geneva (1989) Protocols to the General Agreement on Tariffs and Trade in connection with the Harmonized System introduction, L/6112, L/6222 and L/6292), 34S/5; L/6363, 35S/3; L/6466, 36S/3.
[86]L/6728, BISD 37S/3; L/6987.

the concession was initially granted ... for specific duties paragraph 2(b) of the draft Protocol contains the same idea relating to the depreciation of the currency in which the concession is expressed".[87]

Thus, in the GATT 1947, each concession would have its own "date of this Agreement" for the purpose of the binding on "other duties and charges" under Article II:1(b) or the adjustment of specific duties under Article II:6, and in a Schedule with a number of concessions there could be a number of different and coexisting such "dates of this Agreement".

The Understanding on the Interpretation of Article II:1(b) of the GATT 1994, which is incorporated into the GATT 1994, provides that each

" ... the nature and level of any 'other duties or charges' levied on bound tariff items shall be recorded in the Schedules of concessions annexed to GATT 1994 against the tariff item to which they apply. It is understood that such recording does not change the legal character of 'other duties or charges'.

"The date as of which 'other duties or charges' are bound, for the purposes of Article II, shall be 15 April 1994. 'Other duties or charges' shall therefore be recorded in the Schedules at the levels applying on this date. At each subsequent renegotiation of a concession or negotiation of a new concession the applicable date for the tariff item in question shall become the date of the incorporation of the new concession in the appropriate Schedule. However, the date of the instrument by which a concession on any particular tariff item was first incorporated into GATT 1947 or GATT 1994 shall also continue to be recorded in column 6 of the Loose-Leaf Schedules.

...

"The decision in paragraph 2 regarding the date applicable to each concession for the purposes of paragraph 1(b) of Article II of GATT 1994 supersedes the decision regarding the applicable date taken on 26 March 1980 (BISD 27S/24)."[88]

(7) "directly and mandatorily required to be imposed ... by legislation"

The words "directly and mandatorily" were inserted during the negotiation of the General Agreement in 1947 "to eliminate the case where the rate may be varied by some kind of administrative order under a law in force and to make it necessary that it shall be a direct requirement of the law that that change shall be made". However, the addition of the words "at specified fixed rates" after "imposed thereafter" was not accepted. The main argument against this addition was that this sentence "was designed to deal with measures such as anti-dumping duties and countervailing duties and, for example, marking duties or penalty duties with the effect that it would simply require the administration to impose a penalty which may vary ... if certain violations take place".[89]

The Report of the Sub-Committee on Schedules of the Tariff Agreement Committee during the Geneva session of the Preparatory Committee in 1947, which recommended the inclusion of paragraphs 1(b) and (c) in the text of Article II, noted that this inclusion "would not affect the right of any Delegation to require any other Delegation with which it has entered into negotiations to provide lists or details of legislation referred to in ... each of these paragraphs".[90]

(8) Paragraph 1(c): "preferential treatment"

Under paragraph 1(c) the preferential commitments in Part II of a Schedule may only relate to products "entitled under Article I to receive preferential treatment": i.e. products of those territories listed in Annexes A through F, or of territories benefitting from preferences under Article I:3. The historical preference provisions

---

[87]TAR/W/65/Rev.1, dated 14 January 1987, para. 4.
[88]Understanding on the Interpretation of Article II:1(b) of the GATT 1994, paras. 1, 2, 8.
[89]EPCT/TAC/PV/23, p. 28.
[90]EPCT/201, p. 2.

of paragraphs 2 through 4 of Article I permit certain contracting parties to accord tariff preferences to the products of certain other territories even on unbound items, and set a ceiling on the margin of preference that may be accorded, but do not specify any particular preferential duty rate and do not require that such preferences be accorded. On the other hand, the preferential schedules under Article II:1(c) provide a means for the participants in those historical preference schemes to bargain for commitments enforceable under GATT on the level of the preferential tariff for particular products.

A number of the Schedules negotiated at Geneva in 1947 included a Part II: Australia, Canada, Cuba, India, New Zealand, Pakistan, South Africa, Sri Lanka, the United Kingdom, the United Kingdom for Newfoundland, and the United States. However, none of the contracting parties listed in Annexes B, C, E or F of the General Agreement included a Part II in its Schedule. The United Kingdom Schedule, including its Part II, was withdrawn upon UK accession to the EEC.

See also the discussion under Article I of historical preferences and the effect of m.f.n. duty reductions on the permissible margin of preference; see also under Article XXIV:9. See also the discussion above at page 75 of direct consignment requirements.

3. Paragraph 2

(1) Paragraph 2(a): "a charge equivalent to an internal tax imposed consistently with the provisions of paragraph 2 of Article III"

See Interpretative Note ad Article II, paragraph 2(a).

During the Geneva session of the Preparatory Committee the Legal Drafting Committee agreed that the word "equivalent" means that "for example, if a [charge] is imposed on perfume because it contains alcohol, the [charge] to be imposed must take into consideration the value of the alcohol and not the value of the perfume, that is to say the value of the content and not the value of the whole".[91]

See also the discussion of border tax adjustments under Article III:2.

(2) Paragraph 2(b): "any anti-dumping or countervailing duty applied consistently with the provisions of Article VI"

In the 1962 Panel Report on "Exports of Potatoes to Canada", the Panel examined the complaint of the United States concerning the imposition by Canada of a charge in addition to the specific duty on potatoes bound in 1957, as a result of the application under the Canadian Customs Act (as revised in 1958) of "values for duty" on potatoes imported below a certain price.

"The Panel ... did not consider that the provisions of Article VII were relevant in the context of its examination.

"... The Panel concluded that the imposition of an additional charge could not be justified by Article VI of the General Agreement, since the main requirement laid down in paragraph 1(a) of the Article was not satisfied, namely that the price of the product exported from one country to another was less than the comparable price, in the ordinary course of trade, for the like product when destined for consumption in the exporting country.

"The Panel came to the conclusion that the measure introduced by the Canadian Government amounted to the imposition of an additional charge on potatoes which were imported at a price lower than Can.$2.67 per 100 lbs. The Panel considered that this charge was in addition to the specific import duty which had been bound at a rate of Can.$0.375 per 100 lbs. Since no provisions of the General Agreement had been

---

[91] EPCT/TAC/PV/26, p. 21; see also reference to this passage in the Panel Report on "United States - Taxes on Petroleum and Certain Imported Substances", adopted on 17 January 1987, 34S/136, 162, para. 5.2.7.

brought forward for the justification of the imposition of an additional charge above the bound import duty, the Panel considered that the Canadian Government had failed to carry out its obligations under paragraph 1(a) of Article II".[92]

(3) Paragraph 2(c): "fees or other charges commensurate with the cost of services rendered"

The 1978 Panel Report on "EEC - Programme of Minimum Import Prices, Licences and Security Deposits for Certain Processed Fruits and Vegetables" (referred to above at page 80) found that the interest charges and costs connected with the security deposit associated with the import certificate were limited in amount to the approximate costs of administration in accordance with the provisions of Article VIII:l(a). "The Panel considered that the term 'fees or other charges commensurate with the cost of services rendered' in Article II:2(c) would include these costs of administration. Therefore, the Panel concluded that the interest charges and costs in connection with the lodging of the security associated with the import certificate were not inconsistent with the obligations of the Community under Article II".[93]

The 1988 Panel Report on "United States - Customs User Fee" examined a fee charged for processing of commercial cargo by the U.S. Customs Service, in relation to Articles II:2(c) and VIII:1(a). The Panel noted that:

"Article II:2(c) is a rather extraordinary exception. It authorizes governments to impose new charges on imports in excess of the ceiling established by a tariff binding. Given the central importance assigned by the General Agreement to protecting the commercial value of tariff bindings, any such exceptions would require strict interpretation. The exception stated in Article II:2(c) requires particularly strict interpretation, however, because it does not conform to the policy justification normally given for such exceptions. In the words of an explanation of Article II:2 contained in a 1980 proposal by the Director-General (27S/24), the policy justification for the three types of border charges permitted by Article II:2 was that they did not "discriminate against imports". If the import fees authorized by Article II:2(c) were in fact fees for beneficial services, this justification would be valid. But given the reality that most such fees are simply an ordinary tax on imports, it cannot be said that such fees do not disadvantage imports vis-a-vis domestic products. In simple terms, Article II:2(c) authorizes governments to impose new protective charges in addition to the bound tariff rate. As such, it is an exception which should be doubly guarded against enlargement by interpretation".[94]

See also below at page 99 regarding the relationship between Article II:2(c) and Article VIII:1, and see further under Article VIII concerning fees for services.

4. Paragraph 3: impairment of concessions by alteration in valuation or currency conversion

In June 1953, Czechoslovakia gave notice that in conjunction with its May 1953 revaluation of the Czechoslovak crown, the Government of Czechoslovakia had decided to reduce its bound specific duties by an amount equivalent to the revaluation, in order "not [to] impair the value of any of the concessions provided for in the Schedule and thus afford protection in excess of the amount of protection provided for in the Schedule". The Working Party which examined the case reported that it had "considered the question of the adjustments of the Czechoslovak specific duties from the angle of the provisions of paragraph 3 of Article II" and that it had "noted that no contracting party offered any objection on the basis of those provisions to the alterations made by the Czechoslovak Government. In view of the fact that these changes do not modify the legal position which is defined in the first sentence of Article II:6(a) ... the Working Party felt that it would be sufficient for the CONTRACTING PARTIES to take note of the adjustments made ...".[95]

---

[92] L/1927, adopted on 16 November 1962, 11S/88, 93, paras. 16-18.
[93] L/4687, adopted on 18 October 1978, 25S/68, 97-98, para. 4.6.
[94] L/6264, adopted on 2 February 1988, 35S/245, 278, para. 84.
[95] G/62, 2S/64, 66, discussed at SR.8/20 p. 4-5; see also request of Czechoslovakia and Secretariat note, L/100, L/136, and Sec/53/126 and Rev.1-2. In the case in question the revaluation had not been approved by the International Monetary Fund.

See also the material under Article XXIV:8(a)(ii) concerning the 1978 EEC change in the unit of account for specific duties in its common customs tariff, which was stated to be consistent with Article II:3.

See also the material from the 1962 Panel Report on "Exports of Potatoes to Canada" on application of a "value for duty" statute, at page 86.

The 1980 Report of the Working Party on "Specific Duties" notes that

"The Working Party examined the question of whether the application of Article II:6(a) should in the present monetary situation be symmetrical, that is whether contracting parties whose currency appreciated should be required to reduce their specific duties. ... The Working Party decided not to pursue this matter noting that ... contracting parties could resort to Article XXII and XXIII of the General Agreement if they considered that an appreciation impaired in a particular case the value of specific duty concessions".[96]

5. Paragraph 4

The text of this paragraph was drafted by a Sub-Committee of the Tariff Agreement Committee during the Geneva session of the Preparatory Committee. In introducing the text, the chairman of the Sub-Committee stated:

"... the Sub-Committee primarily aimed at covering three points. First ... where there had been tariff negotiations between the two parties and where one of the two parties had an import monopoly and where the parties agreed to a very definite and exact agreement as to any price margin, whether in percentages or in amounts ... That was case number 1. This is provided for in the text ... where it says 'except as provided in the Schedule or as otherwise agreed between the parties [which initially negotiated] the concession'.

"The second case we had in mind was the one where there is an import monopoly, but where the negotiations for tariff binding or reduction had only resulted in the binding of the tariff but not in any concrete arrangement regarding the margin for the sale of the goods in question in domestic markets. In that case, the Committee considered that the principles of the Charter would apply, especially the rules laid down in Article 31 of the Charter.

"Thirdly, we had in mind the case where an import duty has been fixed in a case where, at present, there is no import monopoly, but where ... an import monopoly might be established in the future. There the Sub-Committee considered that the tariff duty already fixed should ... stand, and that all sales in the domestic markets of products covered by that tariff item should be covered by the principles of the Charter especially, of course, Article 31.

"... in the last sentence ... by the reference to 'this Agreement' we had in mind the General Agreement, and also the Protocol, and especially ... we had in mind Article 31 of the Charter".[97]

(1) "a monopoly of the importation of any product described in the appropriate Schedule"

The 1988 Panel Report on "Canada - Import, Distribution and Sale of Alcoholic Drinks by Canadian Provincial Marketing Agencies" examined the practices of provincial liquor boards with respect to alcoholic beverages. Noting that "Canada's Schedule of Concessions includes tariff bindings on all imported alcoholic beverages", the Panel "recalled that Canada and the European Communities agreed on the fact that Canada had, through the Importation of Intoxicating Liquors Act, authorized a monopoly of the importation of alcoholic beverages. The Panel noted therefore that the amount of protection admissible under Article II:4 was thus either the amount provided for in the Canadian Schedule or 'as otherwise agreed between the parties which had initially negotiated the concession'".[98]

---

[96]L/4858, adopted 29 January 1980, 27S/149, 154, para. 14.
[97]EPCT/TAC/PV/16 p. 35-37, discussing Sub-Committee report at EPCT/191; see further discussion at EPCT/TAC/PV/16 p. 37-49..
[98]L/6304, adopted on 22 March 1988, 35S/37, 85, paras. 4.3-4.4.

Three Panel Reports in 1989 on the complaints of Australia, New Zealand and the United States regarding "Republic of Korea - Restrictions on Imports of Beef"[99] examined challenges by Australia, New Zealand and the United States of Korean beef import restrictions on the ground, *inter alia,* that these contravened Article II:4. All three applicant contracting parties argued that the application of the price mark-up on imports by the Korean Livestock Products Marketing Organization (LPMO) was in contravention of Article II:4 and in excess of the amount of protection provided for in Korea's schedule under which a protective import tariff on beef was bound at 20 per cent ad valorem; in Korea's view, the operation of the LPMO was consistent with the provisions of Article II:4. Each Report provides that "The Panel noted that the LPMO was a beef import monopoly ... with exclusive privileges for the administration of both the beef import quota set by the Korean Government and the resale of the imported beef to wholesalers or in certain cases directly to end users such as hotels".[100]

(2) *"except as provided for in that Schedule or as otherwise agreed": concessions on the operations of import monopolies*

The Schedules of Benelux and France negotiated at Geneva in 1947 and at Torquay in 1950 contained certain concessions on monopoly duties, minimum imports by an import monopoly, or domestic selling prices of products subject to a monopoly.[101]

The 1988 Panel Report on "Canada - Import, Distribution and Sale of Alcoholic Drinks by Canadian Provincial Marketing Agencies" examined the application of Article II:4 in relation to a "Provincial Statement of Intentions with Respect to Sales of Alcoholic Beverages by Provincial Marketing Agencies in Canada" (which was negotiated by Canada on behalf of its provinces in the Tokyo Round and set out specific undertakings with respect to mark-ups, listing and distribution practices) and related letters exchanged between Canada and the EC.

"... The Panel examined ... whether the parties had, by a Provincial Statement of Intentions and the related exchange of letters, 'otherwise agreed' in the sense of Article II:4, as claimed by Canada, on an amount of protection different from that provided for in the Canadian Schedule.

"The Canadian Government's letter of 5 April 1979 made it clear that the Provincial Statement of Intentions was put forward on behalf of the provincial authorities. The title and wording of the Provincial Statement of Intentions indicated that it expressed 'intentions' and was, as confirmed in the letter, 'necessarily non-contractual in nature'. The only undertaking expressed by the Government of Canada in the letter of 5 April 1979 was that it 'will be prepared to use its good offices with the provincial authorities concerned regarding any problem which may arise with respect to the application of provincial policies and practices set forth in the statement'. Canada's emphasis on the non-binding nature of the undertaking seemed to indicate that it was not meant to affect Canada's rights and obligations under Article II:4. Nor did the letters of the EC Commission, dated 5 April and 29 June 1979, express an acceptance of an agreement concerning its rights and obligations under Article II:4. The first of these letters restricted itself to acknowledging the receipt of the Canadian letter and the second only expressed 'some disquiet' concerning the terms 'normal commercial considerations' in the Provincial Statement of Intentions.

"The Panel noted that the Provincial Statement of Intentions and related letters had not been included among the texts listed in the Procès-Verbal embodying the results of the Tokyo Round, that the letters were classified as confidential and had not been notified to the CONTRACTING PARTIES. While the Council has stated in the terms of reference of the Panel that the Provincial Statement had been 'concluded in the context of the Tokyo Round of Multilateral Trade Negotiations' it appeared to the Panel that for the Statement to satisfy the conditions of Article II:4, it would have had to be binding to the same extent as the concession in the Schedule which it was intended to supersede.

---

[99]L/6503, L/6504, L/6505, adopted on 7 November 1989, 36S/202, 234, 268.
[100]*Ibid.*, at 36S/228-229, para. 102; 36S/266, para. 118; 36S/304, para. 124.
[101]Benelux: binding of monopoly duties for various food-related items (59, 70, 75, 84, ex 100, etc.); France: Note Ad item 235A (minimum imports of leaf tobacco and cigarettes by SEITA; selling price of foreign cigarettes).

"The Panel therefore *concluded* that the Provincial Statement of Intentions and the related exchange of letters could not be held to constitute an agreement in terms of Article II:4 and did not, therefore, modify Canada's obligations arising from the inclusion of alcoholic beverages in its GATT Schedule".[102]

(3) "in the light of the provisions of Article 31 of the Havana Charter"

(a) Application of the Interpretative Note

The Panel Report on "Japan - Restrictions on Imports of Certain Agricultural Products" examined, *inter alia*, the import quota maintained by Japan on prepared beef products and administered by the Livestock Industry Promotion Corporation (LIPC), a state corporation holding an import monopoly.

"The Panel noted the view of Japan that Article XI:1 did not apply to import restrictions made effective through an import monopoly. According to Japan, the drafters of the Havana Charter for an International Trade Organization intended to deal with the problem of quantitative trade limitations applied by import monopolies through a provision under which a monopoly of the importation of any product for which a concession had been negotiated would have "to import and offer for sale such quantities of the product as will be sufficient to satisfy the full domestic demand for the imported product" (Article 31:5 of the Havana Charter) . Japan contended that that provision had not been inserted into the General Agreement and that quantitative restrictions made effective through import monopolies could therefore not be considered to be covered by Article XI:1 of the General Agreement ...

"The Panel examined this contention and noted the following: Article XI:1 covers restrictions on the importation of any product, 'whether made effective through quotas, import ... licences or other *measures*' (emphasis added). The wording of this provision is comprehensive, thus comprising restrictions made effective through an import monopoly. This is confirmed by the note to Articles XI, XII, XIII, XIV and XVIII, according to which the term 'import restrictions' throughout these Articles covers restrictions made effective through state-trading operations. The basic purpose of this note is to extend to state-trading the rules of the General Agreement governing private trade and to ensure that the contracting parties cannot escape their obligations with respect to private trade by establishing state-trading operations. This purpose would be frustrated if import restrictions were considered to be consistent with Article XI:1 only because they were made effective through import monopolies. The note to Article II:4 of the General Agreement specifies that that provision 'will be applied in the light of the provisions of Article 31 of the Havana Charter.' The obligation of a monopoly importing a product for which a concession had been granted 'to import and offer for sale such quantities of the product as will be sufficient to satisfy the full domestic demand for the imported product' is thus part of the General Agreement. The Panel could therefore not follow the arguments of Japan based on the assumption that Article 31:5 of the Havana Charter was *not* included in the General Agreement. The Panel found for these reasons that the import restrictions applied by Japan fell under Article XI independent of whether they were made effective through quotas or through import monopoly operations."[103]

In the three parallel Panel Reports in 1989 on the complaints of Australia, New Zealand and the United States regarding "Republic of Korea - Restrictions on Imports of Beef":[104]

"In examining Article II:4, the Panel noted that, according to the interpretative note to Article II:4, the paragraph was to be applied 'in the light of the provisions of Article 31 of the Havana Charter'. Two provisions of the Havana Charter, Article 31:4 and 31:5, were relevant. Article 31:4 called for an analysis of the import costs and profit margins of the import monopoly. However, Article 31:5 stated that import monopolies would 'import and offer for sale such quantities of the product as will be *sufficient to satisfy the full domestic demand* for the imported product...' (emphasis added). In the view of the panel, Article 31:5 clearly implied that Article 31:4 of the Havana Charter and by implication Article II:4 of the General

---

[102] L/6304, adopted on 22 March 1988, 35S/37, 85-86, paras. 4.5-4.8.
[103] L/6253, adopted on 2 February 1988, 35S/163, 229, paras. 5.2.2.1-5.2.2.2.
[104] L/6503, L/6504, L/6505, adopted on 7 November 1989, 36S/202, 234, 268.

Agreement were intended to cover import monopolies operating in markets not subject to quantitative restrictions.

"Bearing in mind Article 31:5 of the Havana Charter, the Panel considered that in view of the existence of quantitative restrictions, it would be inappropriate to apply Article II:4 of the General Agreement in the present case. The price premium obtained by the LPMO through the setting of a minimum bid price or derived sale price was directly afforded by the situation of market scarcity arising from the quantitative restrictions on beef. The Panel concluded that because of the presence of the quantitative restrictions, the level of the LPMO's mark-up of the price for imported beef to achieve the minimum bid price or other derived price was not relevant in the present case. Furthermore, once these quantitative restrictions were phased out, as recommended by the Panel … this price premium would disappear.

"The Panel stressed, however, that in the absence of quantitative restrictions, an import monopoly was not to afford protection, on the average, in excess of the amount of protection provided for in the relevant schedule, as set out in Article II:4 of the General Agreement. Furthermore, in the absence of quantitative restrictions, an import monopoly was not to charge on the average a profit margin which was higher than that 'which would be obtained under normal conditions of competition (in the absence of the monopoly)'…. The Panel therefore expected that once Korea's quantitative restrictions on beef were removed, the operation of the LPMO would conform to these requirements".[105]

(b)   Article 31

The Interpretative Note ad Paragraph 4 refers to Article 31 of the Havana Charter, which provides as follows:

"*Article 31*

Expansion of Trade

"1.   If a Member establishes, maintains or authorizes, formally or in effect, a monopoly of the importation or exportation of any product, the Member shall, upon the request of any other Member or Members having a substantial interest in trade with it in the product concerned, negotiate with such other Member or Members in the manner provided for under Article 17 in respect of tariffs, and subject to all the provisions of this Charter with respect to such tariff negotiations, with the object of achieving:

"(a)   in the case of an export monopoly, arrangements designed to limit or reduce any protection that might be afforded through the operation of the monopoly to domestic users of the monopolized product, or designed to assure exports of the monopolized product in adequate quantities at reasonable prices;

"(b)   in the case of an import monopoly, arrangements designed to limit or reduce any protection that might be afforded through the operation of the monopoly to domestic producers of the monopolized product, or designed to relax any limitation on imports which is comparable with a limitation made subject to negotiation under other provisions of this Chapter.

"2.   In order to satisfy the requirements of paragraph 1(b), the Member establishing, maintaining or authorizing a monopoly shall negotiate:

"(a)   for the establishment of the maximum import duty that may be applied in respect of the product concerned; or

---

[105] L/6504, 36S/229, paras. 104, 105, 106; L/6505, 36S/266, 267, paras. 120, 121, 122; L/6503, 36S/305, paras. 126, 127, 128.

"(b)   for any other mutually satisfactory arrangement consistent with the provisions of this Charter, if it is evident to the negotiating parties that to negotiate a maximum import duty under sub-paragraph (a) of this paragraph is impracticable or would be ineffective for the achievement of the objectives of paragraph 1; any Member entering into negotiations under this sub-paragraph shall afford to other interested Members an opportunity for consultation.

"3. In any case in which a maximum import duty is not negotiated under paragraph 2(a), the Member establishing, maintaining or authorizing the import monopoly shall make public, or notify the Organization of, the maximum import duty which it will apply in respect of the product concerned.

"4. The import duty negotiated under paragraph 2, or made public or notified to the Organization under paragraph 3, shall represent the maximum margin by which the price charged by the import monopoly for the imported product (exclusive of internal taxes conforming to the provisions of Article 18, transportation, distribution and other expenses incident to the purchase, sale or further processing, and a reasonable margin of profit) may exceed the landed cost; Provided that regard may be had to average landed costs and selling prices over recent periods; and Provided further that, where the product concerned is a primary commodity which is the subject of a domestic price stabilization arrangement, provision may be made for adjustment to take account of wide fluctuations or variations in world prices, subject where a maximum duty has been negotiated to agreement between the countries parties to the negotiations.

"5. With regard to any product to which the provisions of this Article apply, the monopoly shall, wherever this principle can be effectively applied and subject to the other provisions of this Charter, import and offer for sale such quantities of the product as will be sufficient to satisfy the full domestic demand for the imported product, account being taken of any rationing to consumers of the imported and like domestic product which may be in force at that time.

"6. In applying the provisions of this Article, due regard shall be had for the fact that some monopolies are established and operated mainly for social, cultural, humanitarian or revenue purposes.

"7. This Article shall not limit the use by Members of any form of assistance to domestic producers permitted by other provisions of this Charter.

Ad Article 31

"*Paragraphs 2 and 4*

"The maximum import duty referred to in paragraphs 2 and 4 would cover the margin which has been negotiated or which has been published or notified to the Organization, whether or not collected, wholly or in part, at the custom house as an ordinary customs duty.

"*Paragraph 4*

"With reference to the second proviso, the method and degree of adjustment to be permitted in the case of a primary commodity which is the subject of a domestic price stabilization arrangement should normally be a matter for agreement at the time of the negotiations under paragraph 2 (*a*)."

Concerning Article 17 of the Charter, see the material under Article XXVIII*bis* of this Index.

(c)   *Interpretative Note Ad Article II:4*

During the Review Session of 1954-55, the Review Working Party on Other Barriers to Trade considered proposals for amending the state trading provisions of the General Agreement either by consolidating them or by adopting Articles 29-31 of the Havana Charter. The Report of the Working Party notes: "The conclusion reached by the majority of the Working Party, however, was in general to retain the present structure of the Agreement with respect to state trading. ... The Working Party undertook to redraft the existing interpretative note to paragraph 4 of Article II, both so as to eliminate the cross reference to the Havana Charter and so as to clarify the meaning ...".[106] The interpretative note would have been replaced by the following text:

"The provisions of this paragraph will be applied in the light of the following:

"1. The protection afforded through the operation of an import monopoly in respect of products described in the appropriate schedule shall be limited by means of:

"(a) a maximum import duty that may be applied in respect of the product concerned; or

"(b) any other mutually satisfactory arrangement consistent with the provisions of this Agreement; any contracting party entering into negotiations with a view to concluding such arrangement shall afford to other interested contracting parties an opportunity for consultation.

"2. The import duty mentioned in 1(a) above shall represent the margin by which the price charged by the import monopoly for the imported product (exclusive of internal taxes conforming to the provisions of Article III, transportation, distribution, and other expenses incident to the purchase, sale or further processing, and a reasonable margin of profit) exceeds the landed cost; *Provided* that regard may be had to average landed costs and selling prices over recent periods; and *Provided* further that, where the product concerned is a primary commodity which is the subject of a domestic price stabilization arrangement, provisions may be made for adjustment to take account of wide fluctuations or variations in world prices, subject to agreement between the countries parties to the negotiations".

However, this change was effected through the Protocol Amending Part I and Article XXIX and XXX, which failed to gain the requisite unanimous approval, and was abandoned.[107]

(4) *"protection on the average in excess of the amount of protection provided for in that Schedule"*

The 1988 Panel Report on "Canada - Import, Distribution and Sale of Alcoholic Drinks by Canadian Provincial Marketing Agencies" examined the application of Article II:4 :

"The Panel then proceeded to examine whether the mark-ups imposed on imported alcoholic beverages plus the import duties, which were collected at the bound rate, afforded protection on the average in excess of the amount of protection provided for in Canada's Schedule contrary to Article II:4, as claimed by the European Communities. The Panel noted that according to the interpretative note to Article II:4 the paragraph was to be applied 'in the light of the provisions of Article 31 of the Havana Charter.' ...

"The Panel noted that Article II:4, applied in the light of Article 31:4, prohibited the charging of prices by the provincial liquor boards for imported alcoholic beverages which (regard being had to average landed costs and selling prices over recent periods) exceeded the landed costs; plus customs duties collected at the rates bound under Article II; plus transportation, distribution and other expenses incident to the purchase, sale or further processing; plus a reasonable margin of profit; plus internal taxes conforming to the provisions of Article III. ...[108]

"The Panel considered that differential mark-ups could be justified to offset any additional costs of transportation, distribution and other expenses incident to the purchase, sale or further processing, such as storage, necessarily associated with importing products and that such calculations could be made on the basis of average costs over recent periods.

"The Panel noted Canada's statement that, in some instances, the differential mark-ups also reflected a policy of revenue maximization on the part of the provincial liquor boards, which charged higher mark-ups

---

[106]L/334 and Addendum, adopted on 3 March 1955, 3S/222, 228, para. 26.
[107]15S/65.
[108]35S/86, paras. 4.9, 4.10.

on imported than on domestic alcoholic beverages because they marketed imported products as premium products and exploited less price elastic demand for these products, and that this policy was in accordance with the General Agreement because revenue maximization was justified by normal commercial considerations.

"The Panel considered that a monopoly profit-margin on imports resulting from policies of revenue maximization by provincial liquor boards could not normally be considered as a 'reasonable margin of profit' in the sense of Article II:4, especially if it were higher on imported products than on domestic products.

"The Panel considered that the phrase 'a reasonable margin of profit' should be interpreted in accordance with the normal meaning of these words in their context of Article II and Article 31 of the Havana Charter and that 'a reasonable margin of profit' was a margin of profit that would be obtained under normal conditions of competition (in the absence of the monopoly). The margin of profit would have on the average to be the same on both domestic and the like imported products so as not to undermine the value of tariff concessions under Article II.

"The Panel also noted Canada's argument that the drafting history implied that a reasonable margin of profit was a margin which 'should not be so excessive as to restrict the volume of trade in the product concerned', and that since the volume of imports from the European Communities of the products in question had not declined, the margin of profit was a reasonable one. The Panel noted that the fact that these imports had not declined did not say anything about what they would have been in the absence of a policy of monopolistic profit maximization by the provincial liquor boards.

"The Panel examined Canada's reference to normal commercial considerations and noted that the term 'commercial considerations' was mentioned in Article XVII:1(b). It considered that this reference was not relevant to its examination of Article II:4 as the context in which the term 'commercial considerations' had been used was different.

"The Panel therefore *concluded* that the mark-ups which were higher on imported than on like domestic alcoholic beverages (differential mark-ups) could only be justified under Article II:4, to the extent that they represented additional costs necessarily associated with marketing of the imported products, and that calculations could be made on the basis of average costs over recent periods. The Panel also *concluded* that the burden of proof would be on Canada if it wished to claim that additional costs were necessarily associated with marketing of the imported products".[109]

In Council discussions on the adoption of the Panel Report the representative of Canada stated that "with respect to the Panel's conclusions in paragraph 4.16 of the report, Canada could not agree that the margin of profit would on average have to be the same on both the domestic and the like imported product so as not to undermine the value of tariff concessions under Article II. His authorities considered that the Panel's interpretation did not accord with normal conditions of competition or reflect the realities of the market place".[110]

In the 1992 Panel Report on "Canada - Import, Distribution and Sale of Certain Alcoholic Drinks by Provincial Marketing Agencies", the same Panel again examined the practices of provincial liquor boards in Canada.

"The Panel noted that the Panel which had examined in 1988 the practices of the Canadian liquor boards had concluded that 'mark-ups which were higher on imported than on like domestic alcoholic beverages (*differential mark-ups*) could only be justified under Article II:4, to the extent that they represented *additional costs necessarily associated with marketing of the imported products*, and that calculations could be made on the basis of average costs over recent periods'. That Panel had also concluded that 'the burden of proof would be on Canada if it wished to claim that additional costs were

---

[109] 35S/87, paras. 4.13 - 4.19.
[110] C/M/218, p. 5.

necessarily associated with marketing of the imported products'. The Panel noted that the United States and Canada did not agree on which costs incurred by the liquor boards constituted 'additional costs n necessarily associated with marketing of imported products' and requested guidance from the Panel on this issue.

"The Panel considered that, in determining which costs were 'additional costs necessarily associated with the marketing of imported products', four situations had to be distinguished. The costs could be 'additional' because they were incurred as a result of activities of the liquor boards that were specific to imported products; such costs were, for instance, the expenses arising from customs clearance or warehouse handling (e.g. palletization). The costs could also be 'additional' because, although they arose both for imported and domestic products, they were higher for imported products; such costs were, for instance, storage or imputed inventory finance costs, where inventory turnover for imported products was slower than for domestic products. On the other hand there were costs, such as general or administrative expenses, which could not be considered 'additional', since they were not necessarily associated with the marketing of the imported product, but rather with the overall operation of the liquor monopoly. Nor could costs be considered 'additional' which were incurred in respect of services prescribed for imported products but not for domestic products inconsistently with the General Agreement.

"Taking into account the four situations outlined above, the Panel also recalled that, in view of Article 31:4 of the Havana Charter, import monopolies were authorized to charge for transportation, distribution and other expenses incident to the purchase and sale of imported products. The Panel then considered how the liquor boards could and should compute the 'differential mark-up' i.e. the difference in the mark-ups on imported and domestic products. It believed that the liquor boards, as commercial enterprises, were entitled to recover both variable and fixed costs arising from their commercial activities incident to the purchase and sale of imported products. Thus, in line with the categorization in the previous paragraph, the Panel considered that the differential mark-up on imported beer should allow the recovery of those costs that were directly associated with the handling of imported beer (variable costs), and of charges for fixed assets employed that were calculated in proportion to the use of these assets by the imported product. All other expenses (e.g. general or administrative expenses) would have to be recovered through mark-ups uniformly applied to both domestic and imported beer.

"The Panel noted in this context that the disagreements between the United States and Canada appeared to arise primarily from the fact that Canada regarded as additional costs all costs arising from services performed by the liquor boards for imported beer that they did not perform for domestic beer, such as the cost of delivering imported beer to the points of sale. The Panel recalled its finding in paragraphs 5.12-5.16 above that, under Article III:4 of the General Agreement, Canada would have to apply the same delivery system to both domestic and imported beer or permit imported beer to be delivered privately if it had done so for domestic beer. In this context the Panel had noted that, in the situation in which the liquor boards authorized the private delivery of domestic beer to the points of sale but prohibited the private delivery of imported beer, a charge on imported beer for delivery to points of sale which corresponded to their actual costs of delivering such beer was not necessarily consistent with Article III:4. The Panel considered that strict observation of the national treatment principle in respect of the services performed by the liquor boards (i.e. identical treatment of imported and domestic beer) would, to a large extent, eliminate the uncertainties as to the proper allocation of the costs of the liquor boards. The Panel considered further that application of the national treatment principle in terms of affording effective equality of opportunities (i.e. permitting imported beer to be treated in the same way as domestic beer) would eliminate any problems with respect to liquor board charges for the services performed; in this situation, the foreign brewers' choice of distribution system would be made on purely commercial grounds.

"The Panel then examined the mark-up practices of the liquor boards in the light of the principles set out above. The Panel noted that most liquor boards had, subsequent to the adoption of the 1988 Panel report, introduced so-called 'cost-of-service charges' and that the cost-of-service differential between imported and domestic products was in fact equivalent to the differential mark-up defined in the 1988 Panel report. It further noted that, in seven of the 10 provinces, the differential mark-ups as computed on the basis of cost-of-service charges did not conform to the principles set out above and included additional costs incurred by the liquor boards not necessarily associated with the marketing of imported beer. Two provinces, New Brunswick and Newfoundland, did not introduce separate cost-of-service charges but maintained differential mark-ups. In New Brunswick, this differential again included costs that were not necessarily associated with the marketing of imported beer. In the case of Newfoundland, no audit of the mark-ups had been provided. Only in Prince Edward Island, where no beer was brewed, no differential mark-up was maintained. The Panel therefore *concluded* that the differential mark-ups currently levied by the liquor boards (with the exception of Prince Edward Island), including differential mark-ups based on cost-of-service charges, were inconsistent with Article II:4 of the General Agreement.

"The Panel then considered how Canada could best meet its burden of proving that the differential mark-ups consisted only of additional costs necessarily associated with the marketing of imported beer. The Panel considered that one possibility was for Canada to submit audited cost-of-service accounts prepared by independent reputable auditors who were made aware of Canada's obligations under the General Agreement in respect of mark-ups, in particular the obligation under Article II:4 not to afford protection on the average in excess of the amount of protection provided for in Canada's Schedule of Concessions. The Panel noted in this context that, in respect of wine and distilled spirits, the United States and Canada had agreed to rely on audited cost-of-service accounts. The Parties might, therefore, wish to agree on the instructions to be given to the auditors or, alternatively, to entrust an independent expert with the task of drawing up such instructions".[111]

See also the reference to "protection, on the average, in excess of the amount of protection provided for" in the three parallel Panel Reports in 1989 on the complaints of Australia, New Zealand and the United States regarding "Republic of Korea - Restrictions on Imports of Beef"[112] excerpted above at pages 82, 90, 96.

Concerning "other charges and fees" charged by import monopolies, see the finding from the same Panel Reports excerpted above at page 82.

See also the definition of the term "import mark-up" in the Interpretative Note ad Article XVII, paragraph 4(b).

6. Paragraph 5

In 1956, Germany complained that the Greek government had imposed a tariff rate of 40 to 60 per cent ad valorem on long-playing gramophone records, despite the fact that "gramophone records" were bound in the Greek Schedule with a per-kilogram specific duty.[113] Greece considered the introduction of the new long-playing records as the creation of a completely new item since they were made of a different material. A Group of Experts that considered the complaint found that when granting the specific duty concession on "gramophone records" the Greek government had not attached any qualification to the description of the product; the experts considered that long-playing records fell within that item and were covered by the concession. "The Group agreed that the practice generally followed ... was to apply the tariff item ... that specified the products by name, or, if no such item existed, to assimilate the new products to existing items in accordance with the principles established by the national tariff legislation ...".[114] The case was ultimately settled bilaterally.[115]

The only instance in which the Secretariat has been informed of negotiations completed under Article II:5 was in 1969, involved Canada and the European Communities and concerned "compensatory adjustment in connection with the impairment of the concession on flash guns in Schedule V (Canada) resulting from the decision of the Tariff Board of 17 May 1965, on the classification of electronic flash apparatus".[116] A 1980 Note by the Secretariat for the Committee on Tariff Concessions on reclassification issues observes that "It would seem that questions of this kind have come up from time to time in connexion with reclassification questions by the

---

[111]DS17/R, adopted on 18 February 1992, 39S/27, 80-82, paras. 5.17-5.22.
[112]L/6503, L/6504, L/6505, adopted on 7 November 1989, 36S/202, 234, 268.
[113]L/575; SR.11/12 p. 115-116.
[114]L/580, SR.11/16 p. 168-170.
[115]L/765.
[116]SECRET/193, TAR/W/14.

Customs Co-operation Council, but up to now they have presumably been settled bilaterally or did not involve changes of substance".[117]

See also the discussion above of the difference between maintenance of "treatment" and modification of a concession; see generally the chapter on Article XXVIII; and see paragraphs 4 and 5 of the Understanding on the Interpretation of Article XXVIII of the GATT 1994.

7. Paragraph 6

(1) "currency at the par value accepted or provisionally recognized"

Article IV of the original Articles of Agreement of the International Monetary Fund required each member of the Fund to state a par value for its currency in terms of gold or U.S. dollars of a fixed gold value, as part of a system of fixed exchange rates. A change in the par value of a member's currency could be made only after consultation with the Fund. The words "or provisionally recognized" were inserted in paragraph 6(a) during the Geneva session of the Preparatory Committee to meet the case of Brazil, which had not established a par value at the time when the paragraph was drafted.[118]

During the Review Session of 1954-55 the CONTRACTING PARTIES agreed to amend paragraph 6(a) by using the words "... at the par value accepted or at the rate of exchange recognized by the Fund" on the ground that "these words correspond more closely to the Fund's practices under its Articles of Agreement and cover cases not provided for in the present text". The Working Party Report on these changes noted that in the case of Canada, for example, the established par value accepted by the Fund was no longer the effective rate, and the Fund recognized the fluctuating rate for its own accounting purposes. The wording was also changed so as to refer to "the" par value instead of "this" par value, in order to permit an adjustment of duties after a second devaluation of a currency. However, this amendment was included in the Protocol Amending Part I and Articles XXIX and XXX, which did not enter into force.[119]

As revised in 1978, Article IV of the IMF Articles no longer requires the stating of par values and instead provides that "each member undertakes to collaborate with the Fund and other members to assure orderly exchange arrangements and to promote a stable system of exchange rates".[120]

In 1978-80 the Working Party on Specific Duties examined the modalities for the application of Article II:6(a) in the monetary situation of increased flexibility of exchange rates.

"The Working Party noted that the rules for the adjustment of bound specific duties in Article II:6(a) of the General Agreement were drafted on the assumption that the members of the International Monetary Fund maintain par values for their currencies. However, under the present Articles of Agreement of the Fund, as amended on 1 April 1978, Fund members are no longer obliged to maintain par values but have the right to adopt exchange arrangements of their choice. Some Fund members have floating exchange rates, and other maintain the exchange rate against one other currency, a basket of currencies or an international unit of account. The Working Party concluded that the right to adjust specific duties in the present monetary

---

[117]TAR/W/14, dated 29 August 1980, para. 5.
[118]EPCT/TAC/PV/24, p. 43-44.
[119]L/329, Report of the Review Working Party on "Schedules and Customs Administration", adopted on 26 February 1955, 3S/205, 209-210, para. 8; *ibid.*, 3S/214, para. 18. The Protocol Amending Part I and Articles XXIX and XXX was abandoned due to lack of the requisite unanimous acceptance; see 15S/65. Concerning the Review Session amendments to Article II:6 see further SR.9/16 and W.9/109+Rev.1, 163, 193, 200 and 212.
[120]Section 4 of Article IV as revised provides that "The Fund may determine, by an 85 per cent majority of the total voting power, that international economic conditions permit the introduction of a widespread system of exchange arrangements based on stable but adjustable par values. ... Upon making such determination, the Fund shall notify members that the provisions of Schedule C [on Par Values] apply". Articles of Agreement of the International Monetary Fund, 2 UNTS 39 (1947) as amended 1 April 1978.

situation could not be called into question but that the modalities for the application of Article II:6(a) needed to be adjusted to take into account the changes in the international monetary system".[121]

The Working Party on Specific Duties drafted "Guidelines for Decisions under Article II:6(a) of the General Agreement", which were adopted on 29 January 1980. See also the material under Article XXIV:8(a)(ii) concerning the 1978 EEC change in the unit of account for specific duties in its common customs tariff.

(2) Adjustment of specific duties in accordance with paragraph 6(a)

The Decisions of the CONTRACTING PARTIES under Article II:6 are listed in the accompanying table. The "Guidelines for Decisions under Article II:6(a) of the General Agreement", adopted on 29 January 1980, provide that:

"In the present monetary situation the CONTRACTING PARTIES shall apply the provisions of Article II:6(a) as set out below unless they consider that this would not be appropriate in the circumstances of the particular case, for example because it would lead to an impairment of the value of a specific duty concession ...

"If a contracting party, in accordance with Article II:6(a) of the General Agreement, requests the CONTRACTING PARTIES to concur with the adjustment of bound specific duties to take into account the depreciation of its currency, the CONTRACTING PARTIES shall ask the International Monetary Fund to calculate the size of the depreciation of its currency and to determine the consistency of the depreciation with the Fund's Articles of Agreement. ...

"The CONTRACTING PARTIES shall be deemed to have authorized the contracting party to adjust its specific duties ... if the International Monetary Fund advises the CONTRACTING PARTIES that the depreciation calculated as set out above ... is in excess of 20 per cent and consistent with the Fund's Articles of Agreement and if, during the sixty days following the notification of the Fund's advice to the contracting parties, no contracting party claims that a specific duty adjustment to take into account the depreciation would impair the value of a concession ...".[122]

Decisions of the CONTRACTING PARTIES under Article II:6(a) to authorize adjustment of specific duties

Benelux	Decision of 15 December 1950	II/12
Finland	Decisions of 3 March 1955, 15 November 1957, 20 November 1967	3S/28, 6S/22, 15S/66
Greece	Decision of 24 October 1953	2S/24
Israel	Decision of 3 February 1975	C/M/103, 124, 125, 138
Turkey	Decision of 10 April 1959	8S/24
Uruguay	Decisions of 18 May 1961, 25 March 1965	10S/34, 13S/20

The Decision provides rules for calculating the size of the depreciation, in the case of one contracting party or in the case of contracting parties members of a customs union which define their common specific duties in terms of a unit of account composed of the currencies of the members.

(3) "date of this Agreement"

See the discussion of "date of this Agreement" at page 83 above.

---

[121]L/4858, adopted on 29 January 1980, 27S/149, 150, para. 5.
[122]L/4938, adopted on 29 January 1980, 27S/28-29.

(4) Article II:6(b)

The Working Party on "Specific Duties" also examined which procedures should apply to requests submitted under Article II:6(a) by contracting parties that are not members of the Fund. It noted that this matter was dealt with in Article II:6(b) and in accession protocols of contracting parties that were not members of the Fund, and considered that no proposals were necessary, it being understood that all contracting parties have access to Article II:6(a).[123]

8. Paragraph 7: "an integral part of Part I of this Agreement"

The Schedules were included in Part I of the General Agreement as it was intended that Part II would be immediately superseded by the Charter provisions when the Charter entered into force. See Section III below.

In 1949, Cuba challenged the reduction of most-favoured-nation tariff rates by the United States on products with respect to which Cuba benefited from preferential tariff rates under bilateral trade agreements with the US. Cuba argued, *inter alia*, that the inclusion of a rate of duty in Part I of any Schedule legally prevented the reduction of that rate otherwise than by an amendment in accordance with Article XXX requiring acceptance by all the contracting parties as a condition of its becoming effective.[124] So as to clarify that the wording of Article II meant that the rates of duty contained in the Schedules were only maximum, and not also minimum, rates of duty, the CONTRACTING PARTIES, in a Decision of 9 August 1949, ruled,

"The reduction of the rate of duty on a product, provided for in a schedule to the General Agreement, below the rate set forth therein, does not require unanimous consent of the CONTRACTING PARTIES in accordance with the provisions of Article XXX".[125]

See also the term "in excess of" in paragraph 1(b); see also the material on modification and rectification of Schedules below and under Article XXX.

B. RELATIONSHIP BETWEEN ARTICLE II AND OTHER GATT ARTICLES

1. Article III

See under Article III.

2. Article VIII

In the 1988 Panel Report on "United States - Customs User Fee" the Panel examined the general meaning, drafting history and differences in wording in Articles II:2(c) and VIII:1(a).

"Two questions of general interpretation had to be answered before addressing the specific issues raised by the complainants. First, it was necessary to decide whether there was any legal significance in the slight difference in wording between the two 'cost of services' limitations stated in Articles II:2(c) and VIII:1(a), i.e. 'commensurate with the cost of services rendered' and 'limited in amount to the approximate cost of services rendered.' The words themselves suggested no immediately apparent difference in meaning. After reviewing both the drafting history and the subsequent application of these provisions, the Panel concluded that no difference of meaning had been intended. The difference in wording appears to be explained by the somewhat different paths by which each provision entered the General Agreement. The text which was to become Article VIII:1(a) appeared in the very first draft submitted to the negotiating conference by the United States, whereas the text of Article II:2(c) originated as a standard term to be

---

[123]L/4858, adopted on 29 January 1980, 27S/149, 156, para. 18.
[124]CP.3/59, CP.3/SR.34-38; Working Party Report on "Accession at Annecy", GATT/CP.3/37, II/148, 152-153, para. 25.
[125]Vol. II/11.

incorporated in each contracting party's schedule of concessions (see E/PC/T/153) and was not raised to the text of Article II until some time later (E/PC/T/201)".[126]

A footnote to this paragraph provides:

"A collateral issue which the Panel considered but was not required to answer was whether the form of words utilized in Article II:2(c) might not have been intended as a reference to exactly the same fees permitted by Article VIII:1(a) - in other words, whether Article II:2(c) incorporates all three of the criteria in Article VIII:1(a). The following considerations had raised the issue: (i) The text of Article II:2(c) was in fact developed after the draft text of Article VIII:1(a) had been established. (ii) Article II:2(c) sets the standards for determining when 'service' fees may be imposed in excess of tariff bindings, whereas Article VIII:1(a) is a general provision relating to fees on all products. (iii) At least two Article XXIII complaints in the past had claimed that an import fee used for a 'fiscal purpose' had constituted a violation of Article II, and in both cases the contracting party complained against had agreed and had withdrawn the fee (L/64; SR.8/7 (page 10); L/410; SR.10/5 (pages 51-52)".[127]

See the material from this Panel Report cited *in extenso* under Article VIII.

3. Articles XI and XIII

In a dispute concerning EEC restrictions on imports of apples from Chile, Chile maintained that the EEC quantitative protective measure against Chile contravened Article II:1(a) and (b), in that the EEC measure involved treatment less favourable than that provided for in tariff concessions granted by the EEC for apples and had the effect of being an absolute or infinite duty completely nullifying the concession granted. In the 1980 Panel Report on "EEC Restrictions on Imports of Apples from Chile",

"the Panel considered that the EEC import suspension did affect the value of the EEC tariff binding to Chile on apples. With reference to II:1(b), however, the Panel considered that the EEC measure was not strictly speaking a duty or charge in excess of the tariff concession provided in the EEC schedule. Therefore, the Panel considered that it was more appropriate to examine the EEC measure in the context of Article XI".[128]

The 1984 Panel Report on "United States - Imports of Sugar from Nicaragua" concluded, *inter alia,* that:

"Having found the reduction of the quota to be inconsistent with the obligations of the United States under Article XIII, the Panel did not deem it necessary to examine whether the action was also inconsistent with any other obligations on quota allocations which the United States might have assumed under Article II in its schedule of concessions".[129]

In the 1984 Report of the "Panel on Newsprint", the Panel did not share the argument advanced by the EC that their opening of a duty-free tariff quota of 500,000 tonnes for newsprint, whereas the commitment of the EC in its GATT Schedule LXXII provided for an annual duty-free tariff quota of 1.5 million tonnes, was merely a change in the administration or management of the tariff quota which was permissible under Article XIII of the GATT.

"The Panel considered the arguments advanced by the EC relating to Article XIII, but concluded that the conditions for its application had not been fulfilled. In examining the EEC Regulation 3684/83, the Panel found that it did not in fact constitute a change in the administration or management of the tariff quota from a global quota system to a system of country shares, as had been asserted by the EC. The Regulation in its Article 1.1 simply opens a quota of 500,000 tonnes and stipulates in Article 1.3 that imports shall not be charged against this quota if they are already free of customs duties under other preferential tariff treatment. It does not provide an allocation of country shares to individual m.f.n. suppliers, nor has a

---

[126] L/6264, adopted on 2 February 1988, 35S/245, 275, para. 75.
[127] *Ibid.*, footnote 1 at 35S/275.
[128] L/5047, adopted on 10 November 1980, 27S/98, 112, para. 4.2.
[129] L/5607, adopted on 13 March 1984, 31S/67, 74, para. 4.5.

separate quota (global or otherwise) for the EFTA countries been established, as Article XIII requires ... It is in the nature of a duty-free tariff quota to allow specified quantities of imports into a country duty-free which would otherwise be dutiable, which is not the case for EFTA imports by virtue of the free-trade agreements. Imports which are already duty-free, due to a preferential agreement, cannot by their very nature participate in an m.f.n. duty-free quota."[130]

4. Article XXIII

See under Article XXIII:1(b) on non-violation cases and the relevance of tariff concessions.

5. Article XXVIII

Concerning the relationship between Article XXVIII negotiations and the status of tariff bindings, see the unadopted panel report of 1994 on "EEC - Import Régime for Bananas".[131]

C. EXCEPTIONS AND DEROGATIONS

1. Article II:2

See pages 86-87 above. The 1988 Panel Report on "United States - Customs User Fee" notes that "Paragraph 1(b) of Article II establishes a general ceiling on the charges that can be levied on a product whose tariff is bound; it requires that the product be exempt from all tariffs in excess of the bound rate, and from all other charges in excess of those (i) in force on the date of the tariff concession, or (ii) directly and mandatorily required by legislation in force on that date. Article II:2 permits governments to impose, above this ceiling, three types of non-tariff charges, of which the third, permitted by sub-paragraph (c), is 'fees or other charges commensurate with the cost of services rendered'."[132]

2. Protocol of Provisional Application

The Note Ad Article I:1 provides that "The obligations incorporated in ... paragraph 2(b) of Article II by reference to Article VI shall be considered as falling within Part II for the purposes of the Protocol of Provisional Application". An identical provision is included in the standard text of accession Protocols.

3. Other Protocols of accession

The Report of the Working Party on "Accession of the United Arab Republic" notes that "The Working Party discussed the 10 per cent 'consolidation of economic development tax' imposed on imports into the United Arab Republic. ... The Working Party noted that this tax was not to be considered as a charge for services rendered. Nor, in the view of the representative of the United Arab Republic, were the provisions of Article III applicable, since there was no question of national treatment. The tax was applied only on imports and as such had an effect equivalent to that of a customs duty".[133] The accession protocol of the United Arab Republic provided that "The temporary 'consolidation of economic development tax' may be maintained in effect, at rates not exceeding the rates in force at the date of this Protocol, on bound duties until 31 December 1975, by which time, if the measure is still in effect, the matter shall be reviewed by the CONTRACTING PARTIES".[134] This deadline was extended to 31 December 1980,[135] to 31 December 1985,[136] and to 31 December 1990[137] and has expired.

---

[130] L/5680, adopted on 20 November 1984, 31S/114, 31S/131-2 para. 51, 31S/133 para. 55.
[131] DS38/R, dated 11 February 1994, para. 133.
[132] L/6264, adopted on 2 February 1988, 35S/245, 273, para. 70.
[133] L/3362, adopted on 27 February 1970, 17S/33, 37, para. 16.
[134] 17S/2, 4, para. 6.
[135] L/4264, Decision of 26 November 1975, 22S/8.
[136] L/5083, Decision of 25 November 1980, 27S/16.
[137] L/5923, Decision of 26 November 1985, 32S/15.

4. Waivers under Article XXV:5

For a list of waivers of Article II, see the table of waivers following Article XXV. Recent supplements to the BISD have included a list of waivers related to implementation of the Harmonized System and other schedule-related waivers.[138]

The CONTRACTING PARTIES have decided on a number of occasions to grant waivers suspending the application of Article II of the General Agreement to enable a contracting party to implement a modified Schedule in advance of completion of negotiations under Article XXVIII, subject to specified conditions. In recent years, typical conditions have included:

"1. The Government of [contracting party] will as soon as possible enter into negotiations or consultations pursuant to paragraphs 1 to 3 of Article XXVIII.

"2. The negotiations or consultations mentioned above shall be completed not later than [date].

"3. Pending the entry into force of the results of the negotiations or consultations mentioned above, the other contracting parties will be free to suspend concessions initially negotiated with [contracting party] to the extent that they consider that adequate compensation is not offered by the Government of [contracting party]".[139]

See also discussion of such waivers under Article XXVIII.

During 1993 the matter of renewal of waivers of Article II associated with the introduction of the Harmonized System was raised in the Council. The 1993 Report of the Committee on Tariff Concessions notes that the Committee at its December 1993 meeting agreed to the following proposal:

"The Committee shall report twice a year on its activities to the Council. Under the item related to 'Ongoing negotiations and submission of HS documentation by contracting parties under waivers', the following factual information shall be included:

"- Date of original waiver.

"- Date of submission of documents relevant to the HS implementation (if no documents have been circulated, reasons therefor).

"- Number of extensions and dates when granted.

"- Number of countries with which Article XXVIII negotiations have been initiated.

"- Number of countries with which Article XXVIII negotiations have been concluded.

"- Status of outstanding Article XXVIII negotiations as well as a general outline of relevant problems, if any.

"- Outlook for concluding the process."[140]

---

[138]See, e.g., 37S/295, 38S/78.

[139]See, e.g., Waiver decisions on "Indonesia - Establishment of a new Schedule XXI", L/6331, Decision of 22 April 1988, 35S/347; "Bangladesh - Establishment of a New Schedule LXX", L/6374, Decision of 18 July 1988, 35S/348; "Mexico - Establishment of a New Schedule LXXVII", L/6377, Decision of 18 July 1988, 35S/351.

[140]TAR/243, adopted on 25-26 January 1994, Annex II. See also Council discussion at C/M/264 and proposal at TAR/W/88.

5. Coexistence of the GATT 1947 and the WTO Agreement

On 8 December 1994, the Preparatory Committee for the WTO, meeting on the occasion of the Implementation Conference, adopted a Decision on "Coexistence of the General Agreement on Tariffs and Trade 1947 and the World Trade Organization". The CONTRACTING PARTIES meeting in Special Session on the same date also adopted this decision, which provides *inter alia*:

> "The CONTRACTING PARTIES to the General Agreement on Tariffs and Trade (hereinafter referred to as 'GATT 1947'),
>
>> *"Noting* that not all contracting parties to the GATT 1947 meeting the conditions for original membership in the World Trade Organization ... will be able to accept the Marrakesh Agreement Establishing the WTO ... as of its date of entry into force, and that the stability of multilateral trade relations would therefore be furthered if the GATT 1947 and the WTO Agreement were to co-exist for a limited period of time;
>>
>> *"Considering* that, during that period of co-existence, a contracting party which has become a Member of the WTO should not be under a legal obligation to extend the benefits accruing solely under the WTO Agreement to contracting parties that have not yet become WTO Members and should have the right to act in accordance with the WTO Agreement notwithstanding its obligations under the GATT 1947; ...
>
> *"Decide as follows:*
>
> "1. The contracting parties that are Members of the WTO may, notwithstanding the provisions of the GATT 1947,
>
>> "(a) accord to products originating in or destined for a Member of the WTO the benefits to be accorded to such products solely as a result of concessions, commitments or other obligations assumed under the WTO Agreement without according such benefits to products originating in or destined for a contracting party that has not yet become a Member of the WTO; and
>>
>> "(b) maintain or adopt any measure consistent with the provisions of the WTO Agreement."[141]

Concerning the transition to the WTO, see further in the chapter on institutions and procedure in this book.

D. TARIFF PROTOCOLS, SCHEDULES OF CONCESSIONS, AND NATIONAL TARIFF SCHEDULES

1. Schedules in general

The "Procedures for Giving Effect to Certain Provisions of the Charter of the International Trade Organization by Means of a General Agreement on Tariffs and Trade Among the Members of the Preparatory Committee", which were drawn up during the London session of the Preparatory Committee, provided:

> "It is contemplated that the tariff negotiations among the members of the Preparatory Committee will be multilateral, both in scope and in legal application. Thus, there would result from the negotiations a total of sixteen schedules of tariff concessions, each schedule setting forth a description of the products and of the maximum (concession) rates of duty thereon which would be applicable in respect of the imports into a particular country. In this way each member of the Committee would be contractually entitled, in its own right and independently of the most-favoured-nation clause, to each of the concessions in each of the schedules of the other members.

---

[141] PC/12, L/7583, preamble and para. 1.

"The multilateral form of the schedules is designed to provide more stability than has existed in the past under bilateral tariff agreements, to assure certainty of broad action for the reduction of tariffs and to give to countries a right to tariff concessions on particular products which such countries might wish to obtain, but could not obtain under bilateral agreements, because of their relatively less important position as a supplier of the product concerned. The multilateral form also gives expression to the fact that each country stands to gain when another country grants tariff reductions on any product, even though primarily supplied by a third country ...".[142]

2. Protocols of concessions

A 1985 Secretariat Note for the Committee on Tariff Concessions on "Loose-leaf Schedules Based on Harmonized System Nomenclature" notes as follows:

"*Tariff protocols* which were established at the end of multilateral rounds of trade negotiations have, subsequent to 1959, been signed only by those contracting parties whose schedules were annexed to the protocol. This applied not only to those cases where the new schedules contained exclusively tariff reductions, but also to a case such as the Dillon Round Protocol in which both tariff reductions and tariff increases (resulting from Article XXVIII and Article XXIV:6 negotiations) were embodied.

"Contracting parties have as a general rule submitted the results of their tariff negotiations for inclusion in a protocol at a time when they had concluded all, or at least most, of their bilateral negotiations. The results of negotiations which had not yet been terminated at that time, as well as improvements in the concessions initially granted, were incorporated in supplementary protocols established after the end of a tariff conference. In the context of a Harmonized System exercise ... supplementary protocols would become necessary as not all contracting parties changing over to the Harmonized System will be ready to submit their new schedules at the time the main protocol is opened for signature.

"It should be recalled that annexing schedules to a protocol is only binding on the contracting parties in question which thereby commit themselves to apply in the future the new (normally reduced) rates of duty. This does not, on the other hand, commit other contracting parties which, in the case of increased duty rates and in the absence of an agreement, retain their right to withdraw substantially equivalent concessions (e.g. under Article XXVIII:3 in the case of the Dillon Round or in the Harmonized System negotiations).

"It follows from the above that a protocol (together with the schedules attached) does not require the approval or signature of other contracting parties than those that have schedules annexed to it. The rights of these other contracting parties are, as mentioned above, protected in all cases where agreement could not be reached. However, in order to avoid that technical errors find their way into the new schedules, the practice has been to provide countries which have participated in the negotiations the opportunity to verify that the results of the negotiations have been correctly incorporated into the schedules that are to be annexed to the protocol. In the Tokyo Round, for instance, contracting parties were invited to circulate their draft schedules to the countries with which they had negotiated not later than 1 June 1979, the period of verification having been limited until 22 June, by which date the contracting parties in question had to transmit to the secretariat the necessary number of copies of their final schedules for distribution to all MTN participants; the Geneva (1979) Protocol was opened for signature on 30 June 1979 by the contracting parties having annexed their schedules to it".[143]

See also a 1990 Secretariat Note on the "Uruguay Round Tariff Protocol", concerning technical issues such as timetable, opening for signature, schedule format, preparation of revised loose-leaf schedules, and issues to

---

[142]London Report, Annexure 10, p. 49-50, "Form of Tariff Schedules". See also generally the records of the Sub-Committee on Procedures, EPCT/C.II/PRO/PV/5-15 and summary records in the series EPCT/C.II/W/2-31.
[143]TAR/W/55/Add.1, dated 28 November 1985, paras. 1-4.

be decided concerning implementation of the tariff concessions[144], as well as a 1993 Note on "Preparation of the Uruguay Round Schedules of Concessions on Market Access".[145]

See also the material below on certifications of rectifications and modifications.

3. Consolidated Schedules

The inclusion of successive concessions in Schedules and in tariff protocols has meant that in order to determine the applicable concession rates for a given tariff line, it was often necessary to examine a number of instruments. However, there have been a number of efforts to reform this system. In the early years of the GATT, the proposal was made that, for each contracting party, its successive Schedules of concessions would be replaced by one consolidated Schedule. A consolidation was carried out in 1951 incorporating the results of the Geneva (1947), Annecy and Torquay Rounds. The question of giving legal status to consolidated Schedules was discussed at the Thirteenth Session in 1958. At that time, the Working Party on Schedules recommended as follows:

"(a) any contracting party, wishing to prepare a consolidated schedule to replace its separate schedules annexed to the various Protocols, may do so, provided a draft consolidated schedule is submitted to the CONTRACTING PARTIES for approval under the normal rectification procedures;

"(b) such a contracting party should give due notice of its intention and should submit copies early enough before the usual protocol of rectifications and modifications is prepared, to allow for adequate checking by all contracting parties;

"(c) the contracting party to which the consolidated schedule relates, should be expected to accept the understanding that earlier schedules and - as has always been the case in the past - negotiating records, would be considered as proper sources in interpreting concessions contained in legal consolidated schedules".[146]

A number of contracting parties submitted Consolidated Schedules under these rules, and updated Schedules were certified in a number of instances. The introduction of the loose-leaf system and the conversion of Schedules to the Harmonized System nomenclature have each entailed a consolidation of past Schedules, and consolidated Schedules are now submitted under the rules and practices pertaining to these two exercises.

4. Loose-leaf Schedules

On 26 March 1980 the Council adopted a proposal by the Director-General on the introduction of a loose-leaf system for the Schedules of Tariff Concessions.[147] The proposal stated:

"... the existing system for the publication of the tariff concessions has become outdated. There are at present more than forty legal instruments (Protocols, Certifications) containing valid tariff concessions. Extensive and time-consuming efforts are necessary under the present system to find out the status of a particular concession.

"In view of this, I suggest that henceforth the schedules of tariff concessions be published in the form of a loose-leaf system which can continuously be kept up to date when rectifications, modifications, withdrawals and new concessions are made ...

"... The basis for the creation of a loose-leaf system for the schedules of tariff concessions must be a general consolidation of tariff schedules. I would consequently propose that the *Council agree that*

---

[144]MTN.GNG/NG1/W/56, dated 24 October 1990..
[145]MTN.GNG/MA/W/25, dated 22 December 1993.
[146]L/934, Report on "Rectification and Modification of Schedules and Consolidation of Schedules", adopted on 22 November 1958, 7S/113, 115-116, para. 8.
[147]27S/22; see also discussion at C/M/138 p. 10-11, C/M/139 p. 4-6.

contracting parties submit consolidated schedules of tariff concessions as soon as possible and not later than 30 September 1980 ...

"... I would suggest that *the Council agree on a format for the schedules as set out in the Annex to document L/4821/Add.1.*

"The schedules should comprise a complete description of the products covered... the entries in the schedules should, as far as possible, correspond with the entries in the customs tariffs, not only for the descriptions but also in respect of the numeration used. For example, if a heading is only partially bound, then sub-headings should be created and should have their own numbers".[148]

See also the minutes of the Committee on Tariff Concessions concerning discussions of the legal status of loose-leaf schedules and of initial negotiating rights regarding earlier bindings.[149]

The Secretariat has issued periodic Notes for the Committee on Tariff Concessions on the status of loose-leaf and other Schedules.[150]

5. Implementation of the Harmonized System

(1) *Conversion of schedules to Harmonized System nomenclature*

The International Convention on the Harmonized Commodity Description and Coding System, established under the auspices of the Customs Co-operation Council, entered into force on 1 January 1988. The Convention requires each party thereto to conform its customs tariff and statistical nomenclature to the Harmonized Commodity Description and Coding System ("Harmonized System") nomenclature and to any future amendments thereto.[151] The distinguishing feature of the Harmonized System nomenclature is its multi-functional design, which allows it to serve the needs of tariff classification and trade statistics, while providing a basis for future applications such as freight tariffs and production statistics.

The Ministerial Decision adopted 29 November 1982 on "Tariffs" provides, *inter alia*, that "The CONTRACTING PARTIES decide ...

"That wide acceptance of a common system for classifying products for tariff and statistical purposes would facilitate world trade and therefore recommend prompt action towards the introduction of such a system. They take note of the ongoing work to this end in the Customs Co-operation Council. They further agree that, if such a system is introduced, the general level of benefits provided by GATT concessions must be maintained, that existing concessions should normally remain unchanged and that any negotiations that should prove necessary should be initiated promptly so as to avoid any undue delay in the implementation of a system. They also agree that technical support shall be provided by the GATT secretariat to developing contracting parties in order to fully assist their participation in such a process".[152]

On 12 July 1983 the Council approved a Decision on "GATT Concessions under the Harmonized Commodity Description and Coding System" which includes, *inter alia*, the following general principles:

"1.2 In addition to the benefits for trade facilitation and analysis of trade statistics, from a GATT point of view adoption of the Harmonized System would ensure greater uniformity among countries in customs

---

[148]C/107/Rev.1, 27S/22, 22-23, paras. 1-5.
[149]TAR/M/1 et seq., TAR/W/30, 33, 34.
[150]See TAR/W/23/Rev.21, "Status of Pre-HS Loose-leaf Schedules", dated 4 October 1990 (or later revisions); TAR/W/40/Rev.13, "Tariff Information Available in the Secretariat", dated 13 November 1994 (or later revisions); TAR/W/85, "Status of Schedules of Contracting Parties to the GATT", dated 16 October 1992. See also notes referred to below on the Harmonized System schedules.
[151]Delayed application of these obligations is permitted for developing country parties to the Convention.
[152]L/5424, 29S/18, para. 2.

classification and thus a greater ability for countries to monitor and protect the value of tariff concessions. ...

"2.1 The main principle to be observed in connexion with the introduction of the Harmonized System in national tariffs is that existing bindings should be maintained unchanged. The alteration of existing bindings should only be envisaged where their maintenance would result in undue complexity in the national tariffs and should not involve a significant or arbitrary increase in customs duties collected on a particular product.

"2.2 In order to avoid complicating the introduction of the Harmonized System, contracting parties should endeavour to avoid modifying or renegotiating, in the context of the introduction of the Harmonized System, their bindings for reasons not associated with the System.

"2.3 In light of paragraphs 2.1 and 2.2 contracting parties should be ready to explain and discuss the reason for their proposed changes when requested. Interested contracting parties will be free to raise specific cases, which the party which has notified the change will examine, taking into account all relevant factors with a view to finding a mutually acceptable solution. If such agreement cannot be reached, the contracting party which has notified the change shall proceed under Article XXVIII ...

"2.4 To the extent that the value of existing concessions is not impaired, the conversion of present nomenclatures to the Harmonized System can be done through the rectification procedure.[153]

This Decision also specifies requirements for information to be provided to the GATT Secretariat by each contracting party adopting the Harmonized System; specifies rules to be used for conversion of duty rates if concessions must be modified if headings or parts of headings are combined in the process of implementing the Harmonized System; and provides for the procedures to be used in the event of renegotiation under Article XXVIII. See also material from this Decision in the chapter on Article XXVIII. Prior to the adoption of the Decision, it was stated "that, under this document, any contracting party was entitled to request the maintenance of particular tariff items of interest to it in the new nomenclature, whenever tariff lines with different bound rates were combined or whenever bound rates were combined with unbound rates. This understanding was in keeping with the basic principle stated in paragraph 2.1 [of the Decision,] namely that 'existing GATT bindings should be maintained unchanged'".[154] Procedures for the conversion of contracting parties' schedules of concessions into the Harmonized System nomenclature were also discussed in the Committee on Tariff Concessions.[155]

As schedules under the Harmonized System have been finalized, they have been annexed to successive Protocols of tariff concessions: the First, Second, and Third Geneva (1987) Protocols; the Geneva (1988) Protocol; the Geneva (1989) Protocol; the Geneva (1992) Protocol; the Geneva (1993) Protocol; and the Geneva (1994) Protocol.[156] In addition, some HS conversions were completed during the Uruguay Round and the resulting schedules attached to the Marrakesh Protocol to the GATT 1994.

The minutes of the October 1994 meeting of the Committee on Tariff Concessions note that as of that date, all but a very few contracting parties had implemented the Harmonized System in their national tariffs and more than 90 percent of contracting parties' trade was covered by the HS. However, of 84 GATT 1947 contracting

---

[153]L/5470/Rev.1, 30S/17, 17-18.
[154]C/M/170, p. 15.
[155]TAR/M/4, point 7. For a list of documentation submitted by delegations in the context of Harmonized System negotiations and the certification of schedules, see the latest revision of TAR/W/67.
[156]First, Second, and Third Geneva (1987) Protocols, L/6112, L/6222, L/6292, 34S/5; Geneva (1988) Protocol, L/6363, 35S/3; Geneva (1989) Protocol, L/6466, 36S/3; Geneva (1992) Protocol, L/6987, 39S/3; Geneva (1993) Protocol, L/7195, L/7195/Corr.1 and L/7195/Add.1-5. A Geneva (1990) Protocol (L/6728, 37S/3) was done but no schedules were concluded during the relevant period. Concerning status of the Harmonized System Schedules, see the most recent revision of TAR/W/74.

parties with a GATT Schedule, only 25, plus the European Communities, had a certified schedule in the nomenclature of the Harmonized System, and only 12 of these were complete, with all 12 columns completed.[157]

The Secretariat has issued periodic Notes for the Committee on Tariff Concessions on the status of Harmonized System Schedules and the associated Article XXVIII negotiations.[158] A Secretariat Note of 13 October 1994 on "Transposition of Schedules into the 1996 Harmonized System and Establishment of Loose-Leaf Schedules" assesses the status of schedules as of that date, grouping participants in the Uruguay Round into eight categories as follows. The number of participants is indicated after each category; since October 1994, a number of developing participants have submitted their Uruguay Round schedules which have been annexed to the Marrakesh Protocol.[159]

A. Uruguay Round participants which have adopted the Harmonized System, including:

(1) Participants which have an HS consolidated schedule annexed to the Marrakesh Protocol that is not in loose-leaf format and does not include the HS 1996 changes: (44)

(2) Participants which have a GATT pre-Uruguay Round schedule in loose-leaf format which has been certified, and also have a Uruguay Round HS schedule annexed to the Marrakesh Protocol: (21)

(3) Participants maintaining an HS schedule under waiver which have submitted required HS documentation for transposition of pre-UR GATT schedules into the HS, have not yet concluded Article XXVIII negotiations with respect to that schedule, but have a UR HS schedule annexed to the Marrakesh Protocol: (9)

(4) Participants which are under waiver, have not submitted the required HS documentation for transposition of pre-UR GATT schedules into the HS, but have a UR HS Schedule annexed to the Marrakesh Protocol: (10)

(5) Participants which have a GATT pre-UR schedule not in HS and a UR schedule in HS, and which have not taken any action concerning the transposition of their pre-UR schedules into HS: (11)

(6) Participants which have no GATT pre-UR schedule and have not submitted a UR schedule: (7)

B. Participants where it is not certain that they have adopted the HS system

(1) Participants which have a GATT pre-UR schedule and have not submitted a UR Schedule: (3)

(2) Participants which have no GATT pre-UR schedule and have not submitted a UR Schedule: (6)

(2) Implementation in GATT schedules of amendments to Harmonized System nomenclature

On 8 October 1991 the Council adopted simplified "Procedures to Implement Changes in the Harmonized System"[160] to provide for changes to the Harmonized System planned to enter into force on 1 January 1992 and any changes in the future:

"Contracting parties to the GATT which are also contracting parties to the International Convention on the Harmonized Commodity Description and Coding System (Harmonized System), in order to keep the authentic texts of their GATT schedules up to date and in conformity with their national customs tariffs, adopt the following procedures:

---

[157] TAR/M/38.
[158] See TAR/W/67/Rev.13, "Harmonized System and Article XXVIII Negotiations", dated 28 September 1993 (or later revisions); TAR/W/74/Rev.10, "Status of the Harmonized System Schedules", dated 27 September 1993 (or later revisions). See also notes concerning status of loose-leaf schedules referred to above.
[159] TAR/W/93.
[160] L/6905, 39S/300-301.

"1. The implementation of revisions of the nomenclature of the Harmonized System adopted by the Customs Co-operation Council (CCC) shall not involve any alteration in the scope of concessions nor any increase in bound rates of duty unless their maintenance results in undue complexity in the national tariffs. In such cases the contracting parties concerned shall inform the other contracting parties of the technical difficulties in question, e.g. why it has not been possible to create a new subheading to maintain the existing concession on a product or products transferred from within one HS 6-digit heading to another.

"2. No later than 120 days after the circulation by the secretariat of both

    (1) a communication concerning the acceptance by the CCC of a recommendation to revise the Harmonized System nomenclature made in accordance with Article 16 of the Harmonized System Convention, and

    (2) correlation tables prepared by the CCC secretariat,

contracting parties shall submit to the GATT secretariat a notification which includes the pages of their loose-leaf schedules containing proposed changes. The relevant pages of the loose-leaf schedules shall be presented as follows:

(a) Items in relation to which the proposed changes do not, in the view of the contracting party in question, alter the scope of a concession (e.g. changes or other rectifications of a purely formal character) ...

(b) Items in relation to which the proposed changes will, in the view of the contracting party in question, alter the scope of a concession (e.g. through an increase in the bound rate of duty or a change in the product description of the item) ...

"4. A proposed change in the authentic text of a GATT schedule described in paragraph 2(a) above shall be certified provided no objection has been raised by a contracting party within ninety days on the ground that the proposed change or rectification is not of a purely formal character. If such objection is raised and in the absence of agreement among the contracting parties concerned, the contracting party in question shall without delay submit to the secretariat, for circulation to all contracting parties, the documentation described in paragraph 2(b) above.

"5. A proposed change in the authentic text of a GATT schedule described in paragraph 2(b) above shall be certified provided no request for negotiation or consultation under Article XXVIII has been made to the contracting party in question within ninety days following the circulation of the documentation described in paragraph 2(b) above.

"6. In cases where an objection under paragraph 4 above is raised or where a request for negotiation or consultation under paragraph 5 has been made, the Procedures for Negotiations Under Article XXVIII (BISD 27S/26) shall apply. Any such objection or request shall at the same time be sent to the secretariat. After the completion of these procedures, a comprehensive list of all changes and the corresponding amended pages of the GATT schedule shall be sent to the secretariat for certification."

A Secretariat Note of 13 October 1994 on "Transposition of Schedules into the 1996 Harmonized System and Establishment of Loose-Leaf Schedules" (TAR/W/93) notes these procedures and states that "It is expected that the whole of 1995 will be dedicated to the preparation of the new schedules, including the necessary Article XXVIII renegotiations. While it is hoped that this work will be completed during 1995, there is no time-limit set for carrying out Article XXVIII renegotiations. After the completion of the required procedures the new consolidated HS loose-leaf schedules will need to be submitted to the Secretariat for certification; the submission should be in printed form as well as on diskette in spreadsheet format (Lotus 1-2-3 or Excel)." The Note also discusses the procedures required for participants in each of the eight categories listed at the end of in the preceding section.[161]

6. Concessions in schedules

(1) Authentic texts of Schedules

During discussions on the draft General Agreement at Geneva in 1947 it was agreed that "each Schedule would be authentic in either English or French or in both languages, at the option of the country whose Schedule was concerned. The way it was decided to provide for this was to put in parentheses at the top of the Schedule the words: 'Authentic in the English text only' or 'Authentic in the French text only,' if it was to be authentic only in one of these two languages. For that reason it was not considered necessary" to refer to the language in which Schedules would be authentic, either in Article II or in the paragraph corresponding to the present Article XXVI:3.[162]

The standard text of accession protocols now provides that the English, French and Spanish texts of the protocol will each be authentic, "except as otherwise specified with respect to the Schedule annexed thereto".[163] Tariff protocols such as the Geneva (1992) Protocol or the Marrakesh Protocol provide that "The Schedules annexed hereto are authentic in the English, French or Spanish language as specified in each Schedule".[164]

(2) Description of concessions

The Decision of 26 March 1980 on "Introduction of a Loose-leaf System for the Schedules of Tariff Concessions" provides that "The schedules should comprise a complete description of the products covered" and provides for submission of schedules in a specified format.[165] In discussion in the Committee on Tariff Concessions in 1987, the Chairman stated that "in supplying a schedule for annexation to a protocol, the minimum information required would be to complete the first four columns; concerning the fifth and seventh columns referring to current and historical INRs, it was understood that as long as the minimum information was provided in the schedules to be annexed to protocols, the schedules would be considered as authentic for the purpose of the protocols but incomplete as far as the requirements of the loose-leaf system were concerned. When countries would be in a position to provide the missing information, the matter could be dealt with under the certification procedure".[166] In 1988, the Chairman confirmed that "in order to comply with the Council Decision of 26 March 1980 on the introduction of the loose-leaf system, all the columns of a schedule had to be completed". The Chairman recalled that "the Harmonized System schedules annexed to the protocols which did not contain entries in all seven columns were considered as legally valid, but incomplete consolidated schedules".[167]

(3) Legal basis for determining initial negotiating rights (INRs)

The Director-General's proposal adopted on 26 March 1980 on "Introduction of a Loose-leaf System for the Schedules of Tariff Concessions" provides:

---

[161]TAR/W/93, paras. 8-9; see also TAR/W/81: "Amendment of the Harmonized Commodity Description and Coding System 1992) - Note by the Secretariat", dated 30 April 1991; TAR/W/81/Add.1 containing the correlation tables between HS 1988 and HS 1992", dated 2 July 1991; L/6905: "Procedures to Implement Changes in the Harmonized System", dated 20 September 1991; TAR/W/89: "Changes in the Harmonized System to be introduced on 1 January 1996 - Note by the Secretariat", dated 4 May 1993; TAR/W/91: "Changes in the Harmonized System to be Introduced on 1 January 1996 - Correlation Tables", dated 20 June 1994; and CCC document No. 38700: "Amendments to the Nomenclature appended as an Annex to the Convention accepted pursuant to the Recommendation of 6 July 1993 of the Customs Co-operation Council".

[162]EPCT/TAC/PV/25, p. 13-14.

[163]See, e.g. Protocols for the Accession of Bolivia, L/6562, 37S/5, 6, para. 10, or Costa Rica, L/6626, 37S/7, 9, para. 12.

[164]L/6987, para. 5; Marrakesh Protocol, para. 8.

[165]C/107/Rev.1, 27S/22, 23, para. 5; format appears in Annex to L/4821/Add.1.

[166]TAR/M/25, p. 5-6, para. 7.4.

[167]TAR/M/26, p. 3, para. 4.1.

"So far, initial negotiating rights (INRs) have only been indicated in working documents on schedules in connexion with renegotiations or with consolidation of schedules. In the final, published schedules the indication of INRs has so far been deleted. In order to make the loose-leaf system as transparent as possible and to remove the need for contracting parties to consult underlying documents, I propose that *the INRs be indicated in the loose-leaf schedules* as foreseen in the fifth column of the proposed format annexed to L/4821/Add.1 ...

"There is an understanding in the GATT concerning consolidated schedules that earlier schedules and negotiating records should be considered as proper sources in interpreting concessions in consolidated schedules (7S/115-116). This understanding is valid *inter alia* for INRs regarding earlier bindings made at a higher level than the present bound rate on a certain item. ... I propose that *this understanding will cease to be valid as regards the previous INRs when the loose-leaf schedules have been established and that all these previous INRs must, in order to maintain a legal value, be indicated in the loose-leaf schedules.* As the incorporation of previous INRs into the Schedules will necessitate time-consuming research in old negotiating records, I suggest that ... earlier schedules and negotiating records will remain proper sources for interpreting concessions until 1 January 1987."[168]

A Secretariat Note of 1982 on "Submission of Loose-leaf Schedules - Initial Negotiating Rights regarding Earlier Bindings" notes that "the way of presenting previous INRs is a purely bilateral matter" and states as follows:

"In the course of the preparation of loose-leaf schedules, it was found that a complete listing of previous INRs in respect of concessions given in different nomenclatures and at different rates could be very complicated and in some cases could amount to several pages of INRs in respect of one tariff line ...

"It appears ... that the best solution would be to permit a country submitting a schedule to examine bilaterally with countries having INRs in respect of earlier concessions if simplifications could be made in the presentation of the INRs. INRs at different levels and with different item descriptions could thus, for example, be condensed into only one INR at a level to be mutually agreed upon and expressed in the present nomenclature. Such a solution would, however, have to be agreed upon by the two sides. If the INR holder requests, the country submitting the schedule would have to fill in column 7 in full detail."[169]

On 6 November 1986, the Council agreed, in response to a request from the Committee on Tariff Concessions, to change the wording of paragraph 8 of the decision of 26 March 1980 from "until 1 January 1987" to read "until a date to be established by the Council".[170] The Council has not subsequently established any such date.

The Tariff Division of the Secretariat maintains a complete archive of all bilateral agreements regarding concessions since 1947.

Concerning the definition and application of initial negotiating rights, see Article XXVIII.

7. Application of concessions

(1) National tariff schedules

The Procedures for Rectification and Modification of Schedules agreed on 26 March 1980 provide that:

"... *Considering* the importance of keeping the authentic texts of Schedules annexed to the General Agreement up to date and of ensuring that they tally with the texts of corresponding items in national customs tariffs; ...

---

[168]C/107/Rev.1, 30S/22, 23-24, paras. 7-8.
[169]TAR/W/30, dated 23 June 1982, paras. 2, 4-5.
[170]Report by Vice-Chairman of the Committee to the Council on 6 November 1986, TAR/132, 33S/133, 135 para. 10.

"The CONTRACTING PARTIES decide that ...

"2. Changes in the authentic texts of Schedules shall be made when amendments or rearrangements which do not alter the scope of a concession are introduced in national customs tariffs in respect of bound items. Such changes and other rectifications of a purely formal character shall be made by means of Certifications. A draft of such changes shall be communicated to the Director-General where possible within three months but not later than six months after the amendment or rearrangement has been introduced in the national customs tariff ... ."[171]

The Secretariat has issued periodically for the Committee on Tariff Concessions lists of information available in the Secretariat on national tariff schedules.[172]

(2) Changes in tariff nomenclature

It was agreed in 1955 that the adoption of the Brussels Tariff Nomenclature as such presented no basic problem so far as schedules to the General Agreement are concerned. Since such a change would not necessarily impair concessions, the contracting party wishing merely to change the nomenclature of its schedule could resort to the normal rectification procedures; see at page 70 above.[173] See also the material above on introduction of the Harmonized System.

(3) Provisional accession to the General Agreement

The Declarations on the provisional accession of certain contracting parties to the General Agreement stated that the contracting party in question "shall not have any direct rights with respect to the concessions contained in the schedules annexed to the General Agreement either under the provisions of Article II or under the provisions of any other Article of the General Agreement".[174]

See also the discussion of provisional accession under Article XXXIII.

8. Modification of concessions

See Article XXVIII and the material above on paragraph 1 of Article II.

9. Modification and rectification of Schedules

The General Agreement provides for various types of tariff negotiations among contracting parties (Article XXVIII *bis*) or with acceding governments (Article XXXIII) as well as for renegotiations (Article XXVIII:1, 4, 5, Article XVIII:7, XXIV:6), or withholding or withdrawal of concessions (Article XXVII). Each modification of concessions brings a corresponding modification of Schedules.

(1) Procedures for modification or rectification of Schedules

In the early years of the GATT, modification and rectification of Schedules was carried out by means of Protocols. See the material on this subject under Article XXX.

---

[171]L/4962, 27S/25, para. 2.
[172]See TAR/W/40/Rev.13, "Tariff Information Available in the Secretariat", dated 13 November 1994 (or later revisions); TAR/W/85, "Status of Schedules of Contracting Parties to the GATT", dated 16 October 1992.
[173]Report on "Transposition of Schedule XXXVII - Turkey", L/294, adopted on 20 December 1954, 3S/127, para. 2.
[174]See, e.g., 8S/10, 20S/9.

Procedures for modification and rectification of Schedules were agreed in the following decisions: Decision of 17 November 1959;[175] Decision of 19 November 1968;[176] Decision of 26 March 1980.[177] The latter Decision provides, *inter alia*, that:

"1. Changes in the authentic texts of Schedules annexed to the General Agreement which reflect modifications resulting from action under Article II, Article XVIII, Article XXIV, Article XXVII or Article XXVIII shall be certified by means of Certifications. A draft of such change shall be communicated to the Director-General within three months after the action has been completed.

"2. Changes in the authentic texts of Schedules shall be made when amendments or rearrangements which do not alter the scope of a concession are introduced in national customs tariffs in respect of bound items. Such changes and other rectifications of a purely formal character shall be made by means of Certifications. A draft of such changes shall be communicated to the Director-General where possible within three months but not later than six months after the amendment or rearrangement has been introduced in the national customs tariff or in the case of other rectifications, as soon as circumstances permit.

"3. The draft containing the changes described in paragraphs 1 and 2 shall be communicated by the Director-General to all the contracting parties and shall become a Certification provided that no objection has been raised by a contracting party within three months on the ground that, in the case of changes described in paragraph 1, the draft does not correctly reflect the modifications or, in the case of changes described in paragraph 2, the proposed rectification is not within the terms of that paragraph.

"4. Whenever practicable Certifications shall record the date of entry into force of each modification and the effective date of each rectification.

"5. The procedure of Certification under this Decision may be applied for the establishment of consolidated Schedules or of new Schedules under paragraph 5(c) of Article XXVI, wherein all changes are modifications or rectifications referred to in paragraphs 1 or 2.

"6. This Decision supersedes the Decision of 19 November 1968."

The following certifications of changes to Schedules have been issued:

First Certification of Changes to Schedules	12 July 1969	17S/12
Second Certification of Changes to Schedules	9 January 1974	21S/19
Third Certification of Changes to Schedules	23 October 1974	21S/20
Fourth Certification of Changes to Schedules	20 April 1979	26S/198
Fifth Certification of Changes to Schedules	7 August 1981	28S/10
Sixth Certification of Changes to Schedules	28 November 1987	35S/4

Since the Sixth Certification, changes to schedules have been made and certified on an ad hoc basis: see directly below.

(2) Certifications of rectifications and modifications

Certifications are governed by the Decision of 26 March 1980 on "Procedures for Modifications and Rectifications of Schedules of Tariff Concessions". A 1985 Secretariat Note on "Loose-leaf Schedules Based on Harmonized System Nomenclature" describes practice with regard to certifications.

---

[175] 8S/25.
[176] 16S/16.
[177] 27S/25.

"The general practice for *certifications* ... has been that notifications received (at irregular intervals) from contracting parties concerning changes in tariff schedules are circulated to all contracting parties in a TAR- document. In this document it is indicated that if no objection is notified to the secretariat within three months, the respective change in the tariff schedule (modification or rectification) will be deemed to be approved and will be included in the next certification of changes to schedules. When a sufficient number of notifications have been approved, a (collective) draft certification is prepared and circulated by the secretariat to all contracting parties. This draft certification contains a proviso to the effect that if no objection is raised by a contracting party within three months from the date of its circulation on the ground that the draft does not correctly reflect modifications which have (already) entered into force, or that the rectifications (included in the draft) are not of a purely formal character, the draft will become a draft certification under paragraph 3 of the 1980 Decision ...

"In the context of the discussions leading to the establishment of a loose-leaf system of tariff schedules ... it was understood ... that in order to simplify and accelerate the certification process, a consolidated loose-leaf schedule - and subsequent amendments to it - would be certified if, upon its initial circulation in a TAR- document, no objections had been raised within the three-month period mentioned above, thus obviating the need for a second circulation of a (collective) draft certification ...

"... *Certifications* ... require the tacit approval of all contracting parties before being approved, by virtue of the (first) three-month period during which objections against proposed changes in tariff schedules can be raised. A contracting party with which agreement concerning the proposed changes has not been reached can thus indefinitely block the entry into force of the certification."[178]

The most recent Certification to enter into force is the Sixth Certification of Changes to Schedules to the General Agreement on Tariffs and Trade, of 28 November 1987.[179]

Since the Sixth Certification was issued, it was agreed that because of the introduction of the loose-leaf system, changes to schedules would be made on an ad hoc basis. These changes are circulated in documents in the TAR/ series under the Decision of 26 March 1980 on Procedures for Modifications and Rectifications of Schedules of Tariff Concessions, and are certified through documents in the Let/ series.[180]

(3) Legal effect of certification

The Sixth Certification provides that "it is hereby certified (i) that the authentic texts of Schedules to the General Agreement are changed to reflect the rectifications of a purely formal character or the modifications resulting from action taken under paragraph 6 of Article II, Article XVIII, Article XXIV, Article XXVII or Article XXVIII of the General Agreement as set out in Annex A; and (ii) that Schedules in Annex B are established in conformity with paragraph 5 of the Decision [of 26 March 1980] and that, in each case in which Article II of the General Agreement refers to the date of the Agreement, the applicable date in respect of any concession contained in these Schedules shall be the date of the instrument by which the concession was first incorporated in the relevant Schedule to the General Agreement ...".[181]

A 1987 Secretariat Note on "Harmonized System Negotiations under Article XXVIII" states that: "Although the uncertified loose-leaf schedules represent important sources of information and bases for negotiations, they have no legal status. It follows that past protocols and other legal instruments continue to keep their legal status

---

[178]TAR/W/55/Add.1, p. 2-3, paras. 5-7.
[179]TAR/138, and Add.1 & 2, 35S/4; for a list of all previous Protocols and Certifications of rectifications and modifications, see the index to the annual Supplements to the BISD under "Schedules".
[180]See, for instance, TAR/172, dated 5 January 1989 (notification by Austria of results of Article XXVIII negotiations with Japan and modification of Schedule XXXII - Austria, together with sets of replacement loose-leaf pages), and Let/1631 dated 5 June 1989 (transmission of certified true copy of Certification of Modification and Rectifications relating to Schedule XXXII - Austria, done at Geneva on 31 May 1989).
[181]TAR/138 and Add.1 & 2, 35S/4-5.

until the time of certification of the respective loose-leaf schedules or their entry into force by means of a Protocol".[182]

(4) Application of rectification procedures in other agreements

On 16/17 December 1980, the Committee on Trade in Civil Aircraft decided to apply the Council's Decision of 26 March 1980 on Modification and Rectification of Schedules (27S/25) in respect of the Annex to the Agreement on Trade in Civil Aircraft.[183] The Agreement on Government Procurement provides simplified procedures for rectifications of a purely formal nature and minor amendments relating to Annexes I-IV, and a more elaborate procedure for modifications to lists of entities.[184] On 27 April 1982, the Government of Switzerland added the "Government of the Principality of Liechtenstein" to its list of covered entities annexed to the Agreement on Government Procurement. A Secretariat legal opinion of 12 June 1992 concluded that since this addition would not appear to add new obligations for other Parties, no re-establishment of the balance of rights and obligations would be necessary; since the purpose of the more elaborate procedures in sub-paragraph (b) was to permit re-establishment of this balance, the case in question would fit more appropriately under the simplified procedures of sub-paragraph (a). At its meeting of 26 June 1992 the Committee on Government Procurement noted that the addition in question had been correctly notified under Article IX:5(a).[185]

10. Withholding or withdrawal of concessions

Tariff protocols concluding rounds of multilateral trade negotiations in which one or more governments have negotiated accession to the GATT have included provisions regarding the application of Article XXVII. For instance, both the Geneva (1979) Protocol to the General Agreement on Tariffs and Trade and the Protocol Supplementary to the Geneva (1979) Protocol to the General Agreement on Tariffs and Trade included the following provision on withholding or withdrawal of concessions.

"After the schedule of tariff concessions annexed to this Protocol relating to a participant has become a Schedule to the General Agreement pursuant to the provisions of paragraph 1, such participant shall be free at any time to withhold or to withdraw in whole or in part the concession in such schedule with respect to any product for which the principal supplier is any other participant or any government having negotiated for accession during the Multilateral Trade Negotiations, but the schedule of which, as established in the Multilateral Trade Negotiations, has not yet become a Schedule to the General Agreement. Such action can, however, only be taken after written notice of any such withholding or withdrawal of a concession has been given to the CONTRACTING PARTIES and after consultations have been held, upon request, with any participant or any acceding government, the relevant schedule of tariff concessions relating to which has become a Schedule to the General Agreement and which has a substantial interest in the product involved. Any concessions so withheld or withdrawn shall be applied on and after the day on which the schedule of the participant or the acceding government which has the principal supplying interest becomes a Schedule to the General Agreement."[186]

11. Notification of national tariff schedules, the Tariff Study and the Integrated Data Base

The "IDB User Reference Manual" issued by the Secretariat on 19 April 1994 notes that:

"The GATT Secretariat has maintained a data base on tariffs and trade since the early seventies. The first GATT data base, known as the Tariff Study, contained information on customs tariffs and imports of eleven OECD markets (including the European Communities counted as one market). The Tariff Study was designed to analyze the tariff situation in the developed markets after the Kennedy Round. Under the guidance of a group of technical experts from governments, the Secretariat prepared several analyses of the

---

[182]TAR/W/65/Rev.1, dated 14 January 1987, para. 1.
[183]L/5094, L/5225, 28S/43, para. 4; see also AIR/41, AIR/M/3 and AIR/M/9.
[184]26S/33, 53, Article IX:5. For examples see, e.g., GPR/46-52, 54-55, 58-59.
[185]GPR/68, dated 13 July 1992, referring to Secretariat opinion in GPR/W/114 dated 12 June 1992.
[186]26S/4. See also corresponding provisions in the Geneva (1967) Protocol to the General Agreement, 15S/6, para. 3.

tariff situation during the early seventies. A final analysis was published before the Tokyo Round in four volumes known as 'the Basic Documentation for the Tariff Study'.

"During the Tokyo Round, the Tariff Study exercise was continued to assist the participants in the negotiations. Access to the Tariff Study data was restricted to the 11 contracting parties participating in the exercise. However, during and after the Tokyo Round, the participants authorised the Secretariat to provide developing countries with summary information extracted from the Tariff Study files concerning products of export interest to them.

"Between 1980 and 1987, the Tariff Study files continued to be updated on an annual basis to follow the application of the Tokyo Round concessions which were implemented in eight annual stages starting 1 January 1980.

"In 1983, a group of technical experts from governments was convened to analyze the feasibility of establishing a data base containing information to be used in Article XXVIII negotiations which were necessary before the Harmonized System could be implemented. ... The Secretariat established, in parallel with the Tariff Study, the HS common data base in which only the five major developed markets participated.

"From 1986, the Group of experts on the HS data base studied the feasibility of replacing the Tariff Study exercise by a new data base in which all GATT Contracting Parties would be invited to participate and which would cover not only customs tariffs and imports but also non-tariff measures and, if feasible in the future, any additional statistics which could be "integrated" with the above three areas.

"In November 1987, the GATT Council launched the Integrated Data Base (IDB) and the Group of experts on the HS data base became the Informal Advisory Group (IAG) on the IDB in which experts from *all contracting parties* were invited to participate with a view to guiding the Secretariat in the preparation of the IDB and reporting to the Council on the progress of the work. ..."[187]

On 10 November 1987 the Council agreed to a Decision on an "Integrated Data Base", providing that the Secretariat would begin work on setting up an integrated data base, and noting that the information would initially be restricted to three categories of data, each at the tariff line level: imports, tariffs and quantitative restrictions. The Decision noted as well that "with respect to the data elements ... contracting parties have already agreed to notification requirements affecting quantitative restrictions ... and bound tariffs. [The Council a]grees that, for the purposes of the integrated data base, contracting parties should also submit annually to the secretariat, by tariff line, tariff data for unbound items and import data for all bound and unbound items."[188] The Council decision also recommends that, when the IDB is operational, all contracting parties will have access to the data base, including the tariff study data base. The IDB User Reference Manual notes that as of April 1994, 45 contracting parties (the EC being counted as one) participated in the IDB, accounting for over 97 percent of total merchandise trade of GATT contracting parties.[189]

III. PREPARATORY WORK AND SUBSEQUENT MODIFICATIONS

Differences from Havana Charter text: The Havana Charter did not itself provide for the scheduling of tariff concessions. Article 17 of the Charter on "Reduction of Tariffs and Elimination of Preferences" obligated each ITO Member to negotiate on request concerning reduction of tariffs, other charges and preferences; paragraph 3 provided that the Geneva negotiations leading to the GATT would be deemed to be negotiations under Article 17. Concessions made in Article 17 negotiations would be incorporated in the GATT on terms

---

[187] IDB/URM/1, dated 19 April 1994.

[188] L/6290, 34S/66, para. 3, referring to: Decision of 30 November 1984, L/5754/Rev.1, 31S/12, adopting *inter alia* recommendations in para. 44 of the Report on "Quantitative Restrictions and Other Non-Tariff Measures", L/5713, 31S/211; and Director-General's proposal adopted 26 March 1980 on "Introduction of a Loose-Leaf System for the Schedules of Tariff Concessions".

[189] IDB/URM/1, dated 19 April 1994.

to be agreed with the GATT contracting parties. Hence, the scheduling provisions of the GATT were located in Part I, which under Article XXIX:2 would not be superseded by the Charter when the Charter entered into force.

Preparatory work of Article II: During the London session of the Preparatory Committee, the Procedures Sub-Committee of Committee II drew up a "Resolution Regarding the Negotiation of a Multilateral Trade Agreement Embodying Tariff Concessions"[190], and "Procedures for Giving Effect to Certain Provisions of the Charter of the International Trade Organization by Means of a General Agreement on Tariffs and Trade Among the Members of the Preparatory Committee".[191] The Resolution, noting that the United States government had invited the members of the Preparatory Committee "to meet to negotiate concrete arrangements for the relaxation of tariffs and trade barriers of all kinds and the invitation has been accepted", recommended "that the meeting envisaged by the invitations ... should be held under the sponsorship of the Preparatory Committee in connection with, and as a part of, the Second Session of the Committee". The Procedures provided negotiating rules, as well as specific provisions on the use of the principal supplier rule in negotiations, the form of tariff schedules (see page 103 above) and the status of preferential rates of duty; they also provided a draft outline of a General Agreement on Tariffs and Trade, of which Article III provided that "Each signatory government shall accord to the commerce of the customs territories of the other signatory governments the treatment provided for in the appropriate Schedule annexed to this Agreement and made an integral part thereof".[192]

The General Agreement was then discussed at the Drafting Committee in New York. Article VIII of the draft of the General Agreement in the Drafting Committee Report included paragraphs corresponding to the present paragraphs 1(a), 3 and 4 of Article II; a footnote to Article VIII stated that it was contemplated that at an appropriate place in each schedule of concessions, notes would be included, the text of which corresponded to the present paragraphs 1(b), 2(a) and 5 of Article II. There were no provisions on renegotiation of concessions.

At the Geneva session of the Preparatory Committee, the text of the General Agreement was principally negotiated in the meetings of the Tariff Agreement Committee, which discussed (*inter alia*) scheduling provisions, the contents of schedules, and formalities for putting the General Agreement into effect. The headnote to the first draft model schedule included the provisions now in paragraphs 1(b) and (c) and 2 of Article II, which were later moved into the Article.[193]

Article II has been amended only once, in 1948, when the reference to Article III in paragraph 2(a) was altered as a conforming change associated with the replacement of the original text of Article III by the text of Article 18 of the Havana Charter. This change was effected by the Protocol Modifying Part I and Article XXIX, which entered into force on 24 September 1952.

During the Review Session of 1954-55, it was agreed to amend paragraphs 1(b) and 1(c) to include references to charges on the transfer of payments (see page 81); to amend paragraph 6(a) (see page 97); to delete the interpretative note to paragraph 2(a) as outdated; and to redraft the interpretative note to paragraph 4 (see page 92). However, these amendments were made in the Protocol Amending Part I and Articles XXIX and XXX, which failed to gain the requisite unanimous approval and was abandoned.[194]

---

[190]London Report, Annexure 7, p. 47-48.
[191]London Report, Annexure 10, p. 48-52. See also generally the verbatim records of the Sub-Committee on Procedures, EPCT/C.II/PRO/PV/5-15 and its summary records in the series EPCT/C.II/W/2-31.
[192]*Ibid.* p. 52.
[193]EPCT/153; discussion at EPCT/TAC/PV/21, p. 16ff; EPCT/201; discussion at EPCT/TAC/PV/23 p. 15ff.
[194]15S/65.

IV. RELEVANT DOCUMENTS

New York

Reports:	EPCT/C.6/74, 79
Other:	EPCT/C.6/W.58

Geneva

Discussion:	EPCT/TAC/PV/8, 9, 16, 21, 23, 24, 26, 27, 28
Reports:	EPCT/135, 153, 191, 201, 208, 211, 214/Add.1/Rev.1
Other:	EPCT/189+Corr.2, 196, 238 EPCT/W/272, 287, 312, 318, 321, 341

Review Session

Discussion:	SR.9/16, 18, 20, 36
Reports:	W.9/124, 177, 193, 200, 212+Corr.1, 217+Corr.1, 236
Other:	L/189, 261/Add.1 W.9/45, 70, 109/Rev.1, 113, 118, 223 Spec/4/55, 85/55, 94/55

V. SCHEDULES OF CONTRACTING PARTIES TO THE GATT 1947

Contracting party	Schedule
Argentina	LXIV
Australia	I
Austria	XXXII
Bangladesh	LXX
Belgium	EC
Benelux (Part D only)	II
Part D - Netherlands Antilles	
Benin	XLVIII
Bolivia	LXXXIV
Brazil	III
Burkina Faso	XLVI
Burundi	LV
Canada (E/F)	V
Chile (E/S)	VII
Colombia (E/S)	LXXVI
Costa Rica	LXXXV
Côte d'Ivoire	LII
Cuba	IX
Czech Republic	XCII
Denmark	EC
Djibouti	CXXXVII
Dominican Republic	XXIII
European Communities (E/F) (12)	LXXX
Egypt	LXIII
El Salvador	LXXXVII
Finland	XXIV
France	EC
France (Parts E, H, K, M only)	XI
Part E - French Establishments in Oceania	
Part H - Indo-China	
Part K - New Caledonia and Dependencies	
Part M - St.Pierre and Miquelon	
Gabon	XLVII
Germany	EC
Greece	EC
Guatemala	LXXXVIII
Guinea	CXXXVI
Haiti	XXVI
Honduras	XCV
Hong Kong	LXXXII
Hungary	LXXI
Iceland	LXII
India	XII
Indonesia	XXI
Ireland	EC
Israel	XLII
Italy	EC
Jamaica	LXVI
Japan	XXXVIII
Korea, Republic of	LX
Luxembourg	EC
Macau	LXXXIX
Madagascar	LI
Malawi	LVIII
Malaysia	XXXIX
Mali	XCIV
Mauritania	L
Mexico	LXXVII
Morocco	LXXXI
Myanmar	IV
Namibia	XC
Netherlands	EC
New Zealand	XIII
Nicaragua	XXIX
Niger	LIII
Nigeria	XLIII
Norway	XIV
Pakistan	XV
Paraguay	XCI
Peru	XXXV
Philippines	LXXV
Poland	LXV
Portugal	EC
Romania	LXIX
Rwanda	LVI
Senegal	XLIX
Singapore	LXXIII
Slovak Republic	XCIII
Slovenia	
South Africa	XVIII
Spain	EC
Sri Lanka	VI
Surinam	LXXIV
Sweden	XXX
Switzerland (including Liechtenstein)	LIX
Thailand	LXXIX
Trinidad & Tobago	LXVII
Tunisia	LXXXIII
Turkey	XXXVII
United Kingdom	EC
United Kingdom (Part B only)	XIX
Part B - Bahamas	
United States	XX
Uruguay	XXXI
Venezuela	LXXXVI
Yugoslavia	LVII
Zaire	LXVIII
Zambia	LXXVIII
Zimbabwe	LIV

Notes:

A summary of the status of Schedules of contracting parties appears in TAR/W/85 dated 16 October 1992.

1. Schedule II - Benelux, Part D (Netherlands Antilles) remains in force.
2. The concessions in Schedule XI - France, Parts E, H, K, M (French Establishments in Oceania, Indo-China, New Caledonia and Dependencies, St.Pierre and Miquelon) remain in force. Part H was terminated for Laos and Vietnam upon expiry of their *de facto* application of the General Agreement but is applied *de facto* by Cambodia pending decision on accession to the General Agreement.
3. The status of Schedule XLVII - Gabon is uncertain, Gabon not having recognized the concessions in the former Schedule XVI - France, Part B when it acceded under Article XXVI:5(c) in 1963; see L/2169, 12S/75-76.
4. The concessions in Schedule XIX - United Kingdom, Part B (Bahamas) are applied by the Bahamas *de facto* pending decision on accession to the General Agreement.

PART II

ARTICLE III

NATIONAL TREATMENT ON INTERNAL TAXATION AND REGULATION

I.	TEXT OF ARTICLE III AND INTERPRETATIVE NOTE AD ARTICLE III			122
II.	INTERPRETATION AND APPLICATION OF ARTICLE III			124
	A.	SCOPE AND APPLICATION OF ARTICLE III		124
		1.	General	124
			(1) Scope of Article III	124
			(2) Purpose of Article III	125
			(3) Relevance of tariff concessions	127
			(4) Relevance of policy purpose of internal measures	127
			(5) Relevance of trade effects	128
			(6) Application of Article III to regional and local governments and authorities within the territory of a contracting party	130
			(7) Application of Article III with regard to State trading monopolies	131
			(8) Mandatory versus discretionary legislation; non-enforcement	133
		2.	Interpretative Note Ad Article III: measures imposed at the time or point of importation	136
			(1) "collected or enforced … at the time or point of importation"	136
			(2) "which applies to an imported product and to the like domestic product"	137
		3.	Paragraph 1	139
			(1) "should not be applied to imported or domestic products so as to afford protection to domestic production"	139
			(2) Note Ad paragraph 1: Application of paragraph 1 to internal taxes imposed by local governments and authorities	141
		4.	Paragraph 2: internal taxes or other internal charges of any kind	141
			(1) "directly or indirectly"	141
			(2) "internal taxes"	141
			(a) Excise taxes, indirect taxes and consumption taxes	141
			(b) Fiscal measures versus enforcement measures	142
			(c) Income taxes, exemptions from income taxes and credits against income taxes	144
			(d) Border tax adjustments; border adjustment of taxes and charges	144
			(3) "or other internal charges of any kind": charges on the transfer of payments for imports or exports	149
			(4) "in excess of those applied"	150
			(a) Discriminatory rates of tax	150
			(b) Methods of taxation	150
			(c) Exemption or remission of taxes	152
			(d) Exposure of imported products to a risk of discrimination	154
			(5) "like domestic products"	155
			(6) "a directly competitive or substitutable product" (Ad Article III paragraph 2)	159
			(7) Taxes collected or enforced at the point of importation	161
		5.	Paragraph 3	161
		6.	Paragraph 4	162
			(1) "treatment no less favourable"	162
			(a) Equality of competitive opportunities	164
			(b) Formally identical legal requirements versus formally different legal requirements	168
			(c) Application of legal requirements to individual cases and "balancing"	169
			(2) "than that accorded to like products of national origin"	171
			(3) "in respect of all laws, regulations and requirements"	173
			(a) Requirements applied in individual cases	173
			(b) Subsidies and other benefits as "requirements"	173
			(c) Requirements associated with the regulation of international investment	174
			(4) "affecting"	175
			(5) "internal sale, offering for sale, purchase, transportation, distribution or use"	177
			(a) Standardization of products	177
			(b) Minimum and maximum price regulations	177
			(c) Requirements affecting internal offering for sale	178
			(d) Regulations on quality or quantity of products consumed	179
			(e) Marking requirements	181
			(f) Measures affecting internal transportation	181

			(6)	"differential internal transportation charges": second sentence of paragraph 4	183
		7.		Paragraphs 5, 6 and 7: internal quantitative regulations (mixing regulations)	183
			(1)	Scope of paragraph 5	183
			(2)	"otherwise apply internal quantitative regulations in a manner contrary to the principles set forth in paragraph 1"	186
			(3)	Special customs treatment granted conditional on mixing or use of the imported product with domestic products	187
			(4)	Application of mixing regulations in time of shortages	187
			(5)	Paragraph 6: existing mixing regulations and their alteration	187
			(6)	Paragraph 7	189
			(7)	Relationship between provisions on mixing regulations and other provisions of Article III	189
		8.		Paragraph 8	190
			(1)	Paragraph 8(a): "procurement by governmental agencies"	190
				(a) "governmental"	191
				(b) "not with a view to commercial resale or with a view to use in the production of goods for commercial sale"	193
				(c) Tied loans	194
			(2)	Paragraph 8(b): "payment of subsidies exclusively to domestic producers"	194
		9.		Paragraph 9	197
		10.		Paragraph 10	197
	B.	RELATIONSHIP WITH OTHER ARTICLES OF THE GENERAL AGREEMENT			197
		1.		Article I	197
		2.		Article II	198
		3.		Article XI	201
		4.		Article XVII	204
		5.		Article XX(d)	204
		6.		Article XXIV:12	204
		7.		Part IV	204
	C.	EXCEPTIONS AND DEROGATIONS			204
		1.		Exceptions to the scope of the national treatment requirement	204
		2.		Protocol of Provisional Application	204
		3.		Protocols of accession	205
III.	PREPARATORY WORK AND SUBSEQUENT MODIFICATIONS				205
IV.	RELEVANT DOCUMENTS				207

I. TEXT OF ARTICLE III AND INTERPRETATIVE NOTE AD ARTICLE III

Article III*

National Treatment on Internal Taxation and Regulation

1. The contracting parties recognize that internal taxes and other internal charges, and laws, regulations and requirements affecting the internal sale, offering for sale, purchase, transportation, distribution or use of products, and internal quantitative regulations requiring the mixture, processing or use of products in specified amounts or proportions, should not be applied to imported or domestic products so as to afford protection to domestic production.*

2. The products of the territory of any contracting party imported into the territory of any other contracting party shall not be subject, directly or indirectly, to internal taxes or other internal charges of any kind in excess of those applied, directly or indirectly, to like domestic products. Moreover, no contracting party shall otherwise apply internal taxes or other internal charges to imported or domestic products in a manner contrary to the principles set forth in paragraph 1.*

3. With respect to any existing internal tax which is inconsistent with the provisions of paragraph 2, but which is specifically authorized under a trade agreement, in force on April 10, 1947, in which the import duty on the taxed product is bound against increase, the contracting party imposing the tax shall be free to postpone the application of the provisions of paragraph 2 to such tax until such time as it can obtain release from the

obligations of such trade agreement in order to permit the increase of such duty to the extent necessary to compensate for the elimination of the protective element of the tax.

4. The products of the territory of any contracting party imported into the territory of any other contracting party shall be accorded treatment no less favourable than that accorded to like products of national origin in respect of all laws, regulations and requirements affecting their internal sale, offering for sale, purchase, transportation, distribution or use. The provisions of this paragraph shall not prevent the application of differential internal transportation charges which are based exclusively on the economic operation of the means of transport and not on the nationality of the product.

5. No contracting party shall establish or maintain any internal quantitative regulation relating to the mixture, processing or use of products in specified amounts or proportions which requires, directly or indirectly, that any specified amount or proportion of any product which is the subject of the regulation must be supplied from domestic sources. Moreover, no contracting party shall otherwise apply internal quantitative regulations in a manner contrary to the principles set forth in paragraph 1.*

6. The provisions of paragraph 5 shall not apply to any internal quantitative regulation in force in the territory of any contracting party on July 1, 1939, April 10, 1947, or March 24, 1948, at the option of that contracting party; *Provided* that any such regulation which is contrary to the provisions of paragraph 5 shall not be modified to the detriment of imports and shall be treated as a customs duty for the purpose of negotiation.

7. No internal quantitative regulation relating to the mixture, processing or use of products in specified amounts or proportions shall be applied in such a manner as to allocate any such amount or proportion among external sources of supply.

8. (*a*) The provisions of this Article shall not apply to laws, regulations or requirements governing the procurement by governmental agencies of products purchased for governmental purposes and not with a view to commercial resale or with a view to use in the production of goods for commercial sale.

(*b*) The provisions of this Article shall not prevent the payment of subsidies exclusively to domestic producers, including payments to domestic producers derived from the proceeds of internal taxes or charges applied consistently with the provisions of this Article and subsidies effected through governmental purchases of domestic products.

9. The contracting parties recognize that internal maximum price control measures, even though conforming to the other provisions of this Article, can have effects prejudicial to the interests of contracting parties supplying imported products. Accordingly, contracting parties applying such measures shall take account of the interests of exporting contracting parties with a view to avoiding to the fullest practicable extent such prejudicial effects.

10. The provisions of this Article shall not prevent any contracting party from establishing or maintaining internal quantitative regulations relating to exposed cinematograph films and meeting the requirements of Article IV.

Interpretative Note *Ad* Article III from Annex I

Any internal tax or other internal charge, or any law, regulation or requirement of the kind referred to in paragraph 1 which applies to an imported product and to the like domestic product and is collected or enforced in the case of the imported product at the time or point of importation, is nevertheless to be regarded as an internal tax or other internal charge, or a law, regulation or requirement of the kind referred to in paragraph 1, and is accordingly subject to the provisions of Article III.

Paragraph 1

The application of paragraph 1 to internal taxes imposed by local governments and authorities within the territory of a contracting party is subject to the provisions of the final paragraph of Article XXIV. The term "reasonable measures" in the last-mentioned paragraph would not require, for example, the repeal of existing national legislation authorizing local governments to impose internal taxes which, although technically inconsistent with the letter of Article III, are not in fact inconsistent with its spirit, if such repeal would result in a serious financial hardship for the local governments or authorities concerned. With regard to taxation by local governments or authorities which is inconsistent with both the letter and spirit of Article III, the term "reasonable measures" would permit a contracting party to eliminate the inconsistent taxation gradually over a transition period, if abrupt action would create serious administrative and financial difficulties.

Paragraph 2

A tax conforming to the requirements of the first sentence of paragraph 2 would be considered to be inconsistent with the provisions of the second sentence only in cases where competition was involved between, on the one hand, the taxed product and, on the other hand, a directly competitive or substitutable product which was not similarly taxed.

Paragraph 5

Regulations consistent with the provisions of the first sentence of paragraph 5 shall not be considered to be contrary to the provisions of the second sentence in any case in which all of the products subject to the regulations are produced domestically in substantial quantities. A regulation cannot be justified as being consistent with the provisions of the second sentence on the ground that the proportion or amount allocated to each of the products which are the subject of the regulation constitutes an equitable relationship between imported and domestic products.

II. INTERPRETATION AND APPLICATION OF ARTICLE III

A. SCOPE AND APPLICATION OF ARTICLE III

1. General

(1) Scope of Article III

The 1958 Panel Report on "Italian Discrimination against Imported Agricultural Machinery," which examined an Italian law providing special credit terms for the purchase of agricultural machinery produced in Italy, notes that the Panel examined the argument of Italy that "the General Agreement was a trade agreement and its scope was limited to measures governing trade ... the commitment undertaken by the CONTRACTING PARTIES under [Article III:4] was limited to qualitative and quantitative regulations to which goods were subjected, with respect to their sale or purchase on the domestic market."[1] The Panel found as follows.

> "The Panel ... noted that if the Italian contention were correct, and if the scope of Article III were limited in the way the Italian delegation suggested to a specific type of law and regulations, the value of the bindings under Article II of the Agreement and of the general rules of non-discrimination as between imported and domestic products could be easily evaded.

> "The Panel recognized ... that it was not the intention of the General Agreement to limit the right of a contracting party to adopt measures which appeared to it necessary to foster its economic development or to protect a domestic industry, provided that such measures were permitted by the General Agreement. The GATT offered a number of possibilities to achieve these purposes through tariff measures or otherwise. The Panel did not appreciate why the extension of the credit facilities in question to the purchasers of imported tractors as well as domestically produced tractors would detract from the attainment of the objectives of the Law, which aimed at stimulating the purchase of tractors mainly by small farmers and co-operatives in the interests of economic development. If, on the other hand, the objective of the Law, although not specifically stated in the text thereof, were to protect the Italian agricultural machinery industry, the Panel considered that such protection should be given in ways permissible under the General Agreement rather than by the extension of credit exclusively for purchases of domestically produced agricultural machinery."[2]

The 1984 Panel Report on "Canada - Administration of the Foreign Investment Review Act" examined written purchase and export undertakings under the Foreign Investment Review Act of Canada, submitted by investors regarding the conduct of the business they were proposing to acquire or establish, conditional on

---

[1] L/833, adopted 23 October 1958, 7S/60, 63, para. 6.
[2] *Ibid.*, 7S/64-65, paras. 15-16.

approval by the Canadian government of the proposed acquisition or establishment. Written undertakings are legally binding on the investor if the investment is allowed. The Panel noted:

"... the Panel does not consider it relevant nor does it feel competent to judge how the foreign investors are affected by the purchase requirements, as the national treatment obligations of Article III of the General Agreement do not apply to foreign persons or firms but to imported products and serve to protect the interests of producers and exporters established on the territory of any contracting party".[3]

(2)   Purpose of Article III

The 1958 Panel Report on "Italian Discrimination against Imported Agricultural Machinery" provides that "It was considered ... that the intention of the drafters of the Agreement was clearly to treat the imported products in the same way as the like domestic products once they had been cleared through customs. Otherwise indirect protection could be given".[4]

The Panel Report on "United States - Section 337 of the Tariff Act of 1930" notes that "... the purpose of Article III ... is to ensure that internal measures 'not be applied to imported or domestic products so as to afford protection to domestic production' (Article III:1)".[5] The same Panel "rejected any notion of balancing more favourable treatment of some imported products against less favourable treatment of other imported products. ... Such an interpretation would lead to great uncertainty about the conditions of competition between imported and domestic products and thus defeat the purposes of Article III".[6]

The 1987 Panel Report on "United States - Taxes on Petroleum and Certain Imported Substances" notes that "Article III:2, first sentence, obliges contracting parties to establish certain competitive conditions for imported products in relation to domestic products. Unlike some other provisions in the General Agreement, it does not refer to trade effects".[7] See further on page 128. Concerning another issue examined by the panel, the same panel report provides:

"... The general prohibition of quantitative restrictions under Article XI ... and the national treatment obligation of Article III ... have essentially the same rationale, namely to protect expectations of the contracting parties as to the competitive relationship between their products and those of the other contracting parties. Both articles are not only to protect current trade but also to create the predictability needed to plan future trade".[8]

The 1991 Panel Report on "United States - Restrictions on Imports of Tuna," which has not been adopted, notes with regard to Article III:

"... While restrictions on importation are prohibited by Article XI:1, contracting parties are permitted by Article III:4 and the Note Ad Article III to impose an internal regulation on products imported from other contracting parties provided that it: does not discriminate between products of other countries in violation of the most-favoured-nation principle of Article I:1; is not applied so as to afford protection to domestic production, in violation of the national treatment principle of Article III:1; and accords to imported products treatment no less favourable than that accorded to like products of national origin, consistent with Article III:4....

"The text of Article III:1 refers to the application to imported or domestic products of 'laws, regulations and requirements affecting the internal sale ... of *products*' and 'internal quantitative regulations requiring the mixture, processing or use of *products*'; it sets forth the principle that such regulations on *products* not be applied so as to afford protection to domestic production. Article III:4 refers solely to laws,

---

[3] L/5504, adopted 7 February 1984, 30S/140, 167, para. 6.5.
[4] L/833, adopted on 23 October 1958, 7S/60, 63-64, para. 11.
[5] L/6439, adopted on 7 November 1989, 36S/345, 385, para. 5.10.
[6] 36S/387, para. 5.14.
[7] L/6175, adopted 17 June 1987, 34S/136, 158, para. 5.1.9.
[8] *Ibid.*, 34S/160, para. 5.2.2.

regulations and requirements affecting the internal sale, etc. of *products*. This suggests that Article III covers only measures affecting products as such. Furthermore, the text of the Note Ad Article III refers to a measure 'which applies to an imported *product* and the like domestic *product* and is collected or enforced in the case of the imported *product* at the time or point of importation'. This suggests that this Note covers only measures applied to imported products that are of the same nature as those applied to the domestic products, such as a prohibition on importation of a product which enforces at the border an internal sales prohibition applied to both imported and like domestic products.

"A previous panel had found that Article III:2, first sentence, 'obliges contracting parties to establish certain competitive conditions for imported *products* in relation to domestic *products*'.[9] Another panel had found that the words 'treatment no less favourable' in Article III:4 call for effective equality of opportunities for imported *products* in respect of the application of laws, regulations or requirements affecting the sale, offering for sale, purchase, transportation, distribution or use of *products*, and that this standard has to be understood as applicable to each individual case of imported *products*.[10] It was apparent to the Panel that the comparison implied was necessarily one between the measures applied to imported products and the measures applied to like domestic products".[11]

The 1992 Panel Report on "United States - Measures Affecting Alcoholic and Malt Beverages" noted with respect to the application of the Article III rules which compare the tax treatment accorded to "like products":

"The basic purpose of Article III is to ensure, as emphasized in Article III:1,

'that internal taxes and other internal charges, and laws, regulations and requirements affecting the internal sale, purchase, transportation, distribution or use of products ... should not be applied to imported or domestic products so as to afford protection to domestic production'.

"The purpose of Article III is thus not to prevent contracting parties from using their fiscal and regulatory powers for purposes other than to afford protection to domestic production. Specifically, the purpose of Article III is not to prevent contracting parties from differentiating between different product categories for policy purposes unrelated to the protection of domestic production. The Panel considered that the limited purpose of Article III has to be taken into account in interpreting the term 'like products' in this Article. Consequently, in determining whether two products subject to different treatment are like products, it is necessary to consider whether such product differentiation is being made 'so as to afford protection to domestic production'. While the analysis of 'like products' in terms of Article III:2 must take into consideration this objective of Article III, the Panel wished to emphasize that such an analysis would be without prejudice to the 'like product' concepts in other provisions of the General Agreement, which might have different objectives and which might therefore also require different interpretations".[12]

In the same Report, referring to regulatory treatment of "like products",

"... The Panel recalled ... its earlier statement on like product determinations and considered that, in the context of Article III, it is essential that such determinations be made not only in the light of such criteria as the products' physical characteristics, but also in the light of the purpose of Article III, which is to ensure that internal taxes and regulations 'not be applied to imported or domestic products so as to afford protection to domestic production'. The purpose of Article III is not to harmonize the internal taxes and regulations of contracting parties, which differ from country to country. In light of these

---

[9] A footnote to this paragraph refers to the Panel Report on "United States - Taxes on Petroleum and Certain Imported Substances", adopted 17 June 1987, BISD 34S/136, 158, para. 5.1.9.

[10] A footnote to this paragraph refers to the Panel Report on "United States - Section 337 of the Tariff Act of 1930," adopted 7 November 1989, BISD 36S/345, 386-7, paras. 5.11, 5.14.

[11] DS21/R, 3 September 1991, 39S/155, 193-194, paras. 5.9, 5.11-5.12.

[12] DS23/R, adopted 19 June 1992, 39S/206, 276, para. 5.25.

considerations, the Panel was of the view that the particular level at which the distinction between high alcohol and low alcohol beer is made in the various states does not affect its reasonings and findings.

"The Panel recognized that the treatment of imported and domestic products as like products under Article III may have significant implications for the scope of obligations under the General Agreement and for the regulatory autonomy of contracting parties with respect to their internal tax laws and regulations: once products are designated as like products, a regulatory product differentiation, e.g. for standardization or environmental purposes, becomes inconsistent with Article III even if the regulation is not 'applied ... so as afford protection to domestic production'. In the view of the Panel, therefore, it is imperative that the like product determination in the context of Article III be made in such a way that it not unnecessarily infringe upon the regulatory authority and domestic policy options of contracting parties".[13]

(3) Relevance of tariff concessions

The first Report of the Working Party on "Brazilian Internal Taxes" notes that "The working party agreed that a contracting party was bound by the provisions of Article III whether or not the contracting party in question had undertaken tariff commitments in respect of the goods concerned".[14]

In the 1990 Panel Report on "EEC - Regulation on Imports of Parts and Components," in connection with the Panel's examination of whether anti-circumvention duties levied by the EEC were import duties under Article II or internal taxes under Article III:

"... The Panel recalled that the distinction between import duties and internal charges is of fundamental importance because the General Agreement regulates ordinary customs duties, other import charges and internal taxes differently: the imposition of 'ordinary customs duties' for the purpose of protection is allowed unless they exceed tariff bindings; all other duties or charges of any kind imposed on or in connection with importation are in principle prohibited in respect of bound items (Article II:1(b)). By contrast, internal taxes that discriminate against imported products are prohibited, whether or not the items concerned are bound (Article III:2)".[15]

(4) Relevance of policy purpose of internal measures

The 1952 Panel Report on "Special Import Taxes Instituted by Greece" states: "It appeared to the Panel that the principal question arising for determination was whether or not the Greek tax was an internal tax or charge on imported products within the meaning of paragraph 2 of Article III. If the finding on this point were affirmative, the Panel considered that it would be subject to the provisions of Article III whatever might have been the underlying intent of the Greek Government in imposing the tax".[16]

See also the discussion of eligibility for border tax adjustment in the 1987 Panel Report on "United States - Taxes on Petroleum and Certain Imported Substances".[17] See also the material above from the 1992 Panel Report on "United States - Measures Affecting Alcoholic and Malt Beverages"[18], and the unadopted Panel Report of 1994 on "United States - Taxes on Automobiles."[19]

---

[13]*Ibid.*, 39S/293-294, paras. 5.71-5.72.
[14]GATT/CP.3/42, adopted 30 June 1949, II/181, 182, para. 4.
[15]L/6657, adopted on 16 May 1990, 37S/132, 191-192, para. 5.4.
[16]G/25, adopted 3 November 1952, 1S/48, 49, para. 5.
[17]L/6175, adopted 17 June 1987, 34S/136, para. 5.2.3ff; see below at page 147.
[18]DS23/R, adopted 19 June 1992, 39S/206, 276, 293-294, paras. 5.25, 5.71-5.72.
[19]DS31/R, dated 11 October 1994, paras. 5.5-5.16, 5.23-5.36.

(5) Relevance of trade effects

The 1949 Working Party Report on "Brazilian Internal Taxes" notes that

"... the delegate of Brazil submitted the argument that if an internal tax, even though discriminatory, does not operate in a protective manner the provisions of Article III would not be applicable. He drew attention to the first paragraph of Article III, which prescribes that such taxes should not be applied 'so as to afford protection to domestic production'.... The delegate of Brazil .... suggested that where there were no imports of a given commodity or where imports were small in volume, the provisions of Article III did not apply. [The majority of the working party] argued that the absence of imports from contracting parties during any period of time that might be selected for examination would not necessarily be an indication that they had no interest in exports of the product affected by the tax, since their potentialities as exporters, given national treatment, should be taken into account. These members of the working party therefore took the view that the provisions of the first sentence of Article III, paragraph 2, were equally applicable whether imports from other contracting parties were substantial, small or non-existent".[20]

The 1987 Panel Report on "United States - Taxes on Petroleum and Certain Imported Substances" found, *inter alia*, that an excise tax on petroleum was imposed at a higher rate on imported products than on the like domestic product, and therefore was inconsistent with Article III:2, first sentence (see page 150 below); the Panel examined the argument of the United States that the tax differential of 3.5 US cents per barrel was so small that it did not nullify or impair benefits accruing to Canada, the EEC and Mexico under the General Agreement. The Panel noted with respect to Article III:2:

"An acceptance of the argument that measures which have only an insignificant effect on the volume of exports do not nullify or impair benefits accruing under Article III:2, first sentence, implies that the basic rationale of this provision - the benefit it generates for the contracting parties - is to protect expectations on export volumes. That, however, is not the case. Article III:2, first sentence, obliges contracting parties to establish certain competitive conditions for imported products in relation to domestic products. Unlike some other provisions in the General Agreement, it does not refer to trade effects. The majority of the members of the Working Party on the 'Brazilian Internal Taxes' therefore correctly concluded that the provisions of Article III:2, first sentence, 'were equally applicable, whether imports from other contracting parties were substantial, small or non-existent' (BISD Vol. II/185). The Working Party also concluded that 'a contracting party was bound by the provisions of Article III whether or not the contracting party in question had undertaken tariff commitments in respect of the goods concerned' (BISD Vol. II/182), in other words, the benefits under Article III accrue independent of whether there is a negotiated expectation of market access or not. Moreover, it is conceivable that a tax consistent with the national treatment principle (for instance, a high but non-discriminatory excise tax) has a more severe impact on the exports of other contracting parties than a tax that violates that principle (for instance a very low but discriminatory tax). The case before the Panel illustrates this point: the United States could bring the tax on petroleum in conformity with Article III:2, first sentence, by raising the tax on domestic products, by lowering the tax on imported products or by fixing a new common tax rate for both imported and domestic products. Each of these solutions would have different trade results, and it is therefore logically not possible to determine the difference in trade impact between the present tax and one consistent with Article III:2, first sentence, and hence to determine the trade impact resulting from the non-observance of that provision. For these reasons, Article III:2, first sentence, cannot be interpreted to protect expectations on export volumes; it protects expectations on the competitive relationship between imported and domestic products. A change in the competitive relationship contrary to that provision must consequently be regarded ipso facto as a nullification or impairment of benefits accruing under the General Agreement. A demonstration that a measure inconsistent with Article III:2, first sentence, has no or insignificant effects would therefore in the view of the Panel not be a sufficient demonstration that the benefits accruing under that provision had not been nullified or impaired even if such a rebuttal were in principle permitted".[21]

---

[20]GATT/CP.3/42, adopted 30 June 1949, II/181, 185, para. 16.
[21]L/6175, adopted 17 June 1987, 34S/136, 158, para. 5.1.9.

The 1992 Panel Report on "United States - Measures Affecting Alcoholic and Malt Beverages" examined an argument that since only 1.5 percent of domestic beer in the United States was eligible for a reduction in the excise tax on beer and less than one percent of domestic beer benefited from the tax reduction, "the federal excise tax neither discriminated against imported beer nor provided protection to domestic production".

> "The Panel noted the United States argument that the total number of barrels currently subject to the lower federal excise tax rate represented less than one per cent of total domestic beer production, that over 99 per cent of United States beer was subject to the same federal excise tax as that imposed on imported beer, and that therefore the federal excise tax neither discriminated against imported beer nor provided protection to domestic production. The Panel further noted that although Canada did not accept the United States estimate that the tax exemption applied to only one per cent of United States production, it pointed out that this figure nonetheless equalled total Canadian exports of beer to the United States. In accordance with previous panel reports adopted by the CONTRACTING PARTIES, the Panel considered that Article III:2 protects competitive conditions between imported and domestic products but does not protect expectations on export volume. In the view of the Panel, the fact that only approximately 1.5 per cent of domestic beer in the United States is eligible for the lower tax rate cannot justify the imposition of higher internal taxes on imported Canadian beer than on competing domestic beer. The prohibition of discriminatory taxes in Article III:2, first sentence, is not conditional on a 'trade effects test' nor is it qualified by a *de minimis* standard. ... Thus, in the view of the Panel, the fact that only approximately 1.5 per cent of domestic beer in the United States is eligible for the lower tax rate does not immunize this United States measure from the national treatment obligation of Article III."[22]

The same Panel examined a similar argument with respect to paragraph 4 of Article III.

> "With respect to Vermont and Virginia, the Panel noted that certain imported wines cannot be sold in state-operated liquor stores whereas the like domestic wine can. The Panel recalled the United States argument that the number of state-operated sales outlets was relatively small compared to the number of private outlets. The Panel considered that although Canadian wine has access to most of the available sales outlets in these states, it is still denied competitive opportunities accorded to domestic like products with respect to sales in state-operated outlets. Therefore, the Panel considered that the Vermont and Virginia measures are inconsistent with Article III:4."[23]

In 1994, the Panel on "United States - Measures Affecting the Importation, Internal Sale and Use of Tobacco" noted, in relation to an argument regarding a difference in the amount of nonrefundable marketing assessment, termed "budget deficit assessment" ("BDA") charged on imported tobacco and on domestically produced tobacco:

> "The Panel ... recalled the U.S. argument that the discriminatory impact of the BDA differential was so small as to be of no commercial consequence. Here, the Panel noted that previous panels had rejected arguments of de minimis trade consequences and had found that the size of the trade impact of a measure was not relevant to its consistency with Article III.[24] The CONTRACTING PARTIES had recognized that Article III protected expectations on the competitive relationship between imported and domestic products, not export volumes.[25] In accordance with these past panel rulings, the Panel considered that it was not permissible to impose higher internal taxes on imported products than on like

---

[22] DS23/R, adopted 19 June 1992, 39S/206, 270-271, para. 5.6.
[23] *Ibid.*, 39S/292, para. 5.65.
[24] The footnote to this sentence in the panel report provides: "See, *e.g.*, report of the panel on United States - Taxes on Petroleum and Certain Imported Substances, adopted on 17 June 1987, BISD 34S/136, 155-159; report of the panel on United States - Section 337 of the Tariff Act of 1930, adopted on 7 November 1989, BISD 36S/345, 386-387".
[25] The footnote to this sentence in the panel report refers to the panel report on "United States - Taxes on Petroleum and Certain Imported Substances", adopted on 17 June 1987, BISD 34S/136, 158 ("Article III:2, first sentence, obliges contracting parties to establish certain competitive conditions for imported products in relation to domestic products. Unlike some other provisions of the General Agreement, it does not refer to trade effects") and also to the panel report on "United States - Measures Affecting Alcoholic and Malt Beverages", adopted on 19 June 1992, BISD 39S/206, 271.

domestic products, even where the difference was minimal or of no commercial consequence.[26] The Panel thus rejected this particular U.S. defense of the BDA.

"... the Panel concluded that the BDA subjected imported tobacco to an internal tax or charge in excess of that applied to like domestic tobacco."[27]

(6) Application of Article III to regional and local governments and authorities within the territory of a contracting party

See the Note *ad* Article III:1, which provides that the application of paragraph 1 to internal taxes imposed by local governments and authorities within the territory of a contracting party is subject to the provisions of the final paragraph of Article XXIV, and adds certain qualifying conditions. This Note was added at the Havana Conference. In response to a request for an explanation of which internal taxes might be considered "technically inconsistent with the letter but not inconsistent with the spirit of Article III" in terms of the Note, the representative of Colombia replied that "the first part of the interpretative note had been drafted to cover certain problems of Colombia connected with domestic products, subject to prices fixed by local public monopolies, which could not be taxed in the same manner as the like imported products, which were subject to a consumption tax, without grave political and administrative consequences".[28]

The 1992 Panel Report on "Canada - Import, Distribution and Sale of Certain Alcoholic Drinks by Provincial Marketing Agencies" considered measures of provincial liquor boards which applied both to beer originating outside Canada and beer from other provinces of Canada. A note to the Panel findings provides that "Throughout these findings the reference to domestic beer is a reference to the domestic beer which receives the most favourable treatment by Canada in the province in question, that is in most instances the beer brewed in that province".[29]

The 1992 Panel Report on "United States - Measures Affecting Alcoholic and Malt Beverages" observed with respect to differential excise taxes levied by US states:

"The Panel did not consider relevant the fact that many of the state provisions at issue in this dispute provide the same treatment to products of other states of the United States as that provided to foreign products. The national treatment provisions require contracting parties to accord to imported products treatment no less favourable than that accorded to any like domestic product, whatever the domestic origin. Article III consequently requires treatment of imported products no less favourable than that accorded to the most-favoured domestic products".[30]

The same Panel also examined the listing requirements of state-operated liquor stores in certain states.

"Having regard to the past panel decisions and the record in the instant case, the present Panel was of the view that the listing and delisting practices here at issue do not affect importation as such into the United States and should be examined under Article III:4. The Panel further noted that the issue is not whether the practices in the various states affect the right of importation as such, in that they clearly apply to both domestic (out-of-state) and imported wines; rather, the issue is whether the listing and delisting practices accord less favourable treatment -- in terms of competitive opportunities -- to imported wine than that accorded to the like domestic product. Consequently, the Panel decided to analyze the state listing and delisting practices as internal measures under Article III:4."[31]

See also generally Article XXIV:12.

---

[26]The footnote to this sentence in the panel report refers to the panel report on "United States - Taxes on Petroleum and Certain Imported Substances", adopted on 17 June 1987, BISD 34S/136, 158-159.
[27]DS44/R, adopted on 4 October 1994, paras. 99-100.
[28]E/CONF.2/C.3/SR.40, p. 2; see also E/CONF.2/C.3/A/W.30, p. 1.
[29]DS17/R, adopted 18 February 1992, 39S/27, 75, note to finding in para. 5.4 applying Article III:4.
[30]DS23/R, adopted 19 June 1992, 39S/206, 274, para. 5.17.
[31]*Ibid.*, 39S/292, para. 5.63.

ARTICLE III - NATIONAL TREATMENT ON INTERNAL TAXATION AND REGULATION

(7) Application of Article III with regard to State trading monopolies

During discussions in Sub-Committee A of the Third Committee at the Havana Conference, it was agreed that "state monopolies importing products for commercial resale were not excepted from the provisions of Article 18".[32] Also during the Havana Conference, in order to make it clear that an internal tax levied by a State monopoly, if treated as a negotiable monopoly margin, would not fall within the scope of Article 18 [III], the following Interpretative Note was added to Article 31 of the Charter:[33]

> "The maximum import duty referred to in paragraph 2 and 4 [of Article 31] would cover the margin which has been negotiated or which has been published or notified to the Organization, whether or not collected, wholly or in part, at the custom house as an ordinary customs duty".[34]

The 1988 Panel Report on "Canada - Import, Distribution and Sale of Alcoholic Drinks by Canadian Provincial Marketing Agencies" examined, *inter alia*, mark-up practices of provincial marketing agencies, or "liquor boards" which have a monopoly of the supply and distribution of alcoholic beverages in Canada.

> "The Panel ... noted that the retail prices charged by the provincial liquor boards for imported alcoholic beverages were composed of the invoice price; *plus* federal customs duties collected at the bound rates; *plus* standard freight to a set destination; *plus* additional price increases ('mark-ups') which were sometimes higher on imported than on like domestic alcoholic beverages ('differential mark-ups'); *plus* federal and provincial sales taxes. ...

> "... It noted that federal and provincial sales taxes were levied on alcoholic beverages and asked itself whether the fiscal elements of mark-ups, which produced revenue for the provinces, could also be justified as 'internal taxes conforming to the provisions of Article III', noting that Article III:2 itself referred, not only to internal taxes, but also to 'other internal charges'. The Panel was of the view that to be so considered, the fiscal element of mark-ups must of course meet the requirements of Article III, e.g. they must not be applied to imported or domestic products so as to afford protection to domestic production. The Panel also considered it important that, if fiscal elements were to be considered as internal taxes, mark-ups would also have to be administered in conformity with other provisions of the General Agreement, in particular Article X dealing with the Publication and Administration of Trade Regulations."[35]

In regard to its examination of the listing practices of provincial liquor boards:

> "... the Panel saw great force in the argument that Article III:4 was also applicable to state-trading enterprises at least when the monopoly of the importation and monopoly of the distribution in the domestic markets were combined, as was the case of the provincial liquor boards in Canada. This interpretation was confirmed *e contrario* by the wording of Article III:8(a)".[36]

The 1989 Panel Report on "Thailand - Restrictions on Importation of and Internal Taxes on Cigarettes" notes as follows:

> "The Panel ... examined how Thailand might restrict the *supply* of cigarettes in a manner consistent with the General Agreement. The Panel noted that contracting parties may maintain governmental monopolies, such as the Thai Tobacco Monopoly, on the importation and domestic sale of products.[37] The Thai Government may use this monopoly to regulate the overall supply of cigarettes, their prices and their retail availability provided it thereby does not accord imported cigarettes less

---

[32] E/CONF.2/C.3/A/W.50, p. 1.
[33] Havana Reports, p. 67, para. 74.
[34] Havana Charter, Interpretative Note to Article 31. The General Agreement contains no corresponding interpretative note.
[35] L/6304, adopted 22 March 1988, 35S/37, 87, para. 4.11 and 88-89, para. 4.20.
[36] L/6304, adopted on 22 March 1988, 35S/37, 90, para. 4.26.
[37] Note 1 on page 37S/225 provides: "Cf. Articles III:4, XVII and XX(d)".

favourable treatment than domestic cigarettes or act inconsistently with any commitments assumed under its Schedule of Concessions.[38]

The 1992 Panel Report on "Canada - Import, Distribution and Sale of Certain Alcoholic Drinks by Provincial Marketing Agencies" found as follows concerning Article III.

> "The Panel ... turned to Canada's argument that its right to deliver imported beer to the points of sale was an inherent part of Canada's right to establish an import monopoly in accordance with Article XVII of the General Agreement which was not affected by its obligations under Article III:4. The Panel noted that the issue before it was not whether Canada had the right to create government monopolies for the importation, internal delivery and sale of beer. The Panel fully recognized that there was nothing in the General Agreement which prevented Canada from establishing import and sales monopolies that also had the sole right of internal delivery. The only issue before the Panel was whether Canada, having decided to establish a monopoly for the internal delivery of beer, might exempt domestic beer from that monopoly. The Panel noted that Article III:4 did not differentiate between measures affecting the internal transportation of imported products that were imposed by governmental monopolies and those that were imposed in the form of regulations governing private trade. Moreover, Articles II:4, XVII and the Note Ad Articles XI, XII, XIII, XIV and XVIII clearly indicated the drafters' intention not to allow contracting parties to frustrate the principles of the General Agreement governing measures affecting private trade by regulating trade through monopolies. Canada had the right to take, in respect of the privately delivered beer, the measures necessary to secure compliance with laws consistent with the General Agreement relating to the enforcement of monopolies. This right was specifically provided for in Article XX(d) of the General Agreement. The Panel recognized that a beer import monopoly that also enjoyed a sales monopoly might, in order properly to carry out its functions, also deliver beer but it did not for that purpose have to prohibit unconditionally the private delivery of imported beer while permitting that of domestic beer. For these reasons the Panel *found* that Canada's right under the General Agreement to establish an import and sales monopoly for beer did not entail the right to discriminate against imported beer inconsistently with Article III:4 through regulations affecting its internal transportation."[39]

With respect to the issue of mark-ups:

> "The Panel noted that Canada taxed both imported and domestic beer by assessing mark-ups through the liquor boards and by levying provincial sales taxes and the federal Goods and Services Tax at the retail level. ...
>
> "The Panel noted that, according to Article III:2, first sentence, imported products
>
> > 'shall not be subject, directly or indirectly, to internal taxes or other internal charges of any kind in excess of those applied, directly or indirectly, to like domestic products'.
>
> "The Panel considered that this provision applied not only to the provincial and federal sales taxes but also to the mark-ups levied by the liquor boards because they also constituted internal governmental charges borne by products".[40]

The Panel also found that the following requirements maintained by Canadian provincial liquor boards fell under Article III:4: the practice of the liquor boards of Ontario to limit listing of imported beer to the six-pack size while according listings in different package sizes to domestic beer; restrictions on private delivery of beer, including levies for delivering imported beer; and application of minimum prices to domestic and imported beer.

---

[38]DS10/R, adopted on 7 November 1990, 37S/200, 225, para. 79. Note 2 on page 37S/225, to this sentence, provides: "Cf. Articles III:2 and 4 and II:4".
[39]DS17/R, adopted 18 February 1992, 39S/27, 79-80, para. 5.15.
[40]*Ibid.*, 39S/83, paras. 5.23-5.24.

In the 1992 Panel Report on "United States - Measures Affecting Alcoholic and Malt Beverages" the Panel found that listing and delisting requirements maintained by liquor stores operated by certain US states fell under Article III:4.[41]

See also the Note *Ad* Article XVII:1.

(8) Mandatory versus discretionary legislation; non-enforcement

The 1987 Panel Report on "United States - Taxes on Petroleum and Certain Imported Substances" examined excise taxes on imported petroleum and certain imported chemical substances ("Superfund taxes"), which had been enacted as a revenue source for the US "Superfund" hazardous-waste cleanup program. The tax on certain imported substances, enacted in October 1986, provided that it would not enter into effect until 1 January 1989; regulations implementing it had not been drafted or put into effect.

"The Panel noted that the United States objected to an examination of this tax because it did not go into effect before 1 January 1989, and - having no immediate effect on trade and therefore not causing nullification or impairment - fell outside the framework of Article XXIII. The Panel examined this point and concluded the following.

"... The general prohibition of quantitative restrictions under Article XI ... and the national treatment obligation of Article III ... have essentially the same rationale, namely to protect expectations of the contracting parties as to the competitive relationship between their products and those of the other contracting parties. Both articles are not only to protect current trade but also to create the predictability needed to plan future trade. That objective could not be attained if contracting parties could not challenge existing legislation mandating actions at variance with the General Agreement until the administrative acts implementing it had actually been applied to their trade. Just as the very existence of a regulation providing for a quota, without it restricting particular imports, has been recognized to constitute a violation of Article XI:1, the very existence of mandatory legislation providing for an internal tax, without it being applied to a particular imported product, should be regarded as falling within the scope of Article III:2, first sentence. The Panel noted that the tax on certain imported substances had been enacted, that the legislation was mandatory and that the tax authorities had to apply it after the end of next year and hence within a time frame within which the trade and investment decisions that could be influenced by the tax are taken. The Panel therefore concluded that Canada and the EEC were entitled to an investigation of their claim that this tax did not meet the criteria of Article III:2, first sentence."[42]

The 1987 Panel Report on "United States - Taxes on Petroleum and Certain Imported Substances" also examined, with respect to the tax on certain imported substances, the requirement that importers supply sufficient information regarding the chemical inputs of taxable substances to enable the tax authorities to determine the amount of tax to be imposed; otherwise a penalty tax would be imposed in the amount of five percent ad valorem, or a different rate to be prescribed by the Secretary of the Treasury which would equal the amount that would be imposed if the substance were produced using the predominant method of production. The Panel noted concerning the penalty rate:

"... the Superfund Act permits the Secretary of the Treasury to prescribe by regulation, in lieu of the 5 per cent rate, a rate which would equal the amount that would be imposed if the substance were produced using the predominant method of production.... These regulations have not yet been issued. Thus, whether they will eliminate the need to impose the penalty tax and whether they will establish complete equivalence between domestic and imported products, as required by Article III:2, first sentence, remain open questions. From the perspective of the overall objectives of the General Agreement it is regrettable that the Superfund Act explicitly directs the United States tax authorities to impose a tax inconsistent with the national treatment principle but, since the Superfund Act also gives them the possibility to avoid the need to impose that tax by issuing regulations, the existence of the

---

[41] DS23/R, adopted 19 June 1992, 39S/206, 291-293, paras. 5.62-5.69.
[42] L/6175, adopted 17 June 1987, 34S/136, 160, paras. 5.2.1-5.2.2.

penalty rate provisions as such does not constitute a violation of the United States obligations under the General Agreement. The Panel noted with satisfaction the statement of the United States that, given the tax authorities' regulatory authority under the Act, 'in all probability the 5 per cent penalty rate would never be applied'".[43]

In the 1990 Panel Report on "EEC - Regulation on Imports of Parts and Components" the Panel also examined an argument of Japan concerning the anti-circumvention provision in the EEC anti-dumping legislation:

"Japan considers not only the measures taken under the anticircumvention provision but also the provision itself to be violating the EEC's obligations under the General Agreement. Japan therefore asked the Panel to recommend to the CONTRACTING PARTIES that they request the EEC not only to revoke the measures taken under the provision but also to withdraw the provision itself. The Panel therefore examined whether the mere existence of the anti-circumvention provision is inconsistent with the General Agreement. The Panel noted that the anti-circumvention provision does not mandate the imposition of duties or other measures by the EEC Commission and Council; it merely authorizes the Commission and the Council to take certain actions. Under the provisions of the General Agreement which Japan claims to have been violated by the EEC contracting parties are to avoid certain measures; but these provisions do not establish the obligation to avoid legislation under which the executive authorities may possibly impose such measures. ...

"In the light of the above the Panel found that the mere existence of the anti-circumvention provision in the EEC's anti-dumping Regulation is not inconsistent with the EEC's obligations under the General Agreement. Although it would, from the perspective of the overall objectives of the General Agreement, be desirable if the EEC were to withdraw the anti-circumvention provision, the EEC would meet its obligations under the General Agreement if it were to cease to apply the provision in respect of contracting parties".[44]

The 1990 Panel Report on "Thailand - Restrictions on Importation of and Internal Taxes on Cigarettes" examined, *inter alia*, whether excise taxes which could be levied by Thai authorities on foreign cigarettes, as well as the exemption from Thai business and municipal taxes accorded in respect of cigarettes made from domestic leaf, were consistent with Article III. While the ceiling tax rates permitted under law were higher for imported than for domestic cigarettes, and the tax rate applied until 11 July 1990 varied in proportion to foreign tobacco content, the Thai Ministry of Finance had issued a regulation on 11 July 1990 to provide a uniform excise tax rate for all cigarettes. On 18 August 1990 Thailand modified its regulations to exempt all cigarettes from business and municipal taxes.

"... The United States argued that it was not sufficient under Article III for the rates effectively levied to be the same; the maximum rates that could be levied under the legislation also had to be non-discriminatory. The Panel noted that previous panels had found that legislation mandatorily requiring the executive authority to impose internal taxes discriminating against imported products was inconsistent with Article III:2, whether or not an occasion for its actual application had as yet arisen; legislation merely giving the executive the possibility to act inconsistently with Article III:2 could not, by itself, constitute a violation of that provision.[45] The Panel agreed with the above reasoning and found that the possibility that the Tobacco Act might be applied contrary to Article III:2 was not sufficient to make it inconsistent with the General Agreement.[46]

"... The Panel observed that the new Thai measure, by eliminating business and municipal taxes on cigarettes, removed the internal taxes imposed on imported cigarettes in excess of those applied to

---

[43]*Ibid.*, 34S/163-164, para. 5.2.9.

[44]L/6657, adopted 16 May 1990, 37S/132, 198-199, para. 5.25-5.26.

[45]A footnote to this paragraph refers to Report of the Panel on "EEC - Regulation on Imports of Parts and Components" (L/6657 at paragraph 5.25, adopted on 16 May 1990). Report of the panel on "United States - Taxes on Petroleum and Certain Imported Substances" (BISD 34S/160, 164, adopted on 17 June 1987).

[46]DS10/R, adopted on 7 November 1990, 37S/200, 227, para. 84.

domestic cigarettes. The Panel noted that, as in the case of the excise tax, the Tobacco Act continued to enable the executive authorities to levy the discriminatory taxes. However, the Panel, recalling its findings on the issue of excise taxes, found that the possibility that the Tobacco Act might be applied contrary to Article III:2 was, by itself, not sufficient to make it inconsistent with the General Agreement."[47]

The Panel concluded that "The current regulations relating to the excise, business and municipal taxes on cigarettes are consistent with Thailand's obligations under Article III of the General Agreement".[48]

The 1992 Panel Report on "United States - Measures Affecting Alcoholic and Malt Beverages" examined arguments that certain legislation, while it might be mandatory, was not actually being enforced. With respect to legislation exempting local producers from requirements to distribute through wholesalers, which the Panel ruled was inconsistent with Article III:4 (see page 178):

"The Panel then proceeded to consider the United States argument that the provisions in the state of Illinois permitting manufacturers to sell directly to retailers were not given effect. In this regard, the Panel recalled the decisions of the CONTRACTING PARTIES on the relevance of the non-application of laws in dispute. Recent panels addressing the issue of mandatory versus discretionary legislation in the context of both Articles III:2 and III:4[49] concluded that legislation mandatorily requiring the executive authority to take action inconsistent with the General Agreement would be inconsistent with Article III, whether or not the legislation were being applied, whereas legislation merely giving the executive authority the possibility to act inconsistently with Article III would not, by itself, constitute a violation of that Article. The Panel agreed with the above reasoning and concluded that because the Illinois legislation in issue allows a holder of a manufacturer's license to sell beer to retailers, without allowing imported beer to be sold directly to retailers, the legislation mandates governmental action inconsistent with Article III:4".[50]

With respect to the local option law in the state of Mississippi, which the Panel found to be inconsistent with Article III:4 (see page 178):

"The Panel then proceeded to consider the United States argument that the Mississippi law was not being applied. In this regard, the Panel recalled its previous discussion of this issue. ... The Panel noted that the option law in Mississippi provides discretion only for the reinstatement of prohibition, but not for the discriminatory treatment of imported wines. The Panel concluded, therefore, that because the Mississippi legislation in issue, which permits native wines to be sold in areas of the state which otherwise prohibit the sale of alcoholic beverages, including imported wine, mandates governmental action inconsistent with Article III:4, it is inconsistent with that provision whether or not the political subdivisions are currently making use of their power to reinstate prohibition".[51]

With respect to the Massachusetts and Rhode Island "price affirmation" (maximum price) laws:

"In respect of the United States contention that the Massachusetts measure was not being enforced and that the Rhode Island measure was only nominally enforced, the Panel recalled its discussion of mandatory versus discretionary laws in the previous section. The Panel noted that the price affirmation measures in both Massachusetts and Rhode Island are mandatory legislation. Even if Massachusetts may not currently be using its police powers to enforce this mandatory legislation, the measure continues to be mandatory legislation which may influence the decisions of economic operators. Hence, a non-enforcement of a mandatory law in respect of imported products does not ensure that imported beer

---

[47]*Ibid.*, 37S/227 para. 86.

[48]*Ibid.*, 37S/228 para. 88.

[49]Note 11 to this paragraph refers to the Report of the Panel on "Thailand - Restrictions on Importation of and Internal Taxes on Cigarettes", adopted on 7 November 1990, BISD 37S/200, 227; Report of the Panel on "EEC - Regulation on Imports of Parts and Components", adopted on 16 May 1990, BISD 37S/132, 198; and Report of the Panel on "United States - Taxes on Petroleum and Certain Imported Substances", adopted on 17 June 1987, BISD 34S/136, 160.

[50]DS23/R, adopted 19 June 1992, 39S/206, 281-282, para. 5.39.

[51]*Ibid.*, 39S/289, para. 5.57.

and wine are not treated less favourably than like domestic products to which the law does not apply. Similarly, the contention that Rhode Island only 'nominally' enforces its mandatory legislation a fortiori does not immunize this measure from Article III:4. The mandatory laws in these two states by their terms treat imported beer and wine less favourably than the like domestic products. Accordingly, the Panel found that the mandatory price affirmation laws in Massachusetts and Rhode Island are inconsistent with Article III:4, irrespective of the extent to which they are being enforced".[52]

See also the material on discretionary legislation, measures not yet in effect, and measures no longer in effect, under Article XXIII.

2. Interpretative Note Ad Article III: measures imposed at the time or point of importation

(1) "collected or enforced ... at the time or point of importation"

The Interpretative Note *ad* Article III was added at Havana. It makes clear that the mere fact that an internal charge or regulation is collected or enforced in the case of the imported product at the time or point of importation does not prevent it from being an "internal tax or other internal charge" and from being subject to the provisions of Article III. During discussions at Havana on the proposal to add the Note, it was stated that "the proposed additional paragraph was intended to cover cases where internal excise taxes were, for administrative reasons, collected at the time of importation, as well as 'mixing' regulations also enforced at that stage".[53] The Report of Sub-Committee A of the Third Committee at the Havana Conference, which considered Article 18 of the Charter (on national treatment), states as follows:

> "The delegations of Chile, Lebanon, and Syria inquired whether certain charges imposed by their countries on imported products would be considered as internal taxes under Article 18. The Sub-Committee, while not attempting to give a general definition of internal taxes, considered that the particular charges referred to are import duties and not internal taxes because according to the information supplied by the countries concerned (a) they are collected at the time of, and as a condition to, the entry of the goods into the importing country, and (b) they apply exclusively to imported products without being related in any way to similar charges collected internally on like domestic products. The fact that these charges are described as internal taxes in the laws of the importing country would not in itself have the effect of giving them the status of internal taxes under the Charter".[54]

See also the discussion of border tax adjustments below at page 144.

The 1978 Panel Report on "EEC - Measures on Animal Feed Proteins" examined an EEC scheme requiring importers and producers of vegetable proteins to purchase and denature surplus skimmed milk powder from EEC intervention stocks. The scheme allowed persons subject to this requirement to provide a security deposit or a bank guarantee instead of documents providing proof of the purchase and the denaturing of the skimmed milk powder; the deposit or guarantee was refunded interest-free upon presentation of the required documents but forfeited otherwise. The Panel examined the argument that this security deposit scheme was a charge enforced at the border under Article II:2(a) and the Note *ad* Article III.

> "The Panel was of the opinion that the security deposit was not of a fiscal nature because, if it had been, it would have defeated the stated purpose of the EEC Regulation which was to increase utilization of denatured skimmed milk powder. In addition the revenue from the security deposit accrued to EEC budgetary authorities only when the buyer of vegetable proteins had not fulfilled the purchase obligations. The Panel further noted that less than 1 per cent of the security deposits paid, were not released, indicating compliance with the purchase obligation. The Panel therefore considered that the

---

[52]*Ibid.*, 39S/290, para. 5.60; see also similar finding with respect to non-enforcement of New Hampshire statute requiring preferential treatment for listing of wine manufactured or bottled in New Hampshire, *ibid.*, 39S/292, para. 5.66.
[53]E/CONF.2/C.3/SR.11 p. 1; proposal at E/CONF.2/C.3/1/Add.21. See also E/CONF.2/C.3/A/W.33, p. 1.
[54]Havana Reports, p. 62, para. 42; E/CONF.2/C.3/A/W.30, p. 2. The text of Article 18 as amended at Havana was taken into the General Agreement; see the discussion of negotiating history in section III below.

security deposit, including any associated cost, was only an enforcement mechanism for the purchase requirement and, as such, should be examined with the purchase obligation."[55]

The 1983 Panel Report on "United States - Imports of Certain Automotive Spring Assemblies" notes the view of Canada that "The institution of a bonding requirement, pursuant to Section 337 [of the Tariff Act of 1930] was applied to imports but did not apply to like domestic products and was thus inconsistent with the requirements of Article III:1 and 2. Even if the bonding requirement did not contravene Article III because it was a border measure as contended by the United States delegation, it would still contravene Article II:1(b), the last sentence of which had to be read in conjunction with paragraph 2 of the same Article"[56] and the view of the United States that "as a matter of GATT interpretation ... Article III:2 would not apply to temporary bonding requirements imposed as a condition of importation".[57] The Panel found Article XX(d) to apply and "considered that an examination of the United States action in the light of the other GATT provisions referred to ... above was not required".[58] The same statute was again examined in the 1989 panel decision on "United States - Section 337 of the Tariff Act of 1930".[59]

In the 1990 Panel Report on "EEC - Regulation on Imports of Parts and Components," the Panel examined the argument of the EEC that the anti-circumvention duties at issue were customs or other duties imposed "on or in connection with importation" under Article II:1(b), or internal taxes or charges falling under Article III:2. See the excerpts from this report below at page 200.[60]

(2)   "which applies to an imported product and to the like domestic product"

The 1991 Panel Report on "United States - Restrictions on Imports of Tuna," which has not been adopted, examined the United States prohibition of imports of tuna and tuna products from Mexico under the provisions of the US Marine Mammal Protection Act (MMPA) relating to fishing of yellowfin tuna in the Eastern Tropical Pacific Ocean (ETP).

"The Panel noted that Mexico had argued that the measures prohibiting imports of certain yellowfin tuna and yellowfin tuna products from Mexico imposed by the United States were quantitative restrictions on importation under Article XI, while the United States had argued that these measures were internal regulations enforced at the time or point of importation under Article III:4 and the Note Ad Article III, namely that the prohibition of imports of tuna and tuna products from Mexico constituted an enforcement of the regulations of the MMPA relating to the harvesting of domestic tuna.

"The Panel examined the distinction between quantitative restrictions on importation and internal measures applied at the time or point of importation, and noted the following. While restrictions on importation are prohibited by Article XI:1, contracting parties are permitted by Article III:4 and the Note Ad Article III to impose an internal regulation on products imported from other contracting parties provided that it: does not discriminate between products of other countries in violation of the most-favoured-nation principle of Article I:1; is not applied so as to afford protection to domestic production, in violation of the national treatment principle of Article III:1; and accords to imported products treatment no less favourable than that accorded to like products of national origin, consistent with Article III:4. ...

"The Panel noted that the United States had claimed that the direct import embargo on certain yellowfin tuna and certain yellowfin tuna products of Mexico constituted an enforcement at the time or point of importation of the requirements of the MMPA that yellowfin tuna in the ETP be harvested with fishing techniques designed to reduce the incidental taking of dolphins. The MMPA did not regulate tuna products as such, and in particular did not regulate the sale of tuna or tuna products. Nor did it

---

[55]L/4599, adopted on 14 March 1978, 25S/49, 64, para. 4.4.
[56]L/5333, adopted on 26 May 1983 subject to an understanding (C/M/168), 30S/107, 119, para. 35.
[57]*Ibid.*, 30S/123, para. 46.
[58]*Ibid.*, 30S/126, para. 61.
[59]L/6439, adopted on 7 November 1989, 36S/345.
[60]L/6657, adopted on 16 May 1990, 37S/132, 192-93, paras. 5.5-5.8.

prescribe fishing techniques that could have an effect on tuna as a product. This raised in the Panel's view the question of whether the tuna harvesting regulations could be regarded as a measure that 'applies to' imported and domestic tuna within the meaning of the Note Ad Article III and consequently as a measure which the United States could enforce consistently with that Note in the case of imported tuna at the time or point of importation. The Panel examined this question in detail and found the following.

"The text of Article III:1 refers to the application to imported or domestic products of laws, regulations and requirements affecting the internal sale ... of products and internal quantitative regulations requiring the mixture, processing or use of products; it sets forth the principle that such regulations on products not be applied so as to afford protection to domestic production. Article III:4 refers solely to laws, regulations and requirements affecting the internal sale, etc. of products. This suggests that Article III covers only measures affecting products as such. ...

"A previous panel had found that Article III:2, first sentence, 'obliges contracting parties to establish certain competitive conditions for imported *products* in relation to domestic *products*'.[61] Another panel had found that the words 'treatment no less favourable' in Article III:4 call for effective equality of opportunities for imported *products* in respect of the application of laws, regulations or requirements affecting the sale, offering for sale, purchase, transportation, distribution or use of *products*, and that this standard has to be understood as applicable to each individual case of imported *products*.[62] It was apparent to the Panel that the comparison implied was necessarily one between the measures applied to imported products and the measures applied to like domestic products. ...

"The Panel considered that, as Article III applied the national treatment principle to both regulations and internal taxes, the provisions of Article III:4 applicable to regulations should be interpreted taking into account interpretations by the CONTRACTING PARTIES of the provisions of Article III:2 applicable to taxes. The Panel noted in this context that the Working Party Report on Border Tax Adjustments, adopted by the CONTRACTING PARTIES in 1970, had concluded that

'... there was convergence of views to the effect that taxes directly levied on products were eligible for tax adjustment ... Furthermore, the Working Party concluded that there was convergence of views to the effect that certain taxes that were not directly levied on products were not eligible for adjustment, [such as] social security charges whether on employers or employees and payroll taxes'.

Thus, under the national treatment principle of Article III, contracting parties may apply border tax adjustments with regard to those taxes that are borne by products, but not for domestic taxes not directly levied on products (such as corporate income taxes). Consequently, the Note Ad Article III covers only internal taxes that are borne by products. The Panel considered that it would be inconsistent to limit the application of this Note to taxes that are borne by products while permitting its application to regulations not applied to the product as such.

"The Panel concluded from the above considerations that the Note Ad Article III covers only those measures that are applied to the product as such. The Panel noted that the MMPA regulates the domestic harvesting of yellowfin tuna to reduce the incidental taking of dolphin, but that these regulations could not be regarded as being applied to tuna products as such because they would not directly regulate the sale of tuna and could not possibly affect tuna as a product. Therefore, the Panel found that the import prohibition on certain yellowfin tuna and certain yellowfin tuna products of Mexico and the provisions of the MMPA under which it is imposed did not constitute internal regulations covered by the Note Ad Article III."[63]

---

[61] The footnote to this sentence refers to the Panel Report on "United States - Taxes on Petroleum and Certain Imported Substances", adopted on 17 June 1987, 34S/136, 158, para. 5.1.9.
[62] The footnote to this sentence refers to the Panel Report on "United States - Section 337 of the Tariff Act of 1930", adopted on 7 November 1989, 36S/345, 386-7, paras. 5.11, 5.14.
[63] DS21/R (unadopted) dated 3 September 1991, 39S/155, 193-195, paras. 5.8-5.14.

See also the references to this report at pages 164 and 175; in this connection see also the unadopted Panel Report of 1994 on "United States - Restrictions on Imports of Tuna"[64] and the related findings in the unadopted Panel Report of 1994 on "United States - Taxation of Automobiles".[65]

3. Paragraph 1

(1) *"should not be applied to imported or domestic products so as to afford protection to domestic production"*

The 1978 Panel Report on "EEC - Measures on Animal Feed Proteins" examined an EEC scheme requiring domestic producers or importers of oilseeds, cakes and meals, dehydrated fodder and compound feeds and importers of corn gluten feed to purchase a certain quantity of surplus skimmed milk powder held by intervention agencies and to have it denatured for use as feed for animals other than calves. The Panel, having concluded that these vegetable proteins and skimmed milk powder were substitutable in terms of their final use (see page 160), noted as follows.

> "... The Panel ... considered that the EEC Regulation was an 'internal quantitative regulation' in the sense of Article III:5. However, the Panel found that this 'internal quantitative regulation' as such was not related to "the mixture, processing or use ... in specified amounts or proportions" within the meaning of Article III:5 because, at the level of its application, the EEC Regulation introduced basically an obligation to purchase a certain quantity of skimmed milk powder and the purchase obligation falls under Article III:1.

> "Given the reference in Article III:5, second sentence, to Article III:1, the Panel then examined the consistency of the EEC Regulation as an internal quantitative regulation with provisions of Article III:1, particularly as to whether the Regulation afforded protection to domestic production. The Panel noted that the EEC Regulation considered, in its own terms, that denatured skimmed milk powder was an important source of protein which could be used in feedingstuffs. The Panel also noted that surplus stocks could originate either from domestic production or imports, but that the intervention agencies from which the buyers of vegetable proteins had to purchase a certain quantity of denatured skimmed milk powder only held domestically produced products. The Panel further noted that, although globally about 15 percent of the EEC apparent consumption of vegetable protein was supplied from domestic sources, not all the individual products subject to the EEC measures were produced domestically in substantial quantities.

> "The Panel concluded that the measures provided for by the Regulation with a view to ensuring the sale of a given quantity of skimmed milk powder protected this product in a manner contrary to the principles of Article III:1 and to the provisions of Article III:5, second sentence."[66]

During the discussion in the Council of the 1981 Panel Report on "Spain - Measures concerning Domestic Sale of Soyabean Oil"[67] many contracting parties stated that neither the language of Article III nor past interpretations of that provision supported an interpretation that internal regulations which protect domestic production must have restrictive effects on directly competitive or substitutable products in order to be found contrary to Article III:1. Some representatives also noted that adverse effects could not only be measured by direct effects on import volume in the country maintaining the measure but could manifest themselves as well by other trade distorting consequences, including possible suppression of growth of trade. The Council took note of this panel report and of the statements made concerning it, and did not adopt the report.[68]

---

[64] DS29/R, dated 16 June 1994, paras.5.8-5.10.
[65] DS31/R, dated 11 October 1994, paras. 5.51-5.55.
[66] L/4599, adopted 14 March 1978, 25S/49, 64-65, paras. 4.6-4.8.
[67] L/5142 and Corr.1, dated 17 June 1981, unadopted.
[68] C/M/152 p. 7-19; L/5161, L/5188.

The 1987 Panel Report on "Japan - Customs Duties, Taxes and Labelling Practices on Imported Wines and Alcoholic Beverages" examined, *inter alia*, the application of Article III:1.

"... The Panel noted that, whereas under the first sentence of Article III:2 the tax on the imported product and the tax on the like domestic product had to be equal in effect, Article III:1 and 2, second sentence, prohibited only the application of internal taxes to imported or domestic products in a manner 'so as to afford protection to domestic production'. The Panel was of the view that also small tax differences could influence the competitive relationship between directly competing distilled liquors, but the existence of protective taxation could be established only in the light of the particular circumstances of each case and there could be a *de minimis* level below which a tax difference ceased to have the protective effect prohibited by Article III:2, second sentence. ... Since it has been recognized in GATT practice that Article III:2 protects expectations on the competitive relationship between imported and domestic products rather than expectations on trade volumes (see L/6175, paragraph 5.1.9), the Panel did not consider it necessary to examine the quantitative trade effects of this considerably different taxation for its conclusion that the application of considerably lower internal taxes by Japan on shochu than on other directly competitive or substitutable distilled liquors had trade-distorting effects affording protection to domestic production of shochu contrary to Article III:1 and 2, second sentence."[69]

The 1992 Panel Report on "United States - Measures Affecting Alcoholic and Malt Beverages" notes as follows.

"The Panel began its examination with Canada's claim that the application of a lower rate of federal excise tax on domestic beer from qualifying (small) United States producers, which lower rate was not available to imported beer, was inconsistent with Articles III:1 and III:2 of the General Agreement. The Panel noted that because Article III:1 is a more general provision than either Article III:2 or III:4, it would not be appropriate for the Panel to consider Canada's Article III:1 allegations to the extent that the Panel were to find United States measures to be inconsistent with the more specific provisions of Articles III:2 and III:4."[70]

The same Panel examined the argument that laws in certain states restricting the points of sale, distribution and labelling of beer above a certain percent of alcohol by weight contravened Articles III:1 and III:4. Having found that low alcohol beer and high alcohol beer need not be considered as ' like products' in terms of Article III:4 (see page 171):

"The Panel ... proceeded to examine whether the laws and regulations in the above-mentioned states affecting the alcohol content of beer are applied to imported or domestic beer so as to afford protection to domestic production in terms of Article III:1. In this context, the Panel recalled its finding in paragraph 5.74 regarding the alcohol content of beer and concluded that the evidence submitted to it does not indicate that the distinctions made in the various states with respect to the alcohol content of beer are applied so as to favour domestic producers over foreign producers. Accordingly, the Panel found that the restrictions on points of sale, distribution and labelling based on the alcohol content of beer maintained by the states of Alabama, Colorado, Florida, Kansas, Minnesota, Missouri, Oklahoma, Oregon and Utah are not inconsistent with Article III:1".[71]

With regard to the interpretation of paragraph 1 in the context of the second sentence of paragraph 2, see below under "a directly competitive or substitutable product" (page 159 and following). See also the discussion of this provision in the context of paragraph 5 of Article III.

See also the excerpt from the Working Party Report on "Brazilian Internal Taxes" above at page 128; see also above under "purpose of Article III".

---

[69] L/6216, adopted on 10 November 1987, 34S/83, 122-123, para. 5.11.
[70] DS23/R, adopted 19 June 1992, 39S/206, 270, para. 5.2.
[71] *Ibid.*, 39S/295, para. 5.76.

(2) Note Ad paragraph 1: Application of paragraph 1 to internal taxes imposed by local governments and authorities

See above at page 130.

The Panel Report on "Canada - Measures Affecting the Sale of Gold Coins," which has not been adopted, examined the application of a retail sales tax on gold coins by the Province of Ontario, and the question of whether the Canadian federal government had, as required by Article XXIV:12, taken "such reasonable measures as may be available to it to ensure observance of the provisions of [the General Agreement]" by Ontario.

"The Panel ... examined what meaning should be given to the term 'reasonable'. The Panel noted that the only indication in the General Agreement of what was meant by 'reasonable' was contained in the interpretative note to Article III:1, which defined the term 'reasonable measures' for the case of national legislation authorizing local governments to impose taxes. According to this note the question of whether the repeal of such enabling legislation would be a reasonable measure required by Article XXIV:12 should be answered by taking into account the spirit of the inconsistent local tax laws, on the one hand, and the administrative or financial difficulties to which the repeal of the enabling legislation would give rise, on the other. The basic principle embodied in this note is, in the view of the Panel, that in determining which measures to secure the observance of the provisions of the General Agreement are 'reasonable' within the meaning of Article XXIV:12, the consequences of their non-observance by the local government for trade relations with other contracting parties are to be weighed against the domestic difficulties of securing observance. While recognizing that this note refers to the case of national enabling legislation, the Panel considered that the basic principle embodied therein was applicable to the present case."[72]

4. Paragraph 2: internal taxes or other internal charges of any kind

(1) "directly or indirectly"

In initial discussions at the London session of the Preparatory Committee, it was suggested that while this phrase in the US Draft Charter referred to "taxes and other internal charges imposed on or in connection with like products", the rapporteurs in the Working Party on Technical Articles had used the phrase 'directly or indirectly' instead, owing to the difficulty of obtaining the exact equivalent in the French text.[73] In later discussions in Commission A at the London session of the Preparatory Committee, it was stated that the word "indirectly" would cover even a tax not on a product as such but on the processing of the product.[74]

(2) "internal taxes"

(a) Excise taxes, indirect taxes and consumption taxes

It was stated during discussions in the Third Committee at the Havana Conference that "the provisions relating to internal taxes were not designed to limit the degree of protection, but merely to determine the form which that protection should take. Any country was free to replace internal taxes by import tariffs which were subject to the negotiations referred to in Article 17. There was no general binding or limitations on tariffs as such".[75]

The 1987 Panel Report on "United States - Taxes on Petroleum and Certain Imported Substances" examined excise taxes on imported petroleum and certain imported chemical substances ("Superfund taxes"), which had been enacted as a revenue source for the US "Superfund" hazardous-waste cleanup program.

---

[72] L/5863, para. 69.
[73] Proposal by UK, EPCT/C.II/11; discussion at EPCT/C.II/W.5, p. 5.
[74] EPCT/A/PV/9 p. 19; EPCT/W/181, p. 3.
[75] E/CONF.2/C.3/SR.11, p. 3; Article 17 was the Charter article on multilateral trade negotiations, some elements of which were incorporated into Article XXVIIIbis.

"The Panel examined the tax on petroleum in the light of the obligations the United States assumed under the General Agreement and found the following: The tax on petroleum is an excise tax levied on imported and domestic goods. Such taxes are subject to the national treatment requirement of Article III:2, first sentence, which reads: 'The products of the territory of any contracting party imported into the territory of any other contracting party shall not be subject, directly or indirectly, to internal taxes or other internal charges of any kind in excess of those applied, directly or indirectly, to like domestic products'."[76]

The 1992 Panel Report on "United States - Measures Affecting Alcoholic and Malt Beverages" examined, inter alia, excise taxes on beer and wine at the federal and state level in the United States, and the relationship between exemptions granted from such taxes and the exception in Article III:8(b): see below at page 195.

(b) Fiscal measures versus enforcement measures

The Panel Report on "United States - Measures Affecting the Importation, Internal Sale and Use of Tobacco" examined a claim that the penalty provisions of the Domestic Marketing Assessment ("DMA") under Section 1106(a) of the US 1993 Budget Act, and rules of the U.S. Department of Agriculture ("USDA"), were inconsistent with the first sentence of Article III:2. These provisions, consisting of a nonrefundable marketing assessment and a requirement to purchase additional quantities of domestic burley and flue-cured tobacco, were applicable where a domestic manufacturer failed to provide a required certification of the percentage of domestically-produced tobacco used by it to produce cigarettes each year, or to use annually a minimum of 75 per cent domestic tobacco in the manufacture of cigarettes.

"In the Panel's view, the Article III:2 claim raised the question of whether the DMA's penalty provisions were separate fiscal measures or enforcement measures for the domestic content requirement of the DMA. The Panel noted in this regard that previous panels, consistent with the practice of international tribunals, had refrained from engaging in an independent interpretation of domestic laws, and had treated the interpretation of such laws as questions of fact.[77] The Panel considered that it should approach its analysis of the complainants' Article III:2 claims in conformity with this practice and, therefore, to treat the interpretation of Section 1106(a) of the 1993 Budget Act as a question of fact. As the basis for such an analysis, the Panel considered that it should seek guidance from the manner in which the United States, as author of the legislation, itself interpreted these provisions.

"The Panel considered as significant that the subsection of the DMA provision which set forth the additional marketing assessment and purchase requirements was entitled 'Penalties'. Thus, the ordinary meaning of the title of the provision suggested to the Panel that the additional assessment and purchase requirements were treated under U.S. domestic law as penalties, not as separate fiscal measures.

"The Panel recalled once again that the DMA provision, in relevant part, read as follows:

'*PENALTIES*. In General. Subject to subsection (f), a domestic manufacturer of cigarettes that has failed, as determined by the Secretary after notice and opportunity for a hearing, to use in the manufacture of cigarettes during a calendar year a quantity of tobacco grown in the United States that is at least 75 percent of the total quantity of tobacco used by the manufacturer or to comply with subsection (a) [certification requirement], shall be subject to the requirements of subsections (c) [*nonrefundable marketing assessment*], (d) [*purchase of additional quantities of domestic burley tobacco*] and (e) [*purchase of additional quantities of domestic flue-cured tobacco*]'. *(emphasis added)*

---

[76]L/6175, adopted on 17 June 1987, 34S/136, 154, para. 5.1.1.

[77]The footnote to this sentence in the panel report provides: "See, e.g., report of the panel on United States - Measures Affecting Alcoholic and Malt Beverages, adopted on 19 June 1992, BISD 39S/206, 284-287, 296-297".

"The Panel further recalled that USDA's Proposed Rules implementing Section 1106(a) of the 1993 Budget Act set out the penalty provisions under Section 723.502(b), entitled "Failure to Comply". The text of these Proposed Rules provided the following:

'Each domestic manufacturer of cigarettes who *fails to comply* with the requirements of this section *shall pay* a domestic marketing assessment and *shall purchase* loan stocks of tobacco in accordance with Sections 723.503 and 723.504'.[78] *(emphasis added)*

"The Panel noted in addition that the text accompanying the Proposed Rules suggested that the additional marketing assessment and purchase requirements were in the nature of penalties. For example, the Panel noted that the following explanation was provided:

'Section 320C(c) of the Act provides that *if the quantity of imported tobacco* used by a domestic manufacturer for making cigarettes for the year *exceeds 25 percent, such manufacturer must pay a domestic marketing assessment* on each pound of imported tobacco used in excess of 25 percent. In addition, as provided in section 320C(d) and (e), *such manufacturer must purchase tobacco* from the existing burley and flue-cured tobacco inventories of producer owned cooperative marketing associations in an amount equal to the weight of imported tobacco used in excess of 25 percent'.[79] *(emphasis added)*

"The accompanying text further provided:

'Where a domestic content *violation* has occurred, the *compensatory* purchases of tobacco ... must be from the inventories of producer owned cooperative marketing associations that handle price support loans for tobacco'.[80] *(emphasis added)*

"It was thus the Panel's understanding that the U.S. Government treated these DMA provisions as penalty provisions for the enforcement of a domestic content requirement for tobacco, not as separate fiscal measures, and that such interpretation corresponded to the ordinary meaning of the terms used in the relevant statute and proposed rules. Further, it appeared that these penalty provisions had no separate *raison d'être* in the absence of the underlying domestic content requirement. The above factors suggested to the Panel that it would not be appropriate to analyze the penalty provisions separately from the underlying domestic content requirement.

"The Panel further noted that prior panel decisions also supported the view that the additional marketing assessment and purchase requirements should be treated as enforcement measures, and not be analyzed separately as internal charges. The Panel recalled that one such panel, in examining a regulation according to which buyers of vegetable proteins had the possibility of providing a security as an alternative to the required purchase of a certain quantity of skimmed milk powder, had determined that the security deposit was not a fiscal measure because, *inter alia*,

'the revenue from the security deposit accrued to EEC budgetary authorities only when the buyer of vegetable proteins had not fulfilled the purchase obligation. The Panel therefore considered that the security deposit, including any associated cost, was only an enforcement mechanism for the purchase requirement and, as such, should be examined with the purchase obligation'.[81]

"In a similar vein, another more recent panel had first examined the underlying measure at issue (differing systems for the internal distribution of imported and domestic beer), and considered it

---

[78] The footnote to this sentence in the panel report refers to 59 Federal Register 1493, 1497 (11 January 1994).
[79] The footnote to this sentence in the panel refers to 59 Federal Register 1493, 1495 (11 January 1994).
[80] The footnote to this sentence in the panel report refers to 59 Federal Register 1493, 1495 (11 January 1994).
[81] The footnote to this paragraph in the panel report provides: "Report of the panel on EEC - Measures on Animal Feed Proteins, adopted on 14 March 1978, BISD 25S/49, 64. See also report of the panel on EEC - Programme of Minimum Import Prices, Licences and Surety Deposits for Certain Processed Fruits and Vegetables, adopted on 18 October 1978, BISD 25S/68, 98".

unnecessary to examine certain enforcement measures (charges on beer containers).[82] The Panel did not consider that there were any elements in the case before it which would justify a different approach from that adopted in these earlier cases.

"In view of the Panel's analysis in paragraphs II.A.4.(2)(b) - II.A.4.(2)(b) above, the Panel considered that the evidence did not support the complainants' claim that the DMA's penalty provisions were separate taxes or charges within the meaning of Article III:2.[83]

In this connection see also the unadopted Panel Report of 1994 on "United States - Taxes on Automobiles".[84]

(c)   Income taxes, exemptions from income taxes and credits against income taxes

See also the material below at page 152 and under paragraph 8(b).

During discussions in Sub-Committee A of the Third Committee at the Havana Conference, which considered Article 18 of the Charter (on national treatment), it was stated that the sub-committee on Article 25 [XVI] "had implied that exemptions from income taxes would constitute a form of subsidy permissible under Article 25 [XVI] and therefore not precluded by Article 18." It was agreed that "neither income taxes nor import duties came within the scope of Article 18 [III] since this Article refers specifically to internal taxes on products".[85]

In October 1952, Austria brought a complaint that the Italian authorities granted a remission of income tax to firms that used domestically-produced ship's plate.[86]

The 1971 Working Party on the United States Temporary Import Surcharge held an exchange of views on the Job Development Tax Credit, a credit against United States income taxes which was allowed in the year that certain new capital equipment was placed in service, and was not allowed with respect to foreign-produced property ordered by the taxpayer while the import surcharge was in effect. Foreign-produced property was defined as property manufactured outside the US or property manufactured in the US with 50 percent or more foreign components. Several members of the Working Party stated that the provision under which only goods of United States origin were eligible for the exemption from a direct tax was inconsistent with Article III of the GATT.[87]

In early 1987, the EEC brought a complaint concerning US income tax legislation passed in 1986 which, while eliminating provisions for certain tax credits and special depreciation for capital goods, permitted the temporary use of these provisions for passenger aircraft assembled in certain states of the US if ordered and delivered before a date in late 1986.[88]

(d)   Border tax adjustments; border adjustment of taxes and charges

See paragraph 2(a) of Article II. See also the discussion of the Note *ad* Article III above.

The 1955 Report of Review Working Party II on Schedules and Customs Administration notes that during the Review Session of 1954-55, Germany (which at the time had a system of border tax adjustment for cascading internal indirect taxes) "proposed insertion of the following interpretative note to Article III:2:

---

[82]The footnote to this sentence in the panel report refers to "Report of the panel on Canada - Import, Distribution and Sale of Certain Alcoholic Drinks by Provincial Marketing Agencies, adopted on 18 February 1992, BISD 39S/27, 85".
[83]DS44/R, adopted on 4 October 1994, paras. 75-82.
[84]DS31/R, dated 11 October 1994, paras. 5.42-5.43.
[85]E/CONF.2/C.3/A/W/32, p. 1-2; statement repeated in Havana Reports, p. 63, para. 44. See also E/CONF.2/C.3/SR.13, p. 1.
[86]L/875; see SR.13/12, SR.15/17, SR.16/9, SR.17/5. The tax remission was extended for all purchases in May 1961: see SR.18/4.
[87]L/3575.
[88]L/6153, C/M/208, C/M/209.

"'the words 'internal taxes or other internal charges of any kind in excess of those applied, directly or indirectly, to like domestic products', as employed in the first sentence of paragraph 2, shall be construed to denote the overall charge, including the charges borne by like domestic products through being subjected to internal taxes or other internal charges at various stages of their production (charges borne by the raw materials, semifinished products, auxiliary materials, etc. incorporated in, and by the power consumed for the production of, the finished products)'.

"The Working Party considered the significance of the phrase 'internal taxes or other internal charges' in relation to taxes which are levied at various stages of production, and in particular whether the rule of national treatment would allow a government to tax imported products at a rate calculated to be the equivalent of the taxes levied at the various stages of production of the like domestic product or only at the rate of the tax levied at the last stage. Several representatives supported the former interpretation, while the representative of the United States, on the other hand, thought the reference to internal taxes covered only a tax levied on the final product competitive with the imported article. Against the latter view it was argued that that interpretation would establish a discrimination against countries which chose to levy taxes at various stages and in favour of those which levy a single turnover tax on finished products. Some other representatives were of the opinion that the equivalent of the taxes on the final product and on its components and ingredients would be permitted, but not taxes on power consumed in manufacture, etc. In view of these differences of opinion, the Working Party does not recommend the insertion of an interpretative note, it being understood that the principle of equality of treatment would be upheld in the event of a tax on imported products being challenged under the consultation or complaint procedure of the Agreement."[89]

The Working Party on "Border Tax Adjustments" in 1968-70 examined the tax adjustment practices of contracting parties, their trade effects and relevant provisions of the General Agreement, and in particular the changeover in certain countries from cascade tax systems to the value-added tax. The Working Party used the definition of border tax adjustments applied in the OECD: "any fiscal measures which put into effect, in whole or in part, the destination principle (i.e. which enable exported products to be relieved of some or all of the tax charged in the exporting country in respect of similar domestic products sold to consumers on the home market and which enable imported products sold to consumers to be charged with some or all of the tax charged in the importing country in respect of similar domestic products)". The Working Party considered, on the import side, Articles II and III and on the export side, Article XVI; other articles deemed relevant included Articles I, VI and VII. The 1970 Report of the Working Party notes as follows:

"There was general agreement that the main provisions of the GATT represented the codification of practices which existed at the time these provisions were drafted, re-examined and completed. ...

"Most members argued that there seemed to have been a coherent approach when the relevant articles of the GATT were drafted and that there were no inconsistencies of substance between the different provisions even if the question of tax adjustments was dealt with in different articles. They added that the philosphy behind these provisions was the ensuring of a certain trade neutrality. ...

"The Working Party also noted that there were differences in the terms used in these articles, in particular with respect to the provisions regarding importation and exportation: for instance, the terms 'borne by' and 'levied on'. It was established that those differences in wording had not led to any differences in interpretation of the provisions. It was agreed that GATT principles on tax adjustment applied the principle of destination identically to imports and exports.

"It was further agreed that these provisions set maxima limits for adjustment (compensation) which were not to be exceeded, but below which each contracting party was free to differentiate in the degree of compensation applied, provided that such action was in conformity with other provisions of the General Agreement."[90]

---

[89] L/329, adopted on 26 February 1955, 3S/205, 210-11, para. 10.
[90] L/3464, adopted on 2 December 1970, 18S/97, 99-100, paras. 8-11. See also documents L/3389 (Consolidated document on the examination of practices of contracting parties in relation to border tax adjustments); COM.IND/W/98; L/3272; Spec(68)57 and Add.1-2.

"On the question of eligibility of taxes for tax adjustment under the present rules, the discussion took into account the term 'directly or indirectly ...' (*inter alia* Article III:2). The Working Party concluded that there was convergence of views to the effect that taxes directly levied on products were eligible for tax adjustment. Examples of such taxes comprised specific excise duties, sales taxes and cascade taxes and the tax on value added. It was agreed that the TVA, regardless of its technical construction (fractioned collection), was equivalent in this respect to a tax levied directly - a retail or sales tax. Furthermore, the Working Party concluded that there was convergence of views to the effect that certain taxes that were not directly levied on products were not eligible for tax adjustment. Examples of such taxes comprised social security charges whether on employers or employees and payroll taxes.

"The Working Party noted that there was a divergence of views with regard to the eligibility for adjustment of certain categories of tax and that these could be sub-divided into

(a) 'Taxes occultes' which the OECD defined as consumption taxes on capital equipment, auxiliary materials and services used in the transportation and production of other taxable goods. Taxes on advertising, energy, machinery and transport were among the more important taxes which might be involved. It appeared that adjustment was not normally made for taxes occultes except in countries having a cascade tax;

(b) Certain other taxes, such as property taxes, stamp duties and registration duties ... which are not generally considered eligible for tax adjustment. Most countries do not make adjustments for such taxes ...

It was generally felt that while this area of taxation was unclear, its importance - as indicated by the scarcity of complaints reported in connexion with adjustment of taxes occultes - was not such as to justify further examination.

"The Working Party noted that there were some taxes which, while generally considered eligible for adjustment, presented a problem because of the difficulty of calculating exactly the amount of compensation. Examples of such difficulties were encountered in cascade taxes. ... Other examples included composite goods which, on export, contained ingredients for which the Working Party agreed in principle it was administratively sensible and sufficiently accurate to rebate by average rates for a given class of goods.

"It was generally agreed that countries adjusting taxes should, at all times, be prepared, if requested, to account for the reasons for adjustment, for the methods used, for the amount of compensation and to furnish proof thereof."[91]

Based on the recommendations of this Working Party the Council introduced a notification procedure on a provisional basis in December 1970, whereby contracting parties would report changes in their tax adjustments. The notifications are to report any major changes in tax adjustment legislation and practices involving international trade, and bring periodically up to date the information contained in the consolidated document on contracting parties' practices (L/3389) on tax adjustments drawn up in the course of the Working Party's work. Notifications under this procedure are currently distributed as addenda to document L/3518.[92]

The 1987 Panel Report on "Japan - Customs Duties, Taxes and Labelling Practices on Imported Wines and Alcoholic Beverages" examined the argument of Japan that different tax treatment of liqueurs and sparkling wines according to alcohol and extract contents was consistent with Article III:2.

"The Panel noted ... that GATT Article II:2 permitted the non-discriminatory taxation 'of an article from which the imported product has been manufactured or produced in whole or in part', and that such

---

[91]*Ibid.*, 18S/100-101, paras. 14-17.
[92]18S/108; see discussion on Notification in the GATT under Article X.

a non-discriminatory alcohol tax on like alcoholic beverages with different alcohol contents could result in differential tax rates on like products. ... Having found that

- liqueurs and sparkling wines with high raw material contents, imported into Japan, were subject to internal taxes in excess of those applied to like domestic liqueurs and sparkling wines with lower raw material contents ... and that

- this differential taxation of like products depending on their extract and raw material content had not been, and apparently could not be, justified as resulting from a non-discriminatory internal tax on the raw material content concerned or as justifiable under any of the exception clauses of the General Agreement,

the Panel concluded that this imposition of higher taxes on 'classic' liqueurs and sparkling wines with higher raw material content was inconsistent with Article III:2, first sentence."[93]

The 1987 Panel Report on "United States - Taxes on Petroleum and Certain Imported Substances" noted that the legislation at issue (the Superfund Amendments and Reauthorization Act) provided for an excise tax per ton on sale of certain chemicals. The legislation also provided for an excise tax on certain downstream imported chemical substances which were derivatives of taxable chemicals. The amount of the tax on any of the downstream imported substances was to equal the amount of the excise taxes which would have been imposed on the upstream chemicals used as materials in the production of the imported substance if those upstream chemicals had been sold in the United States for use in the manufacture of the downstream imported substance.

"The Panel noted that the United States justified the tax on certain imported substances as a border tax adjustment corresponding in its effect to the internal tax on certain chemicals from which these substances were derived ... The Panel further noted that the EEC considered the tax on certain chemicals not to be eligible for border tax adjustment because it was designed to tax polluting activities that occurred in the United States and to finance environmental programmes benefitting only United States producers. Consistent with the Polluter-Pays Principle, the United States should have taxed only products of domestic origin because only their production gave rise to environmental problems in the United States. ... The Panel therefore first examined whether the tax on certain chemicals was eligible for border tax adjustments.

"... As [the conclusions of the Border Tax Adjustments Working Party] clearly indicate, the tax adjustment rules of the General Agreement distinguish between taxes on products and taxes not directly levied on products; they do not distinguish between taxes with different policy purposes. Whether a sales tax is levied on a product for general revenue purposes or to encourage the rational use of environmental resources, is therefore not relevant for the determination of the eligibility of a tax for border tax adjustment. For these reasons the Panel concluded that the tax on certain chemicals, being a tax directly imposed on products, was eligible for border tax adjustment independent of the purpose it served. The Panel therefore did not examine whether the tax on chemicals served environmental purposes and, if so, whether a border tax adjustment would be consistent with these purposes. ...

"The Panel, having concluded that the tax on certain chemicals was in principle eligible for border tax adjustment, then examined whether the tax on certain imported substances meets the national treatment requirement of Article III:2, first sentence. This provision permits the imposition of an internal tax on imported products provided the like domestic products are taxed, directly or indirectly, at the same or a higher rate. Such internal taxes may be levied on imported products at the time or point of importation (Note ad Article III). Paragraph 2(a) of Article II therefore clarifies that a tariff concession does not prevent the levying of

---

[93] L/6216, adopted 10 November 1987, 34S/83, 120-121, para. 5.9(d).

'a charge equivalent to an internal tax imposed consistently with the provisions of paragraph 2 of Article III in respect of the like domestic product or in respect of an article from which the imported product has been manufactured or produced in whole or in part'.

"The drafters of the General Agreement explained the word 'equivalent' used in this provision with the following example:

'If a charge is imposed on perfume because it contains alcohol, the charge to be imposed must take into consideration the value of the alcohol and not the value of the perfume, that is to say the value of the content and not the value of the whole' (EPCT/TAC/PV/26, page 21).

"The tax on certain imported substances equals in principle the amount of the tax which would have been imposed under the Superfund Act on the chemicals used as materials in the manufacture or production of the imported substance if these chemicals had been sold in the United States for use in the manufacture or production of the imported substance. In the words which the drafters of the General Agreement used in the above perfume-alcohol example: The tax is imposed on the imported substances because they are produced from chemicals subject to an excise tax in the United States and the tax rate is determined in principle in relation to the amount of these chemicals used and not in relation to the value of the imported substance. The Panel therefore concluded that, to the extent that the tax on certain imported substances was equivalent to the tax borne by like domestic substances as a result of the tax on certain chemicals the tax mat the national treatment requirement of Article III:2, first sentence."[94]

The "Superfund" legislation also provided with respect to the tax on certain imported substances that importers would be required to provide sufficient information regarding the chemical inputs of taxable substances to enable the tax authorities to determine the amount of tax to be imposed; otherwise a penalty tax would be imposed in the amount of five percent ad valorem, or a different rate to be prescribed by the Secretary of the Treasury which would equal the amount that would be imposed if the substance were produced using the predominant method of production. The Panel, examining this penalty rate, noted as follows.

"According to the Superfund Act, the tax on certain imported substances will however not necessarily be equal to the tax on the chemicals used in their production. If an importer fails to furnish the information necessary to determine the amount of tax to be imposed, a penalty tax of 5 per cent of the appraised value of the imported substance shall be imposed. Since the tax on certain chemicals subjects some of the chemicals only to a tax equivalent to 2 per cent of the 1980 wholesale price of the chemical, the 5 per cent penalty tax could be much higher than the highest possible tax that the importer would have to pay if he provided sufficient information.... The imposition of a penalty tax on the basis of the appraised value of the imported substance would not conform with the national treatment requirement of Article III: 2, first sentence, because the tax rate would in that case no longer be imposed in relation to the amount of taxable chemicals used in their production but the value of the imported substance. Thus it would not meet the requirement of equivalence which the drafters explained in the perfume-alcohol example mentioned in the preceding paragraph. ..."[95]

In the 1990 Panel Report on "EEC - Regulation on Imports of Parts and Components" the Panel examined the application of Article 13:10 of the EEC's anti-dumping regulation (Council Regulation No. 2176/84), under which anti-circumvention duties were levied on products assembled or produced in the EEC. Having found that the anti-circumvention duties were not customs duties within the meaning of Article II:1(b) (see excerpts starting at page 200), the Panel examined them in the light of the first sentence of Article III:2.

"The Panel noted that, in the cases in which anti-circumvention duties had been applied, the EEC followed sub-paragraph (c) of the anti-circumvention provision, according to which 'the amount of duty collected shall be proportional to that resulting from the application of the rate of the anti-dumping duty

---

[94]L/6175, adopted on 17 June 1987, 34S/136, 160-163, paras. 5.2.3, 5.2.4, 5.2.7, 5.2.8.
[95]*Ibid.*, 34S/163, para. 5.2.9.

applicable to the exporter of the complete products on the c.i.f. value of the parts or materials imported'. The Panel further noted that like parts and materials of domestic origin are not subject to any corresponding charge. The Panel therefore found that the anti-circumvention duties on the finished products subject imported parts and materials indirectly to an internal charge in excess of that applied to like domestic products and that they are consequently contrary to Article III:2, first sentence".[96]

In the 1994 Panel Report on "United States - Measures Affecting the Importation, Internal Sale and Use of Tobacco", "The Panel ... turned to the claim of the United States that the internal tax on imported tobacco was a border tax adjustment applied consistently with Article III:2 due to the existence of a similar internal tax applied to domestic tobacco. Addressing this claim, the Panel noted that the BDA could only be subject to border tax adjustment if it were an internal tax or charge consistent with Article III:2".[97] See also the material from this report at page 153 concerning the claim that the "No Net Cost Assessments" on imported burley and flue-cured tobacco were permissible border tax adjustments consistent with Article III:2.[98]

See also under the Note *ad* Article III and see the discussion below of the phrase "in excess of those applied".

(3) *"or other internal charges of any kind": charges on the transfer of payments for imports or exports*

The Report of Sub-Committee A of the Third Committee at the Havana Conference, which considered Article 18 of the Charter, states as follows.

> "The Sub-Committee [A] considered that charges imposed in connection with the international transfer of payments for imports or exports, particularly the charges imposed by countries employing multiple currency practices, where such charges are imposed not inconsistently with the Articles of Agreement of the International Monetary Fund, would not be covered by Article 18. On the other hand, in the unlikely case of a multiple currency practice which takes the form of an internal tax or charge, such as an excise tax on an imported product not applied on the like domestic product, that practice would be precluded by Article 18. It may be pointed out that the possible existence of charges on the transfer of payments insofar as these are permitted by the International Monetary Fund is clearly recognized by Article 16."[99]

The foregoing passage was referred to in the 1952 Panel Report on "Special Import Taxes Instituted by Greece". In this connection, the Panel observed:

> "... the principal question arising for determination was whether or not the Greek tax was an internal tax or charge on imported products within the meaning of paragraph 2 of Article III. If the finding on this point were affirmative, the panel considered that it would be subject to the provisions of Article III whatever might have been the underlying intent of the Greek Government in imposing the tax. ... On the other hand, if the contention of the Greek Government were accepted that the tax was not in nature of a tax or charge on imported goods, but was a tax on foreign exchange allocated for the payment of imports, the question would arise whether this was a multiple currency practice, and, if so, whether it was in conformity with the Articles of Agreement of the International Monetary Fund. These matters would be for the determination of the International Monetary Fund. If the Fund should find that the tax system was a multiple currency practice and in conformity with the Articles of Agreement of the International Monetary Fund, it would fall outside the scope of Article III.

---

[96] L/6657, adopted on 16 May 1990, 37S/132, 193, para. 5.9.

[97] DS44/R, adopted on 4 October 1994, para. 89; the footnote to this paragraph refers to the panel reports on "United States - Taxes on Petroleum and Certain Imported Substances", adopted on 17 June 1987, BISD 34S/136, 155-159, and "United States - Section 337 of the Tariff Act of 1930", adopted on 7 November 1989, BISD 36S/345, 386-387.

[98] DS44/R, adopted on 4 October 1994, paras. 102-112.

[99] Havana Reports, p. 62, para. 39, repeating an understanding arrived at during the Geneva session of the Preparatory Committee (see EPCT/174, p. 7). See also Havana discussion of this understanding at E/CONF.2/C.3/A/W.33, p. 3. The text of Article 18 as revised at Havana was taken into the GATT; see the discussion of negotiating history in section III below. Article 16 corresponded to Article I of the General Agreement.

"Even if it were found that the tax did not fall within the ambit of Article III the further question might arise under Article XV:4 whether the action of the Greek Government constituted frustration by exchange action of the intent of the provisions of Article III of the General Agreement".[100]

(4)   "in excess of those applied"

The summary records of the Third Committee at the Havana Conference note the statement that "internal taxes on imported products could be increased if the tax on the domestic products was also increased; the requirement was that the tax should be the same on both imported and domestic products".[101]

The 1992 Panel Report on "Canada - Import, Distribution and Sale of Certain Alcoholic Drinks by Provincial Marketing Agencies" notes with respect to taxes on beer containers:

"The Panel noted that Canada levied in the provinces of Manitoba and Ontario a charge on all beverage alcohol containers, domestic and imported, which were not part of a deposit/return system; in Nova Scotia, a charge was levied on non-refillable containers, domestic and imported, shipped to the liquor board. The United States considered these charges to be inconsistent with Article III since they were in practice applied only to imported beer because imported beer could not be delivered by the brewers to the points of sale and the establishment of a separate container collection system was, therefore, prohibitively expensive. The Panel noted that it was not the charges on containers as such that the United States considered to be inconsistent with Article III but rather their application in a situation where different systems for the delivery of beer to the points of sale applied to imported and domestic beer. The Panel, therefore, considered that its findings on restrictions on private delivery [see page 181 below] dealt with this matter".[102]

(a)   Discriminatory rates of tax

In October 1955 the United Kingdom complained that the Italian government's imposition of a general turnover tax on pharmaceuticals at one rate for domestic products and a different and higher rate for imported products was inconsistent with Article III.[103]

The 1987 Panel Report on "United States - Taxes on Petroleum and Certain Imported Substances," examining an excise tax on petroleum, found that "The rate of tax applied to the imported products is 3.5 cents per barrel higher than the rate applied to the like domestic products. ... The tax on petroleum is ... inconsistent with the United States' obligations under Article III:2".[104] See also the discussion of this case above under "Border tax adjustments".

The 1992 Panel Report on "United States - Measures Affecting Alcoholic and Malt Beverages" "considered that the application of a lower rate of federal excise tax on domestic beer from qualifying United States producers, which lower rate is not available in the case of imported beer, constitutes less favourable treatment to the imported product in respect of internal taxes and is therefore inconsistent with the national treatment provision of Article III:2, first sentence". The Panel reached the same conclusion with respect to federal excise taxes on wine and cider and floor stocks of wine.[105]

(b)   Methods of taxation

The 1987 Panel Report on "Japan - Customs Duties, Taxes and Labelling Practices on Imported Wines and Alcoholic Beverages" examined Japanese excise taxes on alcoholic beverages, which provided different tax rates for different types of beverages, different quality grades of the same beverage, and beverages above

---

[100]G/25, adopted on 3 November 1952, 1S/48, 49-50, paras. 5, 7, 8.
[101]E/CONF.2/C.3/SR.42, p. 4.
[102]DS17/R, adopted 18 February 1992, 39S/27, 85, para. 5.33.
[103]L/421, SR.10/5.
[104]L/6175, adopted on 17 June 1987, 34S/136, 155, para. 5.1.1.
[105]DS23/R, adopted on 19 June 1992, 39S/206, 270, 273, paras. 5.5 (beer), 5.14 (wine, cider and floor stocks of wine).

and below a price threshold. The Panel compared the fiscal burden on the various alcoholic beverages that the Panel had determined to be "like products" or "directly competitive or substitutable products" (see below).

"... The Panel further found that the wording 'directly or indirectly' and 'internal taxes ... *of any kind*' implied that, in assessing whether there is tax discrimination, account is to be taken not only of the rate of the applicable internal tax but also of the taxation methods (e.g. different kinds of internal taxes, direct taxation of the finished product or indirect taxation by taxing the raw materials used in the product during the various stages of its production) and of the rules for the tax collection (e.g. basis of assessment).

"The Panel then examined the European Communities' contention ... that Japanese internal taxes on whiskies, brandies, still wines, sparkling wines, spirits and liqueurs imported from the EEC were in excess of those applied to like Japanese products, and reached the following conclusions:

"a) *Whiskies and brandies subject to the grading system:* The Panel noted that the Japanese specific tax rates on imported and Japanese whiskies/brandies special grade (2,098,100 yen/kl) were considerably higher than the Japanese specific tax rates on whiskies/brandies first grade (1,011,400 yen/kl) and second grade (296,200 yen/kl). The Panel was unable to find that these tax differentials corresponded to objective differences of the various distilled liquors, for instance that they could be explained as a non-discriminatory taxation of their respective alcohol contents. ... almost all whiskies/brandies imported from the EEC were subject to the higher rates of tax whereas more than half of whiskies/brandies produced in Japan benefited from considerably lower rates of tax. The Panel concluded, therefore, that (special and first grade) whiskies/brandies imported from the EEC were subject to internal Japanese taxes 'in excess of those applied ... to like domestic products' (i.e. first and second grade whiskies/brandies) in the sense of Article III:2, first sentence.

"b) *Wines, spirits and liqueurs subject to the 'mixed' system of specific tax and ad valorem tax:* The Panel noted that imported and domestic wines, whiskies, brandies, spirits and liqueurs were subject to *ad valorem* taxes in lieu of the specific tax when the manufacturer's selling price (CIF and customs duty for imported products) exceeded a specified threshold. ... The Panel was of the view that a 'mixed' system of specific and ad valorem liquor taxes was as such not inconsistent with Article III:2, which prohibits only discriminatory or protective taxation of imported products but not the use of differentiated taxation methods as such, provided the differentiated taxation methods do not result in discriminatory or protective taxation. ... since liquors above the non-taxable thresholds were subjected to *ad valorem* taxes in excess of the specific taxes on ' like' liquors below the threshold ... the imposition of ad valorem taxes on wines, spirits and liqueurs imported from the EEC, which are considerably higher than the specific taxes on ' like' domestic wines, spirits and liqueurs, was inconsistent with Article III:2, first sentence.

"c) *The different methods of calculating ad valorem taxes on imported and domestic liquors:* The Panel shared the view expressed by both parties that Article III:2 does not prescribe the use of any specific method or system of taxation. The Panel was further of the view that there could be objective reasons proper to the tax in question which could justify or necessitate differences in the system of taxation for imported and for domestic products. The Panel found that it could be also compatible with Article III:2 to allow two different methods of calculation of price for tax purposes. Since Article III:2 prohibited only discriminatory or protective tax burdens on imported products, what mattered was, in the view of the Panel, whether the application of the different taxation methods actually had a discriminatory or protective effect against imported products. The Panel could therefore not agree with the European Community's view that the mere fact that the so-called 'fixed subtraction system' was available only for domestic liquors constituted in itself a discrimination contrary to Article III:2 or 4".[106]

---

[106] L/6216, adopted 10 November 1987, 34S/83, 118-120, paras. 5.8-5.9.

The 1992 Panel Report on "Canada - Import, Distribution and Sale of Certain Alcoholic Drinks by Provincial Marketing Agencies" noted with respect to the markups charged by provincial liquor boards:

"... The Panel ... considered that Article III:2 required that the computations of the base value for the purposes of assessing these charges be no less favourable for imported beer than for domestic beer. This requirement was met if this value was computed for both imported and domestic beer on the basis of the full cost of the beer, which in the case of the imported beer included charges for cost of services levied by the liquor boards consistently with the General Agreement.

"The Panel further noted that Article III:2 applied to internal taxes levied on imported products, that is products on which duties levied in connection with importation had already been assessed. The Panel therefore *found* that Canada could, consistently with Article III:2, levy the provincial and federal sales taxes on the basis of the duty-paid value of imported beer.

"In the light of these considerations the Panel *found* that Canada's methods of assessing mark-ups and taxes on imported beer were not inconsistent with Article III:2".[107]

See also the material on border tax adjustments at page 144 *et seq.*

(c) *Exemption or remission of taxes*

In 1950 the Netherlands brought a complaint concerning the "utility" system in the United Kingdom, under which goods satisfying certain quality and price criteria were exempted from the UK purchase tax, but imported articles of comparable quality and price were not so exempted. Other representatives stated that the utility system applied only to goods produced in the UK, and that the purchase tax was collected on many imported goods where the identical UK product was exempted. The UK representative agreed that this discrimination had a protective effect. In 1952 the UK authorities notified that the system had been changed so as to exempt from purchase tax all listed textiles, clothing and footwear below specified price levels.[108]

The 1985 Panel Report on "Canada - Measures Affecting the Sale of Gold Coins," which has not been adopted, examined taxes imposed by the Province of Ontario on the Maple Leaf (Canadian) and Krugerrand (South African) gold coins. Having found that the Maple Leaf and Krugerrand were "like products" (see below), the Panel found that "Ontario had exempted the Maple Leaf gold coin from its retail sales tax but not the Krugerrand gold coin. The internal taxes to which Krugerrand gold coins imported into Canadian territory were subject in Ontario were thus in excess of those applied to a like domestic product".[109]

In the 1994 dispute on "United States - Measures Affecting the Importation, Internal Sale and Use of Tobacco", the Panel examined the "No Net Cost Assessment" ("NNCA"), a tax applied to both domestic and imported burley and flue-cured tobacco, the proceeds of which were deposited in an account used to reimburse the U.S. Government for any losses resulting from the operation of the domestic tobacco price-support programme.

"The Panel recalled the claim of the complainants that the NNCA was inconsistent with Article III:2, first sentence, because the net charge of the NNCA on imported tobacco was greater than that on like domestic tobacco. The Panel further recalled the complainants' claim that the NNCA was inconsistent with Article III:2, second sentence, because the NNCA charged on imported tobacco reduced the cost of the price support programme to the domestic tobacco producer, without providing any benefit to imported tobacco. The Panel also recalled the defense of the United States that the NNCA was a border tax adjustment consistent with Article III.

...

---

[107]DS17/R, adopted 18 February 1992, 39S/27, 83, paras. 5.24-5.26.
[108]GATT/CP.5/12 (Netherlands complaint), GATT/CP.5/SR.20, p. 1-5 (discussion at Fifth Session), GATT/CP.6/SR.7 (interim report by UK), G/18 (UK notification of elimination of discrimination).
[109]L/5863, para. 51.

"In examining the parties' claims as to the NNCA in the light of Article III:2, first sentence, the Panel first noted that the record indicated, and all parties to the dispute agreed, that the tax applied to imported burley and flue-cured tobacco was not in excess of - indeed was identical to - the tax applied to domestic burley and flue-cured tobacco, respectively.

"The Panel then examined the complainants' claim that the net rate of the NNCA on imported tobacco was higher than that of the NNCA on domestic tobacco because the latter in effect benefitted from a tax remission through the operation of the tobacco price support programme.

"On this point, the Panel first noted that Article III is concerned with ensuring national treatment of products, not of producers.[110] The Panel then noted that the same rate of tax was imposed via the NNCA on both imported and domestic tobacco. Both in the case of imported and domestic burley and in the case of imported and domestic flue-cured, respectively, the identical rate of tax was paid to the CCC on each pound of such tobacco sold in the United States. What was different in the case of domestic tobacco subject to NNCAs was that its producers benefitted from the U.S. Government's tobacco price support programme. In the view of the Panel, this distinction did not transform the NNCA paid on domestic tobacco into a remission of a tax on a product. The Panel here agreed with the United States that whether or not the use of the revenue derived from the NNCA might ultimately benefit domestic rather than imported tobacco was not relevant to the Panel's analysis under Article III:2.

"The Panel noted, moreover, that Article III:8(b) explicitly recognizes that

'[t]he provisions of this Article shall not prevent the payment of subsidies exclusively to domestic producers, including *payments to domestic producers derived from the proceeds of internal taxes or charges* applied consistently with the provisions of this Article and subsidies effected through governmental purchases of domestic products.' *(emphasis added)*

"It appeared to the Panel that the complainants were in essence arguing that Article III:2 was violated because U.S. producers benefitted from a payment of a subsidy derived from the proceeds of the internal tax, but that importers did not benefit in a like manner.

"The Panel was cognizant of the fact that a remission of a tax on a product and the payment of a producer subsidy out of the proceeds of such a tax could have the same economic effects. However, the Panel noted that the distinction in Article III:8(b) is a formal one, not one related to the economic impact of a measure. Thus, in view of the explicit language of Article III:8(b), which recognizes that the product-related rules of Article III 'shall not prevent the payment of subsidies exclusively to domestic producers', the Panel did not consider, as argued by the complainants, that the payment of a subsidy to tobacco producers out of the proceeds of the NNCA resulted in a form of tax remission inconsistent with Article III:2.[111]

...

"... the Panel rejected the complainants' claims of inconsistency of the NNCA with Article III:2, first and second sentence. In addition, the Panel concurred with the United States that the NNCAs on imported burley and flue-cured tobacco were permissible border tax adjustments consistent with Article III:2."[112]

---

[110] The footnote to this paragraph in the panel report notes: "See report of the panel on United States - Section 337 of the Tariff Act of 1930, adopted on 7 November 1989, BISD 36S/345, 387, citing report of the panel on United States - Taxes on Petroleum and Certain Imported Substances, adopted on 17 June 1987, BISD 34S/136, 158."

[111] The footnote to this paragraph notes: "See report of the panel on United States - Measures Affecting Alcoholic and Malt Beverages, adopted on 19 June 1992, BISD 39S/206, 271-273 for a discussion of the reasons for the distinction in GATT between tax exemptions and remissions on the one hand and producer subsidies on the other."

[112] DS44/R, adopted on 4 October 1994, paras. 103, 105-109, 112.

(d) Exposure of imported products to a risk of discrimination

The 1994 Panel Report on "United States - Measures Affecting the Importation, Internal Sale and Use of Tobacco" notes, in relation to the budget deficit assessment ("BDA") charge assessed on domestic and imported tobacco:

"The Panel recalled that the BDA, applicable to all domestic tobacco for which price support was available, was calculated at the rate of one per cent of the average price support level for each such tobacco type in the previous crop year. The Panel then recalled that the BDA on all types of imported tobacco was calculated as the average of the BDA on domestic burley and domestic flue-cured tobacco.

"The Panel further noted that the application of these two different statutorily prescribed formulas to tobacco in the current year, at least in the case of flue-cured tobacco, resulted in an internal tax on imported tobacco that was higher than that on like domestic tobacco. ...

...

"The Panel thus considered that this imposition of an internal tax on imported flue-cured tobacco at a higher rate than on domestic flue-cured tobacco, as well as the fact that some domestic tobacco was entirely exempt from such tax, each presented cases of less favourable tax treatment inconsistent with Article III:2, first sentence.[113]

"The Panel recognized that a change in the price support levels for domestic burley and flue-cured tobacco could result in a given year in the elimination of the discriminatory tax treatment against imported flue-cured tobacco. However, beyond the immediate circumstance of a higher assessment on imported flue-cured tobacco than on like domestic tobacco, the Panel considered that the U.S. statutorily prescribed averaging method for calculation of the BDA on imported tobacco contained an inherent risk of a higher assessment on some types of imported tobacco than on like domestic tobacco. The Panel agreed with the argument of the complainants that, mathematically, given the statutorily mandated averaging formula, the BDA would always be higher on imported tobacco than on one type of domestic tobacco so long as there was any price differential between the average support price of burley and flue-cured tobacco.

"The Panel noted that an internal regulation which merely exposed imported products to a risk of discrimination had previously been recognized by a GATT panel to constitute, by itself, a form of discrimination, and therefore less favourable treatment within the meaning of Article III.[114] The Panel agreed with this analysis of risk of discrimination as enunciated by this earlier panel.

"The Panel thus considered that the system for calculation of the BDA on imported tobacco itself, not just the manner in which it was currently applied, was inconsistent with Article III:2 because it carried with it the risk of discriminatory treatment of imports in respect of internal taxes.

"The Panel recalled the U.S. defense that even if the BDA was higher on imported flue-cured tobacco than on like domestic tobacco, the method of calculation of the BDA for imports - averaging the BDA on domestic burley and flue-cured tobacco - was a reasonable method and should not be subject to challenge before this Panel. However, the Panel could not see how such a method of calculation could be termed 'reasonable' in the context of the General Agreement if it mandated and inevitably resulted in discriminatory treatment of imported tobacco in respect of internal taxes. The Panel recalled in this regard that a prior GATT panel had ruled that in assessing whether there was tax discrimination, account was to be taken not only of the rate of the applicable internal tax but also of the taxation methods,

---

[113] The footnote to this sentence notes: "See, *e.g.*, report of the panel on United States - Taxes on Petroleum and Certain Imported Substances, adopted on 17 June 1987, BISD 34S/136, 155; report of the panel on United States - Measures Affecting Alcoholic and Malt Beverages, adopted on 19 June 1992, BISD 39S/206, 270".

[114] The footnote to this sentence notes: "See, *e.g.*, report of the panel on EEC - Payments and Subsidies Paid to Processors and Producers of Oilseeds and Related Animal Feed Protein, adopted on 25 January 1990, BISD 37S/86, 125".

including the basis of assessment.[115] Another Article III panel had ruled that more favourable treatment as to some products could not be balanced against less favourable treatment as to others.[116] It had noted that '[s]uch an interpretation would lead to great uncertainty about the conditions of competition between imported and domestic products and thus defeat the purposes of Article III'.[117] The Panel agreed with these earlier rulings and rejected the U.S. defense of 'reasonableness' of the BDA's method of calculation. In accordance with the national treatment provisions of Article III:2, each pound of tobacco imported into the United States had to be accorded treatment no less favourable in respect of internal taxes than that accorded to like domestic tobacco."[118]

In this connection see also the unadopted Panel Report of 1994 on "United States - Taxes on Automobiles".[119]

(5) "like domestic products"

See also the material on "like product" under Article I and paragraph 4 of Article III.

The 1970 Working Party Report on "Border Tax Adjustments" observed that "With regard to the interpretation of the term 'like or similar products', which occurs some sixteen times throughout the General Agreement, it was recalled that considerable discussion had taken place ... but that no further improvement of the term had been achieved. The Working Party concluded that problems arising from the interpretation of the terms should be examined on a case-by-case basis. This would allow a fair assessment in each case of the different elements that constitute a 'similar' product. Some criteria were suggested for determining, on a case-by-case basis, whether a product is 'similar': the product's end-uses in a given market; consumers' tastes and habits, which change from country to country; the product's properties, nature and quality. ..."[120]

The 1985 Panel Report on "Canada - Measures Affecting the Sale of Gold Coins," which has not been adopted, examined taxes imposed by the Province of Ontario on the Maple Leaf (Canadian) and Krugerrand (South African) gold coins.

"The Panel ... examined the Ontario measure in the light of the provisions of Article III and reached the following conclusions: (a) Both the Maple Leaf and the Krugerrand are legal tender in their respective countries of origin. However, they are normally purchased as investment goods. The Panel therefore considered that the Maple Leaf and Krugerrand gold coins were not only means of payment but also 'products' within the meaning of Article III:2. (b) The Maple Leaf and Krugerrand gold coins are produced to very similar standards, have the same weight in gold, and therefore compete directly with one another in international markets. The Panel therefore considered that the Maple Leaf and Krugerrand gold coins were 'like' products within the meaning of Article III:2, first sentence."[121]

The 1987 Panel Report on "United States - Taxes on Petroleum and Certain Imported Substances" examined, *inter alia*, a tax on petroleum, applied at US$0.082 per barrel for "crude oil received at a United States refinery" and US$0.117 per barrel for "petroleum products entered into the United States for consumption, use or warehousing". The panel findings note as follows.

"... The CONTRACTING PARTIES have not developed a definition of the term 'like products' in [Article III:2, first sentence]. In the report of the Working Party on Border Tax Adjustments, adopted by the CONTRACTING PARTIES in 1970, it was suggested that the problems arising from the interpretation of

---

[115] The footnote to this sentence refers to the panel report on "Japan - Customs Duties, Taxes and Labelling Practices on Imported Wines and Alcoholic Beverages", adopted on 10 November 1987, BISD 34S/83, 118-120.
[116] The footnote to this sentence refers to the panel report on "United States - Section 337 of the Tariff Act of 1930", adopted on 7 November 1989, BISD 36S/345, 387.
[117] The footnote to this sentence refers to the panel report on "United States - Section 337 of the Tariff Act of 1930", adopted on 7 November 1989, BISD 36S/345, 387.
[118] DS44/R, adopted on 4 October 1994, paras. 92-93, 95-98.
[119] DS31/R, dated 11 October 1994, paras. 5.10, 5.14, 5.27-5.32.
[120] L/3464, adopted on 2 December 1970, 18S/97, 102, para. 18.
[121] L/5863, para. 51.

this term should be examined on a case-by-case basis and that one of the possible methods for determining whether two products were like products was to compare their end-uses in a given market (BISD 18S/102). The domestic products subject to the tax are: crude oil, crude oil condensates, and natural gasoline. The imported products subject to the tax are: crude oil, crude oil condensates, natural gasoline, refined and residual oil, and certain other liquid hydrocarbon products. The imported and domestic products are thus either identical or, in the case of imported liquid hydrocarbon products, serve substantially identical end-uses. The imported and domestic products subject to the tax on petroleum are therefore in the view of the Panel 'like products' within the meaning of Article III:2. ..."[122]

In the 1987 Panel Report on "Japan - Customs Duties, Taxes and Labelling Practices on Imported Wines and Alcoholic Beverages" the Panel examined the arguments of the parties regarding the application of Article III:2 to the liquor tax system applied to various types of domestic and imported alcoholic beverages in Japan.

"The *text of the first sentence of Article III:2* clearly indicates that the comparison to be made is between internal taxes on imported products and 'those applied ... to like domestic products'. The wording 'like' products (in the French text: 'produits similaires') has been used also in other GATT Articles on non-discrimination (*e.g.* Article I:1) in the sense not only of 'identical' or 'equal' products but covering also products with similar qualities (see, for instance, the 1981 Panel Report on Tariff Treatment by Spain of Imports of Unroasted Coffee, BISD 28S/102, 112).

"The *context of Article III:2* shows that Article III:2 supplements, within the system of the General Agreement, the provisions on the liberalization of customs duties and of other charges by prohibiting discriminatory or protective taxation against certain products from other GATT contracting parties. The Panel found that this context had to be taken into account in the interpretation of Article III:2. For instance, the prohibition under GATT Article I:1 of different tariff treatment for various types of 'like' products (such as unroasted coffee, see BISD 28S/102, 112) could not remain effective unless supplemented by the prohibition of different internal tax treatment for various types of 'like' products. Just as Article I:1 was generally construed, in order to protect the competitive benefits accruing from reciprocal tariff bindings, as prohibiting 'tariff specialization' discriminating against 'like' products, only the literal interpretation of Article III:2 as prohibiting 'internal tax specialization' discriminating against 'like' products could ensure that the reasonable expectation, protected under GATT Article XXIII, of competitive benefits accruing under tariff concessions would not be nullified or impaired by internal tax discrimination against like products. It had therefore been correctly stated in another Panel Report recently adopted by the CONTRACTING PARTIES that 'Article III:2, first sentence, obliges contracting parties to establish certain competitive conditions for imported products in relation to domestic products' (L/6175, paragraph 5.1.9). And it had been for similar reasons that, during the discussion in the GATT Council of the panel report on Spain's restrictions on the domestic sale of soyabean oil which had not been adopted by the Council, several contracting parties, including Japan, had emphasized 'with regard to Article III:4 that the interpretation of the term "like products" in the Panel Report as meaning 'more or less the same product' was too strict an interpretation' (C/M/152 at page 16).

"The *drafting history* confirms that Article III:2 was designed with 'the intention that internal taxes on goods should not be used as a means of protection' ... This accords with the broader objective of Article III 'to provide equal conditions of competition once goods had been cleared through customs' (BISD 7S/64), and to protect thereby the benefits accruing from tariff concessions. This object and purpose of Article III:2 of promoting non-discriminatory competition among imported and like domestic products could not be achieved if Article III:2 were construed in a manner allowing discriminatory and protective internal taxation of imported products in excess of like domestic products.

"*Subsequent GATT practice* in the application of Article III further shows that past GATT panel reports adopted by the CONTRACTING PARTIES have examined Article III:2 and 4 by determining, firstly, whether the imported and domestic products concerned were 'like' and, secondly, whether the internal taxation or other regulation discriminated against the imported products ... Past GATT practice has

---

[122]L/6175, adopted on 17 June 1987, 34S/136, 154-155, para. 5.1.1.

clearly established that 'like' products in terms of Article III:2 are not confined to identical products but cover also other products, for instance if they serve substantially identical end-uses. ...

"The Panel concluded that the ordinary meaning of Article III:2 in its context and in the light of its object and purpose supported the past GATT practice of examining the conformity of internal taxes with Article III:2 by determining, firstly, whether the taxed imported and domestic products are 'like' or 'directly competitive or substitutable' and, secondly, whether the taxation is discriminatory (first sentence) or protective (second sentence of Article III:2). The Panel decided to proceed accordingly also in this case."[123]

"The CONTRACTING PARTIES have never developed a general definition of the term 'like products' in Article III:2. Past decisions on this question have been made on a case-by-case basis after examining a number of relevant factors. ... The Panel was aware of the more specific definition of the term 'like product' in Article 2:2 of the 1979 Antidumping Agreement ... but did not consider this very narrow definition for the purpose of antidumping proceedings to be suitable for the different purpose of GATT Article III:2. The Panel decided, therefore, to examine the table of 'like products' submitted by the EEC [in the dispute] on a product-by-product basis using the above-mentioned criteria as well as others recognized in previous GATT practice (see BISD 25S/49, 63), such as the Customs Cooperation Council Nomenclature (CCCN) for the classification of goods in customs tariffs which has been accepted by Japan. The Panel found that the following alcoholic beverages should be considered as 'like products' in terms of Article III:2 in view of their similar properties, end-uses and usually uniform classification in tariff nomenclatures:

- imported and Japanese-made *gin*;
- imported and Japanese-made *vodka*;
- imported and Japanese-made *whisky* (including all grades classified as 'whisky' in the Japanese Liquor Tax Law) and 'spirits similar to whisky in colour, flavour and other properties' as described in the Japanese Liquor Tax Law;
- imported and Japanese-made *grape brandy* (including all grades classified as 'brandy' in the Japanese Liquor Tax Law);
- imported and Japanese-made *fruit brandy* (including all grades classified as 'brandy' in the Japanese Liquor Tax Law);
- imported and Japanese-made *'classic' liqueurs* (not including, for instance, medicinal liqueurs);
- imported and Japanese-made unsweetened *still wine*;
- imported and Japanese-made *sparkling wines*."[124]

The 1992 Panel Report on "United States - Measures Affecting Alcoholic and Malt Beverages" examined the excise tax exemption accorded by the state of Mississippi to wine made from scuppernong grapes (*vitis rotundifolia*).

"The Panel ... examined the claim by Canada that the state of Mississippi applied a lower tax rate to wines in which a certain variety of grape was used, contrary to Articles III:1 and III:2. The Panel recalled the United States argument that the tax provision in Mississippi was applicable to all qualifying wine produced from the specified variety of grape, regardless of the point of origin.

"The Panel considered that Canada's claim depends upon whether wine imported from Canada is 'like' the domestic wine in Mississippi made from the specified variety of grape, within the meaning of Article III:2. In this regard, the Panel noted that the CONTRACTING PARTIES have not developed a general definition of the term 'like products', either within the context of Article III or in respect of other Articles of the General Agreement. Past decisions on this question have been made on a case-by-case basis after examining a number of relevant criteria, such as the product's end-uses in a given

---

[123]L/6216, adopted on 10 November 1987, 34S/83, 113-115, para. 5.5.
[124]*Ibid.*, 34S/115-116, para. 5.6.

market, consumers tastes and habits, and the product's properties, nature and quality. The Panel considered that the like product determination under Article III:2 also should have regard to the purpose of the Article."

"The basic purpose of Article III is to ensure, as emphasized in Article III:1,

'that internal taxes and other internal charges, and laws, regulations and requirements affecting the internal sale, purchase, transportation, distribution or use of products ... should not be applied to imported or domestic products so as to afford protection to domestic production'.

"The purpose of Article III is thus not to prevent contracting parties from using their fiscal and regulatory powers for purposes other than to afford protection to domestic production. Specifically, the purpose of Article III is not to prevent contracting parties from differentiating between different product categories for policy purposes unrelated to the protection of domestic production. The Panel considered that the limited purpose of Article III has to be taken into account in interpreting the term 'like products' in this Article. Consequently, in determining whether two products subject to different treatment are like products, it is necessary to consider whether such product differentiation is being made 'so as to afford protection to domestic production'. While the analysis of 'like products' in terms of Article III:2 must take into consideration this objective of Article III, the Panel wished to emphasize that such an analysis would be without prejudice to the 'like product' concepts in other provisions of the General Agreement, which might have different objectives and which might therefore also require different interpretations.

"Applying the above considerations to the Mississippi wine tax, the Panel noted that the special tax treatment accorded in the Mississippi law to wine produced from a particular type of grape, which grows only in the southeastern United States and the Mediterranean region, is a rather exceptional basis for a tax distinction. Given the limited growing range of the specific variety of grape, at least in North America, the Panel was of the view that this particular tax treatment implies a geographical distinction which affords protection to local production of wine to the disadvantage of wine produced where this type of grape cannot be grown. The Panel noted that a previous panel concerning Article III treatment of wines and alcoholic beverages found imported and Japanese unsweetened still wines to be like products. The Panel agreed with the reasoning of this previous panel and was of the view that tariff nomenclatures and tax laws, including those at the United States federal and state level, do not generally make such a distinction between still wines on the basis of the variety of grape used in their production. The Panel noted that the United States did not claim any public policy purpose for this Mississippi tax provision other than to subsidize small local producers. The Panel concluded that unsweetened still wines are like products and that the particular distinction in the Mississippi law in favour of still wine of a local variety must be presumed, on the basis of the evidence submitted to the Panel, to afford protection to Mississippi vintners. Accordingly, the Panel found that the lower rate of excise tax applied by Mississippi to wine produced from the specified variety of grape, which lower rate is not available to the imported like product from Canada, is inconsistent with Article III:2, first sentence."[125]

See also the similar treatment of "like product" in the same Panel Report with respect to an Article III:4 claim regarding regulation of beer according to alcohol content (cited below at page 171).

In the 1994 Panel Report on "United States - Measures Affecting the Importation, Internal Sale and Use of Tobacco", the panel examined

"The Panel recalled the complainants's subsidiary argument under Article III:2, second sentence, as to the protective effect of the differing tax liability mandated by the BDA. On this point, the Panel noted that the second sentence of Article III:2 is subsidiary to the first sentence thereof: the second sentence only becomes relevant where a contracting party is '*otherwise* apply[ing] internal taxes or other internal charges to imported or domestic products in a manner contrary to the principles set forth in

---

[125]DS23/R, adopted 19 June 1992, 39S/206, 276-277, paras. 5.23-5.26.

paragraph 1', *i.e.* 'so as to afford protection to domestic production'. However, in the present case, because the Panel had already determined that the BDA was inconsistent with Article III:2, first sentence, the Panel considered that it would not be necessary to examine the consistency of the BDA with Article III:2, second sentence."[126]

In this connection see also the unadopted Panel Report of 1994 on "United States - Taxes on Automobiles".[127]

(6) "a directly competitive or substitutable product" (Ad Article III paragraph 2)

During discussions in Commission A in the Geneva session of the Preparatory Committee, the following explanation was offered of this provision.

"... Let us suppose that ... Country A gets a ... binding of oranges from Country B. Now Country B after that can proceed to put on an internal duty of any height at all on oranges, seeing that it grows no oranges itself. But by putting on that very high duty on oranges, it protects the apples which it grows itself. The consequence is that the binding duty which Country A has secured from Country B on its oranges is made of no effect, because in fact the price of oranges is pushed up so high by this internal [tax] that no one can buy them. The consequence is that the object of that binding is defeated".[128]

An ad-hoc Sub-committee which then examined the national treatment provisions of the draft Charter, and redrafted that article, included the following in its report.

"The Sub-committee considered a suggestion by the Sub-committee on Articles 25 [XI] and 27 [XIII] that the expression 'directly competitive or substitutable' used in [Article III] should conform with the wording adopted for Article 25(2)(c) [XI:2(c)]. In view of the difference in significance between the somewhat comparable expressions used in Articles 15 [III] and Article 25 [XI], it was the opinion of the Sub-committee that there was no necessity for the language of the two articles to be identical in this respect."[129]

The Report of Sub-Committee A of the Third Committee at the Havana Conference, which considered Article 18 of the Charter (on national treatment), states that

"The Sub-Committee (A) agreed that a general tax, imposed for revenue purposes, uniformly applicable to a considerable number of products, which conformed to the requirements of the first sentence of paragraph 2 would not be considered to be inconsistent with the second sentence. ... It was agreed further that a tax applying at a uniform rate to a considerable number of products was to be regarded as a tax of the kind referred to in the preceding paragraph ... notwithstanding the fact that the legislation under which the tax was imposed also provided for other rates of tax applying to other products".[130]

The summary records of discussions in the Third Committee at the Havana Conference include the following statements.

-- It was stated by one of the drafters that

"... the second sentence of [the Article], far from being a departure from the principle of national treatment, was intended to strengthen that principle and prevent its abuse. Illustrating the case of tung oil and linseed oil, which could be considered as competitive and substitutable, he stated that the United States, under the first sentence of paragraph 1 of the Article, would be required to apply the same

---

[126]DS44/R, adopted on 4 October 1994, para. 101.
[127]DS31/R, dated 11 October 1994, paras. 5.4-5.16, 5.23-5.32, 5.33-5.37.
[128]EPCT/A/PV/9, p. 7.
[129]EPCT/174, p. 6.
[130]Havana Reports, p. 62, para. 40-41.

taxation policy to a domestic product as to a like imported product. The first sentence was, however, qualified by the second because if no substantial domestic production existed, a tax could not be placed on tung oil in order to protect linseed oil which was not similarly taxed".[131]

-- It was stated that it would not be permissible to impose a tax on imported natural rubber in order to assist the production of synthetic rubber.[132]

The 1978 Panel Report on "EEC - Measures on Animal Feed Proteins" examined an EEC Regulation requiring domestic producers or importers of oilseeds, cakes and meals, dehydrated fodder and compound feeds and importers of corn gluten feed to purchase a certain quantity of surplus skimmed milk powder held by intervention agencies and to have it denatured for use as feed for animals other than calves. The Panel concluded that skimmed milk powder and vegetable proteins for animal feedingstuffs could not be considered as "like products" (see page 171):

> "The Panel noted that the General Agreement made a distinction between 'like products' and 'directly competitive and substitutable' products. The Panel therefore also examined whether these products should be considered as directly competitive and substitutable within the meaning of Article III. In this regard the Panel noted that both the United States and the EEC considered most of these products to be substitutable under certain conditions. The Panel also noted that the objective of the EEC Regulation during the period of its application, in its own terms, was to allow for increased utilization of denatured skimmed milk powder as a protein source for use in feedingstuffs for animals other than calves. Furthermore, the Panel noted that the security deposit had been fixed at such a level as to make it economically advantageous to buy denatured skimmed milk powder rather than to provide the security, thus making denatured skimmed milk powder competitive with these products. The Panel concluded that vegetable proteins and skimmed milk powder were technically substitutable in terms of their final use and that the effects of the EEC measures were to make skimmed milk powder competitive with these vegetable proteins".[133]

In the 1987 Panel Report on "Japan - Customs Duties, Taxes and Labelling Practices on Imported Wines and Alcoholic Beverages," as noted above the Panel concluded that "the ordinary meaning of Article III:2 in its context and in the light of its object and purpose supported the past GATT practice of examining the conformity of internal taxes with Article III:2 by determining, firstly, whether the taxed imported and domestic products are 'like' or 'directly competitive or substitutable' and, secondly, whether the taxation is discriminatory (first sentence) or protective (second sentence of Article III:2)."[134]

> "... In the view of the Panel there existed - even if not necessarily in respect of all the economic uses to which the product may be put - direct competition or substitutability among the various distilled liquors, among various liqueurs, among unsweetened and sweetened wines, and among sparkling wines. The increasing imports of 'Western-style' alcoholic beverages into Japan bore witness to this lasting competitive relationship and to the potential products substitution through trade among various alcoholic beverages. Since consumer habits vis-a-vis these products varied in response to their respective prices, their availability through trade and their other competitive inter-relationships, the Panel concluded that the following alcoholic beverages could be considered to be '*directly competitive or substitutable products*' in terms of Article III:2, second sentence:
>
>> imported and Japanese-made distilled liquors, including all grades of whiskies/brandies, vodka and shochu Groups A and B, among each other; imported and Japanese-made liqueurs among each other; imported and Japanese-made unsweetened and sweetened wines among each other; and imported and Japanese-made sparkling wines among each other.[135]

---

[131]E/CONF.2/C.3/SR.11 p. 1 and Corr.2.
[132]E/CONF.2/C.3/SR.11 p. 3.
[133]L/4599, adopted on 14 March 1978, 25S/49, 63-64, para. 4.3.
[134]L/6216, adopted 10 November 1987, 34S/83, 115, para. 5.5.
[135]*Ibid.*, 34S/117, para. 5.7.

"... The Panel noted that shochu was not subject to ad valorem taxes and that the specific tax rates on shochu were many times lower than the specific tax rates on whiskies, brandies and other spirits. The Panel noted that, whereas under the first sentence of Article III:2 the tax on the imported product and the tax on the like domestic product had to be equal in effect, Article III:1 and 2, second sentence, prohibited only the application of internal taxes to imported or domestic products in a manner 'so as to afford protection to domestic production'. The Panel was of the view that also small tax differences could influence the competitive relationship between directly competing distilled liquors, but the existence of protective taxation could be established only in the light of the particular circumstances of each case and there could be a *de minimis* level below which a tax difference ceased to have the protective effect prohibited by Article III:2, second sentence. ... Since it has been recognized in GATT practice that Article III:2 protects expectations on the competitive relationship between imported and domestic products rather than expectations on trade volumes (see L/6175, paragraph 5.1.9), the Panel did not consider it necessary to examine the quantitative trade effects of this considerably different taxation for its conclusion that the application of considerably lower internal taxes by Japan on shochu than on other directly competitive or substitutable distilled liquors had trade-distorting effects affording protection to domestic production of shochu contrary to Article III:1 and 2, second sentence."[136]

A request for consultations in 1989 by the EEC concerning "Chile - Internal Taxes on Spirits" states that "The Government of Chile levies an additional sales tax of 70% on imported whisky, compared with the rate of 25% for pisco. In the view of the European Communities this situation constitutes a breach of Chile's obligations under Article III:2 ... Whisky and pisco, while they may not be 'like products', are directly competitive or substitutable products, and in this connection the panel on Japanese customs duties, taxes etc. on alcoholic drinks (L/6216) has made very clear findings and constitutes a precedent applicable in the present instance to Chilean taxation of spirits".[137]

The 1992 Panel Report on "United States - Measures Affecting Alcoholic and Malt Beverages," in examining an excise tax exemption accorded by the state of Mississippi to wine made from scuppernong grapes (*vitis rotundifolia*), found that the lower excise tax rate applying to such wine was inconsistent with Article III:2, first sentence, and further noted as follows:

"... The Panel wished to point out that even if the wine produced from the special variety of grape were considered unlike other wine, the two kinds of wine would nevertheless have to be regarded as 'directly competitive' products in terms of the Interpretative Note to Article III:2, second sentence, and the imposition of a higher tax on directly competing imported wine so as to afford protection to domestic production would be inconsistent with that provision".[138]

See also the material above at page 139-140 on paragraph 1 of Article III.

(7) Taxes collected or enforced at the point of importation

See the discussion above at page 136 *et seq.* of the Interpretative Note ad Article III.

5. Paragraph 3

Paragraph 3 of Article III was inserted into the General Agreement in 1948 when the original text of Article III was replaced by the text of Article 18 of the Havana Charter. The corresponding provision in the Charter had been inserted at the Havana Conference in response to a proposal by Venezuela.[139] It was stated during discussions at the Havana Conference that "if the import duty on the product in question was not bound, the margin of protection afforded by internal taxation could be transferred to the customs duty; even if

---

[136]*Ibid.*, 34S/122-123, para. 5.11; the reference is to the "Superfund" case.
[137]DS9/1, communication dated 31 October 1989.
[138]DS23/R, adopted 19 June 1992, 39S/206, 277, para. 5.26.
[139]Venezuelan proposal: E/CONF.2/C.3/6/Corr.2; see discussion at E/CONF.2/C.3/A/W.22, W.30.

it were bound, under paragraph 3 of Article 18 [III] it was possible to postpone the transfer until such time as it was possible for the member to obtain a release from its trade agreement obligations".[140]

Paragraph 3 of Article III applies only to the situation in which a contracting party may maintain discriminatory internal taxes on a particular item, but cannot simply transfer the discriminatory element into an import tariff because the tariff on the item in question is bound in a bilateral trade agreement that was in existence on 10 April 1947 (the opening date for the Second Session (at Geneva) of the Preparatory Committee for the Havana Conference). Paragraph 3 permits maintenance of the internal tax discrimination until the contracting party in question can obtain a release from its *bilateral* obligations with respect to the tariff.

6. Paragraph 4

(1) "treatment no less favourable"

Australia complained in 1955 that a Hawaiian regulation requiring firms which sold imported eggs to display a placard stating: "We sell foreign eggs" violated paragraph 4 of Article III.[141] The complaint was withdrawn when a domestic court decision declared the law unconstitutional and contrary to paragraph 4 of Article III.[142]

The 1958 Panel Report on "Italian Discrimination against Imported Agricultural Machinery", which examined the consistency with Article III:4 of an Italian law providing special credit facilities to farmers for the purchase of agricultural machinery produced in Italy:

> "The Panel ... had the impression that the contention of the Italian Government might have been influenced in part by the slight difference of wording which existed between the French and the English texts of paragraph 4 of Article III. The French text which had been submitted to the Italian Parliament for approval provided that the imported products '*ne seront pas soumis à un traitement moins favorable*' whereas the English text reads 'the imported product shall be accorded treatment no less favourable'. It was clear from the English text that any favourable treatment granted to domestic products would have to be granted to like imported products and the fact that the particular law in question did not specifically prescribe conditions of sale or purchase appeared irrelevant in the light of the English text. It was considered, moreover, that the intention of the drafters of the Agreement was clearly to treat the imported products in the same way as the like domestic products once they had been cleared through customs. Otherwise indirect protection could be given".[143]

The 1978 Panel Report on "EEC - Measures on Animal Feed Proteins" examined an EEC Regulation requiring domestic producers or importers of oilseeds, cakes and meals, dehydrated fodder and compound feeds and importers of corn gluten feed to purchase a certain quantity of surplus skimmed milk powder held by intervention agencies and to have it denatured for use as feed for animals other than calves. The Regulation was not applied to domestic producers of corn gluten, and was not applicable to animal, fish and synthetic proteins. The Panel examined the consistency with Article III:4 of these aspects of the Regulation and of the requirement to produce either a protein certificate (certifying the purchase and denaturing of a certain quantity of milk powder) or a security deposit.

> "The Panel ... examined whether the EEC measures accorded imported products less favourable treatment than that accorded to like products of EEC origin within the meaning of Article III:4. In this regard the Panel noted the economic considerations, including the level of domestic production and of the applicable security deposit, put forward by the EEC to justify the application of the measures to corn gluten of foreign origin only. The Panel was not convinced that these considerations justified the non-application of these measures to domestic corn gluten and therefore concluded that the measures

---

[140]E/CONF.2/C.3/SR.40, p. 3.
[141]L/411.
[142]SR.10/13.
[143]L/833, adopted on 23 October 1958, 7S/60, 63-64, para. 11.

accorded imported corn gluten less favourable treatment than that accorded corn gluten of national origin in violation of Article III:4.

"The Panel also examined whether the fact that the EEC measures were not applicable to animal, fish and synthetic proteins was consistent with the provisions of Article III:4. Having regard to its own conclusion with regard to 'like products', the Panel was satisfied that animal, fish and synthetic proteins could not be considered as 'like products' for the sake of Article III:4. Since the obligations under Article III:4 relate to 'like products', the Panel concluded that the non-application of the EEC measures to these products was not inconsistent with the EEC obligations under the Article.

The Panel examined whether the protein certificate requirement and other specific administrative requirements accorded to imported products treatment less favourable than that accorded to 'like products' of EEC origin in respect of the purchase, sale and distribution of the products in the EEC within the meaning of Article III:4. The Panel was of the opinion that these requirements should be considered as enforcement mechanisms to ensure that the obligation, of either purchasing a certain quantity of denatured skimmed milk powder or of providing a security, had been complied with. The Panel noted that the protein certificate applied only to imports but that there was an equivalent document required for products of national origin except for a relatively short period at the beginning of the application of the EEC measures. The Panel concluded that the various administrative requirements, including the protein certificate, were not inconsistent with the EEC obligations under Article III:4."[144]

The 1981 Panel Report on "EEC - United Kingdom Application of EEC Directives to Imports of Poultry from the United States" notes that this panel was established in 1980 to examine the US complaint that the UK had prevented the importation of US poultry not in compliance with legislation implementing an EEC Directive, which required that slaughtered poultry be cooled by the "spin-chill" method. As poultry produced in the United Kingdom was by derogation exempted from the requirements of the legislation (permitting it to be chilled by other methods) the US considered the UK action to be a violation of Article III. After formation of the panel, the complaint was withdrawn.[145]

In a 1982 request for consultations under Article XXII:1, the United States cited the differential postal rates applicable to second class printed matter in Canada:

"We consider that such differentiated rates which distinguish between Canadian newspapers and periodicals, non-Canadian printed-in-Canada publications, and non-Canadian mailed-in-Canada publications constitute regulations which accord treatment to imported products less favourable than that accorded to like products of national origin, and that these regulations are therefore contrary to Canada's obligations under Article III of the GATT".[146]

The 1983 Panel Report on "United States - Imports of Certain Automotive Spring Assemblies" examined the consistency with Articles III and XX of Section 337 of the Tariff Act of 1930, a US statutory provision providing (*inter alia*) for enforcement of patent infringement claims when imported goods are alleged to infringe a US patent. The Panel Report notes the Canadian view that the use of Section 337 "in cases of alleged patent infringement granted to holders of United States patents a remedy in addition to that provided by the United States patent laws, which was available only in the context of import trade. This constituted a denial of national treatment under Article III:1 and 4 of the General Agreement. Foreign producers were treated less favourably because, instead of being subject only to the procedures under United States patent law, they had to face separate proceedings in separate bodies. This was not the case for domestic producers unless they engaged in import trade. In the Canadian view this dual system was of a discriminatory nature".[147] The Panel found that "Since Article XX(d) had been found to apply, the Panel considered that an examination of the United States action in the light of the other GATT provisions ... was not required".[148]

---

[144] L/4599, adopted 14 March 1978, 25S/49, 65-66, paras. 4.10-4.12.
[145] L/5155, adopted 11 June 1981, 28S/90.
[146] L/5359.
[147] L/5333, adopted on 26 May 1983 subject to an understanding (C/M/168), 30S/107, 119, para. 34.
[148] *Ibid.*, 30S/126-127, para. 61.

This Panel Report was adopted subject to an understanding that its adoption "shall not foreclose future examination of the use of Section 337 to deal with patent infringement cases from the point of view of consistency with Articles III and XX of the General Agreement".[149] The same statute was again examined in the 1989 panel decision on "United States - Section 337 of the Tariff Act of 1930".[150]

The 1991 Panel Report on "United States - Restrictions on Imports of Tuna," which has not been adopted, examined a prohibition on imports of tuna and tuna products from Mexico imposed under the US Marine Mammal Protection Act (MMPA), and found that

"... even if the provisions of the MMPA enforcing the tuna harvesting regulations (in particular those providing for the seizure of cargo as a penalty for violation of the Act) were regarded as regulating the sale of tuna as a product, the United States import prohibition would not meet the requirements of Article III. As pointed out in paragraph 5.12 above, Article III:4 calls for a comparison of the treatment of imported tuna *as a product* with that of domestic tuna *as a product*. Regulations governing the taking of dolphins incidental to the taking of tuna could not possibly affect tuna as a product. Article III:4 therefore obliges the United States to accord treatment to Mexican tuna no less favourable than that accorded to United States tuna, whether or not the incidental taking of dolphins by Mexican vessels corresponds to that of United States vessels.

"The Panel noted that Mexico had argued that the MMPA requirements with respect to production of yellowfin tuna in the ETP, and the method of calculating compliance with these requirements, provided treatment to tuna and tuna products from Mexico that was less favourable than the treatment accorded to like United States tuna and tuna products. It appeared to the Panel that certain aspects of the requirements could give rise to legitimate concern, in particular the MMPA provisions which set a prospective absolute yearly ceiling for the number of dolphins taken by domestic tuna producers in the ETP, but required that foreign tuna producers meet a retroactive and varying ceiling for each period based on actual dolphin taking by the domestic tuna fleet in the same time period. However, in view of its finding in the previous paragraph, the Panel considered that a finding on this point was not required."[151]

See also the material from this report at pages 137 and 175. See also the unadopted Panel Reports of 1994 on "United States - Restrictions on Imports of Tuna"[152] and "United States - Taxation of Automobiles".[153]

(a) Equality of competitive opportunities

The Panel Report on "Italian Discrimination against Imported Agricultural Machinery" examined an Italian law providing special credit terms to farmers for the purchase of agricultural machinery, conditional on the purchase of machinery produced in Italy. The Panel Report found, *inter alia*, that

"... the intention of the drafters of the Agreement was clearly to treat the imported products in the same way as the like domestic products once they had been cleared through customs. Otherwise indirect protection could be given.

"In addition, the text of paragraph 4 referred ... to laws and regulations and requirements *affecting* internal sale, purchase, etc., and not to laws, regulations and requirements governing the conditions of sale or purchase. The selection of the word 'affecting' would imply, in the opinion of the Panel, that the drafters of the Article intended to cover in paragraph 4 not only the laws and regulations which directly governed the conditions of sale or purchase but also any laws or regulations which might adversely modify the conditions of competition between the domestic and imported products on the internal market.

---

[149] C/M/168.
[150] L/6439, adopted on 7 November 1989, 36S/345.
[151] DS21/R (unadopted), 39S/155, 195-196, paras. 5.15-5.16.
[152] DS29/R, dated 16 June 1994, paras. 5.8-5.9.
[153] DS31/R, dated 11 October 1994, paras. 5.51-5.55.

"... The fact that the drafters of Article III thought it necessary to include [the Article III:8(b)] exemption for production subsidies would indicate that the intent of the drafters was to provide equal conditions of competition once goods had been cleared through the customs".[154]

The 1984 Panel Report on "Canada - Administration of the Foreign Investment Review Act" examined written purchase and export undertakings under the Foreign Investment Review Act of Canada, submitted by investors regarding the conduct of the business they were proposing to acquire or establish, conditional on approval by the Canadian government of the proposed acquisition or establishment. Written undertakings are legally binding on the investor if the investment is allowed. The Panel first determined that the undertakings were to be considered "laws, regulations or requirements" within the meaning of Article III:4 (see page 173 below).

"The Panel then examined the question whether less favourable treatment was accorded to imported products than that accorded to like products of Canadian origin in respect of requirements affecting their purchase. For this purpose the Panel distinguished between undertakings to purchase goods of Canadian origin and undertakings to use Canadian sources or suppliers (irrespective of the origin of the goods), and for both types of undertakings took into account the qualifications 'available', 'reasonably available', or 'competitively available'.

"The Panel found that undertakings to purchase *goods of Canadian origin* without any qualification exclude the possibility of purchasing available imported products so that the latter are clearly treated less favourably than domestic products and that such requirements are therefore not consistent with Article III:4. This finding is not modified in cases where undertakings to purchase goods of Canadian origin are subject to the qualification that such goods be 'available'. It is obvious that if Canadian goods are not available, the question of less favourable treatment of imported goods does not arise.

"When these undertakings are conditional on goods being 'competitively available' (as in the majority of cases) the choice between Canadian or imported products may frequently coincide with normal commercial considerations and the latter will not be adversely affected whenever one or the other offer is more competitive. However, it is the Panel's understanding that the qualification 'competitively available' is intended to deal with situations where there are Canadian goods available on competitive terms. The Panel considered that in those cases where the imported and domestic product are offered on equivalent terms, adherence to the undertaking would entail giving preference to the domestic product. Whether or not the foreign investor chooses to buy Canadian goods in given practical situations, is not at issue. The purpose of Article III:4 is not to protect the interests of the foreign investor but to ensure that goods originating in any other contracting party benefit from treatment no less favourable than domestic (Canadian) goods, in respect of the requirements that affect their purchase (in Canada). On the basis of these considerations, the Panel found that a requirement to purchase goods of Canadian origin, also when subject to 'competitive availability', is contrary to Article III:4. The Panel considered that the alternative qualification 'reasonably available' which is used in some cases, is *a fortiori* inconsistent with Article III:4, since the undertaking in these cases implies that preference has to be given to Canadian goods also when these are not available on entirely competitive terms.

"The Panel then turned to the undertakings to buy from *Canadian suppliers*. The Panel did not consider the situation where domestic products are not available, since such a situation is not covered by Article III:4. The Panel understood the choice under this type of requirement to apply on the one hand to imported goods if bought through a Canadian agent or importer and on the other hand to Canadian goods which can be purchased either from a Canadian 'middleman' or directly from the Canadian producer. The Panel recognized that these requirements might in a number of cases have little or no effect on the choice between imported or domestic products. However, the possibility of purchasing imported products *directly* from the foreign producer would be excluded and as the conditions of purchasing imported products through a Canadian agent or importer would normally be less advantageous, the imported product would therefore have more difficulty in competing with Canadian

---

[154] L/833, adopted 23 October 1958, 7S/60, 64, paras. 11-13.

products (which are not subject to similar requirements affecting their sale) and be treated less favourably. For this reason, the Panel found that the requirements to buy from Canadian suppliers are inconsistent with Article III:4.

"In case undertakings to purchase from Canadian suppliers are subject to a 'competitive availability' qualification, as is frequent, the handicap for the imported product is alleviated as it can be obtained directly from the foreign producer if offered under more competitive conditions than via Canadian sources. In those cases in which Canadian sources and a foreign manufacturer offer a product on equivalent terms, adherence to the undertaking would entail giving preference to Canadian sources, which in practice would tend to result in the purchase being made directly from the Canadian producer, thereby excluding the foreign product. The Panel therefore found that requirements to purchase from Canadian suppliers, also when subject to competitive availability, are contrary to Article III:4. As before (paragraph 5.9), the Panel considered that the qualification 'reasonably available' is *a fortiori* inconsistent with Article III:4."[155]

The Panel noted in its conclusions that

"The Panel sympathizes with the desire of the Canadian authorities to ensure that Canadian goods and suppliers would be given a fair chance to compete with imported products. However, the Panel holds the view that the purchase requirements under examination do not stop short of this objective but tend to tip the balance in favour of Canadian products, thus coming into conflict with Article III:4. ...

"As to the extent to which the purchase undertakings reflect plans of the investors, the Panel does not consider it relevant nor does it feel competent to judge how the foreign investors are affected by the purchase requirements, as the national treatment obligations of Article III of the General Agreement do not apply to foreign persons or firms but to imported products and serve to protect the interests of producers and exporters established on the territory of any contracting party. Purchase requirements applied to foreign investors in Canada which are inconsistent with Article III:4 can affect the trade interests of all contracting parties, and impinge upon their rights".[156]

The 1989 Panel Report on "United States - Section 337 of the Tariff Act of 1930" again examined the consistency with Articles III and XX of Section 337, a US statute providing procedures for enforcing patent infringement claims which only applies to imported goods alleged to infringe a US patent. The Panel examined in particular the application of Article III:4. Having found that the procedures of Section 337 fell within the scope of "laws, regulations and requirements" (see page 175), the Panel turned to the "no less favourable treatment" standard, examining the United States argument that in certain instances Section 337 proceedings were more favourable to imported products than the alternative of enforcement of a patent in federal district court.

"The Panel noted that, as far as the issues before it are concerned, the 'no less favourable' treatment requirement set out in Article III:4, is unqualified. These words are to be found throughout the General Agreement and later agreements negotiated in the GATT framework as an expression of the underlying principle of equality of treatment of imported products as compared to the treatment given either to other foreign products, under the most favoured nation standard, or to domestic products, under the national treatment standard of Article III. The words 'treatment no less favourable' in paragraph 4 call for effective equality of opportunities for imported products in respect of the application of laws, regulations and requirements affecting the internal sale, offering for sale, purchase, transportation, distribution or use of products. This clearly sets a minimum permissible standard as a basis. ...

"The Panel noted the differing views of the parties on how an assessment should be made as to whether the differences between Section 337 and federal district court procedures do or do not accord imported products less favourable treatment than that accorded to products of United States origin. ... In brief, the United States believed that this determination could only be made on the basis of an

---

[155]L/5504, adopted 7 February 1984, 30S/140, 159-161, paras. 5.7-5.11.
[156]*Ibid.*, 30S/166-167, paras. 6.3, 6.5.

examination of the *actual results* of past Section 337 cases. It would follow from this reasoning that any unfavourable elements of treatment of imported products could be offset by more favourable elements of treatment, provided that the results, as shown in past cases, have not been less favourable. The Community's interpretation of Article III:4 would require that Section 337 not be *capable* of according imported products less favourable treatment; elements of less and more favourable treatment could thus only be offset against each other to the extent that they always would arise in the same cases and necessarily would have an offsetting influence on each other.

"The Panel examined these arguments carefully. It noted that a previous Panel had found that the purpose of the first sentence of Article III:2, dealing with internal taxes and other internal charges, is to protect 'expectations on the competitive relationship between imported and domestic products'.[157] Article III:4, which is the parallel provision of Article III dealing with the 'non-charge' elements of internal legislation, has to be construed as serving the same purpose. Article III:4 would not serve this purpose if the United States interpretation were adopted, since a law, regulation or requirement could then only be challenged in GATT after the event as a means of rectifying less favourable treatment of imported products rather than as a means of forestalling it. In any event, the Panel doubted the feasibility of an approach that would require it to be demonstrated that differences between procedures under Section 337 and those in federal district courts had actually caused, in a given case or cases, less favourable treatment. The Panel therefore considered that, in order to establish whether the 'no less favourable' treatment standard of Article III:4 is met, it had to assess whether or not Section 337 in itself may lead to the application to imported products of treatment less favourable than that accorded to products of United States origin. It noted that this approach is in accordance with previous practice of the CONTRACTING PARTIES in applying Article III, which has been to base their decisions on the distinctions made by the laws, regulations or requirements themselves and on their potential impact, rather than on the actual consequences for specific imported products."[158]

In the 1992 Panel Report on "Canada - Import, Distribution and Sale of Certain Alcoholic Drinks by Provincial Marketing Agencies," the Panel examined restrictions imposed by provincial liquor authorities on access for imported beer to points of sale (with respect to which Canada invoked the Protocol of Provisional Application):

"... The Panel recalled that the CONTRACTING PARTIES had decided in a number of previous cases that the requirement of Article III:4 to accord imported products treatment no less favourable than that accorded to domestic products was a requirement to accord imported products competitive opportunities no less favourable than those accorded to domestic products. The Panel found that, by allowing the access of domestic beer to points of sale not available to imported beer, Canada accorded domestic beer competitive opportunities denied to imported beer. For these reasons the present Panel saw great force in the argument that the restrictions on access to points of sale were covered by Article III:4. However, the Panel considered that it was not necessary to decide whether the restrictions fell under Article XI:1 or Article III:4 because Canada was not invoking an exception to the General Agreement applicable only to measures taken under Article XI:1 (such as the exceptions in Articles XI:2 and XII) and the question of whether the restrictions violated Article III:4 or Article XI:1 of the General Agreement was therefore of no practical consequence in the present case".[159]

The 1992 Panel Report on "United States - Measures Affecting Alcoholic and Malt Beverages" examined the requirement, imposed by certain states in the US, that imported beer and wine be sold only through in-state wholesalers or other middlemen, while some in-state like products were permitted to be sold directly to retailers, and in some cases at retail on producers' premises.

---

[157]Note 1 to this paragraph refers to the Panel Report on "United States - Taxes on Petroleum and Certain Imported Substances", L/6175, paragraph 5.1.9), adopted on 17 June 1987, 34S/136.

[158]36S/386-387, paras. 5.11-5.13. Note 2 to this paragraph provides: "For example: Working Party on Brazilian Internal Taxes (BISD II/184-5, paragraph 13-16); Panel on Italian Discrimination against Imported Agricultural Machinery (BISD 7S/63-64, paragraphs 11-12); Panel on EEC - Measures on Animal Feed Proteins (BISD 25S/65, paragraph 4.10); Panel on Canada - Administration of the Foreign Investment Review Act (BISD 30S/167, paragraph 6.6); Panel on United States - Taxes on Petroleum and Certain Imported Substances (L/6175, paragraphs 5.1.1-5.1.9)".

[159]DS21/R, adopted on 18 February 1992, 39S/27, 75-76, para. 5.5.

"... The Panel recalled that the CONTRACTING PARTIES have consistently interpreted the requirement of Article III:4 to accord imported products treatment no less favourable than that accorded to domestic products as a requirement to accord imported products competitive opportunities no less favourable than those accorded to domestic products.[160]

"The Panel considered as irrelevant to the examination under Article III:4 the fact that many -- or even most -- in-state beer and wine producers 'preferred' to use wholesalers rather than to market their products directly to retailers. The Article III:4 requirement is one addressed to relative competitive opportunities created by the government in the market, not to the actual choices made by enterprises in that market. Producers located in the states in question have the opportunity to choose their preferred method of marketing. The Panel considered that it is the very denial of this opportunity in the case of imported products which constitutes less favourable treatment. The Panel then recalled the finding of a previous panel[161] that a requirement to buy from domestic suppliers rather than from the foreign producer was inconsistent with Article III:4:

"Similarly, in the present case the Panel considered that the choice available to some United States producers to ship their beer and wine directly to in-state retailers may provide such domestic beer and wine with competitive opportunities denied to the like imported products. Even if in some cases the in-state exemption from the wholesaler requirement is available only to small wineries and small breweries, this fact does not in any way negate the denial of competitive opportunities to the like imported products. In so finding, the Panel recalled its earlier finding, in paragraph 5.19, that beer from large breweries is not unlike beer from small breweries.

"In the view of the Panel, therefore, the requirement that imported beer and wine be distributed through in-state wholesalers or other middlemen, when no such obligation to distribute through wholesalers exists with respect to in-state like domestic products, results in 'treatment ... less favourable than that accorded to like products' from domestic producers, inconsistent with Article III:4. The Panel considered that even where Canadian producers have the right to establish in-state wholesalers, as is the case in some states, subject to varying conditions, the fact remains that the wholesale level represents another level of distribution which in-state product is not required to use.

"The Panel ... recalled the argument of the United States that the wholesaling requirement was consistent with Article III:4 because in-state breweries and wineries not subject to the wholesaling requirement bore the same costs as did wholesalers in respect of record keeping, audit, inspection and tax collection. The Panel noted that this factual contention -- that imported products are not in fact disadvantaged vis-à-vis domestic like products in spite of different requirements -- was disputed by Canada and was similar to the position taken by the United States with respect to imported products being subject to the 'preferred' wholesaling method of distribution. As previously noted, the Panel considered that the inconsistency with Article III:4 stems from the denial to the imported products of competitive opportunities accorded to the domestic like products. Whereas domestic beer and wine may be shipped directly from the in-state producer to the retailer, or sold directly at retail, this competitive advantage is denied to imported beer and wine."[162]

(b) Formally identical legal requirements versus formally different legal requirements

The 1989 Panel Report on "United States - Section 337 of the Tariff Act of 1930" further provided:

"... The words 'treatment no less favourable' in paragraph 4 call for effective equality of opportunities for imported products in respect of the application of laws, regulations and requirements affecting the

---

[160]Note 8 to the Panel Report provides: "See, for example, the Report of the Panel on 'United States - Section 337 of the Tariff Act of 1930', adopted on 7 November 1989, BISD 36S/345, 386; and the Report of the Panel on 'Canada - Import, Distribution and Sale of Certain Alcoholic Drinks by Provincial Marketing Agencies', [not yet considered by the Council,] DS17/R, page 55".
[161]Note 9 to the Panel Report provides: "Report of the Panel on 'Canada - Administration of the Foreign Investment Review Act', adopted on 7 February 1984, BISD 30S/140, 160-61".
[162]DS23/R, adopted 19 June 1992, 39S/206, 279-280, paras. 5.30-5.33.

internal sale, offering for sale, purchase, transportation, distribution or use of products. This clearly sets a minimum permissible standard as a basis. On the one hand, contracting parties may apply to imported products different formal legal requirements if doing so would accord imported products more favourable treatment. On the other hand, it also has to be recognised that there may be cases where application of formally identical legal provisions would in practice accord less favourable treatment to imported products and a contracting party might thus have to apply different legal provisions to imported products to ensure that the treatment accorded them is in fact no less favourable. For these reasons, the mere fact that imported products are subject under Section 337 to legal provisions that are different from those applying to products of national origin is in itself not conclusive in establishing inconsistency with Article III:4. In such cases, it has to be assessed whether or not such differences in the legal provisions applicable do or do not accord to imported products less favourable treatment. Given that the underlying objective is to guarantee equality of treatment, it is incumbent on the contracting party applying differential treatment to show that, in spite of such differences, the no less favourable treatment standard of Article III is met".[163]

The 1992 Panel Report on "Canada - Import, Distribution and Sale of Certain Alcoholic Drinks by Provincial Marketing Agencies" also examined the application of Article III:4 with respect to formally identical requirements (in the case of minimum prices applied to all beer: see page 177) and formally different requirements (in the case of internal transportation of beer: see page 181).

(c) *Application of legal requirements to individual cases and "balancing"*

The 1989 Panel Report on "United States - Section 337 of the Tariff Act of 1930" further provides:

"The Panel further found that the 'no less favourable' treatment requirement of Article III:4 has to be understood as applicable to each individual case of imported products. The Panel rejected any notion of balancing more favourable treatment of some imported products against less favourable treatment of other imported products. If this notion were accepted, it would entitle a contracting party to derogate from the no less favourable treatment obligation in one case, or indeed in respect of one contracting party, on the ground that it accords more favourable treatment in some other case, or to another contracting party. Such an interpretation would lead to great uncertainty about the conditions of competition between imported and domestic products and thus defeat the purposes of Article III".[164]

After a detailed comparison between Section 337 procedures and those in federal district court,

"The Panel *found* that Section 337, inconsistently with Article III:4 of the General Agreement, accords to imported products alleged to infringe United States patents treatment less favourable than that accorded under federal district court procedures to like products of United States origin as a result of the following factors:

(i)   the availability to complainants of a choice of forum in which to challenge imported products, whereas no corresponding choice is available to challenge products of United States origin;

(ii) the potential disadvantage to producers or importers of challenged products of foreign origin resulting from the tight and fixed time-limits in proceedings under Section 337, when no comparable time-limits apply to producers of challenged products of United States origin;

(iii) the non-availability of opportunities in Section 337 proceedings to raise counterclaims, as is possible in proceedings in federal district court;

---

[163]L/6439, adopted 7 November 1989, 36S/345, 386, para. 5.11.
[164]L/6439, adopted on 7 November 1989, 36S/345, 387, para. 5.14. See also similar finding with respect to Article I in the Panel Report on "United States - Denial of Most-favoured-nation Treatment as to Non-Rubber Footwear from Brazil", DS18/R, adopted on 19 June 1992, 39S/128, 151, para. 6.10.

(iv) the possibility that general exclusion orders may result from proceedings brought before the USITC under Section 337, given that no comparable remedy is available against infringing products of United States origin;

(v) the automatic enforcement of exclusion orders by the United States Customs Service, when injunctive relief obtainable in federal court in respect of infringing products of United States origin requires for its enforcement individual proceedings brought by the successful plaintiff;

(vi) the possibility that producers or importers of challenged products of foreign origin may have to defend their products both before the USITC and in Federal district court, whereas no corresponding exposure exists with respect to products of United States origin".[165]

In the 1990 Panel Report on "EEC - Payments and Subsidies Paid to Processors and Producers of Oilseeds and Related Animal-Feed Proteins" the Panel examined EEC legislation providing for payment of subsidies to processors of oilseeds whenever they established by documentary evidence that they had transformed oilseeds of Community origin. Discussing as well the relationship between paragraphs 4 and 8(b) of Article III (see page 194 below),

"... The Panel noted that ... if the economic benefits generated by the payments granted by the Community can at least partly be retained by the processors of Community oilseeds, the payments generate a benefit conditional upon the purchase of oilseeds of domestic origin inconsistently with Article III:4. ...

"... The Panel concluded that the Community Regulations do not ensure that the payments to processors are based on prices processors actually have to pay when purchasing Community oilseeds ... [nor that] the subsidy payments are based on prices that the subsidy recipients would actually have paid had they chosen to buy imported rather than domestic products.

"For the reasons indicated in the preceding paragraphs, the Panel found that subsidy payments made to processors can be greater than the difference between the price processors actually pay to producers and the price that processors would have to pay for imported oilseeds. Whether such over-compensation creating an incentive to purchase domestic rather than imported products takes place depends on the circumstances of the individual purchase. The Community Regulations are thus capable of giving rise to discrimination against imported products though they may not necessarily do so in the case of each individual purchase.

"Having made this finding the Panel examined whether a purchase regulation which does not necessarily discriminate against imported products but is capable of doing so is consistent with Article III:4. The Panel noted that the exposure of a particular imported product to a risk of discrimination constitutes, by itself, a form of discrimination. The Panel therefore concluded that purchase regulations creating such a risk must be considered to be according less favourable treatment within the meaning of Article III:4. The Panel found for these reasons that the payments to processors of Community oilseeds are inconsistent with Article III:4".[166]

In the 1992 Followup on this Panel Report, the members of the Reconvened Oilseeds Panel noted that "The facts before the Panel, which were not challenged by the United States, indicated that ... the payments to processors conditional on the purchase of domestic oilseeds that had given rise to the inconsistency found by the original Panel had been superseded, there being no provision for such payments under the new support system other than in the transitional arrangements»[167] and concluded that "... the Panel suggests that the CONTRACTING PARTIES take note of the Community's statement that the new support system for oilseeds

---

[165] Ibid., 36S/391, para. 5.20.
[166] L/6627, adopted on 25 January 1990, 37S/86, 124-125, paras. 137-141.
[167] DS28/R, dated 31 March 1992, 39S/91, 113, para. 74.

under Regulation N° 3766/91 was intended to eliminate any inconsistency with Article III:4 by the discontinuation of payments to processors conditional on the purchase of domestic oilseeds".[168]

In this connection, see also the unadopted Panel Report of 1994 on "United States - Taxes on Automobiles".[169]

(2) "than that accorded to like products of national origin"

See also the discussion of "like product" above in this chapter and under Article I.

The 1978 Panel Report on "EEC - Measures on Animal Feed Proteins" examined an EEC Regulation requiring domestic producers or importers of oilseeds, cakes and meals, dehydrated fodder and compound feeds and importers of corn gluten feed to purchase a certain quantity of surplus skimmed milk powder held by intervention agencies and to have it denatured for use as feed for animals other than calves. The Panel examined the consistency of the EEC measures with, *inter alia*, Article III:1, III:4 and III:5.

> "The Panel began by examining whether all products used for the same purpose of adding protein to animal feeds should be considered as 'like products' within the meaning of Articles I and III. Having noted that the General Agreement gave no definition of the concept of 'like product' the Panel reviewed how it had been applied by the CONTRACTING PARTIES in previous cases.[170]

> "The Panel noted, in this case, such factors as the number of products and tariff items carrying different duty rates and tariff bindings, the varying protein contents and the different vegetable, animal and synthetic origins of the protein products before the Panel - not all of which were subject to the EEC measures. Therefore, the Panel concluded that these various protein products could not be considered as 'like products' within the meaning of Articles I and III."[171]

During the discussion in the Council of the Panel Report on "Spain - Measures concerning Domestic Sale of Soyabean Oil"[172] which was noted by the Council and not adopted, representatives of several contracting parties criticized the Panel's conclusion in respect of Article III:4, that the term "like products" meant "more or less the same product", on the basis that this general definition in the Panel Report was too narrow and that past decisions on this term had been made on a case-by-case basis after examining a number of relevant factors.[173]

In the 1992 Panel Report on "United States - Measures Affecting Alcoholic and Malt Beverages"

> "The Panel began its examination of these beer alcohol content distinctions in the named states by considering whether, in the context of Article III:4, low alcohol beer and high alcohol beer should be considered 'like products'. The Panel recalled in this regard its earlier statement on like product determinations and considered that, in the context of Article III, it is essential that such determinations be made not only in the light of such criteria as the products' physical characteristics, but also in the light of the purpose of Article III, which is to ensure that internal taxes and regulations 'not be applied to imported or domestic products so as to afford protection to domestic production'. The purpose of Article III is not to harmonize the internal taxes and regulations of contracting parties, which differ from country to country. In light of these considerations, the Panel was of the view that the particular level at which the distinction between high alcohol and low alcohol beer is made in the various states does not affect its reasonings and findings.

---

[168]*Ibid.*, 39S/118, para. 89.
[169]DS31/R, dated 11 October 1994, paras. 5.47-5.49.
[170]Note 1 at 25S/63 provides: "See for instance BISD II/188, BISD IS/53, BISD II/181, 183."
[171]L/4599, adopted on 14 March 1978, 25S/49, 63, paras. 4.1-4.2. See also material on this report at pages 162, 199 and 160 in this chapter.
[172]L/5142.
[173]C/M/152.

"The Panel recognized that the treatment of imported and domestic products as like products under Article III may have significant implications for the scope of obligations under the General Agreement and for the regulatory autonomy of contracting parties with respect to their internal tax laws and regulations: once products are designated as like products, a regulatory product differentiation, e.g. for standardization or environmental purposes, becomes inconsistent with Article III even if the regulation is not 'applied ... so as afford protection to domestic production'. In the view of the Panel, therefore, it is imperative that the like product determination in the context of Article III be made in such a way that it not unnecessarily infringe upon the regulatory authority and domestic policy options of contracting parties. The Panel recalled its earlier statement that a like product determination under Article III does not prejudge like product determinations made under other Articles of the General Agreement or in other legislative contexts.

"The Panel recognized that on the basis of their physical characteristics, low alcohol beer and high alcohol beer are similar. It then proceeded to examine whether, in the context of Article III, this differentiation in treatment of low alcohol beer and high alcohol beer is such 'as to afford protection to domestic production'. The Panel first noted that both Canadian and United States beer manufacturers produce both high and low alcohol content beer. It then noted that the laws and regulations in question in the various states do not differentiate between imported and domestic beer as such, so that where a state law limits the points of sale of high alcohol content beer or maintains different labelling requirements for such beer, that law applies to all high alcohol content beer, regardless of its origin. The burdens resulting from these regulations thus do not fall more heavily on Canadian than on United States producers. The Panel also noted that although the market for the two types of beer overlaps, there is at the same time evidence of a certain degree of market differentiation and specialization: consumers who purchase low alcohol content beer may be unlikely to purchase beer with a higher alcohol content and vice-versa, and manufacturers target these different market segments in their advertising and marketing.

"The Panel then turned to a consideration of the policy goals and legislative background of the laws regulating the alcohol content of beer. In this regard, the Panel recalled the United States argument that states encouraged the consumption of low alcohol beer over beer with a higher alcohol content specifically for the purposes of protecting human life and health and upholding public morals. The Panel also recalled the Canadian position that the legislative background of laws regulating the alcohol content of beer showed that the federal and state legislatures were more concerned with raising tax revenue than with protecting human health and public morals. On the basis of the evidence submitted, the Panel noted that the relevant laws were passed against the background of the Temperance movement in the United States. It noted further that prior to the repeal of the Eighteenth Amendment of the United States Constitution authorizing Prohibition, amendments to the federal Volstead Act -- the Act which implemented the Eighteenth Amendment -- authorized the sale of low alcohol beer, and that the primary focus of the drafters of these amendments may have been the establishment of a brewing industry which could serve as a new source of tax revenue. However, irrespective of whether the policy background to the laws distinguishing alcohol content of beer was the protection of human health and public morals or the promotion of a new source of government revenue, both the statements of the parties and the legislative history suggest that the alcohol content of beer has not been singled out as a means of favouring domestic producers over foreign producers. The Panel recognized that the level at which the state measures distinguished between low and high alcohol content could arguably have been other than 3.2 per cent by weight. Indeed, as the Panel previously noted, Alabama and Oregon make the distinction at slightly different levels. However, there was no evidence submitted to the Panel that the choice of the particular level has the purpose or effect of affording protection to domestic production".[174]

See also the similar treatment of "like product" in the same Report with regard to an Article III:2 claim concerning the Mississippi excise tax exemption for wine made from scuppernong grapes (page 157).

---

[174] DS23/R, adopted 19 June 1992, 39S/206, 293-294, para. 5.71-5.74.

(3) "in respect of all laws, regulations and requirements"

(a) Requirements applied in individual cases

The 1984 Panel Report on "Canada - Administration of the Foreign Investment Review Act" notes as follows.

> "The Panel could not subscribe to the Canadian view that the word 'requirements' in Article III:4 should be interpreted as 'mandatory rules applying across-the-board' because this latter concept was already more aptly covered by the term 'regulations' and the authors of this provision must have had something different in mind when adding the word 'requirements'. The mere fact that the few disputes that have so far been brought before the CONTRACTING PARTIES regarding the application of Article III:4 have only concerned laws and regulations does not in the view of the Panel justify an assimilation of 'requirements' with 'regulations'. The Panel also considered that, in judging whether a measure is contrary to obligations under Article III:4, it is not relevant whether it applies across-the-board or only in isolated cases. Any interpretation which would exclude case-by-case action would, in the view of the Panel, defeat the purposes of Article III:4.

> "The Panel carefully examined the Canadian view that the purchase undertakings should be considered as private contractual obligations of particular foreign investors vis-à-vis the Canadian government ... The Panel felt ... that ... private contractual obligations entered into by investors should not adversely affect the rights which contracting parties, including contracting parties not involved in the dispute, possess under Article III:4 of the General Agreement and which they can exercise on behalf of their exporters. This applies in particular to the rights deriving from the national treatment principle, which - as stated in Article III:1 - is aimed at preventing the use of internal measures 'so as to afford protection to domestic production'."[175]

(b) Subsidies and other benefits as "requirements"

The 1958 Panel Report on "Italian Discrimination against Imported Agricultural Machinery" examined an Italian law providing special credit terms to farmers for the purchase of agricultural machinery, conditional on the purchase of machinery produced in Italy.[176] The United Kingdom also complained in October 1957 concerning a subsidy granted by the French government to purchasers of agricultural machinery, conditional on the purchase of domestically-produced machinery.[177]

The Panel Report on "Canada - Administration of the Foreign Investment Review Act" provides as follows.

> "... As both parties had agreed that the Foreign Investment Review Act and the Foreign Investment Review Regulations - whilst providing for the possibility of written undertakings - did not make their submission obligatory, the question remained whether the undertakings given in individual cases are to be considered 'requirements' within the meaning of Article III:4. In this respect the Panel noted that Section 9(c) of the Act refers to 'any written undertakings relating to the proposed or actual investment given by any party thereto conditional upon the allowance of the investment' and that Section 21 of the Act states that 'where a person who has given a written undertaking... fails or refuses to comply with such undertaking' a court order may be made 'directing that person to comply with the undertaking'. The Panel noted that written purchase undertakings - leaving aside the manner in which they may have been arrived at (voluntary submission, encouragement, negotiation, etc.) - once they were accepted, became part of the conditions under which the investment proposals were approved, in which case compliance could be legally enforced. The Panel therefore found that the word 'requirements' as used in Article III:4 could be considered a proper description of existing undertakings."[178]

---

[175] L/5504, adopted on 7 February 1984, 30S/140, 159, paras. 5.5-5.6.
[176] L/833, adopted on 23 October 1958, 7S/60.
[177] L/695, SR.12/5.
[178] L/5504, adopted on 7 February 1984, 30S/140, 158, para. 5.4.

In the Panel Report on "EEC - Regulation on Imports of Parts and Components" the Panel examined, *inter alia*, the EEC's acceptance of undertakings under anti-circumvention rules in its anti-dumping legislation, examining whether acceptance of such undertakings to limit the use of imported parts and materials constituted a "requirement" according treatment to imported products less favourable than that accorded to domestic products contrary to Article III:4.

"The Panel recalled that, during the period June 1987 to October 1988, eleven undertakings by parties related to or associated with Japanese manufactures had been accepted by the EEC in investigations under the anti-circumvention provision and that, according to the relevant Commission decisions published in the Official Journal of the European Communities, these undertakings related, *inter alia*, to changes in the sourcing of parts and materials used in assembly or production operations in the Community. The Panel noted that there is no obligation under the EEC's anti-dumping Regulation to offer parts undertakings, to accept suggestions by the EEC Commission to offer such undertakings and to maintain the parts undertakings given. However, the consequence of not offering an undertaking, or of withdrawing an existing undertaking, can be the continuation of procedures that may lead to the imposition of the anti-circumvention duties. Article 10 of Regulation N° 2324/88 states that 'where an undertaking has been withdrawn or where the Commission has reason to believe that it has been violated ... it may ... apply ... antidumping ... duties forthwith on the basis of the facts established before the acceptance of the undertaking'.

"The Panel noted that Article III:4 refers to 'all laws, regulations or requirements affecting (the) internal sale, offering for sale, purchase, transportation, distribution or use'. The Panel considered that the comprehensive coverage of '*all* laws, regulations or requirements *affecting*' (emphasis added) the internal sale, etc. of imported products suggests that not only requirements which an enterprise is legally bound to carry out, such as those examined by the 'FIRA Panel' (BISD 30S/140, 158), but also those which an enterprise voluntarily accepts in order to obtain an advantage from the government constitute 'requirements' within the meaning of that provision. The Panel noted that the EEC made the grant of an advantage, namely the suspension of proceedings under the anti-circumvention provision, dependent on undertakings to limit the use of parts or materials of Japanese origin without imposing similar limitations on the use of like products of EEC or other origin, hence dependent on undertakings to accord treatment to imported products less favourable than that accorded to like products of national origin in respect of their internal use. The Panel therefore concluded that the decisions of the EEC to suspend proceedings under Article 13:10 conditional on undertakings by enterprises in the EEC to limit the use of parts or materials originating in Japan in their assembly or production operations are inconsistent with Article III:4."[179]

In this connection see also the unadopted 1994 Panel Report on "EEC - Import Régime for Bananas".[180]

(c) Requirements associated with the regulation of international investment

The 1984 Panel Report on "Canada - Administration of the Foreign Investment Review Act" examined, *inter alia*, the argument of Canada that in accordance with Article XXIX:1 of the General Agreement, the word "requirements" in Article III:4 of the General Agreement should be interpreted in the light of Article 12 of the Havana Charter concerning the right to regulate foreign investment.

"... the Panel could not subscribe to the assumption that the drafters of Article III had intended the term 'requirements' to exclude requirements connected with the regulation of international investments and did not find anything in the negotiating history, the wording, the objectives and the subsequent application of Article III which would support such an interpretation."[181]

---

[179]L/6657, adopted on 16 May 1990, 37S/132, 197, para. 5.20-5.21.
[180]DS38/R, dated 11 February 1994, paras. 143-148.
[181]L/5504, adopted on 7 February 1984, 30S/140, 162, para. 5.12.

(4) "affecting"

The 1958 Panel Report on "Italian Discrimination Against Imported Agricultural Machinery," which examined the consistency with Article III:4 of an Italian law providing special credit facilities to farmers for the purchase of agricultural machinery produced in Italy, noted that

> "... the text of paragraph 4 referred both in English and French to laws and regulations and requirements *affecting* internal sale, purchase, etc., and not to laws, regulations and requirements governing the conditions of sale or purchase. The selection of the word 'affecting' would imply, in the opinion of the Panel, that the drafters of the Article intended to cover in paragraph 4 not only the laws and regulations which directly governed the conditions of sale or purchase but also any laws or regulations which might adversely modify the conditions of competition between the domestic and imported products on the internal market".[182]

The 1989 Panel Report on "United States - Section 337 of the Tariff Act of 1930" also addressed the meaning of "affecting" in Article III:4.

> "... The Panel first addressed the issue of whether only substantive laws, regulations and requirements or also procedural laws, regulations and requirements can be regarded as 'affecting' the internal sale of imported products. The positions of the United States and the Community on this were different. The Panel noted that the text of Article III:4 makes no distinction between substantive and procedural laws, regulations or requirements and it was not aware of anything in the drafting history that suggests that such a distinction should be made. A previous Panel had found that 'the selection of the word 'affecting' would imply ... that the drafters of the Article intended to cover in paragraph 4 not only the laws and regulations which directly governed the conditions of sale or purchase but also any laws or regulations which might adversely modify the conditions of competition between the domestic and imported products on the internal market.'[183] In the Panel's view, enforcement procedures cannot be separated from the substantive provisions they serve to enforce. If the procedural provisions of internal law were not covered by Article III:4, contracting parties could escape the national treatment standard by enforcing substantive law, itself meeting the national treatment standard, through procedures less favourable to imported products than to like products of national origin. The interpretation suggested by the United States would therefore defeat the purpose of Article III, which is to ensure that internal measures 'not be applied to imported or domestic products so as to afford protection to domestic production' (Article III:1). The fact that Section 337 is used as a means for the enforcement of United States patent law at the border does not provide an escape from the applicability of Article III:4; the interpretative note to Article III states that any law, regulation or requirement affecting the internal sale of products that is enforced in the case of the imported product at the time or point of importation is nevertheless subject to the provisions of Article III. Nor could the applicability of Article III:4 be denied on the ground that most of the procedures in the case before the Panel are applied to persons rather than products, since the factor determining whether persons might be susceptible to Section 337 proceedings or federal district court procedures is the source of the challenged products, that is whether they are of United States origin or imported. For these reasons, the Panel found that the procedures under Section 337 come within the concept of 'laws, regulations and requirements' affecting the internal sale of imported products, as set out in Article III of the General Agreement."[184]

In this connection see also the unadopted Panel Report of 1994 on "United States - Taxes on Automobiles".[185]

The 1991 Panel Report on "United States - Restrictions on Imports of Tuna," which has not been adopted, examined a US prohibition on the imports of tuna and tuna products from Mexico imposed under the

---

[182] L/833, adopted on 23 October 1958, 7S/60, 64, para. 12.

[183] The note to this sentence refers to the Panel Report on "Italian Discrimination Against Imported Agricultural Machinery," adopted on 23 October 1958, 7S/60, para. 12.

[184] L/6439, adopted on 7 November 1989, 36S/345, 385-386, para. 5.10.

[185] DS31/R, dated 11 October 1994, paras. 5.45-5.46.

US Marine Mammal Protection Act because of the incidental taking of dolphins during tuna fishing by the Mexican tuna fleet. The Panel found that

"... The text of Article III:1 refers to the application to imported or domestic *products* of 'laws, regulations and requirements affecting the internal sale ... of *products*' and 'internal quantitative regulations requiring the mixture, processing or use of *products*'; it sets forth the principle that such regulations on *products* not be applied so as to afford protection to domestic production. Article III:4 refers solely to laws, regulations and requirements affecting the internal sale, etc. of *products*. This suggests that Article III covers only measures affecting products as such. ...

"A previous panel had found that Article III:2, first sentence, 'obliges contracting parties to establish certain competitive conditions for imported *products* in relation to domestic *products*'.[186] Another panel had found that the words 'treatment no less favourable' in Article III:4 call for effective equality of opportunities for imported *products* in respect of the application of laws, regulations or requirements affecting the sale, offering for sale, purchase, transportation, distribution or use of *products*, and that this standard has to be understood as applicable to each individual case of imported *products*.[187] It was apparent to the Panel that the comparison implied was necessarily one between the measures applied to imported products and the measures applied to like domestic products.

"The Panel considered that, as Article III applied the national treatment principle to both regulations and internal taxes, the provisions of Article III:4 applicable to regulations should be interpreted taking into account interpretations by the CONTRACTING PARTIES of the provisions of Article III:2 applicable to taxes. The Panel noted in this context that the Working Party Report on Border Tax Adjustments, adopted by the CONTRACTING PARTIES in 1970, had concluded that

'... there was convergence of views to the effect that *taxes directly levied on products were eligible for tax adjustment* ... Furthermore, the Working Party concluded that there was convergence of views to the effect that certain taxes that were not directly levied on products were not eligible for adjustment, [such as] social security charges whether on employers or employees and payroll taxes.'[188]

"Thus, under the national treatment principle of Article III, contracting parties may apply border tax adjustments with regard to those taxes that are borne by products, but not for domestic taxes not directly levied on products (such as corporate income taxes). Consequently, the Note Ad Article III covers only internal taxes that are borne by products. The Panel considered that it would be inconsistent to limit the application of this Note to taxes that are borne by products while permitting its application to regulations not applied to the product as such.

"The Panel further concluded that, even if the provisions of the MMPA enforcing the tuna harvesting regulations (in particular those providing for the seizure of cargo as a penalty for violation of the Act) were regarded as regulating the sale of tuna as a product, the United States import prohibition would not meet the requirements of Article III. As pointed out ... above, Article III:4 calls for a comparison of the treatment of imported tuna *as a product* with that of domestic tuna *as a product*. Regulations governing the taking of dolphins incidental to the taking of tuna could not possibly affect tuna as a product. Article III:4 therefore obliges the United States to accord treatment to Mexican tuna no less favourable than that accorded to United States tuna, whether or not the incidental taking of dolphins by Mexican vessels corresponds to that of United States vessels."[189]

---

[186] A note to this paragraph refers to the Panel report on "United States - Taxes on Petroleum and Certain Imported Substances", adopted 17 June 1987, BISD 34S/136, 158, para. 5.1.9.

[187] A note to this paragraph refers to the Panel Report on "United States - Section 337 of the Tariff Act of 1930", adopted 7 November 1989, BISD 36S/345, 386-7, paras. 5.11, 5.14.

[188] A note to this paragraph refers to 18S/97, 100-101, para. 14.

[189] DS21/R (unadopted), dated 3 September 1991, 39S/155, 194-195, paras. 5.11-5.13, 5.15.

In this connection see also the unadopted Panel Report of 1994 on "United States - Taxes on Automobiles".[190]

(5) "internal sale, offering for sale, purchase, transportation, distribution or use"

(a) Standardization of products

The Report of Sub-Committee A of the Third Committee at the Havana Conference, which considered Article 18 of the Charter (on national treatment), notes as follows:

> "The Norwegian delegation had proposed to insert a new paragraph in Article 18 to make sure that the provisions of this Article would not apply to laws, regulations and requirements which have the purpose of standardizing domestic products in order to improve the quality or to reduce costs of production, or have the purpose of facilitating an improved organization of internal industry, provided they have no harmful effect on the expansion of international trade. The Sub-Committee was of the opinion that this amendment would not be necessary because the Article as drafted would permit the use of internal regulations required to enforce standards".[191]

(b) Minimum and maximum price regulations

The 1992 Panel Report on "Canada - Import, Distribution and Sale of Certain Alcoholic Drinks by Provincial Marketing Agencies" examined minimum prices maintained in certain provinces of Canada. The Panel found that the minimum price requirement fell under Article III, not Article XI (see page 203 below).

> "The Panel noted that minimum prices applied equally to imported and domestic beer did not necessarily accord equal conditions of competition to imported and domestic beer. Whenever they prevented imported beer from being supplied at a price below that of domestic beer, they accorded in fact treatment to imported beer less favourable than that accorded to domestic beer: when they were set at the level at which domestic brewers supplied beer - as was presently the case in New Brunswick and Newfoundland - they did not change the competitive opportunities accorded to domestic beer but did affect the competitive opportunities of imported beer which could otherwise be supplied below the minimum price. The Panel noted, moreover, that one of the basic purposes of Article III was to ensure that the contracting parties' internal charges and regulations were not such as to frustrate the effect of tariff concessions granted under Article II ...

> "The Panel considered that the case before it did not require a general finding on the consistency of minimum prices with Article III:4. However, it did consider that the above considerations justified the conclusion that the maintenance by an import and sales monopoly of a minimum price for an imported product at a level at which a directly competing, higher-priced domestic product was supplied was inconsistent with Article III:4."[192]

The 1992 Panel Report on "United States - Measures Affecting Alcoholic and Malt Beverages" examined "price affirmation requirements" (maximum price levels) in the states of Massachusetts and Rhode Island.

> "The Panel noted that the price affirmation measures apply with respect to sales of alcoholic beverages to wholesalers, and that in-state producers are not required to sell through wholesalers whereas out-of-state and foreign producers are required to do so. ... The Panel considered that the price affirmation measures of Massachusetts and Rhode Island prevent the imported alcoholic beverages from being priced in accordance with commercial considerations in that imported products may not be

---

[190] DS31/R, dated 11 October 1994, paras. 5.52-5.55.
[191] Havana Reports, p. 64, para. 49, reflecting E/CONF.2/C.3/A/W.35, p. 1-2 (withdrawal of Norwegian amendment relating to mixing requirements used to enforce standards (see page 183) on the understanding that this statement would be inserted in the Sub-Committee's Report).
[192] DS17/R, adopted 18 February 1992, 39S/27, 84-85, paras. 5.30-5.31.

offered below the price of these products in neighbouring states. In the view of the Panel, these measures thus accord less favourable treatment to imported products than to the like domestic products with respect to their internal sale and offering for sale, inconsistent with Article III:4."[193]

(c)   Requirements affecting internal offering for sale

The 1988 Panel Report on "Canada - Import, Distribution and Sale of Alcoholic Drinks by Canadian Provincial Marketing Agencies" examined, *inter alia*, the application by provincial liquor boards of practices concerning listing and delisting of alcoholic beverages for sale, and availability of points of sale, which discriminated against imported alcoholic beverages. The Panel treated these measures as restrictions made effective through state-trading operations contrary to Article XI:1 and considered that it was therefore not necessary to decide whether the practices were contrary to Article III:4. "However, the Panel saw great force in the argument that Article III:4 was also applicable to state-trading enterprises at least when the monopoly of the importation and monopoly of the distribution in the domestic markets were combined, as was the case of the provincial liquor boards in Canada. This interpretation was confirmed *e contrario* by the wording of Article III:8(a)".[194]

The 1992 Panel Report on "Canada - Import, Distribution and Sale of Certain Alcoholic Drinks by Provincial Marketing Agencies" notes as follows.

> "The Panel ... turned to the United States claim that the practice of the liquor boards of Ontario to limit listing of imported beer to the six-pack size while according listings in different package sizes to domestic beer was inconsistent with the General Agreement. The Panel noted that this package-size requirement, though implemented as a listing requirement, was in fact a requirement that did not affect the importation of beer as such but rather its offering for sale in certain liquor board outlets. The Panel therefore considered that this requirement fell under Article III:4. ... The Panel *found* that the imposition of the six-pack configuration requirement on imported beer but not on domestic beer was inconsistent with that provision."[195]

The 1992 Panel Report on "United States - Measures Affecting Alcoholic and Malt Beverages" examined the requirement, imposed by certain states in the US, that imported beer and wine be sold only through in-state wholesalers or other middlemen, while some in-state like products were permitted to be sold directly to retailers, and in some cases at retail on producers' premises.

> "In the view of the Panel, therefore, the requirement that imported beer and wine be distributed through in-state wholesalers or other middlemen, when no such obligation to distribute through wholesalers exists with respect to in-state like domestic products, results in 'treatment ... less favourable than that accorded to like products' from domestic producers, inconsistent with Article III:4. The Panel considered that even where Canadian producers have the right to establish in-state wholesalers, as is the case in some states, subject to varying conditions, the fact remains that the wholesale level represents another level of distribution which in-state product is not required to use."[196]

See also at page 167 above. The same Panel also examined the exemption of Mississippi-produced wine from "local option" rules prohibiting sale of alcoholic beverages in "dry" subdivisions of the state of Mississippi.

> " ... The Panel noted that the local option law in Mississippi permits wines produced in the state to continue to be sold in those political subdivisions of the state that choose to reinstate prohibition laws, while prohibiting out-of-state and imported wines from being sold in those same subdivisions. The Panel considered that the Mississippi local option law, on its face, accords less favourable treatment to imported wine than to wine of domestic origin, because domestic wine produced in-state may continue to

---

[193]DS23/R, adopted 19 June 1992, 39S/206, 290, para. 5.59.
[194]L/6304, adopted 22 March 1988, 35S/37, 90, para. 4.26.
[195]DS17/R, adopted 18 February 1992, 39S/27, 75, para. 5.4.
[196]DS23/R, adopted 19 June 1992, 39S/206, 280, para. 5.32.

be sold even where a local political subdivision prohibits the sale of imported wine. The Mississippi law would therefore appear to be inconsistent with Article III:4."[197]

The same Panel also examined the listing requirements of state-operated liquor stores in certain US states.

"Having regard to the past panel decisions and the record in the instant case, the present Panel was of the view that the listing and delisting practices here at issue do not affect importation as such into the United States and should be examined under Article III:4. The Panel further noted that the issue is not whether the practices in the various states affect the right of importation as such, in that they clearly apply to both domestic (out-of-state) and imported wines; rather, the issue is whether the listing and delisting practices accord less favourable treatment -- in terms of competitive opportunities -- to imported wine than that accorded to the like domestic product. Consequently, the Panel decided to analyze the state listing and delisting practices as internal measures under Article III:4."[198]

(d) Regulations on quality or quantity of products consumed

The 1990 Panel Report on "Thailand - Restrictions on importation of and internal taxes on cigarettes" examined the argument of the United States that Thailand could achieve its public health objectives through internal measures consistent with Article III:4 and that the inconsistency with Article XI:1 could therefore not be considered to be 'necessary' within the meaning of Article XX(b).

"The Panel noted that the principal health objectives advanced by Thailand to justify its import restrictions were to protect the public from harmful ingredients in imported cigarettes, and to reduce the consumption of cigarettes in Thailand. The measures could thus be seen as intended to ensure the quality and reduce the quantity of cigarettes sold in Thailand.

"The Panel then examined whether the Thai concerns about the *quality* of cigarettes consumed in Thailand could be met with measures consistent, or less inconsistent, with the General Agreement. It noted that other countries had introduced strict, non-discriminatory labelling and ingredient disclosure regulations which allowed governments to control, and the public to be informed of, the content of cigarettes. A non-discriminatory regulation implemented on a national treatment basis in accordance with Article III:4 requiring complete disclosure of ingredients, coupled with a ban on unhealthy substances, would be an alternative consistent with the General Agreement. The Panel considered that Thailand could reasonably be expected to take such measures to address the quality-related policy objectives it now pursues through an import ban on all cigarettes whatever their ingredients.

"The Panel then considered whether Thai concerns about the *quantity* of cigarettes consumed in Thailand could be met by measures reasonably available to it and consistent, or less inconsistent, with the General Agreement. The Panel first examined how Thailand might reduce the *demand* for cigarettes in a manner consistent with the General Agreement. The Panel noted the view expressed by the WHO that the demand for cigarettes, in particular the initial demand for cigarettes by the young, was influenced by cigarette advertisements and that bans on advertisement could therefore curb such demand. At the Forty-third World Health Assembly a resolution was approved stating that the WHO is:

'Encouraged by ... recent information demonstrating the effectiveness of tobacco control strategies, and in particular ... comprehensive legislative bans and other restrictive measures to effectively control the direct and the indirect advertising, promotion and sponsorship of tobacco'.[199]

---

[197]*Ibid.*, 39S/289, para. 5.56.
[198]DS23/R, adopted 19 June 1992, 39S/206, 292, para. 5.63.
[199]Note 3 to this paragraph provides: "Forty-third World Health Assembly, Fourteenth plenary meeting, Agenda Item 10, 17 May 1990 (A43/VR/14; WHA43.16)."

"The resolution goes on to urge all member states of the WHO

'to consider including in their tobacco control strategies plans for legislation or other effective measures at the appropriate government level providing for: ...

'(c) progressive restrictions and concerted actions to eliminate eventually all direct and indirect advertising, promotion and sponsorship concerning tobacco'

"A ban on the advertisement of cigarettes of both domestic and foreign origin would normally meet the requirements of Article III:4. It might be argued that such a general ban on all cigarette advertising would create unequal competitive opportunities between the existing Thai supplier of cigarettes and new, foreign suppliers and was therefore contrary to Article III:4.[200] Even if this argument were accepted, such an inconsistency would have to be regarded as unavoidable and therefore necessary within the meaning of Article XX(b) because additional advertising rights would risk stimulating demand for cigarettes. The Panel noted that Thailand had already implemented some non-discriminatory controls on demand, including information programmes, bans on direct and indirect advertising, warnings on cigarette packs, and bans on smoking in certain public places.

"The Panel then examined how Thailand might restrict the *supply* of cigarettes in a manner consistent with the General Agreement. The Panel noted that contracting parties may maintain governmental monopolies, such as the Thai Tobacco Monopoly, on the importation and domestic sale of products.[201] The Thai Government may use this monopoly to regulate the overall supply of cigarettes, their prices and their retail availability provided it thereby does not accord imported cigarettes less favourable treatment than domestic cigarettes or act inconsistently with any commitments assumed under its Schedule of Concessions.[202] As to the pricing of cigarettes, the Panel noted that the Forty-third World Health Assembly, in its resolution cited above, stated that it was:

'Encouraged by ... recent information demonstrating the effectiveness of tobacco control strategies, and in particular ... policies to achieve progressive increases in the real price of tobacco'.

"It accordingly urged all member states

'to consider including in their tobacco control strategies plans for ... progressive financial measures aimed at discouraging the use of tobacco'[203]

"For these reasons the Panel could not accept the argument of Thailand that competition between imported and domestic cigarettes would necessarily lead to an increase in the total sales of cigarettes and that Thailand therefore had no option but to prohibit cigarette imports.

"The Panel then examined further the resolutions of the WHO on smoking which the WHO made available. It noted that the health measures recommended by the WHO in these resolutions were non-discriminatory and concerned all, not just imported, cigarettes. The Panel also examined the Report of the WHO Expert Committee on Smoking Control Strategies in Developing Countries. The Panel observed that a common consequence of import restrictions was the promotion of domestic production and the fostering of interests in the maintenance of that production and that the WHO Expert Committee had made the following recommendation relevant in this respect:

'Where tobacco is already a commercial crop every effort should be made to reduce its role in the national economy, and to investigate alternative uses of land and labour. The existence of a

---

[200]Note 2 to this sentence provides: "On the requirement of equal competitive opportunities, see the Report of the panel on 'United States - Section 337 of the Tariff Act of 1930' (L/6439, paragraph 5.26, adopted on 7 November 1989)."

[201]Note 1 on page 37S/225 provides: "Cf. Articles III:4, XVII and XX(d)."

[202]Note 2 on page 37S/225 provides: "Cf. Articles III:2 and 4 and II:4."

[203]Note 3 on page 37S/225 provides: "Forty-third World Health Assembly, Fourteenth plenary meeting, Agenda Item 10, 17 May 1990 (A43/VR/14; WHA43.16)."

tobacco industry of any kind should not be permitted to interfere with the implementation of educational and other measures to control smoking'.[204]

"In sum, the Panel considered that there were various measures consistent with the General Agreement which were reasonably available to Thailand to control the quality and quantity of cigarettes smoked and which, taken together, could achieve the health policy goals that the Thai government pursues by restricting the importation of cigarettes inconsistently with Article XI:1. The Panel found therefore that Thailand's practice of permitting the sale of domestic cigarettes while not permitting the importation of foreign cigarettes was an inconsistency with the General Agreement not 'necessary' within the meaning of Article XX(b)."[205]

In the November 1990 Council discussion on adoption of this Panel Report, the representative of Thailand stated that "Thailand took heart from the report that a set of GATT-consistent measures could be taken to control both the supply of and demand for cigarettes, as long as they were applied to both domestic and imported cigarettes on a national-treatment basis".[206]

(e) Marking requirements

The 1956 Working Party Report on "Certificates of Origin, Marks of Origin, Consular Formalities" notes "that the question of additional marking requirements, such as an obligation to add the name of the producer or the place of origin or the formula of the product, should not be brought within the scope of any recommendation dealing with the problem of marks of origin. The point was stressed that requirements going beyond the obligation to indicate origin would not be consistent with the provisions of Article III, if the same requirements did not apply to domestic producers of like products".[207] See also the 1955 complaint referred to above at page 162 regarding a requirement to display a placard stating "We sell foreign eggs".

See also Article IX.

(f) Measures affecting internal transportation

During discussions on this provision at Geneva in 1947 it was stated that "transportation" referred to "all kinds of transportation, from a man's back to jet-propelled rockets".[208] At the Havana Conference, a proposal to delete the references to transportation in Article III received no support, "on the grounds that these provisions were necessary to prevent indirect protection to domestic products by means of differential transportation charges".[209]

The 1992 Panel Report on "Canada - Import, Distribution and Sale of Certain Alcoholic Drinks by Provincial Marketing Agencies" also examined practices concerning the internal transportation of beer in Canada. The delivery of beer in Canada is controlled or conducted by the provincial liquor boards, which require or permit the delivery of domestic beer by the brewer to the point of sale. Except for two provinces, imported beer must be sold to the provincial liquor board which either require or arrange delivery of the beer to their own distribution centres; the cost of delivery to the point of sale was included in the markup charged on imported beer.

"The Panel first examined the question of whether Article III:4 of the General Agreement permitted contracting parties to apply regulations to imported products that were different from those applied to domestic products. ... The Panel ... considered that the mere fact that imported and domestic beer were subject to different delivery systems was not, in itself, conclusive in establishing inconsistency

---

[204]Note 4 on page 37S/225 provides: "1982 Expert Committee on 'Smoking Control Strategies in Developing Countries', page 69; cited at page 16 in the WHO Submission to the Panel of 19 July 1990."
[205]DS10/R, adopted 7 November 1990, 37S/200, 223-226, paras. 76-81.
[206]C/M/246, 23 November 1990.
[207]L/595, adopted on 17 November 1956, 5S/102, 105-106, para. 13.
[208]EPCT/A/PV/9, p. 43.
[209]E/CONF.2/C.3/A/W.34, p. 4.

with Article III:4 of the General Agreement. The Panel then examined whether the application by Canada of the different delivery systems accorded imported beer treatment no less favourable than that accorded to domestic beer. The Panel ... considered that Article III:4 required Canada to ensure that its regulations affecting the internal transportation of imported beer to points of sale accorded imported beer competitive opportunities at least equal to those accorded to domestic beer and that it was up to Canada to demonstrate that, in spite of the application of different transportation regulations to imported and domestic beer, imported beer was accorded no less favourable treatment in this respect.

"The Panel noted that Canada claimed that it met the requirements of Article III:4 by levying charges for the delivery of imported beer to the points of sale which were no higher than the costs actually incurred by the liquor boards. The Panel, therefore, examined whether Canada, by subjecting imported beer to a levy that corresponded to the actual cost of delivery by the liquor board, offered competitive opportunities to imported beer that were equivalent to the opportunities which would result from the application of the same delivery system to both imported and domestic beer. The Panel noted that such a levy did not necessarily correspond to the cost that the liquor board would incur for the delivery of imported beer if it delivered not only imported but also domestic beer. It could reasonably be assumed that it would, in that case, make economies of scale from which also imported beer could benefit. Nor did such a levy necessarily correspond to the cost of private delivery of imported beer. It could reasonably be assumed that the structure and efficiency of private delivery systems would be different from the systems operated by the liquor boards.

"The Panel further noted that, in order to prove that the levies charged by the liquor boards for delivering imported beer to the points of sale did not exceed the cost of private delivery of such beer, Canada could not base itself on the transportation costs actually incurred by the liquor boards or the domestic breweries; it would have to determine the costs of transporting beer under delivery systems not presently in existence. The Panel felt that, given the inherent difficulties in making such a determination, its result would always be open to challenge. The Panel also noted that, in order to meet its national treatment obligations, Canada did not have to abandon the delivery of imported beer by the liquor boards; it merely had to provide competitive opportunities to imported beer that were at least equal to those accorded to domestic beer, in other words allow for the possibility of private delivery of imported beer. This would enable foreign brewers to choose between liquor-board services and private delivery on purely commercial grounds. If, as claimed by Canada, imported beer did enjoy national treatment, there was no need to prohibit the private delivery of imported beer because the services of the liquor boards would be available at a price at which they could compete successfully with private delivery systems. ..."[210]

The 1992 Panel Report on "United States - Measures Affecting Alcoholic and Malt Beverages" examined the requirement imposed by certain states that alcoholic beverages imported into the state be transported by common carriers authorized to operate as such within the state whereas in-state producers of alcoholic beverages could deliver their product to customers in their own vehicles.

"The Panel noted that Article III:4 requires that imported products be granted treatment no less favourable than that afforded to like domestic products with respect to laws and regulations affecting their transportation. In the view of the Panel, the requirement for imported beer and wine to be transported by common carrier, whereas domestic in-state beer and wine is not so required, may result in additional charges to transport these imported products and therefore prevent imported products from competing on an equal footing with domestic like products. Accordingly, the Panel found the requirement that imported beer and wine be transported by common carrier into the states of Arizona, California, Maine, Mississippi and South Carolina, which requirement does not exist in such states for in-state beer and wine, is inconsistent with Article III:4."[211]

---

[210]DS17/R, adopted 18 February 1992, 39S/27, 78-79, paras. 5.12-5.14.
[211]DS23/R, adopted 19 June 1992, 39S/206, 287, para. 5.50.

(6) "differential internal transportation charges": second sentence of paragraph 4

The second sentence of paragraph 4 was drafted during the discussions of the Preparatory Committee at Geneva by a sub-committee which reviewed (*inter alia*) the Charter article on national treatment. The Report of this sub-committee states:

> "The South African Delegation had objected to the inclusion of the word 'transportation' [in the first sentence of this paragraph] but agreed to its retention subject to the addition of a new sentence clarifying the intention that this paragraph should not be construed to prevent differential transport charges which are based on economic operation of the means of transport and not on the nationality of the product concerned. ... Since the present paragraph 2 [4] relates solely to the question of differential treatment between imported and domestic goods, the inclusion of the last sentence in that paragraph should not be understood to give sanction to the use of artificial measures in the form of differential transport charges designed to divert traffic from one port to another".[212]

The same statement regarding differential transport charges designed to divert traffic from one port to another is repeated in the report of Sub-Committee A of the Third Committee, which considered the national treatment article of the Charter at the Havana Conference.[213] The report also notes: "The Sub-Committee inserted the word 'internal' to make it clear that the phrase 'differential transportation charges' does not refer to international shipping".[214] The Sub-Committee also rejected a proposal to delete the word 'transportation' in the first sentence and delete the second sentence.[215]

Concerning discriminatory internal transportation charges constituting a subsidy, see Article XVI.

7. Paragraphs 5, 6 and 7: internal quantitative regulations (mixing regulations)

(1) Scope of paragraph 5

During discussions at the Geneva session of the Preparatory Committee for the Havana Conference, the representative of Norway stated in connection with one of the proposals to amend this paragraph, "In Norway we would normally have a regulation to define that margarine would include a certain amount of butter. ... For practical purposes [margarine] is produced in Norway ... With regard to butter ... if we decided that, for example, margarine should include 20 percent butter, we would not lay down that that should be totally Norwegian butter, to the exclusion of foreign butter, but, whether or Norwegian or foreign origin, it would be on an equal footing ...".[216] It was stated in reply that

> "The mixing regulation described ... could not be classed as protective in purpose. ... The case presented ... is that of a mixing regulation which may be described as follows:
>
>> "A regulation requiring a product be composed of two or more materials in specified proportions, where all the materials in question are produced domestically in substantial quantities, and where there is no requirement that any specified quantity of any of the materials be of domestic origin.
>
> "Stated in this way, it seems obvious that this case is not intended to be covered by Article [III].
>
>> "The opposite case of mixing regulations ... is where the regulation requires that a certain percentage of a product of domestic origin be used in the production of another product (e.g. that 25 percent domestic wheat be used in making flour). Such a regulation would limit the use of the like foreign product and, hence, would under any interpretation be contrary to [Article III:5].

---

[212]Report to Commission A by the Sub-Committee on Articles 14, 15 and 24, EPCT/174, pp. 6-7.
[213]Havana Reports, p. 64, para. 51; see E/CONF.2/C.3/SR.11 p. 2 (proposal to pick up this statement, citing prewar *Seehafen-Ausnahmstarife* of Germany).
[214]*Ibid.*, para. 50.
[215]*Ibid.*, para. 52.
[216]EPCT/A/PV/9, p. 52-53.

"A third and more difficult case of mixing regulations are regulations which require that in producing an article a certain percentage of a specified material produced domestically be used when there is a competitive imported material which is not produced domestically in substantial quantities. It corresponds in the field of mixing regulations to the type of excise tax sought to be prohibited ... [by Article III:2, second sentence]".[217]

This and other questions were referred to an ad-hoc Sub-committee, the report of which noted:

"The Sub-committee was ... in agreement that under the provisions of Article 18 [III] regulations and taxes would be permitted which, while perhaps having the effect of assisting the production of a particular domestic product (say, butter), are directed as much against the domestic production of another product (say, domestic oleomargarine), of which there was a substantial domestic production, as they are against imports (say, imported oleomargarine)".[218]

This statement was reiterated in the reports adopted at the Havana Conference.

Later, in discussions in the Third Committee at Havana, it was clarified in a statement that:

"... requiring flour mills, for instance, to use twenty-five percent wheat of domestic origin would be considered an internal quantitative regulation relating to 'use' under paragraph 5. The paragraph was also intended to relate to mixing regulations such as the mixture of alcohol and gasoline in the manufacture of motor fuel. ... paragraph 5 would not preclude regulations designed to eke out supplies of short materials or to enforce objective standards".[219]

It was also stated that "If a Member required that fifty percent of the timber used in building should come from domestic sources, the regulation was not related to the mixture nor to the processing of the timber, but to its use".[220]

During the Review Session in 1954-55, "the delegate for Sweden proposed an interpretative note for paragraph 5, on the lines of the statement adopted at the Havana Conference [including the example on butter and oleomargarine] ... After discussion the representative of Sweden expressed his willingness to withdraw his proposal but desired that the Working Party's report should record his statement that the system of levying internal fees on home-produced and imported raw materials for oleomargarine manufacture, as well as on imports of oleomargarine, in order to help in the stabilization of the marketing of butter - which was mentioned in the report of Sub-Committee A of Committee III at Havana and found by that Sub-Committee to be consistent with the terms of Article 18 (Article III of GATT) was still in force. The Working Party took note of the Swedish statement".[221]

In the 1994 panel report on "United States - Measures Affecting the Importation, Internal Sale and Use of Tobacco", the panel examined a claim that the US' Domestic Marketing Assessment ("DMA") was inconsistent with Article III:5. The DMA legislation required each "domestic manufacturer of cigarettes", as defined in the legislation, to certify to the Secretary of the U.S. Department of Agriculture ("USDA") for each calendar year, the percentage of domestically produced tobacco used by such manufacturer to produce cigarettes during the year. A domestic manufacturer that failed to make such a certification or to use at least 75 per cent domestic tobacco was subject to penalties in the form of a nonrefundable marketing assessment (i.e. the DMA) and was required to purchase additional quantities of domestic burley and flue-cured tobacco.

---

[217] EPCT/A/SR/10 p. 2-3, EPCT/W/181, p. 10.
[218] EPCT/174, p. 8-9; statement repeated verbatim in Havana Reports, p. 64, para. 54.
[219] E/CONF.2/C.3/SR.40, p. 6.
[220] *Ibid.*, p. 7.
[221] L/329, Report of the Review Working Party on "Schedules and Customs Administration", adopted 26 February 1955, 3S/205, 210, para. 9.

"As to the applicability of Article III:5, first sentence, to the DMA, the Panel considered that it first had to determine whether the United States had established an 'internal quantitative regulation relating to the mixture, processing or use of products in specified amounts or proportions ...'. The Panel noted the following in this respect:

"(a) First, the DMA was established by an Act of the U.S. Congress, Section 1106(a) of the 1993 Budget Act, and was implemented through regulations of USDA. The effective date for the DMA was 1 January 1994. It thus constituted a *regulation* within the meaning of Article III:5.

"(b) Second, the Panel noted that the opening sentence of the DMA legislative provision, Section 1106(a) of the 1993 Budget Act, stated:

> 'CERTIFICATION. A *domestic manufacturer* of cigarettes *shall certify* to the Secretary, for each calendar year, the percentage of the quantity of tobacco used by the manufacturer to produce cigarettes during the year that is produced in the United States'. (*emphasis added*)

"The DMA was thus an internal regulation imposed on domestic manufacturers of cigarettes.

"(c) Third, the Panel noted that the second sub-paragraph of the DMA legislative provision stated:

> 'PENALTIES. In General. Subject to subsection (f) [exception for crop losses due to natural disasters], a *domestic manufacturer of cigarettes that has failed*, as determined by the Secretary after notice and opportunity for a hearing, to *use in the manufacture of cigarettes* during a calendar year a *quantity of tobacco grown in the United States that is at least 75 percent of the total quantity of tobacco used* by the manufacturer or to comply with subsection (a) [certification requirement], *shall be subject to* the requirements of subsections (c), (d) and (e) [*penalties* in the form of a nonrefundable marketing assessment and a required purchase of additional quantities of domestic burley and flue-cured tobacco]'. (*emphasis added*)

"The DMA was thus a *quantitative* regulation in that it set a minimum *specified proportion* of 75 per cent for the use of U.S. tobacco in manufacturing cigarettes.

"(d) Fourth, the DMA was an internal quantitative regulation relating to the *use* of a product, in that it *required the use* of U.S. domestically grown tobacco.

"The Panel thus found that the DMA was an 'internal quantitative regulation relating to the ... use of products in specified amounts or proportions ...', within the meaning of the first part of the first sentence of Article III:5.

"The Panel then turned to a consideration of whether the DMA 'requires, directly or indirectly, that any specified amount or proportion of any product which is the subject of the regulation must be supplied from domestic sources', as provided in the second part of the first sentence of Article III:5. The Panel noted the following in this respect:

"(a) The DMA required each domestic manufacturer of cigarettes to certify to the Secretary of USDA, for each calendar year, the percentage of the quantity of tobacco used by the manufacturer to produce cigarettes during the year that was produced in the United States.

"(b) Subject to an exception dealing with crop losses due to disasters, a domestic manufacturer that failed to make the required certification or to use at least 75 per cent domestic tobacco was subject to penalties including the required purchase of additional domestic tobacco.

"The Panel thus concluded that the DMA was an internal quantitative regulation relating to the use of tobacco in specified amounts or proportions which required, directly or indirectly, that a minimum specified proportion of tobacco be supplied from domestic sources, inconsistently with Article III:5, first sentence."[222]

(2) *"otherwise apply internal quantitative regulations in a manner contrary to the principles set forth in paragraph 1"*

See Interpretative Note *ad* Article III, paragraph 5.

The 1978 Panel Report on "EEC - Measures on Animal Feed Proteins" examined the measures in question in relation to this paragraph.

"Given the reference in Article III:5, second sentence, to Article III:1, the Panel then examined the consistency of the EEC Regulation as an 'internal quantitative regulation' with the provisions of Article III:1, particularly as to whether the Regulation afforded protection to domestic production. The Panel noted that the EEC Regulation considered, in its own terms, that denatured skimmed milk powder was an important source of protein which could be used in feedingstuffs. The Panel also noted that surplus stocks could originate either from domestic production or imports, but that the intervention agencies from which the buyers of vegetable proteins had to purchase a certain quantity of denatured skimmed milk powder only held domestically produced products. The Panel further noted that, although globally about 15 per cent of the EEC apparent consumption of vegetable protein was supplied from domestic sources, not all the individual products subject to the EEC measures were produced domestically in substantial quantities.

"The Panel concluded that the measures provided for by the Regulation with a view to ensuring the sale of a given quantity of skimmed milk powder protected this product in a manner contrary to the principles of Article III:1 and to the provisions of Article III:5, second sentence."[223]

The interpretation of the second sentence of Article III:5 was the subject of the Panel Report on "Spain - Measures concerning Domestic Sale of Soyabean Oil",[224] which was not adopted, and of subsequent discussions in the Council. Several contracting parties expressed reservations with regard to the Panel's interpretation of Article III. The Council took note of the Report as well as of the statements made in the discussion.[225]

In Council discussions in 1982, the European Communities expressed the view that Finland's decision to make exports of leather footwear to the Soviet Union subject, *inter alia*, to the condition that the soles incorporated in such footwear should be of domestic origin, was a violation of certain provisions of the General Agreement, particularly Article III.[226] Finland considered the claim to be without legal justification and stated, inter alia, that "the economic rationale of restricting third country participation in bilateral clearing trade in non-convertible currencies with a non-contracting party ought to be evident".[227]

In the 1994 Panel Report on "United States - Measures Affecting the Importation, Internal Sale and Use of Tobacco"

"... the Panel noted that the second sentence of Article III:5 is subsidiary to the first sentence thereof, as the second sentence only becomes relevant where a contracting party is '*otherwise* apply[ing] internal quantitative regulations in a manner contrary to the principles set forth in paragraph 1", *i.e.* 'so as to afford protection to domestic production'. The Panel was therefore of the view that, in light of the

---

[222]DS44/R, adopted on 4 October 1994, paras. 67-68.
[223]L/4599, adopted on 14 March 1978, 25S/49, 65, paras. 4.7-4.8.
[224]L/5142.
[225]C/M/152, L/5142, L/5161, L/5188.
[226]C/M/161, L/5369.
[227]C/M/161, L/5394.

finding of inconsistency of the DMA with Article III:5, first sentence, it would not be necessary to examine the consistency of the DMA with Article III:5, second sentence.[228]

(3) Special customs treatment granted conditional on mixing or use of the imported product with domestic products

The Report of Sub-Committee A of the Third Committee at the Havana Conference, which considered Article 18 of the Charter (on national treatment), notes as follows:

"The Sub-Committee is of the opinion that paragraph 5 ... would not prohibit the continuance of a tariff system which permits the entry of the product at a rate of duty lower than the normal tariff rate, provided the product is mixed or used with a certain proportion of a similar product of national origin. The Sub-Committee considered that such a provision would not be regarded as an internal quantitative regulation in terms of this paragraph for the reason that the use of a percentage of the local product is not made compulsory, nor is the import of the product in any way restricted".[229]

(4) Application of mixing regulations in time of shortages

The question of the application of mixing regulations in time of shortages was fully discussed at Havana.[230] The main points made in the course of the discussion were as follows.

-- "... provided the regulation did not require that the product to be mixed had to be of domestic origin, or provided that the regulation was not imposed for protective purposes, then such a regulation would not contravene the Article."[231]

-- In the event that regulations imposed in respect of shortages of raw materials had protective effects, "they would be covered by Article 43" [XX].[232]

Further, a clarification was given in the following statement:

"... under paragraph 5 a Member could not establish a mixing regulation which protected a domestic product as against an imported product during periods when there was no shortage in order that the industry in question would be in existence in the event of a future shortage".[233]

(5) Paragraph 6: existing mixing regulations and their alteration

The report of the ad-hoc Geneva Sub-committee which examined the national treatment provisions of the Charter notes:

"The [New York Draft provision] is aimed at preventing only those internal quantitative regulations which are clearly directed against imported products for the purposes of protecting domestic products. The new text removes the requirement that existing internal quantitative regulations not expressly approved by the Organization should be terminated at the expiration of one year after the entry into force of the Charter. The revised draft would permit the continuation of regulations in force on 1 July 1939 or 10 April 1947, whichever date the Member selects, subject to the requirement that such requirements as are retained shall be negotiable and shall not be altered to the detriment of imports. The

---

[228] DS44/R, adopted on 4 October 1994, para. 69. The footnote to this paragraph provides: "Cf. Report of the panel on United States - Measures Affecting Alcoholic and Malt Beverages, adopted on 19 June 1992, BISD 39S/206, 270, where that panel found that it would not be appropriate to consider Canada's Article III:1 allegations to the extent that it found the U.S. measures to be inconsistent with the more specific provisions of Articles III:2 and III:4."

[229] EPCT/174, p. 8.

[230] E/CONF.2/C.3/SR.40, pp. 5-8; also earlier discussion at E/CONF.2/C.3/A/W.38, p. 1-2 (discussing regulation requiring mixing of imported gasoline with domestic alcohol).

[231] E/CONF.2/C.3/SR.40, p. 6.

[232] E/CONF.2/C.3/SR.40, p. 5.

[233] E/CONF.2/C.3/SR.40, p. 7.

alternative dates were thought desirable by the Sub-Committee in order particularly to take account of the departures from normal pre-war practices rendered necessary by war-time or post-war emergencies".[234]

10 April 1947 was the opening date of the Second Session of the Preparatory Committee at Geneva. During the Havana Conference, it was decided to add a third alternative date for existing mixing regulations, the date of the signing of the Havana Conference Final Act (24 March 1948).[235] This date was chosen rather than the date of entry into force of the Charter "to avoid giving Members an opportunity to impose new regulations which would be contrary to paragraph [5]".[236]

The Report of Sub-Committee A of the Third Committee at the Havana Conference, which considered Article 18 of the Charter (on national treatment), notes that "a Member would be free to alter the details of an existing regulation provided that such alterations do not result in changing the overall effect of the regulation to the detriment of imports".[237] During the Review Session of 1954-55, it was proposed that an interpretative note to Article III:6 be added on the lines of this statement; however,

> "The Working Party considered that it was not necessary to insert a note in the Agreement as paragraph 6 is to be interpreted in this sense, with the understanding that such changes would be of a minor character and would not apply to a concession provided for in a schedule to the General Agreement".[238]

Sub-Committee A at Havana also noted in its report that:

> "The delegate from Ireland inquired whether the phrase 'shall not be modified to the detriment of imports' would permit changes in the amounts or proportions of a product required to be mixed under an existing regulation in Ireland, which changes are the result of changes in crops from year to year. The Sub-Committee decided that since the regulation in question clearly contemplates such changes, the changes would not be precluded by paragraph 6 …".[239]

The Working Party on "The Haitian Tobacco Monopoly" in 1955 examined whether the licensing of tobacco imports by the Tobacco Régie required a release under the provisions of Article XVIII:12 (prior to the Review Session amendments to Article XVIII). "The representative of Haiti declared that the licensing system served solely to enforce the internal quantitative regulations of the Régie and did not impose any additional limitation of the quantity that may be imported. The Working Party therefore took the view that in these circumstances Article XI would not apply, that the import control should be considered under the terms of the exception in Article [XX:(d)] and that the internal regulation to which it relates should be considered under paragraphs 5 and 6 of Article III." The mixing regulation on tobacco was found to have been in effect on one of the dates specified in Article III:6. "The representative of Haiti also informed the Working Party that the provisions of paragraph 6 were fully complied with in that the regulation in force on the base date had not been altered to the detriment of imports. In these circumstances the Working Party did not see anything in paragraphs 5 or 6 of Article III which required a release under Article XVIII for these measures."[240]

---

[234]EPCT/174, p. 7-8.
[235]Havana Reports, p. 65, para. 60.
[236]E/CONF.2/C.3/SR.40, p. 9.
[237]Havana Reports, p. 65, para. 58.
[238]Report of the Review Working Party on "Schedules and Customs Administration", L/329, adopted on 26 February 1955, 3S/205, 211, para. 11.
[239]Havana Reports, p. 65, para. 59; see also E/CONF.2/C.3/W.35 p. 4 (regulation in question required mixing of imported petroleum with industrial alcohol made from domestic potatoes).
[240]L/454, adopted on 22 November 1955, 4S/38, 39-40, paras. 9-10. Before the revision of Article XVIII in the Review Session, Article XVIII:12 provided for notification and concurrence with regard to certain measures affecting imports which were not otherwise permitted by the General Agreement.

(6) Paragraph 7

Article 22 of the Geneva Draft Charter (corresponding to GATT Article XIII) provided in its paragraph 5 that internal quantitative restrictions would be included within its scope. The chairman of the working party of Sub-Committee A which redrafted Article 18 at Havana explained that "in the Working Party's view it would not be feasible or desirable to allocate between sources of supply by internal quantitative restrictions, as implied by paragraph 5 of Article 22. Article 18 was concerned with allocation between domestic and foreign sources of supply and the word 'external' had been inserted before 'sources of supply' in order to ensure most-favoured-nation treatment. For this reason the Working Party had recommended new paragraph 7 and the deletion of the reference to Article 18 in paragraph 5 of Article 22".[241]

In later discussions at Havana, it was stated that "the objectives of the Geneva draft and paragraph 7 were the same, i.e., to secure non-discrimination as between foreign suppliers with respect to products subject to internal mixing regulations. The Sub-Committee had thought that the best way to assure non-discrimination was to permit free competition. In the case of import quotas this was not always possible, so Article 22 [XIII] permitted allocation in accordance with certain rules. The same reasons of practicality did not apply, however, in the case of internal quantitative regulations, and therefore paragraph 7 had been inserted as the best method of securing most-favoured-nation treatment".[242]

(7) Relationship between provisions on mixing regulations and other provisions of Article III

During discussions in Sub-Committee A at Havana, it was stated that "there was some inconsistency between the language of paragraphs 2 [III:4] and 3 [III:5], in that paragraph 2 refers only to 'like' products whereas it was not the intention of the drafters that paragraph 3 should be restricted to 'like' products".[243]

The 1978 Panel Report on "EEC - Measures on Animal Feed Proteins" examined an EEC Regulation requiring domestic producers or importers of oilseeds, cakes and meals, dehydrated fodder and compound feeds and importers of corn gluten feed to purchase a certain quantity of surplus skimmed milk powder held by intervention agencies and to have it denatured for use as feed for animals other than calves.

"The Panel examined the obligation under the EEC Regulation, to purchase a certain quantity of denatured skimmed milk powder from intervention agencies, in terms of the provisions of Article III:5, that is whether the EEC measures constituted an 'internal quantitative regulation relating to the mixture, processing or use' within the meaning of Article III:5.

"The Panel noted that the Council Regulation (EEC) No. 563/76 referred, in its stated considerations, to the considerable stocks of skimmed milk powder held by intervention agencies and to the objective of increasing the utilization of skimmed milk powder as a protein in feedingstuffs for animals other than calves. In other words, the Regulation was intended to dispose on the internal market ('utilization') of a given quantity ('stocks') of skimmed milk powder in a particular form ('denatured' i.e. utilizable only for the intended purposes). The Panel therefore considered that the EEC Regulation was an 'internal quantitative regulation' in the sense of Article III:5. However, the Panel found that this 'internal quantitative regulation' as such was not related to the 'mixture, processing and use ... in specified amounts or proportions' within the meaning of Article III:5 because, at the level of its application, the EEC Regulation introduced basically an obligation to purchase a certain quantity of skimmed milk powder and the purchase obligation falls under Article III:1."[244]

The 1984 Panel Report on "Canada - Administration of the Foreign Investment Review Act" examined also a claim by the United States that purchase undertakings (see pages 124, 165 above) which obliged the

---

[241] E/CONF.2/C.3/A/W.49, p. 2.
[242] E/CONF.2/C.3/SR.41, p. 2.
[243] E/CONF.2/C.3/A/W.38, p. 2.
[244] L/4599, adopted on 14 March 1978, 25S/49, 64-65, paras. 4.5-4.6.

investor to purchase in Canada a specified amount or proportion of his requirements were contrary to Article III:5.

> "... The Panel noted that these cases had been characterized by both parties as *purchase* undertakings ... and had also been presented as such by the United States. ... In this regard the Panel noted that in paragraph 5 of Article III the conditions of purchase are not at issue but rather the existence of internal quantitative regulations relating to the mixture, processing or use of products (irrespective of whether these are purchased or obtained by other means). On the basis of the presentations made, the Panel (which was unable to go into a detailed examination of individual cases where purchase undertakings referred to percentages or specific amounts) therefore did not find sufficient grounds to consider the undertakings in question in the light of Article III:5, but came to the conclusion that they fell under the purchase requirements that had been found inconsistent with Article III:4."[245]

In the 1994 Panel Report on "United States - Measures Affecting the Importation, Internal Sale and Use of Tobacco",

> "The Panel noted that both Article III:5 and Article III:4 deal with internal regulations, but that Article III:5 is the more specific of the two provisions. In view of the Panel's finding of inconsistency of the DMA with Article III:5, and following the reasoning enunciated in paragraph II.A.7.(2), the Panel considered that it would not be necessary to examine the consistency of the DMA with Article III:4."[246]

8. Paragraph 8

(1) Paragraph 8(a): "procurement by governmental agencies"

The ITO Charter, as proposed in the original United States draft, would have provided for national and most-favoured-nation treatment in respect of governmental purchases of supplies for governmental use. However, this provision was deleted from the London Draft Charter "as it appears to the Preparatory Committee that an attempt to reach agreement on such a commitment would lead to exceptions almost as broad as the commitment itself".[247] See also the material on the drafting history of Article XVII:2 under that provision.

During discussions in Sub-Committee A at Havana, it was agreed that "paragraph 5 [III:8] was an exception to the whole of Article 18 [III]".[248] It was noted later that "the Sub-Committee had considered that the language of paragraph 8 would except from the scope of Article 18 [III] and hence from Article 16 [I], laws, regulations and requirements governing purchases effected for governmental use where resale was only incidental".[249]

During discussions at Havana, in response to a question regarding the case of a government which received tied loans and purchased equipment from the countries granting the loans, and which might resell such equipment later to private enterprises, it was stated that paragraph 8 "had been redrafted by the Sub-Committee specifically to cover purchases made originally for governmental purposes and not with a view to commercial resale, which might nevertheless later be sold; nor ... [could] Article 18 [III] be construed as applying to contracts for purchases in foreign countries, since paragraph 8 refers only to laws, regulations or requirements relating to mixture, processing or use, which might grant protection or give more favourable treatment to domestic as opposed to foreign products".[250]

---

[245]L/5504, adopted on 7 February 1984, 30S/140, 162, para. 5.13.

[246]DS44/R, adopted on 4 October 1994, para. 72. The footnote to this paragraph provides as follows: "Cf. Report of the panel on United States - Measures Affecting Alcoholic and Malt Beverages, adopted on 19 June 1992, BISD 39S/206, 270, where that panel found that it would not be appropriate to consider Canada's Article III:1 allegations to the extent that it found the U.S. measures to be inconsistent with the more specific provisions of Articles III:2 and III:4."

[247]London Report, p. 9, para. (d)(iv).

[248]E/CONF.2/C.3/A/W.39, p. 1.

[249]E/CONF.2/C.3/SR.41, p. 3.

[250]E/CONF.2/C.3/SR.41.

The 1979 Agreement on Government Procurement negotiated in the Tokyo Round of Trade Negotiations, as amended in 1988, provides in Article II:

"1. With respect to all laws, regulations, procedures and practices regarding government procurement covered by this Agreement, the Parties shall provide immediately and unconditionally to the products and suppliers of other Parties offering products originating within the customs territories (including free zones) of the Parties, treatment no less favourable than:

   (a)   that accorded to domestic products and suppliers; and

   (b)   that accorded to products and suppliers of any other Party.

"2. With respect to all laws, regulations, procedures and practices regarding government procurement covered by this Agreement, the Parties shall ensure:

   (a)   that their entities shall not treat a locally-established supplier less favourably than another locally-established supplier on the basis of degree of foreign affiliation or ownership;

   (b)   that their entities shall not discriminate against locally-established suppliers on the basis of the country of production of the good being supplied, provided that the country of production is a Party to the Agreement in accordance with the provisions of paragraph 4 of this Article.

"3. The provisions of paragraph 1 shall not apply to customs duties and charges of any kind imposed on or in connexion with importation, the method of levying such duties and charges, and other import regulations and formalities."[251]

(a)   "governmental"

The report of the Sub-committee which examined the national treatment articles of the Charter at Geneva provides that this "word was intended to include all governmental bodies, including local authorities".[252]

The 1952 Panel Report on "Belgian Family Allowances" examined a Belgian law imposing a 7.5 per cent levy on foreign goods purchased by public bodies when these goods originated in countries whose system of family allowances did not meet specific requirements. Having found that this levy was an internal charge under Article III:2, and further that the m.f.n. requirements of Article I:1 applied to the exemptions from the levy, the Panel further observed that:

"[the] undertaking to extend an exemption of an internal charge unconditionally is not qualified by any other provision of the Agreement. The Panel did not feel that the provisions of paragraph 8(a) of Article III were applicable in this case as the text of the paragraph referred only to laws, regulations and requirements and not to internal taxes or charges. As regards the exception contained in paragraph 2 of Article XVII, it would appear that it referred only to the principle set forth in paragraph 1 of that Article, i.e. the obligation to make purchases in accordance with commercial considerations, and did not extend to matters dealt with in Article III".[253]

See also Article I:1(c) and 2 of the Agreement on Government Procurement of 1979.[254]

The Panel Report on "United States - Procurement of a Sonar Mapping System", which has not been adopted, examined as a threshold issue whether the acquisition of a sonar mapping system by a private company, Antarctic Support Associates (ASA), in connection with a contract between ASA and the US

---

[251] 26S/33, 35 and 34S/12, 13.
[252] EPCT/174, p. 9.
[253] G/32, adopted on 7 November 1952, 1S/59, 60, para. 4.
[254] 26S/34.

National Science Foundation (NSF), was a government procurement subject to the obligations of the Agreement on Government Procurement or a private procurement subject to the disciplines of the GATT.

"The Panel noted that there was no definition of government procurement in the Agreement. The scope of the Agreement was instead determined by the wording of Article I which spoke of 'any procurement of products ... by' covered entities. It specified further that procurement could be 'through such methods as purchase or as lease, rental or hire-purchase, with or without an option to buy'. The Panel considered that, since these methods were all means of obtaining the use or benefit of a product, the word 'procurement' could be understood to refer to the obtaining of such use or benefit. At the same time, the wording of Article I:1(a) made it clear that such use was to be obtained through procurement 'by' an entity, which suggests that the entity has some form of controlling influence over the obtaining of the product.

"Some guidance as to the meaning of government procurement can be obtained from examination of those provisions of the General Agreement in which reference is made to it. The Panel noted that the General Agreement, in referring to government procurement, spoke in terms of 'products for immediate or ultimate consumption in governmental use' (Article XVII:2), and 'procurement by governmental agencies of products purchased for governmental purposes' (Article III:8(a)). The Panel noted that the emphasis in these provisions on the concepts of governmental use, governmental purposes and procurement by government agencies supported its own understanding of the concept of government procurement as explained in paragraph 4.7 below.

"While not intending to offer a definition of government procurement within the meaning of Article I:1(a), the Panel felt that in considering the facts of any particular case the following characteristics, none of which alone could be decisive, provide guidance as to whether a transaction should be regarded as government procurement within the meaning of Article I:1(a): payment by government, governmental use of or benefit from the product, government possession and government control over the obtaining of the product.

"In the present case the European Community suggested that the fact that the procurement of the sonar mapping system would take place by means of a contract between two private companies could lead to the conclusion that it is a private transaction outside the scope of the Agreement. The Panel concurred with the Community's view that this would normally be the case; the purchase by service contractors of products they need in order to be able to render the services contracted for would not normally be government procurement. The fact that government money was used would not necessarily overturn such a view. Nor would the fact that a number of conditions and guarantees relating to the procurement were required by the government necessarily lead to the conclusion that it was procurement by the government; they could simply reflect normal concern for the proper use of government funds.

"However, there were a number of factors in this case which, when taken together, led the Panel to conclude that it was indeed a case of government procurement. The Panel noted first that payment for the system would be made with government money; due to the contractually-prescribed reimbursement of ASA's costs by the NSF, the purchase money for the system remained government money. The amount of the purchase was also specifically determined by the government, with the maximum permissible price legislatively prescribed (Section 307 of P.L. 101-302).

"Secondly, the NSF would take title to the sonar mapping system as of the time of its delivery; at no stage would it become the property of ASA. Having obtained title at the moment of the purchase the NSF, at the expiry of the contract with ASA, would be able to choose whether to continue to use, or to dispose of, the system. Whereas ownership is not a necessary element of government procurement, as is clear from the various methods of procurement mentioned in Article I:1(a), transfer of title to the Government is a strong indication that government procurement is involved. The NSF would also enjoy the benefits of the system's purchase - Antarctic research and the preparation of seabed maps - which were clearly for government purposes, and the Government can thus be regarded as the ultimate beneficiary of the system.

"Thirdly, the Panel noted that the selection of the system was subject to the final approval of the NSF, which also retained the right to cancel the contract between ASA and the supplier of the sonar mapping system, with compensation, at its convenience. Other indicators of the extent of the Government's control of the procurement, perhaps less significant, include the fact that the NSF attached to the procurement many non-technical requirements, some of which could influence the final selection of the system. These requirements include the application of numerous Federal Acquisition Regulations (FARs), including the 'Buy American' domestic sourcing rules, implementing various social and political objectives of the United States Government.

"Fourthly, the Panel noted that the nature of the contract between the NSF and ASA meant that ASA would have no commercial interest in the transaction in the sense of a profit motive or a commercial risk, since it would not directly profit from the selection of the lowest-cost bid among competing manufacturers of sonar mapping systems. In making its selection therefore ASA would be functioning less like a private buyer than like a procurement agency acting on behalf of a third party.

"The Panel concluded that, in the light of the Government's payment for, ownership and use of the sonar mapping system and given the extent of its control over the obtaining of the system, the acquisition of the sonar mapping system was government procurement within the meaning of Article I:1(a), first sentence, and not 'private' procurement outside the Agreement as proposed in the alternative by the European Community."[255]

(b) *"not with a view to commercial resale or with a view to use in the production of goods for commercial sale"*

At Havana, paragraph 8(a) of Charter Article 18 on national treatment was revised by adding the word "commercial" before "resale" and "sale". This change was brought into the General Agreement in 1948 when the original text of Article III was replaced by the text of Article 18 of the Charter; however, the parallel changes which were made at Havana to paragraph 2 of Article 29 (on government procurement) were not brought over into the text of paragraph 2 of Article XVII.[256]

See also the Interpretative Note to paragraph 2 of Article XVII (non-application of state trading obligations to government procurement) where it is stated in respect of the terms "production of goods" that "The term 'goods' is limited to products as understood in commercial practice, and is not intended to include the purchase or sale of services".

The Report of the Working Party on "Accession of Venezuela" notes that

"Referring to the purchases by state enterprises, some members questioned whether the buy national provisions of Decree 1182 were consistent with the provisions of Articles XVII and III of the General Agreement. A member added that in order to conform to Article III obligations the preference provided by Decree 1182 should only be applied to imports by the State for its own consumption and not to imports by enterprises engaged in normal commerce. ... The representative of Venezuela ... confirming that Decree 1182 provided a buy-Venezuela preference ... noted that its provisions did not distinguish between Government purchases for governmental use and purchases by State enterprises for commercial purposes.

"The representative of Venezuela ... stated that by 30 June 1994, his Government would ensure that Decree 1182 will be brought into conformity with Article III of the General Agreement, and that its application to purchases other than those for ultimate consumption in governmental use would not deny the benefits of Article III to imports from other contracting parties. The representative of Venezuela also stated that if Decree 1182 was still in effect at that time without the above-mentioned actions having been taken, the matter will be reviewed by the CONTRACTING PARTIES. The representative of Venezuela

---

[255]GPR.DS1/R, dated 23 April 1992 (unadopted), paras. 4.5-4.13.
[256]Working Party Report on "Modifications to the General Agreement", GATT/CP.2/22/Rev.1, adopted 1-2 September 1948, II/39.

further confirmed that his Government would, if requested, consult with interested contracting parties concerning the effect of Decree 1182 on their trade".[257]

(c)   Tied loans

See the reference to tied loans above at page 190. A Brazilian proposal in the Review Session that the General Agreement be amended to prohibit tied loans so that funds could be spent in the cheapest markets was not adopted.[258]

See also Interpretative Note ad Article XVII, paragraph 1(b).

A Note relating to Article I:1 of the Agreement on Government Procurement states:

"Having regard to general policy considerations relating to tied aid, including the objective of developing countries with respect to the untying of such aid, this Agreement does not apply to procurement made in furtherance of tied aid to developing countries so long as it is practised by Parties".[259]

(2)   Paragraph 8(b): *"payment of subsidies exclusively to domestic producers"*

The chairman of the working party of Sub-Committee A which redrafted Article 18 at Havana explained that "the Working Party had tried to clarify the wording of sub-paragraph (b). This provision had been added to the Geneva draft because it was felt that if subsidies were paid on domestic and not on imported products, it might be construed that Members were not applying the 'national treatment' rule".[260]

The Report of the Sub-Committee at the Havana Conference which examined Article 18 of the Charter (the text of which constitutes Article III of the General Agreement) notes with respect to paragraph 8(b) that

"This sub-paragraph was redrafted in order to make it clear that nothing in Article 18 could be construed to sanction the exemption of domestic products from internal taxes imposed on like imported products or the remission of such taxes. At the same time the Sub-Committee recorded its view that nothing in this sub-paragraph or elsewhere in Article 18 would override the provisions of Section C of Chapter IV [on Subsidies]".[261]

The 1958 Panel Report on "Italian Discrimination against Agricultural Machinery," which examined the consistency with Article III:4 of an Italian law providing special credit facilities to farmers for the purchase of agricultural machinery produced in Italy, notes that the "Panel agreed with the contention of the United Kingdom delegation that in any case the provisions of paragraph 8(b) would not be applicable to this particular case since the credit facilities provided under the Law were granted to the purchasers of agricultural machinery and could not be considered as subsidies accorded to the producers of agricultural machinery".[262]

The 1990 Panel Report on "European Economic Community - Payments and Subsidies paid to Processors and Producers of Oilseeds and related Animal-Feed Proteins" examined EEC legislation providing for payment of subsidies to processors of oilseeds whenever they established by documentary evidence that they had transformed oilseeds of Community origin.

"The Panel first examined the United States' claim that the payments to processors generate an incentive to purchase domestic rather than imported oilseeds inconsistently with Article III:4. The Panel noted that the Community considers the payments made to processors to be covered by Article III:8(b) which provides that Article III '... shall not prevent the payment of subsidies exclusively to domestic

---

[257] L/6696, adopted on 11 July 1990, 37S/43, 65-66, paras. 70-71.
[258] SR.9/18, p. 1; see also 3S/243, para. 37.
[259] 26S/55.
[260] E/CONF.2/C.3/A/W.49, p. 2.
[261] Havana Reports, p. 66, para. 69; see also E/CONF.2/C.3/SR.13 p. 1-2.
[262] L/833, adopted on 23 October 1958, 7S/60, 64, para. 14.

producers ...' The Community argues that the payments to processors are made conditional upon the transformation or purchase of domestic oilseeds sold at prices determined by the Community Regulations, are therefore passed on to the producers of domestic oilseeds and consequently constitute producer subsidies within the meaning of that provision.

"The Panel noted that Article III:8(b) applies only to payments made *exclusively* to domestic producers and considered that it can reasonably be assumed that a payment not made directly to producers is not made 'exclusively' to them. It noted moreover that, if the economic benefits generated by the payments granted by the Community can at least partly be retained by the processors of Community oilseeds, the payments generate a benefit conditional upon the purchase of oilseeds of domestic origin inconsistently with Article III:4. Under these circumstances Article III:8(b) would not be applicable because in that case the payments would not be made exclusively to domestic producers but to processors as well."[263]

The 1992 Panel Report on "United States - Measures Affecting Alcoholic and Malt Beverages" examined a United States tax measure providing a credit against excise taxes for small United States producers of beer and wine, which was not available for imported beer and wine. The Panel found that this tax law operated to create lower tax rates on domestic beer and wine than on like imported products.

"The Panel then considered the additional argument of the United States that the lower federal excise tax rate was allowable as a subsidy to domestic producers under Article III:8(b). The United States maintained that the clear intent of the lower tax was to subsidize small producers and that reduction in the rate of the excise tax was a GATT-consistent means of providing such a subsidy....

"The Panel noted that in contrast to Article III:8(a), where it is stated that 'this Article *shall not apply to* ... [government procurement]', the underlined words are not repeated in Article III:8(b). The ordinary meaning of the text of Article III:8(b), especially the use of the words 'shall not prevent', therefore suggests that Article III does apply to subsidies, and that Article III:8(b) only clarifies that the *product-related* rules in paragraphs 1 through 7 of Article III 'shall not prevent the payment of subsidies exclusively to domestic *producers*' (emphasis added). The words 'payment of subsidies' refer only to direct subsidies involving a payment, not to other subsidies such as tax credits or tax reductions. The specific reference to 'payments .... derived from the proceeds of internal taxes ... applied consistently with the provisions of this Article' relates to after-tax-collection payments and also suggests that tax credits and reduced tax rates inconsistent with Article III:2, which neither involve a 'payment' not result in 'proceeds of internal taxes applied consistently with ... this Article', are not covered by Article III:8(b).

"This textual interpretation is confirmed by the context, declared purpose and drafting history of Article III. The context of Article III shows its close interrelationship with the fundamental GATT provisions in Articles I and II and the deliberate separation of the comprehensive national treatment requirements in Article III from the subsidy rules in Article XVI. The most-favoured-nation requirement in Article I, and also tariff bindings under Article II, would become ineffective without the complementary prohibition in Article III on the use of internal taxation and regulation as a discriminatory non-tariff trade barrier. The additional function of the national treatment requirements in Article III to enhance non-discriminatory conditions of competition between imported and domestic products could likewise not be achieved. As any fiscal burden imposed by discriminatory internal taxes on imported goods is likely to entail a trade-distorting advantage for import-competing domestic producers, the prohibition of discriminatory internal taxes in Article III:2 would be ineffective if discriminatory internal taxes on imported products could be generally justified as subsidies for competing domestic producers in terms of Article III:8(b).

"Article III:8(b) limits, therefore, the permissible producer subsidies to 'payments' after taxes have been collected or payments otherwise consistent with Article III. This separation of tax rules, e.g. on

---

[263] L/6627, adopted on 25 January 1990, 37S/86, 124, paras. 136-137.

tax exemptions or reductions, and subsidy rules makes sense economically and politically. Even if the proceeds from non-discriminatory product taxes may be used for subsequent subsidies, the domestic producer, like his foreign competitors, must pay the product taxes due. The separation of tax and subsidy rules contributes to greater transparency. It also may render abuses of tax policies for protectionist purposes more difficult, as in the case where producer aids require additional legislative or governmental decisions in which the different interests involved can be balanced.

"The Panel considered that the drafting history of Article III confirms the above interpretation. The Havana Reports recall in respect of the provision corresponding to Article III:8(b):

> 'This sub-paragraph was redrafted in order to make it clear that nothing in Article [III] could be construed to sanction the exemption of domestic products from internal taxes imposed on like imported products or the remission of such taxes. At the same time the Sub-Committee recorded its view that nothing in this sub-paragraph or elsewhere in Article [III] would override the provisions [of Article XVI]'.[264]

"The drafters of Article III explicitly rejected a proposal by Cuba at the Havana Conference to amend the Article to read:

> 'The provisions of this Article shall not preclude the exemption of domestic products from internal taxes as a means of indirect subsidization in the cases covered under Article [XVI]'.[265]

"The Panel found, therefore, that the expansive interpretation of Article III:8(b) suggested by the United States is not supported by the text, context, declared purpose and drafting history of Article III and, if carried to its logical conclusion, such an interpretation would virtually eliminate the prohibition in Article III:2 of discriminatory internal taxation by enabling contracting parties to exempt all domestic products from indirect taxes. The Panel accordingly found that the reduced federal excise tax rates on beer are not covered by Article III:8(b)."[266]

In the 1994 Panel Report on "United States - Measures Affecting the Importation, Internal Sale and Use of Tobacco", the panel examined a claim regarding the No Net Cost Assessment ("NNCA") levied on domestic and imported tobacco, the proceeds of which were deposited in an account used to reimburse the U.S. Government for any losses resulting from the domestic tobacco price-support programme.

"The Panel was cognizant of the fact that a remission of a tax on a product and the payment of a producer subsidy out of the proceeds of such a tax could have the same economic effects. However, the Panel noted that the distinction in Article III:8(b) is a formal one, not one related to the economic impact of a measure. Thus, in view of the explicit language of Article III:8(b), which recognizes that the product-related rules of Article III 'shall not prevent the payment of subsidies exclusively to domestic producers', the Panel did not consider, as argued by the complainants, that the payment of a subsidy to tobacco producers out of the proceeds of the NNCA resulted in a form of tax remission inconsistent with Article III:2.[267]

...

"The Panel then considered the complainants' claim that the NNCA was inconsistent with Article III:2, second sentence, because the NNCAs charged on imported tobacco reduced the cost of the price support programme to the domestic tobacco producer, without providing any benefit to imported tobacco. The Panel did not consider that it needed to examine this claim in view of the fact that

---

[264]The footnote to this paragraph refers to Havana Reports, page 66.
[265]The footnote to this paragraph refers to E/CONF.2/C.3/6, page 17; E/CONF.2/C.3/A/W.32, page 2.
[266]DS23/R, adopted 19 June 1992, 39S/206, 271-273, paras. 5.7-5.12.
[267]The footnote to this paragraph notes: "See report of the panel on United States - Measures Affecting Alcoholic and Malt Beverages, adopted on 19 June 1992, BISD 39S/206, 271-273 for a discussion of the reasons for the distinction in GATT between tax exemptions and remissions on the one hand and producer subsidies on the other."

Article III:8(b), which explicitly recognizes that subsidies to domestic producers are not subject to the national treatment rules of Article III, applies to all provisions of Article III, including that of Article III:2, second sentence."[268]

See also material on this panel report above.

9. Paragraph 9

During discussions on this paragraph at Havana it was agreed to retain it in Article 18 [III] "on the grounds that 'internal maximum price control measures' were internal regulations within the terms of paragraphs 1 and 4 of Article 18".[269] At Havana it was also stated that "this provision would apply in the case of a country establishing a maximum control price for a commodity of which that country was such an important consumer that its price was likely to become the effective world price. If such a price were too low, it would be prejudicial to the interests of exporting countries".[270]

The Report of the Working Party on "Accession of El Salvador" contains, *inter alia*, the statement of the representative of El Salvador that "from the date of accession, price regulations would be applied in conformity with Article III:9 of the General Agreement".[271]

10. Paragraph 10

See the chapter on Article IV regarding the background of paragraph 10 and Article IV. The exception in Paragraph 10 to the general provisions of Article III is defined therein as applying to "internal quantitative regulations relating to exposed cinematograph films and meeting the requirements of Article IV". As for taxes on films, the Report of the Working Party on "Accession of the United Arab Republic" discusses a "film tax" in relation to Article III:2 and the Protocol of Provisional Accession.[272] See also references to the New Zealand film hire tax and renters' film quota in Annex A of the General Agreement.

B. RELATIONSHIP WITH OTHER ARTICLES OF THE GENERAL AGREEMENT

1. Article I

The unconditional most-favoured-nation clause in Article I:1 includes within its scope "all matters referred to in paragraphs 2 and 4 of Article III". In response to a request for an interpretation of paragraph 1 of Article I with respect to rebates of excise duties, the Chairman of the CONTRACTING PARTIES ruled on 24 August 1948 that "the most-favoured-nation treatment principle embodied in that paragraph would be applicable to any advantage, favour, privilege or immunity granted with respect to internal taxes".[273] Under the Protocol Amending Part I and Articles XXIX and XXX of the General Agreement, which was agreed in the Review Session of 1954-55, the words "and with respect to the application of internal taxes to exported goods" would have been included in paragraph 1 to remove any uncertainty as to the application of Article I to discrimination in the exemption of exports from the levy of an excise tax.[274] See further under Article I:1.

The 1952 Panel Report on "Belgian Family Allowances" examined a Belgian law providing for a charge to be levied on foreign goods purchased by public bodies when these goods originated in a country whose system of family allowances did not meet specific requirements. Having found that this charge was an internal charge under Article III:2 (see below), the Panel noted:

---

[268] DS44/R, adopted 4 October 1994, para. 109, 111.
[269] E/CONF.2/C.3/A/W.49, p. 3; see also E/CONF.2/C.3/A/W.46 and E/CONF.2/C.3/A/W.48 p. 1-2.
[270] E/CONF.2/C.3/A/W.46 p. 3.
[271] L/6771, adopted on 12 December 1990, 37S/9, 21, para. 36.
[272] L/3362, adopted on 27 February 1970, 17S/33, 37, para. 17.
[273] II/12, CP.2/SR.11, CP.3/SR.19.
[274] 3S/206, para. 3. This Protocol was abandoned as of 31 December 1967; see 15S/65.

"Belgium has granted exemption from the levy under consideration to products purchased by public bodies when they originate in Luxemburg and the Netherlands, as well as in France, Italy, Sweden and the United Kingdom. If the General Agreement were definitively in force in accordance with Article XXVI, that exemption would have to be granted unconditionally to all other contracting parties. ... The consistency or not of the system of family allowances in force in the territory of a given contracting party with the requirements of the Belgian law would be irrelevant in this respect, and the Belgian legislation would have to be amended insofar as it introduced a discrimination between countries having a given system of family allowances and those which had a different system or no system at all, and made the granting of an exemption dependent on certain conditions".[275]

See also the Note *Ad* Article I:1, which provides that "The obligations incorporated in paragraph 1 of Article I by reference to paragraphs 2 and 4 of Article III ... shall be considered as falling within Part II for the purposes of the Protocol of Provisional Application". See further on page 204 below.

The 1987 Panel Report on "Japan - Customs Duties, Taxes and Labelling Practices on Imported Wines and Alcoholic Beverages" examined, *inter alia*, a claim by the EEC under Article III:1 and 2 with respect to these duties, taxes and labelling practices. In interpreting Article III:2, the Panel examined its context:

"The *context* of Article III:2 shows that Article III:2 supplements, within the system of the General Agreement, the provisions on the liberalization of customs duties and of other charges by prohibiting discriminatory or protective taxation against certain products from other GATT contracting parties. ... For instance, the prohibition under GATT Article I:1 of different tariff treatment for various types of 'like' products (such as unroasted coffee, see BISD 28S/102, 112) could not remain effective unless supplemented by the prohibition of different internal tax treatment for various types of 'like' products. ... Article I:1 was generally construed, in order to protect the competitive benefits accruing from reciprocal tariff bindings, as prohibiting 'tariff specialization' discriminating against 'like' products".[276]

The 1990 Panel Report on "EEC - Regulation on Imports of Parts and Components" examined, *inter alia*, a claim by Japan that since the EEC Regulation at issue provided for imposition of duties on products produced or assembled in the EEC on the basis of the proportion of parts imported from Japan used in production or assembly of such products, imposition of duties or acceptance of undertakings under that Regulation was inconsistent with Articles I and II or III. The Panel "found that the anti-circumvention duties are not levied 'on or in connection with importation' within the meaning of Article II:1(b), and therefore do not constitute customs duties within the meaning of that provision".[277] It then "found that the anti-circumvention duties are inconsistent with Article III:2, first sentence, [and] saw no need for examining whether the anti-circumvention duties are also inconsistent with the obligations of the EEC under Article III:2, second sentence, and Article I:1".[278] The Panel "found the acceptance by the EEC of parts undertakings limiting the use of imported parts and components to be inconsistent with Article III:4, [and therefore] saw no need for examining whether the acceptance of such undertakings is also inconsistent with Article I:1 of the General Agreement".[279]

See also the discussion of the relation between Article I and III in the unadopted 1994 Panel Report on "EEC - Import Régime for Bananas".[280]

2. Article II

A number of panels have examined whether a measure was an internal tax or charge (under Article III) or a duty or charge "imposed on or in connection with importation" (under Article II). In the 1952 Panel

---

[275]G/32, adopted on 7 November 1952, 1S/59, 60, para. 3.
[276]L/6216, adopted on 10 November 1987, 34S/83, 113-114, para. 5.5(b).
[277]L/6657, adopted on 16 May 1990, 37S/132, 193 para. 5.8.
[278]*Ibid.*, 37S/193-194, para. 5.10.
[279]*Ibid.*, 37S/197-198, para. 5.22.
[280]DS38/R, dated 11 February 1994, paras. 143-148.

Report on "Belgian Family Allowances" the Panel began by examining the nature of the Belgian law in question:

> "After examining the legal provisions regarding the methods of collection of that charge, the Panel came to the conclusion that the 7.5 per cent levy was collected only on products purchased by public bodies for their own use and not on imports as such, and that the levy was charged, not at the time of importation, but when the purchase price was paid by the public body. In those circumstances, it would appear that the levy was to be treated as an 'internal charge' within the meaning of paragraph 2 of Article III of the General Agreement, and not as an import charge within the meaning of paragraph 2 of Article II".[281]

The 1978 Panel Report on "EEC - Measures on Animal Feed Proteins" examined an EEC Regulation requiring domestic producers or importers of oilseeds, cakes and meals, dehydrated fodder and compound feeds and importers of corn gluten feed to purchase a certain quantity of surplus skimmed milk powder held by intervention agencies and to have it denatured for use as feed for animals other than calves. The Panel examined the consistency with Articles II and III of these aspects of the Regulation and of the requirement for producers and importers to present either a protein certificate (certifying the purchase and denaturing of a certain quantity of milk powder) or a security deposit.

> "The Panel ... considered the question of whether the EEC measures should be examined both as internal measures under Article III and border measures under Article II. In this regard, the Panel reviewed the drafting history of Articles II and III and their subsequent application by contracting parties, particularly with a view to ascertaining the relationship between these two Articles...

> "The Panel also recalled its own findings that (a) the EEC measures applied to both imported and domestically produced vegetable proteins (except in the case of corn gluten); (b) the EEC measures basically instituted an obligation to purchase a certain quantity of skimmed milk powder and, as an 'internal quantitative regulation' fell under Article III:1; (c) the EEC security deposit and protein certificate were enforcement mechanisms for the purchase obligation.

> "Having regard to the legal considerations referred to above and taking account of its own findings in relation to Article III:5 and Article III:1 that the EEC measures were an 'internal quantitative regulation', the Panel concluded that the EEC measures should be examined as internal measures under Article III and not as border measures under Article II".[282]

In the 1985 Panel Report on "Canada - Measures Affecting the Sale of Gold Coins," which has not been adopted,

> "The Panel noted that Articles III and II of the General Agreement distinguish between charges applied to products 'imported into the territory of any other contracting party' (Article III:2) and charges 'imposed on or in connection with importation' (Article II:1(b) ... The Panel noted that the Ontario retail sales tax is levied at the time of retail sale of goods within the province, not at the time of importation into Canadian territory (see para. 5 above). The Ontario measure thus affects the internal retail sale of gold coins rather than the importation of Krugerrands as such. The Panel therefore considered that the tax was an 'internal tax' to be considered under Article III and not an 'import charge' to be considered under Article II".[283]

The 1988 Panel Report on "Canada - Import, Distribution and Sale of Alcoholic Drinks by Canadian Provincial Marketing Agencies"

> "noted that Article 31:6 of the Havana Charter provided that 'in applying the provisions of this Article, due regard shall be had for the fact that some monopolies are established and operated mainly

---

[281] G/32, adopted on 7 November 1952, 1S/59, 60, para. 2. See also page 191, 197 above.
[282] L/4599, adopted on 14 March 1978, 25S/49, 66-67, paras. 4.15, 4.17, 4.18.
[283] L/5863, unadopted, dated 17 September 1985, para. 50.

for social, cultural, humanitarian or revenue purposes'. While the drafting history indicated that Article 31 should be applied to the extent that it was relevant to the context of the General Agreement, the Panel considered that Canada had the right to use import monopolies to raise revenue for the provinces, consistently with the provisions of the General Agreement. The Panel also considered that its conclusions on Article II:4 did not affect this right, because Article II:4, applied in the light of Article 31:4 of the Charter, permitted the charging of internal taxes conforming to the provisions of Article III. It noted that federal and provincial sales taxes were levied on alcoholic beverages and asked itself whether the fiscal elements of mark-ups, which produced revenue for the provinces, could also be justified as 'internal taxes conforming to the provisions of Article III', noting that Article III:2 also referred, not only to 'internal taxes', but also to 'other internal charges.' The panel was of the view that to be so considered, the fiscal element of mark-ups must of course meet the requirements of Article III, e.g., they must not be applied to imported or domestic products so as to afford protection to domestic production. The Panel also considered it important that, if fiscal elements were to be considered as internal taxes, mark-ups would also have to be administered in conformity with other provisions of the General Agreement, in particular Article X dealing with the Publication and Administration of Trade Regulations".[284]

In the 1990 Panel Report on "EEC - Regulation on Imports of Parts and Components," the Panel examined the argument of the EEC that the anti-circumvention duties at issue were customs or other duties imposed "on or in connection with importation" under Article II:1(b), or internal taxes or charges falling under Article III:2.

"The Panel noted that the anti-circumvention duties are levied, according to Article 13:10(a), 'on products that are introduced into the commerce of the Community after having been assembled or produced in the Community'. The duties are thus imposed, as the EEC explained before the Panel, not on imported parts or materials but on the finished products assembled or produced in the EEC. They are not imposed conditional upon the importation of a product or at the time or point of importation. The EEC considers that the anti-circumvention duties should, nevertheless, be regarded as customs duties imposed 'in connection with importation' within the meaning of Article II:1(b). The main arguments the EEC advanced in support of this view were: firstly, that the purpose of these duties was to eliminate circumvention of anti-dumping duties on finished products and that their nature was identical to the nature of the anti-dumping duties they were intended to enforce; and secondly, that the duties were collected by the customs authorities under procedures identical to those applied for the collection of customs duties, formed part of the resources of the EEC in the same way as customs duties and related to parts and materials which were not considered to be 'in free circulation' within the EEC.

"In the light of the above facts and arguments, the Panel first examined whether the *policy purpose of a charge* is relevant to determining the issue of whether the charge is imposed 'in connection with importation' within the meaning of Article II:1(b). The text of Articles I, II, III and the Note to Article III refers to charges 'imposed on importation', 'collected ... at the time or point of importation' and applied 'to an imported product and to the like domestic product'. The relevant fact, according to the text of these provisions, is not the policy purpose attributed to the charge but rather whether the charge is due on importation or at the time or point of importation or whether it is collected internally. This reading of Articles II and III is supported by their drafting history and by previous panel reports (e.g. BISD 1S/60; 25S/49, 67). ... The Panel further noted that the policy purpose of charges is frequently difficult to determine objectively. Many charges could be regarded as serving both internal purposes and purposes related to the importation of goods. Only at the expense of creating substantial legal uncertainty could the policy purpose of a charge be considered to be relevant in determining whether the charge falls under Article II:1(b) or Article III:2. The Panel therefore concluded that the policy purpose of the charge is not relevant to determining the issue of whether the charge is imposed in 'connection with importation' within the meaning of Article II:1(b).

---

[284] L/6304, adopted on 22 March 1988, 35S/37, 88-89, para. 4.20.

"The Panel proceeded to examine whether the mere *description or categorization of a charge under the domestic law* of a contracting party is relevant to determining the issue of whether it is subject to requirements of Article II or those of Article III:2. The Panel noted that if the description or categorization of a charge under the domestic law of a contracting party were to provide the required 'connection with importation', contracting parties could determine themselves which of these provisions would apply to their charges. They could in particular impose charges on products after their importation simply by assigning the collection of these charges to their customs administration and allocating the revenue generated to their customs revenue. With such an interpretation the basic objective underlying Articles II and III, namely that discrimination against products from other contracting parties should only take the form of ordinary customs duties imposed on or in connection with importation and not the form of internal taxes, could not be achieved. The same reasoning applies to the *description or categorization of the product subject to a charge*. The fact that the EEC treats imported parts and materials subject to anti-circumvention duties as not being 'in free circulation' therefore cannot, in the view of the Panel, support the conclusion that the anti-circumvention duties are being levied 'in connection with importation' within the meaning of Article II:1(b).

"In the light of the above, the Panel found that the anti-circumvention duties are not levied 'on or in connection with importation' within the meaning of Article II:1(b), and consequently do not constitute customs duties within the meaning of that provision."[285]

3. Article XI

The Working Party on "The Haitian Tobacco Monopoly" in 1955 examined whether the licensing of tobacco imports by the Tobacco Régie required a release under the provisions of Article XVIII:12 (prior to the Review Session amendments to Article XVIII). "The representative of Haiti declared that the licensing system served solely to enforce the internal quantitative regulations of the Régie and did not impose any additional limitation of the quantity that may be imported. The Working Party therefore took the view that in these circumstances Article XI would not apply, that the import control should be considered under the terms of the exception in Article [XX:(d)] and that the internal regulation to which it relates should be considered under paragraphs 5 and 6 of Article III."[286] See also the references to this case above in the material on mixing regulations; see also the reference to border enforcement of mixing regulations under the Interpretative Note Ad Article III.

The 1984 Panel Report on "Canada - Administration of the Foreign Investment Review Act" notes that

"The Panel shares the view of Canada that the General Agreement distinguishes between measures affecting the 'importation' of products, which are regulated in Article XI:1, and those affecting 'imported products', which are dealt with in Article III. If Article XI:1 were interpreted broadly to cover also internal requirements, Article III would be partly superfluous. Moreover, the exceptions to Article XI:1, in particular those contained in Article XI:2, would also apply to internal requirements restricting imports, which would be contrary to the basic aim of Article III. The Panel did not find, either in the drafting history of the General Agreement or in previous cases examined by the CONTRACTING PARTIES, any evidence justifying such an interpretation of Article XI. For these reasons, the Panel, noting that purchase undertakings do not prevent the importation of goods as such, reached the conclusion that they are not inconsistent with Article XI:1".[287]

The 1987 Panel Report on "United States - Taxes on Petroleum and Certain Imported Substances" provides that "The general prohibition of quantitative restrictions under Article XI .... and the national

---

[285] L/6657, adopted on 16 May 1990, 37S/132, 192-93, paras. 5.5-5.8. The "previous panel reports" referred to in para. 5.6 are the Reports on "Belgian Family Allowances", G/32, adopted on 7 November 1952, 1S/59, 60, para. 2, and "EEC - Measures on Animal Feed Proteins", L/4599, adopted on 14 March 1978, 25S/49, 67, paras. 4.16-4.18.

[286] L/454, adopted on 22 November 1955, 4S/38, 39, para. 9. Before the revision of Article XVIII in the Review Session, Article XVIII:12 provided for notification and concurrence with regard to certain measures affecting imports which were not otherwise permitted by the General Agreement.

[287] L/5504, adopted on 7 February 1984, 30S/140, 162-163, para. 5.14.

treatment obligation of Article III ... have essentially the same rationale, namely to protect expectations of the contracting parties as to the competitive relationship between their products and those of other contracting parties. Both articles are not only to protect current trade but also create the predictability needed to plan future trade".[288]

A series of three cases in 1988 and 1992 examined the application of Articles III and XI to regulations affecting imported alcoholic beverages in Canada and the United States. The 1988 Panel Report on "Canada - Import, Distribution and Sale of Alcoholic Drinks by Provincial Marketing Agencies" provides that

> "The Panel ... *concluded* that the practices concerning listing/delisting requirements and the availability of points of sale which discriminate against imported alcoholic beverages were restrictions made effective through state-trading operations contrary to Article XI:1. ...
>
> "The Panel then examined the contention of the European Communities that the practices complained of were contrary to Article III. The Panel noted that Canada did not consider Article III to be relevant to this case, arguing that the Interpretative Note to Articles XI, XII, XIII, XIV and XVIII made it clear that provisions other than Article XVII applied to state-trading enterprises by specific reference only. The Panel considered that it was not necessary to decide in this particular case whether the practices complained of were contrary to Article III:4 because it had already found that they were inconsistent with Article XI. However, the Panel saw great force in the argument that Article III:4 was also applicable to state-trading enterprises at least when the monopoly of the importation and monopoly of the distribution in the domestic markets were combined, as was the case of the provincial liquor boards in Canada. This interpretation was confirmed *e contrario* by the wording of Article III:8(a)".[289]

The 1992 Panel Report on "Canada - Import, Distribution and Sale of Certain Alcoholic Drinks by Provincial Marketing Agencies" examined a United States claim that the practice of the liquor boards of Ontario to limit listing of imported beer to the six-pack size while according listings in different package sizes to domestic beer was inconsistent with the General Agreement.

> "... The Panel noted that this package-size requirement, though implemented as a listing requirement, was in fact a requirement that did not affect the importation of beer as such but rather its offering for sale in certain liquor-board outlets. The Panel therefore considered that this requirement fell under Article III:4 of the General Agreement, which required, *inter alia*, that contracting parties accord to imported products '... treatment no less favourable than that accorded to like products of national origin in respect of all laws, regulations and requirements affecting their internal ... offering for sale ...'. The Panel *found* that the imposition of the six-pack configuration requirement on imported beer but not on domestic beer was inconsistent with that provision."[290]

With respect to restrictions imposed by provincial liquor authorities on access for imported beer to points of sale (with respect to which Canada invoked the Protocol of Provisional Application):

> "The Panel which had examined in 1988 the practices of the Canadian liquor boards had analysed the restrictions on access to points of sale under Articles III:4 and XI:1 of the General Agreement. While that Panel had found these restrictions to be inconsistent with Canada's obligations under Article XI:1, it had also pointed out that it 'saw great force in the argument that Article III:4 was also applicable to State-trading enterprises at least when the monopoly of the importation and monopoly of the distribution in the domestic markets were combined, as was the case of the provincial liquor boards in Canada'. The present Panel, noting that Canada now considered Article III:4 to be applicable to practices of the liquor boards, examined this issue again. ... The Panel found that, by allowing the access of domestic beer to points of sale not available to imported beer, Canada accorded domestic beer

---

[288] L/6175, adopted on 17 June 1987, 34S/136, 160, para. 5.2.2; see also reference to this passage in Panel Report on "European Economic Community - Payments and Subsidies paid to Processors and Producers of Oilseeds and related Animal-Feed Proteins", L/6627, adopted on 25 January 1990, 37S/86, 130, para. 150.
[289] L/6304, adopted 22 March 1988, 35S/37, 89-90, paras. 4.25-4.26.
[290] DS17/R, adopted 18 February 1992, 39S/27, 75, para. 5.4.

competitive opportunities denied to imported beer. For these reasons the present Panel saw great force in the argument that the restrictions on access to points of sale were covered by Article III:4. However, the Panel considered that it was not necessary to decide whether the restrictions fell under Article XI:1 or Article III:4 because Canada was not invoking an exception to the General Agreement applicable only to measures taken under Article XI:1 (such as the exceptions in Articles XI:2 and XII) and the question of whether the restrictions violated Article III:4 or Article XI:1 of the General Agreement was therefore of no practical consequence in the present case".[291]

The Panel also examined minimum prices maintained for beer in certain provinces of Canada.

"The Panel first examined whether the minimum prices fell under Article XI:1 or Article III:4. The Panel noted that according to the Note Ad Article III a regulation is subject to the provisions of Article III if it 'applies to an imported product and to the like domestic product' even if it is 'enforced in case of the imported product at the time or point of importation'. The Panel found that, as the minimum prices were applied to both imported and domestic beer, they fell, according to this Note under Article III."[292]

The 1992 Panel on "United States - Measures Affecting Alcoholic and Malt Beverages" examined the listing requirements of state-operated liquor stores in certain US states:

"Having regard to the past panel decisions and the record in the instant case, the present Panel was of the view that the listing and delisting practices here at issue do not affect importation as such into the United States and should be examined under Article III:4. The Panel further noted that the issue is not whether the practices in the various states affect the right of importation as such, in that they clearly apply to both domestic (out-of-state) and imported wines; rather, the issue is whether the listing and delisting practices accord less favourable treatment -- in terms of competitive opportunities -- to imported wine than that accorded to the like domestic product. Consequently, the Panel decided to analyze the state listing and delisting practices as internal measures under Article III:4".[293]

The 1991 Panel Report on "United States - Restrictions on Imports of Tuna," which has not been adopted, examined the relationship between Articles III and XI, and found that the restrictions at issue were governed not by Article III but by Article XI.

"The Panel noted that Mexico had argued that the measures prohibiting imports of certain yellowfin tuna and yellowfin tuna products from Mexico imposed by the United States were quantitative restrictions on importation under Article XI, while the United States had argued that these measures were internal regulations enforced at the time or point of importation under Article III:4 and the Note *Ad* Article III, namely that the prohibition of imports of tuna and tuna products from Mexico constituted an enforcement of the regulations of the MMPA relating to the harvesting of domestic tuna.

"The Panel examined the distinction between quantitative restrictions on importation and internal measures applied at the time or point of importation, and noted the following. While restrictions on importation are prohibited by Article XI:1, contracting parties are permitted by Article III:4 and the Note *Ad* Article III to impose an internal regulation on products imported from other contracting parties provided that it: does not discriminate between products of other countries in violation of the most-favoured-nation principle of Article I:1; is not applied so as to afford protection to domestic production, in violation of the national treatment principle of Article III:1; and accords to imported products treatment no less favourable than that accorded to like products of national origin, consistent with Article III:4. ...

"... The Panel noted that the MMPA regulates the domestic harvesting of yellowfin tuna to reduce the incidental taking of dolphin, but that these regulations could not be regarded as being applied to tuna

---

[291]*Ibid.*, 39S/75-76, para. 5.6.
[292]*Ibid*, 39S/84, para. 5.28.
[293]DS23/R, adopted 19 June 1992, 39S/206, 292, para. 5.63.

products as such because they would not directly regulate the sale of tuna and could not possibly affect tuna as a product. Therefore, the Panel found that the import prohibition on certain yellowfin tuna and certain yellowfin tuna products of Mexico and the provisions of the MMPA under which it is imposed did not constitute internal regulations covered by the Note *Ad* Article III."[294]

In this connection see also the unadopted panel report of 1994 on "United States - Restrictions on Imports of Tuna".[295]

4. Article XVII

See under Article XVII.

5. Article XX(d)

See under Article XX.

6. Article XXIV:12

See under Article XXIV.

7. Part IV

See under Part IV.

C. EXCEPTIONS AND DEROGATIONS

1. Exceptions to the scope of the national treatment requirement

See discussion above of paragraphs 3, 6, 8 and 10 of Article III.

2. Protocol of Provisional Application

The Report of the Working Party on "Brazilian Internal Taxes" notes that the majority of the members of the Working Party took the view

> "... that the Protocol of Provisional Application limited the operation of Article III only in the sense that it permitted the retention of an absolute difference in the level of taxes applied to domestic and imported products, required by existing legislation, and that no subsequent change in legislation should have the effect of increasing the absolute margin of difference".[296]

The Interpretative Note to Article I paragraph 1 provides that "The obligations incorporated in paragraph 1 of Article I by reference to paragraphs 2 and 4 of Article III ... shall be considered as falling within Part II for the purposes of the Protocol of Provisional Application". The objective of this provision, which was based on a proposal by the US delegation, was to reserve legislation regarding preferential internal taxes until definitive acceptance of the Agreement.[297] Similar provisions appear in the standard text of protocols of access; see discussion under Article I.

---

[294] DS21/R (unadopted) dated 3 September 1991, 39S/155, 193, 195, paras. 5.8-5.9, 5.14.
[295] DS29/R, dated 16 June 1994, para. 5.8-5.9.
[296] GATT/CP.3/42, adopted 30 June 1949, II/181, 183, para. 12.
[297] Proposal at EPCT/W/343; discussion at EPCT/TAC/PV/26, p. 9-11 (referring to preferential internal tax on processing of coconut oil from the Philippines, later notified as measure under the Protocol of Provisional Application; see L/309/Add.2).

3. Protocols of accession

Paragraph 3 of the Protocol for the Accession of the Philippines to the General Agreement provides as follows.

> "The Philippines intends to bring into line with Article III of the General Agreement, the sales and specific taxes with respect to the items listed in document L/4724/Add.1 whose rates, in accordance with the relevant sections of Titles IV and V of the Philippines Internal Revenue Code in force on the date of this Protocol, vary according to whether the items are locally manufactured or imported and will endeavour to do so as soon as possible in the light of its development, financial and trade needs. If by 31 December 1984, the above-mentioned taxes are still in effect with differential rates for imported items, the matter will be reviewed by the CONTRACTING PARTIES."[298]

A Decision of the CONTRACTING PARTIES of 27 November 1984[299] extended this time-limit until 31 December 1989; a Decision of 4 December 1989[300] further extended this time-limit until 31 December 1991 at which point it lapsed; consensus was not reached on a further extension.[301]

Paragraph 3 of the Protocol for the Accession of Thailand to the General Agreement provides as follows.

> "Thailand intends to bring into line with Article III of the General Agreement, the business and excise taxes with respect to items on which the incidence of these taxes varies according to whether the items are locally produced or imported, and will endeavour to do so as soon as possible in the light of the provisions of Part IV, and in particular Thailand's development, financial and trade needs. If by 30 June 1987, the incidence of the above-mentioned taxes still varies as between locally produced and imported items, the matter will be reviewed by the CONTRACTING PARTIES."[302]

A Decision of the CONTRACTING PARTIES of 17 June 1987[303] extended this time-limit to 30 June 1990; a Decision of 3 October 1990[304] retroactively extended this time-limit until 31 December 1991 at which point it lapsed.

III. PREPARATORY WORK AND SUBSEQUENT MODIFICATIONS

The US-UK *Proposals* provided in section III.A that "Members should undertake: 1. To accord to products imported from other members treatment no less favorable than that accorded to domestic products with regard to matters affecting the internal taxation and regulation of the trade in goods". This principle was elaborated in Article 9 of the US Draft Charter. These provisions were debated at London in the Technical Sub-Committee of Committee II and were redrafted by an ad-hoc group of rapporteurs; however, no national treatment article appeared in the London Draft Charter, as the drafting of this and most of the other general commercial provisions was deferred until the New York meetings of the Drafting Committee. After further work in the Drafting Committee, provisions on national treatment appeared as Article 15 of the New York Draft Charter. At Geneva, the national treatment article was considered in the plenary sessions of Commission A and in an ad-hoc Sub-Committee on the Charter articles on most-favoured-nation treatment, national treatment and tariff negotiations; this article appeared as Article 18 of the Geneva Charter. It was at this time that the provisions on films were separated into a different article. Article III of the original General Agreement text of 30 October 1947 corresponded almost exactly to Article 18 of the Geneva Draft Charter.

---

[298]26S/193, para. 3.
[299]L/5741, 31S/7; see C/M/183.
[300]L/6619, 36S/44; see C/M/237.
[301]W.47/23, SR.47/3 p. 6, C/W/694, C/M/254, p. 6-7.
[302]29S/4, para. 3.
[303]L/6190, 34S/28; see C/M/211.
[304]L/6736, 37S/29; see C/M/243, C/M/244, C/M/245 p. 22.

At the Havana Conference, extensive debates on this provision of the Charter took place in the Third Committee, in its Sub-Committee A on Tariff Negotiations, Internal Taxation and Regulation, and Working Party 3 of the Sub-Committee which focused exclusively on national treatment. As the Chairman of Sub-Committee A stated:

> "... the text of Article 18 had been recast, because the Geneva text, in itself the result of many compromises, was somewhat cryptic and obscure. The text recommended by the Sub-Committee differed considerably in form from the original, but there was only one important change of substance. In the Geneva text discriminatory internal taxes which afforded protection to directly competitive or substitutable products in cases in which there was no substantial domestic production of the like product could be maintained subject to negotiations, but the Sub-Committee recommended their outright elimination as a sounder principle. Members would, of course, be free to convert the protective element of such taxes into customs duties".[305]

The Report of Sub-Committee A adds that "The new form of the Article makes clearer than did the Geneva text the intention that internal taxes on goods should not be used as a means of protection".[306]

The CONTRACTING PARTIES at their Second Session in September 1948 decided to replace the original text of Article III with the text of Article 18 of the Charter *mutatis mutandis*. The Working Party on "Modifications to the General Agreement" "noted that administrative difficulties might arise in the case of countries which would have to change their fiscal regulations twice - on acceptance of the Agreement, and again on ratification of the Charter. ... it recognized that the wording adopted at Havana was clearer and more precise than the text as it now stood".[307] These changes were effected through the Protocol Modifying Part II and Article XXVI, which entered into force 14 December 1948. Article III has not been amended since that date.

The Review Session Working Party on "Schedules and Customs Administration" in 1954-55 considered and rejected various proposals for the insertion of interpretative notes to Article III; see above at pages 144, 184 and 188.[308] It was agreed at the Review Session to insert the provisions of Article IV (on cinematographic films) into paragraph 10 of Article III with no substantive change.[309] However, as this amendment was made contingent on the entry into force of the Protocol Amending Part I and Article XXIX, which did not achieve the requisite unanimous approval and was abandoned, this amendment never entered into force.

---

[305] E/CONF.2/C.3/SR.40 p. 1.
[306] Havana Reports, p. 61, para. 36.
[307] GATT/CP.2/22/Rev.1, adopted 1 and 2 September 1948, II/39, 40-41, para. 11.
[308] See also Report of this Working Party, L/329, adopted 26 February 1955, 3S/205, 210-211, paras. 9-11.
[309] See W.9/236 (changes proposed by the Legal and Drafting Committee).

IV. RELEVANT DOCUMENTS

London

Discussion:	EPCT/C.II/PV/10 (p. 53), 13 (p. 51)
Reports:	EPCT/C.II/64, EPCT/C.II/54/Rev.1, pp. 4-5
Other:	EPCT/C.II/W.2, 5, 14

New York

Discussion:	EPCT/C.6/6, 8, 84
Reports:	EPCT/C.6/55/Rev.1, 97/Rev.1

Geneva

Discussion:	EPCT/EC/SR.2/3, 22 EPCT/A/SR/9+Corr.1, 10+Corr.1-4, 22, 23, 26, 43 EPCT/A/PV/22+Corr.1-5, 23+Corr.1-2, 26+Corr.1-3 EPCT/B/SR.22 EPCT/WP.1/SR/11 EPCT/TAC/SR.10 EPCT/TAC/PV/26 (p.29)
Reports:	EPCT/127, 162, 174, 178, 180, 186
Other:	EPCT/W/23, 25, 26, 28, 29, 30, 48, 56, 62, 79, 92, 99, 106, 112, 147, 149, 150, 181, 267, 272, 280, 301, 309, 313

Havana

Discussion:	E/CONF.2/C.3/SR.9, 11, 13, 40, 41, 42
Reports:	E/CONF.2/C.3/59, 71
Other:	E/CONF.2/C.3/A/W.30 to 35, 38, 39, 46 to 50

CONTRACTING PARTIES

Discussion:	GATT/CP.3/SR.9, 10, 30 GATT/CP.5/SR.6/21
Reports:	GATT/CP.3/42 GATT/CP.5/37 G/25

Review Session

Discussion:	SR.9/18, 20
Reports:	W.9/193+Corr.1, 200, 212+Corr.1, 236+Add.1, L/329, 3S/205
Other:	L/189+Add.1, 261/Add.1, 275 W.9/45 Spec/3/55, 85/55, 94/55

ARTICLE IV

SPECIAL PROVISIONS RELATING TO CINEMATOGRAPH FILMS

I. TEXT OF ARTICLE IV 209
II. INTERPRETATION AND APPLICATION OF ARTICLE IV 209
    (1) *"cinematograph films"* 209
    (2) *Discrimination between films* 210
    (3) *Concessions on screen quotas* 210
    (4) *Relationship with Article III* 210
III. PREPARATORY WORK AND SUBSEQUENT MODIFICATIONS 210
IV. RELEVANT DOCUMENTS 211

I. TEXT OF ARTICLE IV

Article IV

Special Provisions relating to Cinematograph Films

If any contracting party establishes or maintains internal quantitative regulations relating to exposed cinematograph films, such regulations shall take the form of screen quotas which shall conform to the following requirements:

(*a*) Screen quotas may require the exhibition of cinematograph films of national origin during a specified minimum proportion of the total screen time actually utilized, over a specified period of not less than one year, in the commercial exhibition of all films of whatever origin, and shall be computed on the basis of screen time per theatre per year or the equivalent thereof;

(*b*) With the exception of screen time reserved for films of national origin under a screen quota, screen time including that released by administrative action from screen time reserved for films of national origin, shall not be allocated formally or in effect among sources of supply;

(*c*) Notwithstanding the provisions of sub-paragraph (*b*) of this Article, any contracting party may maintain screen quotas conforming to the requirements of sub-paragraph (*a*) of this Article which reserve a minimum proportion of screen time for films of a specified origin other than that of the contracting party imposing such screen quotas; *Provided* that no such minimum proportion of screen time shall be increased above the level in effect on April 10, 1947;

(*d*) Screen quotas shall be subject to negotiation for their limitation, liberalization or elimination.

II. INTERPRETATION AND APPLICATION OF ARTICLE IV

(1) "cinematograph films"

In discussions in the early 1960s, the United States stated that restrictions against showing foreign television programmes were technically a violation of Article III:4, but that some of the principles of Article IV might apply to them.[1] A Working Party was unable to come to any agreement on the subject.[2] Several Draft Resolutions proposed in 1962/63 were not adopted.[3]

In 1991, the United States requested consultations under Article XXII:1 concerning certain measures restricting the showing of non-European films on television. The EEC stated that the question of broadcasting, whether by television or by any other means, belonged essentially to the area of services.[4]

(2) Discrimination between films

At Havana an amendment to the Charter provision corresponding to Article IV was withdrawn in view of the interpretation that "The date fixed in sub-paragraph (c) clearly relates only to discriminatory measures as between foreign films, not as between domestic and foreign films".[5]

(3) Concessions on screen quotas

Additional note 2 *ad* item 3708 of the Torquay Schedule XXXIII of the Federal Republic of Germany provided: "Should the Federal Republic of Germany establish a screen quota for the exhibition of films of foreign origin, the Federal Republic would then not maintain or establish any prohibitions or restrictions (other than non-discriminatory rates or charges), whether made effective through quotas, import or export licenses or other measures, on the importation of films which are the product of any other contracting party. Furthermore, should the Federal Republic of Germany establish such screen quota, this should not exceed 27 per cent. It is, however, confirmed herewith that, should a screen quota be instituted as indicated above, and in case the German foreign exchange position demands prohibitions or restrictions, these can only be effected through the non-transfer of proceeds". In 1956 this concession was withdrawn pursuant to negotiations under Article XXVIII.[6]

(4) Relationship with Article III

See Article III:10.

III. PREPARATORY WORK AND SUBSEQUENT MODIFICATIONS

The corresponding provisions in the Havana Charter appear in Article 19, in the New York Draft in Article 15(4) and in the Geneva Draft in Article 19. Article 9 of the US Draft Charter, on national treatment, proposed to treat internal quantitative restrictions on exhibition as a prohibited mixing requirement. While the London Draft Charter included no agreed national treatment provisions (as resolution of these issues was deferred), the New York Drafts of the Charter and the General Agreement dealt with internal quantitative regulations on distribution or exhibition of cinematograph films in a separate paragraph of the article on national treatment.

After discussion at the Geneva session of the Preparatory Committee, provisions substantially identical to those in the present GATT Article IV were drafted by a Special Subcommittee on Films. "The Sub-Committee agreed that the New Zealand renters' quota is in purpose and effect the equivalent of a screen quota ... This particular quota is in fact a preferential quota of the type referred to in [the Charter provision corresponding to

---

[1] L/1615, L/1646, L/1686.
[2] L/1741.
[3] L/1908, L/2120.
[4] C/M/236 p. 34.
[5] Havana Reports, p. 68, para. 80.
[6] SECRET/27, Spec/86/56.

GATT Article XIV:5(b).]" A note was therefore added to Annex A treating this film quota as a screen quota under Article IV.[7] The date of 10 April 1947 referred to in sub-paragraph (c) was the opening date of the Geneva session.

At the Review Session, it was agreed to incorporate Article IV into Article III:10, as an amendment contingent on the entry into force of the Protocol Amending Part I and Articles XXIX and XXX of the General Agreement.[8] However, this Protocol never entered into effect and was formally abandoned at the end of 1967.[9]

IV. RELEVANT DOCUMENTS

London

Other: EPCT/C.II/W.5, 14

New York

Discussion: EPCT/C.6/8
Reports: EPCT/C.6/97 (p. 11)

Geneva

Discussion: EPCT/A/SR.9, 10 (pp. 18-30), 43
               EPCT/EC/PV.2/22
               EPCT/TAC/SR.10
               EPCT/TAC/PV/10+Corr.1, 26
Reports: EPCT/175, 189, 196, 212, 214/Add.1/Rev.1
Other: EPCT/W/312

Havana

Discussion: E/CONF.2/C.3/SR.13, 41
Reports: E/CONF.2/C.3/59

Review Session

Reports: W.9/236, 3S/25

---

[7] Report of the Special Sub-Committee on Films, EPCT/175.
[8] Protocol Amending the Preamble and Parts II and III of the General Agreement, para. 1(B).
[9] 15S/65.

ARTICLE V

FREEDOM OF TRANSIT

I.	TEXT OF ARTICLE V AND INTERPRETATIVE NOTE AD ARTICLE V	213
II.	INTERPRETATION AND APPLICATION OF ARTICLE V	214
	A. Scope and Application of Article V	214
	1. Scope of Article V	214
	2. Paragraph 1: "traffic in transit"	214
	3. Paragraph 2	215
	(1) *Freedom of transit*	215
	(2) *Neighbouring countries*	215
	4. Paragraphs 3, 4 and 5: "charges"	215
	5. Paragraph 6	216
	(1) *"products which have been in transit"*	216
	(2) *"date of this Agreement"*	216
	B. Exceptions and Derogations	216
III.	PREPARATORY WORK	217
IV.	RELEVANT DOCUMENTS	217

I. TEXT OF ARTICLE V AND INTERPRETATIVE NOTE AD ARTICLE V

Article V

Freedom of Transit

1. Goods (including baggage), and also vessels and other means of transport, shall be deemed to be in transit across the territory of a contracting party when the passage across such territory, with or without transshipment, warehousing, breaking bulk, or change in the mode of transport, is only a portion of a complete journey beginning and terminating beyond the frontier of the contracting party across whose territory the traffic passes. Traffic of this nature is termed in this article "traffic in transit".

2. There shall be freedom of transit through the territory of each contracting party, via the routes most convenient for international transit, for traffic in transit to or from the territory of other contracting parties. No distinction shall be made which is based on the flag of vessels, the place of origin, departure, entry, exit or destination, or on any circumstances relating to the ownership of goods, of vessels or of other means of transport.

3. Any contracting party may require that traffic in transit through its territory be entered at the proper custom house, but, except in cases of failure to comply with applicable customs laws and regulations, such traffic coming from or going to the territory of other contracting parties shall not be subject to any unnecessary delays or restrictions and shall be exempt from customs duties and from all transit duties or other charges imposed in respect of transit, except charges for transportation or those commensurate with administrative expenses entailed by transit or with the cost of services rendered.

4. All charges and regulations imposed by contracting parties on traffic in transit to or from the territories of other contracting parties shall be reasonable, having regard to the conditions of the traffic.

5. With respect to all charges, regulations and formalities in connection with transit, each contracting party shall accord to traffic in transit to or from the territory of any other contracting party treatment no less favourable than the treatment accorded to traffic in transit to or from any third country.*

6. Each contracting party shall accord to products which have been in transit through the territory of any other contracting party treatment no less favourable than that which would have been accorded to such products had they been transported from their place of origin to their destination without going through the territory of such other contracting party. Any contracting party shall, however, be free to maintain its requirements of direct consignment existing on the date of this Agreement, in respect of any goods in regard to which such direct consignment is a requisite condition of eligibility for entry of the goods at preferential rates of duty or has relation to the contracting party's prescribed method of valuation for duty purposes.

7. The provisions of this Article shall not apply to the operation of aircraft in transit, but shall apply to air transit of goods (including baggage).

Interpretative Note *Ad* Article V from Annex I

Paragraph 5

With regard to transportation charges, the principle laid down in paragraph 5 refers to like products being transported on the same route under like conditions.

II. INTERPRETATION AND APPLICATION OF ARTICLE V

A. SCOPE AND APPLICATION OF ARTICLE V

Paragraph 1 and the last sentence of paragraph 2 were based on the text of the Barcelona Convention and Statute on Freedom of Transit of 20 April 1921. Notes to the New York Draft Charter 16 (which corresponds to Article V) state that there is no apparent inconsistency between that Article and the Barcelona Convention.[1] As of 31 December 1994, the Barcelona Convention was still in force and had 46 parties.[2]

1. Scope of Article V

The Report of the New York Drafting Committee on Article 16 of the New York Draft Charter (which corresponded to Article V) states:

"The original text referred in general to persons, goods and means of transport. The text recommended by the Drafting Committee refers to goods and means of transport only, since the transit of persons was considered not to be within the scope of the Charter, and since traffic of persons is subject to immigration laws and may properly be the concern of an international agency other than the organization."[3]

The operation of aircraft in transit was exempted as a subject that would be dealt with by the International Civil Aviation Organization (ICAO), but air transit of goods, including baggage, is covered by paragraph 7.[4] A working party at the Geneva session of the Preparatory Committee discussed whether the principle of freedom of transit applied to goods consigned to a country in bond without a final destination. There was some difference of opinion and the working party did not pursue the matter.[5] Minutes of the discussions of Sub-Committee C of the Third Committee at the Havana Conference note that: "In the opinion of the Sub-Committee the case of grazing livestock ... was not considered as coming within the ambit of this Article."[6]

---

[1]7 LNTS 11; see comment p. 12 of New York Report, which notes also that "Should the question of a new transit convention be raised, the Committee felt that the Organization might wish to co-operate." See also EPCT/C.II/W.11 (comparison of the Statute Annex to the Barcelona Convention and Article 10 of the Proposed Charter); EPCT/34/Rev.1, p. 12; EPCT/C.II/PV.2, p. 63; EPCT/C.II/PV.10, p. 3.
[2]*Multilateral Treaties Deposited with the Secretary-General: Status as at 31 December 1994*, UN Doc. ST/LEG/SER.E/13 (1995).
[3]New York Report, p. 12; similar statement appears at EPCT/C.II/54/Rev.1, p. 8.
[4]EPCT/C.II/54/Rev.1, p. 7.
[5]EPCT/A/SR.20, p. 3; EPCT/109.
[6]E/CONF.2/C.3/C/W.5 p. 1 (transit facilities for grazing livestock; exemption for "seasonal nomads").

2. Paragraph 1: "traffic in transit"

At the Havana Conference it was agreed to add an interpretative note to paragraph 1 of Article 33 of the Havana Charter, as follows: "The assembly of vehicles and mobile machinery arriving in a knocked-down condition or the disassembly (or disassembly and subsequent reassembly) of bulky articles shall not be held to render the passage of such goods outside the scope of 'traffic in transit,' provided that any such operation is undertaken solely for convenience of transport".[7] The 1948 Working Party Report on "Modifications to the General Agreement" notes that while the working party considered a proposal for the insertion into the General Agreement of this interpretative note, the working party "came to the conclusion that such insertion was not necessary, since the text of Article 33, paragraph 1, of the Charter tallied with that of Article V, paragraph 1, of the General Agreement, and the CONTRACTING PARTIES, who all signed the Final Act of the conference of Havana, could not interpret these provisions in any way other than that laid down in the note Ad Article 33 of the Charter".[8]

Also at Havana, Sub-Committee C of the Third Committee on Articles 32-39 "agreed to state in its report that a movement between two points in the same country passing through another country was clearly 'in transit' through the other country within the meaning of paragraph 1".[9]

3. Paragraph 2

(1) Freedom of transit

At the Forty-fifth Session Austria informed the CONTRACTING PARTIES that with effect from 1 December 1989, Austria had limited traffic of certain heavy trucks during night hours on certain Austrian roads. This measure applied to trucks of all nationalities, including Austrian trucks. On 28 February 1990 Austria requested consultations under Article XXII:1 with respect to a measure by the Federal Republic of Germany banning the circulation of 212,000 Austrian lorries during night hours in the entire territory of the Federal Republic. The German measure applied only against Austrian trucks, and, in the view of Austria, was inconsistent with, *inter alia*, Article V.[10]

See also the reference to freedom of transit and Article V in the Working Party Report on "Accession of the United Arab Republic".[11]

(2) Neighbouring countries

At Havana, a proposal to append a note to the corresponding paragraph of the Charter article on transit "to the effect that this Article does not preclude agreements between neighbouring countries for the regulation of transit in respect of their own trade was not approved because such agreements are clearly permissible under the terms of the Article if they do not prejudice the interests of other members in violation of the most-favoured-nation provisions of the Charter, and if they do not limit freedom of transit for other Members".[12] See also under Article XXIV:3(a).

The Interpretative Note *Ad* Paragraph 6 of Article 33 of the Charter provided: "If, as a result of negotiations in accordance with paragraph 6 [not included in the GATT], a member grants to a country which has not direct access to the sea more ample facilities than those already provided for in other paragraphs of Article 33 [V], such special facilities may be limited to the landlocked country concerned unless the Organization finds, on the complaint of any other member, that the withholding of the special facilities from the complaining member contravenes the most-favoured-nation provisions of this Charter".

---

[7] Havana Reports, p. 71, para. 9.
[8] GATT/CP.2/22/Rev.1, adopted on 1 and 2 September 1948, II/39, 44, para. 26.
[9] Havana Reports, p. 71, para. 10.
[10] DS14/1, C/M/241 p. 29.
[11] L/3362, adopted on 27 February 1970, 17S/33, 41, para. 27.
[12] Havana Reports, p.72, para. 12.

4. Paragraphs 3, 4 and 5: "charges"

It was stated by one delegation during the London session of the Preparatory Committee that "the words 'or similar charges' should not be held to imply that traffic in transit shall be exempted from the charges imposed alike on domestic and in transit traffic".[13] The Report of the Technical Subcommittee which considered the general commercial provisions of the draft Charter during discussions at London stated:

"It is understood that the word 'charges' in [paragraph 4] includes charges for transportation by Government-owned railroads or Government-owned modes of transportation. Since this paragraph only provides that such charges shall be 'reasonable', it is believed that the question of preferential rail rates comes under paragraph 5".[14]

The Interpretative Note *Ad* Paragraphs 3, 4 and 5 of Article 33 of the Havana Charter stated: "The word 'charges' as used in the English text of paragraph(s) 3, 4 and 5 shall not be deemed to include transportation charges". It was agreed during discussion of this provision "that transportation charges on traffic in transit did not come within the purview of Article 32 [V], but were subject to the provisions of paragraph 2 of Article 18 [III] …".[15]

See also the reference to internal transportation charges in Article III:4, as well as the Interpretative Note *Ad* Article V:5.

5. Paragraph 6

(1) "products which have been in transit"

The Report of the Technical Subcommittee which examined the general commercial provisions of the draft Charter during the discussions at London states that "… it is understood that paragraphs 2-5 of this Article cover the treatment to be given by a member country to products in transit through its territory between any other member country and any third country, and paragraph 6 covers the treatment to be given by a member country to product cleared from customs within its territory after transit through any other member country".[16]

(2) "date of this Agreement"

The proviso for direct consignment requirements existing on the "date of this Agreement" was added in order to provide for the difficulties of certain countries which required that goods benefiting from historical preferences accorded by them be shipped directly to them from the country of origin.[17] See also the last sentence of Article II:1(c) and the material on it in this volume.

Article XXVI:1 provides that "The date of this Agreement shall be 30 October 1947". This date applies for the obligations under Article V:6 of the original contracting parties; of the former territories of the original contracting parties which, after attaining independence or commercial autonomy, succeeded to contracting party status under Article XXVI:5(c); and of Chile. When the modalities of accession to the General Agreement were first considered, at the Third Session in Annecy in 1949, the Working Party decided to draft the Annecy Protocol of Terms of Accession using instead the date of the Havana Final Act, 24 March 1948, and this approach was followed for the next group of accessions in the Torquay Protocol of 1951.[18] Since the next accession thereafter, which was the accession of Japan in 1955, the standard terms in accession protocols have provided that the "date of this Agreement" for the purposes of Article V:6 shall be the date of the protocol of accession or (where the acceding government had previously acceded provisionally) the date of the declaration on provisional accession.[19]

---

[13] EPCT/C.II/54/Rev.1, p. 10.
[14] EPCT/C.II/54/Rev.1 p. 10.
[15] Havana Reports p. 72, para. 13.
[16] EPCT/C.II/54/Rev.1 p. 11.
[17] EPCT/C.II/42 p. 5-6; EPCT/C.II/54/Rev.1 p. 11.
[18] Annecy Protocol, dated 10 October 1949, I/79, 81, para. 5(b); Torquay Protocol, dated 21 April 1951, I/86, 88, para. 5(b).
[19] E.g. Protocol for the Accession of Bolivia, L/6562, 37S/5.

B. EXCEPTIONS AND DEROGATIONS

See Article V:7. With regard to frontier traffic, see also Article XXIV:3.

The Rapporteurs' Report on the Charter Article corresponding to Article V during the London session of the Preparatory Committee notes, in response to a suggestion that a member be permitted to divert in-transit traffic from the most convenient route if conditions such as a famine required reservation of that route for other use: "It would seem that Article 32(b) and (e) [GATT XX(b) and XXI(b)(iii)] afford ample protection for cases in which transit must be suspended or diverted for humanitarian or security reasons."[20]

III. PREPARATORY WORK

Article V of the GATT corresponds to Article 33 of the Havana Charter. Relevant provisions in the US-UK *Proposals* appear in Chapter III-2. The corresponding Article in the US Draft is Article 10, in the New York Draft Article 16 and in the Geneva Draft Article 32.

The Interpretative Note in the General Agreement does not appear in the Havana Charter. On the other hand, the General Agreement does not include paragraph 6 of Article 33 of the Charter, a provision inserted at the Havana Conference "in view of the great importance of this matter to many countries, particularly to those countries which have no access to the sea"[21], nor does it include three interpretative notes annexed to Article 33 of the Havana Charter. These provisions were not picked up in 1948 when the Working Party on Modifications to the General Agreement in the Second Session considered which of the changes made at Havana should be taken into the General Agreement. Article V has never been amended.

IV. RELEVANT DOCUMENTS

See below at the end of Article X.

---

[20] EPCT/C.II/W.11 p. 1.
[21] Havana Reports, p. 3, para. 16.

Do
(03) 246-5700

ARTICLE VI

ANTI-DUMPING AND COUNTERVAILING DUTIES

I.	TEXT OF ARTICLE VI AND INTERPRETATIVE NOTE AD ARTICLE VI	220
II.	INTERPRETATION AND APPLICATION OF ARTICLE VI	222
	A. SCOPE AND APPLICATION OF ARTICLE VI	222
	1. Institutional background	222
	2. Scope of Article VI	222
	(1) "Dumping"	222
	(2) Measures under Article VI	223
	3. Paragraph 1	223
	(1) "dumping ... is to be condemned if it causes or threatens material injury ..."	223
	(2) "the price of the product exported"	223
	(a) "hidden dumping by associated houses"	224
	(b) Indirect dumping	224
	(3) "normal value"	225
	(a) Criteria for determining normal value	225
	(b) "the comparable price ... for consumption in the exporting country"	225
	(c) "the cost of production in the country of origin plus a reasonable addition for selling cost and profit"	226
	(d) "like product"	227
	(e) Note 2 Ad Paragraph 1: "imports from a country which has a complete or substantially complete monopoly of its trade and where all domestic prices are fixed by the State"	228
	(f) Special problems of developing countries	229
	(4) Comparisons between normal value and export price	230
	(5) "introduced into the commerce"	230
	4. Paragraph 2	231
	(1) "a contracting party may levy on any dumped product an anti-dumping duty"	231
	(2) Basic price systems	232
	(3) Initiation of investigations	233
	(4) Provisional measures	236
	(5) Retroactive effect of an anti-dumping duty	237
	(6) Duration of validity of anti-dumping duties	237
	(7) Use of measures against dumping or subsidization other than anti-dumping or countervailing duties on imports	237
	5. Paragraph 3	239
	(1) "bounty or subsidy"	239
	(2) "the estimated bounty or subsidy determined to have been granted, directly or indirectly, on the manufacture, production or export of such product in the country of origin or exportation"	239
	(3) Multiple currency practices	240
	6. Paragraph 4	240
	(1) "exemption ... from duties or taxes"	240
	(2) "borne by the like product"	241
	7. Paragraph 6	241
	(1) "it determines ... material injury"	241
	(2) Threat of material injury	242
	(3) "to retard materially the establishment"	243
	(4) "to cause ... material injury"	244
	(5) "domestic industry"	245
	(6) Sub-paragraphs 6(b) and 6(c): Anti-dumping and countervailing duties based on material injury to the industry in a third country	247
	8. Paragraph 7	248
	B. RELATIONSHIP BETWEEN ARTICLE VI AND OTHER GATT ARTICLES	249
	1. Article I	249
	2. Article II	250
	3. Article XVI	250
	4. Article XXIII	252
	C. AGREEMENT ON IMPLEMENTATION OF ARTICLE VI AND AGREEMENT ON INTERPRETATION AND APPLICATION OF ARTICLES VI, XVI AND XXIII	252
	1. Work done under the 1979 Agreements	252
	2. Co-existence of the 1979 Agreements and the WTO Agreement	253
III.	PREPARATORY WORK AND SUBSEQUENT MODIFICATIONS	255

IV. **RELEVANT DOCUMENTS** 256

I. TEXT OF ARTICLE VI AND INTERPRETATIVE NOTE AD ARTICLE VI

Article VI

Anti-dumping and Countervailing Duties

1. The contracting parties recognize that dumping, by which products of one country are introduced into the commerce of another country at less than the normal value of the products, is to be condemned if it causes or threatens material injury to an established industry in the territory of a contracting party or materially retards the establishment of a domestic industry. For the purposes of this Article, a product is to be considered as being introduced into the commerce of an importing country at less than its normal value, if the price of the product exported from one country to another

  (*a*) is less than the comparable price, in the ordinary course of trade, for the like product when destined for consumption in the exporting country, or,

  (*b*) in the absence of such domestic price, is less than either

   (i) the highest comparable price for the like product for export to any third country in the ordinary course of trade, or

   (ii) the cost of production of the product in the country of origin plus a reasonable addition for selling cost and profit.

Due allowance shall be made in each case for differences in conditions and terms of sale, for differences in taxation, and for other differences affecting price comparability.*

2. In order to offset or prevent dumping, a contracting party may levy on any dumped product an anti-dumping duty not greater in amount than the margin of dumping in respect of such product. For the purposes of this Article, the margin of dumping is the price difference determined in accordance with the provisions of paragraph 1.*

3. No countervailing duty shall be levied on any product of the territory of any contracting party imported into the territory of another contracting party in excess of an amount equal to the estimated bounty or subsidy determined to have been granted, directly or indirectly, on the manufacture, production or export of such product in the country of origin or exportation, including any special subsidy to the transportation of a particular product. The term "countervailing duty" shall be understood to mean a special duty levied for the purpose of offsetting any bounty or subsidy bestowed, directly, or indirectly, upon the manufacture, production or export of any merchandise.*

4. No product of the territory of any contracting party imported into the territory of any other contracting party shall be subject to anti-dumping or countervailing duty by reason of the exemption of such product from duties or taxes borne by the like product when destined for consumption in the country of origin or exportation, or by reason of the refund of such duties or taxes.

5. No product of the territory of any contracting party imported into the territory of any other contracting party shall be subject to both anti-dumping and countervailing duties to compensate for the same situation of dumping or export subsidization.

6. (*a*) No contracting party shall levy any anti-dumping or countervailing duty on the importation of any product of the territory of another contracting party unless it determines that the effect of the dumping or subsidization, as the case may be, is such as to cause or threaten material injury to an established domestic industry, or is such as to retard materially the establishment of a domestic industry.

(b) The CONTRACTING PARTIES may waive the requirement of sub-paragraph (a) of this paragraph so as to permit a contracting party to levy an anti-dumping or countervailing duty on the importation of any product for the purpose of offsetting dumping or subsidization which causes or threatens material injury to an industry in the territory of another contracting party exporting the product concerned to the territory of the importing contracting party. The CONTRACTING PARTIES shall waive the requirements of sub-paragraph (a) of this paragraph, so as to permit the levying of a countervailing duty, in cases in which they find that a subsidy is causing or threatening material injury to an industry in the territory of another contracting party exporting the product concerned to the territory of the importing contracting party.*

(c) In exceptional circumstances, however, where delay might cause damage which would be difficult to repair, a contracting party may levy a countervailing duty for the purpose referred to in sub-paragraph (b) of this paragraph without the prior approval of the CONTRACTING PARTIES; *Provided* that such action shall be reported immediately to the CONTRACTING PARTIES and that the countervailing duty shall be withdrawn promptly if the CONTRACTING PARTIES disapprove.

7. A system for the stabilization of the domestic price or of the return to domestic producers of a primary commodity, independently of the movements of export prices, which results at times in the sale of the commodity for export at a price lower than the comparable price charged for the like commodity to buyers in the domestic market, shall be presumed not to result in material injury within the meaning of paragraph 6 if it is determined by consultation among the contracting parties substantially interested in the commodity concerned that:

(a) the system has also resulted in the sale of the commodity for export at a price higher than the comparable price charged for the like commodity to buyers in the domestic market, and

(b) the system is so operated, either because of the effective regulation of production, or otherwise, as not to stimulate exports unduly or otherwise seriously prejudice the interests of other contracting parties.

Interpretative Note *Ad* Article VI from Annex I

Paragraph 1

1. Hidden dumping by associated houses (that is, the sale by an importer at a price below that corresponding to the price invoiced by an exporter with whom the importer is associated, and also below the price in the exporting country) constitutes a form of price dumping with respect to which the margin of dumping may be calculated on the basis of the price at which the goods are resold by the importer.

2. It is recognized that, in the case of imports from a country which has a complete or substantially complete monopoly of its trade and where all domestic prices are fixed by the State, special difficulties may exist in determining price comparability for the purposes of paragraph 1, and in such cases importing contracting parties may find it necessary to take into account the possibility that a strict comparison with domestic prices in such a country may not always be appropriate.

Paragraphs 2 and 3

1. As in many other cases in customs administration, a contracting party may require reasonable security (bond or cash deposit) for the payment of anti-dumping or countervailing duty pending final determination of the facts in any case of suspected dumping or subsidization.

2. Multiple currency practices can in certain circumstances constitute a subsidy to exports which may be met by countervailing duties under paragraph 3 or can constitute a form of dumping by means of a partial depreciation of a country's currency which may be met by action under paragraph 2. By "multiple currency practices" is meant practices by governments or sanctioned by governments.

Paragraph 6 (b)

Waivers under the provisions of this sub-paragraph shall be granted only on application by the contracting party proposing to levy an anti-dumping or countervailing duty, as the case may be.

II. INTERPRETATION AND APPLICATION OF ARTICLE VI

A. SCOPE AND APPLICATION OF ARTICLE VI

1. Institutional background

In the Kennedy Round of multilateral trade negotiations, the 1967 Agreement on Implementation of Article VI was negotiated, and entered into force on 1 July 1968. In the Tokyo Round of multilateral trade negotiations, two agreements relating to Article VI were negotiated, and entered into force on 1 January 1980: the 1979 Agreement on Implementation of Article VI, and the 1979 Agreement on Interpretation and Application of Articles VI, XVI and XXIII. The 1967 agreement was limited in participation to those contracting parties and the EEC which had accepted it; the 1979 agreements were limited in participation to contracting parties that had accepted them, or governments not contracting parties to the GATT which had acceded to them.

In the Uruguay Round of multilateral trade negotiations, new agreements were negotiated, which are included in Annex 1A of the WTO Agreement, entered into force with it on 1 January 1995, and bind all Members of the WTO: the 1994 Agreement on Implementation of Article VI, and the Agreement on Subsidies and Countervailing Measures. Information is provided in this chapter from relevant panel reports and decisions under the 1967 and 1979 agreements and in GATT practice, but not on the WTO agreements.

See further at page 252.

2. Scope of Article VI

(1) "Dumping"

During the London meetings of the Preparatory Committee, in the discussions of the Technical Sub-Committee on Article 11 of the US proposed Charter on anti-dumping duties, it was stated that "the discussion had shown that there were four types of dumping: price, service, exchange and social. Article 11 permitted measures to counteract the first type. It would obligate members not to impose anti-dumping duties with respect to the other three types. It seemed to be generally agreed that exchange dumping was a question for the Fund to consider. Social dumping was a matter for consideration by the Committee studying industrialization".[1]

The Report of the Sub-Committee at the Havana Conference which considered and extensively debated the article of the Charter on anti-dumping and countervailing duties noted regarding the text of this Article, "The Article as agreed to by the Sub-Committee condemns injurious 'price dumping' as defined therein and does not relate to other types of dumping".[2] The Report of another Sub-Committee which considered the general exceptions to Chapter IV, the commercial policy chapter of the Charter, noted as well that, in discussing an amendment to the provision corresponding to GATT Article XX(d), "designed to exempt measures against so-called 'social dumping' from the provisions of Chapter IV, the Sub-Committee expressed the view that this objective was covered for short-term purposes by paragraph 1 of Article 40 [XIX] and for long-term purposes by Article 7 [on worker rights] in combination with Articles 93, 94 and 95 [on dispute settlement]".[3]

The 1960 Second Report of the Group of Experts on "Anti-Dumping and Countervailing Duties" notes that "the Group decided that what was generally known as freight dumping did not fall under the provisions of Article VI".[4]

---

[1] EPCT/C.II/48, p. 1.
[2] Havana Reports, p. 74, para. 23; see also E/CONF.2/C.3/C/18, p. 3. In 1948 this Article of the Havana Charter was brought into the General Agreement and replaced the prior text of Article VI; see Section III below.
[3] Havana Reports, p. 84, para. 19.
[4] L/1141, adopted on 27 May 1960, 9S/194, 199, para. 27; concerning freight dumping see further SR.13/16, Spec/326/58, and Spec/343/58.

(2) Measures under Article VI

See the material below at page 237 on "Use of measures against dumping or subsidization other than anti-dumping or countervailing duties on imports".

3. Paragraph 1

(1) *"dumping ... is to be condemned if it causes or threatens material injury ..."*

The first sentence of Article VI:1 was drafted at the Havana Conference "as a preamble to Article [VI] ... which would, in effect, constitute a general condemnation of the practice of dumping".[5] In discussions at the Review Session in 1954-55, in connection with the rejection of a proposal to add a clause specifically obligating contracting parties to prevent dumping by their commercial enterprises, it was agreed to add the following statement to the Working Party's Report:

> "In connexion with the effect of Article VI on the practice of dumping itself, they agreed that it follows from paragraph 1 of Article VI that contracting parties should, within the framework of their legislation, refrain from encouraging dumping, as defined in that paragraph, by private commercial enterprises".[6]

(2) *"the price of the product exported"*

In the 1959 Report of the Group of Experts on "Anti-Dumping and Countervailing Duties"

> "... the Group noted that although paragraph 1 of Article VI of the General Agreement refers to the price at which products are introduced into the commerce of another country, the same paragraph later speaks of the price of the product 'exported'. The Group concluded that the latter was a guide as to how the 'dumped price' should most appropriately be established. The Group further noted that Article VI also stipulated that 'due allowance shall be made in each case for differences in conditions and terms of sale, for differences in taxation, and for other differences affecting price comparability'. In view of this, it seemed that the essential aim was to make an effective comparison between the normal domestic price in the exporting country and the price at which the like product left that country.

> "The Group took the view that it was the export price that had to be compared with the normal domestic price and agreed that the export price would ideally be the ex-factory price on sales for export; an equally satisfactory price would be the f.o.b. price, port of shipment. In the exceptional case where the actual f.o.b. price on an invoice could not appropriately be used (for example, where the export sale was between associated houses), the export price might be taken to be a notional f.o.b. price calculated by making adjustments such as would normally be made to convert a c.i.f. or other price to f.o.b. The aim should in any event be to arrive at a price which was genuinely comparable with the domestic price in the exporting country".[7]

In the Second Report of the Group of Experts on "Anti-Dumping and Countervailing Duties"

> "It was noted that it sometimes happened that importers sold imported products at a loss, for example, in order to gain a foothold in a market. However, provided that the f.o.b. export price of the article was not below the normal domestic value of the comparable article in the country of export, this was not dumping in the GATT sense. It could become dumping if the importer were in some way recompensed for his loss by the exporter. If a refund or any other consideration was given by the exporter, this should be taken into account in determining the export price and if the consequent export price was less than the normal value, the result would be a dumping price".[8]

---

[5] E/CONF.2/C.3/C/18, p. 2.
[6] L/334 and Addendum, adopted on 3 March 1955, 3S/222, 223, para. 4; discussion at SR.9/41 p. 2.
[7] L/978, adopted on 13 May 1959, 8S/145, 146, paras. 5-6.
[8] L/1141, adopted on 27 May 1960, 9S/194, 199, para. 28.

(a) "hidden dumping by associated houses"

See Interpretative Note to paragraph 1. See also Articles 2(e) and 2.5 of the Agreements on Implementation of Article VI of the General Agreement on Tariffs and Trade of 1967 and 1979 respectively[9] which provide: "In cases where there is no export price or where it appears to the authorities concerned that the export price is unreliable because of association or a compensatory arrangement between the exporter and the importer or a third party, the export price may be constructed on the basis of the price at which the imported products are first resold to an independent buyer, or if the products are not resold to an independent buyer, or not resold in the condition as imported, on such reasonable basis as the authorities may determine".[10]

(b) Indirect dumping

The Report of the Review Working Party on "Other Barriers to Trade" provides as follows:

"The Working Party also agreed that in the case where goods are not imported directly from the country of origin but are consigned to the country of importation from an intermediate territory, it would be in accordance with the terms of Article VI to determine the margin of dumping by comparing the price at which the goods are sold from the country of consignment to the country of importation with the comparable price (as defined in paragraph 1 of Article VI) in either the country of consignment or the country of origin of the goods. It is of course understood that where goods are merely transhipped through a third country without entering into the commerce of that country, it would not be permissible to apply anti-dumping duties by reference to prices of like goods in the country".[11]

The Report of the Group of Experts on "Anti-Dumping and Countervailing Duties" notes that:

"In their examination of the problem of the determination of the normal value or the domestic market price in the exporting country the Group then considered the question of dumping of goods where the exporting country is not the producing country of the goods concerned... The Group noted that since the wording of Article VI, paragraph 1(a), referred only to the comparable price in the exporting country, there was some doubt whether action against indirect dumping was strictly in accordance with the letter of the Agreement. However, despite this doubt, the Group were generally of the opinion that it was reasonable for countries to have the right to protect themselves against indirect dumping (whether of processed or unprocessed goods), particularly in view of the provision of Article VI which permits the imposition of countervailing duties to offset the effects of subsidies whether these are granted in the producing country or the exporting country, and in this connection the Group noted the conclusions recorded in paragraph 5 of the report of the Review Working Party on Other Barriers to Trade (BISD, Third Supplement, page 223)".[12]

See also Articles 2(c) and 2:3 of the Agreement on Implementation of Article VI of the General Agreement of 1967 and 1979 respectively[13], which provide: "In the case where products are not imported directly from the country of origin but are exported to the country of importation from an intermediate country, the price at which the products are sold from the country of export to the country of importation shall normally be compared with the comparable price in the country of export. However, comparison may be made with the price in the country of origin, if, for example, the products are merely transhipped through the country of export, or such products are not produced in the country of export, or there is no comparable price for them in the country of export". Similarly, Article 2:11 of the 1979 Agreement on Interpretation and Application of Articles VI, XVI and XXIII provides that "In cases where products are not imported directly from the country of origin but are exported to the country of importation from an intermediate country, the provisions of this Agreement shall be fully applicable

---

[9] 15S/25; 26S/172.
[10] 26S/173.
[11] L/334, adopted on 3 March 1955, 3S/222ff.
[12] L/978, adopted on 13 May 1959, 8S/148, 149, para. 11.
[13] 15S/24, 25; 26S/171, 172.

and the transaction or transactions shall, for the purposes of this Agreement, be regarded as having taken place between the country of origin and the country of importation".[14]

(3) "normal value"

(a) Criteria for determining normal value

Paragraph 1 of Article VI sets out three ways to determine the normal value of the exported goods. The Panel Report on "Swedish Anti-Dumping Duties" notes in this respect:

> "The Panel was of the opinion that if the Swedish authorities considered that it was not possible to find 'a comparable price in the ordinary course of trade for the like product when destined for consumption in the exporting country', no provision in the General Agreement would prevent them from using one of the other two criteria laid down in Article VI".[15]

The Report of the Group of Experts on "Anti-Dumping and Countervailing Duties" contains a discussion of the order in which the criteria of paragraph 1 of Article VI should be used:

> "The Group had some discussion on whether the criteria in paragraph 1(b)(i) and paragraph 1(b)(ii) of Article VI were alternative and equal criteria to be used at the discretion of the importing country, or whether paragraph 1(b)(ii) could only be used in cases where it had not been possible to determine a normal market value under paragraph 1(a) or paragraph 1(b)(i) of Article VI. The Group was of the opinion that paragraph 1(b)(i) and paragraph 1(b)(ii) laid down alternative and equal criteria to be used at the discretion of the importing country but only after it had failed to establish a normal market value under paragraph 1(a) of Article VI ... The Group thought that no order of priority for these two criteria could be imposed but, though it might often be easier to collect the necessary information for the use of the criterion under paragraph 1(b)(i), the use of the criterion under paragraph 1(b)(ii) was sometimes preferable in that, since it was normal and reasonable for different prices to be charged in different markets, the use of the criterion under paragraph 1(b)(i) could often produce misleading results. The Group agreed that the criteria under paragraph 1(b) of Article VI could only be used where no domestic price existed as defined in paragraph 1(a) or in cases where there were sales to the home market but where it was not possible to determine normal value from these sales, for example because they did not fall within 'the ordinary course of trade' as required in paragraph 1(a)".[16]

See also Articles 2(d) and 2.4 of the 1967 and 1979 Agreements on Implementation of Article VI respectively: "When there are no sales of the like product in the ordinary course of trade in the domestic market of the exporting country or when, because of the particular market situation, such sales do not permit a proper comparison, the margin of dumping shall be determined by comparison with a comparable price of the like product when exported to any third country which may be the highest such export price but should be a representative price, or with the cost of production in the country of origin plus a reasonable amount for administrative, selling and any other costs and for profits. As a general rule, the addition for profit shall not exceed the profit normally realized on sales of products of the same general category in the domestic market of the country of origin".[17]

(b) "the comparable price ... for consumption in the exporting country"

The 1959 Report of the Group of Experts on "Anti-Dumping and Countervailing Duties" notes:

> "The Group discussed the problems that arose from the fact that rarely was there only one selling price of a product on the domestic market. More frequently, there was a whole range of different domestic prices for a particular product, varying according to the quantity sold and the terms of individual contracts. The

---

[14] 26S/59.
[15] L/328, adopted on 26 February 1955, 3S/81, 89, para. 28.
[16] L/978, adopted on 13 May 1959, 8S/145, 148, para. 10.
[17] 15S/24, 25; 26S/171, 172.

Group agreed that, despite the difficulties of determining the normal domestic price in the exporting country where these circumstances occurred, it would not be desirable to adopt a uniform system of averaging of relevant price quotations; such a system could in certain circumstances nullify attempts to deal with genuine dumping and could in other circumstances lead the importing country to conclude that there was a margin of dumping where in fact dumping had not occurred. The Group agreed that the use of weighted averages should be confined to cases where it was impossible to use a more direct method of establishing the normal domestic price".[18]

In the 1962 Panel Report on "Exports of Potatoes to Canada," the Panel examined a complaint by the United States concerning the imposition by Canada of an import charge on potatoes in addition to the bound specific duty, as a result of the application under the Canadian Customs Act of "values for duty" on potatoes imported below a certain price.

"The Panel ... considered that there was no basic difference between the price, in the ordinary course of trade, of exported potatoes and potatoes intended for domestic consumption in the United States. The Panel felt that the problem for Canadian producers was caused by specific climatic differences which could in certain years give rise to exceptional difficulties. The Panel concluded that the imposition of an additional charge could not be justified by Article VI of the General Agreement, since the main requirement laid down in paragraph 1(a) of the Article was not satisfied, namely that the price of the product exported from one country to another was less than the comparable price, in the ordinary course of trade, for the like product when destined for consumption in the exporting country.[19]

(c) *"the cost of production in the country of origin plus a reasonable addition for selling cost and profit"*

The Panel on "Swedish Anti-Dumping Duties" notes, concerning the anti-dumping measures examined by the panel:

"The Panel concluded that, in effect, the Swedish authorities were relying on the third criterion [in Article VI] which related to the cost of production. The Panel felt that the use by the Swedish authorities of a weighted average as between the Italian prices could only give a rough estimate of the normal price and that if this approach were retained, it would be reasonable to expect that, if the average included not only the 'unmarked' and 'marked' first-choice stockings of a given type, but also the second and third choices of the same type, the results would be more accurate".[20]

The Second Report of the Group of Experts on "Anti-Dumping and Countervailing Duties" notes:

"It was presumed by the Group that the term 'production costs' included all those items involved, directly or indirectly, in the cost of producing an article. While the precise apportionment of these costs to various headings might differ in various countries, the term would normally cover such items as, for example, the cost of materials and components, labour, general over-heads, depreciation on plant and machinery and interest on capital investment.

"The Group noted the provision in paragraph 1(b)(ii) of Article VI that to the cost of production, when this criterion was being used for the determination of normal value, there was to be 'a reasonable addition for selling costs and profit'. The effect of this was to construct what might be regarded as a national ex-factory sales price on the domestic market of the exporting country in circumstances where there was no such actual price or not one that could be used for the determination of normal value. As in the case of 'production costs', the practices of various countries differed on the items to be included under the heading of 'selling costs'. Typical examples were such items as advertising costs and sales commission. The Group agreed, however, that whatever the particular method used for determining both production and sales costs the aim should always be to arrive at a normal value which was genuinely comparable with the export price.

---

[18]L/978, adopted on 13 May 1959, 8S/145, 147, para. 9.
[19]L/1927, adopted on 16 November 1962, 11S/88, 93, para. 17.
[20]L/328, adopted 26 February 1955, 3S/81, 89 para. 30.

Only thus could it be properly determined whether or not merchandise was being sold at less than its normal value in the meaning of Article VI".[21]

The Panel Report on "New Zealand - Imports of Electrical Transformers from Finland" examined the imposition of anti-dumping duties in respect of a sale of two custom-built large power transformers.

"... The Panel noted that - in the absence of a domestic price in Finland for custom-built transformers of this kind - the New Zealand authorities had based their determination of normal value on the cost-of-production method foreseen in Article VI:1(b)(ii). The Panel also noted that Finland, while not objecting to the use of this method as such, had contested the individual elements of the calculation as being too high, resulting in a constructed price much higher than the actual price of the Finnish exporter. In the Finnish view, the New Zealand authorities should have instead used the cost elements provided by the exporter. The Panel, having heard the arguments put forward by both sides and having perused the documents submitted, concluded that the Finnish exporter, whether through its own fault or not, had not provided all of the necessary cost elements which would have enabled the New Zealand authorities to carry out a meaningful cost-of-production calculation on the basis of the information supplied by the exporter alone. ... In the view of the Panel, the New Zealand authorities were therefore justified in making a cost calculation, where necessary, on the basis of price elements obtained from other sources.

"The Panel then considered the evidence put forward by both sides as to the appropriateness of the cost elements used by the New Zealand authorities in arriving at their decision that dumping had occurred. The Panel noted that this evidence was of a highly technical nature, especially because it related to complicated custom-built products. It also noted that Article VI did not contain any specific guidelines for the calculation of cost-of-production and considered that the method used in this particular case appeared to be a reasonable one. In view of this and having noted the arguments put forward by both sides as regards the costing of certain inputs used in the manufacture of the transformers, the Panel considered that there was no basis on which to disagree with the New Zealand authorities' finding of dumping ...".[22]

(d) "like product"

During discussions at the Havana Conference it was stated that the words "like product" "meant in this instance the same product".[23] The 1959 Report of the Group of Experts on "Anti-Dumping and Countervailing Duties" notes as follows:

"In discussing the meaning of the term 'like product', the Group agreed that this term should be interpreted as a product which is identical in physical characteristics subject, however, to such variations in presentation which are due to the need to adapt the product to special conditions in the market of the importing country (i.e., to accommodate different tastes or to meet specific legal or statutory requirements). Some members drew attention to the fact that such an approach was also in conformity with the [statement cited above] concerning the term 'like product' ... where it is stated that the words '"like product" meant in this instance the same product'. For the purpose of an adjustment as mentioned above, however, downward or upward corrections of the price of the like product should be permitted so as to take into account the differences in the type of the products destined for the home market and for the various export markets.

"The Group pointed out that the meaning of 'like product' as agreed by them should not be interpreted either too broadly so as to cover products of a different kind with higher prices on the internal market, nor too stringently so as to elude the application of paragraph 1(a) of Article VI.

"During the discussion of the term 'like product' the Group found some discrepancy in the English and French texts of paragraph 1 of Article VI. In the English text the words '*the* like product' are used and in the French text the words '*un* produit similaire', which are slightly vaguer, are used. The Group

---

[21]L/1141, adopted on 27 May 1960, 9S/194, 196, paras. 12-13.
[22]L/5814, adopted on 18 July 1985, 32S/55, 66-67, paras. 4.2-4.3.
[23]E/CONF.2/C.3/SR.30, p. 5.

nevertheless thought that this slight discrepancy between the two texts would have no practical effect if the term 'like product' were interpreted as suggested by the Group".[24]

Articles 2(b) and 2:2 of the 1967 and 1979 Agreements on Implementation of Article VI of the General Agreement respectively, as well as a footnote to Article 6:1 of the 1979 Agreement on Interpretation and Application of Articles VI, XVI and XXIII of the General Agreement, contain the following definition:

"Throughout this Code [Agreement] the term 'like product' ('produit similaire') shall be interpreted to mean a product which is identical, i.e. alike in all respects to the product under consideration, or in the absence of such a product, another product which, although not alike in all respects, has characteristics closely resembling those of the product under consideration".[25]

See also the material on "domestic industry" below at page 245.

(e) *Note 2 Ad Paragraph 1: "imports from a country which has a complete or substantially complete monopoly of its trade and where all domestic prices are fixed by the State"*

The addition of Note 2 *Ad* Paragraph 1 was agreed in the Review Session of 1954-55. The Report of the Review Working Party on "Other Barriers to Trade" notes that "The Working Party considered a proposal by Czechoslovakia for amending sub-paragraph 1(b) to deal with the special problem of finding comparable prices for the application of that sub-paragraph to the case of a country all, or substantially all, of whose trade is operated by a state monopoly. The Working Party was not prepared to recommend the amendment of the Article in this respect, but agreed to an interpretative note to meet the case".[26]

The Report of the Working Party on the "Accession of Poland" records:

"With regard to the implementation, where appropriate, of Article VI of the General Agreement with respect to imports from Poland, it was the understanding of the Working Party that the second Supplementary Provision in Annex I to paragraph 1 of Article VI of the General Agreement, relating to imports from a country which has a complete or substantially complete monopoly of its trade and where all domestic prices are fixed by the State, would apply. In this connexion it was recognized that a contracting party may use as the normal value for a product imported from Poland the prices which prevail generally in its markets for the same or like products or a value for that product constructed on the basis of the price for a like product originating in another country, so long as the method used for determining normal value in any particular case is appropriate and not unreasonable".[27]

The same text appears in the Report of the Working Party on "Accession of Romania";[28] a text similar to the second sentence of this paragraph appears in the Report of the Working Party on "Accession of Hungary".[29] See also Articles 2(g) and 2:7 of the 1967 and 1979 Agreements on Implementation of Article VI of the General Agreement respectively, which provide that "This Article is without prejudice to the Second Supplementary Provision to paragraph 1 of Article VI in Annex I of the General Agreement".[30] See also Article 15 of the 1979 Agreement on Interpretation and Application of Articles VI, XVI and XXIII of the General Agreement.[31]

---

[24] L/978, adopted on 13 May 1959, 8S/145, 149, paras. 12-14.
[25] 15S/24, 25; 26S/171, 172; 26S/56, 65 fn. 1.
[26] L/334, adopted 3 March 1955, 3S/222, 223 para. 6; see also proposals at W.9/86, Spec/93/55.
[27] L/2806, adopted on 26 June 1967, 15S/109, 111, para. 13.
[28] L/3557, adopted on 6 October 1971, 18S/94, 96 para. 13.
[29] L/3889, adopted on 30 July 1973, 20S/34, 37, para. 18.
[30] 15S/24, 26; 26S/171, 173.
[31] 26S/56, 74-75.

(f)   Special problems of developing countries

The 1975 Report of the Working Party on "Acceptance of the Anti-Dumping Code" records that:

"It appeared from communications from developing countries and from the discussion in the Working Party that the fundamental problem for developing countries in respect of possible anti-dumping measures against their exports was that the home market prices in developing countries for domestically manufactured products were, for various reasons, in most cases higher than those obtainable in the export markets. In order to find outlets abroad for their manufactures, developing countries were thus compelled to sell at prices which could be termed 'dumped' under the criteria of Article VI of GATT and the Anti-Dumping Code, although there were no intentions of causing injury or of dumping in the traditional sense of the word on the side of the exporters. A solution would therefore have to be based on the recognition that in the cases of developing countries it was not reasonable to use home market prices or production costs as normal values in dumping investigations".

...

"The Working Party, not being able to agree on a solution to the problems referred to it by the Council, considered that it should limit itself to reporting to the Council the opinions expressed in the course of its deliberations."[32]

Article 13 of the 1979 Agreement on Implementation of Article VI of the General Agreement on Tariffs and Trade, which was agreed in the Tokyo Round, provides that:

"It is recognized that special regard must be given by developed countries to the special situation of developing countries when considering the application of anti-dumping measures under this Code. Possibilities of constructive remedies provided for by this Code shall be explored before applying anti-dumping duties where they would affect the essential interests of developing countries".[33]

On 5 May 1980 the Committee on Anti-Dumping Practices established under the 1979 Agreement adopted decisions concerning the application and interpretation of the Agreement, including the following:

"The Committee, cognizant of the commitment in Article 13 of the Agreement on Implementation of Article VI of the General Agreement on Tariffs and Trade that special regard must be given by developed countries to the special situation of developing countries when considering the application of anti-dumping measures under the Agreement, takes the following decision concerning the application and interpretation of the Agreement in relation to developing countries:

"(i) In developing countries, governments play a large rôle in promoting economic growth and development in accordance with their national priorities, and their economic regimes for the export sector can be different from those relating to their domestic sectors resulting *inter alia* in different cost structures. The Agreement is not intended to prevent developing countries from adopting measures in this context, as long as they are used in a manner which is consistent with the provisions of the General Agreement on Tariffs and Trade, as applicable to these countries.

"(ii) In the case of imports from a developing country, the fact that the export price may be lower than the comparable price for the like product when destined for domestic consumption in the exporting country does not *per se* justify an investigation or the determination of dumping unless the other factors mentioned in Article 5:1 are also present. Due consideration should be given to all cases where, because special economic conditions affect prices in the home market, these prices do not provide a commercially realistic basis for dumping calculations. In such cases the normal value for the purposes of ascertaining whether the goods are being dumped shall be determined by methods such as a comparison of the export price with the comparable price of the like product when exported to any third country or with the cost of production of

---

[32] L/4239, adopted on 21 November 1975, 22S/27, 28, paras. 4 and 14.
[33] 26S/184. See also references to "special regard" in Article XXXVII of the General Agreement.

the exported goods in the country of origin plus a reasonable amount for administrative, selling and other costs".[34]

(4)   Comparisons between normal value and export price

The Report of the Group of Experts on "Anti-Dumping and Countervailing Duties" discusses adjustments for differences affecting price comparability:

"The Group first considered the problem of the determination of the normal value or the domestic market price in the exporting or producing country in the light of the definition in paragraph 1(a) of Article VI [price-to-price comparisons]. ... some members of the Group took the view that if there were differences in [quantities sold in the home market and quantities exported] these should be taken into account in order to meet fully the requirement in paragraph 1 of Article VI that 'due allowance shall be made in each case for differences in conditions and terms of sale'. The Group recognized that, while it was logical and reasonable to make adjustments to take account of different quantities and that countries should follow the general principle of adjustments in each case, difficulties might nevertheless arise in securing the necessary information on which such adjustments should be based. Furthermore, it was thought that each case had to be considered on its merits in the light of the objective of comparison of like quantities.

"The Group further agreed that in order to effect a true comparison between the export price and the normal value of the product in the home market, countries should aim at a comparison of prices at the same level in the trade - e.g., wholesale - and at the same date or dates as near to each other as possible. They should also take into account any such relevant factors as differences in taxation."[35]

"... For the purposes of an adjustment ... downward or upward corrections of the price of the like product should be permitted so as to take into account the differences in the type of the products destined for the home market and for the various export markets".[36]

See also Articles 2(f) and 2.6 of the 1967 and 1979 Agreements on Implementation of Article VI of the General Agreement respectively:

"In order to effect a fair comparison between the export price and the domestic price in the exporting country (or the country of origin) or, if applicable, the price established pursuant to the provisions of Article VI:1(b) of the General Agreement, the two prices shall be compared at the same level of trade, normally at the ex-factory level, and in respect of sales made at as nearly as possible the same time. Due allowance shall be made in each case, on its merits, for the differences in conditions and terms of sale, for the differences in taxation, and for the other differences affecting price comparability. In the cases referred to in paragraph [(e)][5] of Article 2 allowance for costs, including duties and taxes, incurred between importation and resale, and for profits accruing, should also be made".[37]

(5)   "introduced into the commerce"

Canada initiated anti-dumping proceedings against certain electric generators exported by Italy, on the basis of prices bid in response to requests for tenders, but before the generators in question had been imported. In a Request for conciliation under Article 15:3 of the 1979 Agreement on Implementation of Article VI concerning this action by Canada, the EEC referred to the terms of Article 2:1 of the Agreement ("if the export price of the product concerned") and from this drew the conclusion that "this implies that there must have been exports of the product concerned before there can be dumping".[38] The Canadian representative maintained "that both Article VI of the GATT and Article 2 [of the Agreement] were clear in that dumping was regarded as pertaining to the situation where a product of one country was introduced into the commerce of another country at an export

---

[34]ADP/2, Decisions of 5 May 1980, 27S/16, 17.
[35]L/978, adopted on 13 May 1959, 8S/145, 146-147, paras. 7-8.
[36]*Ibid.*, 8S/149, para. 12.
[37]15S/26, 26S/173. See also discussion at 26S/270-271.
[38]ADP/M/11, para. 53; ADP/16, p. 3.

price which was less than the comparable price in the country of exportation. In the case of the bids, both of these conditions were fulfilled. He added that the effective implementation of Article VI and the [Agreement] would be frustrated if importing authorities were unable to deal with such contractual arrangements at time of tender".[39]

4. Paragraph 2

(1) "a contracting party may levy on any dumped product an anti-dumping duty"

The 1955 Panel Report on "Swedish Anti-Dumping Duties" examined a Swedish Decree imposing a basic price scheme under which an anti-dumping duty was levied on imports of nylon stockings whenever the invoice price was lower than a minimum price fixed by the Swedish Government. The Panel noted:

"... Article VI does not oblige an importing country to levy an anti-dumping duty whenever there is a case of dumping, or to treat in the same manner all suppliers who resort to such practices. The wording of paragraph 6 supports that view. The importing country is only entitled to levy an anti-dumping duty when there is material injury to a domestic industry or at least a threat of such an injury".[40]

As regards the burden of proof of facts justifying the imposition of anti-dumping duties, the same Panel Report notes:

"The Panel ... considered the argument developed by the Italian representative to the effect that the Swedish Decree [on a basic price scheme for stocking imports] reversed the onus of proof since the customs authorities can act without being required to prove the existence of dumping practices or even to establish a *prima facie* case of dumping. ... it was clear from the wording of Article VI that no anti-dumping duties should be levied unless certain facts had been established. As this represented an obligation of the contracting party imposing such duties, it would be reasonable to expect that that contracting party should establish the existence of these facts when its action is challenged."[41]

"... The Italian delegation contended that the main injury suffered by exporters was due to the fact that the Swedish Government was levying an anti-dumping duty on Italian stockings although it had not established that the export prices of the products were less than the normal value of those products as required in Article VI of the GATT. The Panel agreed that if the Swedish Decree was being applied in such a manner as to impose an anti-dumping levy in the absence of dumping practices, the Italian Government ... could claim an impairment of benefits.

"The Swedish representative stated that it appeared doubtful to his delegation that the CONTRACTING PARTIES could consider that question and that it was the right of the national authorities to decide whether dumping had really taken place. The Panel agreed that no provision of the General Agreement could limit in any way the rights of national authorities in that respect. But for the reason set forth in paragraph 15 above, it would be reasonable to expect from the contracting party which resorts to the provisions of Article VI, if such action is challenged, to show to the satisfaction of the CONTRACTING PARTIES that it had exercised its rights consistently with those provisions".[42]

In the Report of the Group of Experts on "Anti-Dumping and Countervailing Duties," "the Group agreed that it was essential that countries should avoid immoderate use of anti-dumping and countervailing duties, since this would reduce the value of the efforts that had been made since the war to remove barriers to trade. These duties were to be regarded as exceptional and temporary measures to deal with specific cases of injurious dumping or subsidization".[43] The Report sets out "understandings on various points" in the field of anti-dumping. The Report of the Group of Experts on "Anti-Dumping and Countervailing Duties" notes that "There was agreement

---

[39] ADP/M/11, para. 54.
[40] L/328, adopted on 26 February 1955, 3S/81, 83, para. 8.
[41] *Ibid.*, 3S/85-86, para. 15.
[42] *Ibid.*, 3S/87-88, para. 22-23.
[43] L/978, adopted on 13 May 1959, 8S/145, para. 4.

that decisions concerning the application of anti-dumping measures should be taken at a high administrative level and that all such decisions should be published in an official form. It was also suggested that the reasons for the decision should be made public ...".[44] See also the discussion in the Second Report of the Group of Experts on Anti-Dumping and Countervailing Duties[45] of investigations in exporting countries, governmental or administrative hearings in importing countries, and contacts between governments concerned prior to the imposition of anti-dumping or countervailing duties.

See also Articles 8 ("Imposition and Collection of Anti-Dumping Duties") and 9 ("Duration of Anti-Dumping Duties") of the 1967 and 1979 Agreements on Implementation of Article VI of the General Agreement and Article 4 ("Imposition of Countervailing Duties") of the 1979 Agreement on Interpretation and Application of Articles VI, XVI and XXIII of the General Agreement.[46]

(2) Basic price systems

The Panel Report on "Swedish Anti-dumping Duties" examined two variations on a "basic price" system for anti-dumping proceedings. At first, "an anti-dumping duty was levied whenever the invoice price was lower than the relevant minimum price fixed by the Swedish Government, the importer being entitled to obtain a refund of that duty if the case of dumping was not established. [In a later system] basic prices ... were retained as an administrative device enabling the Swedish Customs Authorities to exempt from anti-dumping enquiries any consignment the price of which was higher that the basic price: the actual determination of dumping policies and the levying of the anti-dumping duty were related to the concept of normal value ... The anti-dumping duty is assessed in relation to the basic price only when that price is lower than the normal value of the imported product". The Panel found as follows:

> "The Panel recognized ... that the basic price system would have a serious discriminatory effect if consignments of the goods exported by the low-cost producers had been delayed and subjected to uncertainties by the application of that system and the case for dumping were not established in the course of the enquiry. ...
>
> "As regards the second argument relating to the fact that the basic price system is unrelated to the actual prices on the domestic markets of the various exporting countries, the Panel was of the opinion that this feature of the scheme would not necessarily be inconsistent with the provisions of Article VI so long as the basic price is equal to or lower than the actual price on the market of the lowest cost producer. If that condition is fulfilled, no anti-dumping duty will be levied contrary to the provisions of Article VI".[47]

The Second Report on "Anti-Dumping and Countervailing Duties" discusses "pre-selection systems" (in which an anti-dumping investigation is conducted with respect to imports below a particular price, and anti-dumping duties are applied only after a specific complaint has been investigated and a finding of dumping and material injury made); and "basic price systems".

> "The Group recognized that, where basic price systems were operated so as to limit anti-dumping action in a particular case to the margin of dumping judged to be materially injurious, these systems were fully within the terms of Article VI and in fact constituted part of a pre-selection system. Nevertheless, the majority of the Group considered that such systems might be open to abuse and they were not therefore in favour of their adoption. Most members of the Group felt that it was, in any case, understood that the basic price system was satisfactory only provided that:
>
> (a) the basic price was less than, or at most equal to the lowest normal price in any of the supplying countries;

---

[44]*Ibid.*, 8S/145, 151, para. 21.
[45]L/1141, adopted on 27 May 1960, 9S/194.
[46]15S/31-32, 26S/180-181, 26S/61-62.
[47]L/328, adopted 26 February 1955, 3S/81, 84, paras. 9-10.

(b) domestic importers or foreign exporters had in all cases the opportunity to demonstrate that their products, although they were sold below the basic price, were not sold at a dumping price; and

(c) the governments using this system periodically revised the basic price on the basis of the fluctuations of the lowest normal price in any of the supplying countries".[48]

Article 8(d) of the 1967 Agreement and paragraph 8:4 of the 1979 Agreement on Implementation of Article VI of the General Agreement set out rules for the application of a "basic price system". In October 1981, the Committee on Anti-Dumping Practices adopted an Understanding on Article 8:4 of the Agreement providing, *inter alia*, that

"The Committee agreed that basic price systems as provided for in Article 8:4 were intended exclusively as a device to facilitate the calculation and collection of anti-dumping duties following a full investigation for each country and product concerned, and for supplies concerned, resulting in a finding of injurious dumping. However, the Committee recognized that the wording of Article 8:4 contained ambiguities and, in the light of different possible interpretations, concluded that Article 8:4 is not essential to the effective operation of the Agreement and shall not provide the basis for any anti-dumping investigation or for imposition and collection of anti-dumping duties.

"At the same time, the Committee discussed special monitoring schemes, in so far as they are related to anti-dumping systems. The Committee recognizes that such schemes are not envisioned by Article VI of the GATT or the Agreement and it is of the view that they give cause for concern in that they could be used in a manner contrary to the spirit of the Agreement. The Committee agreed that such schemes shall not be used as a substitute for initiating and carrying out anti-dumping investigations in full conformity with all provisions of the Agreement ...".[49]

(3) *Initiation of investigations*

The Second Report of the Group of Experts on Anti-Dumping and Countervailing Duties provides that: "The Group agreed that, since the criterion of material injury was one of the two factors required to allow anti-dumping action, the initiative for such action should normally come from domestic producers who considered themselves injured or threatened with injury by dumping. Governments would, however, have the right to take such initiative when the conditions set forth in Article VI existed".[50]

The Report of the Panel, under the Agreement on Implementation of Article VI, on United States - Anti-dumping Duties on Gray Portland Cement and Cement Clinker from Mexico", which has not been adopted, examined the initiation of the anti-dumping investigation which had led to the measures in question. The investigation had been initiated on the basis of a petition which alleged that domestic industries in two regions of the United States had been injured or threatened with injury by dumped imports of gray portland cement and cement clinker from Mexico, and asserted that the petitioners accounted for a majority of domestic production of gray portland cement in the markets in those regions. The Panel examined this matter on the basis of Article 5:1 of the Agreement, which provides: "An investigation to determine the existence, degree and effect of any alleged dumping shall normally be initiated upon a written request by or on behalf of the industry[9] affected ...". Footnote 9 declares: "As defined in Article 4". Article 4 in turn provides a definition of "industry". The Panel found that "in Article 5:1, the term 'on behalf of' involved a notion of agency or representation, and that a petition had to have the authorization or approval of the industry affected, the term 'industry' being defined in Article 4".[51] The Panel also found that "'the producers of ... almost all of the production within such market' would satisfy the definition of 'industry' for the purpose of initiation".[52]

---

[48]L/1141, adopted on 27 May 1960, 9S/194, 195-196, para. 11.
[49]ADP/M/6, 30S/68 (adoption); 28S/52 (text). See also discussion of various systems in the Committee on Anti-Dumping Practices, 25S/18-21.
[50]L/1141, adopted on 27 May 1960, 9S/194 para. 5.
[51]ADP/82 (unadopted), dated 7 September 1992, para. 5.20.
[52]*Ibid.*, para. 5.23.

"The Panel ... noted that the term 'on behalf of' involved a notion of agency or representation and that Article 4 provided the definition of the term 'industry' in Article 5:1, on behalf of which the petition had to be made. In the case of a national market, one of the two definitions of industry according to Article 4:1 was domestic producers whose collective output of the like products constituted a major proportion of the total domestic production of those products. Thus, in a national market, evidence of 'support by a major proportion' would meet the requirement under Article 5:1 because there would be evidence of support for the petition by the industry concerned. However, the Panel considered that in view of the fact that Article 5:1 required that an industry in a regional market be defined as 'producers of all or almost all of the production within such market', support for a petition by producers accounting for a major proportion of the production in that market would not be adequate to satisfy the requirement that a petition had to have the authorization or approval of the producers of all or almost all of the production in the regional market. ...

"Accordingly, the Panel concluded that the producers in a regional market in respect of whom injury had to be found, namely 'the producers of all or almost all of the production within such market', were the producers by or on behalf of which the request for initiating an anti-dumping investigation in a regional market had to be made under Article 5:1.[53]

"... the Panel concluded that the United States' initiation of the anti-dumping investigation on gray portland cement and cement clinker imported from Mexico was inconsistent with Article 5:1 because the United States' authorities did not satisfy themselves prior to initiation that the petition was on behalf of producers of all or almost all of the production in the regional market. ..."[54]

The 1993 Panel Report on "United States - Measures Affecting the Imports of Softwood Lumber from Canada" examined the consistency with the 1979 Agreement on Interpretation and Application of Articles VI, XVI and XXIII of a decision to self-initiate a countervailing duty investigation:

"The Panel noted that the self-initiation of a countervailing duty investigation was subject to the provisions of Article 2:1 of the Agreement. This Article provided in relevant part:

'An investigation to determine the existence, degree and effect of any alleged subsidy shall normally be initiated upon a written request by or on behalf of the industry affected. The request shall include *sufficient evidence* of the existence of (a) a subsidy and, if possible, its amount, (b) injury within the meaning of Article VI of the General Agreement as interpreted by this Agreement[6] and (c) a causal link between the subsidized imports and the alleged injury. If in *special circumstances* the authorities concerned decide to initiate an investigation without having received such a request, they shall proceed only if they have *sufficient evidence* on all points under (a) to (c) above'. (emphasis added)

"Whereas the Agreement called for 'sufficient evidence' and identified the subject matter on which such evidence was to be adduced, the Panel noted that no specific guidance was given as to what might constitute sufficient evidence. The Panel thus proceeded to consider the meaning of the term "sufficient evidence" in Article 2:1 guided by the customary principles of international law on treaty interpretation, according to which treaty terms were to be given their ordinary meaning in their context and in the light of the treaty's object and purpose.

"The Panel considered that the concept of sufficiency of evidence had to be judged in relation to the particular action contemplated in Article 2:1 of the Agreement, that of initiating a countervailing duty investigation, as was made clear in Article 2:3 which referred to 'sufficient evidence *to justify initiating an investigation*'. (emphasis added) In the view of the Panel, the initiation requirement in Article 2:1 reflected a careful balancing of the rights and obligations of the parties, in particular between (1) the interest of the import-competing domestic industry in the importing country in securing the initiation of a countervailing duty investigation and (2) the interest of the exporting country in avoiding the potentially burdensome consequences of a countervailing duty investigation initiated on an unmeritorious basis. With regard to the

---

[53]*Ibid.*, paras. 5.26, 5.28.
[54]*Ibid.*, para. 5.34.

second of these, the Panel considered that in applying the appropriate standard to a review of the decision of a national authority to initiate a countervailing duty investigation, it should in particular be sensitive to the intended anti-harassment function of Article 2:1.

"In analysing further what was meant by the term 'sufficient evidence', the Panel noted that the quantum and quality of evidence to be required of an investigating authority prior to initiation of an investigation would necessarily have to be less than that required of that authority at the time of making a final determination. At the same time, it appeared to the Panel that 'sufficient evidence' clearly had to mean more than mere allegation or conjecture, and could not be taken to mean just any of the national investigative authorities and this factual basis had to be susceptible to review under the Agreement. Whereas the quantum and quality of evidence required at the time of initiation was less than that required to establish, pursuant to investigation, the required Agreement elements of subsidy, subsidized imports, injury and causal linkage between subsidized imports and injury, the Panel was of the view that the evidence required at the time of initiation nonetheless had to be relevant to establishing these same Agreement elements.

"The Panel recalled Canada's position that 'sufficient evidence' in the context of initiation meant 'that amount of proof which ordinarily satisfies an unprejudiced mind'. The Panel further recalled the United States' position that 'sufficient evidence' meant 'evidence that provides a reason to believe that subsidies may exist and that the domestic industry may be injured by reason of the subsidized imports'. The Panel was not persuaded of the correctness of either of these proposed standards. In the Panel's view, the Canadian proposed standard suggested a level of proof more suitable to a determination made at a stage of the process subsequent to initiation rather than to the initiation itself. As for the United States' proposed standard, the Panel agreed that 'reason to believe' was an appropriate yardstick, but that it was not the *potentiality* of the existence of subsidy or injury for which there had to be a reason to believe but rather a reason to believe that those two elements *existed*. This interpretation was confirmed by the wording of the last sentence of Article 2:1 which made clear that the investigating authorities 'shall proceed only if they have sufficient evidence [of the *existence* of subsidy, injury and causation]'. In the view of the Panel, therefore, the term 'sufficient evidence' in the context of initiation of a countervailing duty investigation was to be interpreted to mean 'evidence that provides a reason to believe that a subsidy exists and that the domestic industry is injured as a result of subsidized imports'.

"The Panel noted that it was the rôle of the national investigating authority in the importing country, not that of the Panel, to make the necessary determinations in connection with the initiation of a countervailing duty case. This point was underlined by the language in Article VI:6(a) of the General Agreement, which provided:

'No contracting party shall levy any ... countervailing duty on the importation of any product of the territory of another contracting party unless *it determines* that the effect of the ... subsidization ... is such as to cause or threaten material injury ...'. (emphasis added)

"The rôle of the Panel was thus not to determine whether there was sufficient evidence for initiation but to review whether the national authorities in the importing country had made the initiation determination in accordance with relevant provisions of the Agreement.

"The Panel considered that in reviewing the action of the United States authorities in respect of determining the existence of sufficient evidence to initiate, the Panel was not to conduct a *de novo* review of the evidence relied upon by the United States authorities or otherwise to substitute its judgment as to the sufficiency of the particular evidence considered by the United States authorities. Rather, in the view of the Panel, the review to be applied in the present case required consideration of whether a reasonable, unprejudiced person could have found, based upon the evidence relied upon by the United States at the time of initiation, that sufficient evidence existed of subsidy, injury and causal link to justify initiation of the investigation.

"The Panel noted the argument of Canada that Article 2:1 required a higher standard of sufficient evidence to self-initiate a countervailing duty investigation than to initiate based upon a petition. The Panel noted that the relevant portion of Article 2:1 stated the following:

'If in special circumstances the authorities concerned decide to initiate an investigation without having received such a request, they shall proceed only if they have sufficient evidence on all points under (a) to (c) above.'

"In the view of the Panel, Canada's claim was not well-founded in that there was nothing in the text of Article 2:1 to suggest a different level of evidence for self-initiation than for initiation pursuant to petition. Moreover, the Panel could not discern any purpose under the Agreement which could be served by a different level of 'sufficient evidence' in the case of self-initiation. The Panel recalled Canada's contention that the words 'only if' in the sentence cited above suggested a higher standard for self-initiation than for initiation based upon a petition. However, the Panel considered that the words 'only if' in the above context referred only to the elements mentioned in the second sentence of Article 2:1, not to a different level of 'sufficient evidence'. What was required in addition to 'sufficient evidence' was the existence of 'special circumstances'."[55]

The 1994 Panel Report on "United States - Imposition of Anti-Dumping Duties on Imports of Fresh and Chilled Atlantic Salmon from Norway" also addressed the issue of initiation of an investigation, finding that "A 'written request ... on behalf of the industry affected' ... meant a request on behalf of the domestic producers as a whole of the like products or those of them whose collective output of the products constitutes a major proportion of the total domestic production of those products."[56]

"The Panel then turned to the question of the duty incumbent on investigating authorities to ensure that their actions with regard to the treatment of written requests for the initiation of anti-dumping investigations were consistent with their obligations under Article 5:1. The Panel considered that, in light of the requirement in Article 5:1 that a written request be by or on behalf of the industry affected and contain certain evidence, the investigating authorities could not, consistently with Article 5:1, initiate investigations automatically in response to any written request received. The requirements of Article 5:1 clearly implied a duty for the authorities to evaluate each such written request to ascertain whether it contained the required information, and to screen out those requests that failed to provide it. The investigating authorities therefore had to evaluate whether a written request for the initiation of an investigation was made "on behalf of" the industry affected.

...

"The Panel noted that the Agreement did not provide precise guidance as to the procedural steps to be taken for such an evaluation, and considered that the question of how this requirement is to be met depends on the circumstances of each particular case. In the Panel's view, this question, or in this case the steps the United States was required to take as a prerequisite to initiating an investigation, had to be evaluated on the basis of the information before the investigating authorities at the time of the initiation decision. ..."[57]

The Panel concluded on the basis of its evaluation of the facts that "Under these circumstances the Department of Commerce could, in the Panel's view, reasonably treat this request as being 'on behalf of the industry affected' and the initiation was not inconsistent with the United States' obligations under the Agreement.[58]

(4) Provisional measures

See Interpretative Note 1 to paragraphs 2 and 3; this Note was added at Havana "to answer any doubt that a Member could require security for the 'payment of anti-dumping or countervailing duty pending final determination of the facts in cases of suspected dumping or subsidization'".[59]

---

[55]SCM/153, adopted on 27 October 1993, paras. 330-336.
[56]ADP/87, adopted by the Committee on Anti-Dumping Practices on 27 April 1994, para. 357.
[57]*Ibid.*, paras. 358, 360.
[58]*Ibid.*, para. 362.
[59]Havana Reports, p. 75 para. 27.

The Group of Experts on Anti-dumping and Countervailing Duties in its 1959 report discussed, *inter alia*, the question of provisional anti-dumping measures.

"It was recognized that in certain circumstances the use of such measures might be justified in order to limit the material injury to a domestic industry, even though it was noted that Article VI made no mention of them. On the other hand, it was generally felt that provisional measures should be used sparingly and for the shortest possible time in order to interfere as little as possible with normal trade and in order that they should not assume a protectionist character. For this reason, any such measures should preferably be introduced after the responsible administration of the importing country had carried out an initial confidential investigation that revealed that there was a serious case to consider further. Moreover, where possible, the provisional measures should not lead to a situation in which either the exporter or the importer of the product under investigation would suffer if the eventual decision were not to impose an anti-dumping duty. The Group agreed that it was desirable that such provisional measures should not be of retroactive application and that they should preferably take the form of bond or cash deposits as mentioned in Interpretative Note 1 to paragraphs 2 and 3 of Article VI. Furthermore, they should be based on provisions which would, as far as possible, permit the importer to determine the maximum duty which could be assessed".[60]

See also Article 10 ("Provisional Measures") of the 1967 and 1979 Agreements on Implementation of Article VI of the General Agreement and Article 5 ("Provisional Measures and Retroactivity") of the 1979 Agreement on Interpretation and Application of Articles VI, XVI and XXIII of the General Agreement.[61]

(5) Retroactive effect of an anti-dumping duty

The 1959 Report of the Group of Experts on Anti-dumping and Countervailing Duties provides: "The Group stressed that final decisions should not have any retroactive effect, except that in cases where provisional measures were applied it should be permitted to collect anti-dumping duties against the merchandise covered by such provisional measures".[62] See also Article 11 ("Retroactivity") of the 1967 and 1979 Agreements on Implementation of Article VI of the General Agreement and Article 5:9 of the 1979 Agreement on Interpretation and Application of Articles VI, XVI and XXIII of the General Agreement.[63]

(6) Duration of validity of anti-dumping duties

The same Report provides: "It was generally agreed that anti-dumping duties should remain in place only so long as they were genuinely necessary to counteract dumping which was causing or threatening material injury to a domestic industry. In this connexion it was noted that any country imposing a duty would naturally be free to review it and the Group agreed that it might well be desirable for it to do so from time to time in the light of information at its disposal. It was further agreed that it should be open to exporters of the product concerned, if they considered that they had the necessary evidence, to request the importing country to carry out a review of the facts".[64] See also Article 9 ("Duration of Anti-Dumping Duties" of the 1967 and 1979 Agreements on Implementation of Article VI of the General Agreement and Article 4:9 of the 1979 Agreement on Interpretation and Application of Articles VI, XVI and XXIII of the General Agreement.[65]

(7) Use of measures against dumping or subsidization other than anti-dumping or countervailing duties on imports

Paragraph 7 of Article VI in the General Agreement as agreed in October 1947 (and paragraph 6 of the corresponding Article in the Geneva Draft Charter) provided that "No measures other than anti-dumping or countervailing duties shall be applied by any contracting party in respect of any product of the territory of any

---

[60] L/978, adopted on 13 May 1959, 8S/151-152, para. 23.
[61] 15S/24, 32-33; 26S/171, 181-182; 26S/56, 61-62.
[62] 8S/151.
[63] 15S/24, 33-34; 26S/171, 182-183; 26S/56, 62.
[64] *Ibid.*, 8S/151-152, para. 23.
[65] 15S/24, 32; 26S/171, 181; 26S/56, 63.

other contracting party for the purpose of offsetting dumping or subsidization". The record of the discussions at Havana notes: "The Subcommittee [on Article 34 of the Charter] agreed to the deletion of paragraph 6 of the Geneva Draft which expressly prohibited the use of measures other than anti-dumping or countervailing duties against dumping or subsidization. It did so with the definite understanding that measures other than compensatory anti-dumping or countervailing duties may not be applied to counteract dumping or subsidization except insofar as such other measures are permitted under other provisions of the Charter".[66] After the close of the Havana Conference, the Working Party in the Second Session on "Modifications to the General Agreement" agreed to take the Havana Charter article into the General Agreement, entirely replacing the original Article VI. The Report of this Working Party notes:

"The working party, endorsing the views expressed by [the Subcommittee on Article 34 at the Havana Conference] agreed that measures other than compensatory anti-dumping and countervailing duties may not be applied to counteract dumping or subsidization except insofar as such other measures are permitted under other provisions of the General Agreement".[67]

The Report of the Review Working Party on "Other Barriers to Trade" includes the following passage:

"With respect to paragraph 3 of Article VI, the Working Party considered a proposal submitted by New Zealand which would have permitted under certain circumstances the use of quantitative restrictions to offset subsidization or dumping. This proposal did not receive the support of the Working Party, and has not been recommended".[68]

Article 16:1 of the 1979 Agreement on Implementation of Article VI of the General Agreement provides that "No specific action against dumping of exports from another Party can be taken except in accordance with the provisions of the General Agreement, as interpreted by this Agreement"; Article 19:1 of the 1979 Agreement on Interpretation and Application of Articles VI, XVI and XXIII of the General Agreement provides that "No specific action against a subsidy of another signatory can be taken except in accordance with the provisions of the General Agreement, as interpreted by this Agreement". Identical footnotes to each of these paragraphs provide that "This paragraph is not intended to preclude action under other relevant provisions of the General Agreement, where appropriate".[69] The Preamble of the 1979 Agreement on Implementation of Article VII notes that "valuation procedures should not be used to combat dumping".

The Panel Report of 1988 on "Japan - Trade in Semi-Conductors" notes as follows with regard to quantitative restrictions or other measures imposed on exports by an exporting country:

" ... Having found Japan to have acted inconsistently with Article XI:1, the Panel examined Japan's contention that its measures, being designed to prevent dumping, were justified by the spirit of Article VI, which condemned dumping. The Panel noted that Article VI:1 declared that dumping was to be condemned if it caused or threatened material injury to an established industry or materially retarded the establishment of an industry and that Article VI:2 allowed contracting parties to levy a duty on dumped products, subject to certain specified conditions. The provision was silent on actions by exporting countries. The Panel therefore found that Article VI did not provide a justification for measures restricting the exportation or sale for export of a product inconsistently with Article XI:1.

"The Panel proceeded to examine the contention of the EEC that the measures maintained by Japan to prevent dumping were contrary to Article VI because that provision gave the exclusive right of preventing dumping to the importing countries. The Panel noted that Article VI provided importing countries with the right to levy anti-dumping duties subject to certain specific conditions but was silent on actions by exporting countries".[70]

---

[66]Havana Reports, p.74, para. 25; E/CONF.2/C.3/SR.30, p. 6.
[67]II/41, para. 12.
[68]L/334 and Addendum, Report adopted on 3 March 1955, 3S/223.
[69]26S/171, 186; 26S/56, 78.
[70]L/6309, adopted on 4 May 1988, 35S/116, 159, paras. 120-121.

5. Paragraph 3

(1) "bounty or subsidy"

See also the material below concerning the relationship between Article VI and Article XVI, and the material concerning the definition of a subsidy under Article XVI:1.

The Second Report of the Group of Experts on "Anti-Dumping and Countervailing Duties" records:

"With respect to the meaning of the word 'subsidies', a large majority of the experts considered that it covered only subsidies granted by governments or by semi-governmental bodies. Three experts considered that the word should be interpreted in a wider sense and felt that it covered all subsidies, whatever their character and whatever their origin, including also subsidies granted by private bodies. It was agreed that the word 'subsidies' covered not only actual payments, but also measures having an equivalent effect".[71]

The 1994 Panel Report on "United States - Measures Affecting Imports of Softwood Lumber from Canada" examined a claim that the initiation of a countervailing duty investigation was inconsistent with the Agreement on Interpretation and Application of Articles VI, XVI and XXIII because under the circumstances there could be no subsidy from sales of timber from public lands.

"...the Panel recalled Canada's contention that the theory of economic rent taught that the exaction of economic rent - or revenue collection - for access to a natural resource such as timber could not cause any countervailable market distortion, in terms of an increase in the output or a decrease in the price of products made from the timber, which could constitute a subsidy. According to Canada, the granting of the right of access to the land on which the trees were standing and the collection of revenue (stumpage fees) from those granted the right of access was not the sale of a good. The tree became a good only once it was cut down and turned into a log. The Panel further recalled Canada's argument that stumpage fees were a component of the total cost of making logs but that they were not part of the per unit production cost or variable cost of producing the logs in that the stumpage fee did not influence the marginal cost of producing the next unit of product. The Panel then recalled the United States' contention that the administratively set stumpage fees in the Canadian provinces reduced the cost of the input product (logs) to the forest products industries, thus conferring a benefit on those industries.

"Reviewing these arguments, the Panel considered that assuming that Article XVI of the General Agreement and Part II of the Agreement only covered measures that had trade effects and that this trade effects characteristic also applied to countervailable subsidies under Article VI of the General Agreement and Part I of the Agreement, and assuming further that the theory of economic rent was relevant to the question of whether a governmental measure could have trade effects, the applicability of these arguments in the present case was nonetheless an empirical issue, in that it was not possible to determine without further investigation whether stumpage pricing practices in Canada affected the volume or pricing of lumber. The Panel noted in this regard, as argued by the United States, that there were also a number of studies suggesting, contrary to the argument of Canada, that stumpage fees did in fact affect prices and output of lumber. In the Panel's view, whereas the setting of the price for access to the natural resource in and of itself might relate only to the revenue collection function of government and might not constitute a benefit in connection with the harvesting or extraction of that resource, if the conditions of access were such that stumpage was available only to a specific group of enterprises, then the stumpage programme could potentially be considered as a benefit in connection with the right of access to harvest the resource."[72]

(2) "the estimated bounty or subsidy determined to have been granted, directly or indirectly, on the manufacture, production or export of such product in the country of origin or exportation"

The 1959 Report of the Group of Experts on Anti-dumping and Countervailing Duties refers to "the provision of Article VI which permits the imposition of countervailing duties to offset the effects of subsidies

---

[71] L/1141, adopted on 27 May 1960, 9S/194; 200, para. 34.
[72] SCM/162, adopted by the Committee on Subsidies and Countervailing Measures on 27 April 1993, paras. 346-347.

whether these are granted in the producing country or the exporting country".[73] The Second Report in 1960 of the same Group notes as well:

> "Paragraph 3 of Article VI stipulated that no countervailing duty could be collected beyond the 'estimated' amount of the bounty or of the subsidy granted. In order to arrive at this estimate, the majority of the Group considered it normal, and at least desirable, that the country which became aware of the existence of a subsidy and which ascertained the injury which this subsidy caused, should enter into direct contact with the government of the exporting country. It was also desirable that the latter country should give information requested without delay. This would after all be in its own interest in that it would avoid the imposition of a countervailing duty on its exports at a rate which, failing this information, might be fixed at too high a level".[74]

The 1991 Panel Report on "United States - Countervailing Duties on Fresh, Chilled and Frozen Pork from Canada"

> "... noted in this respect that the words in Article VI:3 'to determine' and 'estimated' as well as the practices of the contracting parties under that provision, as reflected in Part I of the Subsidies Code, indicate that the decision as to the existence of a subsidy must result from an examination of all relevant facts. The Panel considered that the issue was not whether the United States had applied a methodology for establishing facts consistent with Article VI:3 but rather whether the facts which the United States did take into account were all the facts relevant for the determination it has made. The Panel therefore proceeded to examine whether the United States, by basing its determination that pork production is subsidized in Canada on a finding that the conditions set out in Section 771B had been met, had demonstrated that it had taken into account all facts necessary to meet the requirements of Article VI:3".[75]

See also the Guidelines on Amortization and Depreciation adopted by the Committee on Subsidies and Countervailing Measures.[76]

(3) Multiple currency practices

See Interpretative Note 2 *Ad* paragraphs 2 and 3, which provides that "Multiple currency practices can in certain circumstances constitute a subsidy to exports ... or a form of dumping by means of partial depreciation of a country's currency ... By 'multiple currency practices' is meant practices by governments or sanctioned by governments'. See also material on multiple exchange rates under Article XVI; see also the memorandum of the International Monetary Fund on multiple currency practices, annexed to the Report of the Review Working Party on "Quantitative Restrictions".[77]

6. Paragraph 4

(1) "exemption ... from duties or taxes"

The Panel on "Swedish Anti-Dumping Duties" examined the application of Article VI:4 where an anti-dumping scheme applied to products benefiting from an export rebate of duties and taxes. "... the Panel noted that there was no disagreement between the parties concerned regarding the obligation to take account of legitimate refund of duties and taxes".[78]

The 1977 Working Party Report on "Suspension of Customs Liquidation by the United States" examined a United States Federal court ruling that remission and exemption by Japan of consumption taxes on exported consumer electronic products was a countervailable export subsidy. Pending appeal of this decision, final duty

---

[73] L/978, adopted 13 May 1959, 8S/145, 149, para. 11.
[74] L/1141, adopted on 27 May 1960, 9S/194, 200, para. 35.
[75] DS7/R, adopted on 11 July 1991, 38S/45.
[76] SCM/64, adopted on 25 April 1985, 32S/154ff.
[77] L/332/Rev. 1 and Addenda, adopted on 2, 4 and 5 March 1955, 3S/170, 200.
[78] L/328, adopted 26 February 1955, 3S/81, 86 para. 16.

payment (liquidation) of entries of these products had been held in suspense. The Working Party Report notes that "All but one member of the Working Party expressed views on the legal aspects of the matter. They agreed that the Japanese tax practices in question were in full accord with the provisions of GATT, its established interpretation as well as established practice of the GATT. They also agreed that, should the court decision be upheld finally and if countervailing duties were imposed, the imposition of such duties would be in contravention of the provisions of the GATT including Article VI:4 and the note to Article XVI, and would constitute a *prima facie* case of nullification or impairment of Japan's rights under the General Agreement".[79]

(2) "borne by the like product"

The Second Report on Anti-dumping and Countervailing Duties noted the view of the Group, in relation to Article VI:4, that "If, however, it were established that the exemption or the reimbursement [of duties and taxes] exceeded the real charge which the product would have to pay in the exporting country, the difference could be considered as constituting a subsidy".[80]

During its consideration of the 1982 complaint by India concerning certain domestic procedures of the United States, the Committee on Subsidies and Countervailing Measures heard differing views concerning the linkage between payment of internal (cascading indirect) taxes and export tax rebates, and the evidence of such linkage which an importing country could require as a condition for making an adjustment to the level of subsidy determined to exist.[81]

See also the Guidelines on Physical Incorporation[82], which were adopted by the Committee on Subsidies and Countervailing Measures, it being stated that these guidelines constituted an understanding on the manner in which signatories intended to calculate the amount of certain subsidies.[83]

7. Paragraph 6

(1) "it determines ... material injury"

In the Report of the Group of Experts on "Anti-Dumping and Countervailing Duties",

"At the outset of their discussions on the injury concept, the Group stressed that anti-dumping measures should only be applied when material injury, i.e. substantial injury, is caused or threatens to be caused. It was agreed that no precise definitions or set of rules could be given in respect of the injury concept, but that a common standard ought to be adopted in applying this criterion and that decisions about injury should be taken by authorities at a high level. It was suggested that legislation which provided for 'injury' only should be applied as if the word 'material' were stated therein....

"In concluding the discussion on the use of the injury concept and in relating it to the term 'industry' it was the general consensus that, before deciding to impose an anti-dumping duty, the importing country should ensure that dumped goods:

(a) are causing material injury to an established industry; or
(b) clearly threaten material injury to an established industry; or
(c) materially retard the establishment of a domestic industry".[84]

---

[79]L/4508, adopted on 16 June 1977, 24S/134, 138, para. 15. The court ruling was reversed by higher US courts.
[80]L/1141, adopted on 27 May 1960, 9S/194, 201 para. 36.
[81]See SCM/M/11, SCM/M/Spec/7.
[82]SCM/68, adopted on 24 October 1985, 32S/156ff.
[83]31S/262 para. 12.
[84]L/978, adopted on 13 May 1959, 8S/145, 150, paras. 15, 17.

See also the provisions on determination of injury for purposes of Article VI, in Article 3 of the 1967 and 1979 Agreements on Implementation of Article VI of the General Agreement and Article 6 of the 1979 Agreement on Interpretation and Application of Articles VI, XVI and XXIII of the General Agreement.[85]

In the Panel Report on "New Zealand - Imports of Electrical Transformers from Finland"

"The Panel noted the view expressed by the New Zealand delegation that the determination of material injury was a matter specifically and expressly reserved, under the terms of Article VI:6(a), for the decision of the contracting party levying the anti-dumping duty. It also noted the contention that other contracting parties might inquire as to whether such a determination had been made, but that the latter could not be challenged or scrutinized by other contracting parties nor indeed by the CONTRACTING PARTIES themselves. The Panel agreed that the responsibility to make a determination of material injury caused by dumped imports rested in the first place with the authorities of the importing contracting party concerned. However, the Panel could not share the view that such a determination could not be scrutinized if it were challenged by another contracting party. On the contrary, the Panel believed that if a contracting party affected by the determination could make a case that the importation could not in itself have the effect of causing material injury to the industry in question, that contracting party was entitled, under the relevant GATT provisions, in particular Article XXIII, that its representations be given sympathetic consideration and that eventually, if no satisfactory adjustment was effected, it might refer the matter to the CONTRACTING PARTIES, as had been done by Finland in the present case. To conclude otherwise would give governments complete freedom and unrestricted discretion in deciding anti-dumping cases without any possibility to review the action taken in the GATT. This would lead to an unacceptable situation under the aspect of law and order in international trade relations as governed by the GATT. The Panel in this connection noted that a similar point had been raised, and rejected, in the report of the Panel on Complaints relating to Swedish anti-dumping duties (BISD 3S/81). The Panel fully shared the view expressed by that panel when it stated that 'it was clear from the wording of Article VI that no anti-dumping duties should be levied until certain facts had been established. As this represented an obligation on the part of the contracting party imposing such duties, it would be reasonable to expect that that contracting party should establish the existence of these facts when its action is challenged' (paragraph 15)".[86]

(2) Threat of material injury

The Report of the Group of Experts on "Anti-Dumping and Countervailing Duties" notes that "With respect to cases where material injury is *threatened* by dumped imports, the Group stressed that the application of anti-dumping measures had to be studied and decided with particular care".[87] See also the provisions on determinations of threat of injury for purposes of Article VI, in Articles 3(e)-(f) and 3:6-7 of the 1967 and 1979 Agreements on Implementation of Article VI of the General Agreement respectively, and in the first footnote to Article 6:1 of the 1979 Agreement on Interpretation and Application of Articles VI, XVI and XXIII of the General Agreement.[88] The Committee on Anti-Dumping Practices has adopted a Recommendation Concerning Determination of Threat of Material Injury.[89]

In the course of its examination of an EEC complaint concerning anti-dumping action by Canada, the Committee on Anti-Dumping Practices, meeting in November 1983, discussed whether injury or a threat of injury can be caused by submission of tenders, even if the contract is awarded to other bidders and the offered goods have not been exported.[90]

The Panel Report on "New Zealand - Imports of Electrical Transformers from Finland" provides the following in this regard:

---

[85] 15S/24, 26; 26S/171, 173; 26S/56, 64.
[86] L/5814, adopted on 18 July 1985, 32S/55, 67-68, para. 4.4.
[87] L/978, adopted on 13 May 1959, 8S/145, 150, para. 16.
[88] 15S/24, 27; 26S/171, 174-175; 26S/56, 64.
[89] ADP/25, adopted 21 October 1985, 32S/182.
[90] ADP/M/11, paras. 53-56.

"The Panel noted that while the decision of the New Zealand Minister of Customs to impose anti-dumping duties was based solely on material injury having been caused by the imports in question, the New Zealand delegation had also alleged before the Panel the existence of threat of material injury. In view of the high import penetration of the New Zealand transformer market, the significant increase in imports from all sources over one single year and the minimal impact of the actual Finnish imports in question, the Panel saw no reason to assume that imports from Finland would in the future change this picture significantly. The Panel noted in addition that at the time the ministerial decision was taken the Finnish exporter had not attempted to make any further sales to the New Zealand market. The Panel could therefore not agree that the imposition of anti-dumping duties could have been based on threat of material injury in terms of Article VI".[91]

The 1993 Panel Report on "Korea - Anti-dumping Duties on Imports of Polyacetal Resins from the United States" examined an injury determination by the Korean authorities which was partially based on a finding of threat of injury:

"... It followed from the text of Article 3:6 that a proper examination of whether a threat of material injury was caused by dumped imports necessitated a prospective analysis of a present situation with a view to determining whether a 'change in circumstances' was 'clearly foreseen and imminent'. Interpreted in conjunction with Article 3:1, a determination of the existence of a threat of material injury under Article 3:6 required an analysis of relevant future developments with regard to the volume, and price effects of the dumped imports and their consequent impact on the domestic industry."

...

"... While Korea had argued that reliance on capacity of foreign producers to supply the Korean market was consistent with the Recommendation of the Committee on Anti-Dumping Practices, this Recommendation provided for the consideration of whether there existed 'sufficient freely disposable capacity of the exporter *indicating the likelihood of substantially increased dumped exports* to the importing country's market taking into account the availability of other export markets to absorb any additional exports.' This indicated that capacity *per se* was not a sufficient factor in considering the likelihood of increased import volumes.[92]

(3) *"to retard materially the establishment"*

At Havana, it was stated that if an industry became economically unprofitable because of dumping, this would be covered by "retard materially".[93]

Article 3(a) of the 1967 Agreement on the Implementation of Article VI provided, *inter alia*, that "In the case of retarding the establishment of a new industry in the country of importation, convincing evidence of the forthcoming establishment of an industry must be shown, for example that the plans for a new industry have reached a fairly advanced stage, a factory is being constructed or machinery has been ordered".[94]

The 1993 Panel Report on "Korea - Anti-dumping Duties on Imports of Polyacetal Resins from the United States" examined an injury determination by the Korean authorities:

"... if the conclusion [on injury issues in the Korean determination] were to be interpreted to mean that the KTC had made a finding of injury based simultaneously on all three standards of injury, this would necessarily mean that the KTC's statement was internally contradictory: the KTC could not logically have found that a domestic industry was being injured by dumped imports (which presupposed that such an industry was already established) and at the same time that the establishment of a domestic industry was materially retarded by those imports.[95]

---

[91] L/5814, adopted on 18 July 1985, 32S/55, 69-70, para. 4.8.
[92] 222. ADP/92 adopted by the Committee on Anti-Dumping Practices on 27 April 1993, paras. 271, 281.
[93] E/CONF.2/C.3/SR.30, p. 5.
[94] 15S/26. There is no parallel provision in Article 3 of the 1979 Agreement on the Implementation of Article VI.
[95] ADP/92, adopted by the Committee on Anti-Dumping Practices on 27 April 1993, para. 222.

industry was already established) and at the same time that the establishment of a domestic industry was materially retarded by those imports.[95]

(4)   "to cause ... material injury"

The Panel Report on "New Zealand - Imports of Electrical Transformers from Finland" provides in this regard:

> "In its examination, the Panel then turned to the question whether the New Zealand transformer industry had suffered material injury as a result of the imports of the two transformers from Finland.... The Panel did not question that this industry had been in a poor economic situation, due to lack of new orders, diminishing orders on hand in certain product categories, declining profitability, a large increase in imports and considerable uncertainty as to new orders. The Panel noted, on the other hand, that the Finnish imports in question ... represented only 2.4 percent of total sales of the New Zealand transformer industry in 1983. In terms of MVA ratings ... the two Finnish transformers taken together ... represented 1.5 percent of the sum of domestic production and imports, or 2.4 percent of total imports. The Panel also considered it significant that imports increased from 1981/82 to 1982/83 by 250 percent in MVA terms ... and that the imports from Finland represented only 3.4 percent of this increase. In view of these facts, the Panel concluded that while the New Zealand transformer industry might have suffered injury from increased imports, the cause of this injury could not be attributed to the imports in question from Finland, which constituted an almost insignificant part in the overall sale of transformers in the period concerned. In this connection, the Panel rejected the contention advanced by the New Zealand delegation that, at least as far as material injury in terms of Article VI was concerned, 'any given amount of profit lost' by the complaining firm was in some sense an 'injury' to a domestic industry. ...
>
> "In view of the reasons contained in the preceding paragraphs, the Panel came to the conclusion that New Zealand had not been able to demonstrate that any injury suffered by its transformer industry had been material injury caused by the imports from Finland. The Panel therefore found that the imposition of anti-dumping duties on these imports was not consistent with the provisions of Article VI:6(a) of the General Agreement".[96]

The 1992 Panel Report under the Agreement on Interpretation and Application of Articles VI, XVI and XXIII on "Canadian Countervailing Duties on Grain Corn from the United States" examined the countervailing duties in question in relation to, *inter alia*, Article 6:4 of the Agreement; this provision requires that "It must be demonstrated that the subsidized imports are, through the effects of the subsidy, causing injury within the meaning of this Agreement. There may be other factors which at the same time are injuring the domestic industry, and the injuries caused by other factors must not be attributed to the subsidized imports".

> "In the view of the Panel, the CIT's findings of injury and causality were themselves largely based on factors other than subsidized imports: in particular, the factor of a dramatic decline in world market prices resulting in large part from a United States subsidy under the 1985 Farm Bill. Clearly, if there is a general and dramatic decline in world market prices for grain corn, this will affect Canadian producers. It will affect Canadian producers even if Canada does not import any grain corn from the United States, even if it imports grain corn from third countries, even if it is completely self-sufficient in grain corn or, indeed, even if it is a net exporter of grain corn, as it was in some crop years during the period of the CIT investigation. In each case, the Canadian price for corn would still be directly impacted -- in a material way -- by the world price decline. Thus, the price depression experienced in the Canadian market would have occurred in all such cases, and the imposition of countervailing duties would be contrary to Article 6.4, which requires that price depression or prevention of price increases caused by other factors must not be attributed to subsidized imports. Since no case was made by the CIT that *subsidized imports* from the United States were responsible for the decline in prices suffered in Canada, the Panel concluded that the CIT determination was inconsistent with the requirements of Article 6 of the Subsidies Agreement.

---

[95] ADP/92, adopted by the Committee on Anti-Dumping Practices on 27 April 1993, para. 222.
[96] L/5814, adopted on 18 July 1985, 32S/55, 69-70, paras. 4.7, 4.9.

"The Panel considered that the purpose of countervailing duties is to allow signatories to counteract injury from subsidized imports, not from a general decline in world market prices. Only a generally applicable import tariff, not however a countervailing duty on imports from a particular country, can normally prove effective in raising the domestic price when there is a general decline in world prices. The fact that in the present case the countervailing duty may have been partially effective in raising the price of grain corn in Canada, in that the United States was the only viable source for imports given the existence of phytosanitary regulations which effectively barred all other imports, does not relieve Canada of the duty of making an injury determination in accordance with Article 6, namely, of showing that subsidized imports are the cause of material injury. ..."[97]

(5) "domestic industry"

The Sub-Committee that considered the Havana Charter article which became Article VI noted in its report: "The Sub-Committee desired it to be understood that, where the word 'industry' is used in the Article, it includes such activities as agriculture, forestry, mining etc., as well as manufacturing".[98]

The Report of the Group of Experts on "Anti-Dumping and Countervailing Duties" further notes:

"The Group discussed the term 'industry' in relation to the concept of injury and agreed that, even though individual cases would obviously give rise to particular problems, as a general guiding principle judgements of material injury should be related to total national output of the like commodity concerned or a significant part thereof. The Group agreed that the use of anti-dumping duties to offset injury to a single firm within a large industry (unless that firm were an important or significant part of the industry) would be protectionist in character, and the proper remedy for that firm lay in other directions".[99]

In the Panel Report on "New Zealand - Imports of Electrical Transformers from Finland"

"The Panel accepted the argument put forward by New Zealand that the complaining company represented the New Zealand transformer industry in terms of Article VI of the GATT since its output accounted for 92 per cent of the total domestic production. It found support for this view in the report of the Group of Experts on Anti-Dumping and Countervailing Duties (BISD 8S/145, paragraph 18) which had discussed the term industry in relation to the concept of injury and had concluded that as a general guiding principle, judgements of material injury should be related to total national output of the like commodity concerned or a significant part thereof. In this connection, the Group of Experts did refer to a single firm that was an important or significant part of the industry.

"In its examination whether the New Zealand transformer industry had suffered injury from the imports in question, the Panel subsequently dealt with the argument put forward by New Zealand that this industry was structured in such a way that there existed four distinguishable ranges of transformers, i.e. transformers between 1-5 MVA, 5-10 MVA, 10-20 MVA, and 20 MVA and above, which for purposes of injury determination had to be considered separately. The Panel was of the view that this was not a valid argument, especially in light of the fact that the complaining company, representing - as indicated above - the New Zealand transformer industry, in the year 1982/83 produced the whole range of transformers, most of which in a range (i.e. above 20 MVA) which was not at all affected by the imports from Finland. ... It was thus, in the Panel's view, the overall state of health of the New Zealand transformer industry which must provide the basis for a judgement whether injury was caused by dumped imports. To decide otherwise would allow the possibility to grant relief through anti-dumping duties to individual lines of production of a particular industry or company - a notion which would clearly be at variance with the concept of industry in Article VI in a case like the present one where both the Finnish exporter and the New Zealand industry were engaged in the manufacture and distribution of power transformers".[100]

---

[97] SCM/140, adopted on 26 March 1992, 39S/411, 435-436, paras. 5.2.9-5.2.10.
[98] Havana Reports, p. 74, para. 24.
[99] L/978, adopted on 13 May 1959, 8S/145, 150, para. 18.
[100] L/5814, adopted on 18 July 1985, 32S/55, 68, paras. 4.5-4.6.

See the definition of "domestic industry" for purposes of determining injury in terms of Article VI of the GATT, in Article 4 of the 1967 and 1979 Agreements on Implementation of Article VI of the General Agreement and Article 6:5 and 6:7-9 of the 1979 Agreement on Interpretation and Application of Articles VI, XVI and XXIII of the General Agreement[101]: these definitions provide:

> "In determining injury, the term 'domestic industry' shall ... be interpreted as referring to the domestic producers as a whole of the like products or to those of them whose collective output of the products constitutes a major proportion of the total domestic production of those products, except that when producers are related to the exporters or importers or are themselves importers of the allegedly subsidized product, the industry may be interpreted as referring to the rest of the producers ...".

A footnote to this paragraph in the 1979 Agreements called for a group of experts to develop a definition of the word "related". The 1981 Report of this group, adopted by the Committee on Anti-Dumping Practices and the Committee on Subsidies and Countervailing Measures, provides that for the purpose of these provisions, "producers shall be deemed to be related to the exporters or importers only if: (a) one of them directly or indirectly controls* the other; (b) both of them are directly or indirectly controlled* by a third person; or (c) together they directly or indirectly control* a third person, provided that there are grounds for believing or suspecting that the effect of the relationship is such as to cause the producer concerned to behave differently from non-related producers". A footnote to the asterisked words provides that "For the purposes of these Articles, one shall be deemed to control another when the former is legally or operationally in a position to exercise restraint or direction over the latter". The report notes that "The experts were of the opinion that the best approach would be to combine certain relevant criteria from the definition in [Article 15 of the Agreement on Implementation of Article VII of the General Agreement] with the requirement that the effect of the relationship was such as to cause the producer concerned to behave differently from non-related producers. At the same time they recognized that, as certain criteria were extremely difficult to evaluate, any such definition should allow sufficient flexibility and should be applied with appropriate care".[102]

The Panel on "United States - Definition of Industry Concerning Wine and Grape Products" under the Agreement on Interpretation and Application of Articles VI, XVI and XXIII of the General Agreement, examined a dispute regarding amendments made in 1984 to the United States anti-dumping and countervailing duty laws which had provided that the definition of "industry" for anti-dumping and countervailing duty investigations in the case of wine and grapes would be as follows: "The term 'industry' means the domestic producers as a whole of a like product, or those producers whose collective output of the like product constitutes a major proportion of the total domestic production of that product; except that in the case of wine and grape products subject to investigation under this Title, the term also means the domestic producers of the principal raw agricultural product (determined on either a volume or value basis) which is included in the like domestic product, if those producers allege material injury, or threat of material injury, as a result of imports of such wine and grape products".

> "The Panel based the consideration of the case before it on Article 6 of the Code, in particular its paragraph 5, and footnote 18 to paragraph 1. It noted that Article 6:5 defines the term 'domestic industry' as the domestic producers as a whole of the like products (or those of them whose collective output of the products constitutes a major proportion of the total domestic production of those products). The Panel also noted that the term 'like product' is defined in footnote 18 to Article 6:1 of the Code, and it shared the view expressed by both parties to the dispute that, because of different physical characteristics, wine and grapes were not 'like products' in the sense of the Code. In view of the precise definition of 'domestic industry', the Panel considered that producers of the like products could be interpreted to comprise only producers of wine.

> "The Panel then addressed the question whether, as a consequence of the close relationship between grape and wine production, the wine-grape growers could be regarded as part of the industry producing wine. It noted in this respect that both delegations had stated before the Panel that in the United States, the structure of the industries was such that wineries did not normally grow their own grapes but bought them

---

[101] 15S/24, 27; 26S/171, 175; 26S/56, 65.

[102] Report to the Committee on Anti-dumping Practices and the Committee on Subsidies and Countervailing Measures, 28S/33, adopted 28-30 October 1981 by both Committees, 28S/47, 28S/28; Agreement on Implementation of Article VII, 26S/116.

from the grape-growers for processing. In view of this situation, the Panel found that, irrespective of ownership, a separate identification of production of wine-grapes from wine in terms of Article 6:6 of the Code was possible and that therefore in fact two separate industries existed in the United States - the growers of wine-grapes on the one hand and the wineries on the other. Bearing in mind its terms of reference, the Panel did not consider it appropriate to examine the structure of the wine industry in other countries or the situation in other product sectors.

"The finding which the Panel reached was supported by the fact that in a previous countervailing duty investigation on wine imports, which had been conducted under the unamended version of Section 771(4)(a) of the US Tariff Act of 1930, the USITC had concluded that it was not appropriate to include grape growers within the scope of the domestic industry. The Panel noted the language of the Conference Report of the US Congress ... which states that producers of products being incorporated into a processed or manufactured article (i.e. intermediate goods or component parts) were generally not included in the scope of the domestic industry that the USITC analysed for the purposes of determining injury. In view of this fact it therefore appeared to the Panel that this had been a reason for the United States to amend the Trade and Tariff Act of 1984, in order to give wine-grape growers standing in countervailing duty proceedings involving wine imports. The Panel thus was of the opinion that it would not have been necessary to change the definition of 'industry' in the US Tariff Act of 1930 if wine-grape growers in the United States were part of the wine industry."[103]

See also the material on "like product" in the context of Article VI, at page 227 above.

(6) Sub-paragraphs 6(b) and 6(c): Anti-dumping and countervailing duties based on material injury to the industry in a third country

The first sentence of paragraph 6(b) was added during discussions at the Geneva session of the Preparatory Committee in 1947.[104] The second sentence of paragraph 6(b) and paragraph 6(c) were agreed during the 1954-55 Review Session, as noted in the Report of the Review Working Party on "Other Barriers to Trade":

"The representatives of Australia and New Zealand originally proposed an extensive amendment to paragraph 6 which would have removed the requirement of prior approval by the CONTRACTING PARTIES before the imposition of a countervailing or anti-dumping measure designed to protect the industry of another exporting country. While this amendment did not receive wide support in its original form, a revised amendment proposed by those two delegations which is confined to countervailing duties, is recommended by the Working Party".[105]

Accordingly, the second sentence of paragraph 6(b) and paragraph 6(c), and the interpretative note to paragraph 6(b), were added to Article VI by the Protocol Amending the Preamble and Parts II and III of the General Agreement, which entered into force in 1957.

The same Working Party Report notes that "During the consideration of this subject by the Working Party, the Netherlands representative presented an oral proposal that the CONTRACTING PARTIES should be given the authority to require contracting parties to impose countervailing and anti-dumping duties against imports of a product from another country which, through the sale of the product concerned at a subsidized or dumping price, causes serious injury to other exporting contracting parties. This proposal was not accepted by the Working Party".[106]

The Second Report of the Group of Experts on Anti-dumping and Countervailing Duties noted the view of the Group that: "As regards the application of anti-dumping duties in the interests of third countries, the Group

---

[103]SCM/71, adopted on 28 April 1992, 39S/436, 446-447, paras. 4.2-4.4. The legislative proviso regarding wine and grape products has since expired; see SCM/M/59 p. 29-31.
[104]See EPCT/103.
[105]3S/223-224; see proposal at W.9/214.
[106]*Ibid.*, 3S/224, para. 11.

was of the opinion that the initiative should come from the third country involved".[107] Further on this subject, the Group's Second Report provides:

> "The Group was of the opinion that the situation of third countries was fully dealt with in Article VI, paragraph 6, which related to cases where countries could levy an anti-dumping duty on behalf of third countries.
>
> "In these circumstances, and contrary to one of the basic principles of Article VI, paragraph 6(a), the imposition of an anti-dumping duty was not contingent upon the existence of injury caused to an industry of the importing country, but upon injury caused or threatened to an industry of one or more third countries which were suppliers of the importing country.
>
> "In order to avoid any misunderstanding, the Group wished to stress that a third country, in order to justify a request to an importing country to impose measures against another country, should produce evidence that the dumping engaged in by the other country was causing material injury to its domestic industry and not only to the exports of the industry of that third country. However, in cases where the importing country granted a request from a third country, anti-dumping measures should not be imposed until and unless the CONTRACTING PARTIES had approved the proposed measure (Article VI, paragraph 6). ...
>
> "In any case, there was no doubt that the initiation of the procedures of resorting to the CONTRACTING PARTIES laid down in Article VI, paragraph 6, should be left to the discretion of the importing country. Consequently, the Group was of the opinion that where the importing country found it impossible or undesirable to grant the request from a third country which claimed injury, the third country had no right to retaliatory measures but could have resort to Articles XXII and XXIII of the General Agreement".[108]

The provisions of sub-paragraph 6(b) and 6(c) have, so far, not been invoked and no waiver from the provisions of paragraph 6(a) has been requested.[109]

The 1967 and 1979 Agreements on the Implementation of Article VI each include in Article 12 provisions on "Anti-dumping action on behalf of a third country".[110]

8. Paragraph 7

The Second Report of the Group of Experts on Anti-dumping and Countervailing Duties notes:

> "The Group felt that the responsibility for ensuring the adequate implementation of international stabilization agreements affecting certain commodities should, in the first instance, be left to the bodies or institutions provided for in such agreements; this applied regardless of whether the agreements provided for floor or ceiling prices. ... Of course if while conforming with such an international agreement products were sold at a dumping price, recourse to the provisions of Article VI of GATT would be justified".[111]

There is no record of Article VI:7 ever having been invoked formally in the GATT so far, although this may signify that the justification of its use by a contracting party has never been challenged during discussions with other interested contracting parties.[112]

---

[107]L/1141, adopted on 27 May 1960, 9S/194, 195 para. 6.
[108]*Ibid.*, 9S/198, paras. 21-23, 25.
[109]C/W/420, p. 2.
[110]15S/24, 34; 26S/171, 183.
[111]L/1141, adopted on 27 May 1960, 9S/194, 199, para. 30.
[112]CG.18/W/59, p. 16.

B. RELATIONSHIP BETWEEN ARTICLE VI AND OTHER GATT ARTICLES

1. Article I

The 1955 Panel Report on "Swedish Anti-Dumping Duties" examined Sweden's application of a basic price scheme on imports of nylon stockings, in which any consignment with an invoice price higher than the basic price determined by the Swedish government was exempted from anti-dumping proceedings, and for other shipments dumping margins were related to the concept of normal value in Article VI. The Panel examined, *inter alia*, the claim by Italy that this scheme was inconsistent with Article I because it would exempt from anti-dumping proceedings imports from high-cost producers which were below normal value but above the basic price, and would deprive the low-cost producers of their competitive advantage to which they were entitled under the most-favoured-nation clause. The Panel Report notes as follows:

> "The Panel considered that this argument was not entirely convincing. If the low-cost producer is actually resorting to dumping practices he foregoes the protection embodied in the most-favoured-nation clause. On the other hand, Article VI does not oblige an importing country to levy an anti-dumping duty whenever there is a case of dumping, or to treat in the same manner all suppliers who resort to such practices. The wording of paragraph 6 supports that view. The importing country is only entitled to levy an anti-dumping duty when there is material injury to a domestic industry or at least a threat of such an injury. If, therefore, the importing country considers that the imports above a certain price are not prejudicial to its domestic industry, the text of paragraph 6 does not oblige it to levy an anti-dumping duty on imports coming from high-cost suppliers, but, on the contrary, prevents it from doing so. On the other hand, if the price at which the imports of the low-cost producers are sold is prejudicial to the domestic industry, the levying of an anti-dumping duty is perfectly permissible, provided, of course, that the case of dumping is clearly established.

> "The Panel recognized however that the basic price system would have a serious discriminatory effect if consignments of the goods exported by the low-cost producers had been delayed and subjected to uncertainties by the application of that system and the case for dumping were not established in the course of the enquiry. The fact that the low-cost producer would thus have been at a disadvantage whereas the high-cost producer would have been able to enter his goods freely even at dumping prices would clearly discriminate against the low-cost producer".[113]

The Second Report of the Group of Experts on Anti-dumping and Countervailing Duties notes:

> "In equity, and having regard to the most-favoured-nation principle the Group considered that where there was dumping to the same degree from more than one source and where that dumping caused or threatened material injury to the same extent, the importing country ought normally to be expected to levy anti-dumping duties equally on all the dumped imports".[114]

See also Articles 8(b) and 8:2 of the 1967 and 1979 Agreements on the Implementation of Article VI[115].

The Report of the Panel on "United States - Definition of Industry Concerning Wine and Grape Products", established under the Agreement on Interpretation and Application of Articles VI, XVI and XXIII of the General Agreement to examine a dispute regarding a provision of the United States anti-dumping and countervailing duty laws, notes that "the Panel held the view that Article VI of the GATT and the corresponding Code provision should, because they permitted action of a non-m.f.n. nature otherwise prohibited by Article I, be interpreted in a narrow way".[116]

The 1991 Report of the Panel on "United States - Countervailing Duties on Fresh, Chilled and Frozen Pork from Canada" contains the following finding:

---

[113] L/328, adopted 26 February 1955, 3S/81, 83-84, paras. 8-9.
[114] L/1141, adopted on 27 May 1960, 9S/194, 198, para. 26.
[115] 15S/24, 31; 26S/171, 180.
[116] SCM/71, adopted on 28 April 1992, 39S/436, 447, para. 4.5.

"... in conducting [its] examination, the Panel took into account that Article VI:3 is an exception to basic principles of the General Agreement, namely that ... charges of any kind imposed in connection with imports must meet the most-favoured-nation standard (Article I:1). The Panel also noted in this context that discriminatory trade measures may under the General Agreement only be taken in expressly defined circumstances (e.g. Article XXIII:2)".[117]

In the 1992 Panel Report on "United States - Denial of Most-favoured-nation Treatment as to Non-rubber Footwear from Brazil," "The Panel considered that the rules and formalities applicable to countervailing duties, including those applicable to the revocation of countervailing duty orders, are rules and formalities imposed in connection with importation, within the meaning of Article I:1".[118]

"The Panel noted that Article I would in principle permit a contracting party to have different countervailing duty laws and procedures for different categories of products, or even to exempt one category of products from countervailing duty laws altogether. The mere fact that one category of products is treated one way by the United States and another category of products is treated another is therefore in principle not inconsistent with the most-favoured-nation obligation of Article I:1. However, this provision clearly prohibits a contracting party from according an advantage to a product originating in another country while denying the same advantage to a *like product* originating in the territories of other contracting parties."[119]

"The Panel found that the United States failed to grant, pursuant to Section 104(b) of the Trade Agreements Act of 1979, to products originating in contracting parties signatories to the Subsidies Agreement the advantage accorded in Section 331 of the Trade Act of 1974 to like products originating in countries beneficiaries of the United States GSP programme, that advantage being the automatic backdating of the revocation of countervailing duty orders issued without an injury determination to the date on which the United States assumed the obligation to provide an injury determination under Article VI:6(a). Accordingly, the Panel concludes that the United States acted inconsistently with Article I:1 of the General Agreement".[120]

2. Article II

In the 1962 Panel Report on "Exports of Potatoes to Canada", the Panel examined a complaint by the United States concerning the imposition by Canada of an import charge on potatoes in addition to the bound specific duty, as a result of the application under the Canadian Customs Act of "values for duty" on potatoes imported below a certain price. The Panel found that "the imposition of an additional charge could not be justified by Article VI of the General Agreement, since the main requirement laid down in paragraph 1(a) of the Article was not satisfied" (see page 226 above).

"The Panel came to the conclusion that the measure introduced by the Canadian Government amounted to the imposition of an additional charge on potatoes which were imported at a price lower than Can.$2.67 per 100 lbs. The Panel considered that this charge was in addition to the specific import duty which had been bound at a rate of Can.$0.375 per 100 lbs. Since no provisions of the General Agreement had been brought forward for the justification of the imposition of an additional charge above the bound import duty, the Panel considered that the Canadian Government had failed to carry out its obligations under paragraph 1(a) of Article II".[121]

---

[117]DS7/R, adopted 11 July 1991, 38S/30, 44, para. 4.4.
[118]DS18/R, adopted on 19 June 1992, 39S/128, 150, para. 6.8.
[119]*Ibid.*, 39S/151, para. 6.11.
[120]*Ibid.*, 39S/154, para. 7.2.
[121]L/1927, adopted on 16 November 1962, 11S/88, 93, para. 18.

3. Article XVI

During discussions at London on Article 11 of the proposed Charter on anti-dumping and countervailing duties, it was stated that "Article 11 would permit countervailing duties to prevent injury, even though the subsidy granted by the exporting country was justified under provisions of the Charter".[122]

The Report of the 1954-55 Review Working Party on "Other Barriers to Trade", which drafted the provisions of Section B of Article XVI, notes that the "Working Party ... agreed ... that nothing in the terms of Section B of Article XVI, relating to export subsidies, should be considered as limiting the scope of consultations envisaged under other provisions of the Agreement or as affecting in any way the right of a contracting party to impose countervailing and anti-dumping duties".[123]

The Second Report of the Group of Experts on Anti-Dumping and Countervailing Duties provides: "The fact that the granting of certain subsidies was authorized by the provisions of Article XVI of the General Agreement clearly did not debar importing countries from imposing, under the terms of Article VI, a countervailing duty on the products on which subsidies had been paid".[124]

The Panel Report on "United States - Countervailing Duties on Fresh, Chilled and Frozen Pork from Canada"

"... noted that the purposes of Article VI and Article XVI were fundamentally different: the former provision provides for a right to react unilaterally to subsidies while the latter sets out rules of conduct and procedures relating to subsidies. It is for these reasons not justified in the view of the Panel to conclude from the references to trade effects in Article XVI:1 that Article VI:3 permits contracting parties to offset the full trade effects caused by a subsidy granted to the producers of a product by levying countervailing duties without it having been determined that subsidies have been bestowed on these other products".[125]

The Panel on "United States - Definition of Industry Concerning Wine and Grape Products", which was established under the Agreement on Interpretation and Application of Articles VI, XVI and XXIII of the General Agreement to examine a dispute regarding a provision of the United States anti-dumping and countervailing duty laws, found, *inter alia*:

"The Panel ... considered the argument made by the US delegation that Article 9 of the Code was no less pertinent to the definition of 'domestic industry' that might be injured by subsidization than to the scope of producers whose exports might be subsidized. The Panel could see no relationship between Article 9 which prohibits the use of export subsidies on non-primary products, on the one hand, and Article 6:5 which contains the definition of 'domestic industry' for countervailing duty purposes, on the other. Quite apart from the fact that the two Code provisions in question had a different basis in the General Agreement itself, i.e. Article XVI in the case of Article 9 of the Code and Article VI in the case of Article 6:5 of the Code, the Panel was of the view that the definition of 'certain primary products' under Article 9 was made for different purposes than defining 'domestic industry' and that it could therefore not be used to interpret an otherwise explicit wording of Article 6:5. The processing permitted under the definition of 'certain primary products' could be, and in many instances was, a separate economic process identifiable in terms of Article 6:6 of the Code. Once such a separate identification was possible (e.g. because of the structure of the production), the economic interdependence between industries producing raw materials or components and industries producing the final product was not relevant for the purposes of the Code. There was therefore, in the Panel's view, no basis for the contention that two products had to be considered as 'like products', and consequently the industries concerned to be one and the same, just because a primary product might continue to be considered a primary product even after processing ...".[126]

---

[122] EPCT/C.II/48, p. 3.
[123] L/334 and Addendum, adopted on 3 March 1955, 3S/222, 226, para. 20.
[124] L/1141, adopted on 27 May 1960, 9S/194, 200, para. 32.
[125] 38S/44.
[126] SCM/71, adopted on 28 April 1992, 39S/436, 447, para. 4.5.

4. Article XXIII

See under Article XXIII.

C. AGREEMENT ON IMPLEMENTATION OF ARTICLE VI AND AGREEMENT ON INTERPRETATION AND APPLICATION OF ARTICLES VI, XVI AND XXIII

1. Work done under the 1979 Agreements

The Agreement on Implementation of Article VI of the General Agreement was negotiated in the Kennedy Round of multilateral trade negotiations in the light of the decision of Ministers in 1963 that the Kennedy Round should "deal not only with tariffs but also with non-tariff barriers".[127] This Agreement entered into force on 1 July 1968. In the Tokyo Round of multilateral trade negotiations revisions to the 1967 Agreement were proposed to take into account the draft text of the Agreement on Interpretation and Application of Articles VI, XVI and XXIII; the 1979 Agreement on Implementation of Article VI entered into force on 1 January 1980.[128] Article 16:5 of the 1979 Agreement provides that "Acceptance of this Agreement shall carry denunciation of the Agreement on Implementation of Article VI, done at Geneva on 30 June 1967". As of 31 December 1979 the 1967 Agreement had been accepted by twenty-five contracting parties including the ten EEC Member States, and by the European Economic Community. Two parties to the 1967 Agreement, Macau and Malta, have not accepted the 1979 Agreement. An updated list of acceptances of the 1979 Agreement appears in the Appendix.

Both the 1967 and 1979 Agreements on the Implementation of Article VI express in their respective preambles the desire of the parties to the Agreement "to interpret the provisions of Article VI of the General Agreement ... and to elaborate rules for their application in order to provide greater uniformity and certainty in their implementation". Accordingly, the respective Articles 1 of both Agreements state: "The imposition of an anti-dumping duty is a measure to be taken only under the circumstances provided for in Article VI of the General Agreement and pursuant to investigations initiated and conducted in accordance with the provisions of this Code." Article 14 of the 1979 Agreement establishes a Committee on Anti-Dumping Practices constituted of the Parties to the Agreement.

The Agreement on Interpretation and Application of Articles VI, XVI and XXIII of the General Agreement was negotiated in the Tokyo Round of multilateral trade negotiations, and entered into force on 1 January 1980.[129] An updated list of acceptances of the Agreement appears in the Appendix tables at the end of this book. In the preamble of this Agreement, the signatories express their desire "to apply fully and to interpret the provisions of Articles VI, XVI and XXIII of the General Agreement on Tariffs and Trade only with respect to subsidies and countervailing measures ... and to elaborate rules for their application in order to provide greater uniformity and certainty in their implementation". Accordingly, Article 1 of the Agreement states: "Signatories shall take all necessary steps to ensure that the imposition of a countervailing duty on any product of the territory of any signatory imported into the territory of another signatory is in accordance with the provisions of Article VI of the General Agreement and the terms of this Agreement". Part I of the Agreement deals with countervailing duties; other provisions of the Agreement deal with subsidies. Article 16 of the Agreement establishes a Committee on Subsidies and Countervailing Measures constituted of the signatories to the Agreement.

The GATT Secretariat has periodically published a collection of legislation under the title of *Anti-Dumping Legislation*.[130] Legislation and regulations of parties to the Agreement on Implementation of Article VI and the

---

[127] Decision of Ministers, 12S/47, para. 3; see Preamble of 1967 Agreement, 15S/24. The 1967 Agreement appears at 15S/24. For the drafting background of the 1967 Agreement, see the documents of the Sub-Committee on Non-Tariff Barriers and other Special Problems, TN.64/SR.1-3, TN.64/NTB/1-; documents of the Group on Anti-Dumping Duties, TN.64/NTB/38-41 and TN.64/NTB/W/1-21; and the draft Code tabled by the United Kingdom in Spec(65)86.

[128] For drafting background on the 1979 Agreement, see documents MTN/NTM/W/232+Corr.1, Add.1/Rev.1, Add.2; MTN/W/241/Rev.1, MTN/NTM/W/232/Rev.1, MTN/NTM/W/248, MTN/NTM/W/258-259 and see generally minutes and documents of the Committee on Anti-Dumping Practices, 1968-1979, in the COM.AD/ series. The text of the 1979 Agreement is at 26S/171.

[129] Text of the Agreement appears at 26S/56. On the drafting history, see documents listed in TA/INF/1/Rev.8, p. 45-50.

[130] *Anti-Dumping Legislation*, published 1958, 1970, 1974, 1977; *Anti-dumping and Countervailing Measures Legislation*, published in looseleaf format; current edition updated to March 1987.

Agreement on Interpretation and Application of Articles VI, XVI and XXIII are notified to the Committee on Anti-Dumping Practices and the Committee on Subsidies and Countervailing Measures.[131]

These two Committees have examined issues relating to administration of anti-dumping and countervailing duty proceedings, and have adopted certain recommendations "constituting an understanding on the manner in which Parties intended to implement certain provisions of the Code. The recommendations have not added new obligations nor have they detracted from the existing obligations under the Code."[132] The Committee on Anti-Dumping Practices has adopted the Recommendation concerning Transparency of Anti-dumping Procedures[133], the Recommendation concerning Procedures for an On-the-spot Investigation[134], the Recommendation concerning the Time-limits Given to Respondents to Anti-dumping Questionnaires[135] and the Recommendation concerning Best Information Available in terms of Article 6:8.[136] The Committee on Subsidies and Countervailing Measures has adopted Guidelines on Physical Incorporation,[137] it being stated that these guidelines constituted an understanding on the manner in which signatories intended to calculate the amount of certain subsidies;[138] Guidelines on Amortization and Depreciation;[139] and Guidelines in the Determination of Substitution Drawback Systems as Export Subsidies.[140] Both Committees adopted in 1981 the Report of a Group of Experts on the definition of the word "related": see above at page 246.

2. Co-existence of the 1979 Agreements and the WTO Agreement

In the Uruguay Round of multilateral trade negotiations, two agreements were reached: the 1994 Agreement on Implementation of Article VI, and the Agreement on Subsidies and Countervailing Measures. These agreements are included in Annex 1A to the WTO Agreement and therefore bind all Members of the WTO. In late 1994, the Preparatory Committee for the WTO discussed arrangements for transition from the 1979 agreements to the 1994 agreements. The Preparatory Committee and the Committee on Anti-Dumping Practices each adopted the following decision on "Transitional Arrangements - Transitional Co-existence of the Agreement on Implementation of Article VI of the General Agreement on Tariffs and Trade and the Marrakesh Agreement Establishing the World Trade Organization":

"The Parties to the Agreement on Implementation of Article VI of the General Agreement on Tariffs and Trade (hereinafter referred to as 'the Agreement'),

"Noting that not all Parties to the Agreement meeting the conditions for original membership in the World Trade Organization ... will be able to accept the Marrakesh Agreement Establishing the WTO ... as of its date of entry into force, and that the stability of multilateral trade relations would therefore be furthered if the Agreement and the WTO Agreement were to co-exist for a limited period of time;

"Considering that, during that period of co-existence, a Party to the Agreement which has become a Member of the WTO should have the right to act in accordance with the WTO Agreement notwithstanding its obligations under the Agreement;

"Desiring to end the period of co-existence on a date agreed in advance so as to provide predictability for policy makers and facilitate an orderly termination of the institutional framework of the Agreement;

---

[131] See the ADP/1/Add. and SCM/1/Add. document series.
[132] 31S/287-288.
[133] 30S/24.
[134] 30S/28.
[135] 30S/30.
[136] 31S/283.
[137] SCM/68, adopted on 24 October 1985, 32S/156ff.
[138] 31S/262 para. 12.
[139] SCM/64, adopted on 25 April 1985, 32S/154ff.
[140] 31S/257.

"(a) to disputes brought against a Party to the Agreement which is a Member of the WTO if the dispute concerns a measure that is identified as a specific measure at issue in the request for the establishment of a panel made in accordance with Article 6 of the Understanding on Rules and Procedures Governing the Settlement of Disputes in Annex 2 of the WTO Agreement and the dispute settlement proceedings following that request are being pursued or are completed; and

"(b) in respect of measures covered by paragraph 1 above.

"3. The Agreement is herewith terminated one year after the date of entry into force of the WTO Agreement. In the light of unforeseen circumstances, the Parties may decide to postpone the date of termination by no more than one year."[141]

On the same date, the Preparatory Committee and the Committee on Anti-Dumping Practices also adopted a decision on "Transitional Arrangements - Committee on Anti-Dumping Practices":

"The Parties to the Agreement on Implementation of Article VI of the General Agreement on Tariffs and Trade ...

"*Recalling* the Ministerial Decision of 15 April 1994 on the Application and Review of the Understanding on Rules and Procedures Governing the Settlement of Disputes,

"*Further recalling* that Parties to the Agreement have the right to withdraw from the Agreement at any time, said withdrawal to take effect upon the expiration of sixty days from the day on which written notice is received by the Director-General to the CONTRACTING PARTIES to GATT 1947;

"*Agree* that, in the event of withdrawal by any Party from the Agreement taking effect on or after the date of entry into force for it of the Marrakesh Agreement Establishing the World Trade Organization ... or in case of termination of the Agreement while this Decision is in effect:

"(a) the Agreement shall continue to apply with respect to any anti-dumping investigation or review which is not subject to application of the Agreement on Implementation of Article VI of the General Agreement on Tariffs and Trade 1994 pursuant to the terms of Article 18:3 of that Agreement.

"(b) Parties that withdraw from the Agreement shall remain Members of the Committee on Anti-Dumping Practices exclusively for the purpose of dealing with any dispute arising out of any anti-dumping investigation or review identified in paragraph (a).

"(c) In case of termination of the Agreement during the period of validity of this Decision the Committee on Anti-Dumping Practices shall remain in operation for the purpose of dealing with any dispute arising out of any anti-dumping investigation or review identified in paragraph (a).

"(d) The rules and procedures for the settlement of disputes arising under the Agreement applicable immediately prior to the date of entry into force of the WTO Agreement shall apply to disputes arising out of any investigation or review identified in paragraph (a). With respect to such disputes for which consultations are requested after the date of this Decision, Parties and panels will be guided by Article 19 of the Understanding on Rules and Procedures Governing the Settlement of Disputes in Annex 2 of the WTO Agreement.

"(e) Parties will make their best efforts to expedite to the extent possible under their domestic legislation investigations and reviews referred to in paragraph (a), and to

---

[141] PC/13, L/7584, ADP/131.

With respect to such disputes for which consultations are requested after the date of this Decision, Parties and panels will be guided by Article 19 of the Understanding on Rules and Procedures Governing the Settlement of Disputes in Annex 2 of the WTO Agreement.

"(e) Parties will make their best efforts to expedite to the extent possible under their domestic legislation investigations and reviews referred to in paragraph (a), and to expedite procedures for the settlement of disputes so as to permit Committee consideration of such disputes within the period of validity of this Decision.

"This Decision shall remain in effect for a period of two years after the date of entry into force of the WTO Agreement. Any Party to the Agreement as of the date of this Decision may renounce this Decision. The renunciation shall take effect upon the expiration of sixty days from the day on which written notice of renunciation is received by the person who performs the depositary function of the Director-General to the CONTRACTING PARTIES to GATT 1947."[142]

On 8 December 1994 the Preparatory Committee and the Committee on Subsidies and Countervailing Measures also adopted two decisions paralleling those cited directly above, concerning coexistence of the WTO Agreement and the Agreement on Interpretation and Application of Articles VI, XVI and XXIII of the General Agreement on Tariffs and Trade.[143]

III. PREPARATORY WORK AND SUBSEQUENT MODIFICATIONS

The corresponding Articles in the Havana Charter are Article 34, in the US proposals Chapter III-3, in the US Draft Article 11, in the New York Draft Article 17 and in the Geneva Draft Article 33.

Article VI in the General Agreement as agreed 30 October 1947 was identical to Article 33 of the Geneva Draft Charter except for the provisions corresponding to the paragraph 7 of the present Article VI. At Havana, this Article was further discussed and amended. After the close of the Havana Conference, the second session Working Party on "Modifications to the General Agreement" agreed to take the Havana Charter article into the General Agreement, entirely replacing the original Article VI. The Report of the Working Party notes in this regard:

"While agreeing that there is no substantive difference between Article VI of the General Agreement and Article 34 of the Charter, the working party recommends the replacement of that article, as the text adopted at Havana contains a useful indication of the principle governing the operation of that article and constitutes a clearer formulation of the rules laid down in that article".[144]

The replacement of Article VI was effected through the Protocol Modifying Part II and Article XXVI, which entered into force on 14 December 1948.

Further amendments to Article VI were considered in the Review Session of 1954-55, in the Working Party on "Other Barriers to Trade". The Report of this Working Party notes that only two amendments were accepted: the amendments to paragraph 6 discussed on page 247 above, and the insertion of the second interpretative note to paragraph 1 discussed on page 228 above. The Review Session amendments to Article VI were effected

---

[142]PC/14, L/7585, ADP/132. The Agreement on the Transfer of Assets, Liabilities, Records, Staff and Functions from the Interim Commission of the International Trade Organization (ICITO) and the GATT to the World Trade Organization, adopted on 8 and 9 December by the Preparatory Committee for the WTO, the GATT CONTRACTING PARTIES and the Executive Committee of ICITO, provides that "The Director-General of the WTO shall perform the depositary functions of the Director-General of the GATT 1947 after the date on which the legal instruments through which the contracting parties apply the GATT 1947 are terminated. On that date the records of the GATT 1947 shall be transferred to the WTO." PC/9, L/7580, ICITO/39, para. 5.

[143]Decisions on "Transitional Arrangements - Transitional Co-existence of the Agreement on Interpretation and Application of Articles VI, XVI and XXIII of the General Agreement on Tariffs and Trade and the Marrakesh Agreement Establishing the World Trade Organization", PC/15, L/7586, SCM/186; "Transitional Arrangements - Committee on Subsidies and Countervailing Measures", PC/16, L/7587, SCM/187.

[144]GATT/CP.2/22/Rev.1, adopted 1-2 September 1948, II/39, 42 para. 12.

through the Protocol Amending the Preamble and Parts II and III of the General Agreement, which entered into force 7 October 1957.

IV. RELEVANT DOCUMENTS

See below at the end of Article X.

ARTICLE VII

VALUATION FOR CUSTOMS PURPOSES

I. TEXT OF ARTICLE VII AND INTERPRETATIVE NOTE AD ARTICLE VII	257
II. INTERPRETATION AND APPLICATION OF ARTICLE VII	259
A. SCOPE AND APPLICATION OF ARTICLE VII	259
1. Paragraph 1	259
(1) "to give effect"	259
(2) "or other charges"	259
(3) "laws or regulations"	259
2. Paragraph 2	260
(1) "actual value" versus "arbitrary or fictitious values"	260
(a) Government contracts	260
(b) Valuation according to fixed values	261
(2) "in the ordinary course of trade ... under fully competitive conditions"	261
3. Paragraph 3: "any internal tax"	262
4. Paragraph 4	262
(1) Par values and conversion rates of exchange	262
(2) "date of this Agreement"	263
5. Paragraph 5	263
(1) "The bases and methods ... should be stable"	263
(2) "sufficient publicity"	263
B. RELATIONSHIP BETWEEN ARTICLE VII AND OTHER ARTICLES	263
1. Article II	263
2. Article XV	263
C. AGREEMENT ON IMPLEMENTATION OF ARTICLE VII	263
III. PREPARATORY WORK	266
IV. RELEVANT DOCUMENTS	266

I. TEXT OF ARTICLE VII AND INTERPRETATIVE NOTE AD ARTICLE VII

Article VII

Valuation for Customs Purposes

1. The contracting parties recognize the validity of the general principles of valuation set forth in the following paragraphs of this Article, and they undertake to give effect to such principles, in respect of all products subject to duties or other charges* or restrictions on importation and exportation based upon or regulated in any manner by value. Moreover, they shall, upon a request by another contracting party review the operation of any of their laws or regulations relating to value for customs purposes in the light of these principles. The CONTRACTING PARTIES may request from contracting parties reports on steps taken by them in pursuance of the provisions of this Article.

2. (a) The value for customs purposes of imported merchandise should be based on the actual value of the imported merchandise on which duty is assessed, or of like merchandise, and should not be based on the value of merchandise of national origin or on arbitrary or fictitious values.*

(b) "Actual value" should be the price at which, at a time and place determined by the legislation of the country of importation, such or like merchandise is sold or offered for sale in the ordinary course of trade under fully competitive conditions. To the extent to which the price of such or like merchandise is governed by the quantity in a particular transaction, the price to be considered should uniformly be related to either (i) comparable quantities, or (ii) quantities not less favourable to importers than those in which the greater volume of the merchandise is sold in the trade between the countries of exportation and importation.*

(*c*)   When the actual value is not ascertainable in accordance with sub-paragraph (*b*) of this paragraph, the value for customs purposes should be based on the nearest ascertainable equivalent of such value.*

3.   The value for customs purposes of any imported product should not include the amount of any internal tax, applicable within the country of origin or export, from which the imported product has been exempted or has been or will be relieved by means of refund.

4.   (*a*)   Except as otherwise provided for in this paragraph, where it is necessary for the purposes of paragraph 2 of this Article for a contracting party to convert into its own currency a price expressed in the currency of another country, the conversion rate of exchange to be used shall be based, for each currency involved, on the par value as established pursuant to the Articles of Agreement of the International Monetary Fund or on the rate of exchange recognized by the Fund, or on the par value established in accordance with a special exchange agreement entered into pursuant to Article XV of this Agreement.

(*b*)   Where no such established par value and no such recognized rate of exchange exist, the conversion rate shall reflect effectively the current value of such currency in commercial transactions.

(*c*)   The CONTRACTING PARTIES, in agreement with the International Monetary Fund, shall formulate rules governing the conversion by contracting parties of any foreign currency in respect of which multiple rates of exchange are maintained consistently with the Articles of Agreement of the International Monetary Fund. Any contracting party may apply such rules in respect of such foreign currencies for the purposes of paragraph 2 of this Article as an alternative to the use of par values. Until such rules are adopted by the CONTRACTING PARTIES, any contracting party may employ, in respect of any such foreign currency, rules of conversion for the purposes of paragraph 2 of this Article which are designed to reflect effectively the value of such foreign currency in commercial transactions.

(*d*)   Nothing in this paragraph shall be construed to require any contracting party to alter the method of converting currencies for customs purposes which is applicable in its territory on the date of this Agreement, if such alteration would have the effect of increasing generally the amounts of duty payable.

5.   The bases and methods for determining the value of products subject to duties or other charges or restrictions based upon or regulated in any manner by value should be stable and should be given sufficient publicity to enable traders to estimate, with a reasonable degree of certainty, the value for customs purposes.

Interpretative Note *Ad* Article VII from Annex I

Paragraph 1

The expression "or other charges" is not to be regarded as including internal taxes or equivalent charges imposed on or in connexion with imported products.

Paragraph 2

1.   It would be in conformity with Article VII to presume that "actual value" may be represented by the invoice price, plus any non-included charges for legitimate costs which are proper elements of "actual value" and plus any abnormal discount or other reduction from the ordinary competitive price.

2.   It would be in conformity with Article VII, paragraph 2 (*b*), for a contracting party to construe the phrase "in the ordinary course of trade ... under fully competitive conditions", as excluding any transaction wherein the buyer and seller are not independent of each other and price is not the sole consideration.

3.   The standard of "fully competitive conditions" permits a contracting party to exclude from consideration prices involving special discounts limited to exclusive agents.

4.   The wording of sub-paragraphs (*a*) and (*b*) permits a contracting party to determine the value for customs purposes uniformly either (1) on the basis of a particular exporter's prices of the imported merchandise, or (2) on the basis of the general price level of like merchandise.

II. INTERPRETATION AND APPLICATION OF ARTICLE VII

A. SCOPE AND APPLICATION OF ARTICLE VII

1. Paragraph 1

(1) "to give effect"

Until the Review Session of 1954-55, the undertaking in the first sentence of Article VII was qualified by the phrase "at the earliest practicable date" and an interpretative note to that phrase. The Review Session Working Party on "Schedules and Customs Administration" recommended deletion of this phrase and its note, "on the assumption that a general provision will be made allowing time for governments to bring their legislation into conformity with the rules".[1]

(2) "or other charges"

The Review Working Party also recommended the addition of the present Note *Ad* Paragraph 1 stating that "The expression 'or other charges' is not to be regarded as including internal taxes or equivalent charges imposed on or in connexion with imported products". The Working Party report notes:

"The new interpretative note to paragraph 1, concerning the words 'or other charges', is intended to make it clearly understood that the wording does not require internal taxes (or their equivalents) which are charged on imported goods to be assessed on the same basis as that established for the purpose of charging customs duties. While some countries assess internal taxes on imported goods on the customs value or the customs value inclusive of duty, certain countries establish the value on which such internal taxes are charged on a different basis, being the same basis as is adopted for the charge of such internal taxes on domestically produced goods. Moreover, Article VII cannot be held to impose any commitment in relation to internal taxes, over and above those contained in Articles I and III".[2]

(3) "laws or regulations"

During the Ninth (Review) Session in 1954-55, a Technical Working Party also examined laws and regulations of contracting parties concerning customs valuation. Its Report, "Comparative Study of Methods of Valuation for Customs Purposes,"[3] describes the main systems of customs valuation at the time in the perspective of the criteria in Article VII, and presents a summary table of replies submitted by governments to a questionnaire.

See also the Agreement Relating Principally to Chemicals, supplementary to the Geneva (1967) Protocol to the General Agreement[4] which was concluded in the Kennedy Round but did not enter into force.

Customs valuation laws and regulations of parties to the Agreement on the Implementation of Article VII, discussed at page 263 below, are reviewed in the Committee on Customs Valuation.

---

[1] L/329, adopted 26 February 1955, 3S/205, 211-212, para. 12. As part of the results of the Review Session it was envisaged that the General Agreement would be brought into force on a definitive basis and in that connection a blanket reservation on acceptance for pre-existing inconsistent legislation was agreed to; see discussion of this reservation in the chapter on Article XXVI.
[2] 3S/212, para. 13.
[3] G/88, adopted 2 March 1955, 3S/103; see also the 1953 interim report on Valuation for Customs Purposes (G/57, 2S/52).
[4] 15S/8.

2. Paragraph 2

(1) "actual value" versus "arbitrary or fictitious values"

See Interpretative Notes 1 and 4 *Ad* Paragraph 2.

The Report of the Working Party on the "Accession of El Salvador" discusses customs valuation as follows:

> "Some members noted that Article VII of the General Agreement which set a basic GATT obligation prohibited the use of indicative, normal or official prices for the valuation of imports and requested that El Salvador commit to apply, in practice, and from the date of accession, the provisions of Articles VII and X in its customs practices and procedures, including customs valuation. In the view of these members, if this was not the case, El Salvador's request for accession might be premature. These members added that ... El Salvador should also state clearly that its customs officials will give first priority in determining customs value to the "actual value" of imports, as provided for in Article VII:2 of the General Agreement, and will avoid the use of administratively determined or constructed prices for customs valuation purposes ..."

> "The representative of El Salvador ... confirmed ... that his Government would give first priority in determining customs value to the 'actual value' of imports, as provided for in Article VII:2 of the General Agreement, and would avoid the use of administratively determined or constructed prices for customs valuation purposes".[5]

The Panel Report on "Exports of Potatoes to Canada" examined the application of a "value for duty" on potatoes under the Canadian Customs Act on 16 October 1962, at a level equal to the amount determined to be the average value, weighted as to quantity, at which potatoes were imported during the three-year period immediately preceding the date of shipment to Canada. Under this Act the difference between the lower export value and the "value for duty" would be levied by the Canadian customs authorities as "dumping duty". The United States claimed that this determination of the value for duties of fresh potatoes constituted a "determination based on arbitrary or fictitious value" inconsistent with the provisions of Article VII:2(a).

> "The Panel, having heard the points of view of the parties concerned, considered that the concept of value for duty as applied presently on imports of potatoes under the Canadian Customs Act was different from the concept of value for customs purposes, which the CONTRACTING PARTIES had in mind in drafting the provisions of Article VII. The Panel, therefore, did not consider that the provisions of Article VII were relevant in the context of its examination".[6]

The Panel also found that the requirements of Article VI were not fulfilled, and concluded that the measure introduced by Canada amounted to the imposition of an additional charge above the bound import duty inconsistent with Article II:1(a).[7]

(a) Government contracts

The Charter text corresponding to the first Interpretative Note to Article VII:2 was amended during the Havana Conference "so as to provide expressly for the presumption that contract prices may represent the basis for establishing 'actual values' in the case of government contracts in respect of primary products".[8] This amendment was not brought into the General Agreement.

---

[5]L/6771, adopted on 12 December 1990, 37S/9, 15, paras. 19-20.
[6]L/1927, adopted on 16 November 1962, 11S/88, 93, para. 16.
[7]*Ibid.* para. 18. See also the material on this dispute under Article VI. See also the table of Article XIX actions for an invocation by Canada of Article XIX with regard to a later imposition of "values for duty" in respect of imports of potatoes into Western Canada.
[8]Havana Reports, p. 76, para. 32.

(b) Valuation according to fixed values

During discussions at the Havana Conference on Article 35 of the Charter (corresponding to GATT Article VII), "it was revealed that in certain countries it had been the practice to apply *ad valorem* tariffs to established values of goods which remain fixed for various periods of time. It was agreed that, in such cases, the *ad valorem* rates are, in practical result, the equivalent of specific duties so long as the established values of goods are not changed. It was agreed that a note recognizing this fact should be appended to paragraph 3 [corresponding to Article VII:2]. However, it was agreed ... that it would not, and should not, be compatible with the letter or spirit of the Article to accept the principle of variable schedules of 'fixed values' for products subject to *ad valorem* rates of duty".[9] The text of the note added was as follows:

"If on the date of this Charter a Member has in force a system under which ad valorem duties are levied on the basis of fixed values the provisions of paragraph 3 of Article 35 shall not apply:

"1. in the case of values not subject to periodical revision in regard to a particular product, as long as the value established for that product remains unchanged;

"2. in the case of values subject to periodical revision, on condition that the revision is based on the average 'actual value' established by reference to an immediately preceding period of not more than twelve months and that such revision is made at any time at the request of the parties concerned or of Members. The revision shall apply to the importation or importations in respect of which the specific request for revision was made, and the revised value so established shall remain in force pending further revision".[10]

This note was not brought into the General Agreement. It was also noted in the summary record of the discussions at Havana that the system of tariff valuation in force in India "for non-ordinary products was in order insofar as the actual value could not be really ascertained under paragraph 3(b) [GATT VII:2(b)] and that paragraph 3(c) [GATT VII:2(c)] met the problem of India in respect of those particular products for which they found it necessary periodically to fix a value".[11]

The 1955 Report of the Technical Working Party on "Comparative Study of Methods of Valuation for Customs Purposes" notes concerning the system of fixed values: "This question was also discussed in the Working Party on Valuation at the eighth session of the CONTRACTING PARTIES in October 1953. The discussion in that Working Party showed that the system of fixed values as operated by India and Pakistan was not inconsistent with the principles of paragraph 2(c) of Article VII".[12]

During the Review Session of 1954-55, the idea of inserting an interpretative note similar to that annexed to the Havana Charter was again examined in the Review Working Party on Schedules and Customs Administration. The suggestion was rejected because of the difficulties of drafting a suitable provision and also because contracting parties then using the fixed values system had not suffered any disability from the absence of such an interpretative Note: the Working Party Report stated that "... the systems practised in Chile, India and Pakistan have been closely examined on a number of occasions and ... it is recognized that they are not inconsistent with the General Agreement".[13]

(2) "in the ordinary course of trade ... under fully competitive conditions"

See Interpretative Notes 2 and 3 to paragraph 2.

---

[9] Havana Reports, pp. 75-76, para. 31.
[10] Havana Charter, Interpretative Note *Ad* Article 35.
[11] E/CONF.2/C.3/SR.30, p.7.
[12] G/88, adopted on 2 March 1955, 3S/103, 109, para. 3.
[13] L/329, adopted on 26 Februaray 1955, 3S/205, 212-213, para. 15; see also discussion of these valuation systems in the Report of the Technical Working Party on "Comparative Study of Methods of Valuation for Customs Purposes" in G/88, adopted on 2 March 1955, 3S/103, 108-109, para. 3.

3. Paragraph 3: "any internal tax"

The Report of the Review Working Party on "Schedules and Customs Administration" records that the Technical Group on Customs Administration agreed

> "that the words 'internal tax' read in conjunction with the words 'from which the imported product has been exempted or has been or will be relieved by means of refund' mean only (i) internal taxes of the kind which are levied directly on the goods exported (or directly on the materials going into the manufacture of such goods), as distinct from (ii) other taxes (income tax, etc.). It follows that the obligation contained in paragraph 3, is limited to internal taxes of the kind mentioned in (i) above; so far as concerns taxes of the kind falling within (ii) above, there is no obligation upon contracting parties and, equally, there is nothing to prevent them from giving imported goods the benefit of more liberal provisions".[14]

See also Articles II:2(a), VI:4 and the Interpretative Note to Article XVI of the General Agreement.

4. Paragraph 4

(1) Par values and conversion rates of exchange

In discussions at the Geneva session of the Preparatory Committee it was agreed that "cases in which an alteration in the rate of exchange, with or without par value, is introduced are adequately covered by paragraphs 4(a) and (b)".[15]

Article IV of the original Articles of Agreement of the International Monetary Fund required each member of the Fund to state a par value for its currency in terms of either gold or U.S. dollars of a fixed gold value, as part of a system of fixed exchange rates. A change in the par value of a member's currency could be made only after consultation with the Fund. As revised in 1978, Article IV no longer requires the stating of par values and instead provides that "each member undertakes to collaborate with the Fund and other members to assure orderly exchange arrangements and to promote a stable system of exchange rates".[16]

The present text of paragraph 4 was agreed during the Review Session of 1954-55. The Report of the Review Working Party on "Schedules and Customs Administration" notes in this connection that:

> "The amendments to paragraph 4(a) and (b), to use the words 'par value as established' and 'rate of exchange recognized' by the Fund, are intended to cover certain exchange situations which are likely to arise in practice and which are not provided for in the present text. For example, in the case of Canada the established par value accepted by the Fund is no longer the effective rate, and the Fund recognizes the fluctuating rate for its own accounting purposes. This type of exchange situation will be covered by the amended text".[17]

Article IV of the IMF Articles, as revised in 1978, does not refer to "recognition" of a Fund member's rate of exchange. However, Article VII:4(b) of the General Agreement provides that "Where no such established par value and no such recognized rate of exchange exist, the conversion rate shall reflect effectively the current value of such currency in commercial transactions".

---

[14] L/329, adopted on 26 February 1955, 3S/205, 213-214, para. 17.

[15] EPCT/A/SR.40(2), p. 16; EPCT/154, p. 25 (note to para. 5).

[16] Section 4 of Article IV as revised provides that "The Fund may determine, by an 85 per cent majority of the total voting power, that international economic conditions permit the introduction of a widespread system of exchange arrangements based on stable but adjustable par values. ... Upon making such determination, the Fund shall notify members that the provisions of Schedule C [on Par Values] apply". Articles of Agreement of the International Monetary Fund, 2 UNTS 39 (1947) as amended April 1, 1978.

[17] L/329, adopted on 26 February 1955, 3S/205, 214, para. 18.

See also the material on Article II:6 in this Index. Concerning exchange matters, special exchange agreements, and relations with the Fund, see Article XV.[18]

(2)   "date of this Agreement"

Article XXVI:1 provides that "The date of this Agreement shall be 30 October 1947". This date applies for the obligations under Article VII:4(d) of the original contracting parties; of the former territories of the original contracting parties which, after attaining independence or commercial autonomy, succeeded to contracting party status under Article XXVI:5(c); and of Chile. When the modalities of accession to the General Agreement were first considered, at the Third Session in Annecy in 1949, the Working Party which drafted the Annecy Protocol of Terms of Accession decided to use instead the date of the Havana Final Act, 24 March 1948, and this approach was followed for the next group of accessions in the Torquay Protocol of 1951.[19] Since the next accession thereafter, which was the accession of Japan in 1955, the standard terms in accession protocols have provided that the "date of this Agreement" for the purposes of Article VII:4(d) shall be the date of the protocol of accession or (where the acceding government had previously acceded provisionally) the date of the declaration on provisional accession.[20]

5.   Paragraph 5

(1)   "The bases and methods ... should be stable"

During the Review Session, the Review Working Party on Schedules and Customs Administration considered a proposal to replace the words "the bases ... should be stable" by the words "the system ... should not constitute an obstacle to the rapid clearance of merchandise, should protect honest importers from unfair competition in the field concerned, should as far as possible be based on trade documents ...". The Report of the Working Party notes that members "expressed sympathy with the ideas underlying this proposal, but did not find it practicable to recommend the amendment. It was desired particularly to retain the requirement that valuation systems shall be stable".[21]

(2)   "sufficient publicity"

See also Article X.

B.   RELATIONSHIP BETWEEN ARTICLE VII AND OTHER ARTICLES

1.   Article II

See the Panel Report on "Exports of Potatoes to Canada" above at page 260.

2.   Article XV

See Article VII:4.

C.   AGREEMENT ON IMPLEMENTATION OF ARTICLE VII

The Agreement on Implementation of Article VII of the General Agreement, negotiated during the Tokyo Round of multilateral trade negotiations, was signed on 12 April 1979[22] and entered into force on 1 January 1981. The Protocol to the Agreement on Implementation of Article VII ("Customs Valuation Protocol"), done on 1

---

[18] Concerning multiple rates of exchange, see the 19 December 1947 Memorandum on decisions by the Executive Board of the Fund on "Multiple Currency Practices", reprinted as an addendum to the Report of the Review Working Party on "Quantitative Restrictions," L/332/Rev.1 and Addenda, adopted on 2, 4 and 5 March 1955, 3S/170, 200-205.
[19] Annecy Protocol, I/81, para. 5(b); Torquay Protocol, dated 21 April 1951, I/86, 88, para. 5(b).
[20] E.g. Protocol for the Accession of Bolivia, L/6562, 37S/5.
[21] L/329, adopted on 26 February 1955, 3S/205, 214, para. 19.
[22] On the drafting history, see documents listed in TA/INF/1/Rev.8, p. 61-68. The text of the Agreement and the Protocol appear at 26S/116.

November 1979, provided that upon entry into force of the Agreement the provisions of the Protocol would be deemed to be part of the Agreement.

The Agreement sets out five valuation methods, which are ranked in a hierarchical order to be followed by customs administrations of parties to the Agreement. The primary basis for customs value under the Agreement is "transaction value" as defined in Article 1: "the price actually paid or payable for the goods when sold for export to the country of importation", subject to certain specified adjustments. When the customs value cannot be determined under the provisions of Article 1, there should normally be a process of consultation between the customs administration and the importer with a view to arriving at a basis of value under Article 2 (transaction value of identical goods) or Article 3 (transaction value of similar goods). When the customs value cannot be determined on this basis, resort may be made to deductive value (Article 5) or computed value (Article 6). Article 7 provides a fall-back method:

"1. If the customs value of the imported goods cannot be determined under the provisions of Articles 1 to 6, inclusive, the customs value shall be determined using reasonable means consistent with the principles and general provisions of this Agreement and of Article VII of the General Agreement and on the basis of data available in the country of importation.

"2. No customs value shall be determined under the provisions of this Article on the basis of:

"(a) the selling price in the country of importation of goods produced in such country;

"(b) a system which provides for the acceptance for customs purposes of the higher of two alternative values;

"(c) the price of goods on the domestic market of the country of exportation;

"(d) the cost of production other than computed values which have been determined for identical or similar goods in accordance with the provisions of Article 6;

"(e) the price of the goods for export to a country other than the country of importation;

"(f) minimum customs values; or

"(g) arbitrary or fictitious values".

Annex I to the Agreement provided extensive interpretative notes to its provisions. The Protocol to the Agreement provides for the possibility of reservations by developing countries to certain provisions of the Agreement; a number of acceptances have been accompanied by such reservations. Article 21 of the Agreement permitted a developing country party to the Agreement to delay application of its provisions for five years from the date of entry into force of the Agreement with respect to it; the Protocol provided for the possibility of further extension of this period of delay. Article 21 also permitted developing country parties a further delay of three years in application of certain provisions of the Agreement. A list of acceptances of the Agreement appears in the Appendix at the end of this book, and indicates those acceptances accompanied by reservations.

Article 18 of the Agreement established two committees: a Committee on Customs Valuation composed of representatives of the parties, and serviced by the GATT Secretariat, and a Technical Committee on Customs Valuation under the auspices of the Customs Co-operation Council. The Committee has discussed the implementation and application of the Agreement by its parties, including difficulties encountered by developing countries in implementation, the use of preshipment inspection companies in customs valuation, and the shifting of the burden of proof in cases where customs administrations have reasons to doubt the truth or accuracy of the declared value.[23] The Committee has made a number of decisions regarding its working procedures and the administration of the Agreement.[24]

The Committee adopted two decisions in 1984 regarding the interpretation of the Agreement: decisions in 1984 on "Treatment of Interest Charges in the Customs Value of Imported Goods"[25] and on "Valuation of Carrier Media Bearing Software for Data Processing Equipment".[26] The Committee has also adopted agreed interpretations of the word "undertaken" used in Article 8.1(b)(iv) of the Agreement;[27] the terms "development" in English, "travaux d'étude" in French and "creación y perfeccionamiento" in Spanish in Article 8.1(b);[28] and has agreed to rectify the French text of paragraph 1 of the Note to Article 2 and the Note to Article 3.[29] The Committee has also discussed the linguistic consistency of the three authentic language texts of the Agreement. Concerning the Committee's activities, see its Annual Reports and the Secretariat Background Documents for the annual reviews of the implementation and operation of the Agreement.[30]

The Technical Committee's terms of reference in Annex II of the Agreement provide for it to, *inter alia*, "examine specific technical problems arising in the day-to-day administration of the customs valuation systems of Parties and to give advisory opinions on appropriate solutions based upon the facts presented; to study, as requested, valuation laws, procedures and practices as they relate to this Agreement and to prepare reports on the results of such studies; to prepare and circulate annual reports on the technical aspects of the operation and status of this Agreement; to furnish such information and advice on any matters concerning the valuation of imported goods for customs purposes as may be requested by any Party or the Committee. Such information and advice may take the form of advisory opinions, commentaries or explanatory notes". The Technical Committee has issued many instruments setting out information and advice (including advisory opinions, commentaries, explanatory notes, case studies or studies).[31] The Technical Committee has also issued reports on national practices with regard to, *inter alia,* treatment of interest for deferred payment,[32] and treatment of valuation of computer software.[33]

The negotiation of the Agreement on Implementation of Article VII followed substantial previous work in this area. In the Kennedy Round of multilateral trade negotiations, the Agreement Relating Principally to Chemicals, supplementary to the Geneva (1967) Protocol to the General Agreement, was negotiated, and included certain provisions on valuation.[34] However, this Agreement was not implemented.

The WTO Agreement includes in its Annex 1A a new Agreement on Implementation of Article VII, which constitutes essentially a rectified text of the 1979 Agreement and the Customs Valuation Protocol. The Final Act of the Uruguay Round also includes two Decisions relating to customs valuation: the Decision Regarding Cases Where Customs Administrations Have Reasons to Doubt the Truth or Accuracy of the Declared Value, and the Decision on Texts Relating to Minimum Values and Imports by Sole Agents, Sole Distributors and Sole Concessionnaires.

---

[23]On preshipment inspection, see VAL/W/41-44, VAL/M/17, VAL/M/19-22; on the burden of proof see statement of India at VAL/W/51, VAL/M/21, VAL/M/22, and Secretariat Note at MTN.GNG/NG8/W/19.

[24]For a complete list of the decisions of the Committee, see G/VAL/W/1, "Decisions Adopted by the Tokyo Round Committee on Vustoms Valuation", dated 28 April 1995.

[25]VAL/6/Rev.1, adopted on 26 April 1984, 31S/273 (rectified (French and Spanish only) on 24 Committee 1984, VAL/M/10); see also VAL/9+Adds. 1-6. See also VAL/M/9, VAL/M/10, VAL/W/8, VAL/W/10, VAL/W/13+Revs. 1-3, VAL/W/16, VAL/W/34+Revs.1-5.

[26]VAL/8, adopted on 24 September 1984, 31S/274; see also VAL/8/Add.1, Chairman's statement in connection with this decision, reprinted at 30S/274; see also VAL/M/10, VAL/W/7, VAL/W/11, VAL/W/14+Rev.1, VAL/W/16, VAL/11+Adds.1-7..

[27]VAL/M/6, adopted on 3 March 1983, 30S/22.

[28]Interpretation adopted on 9-10 May 1985, VAL/M/13, paras. 37-41; see also VAL/M/8, para. 4, VAL/M/9, paras. 30-37, VAL/M/11, paras. 37-41, VAL/W/24, VAL/W/24/Rev.1

[29]VAL/M/26, para. 24, VAL/W/49/Add. 4.

[30]See Reports at 28S/40, 29S/55, 30S/56, 31S/275, 32S/174, 33S/216, 34S/208, 35S/362, 36S/440, 37S/302, 38S/89, 39S/396; background documents at VAL/W/4/Rev.1, VAL/W/12/Rev.1, VAL/W/21/Rev.1, VAL/13, VAL/19, VAL/28, VAL/35, VAL/37, VAL/39, VAL/40, VAL/43, VAL/44.

[31]See list of instruments issued to 1984 in VAL/10, p. 8-9; subsequent instruments are listed in the Secretariat Background Documents for the annual review.

[32]VAL/W/10.

[33]VAL/W/11.

[34]15S/8. See also documents from the Kennedy Round Group on Assessment of Duties, TN.64/30, TN.64/NTB/19, 21, 25, 26, 28, 32, 34, and Secretariat background notes of 12 June 1972, COM.IND/W/79+Add.1, and 29 April 1975, MTN/NTM/W/7.

III. PREPARATORY WORK

Provisions corresponding to Article VII appear in Chapter III-4 of the US-UK *Proposals*, in Article 12 of the US Draft Charter, in Article 18 of the New York Draft Charter, and in Article 34 of the Geneva Draft Charter.

The subject of customs valuation was further discussed at the Havana Conference and a number of amendments were made, including the addition of a new paragraph 1, providing for co-operation toward standardization of definitions of value and of procedures for determining customs value. In paragraph 2 of the Charter article the words "directly affected" are inserted after "upon a request by another Member".[35] Sub-paragraph (d) of paragraph 4 became in the Havana Charter a separate paragraph (6) in order to avoid any misunderstanding of the concept of paragraph 4. Accordingly, the word "paragraph" was replaced by the word "article" in the Havana text.[36] The Working Party on Modifications to the General Agreement, which met at the Second Session in September 1948, did not decide to bring these changes into the General Agreement.

During the early years of the GATT, work was pursued on valuation and other issues relating to customs administration (see also Article VIII). During the Review Session of 1954-55, a number of amendments to Article VII were agreed. The Protocol Amending the Preamble and Parts II and III of the General Agreement, which was done on 10 March 1955 and entered into force on 7 October 1957, deleted the words "at the earliest practicable date" in paragraph 1, amended paragraphs 2(b), 4(a) and (b), and amended the interpretative notes in Annex I relating to Article VII. The amendments are commented upon in the Working Party Report on "Schedules and Customs Administration" adopted on 26 February 1955.[37]

IV. RELEVANT DOCUMENTS

See below at the end of Article X.

---

[35] Havana Reports, p.75, para.30.
[36] Havana Reports, p.76, para.34.
[37] 3S/205, 211-214.

ARTICLE VIII

FEES AND FORMALITIES CONNECTED WITH IMPORTATION AND EXPORTATION

I.	TEXT OF ARTICLE VIII AND INTERPRETATIVE NOTE AD ARTICLE VIII			267
II.	INTERPRETATION AND APPLICATION OF ARTICLE VIII			268
	A.	SCOPE AND APPLICATION OF ARTICLE VIII		268
		1. Paragraph 1		268
			(1) "All fees and charges ... on or in connexion with importation or exportation"	269
			(a) Customs processing fees	269
			(b) Consular fees	270
			(c) Minimum import prices and associated security systems	270
			(d) Multiple exchange rates	271
			(2) "shall be limited in amount to the approximate cost of services rendered"	271
			(a) General: the 'cost of services' limitation in Article VIII:1(a)	271
			(b) "Services rendered"	273
			(c) Ad valorem fees	274
			(d) Various charges	277
			(3) "an indirect protection to domestic products or a taxation of imports or exports for fiscal purposes"	278
			(4) "The contracting parties also recognize the need for minimizing the incidence and complexity of import formalities and for decreasing and simplifying import and export documentation requirements"	278
			(a) Origin of imported goods and requirement of certificates of origin	278
			(b) Documentary requirements for importation of goods	279
			(c) Formalities associated with administration of quantitative restrictions	280
			(d) Abolition of consular formalities	280
			(e) Customs conventions	280
			(f) Facilitation of trade in cultural or health-related products	281
			(g) Preshipment inspection	281
			(h) Testing fees for imported products	281
		2. Paragraph 2		281
		3. Paragraph 3: penalty charges		282
		4. Paragraph 4		282
	B.	RELATIONSHIP BETWEEN ARTICLE VIII AND OTHER ARTICLES		282
		1. Article I		282
		2. Article II:2(c)		282
		3. Article III		283
	C.	EXCEPTIONS AND DEROGATIONS		283
III.	PREPARATORY WORK AND SUBSEQUENT MODIFICATIONS			284
IV.	RELEVANT DOCUMENTS			285

I. TEXT OF ARTICLE VIII AND INTERPRETATIVE NOTE AD ARTICLE VIII

Article VIII

Fees and Formalities connected with Importation and Exportation*

1. (a) All fees and charges of whatever character (other than import and export duties and other than taxes within the purview of Article III) imposed by contracting parties on or in connexion with importation or exportation shall be limited in amount to the approximate cost of services rendered and shall not represent an indirect protection to domestic products or a taxation of imports or exports for fiscal purposes.

(b) The contracting parties recognize the need for reducing the number and diversity of fees and charges referred to in sub-paragraph (a).

(c) The contracting parties also recognize the need for minimizing the incidence and complexity of import and export formalities and for decreasing and simplifying import and export documentation requirements.*

2. A contracting party shall, upon request by another contracting party or by the CONTRACTING PARTIES, review the operation of its laws and regulations in the light of the provisions of this Article.

3. No contracting party shall impose substantial penalties for minor breaches of customs regulations or procedural requirements. In particular, no penalty in respect of any omission or mistake in customs documentation which is easily rectifiable and obviously made without fraudulent intent or gross negligence shall be greater than necessary to serve merely as a warning.

4. The provisions of this Article shall extend to fees, charges, formalities and requirements imposed by governmental authorities in connexion with importation and exportation, including those relating to:

(a) consular transactions, such as consular invoices and certificates;

(b) quantitative restrictions;

(c) licensing;

(d) exchange control;

(e) statistical services;

(f) documents, documentation and certification;

(g) analysis and inspection; and

(h) quarantine, sanitation and fumigation.

Interpretative Note *Ad* Article VIII from Annex I

1. While Article VIII does not cover the use of multiple rates of exchange as such, paragraphs 1 and 4 condemn the use of exchange taxes or fees as a device for implementing multiple currency practices; if, however, a contracting party is using multiple currency exchange fees for balance of payments reasons with the approval of the International Monetary Fund, the provisions of paragraph 9 (a) of Article XV fully safeguard its position.

2. It would be consistent with paragraph 1 if, on the importation of products from the territory of a contracting party into the territory of another contracting party, the production of certificates of origin should only be required to the extent that is strictly indispensable.

II. INTERPRETATION AND APPLICATION OF ARTICLE VIII

A. SCOPE AND APPLICATION OF ARTICLE VIII

1. Paragraph 1

The Panel on "United States - Customs User Fee" examined complaints by Canada and the EC concerning the "merchandise processing fee" levied by the United States Customs Service. This *ad valorem* charge was imposed for the processing of commercial merchandise entering the United States, and receipts from the fee were used to fund certain "commercial operations" of the Customs Service. The Panel findings note the following generally regarding Article VIII:1.

"... Article VIII:1(a) states a rule applicable to all charges levied at the border, except tariffs and charges which serve to equalize internal taxes. It applies to all such charges, whether or not there is a tariff binding to the product in question. The rule of Article VIII:1(a) prohibits all such charges unless they satisfy the three criteria listed in that provision:

(a)   the charge must be 'limited in amount to the approximate cost of services rendered';

(b)   it must not 'represent an indirect protection to domestic products';

(c)   it must not 'represent ... a taxation of imports ... for fiscal purposes'."[1]

(1)   "All fees and charges ... on or in connexion with importation or exportation"

In discussions at the Havana Conference it was agreed that "this Article relates to all payments of any character required by a Member on or in connexion with importation or exportation, other than import and export duties, and other than taxes within the purview of Article 18 [III] of the Geneva draft".[2]

The Panel Report on "United States - Customs User Fee" notes in its findings, regarding the nature of the fees covered by Article VIII:1(a):

"... it was necessary to determine what type of fees were incorporated within the basic concept of 'services rendered' in Articles II:2(c) and VIII:1(a). The Panel concluded that there was a rather well established general understanding of this concept, demonstrated more by practice than by the actual text of the General Agreement. In its original form, as found in Article 13 of the United States' Suggested Charter of September, 1946, Article VIII was explicitly addressed to 'fees, charges, formalities and requirements relating to all customs matters', and this definition was followed by an illustrative list which is virtually the same as the list now included in Article VIII:4. The illustrative list includes various aspects of the customs process such as 'consular transactions', 'statistical services', and 'analysis and inspection'. The text of Article VIII was later changed to enlarge the scope of that provision. Notwithstanding the fact that the enlarged scope gave a different meaning to the illustrative list in paragraph 4, GATT practice since 1948 has tended to interpret that illustrative list according to its original meaning, as a list of those customs-related government activities which the draftsmen meant when they referred to 'services rendered'. Thus, GATT proceedings have treated the following types of import fees as being within Articles II:2(c) or VIII:1(a): consular fees (CP.2/SR.11 (pages 7-8); 1S/25), customs fees (L/245; SR.9/28 (pages 4-5)), and statistical fees (18S/89).

"In referring to these customs-related government activities as 'services rendered', the drafters of Articles II and VIII were clearly not employing the term 'services' in the economic sense. Granted that some government regulatory activities can be considered as 'services' in an economic sense when they endow goods with safety or quality characteristics deemed necessary for commerce, most of the activities that governments perform in connection with the importation process do not meet that definition. They are not desired by the importers who are subject to them. Nor do they add value to the goods in any commercial sense. Whatever governments may choose to call them, fees for such government regulatory activities are, in the Panel's view, simply taxes on imports. It must be presumed, therefore, that the drafters meant the term 'services' to be used in a more artful political sense, i.e., government activities closely enough connected to the processes of customs entry that they might, with no more than the customary artistic licence accorded to taxing authorities, be called a 'service' to the importer in question. No other interpretation can make Articles II:2(c) and VIII:1(a) conform to their generally accepted meaning".[3]

(a)   Customs processing fees

See generally the Panel Report on "United States - Customs User Fee".

---

[1] L/6264, adopted on 2 February 1988, 35S/245, 273 para. 69.
[2] Havana Reports, p. 76, para. 35. See also discussion below of preliminary work and subsequent modifications of Article VIII.
[3] L/6264, adopted on 2 February 1988, 35S/245, 275-276, paras. 76-77.

In the 1990 Report of the Working Party on the "Accession of Venezuela", one member noted that "Article VIII of the General Agreement covered all fees and charges imposed by governmental authorities in connection with importation and exportation" and said that "in the view of her Government, the 5 per cent fee on imports, the 2 per cent postal import fee established in Article 37 of the Regulations of the Customs Law, and the 1 per cent fee on imports into the free trade zones, consistent with a 1987 panel recommendation concerning customs user fees, are customs charges which should conform to Article VIII of the General Agreement".[4]

(b) Consular fees

See the 1948 Chairman's ruling on consular taxes excerpted below on page 282, and the discussion beginning on page 278 regarding work in the GATT on consular fees and formalities.

(c) Minimum import prices and associated security systems

In the 1978 Panel Report on "EEC - Programme of Minimum Import Prices, Licenses and Surety Deposits for Certain Processed Fruits and Vegetables", the Panel examined the EEC system under which the issue of an import certificate for the goods in question was conditional on the lodging of a security to guarantee that imports would take place during the period of validity of the certificate.

> "The Panel noted the argument by the United States representative that, when a security was forfeited because importation did not take place within the seventy-five day validity of the certificate, this forfeiture should be considered as a 'charge in connexion with importation' in violation of Article VIII:1(a), since the importation would likely take place later under a new licence. The Panel further noted the argument by the United States representative that the forfeiture of all or part of this security imposed 'substantial penalties for minor breaches of customs regulations or procedural requirements' in violation of Article VIII:3. The Panel considered that such a forfeiture could not logically be accepted as a charge 'in connection with importation' within the meaning of Article VIII:1(a), since no importation had occurred, but only as a penalty to the importer for not fulfilling his obligation to complete the importation within the seventy-five day time-limit. The Panel further considered that such a penalty should be considered as part of an enforcement mechanism and not as a fee or formality 'in connexion with importation' within the purview of Article VIII. As a result, the Panel considered that Article VIII was not relevant, and therefore concluded that the provision for the forfeiture of the security associated with the import certificate could not be inconsistent with the obligations of the Community under Article VIII.
>
> "... The Panel noted that the importer, when applying for the certificate, must agree to complete the importation within the seventy-five day validity limit of the certificate and to import the quantity stated on the certificate plus or minus 5 per cent. The Panel further noted that the importer was not required to obtain an import certificate when a contract was signed, but could wait until the product was approaching the Community frontier. The Panel ... considered that these obligations, which had to be assumed by the importer, were not onerous enough to violate Article VIII."[5]

The same Panel also examined the aspects of the EEC programme which provided for a minimum import price, and enforced this price by making the issuance of an import certificate conditional on the lodging of an additional security to guarantee that the duty-paid c.i.f. price of the goods would be greater than or equal to the minimum price; the security would be forfeited in proportion to quantities imported below the minimum price. The Panel concluded that the minimum import price and associated additional security system for tomato concentrates was inconsistent with Article XI[6] and concluded that the interest charges and costs associated with the lodging of the additional security associated with the minimum import price for tomato concentrate were inconsistent with Article II:1(b).[7]

---

[4]L/6696, adopted on 11 July 1990, 37S/43, para. 24.
[5]L/4687, adopted on 18 October 1978, 25S/68, 96-97, paras. 4.3-4.4.
[6]*Ibid.*, 25S/103, para. 4.14.
[7]*Ibid.*, 25S/103, para. 4.15.

"The Panel ... examined the status of the interest charges and costs associated with the lodging of the additional security which enforced the minimum import price for tomato concentrates ... The Panel noted the complaint by the representative of the United States that the interest charges and costs associated with the lodging of the additional security were imposed as protection for domestic products contrary to the provisions of Article VIII:1(a). The Panel recalled its earlier conclusions with regard to Article XI and Article II. As a result of these previous conclusions, the Panel considered that this minimum import price and associated additional security system could not also be considered merely as an administrative formality or fee falling under the purview of Article VIII. As a result, the Panel considered that Article VIII was not relevant, and therefore concluded that the interest charges and costs associated with the lodging of the additional security could not be inconsistent with the obligations of the Community under Article VIII.

"The Panel next examined the provision for the forfeiture of all or part of the additional security associated with the minimum import price for tomato concentrates in relation to the obligations of the Community under Article VIII. The Panel noted the argument by the representative of the United States that such a forfeiture, if importation took place at a price below the minimum, imposed a substantial penalty for minor breaches of customs regulations or procedural requirements in violation of Article VIII:3. The Panel noted that the forfeiture of the additional security was a penalty imposed on the importer for not fulfilling an obligation which he had undertaken when he applied for the import certificate. The Panel considered that such a penalty should be considered as part of an enforcement mechanism and not as a fee or formality 'in connexion with importation' within the purview of Article VIII. As a result, the Panel considered that Article VIII was not relevant, and therefore concluded that the provision for the forfeiture of all or part of the additional security associated with the minimum import price for tomato concentrates could not be inconsistent with the obligations of the Community under Article VIII."[8]

See also in this connection the unadopted panel report on "EEC - Import Régime for Bananas".[9]

(d) *Multiple exchange rates*

See paragraph 1 of the Interpretative Note *Ad* Article VIII.

(2) "*shall be limited in amount to the approximate cost of services rendered*"

(a) *General: the 'cost of services' limitation in Article VIII:1(a)*

In the Panel Report on "United States - Customs User Fee":

"The Panel began its consideration of the legal issues by addressing the primary issue raised by Canada and the European Economic Community: whether the structure of the United States merchandise processing fee, in the form of an *ad valorem* charge without upper limits, was consistent with the 'cost of services' limitation in Articles II and VIII ... . The aspect of the United States fee the complainants wished to challenge was its tendency to impose fees exceeding the average cost of processing an individual entry. When the rate of an *ad valorem* fee is calculated by dividing the total costs of customs processing by the total value of the imports processed, the fee will, when imposed without upper limits, automatically exceed the average cost of processing whenever it is applied to entries of greater-than-average value.

"The Panel agreed with the parties that the GATT consistency of this type of *ad valorem* fee turned on the meaning of the 'cost of services' limitation in Article II:2(c) and Article VIII:1(a). The Panel understood the central contentions of the parties to be as follows: Canada and the EEC had argued that 'cost of services rendered' should be interpreted to mean the cost of the customs processing activities ('services') actually rendered to the individual importer with respect to the customs entry in question, or, at least, the average cost of such processing activities for all customs entries of a similar kind. Both complainants had stressed that the normal practice with respect to service fees was to require persons to pay only for the services rendered to them. The United States had argued that the 'cost of services' limitation did not require

---

[8]*Ibid*. 25S/104-105, paras. 4.17-4.18.
[9]DS38/R, dated 11 February 1994, para. 150.

exact conformity between fees and costs, but only that the fee be 'commensurate with' the cost (Article II:2(c)), or limited to the 'approximate' cost (Article VIII:1(a)). It had argued that, stated in these terms, the 'cost of services' requirements would be satisfied if the total revenues from the fee did not exceed the total cost of the government activities in question, and if the fee were otherwise fair and equitable in its application. The United States had stressed that the *ad valorem* structure of the merchandise processing fee was the most equitable and least protective method by which such a fee could be imposed.

"The Panel agreed with Canada and the EEC that the ordinary meaning of the term 'cost of services rendered' would be the cost of those services rendered to the individual importer in question. That meaning was also in keeping with general practice when 'services' are charged for, which is to charge the same fee for the same service received. And, finally, the origins of these provisions in the 'cost of issue' requirements of the 1923 Convention pointed to this meaning as well.

"The United States interpretation, by contrast, presented serious problems. Granted that the terms 'commensurate with' and 'approximate' were intended to confer a certain degree of flexibility in the requirement that fees not exceed costs, the range of fees permitted under the US merchandise processing fee could by no stretch of language be considered a matter of mere flexibility. Moreover, the United States contention that 'cost of services rendered' referred only to the total cost of the relevant government activities would leave Articles II:2(c) and VIII:1(a) without any express standard for apportioning such fees among individual importers, thereby committing the issue of apportionment, at best, to an implied requirement of equitable (or non-protective) apportionment that would be neither predictable nor capable of objective application. Finally, if 'cost of services rendered' meant the total cost of customs operations, the 'fiscal purposes' criterion of Article VIII:1(a) would be rendered largely redundant.

"While the Panel thus found that the text of the General Agreement supported the interpretation advocated by Canada and the EEC, it recognized that this interpretation did not yield a result that was completely satisfying from a policy standpoint. A standard which requires the same fee for the same service would be an appropriate method of charging for government activities which were actually 'services' in the economic sense. As noted above, however, most of the import fees covered by these provisions do not involve any such services. They are ordinary taxes on imports. ...

"The Panel was of the view, however, that the interpretation proposed by the United States presented an equally serious problem with regard to the policy objectives of the General Agreement. The problem was that the United States interpretation would enlarge the 'service fee' authority granted by Articles II:2(c) and VIII:1(a) ... In the Panel's view, the interpretation advocated by the United States would expand the scope of Articles II:2(c), as well as VIII:1(a). It would permit a broader variety of import fees to be imposed, and the greater availability and convenience of such fees would, the Panel believed, lead to an increase in both the number and the level of such fees. The Panel was convinced that the attainment of GATT policy objectives would not be furthered by such an interpretation. Thus, even though the requirement that import fees not exceed the cost of individual entries might increase the protective effect of such fees in a particular case, the Panel was unable to accept the United States argument that such consequences justified a more flexible interpretation. The Panel was satisfied that the text of the General Agreement did impose such a requirement, and that it would not promote the objectives of the General Agreement to relax it in the manner proposed by the United States.

"The Panel concluded that the term 'cost of services rendered' in Articles II:2(c) and VIII:1(a) must be interpreted to refer to the cost of the customs processing for the individual entry in question and accordingly that the *ad valorem* structure of the United States merchandise processing fee was inconsistent with the obligations of Articles II:2(c) and VIII:1(a) to the extent that it caused fees to be levied in excess of such costs."[10]

---

[10]L/6264, adopted on 2 February 1988, 35S/245, 276-279, paras. 78-82, 84-86.

(b) "Services rendered"

The Panel Report on "United States - Customs User Fee" further notes:

"... the Panel ... considered several additional arguments by Canada and the European Economic Community claiming that various costs included in the 'commercial operations' budget of the US Customs Service could not be considered 'services rendered' to those commercial importers who were required to pay the fee. These arguments and the conclusions following from them were separate from the issue raised in the previous section. They would apply to any fee based on a calculation of total costs of customs processing, whether the fee was levied on an ad valorem basis or as a flat charge per entry. For convenience of analysis, the present report divides the arguments relating to different costs into three categories.

"(a) *The cost of certain Customs Service activities.* The first category of costs to be challenged were the costs of certain Customs Service operations which, in the view of the complainant governments, could not be considered as 'services rendered' within the meaning of Articles II:2(c) and VIII:1(a), and thus could not be charged to commercial importers under these provisions. ...

"As noted in the previous section of this report, the Panel was of the view that Articles II:2(c) and VIII:1(a) contained a limitation upon the type of charges that could be imposed under these two provisions, a limitation to be found in the term 'services rendered.' Stated generally, the type of government activities deemed to be 'services' were those activities closely enough connected to the processes of customs entry that they might, with no more than the customary artistic license accorded to taxing authorities, be called 'services' to the importer in question.

"The Panel was aware that, in applying this standard, its capacity to make judgments about the nature and functioning of particular government operations would of necessity be limited by the quality of the information presented to it. The Panel was of the view that the government imposing the fee should have the initial burden of justifying any government activity being charged for. Once a *prima facie* satisfactory explanation had been given, it would then be upon the complainant government to present further information calling into question the adequacy of that explanation. ... the Panel was of the view that, where affected governments consider particular cost items important enough to be challenged, the better solution would be to adhere to the legal requirements and to recommend that the government in question make the necessary budgetary correction. If costs were known well enough to support a claim of *de minimis*, they should be known well enough to permit moving the estimated cost of the challenged activity to another budget item.

"The remaining 'commercial operations' activities questioned by the complainants were all activities that had some relationship to the processing of commercial imports, but in each case one or both of the complainants had raised a question whether the activity was of sufficient proximity to the normal process of customs clearance to be considered a 'service' rendered to the importer. A second and related issue raised by the complainants was whether, assuming that a particular activity (e.g., a customs fraud investigation) were considered a 'service' to the directly affected importer, that activity could also be considered a 'service' to all other importers who were not in fact directly affected by it.

"With respect to all but one of these remaining activities, the Panel was satisfied that the challenged activities were both proximate enough, and of sufficiently general applicability, that their costs could be included in the fee applicable to all commercial importers. In reaching these conclusions, the Panel gave considerable weight to the United States explanation that customs processing in the United States had increasingly moved away from hands-on processing of incoming shipments, towards a highly centralized process which focused on identifying problem transactions and concentrating on them. Under such a system, centralized and specialized activities far removed from the ordinary importer were in fact an essential ingredient to the more rapid handling of the ordinary entry, the ultimate objective of the 'service' that importers were being made to pay for. ...

"*The Panel's conclusion under this first category of challenged costs was that the cost of passenger processing and the cost of handling export documentation could not be included in the cost base of the merchandise processing fee, and that the inclusion of the cost of International Affairs had not been justified.*"[11]

"(b) *The cost of customs processing for exempt imports.* The second category of costs challenged by the complainants was the cost of customs processing for imports that were exempt from the merchandise processing fee. ... In the Panel's view ... none of the reasons for exempting a particular class of imports could provide any justification for the decision to make other importers pay the costs attributable to those imports. *The Panel concluded that processing exempted imports could not be considered as 'services rendered' to the commercial importers paying the merchandise processing fee.*"[12]

"(c) *The cost of 'commercial operations' for the first two months of Fiscal Year 1987*. The third category of costs challenged by the complainants concerned the cost of all 'commercial operations' during the first two months of Fiscal Year 1987, a period when the fee was not in force. ... The Panel found nothing in Articles II or VIII which would authorize retroactive imposition of customs fees. The only plausible reading of the link required between costs and revenues was that revenues must be measured against the costs of the period in which the revenues are collected."[13]

In discussions in the Council in 1991, the representative of the United States stated "that its customs user fee had been revised to address the Panel's findings and recommendations ... and ... met the criteria of Article VIII ... The United States also hoped that other contracting parties currently applying customs fees substantially identical to the US fee, as it had been prior to the changes mentioned, would also alter their own fees to bring them into conformity with Article VIII".[14]

(c) *Ad valorem fees*

The Panel Report on "United States - Customs User Fee" further notes as follows with regard to *ad valorem* fees.

"In reaching this conclusion [that the *ad valorem* structure of the United States merchandise processing fee was inconsistent with the obligations of Articles II:2(c) and VIII:1(a) to the extent that it caused fees to be levied in excess of the cost of the customs processing for the individual entry in question] the Panel had also given careful consideration to another United States' argument based on the GATT's prior legal experience with *ad valorem* customs fees. The United States had argued that *ad valorem* service fees had been widely used throughout GATT's history, and that the absence of any previous challenge to their *ad valorem* character during this long period demonstrated that most contracting parties considered *ad valorem* fees to be consistent with Articles II and VIII. The United States had cited several instances in which the CONTRACTING PARTIES had examined particular *ad valorem* fees without objecting to their *ad valorem* character, and had placed particular stress upon the fact that, notwithstanding the large number of *ad valorem* fees in force in 1955, the governments maintaining such fees had agreed to make Article VIII:1(a) mandatory in the 1955 Review Session amendments.

"The Panel had examined all of the instances cited by the United States, as well as others that came to light during the course of its research. This examination had persuaded the Panel that the evidence did not support the conclusion advocated by the United States. The Panel believed it would be of assistance to include the results of this examination in its report.

"The Panel first noted that a substantial number of the service fees reported in GATT documents appeared to have had excessively high rates, a problem that would normally have led to legal challenges far more readily than questions of *ad valorem* structure. The fact that, for the most part, these rather obvious

---

[11]*Ibid.*, 35S/283-286, paras. 95-106.
[12]*Ibid.*, 35S/286, paras. 107-109.
[13]*Ibid.*, 35S/287, para. 111.
[14]C/M/248, p. 8. See also L/6741 (US notification of "a revision of the U.S. customs user fee, in response to the panel report adopted on February 2, 1988").

legal shortcomings also appeared not to have been challenged suggested that many of these fees had simply not been subject to the rules of Articles II and VIII, or had otherwise escaped attention. The Panel found some support for the former hypothesis in the fact that most service fees existing on the date of a government's accession to GATT were immune from legal scrutiny under both Articles II and VIII. Article II:1(b) states that tariff bindings do not prevent governments from continuing to impose any non-tariff border charges existing at the time tariff concessions were made. Article VIII:1(a) imposed no legal obligations at all from 1947 to 1957 when the Review Session amendments went into force, and thereafter the obligations of Article VIII were subject to the reservation for existing mandatory legislation in the Protocol of Provisional Application. ...

"This same legal immunity would also have made it possible for governments with pre-accession service fees to accept the Review Session amendments making Article VIII:1(a) mandatory for post-accession service fees. Once again, the most evident legal problem at the time would have been the excessive rate of many existing fees, and the fact that the new legal obligation was accepted in spite of these more obvious legal shortcomings would tend to support that conclusion. In addition, it is not accurate to say that all governments accepting the Review Session amendment of Article VIII did so in the belief that their fees were in compliance with it. The working party report recommending the amendment also recommended that "the Agreement ... contain a general provision allowing time for governments to bring their legislation into conformity with the rules." (3S/214-215) The same report went on to note that five governments had reserved their position, proposing instead that the amendment should become effective 'at the earliest practicable date.'

"The Panel found five cases in which individual *ad valorem* service fees had been investigated by the CONTRACTING PARTIES. The Panel found that in three of the cases the *ad valorem* method had not been challenged, but that in each case the failure to challenge it could be accounted for by reasons other than an assumption of its validity, either because the fee was immune from legal attack on that issue, or because the government imposing the fee had promptly agreed to remove it for other reasons.[15] In the fourth case, the report of the working party contained a phrase which could have been a criticism of the *ad valorem* method, although the text was not clear.[16] In the fifth case, the legal consistency of the *ad valorem* method had been expressly questioned.

"The fifth case involved a 1954 complaint by the United States concerning an increase in the rate of a French stamp tax. The stamp tax was calculated as a percentage of the customs duty; the increase in question raised the rate from 1.7% of the customs duty to 2%, an increase said to equal about 0.1% *ad valorem*. France defended the increase on the ground that the tax had been provided for in its consolidated schedule and had not actually been changed in gold or dollar value (in essence, that it was exempt under Article II:1(b)). France also defended the fee on the ground that its current level was commensurate with

---

[15] A footnote to this sentence provides as follows: "In 1948, the Netherlands brought a complaint concerning a discriminatory consular tax imposed by Cuba in which a rate of 5 per cent ad valorem was charged on goods from the Netherlands while a rate of 2 per cent ad valorem was charged on others. Cuba agreed to remove the discriminatory element (CP.2/9; CP.2/SR.11). Given the early date of the complaint, the tax itself almost certainly antedated Cuba's accession, and so would not have been open to challenge under Article II. Article VIII was not then in force.

"In 1952, the United States brought a complaint concerning a French statistical tax of 0.4 per cent ad valorem, on the ground that it was being used to fund social payments to agricultural workers. France agreed that this purpose constituted a violation of Article II, and agreed to remove the tax, thereby rendering moot any other claim of legal inconsistency. (L/64; SR.8/7, page 10).

"In 1955, the United States brought a complaint concerning the increase of a French stamp tax, from 2 per cent of the customs duties to 3 per cent; the revenues from the additional 1 per cent were used to fund social payments to agricultural workers. France immediately agreed that the added 1 per cent was inconsistent with GATT obligations because it was not used to fund customs services, thereby rendering moot any other claim of legal inconsistency. (L/410; SR.10/5, pages 51-52). (As is explained more fully below, the United States had already challenged the ad valorem character of the original 2 per cent tax in a 1954 proceeding.)"

[16] A footnote to this sentence provides as follows: "A 1971 working party report on the accession of Zaire stated that a statistical tax of 3 per cent ad valorem was 'not commensurate with the service rendered and was contrary to the provisions of Article VIII:1(a)'. The report did not specify the specific violation or violations in question. Although Zaire's reply to this finding concentrated on the excessive rate of the tax, the working party's eventual recommendation also asked Zaire to 're-examine its present method of application of the statistical tax ...' a form of expression which was more appropriate to a concern over the form of the tax than to concern over the excessive rate. (18S/89, pages 89-90)."

the cost of customs services rendered, and was thus authorized by Article II:2(c). The reply of the United States delegation was as follows:

> 'Mr. BROWN (United States) thanked the French delegate for his report. The United States Government was particularly concerned with the principle that the maintenance of an *ad valorem* charge alone would not satisfy the requirements of Article II. After the statement and explanation of the intentions and attitude of the French Government, and since there was no substantial injury to United States exports, his delegation was prepared to withdraw the complaint from the Agenda.' (SR.9/28, page 5)

"Finally, to give a more complete view of GATT legal experience on the issue of *ad valorem* service fees, the Panel considered it relevant to note that the *ad valorem* method had in fact been expressly attacked in 1952 and 1957, in two formal recommendations concerning consular fees. (1S/25; 6S/25.) Although these recommendations were initiated at a time when Article VIII:1(a) was merely hortatory, and thus were not a legal ruling as such, they were expressly intended to implement the standards of Article VIII:1(a). In its preamble, the 1952 recommendation noted the 'cost of services' standard stated in Article VIII:1(a), and then observed that 'the [consular] fee charged is in many cases a high percentage of the value of the goods'. The operative part of the recommendation then stated, 'Any consular fee should not be a percentage of the value of the goods but should be a flat charge'. The 1957 recommendation, issued one month after the effective date of the protocol making Article VIII:1(a) mandatory, restated the 1952 recommendation in similar terms. While it is probable that the primary concern with the *ad valorem* method in these recommendations had been its tendency to encourage excessive rates, the text of these recommendations is also consistent with a parallel objection to its cost apportionment consequences. In either event, governments were on notice from an early date that the CONTRACTING PARTIES did not necessarily consider the *ad valorem* method an acceptable structure for the type of fees covered by Article VIII.

"Considering the historical evidence as a whole, the Panel could not agree with the United States argument that the GATT's legal experience with *ad valorem* service fees evidenced a widespread belief that the *ad valorem* method as such was consistent with the obligations of Articles II and VIII. Whether considered individually or as a whole, the events which constitute that history simply do not demonstrate any such understanding. If anything, these events tend to show that the *ad valorem* method has been questioned in those few cases where it has been put in issue."[17]

The 1990 Report of the Working Party on the "Accession of Venezuela" contains, inter alia, a discussion of Venezuela's 5 per cent *ad valorem* customs service fee. The representative of Venezuela stated that this fee "corresponded to the services rendered by the Customs Administration ... With reference to Article VIII:1(a) of the General Agreement, and the 1988 Panel Report on Customs User Fee, the representative of Venezuela indicated that recent experience had shown that the application of any system other than an *ad valorem* fee would be extremely complex and bring in an element of administrative discretion which might lead to undesirable delays or obstacles to imports. Moreover, the administrative cost of operating a transaction-based fee would be very high".[18]

The 1990 Report of the Working Party on the "Accession of Tunisia" contains, inter alia, a discussion of Tunisia's "customs formalities tax".

"A member noted that Article VIII of the General Agreement provides that fees and charges on or in connection with importation and exportation shall be limited in amount to the approximate cost of services rendered. In his view, the customs formalities tax should be levied at a fixed rate. This member reserved his position on the conformity of the 5 per cent customs formalities tax with the General Agreement. The representative of Tunisia said that in the light of the objectives of the VII National Development Plan, the Tunisian authorities had decided to incorporate the customs formalities tax into the customs tariff rates under the framework of the Finance Law of 1988 that will enter into force on 1 January 1988."[19]

---

[17] L/6264, adopted on 2 February 1988, 35S/245, 279-282, para. 87-94.
[18] L/6696, adopted on 11 July 1990, 37S/43, 49, para. 22.
[19] L/6277, adopted on 12 December 1990, 37S/30, 35, para. 21.

(d) Various charges

In a complaint brought against France in 1952, the United States maintained that the French "statistical and customs control" tax on imports and exports infringed Article VIII:1 since the proceeds of this tax were also used for funding social security benefits to farmers.[20] France acknowledged the infringement and subsequently abolished the tax.[21]

In another complaint brought against France in 1955, the United States contended that the French stamp tax violated both Articles II:1 and VIII:1 since proceeds from this tax were used for financing agricultural family allowance and exceeded the "approximate cost of services rendered".[22] The stamp tax was subsequently reduced.[23]

The 1971 Report of the Working Party on the accession of the Democratic Republic of the Congo (now known as Zaire) notes that "Members of the Working Party pointed out that the statistical tax of 3 per cent *ad valorem* applied by the Congolese authorities on imports was not commensurate with the service rendered and was contrary to the provisions of Article VIII:1(a). The representative of the Congo recognized that this tax exceeded the cost of the service, and explained that the surplus revenue from the tax would be employed toward improving the service. His authorities were prepared to consider the adjustment of the statistical tax, in the light of the provisions of Article VIII as soon as they would be in a position to afford it".[24]

In the 1978 Panel Report on "EEC - Programme of Minimum Import Prices, Licenses and Surety Deposits for Certain Processed Fruits and Vegetables", the Panel examined the argument that the interest charges and costs associated with the lodging of the security were imposed as protection for domestic products contrary to the provisions of Article VIII:1(a). "The Panel also noted the contention by the Community representative that the incidence of these charges did not exceed 0.005 per cent. The Panel considered that these interest charges and costs were limited in amount to the approximate costs of administration. The Panel further considered that the term 'cost of services rendered' in Article VIII:1(a) would include these costs of administration. Therefore, the Panel concluded that the interest charges and costs associated with the lodging of the security were not inconsistent with the Community's obligations under Article VIII:1(a)."[25]

The 1990 Report of the Working Party on the "Accession of El Salvador" contains, *inter alia*, a discussion of the tax system for imports. In response to questions the representative of El Salvador

"said that these charges which related to services rendered by the customs administration were modest, would have no effect on the agreed bound levels, did not constitute severe sanctions, and were consistent with Article VIII of the General Agreement. He added that the 30 per cent surcharge contemplated in the San José Protocol was not applicable. A member stated that, in his opinion, these charges are not related to the cost of services rendered, and therefore may be inconsistent with the provisions of Article VIII. This member urged El Salvador to state clearly that its customs penalties and charges applied to imports will be applied in accordance with Article VIII from the date of accession and reserved its rights on this point, in light of the findings and recommendations of a GATT panel that examined United States practices in this area".[26]

See also various references to charges on imports in accession Working Party reports;[27] references to *ad valorem* charges for preshipment inspection;[28] and examination of various charges under Article XXIV:8(a) in working party reports on agreements under Article XXIV:8(a).[29]

---

[20] L/238, SR.8/7, SR.8/10.
[21] SR.9/28.
[22] L/410, L/569, L/720.
[23] L/1412.
[24] L/3541, adopted on 29 June 1971, 18S/89, para.5.
[25] L/4687, adopted on 18 October 1978, 25S/68, 95-96, para. 4.2.
[26] L/6771, adopted on 12 December 1990, 37S/9, 17, para. 23.
[27] See, e.g., report on "Provisional Accession of the United Arab Republic", L/1876, adopted on 13 November 1962, 11S/75, 77, para. 7.
[28] L/7170, dated 28 Jan 1993, memorandum on foreign trade of Zaire.
[29] See the reports cited in this work under Article XXIV:8(a).

(3) "an indirect protection to domestic products or a taxation of imports or exports for fiscal purposes"

In the Panel Report on "United States - Customs User Fee"

"... the Panel then considered whether the arguments of the parties had raised any further issues concerning the US merchandise processing fee under the second and third criteria stated in Article VIII:1(a).

"The only issue raised by the parties under the third criterion prohibiting 'taxation of imports ... for fiscal purposes' was the question of whether total revenues exceeded total attributable costs, an issue which the Panel dealt with fully under the 'cost of services' requirement.

"The only specific issue raised by the parties under the second criterion was whether the 0.22 and 0.17 percent *ad valorem* charges constituted 'an indirect protection to domestic products' due to their effect on certain classes of price-sensitive imports. It was not necessary for the Panel to decide whether the 'indirect protection' criterion actually involved a requirement of no adverse trade effects. The Panel concluded that, even if it did, it had not been demonstrated that these *ad valorem* charges had had a trade distorting effect".[30]

See also the discussion of the Panel Report on "EEC - Programme of Minimum Import Prices, Licenses and Surety Deposits for Certain Processed Fruits and Vegetables", on page 271 above, concerning the claim that the interest charges and costs associated with the lodging of the additional security which enforced the minimum import price for tomato concentrates were imposed as protection for domestic products contrary to Article VIII:1(a).

(4) "The contracting parties also recognize the need for minimizing the incidence and complexity of import formalities and for decreasing and simplifying import and export documentation requirements"

In the early years of the GATT, work was undertaken on matters relating to customs formalities, including documentary requirements, temporary admission for samples, and certification of origin. This work, which built on the work that had been carried out under the auspices of the League of Nations in the interwar years, included the drafting of recommendations for adoption by the CONTRACTING PARTIES and of Conventions on certain of these subjects. See, for instance, the 1951 Report on "Customs Treatment of Samples and Advertising Material, Documentary Requirements for the Importation of Goods, and Consular Formalities: Resolutions of the International Chamber of Commerce",[31] and the 1952 Report on "Documentary Requirements for Imports, Consular Formalities, Valuation for Customs Purposes, Nationality of Imported Goods and Formalities connected with Quantitative Restrictions".[32]

See also in this connection the unadopted 1994 panel report on "EEC - Import Régime for Bananas".[33]

(a) Origin of imported goods and requirement of certificates of origin

During the second session of the Preparatory Committee in 1947, a Sub-Committee studying this issue considered "it to be clear that it is within the province of each importing member country to determine, in accordance with the provisions of its law, for the purposes of applying the most-favoured-nation provision whether goods do in fact originate in a particular country".[34]

Concerning consideration in the early years of the GATT of proposals on harmonization of origin rules, see the 1951 and 1952 Reports cited directly above, and the 1953 Report of a Working Party in the Eighth Session of the CONTRACTING PARTIES on "Nationality of Imported Goods",[35] which examined both the definition of origin

---

[30] L/6264, adopted on 2 February 1988, 35S/245, 289, paras. 118-120.
[31] GATT/CP.6/36, adopted 24 October 1951, II/210.
[32] G/28, adopted 7 November 1952, 1S/100.
[33] DS38/R, dated 11 Feb. 1994, para. 151.
[34] EPCT/174, p. 3-4.
[35] G/61 adopted on 23 October 1953, 2S/53-59.

and proof of origin. The Report also includes Recommendations regarding proof of origin, and includes as an annex Article 11 on Certificates of Origin of the 1923 International Convention Relating to the Simplification of Customs Formalities. These Recommendations were amended in 1956; see the Report of the Working Party on "Certificates of Origin, Marks of Origin and Consular Formalities"[36] and the Recommendation on "Certificates of Origin" as amended.[37]

The Report of a Working Party in the Ninth Session on "Definition of Origin" presents the views of governments regarding a proposed definition submitted to governments by the CONTRACTING PARTIES for review and study.[38] Interpretative Note 2 to Article VIII, which deals with the production of certificates of origin, was added as a result of the Review conducted during the Ninth Session.

Rules of origin for the purpose of eligibility for preferential treatment have been extensively discussed in the context of agreements under Article XXIV: see the material on this subject under Article XXIV in this Index. Such rules of origin were also discussed in the context of the Protocol Relating to Trade Negotiations Among Developing Countries, which contains provisions dealing with this issue,[39] and in the context of discussions of the implementation of the Generalized System of Preferences. A 1981 Note by the Secretariat summarizes the concept and main criteria of rules of origin which form part of trade agreements and arrangements where it is essential to establish the preferential (or non-preferential) origin of goods.[40]

Rules of origin have also been discussed in the context of the administration of textile agreements.[41]

The November 1982 Ministerial Declaration requests the Council "to make arrangements for studies of dual-pricing practices and rules of origin; and to consider what further action may be necessary with regard to these matters when the results of these studies are available."[42]

A 1988 Note by the Secretariat on "Rules of Origin" discusses the administration of rules of origin, related provisions of the General Agreement and past discussions on the subject in the GATT.[43]

See generally the Agreement on Rules of Origin reached in the Uruguay Round.

(b) *Documentary requirements for importation of goods*

The Working Party in the Seventh Session on "Documentary Requirements for Imports, Consular Formalities, Valuation for Customs Purposes, Nationality of Imported Goods and Formalities connected with Quantitative Restrictions" drew up a Code of Standard Practices for Documentary Requirements for the Importation of Goods, which was adopted by the CONTRACTING PARTIES.[44]

See also the various Secretariat Notes prepared in the Tokyo Round on this and related subjects.[45]

---

[36] L/595, adopted 17 November 1956, 5S/102-103.
[37] Recommendation of 23 October 1953 as amended by the Recommendation of 17 November 1956, 5S/33.
[38] G/92 adopted on 2 March 1955, 3S/94-99.
[39] 18S/11, Annex A at 18S/17. Information concerning certification of origin in developing countries participating in the Protocol is circulated in CPC/10 and Addenda thereto.
[40] CG.18/W/48, dated 6 March 1981, and Suppl.1; see also discussion at CG.18/13, CG.18/14.
[41] See 31S/324-339, C/M/181.
[42] L/5424, Declaration adopted by Ministers 29 November 1982, 29S/9, 21; see followup discussion at C/M/165.
[43] MTN.GNG/NG2/W/12, dated 21 June 1988. This Note also states that detailed information on the rules of origin maintained by a number of countries can be found in the Customs Co-operation Council's "Compendium of Origin of Goods" and, for the GSP, the "Digest of Rules of Origin" prepared by UNCTAD and UNDP.
[44] G/28, Report adopted 7 November 1952, 1S/100-101; Decision of 7 November 1952, 1S/23.
[45] "Part 2 of the Inventory of Non-Tariff Measures - Customs and administrative entry procedures", MTN/3B/2; "Import documentation (Task 14 of MTN/2)", MTN/3B/8; "Import documentation - Information required by Countries for Customs Entry Purposes", MTN/3B/13; "Import Documentation - Note on the Work being carried out by other International Organizations", MTN/3B/14; Note on Meeting of May 1974, MTN/3B/11; "Customs Matters background note by the Secretariat", MTN/NTM/W/7; Note on import documentation requirements from various contracting parties, MTN/NTM/W/22+Rev.1+Add.1; "Aligned invoice layout key for international trade", MTN/NTM/W/34; "Import documentation and customs procedures - work of the international organizations", MTN/NTM/W/60; "Customs Co-operation Council", MTN/NTM/W/238.

(c) *Formalities associated with administration of quantitative restrictions*

During their fifth session at Torquay in 1950, the CONTRACTING PARTIES adopted a Code of Standard Practices for the Administration of Import and Export Restrictions and Exchange Controls; concerning this Code see under Article XIII.[46]

In the Tokyo Round of trade negotiations the Agreement on Import Licensing Procedures was negotiated, the preamble of which refers *inter alia* to the desire "to simplify, and bring transparency to, the administrative procedures and practices used in international trade, and to ensure the fair and equitable application and administration of such procedures and practices".[47] Further concerning this Agreement, see under Article XIII.

(d) *Abolition of consular formalities*

The Report of the Working Party in the Seventh Session on "Documentary Requirements for Imports, Consular Formalities, Valuation for Customs Purposes, Nationality of Imported Goods and Formalities connected with Quantitative Restrictions" also proposed a "Recommendation on the Abolition of Consular Formalities", providing for abolition of consular invoices and consular visas not later than 31 December 1956; annexed to this Recommendation is a Code of Standard Practices for Consular Formalities.[48] Later working parties from 1953 through 1962 examined reports from contracting parties on steps taken towards the abolition of consular formalities, and resulted in Decisions on "Consular Formalities" reaffirming the 1952 Recommendation.[49] See the discussion of the 1952 Recommendation and these reports in the Panel Report on "United States - Customs User Fee", excerpted above at page 276.[50]

The 1971 Report of the Committee on Trade in Industrial Products discusses, *inter alia,* possible solutions for the further liberalization of consular formalities and documentation.[51] See also a Secretariat Note from the Tokyo Round on "Consular formalities and fees".[52]

(e) *Customs conventions*

In 1951, a proposal of the International Chamber of Commerce for a convention to facilitate importation of commercial samples and advertising material was referred to the CONTRACTING PARTIES by the United Nations Economic and Social Council, and was examined by a working party in the Sixth Session.[53] A working party in the Seventh Session then redrafted the text of the Convention, entitled the International Convention to Facilitate the Importation of Commercial Samples and Advertising Material; the Convention was adopted by the CONTRACTING PARTIES on 7 November 1952[54] and entered into force on 20 November 1955.[55]

A Group of Experts in 1960 examined and amended a Draft Customs Convention on the Temporary Importation of Packings as transmitted by the Customs Co-operation Council (CCC). The CCC accepted all of the suggestions of the GATT group, together with a series of agreed interpretations, and opened the Convention as amended for signature.[56] The Group of Experts in 1960-1961 also examined and amended Draft Customs

---

[46]GATT/CP.5/30/Rev.1; see also supplementary recommendation regarding contract sanctity at 1S/105-106.
[47]26S/154.
[48]G/28, Report adopted 7 November 1952, 1S/100, 101-102; Recommendation of 7 November 1952, 1S/25.
[49]Reports at 2S/59, 3S/91, 5S/108, 11S/214; Decisions or Recommendations at 5S/33, 6S/25, 11S/59.
[50]L/6264, adopted on 2 February 1988, 35S/245, 282, para. 93.
[51]L/3496, adopted on 22 February 1971, pp. 43-46; see also COM.IND/W/79 +Add.1, Background Note by the Secretariat (1972).
[52]MTN/NTM/W/36 and Rev.1, Corr.1-2 and Add.1-3.
[53]GATT/CP.6/36, adopted on 24 October 1951, II/210; ECOSOC proposal appears in resolution 347(XII) of 7 March 1951, E/1987, p. 7.
[54]G/33, Report on "International Convention to Facilitate the Importation of Commercial Samples and Advertising Material", adopted 7 November 1952, 1S/94. For later GATT work on interpretation of this Convention, see L/466, SR.10/11 p. 119, SR.10/16 p. 175, and L/601.
[55]Text of Convention at 221 UNTS 255. As of November 1994, the Convention was in force in 61 countries: see list in L/7538, dated 8 November 1994, and list of acceptances and reservations in yearly editions of *Multilateral Treaties Deposited with the Secretary-General*, United Nations Publication ST/LEG/SER.E/11 (1993).
[56]L/1208, adopted 2 June 1960, 9S/201; text of Convention and agreed interpretations at 9S/205ff.

Conventions on the Temporary Importation of Professional Equipment, and on the ATA Carnet for the Temporary Admission of Goods, as transmitted by the CCC, and arrived at agreed interpretations of these Conventions.[57]

(f) Facilitation of trade in cultural or health-related products

During the Third Session, the United Nations Educational, Scientific and Cultural Organization (UNESCO) submitted a number of proposals for facilitating international trade in books, newspapers and periodicals.[58] A Working Party during the Annecy trade negotiations drafted an international Agreement on the Importation of Educational, Scientific and Cultural Materials and communicated the text to UNESCO for sponsorship.[59] The Agreement was subsequently adopted and opened for signature by the Fourth Session of the General Conference of UNESCO at Florence, and entered into force on 21 May 1952.[60]

During the Fifth Session, the World Health Organization requested the assistance of the CONTRACTING PARTIES with respect to a draft agreement reducing trade barriers to basic insecticides and apparatus and materials necessary for campaigns against insects carriers of human diseases. While the Working Party drafted an agreement, its Report concluded that views were divided as to the utility of such an approach; one problem cited was the difficulty of limiting the duty-free treatment to be provided, since equipment used in making insecticides was usable for other purposes.[61]

(g) Preshipment inspection

Notes by the Secretariat of 1988 and 1989 on "Preshipment Inspection" provide background on the subject, summarize relevant discussions in various GATT bodies, and outline relevant provisions in the GATT and other international agreements.[62]

See generally the Agreement on Preshipment Inspection reached in the Uruguay Round.

(h) Testing fees for imported products

Article 5.1.3 of the Agreement on Technical Barriers to Trade provides that

"Parties shall ensure that, in cases where a positive assurance is required that products conform with technical regulations or standards ... any fees imposed for testing imported products shall be equitable in relation to any fees chargeable for testing like products of national origin or originating in any other country".[63]

2. Paragraph 2

The Report of the Balance-of-Payments Committee on its work in the period 1970-1974 notes: "Without specifically referring to Article VIII:2 the Committee, in its conclusions in a large number of cases, urged the consulting country to reduce the complexity of its import procedures. In one case (1973, India) the Committee suggested the adoption of a uniform nomenclature for import control and tariff purposes".[64]

---

[57]Draft Convention on Temporary Importation of Professional Equipment: L/1366, Report adopted 18 November 1960 including draft text, 9S/212; L/1476, Report adopted 17 May 1961, 10S/211, including interpretations at 10S/212ff, revised text as opened for signature by CCC at 10S/216ff. Draft Convention on the ATA Carnet for the Temporary Admission of Goods, L/1476, Report adopted 17 May 1961, 10S/211, including interpretations at 10S/214ff, text as opened for signature by the CCC at 10S/226ff.

[58]UNESCO Memorandum and list of items for consideration in negotiations, GATT/CP/12 and Add.1; Draft Agreement submitted by UNESCO, GATT/CP/12/Add.2 and Rev.1; UNESCO Notes on relevant practices in various countries, GATT/CP/12/Add.3-14.

[59]Working Party papers, GATT/TN.1/C/1; Working Party Report, GATT/TN.1/27 and Corr.1.

[60]Letter from Director-General of UNESCO concerning draft Agreement, GATT/TN.1/34, GATT/CP.4/19; discussion, GATT/CP.4/SR.4, 17; letter from UNESCO regarding adoption and signature of Agreement, GATT/CP/81 and Add.1-2; letter on entry into force, L/137.

[61]Letter at GATT/CP/79; Report of WP "D" on the Request of the WHO concerning Insecticides GATT/CP.5/47 and Amend.1; discussion at GATT/CP.5/SR.5 p. 3-5, SR.6 p. 2-3, SR.23 p. 3-4, SR.24 p. 1.

[62]MTN.GNG/NG2/W/11 dated 20 April 1988 and Add.1 dated 19 October 1989.

[63]26S/8, 13, 14.

[64]L/4200, para. 48.

3. Paragraph 3: penalty charges

See the discussion of paragraph 3 in the 1978 Panel Report on "EEC - Programme of Minimum Import Prices, Licenses and Surety Deposits for Certain Processed Fruits and Vegetables", on page 271 above.

The 1990 Report of the Working Party on the "Accession of Venezuela" contains, inter alia, a discussion of *ad valorem* storage charges levied by Venezuelan customs authorities. "A member said that having regard to the fee structure described in the Regulation to the Customs Law no distinction could be made in practice between the *ad valorem* warehouse charges and the penalties applied for non-expeditious customs clearance; both charges were customs charges and should conform to Article VIII of the General Agreement concerning correspondence with the approximate cost of services rendered. Furthermore, in setting the level of penalty charges, the provisions of Article VIII:3 concerning substantial penalties should be observed."[65]

4. Paragraph 4

During discussions of this provision at the Geneva session of the Preparatory Committee in 1947, it was agreed that the provisions of sub-paragraph 4(d) were "without prejudice to the provisions of the Charter relating to safeguarding balance of payments and to exchange control".[66]

B. RELATIONSHIP BETWEEN ARTICLE VIII AND OTHER ARTICLES

1. Article I

During the Second Session of the CONTRACTING PARTIES in 1948, in response to a request for an interpretation of the phrase "charges of any kind" in Article I:1 with respect to consular fees, "The Chairman ruled that consular taxes would be included in 'charges of any kind'; Article VIII merely dealt with the magnitude of such taxes in relation to the cost of services rendered, whereas Article I embodies the principle of non-discrimination".[67]

See also the discussion in paragraphs 121-124 of the Panel Report on "United States - Customs User Fee" concerning the question of whether the exemptions from the US merchandise processing fee granted to imports from certain countries were inconsistent with the MFN obligation of Article I:1.[68]

2. Article II:2(c)

The 1988 Panel Report on "United States - Customs User Fee" notes as follows:

"... the Panel ... addressed the general meaning of Articles II:2(c) and VIII:1(a), and their relationship to each other. Article VIII:1(a) states a rule applicable to all charges levied at the border, except tariffs and charges which serve to equalize internal taxes. It applies to all such charges, whether or not there is a tariff binding on the product in question. The rule of Article VIII:1(a) prohibits all such charges unless they satisfy the three criteria listed in that provision:

(a) the charge must be 'limited in amount to the approximate cost of services rendered' ;

(b) it must not 'represent an indirect protection to domestic products';

(c) it must not 'represent ... a taxation of imports ... for fiscal purposes'.

The first requirement is actually a dual requirement, because the charge in question must first involve a 'service' rendered, and then the level of the charge must not exceed the approximate cost of that 'service'.

---

[65] L/6696, adopted on 11 July 1990, 37S/43, 50, paras. 25-26.
[66] EPCT/103, p. 25.
[67] GATT/CP.2/SR.11 p. 7, reprinted in abridged form at II/12; see GATT/CP.2/9 for request for ruling.
[68] L/6264, adopted on 2 February 1988, 35S/245, 289-290.

"Article II:2(c) is a provision of somewhat narrower scope. Its function is to permit the imposition of certain non-tariff border charges on products which are subject to a bound tariff. Paragraph 1(b) of Article II establishes a general ceiling on the charges that can be levied on a product whose tariff is bound; it requires that the product be exempt from all tariffs in excess of the bound rate, and from all other charges in excess of those (i) in force on the date of the tariff concession, or (ii) directly and mandatorily required by legislation in force on that date. Article II:2 permits governments to impose, above this ceiling, three types of non-tariff charges, of which the third, permitted by sub-paragraph (c), is 'fees or other charges commensurate with the cost of services rendered'.

"In order to help clarify the meaning of Articles II:2(c) and VIII:1(a), the Panel examined the origins and the drafting history of these provisions. ..."[69] [See discussion excerpted below on page 284]

"Two questions of general interpretation had to be answered before addressing the specific issues raised by the complainants. First, it was necessary to decide whether there was any legal significance in the slight difference in wording between the two 'cost of services' limitations stated in Articles II:2(c) and VIII:1(a), i.e. 'commensurate with the cost of services rendered' and 'limited in amount to the approximate cost of services rendered.' The words themselves suggested no immediately apparent difference in meaning. After reviewing both the drafting history and the subsequent application of these provisions, the Panel concluded that no difference of meaning had been intended. The difference in wording appears to be explained by the somewhat different paths by which each provision entered the General Agreement. The text which was to become Article VIII:1(a) appeared in the very first draft submitted to the negotiating conference by the United States, whereas the text of Article II:2(c) originated as a standard term to be incorporated in each contracting party's schedule of concessions (see E/PC/T/153) and was not raised to the text of Article II until some time later (E/PC/T/201).

"Second, it was necessary to determine what type of fees were incorporated within the basic concept of 'services rendered' in Articles II:2(c) and VIII:1(a) ...".[70] [See discussion above, page 269.]

3. Article III

In the 1994 panel report on "United States - Measures Affecting the Importation, Internal Sale and Use of Tobacco", the panel examined a fee charged for inspection of tobacco:

"The Panel ... noted that Article VIII does not apply to taxes within the purview of Article III. The Panel then recalled that no party to the dispute had requested the Panel to examine the consistency of these inspection fees with Article III. Indeed, all parties had argued that the Section 1106(c) inspection fees should be examined in the light of Article VIII. The Panel noted that the consistency of Section 1106(c) could present itself differently under Article III in that the focus of the examination would then be on the inspection fees as internal charges and on whether or not national treatment was accorded in respect of such charges. However, in view of the fact that the parties to the dispute had argued the Section 1106(c) inspection fees in terms of Article VIII, the Panel proceeded to examine this legislative provision under that Article."[71]

C. EXCEPTIONS AND DEROGATIONS

The 1988 Panel Report on "United States - Customs User Fee" further notes:

"... Article VIII:1(a) imposed no legal obligations at all from 1947 to 1957 when the Review Session amendments went into force, and thereafter the obligations of Article VIII were subject to the reservation for existing mandatory legislation in the Protocol of Provisional Application. The relative importance of such legal immunity was indicated in a 1962 working party report on customs formalities:

---

[69]*Ibid.*, 35S/273, paras. 69-71.
[70]*Ibid.*, 35S/275, paras. 75-76.
[71]DS44/R, adopted on 4 October 1994, para. 117.

'The question was raised whether the levying of substantial consular fees by the importing country was in conformity with the obligations of Article VIII of GATT since the rates exceeded the costs of the services rendered and were not the equivalent of an internal charge. It was noted, however, that Article VIII being in Part II of GATT involved obligations only within the arrangements for provisional application of the Agreement. [11S/216]'[72]

See also the Interpretative Note *Ad* Article VIII.

III. PREPARATORY WORK AND SUBSEQUENT MODIFICATIONS

Differences between the General Agreement and the Havana Charter: The corresponding provisions in the Havana Charter are contained in Article 36; in the US Proposals in Chapter III-5; in the US Draft in Article 13; in the New York Draft in Article 19; and in the Geneva Draft in Article 35.

In discussions at the Havana Conference on Article 36, "It was ... agreed that paragraph 1 should be revised and care should be taken in the translation to show definitively that this Article relates to all payments of any character required by a Member on or in connexion with importation or exportation, other than import and export duties, and other than taxes within the purview of Article 18 [III] of the Geneva draft".[73] Accordingly paragraph 1 was revised to include the phrase, "all fees and charges of whatever character (other than import and export duties, and other than taxes within the purview of Article 18)". This wording was later brought into the General Agreement in the Review Session amendments; see below.

Paragraph 2 was amended in Havana to provide that a Member need respond to a request to undertake the review of its laws and regulations only if such a request were made by another Member "directly affected"; this change was not retained in the General Agreement. Paragraph 4 provided for studies by the ITO on measures to simplify and standardize customs formalities, and was not included in the General Agreement, as it related to functions of the ITO. Paragraph 6 of the Charter article relating to tariff discrimination based on the use of regional or geographical names in tariff descriptions is not included in the General Agreement as it did not appear in the Geneva draft. The order of the paragraphs was changed at Havana.[74] The Interpretative Note in the Charter reads "not inconsistent with the Articles of Agreement of the International Monetary Fund", instead of "with the approval of the International Monetary Fund"; the change was made because "the express approval of the Fund was not required in all cases covered by the Note".[75]

Antecedents and drafting history: The Panel Report on "United States - Customs User Fee" includes the following discussion of the antecedents and drafting history of Articles VIII:1 and II:2(c).

"In order to help clarify the meaning of Articles II:2(c) and VIII:1(a), the Panel examined the origins and the drafting history of these provisions. During the drafting of the General Agreement, the previous legal instrument referred to most frequently in connection with these provisions was the *International Convention Relating to the Simplification of Customs Formalities* of 3 November 1923[76]. One of the major purposes of the 1923 convention had been to reduce the number and the level of fees imposed in connection with importation. Governments had agreed to limit certain fees to the actual cost of the government activity in question. Article 10 stated, 'When a visa [for commercial travellers] is required, its cost shall be as low as possible and shall not exceed the cost of the service.' Article 11(8) stated, 'The cost of the [consular] visa must be as low as possible, and must not exceed the cost of issue, especially in the case of consignments of small value.' Article 12 stated, 'The cost of a visa for Consular invoices shall be a fixed charge, which should be as low as possible.' The Convention's two provisions on consular fees were

---

[72]*Ibid.*, 35S/280, para. 89, referring to the Declaration of 15 November 1957 (6S/13) stating that Review Session amendments to Part II of the General Agreement are subject to the reservation for existing mandatory legislation in the Protocol of Provisional Application or applicable protocols of accession; see discussion of this Declaration in the chapter of this Index on provisional application.
[73]Havana Reports, p. 76, para. 35.
[74]Havana Reports, pp. 77-78, paras. 43-45.
[75]Havana Reports, p. 77, para. 41.
[76]A footnote to this sentence provides: "League of Nations Treaty Series vol. 30, p. 372 (1925). The treaty, which was negotiated under League of Nations auspices, entered into force on 27 November 1924".

reaffirmed in the recommendations of the World Economic Conference of 1927, which restated them as follows:

> '(1) Consular fees should be a charge, fixed in amount and not exceeding the cost of issue, rather than an additional source of revenue. Arbitrary or variable consular fees cause not only an increase of charges, which is at times unexpected, but also an unwarrantable uncertainty in trade'.[77]

"The Panel was unable to find specific antecedents to Articles II:2(c) and VIII:1(a). In particular, no such provisions could be found in the United States bilateral trade agreements of 1934-1942, from which the United States had drawn many of the texts proposed for adoption in the General Agreement. Those bilateral agreements had contained no general limitation on non-tariff charges as in Article VIII:1(a), nor had their definition of tariff bindings permitted the imposition of new 'service' fees as in Article II:1(c).

"According to the detailed negotiating history of GATT Articles II:2(c) and VIII:1(a) provided by the United States, proposals to permit such fees, characterized as fees for 'services rendered', appeared in the earliest stages of the GATT/ITO negotiations.[78] The criteria stated in the initial draft texts submitted to the negotiating conference[79] were almost identical to those adopted in the final texts, with the result that the actual negotiations presented no occasions for further elaboration of their meaning.

"When the General Agreement was first adopted in 1947, the requirements of Article VIII:1(a) were merely hortatory, reading 'should' rather than 'shall'. Article VIII:1(a) was made mandatory in the Review Session amendments to Part II of the General Agreement (3S/214), which were adopted in March 1955 and which entered into force in October 1957. Article II:2(c) was included in the original 1947 text of the General Agreement in its present form."[80]

The Report of the Review Working Party on Schedules and Customs Administration, which recommended the Review Session amendments to Article VIII, provided the following explanation of the changes.

"Paragraphs 1 and 2 have been redrafted in order (i) to separate the provisions relating to fees and charges from those relating to formalities, (ii) to make it clear that the expression 'fees and charges' does not pertain to import and export duties or to taxes which fall within the purview of Article III, and (iii) to render the provisions of paragraph 1(a) obligatory by changing the word 'should' to 'shall' and by deleting the qualification that contracting parties need take action in accordance with the principles and objectives of that sub-paragraph only 'at the earliest practicable date'. These amendments are recommended on the assumption that the Agreement will contain a general provision allowing time for governments to bring their legislation into conformity with the rules and on condition that the amendment proposed to the interpretative note is adopted."[81]

These changes, including changes to the title and paragraphs 1 and 2 of Article VIII, were implemented by the Protocol Amending the Preamble and Parts II and III of the General Agreement, and entered into effect on 7 October 1957.

IV. RELEVANT DOCUMENTS

See below at the end of Article X.

---

[77] A footnote to this sentence provides: "League of Nations Document C.356.M.129.1927.II, paragraph 5(1)".
[78] A footnote to this sentence provides: "According to negotiation records in the United States archives, the earliest reference occurred in a document titled 'Agenda Resulting from Informal Exploratory Discussions between officials of the United Kingdom and of the United States...', dated 16 October 1943".
[79] A footnote to this word provides: "Article VIII:1(a) first appeared as Article 13, *Suggested Charter for an International Trade Organization of the United Nations*, submitted by the United States in September 1946. The first document found by the Panel containing the text of what was to become Article II:2(c) was E/PC/T/153 of August 1947. See also E/PC/T/201 of September 1947".
[80] L/6264, adopted on 2 February 1988, 35S/245, 273-274, paras. 71-74.
[81] L/329, adopted 26 February 1955, 3S/205, 214, para. 20.

ARTICLE IX

MARKS OF ORIGIN

I. TEXT OF ARTICLE IX 287
II. INTERPRETATION AND APPLICATION OF ARTICLE IX 288
    A.   SCOPE AND APPLICATION OF ARTICLE IX 288
        1.   Paragraph 1 288
        2.   Paragraph 2 288
            (1)   Marks of origin and other marks 289
            (2)   Truth in marking 289
        3.   Paragraph 4 289
        4.   Paragraph 6 289
    B.   RELATIONSHIP BETWEEN ARTICLE IX AND OTHER ARTICLES 291
    C.   RELATIONSHIP BETWEEN ARTICLE IX AND OTHER AGREEMENTS 291
III. PREPARATORY WORK AND SUBSEQUENT MODIFICATIONS 291
IV. RELEVANT DOCUMENTS 291

I. TEXT OF ARTICLE IX

Article IX

Marks of Origin

1. Each contracting party shall accord to the products of the territories of other contracting parties treatment with regard to marking requirements no less favourable than the treatment accorded to like products of any third country.

2. The contracting parties recognize that, in adopting and enforcing laws and regulations relating to marks of origin, the difficulties and inconveniences which such measures may cause to the commerce and industry of exporting countries should be reduced to a minimum, due regard being had to the necessity of protecting consumers against fraudulent or misleading indications.

3. Whenever it is administratively practicable to do so, contracting parties should permit required marks of origin to be affixed at the time of importation.

4. The laws and regulations of contracting parties relating to the marking of imported products shall be such as to permit compliance without seriously damaging the products, or materially reducing their value, or unreasonably increasing their cost.

5. As a general rule, no special duty or penalty should be imposed by any contracting party for failure to comply with marking requirements prior to importation unless corrective marking is unreasonably delayed or deceptive marks have been affixed or the required marking has been intentionally omitted.

6. The contracting parties shall co-operate with each other with a view to preventing the use of trade names in such manner as to misrepresent the true origin of a product, to the detriment of such distinctive regional or geographical names of products of the territory of a contracting party as are protected by its legislation. Each contracting party shall accord full and sympathetic consideration to such requests or representations as may be made by any other contracting party regarding the application of the undertaking set forth in the preceding sentence to names of products which have been communicated to it by the other contracting party.

II. INTERPRETATION AND APPLICATION OF ARTICLE IX

A. SCOPE AND APPLICATION OF ARTICLE IX

Article IX deals with marking of origin. Concerning the work undertaken in the GATT on rules for determining the origin of goods, and on customs formalities such as certificates of origin or other documentary requirements for the importation of goods, see Article VIII. Concerning marking of products for other characteristics than origin, see Article III:4 (national treatment) and Article I:1 (most-favoured-nation treatment for all matters referred to in Article III:4).

1. Paragraph 1

The 1991 Panel Report on "United States - Restrictions on Imports of Tuna," which has not been adopted, considered a claim by Mexico that the provisions of the Dolphin Protection Consumer Information Act (DPCIA) of the United States, restricting the use on tuna products of the label "Dolphin Safe," was inconsistent with Article IX:1.

"The Panel noted that the title of Article IX is 'Marks of Origin' and its text refers to marking of origin of imported products. The Panel further noted that Article IX does not contain a national-treatment but only a most-favoured-nation requirement, which indicates that this provision was intended to regulate marking of origin of imported products but not marking of products generally. The Panel therefore found that the labelling provisions of the DPCIA did not fall under Article IX:1."[1]

2. Paragraph 2

The addition of Article IX:2 was agreed during the Review Session of 1954-55. The Report of the Review Working Party on "Schedules and Customs Administration" notes that "A new paragraph is proposed for insertion in Article IX whereby the contracting parties will recognize that measures relating to marks of origin should not cause difficulties and inconveniences for other governments".[2]

In 1956 and 1958, two working parties examined proposals of the International Chamber of Commerce regarding, *inter alia*, principles for consideration as a basis for a Recommendation on marks of origin. The Report of the 1956 Working Party on "Certificates of Origin, Marks of Origin and Consular Formalities" notes that "any such recommendation would have to be considered as an elaboration of the principles laid down in Article IX and in other Articles of GATT, and would have to be worded in such a way as to make clear that it does not prevent the application of more liberal regulations".[3] The 1958 Working Party reached agreement on the text of a Recommendation, adopted on 21 November 1958 by the CONTRACTING PARTIES, which sets out "certain rules which would further reduce the difficulties and inconveniences which marking regulations may cause to the commerce and industry of the exporting country".[4] The Recommendation also invites contracting parties to report, before 1 September each year, changes in their legislation, rules and regulations concerning marks of origin. A number of contracting parties complied with this invitation, but since 1961 no further submissions have been received.[5]

---

[1] DS21/R, 3 September 1991, 39S/155, 203, para. 5.41.
[2] L/329, adopted 26 February 1955, 3S/205, 215, para. 21.
[3] L/595, adopted 17 November 1956, 5S/102, 104 para. 4
[4] Recommendation on Marks of Origin, 7S/30; Working Party Report on "Marks of Origin", L/912/Rev.1, adopted 21 November 1958, 7S/117.
[5] C/W/420/Rev.1, p. 15; for notifications regarding origin marking see L/478 of 27 March 1956 and addenda 1-20 dated from 17 May 1956 to 26 October 1960.

(1) Marks of origin and other marks

The Report of the 1956 Working Party on "Certificates of Origin, Marks of Origin and Consular Formalities" notes as follows.

> "The Working Party considered that the question of additional marking requirements, such as an obligation to add the name of the producer or the place of origin or the formula of the product, should not be brought within the scope of any recommendation dealing with the problem of marks of origin. The point was stressed that requirements going beyond the obligation to indicate origin would not be consistent with the requirements of Article III, if the same requirements did not apply to domestic producers of like products."[6]

Paragraph 4 of the 1958 Recommendation states that "The national provisions concerning marks of origin should not contain any other obligation than the obligation to indicate the origin of the imported product". The 1958 Report of the Working Party on "Marks of Origin" states that "In particular it was remarked that [paragraph 4] has to be interpreted so as to invite countries to keep such requirements separate from requirements introduced for other purposes, e.g. to protect the health of the population, etc. In this connection, attention was drawn to Article III of the General Agreement which requires contracting parties to give to imported and domestic products the same treatment and that this obligation, being in Part II of the General Agreement, is governed by the terms of the Protocol of Provisional Application".[7]

(2) Truth in marking

The New York Draft of the ITO Charter noted, with regard to the Charter provision corresponding to Article IX, that "... the right of each country to prohibit the import, export and transit of foreign goods falsely marked as being produced in the country in question was considered to be covered primarily by the words 'deceptive practices'" [in Article XX:(d)].[8] The 1958 Recommendation provides that "The CONTRACTING PARTIES ... *Understand* that no country shall be obliged to alter: (a) any provision protecting the 'truth' of marks, including trade marks and trade descriptions, aiming to ensure that the content of such marks is in conformity with the real situation".[9]

3. Paragraph 4

In Council discussions of the United States Trade and Tariff Act of 1984, the EEC noted that it had requested consultations under Article XXII:1 concerning section 207 of that Act on country of origin marking for certain metal pipes and tubes. A number of delegations expressed the view that in some cases it was impossible to mark the products as this law required without damaging them, and stated that such marking requirements were inconsistent with Article IX:4.[10]

4. Paragraph 6

When the Charter article corresponding to Article IX was discussed at the Havana Conference,

> "... it was agreed that the text of paragraph 7 [GATT Article IX:6] should not have the effect of prejudicing the present situation as regards certain distinctive names of products, provided always that the names affixed to the products cannot misrepresent their true origin. This is particularly the case when the name of the producing country is clearly indicated. It will rest with the governments concerned to proceed to a joint examination of particular cases which might arise if disputes occur as a result of the use of distinctive names

---

[6]L/595, adopted on 17 November 1956, 5S/102, 105-106, para. 13.
[7]L/912/Rev.1, adopted on 21 November 1958, 7S/117, para. 2.
[8]Drafting Committee Report, p.16, para.6(b).
[9]7S/33.
[10]C/M/183, p. 89-90.

of products which may have lost their original significance through constant use permitted by law in the country where they are used".[11]

The Panel Report on "Japan - Customs Duties, Taxes and Labelling Practices on Imported Wines and Alcoholic Beverages" examined, *inter alia*, the claim by the European Communities that wines and alcoholic beverages imported into Japan did not enjoy adequate protection as regards origin marking and that Japan had failed to carry out its obligation under GATT Article IX:6 to "cooperate ... with a view to preventing the use of trade names in such manner as to misrepresent the true origin of a product, to the detriment of such distinctive regional or geographical names of products of the territory of a contracting party as are protected by its legislation," and to "accord full and sympathetic consideration to such requests or representations as may be made by any other contracting party regarding the application of the undertaking set forth in the preceding sentence to names of products which have been communicated to it by the other contracting party".

"The Panel noted from the drafting history relating to Article IX:6 that it had been agreed that the text of Article IX:6

> 'should not have the effect of prejudicing the present situation as regards certain distinctive names of products, provided always that the names affixed to the products cannot misrepresent their true origin. This is particularly the case when the name of the producing country is clearly indicated. It will rest with the governments concerned to proceed to a joint examination of particular cases which might arise if disputes occur as a result of the use of distinctive names of products which may have lost their original significance through constant use permitted by law in the country where they are used'. [Havana Reports, p. 79].

"The Panel noted that the Japanese Law and Cabinet Order concerning Liquor Business Association and Measures for Securing Revenue of Liquor Tax stipulated that 'Any manufacturer of liquors must indicate, at a legible location of the container of liquors ... which are shipped out from the manufacturing premise ..., the name of the manufacturer, the place of the manufacturing premise ..., the capacity of the container ..., the category of liquors ..., the grade of liquors and the following matters according to the category of liquors, in a conspicuous manner', including the alcohol content in the case of wine, whisky, brandy, spirits and liqueurs. The Panel examined a large number of labels, photos, wine bottles and packages submitted by the EEC as evidence. The Panel found that this evidence seemed to confirm the Japanese submission to the Panel that the labels on liquor bottles manufactured in Japan indicated their Japanese origin.

"The Panel examined the view of the European Community that the use of French words, French names, of other European languages and European label styles or symbols by Japanese manufacturers continued to mislead Japanese consumers as to the origin of the liquors, and that the indication of a Japanese manufacturer did not clarify his precise activities because, for instance, wines bottled in Japan could contain as much as 95% imported bulk wine. The Panel inferred from the wording of Article IX:6 that it was confined to an obligation to 'cooperate with each other with a view to preventing the use of trade names in such manner as to misrepresent the true origin of a product, to the detriment of such distinctive regional or geographical names of products of the territory of a contracting party as are protected by its legislation'. The Panel noted that there was no definition of a 'trade name' in the General Agreement, and that there were differences in the laws of various countries as to what might constitute a trade name. The Panel did not consider it necessary to define the term 'trade name' in this case for the following reasons: Article IX:6 was designed to protect 'distinctive regional or geographical names of products of the territory of a contracting party as are protected by its legislation'. The Panel did not dispose of evidence and was unable to find that the use by Japanese manufacturers of labels written partly in English (in the case of whisky and brandy) or in French (in the case of wine) , the use of the names of varieties of grapes (such as 'Riesling' or 'Semillon'), or the use of foreign terms to describe Japanese spirits ('whisky', 'brandy') or Japanese wines ('chateau', 'reserve', 'vin rose') had actually been to the detriment of 'distinctive regional or geographical names of products' produced and legally protected in the EEC. Nor could the Panel find that

---

[11]Havana Reports, p. 79, para. 48.

Japan - given, for example, its participation in the Madrid Agreement for the Repression of False or Deceptive Indications of Source on Goods and its internal laws and regulations on labelling and on the protection of distinctive regional or geographical names (such as 'Armagnac' or 'Chianti') - had failed to meet its obligation to cooperate pursuant to GATT Article IX:6."[12]

B. RELATIONSHIP BETWEEN ARTICLE IX AND OTHER ARTICLES

See the citation from the 1991 Panel Report on "United States - Restrictions on Imports of Tuna" at page 288 above, and the discussion on marks of origin versus other marking requirements on page 289 above.

C. RELATIONSHIP BETWEEN ARTICLE IX AND OTHER AGREEMENTS

The 1994 Annual Report of the Committee on Technical Barriers to Trade to the CONTRACTING PARTIES, concerning developments in the implementation and operation of the Agreement on Technical Barriers to Trade (1979) ("TBT Agreement") notes that "Discussions at the TBT Committee's meetings in 1994 indicated that there is a general understanding among signatories of the TBT Agreement that mandatory marking requirements applied in the context of marking the origin of products are covered by the provisions of the Agreement, but one signatory could not join a consensus on this issue and continues to question the applicability of the provisions of the Agreement to marks-of-origin requirements. These discussions have suggested that there may be value in clarifying the coverage of the provisions of the TBT Agreement with respect to mandatory marking requirements applied in the context of marking the origin of products."[13]

III. PREPARATORY WORK AND SUBSEQUENT MODIFICATIONS

Article IX corresponds to Article 37 in the Havana Charter. The US-UK *Proposals* deal with marks of origin in Chapter III-6 and the U.S. Draft in Article 14. Both were largely based on recommendations of the Economic Committee of the League of Nations in its Report to the Council on the Work of the 35th Session of the Economic Committee held at Geneva on 18-22 June 1931. The corresponding article in the New York Draft Charter is Article 20, and in the Geneva Draft is Article 36.

Article 37 of the Charter included the material in Article IX of the General Agreement, with the addition of paragraph 1, corresponding to the present Article IX:2, a paragraph 5 establishing a work programme on the elimination of unnecessary marking requirements, and a provision in the paragraph corresponding to Article IX:6 permitting the ITO to convene a conference on the protection of appellations of origin. These provisions were not brought into the text of the General Agreement after the Havana Conference. At the Review Session of 1954-55, it was agreed to add paragraph 1 of the Charter Article to Article IX of the General Agreement as the present paragraph 2. This amendment was effected through the Protocol Amending the Preamble and Parts II and III of the General Agreement, which entered into force on 7 October 1957.

IV. RELEVANT DOCUMENTS

See below at the end of Article X.

---

[12] L/6216, adopted on 10 November 1987, 34S/83, 125-126, paras. 5.14-5.15.
[13] L/7558, dated 30 November 1994; see also the discussion in TBT/M/45,TBT/M/46, and statement by Korea in TBT/W/176.

ARTICLE X

PUBLICATION AND ADMINISTRATION OF TRADE REGULATIONS

I. TEXT OF ARTICLE X 293

II. INTERPRETATION AND APPLICATION OF ARTICLE X 294
    A. SCOPE AND APPLICATION OF ARTICLE X 294
        1. Paragraph 1 294
            (1) *"Laws, regulations, judicial decisions and administrative rulings of general application"* 294
            (2) *"published promptly in such a manner as to enable governments and traders to become acquainted with them"* 295
            (3) *"Agreements affecting international trade policy"* 296
            (4) *"confidential information"* 297
        2. Paragraph 2 297
        3. Paragraph 3 297
            (1) *"a uniform, impartial and reasonable manner"* 297
            (2) *"date of this Agreement"* 298
    B. RELATIONSHIP BETWEEN ARTICLE X AND OTHER ARTICLES 298
    C. NOTIFICATION IN GATT 300
        1. General understandings 300
        2. Notifications provided for by specific provisions of the General Agreement or decisions of the CONTRACTING PARTIES 301
    D. TRADE POLICY REVIEW MECHANISM 305
    E. NOTIFICATION PROCEDURES DURING THE TRANSITION TO THE WORLD TRADE ORGANIZATION 308

III. PREPARATORY WORK 309

IV. RELEVANT DOCUMENTS (FOR ARTICLES V-X) 310

I. TEXT OF ARTICLE X

Article X

Publication and Administration of Trade Regulations

1. Laws, regulations, judicial decisions and administrative rulings of general application, made effective by any contracting party, pertaining to the classification or the valuation of products for customs purposes, or to rates of duty, taxes or other charges, or to requirements, restrictions or prohibitions on imports or exports or on the transfer of payments therefor, or affecting their sale, distribution, transportation, insurance, warehousing, inspection, exhibition, processing, mixing or other use, shall be published promptly in such a manner as to enable governments and traders to become acquainted with them. Agreements affecting international trade policy which are in force between the government or a governmental agency of any contracting party and the government or governmental agency of any other contracting party shall also be published. The provisions of this paragraph shall not require any contracting party to disclose confidential information which would impede law enforcement or otherwise be contrary to the public interest or would prejudice the legitimate commercial interests of particular enterprises, public or private.

2. No measure of general application taken by any contracting party effecting an advance in a rate of duty or other charge on imports under an established and uniform practice, or imposing a new or more burdensome requirement, restriction or prohibition on imports, or on the transfer of payments therefor, shall be enforced before such measure has been officially published.

3. (*a*) Each contracting party shall administer in a uniform, impartial and reasonable manner all its laws, regulations, decisions and rulings of the kind described in paragraph 1 of this Article.

(b) Each contracting party shall maintain, or institute as soon as practicable, judicial, arbitral or administrative tribunals or procedures for the purpose, *inter alia*, of the prompt review and correction of administrative action relating to customs matters. Such tribunals or procedures shall be independent of the agencies entrusted with administrative enforcement and their decisions shall be implemented by, and shall govern the practice of, such agencies unless an appeal is lodged with a court or tribunal of superior jurisdiction within the time prescribed for appeals to be lodged by importers; *Provided* that the central administration of such agency may take steps to obtain a review of the matter in another proceeding if there is good cause to believe that the decision is inconsistent with established principles of law or the actual facts.

(c) The provisions of sub-paragraph (b) of this paragraph shall not require the elimination or substitution of procedures in force in the territory of a contracting party on the date of this Agreement which in fact provide for an objective and impartial review of administrative action even though such procedures are not fully or formally independent of the agencies entrusted with administrative enforcement. Any contracting party employing such procedures shall, upon request, furnish the CONTRACTING PARTIES with full information thereon in order that they may determine whether such procedures conform to the requirements of this sub-paragraph.

II. INTERPRETATION AND APPLICATION OF ARTICLE X

A. SCOPE AND APPLICATION OF ARTICLE X

1. Paragraph 1

(1) "Laws, regulations, judicial decisions and administrative rulings of general application"

The Panel Report of 1988 on "Japan - Trade in Semiconductors" examined, *inter alia*, a claim by the EEC that lack of information on a monitoring scheme for export prices to third-country markets, and lack of information concerning conditions for improved access to the Japanese market, contravened Article X. The Panel findings provide as follows.

"The Panel considered the contention of the EEC that the measures applied to exports of semi-conductors to third countries and the measures to improve access to the Japanese market lacked transparency and therefore contravened Article X. The Panel felt, however, that the present case did not call for a decision on that point. The measures under examination had been found to be inconsistent with Article XI. At issue was thus their elimination or bringing them into conformity with GATT, not their publication.

"As for the measures to improve access to the Japanese market, the Panel, on the basis of the evidence analysed in paragraphs 125 and 126 above, was unable to identify any measure constituting a requirement, restriction or prohibition on imports required to be published by Article X."[1]

The 1988 Panel Report on "Canada - Import, Distribution and Sale of Alcoholic Drinks by Provincial Marketing Agencies" examined the operation of provincial liquor monopolies in Canada, and found, *inter alia*, as follows:

"... The Panel considered that Canada had the right to use import monopolies to raise revenue for the provinces, consistently with the relevant provisions of the General Agreement. ... It ... asked itself whether the fiscal elements of mark-ups, which produced revenue for the provinces, could also be justified as 'internal taxes conforming to the provisions of Article III', noting that Article III:2 itself referred, not only to internal taxes, but also to 'other internal charges'. The Panel was of the view that to be so considered, the fiscal element of mark-ups must of course meet the requirements of Article III. ... The Panel also considered it important that, if fiscal elements were to be considered as internal taxes, mark-ups would also

---

[1] L/6309, adopted on 4 May 1988, 35S/116, 161 paras. 128-129.

have to be administered in conformity with other provisions of the General Agreement, in particular Article X dealing with the Publication and Administration of Trade Regulations".[2]

(2) "published promptly in such a manner as to enable governments and traders to become acquainted with them"

The Panel Report of 1989 on "EEC - Restrictions on Imports of Dessert Apples, Complaint by Chile" examined, *inter alia*, the claim by Chile that the licensing and deposit system on dessert apple imports introduced by the EEC on 6 February 1988 and administrative arrangements by the member states putting this into effect were not published promptly in such a manner as to enable governments and traders to become acquainted with them as required under Article X:1 (first sentence).

"The Panel first examined the EEC's system of restrictive licensing applied to imports of apples from April through August 1988 under Article XI, as consistency with this Article was the primary determinant of the conformity of the EEC's system with the General Agreement, before proceeding to consider the measures under Articles XIII and X and Part IV of the Agreement. ...

"The Panel found that the EEC had observed the requirement of Article X:1 to publish the measures under examination 'promptly in such a manner as to enable governments and traders to become acquainted with them' through their publication in the Official Journal of the European Communities. It noted that no time limit or delay between publication and entry into force was specified by this provision. However it interpreted the requirements of this provision as clearly prohibiting the use of back-dated quotas, whose use by the EEC in the case of Chile had already been the subject of a finding under Article XIII (above)".[3]

The 1989 Panel Report on "EEC - Restrictions on Imports of Apples, Complaint by the United States" examined claims by the United States regarding the same EEC measure, including a claim that the publication of notice by the EEC on 21 April 1988 of the imposition of quotas for the period of 15 February to 31 August 1988 was inconsistent with Articles XI:2, X:1 and XIII:3(b). The EEC denied that it had violated any notification or publication requirements or applied a quota retroactively.

"The Panel first examined the EEC's system of restrictive licensing applied to imports of apples from April through August 1988 under Article XI, as consistency with this Article was the primary determinant of the conformity of the EEC's system with the General Agreement, before proceeding to consider the measures under Articles XIII and X of the Agreement. ...

"The Panel recognized that, given its finding that the EEC measures were a violation of Article XI:1 and not justified by Article XI:2(c)(i) or (ii), no further examination of the administration of the measure would normally be required. Nonetheless, and even though the Panel was concerned with measures which had already been eliminated, it considered it appropriate to examine the administration of the EEC measures in respect of [Articles XI:2(c) (last paragraph), X:1 and XIII:3(c)], in view of the questions of great practical interest which had been raised by both parties.

"The Panel found that the EEC had observed the requirement of Article X:1 to publish the measures under examination 'promptly in such a manner as to enable governments and traders to become acquainted with them' through their publication in the Official Journal of the European Communities. It noted that no lapse of time between publication and entry into force was specified by this provision.

"The Panel noted that EEC Commission Regulation 1040/88 of 20 April 1988 published, *inter alia*, a quota allocation of 17,600 tons for 'other countries', including the United States, for the period up to 31 August that year. Use of this quota allocation was measured in terms of applications for import licences. However, licensing of imports had been in effect since 14 February 1988 (Reg. 346/88). Therefore, utilisation of the quota published in April was counted as from 14 February. The quota allocation

---

[2]L/6304, adopted on 22 March 1988, 35S/37, 88-89, para. 4.20.
[3]L/6491, adopted on 22 June 1989, 36S/93; arguments 36S/115-116, paras. 6.1-6.2, findings 36S/133, paras. 12.1, 12.29.

announced on 20 April 1988 thus covered a quota period which began on 14 February 1988 and ended on 31 August 1988.

> "... The Panel therefore considered that the allocation of back-dated quotas did not conform to the requirements of Article XIII:3(b) and (c). It also interpreted the requirements of Article X:1 as likewise prohibiting back-dated quotas. It therefore found that the EEC had been in breach of these requirements since it had given public notice of the quota allocation only about two months after the quota period had begun".[4]

The Panel concluded that "The operation of a back-dated import restriction in respect of 'other countries', including the United States, was inconsistent with Article[s] X and XIII".[5]

The 1992 Panel Report on "Canada - Import, Distribution and Sale of Certain Alcoholic Drinks by Provincial Marketing Agencies" examined an argument regarding Article X:

> "The Panel noted that the United States had claimed that the liquor board of British Colombia had shared with domestic brewers information relating to pricing policy before that information was available to the United States' authorities, that in the province of Ontario, an announcement of a new pricing policy for beer had been made in the legislature only five days before it entered into effect, and that both these practices were inconsistent with Article X of the General Agreement. The Panel noted that Article X imposed requirements relating to the prompt publication of trade regulations but that this provision did not require contracting parties to make information affecting trade available to domestic and foreign suppliers at the same time, nor did it require contracting parties to publish trade regulations in advance of their entry into force. The Panel, therefore, *found* that the measures were not inconsistent with Article X of the General Agreement. The Panel noted that the United States did not claim inconsistency of these measures with any other provision of the General Agreement".[6]

In a number of other instances in which a panel examining a quantitative restriction has found that restriction to be inconsistent with Article XI, the panel has declined to make findings with respect to subsidiary arguments raised concerning the consistency with Article X of the administration of the quantitative restriction, stating, for instance, that Article X "dealt with the administration of quotas that may be applied consistently with the General Agreement".[7] See below at page 298 *et seq*.

The publication of laws and regulations concerning trade, tariffs and customs has been addressed in recent working parties on accession, such as those concerning the accession of Costa Rica[8], El Salvador,[9] Venezuela,[10] and Guatemala.[11]

(3) "Agreements affecting international trade policy"

The 1982 Report of the Working Party on the fourth review under the Protocol of Accession on "Trade with Hungary" notes the requests of members of the working party, referring to Article X, for publication of the lists of products annexed to the trade agreements between Hungary and other CMEA member countries, which "having been signed at the governmental level, conferred intergovernmental authority on contracts concluded between foreign-trade enterprises".[12]

---

[4]L/6513, adopted on 22 June 1989, 36S/135, 166-167, paras. 5-20-5.23.
[5]*Ibid.*, 36S/167, para. 5.26.
[6]DS17/R, adopted on 18 February 1992, 39S/27, 85-86, para. 5.34.
[7]Panel Report on "Japan - Restrictions on Imports of Certain Agricultural Products", L/6253, adopted on 2 February 1988, 35S/163, 242, para. 5.4.2.
[8]L/6589, adopted on 7 November 1989, 36S/26, 42 para. 60.
[9]L/6771, adopted on 12 December 1990, 37S/9, 16, para. 21.
[10]L/6696, adopted on 11 July 1990, 37S/43, 52 para. 32.
[11]L/6770, adopted on 6 February 1991, 38S/3, 6 para. 11.
[12]L/5303, adopted on 31 March 1982, 29S/129, paras. 31, 41, 47, 49.

(4) "confidential information"

During the fourth review under the Protocol of Accession on "Trade with Hungary," the representative of Hungary noted, in response to the inquiry by the EEC referred to above, that the lists attached to the governmental trade agreements "resulted from private negotiations among enterprises in Hungary and in the other countries in question. In view of the latter circumstance, in accordance with the relevant provisions of Article X of the General Agreement, the Hungarian authorities could not be required to disclose information which would prejudice the legitimate commercial interests of particular enterprises, public or private ... in many cases there was only one company involved with the production of a particular product and thus, if the lists were published, they would disclose commercial information which could damage the firm's bargaining position".[13]

The Report of the Working Party on the seventh review under the Protocol of Accession on "Trade with Hungary" records that "The Community and Hungary had further agreed to ensure the publication of comprehensive commercial and financial data as well as information in accordance with Article X of the GATT and to maintain and further improve favourable business regulations and facilities for each other's companies on their respective markets".[14]

2. Paragraph 2

See also Article XIII:3(b).

3. Paragraph 3

(1) "a uniform, impartial and reasonable manner"

A Note by the Director-General, dated 29 November 1968, on the applicability of Article I of the General Agreement to the Agreement on Implementation of Article VI includes the following reference to Article X:

"Paragraph 3(a) of [Article X] provides that all laws, regulations, judicial decisions and administrative rulings pertaining to the classification or the valuation of products for customs purposes, or to rates of duty, taxes or other charges shall be administered in 'a uniform, impartial and reasonable manner'. These last words would not permit, in the treatment accorded to imported goods, discrimination based on country of origin, nor would they permit the application of one set of regulations and procedures with respect to some contracting parties and a different set with respect to the others".[15]

The 1984 Panel Report on "Japanese Measures on Imports of Leather" notes that the argument was made in this dispute that the import quotas for leather were not administered in a "reasonable manner," as a result of, *inter alia*, allocation of import licences to competing domestic producers; see the finding of this panel below at page 298.

The Panel Report on "EEC - Restrictions on Imports of Dessert Apples, Complaint by Chile" examined, *inter alia*, the claim by Chile that differences among the ten member states of the EEC as to the requirements imposed for applications for licences for imports of dessert apples, such as refusal by one member state to accept a licence issued by another, meant that the requirements for licence issue were not "uniform" throughout the Community in terms of Article X:3(a); that the import licensing system was not uniform over time; that the one-month validity period of the import licences was too short, and hence "unreasonable" in terms of Article X:3(a); and that the timing of the scheme was not "impartial" in relation to supplying countries. The EEC noted that the import licensing scheme was administered through an EEC Regulation which, under Article 189 of the Treaty of Rome, had general scope, was binding in its entirety, and was directly applicable in all member States. It was the regulation and the regulation alone which established the legal situation for all persons; the internal administrative provisions which certain member States may have found necessary could not validly modify the rights and obligations of persons. Furthermore, these internal administrative provisions did not have

---

[13]*Ibid.*, 29S/139-40, paras. 32, 34.
[14]L/6535, adopted on 19 July 1989, 36S/416 para. 39.
[15]L/3149; see also reference to this passage in "EEC - Restrictions on Imports of Apples, Complaint by Chile", 36S/93, para. 6.5.

to be published and were not usually brought to the attention of the Commission. The fact that Chilean exporters were the first to send apples to the Community was not proof of discriminatory, non-uniform, partial or unreasonable administration, but simply an objective fact due to the climatic differences among exporting countries. In response, the Panel found as follows:

> "The Panel further noted that the EEC Commission Regulations in question were directly applicable in all of the ten Member States concerned in a substantially uniform manner, although there were some minor administrative variations, e.g. concerning the form in which licence applications could be made and the requirement of pro-forma invoices. The Panel found that these differences were minimal and did not in themselves establish a breach of Article X:3. The Panel therefore did not consider it necessary to examine the question whether the requirement of 'uniform' administration of trade regulations was applicable to the Community as a whole or to each of its Member States individually".[16]

(2) "date of this Agreement"

Article XXVI:1 provides that "The date of this Agreement shall be 30 October 1947". This date applies for the obligations under Article X:3 of the original contracting parties; of the former territories of the original contracting parties which, after attaining independence or commercial autonomy, succeeded to contracting party status under Article XXVI:5(c); and of Chile. When the modalities of accession to the General Agreement were first considered, at the Third Session in Annecy in 1949, the Working Party which drafted the Annecy Protocol of Terms of Accession decided to use instead the date of the Havana Final Act, 24 March 1948, and this approach was followed for the next group of accessions in the Torquay Protocol of 1951.[17] Since the next accession thereafter, which was the accession of Japan in 1955, the standard terms in accession protocols have provided that the "date of this Agreement" for the purposes of Article X:3 shall be the date of the protocol of accession or (where the acceding government had previously acceded provisionally) the date of the declaration on provisional accession.[18]

B. RELATIONSHIP BETWEEN ARTICLE X AND OTHER ARTICLES

See Articles XI:2 and XIII:3.

In a number of instances where consistency with Article X was raised as a subsidiary argument in relation to quantitative restrictions, panels have declined to make findings with respect to this issue when they have found that the quantitative restriction was inconsistent with Article XI.

The 1984 Panel Report concerning the dispute on "Japanese Measures on Imports of Leather" notes that the argument was made, *inter alia*, that the alleged lack of publication of the size of the global quotas for leather, the names of licence holders, the quantity of their licences, and the size of unfilled quota balances contravened Article X:1.

> "The Panel noted that the United States had, as a subsidiary matter, argued that Japan had also nullified or impaired benefits under Articles II, X:1, X:3 and XIII:3. In view of the findings set out in the paragraphs above [that the import quotas were inconsistent with Article XI], the Panel found that it was not necessary for it to make a finding on these matters."[19]

The Panel Report concerning the dispute on "Japan - Restrictions on Imports of Certain Agricultural Products" examined, *inter alia*, the argument that the lack of publication of certain information regarding import restrictions was inconsistent with Articles X and XIII.

> "The Panel noted that the United States had, as a subsidiary matter, argued that Japan had also nullified or impaired benefits under Articles X:1, X:3 and XIII:3. Since these provisions dealt with the

---

[16] L/6491, adopted on 22 June 1989, 36S/93; arguments p. 116-17 paras. 6.3-6.6, findings p. 133 para. 12.30.
[17] Annecy Protocol, I/81, para. 5(b); Torquay Protocol, dated 21 April 1951, I/86, 88, para. 5(b).
[18] E.g. Protocol for the Accession of Bolivia, L/6562, 37S/5.
[19] L/5623, adopted on 15/16 May 1984, 31S/94, 114; arguments at 31S/97-98 paras. 26-27; findings at 31S/114 para. 57.

administration of quotas that may be applied consistently with the General Agreement, the Panel decided that it was not necessary for it to make a finding on these matters with regard to quantitative restrictions maintained contrary to that Agreement."[20]

In the three parallel Panel Reports on "Republic of Korea - Restrictions on Imports of Beef," Complaints by Australia[21], New Zealand[22], and the United States[23] the Panel examined the subsidiary claim by the complainants that Korea had not met its obligations under Articles X and XIII by not providing proper public notice of the import restrictions. The Panel found:

"The Panel noted that [Australia/New Zealand/the United States] had, as a subsidiary matter, claimed that Korea had not met its obligations under Articles X and XIII by not providing proper public notice of the import restrictions. It also noted that Korea had stated that the withdrawal of the measures imposed in 1984/85 and the import levels in 1988 had been widely publicized. In view of the Panel's determinations as concerned the consistency of the Korean measures with Articles II and XI, the Panel did not find it necessary to address these subsidiary issues. The Panel noted, however, the requirement in Article X:1 that 'laws, regulations, judicial decisions and administrative rulings of general application, made effective by any contracting party, pertaining to ... rates of duty, taxes or other charges, or to requirements, restrictions or prohibitions on imports ..., shall be published promptly in such a manner as to enable governments and traders to become acquainted with them'. It also noted the provision in Article XIII:3(b) that '[i]n the case of import restrictions involving the fixing of quotas, the contracting party applying the restrictions shall give public notice of the total quantity or value of the product or products which will be permitted to be imported during a specified future period and of any change in such quantity or value'".[24]

The Panel Report on "Canada - Import Restrictions on Ice Cream and Yoghurt" examined, *inter alia* the claim by the United States that in administering its import restrictions Canada had failed to observe the procedural obligations of Article X:1 and Article X:2 which, it was contended, created distinct obligations in addition to the requirement of public notification arising under Article XI:2(c).

"The Panel observed that the remaining provisions of Article XI:2(c), as concerned public notice and the level of imports, as well as those contained in Articles X and XIII, concerned the operation of the quota. As the Panel had found that the Canadian import quotas for ice cream and yoghurt could not be justified under Article XI:2(c)(i), it did not consider it necessary to examine whether the administration of these quotas was in conformity with the General Agreement." [25]

The Panel Report on "EEC - Regulation on Imports of Parts and Components" examined, *inter alia*, the claim of Japan that while the conditions under which anti-dumping duties could be imposed under the "anti-circumvention" legislation of the EEC were defined in the text of that legislation, the criteria for acceptance of offers of undertakings had not been published and that this was inconsistent with Article X:1. The Panel found as follows:

"The Panel considered the argument of Japan that, in the administration of the anti-circumvention provision, the EEC violated its obligations under Article X:1 and X:3 of the General Agreement, in particular in respect of the criteria for the acceptance of undertakings and the methodology for determining the origin of imported parts and components. Given that the Panel found the anti-circumvention duties and the acceptance of parts undertakings to be inconsistent with Article III:2 and 4, and not justifiable under Article XX(d), and that any further imposition of such duties or acceptance of related undertakings would therefore be inconsistent with the General Agreement, the issue of whether the administration of the anti-circumvention provision is consistent with Article X is no longer relevant".[26]

---

[20]L/6253, adopted on 2 February 1988, 35S/163; arguments at paras. 3.5.1-3.5.3; findings at 35S/242, para. 5.4.2.
[21]L/6504, adopted on 7 November 1989, 36S/202.
[22]L/6505, adopted on 7 November 1989, 36S/234.
[23]L/6503, adopted on 7 November 1989, 36S/268.
[24]Same three panel reports referred to above, at 36S/230, 267, 306, paras. 108, 124, 130 respectively.
[25]L/6568, adopted on 5 December 1989, 36S/68, 92, para. 82.
[26]L/6657, adopted on 16 May 1990, 37S/132, 199, para. 5.27.

C. NOTIFICATION IN GATT

At various times since 1947 notes have been prepared by the Secretariat summarizing the notification obligations of contracting parties under the General Agreement.[27] The question of improvement and streamlining of notification procedures has also been raised at various times in the Council and was also discussed in the Senior Officials' Group and the Preparatory Committee in advance of the Uruguay Round.[28] The 15 April 1994 Final Act of the Uruguay Round includes a Decision on Notification Procedures; see under section D below.

1. General understandings

In March 1964, the CONTRACTING PARTIES adopted two Reports on "Trade Information and Trade Promotion Advisory Service" as well as a Recommendation on "Co-operation in the Field of Trade Information and Trade Promotion".[29] The Recommendation provides, *inter alia*, that "The CONTRACTING PARTIES recommend that contracting parties should forward promptly to the secretariat copies of the laws, regulations, decisions, rulings and agreements of the kind described in paragraph 1 of Article X, together with such other information as they consider relevant to the objectives of this Recommendation".

An "Understanding Regarding Notification, Consultation, Dispute Settlement and Surveillance" was adopted on 28 November 1979 at the close of the Tokyo Round. Paragraphs 2 and 3 of this Understanding, on "Notification", provide as follows:

> "Contracting parties reaffirm their commitment to existing obligations under the General Agreement regarding publication and notification.
>
> "Contracting parties moreover undertake, to the maximum extent possible, to notify the CONTRACTING PARTIES of their adoption of trade measures affecting the operation of the General Agreement, it being understood that such notification would be without prejudice to views on the consistency of measures with or their relevance to obligations under the General Agreement. Contracting parties should endeavour to notify such measures in advance of implementation. In other cases, where prior notification has not been possible, such measures should be notified promptly *ex post facto*. Contracting parties which have reason to believe that such trade measures have been adopted by another contracting party may seek information on such measures bilaterally, from the contracting party concerned".[30]

The text of this Understanding appears in full under Article XXIII. On 26 March 1980 a Proposal by the Director-General on "Notification and Surveillance" was adopted, including a number of suggestions relating to action necessary to implement paragraphs 2 and 3 of the Understanding above. It was suggested that the Council draw the attention of all contracting parties to paragraph 2 of the Understanding, and invite contracting parties to submit notifications in accordance with a calendar set out in an annex. "The attention of contracting parties should be drawn to paragraph 3 of the Understanding. Contracting parties should be invited to submit notifications under this paragraph, in particular when notifications covering the measures are not made under other GATT procedures".[31] The proposal also called for semiannual reviews of developments in the trading system to be conducted by the Council at sessions specially held for that purpose.

---

[27]"Provisions of the Agreement which contemplate submission of information to the CONTRACTING PARTIES," Note of 2 February 1950, GATT/CP.4/16; "Notification requirements in GATT," Annex to the Report by the Group of Experts on Trade Information and Trade Promotion Advisory Services, adopted on 19 March 1964, COM.III/128, 12S/138, 146; "Notifications required from contracting parties," Note by the Secretariat, MTN/FR/W/17; Lists on notification requirements (1) applying to all contracting parties, (2) applying to some government or governments, and list of dates on which regular notifications fall due, attached to the Director-General's proposal for Procedures for the Review of Developments in the Trading System, adopted on 26 March 1980, C/111, 27S/20 (attachments not reproduced in BISD); Notes prepared for semi-annual reviews on developments in the trading system (see below), e.g. C/W/437, C/W/446, C/W/471; tabular presentation of all periodic and ad hoc notifications required under the General Agreement, MTN Agreements, MFA, 1979 Understanding and 1982 Work Programme, PREP.COM(86)W/31/Add.1; "Notification procedures in GATT," Note dated 10 March 1988, MTN.GNG/NG14/W/18.

[28]See Notes from 1984 (C/W/446) and 1985 (C/W/471), C/M/182 and C/M/189; also SR.SOG/10 and 11; Secretariat Note, PREP.COM(86)W/31/Add.1; PREP.COM(86)SR/4, SR/6 and SR/7.

[29]Reports at COM.III/128, 12S/138, and L/2181, Part A, 12S/148; Recommendation at 12S/49.

[30]L/4907, adopted on 28 November 1979, 26S/210, paras. 2-3.

[31]C/111, adopted on 26 March 1980, 27S/20, 22, para. 6.

The Decisions of 12 April 1989 on "Functioning of the GATT System" include a decision to establish an "Overview of Developments in the International Trading Environment," providing that "Such an overview should be undertaken by the Council. It should be assisted by an annual report by the Director-General setting out major GATT activities and highlighting significant policy issues affecting the trading system ... It is understood that this overview by the Council, together with the trade policy review mechanism, would replace the existing reviews in special Council meetings established under paragraph 24 of the 1979 Understanding ...".[32] See also the material below on the Trade Policy Review Mechanism.

2. **Notifications provided for by specific provisions of the General Agreement or decisions of the CONTRACTING PARTIES**

The following table presents the provisions of the General Agreement, or decisions of the CONTRACTING PARTIES, which provide for notification of measures, either as such or in connection with requests made to the CONTRACTING PARTIES.

Tariffs

Proposal on Introduction of a Loose-Leaf System for the Schedules of Tariff Concessions[33]	Submission of consolidated schedules of tariff concessions
Decision on Integrated Data Base[34]	Contracting parties should submit annually to the secretariat, by tariff line, tariff data for unbound items and import data for all bound and unbound tariff items, in accordance with the IDB agreed format
Article II:6(a)	Notification of adjustment of specific duties
Article XVIII:A	Notification of modification or withdrawal of concessions pursuant to Article XVIII:7(a)
Article XXVII	Notification of withholding or withdrawal of concessions initially negotiated with a government that has not become, or has ceased to be, a contracting party
Article XXVIII:1	Notification of modification or withdrawal of a concession to take place during "open season" (not earlier than six months nor later than three months before the termination date of a preceding three-year period as referred to in Article XXVIII:1)
Article XXVIII:4	Request for authorization by CONTRACTING PARTIES to enter into negotiations for modification or withdrawal of a concession at any time in special circumstances
Article XXVIII:5	Notification during Article XXVIII:1 "open season" reserving the right to modify or withdraw concessions during the subsequent three-year period

---

[32]L/6490, Decisions of 12 April 1989 arising from action by the Trade Negotiations Committee, 36S/403, 405-406 para. F.
[33]Proposal by the Director-General adopted on 26 March 1980, C./107/Rev.1, 27S/22.
[34]Decision of 10 November 1987, L/6290, 34S/66, para. 3. See also IDB User Reference Manual dated 19 April 1994, IDB/URM/1.

Quantitative restrictions and other measures affecting trade

Articles XII:4 and XVIII:12[35]	Notification of introduction or intensification of all measures taken for balance-of-payments purposes
Questionnaire on Import Licensing Procedures (L/5640)[36]	Notification of import licensing and similar administrative procedures maintained in and applied with respect to imports into the customs territories to which GATT applies
Data base on quantitative restrictions and other non-tariff measures[37]	Biennial complete notification of quantitative restrictions; notification of details of changes in quantitative restrictions as and when these changes occur
Inventory of Non-Tariff Measures[38]	Notification by contracting parties of measures maintained by other contracting parties which affect their trade
Border tax adjustments[39]	Notification of major changes in tax adjustment legislation and practices involving international trade
Marks of origin[40]	Notification of changes in legislation, rules or regulations concerning marks of origin
Ministerial Decision on Export of Domestically Prohibited Goods[41]	Notification by contracting parties, to the maximum extent feasible, of any goods produced and exported by them but banned by their national authorities for sale on their domestic markets on grounds of human health and safety (circulated in DPG/NOTIF/- series)
Streamlined Mechanism for Reconciling the Interests of Contracting Parties in the Event of Trade-Damaging Acts[42]	Notification by importing contracting parties of measures restricting trade for the purpose of protecting human, animal or plant life or health
Decision concerning Article XXI of the General Agreement[43]	Notification of trade measures taken under Article XXI

---

[35] As interpreted by 1979 Declaration on Trade Measures Taken for Balance-of-payments Purposes, 26S/205.

[36] Agreed at the Twenty-eighth Session of the CONTRACTING PARTIES; see Report of the Committee on Trade in Industrial Products, L/3756, para. 76; SR.28/6. The questionnaire and responses now appear in L/5640 and addenda issued thereto, and were formerly under COM.IND/W/55-COM.AG/W/72. The Annual Reports of the Committee on Import Licensing include a list of responses to this questionnaire (see, e.g., L/7313, dated 19 November 1993).

[37] Recommended in para. 44 of L/5713, Report (1984) of the Group on Quantitative Restrictions and other Non-Tariff Barriers, adopted on 30 November 1984, 31S/211, 222; see also 31S/12. Concerning this inventory and other GATT work on quantitative restrictions, see the material at the end of the chapter on Article XI in this volume.

[38] Procedures established 1980, 27S/18; further format for notifications adopted as part of Report (1985) of the Group on Quantitative Restrictions and Other Non-Tariff Measures, adopted on 28 November 1985, 32S/93.

[39] Procedures recommended in Report of the Working Party on "Border Tax Adjustments" adopted on 2 December 1970, L/3464, 18S/97, 108 para. 40.

[40] Recommendation of 21 November 1958 on "Marks of Origin", 7S/30, 33.

[41] Ministerial Declaration adopted on 29 November 1982, 29S/19.

[42] C/M/236, p. 6-7; 36S/67; for text see under Article XX(b).

[43] L/5426, 29S/23; for text of decision see under Article XXI.

Programme of Work of Committee on Trade in Agriculture[44]	Notification of measures and policies affecting trade in agriculture (circulated in AG/FOR/REV/- series)

Exchange arrangements

Article XV:8	Notification by contracting parties not members of the International Monetary Fund of national trade and financial data within the scope of Article VIII:5 of the IMF Articles of Agreement

Subsidies

Article XVI:1[45]	Notification of any subsidy, including any form of income or price support, which operates directly or indirectly to increase exports of any product from, or to reduce imports of any product into, the territory of a contracting party. Full notification (response to questionnaire) every three years; annual notifications of changes in intervening years

State trading

Article XVII:4[46]	Notification of products imported into or exported from territories of contracting parties by State-trading enterprises or other enterprises which enjoy exclusive or special privileges. Full notification (response to questionnaire) every three years; annual notifications of changes in intervening years
Liquidation of strategic stocks[47]	Advance notification by any contracting party holding stocks of primary products accumulated as part of a national strategic stockpile for purposes of national defense and intending to liquidate a substantial quantity of such stocks

Governmental assistance to economic development (Article XVIII:C and D)

Article XVIII:C[48]	Notification of special difficulties which a contracting party falling under Article XVIII:4(a) meets in achieving the objective in Article XVIII:13; indication of specific measure which it proposes to introduce in order to remedy these difficulties
Article XVIII:D[49]	Application to the CONTRACTING PARTIES for approval of a measure described in Article XVIII:13, by a contracting party falling under Article XVIII:4(b)

---

[44]L/5563, 30S/100, 102.
[45]Questionnaire at 9S/193; see also 11S/59.
[46]Procedures for notifications established 1957, modified 1960 (6S/23, 9S/184). Questionnaire established 11S/58.
[47]Resolution of 4 March 1955 on "Liquidation of Strategic Stocks," 3S/51; see, *e.g.* notifications by Australia at L/3373, L/3432, L/4018.
[48]As modified by the Decision of 28 November 1979 on Safeguard Action for Development Purposes, 26S/209.
[49]Questionnaire for guidance established 1958, 7S/85.

Emergency action on imports of particular products

Article XIX:2	Notice in writing to the CONTRACTING PARTIES as far in advance of action as may be practicable; however, in critical circumstances action may be taken provisionally without prior consultation

Consultations and dispute settlement

Article XXII[50]	Notification of any request for consultations under Article XXII
Article XXIII[51]	Notification of any request for consultations under Article XXIII:1 or request for establishment of a panel under Article XXIII:2

Other institutional and final provisions

Article XXV:5[52]	Notification of request for waivers of obligations
Article XXXI	Notice of withdrawal from the General Agreement (see also references to notice of intent to withdraw in Articles XVIII:12(e) and XXIII:2).
Protocol of Provisional Application	Notice of withdrawal of provisional application of the General Agreement

Customs unions and free-trade areas; regional agreements

Article XXIV:7(a)[53]	Notification by any contracting party deciding to enter into a customs union or free-trade area, or an interim agreement leading to the formation of such a union or area
Article XXIV:7(c)	Communication of any substantial change in a plan or schedule included in an interim agreement for the formation of a customs union or free-trade area
Decision of 26 November 1971[54]	Biennial reporting on regional agreements

Trade and development

Article XXXVII:2[55]	Reports by contracting parties whenever it is considered that effect is not being given to the provisions of Article XXXVII:1

---

[50]"Procedures under Article XXII on Questions Affecting the Interests of a Number of Contracting Parties" adopted on 1958, 7S/24; Decision on "Improvements to the GATT Dispute Settlement Rules and Procedures" adopted on 12 April 1989, L/6489, 36S/61. See also under Article XXII.

[51]Decision on "Improvements to the GATT Dispute Settlement Rules and Procedures" adopted on 12 April 1989, L/6489, 36S/61.

[52]See also "Article XXV - Guiding Principles to be Followed by the CONTRACTING PARTIES in Considering Applications for Waivers from Part I or Other Important Obligations of the General Agreement", adopted on 1 November 1956, L/532, 5S/25 (thirty-day advance notice requirement).

[53]Council Decision of 25 October 1972 on "Procedures" for customs unions and free-trade areas, C/M/81 p. 16, 19S/13.

[54]Programme of Work adopted at 27th Session, L/3641, 18S/37, 38, para. 4(c).

[55]Procedures adopted on 25 March 1965, 13S/78-80.

Decision on
Differential and More
Favourable Treatment,
Reciprocity and Fuller
Participation of
Developing Countries[56]

Notification by any contracting party taking action to introduce, modify or withdraw differential and more favourable treatment specified in the Decision; notifications include, *inter alia*, notifications concerning changes in GSP schemes

D. TRADE POLICY REVIEW MECHANISM

On 12 April 1989 the Council adopted the following Decision creating a Trade Policy Review Mechanism ("TPRM"):

"The CONTRACTING PARTIES *decide* to establish a trade policy review mechanism, as follows:

"A. *Objectives*

"(i) The purpose of the mechanism is to contribute to improved adherence by all contracting parties to GATT rules, disciplines and commitments, and hence to the smoother functioning of the multilateral trading system, by achieving greater transparency in, and understanding of, the trade policies and practices of contracting parties. Accordingly, the review mechanism will enable the regular collective appreciation and evaluation by the CONTRACTING PARTIES of the full range of individual contracting parties' trade policies and practices and their impact on the functioning of the multilateral trading system. It is not, however, intended to serve as a basis for the enforcement of specific GATT obligations or for dispute settlement procedures, or to impose new policy commitments on contracting parties.

"(ii) The assessment to be carried out under the review mechanism will, to the extent relevant, take place against the background of the wider economic and developmental needs, policies and objectives of the contracting party concerned, as well as of its external environment. However, the function of the review mechanism is to examine the impact of a contracting party's trade policies and practices on the multilateral trading system.

"B. *Reporting*

"(i) In order to achieve the fullest possible degree of transparency, each contracting party shall report regularly to the CONTRACTING PARTIES. Initial full reports shall be submitted in the year when the contracting party is first subject to review: however, in no case shall the initial report be submitted later than four years after the introduction of the mechanism. Subsequently, full reports shall be provided in years when the contracting party is due for review. Full reports will describe the trade policies and practices pursued by the contracting party or parties concerned, based on an agreed format to be decided upon by the Council. This format may be revised by the Council in the light of experience. Between reviews, contracting parties will provide brief reports when there are any significant changes in their trade policies; an annual update of statistical information will be provided according to the agreed format. Particular account will be taken of difficulties presented to least-developed contracting parties in compiling their reports. The Secretariat shall make available technical assistance on request to less-developed contracting parties, and in particular to the least-developed contracting parties. Information contained in country reports should to the greatest extent possible be coordinated with notifications made under GATT provisions.

"C. *Frequency of Review*

"(i) The trade policies and practices of all contracting parties will be subject to periodic review. Their impact on the functioning of the multilateral trading system, defined in terms of share of world

---

[56] L/4903, Decision of 28 November 1979, 26S/203, 204 para. 4.

trade in a recent representative period, will be the determining factor in deciding on the frequency of reviews. The first four trading entities so identified (counting the European Communities as one) will be subject to review every two years. The next sixteen will be reviewed every four years. Other contracting parties will be reviewed every six years, except that a longer period may be fixed for least-developed countries. It is understood that the review of entities having a common external policy covering more than one contracting party shall cover all components of policy affecting trade including relevant policies and practices of the individual contracting parties. Exceptionally, in the event of changes in a contracting party's trade policies or practices which may have a significant impact on its trading partners, the contracting party concerned may be requested by the Council after consultation to bring forward its next review.

"(ii) Contracting parties recognize the need to minimize the burden for governments also subject to full consultations under the GATT balance-of-payments provisions. To this end, the Chairman of the Council shall, in consultation with the contracting party or parties concerned, and with the Chairman of the Committee on Balance-of-Payments Restrictions, devise administrative arrangements which would harmonize the normal rhythm of the trade policy reviews with the time-table for balance-of-payments consultations but would not postpone the trade policy review by more than 12 months.

"D. *Review Body*

"(i) Trade policy reviews will be carried out by the Council at periodic special meetings.

"(ii) In the light of the objectives set out in A above, discussions in the meetings of the Council will, to the extent relevant, take place against the background of the wider economic and developmental needs, policies and objectives of the contracting party concerned, as well as of its external environment. The focus of these discussions will be on the contracting party's trade policies and practices which are the subject of the assessment under the review mechanism.

"(iii) The Council will establish a basic plan for the conduct of the reviews. It may also discuss and take note of update reports from contracting parties. The Council will establish a programme of reviews for each year in consultation with the contracting parties directly concerned. In consultation with the contracting party or parties under review, the Chairman may choose discussants who, in their personal capacity, will introduce the discussions in the review body.

"(iv) The Council will base its work on the following documentation:

"(a) The full report, referred to in paragraph B(i) above, supplied by the contracting party or parties under review.

"(b) A report, to be drawn up by the Secretariat on its own responsibility, based on the information available to it and that provided by the contracting party or parties concerned. The Secretariat should seek clarification from the contracting party or parties concerned of their trade policies and practices.

"(v) The reports by the contracting party under review and by the Secretariat, together with the minutes of the respective meeting of the Council, will be published promptly after the review.

"(vi) These documents will be forwarded to the next regular Session of the CONTRACTING PARTIES, which will take note of them.

"E. *Implementation and Reappraisal of the Mechanism*

"The trade policy review mechanism will be implemented on a provisional basis from the date of the adoption of this Decision by the CONTRACTING PARTIES. In the light of the experience gained from its operation, the CONTRACTING PARTIES will review, and if necessary modify, these arrangements at the end of the Uruguay Round."[57]

On 19 July 1989, the Council agreed on an outline format for country reports to be submitted under the TPRM, including a list of matters to be dealt with in country reports and of statistical and tabular data to be submitted.[58] In 1993, the Council agreed to clarified procedures dealing with such matters as timing of review meetings, rôle of discussants, statements in the Council and replies by countries under review.[59]

At the Forty-Ninth Session in December 1994, the CONTRACTING PARTIES agreed that informal consultations should be held on issues relating to the operation of the TPRM. On 10 May 1994, the Council agreed to the following decision on arrangements for continued operation of the TPRM:

"1. The Trade Policy Review Mechanism shall continue in operation until its successor mechanism established in Annex 3 of the Agreement establishing the World Trade Organization (WTO) comes into effect.

"2. Contracting parties agree that a report by the Government of the contracting party or by the entity under review remains a central element of the review process. However, in order to avoid duplication of the material contained in the Secretariat report, and to lighten the burden on delegations, Government reports shall be in the form of policy statements. It would essentially be for the contracting parties and entities concerned to decide on the form and length of such statements, although the Council, or the Trade Policy Review Body to be established under the WTO Agreement, may decide on new guidelines for Government reports.

"3. Contracting parties agree that the principal focus of Secretariat reports should be on the trade policies and practices of the contracting party or entity under review. Contracting parties recognize that trade policies must, to the extent necessary, be seen in the context of overall macro-economic and structural policies.

"4. The existing cycle of reviews shall be maintained, but with a general degree of flexibility of up to six months, if and as may be necessary. Schedules of subsequent reviews shall be established by counting from the date of the previous review meeting.

"5. Documentation relating to each review meeting shall be provided to Council members at the latest four weeks before the date of the review meeting.

"6. Contracting parties recognize that the changes in the procedures for review meetings introduced in 1993 (L/7208) have facilitated a more lively debate. All parties subject to review should co-operate in enabling these procedures to function effectively. Contracting parties also recognize that the rôle of discussants is crucial, especially in triggering the debate on the second day of a review meeting. Delegations are reminded that, where possible, written questions should be submitted to the party under review at least one week before the review meeting, to allow time to prepare replies.

"7. Press arrangements for trade policy reviews should ensure sufficiently complete coverage of the proceedings of review meetings. In the light of suggestions made by individual contracting parties, notably regarding the timing and delivery of documentation to the press, participation in press briefings, and other related questions, the Secretariat is requested to consult further on ways in which this can be achieved, and to make proposals to the Council before the next trade policy review to be held.

---

[57]L/6490, adopted on 12 April 1989, 36S/403.
[58]L/6552, 36S/406.
[59]L/7208, Communication from the Council Chairman, dated 30 April 1993.

"8. Contracting parties agree that the understandings in paragraphs 2 to 6 shall be communicated to the Preparatory Committee for the World Trade Organization for its consideration, with a view to their introduction on the entry into force of the WTO Agreement."[60]

E. **NOTIFICATION PROCEDURES DURING THE TRANSITION TO THE WORLD TRADE ORGANIZATION**

The 15 April 1994 Final Act of the Uruguay Round includes a Decision on Notification Procedures, which calls for a Central Registry of Notifications to be established, and for a review of notification obligations and procedures to be carried out by a working group under the WTO Council on Trade in Goods. The Decision was adopted by Ministers at Marrakesh, and it was further adopted, and the Central Registry was established, by the WTO General Council at its first meeting on 31 January 1995.

On 8 December 1994 the CONTRACTING PARTIES and the Preparatory Committee for the World Trade Organization adopted a Decision on "Transitional Arrangements - Avoidance of Procedural and Institutional Duplication", which provides *inter alia* that the Preparatory Committee:

"Noting that the General Agreement on Tariffs and Trade (hereinafter referred to as "GATT 1947") and the Marrakesh Agreement Establishing the World Trade Organization (hereinafter referred to as "WTO Agreement") are legally distinct and that Members of the WTO may therefore remain contracting parties to the GATT 1947;

"Considering that contracting parties to the GATT 1947 and parties to the Tokyo Round Agreements that are also Members of the WTO should not be subjected to the inconvenience of having to notify and consult on their measures and policies twice;

"Desiring, therefore, that the bodies established under the GATT 1947, the Tokyo Round Agreements and the WTO Agreement coordinate their activities to the extent that their functions overlap;

"Decides to propose the following procedures for adoption by the CONTRACTING PARTIES to the GATT 1947, the Committees established under the Tokyo Round Agreements and the General Council of the WTO:

"In the period between the date of entry into force of the WTO Agreement and the date of the termination of the legal instruments through which the contracting parties apply the GATT 1947 and of the Tokyo Round Agreements the following notification and coordination procedures shall apply under the GATT 1947, the Tokyo Round Agreements and the WTO Agreement:

"1. If a measure is subject to a notification obligation both under the WTO Agreement and under the GATT 1947 or a Tokyo Round Agreement, the notification of such a measure to a WTO body shall, unless otherwise indicated in the notification, be deemed to be also a notification of that measure under the GATT 1947 or the Tokyo Round Agreement. Any such notification shall be circulated by the WTO Secretariat simultaneously to the Members of the WTO and to the contracting parties to the GATT 1947 and/or the parties to the Tokyo Round Agreement. These procedures are without prejudice to any notification procedures applicable in specific areas.

"2. The coordination procedures set out in paragraphs 3 and 4 below shall apply in the relations between the bodies referred to in sub-paragraphs (a) to (d) below: ...

"(d) The GATT 1947 Council of Representatives shall coordinate its trade policy reviews with those of the WTO Trade Policy Review Body.

...

---

[60] L/7458, Decision of 10 May 1994; see also SR.49/1, p. 8-9.

"5. The CONTRACTING PARTIES to the GATT 1947, the Committees established under the Tokyo Round Agreements and the General Council of the WTO may decide independently to terminate the application of the provisions set out in paragraphs 1 to 4 above.[61]

III. PREPARATORY WORK

The preparatory work states that Article X was partially based on Articles 4 and 6 of the 1923 International Convention Relating to the Simplification of Customs Formalities.[62] Corresponding provisions in the Havana Charter were in Article 38; in the US Proposals, Chapter III-8; in the US Draft, Article 15; in the New York Draft, Article 21; and in the Geneva Draft, Article 37.

Article X has the same text as Article 37 of the Geneva Draft Charter, except that a provision in paragraph 1 requiring governments to furnish copies of their laws, regulations and agreements to the Organization was not included in the General Agreement. At the Havana Conference, this Article of the Charter was amended as follows, to become Article 38 of the Havana Charter:

- In Article 38:2 the prohibition on enforcing certain measures of general application "before such measure has been officially published" was changed by substituting "made public" for the word "published" in the Charter article. It was agreed that the text "did not require the prior public issue of an official document, but that the effect could also be accomplished by an official announcement made in the legislature of the country concerned".[63]

- Article 38:3(a) as amended provided that "suitable facilities shall be afforded or traders directly affected by any of those matters [the various laws and regulations] to consult with the appropriate governmental authorities".

However, these changes were not brought into the General Agreement.

---

[61]PC/11, L/7582.
[62]See EPCT/C.II/W.41, EPCT/C.II/54/Rev.1 p. 29.
[63]Havana Reports, p. 79, para. 52.

IV. RELEVANT DOCUMENTS (FOR ARTICLES V-X)

London (Arts. V-X)

Discussion:	EPCT/C.II/QR/PV/5
Reports:	EPCT/C.II/42, 46, 48, 49, 50, 54/Rev.1, 55, 56
Other:	EPCT/C.II/W.5, 31

New York (Arts. V-X)

Discussion:	EPCT/C.6/7, 8, 16, 18, 22, 30, 33, 36, 41, 58, 64, 84, 90.
Reports:	EPCT/C.6/55/Rev.1, 97/Rev.1

Geneva

Articles V-X:

Discussion:	see below: also: EPCT/TAC/PV/10-11, 26-28
Reports:	EPCT/103, 109, 135, 142+Corr. 1, 154, 180. 186, 189, 196, 212, 214/Add.1/Rev.1
Other:	EPCT/W/97, 100, 103, 166, 180, 272, 301, 313, 318

Article V:

Discussion:	EPCT/EC/SR.2/3, PV.2/22 EPCT/A/SR/20, 33, 34 EPCT/WP.1/SR/6, 7, 9, 10 EPCT/WP.1/AC.1/SR.1+Corr.1
Reports:	see above
Other:	EPCT/109 EPCT/W/23, 28, 29, 31, 32, 33, 55, 63, 89

Article VI:

Discussion:	EPCT/EC/SR.2/3, 22 EPCT/A/SR/20, 24, 32, 34 EPCT/WP.1/SR/8, 9, 11
Reports:	see above
Other:	EPCT/W/23, 28, 29, 34, 35+Corr.1, 53, 66, 68, 84, 91, 97

Article VII:

Discussion:	EPCT/EC/SR/3, 22 EPCT/A/SR/31, 32, 34+Corr.1, 40(2) EPCT/WP.1/SR/9, 11
Reports:	see above; also EPCT/W/166, 180
Other:	EPCT/W/23, 24, 28, 36, 37+Corr.1, 57, 58, 78, 90, 100, 104, 134, 152, 158, 247, 251, 262, 283

Article VIII:

Discussion:	EPCT/EC/SR.2/3, 22 EPCT/A/SR/24, 25, 34

	EPCT/WP.1/SR/1, 6, 7, 11
Reports:	see above
Other:	EPCT/W/23, 28, 38, 39, 50, 67, 77, 88, 103

Article IX:

Discussion:	EPCT/EC/SR.2/3, 22
	EPCT/A/SR/24, 34, 40(2)
	EPCT/WP.1/SR/1-3, 6-7, 8+Corr.1-2
Reports:	see above
Other:	EPCT/109
	EPCT/W/23, 28, 29, 40, 52, 80

Article X:

Discussion:	EPCT/EC/SR.2/3, 22
	EPCT/A/SR/24, 25, 30, 34, 40(2)
	EPCT/WP.1/SR/3, 4, 8, 11
	EPCT/WP.1/AC/SR/2, 3
Reports:	see above
Other:	EPCT/109
	EPCT/W/23, 24+Add.1, 28, 41, 42, 43, 51

Havana

(Charter Articles corresponding to Articles V-X)

Discussion:	E/CONF.2/C.3/SR.15, 30-32
Reports:	E/CONF.2/C.3/10, 41
Other:	E/CONF.2/C.3/C/W.5

CONTRACTING PARTIES

(Articles V-X)

Reports:	GATT/CP.2/22/Rev.1 (II/43)

Review Session
Article V

Reports:	W.9/155, 217
Other:	L/189, 273, 275, 276
	W.9/46
	Spec/40/55

Article VI

Discussion:	SR.9/17, 24, 41, 47
Reports:	W.9/122+Corr.1, 217, 220, 231, 236/Add.1;
	L/334;
	3S/222
Other:	L/189, 261/Add.1, 270/Add.1, 273, 275, 276
	W.9/20/Add.1, 28, 41, 46, 68, 86+Rev.1, 214
	Spec/70/55, 93/55, 106/55, 109/55, 111/55

Article VII

Discussion:	SR.9/17, 20, 47
Reports:	W.9/155, 191, 199, 212, 217+Corr.1, 236/Add.1;
	L/329;
	3S/205
Other:	L/189, 261/Add.1, 272, 273, 275, 276
	W.9/46, 54+Add.1, 61, 141, 152, 169/Rev.1, 172
	Spec/40/55

Article VIII

Discussion:	SR.9/18, 47
Reports:	W.9/155, 191, 199, 212, 217, 236/Add.1;
	L/329
	3S/205
Other:	L/189, 261/Add.1
	W.9/46, 69, 120, 125, 168, 172
	Spec/40/55 Article IX

Reports:	W.9/155, 191, 212, 217, 236/Add.1;
	L/329;
	3S/205
Other:	L/189, 261/Add.1, 273, 275, 276
	W.9/46, 87, 172
	Spec/40/55

Article X

Report:	L/327,
	3S/234-235
Other:	L/189, 261/Add.1
	W.9/46, 217
	Spec/47/55

ARTICLE XI

GENERAL ELIMINATION OF QUANTITATIVE RESTRICTIONS

I.	TEXT OF ARTICLE XI AND RELEVANT INTERPRETATIVE NOTES			314
II.	INTERPRETATION AND APPLICATION OF ARTICLE XI			315
	A.	SCOPE AND APPLICATION OF ARTICLE XI		315
		1. Paragraph 1		315
			(1) "prohibitions or restrictions other than duties, taxes or other charges"	315
			(a) Measures under Article XI:1	315
			(b) Relevance of trade effects	316
			(2) "made effective through quotas"	317
			(a) Import quotas	317
			(b) Residual restrictions	317
			(3) "import or export licences"	319
			(4) "or other measures": other examples of restrictions	320
			(a) Import or export prohibitions	320
			(b) Minimum price systems for imports or exports	321
			(c) State-trading operations	321
			(d) Import and export restrictions	324
			(5) Tariff rate quotas	325
		2. Paragraph 2(a)		326
			(1) "export prohibitions or restrictions temporarily applied to prevent or relieve"	326
			(2) "critical shortages of foodstuffs"	326
			(3) "essential to the exporting country"	326
		3. Paragraph 2(b)		326
		4. Paragraph 2(c)		327
			(1) General	327
			(2) Relationship with concessions and other obligations	328
			(3) Elements and burden of proof regarding claims under paragraph 2(c)(i)	329
			(4) Scope and application of Paragraph 2(c)	330
			(a) "Import restrictions"	330
			(b) "on any agricultural or fisheries product"	331
			(c) "the like ... product"	331
			(d) "imported in any form": application of paragraph 2(c) to processed products	334
			(e) "necessary"	337
			(f) "to the enforcement of governmental measures"	339
			(5) Paragraph 2(c)(i)	340
			(a) "restrict the quantities ... permitted to be marketed or produced"	340
			(b) "of the like domestic product"	344
			(6) Paragraph 2(c)(ii)	344
			(a) "temporary surplus"	344
			(7) Paragraph 2(c)(iii)	345
			(a) "the production of which is directly dependent, wholly or mainly"	345
		5. Last sub-paragraph of paragraph 2		345
			(1) "Public notice", miscellaneous or "basket" import quotas and quota administration through discretionary licensing	345
			(2) "during a previous representative period"	346
			(3) Proportionality requirement	346
			(4) "special factors"	347
	B.	RELATIONSHIP BETWEEN ARTICLE XI AND OTHER GATT ARTICLES		348
		1. Article III		348
		2. Article VI		348
		3. Article XXIII		348
		4. Article XXIV:12		348
	C.	RELATIONSHIP BETWEEN ARTICLE XI AND OTHER INTERNATIONAL AGREEMENTS		348
		1. General		348
		2. Arrangement Regarding International Trade in Textiles		349
		3. Agreement on Import Licensing Procedures		349
		4. Agreement on Trade in Civil Aircraft		349
	D.	EXCEPTIONS AND DEROGATIONS		349
		1. Reservations in accession protocols		349
		2. Waivers under Article XXV:5		350

E.	WORK CARRIED OUT IN THE GATT ON QUANTITATIVE RESTRICTIONS MAINTAINED FOR OTHER THAN BALANCE-OF-PAYMENTS REASONS	350
	1. Import restrictions	350
	2. Export restrictions	352
III.	PREPARATORY WORK AND SUBSEQUENT MODIFICATIONS	353
IV.	RELEVANT DOCUMENTS	354

I. TEXT OF ARTICLE XI AND RELEVANT INTERPRETATIVE NOTES

Article XI*

General Elimination of Quantitative Restrictions

1. No prohibitions or restrictions other than duties, taxes or other charges, whether made effective through quotas, import or export licences or other measures, shall be instituted or maintained by any contracting party on the importation of any product of the territory of any other contracting party or on the exportation or sale for export of any product destined for the territory of any other contracting party.

2. The provisions of paragraph 1 of this Article shall not extend to the following:

(*a*) Export prohibitions or restrictions temporarily applied to prevent or relieve critical shortages of foodstuffs or other products essential to the exporting contracting party;

(*b*) Import and export prohibitions or restrictions necessary to the application of standards or regulations for the classification, grading or marketing of commodities in international trade;

(*c*) Import restrictions on any agricultural or fisheries product, imported in any form,* necessary to the enforcement of governmental measures which operate:

   (i) to restrict the quantities of the like domestic product permitted to be marketed or produced, or, if there is no substantial domestic production of the like product, of a domestic product for which the imported product can be directly substituted; or

   (ii) to remove a temporary surplus of the like domestic product, or, if there is no substantial domestic production of the like product, of a domestic product for which the imported product can be directly substituted, by making the surplus available to certain groups of domestic consumers free of charge or at prices below the current market level; or

   (iii) to restrict the quantities permitted to be produced of any animal product the production of which is directly dependent, wholly or mainly, on the imported commodity, if the domestic production of that commodity is relatively negligible.

Any contracting party applying restrictions on the importation of any product pursuant to sub-paragraph (*c*) of this paragraph shall give public notice of the total quantity or value of the product permitted to be imported during a specified future period and of any change in such quantity or value. Moreover, any restrictions applied under (i) above shall not be such as will reduce the total of imports relative to the total of domestic production, as compared with the proportion which might reasonably be expected to rule between the two in the absence of restrictions. In determining this proportion, the contracting party shall pay due regard to the proportion prevailing during a previous representative period and to any special factors* which may have affected or may be affecting the trade in the product concerned.

ARTICLE XI - GENERAL ELIMINATION OF QUANTITATIVE RESTRICTIONS

Interpretative Notes from Annex I

Ad *Article XI*

Paragraph 2 (c)

The term "in any form" in this paragraph covers the same products when in an early stage of processing and still perishable, which compete directly with the fresh product and if freely imported would tend to make the restriction on the fresh product ineffective.

Paragraph 2, last sub-paragraph

The term "special factors" includes changes in relative productive efficiency as between domestic and foreign producers, or as between different foreign producers, but not changes artificially brought about by means not permitted under the Agreement.

Ad *Articles XI, XII, XIII, XIV and XVIII*

Throughout Articles XI, XII, XIII, XIV and XVIII, the terms "import restrictions" or "export restrictions" include restrictions made effective through state-trading operations.

II. INTERPRETATION AND APPLICATION OF ARTICLE XI

A. SCOPE AND APPLICATION OF ARTICLE XI

1. Paragraph 1

(1) "prohibitions or restrictions other than duties, taxes or other charges"

(a) Measures under Article XI:1

The 1988 Panel Report on "Japan - Trade in Semi-conductors" examined *inter alia*, "administrative guidance" by the Japanese government and its status as a "restriction" under Article XI.

"The Panel examined the parties' contentions in the light of Article XI:1 … [text of Article XI:1 omitted] The Panel noted that this wording was comprehensive: it applied to all measures instituted or maintained by a contracting party prohibiting or restricting the importation, exportation or sale for export of products other than measures that take the form of duties, taxes or other charges. …

"The Panel then examined the contention of the Japanese Government that the measures complained of were not restrictions in the sense of Article XI because they were not legally binding or mandatory. In this respect the Panel noted that Article XI:1, unlike other provisions of the General Agreement, did not refer to laws or regulations but more broadly to measures. This wording indicated clearly that any measure instituted or maintained by a contracting party which restricted the exportation or sale for export of products was covered by this provision, irrespective of the legal status of the measure.

"Having reached this finding on the basis of the wording and purpose of the provision, the Panel looked for precedents that might be of further assistance to it on this point. [The Panel discussed the Panel Report on 'Japan - Restrictions on Imports of Certain Agricultural Products' (see below, page 339)] The Panel recognized the differences between Article XI:1 and Article XI:2(c) and the fact that the previous case was not the same in all respects as the case before it, but noted that the earlier case supported its finding that it was not necessarily the legal status of the measure which was decisive in determining whether or not it fell under Article XI:1.

"The Panel recognized that not all non-mandatory requests could be regarded as measures within the meaning of Article XI:1. Government-industry relations varied from country to country, from industry to industry, and from case to case and were influenced by many factors. There was thus a wide spectrum of government involvement ranging from, for instance, direct government orders to occasional government consultations with advisory committees. The task of the Panel was to determine whether the measures taken in this case would be such as to constitute a contravention of Article XI.

"In order to determine this, the Panel considered that it needed to be satisfied on two essential criteria. First, there were reasonable grounds to believe that sufficient incentives or disincentives existed for non-mandatory measures to take effect. Second, the operation of the measures to restrict export of semi-conductors at prices below company-specific costs was essentially dependent on Government action or intervention. The Panel considered each of these two criteria in turn. The Panel considered that if these two criteria were met, the measures would be operating in a manner equivalent to mandatory requirements such that the difference between the measures and mandatory requirements was only one of form and not of substance, and that there could be therefore no doubt that they fell within the range of measures covered by Article XI:1 ..."[1]

"All these factors [discussed in paragraphs 110-116 of the Report] led the Panel to conclude that an administrative structure had been created by the Government of Japan which operated to exert maximum possible pressure on the private sector to cease exporting at prices below company-specific costs. This was exercised through such measures as repeated direct requests by MITI, combined with the statutory requirement for exporters to submit information on export prices, the systematic monitoring of company and product-specific costs and export prices and the institution of the supply and demand forecasts mechanism and its utilization in a manner to directly influence the behaviour of private companies. These measures operated furthermore to facilitate strong peer pressure to comply with requests by MITI and at the same time to foster a climate of uncertainty as to the circumstances under which their exports could take place. The Panel considered that the complex of measures exhibited the rationale as well as the essential elements of a formal system of export control. The only distinction in this case was the absence of formal legally binding obligations in respect of exportation or sale for export of semi-conductors. However, the Panel concluded that this amounted to a difference in form rather than substance because the measures were operated in a manner equivalent to mandatory requirements. The Panel concluded that the complex of measures constituted a coherent system restricting the sale for export of monitored semi-conductors at prices below company-specific costs to markets other than the United States, inconsistent with Article XI:1."[2]

See also the material on "mandatory versus discretionary legislation" under "general scope" in the chapter on Article III, and the material on "measures" and "discretionary legislation" under "scope" in the chapter on Article XXIII.

(b) Relevance of trade effects

The 1962 Report of the Panel on the "Uruguayan Recourse to Article XXIII" concluded that the maintenance of import permit requirements justified an assumption of "nullification or impairment" of benefits accruing under the General Agreement insofar as it had not been established that these measures were being applied consistently with the provisions of the General Agreement.[3]

The 1984 Report of the "Panel on Japanese Measures on Imports of Leather" found that restrictions on imports of leather constituted a *prima facie* case of nullification or impairment:

"The Panel noted that its terms of reference explicitly required it 'to make findings on the question of nullification or impairment'. It noted that since a *prima facie* case had been established, according to established GATT practice it was up to Japan to rebut the presumption that nullification or impairment had actually occurred.

"Against this background the Panel considered Japan's argument that the existence of the quotas themselves did not necessarily mean that nullification or impairment of benefits accruing to the United States

---

[1] L/6309, adopted on 4 May 1988, 35S/116, 153-155, paras. 104-109.
[2] *Ibid.* 35S/157-158, para. 117.
[3] L/1923, adopted on 16 November 1962, 11S/95, 105, 108, 123.

had actually been caused, but that this depended solely upon whether or not the allocation system and its implementation functioned so as to hinder United States' trade. ...

"... the Panel could not escape the conclusion that the import restrictions were maintained in order to restrict imports ...

"In any event, the Panel wished to stress that the existence of a quantitative restriction should be presumed to cause nullification or impairment not only because of any effect it had had on the volume of trade but also for other reasons e.g., it would lead to increased transaction costs and would create uncertainties which could affect investment plans".[4]

The 1990 Panel Report on "European Economic Community - Payments and Subsidies to Processors and Producers of Oilseeds and Related Animal-Feed Proteins" observes that "the CONTRACTING PARTIES have consistently interpreted the basic provisions of the General Agreement on restrictive trade measures as provisions establishing conditions of competition. Thus they decided that an import quota constitutes an import restriction within the meaning of Article XI:1 whether or not it actually impeded imports".[5]

(2) "made effective through quotas"

(a) Import quotas

Import quotas have been examined by Panels on a number of occasions. For instance, the 1962 Panel on "French Import Restrictions"[6] examined import quotas maintained by France; the 1988 Panel Report on "Japan - Restrictions on Imports of Certain Agricultural Products"[7] examined import quotas maintained by Japan; and the 1989 Panel Report on "United States - Restrictions on Imports of Sugar"[8] and the 1991 Panel Report on "United States - Restrictions on the Importation of Sugar and Sugar-Containing Products Applied under the 1955 Waiver and under the Headnote to the Schedule of Tariff Concessions"[9] examined the United States import quota on sugar.

See also the material on import licensing below.

(b) Residual restrictions

The Review Working Party on "Quantitative Restrictions" "considered in detail the type of problems which some contracting parties may have in connection with the elimination of the import restrictions which they have been applying for a number of years for balance-of-payments reasons. The Working Party concluded that it would be undesirable to deal with such problems which are essentially of a temporary nature by means of an amendment to the provisions of the Agreement, even in the form of transitional measures".[10] The Working Party proposed instead adoption of the "Hard-core Waiver" decision on "Problems Raised for Contracting Parties in Eliminating Import Restrictions Maintained During a Period of Balance-of-Payments Difficulties", providing for a temporary waiver of obligations under Article XI (subject to concurrence by the CONTRACTING PARTIES) for contracting parties which would apply for such a waiver.[11] Waivers were granted under this Decision to Belgium and Luxembourg.[12]

In 1960, procedures were approved for dealing with residual import restrictions; contracting parties were invited to notify lists of import restrictions which they were applying contrary to the provisions of the General

---

[4] L/5623, adopted on 15/16 May 1984, 31S/94, 112-113, paras. 47-48, 53, 55.
[5] L/6627, adopted on 25 January 1990, 37S/86, 130, para. 150, referring to Panel Report on Japanese Measures on Imports of Leather, adopted on 15/16 May 1984, 31S/113.
[6] L/1921, adopted on 14 November 1962, 11S/94.
[7] L/6253, adopted on 2 February 1988, 35S/163.
[8] L/6514, adopted on 22 June 1989, 36S/331, 343, para. 5.6.
[9] L/6631, adopted on 7 November 1990, 37S/228, 262, para. 6.
[10] L/332/Rev.1+Adds., adopted on 2, 4 and 5 March 1955, 3S/170, 191, para. 75.
[11] Decision of 5 March 1955, 3S/38; see also material on interpretation of this Decision at 3S/191-195.
[12] S/22, S/27; see table of waivers following chapter on Article XXV.

Agreement, and to notify changes to those lists. The procedures provided for bilateral consultations upon request under Article XXII:1, and if necessary, resort either to Article XXII:2 or Article XXIII:2.[13] In 1962, a Panel appointed by the CONTRACTING PARTIES examined the adequacy of these notifications and put forward certain suggestions on the type of information that should be included in notifications.[14]

The 1962 Panel on "French Import Restrictions" examined certain restrictions, formerly maintained by France under Article XII, which France had disinvoked in 1960. The Panel Report notes that the French government did not contest that the restrictions under consideration were contrary to Article XI:1, and did not invoke any other provisions of the General Agreement in justification of their maintenance.

> "The Panel agreed that the maintenance by a contracting party of restrictions inconsistent with Article XI after the contracting party concerned had ceased to be entitled to have recourse to Article XII constituted nullification or impairment of benefits to which other contracting parties were entitled under GATT and the effects of such nullification or impairment were aggravated if such maintenance of restrictions continued for an extended period of time."[15]

The 1983 Panel Report on "EEC - Quantitative Restrictions Against Imports of Certain Products from Hong Kong" examined restrictions maintained by France *de jure* since 1944 on eight product categories. The EEC stated that all of the restrictions in question were "residual restrictions", i.e. measures for which liberalization had not been possible in the OEEC programme of liberalization of the 1950s, and stated that social and economic factors must be taken into account. The EEC also argued that Article XI did not constitute an absolute prohibition on all residual restrictions, and that the discussions in the GATT on quantitative restrictions showed that they had come to be accepted as negotiable.

> "The Panel considered the arguments put forward by the European Community regarding the social and economic conditions which prevailed in the various product categories under examination. The European Community did not claim any corresponding GATT provision in justification for these arguments. The Panel was of the opinion that such matters did not come within the purview of Articles XI and XIII of the GATT, and in this instance concluded that they lay outside its consideration.
>
> "With regard to Article XI ... the Panel acknowledged that there exist quantitative restrictions which are maintained for other than balance-of-payments reasons. It recognized that restrictions had been in existence for a long time without Article XXIII ever having been invoked by Hong Kong in regard to the products concerned, but concluded that this did not alter the obligations which contracting parties had accepted under GATT provisions. Furthermore the Panel considered it would be erroneous to interpret the fact that a measure had not been subject to Article XXIII over a number of years, as tantamount to its tacit acceptance by contracting parties. In fact, contracting parties and in particular Hong Kong have made it clear that the discussions on quantitative restrictions which have taken place in the GATT over the years were without prejudice to the legal status of the measures or the rights and obligations of GATT contracting parties. ...
>
> "The Panel considered the argument put forward by the European Community that the principle referred to as 'the law-creating force derived from circumstances' could be relevant in the absence of law. It found, however, that in the present case such a situation did not exist, and the matter was to be considered strictly in the light of the provisions of the General Agreement."[16]

The 1984 Panel Report on "Japanese Measures on Imports of Leather" likewise examined restrictions maintained after disinvocation of Article XII.

> "... The Panel considered that the special historical, cultural and socio-economic circumstances referred to by Japan could not be taken into account by it in this context since its terms of reference were to examine

---

[13] Procedures approved 16 November 1960, 9S/18-20.
[14] 11S/206, 210.
[15] L/1921, adopted on 14 November 1962, 11S/94, para. 4.
[16] L/5511, adopted on 12 July 1983, 30S/129, 138-139, paras. 27-29.

the matter 'in the light of the relevant GATT provisions' and these provisions did not provide such a justification for import restrictions ... [Referring to the preceding Panel Report] The Panel therefore found that the Japanese import restrictions at issue, maintained through quotas and import licenses, contravened Article XI:1.

"The Panel noted that Japan had ceased to invoke Article XII regarding balance-of-payment difficulties in 1963. It noted that the Panel Report referred to above had also concluded that the fact that 'restrictions had been in place a long time ... did not alter the obligations which contracting parties had accepted under GATT provisions.' The Panel found this to be valid also in the present case."[17]

See also the discussion below at pages 350-352 of work in the GATT on quantitative restrictions.

(3) "import or export licences"

In 1950, the CONTRACTING PARTIES granted a release for certain aspects of the operation of the Haitian tobacco monopoly under Article XVIII:12 (which at that time provided for notification and concurrence with regard to certain measures affecting imports which were not otherwise permitted by the General Agreement). The Report of the Working Party on "Notification by Haiti under Article XVIII" noted that "After examination the working party was satisfied, and the Haitian representative agreed, that in so far as the law establishing the *Régie* provided that the importation of *tobacco, cigars and cigarettes* should be subject to licences issued by a government authority and that licences should be issued at the discretion of that authority in the light of market requirements, there was an element of restriction in the measure which was contrary to Article XI of the General Agreement".[18] A re-examination of the same measure by the Working Party on "The Haitian Tobacco Monopoly" in 1955 found as follows: "With regard to cigars, cigarettes and other tobacco, the representative of Haiti informed the Working Party that importers act as agents of the Régie and that import licences represent in effect orders by the Régie; further, that the Régie only determines the extent of the market demand and the Law requires that licences be issued to the full extent of such demand. The Working Party considered that under these circumstances there would be no infringement of the provisions of Article XI".[19]

The 1978 Panel Report on "EEC - Programme of Minimum Import Prices, Licences and Surety Deposits for Certain Processed Fruits and Vegetables" found with regard to the import certificate and associated security system at issue:

"The Panel ... noted that, without prejudice to the application of safeguard measures, import certificates were to be issued on the fifth working day following that on which the application was lodged and that import certificates were to be valid for seventy-five days. The Panel considered that, pending results concerning automatic licensing in the Multilateral Trade Negotiations, this system did not depart from systems which other contracting parties claimed were justified as automatic licensing. The Panel also considered that automatic licensing did not constitute a restriction of the type meant to fall under the purview of Article XI:1. Therefore, the Panel concluded that the import certificate and associated security system operated by the Community was not inconsistent with the Community's obligations under Article XI:1".[20]

See also the discussion of import licensing and tariff quotas in the unadopted 1994 panel report on "EEC - Import Régime for Bananas".[21]

See also the material under "Administration of import licensing" in Article XIII.

---

[17]L/5623, adopted on 15/16 May 1984, 31S/94, 111, para. 45.
[18]GATT/CP.5/25, adopted on 27 November 1950, II/87; Decision of the same date, II/27.
[19]L/454, adopted on 22 November 1955, S/38, 40, para. 11.
[20]L/4687, adopted on 18 October 1978, 25S/68, 95, para. 4.1.
[21]DS38/R, dated 11 February 1994, para. 140.

(4) "or other measures": other examples of restrictions

(a) Import or export prohibitions

The Panel on "United States Manufacturing Clause" examined Section 601 of Title 17 of the United States Code (the "Manufacturing Clause" of the copyright law), which prohibited, with certain exceptions, the importation or public distribution in the United States of copies of a work consisting preponderantly of copyrighted non-dramatic literary material in the English language, unless the portions consisting of such material had been manufactured in the United States or Canada. The EC maintained that this clause constituted a breach of Article XI:1; the US did not contest this position, maintaining its legality under the Protocol of Provisional Application.[22] The Panel found that the Manufacturing Clause was inconsistent with Article XI:1.[23]

The 1991 Panel Report on "United States - Restrictions on Imports of Tuna", which has not been adopted, examined the provisions of the US Marine Mammal Protection Act (MMPA) which regulated harvesting of tuna within the jurisdiction of the US, and required that, as a condition of access to the United States market for the yellowfin tuna or yellowfin tuna products caught by its fleet, each country of registry of vessels fishing yellowfin tuna in the Eastern Tropical Pacific Ocean had to prove to the satisfaction of the US authorities that its overall regulatory regime regarding the taking of marine mammals is comparable to that of the US. To meet this requirement, the country in question had to prove that the average rate of incidental taking of marine mammals by its tuna fleet operating in the ETP was not in excess of 1.25 times the average incidental taking rate of US vessels operating in the ETP during the same period. The MMPA also provided that ninety days after imports of yellowfin tuna and yellowfin tuna products from a country had been prohibited as above, importation of such tuna and tuna products from any "intermediary nation" would also be prohibited, unless the intermediary nation proved that it too had acted to ban imports of such tuna and tuna products from the country subject to the direct import embargo. The Panel found that these measures did not constitute internal regulations covered by the Note Ad Article III.

"The Panel noted that the United States had, as mandated by the MMPA, announced and implemented a prohibition on imports of yellowfin tuna and yellowfin tuna products caught by vessels of Mexico with purse seine nets in the ETP. The Panel further noted that under United States customs law, fish caught by a vessel registered in a country was deemed to originate in that country, and that this prohibition therefore applied to imports of products of Mexico. The Panel noted that under the General Agreement, quantitative restrictions on imports are forbidden by Article XI:1 ... The Panel therefore found that the direct import prohibition on certain yellowfin tuna and certain yellowfin tuna products from Mexico and the provisions of the MMPA under which it is imposed were inconsistent with Article XI:1. The United States did not present to the Panel any arguments to support a different legal conclusion regarding Article XI."[24]

"The Panel further noted that the MMPA required that the United States authorities implement a prohibition on imports of yellowfin tuna and yellowfin tuna products from 'intermediary nations', and that the United States was refusing entry to yellowfin tuna unless the importer declared that no yellowfin tuna or yellowfin tuna product in the shipment were harvested with purse-seine nets in the ETP by vessels of Mexico. The Panel therefore found that these measures and the provisions of the MMPA mandating such an embargo were import restrictions or prohibitions inconsistent with Article XI:1. The United States did not present to the Panel any arguments to support a different legal conclusion regarding Article XI."[25]

With regard to import prohibitions in relation to Article XI:2(c), see also the excerpts from the 1982 Panel Report on "United States - Prohibition of Imports of Tuna and Tuna Products from Canada" and the 1988 Panel Report on "Japan - Restrictions on Certain Agricultural Products", below at page 330ff. With regard to export prohibitions under Article XI:2(b), see the excerpts below at page 327 of the 1988 Panel Report on "Canada -

---

[22] L/5609, adopted on 15/16 May 1984, 31S/74, 78, paras. 10-11.
[23] *Ibid*. 31S/91, para. 42(i).
[24] DS21/R (unadopted), 39S/155, 196, paras. 5.17-5.18.
[25] *Ibid*., 39S/201, para. 5.36.

Measures Affecting the Export of Unprocessed Herring and Salmon".[26] See also the material on "prohibitions and restrictions" in the unadopted 1994 panel report on "United States - Restrictions on Imports of Tuna".[27]

(b)   Minimum price systems for imports or exports

The 1978 Panel Report on "EEC - Programme of Minimum Import Prices, Licences and Surety Deposits for Certain Processed Fruits and Vegetables" notes as follows:

> "… The Panel … noted the argument by the representative of the United States that this system prohibited importation of goods below a certain price and was, therefore, a restriction within the meaning of Article XI on the importation of those goods. The Panel also noted the argument by the representative of the Community that this system, as enforced by the additional security, was a non-tariff measure and that, in principle, imports of tomato concentrates into the Community were allowed, but not below the minimum price level. … Finally, the Panel noted the assertion by the representative of the Community that this system was a measure which fell within the purview of Article XI and Article XI alone, and furthermore, that it qualified for the exemption from the provisions of Article XI:1 provided by Article XI:2(c)(i) and (ii). Having noted the foregoing, the Panel considered that the minimum import price system, as enforced by the additional security, was a restriction 'other than duties taxes or other charges' within the meaning of Article XI:1".[28]

The Panel Report on "Japan - Trade in Semi-conductors" provides:

> "The Panel noted that the CONTRACTING PARTIES had decided in a previous case that the import regulation allowing the import of a product in principle, but not below a minimum price level, constituted a restriction on importation within the meaning of Article XI:1 (BISD 25S/99). The Panel considered that the principle applied in that case to restrictions on imports of goods below certain prices was equally applicable to restrictions on exports below certain prices".[29]

See also the 1950 Report of the Working Party on "The Use of Quantitative Restrictions for Protective and Commercial Purposes", cited at page 324 below.

In February 1994, the EC gave notice that under a measure in force since 5 February 1994, importation of certain whitefish from all origins (including cod, haddock, coalfish, hake, monkfish and Alaska pollack) had been made conditional on observance of a reference price for imported fresh, frozen and chilled presentations of these products. The notification stated that the action had been "taken in relation to Community measures aimed at restricting the marketing of like or similar domestic products under Article XI:2 of GATT".[30]

(c)   State-trading operations

See the Interpretative Note to Articles XI, XII, XIII, XIV and XVIII. The material in this note was originally located in Article 26 of the Geneva Draft (corresponding to GATT Article XII); however, as it was considered applicable to the entire section on quantitative restrictions, it was reworded so as to cover export restrictions as well as import restrictions, and was moved to become paragraph 3 of Article XI in the text of the General Agreement agreed 30 October 1947.[31] The text of paragraph 3 read: "Throughout Articles XI, XII, XIII and XIV the terms 'import restrictions' or 'export restrictions' include restrictions made effective through State-trading operations". This text was transferred to the Interpretative Notes and broadened (through addition of a reference to Article XVIII) by the 1955 Protocol Amending the Preamble and Parts II and III of the GATT.

---

[26]L/6268, adopted on 22 March 1988, 35S/98.
[27]DS29/R, dated 16 June 1994, para. 5.10.
[28]L/4687, adopted on 18 October 1978, 25S/68, 99, para. 4.9.
[29]L/6309, adopted on 4 May 1988, 35S/116, 153 para. 105.
[30]L/7413, "European Communities' Trade Measures Affecting the Imports of Whitefish", including text of Commission Regulation (EC) No. 275/94 of 4 February 1994.
[31]EPCT/141, p. 3.

The 1961 Report of the Working Party under Article XXII:2 on "Italian Restrictions Affecting Imports from the United States and Certain other Contracting Parties" notes, with regard to residual restrictions maintained through State-trading agencies operating under Article XVII, that "Insofar as the State-trading operation had the effect of restricting imports, the Italian authorities fully recognized that, by virtue of the interpretative notes *ad* Articles XI, XII, etc. in Annex I to the General Agreement, it constituted an import restriction within the purview of Article XI".[32]

The 1988 Panel Report on "Canada - Import, Distribution and Sale of Alcoholic Drinks by Canadian Provincial Marketing Agencies" examined practices of provincial liquor boards which had a monopoly over distribution and sale of alcoholic beverages within each province; federal legislation restricted the importation of liquor except under conditions established by a provincial liquor board. In respect to Article XI, the Panel examined the liquor boards' practices concerning listing and delisting of products for sale, and the availability of points of sale which discriminated against imported beverages.

"The Panel first examined the relevance of Article XI to these requirements. The Panel noted Canada's claim that the practices referred to were not 'restrictions' in the sense of Article XI because they were not associated with the 'importation' of the products. ...

"... The Panel considered it significant that the note [to Articles XI, XII, XIII, XIV and XVIII] referred to 'restrictions made effective through state-trading operations' and not to 'import restrictions'. It considered that this was a recognition of the fact that in the case of enterprises enjoying a monopoly of both importation and distribution in the domestic market, the distinction normally made in the General Agreement between restrictions affecting the importation of products and restrictions affecting imported products lost much of its significance since both types of restriction could be made effective through decision by the monopoly. The Panel considered that systematic discriminatory practices of the kind referred to should be considered as restrictions made effective through 'other measures' contrary to the provisions of Article XI:1."[33]

The Panel Report adopted in 1992 on "Canada - Import, Distribution and Sale of Certain Alcoholic Drinks by Provincial Marketing Agencies" again examined the practices of Canadian provincial liquor boards. The Panel found that the United States had not substantiated its claim that Canada still maintained listing and delisting practices inconsistent with Article XI, with the exception of listing and delisting practices in Ontario; as for the Ontario liquor board's practice of limiting listing of imported beer to the six-pack size, while according listings in different package sizes to domestic beer, "The Panel noted that this package-size requirement, though implemented as a listing requirement, was in fact a requirement that did not affect the importation of beer as such but rather its offering for sale in certain liquor-board outlets. The Panel therefore considered that this requirement fell under Article III:4 ... The Panel found that the imposition of the six-pack configuration requirement on imported beer but not on domestic beer was inconsistent with that provision".[34] As for the restrictions on access to points of sale, which the 1988 Panel had found to be inconsistent with Article XI:1,

"... the Panel considered that it was not necessary to decide whether the restrictions fell under Article XI:1 or Article III:4 because Canada was not invoking an exception to the General Agreement applicable only to measures taken under Article XI:1 (such as the exceptions in Articles XI:2 and XII) and the question of whether the restrictions violated Article III:4 or Article XI:1 of the General Agreement was therefore of no practical consequence in the present case. The Panel found that the restrictions on access by imported beer to points of sale were contrary to the provisions of the General Agreement".[35]

With respect to restrictions on private delivery of imported beer, and Canada's argument that its right to deliver imported beer to the points of sale was an inherent part of Canada's right to establish an import monopoly in accordance with Article XVII, "The Panel noted that ... Articles II:4, XVII and the Note *Ad* Articles XI, XII, XIII, XIV and XVIII clearly indicated the drafters' intention not to allow contracting parties to frustrate the

---

[32]L/1468, adopted on 16 May 1961, 10S/117, 119, para. 7.
[33]L/6304, adopted on 22 March 1988, 35S/37, 89, para. 4.24.
[34]DS17/R, adopted on 18 February 1992, 39S/27, 74-75, para. 5.3-5.4.
[35]*Ibid.*, 39S/75-76, paras. 5.6-5.7.

principles of the General Agreement governing measures affecting private trade by regulating trade through monopolies. ... The Panel found ... that the practice of the liquor boards of Alberta, British Columbia, Manitoba, New Brunswick, Newfoundland, Nova Scotia, Ontario and Quebec to prohibit the private delivery of imported beer to the points of sale while according domestic brewers the right to deliver their products to the points of sale was inconsistent with Article III:4".[36]

The 1988 Panel Report on "Japan - Restrictions on Imports of Certain Agricultural Products" examined, *inter alia*, import restrictions on prepared and preserved beef and certain dairy products, which Japan argued were justified on the basis of its monopoly import system for certain beef and dairy products, maintained by the Livestock Industry Promotion Corporation (LIPC).

"The Panel noted the view of Japan that Article XI:1 did not apply to import restrictions made effective through an import monopoly. According to Japan, the drafters of the Havana Charter for an International Trade Organization intended to deal with the problem of quantitative trade limitations applied by import monopolies through a provision under which a monopoly of the importation of any product for which a concession had been negotiated would have 'to import and offer for sale such quantities of the product as will be sufficient to satisfy the full domestic demand for the imported product' (Article 31:5 of the Havana Charter). Japan contended that that provision had not been inserted into the General Agreement and that quantitative restrictions made effective through import monopolies could therefore not be considered to be covered by Article XI:1 of the General Agreement (paragraph 3.3.3 above).

"The Panel examined this contention and noted the following: Article XI:1 covers restrictions on the importation of any product, 'whether made effective through quotas, import ... licences *or other measures*' (emphasis added). The wording of this provision is comprehensive, thus comprising restrictions made effective through an import monopoly. This is confirmed by the note to Articles XI, XII, XIII, XIV and XVIII, according to which the term 'import restrictions' throughout these Articles covers restrictions made effective through state-trading operations. The basic purpose of this note is to extend to state-trading the rules of the General Agreement governing private trade and to ensure that the contracting parties cannot escape their obligations with respect to private trade by establishing state-trading operations. This purpose would be frustrated if import restrictions were considered to be consistent with Article XI:1 only because they were made effective through import monopolies. The note to Article II:4 of the General Agreement specifies that that provision 'will be applied in the light of the provisions of Article 31 of the Havana Charter'. The obligation of a monopoly importing a product for which a concession had been granted 'to import and offer for sale such quantities of the product as will be sufficient to satisfy the full domestic demand for the imported product' is thus part of the General Agreement. The Panel could therefore not follow the arguments of Japan based on the assumption that Article 31:5 of the Havana Charter was not included in the General Agreement. The Panel found for these reasons that the import restrictions applied by Japan fell under Article XI independent of whether they were made effective through quotas or through import monopoly operations."[37]

The 1989 Panel Report on "Republic of Korea - Restrictions on Imports of Beef - Complaint by the United States" notes the argument made by the US that the Livestock Products Marketing Organization (LPMO), which was established to administer import restrictions on beef, constituted an import monopoly controlled by domestic producers and that the LPMO constituted a separate "import restriction" within the meaning of Article XI, aside from the restrictions administered by the LPMO. Korea stated that the LPMO administered but did not itself determine quota levels.

"The Panel ... examined the further claim by the United States that the existence, or use, of producer-controlled import monopolies to restrict imports was inconsistent with the provisions of Articles XI:1 and XVII. Korea contested that the existence of a producer-controlled import monopoly in itself constituted an additional barrier to trade. The Panel noted that the LPMO had been granted exclusive privileges as the

---

[36]*Ibid.*, 39S/80, paras. 5.15-5.16.
[37]L/6253, adopted on 2 February 1988, 35S/163, 229, paras. 5.2.2.1-5.2.2.2. For findings applying this rule to individual products see paragraphs 5.3.1.1 and 5.3.9 of the same Report.

sole importer of beef. As such, the LPMO had to comply with the provisions of the General Agreement applicable to state-trading enterprises, including those of Articles XI:1 and XVII.

"Article XI:1 proscribed the use of 'prohibitions or restrictions other than duties, taxes or other charges', including restrictions made effective through state-trading activities, but Article XVII permitted the establishment or maintenance of state-trading enterprises, including enterprises which had been granted exclusive or special privileges. The mere existence of producer-controlled import monopolies could not be considered as a separate import restriction inconsistent with the General Agreement. The Panel noted, however, that the activities of such enterprises had to conform to a number of rules contained in the General Agreement, including those of Article XVII and Article XI:1. The Panel had already found that the import restrictions presently administered by the LPMO violated the provisions of Article XI:1. As the rules of the General Agreement did not concern the organization or management of import monopolies but only their operations and effects on trade, the Panel concluded that the existence of a producer-controlled monopoly could not in itself be in violation of the General Agreement."[38]

See also the material on the Haitian tobacco monopoly at page 319.

(d) Import and export restrictions

The 1950 Report of the Working Party on "The Use of Quantitative Restrictions for Protective and Commercial Purposes"[39] examined the use of both import and export restrictions. The Report provides, *inter alia:*

"... The Working Party noted that there was evidence of a number of types of misuse of import restrictions, in particular:

"(i) The maintenance by a country of balance-of-payment restrictions, which give priority to imports of particular products upon the basis of the competitiveness or non-competitiveness of such imports with a domestic industry, or which favour particular sources of supply upon a similar basis, in a manner inconsistent with the provisions of Articles XII to XIV ... Such type of misuse, for example, might take the form of total prohibitions on the import of products competing with domestic products, or of quotas which are unreasonably small having regard to the exchange availability of the country concerned and to other relevant factors.

"(ii) The imposition by a country of administrative obstacles to the full utilization of balance-of-payment import quotas, e.g., by delaying the issuance of licences against such quotas or by establishing licence priorities for certain imports on the basis of the competitiveness or non-competitiveness of such imports with the products of domestic industry, in a manner inconsistent with the provisions of Articles XII to XIV ... In this connection, the Contracting Parties took note of Article XIII:2(d), which provides that 'no conditions or formalities shall be imposed which would prevent any contracting party from utilising fully the share of any such total quantity or value which has been allotted to it, subject to importation being made within any prescribed period to which the quota may relate'.

"(iii) Quantitative restrictions on imports imposed not on balance-of-payment grounds but as a means of retaliation against a country which has refused to conclude a bilateral trade agreement with the country concerned.

"It appeared to the Working Party that insofar as these types of practice were in fact carried on for the purposes indicated above and were not justified under the provisions of Articles XII to XIV relating to the use of import restrictions to protect the balance of payments or under other provisions of the Agreement specifically permitting the use of import restrictions, they were inconsistent with the provisions of the Agreement, and such misuse of import restrictions might appropriately provide a basis for recourse to the

---

[38] L/6503, adopted on 7 November 1989, 36S/268, 301-302, paras. 114-115.
[39] GATT/CP.4/33, republished as "The Use of Quantitative Restrictions for Protective and Commercial Purposes," Sales No. GATT/1950-3.

procedures laid down in the Agreement for the settlement of disputes. Moreover, it was not particularly relevant to the Agreement whether such practices were determined unilaterally or in the course of bilateral negotiations.

"The Working Party agreed that there did not appear to be any provision in the Agreement which would permit the imposition by a contracting party of quantitative restrictions on imports of a particular product for the purpose of avoiding an increase in the cost to the importing country of maintaining a price support programme for the like product of domestic origin and not for other purposes provided for in the Agreement".[40]

The same Report also sets out the Working Party's examination of "several types of export restrictions ... applied for protective, promotional or other commercial purposes ... which appear to fall outside the exceptions provided for in [Articles XI, XIII, XIV, XV and XX]: (i) export restrictions used by a contracting party for the purpose of obtaining the relaxation of another contracting party's import restrictions; (ii) export restrictions used by a contracting party to obtain a relaxation of another contracting party's export restrictions on commodities in local or general short supply, or otherwise to obtain an advantage in the procurement from another contracting party of such commodities; (iii) restrictions used by a contracting party on the export of raw materials, in order to protect or promote a domestic fabricating industry; and (iv) export restrictions used by a contracting party to avoid price competition among exporters".[41]

"... the Working Party could not find any provisions in the Agreement which would justify the linking of the issue of export licences for a particular product with the purchase by another contracting party of any other particular product. ... It was agreed that the use of export restrictions as a bargaining weapon to obtain the relaxation of import restrictions was inconsistent with the provisions of the Agreement. However, whether any particular export restriction could justly be regarded as having the assumed purposes would depend upon the facts in each particular case."[42]

"The Working Party concluded that the Agreement does not permit the imposition of restrictions upon the export of a raw material in order to protect or promote a domestic industry, whether by affording a price advantage to that industry for the purchase of its materials, or by reducing the supply of such materials available to foreign competitors, or by other means. However, it was agreed that the question of the objective of any given export restriction would have to be determined on the basis of the facts in each individual case."[43]

"The Working Party discussed a wide variety of circumstances in which exportation may be restricted in order to maintain the export price. The cases discussed included a commodity whose value might be greatly reduced if its supply to the world market were not controlled and a commodity whose world price was liable to be impaired by the collusive action of importers. The Working Party concluded that where export restrictions were in fact intended for the purpose of avoiding competition among exporters and not for the purposes set out in the exception provisions of Articles XI and XX, such restrictions were inconsistent with the provisions of the Agreement."[44]

(5) Tariff rate quotas

See the discussion of tariff rate quotas and high secondary tariffs in relation to Article XI:1, in the unadopted 1994 panel report on "EEC - Import Régime for Bananas".[45]

---

[40]*Ibid.*, paras. 21-23.
[41]*Ibid.*, para. 2.
[42]*Ibid.*, para. 6-7.
[43]*Ibid.*, para. 12.
[44]*Ibid.*, paras. 14-15.
[45]DS38/R, dated 11 February 1994, paras. 138, 139.

2. Paragraph 2(a)

(1) *"export prohibitions or restrictions temporarily applied to prevent or relieve"*

The preparatory work indicates that the words "prevent or" were added in Geneva "to enable a member to take remedial action before a critical shortage has actually arisen".[46]

(2) *"critical shortages of foodstuffs"*

In the US proposed Charter in 1946 the phrase used was "conditions of distress". The US representative stated that this phrase did not mean "economic distress but referred to shortages of crops, etc., in cases such as famine".[47] With reference to the term "critical", it was agreed in discussions at Geneva and again at Havana that the Australian export prohibitions on merino sheep were covered by paragraph 2(a).[48]

At the Havana Conference the Sub-Committee on Articles 20 and 22 "was satisfied that the terms of paragraph 2(a) ... are adequate to allow a country to impose temporary export restrictions to meet a considerable rise in domestic prices of foodstuffs due to a rise in prices in other countries".[49] The Report of the Review Working Party on "Quantitative Restrictions" also recorded the view that "to the extent that the rise in prices was associated with acute shortages of the products in question, as it normally would be, [temporary export restrictions applied to meet a considerable rise in domestic prices of food-stuffs due to a rise in prices in other countries], whether affecting foodstuffs or other products, was clearly covered by that sub-paragraph [2(a)]".[50]

(3) *"essential to the exporting country"*

The Sub-Committee at the Geneva session of the Preparatory Committee which considered this provision altered the wording "to indicate the view of the Sub-Committee that for the purposes of this provision the importance of any product should be judged in relation to the particular country concerned".[51]

3. Paragraph 2(b)

The Sub-Committee at the Geneva session of the Preparatory Committee which considered this article widened this paragraph so as to include marketing regulations.[52] It was also agreed in Geneva that this exception would permit the Australian butter marketing scheme, which utilized export licenses to spread exports of butter over time and was "not used in any way that could be reasonably described as restrictive over the period of the operation of the scheme".[53] The Havana Conference Sub-committee which examined the general exceptions to the Charter chapter on commercial policy "expressed the view that governmental measures relating to the orderly marketing of agricultural commodities for which storage facilities in both the country of origin and destination were insufficient, were covered in paragraph 2(b) of Article 20 [corresponding to Article XI:2(b) of the General Agreement]".[54]

The Review Working Party on "Quantitative Restrictions" in 1954-55 considered various proposals to amend Article XI:2. While it considered that it was not desirable to amend these provisions,

> "The Working Party agreed, however, to insert in this report brief agreed statements which would clarify some of the points that the proposed amendments were intended to cover. It might be useful, for instance, to reaffirm that the maintenance or the application of a restriction which went beyond what would

---

[46] EPCT/141, p. 2.
[47] EPCT/C.II/36, p. 9.
[48] EPCT/A/PV/40(1), pp. 4, 6, 8, 9 discussing Australian proposal at EPCT/W/218 (post-drought shortage of sheep); endorsed in Sub-Committee Report in Havana Reports, p. 88, para. 11. See discussion of the interpretation of "critical" at EPCT/A/PV/40(1) p. 4-9.
[49] Havana Reports, p. 88, para. 14.
[50] L/332/Rev.1+Adds., adopted on 2, 4 and 5 March 1955, 3S/170, 191, para. 73.
[51] EPCT/141, p. 2.
[52] EPCT/141, p. 2.
[53] EPCT/A/PV/19, pp. 8-10.
[54] Havana Reports p. 85, para. 24; E/CONF.2/C.3/SR.37, p. 3.

be 'necessary' to achieve the objects defined in paragraph 2(b) or 2(c) of Article XI would be inconsistent with the provisions of that Article. This is made clear in the text of these provisions by the use of the word 'necessary'. Restrictions related to the application of standards or regulations for the classification, grading or marketing of commodities in international trade which go beyond what is necessary for the application of those standards or regulations and thus have an unduly restrictive effect on trade, would clearly be inconsistent with Article XI".[55]

The Panel Report on "Canada - Measures Affecting Exports of Unprocessed Herring and Salmon" examined, *inter alia*, the claim of Canada that its regulations prohibiting the exportation of unprocessed sockeye and pink salmon and herring were permitted under Article XI:2(b), as the fish were "commodities" and the regulations dealt with "standards" and "marketing".

"... The Panel noted that Canada considered it necessary to prohibit the export of certain unprocessed salmon and unprocessed herring to maintain its quality standards for these fish, including the standards for frozen salmon exported from Canada ... The Panel noted that Canada applied quality standards to fish and that it prohibited the export of fish not meeting these standards. The Panel further noted, however, that Canada prohibited export of certain unprocessed salmon and unprocessed herring even if they could meet the standards generally applied to fish exported from Canada. The Panel therefore found that these export prohibitions could not be considered as 'necessary' to the application of standards within the meaning of Article XI:2(b).

"The Panel then examined the Canadian contention that the prohibition of exports of certain unprocessed salmon and unprocessed herring was necessary for the international marketing of processed salmon and herring. Canada had argued that, without these prohibitions, Canadian processors would not have been able to develop a superior quality fish product for marketing abroad and would not have been able to maintain their share of the market for herring roe in Japan. ... The question before the Panel therefore was thus whether the export restrictions on certain unprocessed salmon and unprocessed herring constituted marketing regulations on processed salmon and herring within the meaning of Article XI:2(b). The Panel noted that this provision referred to '... regulations ... for the marketing of commodities in international trade', which suggests that the regulations covered by the provisions are not all regulations that facilitate foreign sales but only those that apply to the marketing as such. The drafters of Article XI:2(b) agreed that this provision would cover export restrictions designed to further the marketing of a commodity by spreading supplies of the restricted product over a longer period of time.[56] During the drafting mention was made only of export restrictions designed to promote foreign sales of the restricted product but not of export restrictions on one commodity designed to promote sales of another commodity. The broad interpretation of the term 'marketing regulation' implied in Canada's argument would have the consequence that any import or export restriction protecting a domestic industry and enabling it to sell abroad would be exempted from the General Agreement's prohibition of import and export restrictions. Such interpretation would therefore expand the scope of the provision far beyond its purpose. The Panel found for these reasons that the export prohibitions on certain unprocessed salmon and unprocessed herring were not 'regulations for the marketing' of processed salmon and herring in international trade within the meaning of Article XI:2(b). In the light of the considerations set out above, the Panel concluded that the export prohibitions were not justified by Article XI:2(b)."[57]

4. Paragraph 2(c)

(1) General

The "Suggested Charter for an International Trade Organization of the United Nations" which was proposed by the United States in 1946 contained a provision corresponding to Article XI:2(c)(i). Except for some refinement and the addition of "fisheries products", this provision remained unchanged through the course of the negotiations of the GATT and the Charter.

---

[55] L/332/Rev.1 and Addenda, adopted on 2, 4 and 5 March 1955, 3S/170, 189-190, para. 67.
[56] A footnote to this sentence refers to EPCT/A/PV/19, p. 8.
[57] L/6268, adopted on 22 March 1988, 35S/98, 112, paras. 4.2-4.3.

It was stated during discussions on this provision at the Geneva session of the Preparatory Committee, in reply to objections that industrial products should also be included in this exception, that

> "... in agriculture and fisheries you have to deal with the capricious bounty of nature, which will sometimes give you a huge catch of fish or a huge crop, which knocks the bottom out of prices. You also have the phenomenon peculiar to agriculture and fisheries of a multitude of small unorganized producers that cannot organize themselves. It often happens that the Government has to step in and organize them. But if it does so, it cannot allow the results of its organization to be frustrated by uncontrolled imports".[58]

On the same occasion it was stated that "we view this not as a means of protection but as a means of making watertight, and making possible the working of, necessary forms of internal control".[59]

At the Havana Conference the Sub-Committee which examined Articles 20 and 22 of the Charter discussed various proposals to widen or narrow paragraph 2(c). It "agreed that paragraph 2(c) was not intended to provide a means of protecting domestic producers against foreign competition, but simply to permit, in appropriate cases, the enforcement of domestic governmental measures necessitated by the special problems relating to the production and marketing of agricultural and fisheries products".[60]

(2) Relationship with concessions and other obligations

The same Sub-Committee at the Havana Conference also noted in its report that "... the Sub-Committee agreed to have it recorded that in its view the freedom given to a Member to apply restrictions under paragraph (2)(c) did not free such Member from a prior obligation to any individual Member".[61]

The Second Report of Committee I, which drew up the rules and procedures for the Dillon Round of trade negotiations which took place during 1960-61, discusses an Australian proposal to make import restrictions maintained under Article XI:2(c) negotiable. In response to comments on this proposal,

> "The Australian representative ... recognized that a distinction should be drawn between restrictions which were 'necessary' in terms of paragraph 2(c) of Article XI and those which, although they might be applied in connection with measures which protected domestic production or marketings, were not necessary to the operation of such arrangements. It was not the intention ... to negotiate on those restrictions which were not an integral part of the protective system and which could not be justified under that provision under the General Agreement. On the other hand, 'necessary' restrictions should be regarded as negotiable in the same way as other elements of the arrangements covered by paragraph 2(c) of Article XI. It could well be that negotiations for the reduction of these restrictions would form part of wider negotiations on the products concerned.
>
> "On ... non-discriminatory application of any concessions, the Australian representative pointed out that the results of such negotiations could take the form of global quotas or of country quotas in conformity with the provisions of Article XIII".[62]

The Dillon Round rules and procedures provided that "Participating countries may ... enter into negotiations in accordance with these rules in respect of the following matters: ... import restrictions as provided in paragraph 2(c) of Article XI".[63]

The 1988 Panel Report on "Japan - Restrictions on Imports of Certain Agricultural Products" notes that "Article XI:2 - unlike some other provisions of the General Agreement permitting restrictive trade measures, such as Articles XVIII:C, XXVIII or XIX - does not provide for compensation for contracting parties adversely

---

[58] EPCT/A/PV/19, p. 42; see also references to this passage at 36S/222, 37S/221-222.
[59] *Ibid.*, p. 44.
[60] Havana Reports, p. 89, para. 16.
[61] *Ibid.*, p. 95, para. 45.
[62] L/1043, adopted on 19 November 1959, 8S/103, 106-107, para. 5.
[63] Annex to *ibid.*, 8S/116, para. II(b)(ii).

affected by the measures taken under it".[64] The 1989 Panel Reports on "EEC - Restrictions on Imports of Dessert Apples - Complaint by Chile", and "EEC - Restrictions on Imports of Apples - Complaint by the United States" each note that

> "... The Panel ... considered that, as one of the basic functions of the General Agreement was to provide a legal framework for the exchange of tariff concessions, great care had to be taken to avoid an interpretation of Article XI:2(c)(i) which would impair this function. The Panel noted that Article XI:2(c)(i) - unlike all provisions of the General Agreement specifically permitting actions to protect domestic producers[65] - did not provide either for compensation to be granted by the contracting party invoking it, or for compensatory withdrawals by contracting parties adversely affected by the invocation. This reflected the fact that Article XI:2(c)(i) was not intended to be a provision permitting protective actions. If Article XI:2(c)(i) could be used to justify import restrictions which were not the counterpart of any governmental measure capable of limiting production, the value of the General Agreement as a legal framework for the exchange of tariff concessions in the agricultural field would be seriously impaired".[66]

(3)   Elements and burden of proof regarding claims under paragraph 2(c)(i)

The 1989 Panel Report on "Canada - Import Restrictions on Ice Cream and Yoghurt" summarizes the elements and burden of proof regarding claims under paragraph 2(c) and 2(c)(i) as follows, drawing on the earlier Panel Report on "Japan - Restrictions on Imports of Certain Agricultural Products":

> "As the party invoking an exception, it was incumbent upon Canada to demonstrate that the measures applied to imports of ice cream and yoghurt met each of the conditions under Article XI:2(c)(i) and XI:2(c) last sub-paragraph, in order to qualify in terms of these provisions for exemption from Article XI:1. These conditions are:
>
> "- the measure on importation must constitute an import restriction (and not a prohibition);
>
> "- the import restriction must be on an agricultural or fisheries product;
>
> "- the import restriction and the domestic marketing or production restriction must apply to 'like' products in any form (or directly substitutable products if there is no substantial production of the like product);
>
> "- there must be governmental measures which operate to restrict the quantities of the domestic product permitted to be marketed or produced;
>
> "- the import restriction must be necessary to the enforcement of the domestic supply restriction;
>
> "- the contracting party applying restrictions on importation must give public notice of the total quantity or value of the product permitted to be imported during a specified future period; and
>
> "- the restrictions applied must not reduce the proportion of total imports relative to total domestic production, as compared with the proportion which might reasonably be expected to rule between the two in the absence of restrictions".[67]

The 1988 Panel Report on "Japan - Restrictions on Imports of Certain Agricultural Products" notes that the Panel "considered ... that the burden of providing the evidence that all the requirements of Article XI:2(c)(i),

---

[64] L/6253, adopted on 2 February 1988, 35S/163, 227, para. 5.1.3.7.
[65] The footnote to this sentence refers to e.g., Articles XVIII:A and C, XIX and XXVIII.
[66] L/6491, adopted on 22 June 1989, 36S/93, 129, para. 12.15, and L/6513, adopted on 22 June 1989, 36S/135, 164, para. 5.15.
[67] L/6568, adopted on 5 December 1989, 36S/68, 85-86, para. 62. See also identical passages in "EEC - Restrictions on Imports of Dessert Apples - Complaint by Chile", L/6491, adopted on 22 June 1989, 36S/93, 124-125, para. 12.3, and in "EEC - Restrictions on Imports of Apples - Complaint by the United States", L/6513, adopted on 22 June 1989, 36S/135, 160, para. 5.3.

including the proportionality requirement, had been met must remain fully with the contracting party invoking that provision".[68]

In the 1989 Panel Report on "Canada - Import Restrictions on Ice Cream and Yoghurt":

"The Panel recalled that it had previously been concluded that a contracting party invoking an exception to the General Agreement bore the burden of proving that it had met all of the conditions of that exception.[69] It also noted, as had previous panels, that exceptions were to be interpreted narrowly and considered that this argued against flexible interpretation of Article XI:2(c)(i).[70] The Panel was aware that the requirements of Article XI:2(c)(i) for invoking an exception to the general prohibition on quantitative restrictions made this provision extremely difficult to comply with in practice.[71] However, any change in the burden of proof could have consequences equivalent to amending Article XI, seriously affecting the balance of tariff concessions negotiated among contracting parties, and was therefore outside the scope of the Panel's mandate".[72]

In this connection see also the unadopted 1993 panel report on "EEC - Member States' Import Régimes for Bananas".[73]

(4) Scope and application of Paragraph 2(c)

(a) "Import restrictions"

The 1982 Panel Report on "United States - Prohibition of Imports of Tuna and Tuna Products from Canada" examined a US embargo of all tuna and tuna products from Canada, imposed following the seizure by Canada of US fishing boats in a dispute over fishing jurisdiction. The Panel found that the US action constituted a prohibition in terms of Article XI:1; as for the claim of the United States that the action fell under the exception in Article XI:2(c), "... the Panel noted the difference in language between Article XI:2(a) and (b) and Article XI:2(c), and it felt that the provisions of Article XI:2(c) could not justify the application of an import prohibition". A footnote to this sentence provides: "In Article XI:2(a) and (b) the words 'prohibitions or restrictions' are used while in Article XI:2(c) mention is only made of 'restrictions'".[74]

The 1988 Panel Report on "Japan - Restrictions on Imports of Certain Agricultural Products" provides: "The Panel notes that Article XI:2(c)(i) does not permit the prohibition of imports but only their restriction. It finds that Japan maintains a de facto prohibition on the importation of evaporated milk (04.02 ex), sweetened condensed milk (04.02 ex), processed cheese (04.04 ex) and certain single-strength fruit juices (20.07 ex) into its general customs territory. The Panel concludes that these prohibitions maintained by Japan are contrary to Article XI".[75] The Panel had earlier found with respect to various of these products that an import quota available only for imports for use in Okinawa, or for use in international tourist hotels and for international shipping vessels travelling between Japan and foreign countries, resulted in a *de facto* prohibition on the importation of the product into the general customs territory of Japan.[76]

The 1989 Panel Reports on "EEC - Restrictions on Imports of Dessert Apples - Complaint by Chile" and "EEC - Restrictions on Imports of Apples - Complaint by the United States" "followed the view that prohibitions

---

[68]L/6253, adopted on 2 February 1988, 35S/163, 227, para. 5.1.3.7.

[69]The footnote to this sentence refers to: Panel Report on "Canada - Administration of the Foreign Investment Review Act", 30S/140, 164, para. 5.20; Panel Report on "Japan - Restrictions on Imports of Certain Agricultural Products", 35S/163, 227, para. 5.1.3.7; Panel Report on "European Economic Community - Restrictions on Imports of Dessert Apples - Complaint by Chile", 36S/93, 124, para. 12.3.

[70]The footnote to this sentence refers to, e.g., the Panel Report on "Japan - Restrictions on Imports of Certain Agricultural Products", L/6253, 35S/163, 226-27, para. 5.1.3.7, and Panel Report on "EEC - Restrictions on Imports of Apples - Complaint by the United States", L/6513, 36S/135, 164, para. 5.13.

[71]The footnote to this sentence refers to, e.g., the Panel Report on "EEC - Restrictions on Imports of Dessert Apples - Complaint by Chile", L/6491.

[72]L/6568, adopted on 5 December 1989, 36S/68, 84-85, para. 59.

[73]DS32/R, dated 3 June 1994, para. 328.

[74]L/5198, adopted on 22 February 1982, 29S/91, 107, para. 4.6.

[75]L/6253, adopted on 2 February 1988, 35S/163, 244, para. 6.4.

[76]*Ibid.*, 35S/230-231, 232, 238, paras. 5.3.1.2, 5.3.2.1, 5.3.10.2.

on imports were not permitted under this part of Article XI" but found that "As the EEC had at no time prohibited all imports of apples, its measures therefore constituted an import restriction, rather than an import prohibition". The question of whether the EEC measures had operated as an effective prohibition of imports from Chile was dealt with under Article XIII.[77]

In this connection see also the unadopted 1993 panel report on "EEC - Member States' Import Régimes for Bananas".[78]

(b) "on any agricultural or fisheries product"

It was agreed at the Geneva session of the Preparatory Committee that a decision as to whether whales were included within fisheries products should be made by the ITO when established.[79]

In discussions during the Havana Conference it was agreed that "the term 'agricultural product' in sub-paragraph 2(c) ... may include, inter alia, sericultural products and certain plant products (a) which are derived from the plant in the natural process of growth, such as gums, resins and syrups, and (b) a major part of the total output of which is produced by small producers".[80]

In the Panel Report on "Japan - Restrictions on Imports of Certain Agricultural Products", the Panel stated: "The General Agreement does not define the term 'agricultural product'. In the past rounds of trade negotiations it was accepted that the products falling under Chapters 1 to 24 in the Customs Co-operation Council Nomenclature could in principle be regarded as agricultural products".[81]

The Panel Report on "Canada - Import Restrictions on Ice Cream and Yoghurt" followed this rule, and "further noted that ice cream and yoghurt were food products generally regarded by consumers and the industry to be agricultural products. The Panel thus found that ice cream and yoghurt were agricultural products within the meaning of Article XI:2(c)".[82] The 1989 Panel Reports on "EEC - Restrictions on Imports of Dessert Apples - Complaint by Chile" and "EEC - Restrictions on Imports of Apples - Complaint by the United States" also followed the same rule referring to CCCN Chapters 1 to 24 and found that the measures involved applied to an agricultural product.[83]

(c) "the like ... product"

(i) General

During discussions at the London session of the Preparatory Committee reference was made to the definition of the term "like product" adopted by the League of Nations, which was "practically identical with another product";[84] however it was also stated that "the expression had different meanings in different contexts of the Draft Charter"[85] and it was later agreed that the definition of this phrase should be left to the ITO.[86] As regards the use of the term "like domestic product" in paragraph 2(c) of Article XI, it was stated that in this context "the words 'like product' are used, but those words definitely do not mean what they mean in other contexts - merely a competing product. In other words, to take an extreme case, if a country restricted its output of apples, it could not restrict importation of bananas because they only compete with them".[87]

---

[77]L/6491 and L/6513, both adopted on 22 June 1989, 36S/93 and 36S/135, at 36S/125 and 36S/161, paras. 12.5 and 5.5.
[78]DS32/R, dated 3 June 1994, paras. 329-330.
[79]EPCT/A/PV/40(1), pp. 12-15.
[80]E/CONF.2/C.3/66 and E.CONF.2/C.3/SR.41, p. 8.
[81]L/6253, adopted on 2 February 1988, 35S/163, 223, para. 5.1.3.2.
[82]L/6568, adopted on 5 December 1989, 36S/68, 86, para. 64.
[83]L/6491 and L/6513, both adopted on 22 June 1989, 36S/93 and 36S/135, at 36S/125 and 36S/161, paras. 12.6 and 5.6.
[84]EPCT/C.II/36, p. 8.
[85]EPCT/C.II/65, p. 2.
[86]EPCT/A/PV/41, p. 14.
[87]EPCT/C.II/PV.12, p. 6.

The 1988 Panel Report on "Japan - Restrictions on Imports of Certain Agricultural Products" refers to this material on "like product" and notes:

> "Thus, the mere fact that a product is competitive with another does not in and of itself make them like products. ... Article XI:2(c) and the note supplementary to it regarding 'in any form' establish different requirements for (a) restrictions on the importation of products that are 'like' the product subject to domestic supply restrictions and (b) restrictions on the importation of products that are *processed* from a product that is 'like' the product subject to domestic supply restrictions. This differentiation would be lost if a product in its original form and a product processed from that product were to be considered to be 'like' products with the meaning of Article XI:2(c)".[88]

The same panel report further notes that "as different requirements were established for restrictions on like products and on the importation of those products processed from a like product, a product in its original form and a product processed from it could not be considered to be 'like products'".[89]

(ii) "Like product" in particular instances

In the 1978 Panel Report on "EEC - Programme of Minimum Import Prices, Licences and Surety Deposits for Certain Processed Fruits and Vegetables"

> "The Panel ... examined the concept of 'the like domestic product' within the meaning of Article XI:2(c)(i) and (ii), and attempted to determine which Community product should be considered as 'the like domestic product' in relation to imported tomato concentrate. Having noted that the General Agreement provided no definition of the terms 'the like domestic product' or 'like product', the Panel reviewed how these terms had been applied by the CONTRACTING PARTIES in previous cases and the discussions relating to these terms when the General Agreement was being drafted. During this review, the Panel noted the League of Nations definition of 'practically identical with another product' and the diverging interpretations of these terms by contracting parties in different contexts. The Panel further noted the definition of 'like product' contained in the GATT Anti-Dumping Code and the definitions of 'identical goods' and 'similar goods' contained in the Customs Co-operation Council's Customs Valuation Explanatory Notes to the Brussels definition of value. On the basis of this review, the Panel considered that tomato concentrate produced within the Community would qualify as 'the like domestic product' but was unable to decide if fresh tomatoes grown within the Community would also qualify. As a pragmatic solution, the Panel decided to proceed to determine if the other conditions set forth in Article XI:2(c)(i) and (ii) were satisfied by the Community system, on the basis that 'the like domestic product' in this case could be domestically-produced tomato concentrate, fresh tomatoes or both".[90]

In the 1980 Panel Report on "EEC Restrictions on Imports of Apples from Chile", the Panel considered "that Chilean apples, although of different varieties, were 'a like product' to Community apples for the purposes of Article XI:2(c)".[91] The 1989 Panels on "EEC - Restrictions on Imports of Dessert Apples - Complaint by Chile" and "EEC - Restrictions on Imports of Apples - Complaint by the United States" each provide with respect to this issue:

> "The Panel examined carefully the arguments of the parties ... including the argument that differences in price, variety and quality between [Chilean and US apples respectively] and EEC apples were such as to make them unlike products in terms of this GATT provision. It concluded that while such differences did exist, as they might for many products, they were not such as to outweigh the basic likeness. Dessert apples whether imported or domestic performed a similar function for the consumer and were both marketed as apples, i.e., as substantially similar products. The Panel therefore found that EEC and [Chilean and US dessert apples respectively] were like products for the purposes of Article XI:2(c)(i)".[92]

---

[88] L/6253, adopted on 2 February 1988, 35S/163, 224-225, para. 5.1.3.4.
[89] *Ibid.*, 35S/231 para. 5.3.1.4.
[90] L/4687, adopted on 18 October 1978, 25S/68, 101, para. 4.12.
[91] L/5047, adopted on 10 November 1980, 27S/98, 112, para. 4.4.
[92] Panel Reports on complaint by Chile, L/6491, 36S/93, 125, para. 12.7; and on complaint by US, L/6513, 36S/135, 161, para. 5.7.

The 1988 Panel Report on "Japan - Restrictions on Imports of Certain Agricultural Products" examined import restrictions on twelve categories of products. The Panel found with respect to restrictions on prepared and preserved milk and cream that fresh milk for manufacturing use was not a "like product" in relation to products prepared from it, particularly evaporated milk, sweetened condensed milk, skimmed milk powder, whole milk powder, prepared whey, and whey powder;[93] imported processed cheese;[94] lactose;[95] and food preparations not elsewhere specified consisting mainly of dairy products (e.g. frozen yoghurt base, ice cream powder and prepared milk powder for infants).[96] The Panel found that imported dried leguminous vegetables were "like" the domestic product within the meaning of Article XI:2(c)[97] and that groundnuts produced in Japan and imported groundnuts were identical in all respects and were, therefore, like products.[98] With respect to the import restrictions on starch and inulin, the Panel observed that "the import restrictions were applied to all starches (except modified starch) and inulin and therefore considered that the Japanese 'like product' in this case would be all starches produced in Japan".[99] The Panel considered that "imported fruit purée and paste, fruit pulp and fruit juice were not 'like' Japanese produced fresh fruit in terms of Article XI:2(c)(i)";[100] that prepared and preserved pineapple was not "like" fresh pineapple in terms of Article XI:2(i)(c);[101] and fresh tomatoes and tomato juice, sauce and ketchup were not "like products".[102]

The 1989 Panel Report on "Canada - Import Restrictions on Ice Cream and Yoghurt" examined import restrictions maintained by Canada on imports of yoghurt, ice cream, ice milk and ice milk novelties, and the claim of Canada that these import restrictions were justified under Article XI:2(c). The Panel determined that

"... the domestic product subject to restrictions had to be the product produced by farmers. In this case the farmers were producing raw milk, not 'industrial' or 'fluid' milk. The Panel found that the relevant Canadian 'fresh' product subject to restriction was total raw milk.

"The Panel next considered whether ice cream and yoghurt were 'like' products to raw milk. In the drafting of this provision it had been stated that the words 'like products' in Article XI:2(c) '... definitely do not mean what they mean in other contexts - merely a competing product' (EPCT/C.II/PV.12). The Japanese Agriculture Panel had observed that Article XI:2(c)(i) and the note supplementary to it regarding 'in any form' established different requirements for (a) restrictions on the importation of products that are 'like' the product subject to domestic supply restrictions and (b) restrictions on the importation of products that are processed from a product that is 'like' the product subject to domestic supply restrictions. The Japanese Agriculture Panel had considered that this differentiation would be lost if a product in its original form and a product processed from the original one were to be considered to be 'like' products within the meaning of Article XI:2(c). This Panel concurred with that observation. It further noted that there was virtually no international trade in raw milk".[103]

In the 1991 Panel Report on "Thailand - Restrictions on Importation and Internal Taxes on Cigarettes" the Panel examined the claim of Thailand that its restrictions on the importation of cigarettes were necessary to enforce domestic marketing or production restrictions for leaf tobacco and cigarettes and that they were therefore justified under Article XI:2(c)(i). The Panel found that

"the reference to 'the fresh product' in this Note [*Ad* Article XI:2(c)] makes clear that the agricultural products subject to marketing or production restrictions must be fresh products. ... this interpretation was borne out by the drafting history, which suggested that the provision was intended to enable governments

---

[93] L/6253, adopted on 2 February 1988, 35S/163, 231, para. 5.3.1.4.
[94] *Ibid.*, 35S/232, para. 5.3.2.2.
[95] *Ibid.*, 35S/233, para. 5.3.3.
[96] *Ibid.*, 35S/233-234 para. 5.3.4.
[97] *Ibid.*, 35S/234, para. 5.3.5.1.
[98] *Ibid.*, 35S/236, para. 5.3.8.1.
[99] *Ibid.*, 35S/235, para. 5.3.6.1.
[100] *Ibid.*, 35S/238, para. 5.3.10.3.
[101] *Ibid.*, 35S/239, para. 5.3.11.
[102] *Ibid.*, 35S/240, para. 5.3.12.1.
[103] L/6568, adopted on 5 December 1989, 36S/68, 87, paras. 66-67; see also Panel Report on "Thailand - Restrictions on Importation and Internal Taxes in Cigarettes", 37S/200, 221, para. 69 (following the Ice Cream panel on this point).

to protect farmers and fishermen who, because of the perishability of their produce, often could not withhold excess supplies of fresh product from the market.

"The Panel found for these reasons that the only domestic marketing and production restrictions that would be relevant under Article XI:2 (c)(i) were those that Thailand claimed to have imposed on the production of leaf tobacco - not those on cigarettes - and that consequently this provision would cover import restrictions only on (a) products that were 'like' domestic leaf tobacco and (b) products processed from such "like" products that met the conditions of the Note ad Article XI:2(c). The Panel not[ed] that 'cigarettes were not 'like' leaf tobacco, but processed from leaf tobacco ...".[104]

(d) *"imported in any form": application of paragraph 2(c) to processed products*

The Interpretative Note to paragraph 2(c) states that "The term 'in any form' in this paragraph covers the same products when in an early stage of processing and still perishable, which compete directly with the fresh product and if freely imported would tend to make the restriction on the fresh product ineffective".

In discussions on this provision at the Geneva session of the Preparatory Committee, it was stated that the term "in any form" was meant to cover only "those earlier stages of processing which result in a perishable product" (e.g. kippers). The drafters stated that it was not the intention "... to extend the [import] control not merely to cured and smoked fish but to things like tinned fish and sardines. All that we have in view is an extension to those earlier stages of processing which result in a perishable product. You cannot keep a kipper indefinitely".[105] and "... what we have in mind here is the perishable kind of processed product, not the kind which is capable of being stocked".[106] While the word "perishable" was used in the Geneva Draft Charter and the General Agreement, at the Havana Conference this note (to Article 20 of the Charter) was redrafted to read:

"imported 'in any form' means the product in the form in which it is originally sold by its producer and such processed forms of the product as are so closely related to the original product as regards utilization that their unrestricted importation would make the restriction on the original product ineffective".[107]

This change was made because "... the term 'perishable' which is inapplicable to many types of agricultural products had unduly narrowed the scope of paragraph 2(c)".[108] The Sub-Committee on Quantitative Restrictions at Havana noted:

"The Sub-Committee, however, wishes to make clear that the omission of the phrase 'when in an early stage of processing and still perishable' is dictated solely by the need to permit greater flexibility in taking into account the differing circumstances that may relate to the trade in different types of agricultural products, having in view only the necessity of not making ineffective the restriction on the importation of the product in its original form and is in no way intended to widen the field within which quantitative restrictions under paragraph 2(c) may be applied. In particular, it should not be construed as permitting the use of quantitative restrictions as a method of protecting the industrial processing of agricultural or fisheries products".[109]

The 1978 Panel Report on "EEC - Programme of Minimum Import Prices, Licences and Surety Deposits for Certain Processed Fruits and Vegetables" examined the EEC's minimum import price and associated additional security system in relation to Article XI:2(c)(i) and (ii). "The Panel considered that tomato concentrate was perishable because after a certain time it would decline in quality and value. The Panel also considered that tomato concentrate could compete directly with fresh tomatoes insofar as a large number of end-uses were

---

[104]DS10/R, adopted on 7 November 1990, 37S/200, 222, paras 69-70.

[105]EPCT/A/PV/19, p. 43.

[106]EPCT/A/PV/19, p. 44; see citation to this passage in L/6253, Panel Report on "Japan - Restrictions on Imports of Certain Agricultural Products", adopted on 2 February 1988, 35S/163, 225, para. 5.1.3.4.

[107]See reference to this Note in L/6253, Panel Report on "Japan - Restrictions on Imports of Certain Agricultural Products", adopted on 2 February 1988, 36S/163, 225, para. 5.1.3.4.

[108]Havana Reports p. 93, para. 38.

[109]*Ibid.*, para. 39.

concerned. Therefore, the Panel concluded that tomato concentrate qualified as an 'agricultural or fisheries product, imported in any form' within the meaning of Article XI:2(c)".[110]

The 1988 Panel Report on "Japan - Restrictions on Imports of Certain Agricultural Products" refers to the passage from the Havana Reports cited directly above and notes that "this extension to cover also products which were not perishable was not incorporated into the General Agreement and the condition of perishability remains in force".[111] The Panel concluded that

"Article XI:2(c)(i) permits restrictions not only on fresh products but also on those processed agricultural and fishery products that are in the early stages of processing and still perishable which compete directly with the fresh product and, if freely imported, would render ineffective the restrictions on the fresh product. It concludes, on the basis of its findings presented above, that the import restrictions maintained by Japan on the following items do not meet all of these conditions and are thus not justified under Article XI:2(c)(i): prepared and preserved milk and cream (04.02), processed cheese (04.04 ex), starch and inulin (11.08), glucose, lactose and other sugars and syrups (17.02 ex), prepared or preserved pineapple (20.06 ex), certain fruit juice and tomato juice (20.07 ex), tomato ketchup and sauce (21.04), and certain food preparations, not elsewhere specified, consisting mainly of milk or of sugar (21.07 ex)".[112]

Some of these products were found to be "not perishable"[113] or "a stable product capable of being stocked";[114] some were found to be a "product not intended for further processing"[115] or "further processed from a processed product"[116] or "consumer-ready prepared foods as opposed to products which had undergone only initial processing".[117] With respect to restrictions on imported processed products when an input of that product is unrestricted, in the case of canned pineapple the Panel "noted that imports of fresh and frozen pineapple were not restricted, and substantial quantities of the latter were imported for processing into canned pineapple. The Panel considered that if imports of frozen pineapple for processing into canned pineapple were presumed not to render ineffective the domestic measures relating to production of fresh pineapples, the importation of the further processed canned pineapple could not have such an effect".[118] With respect to dairy import quotas in particular,

"The Panel ... examined whether [prepared and preserved milk and cream products] met the requirements of products 'in any form', that is, whether these milk products were in an early stage of processing and still perishable, which competed directly with fresh milk and if freely imported would render ineffective the restrictions on fresh milk, as required by the interpretative note to Article XI:2(c). It noted that fresh milk as such was rarely traded internationally because of its bulk and perishability, but rather it was processed into (among other things) the canned, powdered or otherwise prepared milk and cream products in question which rendered it capable of being transported and stocked. The Panel considered that the difficulties regarding transport into Japan of a perishable milk product were such that it was highly unlikely that imports of such a product would of themselves render ineffective the government restriction on the production of fresh milk, nor that restriction of its importation would be necessary to the enforcement of the government program. Thus, although the Panel considered that some of these products might meet some of the requirements of being products in an early stage of processing and still perishable which could compete directly with fresh milk for manufacturing use and whose free importation might render ineffective the

---

[110]L/4687, adopted on 18 October 1978, 25S/68, 100, para. 4.10.
[111]L/6253, adopted on 2 February 1988, 36S/163, 225, para. 5.1.3.4.
[112]Ibid., 35S/244, para. 6.6.
[113]Prepared and preserved milk and cream (35S/231-232, para. 5.3.1.4); lactose (35S/233, para. 5.3.3); fruit juices and those fruit products entering in a canned form (35S/238, para. 5.3.10.3); canned pineapple (35S/239, para. 5.3.11); "tomato juice in the canned form primarily imported into Japan" (35S/240, para. 5.3.12.2).
[114]Prepared and preserved milk and cream (e.g. evaporated milk, sweetened condensed milk, skimmed milk powder, whole milk powder, prepared whey, and whey powder) (35S/231-232, para. 5.3.1.4); processed cheese (35S/232, para. 5.3.2.2); lactose (35S/233, para. 5.3.3); starch (35S/236, para. 5.3.6.2); canned pineapple (35S/239, para. 5.3.11).
[115]Processed cheese (35S/232, para. 5.3.2.2); tomato juice, tomato paste and ketchup (35S/240, para. 5.3.12.2).
[116]Glucose and other sugars and food preparations, not elsewhere specified, consisting mainly of sugar (35S/236, para. 5.3.7).
[117]Food preparations not elsewhere specified consisting mainly of dairy products (35S/233-234, para. 5.3.4); tomato juice, tomato sauce and ketchup (35S/240, para. 5.3.12.3).
[118]Ibid., 35S/239, para. 5.3.11; see also similar findings with respect to processed cheese (35S/232, para. 5.3.2.2), fruit pulp, fruit purée and fruit juice (35S/238-239, para. 5.3.10.3) and tomato sauce and ketchup (35S/240, para. 5.3.12.3).

domestic measures on fresh milk, the Panel did not find that any of the products under consideration in tariff category 04.02 met all of the conditions of Article XI:2(c)(i), particularly that regarding perishability".[119]

In the 1989 Panel Report on "Canada - Import Restrictions on Ice Cream and Yoghurt" the Panel examined "whether ice cream and yoghurt were 'like' products 'in any form' to raw milk. It was recognized in Article XI:2(c)(i) that it might be necessary to restrict not only the fresh product, but also some of its processed forms. However, the scope of this exception from the general prohibition on quantitative restrictions was limited by the interpretative note Ad Article XI ... Thus, the exception could not be extended to all processed forms of the fresh product but only to those which met the specified criteria". Citing the Note to Article 20 as redrafted at Havana (see above at page 334), the Panel noted that

"It was this close relationship with regard to use that justified extension of the exception to some forms of processed products. While the interpretative note to the General Agreement focused more on defining the acceptable forms of the processed product, i.e. those that were in an early stage of processing and still perishable, the concept of a close relationship in terms of use was nonetheless retained in the requirements that the processed product compete directly with the fresh one to the extent that its free importation would render ineffective the restrictions on the fresh product. There was no evidence in either the drafting history nor the texts of the General Agreement itself that the exception was ever meant to apply to all, or even most, of the processed forms of any particular fresh product".[120]

The Panel found that

"The exception to Article XI:1 can be applied only to those processed products which meet all the conditions for 'like' products 'in any form' of the interpretative note Ad Article XI:2(c)(i): are in 'an early stage of processing', 'still perishable', 'compete directly' with the fresh product and if freely imported would 'make the restriction on the fresh product ineffective'. The Panel found that ice cream and yoghurt did not compete directly with raw milk, and that their free importation would not render ineffective the Canadian production measures for raw milk. The Panel did not find it necessary to make findings with regard to the criterion of early stage of processing or perishability".[121]

While the Panel did not make findings with respect to "early stage of processing" or "still perishable", the Report contains an extensive discussion of these issues in relation to modern production methods and rapid changes in technology since the General Agreement was drafted.[122] With respect to "directly competitive" and "would make the restrictions ineffective",

"... The Panel considered that the term 'compete directly with ...' imposed a more limiting requirement than merely 'compete with'. As stated in the US arguments, the concept of 'displacement' was apparently not intended by this provision. The essence of direct competition was that a buyer was basically indifferent if faced with the choice between one product or the other and viewed them as substitutable in terms of their use. Only limited competition existed between raw milk and ice cream and yoghurt. Their marketing was quite different, and as was implied in the Canadian arguments the competition which did exist was related to displacement of raw milk used in Canadian ice cream and yoghurt production. The Panel recalled that this provision was not designed to protect the processing industry. It further recalled its consideration concerning the narrow interpretation of exceptions (paragraph 59 above). The Panel did not consider it appropriate to broaden the scope of this requirement to include the concept of displacement or indirect competition. The Panel thus found that imports of ice cream and yoghurt did not compete directly with raw milk in terms of Article XI:2(c)(i). ...

"The Panel recognized that Canada's concern was with regard to potential import levels, rather than historic ones, and with the accumulated effects of imports of various dairy products and the consequential effects on its domestic milk program. Prior to the imposition of the quantitative restrictions, imports of ice

---

[119]Ibid., 35S/231-232, para. 5.3.1.4.
[120]L/6568, adopted on 5 December 1989, 36S/68, 87-88, paras. 68-69.
[121]Ibid., 36S/90, para. 76.
[122]Ibid., 36S/88-89, paras. 71, 72.

cream and yoghurt into Canada had been very small compared to Canadian production of these items, and these imports amounted to less than ten one-thousandths of one per cent of Canadian raw milk production. The factors cited by Canada could potentially lead to an increase in this import level; however, Canada had not provided evidence sufficient to convince the Panel that there existed an immediate threat of imports at such significantly increased levels as could render ineffective the Canadian dairy supply program. Article XI:2(c)(i) did not provide for the imposition of quantitative restrictions on imports at current levels merely on the basis of some hypothetical future situation. The Panel did not find that the evidence submitted by Canada justified the conclusion that unrestricted imports of ice cream and yoghurt would presently render ineffective the Canadian domestic restrictions on raw milk production".[123]

In the 1991 Panel Report on "Thailand - Restrictions on Importation and Internal Taxes in Cigarettes"

"... The Panel, noting that cigarettes were not 'like' leaf tobacco, but processed from leaf tobacco, examined whether cigarettes fell within the range of products covered by this Note [ad Article XI:2(c)]. It recognized that a central requirement of the Note was that the product processed from the fresh product was still 'in an early stage of processing'. It noted that a previous panel had found that agricultural products not normally intended for further processing such as ketchup could not be regarded as eligible for import restrictions under Article XI:2(c)(i).[124] Since cigarettes could not be described as 'leaf tobacco in an early stage of processing' because they had already undergone extensive processing and, moreover, were not intended for further processing, the Panel found that they were not among the products eligible for import restrictions under Article XI:2(c)(i)".[125]

(e)   "necessary"

The Report on the London session of the Preparatory Committee notes that it was suggested that restrictions imposed under the exception contained in paragraph 2(c) "should not be imposed on seasonal commodities at a time when similar domestic products were not available".[126]

The Report of the Review Session Working Party on "Quantitative Restrictions" notes that the Working Party considered and rejected a number of proposals for revision of Article XI, but agreed to insert in its report brief agreed statements which would clarify some of the points that the proposed amendments were meant to cover, including:

"... the maintenance or the application of a restriction which went beyond that which would be 'necessary' to achieve the objects defined in paragraph 2(b) or 2(c) of Article XI would be inconsistent with the provisions of that Article. This is made clear in the text by the use of the word 'necessary'. ... Moreover, if import restrictions of the type referred to in paragraph 2(c) were to be applied after the governmental measures referred to in that paragraph had ceased to be in force, those restrictions would no longer be necessary for the enforcement of those measures and would therefore be inconsistent with the provisions of that paragraph.

"It was also recognized that if restrictions of the type referred to in paragraph 2(c) were applied to imports during that part of the year in which domestic supplies of the product were not available, such restrictions would be regarded as consistent with the provisions of the Article only to the extent that they were necessary to enforce or to achieve the objectives of the governmental measures relating to control of the domestic product. Finally, it was recognized that it would be an abuse of intent of the provisions under paragraph 2(c)(i) of Article XI if contracting parties were to apply restrictions to processed products exceeding those 'necessary' to secure enforcement of the actual measure restricting production or marketing of the primary product".[127]

---

[123] 36S/89-90, paras. 73, 75.
[124] The footnote to this sentence refers to the Panel Report on "Japan - Restrictions on the Import of Certain Agricultural Products", adopted on 2 February 1988, 35S/163, para. 5.3.12.
[125] DS10/R, adopted on 7 November 1990, 37S/200, 222, para. 70.
[126] London Report, para.(e), p. 12.
[127] L/332/Rev.1 and Addenda, adopted on 2,4 and 5 March 1955, 3S/170, 189-190, paras. 67-68.

In the 1978 Panel Report on "EEC - Programme of Minimum Import Prices, Licences and Surety Deposits for Certain Processed Fruits and Vegetables"

> "The Panel ... noted that the minimum import price and additional security system for tomato concentrates was permanent, i.e. in operation year round. The Panel also noted that the intervention system for fresh tomatoes, while being permanently in force, only operated at certain times of year, i.e. when fresh tomatoes were being marketed in quantities in excess of commercial market requirements. The Panel found that the minimum import price and associated additional security system for tomato concentrates would be 'necessary to the enforcement of' the intervention system for fresh tomatoes essentially during those periods when fresh tomatoes were being bought-in by the intervention organizations, and only to the extent that the system satisfied the other conditions contained in Article XI:2(c)(i) and (ii)".[128]

The 1980 Panel Report on "EEC Restrictions on Imports of Appies from Chile" found that "although the EEC measures occurred outside the EEC domestic production season, imports could have affected the possibilities for the disposal or release of EEC apples out of intervention on to the EEC market at that time".[129]

The 1988 Panel Report on "Japan - Restrictions on Imports of Certain Agricultural Products" found as follows:

> "The Panel observes that import restrictions applied under Article XI:2(c)(i) cannot exceed those 'necessary' for the operation of the domestic governmental measure concerned. Such restrictions can thus not normally be justified if applied to imports during that time of year in which domestic supplies of the product are not available (paragraph 5.1.3.5 above). The Panel further considers that a restriction on imports of a processed product can in general not be considered as necessary if importation of more directly competitive forms of the product, i.e. the fresh product (when economically feasible) or earlier-stage products processed from the fresh product, are not also restricted. For these reasons and in light of its findings in paragraph 5.3.10 above, the Panel concludes that Japanese import restrictions on fruit purees and pastes (20.05 ex), prepared or preserved fruit pulp (20.06 ex), and certain fruit juices (20.07 ex) are not justified under Article XI:2(c)(i)".[130]

However, the Panel did find that import restrictions were "necessary" to secure enforcement of production restrictions for dried leguminous vegetables, as it "noted that the Japanese production restrictions were applied to all categories of dried leguminous vegetables and that the various dried legumes were substitutable in terms of the principal form of their consumption in Japan, namely sweetened bean paste".[131] The same finding was made for groundnuts:

> "The Panel ... noted that Japanese groundnuts and imported groundnuts were essentially identical and perfectly substitutable in terms of their use. It further observed that the marketing period for Japanese groundnuts was not limited to a few weeks or months, but was essentially the entire year. The Panel considered that the absence of restrictions on imports of processed groundnut products was not relevant to this consideration. The Panel found, therefore, that the restrictions maintained by Japan on imports of groundnuts could be reasonably considered as 'necessary' in terms of Article XI:2(c)".[132]

In the Panel Report on "Canada - Import Restrictions on Ice Cream and Yoghurt",

> "... When restrictions on processed products were involved, the Panel found it difficult to separate completely the criterion of 'necessary to the enforcement' from that regarding 'would render ineffective the restriction on the fresh product.' If unrestricted imports would render a government measure ineffective, it would be difficult not to conclude that some restriction of the imports was necessary. ...

---

[128] L/4687, adopted on 18 October 1978, 25S/68, 100, para. 4.11.
[129] L/5047, adopted on 10 November 1980, 27S/98, 112, para. 4.6.
[130] L/6253, adopted on 2 February 1988, 35S/163, 244, para. 6.7.
[131] *Ibid.*, 35S/235, para. 5.3.5.2.
[132] *Ibid.*, 35S/237, para. 5.3.8.2.

"The Panel recognized the merits of Canada's argument that for a product which is traded almost exclusively in its processed forms, such as milk, restrictions on the imports of the processed products might in some sense be 'necessary' to ensure that the restriction on the production of the raw material was not undermined. ... At this time, however, there was not sufficient evidence to believe that future imports of ice cream and yoghurt would achieve such levels as to significantly affect Canadian producers' ability to market raw milk. In the past, unrestricted imports had gained less than a half a percent share of the Canadian ice cream and yoghurt market, and accounted for less than ten one-thousandths of one per cent of total raw milk production. Against this background and in the absence of an imminent threat to the Canadian dairy system, the Panel found that the criterion of 'necessary' to the operation of the governmental restrictions could not be met".[133]

See also at page 334 *et seq.*

(f)   *"to the enforcement of governmental measures"*

The 1988 Panel Report on "Japan - Restrictions on Imports of Certain Agricultural Products" notes, in relation to the argument made that Japan's supply management measures were not "governmental measures" because they were non-legally-binding administrative guidance with which compliance was allegedly voluntary, that

"... in one respect the Panel took into account the special circumstances prevailing in Japan. This concerns the interpretation of the term 'the enforcement of governmental measures' in Article XI:2(c)(i) ... the text of this provision does not specify how the domestic production or marketing restrictions are to be imposed, except that they have to be governmental and the drafting history suggests that the drafters were primarily concerned with the effectiveness of the measures. Although the Panel had some difficulty during its initial proceedings in establishing the exact nature of the domestic restrictions, Japan fully cooperated in providing the necessary detailed information, from which it became clear that the measures did in fact emanate from the government. As regards the method used to enforce these measures the Panel found that the practice of 'administrative guidance' played an important role. Considering that this practice is a traditional tool of Japanese Government policy based on consensus and peer pressure, the Panel decided to base its judgements on the effectiveness of the measures in spite of the initial lack of transparency. In view of the special characteristics of Japanese society the Panel wishes, however, to stress that its approach in this particular case should not be interpreted as a precedent in other cases where societies are not adapted to this form of enforcing government policies".[134]

See also the excerpts from the Panel Report on "Japan - Trade in Semi-Conductors" at page 315ff.

The 1989 Panel Reports on "EEC Restrictions on Imports of Dessert Apples - Complaint by Chile" and "EEC Restrictions on Imports of Apples - Complaint by the United States" examined, *inter alia*, the issue of whether the EEC had "governmental" measures consistent with Article XI:2(c)(i). Each of the two Panel Reports provides as follows:

"... The Panel noted that the EEC did not claim that it restricted production of apples, but that it effectively restricted their marketing, through a system of market withdrawals carried out mainly by producer groups. The Panel also took note of the argument that these could not be considered 'governmental' measures in terms of Article XI:2(c) because of the voluntary basis of the organization and the non-obligatory method of their operation. The Panel recalled that the concept of 'governmental' measure had been previously examined on a number of occasions in respect of different articles of the General Agreement".[135]

These Panel Reports then refer to the Panel findings noted immediately above from the Reports on "Japan - Restrictions on Imports of Certain Agricultural Products" and "Japan - Trade in Semi-Conductors", and to a 1960

---

[133] L/6568, adopted on 5 December 1989, 36S/68, 91-92, paras. 80-81.
[134] L/6253, adopted on 2 February 1988, 35S/163, 242, para. 5.4.1.4; cited in Panel Report on "Japan - Trade in Semi-Conductors", L/6309, 35S/116, 154, para. 107.
[135] L/6491 and L/6513, both adopted on 22 June 1989, 36S/93 and 36S/135, at 36S/126 and 36S/161-162, paras. 12.8 and 5.8.

Panel which, examining the question of whether subsidies financed by a non-governmental levy were notifiable under Article XVI, expressed the view that "... the question ... depends upon the source of the funds and the extent of government action, if any, in their collection".[136]

"The Panel examined the EEC measures in the light of these decisions by the CONTRACTING PARTIES. It noted that the EEC internal régime for apples was a hybrid one, which combined elements of public and private responsibility. Legally there were two possible systems, direct buying-in of apples by Member State authorities and withdrawals by producer groups. Under the system of withdrawals by producer groups, which was the EEC's preferred option, the operational involvement of public authorities was indirect. However, the régime as a whole was established by Community regulations which set out its structure. Its operation depended on Community decisions fixing prices, and on public financing; apples withdrawn were disposed of in ways prescribed by regulation. The Panel therefore found that both the buying-in and withdrawal systems established for apples under EEC Regulation 1035/72 (as amended) could be considered to be governmental measures for the purposes of Article XI:2(c)(i)."[137]

(5) Paragraph 2(c)(i)

(a) "restrict the quantities ... permitted to be marketed or produced"

The report of a sub-committee which considered these provisions during the Geneva session of the Preparatory Committee in 1947 notes that the sub-committee was "unable to accept a proposal that governmental measures operating to regulate prices should be included under sub-paragraph (c)(i)".[138] Two proposals to include governmental measures to stabilize prices were also rejected.[139]

The report of Sub-Committee B of the Third Committee, on Quantitative Restrictions, at the Havana Conference, which considered the Charter provision corresponding to Article XI, notes as follows:

"The Sub-Committee agreed that in interpreting the term 'restrict' for the purposes of paragraph 2(c), the essential point was that the measures of domestic restriction must effectively keep output below the level which it would have attained in the absence of restrictions".[140]

"... the Sub-Committee agreed that it was not the case that subsidies were necessarily inconsistent with restrictions of production and that in some cases they might be necessary features of a governmental programme for restricting production. It was recognized, on the other hand, that there might be cases in which restrictions on domestic production were not effectively enforced and that this, particularly in conjunction with the application of subsidies, might lead to misuse of the provisions of paragraph 2(c). The Sub-Committee agreed that members whose interests were seriously prejudiced by the operation of a domestic subsidy should normally have recourse to the procedure of Article 25 [corresponding to Article XVI] and that this procedure would be open to any member which considered that restrictions on domestic agricultural production applied for the purposes of paragraph 2(c) were being rendered ineffective by the operation of a domestic subsidy. The essential point was that the restrictions on domestic production should be effectively enforced and the Sub-Committee recognized that unless this condition were fulfilled, restrictions on imports would not be warranted".[141]

To meet this point, and also to ensure that paragraph 2(c) should apply only when there was a surplus of production the word "effectively" was inserted after "operate" in the Charter. However, this change was not taken into the General Agreement.[142]

---

[136]L/1160, Report of the Panel on "Review pursuant to Article XVI:5", adopted on 24 May 1960, BISD 9S/188, 192, para. 12.
[137]L/6491 and L/6513, both adopted on 22 June 1989, 36S/93 and 36S/135, at 36S/126-127 and 36S/162, paras. 12.9 and 5.9.
[138]EPCT/141, p. 3.
[139]Proposals at EPCT/W/75, EPCT/W/199, summarized in EPCT/W/223; discussion at EPCT/A/PV/19 p. 14-33.
[140]Havana Reports, p. 89, para. 17.
[141]Havana Reports, p. 90, para. 22.
[142]Havana Reports, p. 90, para. 23.

In 1975 a Working Party on "Canadian Import Quotas on Eggs" was set up to make an advisory ruling on certain questions in connection with Canada's imposition of import quotas for eggs and egg products in connection with its supply management program for eggs. While the US did not agree that the system was effectively able to control production, the other members of the Working Party "agreed with the Canadian view that the operation of the Canadian supply management programme for eggs, as described and explained to the Working Party, was in conformity with the requirements of Article XI:2(c)(i)".[143]

The 1978 Panel on "EEC - Programme of Minimum Import Prices, Licences and Surety Deposits for Certain Processed Fruits and Vegetables" found with respect to the EEC intervention system for fresh tomatoes (under Council Regulation 1035/72) that:

"the Panel considered that there was no effective Community or governmental enforcement of the withdrawals of fresh tomatoes by the producers' organizations; these organizations were merely encouraged to make such withdrawals. The Panel further considered that there was no requirement that tomato producers must create, join or market their production through such producers' organizations. In the case where member States were obligated to buy in tomatoes which had been offered to them, the Panel considered that the provision allowing member States to claim an exemption from this obligation was so liberal that it would constitute a lack of effective enforcement of the intent of this Article of the Regulation. The Panel further considered that, in addition, in light of the fact that the buying-in or withdrawal prices were fixed at about one half of the normal cost of production, the intervention system would not effectively restrict the marketing or production of fresh tomatoes, but simply remove any market surplus after all potential commercial markets, including processing into tomato concentrate, had been saturated. The Panel further considered that, since this system was not considered to be an effective restriction on the marketing and production of fresh tomatoes, then it could not be considered to be an effective restriction on the marketing or production of tomato concentrate. Therefore, the Panel concluded that even if fresh tomatoes were considered to be the 'like domestic product', the intervention system for fresh tomatoes did not qualify as a governmental measure which operated 'to restrict the quantities of the like domestic product permitted to be marketed or produced', or 'to remove a temporary surplus of the like domestic product by making the surplus available to certain groups of domestic consumers free of charge or at prices below the current market level', within the meaning of Article XI:2(c)(i) and (ii)".[144]

The 1980 Panel Report on "EEC Restrictions on Imports of Apples from Chile" found with regard to the EEC domestic supply controls on apples that "As regards XI:2(c)(i), the Panel considered that the EEC grubbing-up programmes in 1969 and 1976 seemed to be isolated actions of production control rather than steps in a continuing long-term policy of the Community to restrict production. The Panel noted that the programmes had not resulted in any significant drop in EEC apple production. The Panel considered that the EEC did restrict quantities of apples permitted to be marketed, through its system of intervention purchases by member States and compensation to producer groups for withdrawing apples from the market".[145]

The 1988 Panel Report on "Japan - Restrictions on Imports of Certain Agricultural Products" found generally, in relation to this issue:

"'To restrict' means, according to the drafters, to 'keep output below the level which [would have been] allowed in the absence of restrictions'. The drafters rejected the proposal that *regulation* of production, through price stabilization programmes, also be an accepted criterion (EPCT/PV/19). They agreed that subsidies were *not* 'necessarily inconsistent with restrictions on production and that in some cases they might be necessary features of a governmental programme for restricting production' (Havana Reports, p. 90). According to the note to Article XI the proportion between imports and domestic production is to be determined by taking into account 'special factors' that may have affected or may be affecting the trade in the product concerned. The note specifically excludes from the definition of the term 'special factors' changes 'artificially brought about by means not permitted under the [General] Agreement,' but not changes artificially brought by legal means such as production subsidies or tariff protection granted within the bounds

---

[143] L/4279, adopted on 17 February 1976, 23S/91, 92, para. 4.
[144] L/4687, adopted on 18 October 1978, 25S/68, 102-103, para. 4.13.
[145] L/5047, adopted on 10 November 1980, 27S/98, 112, paras. 4.5-4.6.

of Article II. It is thus clear that the production restrictions applied under Article XI:2(c)(i) may in principle coexist with production subsidies. This means that it is not necessary to restrict the level of production below the level that would exist in the absence of all government support. It also means that production which exists only because of production subsidies may be effectively restricted by imposing quantitative limits on the availability of subsidies. Other than requiring a government measure, Article XI:2(c)(i) does not specify how the production restriction is to be imposed".[146]

The Panel found specifically with respect to the restrictions on groundnuts that:

"The Panel considered that restrictions on planted area could not be considered the equivalent of restrictions on production or marketing unless they demonstrably had that effect. ... In this regard, the Panel noted that there was no penalty or charge imposed on Japanese producers who exceeded their target cultivation area, but rather they could lose eligibility to receive a benefit in the form of a subsidy or loan. The Panel considered that, as indicated by the drafting history of Article XI:2(c)(i), the important factor was not the methods used in restricting production but their effectiveness. The Panel further found that there were many factors, including the long-standing application of import restrictions, the provision of subsidies or loans for production, the changing pattern of agricultural production, and varieties, cultivation methods and improved yields, which affected historic and current output in often contradictory ways, rendering it virtually impossible to objectively determine what the level of production would have been in the absence of restrictions. The Panel considered, therefore, the actual pattern of quantities produced. It found that production exhibited a long-term trend of decline, and on an in-shell basis, had further declined since the reinforcement of the governmental measures in 1984. The Panel found, therefore, that the Japanese measures in the past had in practice been effective in restricting the quantity of groundnuts produced or marketed. On this basis the Panel considered that it could reasonably be assumed that the current production measures were capable of effectively limiting production".[147]

The 1989 Panel Report on "Canada - Import Restrictions on Ice Cream and Yoghurt" found with respect to Canadian domestic milk marketing programmes that:

"The Panel recalled that the requirement was for the effective *restriction* of production, not merely its *regulation*. A major element of the requirement of restricted production was that the measure, regardless of how operated, had to reduce production below the level it would otherwise have attained. The Panel observed that this concept was difficult to apply in practice. In situations such as the Canadian one, where the government measures had been in place for many years and were interrelated with price support and other production incentives, it was virtually impossible to determine what production levels would be in their absence. This determination would be necessary in order to have an objective basis for comparison with current production levels. In light of its findings in paragraphs 73 to 76 above, the Panel did not consider it necessary to further examine this issue. The Panel, therefore, did not make a finding with regard to whether the Canadian dairy management scheme constituted a government measure which effectively restricted total raw milk production in Canada".[148]

The 1989 Panel Reports on "EEC Restrictions on Imports of Dessert Apples - Complaint by Chile" and "EEC Restrictions on Imports of Apples - Complaint by the United States" examined, *inter alia*, the issue of whether the EEC measures (based on Council Regulation 1035/72) "operated to restrict the quantities of [EEC apples] permitted to be marketed". Each of the Panel Reports notes the 1978 and 1980 Panel findings cited above with respect to the same intervention system for certain horticultural crops, and further notes "While taking careful note of the earlier panel reports, the Panel did not consider they relieved it of the responsibility, under its terms of reference, to carry out its own thorough examination on this important point".[149]

---

[146]L/6253, adopted on 2 February 1988, 35S/163, 223-224, para. 5.1.3.3.

[147]*Ibid.*, 35S/236-137, para. 5.3.8.1.; see also similar findings with respect to restrictions on dried leguminous vegetables, *ibid.*, 35S/234-235, para. 5.3.5.1.

[148]L/6568, adopted on 5 December 1989, 36S/68, 91, para. 79.

[149]L/6491 and L/6513, both adopted on 22 June 1989, 36S/93 and 36S/135, at 36S/127 and 36S/162, paras. 12.10 and 5.10.

"The Panel's scrutiny of the EEC market intervention scheme for apples led it to distinguish a number of features particularly relevant to the application of Article XI:2(c)(i). The system's operation and targets were essentially price-related; it was activated or suspended according to market price movements in relation to target prices fixed by the EEC. This was true of both direct intervention (buying-in) by member states and the decentralized withdrawal of apples from the dessert apple market by producers' organizations which could take place at a slightly higher price level than the former. The system thus operated to provide a price floor to EEC producers. In certain years it had resulted in the withdrawal of substantial quantities of apples from the consumer market for dessert apples; but there was no quantitative target or limit defined by the EEC either for these withdrawals or for the overall quantity marketed. The overall quantity withdrawn in any year was a residual amount, resulting from the interplay of market forces instead of being determined by the EEC authorities. Likewise there was no quantitative restriction on supply by producers - i.e., the quantity they could offer for sale. The EEC régime, in assuring producers a minimum price but prescribing no ceiling on the quantity eligible for this guarantee, could in fact act as an incentive for producers operating at the margin of profitability and thereby increase the total amount of apples offered for sale. As noted in paragraph 12.8 above, marketing restrictions under Article XI:2(c)(i) may be implemented and enforced in various ways; but the Panel considered that the above features of the EEC system raised the more basic issue of whether it constituted a marketing restriction within the meaning of Article XI:2(c)(i) at all.

"The Panel considered it necessary to examine a basic interpretative issue involved in this GATT requirement - i.e., did Article XI:2(c)(i) cover only schemes which set quantitative limits on the amount producers could offer for sale, or did it also cover schemes which could result in a reduction of products reaching the consumer through withdrawals activated by reference to a floor price without quantitative targets? ...

"The Panel noted that Article XI:2(c)(i) referred to governmental measures which 'operated to restrict the quantities' of the domestic products 'permitted to be marketed or produced'. Given the ordinary meanings of 'to permit' (to authorize or allow) and 'to market' (to expose for sale in a market or to sell) the *wording* of the provision suggested in the view of the Panel that the governmental measures must include an effective limitation on the quantity that domestic producers are authorized or allowed to sell. Measures which simply prevented consumers from buying products below certain prices would not appear to be covered by this wording. ...

"As to the *context* in which the provision appears, the Panel noted that the final paragraph of Article XI:2 stipulated that imports may be restricted under Article XI:2(c)(i) only in proportion to domestic *production*, whether the government has chosen to restrict the quantities permitted to be *marketed* or those permitted to be *produced*. It is thus clear that in the case of marketing restrictions, also, imports may only be reduced to the extent that production declines. ... a scheme which imposes no limitations on what producers may sell cannot, by itself, bring about a restriction of production. It therefore follows from the context of the provision that such a scheme would not be covered by Article XI:2(c)(i). The Panel also noted that, unlike Article XI:2(c)(i), Article XI:2(c)(ii), which concerned the removal of a temporary surplus, did not stipulate any restriction on domestic output in order to justify import restrictions. A withdrawal programme not capable of limiting production could possibly come under Article XI:2(c)(ii), provided that the specific requirements of the provision were met. The difference between the two sub-paragraphs was a further contextual indication that Article XI:2(c)(i) could not be interpreted as widely as argued by the EEC.

"Concerning the *purpose* of Article XI:2(c)(i), the Panel recalled that the title of Article XI was 'General Elimination of Quantitative Restrictions'. Article XI:2(c)(i) made an exception to this general rule ... The Panel noted that Article XI:2(c)(i) - unlike all provisions of the General Agreement specifically permitting actions to protect domestic producers [e.g. Articles XVIII:A and C, XIX and XXVIII] - did not provide either for compensation to be granted by the contracting party invoking it, or for compensatory withdrawals by contracting parties adversely affected by the invocation. This reflected the fact that Article XI:2(c)(i) was not intended to be a provision permitting protective actions. If Article XI:2(c)(i) could be used to justify import restrictions which were not the counterpart of any governmental measure capable of limiting production, the value of the General Agreement as a legal frame-work for the exchange of tariff concessions in the agricultural field would be seriously impaired."[150]

"In the light of the considerations set out above, the Panel found that the EEC measures taken under the intervention system for apples did not constitute marketing restrictions of a type which could justify import restrictions under Article XI:2(c)(i)."[151]

In this connection see also the unadopted 1993 panel report on "EEC - Member States' Import Régimes for Bananas".[152]

(b) *"of the like domestic product"*

See at page 331 *et seq.*

(6) **Paragraph 2(c)(ii)**

The 1989 Panel Reports on "EEC - Restrictions on Imports of Dessert Apples - Complaint by Chile" and "EEC - Restrictions on Imports of Apples - Complaint by the United States" also "noted that, unlike Article XI:2(c)(i), Article XI:2(c)(ii), which concerned the removal of a temporary surplus, did not stipulate any restriction on domestic output in order to justify import restrictions. A withdrawal programme not capable of limiting production could possibly come under Article XI:2(c)(ii), provided that the specific requirements of the provision were met".[153]

(a) *"temporary surplus"*

At the Havana Conference, the Sub-Committee on Quantitative Restrictions "agreed that the provisions of paragraph 2(c)(ii) would cover arrangements under which the government concerned made temporary surpluses of grain available as animal feeding stuffs to small holders and similar categories with a low standard of living, free of charge or at prices below the current market level".[154] The Review Working Party on Quantitative Restrictions also agreed that this case was clearly covered by the terms of that provision.[155]

The 1980 Panel Report on "EEC Restrictions on Imports of Apples from Chile" found with respect to a claim by the EEC that the restrictions were justified under Article XI:2(c)(ii):

"As regards XI:2(c)(ii), the Panel found that the EEC was 'making the surplus available to certain groups of domestic consumer free of charge or at prices below the current market level', in so far as the apples withdrawn from the market during 1978/79 went into animal feed as well as were distributed freely to social organizations. The panel thought that the EEC surplus of apples could not be considered 'temporary' as it appeared year after year. However, the Panel noted that the surplus in 1979 was significantly higher than normal and could be considered to be a temporary surplus above the recurring surplus".[156]

The 1989 Panels on the complaints by Chile and the United States on "EEC - Restrictions on Imports of Dessert Apples" also examined the restrictions in question in relation to Article XI:2(c)(ii).

"... The Panel ... took note of the views of the 1980 Panel on this point, noting that that Panel's finding of a 'temporary surplus above the recurring surplus' related only to the situation in 1979. Article XI:2(c)(ii) clearly required the Panel to consider whether the EEC's surplus at the time the import restrictions were

---

[150]*Ibid.*, at 36S/127-129 and 36S/163-165, paras. 12.11-12.15 and 5.11-5.15.
[151]*Ibid.*, 36S/129 and 36S/165, paras. 12.17 and 5.17.
[152]DS32/R, dated 3 June 1993, paras. 331-335.
[153]L/6491 and L/6513, both adopted on 22 June 1989, 36S/93 and 36S/135, at 36S/128 and 36S/164, paras. 12.14 and 5.14.
[154]Havana Reports, p. 93, para. 34.
[155]L/332/Rev.1 and Addenda, adopted on 2,4 and 5 March 1955, 3S/170, 191, para. 73.
[156]L/5047, adopted on 10 November 1980, 27S/98, 114, para. 4.10.

imposed, i.e. April 1988, had been demonstrated to be temporary. The Panel considered that the only practicable way to reach a finding on this point was to compare the EEC's apple surplus in 1988 with that in the previous years. From the statistics available to it ... it observed that while amounts withdrawn had varied in the years up to and including the 1987-88 marketing year, stocks had remained relatively stable at levels which indicated a substantial structural surplus. The Panel thus found that the 1988 surplus could not be considered a temporary one, and that therefore the EEC did not meet the conditions for imposing import restrictions under Article XI:2(c)(ii). In the light of this finding the Panel did not consider it necessary to examine whether the EEC measures were in conformity with the other requirements of this provision."[157]

(7) Paragraph 2(c)(iii)

(a) · *"the production of which is directly dependent, wholly or mainly"*

The Report of the Sub-Committee on Quantitative Restrictions at the Havana Conference provides that

"... It was agreed that under the existing text, in a case for example in which a Member wished to restrict the quantities permitted to be produced of any animal product the production of which was dependent wholly or mainly on two or more imported kinds of feeding stuffs considered together but not necessarily on either kind considered separately, it would be open to that Member to restrict the production of animal products, provided that domestic production of imported kinds of feeding-stuffs were relatively negligible, by treating the imported kinds of feeding-stuffs as a single commodity and applying import restrictions thereto.

"It was further agreed that if the various imported feeding-stuffs were in fact treated as a single commodity, import restrictions thereon should be applied globally on the total combined imports without allocating shares to the individual feeding-stuffs. It was felt that, in cases where this procedure would not be practicable, the import restrictions should take the form of an equal proportionate reduction in the amount permitted to be imported of each of the several feeding-stuffs".[158]

5. Last sub-paragraph of paragraph 2

(1) "Public notice", miscellaneous or "basket" import quotas and quota administration through discretionary licensing

The Report of the Review Working Party on "Quantitative Restrictions" notes the following agreed interpretations:

"The requirement that any contracting party applying restrictions pursuant to paragraph 2(c) should give public notice of the quantities or values to be imported should be construed as requiring that contracting party to send a copy of that notice to the CONTRACTING PARTIES ... which would circulate this information to all contracting parties concerned.

"The Working Party recommends that, whenever practicable, a contracting party intending to introduce restrictions pursuant to paragraph 2(c) of Article XI should give advance notice, on a confidential basis, to interested contracting parties and to the CONTRACTING PARTIES ... to give them an opportunity for consultation".[159]

Various contracting parties have notified trade measures they consider to be in conformity with Article XI:2(c).[160]

In the 1980 Panel Report on "EEC Restrictions on Imports of Apples from Chile", examining the criteria in the last paragraph of Article XI:2, "The Panel noted that the EEC had not given public notice of the quantities

---

[157]L/6491, adopted on 22 June 1989, 36S/93, 129-130, para. 12.19; L/6513, adopted on 22 June 1989, 36S/135, 165, para. 5.19.
[158]Havana Reports, p. 92, paras. 32-33.
[159]L/332/Rev.1 and Addenda, adopted on 2,4 and 5 March 1955, 3S/170, 190, paras. 70-71.
[160]See, e.g., L/3455, L/4187, L/4868.

or values to be imported under the voluntary restraint agreements it had negotiated ... as required by the first sentence of this paragraph".[161]

The 1988 Panel Report on "Japan - Restrictions on Imports of Certain Agricultural Products" found that "import restrictions made effective through a miscellaneous 'basket' quota for which only a global value or quantity was announced could not satisfy the requirements of Article XI:2(c)"[162], and concluded:

> "The Panel recalls that under the last sub-paragraph of Article XI:2(c) a contracting party applying an import restriction must give public notice of the total quantity or value of each product permitted to be imported during a specified future period. This requirement implies that under Article XI:2(c) only those quotas can be applied which define the particular quantity or value for each product subject to quota. The Panel finds that the Miscellaneous Import Quota maintained by Japan precludes the identification of the quantity or value of permitted imports of each product included therein. The Panel therefore concludes that those import restrictions maintained by Japan through the Miscellaneous Import Quota on prepared whey powder (04.02 ex), starch and inulin for special use (11.08 ex), certain prepared and preserved bovine meat products (16.02 ex), lactose, glucose and other sugars and sugar syrups (17.02 ex), certain fruit purees and pastes (20.05 ex), certain fruit juices (20.07 ex), and food preparations not elsewhere specified mainly consisting of dairy or sugar (21.07 ex), are not justified under the provisions of Article XI:2(c)".[163]

The 1989 Panel Report on "Canada - Import Restrictions on Ice Cream and Yoghurt" noted, in connection with a permit system for imports of these products, that the Panel "did observe ... that restrictions applied through discretionary licensing could not meet the requirement in Article XI:2(c) of prior public notice of the quantity or value permitted to be imported".[164]

(2) "during a previous representative period"

In the 1980 Panel Report on "EEC Restrictions on Imports of Apples from Chile"

> "... the Panel looked at total imports into the EEC from Southern Hemisphere suppliers, including Chile, as these were the main EEC suppliers during the marketing season concerned when restraints were in effect. The Panel looked at the proportion of these imports to EEC production 'prevailing during a previous representative period' as provided in the third sentence of the last paragraph of XI:2. In keeping with normal GATT practice, the Panel considered it appropriate to use as a 'representative period' a three-year period previous to 1979, the year in which the EEC measures were in effect. Due to the existence of restrictions in 1976, the Panel held that that year could not be considered as representative, and that the year immediately preceding 1976 should be used instead. The Panel thus chose the years 1975, 1977 and 1978 as a 'representative period'".[165]

See also the discussion of "previous representative period" under Article XIII.

(3) Proportionality requirement

In the 1980 Panel Report on "EEC Restrictions on Imports of Apples from Chile"

> "The Panel noted ... that measures taken under XI:2(c)(i) must also meet the criteria expressed in the last paragraph of XI:2. ... The Panel considered that the evidence before it suggested that the EEC measures did not fulfil the conditions of the second sentence of this paragraph ... The Panel found that the EEC had not maintained this proportion [between 'the total of imports' and 'the total of domestic production']".[166]

---

[161] L/5047, adopted on 10 November 1980, 27S/98, 112-113, para. 4.7.
[162] L/6253, adopted on 2 February 1988, 35S/163, 231, para. 5.3.1.3.
[163] *Ibid.*, 35S/245, para. 6.8; see also 35S/226, para. 5.1.3.6.
[164] L/6568, adopted on 5 December 1989, 36S/68, 93, para. 83.
[165] L/5047, adopted on 10 November 1980, 27S/98, 113, para. 4.8.
[166] L/5047, adopted on 10 November 1980, 27S/98, 113, para. 4.7.

The 1988 Panel Report on "Japan - Restrictions on Imports of Certain Agricultural Products" provides as follows:

> "The Panel noted that in the case before it the import restrictions maintained by Japan had been in place for decades and there was, therefore, no previous period free of restrictions in which the shares of imports and domestic supplies could reasonably be assumed to resemble those which would prevail today. The Panel further noted that the CONTRACTING PARTIES recognized in a previous case that a contracting party invoking an exception to the General Agreement had the burden of demonstrating that the requirements of the exception were fulfilled.[167] The Panel realized that a strict application of this burden of proof rule had the consequence that Article XI:2(c)(i) could in practice not be invoked in cases in which restrictions had been maintained for such a long time that the proportion between imports and domestic supplies that would prevail in the absence of restrictions could no longer be determined on the basis of a previous representative period. The Panel, therefore, examined whether it would be possible to change the burden of proof in such a way that the provision could be resorted to also in such a situation. The Panel noted that one among the possible ways of achieving this aim would be to consider a demonstration that the size of the quota is equivalent to a certain percentage of the quantities marketed or produced in the importing country as a sufficient proof that the proportionality requirement had been met. The Panel however also noted that the practical consequence of such a change in the burden of proof would be to turn the requirement of Article XI:2(c)(i) to fix the size of the import quotas in relation to the reduction in the quantities marketed or produced into a requirement to determine the size of the quota in relation to the quantities actually marketed or produced. The Panel found that the above or any other change in the burden of proof to make Article XI:2(c)(i) operational in the case of long-term import and/or supply restrictions would have consequences equivalent to those of an amendment of this provision and could therefore seriously affect the balance of tariff concessions negotiated among contracting parties. The Panel noted in this context that Article XI:2 - unlike some other provisions of the General Agreement permitting restrictive trade measures, such as Articles XVIII:C, XXVIII or XIX - does not provide for compensation for contracting parties adversely affected by the measures taken under it. The Panel considered for these reasons that the burden of providing the evidence that all the requirements of Article XI:2(c)(i), including the proportionality requirement, had been met must remain fully with the contracting party invoking that provision".[168]

In this connection see also the unadopted 1993 panel report on "EEC - Member States' Import Régimes for Bananas".[169]

(4) "special factors"

See the Interpretative Note to the last sub-paragraph of paragraph 2. See also the discussion of "special factors" under Article XIII:4.

In discussions at the Geneva session of the Preparatory Committee, it was stated that "the term 'special factors' would include real changes in relative productive efficiency as between domestic producers and foreign producers, or as between different foreign producers: in a word, real changes in the competitive situation and not changes artificially introduced or encouraged by government action of a kind which other sections of the Charter would not allow".[170] The Report of the Sub-Committee on Quantitative Restrictions at Havana notes that "... the Sub-Committee agreed that it was desirable to make it clear that changes in relative productive efficiency between the home producers and foreign producers should be taken into consideration in determining the size of import quotas under paragraph 2(c)(i). ... The Sub-Committee, after consideration of the interpretative notes on 'special factors' to Articles 20 and 22 of the Geneva text, agreed that, as stated in those notes, changes artificially brought about since the representative period (assuming that period to have preceded the coming into force of the Charter) were not to be regarded as 'special factors' for the purposes of paragraph 2(c) and Article 22 [corresponding to

---

[167]A footnote to this sentence refers to the Report of the Panel on "Canada - Administration of the Foreign Investment Review Act", 30S/140.
[168]L/6253, adopted on 2 February 1988, 35S/163, 226-227, para. 5.1.3.7.
[169]DS32/R, dated 3 June 1993, paras. 336-339.
[170]EPCT/A/PV/19, p. 45.

Articles XI:2(c) and XIII]".[171] The same Report also notes that "It was ... agreed that in the case of perishable commodities, due regard should be had for the special problems affecting the trade in these commodities".[172]

In the Panel Report on "Japan - Restrictions on Imports of Certain Agricultural Products", the Panel stated that "the last sentence of Article XI:2 prescribes the minimum size of the import quotas that contracting parties may establish in accordance with sub-paragraph (c)(i) of that provision. The quotas must be such as not to reduce the total of imports relative to domestic production as compared with the proportion which might reasonably be expected to rule between the two in the absence of restrictions. In order to determine the size of the import quota the contracting party thus has to estimate what the amount of domestic production and of imports would be during the quota period in the absence of supply and quantitative import restrictions. The General Agreement states that in making this determination contracting parties shall pay 'due regard' to the proportions that prevailed during a previous representative period and to 'special factors' that affected or may be affecting the trade in the product concerned".[173] See also the reference to "special factors" in the excerpt from this panel report at page 341 above.

B. RELATIONSHIP BETWEEN ARTICLE XI AND OTHER GATT ARTICLES

1. Article III

See under Article III.

2. Article VI

During the Geneva discussions of the Preparatory Committee, "The suggestion was made that it should be permissible to use import restrictions, under proper safeguards, as an anti-dumping measure in those cases of intermittent dumping in which import duties did not provide a suitable instrument of control. After consideration it was generally agreed that as far as the establishment of new industries is concerned, the position should be sufficiently covered by the provisions of Chapter IV [Article XVIII]. In respect of the threat of intermittent dumping to established industries, there was wide agreement with the view that the position was probably already adequately covered under Article 34 [XIX]".[174] See also the chapter on Article VI.

3. Article XXIII

See under Article XXIII.

4. Article XXIV:12

See under Article XXIV.

C. RELATIONSHIP BETWEEN ARTICLE XI AND OTHER INTERNATIONAL AGREEMENTS

1. General

The Report of the Havana Conference Sub-Committee on Quantitative Restrictions notes: "... the Sub-Committee agreed to have it recorded that in its view the freedom given to a Member to apply restrictions under paragraph 2(c) did not free such Member from a prior obligation to any individual Member".[175]

---

[171]Havana Reports, p. 94, paras. 42-43.
[172]Havana Reports, p. 91, para. 28.
[173]L/6253, adopted on 2 February 1988, 35S/163, 226, para. 5.1.3.7.
[174]London Report, para.(j), p. 12.
[175]Havana Reports, p. 95, para. 45.

2. Arrangement Regarding International Trade in Textiles

The Arrangement Regarding International Trade in Textiles ("Multi-Fibre Arrangement", or MFA) of 20 December 1973,[176] as extended by various Protocols allows for various quantitative restrictions among participating countries but states in paragraph 6 of Article 1: "The provisions of this Arrangement shall not affect the rights and obligations of the participating countries under the GATT".

3. Agreement on Import Licensing Procedures

See the discussion above on "import and export licences", the discussion under Article XIII:3 on "administration of import licensing", and the material on this Agreement at the end of the chapter on Article XIII.

4. Agreement on Trade in Civil Aircraft

Article 5 of the Agreement on Trade in Civil Aircraft of 12 April 1979 reads:

"5.1   Signatories shall not apply quantitative restrictions (import quotas) or import licensing requirements to restrict imports of civil aircraft in a manner inconsistent with applicable provisions of the GATT. This does not preclude import monitoring or licensing systems consistent with the GATT.

"5.2   Signatories shall not apply quantitative restrictions or export licensing or other similar requirements to restrict, for commercial or competitive reasons, exports of civil aircraft to other Signatories in a manner inconsistent with applicable provisions of the GATT".[177]

D. EXCEPTIONS AND DEROGATIONS

See Article XI:2 above; also Articles XII, XVIII, XIX, XX and XXI.

1. Reservations in accession protocols

Paragraph 4 of the Protocol for the Accession of Switzerland[178] provides that "Switzerland reserves its position with regard to the application of the provisions of Article XI of the General Agreement" to the extent necessary to permit it to apply import restrictions pursuant to certain internal legislation. However, this reservation is qualified by the requirements that Switzerland, so far as is consistent with the implementation of these laws, observe to the fullest possible extent the appropriate provisions of the General Agreement, and endeavour to ensure that they are applied in such a manner as to cause minimum harm to the interests of contracting parties. Annual reports and a triennial review are required; also, paragraph 6 of the Protocol provides that "Switzerland shall enter into consultations pursuant to Articles XXII and XXIII of the General Agreement upon request of any contracting party regarding the reservations mentioned in paragraphs 4 and 5 above". When the text of the Protocol was submitted to the CONTRACTING PARTIES for approval, the Chairman stated that this reservation could be considered analogous to a waiver granted under Article XXV, paragraph 5, "in that such waivers normally contain a clause to the effect that the decision does not preclude the right of affected countries to have recourse to all the provisions of Article XXIII".[179]

The Protocol of Accession of Costa Rica provides that "As indicated in paragraph 50 of document L/6589, Costa Rica will continue to gradually eliminate current import licensing restrictions, and quantitative restrictions, and will complete their elimination four years after the day of Costa Rica's accession to the General Agreement. ... If this is not accomplished, the issue will be reviewed by the CONTRACTING PARTIES".[180]

---

[176] 21S/3.
[177] 26S/162, 165.
[178] 14S/6, 8.
[179] SR.23/7.
[180] L/6626, 37S/7-8, para. 4.

2. Waivers under Article XXV:5

The few waivers which have been granted to Article XI are listed in the table of waivers at the end of the chapter on Article XXV.

E. WORK CARRIED OUT IN THE GATT ON QUANTITATIVE RESTRICTIONS MAINTAINED FOR OTHER THAN BALANCE-OF-PAYMENTS REASONS

1. Import restrictions

The text of Article XII:4(b) in the 30 October 1947 text of the General Agreement required that a review of all restrictions under Article XII be conducted not later than 1 January 1951. This review was carried out in connection with the second review of discriminatory application of import restrictions under Article XIV:1(g), and documents the widespread use of balance-of-payments restrictions at that time.[181] When the balance-of-payments Articles were revised in the Review Session of 1954-55, the revised Article XII:4(b) and Article XVIII:12(b) each called for another review of such restrictions. This review was completed by the CONTRACTING PARTIES in 1958-59.[182]

As for restrictions for other than balance-of-payments purposes, a Report was adopted at the Fourth Session on "The Use of Quantitative Restrictions for Protective and Other Commercial Purposes"; see the material on this Report above at page 324. At the Fifth Session in 1950, it was agreed as a follow-up to this Report to gather information on import and export restrictions maintained as exceptions to Article XI:1, other than those applied for balance-of-payments purposes.[183] A Note was later circulated which summarized the information received.[184]

During the first fifteen years of the GATT, work on progressive liberalization of quantitative import restrictions in Europe was being carried out in the Organization for European Economic Co-operation (OEEC).[185]

In 1955, at the Review Session, the Review Working Party on Quantitative Restrictions considered problems raised by certain contracting parties in eliminating balance-of-payments import restrictions. The Working Party drafted a waiver decision, temporarily waiving Article XI for the "hard core" restrictions (many of them on agricultural products) which these contracting parties considered to be difficult to eliminate immediately. Application of this "hard-core" waiver decision was extended successively until 31 December 1962, and then expired.[186]

In the period following the Review Session, work on quantitative restrictions continued in two directions: one focusing on non-tariff barriers of all types to agricultural trade, and one focusing on other quantitative restrictions, particularly those affecting developing country exports. Under the Programme for Expansion of International Trade initiated in 1958, agricultural policies including subsidies and quantitative restrictions were discussed in Committee II, and barriers to trade in products of interest to developing countries (including quantitative restrictions) were discussed in Committee III.

In 1960, procedures were approved for dealing with residual import restrictions; contracting parties were invited to notify lists of import restrictions which they were applying contrary to the provisions of the General Agreement, and to notify changes to those lists. The procedures provided for bilateral consultations upon request under Article XXII:1, and if necessary, resort either to Article XXII:2 or Article XXIII:2.[187] In 1962, a Panel appointed by the CONTRACTING PARTIES examined the adequacy of these notifications and put forward certain

---

[181] See GATT/CP.6/12/Rev.2 and GATT/CP.6/48, published as *Use of Quantitative Import Restrictions to Safeguard Balances of Payments* (Sales No. GATT/1951-2, out of print).

[182] The results of the review appear in MGT(59)75 of 30 July 1959. See also material under Article XII:4(b) in this Index.

[183] GATT/CP.5/SR.4, GATT/CP.5/SR.25, GATT/CP.5/3, GATT/CP.5/39/Rev.1, GATT/CP/93 (Note inviting notifications).

[184] GATT/CP/93/Add.1, dated 20 October 1951.

[185] See reference in Report of Review Working Party on "Quantitative Restrictions", L/332/Rev.1 and Addenda, adopted on 2, 4 and 5 March 1955, 3S/170, 178-179, paras. 31-33.

[186] *Ibid.*, 3S/191-195, paras. 75-91; Decision of 3 March 1955 on "Problems Raised for Contracting Parties in Eliminating Import Restrictions Maintained During a Period of Balance-of-Payments Difficulties", 3S/38, extended at 7S/33, 8S/27, 9S/35, 10S/35.

[187] Procedures approved 16 November 1960, 9S/18-20.

suggestions on the type of information that should be included in notifications.[188] In 1965 it was suggested to newly-independent countries that, even if they were not yet in a position to determine whether they wished to invoke the provisions of Article XVIII as justification for some or all restrictions in force, they might submit descriptive material relative to their entire import control systems, without prejudice to the consistency of the measures maintained with their GATT obligations.[189] A number of notifications under this procedure were made.

A meeting of the CONTRACTING PARTIES at Ministerial level held in May 1963, which also launched the Kennedy Round of multilateral trade negotiations, adopted an Action Programme and Ministerial Conclusions on the expansion of trade of developing countries. Point (ii) of the Action Programme provided that "Quantitative restrictions on imports from less-developed countries which are inconsistent with the provisions of the GATT shall be eliminated within a period of one year. Where, on consultation between the industrialized and the less-developed countries concerned, it is established that there are special problems which prevent action being taken within this period, the restrictions on such items would be progressively reduced and eliminated by 31 December 1965".[190] Notifications of residual restrictions had been examined in Committee III.[191] This examination was continued in the Action Committee and in the Committee on Trade and Development, and in the Group on Residual Restrictions of the Committee on Trade and Development.[192]

In January 1970 the Council established a Joint Working Group on Import Restrictions (JWG), which submitted a report in March 1971 including a systematic collection of data on quantitative restrictions in eighteen developed countries.[193] In 1971 the Council decided that the data assembled by the JWG should be kept up to date and that the contracting parties concerned should be invited to notify annually by 30 September any changes which should be made concerning the restrictions listed in the consolidated document.[194] This decision was reaffirmed by the Council in March 1980.[195] Accordingly, the consolidated table on import restrictions prepared by the JWG was revised annually until 1982 on the basis of notifications from countries applying restrictions.[196] However, not all contracting parties concerned submitted notifications.

During the Tokyo Round of 1973-79, further discussions took place in the Committee on Industrial Products, the Committee on Trade and Development, and the NTM Subgroup on Quantitative Restrictions.[197] The Agreement on Import Licensing Procedures was negotiated as a result of this process. Negotiations were also conducted on an request-offer basis concerning quantitative restrictions[198] and "non-tariff measures not dealt with multilaterally".[199] Negotiations also took place separately on non-tariff barriers of all types in agricultural trade.

Since 1979, some work on quantitative restrictions has taken place in the context of the Committee on Trade and Development's work on trade liberalization in areas of special interest to developing countries which led to the updating of the data on restrictions applied by developed countries to products of export interest to developing

---

[188] 11S/206, 210.

[189] 14S/161.

[190] Ministerial Conclusions adopted on 21 May 1963, 12S/36-37, para. I.1(ii).

[191] See Report of Committee III, L/1989, 12S/88, 95-97, and Secretariat compilation of restrictions, AC/SC.1/3, 12 November 1963.

[192] See Secretariat notes from 1965-1969 in COM.TD/16, COM.TD/19, COM.TD/W/19, COM.TD/W/43, COM.TD/W/60, COM.TD/W/64, COM.TD/W/68, COM.TD/W/76, COM.TD/W/93, COM.TD/W/95. See also the annual reports of the Committee.

[193] L/3391/Rev.1.

[194] C/M/70.

[195] C/M/139; see C/111, Proposal by the Director-General on "Notification and Surveillance - Procedures for the Review of Developments in the Trading System", adopted on 26 March 1980, 27S/20.

[196] L/5265. The last revised data of the JWG were contained in document L/5415 and Corrigenda.

[197] See documents listed in TA/INF/1/Rev.8, p. 38-44.

[198] See Secretariat Notes on "Technical arrangements for bilateral or plurilateral consultations or discussions on quantitative restrictions" (MTN/NTM/W/13); "Consultations or discussions on QRs: Status report and proposed procedure for reports" (MTN/NTM/W/21) and further status reports in MTN/NTM/W/54; "Information regarding import restrictions" (MTN/NTM/W/30, MTN/NTM/W/77, MTN/NTM/W/131, MTN/NTM/W/199); "Feasibility study of establishment of a list of QRs" (MTN/NTM/W/112) and various other papers in the MTN/NTM/W/ series.

[199] See Secretariat Note on "Negotiations on Non-tariff Measures Not Dealt with Multilaterally", MTN/NTM/W/4; "Notification of Non-tariff Measures Not Dealt with Multilaterally", MTN/NTM/W/82+Adds.; notes on procedures for such negotiations at NTM/W/45, MTN/NTM/W/137; and other papers in the MTN/NTM/W series.

countries.[200] Also, the GATT Committee on Trade in Agriculture established in 1982 drew up documentation on non-tariff measures, including quantitative restrictions, for agricultural products.[201]

A Group on Quantitative Restrictions and Other Non-Tariff Measures was established under the 1982 Ministerial work programme to review existing quantitative restrictions and other non-tariff measures, the grounds on which these were maintained and their conformity with the General Agreement, so as to achieve the elimination of quantitative restrictions which were not in conformity with the General Agreement or their being brought into conformity with the General Agreement, and also to achieve progress in liberalizing other quantitative restrictions and non-tariff measures, adequate attention being given to measures affecting products of export interest to developing countries.[202] It was agreed that:

> "The Group's establishment and any work carried out by it, including the presentation, examination and discussion of quantitative restrictions and other non-tariff measures, were without prejudice to the rights and obligations of contracting parties under the GATT and to any action already taken by the CONTRACTING PARTIES".[203]

The Group drew up an information base comprised of notifications made by contracting parties of the quantitative restrictions which they themselves apply, including information on grounds and GATT justifications.[204] It also kept up to date the Inventory of Non-Tariff Measures (Industrial Products), which contains notifications by contracting parties affected by the measures.[205] Procedures for up-dating the Inventory had been adopted in 1980.[206]

Since 1986, a Technical Group on Quantitative Restrictions and Other Non-Tariff Measures has taken over the task of updating and analysis of the documentation in accordance with the timetable and procedures agreed by the CONTRACTING PARTIES in 1984 and 1985.[207] These procedures provide for contracting parties to notify details of changes in the quantitative restrictions that they maintain as and when these changes occur and to make a complete notification of their quantitative restrictions once every two years; they also specify the content of the notifications, which are to include an indication of the grounds and GATT justification for the measures maintained.[208] The most recent compilation of quantitative restrictions was issued in 1989 and has been periodically updated.[209] Information on quantitative restrictions and non-tariff measures is also included in the Integrated Data Base established by a Council Decision of November 1987.[210]

2. Export restrictions

During 1978-79, the Tokyo Round "Framework" Group drafted an "Understanding regarding export restrictions and charges", which provides:

> "The participants in the Multilateral Trade Negotiations have examined the various existing provisions of the General Agreement relating to export restrictions and charges. The Annex contains a statement of these provisions.

---

[200]COM.TD/W/338/Rev.1.
[201]AG/FOR/- and AG/FOR/REV/- series.
[202]29S/17.
[203]L/5713, adopted on 30 November 1984, 31S/211, 212, para. 4; see also NTM/2.
[204]NTM/W/6/- series.
[205]NTM/INV/I-V and Addenda.
[206]C/110, Proposal by Director-General on "Documentation on Non-Tariff Measures", adopted on 26 March 1980, 27S/18.
[207]L/6200, Action taken on 24-26 November 1986, 33S/54.
[208]L/5713, Report (1984) of the Group on Quantitative Restrictions and Other Non-Tariff Measures, adopted on 30 November 1984, 31S/211, 221-223 and 227-228, paras. 44 and 65; L/5888, Report (1985) of the Group on Quantitative Restrictions and Other Non-Tariff Measures, adopted on 28 November 1985, 32S/91, 92-94, paras. 5-11.
[209]NTM/W/6/Rev.5 dated 31 January 1989, Secretariat compilation of "Quantitative Restrictions" including table by CCCN or HS classification, and Addenda 1-7 (to September 1993).
[210]Decision on "Integrated Data Base" of 10 November 1987, L/6290, 34S/66; see also material on the IDB in the chapter on Article II, and the April 1994 User Reference Manual for the IDB, IDB/URM/1.

"In the light of the examination referred to, participants agree upon the need to reassess in the near future the GATT provisions relating to export restrictions and charges, in the context of the international trade system as a whole, taking into account the development, financial and trade needs of the developing countries. They request the CONTRACTING PARTIES to address themselves to this task as one of the priority issues to be taken up after the Multilateral Trade Negotiations are ended".

This Understanding was adopted by the Trade Negotiations Committee at the end of the Tokyo Round[211] and was submitted to the CONTRACTING PARTIES at their Thirty-fifth Session held in November 1979.[212]

See also a 1974 Technical Note by the Secretariat on "GATT and Export Restrictions"[213] discussing legal mechanisms for negotiation in this area; a Secretariat Note of 1980 on "Export Restrictions and Charges", which also lists known export prohibitions, embargoes and licensing-based restrictions[214]; and a 1989 Background Note by the Secretariat on "Export Restrictions and Charges"[215] providing information on export restrictions and charges, their nature, purpose and coverage, relevant GATT provisions and past GATT work.

III. PREPARATORY WORK AND SUBSEQUENT MODIFICATIONS

Corresponding provisions in the Havana Charter are contained in Article 20; in the US Proposals in Chapter III C-1; in the US Draft in Article 19; in the London & New York Drafts in Article 25; and in the Geneva Draft in Article 20.

Differences from the Havana Charter: Article 20:2(b) of the Charter included a reference to the revision of internationally agreed standards. The drafters of the General Agreement decided not to include it in the General Agreement; it was stated that it would be "unwise to envisage the CONTRACTING PARTIES as being in a position to examine marketing standards and agree on regulations", and that this would be appropriate for the ITO, which would have a staff of experts.[216] Article 20 also included additional safeguards for exporting countries (prior notice and consultation) in the case of invocation of Article 20:2(c); these were inserted at Havana and were not taken into the General Agreement.[217] The Sub-Committee at Havana also inserted an interpretative note to Article 20:2(a) to respond to Greek concerns relating to olive oil production, which permitted export restrictions necessary to maintain domestic stocks to avoid critical shortages, in the case of products which are basic to the diet in the exporting country and are subject to alternate annual shortages and surpluses.[218] This too was not taken into the General Agreement.

The wording of the Interpretative Note to paragraph 2(c) in the General Agreement is different from that in the corresponding Interpretative Note to paragraph 2(c) of Article 20 of the Charter. The wording of the Interpretative Note to the last sub-paragraph of paragraph 2 in the General Agreement is different from that in the corresponding Interpretative Note 3(d) of Article 20 of the Charter: "The words 'or as between different foreign producers' had been deleted from this footnote (in the Charter) because they were pertinent only to the footnote on 'special factors' in Article 22 [XIII]".[219]

The inclusion in the General Agreement of Articles XI-XIV was accepted by certain delegations without the insertion of the Charter Articles 4 and 6 relating to the removal of maladjustments within the balance-of-payments and safeguards for members subject to external inflationary or deflationary pressure, on the understanding that if a situation of the sort envisaged in the chapter relating to employment and economic activity should arise, the provisions on nullification and impairment could be invoked.[220]

---

[211]MTN/FR/6, pp. 5/1-5/10; adopted by TNC at MTN/28 and Corr.1.
[212]L/4884 and Add.1.
[213]MTN/3B/9, dated 1 May 1974.
[214]CG.18/W/43 dated 10 October 1980.
[215]MTN.GNG/NG2/W/40, dated 8 August 1989.
[216]EPCT/TAC/PV/27, p. 18.
[217]Havana Reports, pp. 90-91, paras. 24-28.
[218]Havana Reports p. 88, para. 12.
[219]E/CONF.2/C.3/SR.37, p. 7.
[220]EPCT/TAC/SR.13, pp. 4-5.

Article XI has been amended only once. In the Review Session it was agreed to move the former paragraph 3 of Article XI into an interpretative note and to add a reference in that note to Article XVIII (which had been revised into its present form at the Review Session).[221] A number of other amendments were considered and rejected in the Review Session Working Party on Quantitative Restrictions; see the documents listed below.

IV. RELEVANT DOCUMENTS

London

Discussion:	EPCT/C.II/27, 36, 45; EPCT/C.II/QR/PV/1, 4, 5 (part 3); EPCT/C.II/PV/4, 5, 13
Reports:	EPCT/C.II/36, 43, 59; EPCT/30

New York

Discussion:	EPCT/C.6/17, 20, 21, 27, 64, 106
Reports:	EPCT/C.6/14, 97/Rev.1
Other:	EPCT/C.6/W/5, 16, 17, 29, 43 and Corr.1, 70, 72

Geneva

Discussion:	EPCT/EC/PV.2/22 EPCT/A/SR.19, 21, 22, 23, 26, 30 (p. 6), 40(1); EPCT/A/PV/19, 22 and Corr. 1-5, 23 and Corr. 1-2, 41 EPCT/TAC/SR.11, 13 EPCT/TAC/PV/27, 28
Reports:	EPCT/135, 189, 196, 212, 214/Add.1/Rev.1
Other:	EPCT/141, 162, 163, 164, EPCT/W/64, 75, 196, 199, 208, 217, 218, 223, 272, 280, 301, 313, 318

Havana

Discussion:	E/CONF.2/C.3/SR.10, 12, 14, 16, 18, 19, 37, 41
Reports:	E/CONF.2/19, 23 E/CONF.2/C.3/54, 66
Other:	E/CONF.2/C.3/E/W.3, 11, 16, 18

Review Session

Reports:	Spec/74/55, W.9/230 and Add. 1, L/332/Rev.1 and Adds., 3S/170
Discussion:	SR.9/25, 26, 44
Other:	L/261/Add.1, 273, 282 W.9/24, 66, 88, 89, 116, 126-128, 160, 202 Sec/146/54, 157/54, 161/54 Spec/62/55, 76/55, 95/55 and Rev.1-2, 105/55, 151/55, 167/55, 170/55

---

[221]Protocol Amending the Preamble and Parts II and III of the General Agreement, as rectified by Procès-Verbal of Rectification concerning (*inter alia*) this Protocol; both entered into effect 7 October 1957.

ARTICLE XII

RESTRICTIONS TO SAFEGUARD THE BALANCE OF PAYMENTS

I. TEXT OF ARTICLE XII, RELEVANT INTERPRETATIVE NOTES AND UNDERSTANDING ON THE BALANCE-OF-PAYMENTS PROVISIONS OF GATT 1994 356

II. INTERPRETATION AND APPLICATION OF ARTICLE XII 361
    A. SCOPE AND APPLICATION OF ARTICLE XII 361
        1. General 361
        2. Paragraph 1 361
            (1) "any contracting party": member States of the EEC 361
            (2) "in order to safeguard its external financial position and its balance of payments" 362
            (3) "may restrict the quantity or value of merchandise permitted to be imported": Quantitative and other trade measures for balance-of-payments purposes, including import surcharges and import deposit schemes 362
                (a) Treatment of import surcharges prior to 1979 363
                (b) Treatment of import deposit schemes prior to 1979 364
                (c) Practice since 1979 366
        3. Paragraph 2 367
            (1) "Import restrictions ... shall not exceed those necessary 367
            (2) "a serious decline in its monetary reserves" 367
            (3) "special factors which may be affecting the reserves of such contracting party or its need for reserves" 367
            (4) Disinvocation of Article XII 368
        4. Paragraph 3 368
            (1) Paragraph 3(a): adjustment 368
            (2) Paragraph 3(b): "to give priority to the importation of those products which are more essential" 369
            (3) Paragraph 3(c): application of restrictions under Article XII 369
                (a) Conditions applicable to balance-of-payments measures 369
                (b) "to avoid unnecessary damage to the commercial or economic interests of any other contracting party" 371
                (c) "description of goods 371
                (d) "minimum commercial quantities" 371
            (4) Paragraph 3(d): causes of balance-of-payments problems and their relationship with full employment . 371
                (a) Relationship to paragraph 3(a) 371
                (b) "a contracting party may experience a high level of demand for imports" 372
                (c) "shall not be required to withdraw or modify restrictions" 372
        5. Paragraph 4 372
            (1) Paragraph 4(a): obligation to consult 372
                (a) "alternative corrective measures which may be available" 373
            (2) Paragraph 4(b): Review of restrictions applied under Article XII 373
            (3) Paragraph 4(c) 373
            (4) Paragraph 4(d) 374
                (a) "Consultations" 374
                (b) "prima facie case" 374
            (5) Paragraph 4(e): "due regard to ... external factors" 374
        6. Paragraph 5: "persistent and widespread application of import restrictions ... indicating the existence of a general disequilibrium" 375
    B. RELATIONSHIP BETWEEN ARTICLE XII AND OTHER ARTICLES 376
        1. Articles I and XIII 376
        2. Article XVIII 377
        3. Article XXIII 378
        4. Article XXIV 378
    C. BALANCE-OF-PAYMENTS CONSULTATIONS IN THE GATT 378
        1. Committee on Balance-of-Payments Restrictions 378
        2. Procedures for examination of balance-of-payments measures 379
            (1) General 379
            (2) Scope of consultations 379
            (3) Procedures 379
        3. Notification of balance-of-payments measures 380
        4. Consultations 382
            (1) Timing of balance-of-payments consultations 382
            (2) Simplified consultations under Article XVIII:B 383
            (3) Documentation used in consultations 385

		(4)	Secrecy	387
		(5)	Matters discussed in consultations	388
			(a) External trade factors relating to the balance of payments	389
			(b) External factors: general macroeconomic climate and external debt	389
			(c) Prior consultations on external factors	390
	5.	**Conclusions and recommendations of the Committee**		391
	6.	**Discussion and adoption by the GATT Council of reports by the Committee**		392
III.	**PREPARATORY WORK AND SUBSEQUENT MODIFICATIONS**			392
IV.	**RELEVANT DOCUMENTS**			393
V.	**TABLES**			395
	A.	COUNTRIES CURRENTLY INVOKING ARTICLE XII OR XVIII:B: BALANCE-OF-PAYMENTS CONSULTATIONS CONDUCTED SINCE 1979 DECLARATION		396
	B.	CONTRACTING PARTIES WHICH HAVE DISINVOKED ARTICLE XII OR XVIII:B SINCE 1979		396

I. TEXT OF ARTICLE XII, RELEVANT INTERPRETATIVE NOTES AND UNDERSTANDING ON THE BALANCE-OF-PAYMENTS PROVISIONS OF GATT 1994

Article XII*

Restrictions to Safeguard the Balance of Payments

1. Notwithstanding the provisions of paragraph 1 of Article XI, any contracting party, in order to safeguard its external financial position and its balance of payments, may restrict the quantity or value of merchandise permitted to be imported, subject to the provisions of the following paragraphs of this Article.

2. (*a*) Import restrictions instituted, maintained or intensified by a contracting party under this Article shall not exceed those necessary:

(i) to forestall the imminent threat of, or to stop, a serious decline in its monetary reserves, or

(ii) in the case of a contracting party with very low monetary reserves, to achieve a reasonable rate of increase in its reserves.

Due regard shall be paid in either case to any special factors which may be affecting the reserves of such contracting party or its need for reserves, including, where special external credits or other resources are available to it, the need to provide for the appropriate use of such credits or resources.

(*b*) Contracting parties applying restrictions under sub-paragraph (*a*) of this paragraph shall progressively relax them as such conditions improve, maintaining them only to the extent that the conditions specified in that sub-paragraph still justify their application. They shall eliminate the restrictions when conditions would no longer justify their institution or maintenance under that sub-paragraph.

3. (*a*) Contracting parties undertake, in carrying out their domestic policies, to pay due regard to the need for maintaining or restoring equilibrium in their balance of payments on a sound and lasting basis and to the desirability of avoiding an uneconomic employment of productive resources. They recognize that, in order to achieve these ends, it is desirable so far as possible to adopt measures which expand rather than contract international trade.

(*b*) Contracting parties applying restrictions under this Article may determine the incidence of the restrictions on imports of different products or classes of products in such a way as to give priority to the importation of those products which are more essential.

(*c*) Contracting parties applying restrictions under this Article undertake:

(i) to avoid unnecessary damage to the commercial or economic interests of any other contracting party;*

(ii) not to apply restrictions so as to prevent unreasonably the importation of any description of goods in minimum commercial quantities the exclusion of which would impair regular channels of trade; and

(iii) not to apply restrictions which would prevent the importation of commercial samples or prevent compliance with patent, trade mark, copyright, or similar procedures.

(d) The contracting parties recognize that, as a result of domestic policies directed towards the achievement and maintenance of full and productive employment or towards the development of economic resources, a contracting party may experience a high level of demand for imports involving a threat to its monetary reserves of the sort referred to in paragraph 2 (a) of this Article. Accordingly, a contracting party otherwise complying with the provisions of this Article shall not be required to withdraw or modify restrictions on the ground that a change in those policies would render unnecessary restrictions which it is applying under this Article.

4. (a) Any contracting party applying new restrictions or raising the general level of its existing restrictions by a substantial intensification of the measures applied under this Article shall immediately after instituting or intensifying such restrictions (or, in circumstances in which prior consultation is practicable, before doing so) consult with the CONTRACTING PARTIES as to the nature of its balance of payments difficulties, alternative corrective measures which may be available, and the possible effect of the restrictions on the economies of other contracting parties.

(b) On a date to be determined by them,* the CONTRACTING PARTIES shall review all restrictions still applied under this Article on that date. Beginning one year after that date, contracting parties applying import restrictions under this Article shall enter into consultations of the type provided for in sub-paragraph (a) of this paragraph with the CONTRACTING PARTIES annually.

(c) (i) If, in the course of consultations with a contracting party under sub-paragraph (a) or (b) above, the CONTRACTING PARTIES find that the restrictions are not consistent with provisions of this Article or with those of Article XIII (subject to the provisions of Article XIV), they shall indicate the nature of the inconsistency and may advise that the restrictions be suitably modified.

(ii) If, however, as a result of the consultations, the CONTRACTING PARTIES determine that the restrictions are being applied in a manner involving an inconsistency of a serious nature with the provisions of this Article or with those of Article XIII (subject to the provisions of Article XIV) and that damage to the trade of any contracting party is caused or threatened thereby, they shall so inform the contracting party applying the restrictions and shall make appropriate recommendations for securing conformity with such provisions within the specified period of time. If such contracting party does not comply with these recommendations within the specified period, the CONTRACTING PARTIES may release any contracting party the trade of which is adversely affected by the restrictions from such obligations under this Agreement towards the contracting party applying the restrictions as they determine to be appropriate in the circumstances.

(d) The CONTRACTING PARTIES shall invite any contracting party which is applying restrictions under this Article to enter into consultations with them at the request of any contracting party which can establish a *prima facie* case that the restrictions are inconsistent with the provisions of this Article or with those of Article XIII (subject to the provisions of Article XIV) and that its trade is adversely affected thereby. However, no such invitation shall be issued unless the CONTRACTING PARTIES have ascertained that direct discussions between the contracting parties concerned have not been successful. If, as a result of the consultations with the CONTRACTING PARTIES, no agreement is reached and they determine that the restrictions are being applied inconsistently with such provisions, and that damage to the trade of the contracting party initiating the procedure is caused or threatened thereby, they shall recommend the withdrawal or modification of the restrictions. If the restrictions are not withdrawn or modified within such time as the CONTRACTING PARTIES may prescribe, they may release the contracting party initiating the procedure from such obligations under this Agreement towards the contracting party applying the restrictions as they determine to be appropriate in the circumstances.

(*e*)   In proceeding under this paragraph, the CONTRACTING PARTIES shall have due regard to any special external factors adversely affecting the export trade of the contracting party applying the restrictions.*

(*f*)   Determinations under this paragraph shall be rendered expeditiously and, if possible, within sixty days of the initiation of the consultations.

5.   If there is a persistent and widespread application of import restrictions under this Article, indicating the existence of a general disequilibrium which is restricting international trade, the CONTRACTING PARTIES shall initiate discussions to consider whether other measures might be taken, either by those contracting parties the balances of payments of which are under pressure or by those the balances of payments of which are tending to be exceptionally favourable, or by any appropriate intergovernmental organization, to remove the underlying causes of the disequilibrium. On the invitation of the CONTRACTING PARTIES, contracting parties shall participate in such discussions.

Interpretative Notes from Annex I

Ad Article XII

The CONTRACTING PARTIES shall make provision for the utmost secrecy in the conduct of any consultation under the provisions of this Article.

Paragraph 3 (c)(*i*)

Contracting parties applying restrictions shall endeavour to avoid causing serious prejudice to exports of a commodity on which the economy of a contracting party is largely dependent.

Paragraph 4 (b)

It is agreed that the date shall be within ninety days after the entry into force of the amendments of this Article effected by the Protocol Amending the Preamble and Parts II and III of this Agreement. However, should the CONTRACTING PARTIES find that conditions were not suitable for the application of the provisions of this sub-paragraph at the time envisaged, they may determine a later date; *Provided* that such date is not more than thirty days after such time as the obligations of Article VIII, Sections 2, 3 and 4, of the Articles of Agreement of the International Monetary Fund become applicable to contracting parties, members of the Fund, the combined foreign trade of which constitutes at least fifty per centum of the aggregate foreign trade of all contracting parties.

Paragraph 4 (e)

It is agreed that paragraph 4 (*e*) does not add any new criteria for the imposition or maintenance of quantitative restrictions for balance of payments reasons. It is solely intended to ensure that all external factors such as changes in the terms of trade, quantitative restrictions, excessive tariffs and subsidies, which may be contributing to the balance of payments difficulties of the contracting party applying restrictions, will be fully taken into account.

Ad Articles XI, XII, XIII, XIV and XVIII

Throughout Articles XI, XII, XIII, XIV and XVIII, the terms "import restrictions" or "export restrictions" include restrictions made effective through state-trading operations.

ARTICLE XII - RESTRICTIONS TO SAFEGUARD THE BALANCE OF PAYMENTS

UNDERSTANDING ON THE BALANCE-OF-PAYMENTS PROVISIONS OF THE GENERAL AGREEMENT ON TARIFFS AND TRADE 1994

Members,

Recognizing the provisions of Articles XII and XVIII:B of GATT 1994 and of the Declaration on Trade Measures Taken for Balance-of-Payments Purposes adopted on 28 November 1979 (BISD 26S/205-209, referred to in this Understanding as the "1979 Declaration") and in order to clarify such provisions[1];

Hereby *agree* as follows:

Application of Measures

1. Members confirm their commitment to announce publicly, as soon as possible, time-schedules for the removal of restrictive import measures taken for balance-of-payments purposes. It is understood that such time-schedules may be modified as appropriate to take into account changes in the balance-of-payments situation. Whenever a time-schedule is not publicly announced by a Member, that Member shall provide justification as to the reasons therefor.

2. Members confirm their commitment to give preference to those measures which have the least disruptive effect on trade. Such measures (referred to in this Understanding as "price-based measures") shall be understood to include import surcharges, import deposit requirements or other equivalent trade measures with an impact on the price of imported goods. It is understood that, notwithstanding the provisions of Article II, price-based measures taken for balance-of-payments purposes may be applied by a Member in excess of the duties inscribed in the Schedule of that Member. Furthermore, that Member shall indicate the amount by which the price-based measure exceeds the bound duty clearly and separately under the notification procedures of this Understanding.

3. Members shall seek to avoid the imposition of new quantitative restrictions for balance-of-payments purposes unless, because of a critical balance-of-payments situation, price-based measures cannot arrest a sharp deterioration in the external payments position. In those cases in which a Member applies quantitative restrictions, it shall provide justification as to the reasons why price-based measures are not an adequate instrument to deal with the balance-of-payments situation. A Member maintaining quantitative restrictions shall indicate in successive consultations the progress made in significantly reducing the incidence and restrictive effect of such measures. It is understood that not more than one type of restrictive import measure taken for balance-of-payments purposes may be applied on the same product.

4. Members confirm that restrictive import measures taken for balance-of-payments purposes may only be applied to control the general level of imports and may not exceed what is necessary to address the balance-of-payments situation. In order to minimize any incidental protective effects, a Member shall administer restrictions in a transparent manner. The authorities of the importing Member shall provide adequate justification as to the criteria used to determine which products are subject to restriction. As provided in paragraph 3 of Article XII and paragraph 10 of Article XVIII, Members may, in the case of certain essential products, exclude or limit the application of surcharges applied across the board or other measures applied for balance-of-payments purposes. The term "essential products" shall be understood to mean products which meet basic consumption needs or which contribute to the Member's effort to improve its balance-of-payments situation, such as capital goods or inputs needed for production. In the administration of quantitative restrictions, a Member shall use discretionary licensing only when unavoidable and shall phase it out progressively. Appropriate justification shall be provided as to the criteria used to determine allowable import quantities or values.

Procedures for Balance-of-Payments Consultations

5. The Committee on Balance-of-Payments Restrictions (referred to in this Understanding as the "Committee") shall carry out consultations in order to review all restrictive import measures taken for balance-of-payments purposes. The membership of the Committee is open to all Members indicating their wish to serve on it. The Committee shall follow the procedures for consultations on balance-of-payments restrictions approved on 28 April 1970 (BISD 18S/48-53, referred to in this Understanding as "full consultation procedures"), subject to the provisions set out below.

6. A Member applying new restrictions or raising the general level of its existing restrictions by a substantial intensification of the measures shall enter into consultations with the Committee within four months of the adoption of such measures. The Member adopting such measures may request that a consultation be held under paragraph 4(a) of Article XII or paragraph 12(a) of Article XVIII as appropriate. If no such request has been made, the Chairman of the Committee shall invite the Member to hold such a consultation. Factors that may be examined in the consultation would include, inter alia, the introduction of new types of restrictive measures for balance-of-payments purposes, or an increase in the level or product coverage of restrictions.

---

[1] Nothing in this Understanding is intended to modify the rights and obligations of Members under Articles XII or XVIII:B of GATT 1994. The provisions of Articles XXII and XXIII of GATT 1994 as elaborated and applied by the Dispute Settlement Understanding may be invoked with respect to any matters arising from the application of restrictive import measures taken for balance-of-payments purposes.

7. All restrictions applied for balance-of-payments purposes shall be subject to periodic review in the Committee under paragraph 4(b) of Article XII or under paragraph 12(b) of Article XVIII, subject to the possibility of altering the periodicity of consultations in agreement with the consulting Member or pursuant to any specific review procedure that may be recommended by the General Council.

8. Consultations may be held under the simplified procedures approved on 19 December 1972 (BISD 20S/47-49, referred to in this Understanding as "simplified consultation procedures") in the case of least-developed country Members or in the case of developing country Members which are pursuing liberalization efforts in conformity with the schedule presented to the Committee in previous consultations. Simplified consultation procedures may also be used when the Trade Policy Review of a developing country Member is scheduled for the same calendar year as the date fixed for the consultations. In such cases the decision as to whether full consultation procedures should be used will be made on the basis of the factors enumerated in paragraph 8 of the 1979 Declaration. Except in the case of least-developed country Members, no more than two successive consultations may be held under simplified consultation procedures.

Notification and Documentation

9. A Member shall notify to the General Council the introduction of or any changes in the application of restrictive import measures taken for balance-of-payments purposes, as well as any modifications in time-schedules for the removal of such measures as announced under paragraph 1. Significant changes shall be notified to the General Council prior to or not later than 30 days after their announcement. On a yearly basis, each Member shall make available to the Secretariat a consolidated notification, including all changes in laws, regulations, policy statements or public notices, for examination by Members. Notifications shall include full information, as far as possible, at the tariff-line level, on the type of measures applied, the criteria used for their administration, product coverage and trade flows affected.

10. At the request of any Member, notifications may be reviewed by the Committee. Such reviews would be limited to the clarification of specific issues raised by a notification or examination of whether a consultation under paragraph 4(a) of Article XII or paragraph 12(a) of Article XVIII is required. Members which have reasons to believe that a restrictive import measure applied by another Member was taken for balance-of-payments purposes may bring the matter to the attention of the Committee. The Chairman of the Committee shall request information on the measure and make it available to all Members. Without prejudice to the right of any member of the Committee to seek appropriate clarifications in the course of consultations, questions may be submitted in advance for consideration by the consulting Member.

11. The consulting Member shall prepare a Basic Document for the consultations which, in addition to any other information considered to be relevant, should include: (a) an overview of the balance-of-payments situation and prospects, including a consideration of the internal and external factors having a bearing on the balance-of-payments situation and the domestic policy measures taken in order to restore equilibrium on a sound and lasting basis; (b) a full description of the restrictions applied for balance-of-payments purposes, their legal basis and steps taken to reduce incidental protective effects; (c) measures taken since the last consultation to liberalize import restrictions, in the light of the conclusions of the Committee; (d) a plan for the elimination and progressive relaxation of remaining restrictions. References may be made, when relevant, to the information provided in other notifications or reports made to the WTO. Under simplified consultation procedures, the consulting Member shall submit a written statement containing essential information on the elements covered by the Basic Document.

12. The Secretariat shall, with a view to facilitating the consultations in the Committee, prepare a factual background paper dealing with the different aspects of the plan for consultations. In the case of developing country Members, the Secretariat document shall include relevant background and analytical material on the incidence of the external trading environment on the balance-of-payments situation and prospects of the consulting Member. The technical assistance services of the Secretariat shall, at the request of a developing country Member, assist in preparing the documentation for the consultations.

Conclusions of Balance-of-Payments Consultations

13. The Committee shall report on its consultations to the General Council. When full consultation procedures have been used, the report should indicate the Committee's conclusions on the different elements of the plan for consultations, as well as the facts and reasons on which they are based. The Committee shall endeavour to include in its conclusions proposals for recommendations aimed at promoting the implementation of Articles XII and XVIII:B, the 1979 Declaration and this Understanding. In those cases in which a time-schedule has been presented for the removal of restrictive measures taken for balance-of-payments purposes, the General Council may recommend that, in adhering to such a time-schedule, a Member shall be deemed to be in compliance with its GATT 1994 obligations. Whenever the General Council has made specific recommendations, the rights and obligations of Members shall be assessed in the light of such recommendations. In the absence of specific proposals for recommendations by the General Council, the Committee's conclusions should record the different views expressed in the Committee. When simplified consultation procedures have been used, the report shall include a summary of the main elements discussed in the Committee and a decision on whether full consultation procedures are required.

II. INTERPRETATION AND APPLICATION OF ARTICLE XII

A. SCOPE AND APPLICATION OF ARTICLE XII

1. General

The present text of Articles XII and XVIII was agreed in the 1954-55 Review Session, and entered into effect in October 1957. The principal source concerning the drafting of these provisions is the Report of the Review Working Party on "Quantitative Restrictions"[2]. This Report notes generally concerning Article XII:

> "After a detailed consideration of the various proposals put forward with a view to establishing stricter rules for the introduction and maintenance of quantitative restrictions through the institution of fixed time-limits and approval by the CONTRACTING PARTIES, the Working Party came to the conclusion that such proposals would not find general acceptance among the contracting parties, but that, on the other hand, the general opinion was in favour of strengthening and widening the scope of consultations under Article XII, as well as under Article XIV. Consequently, the new text of the first three paragraphs of Article XII does not involve any change of substance. Their provisions have been rearranged in order to improve the language and to set them out in a better logical sequence ...".[3]

Articles XII and XVIII:B have been amplified by detailed consultation procedures introduced in 1970, by "simplified" consultation procedures for developing countries introduced in 1972, and by provisions on the application of the Articles and consultation procedures laid down in the 1979 Declaration on Trade Measures Taken for Balance-of-Payments Purposes, which extend GATT examination under the balance-of-payments provisions from quantitative restrictions alone to all trade measures taken for balance-of-payments purposes. Section II(C) of this chapter discusses the consultation procedures applicable to such measures generally under Articles XII and XVIII.

2. Paragraph 1

(1) "any contracting party": member States of the EEC

At the Twelfth Session in 1957, four sub-groups were appointed to examine the relevant provisions of the Treaty of Rome in the light of the provisions of the General Agreement. The Report of Sub-Group B, which examined those provisions of the Treaty relating to quantitative restrictions notes as follows:

> "Members of the Sub-Group expressed concern that under the Rome Treaty provisions a Member State would be permitted to use quantitative restrictions not justified by its own balance-of-payments position. They recognized that this cause for concern would be removed if at some future stage the integration of the economies of the Six proceeded to the point that they held their foreign exchange reserves in common.
>
> "The Six [EEC member States] considered that the opening phrase of paragraph 5 of Article XXIV provided a general exception under which they were entitled to deviate from the other provisions of the General Agreement, including Articles XI to XIV, insofar as the application of these provisions would constitute obstacles to the formation of the customs union and to the achievement of its objectives ..."
>
> "Most members of the Sub-Group had a different interpretation of Article XXIV. In their view countries entering a customs union would continue to be governed by the provisions of Article XI prohibiting the use of quantitative restrictions as well as by the other provisions of the Agreement which provided certain exceptions permitting the use of quantitative restrictions where necessary to deal with balance-of-payments difficulties ... Since paragraph 8(a)(i) permitted where necessary the use of quantitative restrictions for balance-of-payments reasons, it followed that the use of quantitative restrictions by individual countries within the union for these reasons could not be regarded as preventing the formation of a customs union as defined in Article XXIV.

---

[2]L/332/Rev.1 and Addenda, adopted on 2, 4 and 5 March 1955, 3S/170-185.
[3]*Ibid.*, 3S/171, para. 4.

"Most members of the Sub-Group could not accept the interpretation of the Six of paragraph 5(a). In their view the use of the term 'regulations' in this paragraph and in paragraph 8(a)(ii) does not include quantitative restrictions imposed for balance-of-payments reasons ... the term 'regulation' does not occur in the balance-of-payments Articles of the General Agreement. The General Agreement prohibits the use of quantitative restrictions for protective purposes and permits their use only in exceptional circumstances and mainly to deal with balance-of-payments difficulties. Accordingly, the notion that paragraph 5(a) would require that temporary quantitative restrictions should be treated in the same way as normal protective measures such as tariffs in determining the trade relations between countries in a customs union and third countries would be contrary to the basic provisions of the Agreement which preclude the use of quantitative restrictions as an acceptable protective instrument.

...

"Most members of the Sub-Group believed that the imposition of common quotas by the Six, quite apart from being contrary to Article XII of the GATT, would be contrary to fundamental economic reasoning unless they held their reserves in common. Common quotas could mean that a member of the customs union in balance-of-payments difficulties would be unable to apply restrictions appropriate to its particular difficulties while other members would be applying restrictions not required or justified by their payments position. ...

"Most members of the Sub-Group emphasized that if the Six were individually no longer to be bound by the balance-of-payments provisions of the Agreement permitting the use of quantitative restrictions only in carefully defined circumstances, then the balance of rights and obligations under the Agreement would be impaired.

...

"The Sub-Group took the view that Member States of the Six as regards their individual use of quantitative restrictions should be subject to the consultation procedures applicable to other contracting parties in like circumstances, and agreed that it would not be proper to envisage special consultation procedures. If in the application of the provisions of the Treaty any Member country found it necessary to take action which would bring into play the consultation provisions of the General Agreement, then the country concerned would fulfil its obligations under GATT."[4]

(2) *"in order to safeguard its external financial position and its balance of payments"*

When this wording was proposed during the Geneva session of the Preparatory Committee, it was indicated that it would eliminate the risk that the provision "could be interpreted to mean that import restrictions were not 'necessary' (and therefore were not permitted) until every other possible corrective measure (such as exchange controls, exchange depreciation, etc.) had been tried and found inadequate"[5]. It was also stated that it remained clear, of course, that the Organization had the right during the course of consultation with the Members fully to discuss and recommend alternative action which a Member might take to meet its difficulties.[6]

(3) *"may restrict the quantity or value of merchandise permitted to be imported": Quantitative and other trade measures for balance-of-payments purposes, including import surcharges and import deposit schemes*

Import surcharges and import deposit schemes for balance-of-payments purposes are governed by the 1979 Declaration on "Trade Measures taken for Balance-of-Payments Purposes"[7] which specifies that "The procedures for examination stipulated in Articles XII and XVIII shall apply to all restrictive import measures taken for balance-of-payments purposes". The history of the treatment of such schemes in the GATT 1947 divides into

---

[4] L/778, adopted on 29 November 1957, 6S/70, 76-80, paras. 2-5, 7-8, 11.
[5] EPCT/W/223, p. 13.
[6] *Ibid.*, p. 15.
[7] L/4904, adopted on 28 November 1979, 26S/205.

two periods, before and after the adoption of the Declaration. In this connection see also the provisions of the Understanding on the Balance-of-Payment Provisions of the GATT 1994.

(a) Treatment of import surcharges prior to 1979

The 1979 Declaration reflected the use of import surcharges and import deposit schemes for balance-of-payments purposes in the fifteen years preceding, as well as the practice developed by the Committee on Balance-of-Payments Restrictions and discussed below. In 1964, the Committee on Legal and Institutional Framework, which prepared the text of Part IV of the General Agreement, had also recommended an amendment to Section B of Article XVIII to permit a less-developed contracting party to use temporary import surcharges, in place of quantitative restrictions, to safeguard its balance of payments.[8] This Recommendation had been referred to the Committee on Trade and Development which debated the question in an Ad Hoc Group on Legal Amendments during 1965-1966, and agreed to defer consideration of the issue indefinitely.[9]

In a review of its work in the 1970-74 period, the Committee on Balance-of-Payments Restrictions reported to the Council in 1975 that:

"Surcharges appear to have been applied in twenty-four cases, involving twenty-three contracting parties. The Balance-of-Payments Committee discussed, examined or generally dealt with ten of these cases. In two cases only did it recommend a waiver - Uruguay and Turkey. Both these cases involved extensions of waivers granted originally in 1961 and 1963, making it difficult for the Committee to depart from established practice. In two other cases - Israel and Yugoslavia - the Committee adopted a new approach by assimilating the surcharge to quantitative restrictions applied for balance-of-payments reasons, thus dispensing with the formalities of a waiver. In the other six cases, the surcharges were discussed, not always in detail, in the course of the consultations. It is not within the Committee's terms of reference to recommend a waiver unless it has been assigned the task by the Council. There seems to be a trend on the part of Committee members towards adopting gradually a more flexible approach, rather than emphasize the legal requirements of GATT.

"Of the twenty-four different surcharges, five cases were dealt with in other GATT bodies (Denmark, India, Indonesia, Pakistan and United States); three of which resulting in waivers. Further, nine cases were not brought to the attention of contracting parties."[10]

"In the case of import surcharges on bound items, the decision to be taken, according to the General Agreement, is whether or not to grant a waiver (Article XXV:5). In examining import surcharges, the Committee's main concern has never been the question of whether or not it should recommend to the CONTRACTING PARTIES the validation of the measure through a waiver. The Committee's conclusions have focused instead on the question of whether the surcharges meet the criteria set forth in the General Agreement for import restrictions. A typical example is the 1970 consultation on the Yugoslav special import charge. Here the Committee decided to recommend to the Council to take note of the surcharge on the understanding 'that all the conditions and criteria embodied in the appropriate provisions of the General Agreement concerning the use of quantitative restrictions for balance-of-payments reasons should be deemed applicable in respect of this import charge'. A similar approach was adopted in three other cases (1971 Israel; 1974 Israel; 1974 Yugoslavia). The Committee's decisions assimilating surcharges to the procedures and criteria for import restrictions were adopted unanimously. In the 1971 Israel consultation, however, the representative of Japan asked to have his view recorded in the conclusions that the case should not be regarded as a precedent.

"The Committee's approach towards import surcharges during the past five years contrasts with a more formal approach of the CONTRACTING PARTIES in the early 1960s when waivers for surcharges, at least when imposed by developing countries, were frequently granted. ...

---

[8] L/2281, para. 7 and Annex II; L/2297, para. 6.
[9] 13S/76; 14S/141. See also COM.TD/F/W/3, Note by the Secretariat done for the Ad-Hoc Group on "The Use of Import Surcharges by Contracting Parties", dated 25 May 1965.
[10] L/4200, paras. 31-32.

"The procedural assimilation of surcharges to import restrictions by the Committee does not, of course, change the rights of contracting parties affected by surcharges. The Committee, in some of its conclusions on surcharges re-affirmed the rights of affected countries by stating that the decision to take note by the Council would in no way preclude recourse to the appropriate provisions of the General Agreement by any contracting party which considered that any benefits accruing to it under Article II of the Agreement in respect of any bound item were nullified or impaired as a consequence of the surcharge."[11]

In 1964 the United Kingdom gave notice of its decision to impose a temporary import surcharge in order to safeguard the external financial position of the United Kingdom and its balance of payments; the United Kingdom invoked the provisions of Article XII as justification while recognizing that "the type of restriction on imports there envisaged was the use of quantitative restrictions". The Council, while "bearing in mind that Article XII envisaged that any necessary restraint on imports would be by way of quantitative restrictions", appointed a Working Party of which the terms of reference were identical to those stated in Article XII:4(a), with the addition: "as to the nature of the measures taken".[12]

In 1971, the United States introduced a temporary import surcharge in conjunction with changes in exchange rate policy and a domestic wage and price freeze. The Report of the Working Party on "United States Temporary Import Surcharge" examined the surcharge and noted that "The United States, taking into account the findings of the IMF, considered itself entitled under Article XII to apply quantitative restrictions to safeguard its external financial position and balance of payments but had chosen instead to apply surcharges which were less damaging to world trade. ... The other members of the Working Party ... noted that the surcharge, to the extent that it raised the incidence of customs charges beyond the maximum rates bound under Article II, was not compatible with the provisions of the General Agreement".[13]

The Report in 1972 of the Working Party on the "Danish Temporary Import Surcharge" notes that "Denmark, taking into account the findings of the International Monetary Fund, considered that, although the implementation of an import surcharge was not explicitly covered by any provision of the GATT, such action had been taken in the spirit of Article XII:2(a). Quantitative restrictions provided for in Article XII would have had a more serious effect on the interests of its trading partners ... The Working Party noted that the surcharge, to the extent that it raised the incidence of customs charges beyond the maximum rates bound under Article II, was not compatible with the provisions of the General Agreement".[14]

(b) *Treatment of import deposit schemes prior to 1979*

In 1978, an import deposit scheme was examined by the Panel on "EEC - Programme of Minimum Import Prices, Licences and Surety Deposits for Certain Processed Fruits and Vegetables". The measure in dispute provided that importation of certain products would be conditional on production of a certificate; the issue of the certificate would be conditional on the lodging of a security to guarantee that the imports in question would be made, and an additional security to guarantee that the imports would be made at a minimum price. The United States argued that the minimum import price system operated as a charge on imports, and that charges in excess of bound duties were levied through lost interest, debt servicing, and clerical and administrative costs associated with the provision of security deposits, and through the forfeiture of security deposits if the importation did not occur within the 75-day validity of the licence or if the minimum import price was not respected.[15] The Report of the Panel notes:

"... The Panel considered that these interest charges and costs were 'other duties or charges of any kind imposed on or in connection with importation' in excess of the bound rate within the meaning of Article II:1(b). Therefore, the Panel concluded that the interest charges and costs in connection with the

---

[11]L/4200, paras. 40-42. See also BOP Committee Reports referred to on Yugoslavia in 1970 (BOP/R/48, p. 10); Israel 1971 (BOP/R/54, page 8 with Japanese reservation at p. 8); Israel 1974 (BOP/R/78, page 6); Yugoslavia 1974 (BOP/R/74 p. 7).
[12]L/2676, adopted on 17 November 1966, 15S/113, 113-114, paras. 2-4.
[13]L/3573, adopted on 16 September 1971, 18S/212, 222-223, para. 41.
[14]L/3648, adopted on 12 January 1972, 19S/120, 129, paras. 36-37.
[15]L/4687, adopted on 18 October 1978, 25S/68, 87-88, para. 3.56.

lodging of the additional security associated with the minimum import price for tomato concentrates were inconsistent with the obligations of the Community under Article II:1(b)".[16]

On the relevance of this Panel finding for the consideration in the Committee on Balance-of-Payments Restrictions of whether import deposit requirements are "charges" in terms of Article II:1(b), see, for example, the 1980 consultations with Israel[17] and the 1981 consultation with Italy on the Italian deposit requirement for purchases of foreign currency.[18]

Concerning the treatment of import deposit schemes prior to 1978, the Balance-of-Payments Committee reported to the Council in its review of its work in 1970-74 that:

"Seventeen different import deposit requirements appear to have been applied involving sixteen contracting parties. The Balance-of-Payments Committee discussed or examined seven different cases. The Committee has generally referred to the measures in its conclusions, though without giving much emphasis; it has either noted or welcomed reduction of rates, or hoped or called for early phase-out or removal. In three cases the import deposits were discussed in the course of the consultations but not mentioned in the conclusions (Argentina, Korea and Uruguay).

"Three cases of import deposits were examined in other GATT bodies - United Kingdom, Italy and Iceland, none of which were invoking Article XII at the time, but all of which invoked balance-of-payments reasons.

"Seven cases were not notified to GATT and were not discussed in GATT bodies".[19]

"... the CONTRACTING PARTIES have not decided whether a deposit requirement in respect of bound items is a 'charge ... imposed on or in connection with importation' or, more generally, a 'treatment ... less favourable than that provided for in the appropriate ... Schedule', and therefore contrary to Article II.

"Possibly as a result of this, the conclusions on import deposits have generally been vague and have avoided any connotation of approval or disapproval. A typical example is the 1974 consultation with Greece in which the Committee merely 'noted the intention of Greece to continue reducing the rates of the prior import deposit scheme'. There was no case where an import deposit scheme was found to be violating the General Agreement's financial or commercial criteria for import restrictions".[20]

In 1968, the United Kingdom introduced an import deposit scheme "as a measure necessary to accelerate progress in bringing the United Kingdom balance of payments into surplus". This measure was examined in the Working Party on "United Kingdom Import Deposits" which consulted with the International Monetary Fund and concluded that "the deposits were not more restrictive than measures that an application of the provisions of Article XII permits".[21] The scheme was terminated on 4 December 1970.[22] The 1974 Report of the Working Party on "Italian Import Deposit" notes that "there was a wide measure of support for the conclusion that the Italian import deposit scheme was not more restrictive than measures that an application of the provisions of Article XII of the GATT permits".[23] In the Report in 1976 of the Working Party on the "New Zealand Import Deposit Scheme" it is noted: "The Working Party agreed that the New Zealand import deposit scheme applied on a temporary basis was not more restrictive than an application of the provisions of Article XII of the General Agreement. Noting that New Zealand was not invoking the provisions of Article XII or any other provision of the General Agreement, the Working Party agreed that this conclusion was without prejudice to the rights and obligations of contracting parties under the General Agreement".[24]

---

[16]*Ibid.*, 25S/103, para. 4.15.
[17]BOP/W/37, para. 8.
[18]BOP/R/119; BOP/W/51, para. 8.
[19]L/4200, p. 11, paras. 34-36.
[20]*Ibid.*, p. 13, paras. 43-44.
[21]L/3193, adopted on 15 April 1969, 17S/144, 149, para. 17.
[22]18S/212.
[23]L/4082, adopted on 21 October 1974, 21S/121, 125, para. 13.
[24]L/4363, adopted on 15 July 1976, 23S/84, 91, para. 24.

(c) Practice since 1979

On 28 November 1979 the CONTRACTING PARTIES adopted the Declaration on "Trade Measures taken for Balance-of-Payments Purposes"[25] which notes in its preamble that "restrictive import measures other than quantitative restrictions have been used for balance-of-payments purposes", and provides:

"1. The procedures for examination stipulated in Articles XII and XVIII shall apply to all restrictive import measures taken for balance-of-payments purposes. The application of restrictive import measures taken for balance-of-payments purposes shall be subject to the following conditions in addition to those provided for in Articles XII, XIII, XV and XVIII without prejudice to other provisions of the General Agreement:

"(a) In applying restrictive import measures contracting parties shall abide by the disciplines provided for in the GATT and give preference to the measure which has the least disruptive effect on trade[26];

"(b) The simultaneous application of more than one type of trade measure for this purpose should be avoided; ...

"The provisions of this paragraph are not intended to modify the substantive provisions of the General Agreement. ...

"4. All restrictive import measures taken for balance-of-payments purposes shall be subject to consultation in the GATT Committee on Balance-of-Payments Restrictions".

Thus, since 1979, in principle, all restrictive import measures, including but not limited to quantitative restrictions, surcharges and import deposit requirements, have been subject to examination in the Committee and not to examination by special working parties. The 1979 Declaration followed on discussions prior to and during the Tokyo Round of multilateral trade negotiations.[27]

The 1981 Report of the Committee on Balance-of-Payments Restrictions on the "Italian Deposit Requirement for Purchases of Foreign Currency" notes the view of the Italian Government "that the GATT rules on trade measures taken for balance-of-payments purposes did not apply to the deposit scheme because it was of a monetary nature and its main and primary effects were financial and monetary". The Committee concluded, *inter alia*, "that the deposit scheme, though monetary in form, had some effect on trade and that, in so far as these trade effects were concerned, the scheme could be considered in the spirit of the Declaration on Trade Measures Taken for Balance-of-Payments Purposes".[28] The deposit scheme was terminated on 7 February 1982.[29]

Surcharges for balance-of-payments reasons were notified under Article XII by the Czech and Slovak Republic in January 1991, by Poland in December 1992, and by the Slovak Republic in March 1994.[30] Surcharges for balance-of-payments reasons were notified under Article XVIII:B by Israel in September 1982 and by South Africa without reference to either Article XVIII:B or Article XII in September 1988.[31]

---

[25]L/4904, adopted on 28 November 1979, 26S/205.

[26]A footnote to paragraph 1(a) of the Declaration states: "It is understood that the less developed contracting parties must take into account their individual development, financial and trade situation when selecting the particular measure to be applied."

[27]See, e.g., CG.18/W/5, 19 February 1976, at p. 3; CG.18/W/7; CG.18/W/8; CG.18/W/9 and Rev.1; 1976-1978 Report of the Consultative Group of Eighteen: L/4429, 23S/38, 43-45, paras. 19-25; L/4585, 24S/58, 59-60, paras. 7-9; L/4715, 25S/37, 38-39, paras. 6-7. See also Tokyo Round negotiating documents including MTN/FR/W/1, MTN/FR/W/2, MTN/FR/W/10, MTN/FR/W/12, MTN/FR/W/13, MTN/INF/16, MTN/INF/25 and Rev.1, MTN/FR/4.

[28]BOP/R/119, adopted on 3 November 1981, C/M/152.

[29]L/5162/Add.3.

[30]Czech and Slovak Republic: see L/6812 and Adds.1-2; see also BOP/R/193, C/W/693, C/M/254. The Czech and Slovak Republic ceased to exist on 31 December 1992 and the surcharge was abolished at that time. Poland: see L/7164, C/RM/G/31, BOP/R/206, notification in L/7461 of extension of surcharge to 17 December 1997, BOP/W/154, BOP/317 and BOP/R/216. Slovak Republic: see L/7428, BOP/W/156, BOP/319, BOP/R/218.

[31]Israel: see L/5361 (notification), BOP/R/195, BOP/307, C/M/254 p. 3-4, L/7092, BOP/R/210, BOP/R/213, BOP/R/215. South Africa: see L/5898 (imposition), L/5898/Add.1-3 (changes); see also L/7084, C/M/259 p. 62-63, C/M/260 p. 12, BOP/R/211. Both Israel and South Africa consulted in the Committee on Balance-of-Payments Restrictions without reference to either Article XII or XVIII; see at page 378 below.

Paragraphs 2 and 3 of the Understanding on the Balance-of-Payments Provisions of the GATT 1994 provide as follows:

> "Members confirm their commitment to give preference to those measures which have the least disruptive effect on trade. Such measures (referred to in this Understanding as 'price-based measures') shall be understood to include import surcharges, import deposit requirements or other equivalent trade measures with an impact on the price of imported goods. It is understood that, notwithstanding the provisions of Article II, price-based measures taken for balance-of-payments purposes may be applied by a Member in excess of the duties inscribed in the Schedule of that Member. Furthermore, that Member shall indicate the amount by which the price-based measure exceeds the bound duty clearly and separately under the notification procedures of this Understanding.

> "Members shall seek to avoid the imposition of new quantitative restrictions for balance-of-payments purposes unless, because of a critical balance-of-payments situation, price-based measures cannot arrest a sharp deterioration in the external payments position. In those cases in which a Member applies quantitative restrictions, it shall provide justification as to the reasons why price-based measures are not an adequate instrument to deal with the balance-of-payments situation. ... It is understood that not more than one type of restrictive import measure taken for balance-of-payments purposes may be applied on the same product."

Concerning import surcharges and import deposit schemes, see also Article II.

3. Paragraph 2

(1) *"Import restrictions ... shall not exceed those necessary"*

Paragraph 4 of the Understanding on the Balance-of-Payments Provisions of the GATT 1994 provides *inter alia* that "Members confirm that restrictive import measures taken for balance-of-payments purposes may only be applied to control the general level of imports and may not exceed what is necessary to address the balance-of-payments situation."

(2) *"a serious decline in its monetary reserves"*

Article XV:2 provides that "The CONTRACTING PARTIES, in reaching their final decision in cases involving the criteria set forth in paragraph 2(a) of Article XII ... shall accept the determination of the Fund as to what constitutes a serious decline in the contracting party's monetary reserves, a very low level of its monetary reserves or a reasonable rate of increase in its monetary reserves, and as to the financial aspects of other matters covered in consultation in such cases".

During discussions at the Havana Conference, it was stated that

> "The seriousness of a decline in reserves depended on a number of factors such as the size of a country, its need for reserves, the variability of its trade and the size of the reserves. Neither the absolute amount of the decline nor the proportionate amount would be valid in all cases as the criterion of the seriousness of the decline".[32]

(3) *"special factors which may be affecting the reserves of such contracting party or its need for reserves"*

The report of discussions at the London session of the Preparatory Committee notes that

> "There are, however, many factors to which due regard must be paid ... There may be special non-recurrent movements of funds affecting a country's reserves, a country may have special credits outside its monetary reserves which it might be expected to use to a proper extent and at a proper rate to meet a strain on its external position, a country which has high reserves may, nevertheless, have high future commitments or

---

[32] E/CONF.2/C.3/SR.38, p. 3.

probable drains upon its resources to meet in the near future. All such factors will have to be taken into account in interpreting movements in a country's reserves".[33]

Also, the report of discussions at the Havana Conference notes that

"It was the view of the Sub-Committee that the present text of Article 21 [XII] made adequate provisions for many of the considerations put forward by the delegates of Venezuela and Uruguay. ... It was pointed out that a country exporting principally a small number of products would, in like conditions, probably be considered to have need for greater reserves than a country exporting a large variety of products, particularly if the exports were exhaustible or subject to considerable fluctuations of supply or price. A country actively embarked on a programme of economic development which is raising levels of production and foreign trade would probably then be considered to have need for greater reserves than when its economic activity was at a lower level".[34]

See also the discussion below under sub-paragraph 4(e) and at page 388 concerning consideration of external factors in balance-of-payments consultations.

(4) Disinvocation of Article XII

Contracting parties having disinvoked Article XII since 1979 are indicated in Table 2 at the end of this chapter. See also the Secretariat Note of 24 June 1988 on "Consultations Held in the Committee on Balance-of-Payments Restrictions under Articles XII and XVIII:B since 1975".[35]

4. Paragraph 3

(1) Paragraph 3(a): adjustment

The 1950 Report of the Working Party on "The Use of Quantitative Restrictions for Protective and Commercial Purposes"[36] notes that

"In discussing the application of the Agreement to import restrictions applied for protective, promotional or other commercial purposes, the Working Party devoted its main attention to two points:

"(a) The fact that balance-of-payment restrictions almost inevitably have the incidental effect of protecting those domestic industries which produce the types of goods subject to restriction and of stimulating the development of those industries. Any consequent development of uneconomic production could interfere with the process of removing balance-of-payment restrictions as and when the justification for such restrictions under the Agreement disappears ...".

The report recommended a number of "methods whereby the undesirable incidental protective effects of balance-of-payment restrictions can be minimised": see below under paragraph 3(c).

The 1955 Report of the Review Working Party on "Quantitative Restrictions" notes that

"The Working Party considered a proposal to the effect that a provision be included in paragraph 3(c) requiring contracting parties to minimize the incidental protective effects of the restrictions. The Working Party, while in general agreement with the intent of the proposal, considered such a provision unnecessary; it was of the view that this had been adequately addressed by other provisions in the revised Article, including paragraph 3(a), which requires contracting parties to pay due regard to the desirability of avoiding uneconomic employment of productive resources, and paragraph 3(c)(i) under which contracting parties

---

[33] London Report, p. 13, para. (c).
[34] Havana Reports, p. 105, para. 11; see also E/CONF.2/C.3/SR.38, pp. 2-3.
[35] MTN.GNG/NG7/W/46, para. 30.
[36] GATT/CP.4/33 (Sales No. GATT/1950-3).

undertake to avoid unnecessary damage to the commercial and economic interests of any other contracting party".[37]

In the "Uruguayan Recourse to Article XXIII" in 1962, the complaint of Uruguay included, *inter alia*, balance-of-payments measures maintained by Denmark, Finland, and Japan. In each instance, the Panel Report noted that "the Panel would recall the view of contracting parties, as expressed in the consultations under Article XII:4, that the Government of [Denmark/Finland/Japan] should endeavour to ensure that the quantitative restrictions maintained under Article XII did not have incidental protective effects which would render their removal difficult when [Denmark/Finland/Japan] no longer had need to have recourse to Article XII".[38]

Paragraph 4 of the Understanding on the Balance-of-Payments Provisions of the GATT 1994 provides *inter alia* that "In order to minimize any incidental protective effects, a Member shall administer restrictions in a transparent manner."

(2) *Paragraph 3(b): "to give priority to the importation of those products which are more essential"*

The report of discussions at the London session of the Preparatory Committee notes that permission to give priority for the importation of certain more-essential products was expressly laid down "so that a Member can, if necessary, restrict the importation of consumer goods without restricting the importation of capital goods".[39]

Paragraph 4 of the Understanding on the Balance-of-Payments Provisions of the GATT 1994 provides *inter alia* that:

"Members confirm that restrictive import measures taken for balance-of-payments purposes may only be applied to control the general level of imports … . The authorities of the importing Member shall provide adequate justification as to the criteria used to determine which products are subject to restriction. As provided in paragraph 3 of Article XII and paragraph 10 of Article XVIII, Members may, in the case of certain essential products, exclude or limit the application of surcharges applied across the board or other measures applied for balance-of-payments purposes. The term 'essential products' shall be understood to mean products which meet basic consumption needs or which contribute to the Member's effort to improve its balance-of-payments situation, such as capital goods or inputs needed for production. …

(3) *Paragraph 3(c): application of restrictions under Article XII*

(a) *Conditions applicable to balance-of-payments measures*

The Report of the Working Party on "The Use of Quantitative Restrictions for Protective and Commercial Purposes",[40] adopted at the Fourth Session in 1951, recommended the following "methods by which countries applying balance-of-payment restrictions can seek to minimise the undesirable incidental protective effects resulting from such restrictions … which countries might where possible employ in their own interests and in the spirit of the Agreement in order to stimulate efficiency on the part of their domestic industries and to prepare them for the time when import restrictions can be relaxed or removed":

"(a) avoiding encouragement of investment in enterprises which could not survive without this type of protection beyond the period in which quantitative restrictions may be legitimately maintained;

"(b) finding frequent opportunities to impress upon producers who are protected by balance-of-payment restrictions the fact that these restrictions are not permanent and will not be maintained beyond the period of balance-of-payment difficulties;

---

[37]L/332/Rev.1 and Addenda, adopted on 2, 4 and 5 March 1955, 3S/170, 171, para. 5.
[38]L/1923, adopted on 16 November 1962, 11S/95, Annexes E, F and J, at 11S/116 para. 4, 11S/119 para. 4, and 11S/133 para. 4.
[39]London Report, p. 14, para. (r); see also EPCT/C.II/PV/13 p. 10.
[40]GATT/CP.4/33 (Sales No. GATT/1950-3).

"(c) administering balance-of-payment restrictions on a flexible basis and adjusting them to changing circumstances, thereby impressing upon the protected industries the impermanent character of the protection afforded by the restrictions;

"(d) allowing the importation of 'token' amounts of products, which otherwise would be excluded on balance-of-payment grounds, in order to expose domestic producers of like commodities to at least some foreign competition and to keep such producers constantly aware of the need ultimately to be prepared to meet foreign competition;

"(e) avoiding, as far as balance-of-payment and technical considerations permit, the allocation of quotas among supplying countries in favour of general licences unrestricted in amount or unallocated quotas applying non-discriminatorily to as many countries as possible; and

"(f) avoiding as far as possible narrow classifications and restrictive definitions of products eligible to enter under any given quota."[41]

"... the Working Party noted that there was evidence of a number of types of misuse of import restrictions, in particular:

"(i) The maintenance by a country of balance-of-payment restrictions, which give priority to imports of particular products upon the basis of the competitiveness or non-competitiveness of such imports with a domestic industry, or which favour particular sources of supply upon a similar basis, in a manner inconsistent with the provisions of Articles XII to XIV. ... Such type of misuse, for example, might take the form of total prohibitions on the import of products competing with domestic products, or of quotas which are unreasonably small having regard to the exchange availability of the country concerned and to other relevant factors.

"(ii) The imposition by a country of administrative obstacles to the full utilization of balance-of-payment import quotas, e.g., by delaying the issuance of licences against such quotas or by establishing licence priorities for certain imports on the basis of the competitiveness or non-competitiveness of such imports with the products of domestic industry, in a manner inconsistent with the provisions of Articles XII to XIV ...".[42]

See also the discussion of the relationship between Article XXIII and Articles XII and XVIII, under Article XXIII.

In late 1950, at the Torquay Session the CONTRACTING PARTIES adopted a Working Party Report on a proposal for a Code of Standard Practices for the Administration of Import and Export Restrictions and Exchange Controls,[43] including the recommendations therein that the CONTRACTING PARTIES "approve the draft standards set out in the Annex to this Report [and] recommend these practices to the individual contracting parties as a code which they should endeavour to adopt to the maximum practicable extent". The Report further provides:

"The Working Party considered that the proposed standards ... should be regarded as a code for the guidance of contracting parties and not as additional obligations imposed upon them under the General Agreement ... it was recognised that, where there are clear and overriding considerations, or in individual cases where there is good reason to suspect the bona fides of transactions in question, it may be necessary for contracting parties to depart from the precise terms of these recommendations".

---

[41]*Ibid.*, para. 19.
[42]*Ibid.*, para. 21.
[43]GATT/CP.5/30/Rev.1; adopted on 30 November 1950, GATT/CP.5/SR.16 p. 2-4; preliminary draft at GATT/CP.5/8, discussion also at GATT/CP.5/SR.8, SR.9.

The provisions of this Code appear *in extenso* under Article XIII:3.

See also the provisions of the 1979 Declaration on "Trade Measures Taken for Balance-of-Payments Purposes" above at page 366 and paragraphs 1-4 of the Understanding on the Balance-of-Payments Provisions of the GATT 1994.

(b) *"to avoid unnecessary damage to the commercial or economic interests of any other contracting party"*

See the Interpretative Note to paragraph 3(c)(i).

The 1979 Declaration on Trade Measures Taken for Balance-of-Payments Purposes also provides that "If, notwithstanding the principles of this Declaration, a developed contracting party is compelled to apply restrictive import measures for balance-of-payments purposes, it shall, in determining the incidence of its measures, take into account the export interests of the less-developed contracting parties and may exempt from its measures products of export interest to those contracting parties".[44]

In the Fifth Session in 1950, Belgium reported that it had carried out consultations under Article XXIII, and had reached a satisfactory resolution, concerning quantitative restrictions applied by the United Kingdom and France for protectionist purposes and which, in the view of the Belgian Government, were unnecessarily causing damage to the Belgian economy.[45]

(c) *"description of goods"*

During discussions at the Geneva session of the Preparatory Committee, it was stated that "whether you mean fountain pens as a class or each brand of fountain pen ... you certainly do not mean the importation of one particular kind".[46]

(d) *"minimum commercial quantities"*

During discussions at the Geneva session of the Preparatory Committee, it was stated that "the object ... is to keep open the channels of trade, to make it just worthwhile for the exporter to keep his sales organization together in the overseas market".[47] Although it was recognized that the phrase was open to a wide interpretation, it was stressed as being a matter of common sense on which Members in good faith ought not to disagree very seriously. It was agreed in these discussions to record the statement that "there should be an understood priority for the importation of spare parts, because in prohibiting the importation of spare parts into a country, you are making it impossible for other countries to export machinery".[48]

See also the reference above to "token" imports.

(4) Paragraph 3(d): causes of balance-of-payments problems and their relationship with full employment

(a) *Relationship to paragraph 3(a)*

The Report of the Review Working Party on "Quantitative Restrictions" notes:

"... As regards the redraft of paragraph 3(d), the Working Party wishes to place on record that the provisions of that sub-paragraph should be interpreted, *inter alia*, in the light of the undertaking set forth in sub-paragraph 3(a)."[49]

---

[44]L/4904, adopted on 28 November 1979, 26S/205, 206, para. 2.
[45]GATT/CP.5/SR.25 p. 3.
[46]EPCT/A/PV/28, p. 19.
[47]EPCT/A/PV/28, p. 10.
[48]EPCT/A/PV/41, p. 28.
[49]L/332/Rev.I and Addenda, adopted on 2, 4 and 5 March 1955, 3S/170, 171, para. 5.

During the Fifth Session it was proposed to amend the General Agreement to add Articles 3, 4, and 6 of the Havana Charter Chapter II on employment and economic activity; however, this suggestion did not gain general support.[50] At the 1954-55 Review Session it was proposed to include in the General Agreement an article on full employment. However, the Report of the Review Working Party on "Organizational and Functional Questions" notes that the Working Party considered such an insertion unnecessary since the objectives sought through the proposed amendment were already covered in existing or proposed new Articles of the Agreement.[51]

(b)   "a contracting party may experience a high level of demand for imports"

The meaning of this provision was discussed thoroughly at Havana. As a result the provision was amplified in the Havana Charter as follows (paragraph 4(b)): "Such a Member may find that demands for foreign exchange on account of imports and other current payments are absorbing the foreign exchange resources currently available to it in such a manner as to exercise pressure on its monetary reserves which would justify the institution or maintenance of restrictions under paragraph 3 in this Article".[52] The Interpretative Note *Ad* Article 21 of the Havana Charter provided:

"With regard to the special problems that might be created for Members which, as a result of their programmes of full employment, maintenance of high and rising levels of demand and economic development, find themselves faced with a high level of demand for imports, and in consequence maintain quantitative regulation of their foreign trade, it was considered that the text of Article 21 [XII], together with the provision for export controls in certain parts of this Charter, for example, in Article 45 [XX], fully meet the position of these economies".

However, these provisions were not taken into Article XII, either in 1948 or in the Review Session.

(c)   "shall not be required to withdraw or modify restrictions"

In the course of the discussion at the Geneva session of the Preparatory Committee in 1947 it was suggested that paragraphs 3(b)(i) and 4(d) of Article 26 of the Draft Charter (corresponding to the present GATT Article XII:3(d) and XII:4(d)) were contradictory. The following statement was made in reply:

"If [the restrictions] are necessary in the sense of meeting the criteria in paragraph 2 [XII:2], if they are administered in a way which is in accord with the undertakings in paragraph 3(c), [XII:3(a) and (c)] then you cannot be required to withdraw them on the grounds that if you adopted a policy of deflation or ceased reconstruction, you would no longer be in difficulties, but if you undertake restrictions which do not meet the criteria of paragraph 2, or if you break the undertakings given in paragraph 3(c), then you may be required to withdraw the restrictions".[53]

5.   Paragraph 4

(1)   Paragraph 4(a): obligation to consult

The Report of the Review Working Party on "Quantitative Restrictions" notes:

"… Paragraph 4(a) … has been redrafted for the sake of brevity, but the intent remains unchanged. The reference to 'new restrictions' covers the case described in paragraph 4(a) of the present Article, that of a contracting party which was not applying restrictions under the Article but finds it necessary to introduce restrictions on imports. On the other hand, the phrase: 'raising the general level of its existing restrictions by a substantial intensification of the measures applied under this Article shall …' corresponds to the second part of the first sentence of paragraph 4(b) of the present Article. The language adopted, and in particular the use of the word 'measures' is meant to convey the idea that the intensification referred to in this

---

[50]Proposal at GATT/CP.5/23, discussion at GATT/CP.5/SR.10 p. 2-4.
[51]L/327, adopted on 28 February, 5 and 7 March 1955, 3S/231, 240-242, paras. 27-32.
[52]E/CONF.2/C.3/82.
[53]EPCT/A/PV/41, p. 20.

paragraph may be achieved either by increasing the restrictive effect of the restrictions applied to products the import of which is already limited, or by the institution of new restrictions on products the import of which was not yet subject to limitations."[54]

Paragraph 6 of the Understanding on the Balance-of-Payments Provisions of the GATT 1994 provides as follows:

"A Member applying new restrictions or raising the general level of its existing restrictions by a substantial intensification of the measures shall enter into consultations with the Committee within four months of the adoption of such measures. The Member adopting such measures may request that a consultation be held under paragraph 4(a) of Article XII or paragraph 12(a) of Article XVIII as appropriate. If no such request has been made, the Chairman of the Committee shall invite the Member to hold such a consultation. ..."

(a) *"alternative corrective measures which may be available"*

In discussions during the London session of the Preparatory Committee in 1946, it was stated that "the purpose of this paragraph as we see it is to make sure that before a member puts on import restrictions it should also adequately consider with the international organisations concerned other possible remedial measures such as exchange depreciation, exchange restrictions, special grants from the Fund, special loans from the Bank, and all this kind of thing".[55]

(2) *Paragraph 4(b): Review of restrictions applied under Article XII*

The text of paragraph 4(b) in the 30 October 1947 text of the General Agreement required that a review of all restrictions under Article XII be conducted not later than 1 January 1951. This review was carried out in connection with the second review of discriminatory application of import restrictions under Article XIV:1(g).[56] Article XII:4(b) was then revised in the Review Session of 1954-55, to call for an additional review of restrictions applied under Article XII. The review required by the provisions of paragraph 4(b) as revised, the timing of which is the subject of an Interpretative Note, was carried out by the CONTRACTING PARTIES in 1958-59. Part I of the resulting document discusses the financial background of the restrictions and discriminations, recent changes in the use of restrictions and the then-current level of restrictions and discrimination in the use of restrictions. Part II contains separate notes describing the restrictions in force as at the end of 1958 or early in 1959, in the twenty-five contracting parties resorting to Article XII or Article XVIII:B at that time.[57]

See also section C below on balance-of-payments consultations in the GATT.

(3) *Paragraph 4(c)*

The Report of the Review Working Party on "Quantitative Restrictions" notes that

"... Sub-paragraph (c)(i) is meant to apply to inconsistencies [with Articles XII-XIV] of a minor or technical nature. It is expected that if, during the course of consultations, the CONTRACTING PARTIES should find that such inconsistencies exist in the restrictions maintained by a particular contracting party, they would draw the attention of the contracting party to them, and, in their discretion, advise how they might be suitably modified; no other action is envisaged. It is envisaged that the provisions of (c)(i) will cover the majority of cases in which the consultations may bring to light inconsistencies with the relevant provisions of the Agreement.

---

[54] L/332/Rev.1 and Addenda, adopted on 2, 4 and 5 March 1955, 3S/170, 171, para. 6.
[55] EPCT/C.II/QR/PV/3 p. 26.
[56] See GATT/CP.6/12/Rev.2 and GATT/CP.6/48, published as *Use of Quantitative Restrictions to Safeguard Balances of Payments* (Sales No. GATT/1951-2, out of print).
[57] MGT(59)76, dated 30 July 1959; see also material on the background of this review at 6S/39-40, paras. 13-16.

"Sub-paragraph (c)(ii) deals with cases where the CONTRACTING PARTIES find serious inconsistencies in the application of the restrictions, and moreover, that those inconsistencies are of such a nature as to cause or threaten damage to other parties. In those cases, the CONTRACTING PARTIES would be required to make recommendations to remove the inconsistencies and to set up a time-limit for the removal or modification of the restrictions. If their recommendations are not complied with, the CONTRACTING PARTIES may then release a contracting party affected from certain obligations according to a procedure similar to that of Article XXIII".[58]

(4) Paragraph 4(d)

(a) "Consultations"

The Report of the Review Working Party on "Quantitative Restrictions" notes:

"... Although the changes are more of emphasis than of substance, the new text brings out clearly that the action of the contracting parties adversely affected by an application of restrictions which would not conform to the provisions of the Article, takes the form of a request for consultations rather than of a challenge".[59]

(b) "prima facie case"

The records of discussions of this provision during the London session of the Preparatory Committee indicate that these words were inserted to exclude frivolous complaints and to oblige countries to document to some extent any case presented.[60] As to the relation between sub-paragraph 4(d) and the balance-of-payments consultation process, the rapporteur in those discussions explained that "the Organization ... would have approved a certain restriction of total imports, and a country which was hurt under 3(b) [XII:4(a)] could therefore say 'You are unnecessarily damaging my interests by choosing [to restrict] combs rather than toothbrushes'".[61]

The Report of the Working Party in 1956 on "Accession of Switzerland" notes that:

"it would be appropriate for the CONTRACTING PARTIES to receive a complaint on the part of Switzerland under the provisions of paragraph 4(d) of Article XII if a contracting party which was otherwise entitled to resort to the provisions of Article XII imposed restrictions on Swiss exports which were of such a character as to cause damage to the commercial and economic interests of Switzerland, and in considering such a complaint to pay special attention to the question whether these particular restrictions were necessary. The Working Party in this connexion had particularly in mind the provisions of paragraph 3(c)(iii) of Article XII".[62]

(5) Paragraph 4(e): "due regard to ... external factors"

The Report of the Review Working Party on "Quantitative Restrictions" notes with respect to the drafting of this sub-paragraph:

"It was agreed that the scope of consultations under Articles XII and XIV should include external as well as internal causes of balance-of-payments difficulties, with a view to finding ways and means of eliminating them. In order to make that clear the Working Party agreed to insert a new paragraph ... This insertion was agreed on the understanding that it would not introduce any new criteria for the resort to restrictions under this Article. The intent of the sub-paragraph is clarified by an interpretative note".[63]

---

[58] L/332/Rev.1 and Addenda, adopted on 2, 4 and 5 March 1955, 3S/170, 173, paras. 9-10.
[59] *Ibid.*, 3S/173, para. 11.
[60] EPCT/C.II/QR/PV/5, p. 21. Concerning paragraph 4(d) see generally *ibid.* pp. 16-27.
[61] EPCT/C.II/QR/PV/3 p. 35.
[62] L/598, adopted on 17 November 1956, 5S/40, 42-43, para. 10. See also *inter alia* Havana Reports p. 102-105, GATT/TN.2/3/Add.1, GATT/CP.4/40 and GATT/CP/67 on concerns raised previously by Switzerland in this connection.
[63] L/332/Rev.1 and Addenda, adopted on 2, 4 and 5 March 1955, 3S/170, 173, para. 12.

The Resolution of 17 November 1956 on "Particular Difficulties Connected with Trade in Primary Commodities" provides, *inter alia*, that:

> "the [CONTRACTING PARTIES] shall in the course of consultations undertaken under Article XII and ... under Article XVIII:B, take account of problems relating to international commodity trade among other difficulties which may be contributing to the disequilibrium of the balance of payments and compelling certain contracting parties to maintain import restrictions".[64]

See also the material on "expanded" consultations at page 388 below. See also the discussion under Article XVIII:5.

6. Paragraph 5: "persistent and widespread application of import restrictions ... indicating the existence of a general disequilibrium"

Paragraph 5 was incorporated into the text during the London session of the Preparatory Committee; its source was a United Kingdom proposal.[65] The Report of the 1949 Working Party on "Consultation Procedures under Articles XII, XIII and XIV - other than Article XII:4(a)" notes regarding procedures for the use of Article XII:5: "Because of the broad nature of such discussions the working party considered that generally these issues would be dealt with in regular or special sessions of the CONTRACTING PARTIES".[66]

Discussions under paragraph 5 have been proposed only once, in July 1949 in connection with an agreement by Commonwealth countries to endeavour to reduce dollar-area imports by 25 percent from 1948 levels in order to halt a severe drain on their central reserves. Action was deferred in view of pending discussions in the International Monetary Fund; these discussions led to the September 1949 round of devaluations of sterling and other currencies against the dollar.[67]

The Report of the Review Working Party on "Quantitative Restrictions" notes that during the Review Session, various proposals were made to amend the General Agreement to provide for joint action to restore equilibrium in the system of world trade and payments in the event that that system became seriously unbalanced, and to avoid the imposition of unnecessarily severe restrictions on international trade. In relation to two "scarce currency" proposals, designed for a situation where some large and commercially important country might develop a persistent surplus in its balance of payments with the rest of the world, place a strain on other countries' reserves, and cause a general scarcity of its currency:

> "There was general agreement in the Working Party that such a situation might arise from a variety of different circumstances and that the prime responsibility for the state of unbalance might rest either with the surplus or the deficit countries.
>
> "It was noted that provisions are already contained in the General Agreement and also in the Articles of Agreement of the International Monetary Fund to enable consultation to take place on the measures that might appropriately be adopted to meet such situations.
>
> "In particular it was noted that Article XII:5 of the GATT lays an obligation on the CONTRACTING PARTIES to initiate discussions ...

---

[64] 5S/26, 27, para. 2.
[65] Proposal at EPCT/C.II/W.22; discussion at EPCT/C.II/QR/PV/3 p. 41-42.
[66] GATT/CP.3/50/Rev.1, adopted on 4 July 1949, II/95, 99, para. 21.
[67] GATT/CP.3/SR.42, p. 19-21; see UK notification of agreement at GATT/CP.3/68, and reference in paragraph 10 of Working Party Report on "Balance-of-Payments Questions", GATT/CP.4/38, adopted on 1 April 1950, II/103, 106-107; see also ICITO/1/14, ICITO/1/17 (referring also to Articles 4 and 21(b) of the Havana Charter) and Annecy Press Release No. 59.

"In the discussion of this matter in the Working Party a number of contracting parties stressed the desirability of providing for continuous co-operation and consultation between the GATT and the International Monetary Fund with a view to keeping the world economic situation under constant review and to enabling action to be concerted in good time to prevent any serious disequilibrium in world trade and payments from developing ..."[68]

See also the material under Article XIV:5(a).

B. RELATIONSHIP BETWEEN ARTICLE XII AND OTHER ARTICLES

1. Articles I and XIII

The Reports of the Working Parties on "United Kingdom Temporary Import Charges"[69] and "United States Temporary Import Surcharge"[70] each note the arguments of developing countries in favour of exempting from the surcharge products of developing countries or products of which developing countries were the principal supplier. These Reports also note the arguments in response that special exemption of imports by origin would produce trade diversion and, to the extent that it encouraged imports, delay removal of the surcharge.[71] The Report in 1971 of the Group of Three (constituted of the Chairmen of the CONTRACTING PARTIES, the Council and the Committee on Trade and Development) recommended that if the United States surcharge were maintained beyond 1 January 1972, "the United States Government should take steps to exempt imports from developing countries from the charge", and that the Danish temporary surcharge should exempt products covered by the Danish preference scheme for imports from developing countries.[72] In the Working Party Report on the "Danish Temporary Import Surcharge", "Without prejudice to the legal issues involved, the Working Party noted that as from the introduction of the Danish general preference scheme on 1 January 1972, products included in that scheme would be exempted from the surcharge when imported from members of the Group of Seventy-Seven. Several members of the Working Party welcomed this decision of the Danish Government noting that this had been one of the recommendations of the Group of Three. Other members expressed concern that the exemption did not extend to all developing countries. Some other members said that the discrimination created by these exemptions gave their delegations cause for concern".[73]

Paragraph 2 of the 1979 Declaration on "Trade Measures Taken for Balance-of-Payments Purposes" provides that:

"If, notwithstanding the principles of this Declaration, a developed contracting party is compelled to apply restrictive import measures for balance-of-payments purposes, it shall, in determining the incidence of its measures, take into account the export interests of the less-developed contracting parties and may exempt from its measures products of export interest to those contracting parties".[74]

A 1984 Statement by the Chairman of the Committee on Balance-of-Payments Restrictions to the Council, summarizing the result of discussions in 1982-83 concerning the work of the Committee and the role therein of balance-of-payments problems confronting heavily-indebted developing countries, notes *inter alia* that these discussions had endorsed the view that "any action taken in the balance-of-payments field should be consistent with the multilateral principles embodied in the General Agreement"[75] and adds:

---

[68]L/332/Rev.1 and Addenda, adopted on 2, 4 and 5 March 1955, 3S/170, 174-176, paras. 16-18, 23.
[69]L/2676, adopted on 17 November 1966, 15S/113, 115, para. 10.
[70]L/3573, adopted on 16 September 1971, 18S/212, 220-222, paras. 34-38.
[71]15S/115-116, para. 10; 18S/218, para. 25.
[72]L/3610, 18S/70, 74, para. 17(ii) (US surcharge); 75, para. 20 (Danish surcharge).
[73]L/3648, adopted on 12 January 1972, 19S/120, 126, 129 (identical text in paras. 22 and 41).
[74]26S/206, 207; for background to this provision see, *e.g.*, Report of the Working Party on "United States Temporary Import Surcharge", L/3573, adopted on 16 September 1971, 18S/212, 220-223, paras. 34-38, 40.
[75]C/125, dated 13 March 1984, approved by the Council on 15/16 May 1984 (C/M/178, p. 26), 31S/56, 60, para. 13.

Article XII - Restrictions to Safeguard the Balance of Payments

Comparison of the provisions of Article XII and Article XVIII:B

	Art. XII	Art. XVIII:B	Significant differences
Special considerations for developing contracting parties	...	2(b) and 8	For developed countries see Article XII:3(d).
General statement on the use of restrictions	1	9	
Limits of application of the provisions	2(a)	9 proviso	Criteria in Article XII relate to "imminent threat" and "very low reserves", and in Article XVIII:B to "threat" and "inadequate reserves".
Relaxation and elimination of restrictions	2(b)	11 second sentence	See precautionary clause in interpretative note *ad* Article XVIII:11.
Right to choose goods to restrict	3(b)	10	
Conditions and undertakings	3(c)	10 provisos	
Domestic policy considerations	3(a) and 3(d)	11 first sentence and proviso	Different arrangements of clauses reflect differences in emphasis
Review and consultation procedures	4(a) to (d)	12(a) to (d)	Interval between regular consultations under (b) is one year in Article XII, two years in Article XVIII:B: also note proviso to Article XVIII:12(b).
Consideration of special factors in consultations	4(e)	12(f) first sentence	Consideration in Article XII relates to external factors (see note *ad* Article XII:4(e)) and in Article XVIII to factors in Article XVIII:2
Expeditiousness in making determinations	4(f)	12(f) second sentence	
Right to withdraw on shorter notice, upon unfavourable determination	...	12(e)	When GATT is definitively applied under Art. XXVI, withdrawal is governed by Article XXXI and requires six months' notice
Non-discriminatory application			Article XIII
Deviation from rule of non-discrimination			Article XIV

"In clear language this means that actions should be taken on a most-favoured-nation basis or, pursuant to the provisions of Part IV of the General Agreement (particularly Article XXXVII) and the 1979 Decision on Differential and More Favourable, Treatment, Reciprocity and Fuller Participation of Developing Countries, in a manner consistent with that decision, including special treatment for the least-developed among the developing countries. It was noted that Paragraph 2(c) of the Decision allows for the possibility of more favourable treatment to be accorded among developing contracting parties. ...

"In view of the consensus to respect multilateral principles in responding to the needs of countries experiencing severe balance-of-payments difficulties, the possibility of focusing trade actions on such countries would depend on the choice of products for which a particular country is a principal or substantial supplier to a particular market, or on the choice of specific measures which would particularly benefit that country, it being understood that the implementation of each particular measure would be consistent with the multilateral principles referred to".[76]

2. Article XVIII

The table above presents a simplified comparison of the provisions of Article XII and Article XVIII:B.

In a few instances consultations have been conducted concerning balance-of-payments measures without reference to either Article XII or Article XVIII.[77] In another instance a contracting party has consulted concerning the same measures under Article XVIII:B and subsequently under Article XII.[78]

In the 1958 Working Party Report on "Consultations and Review Regarding Balance-of-Payments Restrictions", the Working Party "noted the recommendation of the Chairman of the CONTRACTING PARTIES that it be placed on record that twelve of the contracting parties applying balance-of-payments import restrictions at present fulfil the requirements of Article XVIII:4 and that their restrictions be considered as being applied under Article XVIII:B rather than Article XII; consequently, the other fourteen contracting parties applying restrictions are considered as acting under Article XII, and are therefore required to consult under Article XII:4(b) in 1959".[79]

3. Article XXIII

See Article XXIII.

4. Article XXIV

See Article XXIV.

C. BALANCE-OF-PAYMENTS CONSULTATIONS IN THE GATT

1. Committee on Balance-of-Payments Restrictions

Prior to 1958, consultations under the balance-of-payments Articles of the General Agreement were conducted in a series of working parties established by the CONTRACTING PARTIES for that purpose. When the balance-of-payments Articles were revised during the Review Session, it was agreed to study improvement of the arrangements for consultations.[80] The Committee on Balance-of-Payments Restrictions was established on 22 November 1958. Its present terms of reference are as follows:

"To conduct the consultations under Article XII:4(b) and Article XVIII:12(b) as well as any such consultations as may be initiated under Article XII:4(a) or Article XVIII:12(a).

"Pursuant to paragraph 4 of the Declaration on Trade Measures Taken for Balance-of-Payments Purposes, adopted by the CONTRACTING PARTIES on 28 November 1979, 'all restrictive import measures taken for balance-of-payments purposes shall be subject to consultation in the GATT Committee on Balance-of-Payments Restrictions'".[81]

In April 1978, one contracting party raised the question of the balance of representation in the Balance-of-Payments Committee, and suggested that the membership should reflect a suitable balance between developed and

---

[76]*Ibid.*, 31S/60-61, paras. 14, 16.
[77]Israel (BOP/R/90, BOP/R/101, BOP/R/113, BOP/R/129, BOP/R/142, BOP/R/155, BOP/R/170, BOP/R/187, BOP/R/195, BOP/R/210); Portugal (BOP/R/62, BOP/R/93, BOP/R/106, BOP/R/111, BOP/R/118, BOP/R/125, BOP/R/134, BOP/R/145, BOP/R/152); South Africa (BOP/R/92, BOP/R/211).
[78]Greece (consultations under Article XVIII:B in BOP/R/89, BOP/R/100, BOP/R/114, BOP/R/123; Article XVIII:B disinvoked, 1984; consultation under Article XII, BOP/R/160; Article XII disinvoked 1987).
[79]L/931, adopted on 22 November 1958, 7S/90, 92, para. 8. The twelve contracting parties referred to are: Brazil, Chile, Ghana, Greece, India, Indonesia, Malaysia, Myanmar, Pakistan, Sri Lanka, Turkey and Uruguay.
[80]3S/179, para. 34.
[81]L/6526/Rev.4, dated 22 April 1993 (also listing the members of the Committee as of that date).

developing contracting parties. In response the Director-General pointed out that members of the Committee were designated by the Council, which had never refused an application for membership.[82]

The 1979 "Declaration on Trade Measures Taken for Balance-of-Payments Purposes" (referred to below as the "1979 Declaration") also provides: "The membership of the Committee is open to all contracting parties indicating their wish to serve on it. Efforts shall be made to ensure that the composition of the Committee reflects as far as possible the characteristics of the contracting parties in general in terms of their geographical location, external financial position and stage of economic development."[83]

A 1984 Statement by the Chairman of the Committee on Balance-of-Payments Restrictions to the Council, summarizing the result of discussions in 1982-83 concerning the work of the Committee and the role therein of balance-of-payments problems confronting heavily-indebted developing countries, notes *inter alia* that: "The need for more active participation in the Balance-of-Payments Committee by both developed and developing countries was recognized. In this connection, it may be recalled that the Committee is open-ended and that any contracting party may become a member of the Committee simply by informing the Director-General of its wish to do so. The level of representation in the Committee was considered as a matter for individual governments' decision".[84]

Paragraph 5 of the Understanding on the Balance-of-Payments Provisions of the GATT 1994 provides *inter alia*: "The Committee on Balance-of-Payments Restrictions ... shall carry out consultations in order to review all restrictive import measures taken for balance-of-payments purposes. The membership of the Committee is open to all Members indicating their wish to serve on it. ... "

2. **Procedures for examination of balance-of-payments measures**

(1) General

The Report of the Review Working Party on "Quantitative Restrictions" notes that the main difference between the provisions of Article XVIII:12 and the corresponding provisions of Article XII:4 "relates to the periodicity of the consultations under sub-paragraph (b)" and further notes that "The remarks and agreed statements referring to consultations under Article XII and which are reproduced in paragraphs 6 to 11 of this report apply also to consultations under paragraph 12 of Article XVIII".[85]

(2) Scope of consultations

The 1979 Declaration provides that "The procedures for examination stipulated in Articles XII and XVIII shall apply to all restrictive import measures taken for balance-of-payments purposes."[86] Thus, the scope of consultations includes both quantitative restrictions for balance-of-payments purposes and other restrictive import measures, such as import surcharges and import deposits, taken for balance-of-payments purposes. See the discussion above at page 366 on the treatment of import surcharges and import deposit measures in balance-of-payments consultations since the 1979 Declaration. Paragraph 5 of the Understanding on the Balance-of-Payments Provisions of the GATT 1994 also provides that the Committee "... shall carry out consultations in order to review all restrictive import measures taken for balance-of-payments purposes. ..."

In the period before 1979, the Committee did not routinely examine non-quantitative balance-of-payments measures. However, in certain instances the Council requested that the Committee examine non-quantitative measures when the Council viewed such measures as appropriately considered in conjunction with existing balance-of-payments quantitative restrictions: these included import surcharges and/or deposits applied by Brazil,

---

[82]C/M/124, p. 4-5.
[83]L/4904, adopted on 28 November 1979, 26S/205, 207, para. 5.
[84]C/125, dated 13 March 1984, approved by the Council on 15/16 May 1984 (C/M/178, p. 26), 31S/56, 59, para. 10.
[85]L/332/Rev.1 and Addenda, adopted on 2, 4 and 5 March 1955, 3S/170, 183-84, para. 46.
[86]L/4904, adopted on 28 November 1979, 26S/205, para. 1.

Finland, Israel, Portugal, South Africa and Yugoslavia. The Committee also examined the extension of the waiver decisions for the stamp duty applied by Turkey as a balance-of-payments measure.[87]

(3) Procedures

The 1979 Declaration states, with regard to examination of balance-of-payments measures in the Committee on Balance-of-Payments Restrictions, that "The Committee shall follow the procedures for consultations on balance-of-payments restrictions approved by the Council on 28 April 1970 (18S/48-53, hereinafter referred to as 'full consultations procedures') or the procedures for regular consultations on balance-of-payments restrictions with developing countries approved by the Council on 19 December 1972 (20S/47-49, hereinafter referred to as 'simplified consultation procedures') subject to the provisions set out below."[88] Paragraph 5 of the Understanding on the Balance-of-Payments Provisions of the GATT 1994 also provides that "… The Committee shall follow the procedures for consultations on balance-of-payments restrictions approved on 28 April 1970 (BISD 18S/48-53, referred to in this Understanding as 'full consultation procedures'), subject to the provisions set out below".

The 1970 "full consultations procedures" referred to in the 1979 Declaration describe the arrangements and procedures originally agreed in 1958 for consultations under Article XII:4(b) and Article XVIII:12(b) as revised in the Review Session, as they had evolved to 1970. The 1970 procedures deal with the contents of the consultations, the documentation for the consultations, the time schedule for the consultations, arrangements for consultation with the International Monetary Fund, the composition of the Committee on Balance-of-Payments Restrictions, and the reports to be prepared on the consultations. Attached to the 1970 procedures are a plan of discussion for balance-of-payments consultations, and a list of points to be covered in the basic document for the consultations.[89]

See also the "Procedures for dealing with new import restrictions applied for balance-of-payments reasons" adopted by the CONTRACTING PARTIES on 16 November 1960,[90] and earlier procedural decisions on examination of balance-of-payments measures.[91]

The first and second reports of the CG-18 to the Council note the discussions in the Group during 1975 through 1977 on procedural improvements concerning examination of balance-of-payments measures.[92]

3. Notification of balance-of-payments measures

In 1952 the Working Party on "Procedures for Report and Consultations in 1953 on the Discriminatory Application of Import Restrictions" examined intersessional procedures for initiation of consultations under Article XII. The Report of the Working Party notes that "It was … agreed to amend the procedure for consultations so as to require a contracting party modifying its import restrictions to furnish detailed information promptly to the Executive Secretary for immediate circulation to other contracting parties … the Working Party

---

[87]See L/2824, adopted on 6 November 1967, 15S/195; L/3229, adopted on 23 July 1969, 17S/151; L/3787, adopted on 19 December 1972, 20S/229.
[88]26S/207, para. 6.
[89]L/3388, presented to the Council on 28 April 1970, 18S/48.
[90]9S/18, paras.1-6.
[91]Concerning consultations under the pre-Review Session provisions of Articles XII and XIV, see Working Party Reports on "Consultation Procedure under Article XII:4(a)", GATT/CP.3/30/Rev.1, adopted on 20 June 1949, II/89; "Procedures for Action on Matters Arising Under Articles XII to XIV between Sessions of the CONTRACTING PARTIES", adopted on 26 October 1952, II/101; "Procedures for Report and
Consultations in 1953 on the Discriminatory Application of Import Restrictions", L/55, adopted on 7 November 1952, 1S/43, section on Article XII at 1S/45-46; "Consultations at the Tenth Session", L/465, adopted on 2 December 1955, 4S/43-46; "Plans for Consultations in 1957", L/597, adopted on 17 November 1956, 5S/48-56; and "Consultations under Article XII:4(b); Etc; Implementation of Revised Provisions of Articles XII and XVIII:B", L/769, adopted on 30 November 1957, 6S/36. On the implementation of the Review Session revision of Articles XII and XVIII, see the last of these reports and the Working Party Report on "Consultations and Review regarding Balance-of-Payments Restrictions", L/931, adopted on 22 November 1958, 7S/90.
[92]L/4429, 23S/38, 43-45, paras. 21-25; L/4585, 24S/58, 60, para. 9. The Mandate of the Consultative Group of Eighteen (CG-18), as adopted in 1975 and confirmed in 1979, provides that "The task of the Group is to facilitate the carrying out, by the CONTRACTING PARTIES, of their responsibilities, particularly with respect to … the international adjustment process …" L/4204, Decision of the Council of 11 July 1975, 22S/15.

recommends that the Executive Secretary be authorized to communicate with any contracting party which he has reason to believe may have significantly modified its restrictions so as to obtain all the information which he and the Chairman require to carry out their responsibilities".[93]

The "Procedures for dealing with new import restrictions applied for balance-of-payments reasons" adopted in 1960 provide that "any contracting party modifying its import restrictions is required to furnish detailed information promptly to the Executive Secretary, for circulation to the contracting parties." A footnote to this paragraph notes: "Under established procedures, contracting parties should furnish such information not only when they wish to initiate a consultation pursuant to Articles XII:4(a) or XVIII:12(a) but whenever any significant changes are made in their restrictive systems".[94]

The 1972 Decision on simplified procedures for balance-of-payments consultations under Article XVIII:12(b) (cited below *in extenso*) noted that "There are a number of developing contracting parties, mostly the newly independent countries, which maintain import restrictions. ... the adoption of the 'streamlined' procedures set forth in paragraph 3 above should contribute substantially to easing the way for all developing countries to define their position regarding their restrictions in relation to the GATT provisions. It is therefore proposed that, upon approval of the new procedures, the secretariat be instructed to enquire and discuss with each of these developing countries with a view to establishing a complete list of the contracting parties invoking Section B of Article XVIII of the Agreement".[95]

Paragraph 3 of the 1979 Declaration provides: "Contracting parties shall promptly notify to the GATT the introduction or intensification of all restrictive import measures taken for balance-of-payments purposes. Contracting parties which have reason to believe that a restrictive import measure applied by another contracting party was taken for balance-of-payments purposes may notify the measure to the GATT or may request the GATT secretariat to seek information on the measure and make it available to all contracting parties if appropriate".[96] In addition, paragraph 3 of the 1979 "Understanding regarding Notification, Consultation, Dispute Settlement and Surveillance" provides that "Contracting parties ... undertake, to the maximum extent possible, to notify the CONTRACTING PARTIES of their adoption of trade measures affecting the operation of the General Agreement, it being understood that such notification would of itself be without prejudice to views on the consistency of measures with or their relevance to rights and obligations under the General Agreement. Contracting parties should endeavour to notify such measures in advance of implementation. In other cases, where prior notification has not been possible, such measures should be notified promptly *ex post facto*. Contracting parties which have reason to believe that such trade measures have been adopted by another contracting party may seek information on such measures bilaterally, from the contracting party concerned".[97]

In its Report on the simplified consultation held with Sri Lanka in 1994, the Committee came to the following "interim conclusion": "In the absence of precise information on import restrictions maintained for balance-of-payments purposes, the Committee was unable to conclude the simplified consultation with Sri Lanka. The Committee requested Sri Lanka to notify, by tariff line, import restrictions, if any, maintained for BOP purposes, or to disinvoke Article XVIII:B. ..." Sri Lanka made the requested notification in October 1994.[98]

Paragraphs 9 and 10 of the Understanding on the Balance-of-Payments Provisions of the GATT 1994 provide as follows:

"A Member shall notify to the General Council the introduction of or any changes in the application of restrictive import measures taken for balance-of-payments purposes, as well as any modifications in time-schedules for the removal of such measures as announced under paragraph 1. Significant changes shall be notified to the General Council prior to or not later than 30 days after their announcement. On a yearly

---

[93] L/55, adopted on 7 November 1952, 1S/43, 45-56, paras. 10, 11.
[94] Procedures approved on 16 November 1960, 9S/18, para. 2.
[95] L/3772/Rev.1, approved by the Council on 19 December 1972, 20S/47, 49, para. 5.
[96] L/4904, adopted on 28 November 1979, 26S/205, 207, para. 3. See also CG.18/W/9/Rev.1, 22 October 1976. Nigeria began consulting in the Committee on Balance-of-Payments Restrictions in 1984 following a "reverse notification" by another contracting party.
[97] L/4907, adopted on 28 November 1979, 26S/210, 210-211, para. 3.
[98] Report, BOP/R/219; notification, L/7542.

basis, each Member shall make available to the Secretariat a consolidated notification, including all changes in laws, regulations, policy statements or public notices, for examination by Members. Notifications shall include full information, as far as possible, at the tariff-line level, on the type of measures applied, the criteria used for their administration, product coverage and trade flows affected.

"At the request of any Member, notifications may be reviewed by the Committee. Such reviews would be limited to the clarification of specific issues raised by a notification or examination of whether a consultation under paragraph 4(a) of Article XII or paragraph 12(a) of Article XVIII is required. Members which have reasons to believe that a restrictive import measure applied by another Member was taken for balance-of-payments purposes may bring the matter to the attention of the Committee. The Chairman of the Committee shall request information on the measure and make it available to all Members. Without prejudice to the right of any member of the Committee to seek appropriate clarifications in the course of consultations, questions may be submitted in advance for consideration by the consulting Member."

For instances of "reverse notification" of restrictions, or requests to the Secretariat to seek information on restrictions maintained by another contracting party, see the 1987 Note by the Secretariat on "Articles XII, XIV, XV and XVIII".[99]

In 1965, procedures were adopted relating to import restrictions maintained by newly-independent countries; it was suggested to such countries that "even if they were not yet in a position to determine whether they wished to invoke the provisions of Article XVIII as justification for some or all restrictions in force, they might submit descriptive material relative to their entire import control system, without prejudice to the consistency of the measures maintained with their obligations under GATT".[100]

---

[99] MTN.GNG/NG7/W/14, dated 11 August 1987, para. 36.
[100] 14S/161.

ARTICLE XII - RESTRICTIONS TO SAFEGUARD THE BALANCE OF PAYMENTS

4. Consultations

(1) Timing of balance-of-payments consultations

Sub-paragraph (a) of Articles XII:4 and XVIII:12 provides that "Any contracting party applying new restrictions or raising the general level of its existing restrictions by a substantial intensification of the measures applied under [Article XII or Article XVIII:B respectively] shall immediately after instituting or intensifying such restrictions (or, in circumstances in which prior consultation is practicable, before doing so) consult with the CONTRACTING PARTIES as to the nature of its balance-of-payments difficulties, alternative corrective measures which may be available, and the possible effect of the restrictions on the economies of other contracting parties".

Article XII:4(b) provides that "contracting parties applying import restrictions under this Article shall enter into consultations of the type provided for in sub-paragraph (a) of this paragraph with the CONTRACTING PARTIES annually." Article XVIII:12(b) provides that "contracting parties applying restrictions under this Section shall enter into consultations of the type provided for in sub-paragraph (a) of this paragraph with the CONTRACTING PARTIES at intervals of approximately, but not less than, two years according to a programme to be drawn up each year by the CONTRACTING PARTIES".

The 1972 statement on "Procedures for Regular Consultations on Balance-of-Payments Restrictions with Developing Countries", which introduced the concept of "simplified consultations" for certain consultations under Article XVIII:B, provides that "Consultations under Article XVIII:12(a) will continue to follow the existing rules. Consultations with developed countries acting under Article XII will be held annually in the usual manner."[101] Thus, the "full consultation procedures" agreed in 1970 apply to all consultations under Article XII or Article XVIII:12(a); in certain cases the "simplified consultation procedures" agreed in 1972 apply to periodic consultations under Article XVIII:12(b). See below.

Contracting parties consulting with the BOP Committee: Date of last consultation (Art. XII) or full consultation (Art. XVIII:B)

Bangladesh	none
Egypt	1992
India	1992
Israel*	1993
Nigeria	1993
Pakistan	1989
Philippines	1993
Poland (Art. XII)	1994
South Africa*	1993
Sri Lanka	1971
Tunisia	1992
Turkey	1993
Yugoslavia	1991

Status as of 1 September 1993.

* Israel and South Africa consult with the Committee on Balance-of-Payments Restrictions without specifying whether restrictions are under Article XII or under Article XVIII:B.

The 1970 "full consultation procedures" provide that "Every January, the secretariat should circulate and submit to the Council a time schedule for the consultations to be held in that year. This should be drawn up in consultation with the contracting parties concerned, and in the light of the programme and progress of the consultations of the International Monetary Fund with the governments concerned, so as to ensure that the most up-to-date and meaningful possible data form part of the Fund's contribution to these consultations in GATT. The time schedule may be modified as necessary in the light of changing circumstances. Normally the consultations to be held in one year will be grouped so that they can be taken up at two to four continuous sessions of the Committee on Balance-of-Payments Restrictions".[102] The provisions establishing the Trade Policy Review Mechanism in the Decision of 12 April 1989 on "Functioning of the GATT System" provide that "the Chairman of the Council shall, in consultation with the contracting party or parties concerned, and with the Chairman of the Committee on Balance-of-Payments Restrictions, devise administrative arrangements which would harmonize the normal rhythm of the trade policy reviews with the time-table for balance-of-payments consultations but would not postpone the trade policy review by more than 12 months".[103] The schedule for balance-of-payments consultations is regularly circulated to the Council each January.[104]

At the March 1993 Council meeting, the Chairman of the Committee on Balance-of-Payments Restrictions announced that in view of the frequent postponements of balance-of-payments consultations experienced in recent

---

[101]L/3772/Rev.1, adopted on 19 December 1972, 20S/47, 49, para. 4.
[102]18S/50-51, paras. 6-7.
[103]L/6490, adopted on 12 April 1989, 36S/403, 404-405, para. I.C(ii).
[104]See, e.g., C/W/727, schedule of consultations for 1993 dated 29 January 1993.

years, the Committee had decided that this matter should be subject to greater discipline. Accordingly, the Committee had decided that if in future, a consulting country wished to request postponement of its consultation, the request should be submitted to the Committee and that the consultation could only be postponed with the consent of the Committee.[105]

Paragraphs 6 and 7 of the Understanding on the Balance-of-Payments Provisions of the GATT 1994 provide as follows:

"A Member applying new restrictions or raising the general level of its existing restrictions by a substantial intensification of the measures shall enter into consultations with the Committee within four months of the adoption of such measures. The Member adopting such measures may request that a consultation be held under paragraph 4(a) of Article XII or paragraph 12(a) of Article XVIII as appropriate. If no such request has been made, the Chairman of the Committee shall invite the Member to hold such a consultation. Factors that may be examined in the consultation would include, *inter alia*, the introduction of new types of restrictive measures for balance-of-payments purposes, or an increase in the level or product coverage of restrictions.

"All restrictions applied for balance-of-payments purposes shall be subject to periodic review in the Committee under paragraph 4(b) of Article XII or under paragraph 12(b) of Article XVIII, subject to the possibility of altering the periodicity of consultations in agreement with the consulting Member or pursuant to any specific review procedure that may be recommended by the General Council."

(2)   Simplified consultations under Article XVIII:B

In December 1972 the Council approved modified "Procedures for Regular Consultations on Balance-of-Payments Restrictions with Developing Countries", and an accompanying statement, as follows:

"At the Council meeting of 6 October 1971, the retiring Chairman of the Committee on Balance-of-Payments Restrictions referred to the difficulties in arranging Article XVIII:12(b) consultations in 1971 ...

"... Some delegations feel that detailed discussions of the external financial justification of the restrictions every two years may not be necessary in all cases and a consultation may become a formality for which adequate preparation may require an amount of energy and attention disproportionate to its value. On the other hand, the consultations are specifically provided for in the General Agreement for well-defined purposes and for sound reasons, and many contracting parties would have serious misgivings if these GATT provisions were to be ignored while there were no insurmountable obstacles to their implementation. ...

"In the light of these considerations, it is proposed that the following modified procedures be adopted for the implementation of Article XVIII:12(b) concerning *regular consultations* on balance-of-payments restrictions with *developing countries*:

"(a)   each year, the secretariat establishes a schedule showing the contracting parties acting under Article XVIII:B which are required to consult under paragraph 12(b) that year;

"(b)   each of these contracting parties should submit to the CONTRACTING PARTIES a concise written statement on the nature of the balance-of-payments difficulties, the system and methods of restriction (with particular reference to any discriminatory features and changes in past two years), the effects of the restrictions and prospects of liberalization;

"(c)   the statements received will be circulated to all contracting parties and presented to the Committee on Balance-of-Payments Restrictions for prior consideration, so that the Committee may determine whether a full consultation is desirable. If it decides that such a consultation is not desirable, the Committee will recommend to the Council that the contracting party be deemed to have consulted with

---

[105]C/M/263, p. 7, BOP/R/208.

the CONTRACTING PARTIES and to have fulfilled its obligations under Article XVIII:12(b) for that year. Otherwise, the CONTRACTING PARTIES will consult the International Monetary Fund, and the Committee will follow the procedures applicable hitherto for a full consultation; and

"(d) arrangements will be made with the International Monetary Fund for the supply of balance-of-payments statistics for each country submitting a statement in accordance with paragraph (b) above."[106]

"It should be noted that this proposal relates only to the periodic consultations provided for in Article XVIII:12(b). Consultations under Article XVIII:12(a) will continue to follow the existing rules. Consultations with developed countries acting under Article XII will be held annually in the usual manner".[107]

The 1977 report of the Consultative Group of Eighteen notes that "The Group exchanged views on ... whether the simplified procedures adopted in 1972 were an exception to the full procedures adopted in 1970 in the sense that, while the simplified procedures would in practice normally apply to balance-of-payments consultations with a developing country, another contracting party might nevertheless require as of right that the full procedures be followed".[108] This question was also discussed in the Council in 1977 where the Chairman of the Committee on Balance-of-Payments Restrictions stated his view that "the simplified procedure was clearly an exception to the general rule, and could only apply if there was a consensus in the Committee. If there was no consensus, i.e. if one or several members requested that a full consultation be held, such consultation would take place automatically. The rule was clear and the practice had so far been in conformity with this rule". A number of contracting parties expressed their view "that the simplified procedures should be the general rule for consultations with developing countries. Consequently, an absolute consensus to decide that a full consultation was not desirable, should not be required. It did not appear reasonable if, on the basis of the opinion of a single member, the Committee would determine that a full consultation was to be held".[109]

The 1979 Declaration provides with respect to the choice of procedure:

"In the case of consultations under Article XVIII:12(b) the Committee shall base its decision on the type of procedure on such factors as the following:

"(a) the time elapsed since the last full consultations;

"(b) the steps the consulting contracting party has taken in the light of conclusions reached on the occasion of previous consultations;

"(c) the changes in the overall level or nature of the trade measures taken for balance-of-payments purposes;

"(d) the changes in the balance-of-payments situation or prospects;

"(e) whether the balance-of-payments problems are structural or temporary in nature.

"A less-developed contracting party may at any time request full consultations".[110]

A 1988 Note by the Secretariat on "Consultations Held in the Committee on Balance-of-Payments Restrictions under Articles XII and XVIII:B since 1975" states that in the period 1975 through June 1988, there had been 106 consultations under Article XVIII:B, of which 77 had taken the simplified form. In 17 of these,

---

[106] 20S/47-49, paras. 1-3.
[107] Ibid., para. 4.
[108] L/4585, 24S/58, 60, para. 9.
[109] C/M/122, p. 4.
[110] L/4904, adopted on 28 November 1979, 26S/205, 207-208, paras. 8-9.

the Committee had, in its report on a simplified consultation, recommended full consultations. Before 1979, the reason for such a recommendation was not indicated; since that date it had always done so.[111]

Paragraph 8 of the Understanding on the Balance-of-Payments Provisions of the GATT 1994 provides as follows:

"Consultations may be held under the simplified procedures approved on 19 December 1972 (BISD 20S/47-49, referred to in this Understanding as 'simplified consultation procedures') in the case of least-developed country Members or in the case of developing country Members which are pursuing liberalization efforts in conformity with the schedule presented to the Committee in previous consultations. Simplified consultation procedures may also be used when the Trade Policy Review of a developing country Member is scheduled for the same calendar year as the date fixed for the consultations. In such cases the decision as to whether full consultation procedures should be used will be made on the basis of the factors enumerated in paragraph 8 of the 1979 Declaration. Except in the case of least-developed country Members, no more than two successive consultations may be held under simplified consultation procedures."

(3) Documentation used in consultations

The 1979 Declaration includes the following provisions concerning documentation:

"The GATT secretariat, drawing on all appropriate sources of information, including the consulting contracting party, shall with a view to facilitating the consultations in the Committee prepare a factual background paper describing the trade aspects of the measures taken, including aspects of particular interest to less-developed contracting parties. The paper shall also cover such other matters as the Committee may determine. The GATT secretariat shall give the consulting contracting party the opportunity to comment on the paper before it is submitted to the Committee."

"The technical assistance services of the GATT secretariat shall, at the request of a less-developed consulting contracting party, assist it in preparing the documentation for the consultations."[112]

Since the entry into force of the 1979 Declaration the material prepared for each full consultation has consisted of three basic documents: (i) a "Basic Document" prepared by the consulting country in case of a full consultation, or a "Written Statement" prepared also by the consulting country in case of a simplified consultation; (ii) a "Background Paper" prepared by the GATT Secretariat; and (iii) a "Recent Economic Developments" document prepared by the IMF.

The 1970 "full consultation procedures" provide that the following points are to be covered in the Basic Document for a full consultation under Articles XII:4(b) or XVIII:12(b):

"(a) Legal and administrative basis of the import restriction.

"(b) Methods used in restricting imports.

"(c) Treatment of imports from different sources including information on the use of bilateral agreements.

"(d) Commodities, or groups of commodities, affected by the various forms of import restrictions.

"(e) State trading, or government monopoly, used as a measure to restrict imports for balance-of-payments reasons.

"(f) Measures taken since the last consultation in relaxing or otherwise modifying import restrictions.

"(g) Effects of the import restriction on trade.

---

[111]MTN.GNG/NG7/W/46, dated 24 June 1988, pp. 11-12, paras. 32-33.
[112]L/4904, adopted on 28 November 1979, 26S/205, 207-208, paras. 7 and 10.

"(h) General policy in the use of restrictions for balance-of-payments reasons".[113]

In 1982-83 discussions took place concerning the treatment in the work of the Committee on Balance-of-Payments Restrictions of balance-of-payments problems confronting heavily-indebted developing countries. A 1984 Statement by the Chairman of the Committee on Balance-of-Payments Restrictions to the Council summarized the result of these discussions, stating *inter alia*, that:

"As regards the preparation of documents for balance-of-payments consultations, it would be advisable for consulting countries which wish to have particular attention paid to their external trading environment to indicate this to the secretariat in good time. In these cases, the consulting country should, in its basic document, provide the Committee with any information on external factors which it deems relevant and indicate specific measures and products, relative to any external market, on which it could consider action to be of particular importance. In this connection it was recalled that the technical assistance of the secretariat is available, under Paragraph 10 of the 1979 Declaration, to any developing country consulting under Article XVIII:B. The secretariat would also provide adequate information on the trading environment, including any relevant measures affecting the trade of a consulting country, as part of its background note. ... While, as at present, background notes would be prepared on the basis of all relevant information available and in full consultation with the consulting country, the secretariat would retain full responsibility for the content of the note. ...".[114]

Paragraphs 11 and 12 of the Understanding on the Balance-of-Payments Provisions of the GATT 1994 provide as follows:

"The consulting Member shall prepare a Basic Document for the consultations which, in addition to any other information considered to be relevant, should include: *(a)* an overview of the balance-of-payments situation and prospects, including a consideration of the internal and external factors having a bearing on the balance-of-payments situation and the domestic policy measures taken in order to restore equilibrium on a sound and lasting basis; *(b)* a full description of the restrictions applied for balance-of-payments purposes, their legal basis and steps taken to reduce incidental protective effects; *(c)* measures taken since the last consultation to liberalize import restrictions, in the light of the conclusions of the Committee; *(d)* a plan for the elimination and progressive relaxation of remaining restrictions. References may be made, when relevant, to the information provided in other notifications or reports made to the WTO. Under simplified consultation procedures, the consulting Member shall submit a written statement containing essential information on the elements covered by the Basic Document.

"The Secretariat shall, with a view to facilitating the consultations in the Committee, prepare a factual background paper dealing with the different aspects of the plan for consultations. In the case of developing country Members, the Secretariat document shall include relevant background and analytical material on the incidence of the external trading environment on the balance-of-payments situation and prospects of the consulting Member. The technical assistance services of the Secretariat shall, at the request of a developing country Member, assist in preparing the documentation for the consultations."

For further background on the format and contents of the Background Paper by the Secretariat for full and simplified consultations, and the IMF document on "Recent Economic Developments", see the 1988 Note by the Secretariat on "Consultations Held in the Committee on Balance-of-Payments Restrictions under Articles XII and XVIII:B since 1975".[115]

(4) Secrecy

The Note *Ad* Article XII provides that "The CONTRACTING PARTIES shall make provision for the utmost secrecy in the conduct of any consultation under the provisions of this Article." The Note Ad Article XVIII

---

[113]L/3388, 18S/48, 53, Annex II.
[114]C/125 dated 13 March 1984, approved by the Council on 15/16 May 1984 (C/M/178, p. 26), 31S/56, 59-60, para. 11.
[115]MTN.GNG/NG7/W/46, dated 24 June 1988, p. 6-7, paras. 24-25.

provides that "The CONTRACTING PARTIES and the parties concerned shall preserve the utmost secrecy in respect of matters arising under this Article".

The text of Article XII:4(e) before the Review Session read: "It is recognized that premature disclosure of the prospective application, withdrawal or modification of any restriction under this Article might stimulate speculative trade and financial movements which would tend to defeat the purposes of this Article. Accordingly, the CONTRACTING PARTIES shall make provision for the utmost secrecy in the conduct of any consultation under the provisions of this Article". The 1949 Report of the Working Party on "Consultation Procedure under Article XII:4(a)" noted concerning this provision that "The working party ... has been impressed with the wisdom of this requirement and records its opinion that, in default of suitable provisions for secrecy, prior consultation with a country which was faced with a crisis would become virtually impossible".[116]

The same Report also notes with respect to the reports submitted on balance-of-payments consultations to the CONTRACTING PARTIES that "The report should be treated as a secret document. It is suggested, however, that the need for absolute secrecy may only be temporary. Without prejudice to the right of the CONTRACTING PARTIES to organize the distribution of their documents, it is recommended that the Chairman may authorize the distribution of the report or parts of the report as a restricted document, provided that the contracting party which requested the consultation has no objection to such a distribution. The facts and statements communicated by the International Monetary Fund will be kept secret as far and as long as the Fund so desires."[117] A General Arrangement for Co-ordination and Consultation concluded between the Chairman of the CONTRACTING PARTIES and the Fund in 1948 provides, *inter alia*, that "Any request for consultation by either the Fund or the CONTRACTING PARTIES shall be accompanied by available information which would contribute to the effectiveness of the consultation. In such cases, due regard shall be paid to the need to safeguard confidential information and to any special obligations of the Fund and the CONTRACTING PARTIES in this respect."[118]

(5) Matters discussed in consultations

As noted above, the 1970 "full consultation procedures" provide a detailed Plan of Consultations with four main headings: balance-of-payments position and prospects; alternative measures to restore equilibrium; system and methods of the restrictions; and effects of the restrictions.[119] The statement on these procedures provides:

"Consultations under Article XII:4 and XVIII:12 cover the nature of the balance-of-payments difficulties of the contracting party in question, alternative measures that may be available and the possible effect of the restrictions on the economies of other contracting parties. They are intended to provide an opportunity for a free exchange of views contributing to a better understanding of the problems facing the consulting countries, of the various measures taken by them to deal with these problems, and of the possibilities of further progress in the direction of freer, multilateral trade. ... Having regard to the diversity of circumstances, the Plan should not be regarded as a rigid programme, but might require suitable adaptation in individual cases. The special problems of each consulting country relating to its balance of payments should perforce be given careful consideration. Account should be taken of all factors, both internal and external, which affect the balance-of-payments position of the consulting country".[120]

Concerning Committee practice regarding the content of discussions, see the 1988 Note by the Secretariat on "Consultations Held in the Committee on Balance-of-Payments Restrictions under Articles XII and XVIII:B since 1975".[121]

---

[116]GATT/CP.3/30/Rev.1, adopted on 20 June 1949, II/89, 90, para. 5. See also discussion of secrecy in the 1985 Report of the Chairman of the Balance-of-Payments Committee on the Chilean proposal noted above, C/132, 32S/46, 48, para. 6.
[117]*Ibid.*, II/94, para. 18.
[118]I/120, 121, para. (iv), proposed by the Chairman of the CONTRACTING PARTIES by letter dated September 9, 1948 and agreed to by the Fund by letter dated September 28, 1948.
[119]L/3388, 18S/48, 52, Annex I.
[120]*Ibid.*, 18S/49, para. 2.
[121]MTN.GNG/NG7/W/46, dated 24 June 1988, pp. 13-18, paras. 35-52.

(a) External trade factors relating to the balance of payments

Article XII:4(e) refers to "special external factors adversely affecting the export trade of the contracting party applying restrictions". The Report of the Review Working Party on "Quantitative Restrictions" notes that the Working Party agreed

> "that ... the scope of consultations under paragraph 12 of Article XVIII was the same as that of consultations under Article XII and that the clarification contained in paragraph 4(e) of Article XII and in the related interpretative note would apply equally to consultations undertaken under Section B of Article XVIII".[122]

The full consultation procedures agreed in 1970 provide in paragraph 3 that:

> "The CONTRACTING PARTIES have agreed that in the consultations on balance of payments and other trade and development problems of developing countries provided for in GATT, particular attention should be given to the possibilities for alleviating and correcting these problems through measures that contracting parties might take to facilitate an expansion of the export earnings of these countries. Such 'expanded consultations' are to be held with any developing contracting party normally consulting under Article XVIII:12(b) which desires that a particular consultation be held on this basis".[123]

In 1972 the Director-General confirmed that the procedure for "expanded consultations" with a developing contracting party was voluntary and would not take place if it was not requested by the country itself.[124]

The 1979 Declaration provides that

> "... If the Committee finds that the consulting contracting party's measures ... are in important respects related to restrictive trade measures maintained by another contracting party[2] ... it shall so report to the Council which shall take such further action as it may consider appropriate. ...

> "In the course of full consultations with a less-developed contracting party the Committee shall, if the consulting contracting party so desires, give particular attention to the possibilities for alleviating and correcting the balance-of-payments problem through measures that contracting parties might take to facilitate an expansion of the export earnings of the consulting contracting party, as provided for in paragraph 3 of the full consultation procedures".[125]

Footnote 2 to the Declaration provides: "It is noted that such a finding is more likely to be made in the case of recent measures than of measures in effect for some considerable time".

(b) External factors: general macroeconomic climate and external debt

In 1982-83 discussions took place concerning the treatment in the work of the Committee on Balance-of-Payments Restrictions of balance-of-payments problems confronting heavily-indebted developing countries. A 1984 Statement by the Chairman of the Committee on Balance-of-Payments Restrictions to the Council summarized the result of these discussions.[126] The Chairman stated, *inter alia*, that:

> "In discussing the legal framework for consideration of external factors, there appeared to be no need for a new or extended mandate to enable the Balance-of-Payments Committee to take into account the trading environment facing consulting countries. The following provisions, which so far have been rarely invoked,

---

[122] L/332/Rev.1 and Addenda, adopted on 2, 4 and 5 March 1955, 3S/170, 184, para. 49.
[123] L/3388, 18S/48, 49, para. 3. See also Spec(68)102, Note by the Chairman of the Committee on "Expanded Balance-of-Payments Consultations under Article XVIII", dated 11 October 1968 (discussing initial experience with such consultations in 1968).
[124] C/M/83, p. 6.
[125] L/4904, adopted on 28 November 1979, 26S/205, 208-209, paras. 11-12.
[126] C/125 dated 13 March 1984, approved by the Council on 15/16 May 1984 (C/M/178, p. 26), 31S/56. See also discussion at C/M/174, 178, 179, 183, 186.

do not only provide a legal basis but also make it clear that the Committee has a duty to fulfil in this respect:

"(a) Article XII:4(e) of the General Agreement states that in undertaking consultations, the CONTRACTING PARTIES 'shall have due regard to any special external factors adversely affecting the export trade of the contracting party applying restrictions'. This principle is also to be found in paragraph 2 of the 1970 consultation procedures, which applies to all consulting contracting parties, where it is stated, *inter alia*, that 'Account should be taken of all factors, both internal and external, which affect the balance of payments position of the consulting country'.

"(b) Paragraph 12 of the 1979 Declaration drawing on paragraph 3 of the 1970 procedures, instructs the Committee, if a developing consulting country so desires, to give particular attention to possibilities for alleviating the balance-of-payments problems of that country through measures that other contracting parties might take to facilitate an expansion of the export earnings of the consulting country. These provisions are available to any developing country in full consultations, if it so desires.

"(c) While preserving the special character of simplified consultations provided for in the procedures agreed in 1972, there is nothing which prevents countries, under these procedures, from drawing attention to any relevant external factors, and appealing to other contracting parties for remedial action. It would then be for the country concerned and the Committee to decide on the desirability of full consultations in such cases".[127]

The Statement provided further:

"It was recognized that the basic rôle of the Committee remains the examination, in terms of the relevant provisions of the General Agreement, of measures taken for balance-of-payments purposes by a consulting country, and that the widely felt need for more symmetry in the Committee's discussions should not detract from this basic function".[128]

"In the present consultations, the general view was taken that the Committee's task in relation to 'external factors' should be to identify, in its reports to the Council, possible areas in which action might be taken by contracting parties, with a view to alleviating the trade aspect of balance-of-payment problems. It would not be the Committee's intention to duplicate any work in other GATT fora or engage in a negotiating process, but rather, to highlight particular areas and encourage those contracting parties which are in a position to do so, to respond in a positive manner ...".[129]

(c) *Prior consultations on external factors*

At the November 1984 Council meeting, Chile proposed that prior consultations under Article XVIII:12 and XII:4 be used to create opportunities for a country facing balance-of-payments difficulties, when trade barriers seemed to be an important factor, to request its trading partners to consider elimination of such barriers.[130] In March 1985 the Chairman of the Committee on Balance-of-Payments Restrictions reported on consultations held on this proposal with members of the Committee and interested contracting parties. The report provides:

"After some discussion, it was recognized that in view of the text and drafting history of Article XII:4(a) and XVIII:12(a) (BISD 3S/171) there was nothing to prevent a contracting party in balance-of-payments difficulties from holding prior consultations with the Committee, under the normal procedures of these Articles. These procedures appeared adequate to accommodate the basic purpose of the Chilean proposal. Consultations in such cases would be full consultations by the Committee to examine the nature of the balance-of-payments difficulties of the consulting country and alternative corrective measures which may be available, and would take due account of all factors, including external factors, affecting the

---

[127] *Ibid.*, 31S/58-59, para. 7.
[128] *Ibid.*, 31S/59, para. 8.
[129] *Ibid.*, 31S/60, para. 12.
[130] C/M/183.

consulting country's balance-of-payments, as laid down in the relevant procedures established for the Committee's work, including Paragraphs 2 and 3 of the 1970 consultation procedures (BISD 18S/49) and Paragraph 12 of the 1979 Declaration (BISD 26S/208), also bearing in mind the considerations set out in document C/125 which was approved by the Council in May 1984 (C/M/178, pages 24-26). If, following such consultations, the consulting country found it necessary to introduce import restrictive measures for balance-of-payments purposes, further full consultations should be held. Depending on the time elapsed since the prior consultations these might focus more particularly on the scope and effect of the measures. However, this would be up to the Committee to judge depending on the circumstances of individual cases".[131]

5. Conclusions and recommendations of the Committee

The 1979 Declaration provides that:

"The Committee shall report on its consultations to the Council. The reports on full consultations shall indicate:

"(a) the Committee's conclusions as well as the facts and reasons on which they are based;

"(b) the steps the consulting contracting party has taken in the light of conclusions reached on the occasion of previous consultations;

"(c) in the case of less-developed contracting parties, the facts and reasons on which the Committee based its decision on the procedure followed; and

"(d) in the case of developed contracting parties, whether alternative economic policy measures are available.

"If the Committee finds that the consulting contracting party's measures

"(a) are in important respects related to restrictive trade measures maintained by another contracting party[132] or

"(b) have a significant adverse impact on the export interests of a less-developed contracting party,

"it shall so report to the Council which shall take such further action as it may consider appropriate.

...

"If the Committee finds that a restrictive import measure taken by the consulting contracting party for balance-of-payments purposes is inconsistent with the provisions of Articles XII, XVIII:B or this Declaration, it shall, in its report to the Council, make such findings as will assist the Council in making appropriate recommendations designed to promote the implementation of Articles XII and XVIII:B and this Declaration. The Council shall keep under surveillance any matter on which it has made recommendations".[133]

Paragraph 13 of the Understanding on the Balance-of-Payments Provisions of the GATT 1994 provides as follows:

"The Committee shall report on its consultations to the General Council. When full consultation procedures have been used, the report should indicate the Committee's conclusions on the different elements

---

[131] C/132, 32S/46, 47-48, para. 5.
[132] Footnote 2 to the Decision provides: "It is noted that such a finding is more likely to be made in the case of recent measures than of measures in effect for some considerable time."
[133] L/4904, adopted on 28 November 1979, 26S/205, 208, paras. 11 and 13.

of the plan for consultations, as well as the facts and reasons on which they are based. The Committee shall endeavour to include in its conclusions proposals for recommendations aimed at promoting the implementation of Articles XII and XVIII:B, the 1979 Declaration and this Understanding. In those cases in which a time-schedule has been presented for the removal of restrictive measures taken for balance-of-payments purposes, the General Council may recommend that, in adhering to such a time-schedule, a Member shall be deemed to be in compliance with its GATT 1994 obligations. Whenever the General Council has made specific recommendations, the rights and obligations of Members shall be assessed in the light of such recommendations. In the absence of specific proposals for recommendations by the General Council, the Committee's conclusions should record the different views expressed in the Committee. When simplified consultation procedures have been used, the report shall include a summary of the main elements discussed in the Committee and a decision on whether full consultation procedures are required."

See also the Secretariat Note of 24 June 1988 on "Consultations Held in the Committee on Balance-of-Payments Restrictions under Articles XII and XVIII:B since 1975", which reproduces in full all of the paragraphs of the Balance-of-Payments Committee's reports containing the Conclusions and Recommendations of the Committee from 1975 through 1988.[134]

See also the reference at page 381 above to the "interim conclusion" reached by the Committee in its Report on the simplified consultation held with Sri Lanka in 1994.

6. Discussion and adoption by the GATT Council of reports by the Committee

Reports on all consultations in the Balance-of-Payments Committee are submitted to the Council for discussion and adoption. The Council's adoption of the reports, which are introduced by the Chairman of the Committee, gives effect to the recommendations of the Committee. All reports by the Committee have been adopted by the Council.

III. PREPARATORY WORK AND SUBSEQUENT MODIFICATIONS

The corresponding provision in the US/UK *Proposals* appears in Chapter III C-2; in the US Draft in Article 20; in the London and New York Drafts in Article 26; in the Geneva Draft in Article 22; and in the Havana Charter in Article 21. The original US proposal was redrafted at London on the basis of a proposal by the United Kingdom, which largely formed the basis of Article 26 of the London Draft Charter.[135]

Article XII was extensvely debated and amended at the Review Session in 1954-55; the 1947 provisions providing for prior consultation were deleted and emphasis was placed on the balance-of-payments consultation process. See the Review Session documents listed below.

---

[134]MTN.GNG/NG7/W/46, Annex I.
[135]See EPCT/C.II/W.22 (UK proposal), EPCT/C.II/QR/PV/1-5, EPCT/C.II/QR/PV/3 p.2ff (explanation of redraft).

IV. RELEVANT DOCUMENTS

London

Discussion:	EPCT/C.II/PV/5, 6, 8, 13; EPCT/C.II/QR/PV/1, 3, 5, 6; EPCT/C.II/36, 45, 66
Reports:	EPCT/C.II/59; EPCT/30
Other:	EPCT/C.II/34, 44

New York

Discussion:	EPCT/C.6/17+Corr.1-2, 20+Corr.1-2, 23, 27, 34, 105, 106
Reports:	EPCT/C.6/15, 97/Rev.1 (p.62)
Other:	EPCT/C.6/W/5, 11, 17+Corr.1, 30+Corr.1, 34, 43, 81

Geneva

Discussion:	EPCT/EC/PV.2/22 EPCT/A/SR.27, 28, 29 EPCT/A/PV/28, 41 EPCT/TAC/SR/13 EPCT/TAC/PV/27, 28
Reports:	EPCT/135, 163, 171, 180, 186, 189, 196, 212, 214/Rev.1/Add.1 EPCT/W/313
Other:	EPCT/W/64, 73, 136, 194, 209, 211, 213, 215, 216, 217, 223, 231, 256, 272, 301, 318+Add.1

Havana

Discussion:	E/CONF.2/C.3/SR.19, 21, 24, 38, 46
Reports:	E/CONF.2/C.3/57, 82
Other:	E/CONF.2/C.3/F/W.8, 11

CONTRACTING PARTIES

Reports:	GATT/CP.4/10, 31+Corr.1 GATT/CP.5/24 L/24+Add.1, L/51
Other:	Annecy press releases 18, 32, 44 Press release Torquay/19 GATT/96

Review Session:

Discussion:	SR.9/14, 15, 25, 26, 40
Reports:	W.9/106+Corr.2, 126, 130, 174+Add.1, 208, 219, 225, 236/Add.3
Other:	L/189, L/246, L/261/Add.1, L/271, L/272 W.9/18+Add.1, 22, 23, 25, 29, 31, 47, 52, 60, 73, 74, 77/Rev.1, 79, 80+Corr.1, 82, 106, 112, 115, 126, 130, 132, 136, 139, 179, 181, 226 Sec/137/54+Rev.1 Spec/23/55, 43/55, 45/55, 51/55, 53/55+Rev.1, 58/55, 68/55, 90/55, 148/55, 150/55, 172/55, 182/55 MGT/9/55

V. TABLES

Key:

F	=	Full consultation
F	=	Last full consultation
S	=	Simplified consultation
P	=	Postponed
D	=	Disinvocation of Article XII or XVIII:B.

Numbers in parentheses are BOP/R/ report references.
Reference to last full consultation indicated in boldface.

Notes:

1. All countries listed were invoking balance-of-payments provisions as of 1979, unless otherwise noted. Invocations of Article XII or XVIII:B during the reference period are understood to mean either the first invocation by a particular country or a reinvocation after previous disinvocation of the relevant Article. Greece disinvoked Article XVIII in 1984; later consultations are under Article XII.

2. Italy, New Zealand (consultation on deposit requirement for purchases of foreign currency) and South Africa also consulted with the CONTRACTING PARTIES on an *ad hoc* basis in 1974-76, about their imposition of import deposits for balance of payments purposes, but in special Working Parties established for the purpose.

3. In the case of Israel and South Africa the Article under which the consultations are held is not specified.

4. The Czech and Slovak Federal Republic ceased to exist on 31 December 1992.

5. There were no disinvocations of Article XII or XVIII in 1993-94.

A. Countries currently invoking Article XII or XVIII:B: Balance-of-Payments consultations conducted since 1979 Declaration

Country	1980	1981	1982	1983	1984	1985	1986	1987	1988	1989	1990	1991	1992	1993	1994
Bangladesh	S(116)		S(128)		S(147)		S(161)		S(175)		S(188)		S(200)		P
Egypt		S(117)		S(133)		S(157)			F(176)		S(188)		F(201)		P
India	S(112)		S(126)		S(143)		S(163)	F(168)		F(184)		P	F(197)		S(221)
Israel (3)	-113		-129		-142	-155		-170		-187		-195		-210.	-214
Nigeria					F(139)		S(163)		S(179)		P	S(190)		F(209)	
Pakistan	S(112)		S(126)			S(150)		S(169)		F(181)		P	S(198)		S(221)
Philippines	F(115)		S(128)		S(147)		F(164)		S(179)		P	S(190)		F(204)	
Poland (Art.XII)													Art.XII invoked 1992	-206.	-216
S.Africa (3)														-211.	P
Sri Lanka		S(117)		S(133)		S(153)		S(169)		S(186)		P	S(198)		S(219)
Tunisia		S(121)		S(137)		S(157)			S(179)		P	S(190)	F(202)		S(214)
Turkey		S(120)		S(137)		S(153)		S(166)	F(178)		P	S(191)		F(207)	
Yugoslavia		S(117) F(122)			S(143)		S(163)		S(179)		P	F(191)			

B. Contracting Parties which have disinvoked Article XII or XVIII:B since 1979

Country	1980	1981	1982	1983	1984	1985	1986	1987	1988	1989	1990	1991	1992
Argentina							F(159)		S(179)			D	
Brazil	S(116)	F(124)		F(135)		S(157)		F(172)		S(186)		P	D
Colombia	Art. XVIII:B invoked upon accession 1981						F(156)		S(166)		S(185)	P	D
Czech & Slovak Fed. Rep.											Art. XII invoked 12/90	-193	D
Ghana	S(116)		S(128)	F(136)		S(157)		S(169)		D(186)			
Greece	F(114)	F(123)			D		F(160)	D					
Hungary				F(131)	F(141)	D							
Italy		F(119)	D										
Korea		S(117)		S(133)	F(146)		S(163)	F(171)		D(183)			
Peru		S(120)		S(137)			S(161)	F(173)		S(186)		D	
Portugal	F(111)	F(118)	F(125)	F(134)	F(145)	F(152)	D						

ARTICLE XIII

NON-DISCRIMINATORY ADMINISTRATION OF QUANTITATIVE RESTRICTIONS

I.	TEXT OF ARTICLE XIII AND RELEVANT INTERPRETATIVE NOTES	398
II.	INTERPRETATION AND APPLICATION OF ARTICLE XIII	399
	A. SCOPE AND APPLICATION OF ARTICLE XIII	399
	1. Paragraph 1	399
	(1) "of all third countries"	399
	(2) "similarly prohibited or restricted"	400
	2. Paragraph 2	400
	(1) "aim at a distribution of trade"	400
	(2) Paragraph 2(c)	401
	(3) Paragraph 2(d): "in cases in which a quota is allocated among supplying countries"	401
	(a) Allocation of quotas	401
	(b) "representative period"	402
	(c) "special factors"	403
	(d) "No conditions or formalities shall be imposed which would prevent any contracting party from utilizing fully the share ... which has been allotted to it ..."	404
	(4) "subject to importation being made within any prescribed period to which the quota may relate"	405
	3. Paragraph 3(a): Administration of import licensing	405
	4. Paragraph 3(b) and 3(c): Administration of import quotas	407
	(1) "shall give public notice ... of the total quantity or value ... which will be permitted to be imported during a specified time period": public notice requirements and back-dated quotas	407
	(2) "supplies of the good in question which were en route at the time at which public notice were given"	407
	(3) Second proviso to paragraph 3(b)	409
	5. Paragraph 4: "representative period"	409
	6. Paragraph 5	409
	(1) Non-discriminatory administration of tariff quotas	409
	(2) Non-discriminatory administration of export restrictions	410
	B. RELATIONSHIP BETWEEN ARTICLE XIII AND OTHER GATT PROVISIONS	410
	1. Article I	410
	2. Article XI	411
	3. Article XXI	411
	4. Article XXIV	411
	5. Part IV	411
	6. Protocols of Accession	411
	C. RELATIONSHIP BETWEEN ARTICLE XIII AND OTHER AGREEMENTS	412
	D. EXCEPTIONS AND DEROGATIONS	413
	1. Provisions of Protocols of Accession relating to discriminatory quantitative restrictions	413
	2. Waivers under Article XXV:5	413
	3. Other exceptions	414
	E. AGREEMENT ON IMPORT LICENSING PROCEDURES	414
III.	PREPARATORY WORK AND SUBSEQUENT MODIFICATIONS	415
IV.	RELEVANT DOCUMENTS	416

I. TEXT OF ARTICLE XIII AND RELEVANT INTERPRETATIVE NOTES

Article XIII*

Non-discriminatory Administration of Quantitative Restrictions

1. No prohibition or restriction shall be applied by any contracting party on the importation of any product of the territory of any other contracting party or on the exportation of any product destined for the territory of any other contracting party, unless the importation of the like product of all third countries or the exportation of the like product to all third countries is similarly prohibited or restricted.

2. In applying import restrictions to any product, contracting parties shall aim at a distribution of trade in such product approaching as closely as possible the shares which the various contracting parties might be expected to obtain in the absence of such restrictions, and to this end shall observe the following provisions:

   (*a*) Wherever practicable, quotas representing the total amount of permitted imports (whether allocated among supplying countries or not) shall be fixed, and notice given of their amount in accordance with paragraph 3 (*b*) of this Article;

   (*b*) In cases in which quotas are not practicable, the restrictions may be applied by means of import licences or permits without a quota;

   (*c*) Contracting parties shall not, except for purposes of operating quotas allocated in accordance with sub-paragraph (*d*) of this paragraph, require that import licences or permits be utilized for the importation of the product concerned from a particular country or source;

   (*d*) In cases in which a quota is allocated among supplying countries, the contracting party applying the restrictions may seek agreement with respect to the allocation of shares in the quota with all other contracting parties having a substantial interest in supplying the product concerned. In cases in which this method is not reasonably practicable, the contracting party concerned shall allot to contracting parties having a substantial interest in supplying the product shares based upon the proportions, supplied by such contracting parties during a previous representative period, of the total quantity or value of imports of the product, due account being taken of any special factors which may have affected or may be affecting the trade in the product. No conditions or formalities shall be imposed which would prevent any contracting party from utilizing fully the share of any such total quantity or value which has been allotted to it, subject to importation being made within any prescribed period to which the quota may relate.*

3. (*a*) In cases in which import licences are issued in connection with import restrictions, the contracting party applying the restrictions shall provide, upon the request of any contracting party having an interest in the trade in the product concerned, all relevant information concerning the administration of the restrictions, the import licences granted over a recent period and the distribution of such licences among supplying countries; *Provided* that there shall be no obligation to supply information as to the names of importing or supplying enterprises.

   (*b*) In the case of import restrictions involving the fixing of quotas, the contracting party applying the restrictions shall give public notice of the total quantity or value of the product or products which will be permitted to be imported during a specified future period and of any change in such quantity or value. Any supplies of the product in question which were *en route* at the time at which public notice was given shall not be excluded from entry; *Provided* that they may be counted so far as practicable, against the quantity permitted to be imported in the period in question, and also, where necessary, against the quantities permitted to be imported in the next following period or periods; and *Provided* further that if any contracting party customarily exempts from such restrictions products entered for consumption or withdrawn from warehouse for consumption during a period of thirty days after the day of such public notice, such practice shall be considered full compliance with this sub-paragraph.

(c) In the case of quotas allocated among supplying countries, the contracting party applying the restrictions shall promptly inform all other contracting parties having an interest in supplying the product concerned of the shares in the quota currently allocated, by quantity or value, to the various supplying countries and shall give public notice thereof.

4. With regard to restrictions applied in accordance with paragraph 2 (*d*) of this Article or under paragraph 2 (*c*) of Article XI, the selection of a representative period for any product and the appraisal of any special factors* affecting the trade in the product shall be made initially by the contracting party applying the restriction; *Provided* that such contracting party shall, upon the request of any other contracting party having a substantial interest in supplying that product or upon the request of the CONTRACTING PARTIES, consult promptly with the other contracting party or the CONTRACTING PARTIES regarding the need for an adjustment of the proportion determined or of the base period selected, or for the reappraisal of the special factors involved, or for the elimination of conditions, formalities or any other provisions established unilaterally relating to the allocation of an adequate quota or its unrestricted utilization.

5. The provisions of this Article shall apply to any tariff quota instituted or maintained by any contracting party, and, in so far as applicable, the principles of this Article shall also extend to export restrictions.

Interpretative Notes from Annex I

Ad Article XIII

Paragraph 2 (d)

No mention was made of "commercial considerations" as a rule for the allocation of quotas because it was considered that its application by governmental authorities might not always be practicable. Moreover, in cases where it is practicable, a contracting party could apply these considerations in the process of seeking agreement, consistently with the general rule laid down in the opening sentence of paragraph 2.

Paragraph 4

See note relating to "special factors" in connexion with the last sub-paragraph of paragraph 2 of Article XI.

Ad Articles XI, XII, XIII, XIV and XVIII

Throughout Articles XI, XII, XIII, XIV and XVIII, the terms "import restrictions" or "export restrictions" include restrictions made effective through state-trading operations.

II. INTERPRETATION AND APPLICATION OF ARTICLE XIII

A. SCOPE AND APPLICATION OF ARTICLE XIII

Concerning the general scope of Article XIII, see also the unadopted 1994 panel report on "EEC - Import Régime for Bananas".[1]

1. Paragraph 1

(1) "of all third countries"

The 1989 Panel Report on "EEC - Restrictions on Imports of Dessert Apples - Complaint by Chile" examined, *inter alia*, the claim that the administration and allocation of certain quantitative restrictions violated Article XIII.

---

[1] DS38/R, dated 11 February 1994, paras. 141-142.

"The Panel recognized that, given its finding that the EEC measures were a violation of Article XI:1 and not justified by Article XI:2(c)(i) or (ii), no further examination of the administration of the measure would normally be required. Nonetheless, and even though the Panel was concerned with measures which had already been eliminated, in view of the questions of great practical interest raised by both parties it considered it appropriate to examine the administration of the EEC measures in respect of Article XIII.

"The first paragraph of the Article established the general obligation of non-discrimination in the administration of quantitative restrictions. The Panel noted that Commission Regulation 984/88 of 12 April 1988 suspended the issue of import licences in respect only of apples originating in Chile, eight days before the publication of import quotas. The Panel found that this measure constituted a prohibition in terms of Article XIII:1, and that it was applied contrary to that provision since the like products of all third countries had not been similarly prohibited. The Panel then proceeded to consider the EEC administration of the import quotas under Regulation 1040/88 in light of the subsequent provisions which delineated more specific requirements to achieve the aim of Article XIII:1."[2]

(2) "similarly prohibited or restricted"

The 1980 Panel on "EEC Restrictions on Imports of Apples from Chile" examined EEC protective measures suspending imports of apples from Chile. The Panel Report includes the following finding:

"The Panel examined the EEC measures in relation to Article XIII:1. The Panel found that the EEC suspension applied to imports from Chile was not a restriction similar to the voluntary restraint agreements negotiated with the other Southern Hemisphere suppliers on the basis primarily that:

"(a)   there was a difference in transparency between the two types of action;

"(b)   there was a difference in the administration of the restrictions, the one being an import restriction, the other an export restraint; and

"(c)   the import suspension was unilateral and mandatory while the other was voluntary and negotiated".[3]

2. Paragraph 2

(1) "aim at a distribution of trade"

It was pointed out during discussions at the Havana Conference that "global quotas not allocated among supplying countries might sometimes operate in a manner unduly favourable to those countries best able for any reason to take prompt advantage of the global quotas at the opening of the quota period; and it was agreed that Members, in administering import restrictions, should pay due regard to the need for avoiding such a result. It was also agreed that, in the case of perishable commodities, due regard should be had for the special problems affecting the trade in these commodities".[4]

The 1980 Panel Report on "Norway - Restrictions on Imports of Certain Textile Products", which examined an Article XIX action by Norway, notes as follows:

"The Panel was of the view that the type of action chosen by Norway, i.e. the quantitative restrictions limiting the importation of the nine textile categories in question, as the form of emergency action under Article XIX was subject to the provisions of Article XIII which provides for non-discriminatory administration of quantitative restrictions. In this connexion, the Panel noted the introductory part of paragraph 2 which stipulates that in applying an import restriction on a product, a contracting party 'shall aim at a distribution of trade in such a product approaching as closely as possible the share which the

---

[2]L/6491, adopted on 22 June 1989, 36S/93, 130, paras. 12.20-12.21.
[3]L/5047, adopted on 10 November 1980, 27S/98, 114, para. 4.11.
[4]Havana Reports, p. 91, para. 28.

various contracting parties might be expected to obtain in the absence of such restrictions ...'. To this end, paragraph 2(a) of Article XIII further prescribes that wherever practicable, quotas representing the total amount of permitted imports (whether allocated among supplying countries or not) shall be fixed".[5]

The 1989 Panel Report on "EEC - Restrictions on Imports of Dessert Apples - Complaint by Chile" notes

"that the first sentence of Article XIII:2 committed contracting parties applying import restrictions to any product to 'aim at a distribution of trade in such product approaching as closely as possible the shares which the various contracting parties might be expected to obtain in the absence of such restrictions', and sub-paragraph (d) provided more specific requirements for the allocation of quota shares. The Panel considered that it would not be useful for it to make a finding regarding the actual size of quota shares ...".[6]

See also the material below regarding choice of reference period for the purpose of allocating quota shares, at page 402.

(2) Paragraph 2(c)

The question was raised at the Geneva session of the Preparatory Committee "whether a Member was permitted to require an import licence or permit to be utilized for the importation of a product from a particular country or source for balance-of-payments reasons". The Sub-Committee on the quantitative restrictions articles of the Charter considered that provisions for such an exception should not appear in Article 27 [corresponding to Article XIII of the General Agreement]; the Sub-Committee on the balance-of-payments articles of the Charter felt that Article 29:8(ii) [corresponding to Article XV:9(b) of the present text of the General Agreement] took due account of this problem.[7] See also generally Article XIV.

(3) Paragraph 2(d): "in cases in which a quota is allocated among supplying countries"

See the Interpretative Note *Ad* Article XIII:2(d).

(a) Allocation of quotas

The Panel Report on "Norway - Restrictions on Imports of Certain Textile Products" notes that

"In the case before the Panel, Norway had in early 1978 concluded long-term bilateral arrangements with six textile-supplying countries. The Panel noted that Norway had concluded these agreements with the intention of acceding to the MFA and notifying these agreements to the TSB pursuant to the appropriate Article of the MFA. The Panel noted also, however, that in the event Norway had not acceded to the MFA and that for these arrangements no derogation or provision of Parts I-III of GATT had ever been invoked by Norway ... The Panel held that Norway's reservation of market shares for these six countries therefore represented a partial allocation of quotas under an existing régime of import restrictions of the products in question and that Norway must therefore be considered to have acted under Article XIII:2(d). The Panel noted that had the reservation of market shares for the six countries been entered into pursuant to Article XIII:2(d), Norway could have been presumed to have acted under the first sentence of that provision.

"... The Panel was of the view that to the extent that Norway had acted with effect to allocate import quotas for these products to six countries but had failed to allocate a share to Hong Kong, its Article XIX action was not consistent with Article XIII".[8]

---

[5] L/4959, adopted on 18 June 1980, 27S/119, 125, para. 14.b.
[6] L/6491, adopted on 22 June 1989, 36S/93, 130-131, para. 12.22.
[7] EPCT/163, p. 23.
[8] L/4959, adopted on 18 June 1980, 27S/119, 125-126, paras. 15-16.

The 1980 Panel Report on "EEC Restrictions on Imports of Apples from Chile" notes that

"... notwithstanding the Panel's conclusions regarding the lack of similarity of the restrictions with reference to Article XIII:1, and in light of XIII:5, the Panel proceeded to consider the EEC import suspension against Chile and the voluntary restraint agreements with other Southern Hemisphere exporters as 'quotas' for purposes of the Panel's examination of the EEC measure under XIII:2".[9]

The 1984 Report of the "Panel on Newsprint" examined the action of the European Communities in opening a duty-free tariff quota for m.f.n. suppliers of 500,000 tonnes for newsprint for the year 1984 (whereas the EC's commitment in its schedule provided for an annual duty-free quota of 1.5 million tonnes) as the EFTA countries had obtained full duty-free access for newsprint from 1 January 1984 onward.

"The Panel also noted the EC statement that ... the action taken by the EC was merely a change in the administration or management of the tariff quota which was permissible under Article XIII of the GATT, and that therefore renegotiations under Article XXVIII were not called for. ...

"The Panel considered the arguments advanced by the EC relating to Article XIII, but concluded that the conditions for its application had not been fulfilled. In examining the EEC Regulation 3684/83, the Panel found that it did not in fact constitute a change in the administration or management of the tariff quota from a global quota system to a system of country shares, as had been asserted by the EC ... It does not provide an allocation of country shares to individual m.f.n. suppliers, nor has a separate quota (global or otherwise) for the EFTA countries been established, as Article XIII requires."[10]

(b) *"representative period"*

The Report of the Review Working Party on "Quantitative Restrictions" includes the following agreed interpretation of paragraph 2, agreed during the 1954-55 Review Session:

"The Working Party does not propose any change in the text of Article XIII. It considered, however, a suggestion which was put forward to the effect that an interpretative note should be added to clarify the term 'previous representative period' which appears in sub-paragraph 2(d) of Article XIII. The object of this note was to specify that, in cases in which import restrictions on a given product had been enforced for a certain time, the contracting party applying the restriction should grant to the foreign suppliers a share of its market which would correspond to what could reasonably have been expected in the absence of restrictions. The Working Party was not prepared to recommend the inclusion of that note but agreed to recognize that the general rule contained in the introduction to paragraph 2 governed the various sub-paragraphs of that paragraph including those of sub-paragraph (d) to which the note was intended to refer".[11]

The 1980 Panel Report on "EEC Restrictions on Imports of Apples from Chile" considered it appropriate, with regard to both Articles XI:2(c) and XIII:2(d), and

"in keeping with normal GATT practice ... to use as a 'representative period' a three-year period previous to 1979, the year in which the EEC measures were in effect. Due to the existence of restrictions in 1976, the Panel held that that year could not be considered as representative, and that the year immediately preceding 1976 should be used instead. The Panel thus chose the years 1975, 1977 and 1978 as a 'representative period'".[12]

The 1989 Panel Report on "EEC - Restrictions on Imports of Dessert Apples - Complaint by Chile" includes the following finding:

---

[9]L/5047, adopted on 10 November 1980, 27S/98, 114, para. 4.12.
[10]L/5680, adopted on 20 November 1984, 31S/114, 131-132, paras. 49, 51.
[11]L/332/Rev.1 and Addenda, adopted on 2, 4 and 5 March 1955, 3S/170, 176, para. 24.
[12]L/5047, adopted on 10 November 1980, 27S/98, 113, 116, paras. 4.8, 4.16.

"... The Panel considered that it would not be useful for it to make a finding regarding the actual size of quota shares. It observed that the previous three years were normally considered to be the appropriate reference period, with due account taken of relevant special factors. The Panel did not construe 'special factors' applicable to only one, or some, exporters as sufficient reason to change the base period which applied to all - though these special factors should be taken into account in considering individual quota allocations. Therefore the Panel found that the reference period applied by the EEC for the purpose of allocating quota shares - i.e., the previous three years - was consistent with its obligations under Article XIII".[13]

(c) "special factors"

The Sub-Committee at the Havana Conference which considered Articles 20 and 22 of the Charter (corresponding to Articles XI and XIII of the General Agreement) "agreed that the interpretative note on 'special factors' should be retained as a note but should be made more explicit both by the deletion of the cross reference to the note to Article 20 which appears in the Geneva text and by the specific mention of certain additional factors which should be taken into account in the allocation of quotas. The Sub-Committee also agreed that it was desirable to make clear that, in cases where separate import quotas were allotted to the various foreign suppliers, a country whose productive efficiency or ability to export had increased relatively to other foreign suppliers since the representative period on which import quotas were based should receive a relatively larger import quota".[14] It was accordingly agreed to add the following Interpretative Note to paragraphs 2(d) and 4 of Article 22 of the Charter (which correspond to Article XIII:2(d) and 4):

"The term 'special factors' as used in Article 22 includes among other factors the following changes, as between the various foreign producers, which may have occurred since the representative period:

"1. changes in relative productive efficiency;

"2. the existence of new or additional ability to export; and

"3. reduced ability to export".

It was also agreed that "changes artificially brought about since the representative period (assuming that period to have preceded the coming into force of the Charter) by means not permissible under the provisions of the Charter were not to be regarded as 'special factors' for the purposes of paragraph 2(c) and Article 22. The Sub-Committee agreed, however, that it was unnecessary to state this specifically in the text of the Articles or in the interpretative notes."[15]

The 1980 Panel Report on "EEC - Restrictions on Imports of Apples from Chile" refers to these Charter provisions:

"... the Panel noted the fact that exports from Chile into the EEC had been expanding rapidly. ... The Panel believed that Chile's increased export capacity should have been taken into account by the EEC in its allocation of shares among the Southern Hemisphere suppliers. The Panel felt such a consideration was in line with the interpretative note to the term 'special factors' as drafted in the Havana Charter, in particular with reference to the 'existence of new or additional ability to export' as between foreign producers. Moreover, the Panel considered that the fact that Chilean exporters had signed commercial contracts with EEC importers to the amount of 60,500 m.t. further demonstrated Chile's increased export capacity and that these contracts should have been taken into account as a 'special factor' as well".[16]

---

[13]L/6491, adopted on 22 June 1989, 36S/93, 130-131, para. 12.22.
[14]Havana Reports, p. 95, para. 52.
[15]Havana Reports, p. 94, para. 43.
[16]L/5047, adopted on 10 November 1980, 27S/98, 115, para. 4.17.

In the Panel Report on "United States - Imports of Sugar from Nicaragua"

"Nicaragua argued that the United States measures were inconsistent with the provisions of Article XIII of the General Agreement and in particular with paragraph 2 ... The Panel noted that under the sugar quota system established by the United States on 5 May 1982 the share of each supplying country corresponded to its share in the total sugar imports of the United States during a previous representative period, and that Nicaragua had, on this basis, been allocated 2.1 percent of the total import quota, which amounted in the fiscal year 1982/83 to 58,000 short tons. Nicaragua's quota for the fiscal year 1983-84 had been reduced to 6,000 short tons, or about one-tenth of its prior allocation, and this reduction had not been motivated by any factor which might have affected or might be affecting trade in sugar. The Panel therefore concluded that the sugar quota allocated to Nicaragua for the fiscal year 1983-84 was inconsistent with the United States obligations under Article XIII:2."[17]

The 1989 Panel Report on "EEC - Restrictions on Imports of Dessert Apples - Complaint by Chile" includes the Panel findings that:

"Concerning 'special factors', the Panel took into account the Interpretative Note to paragraph 4 of Article XIII, which refers to the Note relating to 'special factors' in connection with the last sub-paragraph of Article XI:2. This reads:

'The term "special factors" includes changes in relative productive efficiency as between domestic and foreign producers, or as between different foreign producers, but not changes artificially brought about by means not permitted under the Agreement.'

"The Panel further recalled that Article XIII:4 permits the party applying the restriction to initially select the representative period and appraise the special factors. It should subsequently consult, upon their request, with contracting parties seeking reappraisal of these factors. The Panel considered that this requirement for consultation was designed to ensure that due account was taken of special factors in terms of Article XIII:2(d) and in the light of the interpretation noted above. The Panel found that the overall trend towards an increase in Chile's relative productive efficiency and export capacity had not been duly taken into account, nor had the temporary reduction in export capacity caused by the 1985 earthquake. On the other hand the Panel did not find any basis in the General Agreement for the EEC taking into account as special factors the 'restraint' alleged to have been exercised in previous years by other suppliers. Therefore the Panel found that the account taken of special factors by the EEC in allocating Chile's quota share did not meet the requirements of Article XIII:2(d)".[18]

(d) *"No conditions or formalities shall be imposed which would prevent any contracting party from utilizing fully the share ... which has been allotted to it ..."*

The 1950 Working Party Report on "The Use of Quantitative Import and Export Restrictions for Protective, Promotional and other Commercial Purposes" provides as follows:

"... the Working Party noted that there was evidence of a number of types of misuse of import restrictions, in particular the following ...

"The imposition by a country of administrative obstacles to the full utilization of balance-of-payments import quotas, e.g. by delaying the issuance of licenses against such quotas by establishing license priorities for certain imports on the basis of the competitiveness or non-competitiveness of such imports with the products of domestic industry, in a manner inconsistent with the provisions of Article XII through XIV ... In this connection, the Working Party took note of Article XIII:2(d), which provides that 'No conditions or formalities shall be imposed which would prevent any contracting party from utilizing fully the share of any

---

[17] L/5607, adopted on 13 March 1984, 31S/67, 73, para. 4.3.
[18] L/6491, adopted on 22 June 1989, 36S/93, para. 12.24.

such total quantity or value which has been allotted to it, subject to importation being made within any prescribed period to which the quota may relate'".[19]

(4) "subject to importation being made within any prescribed period to which the quota may relate"

This condition was added to the Charter Article on non-discriminatory administration of quantitative restrictions when it was first discussed during the London session of the Preparatory Committee. The reason given for this addition was that "it would be very difficult to administer any system of quantitative regulation unless you could have some limitation over the time within which imports could be made".[20]

3. Paragraph 3(a): Administration of import licensing

In 1950 at the Torquay Session the CONTRACTING PARTIES adopted a Working Party Report on a proposal for a Code of Standard Practices for the Administration of Import and Export Restrictions and Exchange Controls,[21] including the recommendations therein that the CONTRACTING PARTIES "approve the draft standards set out in the Annex to this Report [and] recommend these practices to the individual contracting parties as a code which they should endeavour to adopt to the maximum practicable extent". The Report further provides:

> "The Working Party considered that the proposed standards ... should be regarded as a code for the guidance of contracting parties and not as additional obligations imposed upon them under the General Agreement ... it was recognised that, where there are clear and overriding considerations, or in individual cases where there is good reason to suspect the bona fides of transactions in question, it may be necessary for contracting parties to depart from the precise terms of these recommendations.

> "The Working Party confined its attention principally to the formulation of standard practices to be applied by governments imposing import and export restrictions for balance-of-payment reasons. Since, however, international trade in many products is subject to other regulations and orders, the Working Party was of the opinion that, where possible, the principles underlying the set of standard practices ... should also be observed for such regulations and orders".

The Annex provides as follows.

> "1. The grant of an import licence should imply that the necessary foreign exchange will be obtainable if applied for within a reasonable time. When both import licences and exchange permits are required, the operation of the two requirements should be co-ordinated. If more than one rate of exchange applies in payment for imports, the import licence or exchange permit should indicate the type of exchange which will apply in the settlement of the particular transaction.

> "2. Any new or intensified restrictions on importation or exportation should not apply to goods shown to the satisfaction of the control authority to have been en route at the time the change was announced or to have been paid for in substantial part or covered by an irrevocable letter of credit.

> "3. Goods proved to have been covered by adequate confirmed prior order at the time new or intensified restrictions are announced, and not marketable elsewhere without appreciable loss, should receive special consideration on an individual case basis, provided their delivery can be completed within a specified period. Such goods, as well as those covered under paragraph 2, should be accountable against any import or export quota or exchange allocation that may have been established for that particular class of goods.

> "4. The administrative formalities in connection with the issuance of import and export licences or exchange permits should be designed to allow action upon applications within a reasonably short period. A licence or permit should be valid for a sufficient period to allow for the production or delivery of the

---

[19]GATT/CP.4/33, adopted on 3 April 1950, para. 21.
[20]Amendment by New Zealand, EPCT/C.II/PV/13, p. 13.
[21]GATT/CP.5/30/Rev.1; adopted on 30 November 1950, GATT/CP.5/SR.16 p. 2-4; preliminary draft at GATT/CP.5/8, discussion also at GATT/CP.5/SR.8, SR.9.

goods, taking into account the character of the goods and the conditions of transport from the country of origin. The control authorities should not withdraw licences or permits unless they are satisfied that exceptional circumstances necessitate such action, and should give sympathetic consideration to requests for renewal or revalidation of licences or permits when exceptional circumstances prevent their utilisation within the original period.

"5. Under a system involving the fixing of quotas for particular classes of goods or of allocations of exchange in payment for them, any period that may be set, within which applications for such quotas or allocations must be made, should be sufficient to allow for the exchange of communications with likely foreign suppliers and the conclusion of purchase contracts.

"6. When foreign products subject to quantitative limitations are apportioned among importers largely in the light of their past participation in the trade, the control authorities, at their discretion and without undue prejudice to the interests of established importers, should give consideration to requests for licences or permits submitted by qualified and financially responsible newcomers.

"7. If an assurance regarding the issue of an import licence is required as a condition of consular legalization of shipping documents in the country of exportation, a reliable communication giving the number of the import licence should suffice.

"8. The authority given to customs officials should be adequate to allow them, at their discretion, to grant reasonable tolerance for variations in the quantity or value of individual shipments as delivered from that specified in the prior import or export authorization, in accordance with the character of the product involved and any extenuating circumstances.

"9. When, owing to exceptional and unforeseen balance-of-payment difficulties, a country is unable to provide foreign exchange for imports immediately payment becomes due to the supplier, transfers of foreign exchange in respect of goods already imported or licensed for importation should have priority over transfers in respect of new orders, or should at least have a definite and equitable share of the total amounts of foreign exchange currently available for imports."[22]

The following supplement to Article 3 of the Torquay Code of Standard Practices was adopted in 1952.

"The CONTRACTING PARTIES recommend to governments imposing or intensifying import or export restrictions that they should authorize, to the fullest extent permitted by the exigencies of their economic and financial position, the importation or exportation of goods covered by firm and legitimate contracts which are proved to their satisfaction to have been concluded in the course of normal business before the announcement of new or intensified import or export restrictions. Governments should give prompt consideration to all individual cases; special consideration should be given to transactions involving perishable or seasonal commodities."[23]

The CONTRACTING PARTIES at their Twenty-eighth Session in November 1972 decided that the data assembled on licensing systems should be kept up to date and that contracting parties should be invited to notify annually by 30 September any changes which should be made concerning the information on their licensing system. The Secretariat has issued annually an airgram inviting contracting parties to communicate any changes in their licensing systems necessary to bring up to date the individual country data, in accordance with a standard questionnaire.[24]

---

[22] GATT/CP.5/30/Rev.1, paras. 4-5.

[23] "Documentary Requirements for Imports, Consular Formalities, Valuation for Customs Purposes, Nationality of Imported Goods and Formalities Connected with Quantitative Restrictions." Report of the Working Party adopted on 7 November 1952, G/28, 1S/100, 106 para. 22; see also discussion p. 105-106.

[24] The questionnaire was originally issued as L/1335; the version currently in effect is annexed to L/5640/Rev.8. Up to 1981, notifications appeared as addenda and corrigenda to a document with the dual symbol COM.IND/W/55-COM.AG/W/72. As from 1981, notifications appear in the L/ series (e.g. L/5106/Rev.2, L/5640 and Revisions, and Addenda and Corrigenda thereto). The Annual Report of the Committee on Import Licensing contains a status report on replies by its members to the questionnaire; see 38S/93, L/7109.

See also Secretariat background notes prepared during the Tokyo Round on "Import Documentation"[25], "Customs and Administrative Entry Procedures"[26] and "Import Licensing Procedures".[27]

See also the material below at page 414 on the 1979 Agreement on Import Licensing Procedures. In this connection see also the unadopted 1994 panel report on "EEC - Import Régime for Bananas".[28]

4. Paragraph 3(b) and 3(c): Administration of import quotas

(1) "shall give public notice ... of the total quantity or value ... which will be permitted to be imported during a specified time period": public notice requirements and back-dated quotas

The 1989 Panel on "EEC - Restrictions on Imports of Dessert Apples - Complaint by Chile" noted in its Report that

"Concerning the notification of quotas and quota shares, ... Article XIII:3(b) requires that 'in the case of import restrictions involving the fixing of quotas, the contracting party applying the restrictions shall give public notice of the total quantity or value of the product or products which will be permitted to be imported during a specified future period ...'. And Article XIII:3(c) requires that 'in the case of quotas allocated among supplying countries, the contracting party applying the restrictions shall promptly inform all other contracting parties having an interest in supplying the product concerned of the shares in the quota currently allocated, by quantity or value, to the various supplying countries and shall give public notice thereof'. The Panel also took into account the requirement of Article X:1 to publish trade regulations, including prohibitions or restrictions on imports, promptly in such a manner as to enable governments and traders to become acquainted with them. In the context of Article XIII's overall concern with the non-discriminatory application of quantitative restrictions, it interpreted Article XIII:3(b) and (c) together as requiring that both the total quota and shares allocated in it be publicly notified for a specified future period. The Article XIII:3(c) requirement to promptly notify other contracting parties with an interest in supplying the product would otherwise be meaningless, as would the Article XIII:3(b) provision for supplies en route to be counted against quota entitlement.

"The Panel therefore considered that the allocation of back-dated quotas, that is, quotas declared to have already been filled at the time of their announcement, did not conform to the requirements of Article XIII:3(b) and Article XIII:3(c). It found that EEC Commission Regulation 1040/88 constituted a back-dated quota in respect of Chile, since although it published a quota share for Chile it simultaneously declared that share to be filled and, in fact, continued the suspension of imports from Chile enacted eight days before quotas were published. The EEC had therefore not observed the notification requirements of Article XIII:3(b) and (c). Moreover, the fact that such a back-dated quota was allocated to only one supplying country, Chile, resulted in the discriminatory administration of the restriction in violation of Article XIII:1".[29]

Claims under the publication requirements of Articles XIII and X have been made in panel proceedings but (as subsidiary claims) not ruled upon by the panel in question; see below at page 411.

---

[25]MTN/3B/8, MTN/3B/13, MTN/3B/14.
[26]MTN/3B/2 and Adds.
[27]NTM/W/73, NTM/W/73/Rev.1, NTM/W/73/Corr.1, NTM/W/73/Add.1.
[28]DS38/R, dated 11 February 1994, paras. 141-142.
[29]L/6491, adopted on 22 June 1989, 36S/93, 131-132, paras. 12.25-12.26.

(2) "supplies of the good in question which were en route at the time at which public notice were given"

The reference to "goods en route" was inserted into the Charter at the initiative of Chile, in discussions at the London session of the Preparatory Committee in 1946, in connection with the administration of supply-management quotas for agricultural and fisheries products. It was generally agreed at that time that if goods were en route, they must be admitted, but may be counted against a quota.[30] The following example was given in the discussion of the operation of the second sentence of paragraph 3(b):

> "Supposing a boat is arriving and then it is found that it has all the quantity which is allowed on board, and then the next day another boat arrives, if the second boat-load was en route at the time, the goods cannot be excluded and the country in question would go over its quota. ... after notice has been given then an account has to be taken of the goods en route at the time ...".[31]

This "goods en route" provision was reflected in the London Draft Charter as a proviso to the provision which corresponds to Article XI:2(c) of the General Agreement.[32] The Drafting Committee which met at New York between the London and Geneva sessions of the Preparatory Committee moved this proviso to the article of the Charter corresponding to Article XIII. It also inserted the second proviso of paragraph 3(b) "to bring this sub-paragraph into harmony with the provision concerning publication of certain administrative rulings contained in paragraph 3 of Article 21".[33] Article 21:3 of the New York Draft Charter (corresponding to Article X:2 of the General Agreement) provided a similar proviso to the requirement of advance publication of trade regulations, which was eliminated in the Geneva Draft Charter and was not included in the General Agreement.[34]

In the 1980 Panel Report on "EEC - Restrictions on Imports of Apples from Chile"

> "The Panel noted that at the time of the suspension, Chilean exporters had signed commercial contracts for 60,500 m.t. of apples with EEC importers. The panel reviewed the Standard Practices for the Administration of Import and Export Restrictions and Exchange Controls (GATT/CP.5/30/Rev.1) that were approved by the CONTRACTING PARTIES in 1950. These guidelines specify, *inter alia*, that:
>
> (a) 'any new or intensified restrictions on importation or exportation should not apply to goods shown to the satisfaction of the control authority to have been en route at the time the change was announced or to have been paid for in substantial part or covered by an irrevocable letter of credit' and
>
> (b) 'goods proven to have been covered by adequate confirmed prior order at the time new or intensified restrictions are announced, and not marketable elsewhere without appreciable loss should receive special consideration on an individual case basis, provided their delivery can be completed within a specified period.'

> "The Panel noted however that these standard practices 'should be regarded as a code for the guidance of contracting parties and not as additional obligations imposed upon them under the General Agreement' and that individual contracting parties 'should endeavour to adopt them to the maximum practicable extent'.

> "With the above in mind, the Panel examined whether the EEC measure against Chile was 'retroactive' in the context of XIII:3(b) second sentence. The Panel found the EEC to be consistent therewith, as the EEC had not excluded from entry Chilean apples on board and destined for the EEC, at the time the EEC regulation regarding the import suspension was published".[35]

---

[30]See EPCT/C.II/QR/PV/4, p. 7-12 and further discussion at EPCT/C.II/QR/PV/5, p. 67-73.
[31]EPCT/C.II/QR/PV/5, p. 71.
[32]London Draft Charter Art. 25(f); see also London Report p. 12, section III.C.1(d).
[33]New York Report, p. 20, 23.
[34]Geneva Draft Charter Article 37:3(a).
[35]L/5047, adopted on 10 November 1980, 27S/98, 116, paras. 4.19-4.20.

In the 1989 Panel Report on "EEC - Restrictions on Imports of Dessert Apples - Complaint by Chile"

"The Panel went on to examine the EEC's treatment of goods en route, in the light of Article XIII:3(b)'s stipulation that 'any supplies of the product in question which were en route at the time at which public notice was given shall not be excluded from entry'. The Panel also took note of the (non-obligatory) Standard Practices for the Administration of Import and Export Restrictions approved by the CONTRACTING PARTIES in 1950. These state in part that 'any new or intensified restrictions should not apply to goods shown to the satisfaction of the control authority to have been en route at the time the change was announced. ...' The Panel noted that the EEC, in the preamble to Regulation 962/88, suspending the issue of import licences for Chilean apples, had stated that '... no account should be taken of goods being transported to the Community other than those for which import licences have been issued' but the issue of import licences before sailing was not mandatory under EEC Regulations. The Panel found that by allowing entry only to those goods en route for which an import licence had been issued prior to the Regulation's entry into force the EEC had added a requirement for which there was no basis in Article XIII. The wording of the Article clearly meant that apples en route - i.e., on board and destined for the EEC - at the time the suspension of Chilean import licences was published should have been admitted to the EEC. The Panel was also aware of the interim decision of the President of the European Court of Justice, dated 10 June 1988, which suspended the operation of the EEC regulations enacting the measures in question in respect of 89,514 cartons of Chilean apples which had been in transit but for which an import licence had not been issued at the time the issue of such licences was suspended for Chile".[36]

(3) Second proviso to paragraph 3(b)

The material which now appears in the second proviso in paragraph 3(b) was originally inserted into the Charter Article on non-discriminatory administration of quota restrictions, by the Drafting Committee which met in New York between the first and second sessions of the Preparatory Committee. This insertion was made in order to harmonize that provision with paragraph 3 of the New York Draft Charter Article on publication and administration of trade regulations, which provided that no administrative ruling imposing a new or more burdensome requirement, restriction or prohibition on imports would be applied to goods en route as of the date of publication, and had a proviso on the lines of this proviso. In the second session of the Preparatory Committee, the goods en route provision and its proviso was eliminated from the Charter Article on publication, but the proviso was retained in the Charter Article on non-discriminatory administration of quantitative restrictions. The resulting difference between the Charter provisions is reflected in the texts of Articles X:2 and XIII:3 of the General Agreement.[37]

5. Paragraph 4: "representative period"

See Article XI and material on this issue on page 402.

6. Paragraph 5

(1) Non-discriminatory administration of tariff quotas

The "Panel on Newsprint"[38] addressed the consistency of an EEC tariff quota on newsprint with the requirements of Article XIII. See also page 402 above. In this connection see also the unadopted 1994 panel report on "EEC - Import Régime for Bananas".[39]

---

[36] L/6491, adopted on 22 June 1989, 36S/93, 132-133, para. 12.27.
[37] New York (Drafting Committee) Report, p. 17, 23; Geneva Report, p. 23, 34.
[38] L/5680, adopted on 20 November 1984, 31S/114.
[39] DS38/R, dated 11 February 1994, paras. 141-142.

(2) Non-discriminatory administration of export restrictions

In 1949, the Czechoslovak government brought a complaint that US export restrictions were administered in a discriminatory manner; see further on page 414 below.

See the discussion under Article XI of the 1950 Working Party Report on "The Use of Quantitative Import and Export Restrictions for Protective, Promotional and other Commercial Purposes", with regard to the use of export restrictions as selective bargaining leverage. See also the discussion on "voluntary export restraints" in the chapter on Article XIX.

B. RELATIONSHIP BETWEEN ARTICLE XIII AND OTHER GATT PROVISIONS

1. Article I

In the 1980 dispute on "EEC - Restrictions on Imports of Apples from Chile," Chile maintained that as the quantitative restrictions in question affected exclusively apples of Chilean origin they were inconsistent with the most-favoured-nation treatment prescribed in Article I. The Panel Report notes: "The Panel examined the consistency of the EEC measures with the most-favoured-nation principles of the General Agreement. The Panel considered it more appropriate to examine the matter in the context of Article XIII which deals with the non-discriminatory administration of quantitative restrictions rather than Article I:1".[40]

In the 1989 dispute concerning the complaint by Chile on "EEC - Restrictions on Imports of Dessert Apples", the Panel examined a claim made by Chile under Article I with regard to the EEC's import quota on apples. The Panel findings note: "The Panel considered it more appropriate to examine the consistency of the EEC measures with the most-favoured-nation principles of the General Agreement in the context of Article XIII. ... This provision deals with the non-discriminatory administration of quantitative restrictions and is thus the *lex specialis* in this particular case".[41]

In 1961 Uruguay requested a ruling from the CONTRACTING PARTIES concerning whether the application of variable import duties was compatible with the GATT. A Note by the Executive Secretary stated: "The General Agreement contains no provision on the use of 'variable import duties'. ... Apart from the question of consistency with Article II it should be noted that the question might arise as to whether a variable import duty is consistent with the provisions of Article I on the most-favoured-nation treatment. This question can, however, hardly be discussed *a priori* without a knowledge of the exact nature of the measure in question or the manner in which it is operated. It should be noted that if a variable levy system should be accompanied by the imposition of restrictions by specified volume, or a prohibition, of imports such measures would of course be subject to the examinations and considerations [concerning Articles XI, XII, XIII, XIV and XVIII:B]".[42] In the discussion of this question at the Nineteenth Session of the CONTRACTING PARTIES the following views were expressed:

(i) "If the variable levy ... had the effect of exactly equalizing the price of the imported goods with the cost of bringing goods onto the market from domestic sources ... the CONTRACTING PARTIES should treat it as if it were a quantitative restriction or quantitative prohibition on imports."

(ii) "A levy that varied from source to source would be violation of the provisions of the Agreement dealing with non-discrimination".[43]

The 1962 Panel Report on the "Uruguayan Recourse to Article XXIII" notes as follows:

"The Panel was faced with a particular difficulty in considering the status of variable import levies or charges. It noted the discussion which took place at the nineteenth session of the CONTRACTING PARTIES on this subject during which it was pointed out that such measures raised serious questions which had not

---

[40] L/5047, adopted on 10 November 1980, 27S/98, 112, para. 4.1.
[41] L/6491, adopted on 22 June 1989, 36S/93, 133, para. 12.28.
[42] L/1636, dated 21 November 1961.
[43] SR.19/8, pp. 111-120.

been resolved. In these circumstances the Panel has not considered it appropriate to examine the consistency or otherwise of these measures under the General Agreement".[44]

2. Article XI

The 1984 Panel Report on "Japanese Measures on Imports of Leather" dealt with the claim by the United States that the Japanese restrictions were in contravention of Article XI and that, in addition, the restrictions also contravened Articles [X:1 and 3 and] XIII:3.

"The Panel noted that the United States had, as a subsidiary matter, argued that Japan had also nullified or impaired benefits under Articles II, X:1, X:3 and XIII:3. In view of the findings set out in the paragraphs above [concerning inconsistency with Article XI], the Panel found that it was not necessary for it to make a finding on these matters."[45]

The 1988 Panel Report on "Japan - Restrictions on Imports of Certain Agricultural Products" examined the claim that import restrictions on several agricultural products were inconsistent with Article XI:1 because each restriction was inconsistent with one or more of seven criteria listed in Article XI:2(c)(i).

"The Panel noted that the United States had, as a subsidiary matter, argued that Japan had also nullified or impaired benefits under Articles [X:1, X:3] and XIII:3. Since these provisions dealt with the administration of quotas that may be applied consistently with the General Agreement, the Panel decided that it was not necessary for it to make a finding on these matters with regard to quantitative restrictions maintained contrary to that Agreement."[46]

See also references under Article X to similar cases in which claims regarding notice of quota allocations were not reached due to a panel finding that a quantitative restriction was inconsistent with Article XI.

3. Article XXI

See below at page 414.

4. Article XXIV

See material in the chapter on Article XXIV.

5. Part IV

See material in the chapter on Part IV.

6. Protocols of Accession

The Protocol for the Accession of Switzerland provides in its paragraph 4 for a reservation with respect to the application of the provisions of Article XI to the extent necessary to permit Switzerland to apply import restrictions pursuant to certain domestic legislation. However, this paragraph also provides:

"... In applying, under these laws, measures which are not covered by paragraph 1(b) above, Switzerland ... consistently with Article XIII of the General Agreement, shall apply all restrictions imposed under these laws in accordance with the principle of non-discrimination".[47]

---

[44]L/1923, adopted on 16 November 1962, 11S/95, 100, para. 17.
[45]L/5623, adopted on 15/16 May 1984, 31S/94, 114, para. 57.
[46]L/6253, adopted on 2 February 1988, 35S/163, 242, para. 5.4.2.
[47]14S/6, 8.

C. RELATIONSHIP BETWEEN ARTICLE XIII AND OTHER AGREEMENTS

In a Decision on "Margins of Preference" of 9 August 1949 the CONTRACTING PARTIES ruled that "The determination of rights and obligations between governments arising under a bilateral agreement is not a matter within the competence of the CONTRACTING PARTIES." This ruling was subject to a footnote:

> "This Decision by its terms clearly refers only to the determination of the rights and obligations as between the parties to the bilateral agreement and arising from that agreement. It is, however, within the competence of the CONTRACTING PARTIES to determine whether action under such a bilateral agreement would or would not conflict with the provisions of the General Agreement".[48]

The Report of the Review Working Party on "Quantitative Restrictions" records that an amendment was proposed to Article XIV with a view to ensuring that discrimination practised by contracting parties under bilateral agreements was limited to the extent justifiable on currency grounds. "The Working Party considered that this amendment was unnecessary since it was already covered by the provisions of Article XIV which clearly defined the extent to which deviation from the provisions of Article XIII was permitted. ... Moreover it is for the CONTRACTING PARTIES to decide whether the provisions of the Agreement are being complied with and in so far as discrimination is not authorized under the Agreement, it is possible to have recourse to the provisions of Article XII."[49]

The question of the compatibility with the General Agreement of bilateral trade agreements providing for quotas or differential treatment was again discussed in 1961 at the Nineteenth Session of the CONTRACTING PARTIES.[50] According to a Note by the Executive Secretary, which was generally supported in the discussion,

> "The General Agreement contains no provisions dealing specifically with the use of bilateral agreements. If a contracting party concludes a bilateral agreement with another contracting party or a government not party to the GATT, what is relevant for the General Agreement is the effect on the trade of other contracting parties of any measures affecting trade which that government takes to make effective the provisions of the bilateral agreement. ... it is, therefore, necessary to know the nature of the quota obligation provided for in the bilateral agreement and details of any measures affecting imports which are taken for the fulfilment of that bilateral obligation.

> "If the fulfilment of the obligations under the bilateral agreement involves the use of restrictions on imports from any other contracting parties, these restrictions will be matters for examination under the relevant provisions of the Agreement:

> "(a) Obviously, if the contracting party is not entitled under any provisions of the General Agreement to apply import restrictions, the application of these restrictions will be contravening the provisions of Article XI.

> "(b) If the contracting party is entitled to apply import restrictions (e.g. under Article XII or XVIII:B) but has no justification under the GATT to use discrimination, then the restrictions will not be compatible with the provisions of Article XIII unless the quota restriction and the restrictions on imports from other contracting parties are 'similar' (see Article XIII:1) and if the rules and criteria in Article XIII are met".[51]

The Note also stated that these principles were equally applicable to the use of lists of countries in administering quantitative restrictions (according particular treatment to several countries at once). In discussion on the Note, the Executive Secretary stated that "as he saw it, the existence of a bilateral agreement could in no circumstances be justified as a basis for non-observance of the non-discrimination provisions of the General Agreement. ... the

---

[48]II/11, para. 1.
[49]L/332/Rev.1+Adds., adopted on 2, 4, and 5 March 1955, 3S/170, 177, para. 29; see also SR.19/8, p. 112.
[50]SR.19/8, pp. 111-120.
[51]L/1636, p. 2-3, paras. 3-4.

[Note] made no distinction between import and export restrictions which were governed in the same way by the provisions of the General Agreement".[52]

D. EXCEPTIONS AND DEROGATIONS

1. **Provisions of Protocols of Accession relating to discriminatory quantitative restrictions**

The Protocol for the Accession of Poland provides, *inter alia*, that contracting parties may maintain with respect to imports from Poland, during a transitional period, prohibitions or quantitative restrictions which are inconsistent with Article XIII, provided that the discriminatory element in these restrictions is not increased, and progressively relaxed over the transitional period.[53] The Report of the Working Party on the Ninth Review under the Protocol of Accession stated that no agreement had been reached on a date for the termination of the transitional period.[54]

The Protocol for the Accession of Romania provides, *inter alia*, that contracting parties still maintaining prohibitions or quantitative restrictions not consistent with Article XIII shall not increase the discriminatory element in these restrictions, undertake to remove them progressively and shall have as their objective to eliminate them before the end of 1974. "Should this agreed objective not be achieved and, for exceptional reasons, should a limited number of restrictions still be in force as of 1 January 1975, the Working Party provided for in paragraph 5 would examine them with a view to their elimination."[55] The Report of the Working Party on the Sixth Review under the Protocol of Accession noted that certain discriminatory import restrictions continued to be maintained.[56]

The Protocol for the Accession of Hungary provides, *inter alia*, that contracting parties still maintaining prohibitions or quantitative restrictions not consistent with Article XIII on imports from Hungary shall not increase the discriminatory element in them and undertake to remove them progressively. "If, for exceptional reasons, any such prohibitions or restrictions are still in force as of 1 January 1975, the Working Party provided for in paragraph 6 will examine them with a view to their elimination."[57] The Report of the Working Party on the Fourth Review under the Protocol of Accession noted that import restrictions not consistent with Article XIII continue to be maintained.[58] This was reiterated in the Reports of the Working Parties on the Sixth and Seventh Review.[59]

Concerning these Protocols of Accession, see also the material under Article XXIV concerning the relationship between that Article and Article XIII.

2. **Waivers under Article XXV:5**

There is only one instance of a waiver to the provisions of Article XIII: the Decision of 10 November 1952 on the "Waiver granted in connection with the European Coal and Steel Community". This decision provided that the Governments of the member States of the ECSC Treaty, "notwithstanding the provisions of paragraphs 1 and 2 of Article XIII of the General Agreement, will be free to refrain from imposing any prohibitions or restrictions on the importation or exportation of coal and steel products from or to the territories of any other member State, although instituting or maintaining such prohibitions or restrictions upon the territories of other contracting parties; *provided* that the prohibitions or restrictions are in all other respects consistent with the General Agreement".[60]

---

[52] SR.19/8, p. 116.
[53] 15S/46, 47-48, para. 3.
[54] 24S/148.
[55] 18S/5, para. 3.
[56] 35S/337, 339, para. 10.
[57] 20S/3, 4, para. 4.
[58] L/5303, adopted on 31 March 1982, 29S/129, 130.
[59] 33S/136, 145; 36S/416, 423, para. 43.
[60] 1S/17/20, para. 3; see also Working Party report on the waiver, G/35, adopted on 10 November 1952, 1S/85.

A Note by the Executive Secretary on "Questions Relating to Bilateral Agreements, Discrimination and Variable Taxes" mentions "that in no case has a waiver on import restrictions authorized any deviation from the provisions of Article XIII".[61] In the case of waivers of Article XI it has generally been the case that it has been provided either in the Waiver Decision or in the accompanying working party report that the waiver does not extend to discriminatory measures inconsistent with Article XIII.[62] For instance, the 1955 Working Party Report on "Import Restrictions Imposed by the United States under Section 22 of the United States Agricultural Adjustment Act" provides, with regard to the waiver granted to the United States for such restrictions: "In particular, as its obligations under Article XIII are not affected, the United States should acquire no right by virtue of this waiver to deviate from the rule of non-discrimination provided for in that Article".[63] Similarly, the 1985 waiver decision on "Caribbean Basin Economic Recovery Act" provides that "The Government of the United States shall ensure that this waiver will not be used to contravene the principle of non-discriminatory allocation of sugar quotas".[64]

3. Other exceptions

In 1949, the Czechoslovak government brought a complaint that US export restrictions were administered in a discriminatory manner; the US representative cited Article XXI:(b)(iii) in justification. In a decision of 8 June 1949 "The CONTRACTING PARTIES decided to reject the contention of the Czechoslovak delegation that the Government of the United States had failed to carry out its obligations under the Agreement through its administration of the issue of export licences".[65]

The Panel Report on "United States - Imports of Sugar from Nicaragua" includes the following finding: "The Panel noted that the United States had not invoked any of the exceptions provided for in the General Agreement permitting discriminatory quantitative restrictions contrary to Article XIII. The Panel therefore did not examine whether the reduction in Nicaragua's quota could be justified under any such provision".[66]

See also Article XIV (Exceptions to the Rule of Non-discrimination) and accompanying text.

E. AGREEMENT ON IMPORT LICENSING PROCEDURES

The Agreement on Import Licensing Procedures was negotiated during the Tokyo Round of multilateral trade negotiations.[67] The Agreement sets out detailed rules so as to ensure, *inter alia*, "that the administrative procedures used to implement import licensing regimes are in conformity with the relevant provisions of the GATT including its annexes and protocols, as interpreted by this Agreement, with a view to preventing trade distortions that may arise from an inappropriate operation of those procedures, taking into account the economic development purposes and financial and trade needs of developing countries".[68] A list of acceptances of the Agreement appears in the Appendix to this book. Article 4 of the Agreement establishes the Committee on Import Licensing composed of representatives of the parties to the Agreement. The Committee reports annually to the CONTRACTING PARTIES. The basic document for the biennial review conducted by its parties includes information on participation in the Agreement and lists of notifications by parties on their import licensing régimes, public notices of import licensing, and import licensing laws and regulations. The basic document also provides references to information on the automatic and non-automatic licensing systems of parties from the replies to the Questionnaire on Import Licensing Practices.[69] At its eleventh meeting, the Committee adopted a work programme to help it reach a common understanding on the meaning of certain provisions of the Agreement

---

[61] L/1636, p. 2.

[62] In addition to examples cited on this page see Decision on "Problems Raised for Contracting Parties in Eliminating Import Restrictions Maintained During a Period of Balance-of-Payments Difficulties" (the "hard-core" waiver decision), 3S/38, 41, para. 2; Working Party Report on the waiver granted under this Decision to Belgium, L/467, adopted on 3 December 1955, 4S/102, 106-107, paras. 18-19; waiver decision on "German Import Restrictions", 8S/32 and Working Party Report at 8S/160.

[63] L/339, adopted on 5 March 1955, 3S/144.

[64] L/5779, Decision of 15 February 1985, 31S/22.

[65] GATT/CP.3/SR.22, II/28.

[66] L/5607, adopted on 13 March 1984, 31S/67, 74, para. 4.4.

[67] 26S/154. Concerning the negotiation of the Agreement, see documents listed in TA/INF/1/Rev.8, p. 38-44.

[68] 26S/155, Article 1:2..

[69] See LIC/22/Rev.1 (1993 basic document).

formulated in vague terms. The Committee has adopted recommendations which were developed on the application of Articles 1.4, 1.6, 3(c), 3(d), 3(e) and 3(g) of the Agreement.[70] A new Agreement on Import Licensing was agreed in the Uruguay Round and is included in Annex 1A of the WTO Agreement.

III. PREPARATORY WORK AND SUBSEQUENT MODIFICATIONS

The corresponding provision in the Havana Charter is contained in Article 22; in the US-UK *Proposals* in Chapter III C-3; in the US Draft Charter in Article 21; in the London and New York Drafts in Article 26; and in the Geneva Draft in Article 22.

Differences between the Havana Charter and the General Agreement: In the first sentence of paragraph 2(d) there is a drafting difference between Article 22 of the Charter and Article XIII of the General Agreement. Also, the Interpretative Note to this paragraph was deleted in Havana and is not included in the Charter.[71] Paragraph 3(d) of the Charter article is not in the GATT text; it was inserted at Havana in order to enable a Member, trading with a non-Member or non-Members, to be released from its obligations to give public notice under paragraph 3(b) and 3(c).[72] Also, the following Interpretative Note to paragraph 3, which is not in the GATT text, was added at Havana to meet the special case of India:

"The first sentence of paragraph 3(b) is to be understood as requiring the Member in all cases to give, not later than the beginning of the relevant period, public notice of any quota fixed for a specified future period, but as permitting a Member, which for urgent balance-of-payments reasons is under the necessity of changing the quota within the course of a specified period, to select the time of its giving public notice of the change. This in no way affects the obligations of a Member under the provisions of paragraph 3(a), where applicable".[73]

In response to proposals in the Sub-Committee on Articles 20 and 22 at Havana, made with regard to the interpretative note on "special factors" (Note Ad Article XIII:4 of the General Agreement, or Ad Article 22:4 of the Charter), the Sub-Committee agreed to the interpretation and the additional interpretative note which appear on page 403 above with reference to "special factors".

In 1948, the Working Party on "Modifications to the General Agreement" at the Second Session of the CONTRACTING PARTIES considered which of the changes made to the Charter at Havana should be brought into the General Agreement. The Working Party decided to amend the text of paragraph 5.[74] The amendment deleted a reference to internal quantitative restrictions and licensing regulations, consequential to the replacement of the 30 October 1947 text of Article III by the text of Article 18 of the Havana Charter, including the text of the present Article III:7. These changes were effected through the Protocol Modifying Part II and Article XXVI.

During the Review Session, various proposals for changes to Article XIII were considered and rejected. See the paragraph from the Report of the Review Session Working Party on "Quantitative Restrictions" at page 402 above, and the documents cited below.

---

[70]See LIC/M/11, paragraphs 29-34 (decision on work programme); LIC/12 (compilation of recommendations adopted); LIC/M/18 (statements made on adoption); and LIC/M/20, para. 13 (later statements referring to the recommendations). See also discussions in the Committee on the definition of "import licensing" under Article 1.1, in LIC/M/20-25.

[71]Havana Reports, p. 95, para. 51.

[72]Havana Reports, p. 96, para. 54.

[73]Havana Reports, p. 96, para. 53.

[74]GATT/CP.2/22/Rev.1, adopted on 1 and 2 September 1948, II/39, 45, para. 32.

IV. RELEVANT DOCUMENTS

London

Discussion:	EPCT/C.II/QR/PV/2, 4 (p. 25), 5 (p. 95), 6 (Part II), EPCT/C.II/PV/4, 5
Reports:	EPCT/30

New York

Discussion:	EPCT/C.6/17, 20, 21, 23, 27, 51
Reports:	EPCT/C.6/97/Rev.1
Other:	EPCT/W.64, 224, 313

Geneva

Discussion:	EPCT/EC/PV.2/22 EPCT/A/SR.21, 40(1) EPCT/TAC/SR.13 EPCT/TAC/PV/27, 28
Reports:	EPCT/135, 141, 164, 189, 196, 212, 214/Rev.1/Add.1 EPCT/W/313
Other:	EPCT/W/64, 74, 208, 219, 223, 259, 272, 301, 318

Havana

Discussion:	E/CONF.2/C.3/SR.21, 37, 41, 42
Reports:	E/CONF.2/C.3/54
Other:	E/CONF.2/C.3/E/W.19

Review Session

Discussion:	SR.9/14, 15, 40
Reports:	W.9/174+Add.1, 208, L/332/Rev.1+Adds.
Other:	W.9/91, 106, 130, Spec/53/55

ARTICLE XIV

EXCEPTIONS TO THE RULE OF NON-DISCRIMINATION

I.	TEXT OF ARTICLE XIV, RELEVANT INTERPRETATIVE NOTES, AND OTHER RELEVANT PROVISIONS	417
II.	INTERPRETATION AND APPLICATION OF ARTICLE XIV	418
	A. SCOPE AND APPLICATION OF ARTICLE XIV	418
	1. General	418
	2. Paragraph 1	420
	(1) Intent of Paragraph 1	420
	(2) "equivalent effect"	420
	(3) "which that contracting party may at that time apply"	420
	(4) Discrimination resulting from bilateral agreements	421
	3. Paragraph 2	421
	4. Paragraph 3	421
	5. Paragraph 4	422
	6. Paragraph 5	422
	(1) Quantitative restrictions having equivalent effect to certain authorized exchange restrictions	422
	(2) Quota preferences listed in Annex A of the General Agreement	423
	B. RELATIONSHIP WITH OTHER ARTICLES	424
	1. Article XVIII	424
III.	PREPARATORY WORK AND SUBSEQUENT MODIFICATIONS	424
IV.	RELEVANT DOCUMENTS	425

I. TEXT OF ARTICLE XIV, RELEVANT INTERPRETATIVE NOTES, AND OTHER RELEVANT PROVISIONS

Article XIV*

Exceptions to the Rule of Non-discrimination

1. A contracting party which applies restrictions under Article XII or under Section B of Article XVIII may, in the application of such restrictions, deviate from the provisions of Article XIII in a manner having equivalent effect to restrictions on payments and transfers for current international transactions which that contracting party may at that time apply under Article VIII or XIV of the Articles of Agreement of the International Monetary Fund, or under analogous provisions of a special exchange agreement entered into pursuant to paragraph 6 of Article XV.*

2. A contracting party which is applying import restrictions under Article XII or under Section B of Article XVIII may, with the consent of the CONTRACTING PARTIES, temporarily deviate from the provisions of Article XIII in respect of a small part of its external trade where the benefits to the contracting party or contracting parties concerned substantially outweigh any injury which may result to the trade of other contracting parties.*

3. The provisions of Article XIII shall not preclude a group of territories having a common quota in the International Monetary Fund from applying against imports from other countries, but not among themselves, restrictions in accordance with the provisions of Article XII or of Section B of Article XVIII on condition that such restrictions are in all other respects consistent with the provisions of Article XIII.

4. A contracting party applying import restrictions under Article XII or under Section B of Article XVIII shall not be precluded by Articles XI to XV or Section B of Article XVIII of this Agreement from applying measures to direct its exports in such a manner as to increase its earnings of currencies which it can use without deviation from the provisions of Article XIII.

5. A contracting party shall not be precluded by Articles XI to XV, inclusive, or by Section B of Article XVIII, of this Agreement from applying quantitative restrictions:

(a) having equivalent effect to exchange restrictions authorized under Section 3 (b) of Article VII of the Articles of Agreement of the International Monetary Fund, or

(b) under the preferential arrangements provided for in Annex A of this Agreement, pending the outcome of the negotiations referred to therein.

Interpretative Notes from Annex I

Ad Article XIV

Paragraph 1

The provisions of this paragraph shall not be so construed as to preclude full consideration by the CONTRACTING PARTIES, in the consultations provided for in paragraph 4 of Article XII and in paragraph 12 of Article XVIII, of the nature, effects and reasons for discrimination in the field of import restrictions.

Paragraph 2

One of the situations contemplated in paragraph 2 is that of a contracting party holding balances acquired as a result of current transactions which it finds itself unable to use without a measure of discrimination.

Ad Articles XI, XII, XIII, XIV and XVIII

Throughout Articles XI, XII, XIII, XIV and XVIII, the terms "import restrictions" or "export restrictions" include restrictions made effective through state-trading operations.

From Annex A:

...

The preferential arrangements referred to in paragraph 5 (b) of Article XIV are those existing in the United Kingdom on 10 April 1947, under contractual agreements with the Governments of Canada, Australia and New Zealand, in respect of chilled and frozen beef and veal, frozen mutton and lamb, chilled and frozen pork and bacon. It is the intention, without prejudice to any action taken under sub-paragraph (h) of Article XX, that these arrangements shall be eliminated or replaced by tariff preferences, and that negotiations to this end shall take place as soon as practicable among the countries substantially concerned or involved.

...

II. INTERPRETATION AND APPLICATION OF ARTICLE XIV

A. SCOPE AND APPLICATION OF ARTICLE XIV

1. General

The Articles of the General Agreement concerning quantitative restrictions for balance-of-payments purposes were redrafted in the 1954-55 Review Session. The principal source concerning the drafting of these provisions is the Report of the Review Working Party on "Quantitative Restrictions"[1], which notes generally concerning the amendments to Article XIV:

"On the one hand, they amount to a deletion of temporary provisions (i.e. sub-paragraphs 1(a) and 3(b)) which are no longer applicable; on the other hand, they provide for the elimination of alternative rules of procedure (sub-paragraphs 1(c) to (h) and Annex J which were necessary so long as a number of

---

[1] L/332/Rev.1 and Addenda., adopted on 2, 4 and 5 March 1955, 3S/170-185.

countries were governed by the provisions of Article XIV of the IMF Agreement but which will be redundant when many of those countries cease to be governed by those provisions".[2]

The first of these two groups of amendments to Article XIV entered into effect on 7 October 1957 with the other Review Session amendments. The second group entered into effect on 15 February 1961 when the obligations of Sections 2, 3 and 4 of Article VIII of the Articles of Agreement of the International Monetary Fund became applicable to contracting parties, members of the Fund, the combined foreign trade of which constituted at least 50 per cent of the aggregate foreign trade of all contracting parties.

In 1959, the Tenth Annual Report under Article XIV:1(g) on the discriminatory application of import restrictions noted that external convertibility of most of the major currencies had been established at the end of 1958, and further noted:

"The Board of Executive Directors of the International Monetary Fund on 23 October 1959 approved the following decision with regard to the discriminatory restrictions imposed for balance-of-payments reasons:

'The following decision deals exclusively with discriminatory restrictions imposed for balance-of-payments reasons.

'In some countries, considerable progress has already been made towards the elimination of discriminatory restrictions; in others, much remains to be done. Recent international financial developments have established an environment favourable to the elimination of discrimination for balance-of-payments reasons. There has been a substantial improvement in the reserve positions of the industrial countries in particular and widespread moves to external convertibility have taken place.

'Under these circumstances, the Fund considers that there is no longer any balance-of-payments justification for discrimination by members whose current receipts are largely in externally convertible currencies. However, the Fund recognizes that where such discriminatory restrictions have been long maintained a reasonable amount of time may be needed fully to eliminate them. But this time should be short and members will be expected to proceed with all feasible speed in eliminating discrimination against member countries, including that arising from bilateralism.

'Notwithstanding the extensive moves toward convertibility, a substantial portion of the current receipts of some countries is still subject to limitations on convertibility, particularly in payments relations with State-trading countries. In the case of these countries the Fund will be prepared to consider whether balance-of-payments considerations would justify the maintenance of some degree of discrimination, although not as between countries having externally convertible currencies. In this connexion the Fund wishes to reaffirm its basic policy on bilateralism as stated in its decision of 22 June 1955.'

"This decision was communicated to the CONTRACTING PARTIES at their fifteenth session where it was welcomed ..."

"The CONTRACTING PARTIES reaffirmed that the removal of discrimination applied under Article XIV is a vital step towards the achievement of the objectives of the General Agreement and the expansion of international trade. There was a consensus that the remaining discrimination applied under Article XIV of the General Agreement should quickly be eliminated".[3]

Since 1961, no contracting party has invoked Article XIV.

---

[2]*Ibid.*, 3S/176, para. 25.
[3]L/1096, adopted on 10 November 1959, 8S/66, 72, paras. 24-26.

2. Paragraph 1

(1) Intent of Paragraph 1

The Report of the Review Working Party on "Quantitative Restrictions" notes that "As regards the amended text of paragraph 1 of Article XIV, it reproduces the text of sub-paragraph 1(b) of the present Article, except that it refers, not only to Article XIV of the International Monetary Fund as is the case at present, but also to Article VIII. This addition is intended to cover cases where contracting parties are authorized by a decision taken by the International Monetary Fund, in accordance with Article VIII of its Articles of Agreement, to deviate from the rule of non-discrimination".[4]

See also the Interpretative Note to Article XIV and the discussion of paragraph 5(a) below at page 422.

(2) "equivalent effect"

The Report of the Review Working Party on "Quantitative Restrictions" notes:

"For practical reasons, the Working Party has not tried to define the phrase 'equivalent effect' in paragraphs 1 and 5 of Article XIV. It agreed, however, to record their view that a contracting party which is deviating from Article XIII will not be considered to be in breach of its obligations under this paragraph if the International Monetary Fund has stated that corresponding restrictions on payments and transfers would have been authorized under the Articles of Agreement of the Fund or approved by the Fund if the contracting party in question had chosen to proceed by way of exchange restrictions rather than trade restrictions …

"… it was pointed out that under … paragraph 1 of the proposed new Article XIV, a contracting party could deviate from the provisions of Article XIII only in a manner having equivalent effect to restrictions on payments and transfers for current international transactions which that contracting party might at that time apply under the Articles of Agreement of the International Monetary Fund; it was understood that such restrictions could be applied only on currency grounds".[5]

Concerning the distinction between exchange restrictions and trade restrictions, see material under Article XV.

(3) "which that contracting party may at that time apply"

During the 1954-55 Review Session, the Review Working Party on Quantitative Restrictions established a Special Sub-Group on GATT/Fund relations. The report of this Sub-Group notes as follows regarding discrimination permissible under Articles VIII and XIV of the Fund Articles of Agreement:

"… the Fund representatives explained that Fund members which did not avail themselves of the transitional arrangements of Article XIV of the Fund Articles of Agreement had to seek prior approval from the Fund, under paragraph 2(a) (or in respect of discriminatory currency arrangements or multiple currency practices, under paragraph 3) of Article VIII for the imposition of restrictions on the making of transfers and payments for current international transactions. Fund members which availed themselves of the transitional arrangements under Article XIV could, subject to annual consultations with the Fund, continue to maintain exchange restrictions and adapt them to changing circumstances so long as they were needed for balance of payments purposes. The Fund could, if it deemed such action necessary in exceptional circumstances, make representations to such members that conditions were favourable for the withdrawal of any particular restriction, or for the general abandonment of restrictions inconsistent with the provisions of any other Article of the Fund Agreement.

---

[4]L/332/Rev.1 and Addenda, adopted on 2, 4 and 5 March 1955, 3S/170, 176-177, para. 26.
[5]*Ibid.*, 3S/177, paras. 28, 29.

"In relation to multiple exchange rates, the Fund representatives recalled that the Executive Board of the Fund in December 1947, took certain decisions relating to such practices ...".[6]

A copy of the Fund Decision regarding multiple currency practices was annexed to the Sub-Group's Report.[7]

(4) Discrimination resulting from bilateral agreements

A Note by the Executive Secretary on "Questions Relating to Bilateral Agreements, Discrimination and Variable Taxes" of 1961 states, *inter alia*:

"If the fulfilment of the obligations under the bilateral agreement involves the use of restrictions on imports from any other contracting parties, these restrictions will be matters for examination under the relevant provisions of the Agreement" [such as Articles XI to XIV and XVIII:B].

"If the contracting party is entitled to apply import restrictions and, by virtue of Article XIV of the Agreement, is also entitled to use discrimination, then the relative incidence of the bilateral quota restrictions and the restrictions applying to imports from other contracting parties can be the subject of examination under the provisions of that Article. If there is discrimination involved, it will be permitted under this Article provided it does not go beyond the limit laid down in paragraph 1, 2, 3 or 5 of the Article. Under paragraph 1 of that Article, for example, a contracting party is entitled to deviate from the provisions of Article XIII in a manner having equivalent effect to restrictions on payments and transfers for current international transactions which the contracting party is applying under the appropriate provisions of the IMF Agreement".[8]

3. Paragraph 2

It was noted by the Sub-Committee which redrafted Article 23 of the Charter (corresponding to Article XIV) during the Havana Conference, that after the termination of the transitional period for a Member (as defined in Article XIV of the Fund Articles of Agreement) paragraph 2 would provide "subject to the prior approval of the Organization, for limited departures from the rule of non-discrimination."[9] As noted below, the Charter Article was brought into the General Agreement in 1948.

The 1949 Report of the Working Party on "Consultation Procedures under Articles XII, XIII and XIV - other than Article XII:4(a)" notes that a "contracting party applying import restrictions under Article XII may, under the provisions of Article XIV, paragraph 2, with the assent of the CONTRACTING PARTIES, temporarily deviate from the provisions of Article XIII. The working party considered that the consultation procedure adopted for Article XII:4(a) would be appropriate in this case".[10] Article XII:4(a) in 1949 provided that "Any contracting party which is not applying restrictions under this Article, but is considering the need to do so, shall before instituting such restrictions (or, in circumstances in which prior consultation is impracticable, immediately after doing so), consult with the CONTRACTING PARTIES".

See also the Interpretative Note to paragraph 2.

4. Paragraph 3

The London Report notes that "It was generally agreed that there must be the following exceptions from the general rule of non-discrimination in the application of quantitative restrictions. ... A group of territories, which have a common quota in the International Monetary Fund, should be able to impose restrictions against imports

---

[6]*Ibid.*, 3S/196-197, paras. 4-5.
[7]*Ibid.*, 3S/200-205.
[8]L/1636, p. 2, para. 4.
[9]Havana Reports, p. 99, para. 22.
[10]GATT/CP.3/50/Rev.1, adopted on 4 July 1949, II/95, 100, para. 24. For the consultation procedure agreed for Article XII:4(a), see para. 3 of the same Report, at II/95-96.

of other countries in order to protect their common monetary reserves".[11] It was stated during discussions at the London session of the Preparatory Committee that this provision "should only apply where the quantitative restrictions are being applied on balance of payments grounds. If the quantitative restrictions are for other purposes the question of whether the countries are in a common unit in the Monetary Fund is irrelevant".[12]

Article III:1 of the Articles of Agreement of the International Monetary Fund provides that "Each member shall be assigned a quota ..." and under Article II of the Articles of Agreement, membership in the Fund is open only to "countries". Hence, territories can only have a common quota in the Fund if they are under common sovereignty. Article XIV:3 of the General Agreement provides an exception to the non-discrimination requirements of Article XIII:1 of the General Agreement, which apply as between contracting parties. Under Article XXIV:1 of the General Agreement, each separate customs territory on behalf of which the General Agreement is applied is "treated as though it were a contracting party", and thus the non-discrimination requirements of Article XIII:1 of the General Agreement, which apply as between contracting parties, apply as between each separate customs territory even if it is under common sovereignty with another customs territory. The records of the London session of the Preparatory Committee in 1946 indicate that in 1946, for instance, the various territories under French sovereignty in the French Union included some colonies treated as part of the metropolitan customs territory of France, and others which constituted separate customs territories later listed in Annex B of the General Agreement; nevertheless all of these territories, even those with different currencies with different exchange rates versus the dollar or sterling, shared a common quota in the Fund represented by France.[13]

5. Paragraph 4

Paragraph 4 was added to the Charter in Havana, and subsequently incorporated into the GATT in 1948. It was stated at the time that Committee III at Havana adopted this provision that "A country might only be able to attain equilibrium in its balance of payments by increasing its exports to hard currency countries. If such a country were allowed to continue to direct its exports, it might very well be able to cease practising import discrimination under paragraph 1 at an earlier date than would otherwise be possible".[14]

6. Paragraph 5

(1) Quantitative restrictions having equivalent effect to certain authorized exchange restrictions

Article XIV:5(a) permits quantitative restrictions having equivalent effect to exchange restrictions authorized under Article VII:3(b) of the Articles of Agreement of the International Monetary Fund.

Article VII:3(a) of the Fund Articles provides: "If it becomes evident to the Fund that the demand for a member's currency seriously threatens the Fund's ability to supply that currency, the Fund ... shall formally declare such currency scarce and shall thenceforth apportion its existing and accruing supply of the scarce currency ...". Article VII:3(b) of the Fund Articles provides that "A formal declaration under (a) above shall operate as an authorization to any member, after consultation with the Fund, temporarily to impose limitations on the freedom of exchange operations in the scarce currency. Subject to the provisions of Article IV and Schedule C, the member shall have complete jurisdiction in determining the nature of such limitations, but they shall be no more restrictive than is necessary to limit the demand for the scarce currency to the supply held by, or accruing to, the member in question, and they shall be relaxed and removed as rapidly as conditions permit".

No formal declaration under Article VII:3(a) has been made by the Fund, and therefore no exchange restrictions have been authorized under Article VII:3(b) of the Fund Articles of Agreement.

The Report of the Review Working Party on "Quantitative Restrictions" notes that during the Review Session, various proposals were made to amend the General Agreement to provide for joint action to restore equilibrium in the system of world trade and payments in the event that that system became seriously unbalanced,

---

[11]London Report, p. 14, para. III.C.3(d)(ii).
[12]EPCT/C.II/QR/PV/2, p. 21: *see generally* discussion at *ibid.* p. 20-21, and *see also* explanation at EPCT/C.II/PV/4, p. 33.
[13]See description at EPCT/C.II/PV/4 p. 18-20.
[14]E/CONF.2/C.3/SR.47, p. 1.

and to avoid the imposition of unnecessarily severe restrictions on international trade.[15] In relation to two "scarce currency" proposals, designed for a situation where some large and commercially important country might develop a persistent surplus in its balance of payments with the rest of the world, place a strain on other countries' reserves, and cause a general scarcity of its currency:

> "There was general agreement in the Working Party that such a situation might arise from a variety of different circumstances and that the prime responsibility for the state of unbalance might rest either with the surplus or the deficit countries.
>
> "It was noted that provisions are already contained in the General Agreement and also in the Articles of Agreement of the International Monetary Fund to enable consultation to take place on the measures that might appropriately be adopted to meet such situations. ...
>
> "If the CONTRACTING PARTIES were to find that strict application of the non-discrimination provisions of Article XIII would cause an unnecessary contraction in world trade there are already provisions in the GATT and in the International Monetary Fund Agreement which could be invoked to waive temporarily the obligation imposed upon contracting parties under that Article to apply import restrictions in a non-discriminatory manner.
>
> "First, the Fund may, if it finds a general scarcity of a currency under Article VII, Section 1, approve discriminatory measures under Article VIII, Sections 2 and 3. Certain important countries which are members of the Fund and GATT have stated that if they supported a finding under Fund Article VII, Section 1, they would also support appropriate action under Article VIII.
>
> "Secondly, Fund Article VII, Section 3, provides that if it becomes evident that the demand for a member's currency seriously threatens the Fund's ability to supply that currency, the Fund shall formally declare such currency scarce and such a declaration authorizes certain discriminatory limitations on the freedom of exchange operations in that currency. Although this provision has not operated in the past because the Fund's ability to supply a currency has never been threatened, it is to be expected that when the resources of the Fund are being used to support the convertibility of currencies, any serious scarcity of a major currency would be reflected in the holdings of the Fund. These provisions of the Fund Agreement bear directly on the question of trade discrimination; for under Article XIV of the GATT, as at present drafted, a contracting party would be able to apply discriminatory quantitative restrictions having equivalent effect to exchange restrictions authorized by the Fund under Article VIII, Section 3, as well as under Article VII, Section 3(b)".[16]

(2) Quota preferences listed in Annex A of the General Agreement

Both in London and Geneva it was recommended that "certain existing preferential arrangements which were established under international agreements but not effected by the normal method of a difference in rates of duty" and which remained after the conclusion of the Geneva negotiations should be dealt with by a provision in the GATT, to the effect that the member applying these arrangements shall be entitled to continue them or equivalent measures, pending either an international commodity agreement under the Charter, or some other arrangement between the members concerned.[17]

> "It was agreed that only a very limited number of commodities fell under this heading and that the countries concerned should establish the facts about them so that the above recommendation could be taken into account in the forthcoming negotiations. It was further recognized that the concessions or lack of concessions in respect of the items concerned would, for purposes of assessing the results of the

---

[15]See W.19/18, W.9/22, W.9/82, W.9/136, W.9/139, L/325, GATT/174.

[16]L/332/Rev.1 and Addenda, adopted on 2, 4 and 5 March 1955, 3S/170, 174-176, paras. 16-17, 19- 21. See also other Review Session documents on these discussions: W.9/18, W.9/22, W.9/82, W.9/136, W.9/139, L/325, GATT/174.

[17]Discussion at EPCT/C.II/QR/PV/1 p. 14, EPCT/C.II/PV/13 p. 26-28; London Report, p. 12, para. n; EPCT/141, p. 2.

negotiations, stand on the same footing as concessions or lack of concessions in respect of particular tariff or preference items".[18]

The arrangements in question were certain arrangements existing in the United Kingdom on 10 April 1947, under contractual arrangements with the Governments of Canada, Australia and New Zealand, in respect of chilled and frozen beef and veal, frozen mutton and lamb, chilled and frozen pork, and bacon. These arrangements are listed in Annex A of the General Agreement, the relevant parts of which appear at the head of this chapter. Their contractual basis is noted in the preparatory work of this provision.[19] During the Review Session of 1954-55 the United Kingdom delegation requested that this provision be retained as the negotiations referred to had not yet taken place.[20]

B. RELATIONSHIP WITH OTHER ARTICLES

1. Article XVIII

The Review Working Party Report on "Quantitative Restrictions" notes that "Appropriate references to Article XVIII have been introduced in the text of Article XIV; through these insertions, the application of balance-of-payments restrictions by under-developed countries are governed by the provisions of Article XIV as regards deviations from the rule of non-discrimination".[21]

III. PREPARATORY WORK AND SUBSEQUENT MODIFICATIONS

Corresponding provisions in the Havana Charter are contained in Article 23; in the US-UK *Proposals* in Chapter III C-4; in the US Draft in Article 22; in the London and New York Drafts in Article 28; and in the Geneva Draft in Article 23.

The text of Article XIV and the extent of permissible discrimination in balance-of-payments restrictions were the subject of much negotiation in 1946-48. The Article in the Geneva Draft Charter, which was adopted in the 30 October 1947 text of the General Agreement, was substantially rewritten at Havana; as rewritten, it provided additional flexibility for discriminatory measures in the case of non-convertible currencies. At their First Session, held during the Havana Conference, the CONTRACTING PARTIES decided to replace the original text of Article XIV with the Havana Charter Article.[22] This change was effected through the Special Protocol Modifying Article XIV, which entered into effect on 9 May 1949.

The Review Session amendments to paragraph 1 of Article XIV and Annex J, which were provided for in the Protocol Amending the Preamble and Parts II and III, came into effect on 15 February 1961 when the obligations of Sections 2, 3 and 4 of Article VIII of the Articles of Agreement of the International Monetary Fund became applicable to contracting parties, members of the Fund, the combined foreign trade of which constituted at least 50 per cent of the aggregate foreign trade of all contracting parties. Paragraph 1, comprising sub-paragraphs (a) to (h), was replaced by the new paragraph 1, which reproduced, with certain changes, paragraph 1(b) of the previous text. The Interpretative Note to sub-paragraph (g) was replaced by a Note to the new paragraph 1. Annex J and the interpretative Note thereto were deleted.

Other changes agreed upon at the Review Session included the insertion of a reference to Section B of Article XVIII in paragraphs 2, 4 and 5, and a redrafting of paragraph 3; these changes entered into effect on 7 October 1957.

---

[18]London Report, p. 12, para. o.
[19]See EPCT/158, Report on Preferential Arrangements Not Effected by the Method of a Difference in Rates of Duty, and annexed note by UK delegation on agreements with Australia, New Zealand and Canada.
[20]W.9/106, p. 6.
[21]L/332/Rev.1 and Addenda, adopted on 2, 4 and 5 March 1955, 3S/170, 177, para. 27; see also *ibid*. 3S/185, para. 50.
[22]See GATT/1/21, GATT/1/27, GATT/1/55, GATT/1/62 Annex 4, and discussion at GATT/1/SR.10+Corr.1, GATT/1/SR.13, GATT/1/SR.14.

IV. RELEVANT DOCUMENTS

London

Discussion:	EPCT/C.II/PV/4 (p. 32ff), 5, 13 (p. 15ff)
	EPCT/C.II/QR/PV/2, 3 (p. 42ff), 6
Reports:	EPCT/30; EPCT/C.II/59

New York

Discussion:	EPCT/C.6/21, 27
Reports:	EPCT/C.6/97/Rev.1 (p. 82)

Geneva

Discussion:	EPCT/EC/PV.2/22
	EPCT/A/SR.29
	EPCT/A/PV/29/Corr.2, 41 (pp. 42-64)
	EPCT/TAC/SR.13, 21
	EPCT/PV/21, 27, 28
Reports:	EPCT/135, 158, 163, 171, 186, 189, 196, 212, 214/Add.1/Rev.1
	EPCT/W/313
Other:	EPCT/W/64, 194, 214, 216, 223, 256, 272, 301, 318, 327, 329, 331, 336

Havana

Discussion:	E/CONF.2/C.3/SR.22, 23, 39 (p. 6), 47
Reports:	E/CONF.2/C.3/91
Other:	E/CONF.2/C.3/F/W.7, 11, 31/Revs. 1 and 2, 32

CONTRACTING PARTIES

Discussion:	GATT/1/SR.10+Corr.1, 13, 14
Reports:	GATT/1/27, 55, 62 Annex 4
	GATT/CP/6

Review Session

Discussion:	SR.9/14, 15, 26, 40, 47
Reports:	W.9/106, 126, 130, 174+Add.1, 208, 234; L/332/Rev.1+Adds., 3S/170
Other:	L/189, 261/Add.1, 264, 277
	W.9/18+Add.1, 22, 23, 82, 90, 115, 133, 136, 139, 190, 226, 236/Add.3
	Spec/53/55, 58/55, 68/55, 74/55, 90/55, MGT/9/55

ARTICLE XV

EXCHANGE ARRANGEMENTS

I.	TEXT OF ARTICLE XV AND INTERPRETATIVE NOTE AD ARTICLE XV	428
II.	INTERPRETATION AND APPLICATION OF ARTICLE XV	429
	A. SCOPE AND APPLICATION OF ARTICLE XV	429
	1. Paragraph 1	429
	(1) *"jurisdiction"*	429
	(2) *Relationship between trade measures and financial system*	430
	2. Paragraph 2	430
	(1) *"findings of statistical ... facts presented by the Fund"*	430
	(2) *"The CONTRACTING PARTIES, in reaching their final decision"*	431
	(3) *"financial aspects of other matters ..."*	431
	(4) *Application of paragraph 2: role of the International Monetary Fund*	431
	(a) *Balance-of-payments consultations*	431
	(b) *Consultations on other problems involving financial issues*	432
	3. Paragraph 3: Arrangements for consultation with the International Monetary Fund	433
	4. Paragraph 4	435
	(1) *"by exchange action frustrate"*	435
	(2) *Distinction between trade action and exchange action*	435
	(3) *Trade measures equivalent to exchange rate changes*	436
	(4) *Trade measures enforcing permissible exchange controls: Note Ad Article XV:4*	436
	(5) *Relationship between paragraph 9(a) and paragraph 4*	436
	5. Paragraph 5	436
	6. Paragraph 6	437
	(1) *"within a time to be determined"*	437
	(2) *"special exchange agreement"*	437
	(3) *Exceptions and derogations from paragraph 6*	437
	7. Paragraph 8	438
	8. Paragraph 9	438
	B. RELATIONSHIP BETWEEN ARTICLE XV AND OTHER PROVISIONS OF THE GENERAL AGREEMENT	439
	1. Article III	439
	2. Article XXIII	440
	3. Other GATT provisions	440
	C. EXCEPTIONS AND DEROGATIONS	441
III.	PREPARATORY WORK AND SUBSEQUENT MODIFICATIONS	441
IV.	RELEVANT DOCUMENTS	442

I. TEXT OF ARTICLE XV AND INTERPRETATIVE NOTE AD ARTICLE XV

Article XV

Exchange Arrangements

1. The CONTRACTING PARTIES shall seek co-operation with the International Monetary Fund to the end that the CONTRACTING PARTIES and the Fund may pursue a co-ordinated policy with regard to exchange questions within the jurisdiction of the Fund and questions of quantitative restrictions and other trade measures within the jurisdiction of the CONTRACTING PARTIES.

2. In all cases in which the CONTRACTING PARTIES are called upon to consider or deal with problems concerning monetary reserves, balances of payments or foreign exchange arrangements, they shall consult fully with the International Monetary Fund. In such consultations, the CONTRACTING PARTIES shall accept all findings of statistical and other facts presented by the Fund relating to foreign exchange, monetary reserves and balances of payments, and shall accept the determination of the Fund as to whether action by a contracting party in exchange matters is in accordance with the Articles of Agreement of the International Monetary Fund, or with the terms of a special exchange agreement between that contracting party and the CONTRACTING PARTIES. The CONTRACTING PARTIES in reaching their final decision in cases involving the criteria set forth in paragraph 2 (*a*) of Article XII or in paragraph 9 of Article XVIII, shall accept the determination of the Fund as to what constitutes a serious decline in the contracting party's monetary reserves, a very low level of its monetary reserves or a reasonable rate of increase in its monetary reserves, and as to the financial aspects of other matters covered in consultation in such cases.

3. The CONTRACTING PARTIES shall seek agreement with the Fund regarding procedures for consultation under paragraph 2 of this Article.

4. Contracting parties shall not, by exchange action, frustrate* the intent of the provisions of this Agreement, nor, by trade action, the intent of the provisions of the Articles of Agreement of the International Monetary Fund.

5. If the CONTRACTING PARTIES consider, at any time, that exchange restrictions on payments and transfers in connection with imports are being applied by a contracting party in a manner inconsistent with the exceptions provided for in this Agreement for quantitative restrictions, they shall report thereon to the Fund.

6. Any contracting party which is not a member of the Fund shall, within a time to be determined by the CONTRACTING PARTIES after consultation with the Fund, become a member of the Fund, or, failing that, enter into a special exchange agreement with the CONTRACTING PARTIES. A contracting party which ceases to be a member of the Fund shall forthwith enter into a special exchange agreement with the CONTRACTING PARTIES. Any special exchange agreement entered into by a contracting party under this paragraph shall thereupon become part of its obligations under this Agreement.

7. (*a*) A special exchange agreement between a contracting party and the CONTRACTING PARTIES under paragraph 6 of this Article shall provide to the satisfaction of the CONTRACTING PARTIES that the objectives of this Agreement will not be frustrated as a result of action in exchange matters by the contracting party in question.

(*b*) The terms of any such agreement shall not impose obligations on the contracting party in exchange matters generally more restrictive than those imposed by the Articles of Agreement of the International Monetary Fund on members of the Fund.

8. A contracting party which is not a member of the Fund shall furnish such information within the general scope of section 5 of Article VIII of the Articles of Agreement of the International Monetary Fund as the CONTRACTING PARTIES may require in order to carry out their functions under this Agreement.

9. Nothing in this Agreement shall preclude:

(*a*) the use by a contracting party of exchange controls or exchange restrictions in accordance with the Articles of Agreement of the International Monetary Fund or with that contracting party's special exchange agreement with the CONTRACTING PARTIES, or

(*b*) the use by a contracting party of restrictions or controls on imports or exports, the sole effect of which, additional to the effects permitted under Articles XI, XII, XIII and XIV, is to make effective such exchange controls or exchange restrictions.

Interpretative Note Ad Article XV from Annex I

Paragraph 4

The word "frustrate" is intended to indicate, for example, that infringements of the letter of any Article of this Agreement by exchange action shall not be regarded as a violation of that Article if, in practice, there is no appreciable departure from the intent of the Article. Thus, a contracting party which, as part of its exchange control operated in accordance with the Articles of Agreement of the International Monetary Fund, requires payment to be received for its exports in its own currency or in the currency of one or more members of the International Monetary Fund will not thereby be deemed to contravene Article XI or Article XIII. Another example would be that of a contracting party which specifies on an import licence the country from which the goods may be imported, for the purpose not of introducing any additional element of discrimination in its import licensing system but of enforcing permissible exchange controls.

II. INTERPRETATION AND APPLICATION OF ARTICLE XV

A. SCOPE AND APPLICATION OF ARTICLE XV

1. Paragraph 1

(1) "jurisdiction"

In the London draft of the Charter the word used was "competence", but was changed to "jurisdiction" at Geneva. The precise difference between the two words was not clearly defined. In the course of the discussion, it was stated that

"it seems ... that there is a real difference here between saying matters within the jurisdiction of the Fund, which relates ... strictly to the powers the Fund has, whereas matters within the competence of the Fund are matters on which the Fund, by reason of the subject matter which it deals with, is competent to provide the facts or to express an opinion. As one might say in a Government department ... which has certain legal powers in relation to a part of its field and no powers in another, certain things are within the jurisdiction of that government department, but a great many more are within its competence".[1]

In 1954-55, the Review Working Party on Quantitative Restrictions set up a Special Sub-Group on GATT/Fund Relations. The Report of this Sub-Group stated that in general,

"... the group felt that the more important problem was not that of defining the respective jurisdictions of the CONTRACTING PARTIES and the Fund but that of establishing more effective machinery for consultation in accordance with Article XV.

"In this connection, the group agreed that there were two problems. The first was that of ensuring that governments who were members of both bodies should themselves pursue a coordinated policy in relation to the Fund and the GATT, taking full account, in particular, of the implications of exchange

---

[1]EPCT/A/PV/29, p. 46; see also *ibid*. p. 40-41.

measures for countries' obligations under the Agreement. Appropriate action here rests with member governments.

"The second problem is one of developing liaison between the two organizations themselves ...".[2]

Concerning GATT-Fund relations, see also below under paragraph 3.

(2) Relationship between trade measures and financial system

The Tokyo Declaration of 1973 which launched the Tokyo Round of multilateral trade negotiations noted that:

"The policy of liberalizing world trade cannot be carried out successfully in the absence of parallel efforts to set up a monetary system which shields the world economy from the shocks and imbalances which have previously occurred. The Ministers will not lose sight of the fact that the efforts which are to be made in the trade field imply continuing efforts to maintain orderly conditions and to establish a durable and equitable monetary system.

"The Ministers recognize equally that the new phase in the liberalization of trade which it is their intention to undertake should facilitate the orderly functioning of the monetary system".[3]

At their Fortieth Session in 1984, the CONTRACTING PARTIES adopted a Decision on "Exchange Rate Fluctuations and their Effect on Trade" in which they "urge that their concern regarding the relationship between exchange market instability and international trade be taken into account in ongoing efforts within the International Monetary Fund to review the operation of the international monetary system with a view to possible improvements" and "agree that they will keep under consideration through further exchanges of views the relationship between exchange market instability and trade".[4]

Concerning the relationship between the international trading system and the international financial system, and floating exchange rates, see also the 1980 Report of the Working Party on "Specific Duties"[5] and the 1983 and 1984 Reports of the Consultative Group of Eighteen and associated Secretariat notes.[6]

2. Paragraph 2

(1) "findings of statistical ... facts presented by the Fund"

The Report of the Sub-Committee that redrafted the corresponding Article of the Charter during the Geneva session of the Preparatory Committee states:

"The provisions in paragraph 2 ... concerning the responsibility of the Fund in respect of statistical data relating to balances of payment or monetary reserves for the purpose of that Article is independent of any arrangement to be made between the Fund and the United Nations concerning the collection and appreciation of statistical data on balances of payments for other purposes".[7]

In 1978-80 the Working Party on "Specific Duties" examined the modalities for the application of Article II:6(a) in the monetary situation of increased flexibility of exchange rates. Although the Working Party consulted with the International Monetary Fund in this connection, "The representative of the Fund noted that ... the role of the Fund in the activities of the Working Party was to provide technical information to the

---

[2]L/332/Rev.1 and Addenda, adopted on 2, 4, and 5 March 1955, 3S/170, 198, para. 9-11.
[3]MIN(73)1, Declaration of Ministers approved at Tokyo on 14 September 1973, 20S/19, 22, para. 7.
[4]L/5761, adopted on 30 November 1984, 31S/15.
[5]L/4858, adopted on 29 January 1980, 27S/149.
[6]L/5572, 30S/96, 98-99, paras. 9-11; L/5721, 31S/52, 53-54, paras. 7-10; CG.18/W/74, "The Relation between the International Trading System and the International Financial System", dated 26 April 1983.
[7]EPCT/163, p. 22.

CONTRACTING PARTIES; the Fund had no mandate to participate in interpreting the General Agreement. The Fund representative emphasized in particular that it was for the CONTRACTING PARTIES to decide how the provisions of Article II:6 should be applied under the present circumstances".[8]

(2) *"The CONTRACTING PARTIES, in reaching their final decision"*

During discussions at the Havana Conference of paragraphs 2 and 3 of the corresponding Charter Article, Article 24, it was stated that "if the provisions of Article 24 were considered with Article 21 [XII], there was no basis for the fears that the ITO would be subservient to the Fund. The provisions of paragraphs 2(a)(ii) and 3(a) of Article 21 [XII] made it clear that the final decision as to whether restrictions would be instituted or maintained rested with the ITO, notwithstanding determinations made by the IMF".[9]

During Council discussion of the 1973 Report of the Committee on Balance-of-Payments Measures on the consultations with Spain, the representative of Spain stated his view that the Committee, in concluding that in the case of Spain the GATT balance-of-payments provisions were no longer applicable, had followed too strictly the determination of the IMF. The representative of Uruguay stated "that the report of the IMF should be considered as one element, but not the only element to be taken into account. While the IMF report could not be contradicted as to the state of the balance of payments, only the CONTRACTING PARTIES were competent to judge the relationship between the balance-of-payments situation and the necessity for greater liberalization of trade. It was up to GATT to decide whether measures taken were efficient and whether they should be maintained or not".[10] Some other contracting parties stated that in view of the IMF's determination and the provisions of Article XV:2 the Committee's conclusions could not have been different. The Report was adopted by the Council.[11]

(3) *"financial aspects of other matters ..."*

In discussions at the Geneva session of the Preparatory Committee concerning the meaning of "financial aspects of other matters covered in consultation in such cases", one representative gave the example that in the case of imminent threat to the balance of payments of a country

> "matters to be taken into consideration may be almost entirely trade questions, such as, for instance, the imminent threat to Australia's balance of payments through the failure of her wheat crop. I say nothing about what would happen if all the sheep died. Equally there might be, in the case of another country, some financial aspect of the imminent threat on which I should have thought the assistance of the International Monetary Fund would be extremely useful to the ITO."[12]

(4) *Application of paragraph 2: role of the International Monetary Fund*

(a) *Balance-of-payments consultations*

The description of procedures for full consultations on balance-of-payments measures under Article XII:4(b) or Article XVIII:12(b), which was agreed in 1970, provides that

> "Under paragraph 2 of Article XV, the CONTRACTING PARTIES are required to consult with the IMF on the points specified in that paragraph. As soon as the programme of consultations for the year is drawn up and taken note of by the Council, the Director-General should send a communication to invite the IMF to consult with the CONTRACTING PARTIES in connexion with each of the GATT consultations. In each case the GATT-IMF consultations will take place in the Committee on Balance-of-Payments Restrictions prior to the GATT consultation".[13]

---

[8] L/4858, adopted on 29 January 1980, 27S/149.
[9] E/CONF.2/C.3/SR.24, p. 3.
[10] C/M/89, p. 7.
[11] C/M/89, p. 7-8, C/M/90, p. 2-3.
[12] EPCT/A/PV/41, pp. 69-70.
[13] L/3388, 18S/48, 51, para. 8.

These GATT-IMF consultations take place through the delivery of a statement by the IMF representative to the Committee concerning the economic and financial situation of the consulting contracting party. For each full balance-of-payments consultation, the Fund submits a "Recent Economic Developments" report. The 1970 procedures state that:

> "The material supplied by the IMF as part of a consultation between the Fund and GATT should be circulated to the members of the Committee ... A copy may be supplied to any other contracting party which requests it".[14]

In "simplified consultations" under Article XVIII:12(b) and the procedures agreed in 1972, the Fund supplies balance-of-payments statistics but is not consulted unless the result of the consultations is a recommendation by the Committee that full consultations be held.[15]

In 1982-83 discussions took place concerning the treatment of balance-of-payments problems confronting heavily-indebted developing countries. A 1984 Statement by the Chairman of the Committee on Balance-of-Payments Restrictions to the Council, which summarized the result of these discussions, stated, *inter alia*, that:

> "The suggestion, that measures relating to trade policy agreed upon under standby or extended facility arrangements with the IMF could be notified to the GATT, had already been strongly questioned during the discussions in the Consultative Group of 18. During the present informal discussions, there was also clear opposition to the idea that a formal link might be established between commitments undertaken in such a delicate context and the response of other contracting parties in the form of measures designed to facilitate an expansion of the export earnings of the consulting country. It is, however, clear that under Paragraph 4 of the 1970 consultation procedures, consulting parties are required to keep the GATT secretariat regularly informed of any changes in trade measures, whether or not such measures are related to commitments vis-à-vis the Fund. Against this background, there was no evidence of support for the suggestion that there should be greater synchronization between consultations in the Committee and the consultations undertaken by the IMF".[16]

Further concerning the role of the Fund in balance-of-payments consultations, see the 1987 Note by the Secretariat on "Articles XII, XIV, XV and XVIII".[17]

See also the material under Article XVIII:10 from the three parallel Panel Reports on "Republic of Korea - Restrictions on Imports of Beef," complaints by Australia,[18] the United States,[19] and New Zealand.[20]

(b) Consultations on other problems involving financial issues

The First Report of the Working Party on "United Kingdom Import Deposits", which examined the Import Deposit Scheme introduced by the United Kingdom on 27 November 1968, notes that the Working Party decided, in agreement with the representative of the United Kingdom, to consult with the International Monetary Fund in accordance with the provisions of Article XV. At the consultation, the statement presented by the Fund representative concluded: "'In these circumstances, the import deposit scheme does not go beyond the extent necessary, in conjunction with other measures, to achieve a reasonable strengthening of the United Kingdom's reserve position." The Working Party examined matters including the use of the monies collected, the product coverage of the scheme and its trade effect. The Conclusions provided that "The Working Party examined the import deposit scheme ... in the light of the findings of the International Monetary Fund ... Taking into account this finding, the Working Party concluded that the United Kingdom import deposits were not more restrictive than measures that an application of the provisions of Article XII of the General Agreement permits".[21] When the

---

[14]*Ibid.*, 18S/51, para. 9.
[15]L/3772/Rev.1, 20S/47, 49, para. 3; see also section II.C under Article XII.
[16]C/125 dated 13 March 1984, approved by the Council on 15/16 May 1984 (C/M/178, p. 26), 31S/56, 59, para. 9.
[17]MTN.GNG/NG7/W/14, dated 11 August 1987, p. 17-18, paras. 55-56.
[18]L/6504, adopted on 7 November 1989, 36S/202.
[19]L/6503, adopted on 7 November 1989, 36S/268.
[20]L/6505, adopted on 7 November 1989, 36S/234.
[21]L/3193, adopted on 15 April 1969, 17S/144-149, 149, paras. 17-18.

scheme was extended, the Working Party again consulted with the Fund. Its Final Report notes that the United Kingdom terminated the import deposit scheme on 4 December 1970.[22]

The Report of the Working Party on the "United States Temporary Import Surcharge" introduced on 16 August 1971 notes that the Working Party consulted with the Fund. The United States representative referred to Article XV, cited a finding by the International Monetary Fund that "in the absence of other appropriate action and in the present circumstances, the import surcharge can be regarded as being within the bounds of what is necessary to stop a serious deterioration in the United States' balance-of-payments position", and cited a statement to the Working Party by the Fund representative that the Fund had no other alternative measures to suggest at that time.[23] Other members of the Working Party drew attention to the full findings of the Fund; the Working Party examined as well the modalities of the surcharge and its effects on trade. The Conclusions of the Report state, *inter alia*:

"The Working Party took note of the findings of the International Monetary Fund and recognized that the United States had found itself in a serious balance-of-payments situation which required urgent action. While noting the contrary views of the United States, the other members of the Working Party ... considered that the surcharge, as a trade restrictive measure, was inappropriate given the nature of the United States balance-of-payments situation and the undue burden of adjustment placed upon the import account with consequent serious effects on the trade of other contracting parties".[24]

3. Paragraph 3: Arrangements for consultation with the International Monetary Fund

The Havana Conference "Resolution Establishing an Interim Commission for the International Trade Organization" provided that the Interim Commission would have as one of its tasks "to prepare, in consultation with inter-governmental organizations other than the United Nations, for presentation to the first regular session of the Conference, documents and recommendations concerning the implementation of the provisions of paragraphs 1 and 3 of Article 87 of the Charter".[25] In 1948 the Executive Committee of the Interim Commission drew up an agreement between the ITO and the Fund[26], but as the Havana Charter did not enter into force, this agreement was never finalized.

In 1948 and 1949 the CONTRACTING PARTIES and the International Monetary Fund agreed on a general "Arrangement for co-ordination and consultation"[27], and an arrangement on "Co-ordination of public announcements relating to consultations".[28]

In 1954-55, the Review Working Party on Quantitative Restrictions set up a Special Sub-Group on GATT/Fund Relations. The Report of this Sub-Group noted that:

"... the CONTRACTING PARTIES had consulted with the Fund on all matters where consultation was required under Article XV of the General Agreement. It noted that the Articles of the Agreement of the Fund do not contain a comparable requirement for consultation, and also that Fund consultation with the CONTRACTING PARTIES on some exchange matters which might have important trade effects was often not appropriate or feasible for reasons of urgency or secrecy ...

"The group felt that in most cases it would be sufficient that co-ordination would take place between the CONTRACTING PARTIES and the Fund on a staff-to-staff basis. ... This would help not only to ensure

---

[22]L/3526, 18S/210, 212, para. 6.

[23]L/3573, adopted on 16 September 1971, 18S/212, 214, para. 8. The section of the Report dealing with the consultations with the Fund has not been derestricted and does not appear in the BISD.

[24]*Ibid.*, 18S/222, para. 39.

[25]Paragraph 1 of Article 87 of the Havana Charter mandated the ITO to make arrangements for effective co-operation and the avoidance of unnecessary duplication in the activities of inter-governmental organizations.

[26]See ICITO/EC.2/2/Add.2 (draft), ICITO/EC.2/14 Annex A (revision), discussion at ICITO/EC.2/SR.5 p. 5-8, approved with amendments at ICITO/EC.2/SR.14 p. 2.

[27]I/120, proposed by the Chairman of the CONTRACTING PARTIES by letter dated 9 September 1948 and agreed to by the Fund by letter dated 28 September 1948.

[28]I/120-123.

that, in appropriate cases, the Fund staff, in preparing its reports to the Executive Directors, would take full account of any information brought to their attention by the GATT staff regarding the trade aspects of exchange measures but also to ensure that matters of concern to the CONTRACTING PARTIES were brought to the attention of the Executive Directors before they took their decisions."[29]

The Sub-Group recommended that:

"(a) The CONTRACTING PARTIES should draw the attention of the Fund to their intention to have the GATT staff, in appropriate cases and where practicable, discuss with the Fund staff trade matters which had implications for exchange policy, and should inform the Fund that the GATT staff would be prepared, at the request of the Fund, to enter into similar discussions, where practicable, on the trade effects of exchange matters under Fund consideration.

"(b) Pursuant to this intention, the Executive Secretary should be authorized to work out with the Fund procedures for ensuring the maximum practicable degree of cooperation between the two staffs on matters of mutual concern to the CONTRACTING PARTIES and the Fund.

"(c) The Intersessional Committee should be authorized to conduct such consultations with the Fund as might seem appropriate in furtherance of the objectives of paragraph 1 of Article XV.

"(d) The CONTRACTING PARTIES should draw the attention of the International Monetary Fund to the new arrangements with respect to the Intersessional Committee, should explain that this would make consultation between the CONTRACTING PARTIES and the Fund easier and more expeditious than hitherto, and should express the hope that this should improve progressively the efficiency of consultation both ways between them.

"(e) The Executive Secretary should be requested to pursue consultations with representatives of the Fund with a view to preparing a formal agreement between the Fund and the proposed Organization [for Trade Cooperation] for consideration by both parties at a suitable future date".[30]

These recommendations were drawn to the attention of the Fund by the Executive Secretary in April 1955. At the Tenth Session in November 1955, it was agreed that recommendation (e) would be set aside pending the entry into force of the Agreement Establishing the Organization for Trade Cooperation.[31] However, informal discussions between GATT and Fund staff did result in arrangements for the transmission to the Secretariat of IMF documentation, especially in connection with balance-of-payments consultations, which were noted and approved at the Eleventh Session in October 1956.[32]

See also the discussion above at page 431 on the IMF role in consultations on balance-of-payments measures.[33]

The Mandate of the Consultative Group of Eighteen (CG-18), as adopted in 1975 and confirmed in 1979, provides that "The task of the Group is to facilitate the carrying out, by the CONTRACTING PARTIES, of their responsibilities, particularly with respect to ... the international adjustment process and the co-ordination, in this context, between the GATT and the IMF".[34] The first and second reports of the CG-18 to the Council note the discussions in the Group during 1975 through 1977 on measures to improve co-ordination with the Fund.[35]

---

[29]L/332/Rev.1 and Addenda, adopted on 2, 4 and 5 March 1955, 3S/170, 199, paras. 12-13.
[30]*Ibid.*, 3S/199-200, para. 14. In the Review Session, agreement was reached on institutional arrangements including an Agreement Establishing the Organization for Trade Cooperation, but this agreement never entered into force.
[31]SR.10/8.
[32]L/533, SR.11/3.
[33]L/3388, 18S/48, 51, paras. 8-9.
[34]L/4204, Decision of the Council of 11 July 1975, 22S/15.
[35]L/4429, 23S/38, 45, para. 25; L/4585, 24S/58, 59-60, paras. 7-8.

4. Paragraph 4

(1) *"by exchange action frustrate"*

In 1977, a panel was established in response to a complaint of the United States stating that in February 1976 Japanese foreign exchange banks had been instructed not to open any new letters of credit for imports of thrown silk yarn from the United States. The complaint claimed, *inter alia*, that the restrictions were inconsistent with Article XV "by using foreign exchange banks to thwart the principles of the General Agreement." The parties reached a bilateral solution to the dispute.[36]

(2) *Distinction between trade action and exchange action*

A Special Sub-Group set up in 1954 during the Review Session carried out a thorough examination of GATT provisions on balance-of-payments restrictions and GATT-IMF relations. It concluded that "in many instances it was difficult or impossible to define clearly whether a government measure is financial or trade in character and frequently it is both".[37] The Sub-Group however noted that the division of work between the CONTRACTING PARTIES and the Fund was in practice "based on the technical nature of government measures rather than on the effect of these measures on international trade and finance".

The 1981 Secretariat Background Paper on the consultation with Italy concerning the Italian deposit requirement for purchases of foreign currency discusses the question of whether the Italian scheme represents a charge on importation or a charge on the transfer of payments:

> "If the distinction between import and payments measures were made by taking into account the purpose or the effect of the action, the Italian scheme would probably be both a trade and an exchange measure: it is intended to improve Italy's payments position as well as to restrain imports, and it has had an impact both on payments for imports and the imports themselves. If however the distinction were made by looking at the restrictive technique used, the Italian deposit scheme would probably have to be regarded as an exchange measure since it is formulated and operated as a requirement to be fulfilled for the purchase of foreign exchange rather than for importation.

> "The Executive Directors of the International Monetary Fund have decided in 1960 that, for the purposes of Article VIII of the Fund Agreement, the criterion for distinguishing between trade and exchange measures should normally be the technique used. 'The guiding principle', they determined, 'in ascertaining whether a measure is a restriction on payments and transfers for current transactions under Article VIII Section 2, is whether it involved a direct governmental limitation on the availability or use of exchange as such' (Decision No. 1034 - (60/27) of 1 June 1960). In conformity with this principle the Fund has regarded the Italian measures as constituting a restriction on current international transactions requiring Fund approval under Article VIII Section 2, an approval which it has granted until 30 September 1981 (C/M/149, page 12)."[38]

> "In summary it can be said that the CONTRACTING PARTIES - unlike the IMF - have never formally decided how to distinguish between trade and exchange controls ... Their approach has been to examine particular restrictive measures affecting trade independent of the form that these measures took".[39]

The 1981 Report of the Committee on Balance-of-Payments Restrictions on the "Italian Deposit Requirement for Purchases of Foreign Currency" notes the view of the Italian Government "that the GATT rules on trade measures taken for balance-of-payments purposes did not apply to the deposit scheme because it was of a monetary nature and its main and primary effects were financial and monetary". The Committee concluded, *inter alia*, "that the deposit scheme, though monetary in form, had some effect on trade and that, in so far as these

---

[36]L/4530 (complaint) and Council discussion at C/M/122, p. 7-9; see also L/4637, Report of the Panel on "Japanese Restrictions on Imports of Thrown Silk Yarn", adopted on 17 May 1978, 25S/107.
[37]L/332/Rev.1 and Addenda, adopted on 2, 4 and 5 March 1955, 3S/170, 196, para. 2.
[38]BOP/W/51, p. 4, paras. 9-10.
[39]*Ibid.*, p. 5, para. 14.

trade effects were concerned, the scheme could be considered in the spirit of the Declaration on Trade Measures Taken for Balance-of-Payments Purposes".[40] The deposit scheme was terminated on 7 February 1982.[41]

(3) Trade measures equivalent to exchange rate changes

There are only two known examples of trade measures equivalent to changes in the exchange rate for commercial transactions. In late 1968 Germany instituted a special 4 per cent refund on imports together with a 4 per cent turnover tax levy on exports.[42] In 1982, Uruguay imposed a 10 per cent import surcharge and a 10 per cent export rebate.[43]

(4) Trade measures enforcing permissible exchange controls: Note Ad Article XV:4

When the Preparatory Committee examined this article in its Geneva session, one delegation proposed that paragraph 1(c) of Article 28 [XIV] of the New York Draft Charter be transferred to Article 29 [XV], suggesting the following wording: "Nothing in this section is intended to preclude a Member from requiring that its exporters accept only its own currency or the currencies of any one or more members of the International Monetary Fund, as it may specify in payment for exports". The proposal stated that the provision "is misplaced in Article 28, since it does not constitute an exception to the rule of non-discrimination on quotas. As rephrased here, it is clearly an exchange matter rather than a provision involving quantitative restrictions, and would therefore belong most appropriately in Article 29".[44]

The Sub-Committee produced a new text which was approved without any changes and inserted in the Geneva Draft Charter and in the General Agreement.[45] It was, however, considered essential to include "as an official explanation of the text" the Note *Ad* paragraph 4. The second sentence of the Note covers the case mentioned in the original draft quoted above. The last sentence was inserted to meet a request of the Czechoslovak delegation. In the final Geneva draft, and also in the General Agreement text, the interpretative Note refers only to paragraph 4. At Havana the note was attached to the last paragraph (9 in the General Agreement).

(5) Relationship between paragraph 9(a) and paragraph 4

See material under paragraph 9(a), at page 441 below.

5. Paragraph 5

The Report on the "Review on the Work of the Balance-of-Payments Committee: 1970-1974" noted, *inter alia*, that the "CONTRACTING PARTIES have no authority over exchange restrictions" and that "Conclusions concerning exchange measures have been rare when viewed against the fact that most consulting countries were, at the time of the consultations, using exchange measures to control their foreign trade. Only in one case (1970 Egypt) the Committee recommended a timely reform of the exchange system, and in another (1971 Ghana) it urged the consulting country to consider liberalizing controls on profit and dividend repatriation. The Committee never decided to report on exchange measures to the Fund".[46]

---

[40] BOP/R/119, adopted on 3 November 1981, C/M/152.
[41] L/5162/Add.3.
[42] L/3171, "Contribution toward Stabilization of the International Monetary System", dated 6 February 1969; see also German announcement at SR.25/9, p. 155.
[43] L/5355.
[44] EPCT/W/223, p. 35, referring to EPCT/W/216 pp. 5-6.
[45] EPCT/A/PV/41, pp. 72-76.
[46] L/4200, paras. 45-46 (referring to BOP/R/49 (Egypt) and BOP/R/53 (Ghana)).

6. Paragraph 6

(1) "within a time to be determined"

It was stated by the rapporteur of the Sub-committee on Quantitative Restrictions and Exchange Control, which drafted the corresponding Charter provisions at the London session of the Preparatory Committee that: "The Organization's functions relating to the special exchange agreement are to act in collaboration with the International Monetary Fund on all questions which may arise in the working of the agreement. And to seek and accept the opinion of the International Monetary Fund whether the action is permissible".[47] The London Report notes as follows:

> "It is generally considered appropriate that any member of the Organization, which is not also a member of the Fund, should not have full freedom in exchange matters, since by exchange arrangements it might frustrate its trade obligations. There is wide measure of agreement for the suggestion that such a member should enter into a special agreement with the Organization in exchange matters, which would provide that the purposes common to the Organization and the Fund would not be frustrated as a result of action in exchange matters by the member in question ...".[48]

A Resolution of the CONTRACTING PARTIES of 20 June 1949 established the time-limit for entering into a special exchange agreement as 1 November 1949, or four months after accession, or thirty days after a contracting party ceases to be a member of the Fund.[49]

(2) "special exchange agreement"

The Working Party Report adopted on 20 June 1949 on "Text of Special Exchange Agreement and Time-limit for Acceptance" has annexed to it the text of a standard special exchange agreement as contemplated by paragraph 6 of Article XV.[50] The standard agreement provides that it will terminate on the day on which the government concerned becomes a member of the Fund or ceases to be a contracting party. In 1994 a draft special exchange agreement was circulated in the working party on accession of Chinese Taipei.[51]

Special exchange agreements were accepted in the 1950-1952 period by: Sri Lanka (Ceylon), Haiti, Indonesia, and the Federal Republic of Germany. These countries later became members of the International Monetary Fund.[52] Consequently, no special exchange agreement under Article XV is currently in force.

(3) Exceptions and derogations from paragraph 6

At the Havana Conference, Article 24 of the Charter was revised to include a paragraph to meet "the case of a country which does not use its own currency".[53] This provision does not appear in the GATT, but the case is provided for in a Resolution of 20 June 1949 by the CONTRACTING PARTIES providing that "no contracting party shall be required to enter a special exchange arrangement so long as it uses solely the currency of another contracting party and so long as neither the contracting party in question nor the country whose currency is being used maintains exchange restrictions; provided, however, that any contracting party which defers entering into a special exchange arrangement ... shall thereby be deemed to have consented to consult with the CONTRACTING PARTIES at any time on their request on any exchange problem."[54]

---

[47] EPCT/C.II/QR/PV/5 p. 63. See also *ibid.* p. 41-49 concerning origin and purpose of special exchange agreements in UK draft proposal on balance-of-payments measures.

[48] London Report, p. 16, para. III.C.4(f).

[49] II/17.

[50] GATT/CP.3/44, II/117-123.

[51] Spec(94)39, Spec(94)31.

[52] Sri Lanka (Ceylon): agreement at GATT/CP/53, became Fund member 29 August 1950; Haiti: special exchange agreement at GATT/CP/96, Fund membership 8 September 1953; Indonesia: special exchange agreement at GATT/CP/96, became Fund member 15 April 1954 (withdrew effective 17 August 1965, readmitted as Fund member 21 February 1967); Federal Republic of Germany: special exchange agreement at G/12, became Fund member 14 August 1952.

[53] Havana Reports, p. 101, paras. 35-36 (revision in response to proposal by Liberia).

[54] II/18.

Since 1955, *waivers* of indefinite duration were granted under Article XXV:5 relieving the following contracting parties from the obligation to become a member of the International Monetary Fund or to accept a special exchange agreement: New Zealand,[55] Czechoslovakia,[56] Indonesia,[57] and Cuba.[58] The waivers for Czechoslovakia and New Zealand were later amended to dispense with a requirement for annual consultations, due to their special nature.[59] New Zealand subsequently became a member of the International Monetary Fund, and Czechoslovakia and Indonesia resumed their memberships in the Fund.[60]

The protocols of accession of Switzerland,[61] Poland,[62] Romania,[63] and Hungary[64] each contain a *reservation to Article XV:6*. In each of these cases, the reservation was accompanied by an undertaking that, inter alia, "so long as [country] is not a member of the International Monetary Fund, it will act in exchange matters in accordance with the intent of the General Agreement and in a manner fully consistent with the principles laid down in the text of the special exchange agreement as adopted by the CONTRACTING PARTIES in their Resolution of 20 June 1949. [Country] shall report to the CONTRACTING PARTIES promptly on any action taken by it which would have been required to be reported to the CONTRACTING PARTIES had [Country] signed the special exchange agreement. [Country] shall consult with the CONTRACTING PARTIES at any time, subject to thirty days' notice, upon request of any contracting party which considers that [country] has taken exchange action which may have a significant effect on the application of the provisions of the General Agreement or is inconsistent with the principles and objectives of the special exchange agreement. If, as a result of such consultation, the CONTRACTING PARTIES find that [country] has taken exchange action contrary to the intent of the General Agreement, they may determine that the present reservation shall cease to apply and [country] shall thereafter be bound by the provisions of paragraph 6 of Article XV of the General Agreement".[65]

Each of these four contracting parties has since become a member or resumed membership in the International Monetary Fund: Switzerland on 29 May 1992, Poland on 12 June 1986, Romania on 15 December 1972, and Hungary on 6 May 1982.

7. Paragraph 8

In 1950 and 1951 the CONTRACTING PARTIES and the International Monetary Fund agreed on arrangements for "Collection of information required by Article XV:8"[66] and "Rules of procedure for direct consultation between a contracting party and the Fund"[67] applying to contracting parties which are not members of the Fund.

8. Paragraph 9

See section III below concerning the drafting history of paragraph 9.

During the Review Session in 1954, a Special Sub-Group of the Review Working Party on Quantitative Restrictions discussed the question whether Article XV:9(a), which exempts from all GATT obligations "the use ... of exchange controls ... in accordance with the Articles of Agreement of the International Monetary Fund", also relieves contracting parties of their obligation not to frustrate the General Agreement's intent through

---

[55] 3S/42, 6S/32.
[56] 3S/43, 6S/28.
[57] 14S/33.
[58] 13S/23.
[59] Report of the Working Party on "Consultations under Article XII:4(b) etc.", L/769, adopted on 30 November 1957, 6S/36, 38, paras. 8-10.
[60] New Zealand: Fund membership effective 31 August 1961; Czechoslovakia: readmitted as a member of the Fund 20 September 1990, ceased to be a member 1 January 1993 (succeeded on that date by Czech Republic and Slovak Republic); Indonesia: see preceding note.
[61] Protocol for the Accession of Switzerland, 14S/6, 8, para. 5. See also L/598. Report on "Arrangements and Procedures for the Accession of Switzerland", adopted on 17 November 1956, 5S/40, 43, para. 11 concerning reasons for the Swiss reservation.
[62] Protocol for the Accession of Poland, 15S/46, 49, para. 8.
[63] Protocol for the Accession of Romania, 18S/5, 8, para. 9.
[64] Protocol for the Accession of Hungary, 20S/3, 6, para. 8.
[65] See also statement of Switzerland on this reservation at 5S/43, para. 11.
[66] I/123, proposed by the CONTRACTING PARTIES by letter dated 9 February 1951 and agreed to by the Fund by letter dated 26 March 1951.
[67] I/121, proposed by the Fund by letter dated 27 February 1950, and agreed by the CONTRACTING PARTIES by letter dated 22 May 1950.

such actions. The United Kingdom proposed an interpretative note to Article XV:9(a) of the General Agreement which would resolve this issue; however, "the Group agreed that it would be preferable not to try to lay down general principles on the relationship between paragraphs 4 and 9 but to leave this question over for empirical consideration if and when particular points arose which had a bearing on it. ... They further agreed that paragraph 9(a) was not to be interpreted so as to preclude the CONTRACTING PARTIES from discussing with a contracting party the effects on the trade of contracting parties of exchange controls or restrictions imposed or maintained by that contracting party, or from reporting on these matters to the IMF (as indeed was specifically envisaged by paragraph 5 of the Article)".[68]

During the Review Session in 1954-55, Italy brought a complaint concerning action by Turkey providing export bonuses for certain agricultural products and levying special import taxes on certain goods deemed less-essential in order to provide the necessary funds for the bonuses. Italy stated that the export subsidies had not been notified as required by Article XVI:1 and that the import taxes were inconsistent with Article II:1(b). Turkey stated that as part of a reform of its foreign exchange system, it had established an Equalization Fund which was financed by the sale of import permits, and that this system had been approved by the International Monetary Fund. A representative of the Fund confirmed that the practices under question were multiple currency practices under the Fund Articles of Agreement and that in a Decision concerning Turkey the Fund had stated that it did not object to the temporary continuance of these practices and would remain in consultation with Turkey on these practices. The complaint was referred to the Panel on Complaints but was withdrawn later in the session.[69] See also the other material on multiple exchange rate practices under Article XVI in this Index.

In 1976-77, the Working Party on Italian Measures examined a deposit requirement for payments abroad, and a tax on the purchase of foreign exchange, which had been imposed by the Italian government; in accordance with Article XV, the Working Party carried out a consultation with the Fund. The Report on "Monetary Measures" prepared by this Working Party notes that the representative of the EC stressed the monetary and exchange character of the Italian measures, which were applied to all purchases of foreign exchange, whether for imports, services or other purposes. "Members of the Working Party ... noted that Italy was not invoking Article XII. They stressed the importance attached to the careful examination in the appropriate GATT body of all restrictive measures having a direct or indirect effect on trade, be these measures monetary in form or not".[70]

This view prevailed also in the Council discussion leading to the decision to hold consultations in the Balance-of-Payments Committee on the Italian deposit requirement for purchases of foreign currency which was introduced in May 1981.[71]

B. RELATIONSHIP BETWEEN ARTICLE XV AND OTHER PROVISIONS OF THE GENERAL AGREEMENT

1. Article III

The record of discussions at the Havana Conference on Article 18 of the Charter (corresponding to Article III of the General Agreement) notes the following understanding:

"The Sub-Committee [A] considered that charges imposed in connection with the international transfer of payments for imports or exports, particularly the charges imposed by countries employing multiple currency practices, where such charges are imposed not inconsistently with the Articles of Agreement of the International Monetary Fund, would not be covered by Article 18 [III]. On the other hand, in the unlikely case of a multiple currency practice which takes the form of an internal tax or charge, such as an excise tax on an imported product not applied on the like domestic product, that practice would be precluded

---

[68]Report of the Special Sub-Group, 3S/195, 198, para. 8; text of UK proposed note appears as Annex 2 to this Report at 3S/205.
[69]L/214 (complaint); SR.9/7 (discussion of complaint, statements by Italy, Turkey and the Fund, referral to Panel on Complaints); W.9/8 (written statement by Turkey); SR.9/40 (withdrawal of complaint).
[70]L/4442, adopted on 2 March 1977, 24S/129, 131, para. 6.
[71]C/M/149.

by Article 18. It may be pointed out that the possible existence of charges on the transfer of payments insofar as these are permitted by the International Monetary Fund is clearly recognized by Article 16 [I]."[72]

In 1952, the standing Panel on Complaints examined a special "contribution" levied by the Greek Government on certain imported goods, which the Greek delegation stated was "a charge imposed on foreign exchange allocated for the importation of goods from abroad equivalent to a multiple currency practice" considered by the Greek Government as indispensable to cover the widening gap between the official exchange rate and the effective purchasing power of the drachma. The Report of the Panel on "Special Import Taxes Instituted by Greece" referred to the passage directly above, observing as follows:

"... the principal question arising for determination was whether or not the Greek tax was an internal tax or charge on imported products within the meaning of paragraph 2 of Article III. If the finding on this point were affirmative, the Panel considered that it would be subject to the provisions of Article III whatever might have been the underlying intent of the Greek Government in imposing the tax ...

"On the other hand, if the contention of the Greek Government were accepted that the tax was not in nature of a tax or charge on imported goods, but was a tax on foreign exchange allocated for the payment of imports, the question would arise whether this was a multiple currency practice, and, if so, whether it was in conformity with the Articles of Agreement of the International Monetary Fund. These matters would be for the determination of the International Monetary Fund. If the Fund should find that the tax system was a multiple currency practice and in conformity with the Articles of Agreement of the International Monetary Fund, it would fall outside the scope of Article III.

"Even if it were found that the tax did not fall within the ambit of Article III the further question might arise under Article XV:4 whether the action of the Greek Government constituted frustration by exchange action of the intent of the provisions of Article III of the General Agreement."[73]

The Panel suggested that the CONTRACTING PARTIES seek further information and inquire of the Fund whether the Greek "contribution" was a multiple currency practice, and whether it was in conformity with the Fund Articles of Agreement. This would make it possible to consider whether any question arose under Article XV:4.[74] The Greek measure in question was terminated following devaluation of the drachma in April 1953.[75]

2. Article XXIII

The Report of the Special Sub-Group on GATT/Fund Relations in the 1954-55 Review Session notes that the Sub-Group rejected as unnecessary a proposal to add a note to Article XV:9(a) confirming the right to invoke Article XXIII with respect to exchange controls or exchange restrictions which were in accordance with the IMF Articles of Agreement.[76]

3. Other GATT provisions

In addition to the broad obligations of Article XV:4 and 9, commitments relating to exchange controls and currency practices also appear in other GATT Articles including I:1; II:3 and 6; VI:2 and 3; VII:4(a) and (c); VIII:1 and 4, as well as Articles XI to XIV and XVIII:B.

---

[72]Havana Reports, p. 62, para. 39, repeating an understanding arrived at during the Geneva session of the Preparatory Committee (see EPCT/174, p. 7). See also Havana discussion of this understanding at E/CONF.2/C.3/A/W.33, p. 3. The text of Article 18 as revised at Havana was taken into the GATT; see the discussion of negotiating history in section III under Article III. Article 16 corresponded to Article I of the General Agreement.
[73]G/25, adopted on 3 November 1952, 1S/48, 49-50, paras. 5, 7, 8.
[74]Ibid., 1S/50-51, paras. 9-12. Concerning multiple currency practices, see also the Decision of the International Monetary Fund annexed to the Report of the Special Sub-Group on GATT/Fund Relations at 3S/200-205.
[75]SR.8/7 p. 9.
[76]L/332/Rev.1 and Addenda, adopted on 2, 4 and 5 March 1955, 3S/170, 198, para. 8, referring to note proposed by UK reprinted at 3S/205.

C. EXCEPTIONS AND DEROGATIONS

See material on exceptions and derogations to the obligation to enter into special exchange agreements, at page 437 above.

III. PREPARATORY WORK AND SUBSEQUENT MODIFICATIONS

Corresponding provisions in the Havana Charter are contained in Article 24; in the US-UK *Proposals* in Chapter III F-5; in the US Draft in Article 23-24; in the London and New York Drafts in Article 29; and in the Geneva Draft in Article 24. The title of Charter Article 24 is "Relationship with the International Monetary Fund and Exchange Arrangements".

The US Draft Charter articles provided for ITO-IMF co-operation, and would have prohibited some exchange restrictions and all restrictions on payments and transfers for current international transactions consisting of payments due in connection with imports of any product. At London this provision was redrafted in the Sub-Committee on Quantitative Restrictions and Exchange Control, which drafted paragraphs 1, 4, 6, 7(a) and 8. At the Geneva session of the Preparatory Committee, further discussion led to insertion of the paragraphs dealing with the relationship between the ITO and the Fund and the relationship between obligations under the Charter and the Fund Articles of Agreement, paragraphs 2, 3, 5, 7(b) and 9. The Geneva Draft Charter Article and the 30 October 1947 text of the General Agreement were substantially identical except that in the Geneva Draft Charter the procedures provided for in paragraph 3 were made subject to approval by the Conference of the ITO. Paragraph 9 began: "Subject to the provisions of paragraph 4 of this Article".

During the Havana Conference, the third sentence of paragraph 2 of Article 24 was amended in the light of amendments proposed by Australia and New Zealand. The Charter text reads as follows: "When the Organization is examining a situation in the light of relevant considerations under all pertinent provisions of Article 21 [XII] for the purpose of reaching its final decision in cases ...".[77] In support of this change it was stated that "It was administratively unsound to separate responsibility for a decision from the responsibility for action arising from it. Good working relations between the IMF and the ITO would be impaired if the ITO had to adopt a decision against its judgement. The proper procedure was for any decision to be preceded by close personal consultation between the officers of the two Organizations, a consultation which would recognize the special fields of competence of each. Moreover, the respect by Members for the provisions of the Charter would be weakened if the ITO were to impose on Members a determination of the IMF with which it disagreed".[78] In addition, at Havana a sub-paragraph was added to cover the case of a country which does not use its own currency (see page 437 above). The words "whether or not it has entered into a special exchange agreement" were inserted in the paragraph relating to the provision of information by non-members of the IMF (corresponding to GATT Article XV:8). Finally, it was also agreed to delete the phrase "Subject to paragraph 4 of this Article" from the beginning of the paragraph corresponding to GATT Article XV:9, and to take the interpretative note from paragraph 4 and attach it to that paragraph.

At the Second Session, it was decided to amend paragraph 9 of Article XV to delete the phrase "Subject to paragraph 4 of this Article", to conform to the text of Article 24:8 of the Havana Charter.[79] This amendment was effected by the Protocol Amending Part II and Article XXVI, and entered into force on 14 December 1948. During the Review Session Article XV was debated together with the other balance-of-payments Articles, but was not itself revised, except for the addition in paragraph 2 of a reference to paragraph 9(a) of the revised Article XVIII.

---

[77] Havana Reports, p.101, para.34; E/CONF.2/11/Add.11, pp.2-3.
[78] E/CONF.2/C.3/SR.24, p.1.
[79] Report of the Working Party on "Modifications to the General Agreement", GATT/CP.2/22/Rev.1, adopted on 1 and 2 September 1948, II/39, 44, para. 28; see also Havana Reports, p. 98, para. 19.

IV. RELEVANT DOCUMENTS

London

Discussion:	EPCT/C.II/QR/PV/5 (p. 41)
	EPCT/C.II/PV/13 (p. 16)
Reports:	EPCT/C.II/43, 59; EPCT/30

New York

Discussion:	EPCT/C.6/21 (p. 6-7), 23
Reports:	EPCT/C.6/97/Rev.1 (p. 86)

Geneva

Discussion:	EPCT/EC/PV.2/22
	EPCT/A/PV/27 (p. 20), 29 (p. 40ff), 41 (p. 64ff)
	EPCT/TAC/SR/11
	EPCT/TAC/PV/27
Reports:	EPCT/135, 163, 171, 189, 196, 212, 214/Add.1/Rev.1
	EPCT/W/313
Other:	EPCT/W/64, 216, 223, 241, 272, 279, 301, 318, 341

Havana

Discussion:	E/CONF.2/C.3/SR.23 (p. 5), 24, 25, 47
Reports:	E/CONF.2/C.3/91;
	E/CONF.2/11/Add.11
Other:	E/CONF.2/C.3/F/W/17, 22, 25

CONTRACTING PARTIES

Reports:	GATT/CP.2/22/Rev.1, II/39
	GATT/CP/53, CP/96; G/12, G/39

Review Session

Discussion:	SR.9/14, 15
Reports:	W.9/106, 130, 174+Add.1, 208, 234, 3S/197
Other:	L/189/Add.1, L/246, L/270
	W.9/18+Add.1, 22, 23, 60, 63, 73, 130, 142, 167
	Spec/46/55, 53/55, 87/55
	MGT/9/55

ARTICLE XVI

SUBSIDIES

I.	TEXT OF ARTICLE XVI AND INTERPRETATIVE NOTE AD ARTICLE XVI			444
II.	INTERPRETATION AND APPLICATION OF ARTICLE XVI			445
	A.	SCOPE AND APPLICATION OF ARTICLE XVI		445
		1. Paragraph 1		445
			(1) "subsidy"	445
			(2) "including any form of income or price support"	445
			(a) Domestic prices fixed above the world price level	446
			(b) Subsidies financed by a non-governmental levy	446
			(c) Export credit programmes as subsidies	446
			(d) Internal transport charges	447
			(e) Tax exemptions	447
			(f) Multiple exchange rates	447
			(g) Border tax adjustments and duty drawback	448
			(3) "directly or indirectly"	448
			(4) "to increase exports ... or to reduce imports"	448
			(5) "it shall notify the CONTRACTING PARTIES in writing about the extent and nature of the subsidization"	449
			(6) "estimated effect"	449
			(7) "serious prejudice to the interests of any other contracting party is caused or threatened"	450
			(8) "shall, upon request, discuss with the other contracting party or parties concerned"	450
			(9) "the possibility of limiting the subsidization"	451
		2. Paragraph 2: "undue disturbance"		451
		3. Paragraph 3		452
			(1) "primary product"	452
			(2) "any form of subsidy which operates to increase the export of any primary product"	452
			(3) "more than an equitable share of world export trade"	453
			(4) "previous representative period"	456
			(5) "special factors"	456
		4. Paragraph 4		457
			(1) "shall cease to grant ... any form of subsidy on the export"	457
			(a) Illustrative lists of export subsidies	457
			(b) Tax deferral	458
			(c) Taxation of transactions outside the territorial limits of the exporting country	459
			(d) Export inflation insurance schemes	460
			(2) "of any product other than a primary product"	461
			(3) "at a price lower than the comparable price charged for the like product to buyers in the domestic market"	461
			(4) Developing countries	462
		5. Paragraph 5		463
	B.	RELATIONSHIP BETWEEN ARTICLE XVI AND OTHER GATT PROVISIONS		463
		1. Article II		463
		2. Article VI		463
		3. Article XXIII		463
		4. Part IV		463
		5. Protocol of Provisional Application		463
	C.	EXCEPTIONS AND DEROGATIONS		464
	D.	AGREEMENT ON INTERPRETATION AND APPLICATION OF ARTICLES VI, XVI AND XXIII		464
III.	PREPARATORY WORK AND SUBSEQUENT MODIFICATIONS			465
IV.	RELEVANT DOCUMENTS			468

I. TEXT OF ARTICLE XVI AND INTERPRETATIVE NOTE AD ARTICLE XVI

Article XVI*

Subsidies

Section A — Subsidies in General

1. If any contracting party grants or maintains any subsidy, including any form of income or price support, which operates directly or indirectly to increase exports of any product from, or to reduce imports of any product into, its territory, it shall notify the CONTRACTING PARTIES in writing of the extent and nature of the subsidization, of the estimated effect of the subsidization on the quantity of the affected product or products imported into or exported from its territory and of the circumstances making the subsidization necessary. In any case in which it is determined that serious prejudice to the interests of any other contracting party is caused or threatened by any such subsidization, the contracting party granting the subsidy shall, upon request, discuss with the other contracting party or parties concerned, or with the CONTRACTING PARTIES, the possibility of limiting the subsidization.

Section B — Additional Provisions on Export Subsidies*

2. The contracting parties recognize that the granting by a contracting party of a subsidy on the export of any product may have harmful effects for other contracting parties, both importing and exporting, may cause undue disturbance to their normal commercial interests, and may hinder the achievement of the objectives of this Agreement.

3. Accordingly, contracting parties should seek to avoid the use of subsidies on the export of primary products. If, however, a contracting party grants directly or indirectly any form of subsidy which operates to increase the export of any primary product from its territory, such subsidy shall not be applied in a manner which results in that contracting party having more than an equitable share of world export trade in that product, account being taken of the shares of the contracting parties in such trade in the product during a previous representative period, and any special factors which may have affected or may be affecting such trade in the product.*

4. Further, as from 1 January 1958 or the earliest practicable date thereafter, contracting parties shall cease to grant either directly or indirectly any form of subsidy on the export of any product other than a primary product which subsidy results in the sale of such product for export at a price lower than the comparable price charged for the like product to buyers in the domestic market. Until 31 December 1957 no contracting party shall extend the scope of any such subsidization beyond that existing on 1 January 1955 by the introduction of new, or the extension of existing, subsidies.*

5. The CONTRACTING PARTIES shall review the operation of the provisions of this Article from time to time with a view to examining its effectiveness, in the light of actual experience, in promoting the objectives of this Agreement and avoiding subsidization seriously prejudicial to the trade or interests of contracting parties.

Interpretative Note *Ad* Article XVI from Annex I

The exemption of an exported product from duties or taxes borne by the like product when destined for domestic consumption, or the remission of such duties or taxes in amounts not in excess of those which have accrued, shall not be deemed to be a subsidy.

Section B

1. Nothing in Section B shall preclude the use by a contracting party of multiple rates of exchange in accordance with the Articles of Agreement of the International Monetary Fund.

2. For the purposes of Section B, a "primary product" is understood to be any product of farm, forest or fishery, or any mineral, in its natural form or which has undergone such processing as is customarily required to prepare it for marketing in substantial volume in international trade.

Paragraph 3

1. The fact that a contracting party has not exported the product in question during the previous representative period would not in itself preclude that contracting party from establishing its right to obtain a share of the trade in the product concerned.

2. A system for the stabilization of the domestic price or of the return to domestic producers of a primary product independently of the movements of export prices, which results at times in the sale of the product for export at a price lower than the comparable price charged for the like product to buyers in the domestic market, shall be considered not to involve a subsidy on exports within the meaning of paragraph 3 if the CONTRACTING PARTIES determine that:

(*a*) the system has also resulted, or is so designed as to result, in the sale of the product for export at a price higher than the comparable price charged for the like product to buyers in the domestic market; and

(*b*) the system is so operated, or is designed so to operate, either because of the effective regulation of production or otherwise, as not to stimulate exports unduly or otherwise seriously to prejudice the interests of other contracting parties.

Notwithstanding such determination by the CONTRACTING PARTIES, operations under such a system shall be subject to the provisions of paragraph 3 where they are wholly or partly financed out of government funds in addition to the funds collected from producers in respect of the product concerned.

II. INTERPRETATION AND APPLICATION OF ARTICLE XVI

A. SCOPE AND APPLICATION OF ARTICLE XVI

Paragraph 1 of Article XVI was drawn from Article 25 of the draft Charter, and has remained unchanged since the original text agreed in 1947. Section B of Article XVI was drafted in the Review Session, drawing on Articles 26 through 28 of the Havana Charter. The principal sources concerning the drafting of Section B are the Report of the Review Working Party on "Other Barriers to Trade" and the documents of the Review Session.

1. Paragraph 1

(1) "subsidy"

In 1959-61, a "Panel on Subsidies" was established and undertook preparatory work for a review to be conducted on the operation of the provisions of Article XVI. The 1961 Report of this group on "Operation of the Provisions of Article XVI" notes that it "considered that it was neither necessary nor feasible to seek an agreed interpretation of what constituted a subsidy. It would probably be impossible to arrive at a definition which would at the same time include all measures that fall within the intended meaning of the term in Article XVI without including others not so intended ... In any event the Panel felt that the lack of a precise definition had not, in practice, interfered with the operation of Article XVI".[1]

General criteria for the determination of the existence of a subsidy have been discussed in the Committee on Subsidies and Countervailing Measures and were discussed in the Committee on Trade in Agriculture.[2]

(2) "including any form of income or price support"

See Interpretative Note 2 *ad* paragraph 3 of Article XVI; this note corresponds to paragraph 1 of Article 27 of the Havana Charter.

---

[1] L/1442 and Add.1-2, adopted on 21 November 1961, 10S/201, 209, para. 23; see also MTN.GNG/NG10/W/4 at p. 49.
[2] See, e.g., SCM/35 and 36, and AG/W/5, para. 48.

(a) Domestic prices fixed above the world price level

The 1960 Report of the Panel on Subsidies on "Review Pursuant to Article XVI:5" examined the circumstances under which price support systems which fix domestic producer prices at a level higher than the world price level might be considered a subsidy in the meaning of Article XVI.

"It was generally agreed that a system under which a government, by direct or indirect methods, maintains such a price by purchases and resale at a loss is a subsidy. Such purchases would need only to cover part of the production to involve a subsidy and, in determining loss on resale, such expenses as holding stocks should be taken into account. The Panel considered, however, that there could be other cases in which a government maintained a fixed price above the world price without resort to a subsidy. One such case might be that in which a government fixes by law a minimum price to producers which is maintained by quantitative restrictions or a flexible tariff or similar charges. In such a case there would be no loss to the government, and the measure would not be governed by Article XVI."[3]

(b) Subsidies financed by a non-governmental levy

See Interpretative Note 2 *ad* paragraph 3 of Article XVI; the last sentence of this note provides that operations under price stabilization schemes "shall be subject to paragraph 3 where they are wholly or partly financed out of government funds in addition to funds collected from producers in respect of the product concerned". On the drafting history of this note, see Section III below.

The 1960 Report on the "Review Pursuant to Article XVI:5" also examined whether subsidies financed by a non-governmental levy were notifiable under Article XVI. The Panel noted that

"The GATT does not concern itself with such action by private persons acting independently of their governments except insofar as it allows importing countries to take action under other provisions of the Agreement. In general there was no obligation to notify schemes in which a group of producers voluntarily taxed themselves in order to subsidize exports of a product ... On the other hand, there was no doubt that there was an obligation to notify all schemes of levy/subsidy affecting imports or exports in which the government took a part either by making payments into the common fund or by entrusting to a private body the functions of taxation and subsidization with the result that the practice would in no real sense differ from those normally followed by governments. In view of these considerations the Panel feels that the question of notifying levy-subsidy arrangements depends upon the source of the funds and the extent of government action, if any, in their collection. Therefore, rather than attempt to formulate a precisely worded recommendation designed to cover all contingencies, the Panel feels that the CONTRACTING PARTIES should ask governments to notify all levy/subsidy schemes affecting imports or exports which are dependent for their enforcement on some form of government action".[4]

The 1958 Panel Report on "French Assistance to Exports of Wheat and Wheat Flour" concluded that the operation of the French system of price supports, which involved a tax on exporters to partially defray losses in the world market, resulted in the grant of export subsidies because, *inter alia,* governmental budgetary appropriations were necessary to cover at least part of the losses.[5] See further below at page 453.

(c) Export credit programmes as subsidies

The question whether export credit programmes, when in conformity with an international arrangement on official export credits, are to be considered subsidies, was discussed in the Committee on Subsidies and Countervailing Measures during 1982-83. The view that granting of export credits at rates below those which actually prevailed on international capital markets constituted a subsidy to be notified under Article XVI:1 of the General Agreement, was disputed by some contracting parties.[6]

---

[3] L/1160, adopted on 24 May 1960, 9S/188, 191, para. 11.
[4] *Ibid.,* 9S/192, para. 12.
[5] L/924, adopted on 21 November 1958, 7S/46, 50-52, paras. 8-14.
[6] SCM/M/11-13, 16.

(d) Internal transport charges

It was agreed during the meetings of the Preparatory Committee at Geneva in 1947 that the granting of reduced internal transport charges on goods for export "would be subject to the provisions of Article [XVI] if it operates directly or indirectly to increase the exports of any product".[7]

(e) Tax exemptions

It was agreed at Havana that the terms of Article 25 [XVI] were sufficiently wide to cover a system where methods of direct subsidization to domestic industries were not used but whereby "certain domestic industries were exempted from internal taxes payable on imported goods".[8] See also the reference to the Panel on "United States Tax Legislation (DISC)" below at page 449.

(f) Multiple exchange rates

See Interpretative Note 1 *ad* Section B of Article XVI, which was added at the Review Session in 1954-55. The Report of the Review Working Party on "Other Barriers to Trade" notes, concerning the provisions added to Article XVI in the Review Session:

> "A number of members of the Working Party were concerned as to the possible effect of the proposed additional provisions on the right of countries to use multiple exchange rates in accordance with the Articles of Agreement of the International Monetary Fund. The Working Party has therefore recommended an interpretative note to cover this case. It wishes also to record the fact that the draft provisions have been considered by the Working Party on the assumption that paragraph 9(a) of Article XV in the present Agreement will not be altered".[9]

During the Review Session, Italy brought a complaint concerning action by Turkey providing export bonuses for certain agricultural products and levying special import taxes on certain goods deemed less-essential in order to provide the necessary funds for the bonuses. Italy stated that the export subsidies had not been notified as required by Article XVI:1 and that the import taxes were inconsistent with Article II:1(b). Turkey stated that as part of a reform of its foreign exchange system, it had established an Equalization Fund which was financed by the sale of import permits, and that this system had been approved by the International Monetary Fund. A representative of the Fund confirmed that the practices under question were multiple currency practices under the Fund Agreement and that in a Decision concerning Turkey the Fund had stated that it did not object to the temporary continuance of these practices and would remain in consultation with Turkey on these practices. The complaint was referred to the standing Panel on Complaints but was withdrawn later in the session.[10]

The 1960 Report on the "Review Pursuant to Article XVI:5" provides that: "The Panel noted that some contracting parties had interpreted approval by the International Monetary Fund of multiple exchange arrangements as absolving them from the obligation to notify such arrangements under Article XVI. The Panel wished to record its view that interpretative note 1 to Section B of Article XVI was intended not to preclude the use by a country of multiple exchange rates which were approved by the International Monetary Fund, but that there was a clear obligation to notify to the CONTRACTING PARTIES multiple exchange rates which have the effect of a subsidy".[11]

See also Article XV:9 and the material on it in this Index. See also Note 2 to paragraphs 2 and 3 of Article VI, which provides that "Multiple currency practices can in certain circumstances constitute a subsidy to exports which may be met by countervailing duties under [Article VI:3] or can constitute a form of dumping by

---

[7] EPCT/127, p. 1; EPCT/B/SR.22. p. 5-6.
[8] Havana Reports, p. 107, paras. 11-12.
[9] L/334 and Addendum, adopted on 3 March 1955, 3S/222, 226, para. 21.
[10] L/214 (complaint); SR.9/7 (discussion of complaint, statements by Italy, Turkey and the Fund, referral to Panel on Complaints); W.9/8 (written statement by Turkey); SR.9/40 (withdrawal of complaint).
[11] L/1160, adopted on 24 May 1960, 9S/188, 192, para. 13.

means of a partial depreciation of a country's currency which may be met by action under [Article VI:2]. By 'multiple currency practices' is meant practices by governments or sanctioned by governments".[12]

(g) Border tax adjustments and duty drawback

See the general Interpretative Note *ad* Article XVI. This note, added in the 1954-55 Review Session, was drawn from paragraph 2 of Article 26 of the Havana Charter, the text of which appears below at page 465. The records of the Havana Conference note the understanding that paragraph 2 "covers the case of remission of duties or taxes imposed on raw materials and semi-manufactured products subsequently used in the production of exported manufactured goods".[13]

The relevance of Article XVI to border tax adjustments was examined by the Working Party on "Border Tax Adjustments" in 1968-71; the 1971 Report of the Working Party notes that "It was agreed that GATT provisions on tax adjustment applied the principle of destination identically to imports and exports".[14]

The 1977 Report of the Working Party on "Suspension of Customs Liquidation by the United States" examined the compatibility with Article VI:4 of the Japanese practice of exempting exported products from domestic consumption taxes and noted that "All but one member of the Working Party ... agreed that the Japanese tax practices in question were in full accord with the provisions of GATT, its established interpretation as well as established practice of the GATT. They also agreed that ... if countervailing duties were imposed, the imposition of such duties would be in contravention of the provisions of the GATT including Article VI:4 and the note to Article XVI ...".[15]

(3) "directly or indirectly"

The New York Report notes, with regard to the draft Charter provision corresponding to Article XVI:1, "It will be observed that the provision in this sentence as now drafted applies to cases in which the subsidy operates, 'directly or indirectly', to increase exports or reduce imports of any product and can thus not be interpreted as being confined to subsidies operating directly to affect trade in the product under consideration".[16]

(4) "to increase exports ... or to reduce imports"

The Report of the Working Party in 1948 on "Modifications to the General Agreement" notes that the Working Party agreed not to amend Article XVI:1 to incorporate the changes made to the corresponding Charter Article at the Havana Conference, *inter alia* in view of the understanding that

"The phrase 'increased exports' in [Article XVI:1] of the General Agreement was intended to include the concept of maintaining exports at a level higher than would otherwise exist in the absence of a subsidy, as made clear in line 3 of Article 25 of the Havana Charter".[17]

The 1960 Report on the "Review Pursuant to Article XVI:5" provides:

"In the opinion of the Panel, it is not sufficient to consider increased exports or reduced imports only in a historical sense. In this connexion the Panel had in mind [the interpretation which appears directly above]. *Mutatis mutandis* this interpretation must apply to the effect on imports. The criterion is therefore what would happen in the *absence* of a subsidy. While the Panel agreed that in most cases such a judgment cannot be reached only by reference to statistics, nevertheless, a statistical analysis helps to discern the trends of imports and exports and may assist in determining the effects of a subsidy. The Panel considers

---

[12] See also discussion of the drafting of this note at EPCT/A/PV/20, p. 34-36, EPCT/A/PV/24, p. 2-3.
[13] E/CONF.2/C.3/51, p. 4.
[14] L/3464, adopted on 2 December 1970, 18S/97, 100, para. 10.
[15] L/4508, adopted on 16 June 1977, 24S/134, 138, para. 15.
[16] New York Report, p. 26.
[17] GATT/CP.2/22/Rev.1, adopted on 1 and 2 September 1948, II/39, 44.

it fair to assume that a subsidy which provides an incentive to increased production will, in the absence of offsetting measures, e.g., a consumption subsidy, either increase exports or reduce imports".[18]

This finding was referred to in the 1990 Panel Report on "EEC - Payments and Subsidies paid to Processors and Producers of Oilseeds and Related Animal-Feed Proteins".[19]

The Panel Report on "United States Tax Legislation (DISC)" notes: "The Panel considered that, as it had found the DISC legislation to constitute an export subsidy which had led to an increase in exports, it was also covered by the notification obligation in Article XVI:1".[20]

(5) "it shall notify the CONTRACTING PARTIES in writing about the extent and nature of the subsidization"

In 1950 the CONTRACTING PARTIES made arrangements for the reporting of existing subsidies and for the notification of modifications therein and of new measures of subsidization.[21] These arrangements were confirmed in the Report of the Review Working Party on "Other Barriers to Trade".[22] The questionnaire now used for the reporting of subsidies was established in 1960.[23] Procedures for Notifications and Reviews under Article XVI:1, which were adopted in 1962, provide for a new and full notification every third year and, in the intervening years, for a notification of the changes that have occurred.[24]

The 1961 Report on "Operation of the Provisions of Article XVI", examining the kinds of notifiable subsidies, the scope of the notification requirement and the adequacy of notifications received, noted:

"The rôle of Article XVI in providing the CONTRACTING PARTIES with accurate information about the nature and extent of subsidies in individual countries has been partly frustrated by the failure of some contracting parties to notify the subsidies they maintain. To the extent that this is based on the reluctance of contracting parties to expose themselves to charges of non-conformity with the Agreement, it reflects a misinterpretation of Article XVI. Moreover, a contracting party can be required to consult concerning a subsidy, whether or not it has been notified. There seems, therefore, no advantage to a contracting party in refraining from notifying its subsidies; on the contrary, notifications may dispel undue suspicions concerning those subsidies not previously notified".[25]

The question of notification of subsidies has also been examined at a number of meetings of the Committee on Subsidies and Countervailing Measures. The 1986 Report of the Committee on Subsidies and Countervailing Measures refers to a Note by the Secretariat reproducing all decisions by the CONTRACTING PARTIES with respect to notifications under Article XVI:1 of the General Agreement, and notes: "The decisions reproduced in this note are binding on all contracting parties and should be used as guidelines in the preparation of notifications under Article XVI:1".[26]

See also the general notification obligations in paragraphs 2 and 3 of the Understanding Regarding Notification, Consultation, Dispute Settlement and Surveillance of 28 November 1979, which appear *in extenso* in the section on "Notification in GATT" under Article X.

---

[18]L/1160, adopted on 24 May 1960, 9S/188, 191, para. 10.
[19]L/6627, adopted on 25 January 1990, 37S/86, 131, para. 154.
[20]L/3851, adopted on 7-8 December 1981, 23S/98, 114, para. 77.
[21]II/19.
[22]L/334, adopted on 3 March 1955, 3S/222, 225 para. 16.
[23]9S/193.
[24]11S/58. The most recent full notifications under this procedure appear in the addenda to L/7162 of 11 January 1994 (updates in addenda to L/7375 of 11 January 1994 and L/7611 of 11 January 1975).
[25]L/1442 & Add.1-2, adopted on 21 November 1961, 10S/201, 206, para. 19.
[26]L/6089, 33S/197, para. 13, referring to SCM/W/98.

(6) "estimated effect"

The New York Report notes that the Drafting Committee changed the words "anticipated effect" to "estimated effect" "in order to remove the possible impression that the effect of a subsidy on export trade could be accurately predicted".[27]

(7) "serious prejudice to the interests of any other contracting party is caused or threatened"

The report of the Preparatory Committee on its discussions at London on the ITO Charter notes that, in revising the US Draft Charter, "Wherever the Draft Charter has words such as 'injury to the trade of a member', it was thought advisable to say 'prejudice to the trade of a member'. It was felt that this wording would in practice facilitate application".[28]

In the 1979 Panel Report on "European Communities - Refunds on Exports of Sugar - Complaint by Australia"

"The Panel noted ... that the Community system for granting refunds on sugar exports and its application had contributed to depress world sugar prices in recent years and that thereby serious prejudice had been caused indirectly to Australia, although it was not feasible to quantify the prejudice in exact terms.

"The Panel found that the Community system of export refunds for sugar did not comprise any pre-established effective limitations in respect of either production, price or the amounts of export refunds and constituted a permanent source of uncertainty in world sugar markets. It therefore concluded that the Community system and its application constitutes a threat of prejudice in terms of Article XVI:1".[29]

In the 1980 Panel Report on "European Communities - Refunds on Exports of Sugar - Complaint by Brazil"

"The Panel concluded that in view of the quantity of Community sugar made available for export with maximum refunds and the non-limited funds available to finance export refunds, the Community system of granting export refunds on sugar had been applied in a manner which in the particular market situation prevailing in 1978 and 1979, contributed to depress sugar prices in the world market, and that this constituted a serious prejudice to Brazilian interests, in terms of Article XVI:1.

"The Panel found that the Community system of export refunds for sugar did not comprise any pre-established effective limitations in respect of either production, price or the amounts of export refunds and that the Community system had not been applied in a manner so as to limit effectively neither exportable surpluses nor the amount of refunds granted. Neither the system nor its application would prevent the European Communities from having more than an equitable share of world export trade in sugar. The Panel, therefore, concluded that the Community system and its application constituted a permanent source of uncertainty in world sugar markets and therefore constituted a threat of serious prejudice in terms of Article XVI:1".[30]

(8) "shall, upon request, discuss with the other contracting party or parties concerned"

The Report of the Working Party in 1948 on "Modifications to the General Agreement" notes that the Working Party agreed not to amend Article XVI:1 to incorporate the changes made to the corresponding Charter Article at the Havana Conference, *inter alia* in view of the understanding that

---

[27]New York Report p. 26.
[28]London Report p. 16.
[29]L/4833, adopted on 6 November 1979, 26S/290, 319, paras. (g) and (h).
[30]L/5011, adopted on 10 November 1980, 27S/69, 97, paras. (f) and (g).

"The intent of the last sentence of Article XVI of the General Agreement is that consultation shall proceed upon the request of a contracting party when it considers that prejudice is caused or threatened and would not require a prior international determination".[31]

This understanding was confirmed in the Report of the Review Working Party on "Other Barriers to Trade"[32].

The 1961 Panel Report on "Operation of the Provisions of Article XVI" notes:

"If a contracting party decides that it wishes to consult with another concerning a subsidy it may, depending on the circumstances, have recourse to the specific consultation procedures of Article XVI:1 or the provisions of Article XXII or Article XXIII. At the Review Session it was made clear that consultations under Article XVI:1 can be initiated by a contracting party which considers that serious prejudice is being caused or threatened without necessity for prior action by the CONTRACTING PARTIES …".[33]

Regarding the interpretation of "upon request", see also the unadopted 1994 panel report on "EEC - Import Régime for Bananas".[34]

(9) *"the possibility of limiting the subsidization"*

The report of the Preparatory Committee on its discussions at London on the ITO Charter notes that "The word 'limiting' … is used in a broad sense to indicate maintaining the subsidization at as low a level as possible, and the gradual reduction in subsidization over a period of time where this is appropriate".[35]

A Memorandum by Denmark of 1957 on "Export of Subsidized Eggs and Cattle from the United Kingdom" noted *inter alia* that "serious prejudice is being caused to Danish interests by the British subsidization which, moreover, involves questions of principle bearing upon the cooperation envisaged within the framework of the General Agreement. The Danish Government therefore requests that discussions take place with the CONTRACTING PARTIES in accordance with Article XVI with a view to limiting the effect of the subsidization".[36] Following these discussions, the United Kingdom took measures to prevent exports of subsidized eggs from the United Kingdom to traditional markets of Denmark and the Kingdom of the Netherlands.[37]

In November 1980, the Council requested the EEC to discuss with the CONTRACTING PARTIES the possibility of limiting the EEC subsidization of exports of sugar. The Report of the Working Party on these discussions notes the view of Australia that "the intention of the final sentence of paragraph 1 of Article XVI was … to obtain a statement from the subsidizing contracting party of what action it intended to take to remove the serious prejudice or the threat of prejudice"[38] as well as the view of the EEC that as to "undertakings on the level of internal support prices for sugar or on the limitation of quantities of sugar eligible for export refunds … contracting parties have no obligation under Article XVI:1 to make such undertakings".[39] In Council discussion on this matter, the representative of the EEC stated that if, following consultations under Article XVI:1, the respective parties did not reach agreement, "there existed no other possibility under Article XVI:1" and "only other provisions of the General Agreement could be invoked, such as Article XXIII".[40]

2. **Paragraph 2: "undue disturbance"**

In the 1983 Panel Report on "EEC - Subsidies on Export of Wheat Flour", which has not been adopted by the Committee on Subsidies and Countervailing Measures, the Panel concluded, *inter alia*, that

---

[31] GATT/CP.2/22/Rev.1, adopted on 1-2 September 1948, II/39, 44, para. 29(b).
[32] L/334, adopted on 3 March 1955, 3S/222, 225 para. 15.
[33] L/1442 & Add.1-2, adopted on 21 November 1961, 10S/201, 206, para. 20.
[34] DS38/R, dated 11 February 1994, paras. 152-153.
[35] London Report, p. 16, para. (d).
[36] L/627.
[37] 10S/208.
[38] L/5113, adopted on 10 March 1981, 28S/80, 83, para. 11.
[39] *Ibid.*, 28S/85, para. 22.
[40] C/M/143, p. 7.

"The Panel was not convinced ... that the application of EEC export subsidies had not caused undue disturbance to the normal commercial interests of the United States in the sense of Article XVI:2, to the extent that it may well have resulted in reduced sales opportunities for the United States.

"The Panel considered it desirable that the EEC, bearing in mind the provisions of Article XVI:2, make greater efforts to limit the use of subsidies on the exports of wheat flour. The Panel considered that there were a number of practical aspects of the application of the export refund which might be examined to this end".[41]

3. Paragraph 3

For a survey of the drafting history and interpretation of Article XVI:3 in GATT practice see a 1983 Note by the Secretariat.[42]

(1) "primary product"

See the definition of this term provided in Interpretative Note 2 to Section B of Article XVI. Article XVI:3 and its Interpretative Note 2 were drawn from the provisions of Articles 27 and 28 of the Havana Charter; see the discussion of the Havana Charter in section III below. Articles 27 and 28 applied to subsidies on "primary commodities", and were linked to the provisions of Chapter VI on inter-governmental agreements on "primary commodities". The definition of "primary product" in the present interpretative note to the General Agreement is the same as the definition of "primary commodity" in Article 56:1 of the Charter.

The 1958 Panel Report on "French Assistance to Exports of Wheat and Wheat Flour" considered wheat as well as wheat flour to be primary products.[43]

A request of 24 July 1980 for consultations under Article XXII:1 of the General Agreement on "EEC - Export Refunds for Wheat Flour" states that "The United States considers that wheat flour is a non-primary product, on which no export subsidy may be maintained under Article XVI of the General Agreement".[44] In the 1983 Panel Report on "EEC - Subsidies on Export of Wheat Flour", which has not been adopted by the Committee on Subsidies and Countervailing Measures, the Panel examined the EEC subsidies in relation to Article 10 of the Agreement on Interpretation and Application of Articles VI, XVI and XXIII, thereby treating wheat flour as a primary product in the sense of that Article. During the Panel proceedings, the United States had argued that wheat flour is a processed product and not a primary product within the meaning of the Code.[45]

The 1983 Panel Report on "EEC - Subsidies on Export of Pasta Products", which has not been adopted by the Committee on Subsidies and Countervailing Measures, noted that neither the United States nor the Community "had finally contended that pasta was a primary product". The Panel "was of the opinion that pasta was not a primary product but was a processed agricultural product".[46]

(2) "any form of subsidy which operates to increase the export of any primary product"

Interpretative Note 2 *ad* Article XVI:3 specifies under what conditions a domestic price stabilization scheme on a primary product "shall be considered not to involve a subsidy on exports within the meaning of paragraph 3". It is essentially identical to the text of Article 27:1 of the Havana Charter, except for the addition of the final paragraph of the note, concerning operations wholly or partially financed out of government funds, which was drafted during the Review Session.

---

[41] SCM/42 (unadopted), paras. 5.6-5.7.
[42] AG/W/4.
[43] L/924, adopted on 21 November 1958, 7S/46, 52, para. 14.
[44] L/5014.
[45] SCM/42, para. 2.3.
[46] SCM/43, para. 4.2.

The 1958 Panel Report on "French Assistance to Exports of Wheat and Wheat Flour" provides that "The Panel ... found that even if the French system had the characteristics described in paragraph 2 of [Interpretative Note 2 to Article XVI] the exemption provided from the provisions of paragraph 3 of Article XVI would be precluded if operations under such a system were 'wholly or partly financed out of government funds in addition to funds collected from producers in respect of the products concerned'". The Panel further found that the operation of the French system involved financial contributions from the government since part of the export losses was covered by Government funds. Accordingly, "the Panel concluded that the operation of the French system did in fact result in the grant of subsidies on the export of wheat and wheat flour within the terms of paragraph 3 of Article XVI".[47]

(3)   "more than an equitable share of world export trade"

The last sentence of Article XVI:3 was based on Article 28 of the Havana Charter, the text of which appears in section III below. Concerning the drafting of this text and the first interpretative note to Article XVI:3 in the Review Session Working Party on Other Barriers to Trade, the Report of the Working Party notes:

"A number of under-developed countries raised the question of whether the criterion concerning an 'equitable share' would prevent an exporting country which had no exports during the previous representative period from establishing its right to obtain a share in the trade of the product concerned. Accordingly, the Working Party adopted an interpretative note proposed by the representatives of Brazil and Turkey to cover the case.

"The Working Party also agreed that in determining what are equitable shares of world trade the CONTRACTING PARTIES should not lose sight of:

(a) the desirability of facilitating the satisfaction of world requirements of the commodity concerned in the most effective and economic manner, and

(b) the fact that export subsidies in existence during the selected representative period may have influenced the share of the trade obtained by the various exporting countries".[48]

The 1958 Panel on "French Assistance to Exports of Wheat and Wheat Flour" examined a complaint by Australia that as a result of subsidies granted by the French government on exports of wheat and wheat flour, French exports had displaced Australian trade in these products in Australian traditional wheat flour markets. The Panel found that the operation of the French price equalization scheme did result in the grant of subsidies under Article XVI:3 (see above). It then considered whether this had resulted in France obtaining more than an equitable share in world export trade for these products inconsistent with Article XVI:3. The Panel Report provides as follows:

"... The Panel noted that there was no explicit definition in Article XVI of what constituted an 'equitable' share of world export trade in these products. It was recalled, however, that at both Havana and the Review Session when the provisions of this paragraph were discussed it was implicitly agreed that the concept of 'equitable' share was meant to refer to share in 'world' export trade of a particular product and not to trade in that product in individual markets."[49]

"The Panel noted that French exports of wheat and wheat flour began to rise in 1954 in absolute quantity to levels very substantially exceeding the quantities exported in any year since 1934 and have since remained considerably higher than in pre-war or early post-war years. This increase in the absolute quantities of wheat and of wheat flour exported by France also represents an increase in France's share of world exports, especially as regards wheat flour. ... French exporters have been able to quote prices for wheat flour lower than those quoted by other exporters ... Moreover, judging from export unit values, the price charged by French exporters for wheat flour has in recent years barely exceed that charged for wheat ... In these

---

[47]L/924, adopted on 21 November 1958, 7S/46, 51-52, paras. 8, 13, 14.
[48]L/334, adopted on 3 March 1955, 3S/222, 226, para. 18.
[49]L/924, adopted on 21 November 1958, 7S/46, 52, para. 15.

circumstances, it is reasonable to conclude that, while there is no statistical definition of an 'equitable' share in world exports, subsidy arrangements have contributed to a large extent to the increase in France's exports of wheat and of wheat flour, and that the present French share of world export trade, particularly in wheat flour, is more than equitable".[50]

The Panel then examined French trade in particular markets (Sri Lanka, Malaysia and Indonesia) to consider whether French export subsidies had caused injury to Australia's normal commercial interests, and whether such injury represented an impairment of benefits accruing to Australia under the General Agreement. The Panel concluded that

"While other suppliers of wheat flour have recently begun to play a larger part in the Southeast Asian markets, and although it is difficult to estimate to what extent such incursions as these are displacing traditional exporters, it is nevertheless clear that French supplies have in fact to a large extent displaced Australian supplies in the three markets.

...

"Since it is obviously more profitable to export wheat flour rather than wheat, Australia has suffered a direct damage which could be evaluated by applying the price difference between wheat flour and wheat to the quantity of Australian exports that were displaced by French exports. It would, however, be difficult to assess this displacement quantitatively with any precision. In addition to this direct damage, there were other incidental adverse effects upon Australia which cannot be measured ...[51]

"The Panel then directed itself to the question of whether the damage apparent in recent years was likely to recur or be prolonged. ...

"Although the Panel recognized that the French Government's policy [to reduce subsidies] would tend to reduce the effects of the system on world trade, it considered, nevertheless, that the operation of the system was such that when climatic circumstances were favourable there might be substantial quantities of wheat in excess of normal consumption requirements. ... Also experience has shown ... there was no inherent guarantee in the system that it would operate in such a manner as to conform to the limits contemplated in Article XVI:3".[52]

The 1967 Report of the Working Party under Article XXII:2 on "United States - Subsidy on Unmanufactured Tobacco" contains a discussion of the concept of "equitable share", particularly in relation to the trade of a less-developed country.

"The representative of Malawi stated that ... the concept of equitability in this context ... did not refer to the maintenance by the subsidizing contracting party of a predetermined proportionate share of a growing world market ... in view of the provisions of an Interpretative Note to paragraph 3 which allowed for the entry of new exporters, there were grounds for maintaining that 'equitable shares' could vary ...

"The representative of the United States said that ... the United States Government shared the view of the Malawi Government that it would not be desirable to assume that a particular country's share of a market should remain static. It was not the intention of the United States to increase its share beyond an 'equitable level' but it could not be expected to accept the continued erosion of its relative position".[53]

In the 1979 Panel Report on "European Communities - Refunds on Exports of Sugar - Complaint by Australia",

---

[50]*Ibid.*, 7S/53 paras. 17-19.
[51]*Ibid.*, 7S/54-55, para. 23(c), 23(e).
[52]*Ibid.*, 7S/55-56, paras. 24-25.
[53]L/2925, adopted on 22 November 1967, 15S/116, 122-123 paras. 21-22.

"The Panel considered that its examination should be based not on the concept of 'free market' introduced by Australia in presenting its contentions but on the concept of 'world export trade' mentioned in Article XVI:3 of the General Agreement .... the Panel did not consider it necessary for the purpose of determining whether a market share was a 'more than equitable share of world export trade' to establish market shares in relation to concepts other than those of total world exports, taking into account the fact that a consideration of shares of the free market involved methodological difficulties that would make any comparison difficult."[54]

"The Panel noted that no definition of the concept 'equitable share' had been provided, and neither had it in the past been considered absolutely necessary to agree upon a precise definition of the concept. The Panel felt that it was appropriate and sufficient in this case to try to analyse main reasons for developments in individual market shares, and to examine market and price developments, and then draw a conclusion on that basis".[55]

"The Panel was of the opinion that the term 'more than an equitable share of world export trade' should include situations in which the effect of an export subsidy granted by a signatory was to displace the exports of another signatory, bearing in mind the developments in world markets. With regard to new markets, traditional patterns of supply of the product concerned to the world market, region or country, in which the new market is situated should be taken into account in determining what would be 'more than an equitable share of world export trade'".[56]

The Panel Report on "European Communities - Refunds on Exports of Sugar - Complaint by Brazil" examined a complaint submitted under Article XXIII. The Panel report provides:

"The Panel noted that no complete definition of the concept 'equitable share' had been provided, and neither had it in the past been considered absolutely necessary to have an agreed precise definition of the concept. The Panel felt that it was appropriate and sufficient in this case to try to analyze main reasons for developments in individual market shares, and in light of the circumstances related to the present complaint try to determine any causal relationship between the increase in Community exports of sugar, the developments in Brazilian sugar exports and other developments in the world sugar market, and then draw a conclusion on that basis".[57]

The Report analyses the concept "more than equitable share" in terms of, inter alia, market shares, displacement, "special factors" such as the entry into operation of export quotas under the International Sugar Agreement (1977) as well as other special trading arrangements, and the effects of the operation of Community regulations.[58]

See also the provisions of Article 10 of the 1979 Agreement on the Interpretation and Application of Articles VI, XVI and XXIII of the General Agreement, which provides in paragraph 2:

"For purposes of Article XVI:3 of the General Agreement and paragraph 1 above:

"(a) 'more than an equitable share of world export trade' shall include any case in which the effect of an export subsidy granted by a signatory is to displace the exports of another signatory bearing in mind the developments on world markets;

"(b) with regard to new markets traditional patterns of supply of the product concerned to the world market, region or country, in which the new market is situated shall be taken into account in determining 'equitable share of world export trade'".[59]

---

[54]L/4833, adopted on 6 November 1979, 26S/290, 307, para. 4.9.
[55]*Ibid.*, 26S/308, para. 4.11.
[56]*Ibid.*, 26S/310, para. 4.17.
[57]L/5011, adopted on 10 November 1980, 27S/69, 88, para. 4.6.
[58]*Ibid.*, 27S/88-96, paras. 4.6-4.31.
[59]26S/56, 69.

(4) "previous representative period"

The term "previous representative period" is also used elsewhere in the General Agreement. See discussion of base periods under Articles XI:2, XIII:2(d) and XXVIII.

The 1958 Panel on "French Assistance to Exports of Wheat and Wheat Flour" made no specific reference to "previous representative period" in terms of Article XVI:3. It reviewed trade statistics from the pre-war (1934-1938) and post-war (1948-1958) periods, including statistics available for part of the year in which the Panel had been established.[60]

In the 1979 Panel proceeding on the complaint of Australia concerning "European Communities - Refunds on Exports of Sugar", the appropriate "previous representative period" was at issue. The representative of Australia argued that its complaint concerned the post-1975 period (i.e. 1976 to 1978, preliminary data only being available for 1978) and that the entire period 1969-1975 should be considered as a "previous representative period". Reference was also made to the "precedent of the Canadian lead/zinc case" interpreting Article XXVIII, in which case "the Panel did not consider that full statistics for the applicable base period had to be available at the very beginning of the negotiations, provided the data became available later on in the negotiations and that their submission was not unduly delayed".[61] "The representative of the European Communities considered that the years chosen as 'previous representative period' should reflect, if possible, a normal market situation ... one suggestion would be to compare the average for the years 1972-1974 with that for 1975-1977 ... the provisions of Article XVI:3 must be understood to mean that estimates for recent periods, forecasts or projections for future periods of whatever duration must not be used".[62] The Panel findings provide as follows:

"The Panel noted that the Australian complaint referred to the post-1975 period. ... In view of the difficulties involved in selecting what could be considered to be the 'previous representative period', the Panel felt it necessary to consider various alternatives and to make a set of comparisons".[63]

The Panel Report on "European Communities - Refunds on Exports of Sugar - Complaint by Brazil" notes the suggestion by Brazil to compare shares in two periods, 1973-75 and 1976-78.[64] The EC had proposed that the two reference averages be those for 1972-74 and 1975-77 and that the year 1978 be considered separately.[65] The Panel considered the two periods 1971-73 and 1972-74 to qualify as previous representative periods and compared these with shares for the years 1976 to 1979 (preliminary data being available for 1979). The Panel found that whichever of the two previous representative periods was used for comparison, the outcome would be fairly similar.[66]

The 1979 Agreement on Interpretation and Application of Articles VI, XVI and XXIII of the General Agreement provides in paragraph 2(c) of its Article 10 that for purposes of Article XVI:3 of the General Agreement and paragraph 1 of Article 10, "'a previous representative period' shall normally be the three most recent calendar years in which normal market conditions existed".[67]

(5) "special factors"

The 1979 and 1980 Panel Reports on the complaints of Australia and Brazil respectively concerning "European Communities - Refunds on Exports of Sugar" took note of, as "special factors" affecting world sugar trade, the coming into operation of the 1977 International Sugar Agreement, in which Australia and Brazil were members but the EEC was not.[68]

---

[60]L/924, adopted on 21 November 1958, 7S/46, 52, paras. 15-17.
[61]L/4833, adopted on 6 November 1979, 26S/290, 298, paras. 2.22-2.23; reference is to the 1978 Panel Report on "Canada - Withdrawal of Tariff Concessions", L/4636, adopted on 17 May 1978, 25S/42 (see material from this Report under Article XXVIII).
[62]*Ibid.*, 26S/299, paras. 2.24-2.25.
[63]*Ibid.*, 26S/307-308, para. 4.10.
[64]L/5011, adopted on 10 November 1980, 27S/69, 74, para. 2.8.
[65]*Ibid.*, 27S/74, para. 2.10.
[66]*Ibid.*, 27S/89-90, para. 4.9.
[67]26S/69.
[68]26S/305, paras. 3.21, 4.13, 4.15; 27S/86, paras.3.21, 4.16, 4.17.

See also the 1983 Panel Report on "EEC - Subsidies on Export of Wheat Flour", which has not been adopted.[69]

4. Paragraph 4

Article XVI:4 was added as a result of discussions in the Review Session of 1954-55.[70] This paragraph does not specify a date for the entry into force of the first sentence and has entered into force only for the seventeen countries which have accepted the Declaration Giving Effect to the Provisions of Article XVI:4.[71] See below.

(1) "shall cease to grant ... any form of subsidy on the export"

Article XVI:4 states in its first sentence that the cessation of certain export subsidies called for will apply "as from 1 January 1958 or the earliest practicable date thereafter". The second sentence provides for a standstill on such export subsidies in the interim. The Interpretative Note to this provision states that "The intention of paragraph 4 is that the contracting parties should seek before the end of 1957 to reach agreement to abolish all remaining subsidies as from 1 January 1958; or, failing this, to reach agreement to extend the application of the standstill until the earliest date thereafter by which they can expect to reach such agreement".

The Report of the Working Party in 1960 on "Provisions of Article XVI:4" reports on the consideration of what steps should be taken by the CONTRACTING PARTIES to implement this paragraph. It notes that "The only question which was ... left open in paragraph 4 of Article XVI was the date from which the prohibition on subsidies on any product other than a primary product should become effective. Since no agreement on that date has so far been reached by contracting parties, the standstill provision contained in paragraph 4 of Article XVI has ceased to be operative, but a number of contracting parties have agreed to extend it beyond that date by means of a declaration".[72] This same Working Party drafted the "Declaration Giving Effect to the Provisions of Article XVI:4"[73], which provides that the governments subscribing to it "agree that the date on which the aforementioned provisions of paragraph 4 of Article XVI come into force shall be, for each party to this Declaration, the date on which this Declaration enters into force for that party".[74]

Accordingly, the first sentence of Article XVI:4 entered into force on 14 November 1962 and is now in force for the seventeen contracting parties the governments of which have accepted this Declaration. Those contracting parties are Austria, Belgium, Canada, Denmark, France, Federal Republic of Germany, Italy, Japan, Luxembourg, Netherlands, New Zealand, Norway, Sweden, Switzerland, the United Kingdom, the United States and Zimbabwe.[75] The acceptance of the Declaration by the United States was made "with the understanding that this Declaration shall not prevent the United States, as part of its subsidization of exports of a primary product, from making a payment on an exported processed product (not itself a primary product), which has been produced from such primary product, if such payment is essentially limited to the amount of the subsidy which would have been payable on the quantity of such primary product, if exported in primary form, consumed in the production of the processed product".

The "standstill clause" contained in the second sentence of Article XVI:4, which had been extended by a number of declarations,[76] expired on 31 December 1967.

(a) Illustrative lists of export subsidies

The Report of the Working Party in 1960 on "Provisions of Article XVI:4" which prepared the Declaration Giving Effect to the Provisions of Article XVI:4 contains a "detailed list of measures which are considered as forms of export subsidies by a number of contracting parties ... the question was raised whether it was clear that

---

[69] SCM/42.
[70] See U.K. compromise proposal at W.9/240.
[71] 9S/32.
[72] L/1381, adopted on 19 November 1960, 9S/185, 186, para. 2.
[73] 9S/32.
[74] 9S/32, 33 para. 1.
[75] Status of Legal Instruments, p. 11-4.1ff.
[76] 6S/24, 7S/30, 8S/25, 9S/33, 12S/50.

these measures could not be maintained if the provisions of the first sentence of paragraph 4 of Article XVI were to become fully operative".[77] With respect to this "1960 Illustrative List" of eight items, "The Working Party agreed that this list should not be considered exhaustive or to limit in any way the generality of the provisions of paragraph 4 of Article XVI. It noted that the governments prepared to accept the declaration ... agreed that, for the purpose of that declaration, these practices generally are to be considered as subsidies in the sense of Article XVI:4 or are covered by the Articles of Agreement of the International Monetary Fund".[78] The 1960 Illustrative List was based on a Decision of the Council of the Organization for European Economic Cooperation (OEEC) and was adopted in order to ensure that GATT obligations on export subsidies would match obligations under the OEEC.[79]

The 1979 Agreement on Interpretation and Application of Articles VI, XVI and XXIII of the General Agreement, Article 9 of which prohibits export subsidies on products other than certain primary products, contains an Annex with an Illustrative List of twelve items defined as export subsidies subject to this prohibition.[80]

At its meeting in May 1980 the Committee on Subsidies and Countervailing Measures which was established under this Agreement set up a Group of Experts on the Calculation of the Amount of a Subsidy which drew up guidelines on various issues for adoption by the Committee. See the discussion of these guidelines under Article VI.

(b)   Tax deferral

The Panel on "United States Tax Legislation (DISC)" examined legislation providing for deferral of the corporate income tax payable on export profits as long as such profits were held in a Domestic International Sales Corporation (DISC). The Panel Report[81], which was adopted subject to an understanding, provides:

> "The Panel noted that the DISC legislation was intended, in its own terms, to increase United States exports and concluded that, as its benefits arose as a function of profits from exports, it should be regarded as an export subsidy.

> "The Panel examined whether a deferral of tax was 'a remission' in terms of item (c) or 'an exemption' in terms of item (d) of the illustrative list of 1960.

> "The Panel was not convinced that a deferral, simply because it was given for an indeterminate period, was equal to a remission or an exemption. In addition, it noted that the DISC legislation provided for the termination of the deferral under specified circumstances. The Panel further noted, however, that the deferral did not attract the interest component of the tax normally levied for late or deferred payment and therefore concluded that, to this extent, the DISC legislation constituted a partial exemption which was covered by one or both of paragraphs (c) and (d) of the Illustrative List".[82]

After this and the panel reports referred to below on French, Belgian and Netherlands tax practices were circulated in November 1976, discussions continued for some time, both in the Council and in the context of the negotiation in the Tokyo Round of the 1979 Agreement on Interpretation and Application of Articles VI, XVI and XXIII. The Illustrative List of Export Subsidies annexed to that Agreement includes various kinds of tax deferrals (see items (e) and (h)). In Note 2 to item (e) of the 1979 Illustrative List, "The signatories recognize that deferral need not amount to an export subsidy where, for example, appropriate interest charges are collected".[83]

---

[77]L/1381, adopted on 19 November 1960, 9S/185, 186-187, para. 5.
[78]*Ibid.*
[79]L/1260 (Proposal by France identifying the source of the list as OEEC document C(59)202); discussion on adoption, SR.17/3.
[80]26S/56, 80-83. Concerning Article 9 see page 461 below.
[81]L/4422, adopted on 7-8 December 1981, 23S/98.
[82]23S/112-113, paras. 69-71.
[83]26S/82. The note also states that "noting in this text prejudges the disposition by the CONTRACTING PARTIES of the specific issues raised in GATT document L/4422" [the panel report on US Tax Legislation].

(c) Taxation of transactions outside the territorial limits of the exporting country

In 1976, the three Panels on "Income Tax Practices Maintained by France"[84], "Income Tax Practices Maintained by Belgium"[85] and "Income Tax Practices Maintained by the Netherlands"[86] examined corporate income tax systems. In the case of France and Belgium the corporate tax system examined was based on the territoriality principle, which in general taxes income earned domestically but not income arising abroad; in the case of the Netherlands, in effect a credit was provided for Dutch tax on foreign income. The Panel found in each case that the tax principles as applied "allowed some part of export activities, belonging to an economic process originating in the country, to be outside the scope of ... taxes. In this way [these contracting parties] had foregone revenue from this source and created the possibility of a pecuniary benefit to exports in those cases where income and corporation tax provisions were significantly more liberal in foreign countries.

" ... however much the practices may have been an incidental consequence of [the contracting party's] taxation principles rather than a specific policy intention, they nonetheless constituted a subsidy on exports because the above-mentioned benefits to exports did not apply to domestic activities for the internal market. The Panel also considered that the fact that the practices might also act as an incentive to investment abroad was not relevant in this context.

"The Panel also noted that the tax treatment of dividends from abroad ensured that the benefits referred to above were fully preserved.

"In circumstances where different tax treatment in different countries resulted in a smaller total tax bill in aggregate being paid on exports than on sales in the home market, the Panel concluded that there was a partial exemption from direct taxes. [...] The Panel further concluded that the practices were covered by one or both items (c) and (d) of the illustrative list of 1960".[87]

Note 2 to item (e) of the Illustrative List of Export Subsidies annexed to the 1979 Agreement on Interpretation and Application of Articles VI, XVI and XXIII also provides as follows:

"The signatories reaffirm the principle that prices for goods in transactions between exporting enterprises and foreign buyers under their or under the same control should for tax purposes be the prices which would be charged between independent enterprises acting at arm's length. Any signatory may draw the attention of another signatory to administrative or other practices which may contravene this principle and which result in a significant saving of direct taxes in export transactions. In such circumstances the signatories shall normally attempt to resolve their differences using the facilities of existing bilateral tax treaties or other specific international mechanisms, without prejudice to the rights and obligations of signatories under the General Agreement, including the right of consultation created in the preceding sentence.

"Paragraph *(e)* is not intended to limit a signatory from taking measures to avoid the double taxation of foreign source income earned by its enterprises or the enterprises of another signatory.

"Where measures incompatible with the provisions of paragraph *(e)* exist, and where major practical difficulties stand in the way of the signatory concerned bringing such measures promptly into conformity with the Agreement, the signatory concerned shall, without prejudice to the rights of other signatories under the General Agreement or this Agreement, examine methods of bringing these measures into conformity within a reasonable period of time."[88]

---

[84]L/4423, adopted on 7-8 December 1981, 23S/114.
[85]L/4424, adopted on 7-8 December 1981, 23S/127.
[86]L/4425, adopted on 7-8 December 1981, 23S/137.
[87]*Ibid.*, at 23S/125, paras. 47-50 (France); 23S/135, paras. 34-37 (Belgium); 23S/145, paras. 34-37 (Netherlands).
[88]26S/82.

At its meeting on 7-8 December 1981, the Council adopted the four Panel Reports on "United States Tax Legislation (DISC)" and on income tax practices in France, Belgium and the Netherlands on the following understanding:

"The Council adopts these reports on the understanding that with respect to these cases, and in general, economic processes (including transactions involving exported goods) located outside the territorial limits of the exporting country need not be subject to taxation by the exporting country and should not be regarded as export activities in terms of Article XVI:4 of the General Agreement. It is further understood that Article XVI:4 requires that arm's-length pricing be observed, i.e., prices for goods in transactions between exporting enterprises and foreign buyers under their or the same control should for tax purposes be the prices which would be charged between independent enterprises acting at arm's length. Furthermore, Article XVI:4 does not prohibit the adoption of measures to avoid double taxation of foreign source income."

"Following the adoption of these reports the Chairman noted that the Council's decision and understanding does not mean that the parties adhering to Article XVI:4 are forbidden from taxing the profits on transactions beyond their borders, it only means that they are not required to do so. He noted further that the decision does not modify the existing GATT rules in Article XVI:4 as they relate to the taxation of exported goods. He noted also that this decision does not affect and is not affected by the Agreement on the Interpretation and Application of Articles VI, XVI and XXIII. Finally, he noted that the adoption of these reports together with the understanding does not affect the rights and obligations of contracting parties under the General Agreement".[89]

A communication from the United States of 20 April 1982 stated that "in the light of the Understanding adopted by the GATT Council when it adopted the panel reports on DISC and the tax practices of Belgium, France and the Netherlands, the United States does not believe that the DISC is a subsidy".[90] At the July 1982 meeting of the Council, the Chairman stated that "it was the opinion of the majority of the Council members that the United States should take appropriate action to ensure that the DISC legislation was brought into conformity with the General Agreement".[91] In July 1984 the United States announced enactment of a statute replacing the DISC tax provisions with Foreign Sales Corporation provisions.[92]

(d) Export inflation insurance schemes

The 1977 Report of the Working Party on "Export Inflation Insurance Schemes" discussed certain export inflation insurance schemes of contracting parties. Several members of the Working Party held the view that export inflation insurance schemes under examination were subsidies in contravention of Article XVI:4 and should be notified under Article XVI:1. Several other members, especially those operating such schemes, considered that schemes operating in long-term financial equilibrium were not subsidies, and did not believe that any indication of dual pricing had been shown. The Working Party could not reach consensus on whether exchange rate guarantee schemes fell under its terms of reference.[93]

The 1979 Panel on "Export Inflation Insurance Schemes" then examined, pursuant to Article XVI:5, and taking into account the 1977 Report, whether and under what conditions such schemes are export subsidies within the meaning of Article XVI:4. The Report of the Panel notes: "... The Panel agreed that a scheme charging premiums at rates which were 'manifestly inadequate to cover its long-term operating costs and losses' would be a subsidy within the terms of Article XVI:4". The Report discusses criteria for evaluating whether such a scheme is an export subsidy.[94] Item (j) of the Illustrative List of Export Subsidies annexed to the 1979 Agreement on Interpretation and Application of Articles VI, XVI and XXIII classifies as an export subsidy "The provision by governments (or special institutions controlled by governments) of export credit guarantee or insurance

---

[89]L/5271, 28S/114; see also Council discussion at C/M/154.
[90]SCM/19.
[91]C/M/160 p. 9.
[92]C/M/180 p. 5.
[93]L/4552, adopted on 11 November 1977, 24S/116, conclusions 24S/125-126.
[94]L/4813, adopted on 25 July 1979, 26S/330, 333, para. 14.

programmes, of insurance or guarantee programmes against increases in the costs of exported products or of exchange risk programmes, at premium rates, which are manifestly inadequate to cover the long-term operating costs and losses of the programmes."[95]

(2) "of any product other than a primary product"

"Primary product" is defined in Note 2 *ad* Article XVI, Section B, paragraph 2. The same definition of "primary product" appeared in paragraph 1 of Article 56 of the Havana Charter. See also the discussion of Article XVI:3 above.

Article 9 of the 1979 Agreement on Interpretation and Application of Articles VI, XVI and XXIII of the General Agreement on Tariffs and Trade provides that "1. Signatories shall not grant export subsidies on products other than certain primary products. 2. The practices listed in points (a) to (l) in the Annex are illustrative of export subsidies". A footnote to Article 9 states that "for purposes of this Agreement 'certain primary products' means the products referred to in Note ad Article XVI of the General Agreement, Section B, paragraph 2, with the deletion of the words 'or any mineral'".[96]

The Panel Report on "EEC - Subsidies on Export of Pasta Products", which has not been adopted by the Committee on Subsidies and Countervailing Measures, noted that neither the United States nor the Community "had finally contended that pasta was a primary product". The Panel "was of the opinion that pasta was not a primary product but was a processed agricultural product".[97] See also the Panel Report on "Canada - Imposition of Countervailing Duties on Imports of Manufacturing Beef from the EEC", which has not been adopted by the Committee on Subsidies and Countervailing Measures.[98]

As regards the possibility of subsidizing the primary product component of a processed product, the United States proposed at the Twelfth Session of the CONTRACTING PARTIES in 1957 that Article XVI:4 should not prevent a contracting party, in this particular case the United States, from subsidizing exports of processed products (cotton textiles) if such subsidy was essentially the payment that would have been made on the raw material (cotton) used in the production of this processed product had the raw material been exported in its natural form. This interpretation was rejected by several contracting parties.[99] The "Declaration Extending the Standstill Provisions of Article XVI:4 of the General Agreement on Tariffs and Trade"[100] was accepted by the United States in November 1958 "with the understanding that this Declaration shall not prevent the United States as part of its subsidization of exports of a primary product, from making a payment on an exported processed product (not in itself a primary product), which has been produced from such primary product, if such payment is essentially limited to the amount of the subsidy which would have been payable on the quantity of such primary product, if exported in primary form, consumed in the production of the processed product". This understanding was repeated by the United States when in 1961 it signed the "Declaration Giving Effect to the Provisions of Article XVI:4".[101] A discussion of the legal effect of this understanding appears in the Panel Report on "EEC - Subsidies on Export of Pasta Products", which has not been adopted by the Committee on Subsidies and Countervailing Measures.[102]

(3) "at a price lower than the comparable price charged for the like product to buyers in the domestic market"

In the three 1976 Panel Reports on income tax practices maintained by France, Belgium and the Netherlands, which were adopted on 7-8 December 1981,

"The Panel noted that the contracting parties that had accepted the 1960 Declaration had agreed that the practices in the illustrative list were generally to be considered as subsidies in the sense of

---

[95] 26S/81.
[96] 26S/68.
[97] SCM/43 (unadopted), para. 4.2.
[98] SCM/85 (unadopted), dated 13 October 1987.
[99] SR.12/22, p. 192-194.
[100] 6S/24.
[101] 9S/32.
[102] SCM/43 (unadopted).

Article XVI:4. The Panel further noted that these contracting parties considered that, in general, the practices contained in the illustrative list could be presumed to result in bi-level pricing and that this presumption could therefore be applied to the [French, Belgian and Netherlands'] practices. The Panel concluded, however, from the words 'generally to be considered' that these contracting parties did not consider that the presumption was absolute.

"The Panel considered that, from an economic point of view, there was a presumption that an export subsidy would lead to any or a combination of the following consequences in the export sector: (a) lowering of prices, (b) increase of sales effort, and (c) increase of profits per unit. Because [France, Belgium and the Netherlands] were an important supplier in certain export sectors it was to be expected that all of these effects would occur and that, if one occurred, the other two would not necessarily be excluded. A concentration of the subsidy benefits on prices could lead to substantial reductions in prices. The Panel did not consider that a reduction in prices in export markets needed automatically to be accompanied by similar reductions in domestic markets. The Panel added that the extent to which tax havens existed was well known and that they considered this some evidence of the extent to which bi-level pricing had probably occurred.

"The Panel therefore concluded that the ... tax practices in some cases had effects which were not in accordance with ... obligations under Article XVI:4".[103]

Similar findings were made by the Panel on United States Tax Legislation (DISC).[104]

In the 1979 Panel Report on "Export Inflation Insurance Schemes",

"The Panel noted the conclusions of the Panels on United States Tax Legislation (DISC), on Income Tax Practices Maintained by France, by Belgium and by the Netherlands, as presented to the CONTRACTING PARTIES, according to which the contracting parties which had accepted the 1960 Declaration 'considered that, in general, the practices contained in the illustrative list could be presumed to result in bi-level pricing, and considered that this presumption could therefore be applied to' the DISC legislation and to the French, Belgian and Netherlands' practices, while concluding, however, that those contracting parties did not consider that the presumption was absolute. The Panel held the view that the presumption mentioned above applied equally to practices which were not contained in the 1960 list but which had clearly been identified as export subsidies".[105]

(4) Developing countries

The Report of the Working Party on the "Accession of Venezuela" discusses, *inter alia*, Venezuelan export subsidies and the view of certain members of the Working Party that Venezuela should undertake specific commitments to observe all of Article XVI, and to eliminate its export subsidies, especially in sectors which in their view could not be considered as "developing" within the meaning of Article XVIII or the Enabling Clause. "Some members expressed concern with respect to the proposal aimed at the progressive elimination of all export subsidies granted by Venezuela ... The concept of sectoral development would deny the rights and obligations provided by the General Agreement for certain industries of developing countries. These members recalled that subsidies were governed in the main by Article XVI which does not include the concept of sectoral development. In their opinion there were no economic, legal or practical grounds for accepting the early application of the concept of sectoral development for developing countries even though some discussions were proceeding in the Negotiating Group on Subsidies in the framework of the Uruguay Round".[106] See also Article 14 of the 1979 Agreement on Interpretation and Application of Articles VI, XVI and XXIII.

---

[103] L/4423, 23S/114, 125-126, paras. 51-53; L/4424, 23S/127, 135, paras. 38-40; L/4425, 23S/137, 145, paras. 38-40; all adopted on 7-8 December 1981 with understanding, L/5271, 28S/114.

[104] L/4422, 23S/98, 113, paras. 72-74. See also paragraphs 25-26 and 51-59 of this report for a discussion of whether the burden of demonstrating bi-level pricing lies with the complainant country adversely affected by subsidies.

[105] L/4813, adopted on 25 July 1979, 26S/330, 332, para. 12.

[106] L/6696, adopted on 11 July 1990, 37S/43, 62-63, para. 62.

5. Paragraph 5

In 1958 the CONTRACTING PARTIES appointed a Panel to undertake the preparatory work for a review envisaged in paragraph 5. The Panel submitted three reports which were adopted by the CONTRACTING PARTIES in 1960 and 1961, but the conduct of the review was postponed and has never taken place.[107]

The GATT Ministerial Declaration of November 1982 provided for the establishment of a Committee on Trade in Agriculture to examine, *inter alia*, "The operation of the General Agreement as regards subsidies affecting agriculture, especially export subsidies, with a view to examining its effectiveness, in the light of actual experience, in promoting the objectives of the General Agreement and avoiding subsidization seriously prejudicial to the trade or interests of contracting parties. Other forms of export assistance will be included in this examination".[108]

B. RELATIONSHIP BETWEEN ARTICLE XVI AND OTHER GATT PROVISIONS

1. Article II

The Report of the Review Working Party on "Other Barriers to Trade" provides that "The Working Party also agreed that there was nothing to prevent contracting parties, when they negotiate for the binding or reduction of tariffs, from negotiating on matters such as subsidies, which might affect the practical effects of tariff concessions and from incorporating in the appropriate schedule annexed to the Agreement, the results of such negotiations; provided that the results of such negotiations should not conflict with other provisions of the Agreement".[109] See also the discussion on "Subsidies in Negotiations" in the 1961 Report on "Operation of the Provisions of Article XVI,"[110] the material on negotiations on non-tariff measures under Article XXVIII*bis*, the material on concessions on non-tariff measures under Article II, and the material on modification or withdrawal of such concessions under Article XXVIII.

2. Article VI

See under Article VI.

3. Article XXIII

See the material on Article XXIII:1(b), and on the relationship between Article XVI and XXIII, under Article XXIII.

4. Part IV

See under Part IV.

5. Protocol of Provisional Application

By virtue of the "Resolution of 7 March 1955 Expressing the Unanimous Agreement of the CONTRACTING PARTIES to the Attaching of a Reservation on Acceptance pursuant to Article XXVI"[111] and the Declaration of 15 November 1957 on "Statements which Accompanied the Acceptance of the Protocol Amending the Preamble and Parts II and III",[112] Part II of the General Agreement as amended by the 1955 amendments (which were effected by this Protocol) applies to the fullest extent not inconsistent with "existing legislation" on the relevant date. See the chapter on provisional application of the General Agreement.

---

[107] 9S/188, 10S/201.
[108] Adopted on 29 November 1982, 29S/9.
[109] 3S/225, para. 14.
[110] L/1442 and Add.1-2, adopted on 21 November 1961, 10S/201, 209, paras. 24-28.
[111] 3S/48.
[112] 6S/13.

The three Panel Reports on income tax practices maintained by Belgium, France and the Netherlands note the argument by the United States that the 1955 amendments to the General Agreement (including Article XVI:4), and the 1960 Declaration giving effect to Article XVI:4, as well as the Standstill Declaration, meant that the contracting parties adhering to the 1960 Declaration had an obligation to cease granting any subsidies whether or not the subsidies were granted pursuant to legislation existing in 1947, unless a specific reservation was made. The Panel reports state in this respect:

> "The Panel considered that the fact that these arrangements might have existed before the General Agreement was not a justification for them and noted that Belgium [France, Netherlands] had made no reservation with respect to the standstill agreement or to the 1960 Declaration".[113]

C. EXCEPTIONS AND DEROGATIONS

Article XVI has been the subject of a waiver under Article XXV:5 in one instance: "United Kingdom: Special Problems of Dependent Overseas Territories of the United Kingdom".[114]

D. AGREEMENT ON INTERPRETATION AND APPLICATION OF ARTICLES VI, XVI AND XXIII

The Agreement on Interpretation and Application of Articles VI, XVI and XXIII of the General Agreement was negotiated in the Tokyo Round of multilateral trade negotiations, and entered into force for the parties thereto on 1 January 1980.[115] The preamble of this Agreement expresses the desire "to apply fully and to interpret the provisions of Articles VI, XVI and XXIII of the General Agreement on Tariffs and Trade only with respect to subsidies and countervailing measures and to elaborate rules for their application in order to provide greater uniformity and certainty in their implementation". See also the Appendix table of acceptances of the Tokyo Round agreements.

In Council discussion of Brazil's request for a panel on "United States - Denial of Most-favoured-nation Treatment as to Imports of Non-rubber Footwear from Brazil"[116], in relation to a measure concerning which Brazil had earlier pursued dispute settlement under the Agreement on Interpretation and Application of Articles VI, XVI and XXIII, the representative of Brazil stated that

> "a contracting party could not be prevented from seeking a remedy before the GATT Council because it had also sought protection of its interests under a particular Code ... this would mean accepting that the Code Committees somehow bound the Council and the contracting parties, many of which were not signatories to the Codes. ... To lend further support to his arguments, he quoted from a letter of 11 April 1979 sent by the Chairman of the Tokyo Round sub-group on subsidies and countervailing measures to a certain number of negotiators, as follows: 'The provisions of the Agreement on Subsidies and Countervailing Measures interpret and apply the provisions of the GATT in Article XXIII as among signatories to the Agreement with respect to disputes concerning subsidies and countervailing measures under the GATT and in this connection will be used by these signatories to resolve any such dispute. However, delegations pointed out that in their view rights and obligations of the contracting parties under Article XXIII of the GATT are not limited thereby.' He recalled that several other Tokyo Round Codes contained similar provisions under which parties were to complete the dispute settlement procedure under the respective Codes before availing themselves of any rights under the General Agreement".[117]

In the panel proceeding on "EEC - Payments and Subsidies Paid to Processors and Producers of Oilseeds and Related Animal-Feed Proteins" the EEC argued that as between the parties that signed it, the Agreement on Interpretation and Application of Articles VI, XVI and XXIII created a expectation as to the criteria that would be used to judge a complaint of non-violation nullification or impairment of tariff concessions. The Panel Report adopted in 1990 provides:

---

[113]Reports adopted on 7 December 1981, L/4423, 23S/114,126, para. 56; L/4424, 23S/127, 136, para. 43; L/4425, 23S/137,146, para.43.
[114]3S/21, 22.
[115]Text of the Agreement appears at 26S/56. On the drafting history, see documents listed in TA/INF/1/Rev.8, p. 45-50.
[116]C/M/248, p.9.
[117]C/M/248, p. 15.

"The Panel was established to make findings 'in the light of the relevant GATT provisions'; it therefore does not have the mandate to propose interpretations of the provisions of the Subsidies Code which the Community invokes to justify its position. However, the following may be noted in this respect. ... The Panel noted that the purpose of the Subsidies Code is, according to its preamble, 'to apply fully and interpret' provisions of the General Agreement. In the view of the Panel this speaks in favour of interpreting Article 8:4 in conformity with the decisions of the CONTRACTING PARTIES rather than, as the Community suggests, revising these decisions in the light of a particular interpretation of a Code accepted by a portion of the contracting parties".[118]

III. PREPARATORY WORK AND SUBSEQUENT MODIFICATIONS

The provisions on subsidies in the Havana Charter were in Articles 25-28; in the US-UK *Proposals* in Chapter III D-1; in the US Draft in Article 25; in the London and New York Drafts in Articles 30; and in the Geneva Draft in Articles 25-29.

Havana Charter text and the GATT: Although many of the articles in the General Agreement were adapted directly from the corresponding provisions in the Geneva Draft Charter, Article XVI in the 30 October 1947 text of the General Agreement was drawn only from Article 25 of the Geneva Draft Charter, and included only one paragraph, the present-day Article XVI:1. The Geneva Draft Charter Articles 26 through 29, which dealt in more detail with export subsidies, were omitted from the General Agreement.

Article 25 of the Geneva Draft Charter, with some changes, became Article 25 of the Havana Charter. The text of Charter Article 25 reads "... which operates directly or indirectly to *maintain or* increase exports of any product from or to reduce *or prevent an increase in* imports ...", the italicized words having been added at Havana because "it was felt that the Geneva text of the Article failed to cover subsidies which, whilst not increasing a Member's exports nor reducing its imports, might nevertheless affect a Member's share of total trade".[119] Also, at the end of Article 25 the words "it is determined that serious prejudice" were changed in the Charter text to "a Member considers that serious prejudice" because "it was thought that this change was consistent with similar changes in Chapter VI [of the Charter] and would expedite procedure".[120]

The Havana Charter also included Articles 26 through 28. Paragraphs 1 and 2 of Article 26 provided:

"1. No Member shall grant, directly or indirectly, any subsidy on the export of any product, or establish or maintain any other system, which subsidy or system results in the sale of such product for export at a price lower than the comparable price charged for the like product to buyers in the domestic market, due allowance being made for differences in the terms and conditions of sale, for differences in taxation, and for other differences affecting price comparability.

"2. The exemption of exported products from duties or taxes imposed in respect of like products when consumed domestically, or the remission of such duties or taxes in amounts not in excess of those which have accrued, shall not be deemed to be in conflict with the provisions of paragraph 1. The use of the proceeds of such duties or taxes to make payments to domestic producers in general of these products shall be considered as a case under Article 25".

Paragraph 3 of Article 26 provided for Members to give effect to the provisions of paragraph 1 no later than two years from the entry into force of the Charter; paragraph 4 permitted export subsidies "to the extent and for such time as may be necessary to offset a subsidy granted by a non-Member affecting the Member's exports of the product".

Articles 27 and 28 applied to subsidies on "primary commodities", which were defined in Article 56:1 of the Charter. Article 27 provided an exception to Article 26 for certain price stabilization schemes, and other

---

[118]L/6627, adopted on 25 January 1990, 37S/131.
[119]Havana Reports, p. 108, para. 13.
[120]*Ibid.*, para. 14.

provisions linked to the Charter chapter on negotiation of commodity agreements, including a standstill on new or increased export subsidies on a commodity during negotiation of a commodity agreement. Article 28 provided as follows.

"1. Any Member granting any form of subsidy, which operates directly or indirectly to maintain or increase the export of any primary commodity from its territory, shall not apply the subsidy in such a way as to have the effect of maintaining or acquiring for that Member more than an equitable share of world trade in that commodity.

"2. As required under the provisions of Article 25, the Member granting such subsidy shall promptly notify the Organization of the extent and nature of the subsidization, of the estimated effect of the subsidization on the quantity of the affected commodity exported from its territory, and of the circumstances making the subsidization necessary. The Member shall promptly consult with any other Member which considers that serious prejudice to its interests is caused or threatened by the subsidization.

"3. If, within a reasonable period of time, no agreement is reached in such consultation, the Organization shall determine what constitutes an equitable share of world trade in the commodity concerned and the Member granting the subsidy shall conform to this determination.

"4. In making the determination referred to in paragraph 3, the Organization shall take into account any factors which may have affected or may be affecting world trade in the commodity concerned, and shall have particular regard to:

"(a) the Member country's share of world trade in the commodity during a previous representative period;

"(b) whether the Member country's share of world trade in the commodity is so small that the effect of the subsidy on such trade is likely to be of minor significance;

"(c) the degree of importance of the external trade in the commodity to the economy of the Member country granting, and to the economies of the Member countries materially affected by, the subsidy;

"(d) the existence of price stabilization systems conforming to the provisions of paragraph 1 of Article 27;

"(e) the desirability of facilitating the gradual expansion of production for export in those areas able to satisfy world market requirements of the commodity concerned in the most effective and economic manner, and therefore of limiting any subsidies or other measures which make that expansion difficult."

Amendments: At the Second Session of the CONTRACTING PARTIES, after the close of the Havana Conference, a Working Party considered which of the changes made at Havana should be taken into the General Agreement in advance of the anticipated supersession of Part II which would take place under Article XXIX upon entry into force of the Charter. It was proposed that the changes made at Havana to Article 25 be inserted in Article XVI; the Working Party "agreed that the differences between Article XVI of the General Agreement and Article 25 of the Havana Charter are not of a substantive nature"[121] and the text was kept unchanged in light of understandings reached concerning the meaning of "increased exports" and concerning the prerequisites for consultation under Article XVI, noted above at pages 448 and 450 respectively. It was also proposed that Articles 26, 27 and 28 of the Charter be taken into the GATT. The 1948 Working Party Report on "Modifications to the General Agreement" notes in this connection:

---

[121] Working Party Report on "Modifications to the General Agreement", GATT/CP.2/22/Rev.1, adopted on 1-2 September 1948, II/39, 44, para. 29.

"While agreeing in principle that insertion of these articles would be desirable, the majority of the working party felt that, in view of practical difficulties, they could not usefully recommend such inclusion at the present stage. It was of course understood that, in the light of Article XXIX, paragraph 1, the CONTRACTING PARTIES undertake to apply the principles of the Havana Charter relating to export subsidies to the full extent of their executive authority".[122]

At the Review Session in 1954-55, various proposals were made for amendment to Article XVI, including conforming the text to Article 25 of the Charter, and incorporating the text of Articles 26, 27 and 28 into the GATT.[123] The outcome is discussed in the Report of the Review Working Party on "Other Barriers to Trade".[124] Paragraph 3 of Article XVI was based on paragraphs 1 and 4 of Article 28; paragraph 4 was based on paragraphs 1 and 3 of Article 26; the general Note *ad* Article XVI was taken from paragraph 2 of Article 26; the first paragraph of Note 2 *ad* Article XVI:3 was drawn from paragraph 1 of Article 27; and the definition of "primary product" in Note 2 *ad* Section B was taken from paragraph 1 of Article 56 in the Charter chapter on commodity agreements. Paragraph 2 as well as Note 1 *ad* Section B and the final paragraph of Note 2 *ad* paragraph 3 were originally drafted in the Review Session, and the final text of Article XVI:4 and its interpretative note emerged as a compromise proposal during final adoption of the Working Party's report.[125] See the proposals and documents listed below under the Review Session. These amendments were effected through the 1955 Protocol Amending the Preamble and Parts II and III of the General Agreement, which entered into force on 7 October 1957 and is in force for all contracting parties.

As noted above on page 457, under the Declaration of 19 November 1960 "Giving Effect to the Provisions of Article XVI:4",[126] the prohibition of certain export subsidies in Article XVI:4 entered into force on 14 November 1962 and is in force only for the seventeen countries which have accepted the Declaration. These countries are Austria, Belgium, Canada, Denmark, France, Federal Republic of Germany, Italy, Japan, Luxembourg, Netherlands, New Zealand, Norway, Sweden, Switzerland, United Kingdom, United States and Zimbabwe. The "standstill clause" contained in the second sentence of Article XVI:4, which had been extended by a number of declarations,[127] expired on 31 December 1967.

---

[122]*Ibid.*, II/43, para. 24. See discussion at GATT/CP.2/SR.5, p. 4-5; GATT/CP.2/SR.6, p. 4.
[123]See Note on "Subsidies", W.9/20 dated 18 November 1954, summarizing initial proposals.
[124]L/334, adopted 3 March 1955, 3S/222. See also discussion on adoption of the amendments to Article XVI, in SR.9/41, SR.9/43, and SR.9/47.
[125]See W.9/240 (compromise proposal by the United Kingdom delegation), and discussion and adoption at SR.9/41, SR.9/43, SR.9/47.
[126]9S/32.
[127]6S/24, 7S/30, 8S/25, 9S/33, 12S/50.

IV. RELEVANT DOCUMENTS

London

Discussion:	EPCT/C.II/37
Reports:	EPCT/30

New York

Discussion:	EPCT/C.6/23, 24, 46, 105
Reports:	EPCT/34 (p.25)

Geneva

Discussion:	EPCT/EC/PV.2/22
	EPCT/A/PV/22+Corr.1-5, 23+Corr.1-2, 26+Corr.1-3
	EPCT/B/SR.10, 11, 22
	EPCT/TAC/SR.11
	EPCT/TAC/PV/27
Reports:	EPCT/124, 127, 130, 135, 180, 186, 189, 212, 214/Add.1/Rev.1
Other:	EPCT/W/64, 72, 81, 140, 182, 185, 186, 188/Rev.1, 190, 201, 207, 220+Corr.1, 272, 280, 301, 313

Havana

Discussion:	E/CONF.2/C.3/SR.26, 27, 36
Reports:	E/CONF.2/C.3/51

CONTRACTING PARTIES

Discussion:	GATT/CP.2/SR.6
Reports:	GATT/CP.2/22/Rev.1

Review Session

Discussion:	SR.9/17, 23, 24, 41, 42, 43, 47
Reports:	W.9/177, 220, 231
Other:	GATT/174, 183, 184, 187, 197
	L/261+Add.1, 264, 273, 274, 276, 277, 282
	W.9/20, 28, 41, 50, 59, 71, 102, 103, 104, 117, 119, 122, 138, 223, 236/Add.1, 240
	Sec/148/54, 153/54
	Spec/29/55, 36/55, 41/55, 111/55, 126/55, 134/55, 169/55, 179/55, 194/55, 197/55
	MGT/9/55

ARTICLE XVII

STATE TRADING ENTERPRISES

I.	TEXT OF ARTICLE XVII, INTERPRETATIVE NOTE AD ARTICLE XVII AND URUGUAY ROUND UNDERSTANDING ON INTERPRETATION OF ARTICLE XVII	469
II.	INTERPRETATION AND APPLICATION OF ARTICLE XVII	472
	A. Scope and Application of Article XVII	472
	1. General: "State trading enterprises"	472
	2. Paragraph 1	473
	(1) "State enterprise"	473
	(2) "exclusive or special privileges"	474
	(3) "involving either imports or exports"	475
	(4) "act in a manner consistent with the general principles of non-discriminatory treatment"	475
	(5) "having due regard to the other provisions of this Agreement"	476
	(6) "commercial considerations"	476
	(a) Relationship of sub-paragraphs (b) and (c) to sub-paragraph (a)	476
	(b) Charging of different prices	476
	(c) Tied loans	476
	(d) "customary business practice"	477
	(7) Paragraph 1(c): "No contracting party shall prevent any enterprise ... within its jurisdiction"	477
	(8) State trading enterprises in countries maintaining a complete monopoly of their import trade	478
	3. Paragraph 2	479
	(1) "imports of products for immediate or ultimate consumption in governmental use and not otherwise for resale ..."	480
	(2) "goods"	481
	(3) "fair and equitable treatment"	481
	4. Paragraph 3	481
	5. Paragraph 4	481
	(1) "Contracting parties shall notify the CONTRACTING PARTIES"	481
	(2) "import mark-up"	482
	B. Relationship between Article XVII and other GATT Provisions	483
	1. Article II	483
	2. Article III	483
	3. Article XI	484
	4. Articles XII and XVIII	485
	5. Part IV	485
	C. Exceptions and Derogations	485
III.	PREPARATORY WORK AND SUBSEQUENT MODIFICATIONS	485
IV.	RELEVANT DOCUMENTS	486

I. TEXT OF ARTICLE XVII, INTERPRETATIVE NOTE AD ARTICLE XVII AND URUGUAY ROUND UNDERSTANDING ON INTERPRETATION OF ARTICLE XVII

Article XVII

State Trading Enterprises

1.* (*a*) Each contracting party undertakes that if it establishes or maintains a State enterprise, wherever located, or grants to any enterprise, formally or in effect, exclusive or special privileges,* such enterprise shall, in its purchases or sales involving either imports or exports, act in a manner consistent with the general principles of non-discriminatory treatment prescribed in this Agreement for governmental measures affecting imports or exports by private traders.

(*b*) The provisions of sub-paragraph (*a*) of this paragraph shall be understood to require that such enterprises shall, having due regard to the other provisions of this Agreement, make any such purchases or sales solely in accordance with commercial considerations,* including price, quality, availability, marketability, transportation and other conditions of purchase or sale, and shall afford the enterprises of the other contracting parties adequate opportunity, in accordance with customary business practice, to compete for participation in such purchases or sales.

(*c*) No contracting party shall prevent any enterprise (whether or not an enterprise described in sub-paragraph (*a*) of this paragraph) under its jurisdiction from acting in accordance with the principles of sub-paragraphs (*a*) and (*b*) of this paragraph.

2. The provisions of paragraph 1 of this Article shall not apply to imports of products for immediate or ultimate consumption in governmental use and not otherwise for resale or use in the production of goods* for sale. With respect to such imports, each contracting party shall accord to the trade of the other contracting parties fair and equitable treatment.

3. The contracting parties recognize that enterprises of the kind described in paragraph 1 (*a*) of this Article might be operated so as to create serious obstacles to trade; thus negotiations on a reciprocal and mutually advantageous basis designed to limit or reduce such obstacles are of importance to the expansion of international trade.*

4. (*a*) Contracting parties shall notify the CONTRACTING PARTIES of the products which are imported into or exported from their territories by enterprises of the kind described in paragraph 1 (*a*) of this Article.

(*b*) A contracting party establishing, maintaining or authorizing an import monopoly of a product, which is not the subject of a concession under Article II, shall, on the request of another contracting party having a substantial trade in the product concerned, inform the CONTRACTING PARTIES of the import mark-up* on the product during a recent representative period, or, when it is not possible to do so, of the price charged on the resale of the product.

(*c*) The CONTRACTING PARTIES may, at the request of a contracting party which has reason to believe that its interests under this Agreement are being adversely affected by the operations of an enterprise of the kind described in paragraph 1 (*a*), request the contracting party establishing, maintaining or authorizing such enterprise to supply information about its operations related to the carrying out of the provisions of this Agreement.

(*d*) The provisions of this paragraph shall not require any contracting party to disclose confidential information which would impede law enforcement or otherwise be contrary to the public interest or would prejudice the legitimate commercial interests of particular enterprises.

Interpretative Note *Ad* Article XVII from Annex I

Paragraph 1

The operations of Marketing Boards, which are established by contracting parties and are engaged in purchasing or selling, are subject to the provisions of sub-paragraphs (*a*) and (*b*).

The activities of Marketing Boards which are established by contracting parties and which do not purchase or sell but lay down regulations covering private trade are governed by the relevant Articles of this Agreement.

The charging by a state enterprise of different prices for its sales of a product in different markets is not precluded by the provisions of this Article, provided that such different prices are charged for commercial reasons, to meet conditions of supply and demand in export markets.

Paragraph 1 (a)

Governmental measures imposed to insure standards of quality and efficiency in the operation of external trade, or privileges granted for the exploitation of national natural resources but which do not empower the government to exercise control over the trading activities of the enterprise in question, do not constitute "exclusive or special privileges".

Paragraph 1 (b)

A country receiving a "tied loan" is free to take this loan into account as a "commercial consideration" when purchasing requirements abroad.

Paragraph 2

The term "goods" is limited to products as understood in commercial practice, and is not intended to include the purchase or sale of services.

Paragraph 3

Negotiations which contracting parties agree to conduct under this paragraph may be directed towards the reduction of duties and other charges on imports and exports or towards the conclusion of any other mutually satisfactory arrangement consistent with the provisions of this Agreement. (See paragraph 4 of Article II and the note to that paragraph.)

Paragraph 4 (b)

The term "import mark-up" in this paragraph shall represent the margin by which the price charged by the import monopoly for the imported product (exclusive of internal taxes within the purview of Article III, transportation, distribution, and other expenses incident to the purchase, sale or further processing, and a reasonable margin of profit) exceeds the landed cost.

UNDERSTANDING ON THE INTERPRETATION OF ARTICLE XVII OF THE GENERAL AGREEMENT ON TARIFFS AND TRADE 1994

Members,

Noting that Article XVII provides for obligations on Members in respect of the activities of the state trading enterprises referred to in paragraph 1 of Article XVII, which are required to be consistent with the general principles of non-discriminatory treatment prescribed in GATT 1994 for governmental measures affecting imports or exports by private traders;

Noting further that Members are subject to their GATT 1994 obligations in respect of those governmental measures affecting state trading enterprises;

Recognizing that this Understanding is without prejudice to the substantive disciplines prescribed in Article XVII;

Hereby *agree* as follows:

1. In order to ensure the transparency of the activities of state trading enterprises, Members shall notify such enterprises to the Council for Trade in Goods, for review by the working party to be set up under paragraph 5, in accordance with the following working definition:

"Governmental and non-governmental enterprises, including marketing boards, which have been granted exclusive or special rights or privileges, including statutory or constitutional powers, in the exercise of which they influence through their purchases or sales the level or direction of imports or exports."

This notification requirement does not apply to imports of products for immediate or ultimate consumption in governmental use or in use by an enterprise as specified above and not otherwise for resale or use in the production of goods for sale.

2. Each Member shall conduct a review of its policy with regard to the submission of notifications on state trading enterprises to the Council for Trade in Goods, taking account of the provisions of this Understanding. In carrying out such a review, each Member should have regard to the need to ensure the maximum transparency possible in its notifications so as to permit a clear appreciation of the manner of operation of the enterprises notified and the effect of their operations on international trade.

3. Notifications shall be made in accordance with the questionnaire on state trading adopted on 24 May 1960 (BISD 9S/184-185), it being understood that Members shall notify the enterprises referred to in paragraph 1 whether or not imports or exports have in fact taken place.

4. Any Member which has reason to believe that another Member has not adequately met its notification obligation may raise the matter with the Member concerned. If the matter is not satisfactorily resolved it may make a counter-notification to the Council for Trade in Goods, for consideration by the working party set up under paragraph 5, simultaneously informing the Member concerned.

5. A working party shall be set up, on behalf of the Council for Trade in Goods, to review notifications and counter-notifications. In the light of this review and without prejudice to paragraph 4(c) of Article XVII, the Council for Trade in Goods may make recommendations with regard to the adequacy of notifications and the need for further information. The working party shall also review, in the light of the notifications received, the adequacy of the above-mentioned questionnaire on state trading and the coverage of state trading enterprises notified under paragraph 1. It shall also develop an illustrative list showing the kinds of relationships between governments and enterprises, and the kinds of activities, engaged in by these enterprises, which may be relevant for the purposes of Article XVII. It is understood that the

Secretariat will provide a general background paper for the working party on the operations of state trading enterprises as they relate to international trade. Membership of the working party shall be open to all Members indicating their wish to serve on it. It shall meet within a year of the date of entry into force of the WTO Agreement and thereafter at least once a year. It shall report annually to the Council for Trade in Goods.[1]

Note 1: The activities of this working party shall be coordinated with those of the working group provided for in Section III of the Ministerial Decision on Notification Procedures adopted on 15 April 1994.

II. INTERPRETATION AND APPLICATION OF ARTICLE XVII

A. SCOPE AND APPLICATION OF ARTICLE XVII

1. General: "State trading enterprises"

Article XVII makes a distinction between various types of enterprises: a "State enterprise" or "any enterprise" that has been granted "formally or in effect, exclusive or special privileges" (paragraph 1(a)) including "Marketing Boards" (interpretative note to paragraph 1); "any enterprise" under the jurisdiction of a contracting party (paragraph 1(c)); and an "import monopoly" (paragraph 4(b)).

In March 1964, in reaction to a proposal of the representative of Egypt seeking an interpretation of Article XVII, the Committee on the Legal and Institutional Framework of the GATT in Relation to Less-Developed Countries agreed that "there was nothing in Article XVII which prevents a contracting party from establishing or maintaining State-trading enterprises, nor does the General Agreement sanction discrimination against State-trading enterprises which are, in this regard, placed on the same basis as any other enterprise".[1]

The 1989 Panel Report on "Republic of Korea - Restrictions on Imports of Beef - Complaint by the United States" notes the argument made by the US that the Livestock Products Marketing Organization (LPMO), which was established to administer import restrictions on beef, constituted an import monopoly controlled by domestic producers and was in itself a separate "import restriction" within the meaning of Article XI, aside from the restrictions administered by the LPMO. Korea stated that the LPMO administered but did not itself determine quota levels.

"The Panel ... examined the further claim by the United States that the existence, or use, of producer-controlled import monopolies to restrict imports was inconsistent with the provisions of Articles XI:1 and XVII. Korea contested that the existence of a producer-controlled import monopoly in itself constituted an additional barrier to trade. The Panel noted that the LPMO had been granted exclusive privileges as the sole importer of beef. As such, the LPMO had to comply with the provisions of the General Agreement applicable to state-trading enterprises, including those of Articles XI:1 and XVII.

"Article XI:1 proscribed the use of 'prohibitions or restrictions other than duties, taxes or other charges', including restrictions made effective through state-trading activities, but Article XVII permitted the establishment or maintenance of state-trading enterprises, including enterprises which had been granted exclusive or special privileges. The mere existence of producer-controlled import monopolies could not be considered as a separate import restriction inconsistent with the General Agreement. The Panel noted, however, that the activities of such enterprises had to conform to a number of rules contained in the General Agreement, including those of Article XVII and Article XI:1. The Panel had already found that the import restrictions presently administered by the LPMO violated the provisions of Article XI:1. As the rules of

---

[1]L/2281, paras. 9-10 (referring to proposal at L/2147, p. 7, and Secretariat Note at LEGAL/W/3). The proposal, made during the preliminary work on the drafting of Part IV of the General Agreement, was designed to ensure that "in interpreting the provisions contained in Article XVII of the General Agreement, contracting parties should give sympathetic consideration to the need for developing contracting parties to make use of State-trading enterprises as one means of overcoming their difficulties in their early stages of development".

the General Agreement did not concern the organization or management of import monopolies but only their operations and effects on trade, the Panel concluded that the existence of a producer-controlled monopoly could not in itself be in violation of the General Agreement."[2]

See also Article II:4, which applies to "a monopoly of the importation of any product described in the appropriate Schedule annexed to this Agreement".

2. Paragraph 1

(1) "State enterprise"

The US Draft Charter contained the following definition in the section on State trading: "For the purposes of this Article, a State enterprise shall be understood to be any enterprise over whose operations a Member government exercises, directly or indirectly, a substantial measure of control". The London Report states that certain delegates at the London session of the Preparatory Committee wished to add a reference to "effective control over the trading operations of such enterprise" but others "considered that in such circumstances it would be proper that the government conferring the exclusive or special privileges should assume the responsibility of exercising effective control over operations affecting the external trade of such enterprise". Also, "It was agreed that when marketing boards buy or sell they would come under the provisions relating to State-trading; where they lay down regulations governing private trade their activities would be covered by the relevant articles of the Charter. It was understood that the term 'marketing boards' is confined to boards established by express governmental action."[3]

In the London and New York Drafts of the Charter, the article on non-discriminatory administration of State trading enterprises included an explicit definition of "State enterprise". This definition was deleted at Geneva in the view that such enterprises are defined as precisely as practicable in sub-paragraph 1(a).[4] The Sub-Committee at the Havana Conference which considered the Charter articles on state trading noted as follows:

"In the opinion of the Sub-Committee, the term 'state enterprise' in the text did not require any special definition; it was the general understanding that the term includes, *inter alia*, any agency of government that engages in purchasing or selling."[5]

In 1959-60 a Panel on Subsidies and State Trading examined the notifications made under Article XVII:1(a) and made recommendations on improving the procedure for such notifications. The 1959 interim report of this group on "Notifications of State-Trading Enterprises" discusses the scope of paragraph 1(a) in connection with the notification requirements contained in paragraph 4(a).[6] Its Final Report of 1960 notes that

"In discussing which enterprises were covered by Article XVII it was thought that there was sufficient guidance in the Article itself and in the Interpretative Notes. The Panel, however, drew special attention to the following points:

"(a) not only State enterprises are covered by the provisions of Article XVII, but in addition any enterprises which enjoy 'exclusive or special privileges';

"(b) marketing boards engaged directly or indirectly in purchasing or selling are enterprises in the sense of Article XVII, paragraphs 1(a) and 1(b), but the activities of marketing boards which do not purchase or sell must be in accordance with the other provisions of GATT;

"(c) the requirements in paragraph 4(a) of Article XVII that contracting parties should notify products 'imported into or exported from their territories' should be interpreted to mean that countries should notify

---

[2] L/6503, adopted on 7 November 1989, 36S/268, 301-302, paras. 114-115.
[3] London Report, p. 17.
[4] EPCT/160, pp. 4, 6; EPCT/A/PV.15, pp. 9-24.
[5] Havana Reports, p. 114, para. 10.
[6] L/970, adopted on 13 May 1959, 8S/142, 143, para. 16.

enterprises which have the statutory power of deciding on imports and exports, even if no imports or exports in fact have taken place".[7]

With regard to this reference to 'enterprise' in sub-paragraph (c) directly above,

"… the Panel did not use the word 'enterprise' to mean any instrumentality of government. There would be nothing gained in extending the scope of the notification provisions of Article XVII to cover governmental measures that are covered by other articles of the General Agreement. The term 'enterprise' was used to refer either to an instrumentality of government which has the power to buy or sell, or to a non-governmental body with such power and to which the government has granted exclusive or special privileges. The activities of a marketing board or any enterprise defined in paragraph 1(a) of Article XVII should be notified where that body has the ability to influence the level or direction of imports or exports by its buying or selling.

"It is clear from the interpretative note to paragraph 1 of Article XVII that the activities of a marketing board or any enterprise covered by paragraph 1(a) of the Article and not covered by paragraph 21 of this report would not be notifiable solely by virtue of a power to influence exports or imports by the exercise of overt licensing powers; where such measures are taken they would be subject to other Articles of the General Agreement.

"Where, however, an enterprise is granted exclusive or special privileges, exports or imports carried out pursuant to those privileges should be notified even if the enterprise is not itself the exporter or importer."[8]

See also the discussion of the term "State enterprise" in the unadopted 1981 Panel Report on "Spain - Measures Concerning Domestic Sale of Soyabean Oil".[9]

The definition of "State enterprise" within the scope of Article XVII:1(a) was also discussed in the Committee on Trade in Industrial Products in 1970 and 1971[10], in the Group on Quantitative Restrictions and Other Non-Tariff Measures in 1985[11] and in the Council in 1986.[12]

Paragraph 1 of the Uruguay Round Understanding on the Interpretation of Article XVII of GATT 1994 provides the following "working definition" for the purposes of notification under Article XVII:

"Governmental and non-governmental enterprises, including marketing boards, which have been granted exclusive or special rights or privileges, including statutory or constitutional powers, in the exercise of which they influence through their purchases or sales the level or direction of imports or exports."

See also the Interpretative Note *ad* paragraph 1, and, as regards monopolies, paragraph 4 of Article II and paragraph (d) of Article XX.

(2) "exclusive or special privileges"

See the Interpretative Note.

The report of a Sub-Committee which considered the articles of the Charter on State trading during the Geneva session of the Preparatory Committee records that: "It was the understanding of the Sub-Committee that governmental measures imposed to ensure standards of quality and efficiency in the execution of external trade, or privileges granted for the exploitation of national natural resources, did not constitute 'exclusive or special

---

[7]L/1146, adopted on 24 May 1960, 9S/179, 180-181, para. 8.
[8]*Ibid.*, 9S/183-184, paras. 21-23.
[9]L/5142.
[10]L/3496.
[11]NTM/W/13 p. 39.
[12]L/5955, C/W/495, C/M/195 p. 24-25, C/M/196 p. 6-7, C/M/198 p. 11-12.

privileges'" and that "It was the understanding of the Sub-Committee that if a Member Government exempted an enterprise from certain taxes, as compensation for its participation in the profits of this enterprise, this procedure should not be considered as 'granting exclusive privileges'".[13]

(3) *"involving either imports or exports"*

The same Sub-Committee report also records that

"It was the understanding of the Sub-Committee that the intent of these words is to cover, within the terms of this Article, any transactions by a State enterprise through which such enterprise could intentionally influence the direction of total import or export trade in the commodity in a manner inconsistent with the other provisions of the Charter".[14]

(4) *"act in a manner consistent with the general principles of non-discriminatory treatment"*

Under Article 26 of the US Draft Charter, State enterprises were to accord to the commerce of other Members "non-discriminatory treatment, as compared with the treatment accorded to the commerce of any country other than that in which the enterprise is located". In the London Draft Charter, the non-discrimination obligation was reformulated to read: "the commerce of other Members shall be accorded treatment no less favourable than that accorded to the commerce of any country, other than that in which the enterprise is located".[15] At Geneva, the present words "act in a manner consistent with the general principles of non-discriminatory treatment" were inserted in order to allay the doubt that "commercial considerations" (in paragraph 1(b)) meant that exactly the same price would have to exist in different markets.[16] This point is covered in the third paragraph of the interpretative note to paragraph 1.[17] During discussions at Geneva, it was stated that the Article on State trading referred only "to most-favoured-nation treatment and not to national treatment".[18]

The 1952 Panel Report on "Belgian Family Allowances" notes: "As regards the exception contained in paragraph 2 of Article XVII, it would appear that it referred only to the principle set forth in paragraph 1 of that Article, i.e. the obligation to make purchases in accordance with commercial considerations and did not extend to matters dealt with in Article III".[19]

The Working Party Report which examined the "Haitian Tobacco Monopoly" in 1955 found, with respect to an import licensing scheme operated in connection with an import and production monopoly, that "As the representative of Haiti informed the Working Party that the import licenses issued by the Régie may be used for purchases from any source, it was considered that the measure did not conflict with the provisions of Article XVII calling for non-discriminatory treatment."[20]

In the panel proceeding relating to Canada's administration of its Foreign Investment Review Act, arguments were presented concerning both the issue of whether Article XVII:1 requires national treatment, and the distinct question of whether (even if this is not the case) contracting parties are required to conform to Article III in the administration of any laws or regulations bearing on State trading enterprises. The 1984 Panel Report on "Canada - Administration of the Foreign Investment Review Act" notes:

"The Panel saw great force in Canada's argument that only the most-favoured-nation and not the national treatment obligations fall within the scope of the general principles referred to in Article XVII:1(a). However, the Panel did not consider it necessary to decide in this particular case whether the general reference to the principles of non-discriminatory treatment referred to in Article XVII:1 also comprises the national treatment principle since it had already found the purchase undertakings at issue to be inconsistent

---

[13]EPCT/160, p. 3 and p. 4.
[14]*Ibid.*, p. 4.
[15]London Report, p. 32.
[16]EPCT/160, p. 5-6; EPCT/A/PV.14, p. 24.
[17]EPCT/A/SR.14, p. 3.
[18]EPCT/A/SR.10, p. 34.
[19]G/32, adopted on 7 November 1952, 1S/59, 60, para. 4.
[20]L/454, adopted on 22 November 1955, 4S/38, 39, para. 8; see also earlier decision and report on the same measure, II/27, II/87.

with Article III:4 which implements the national treatment principle specifically in respect of purchase requirements".[21]

The 1988 Panel Report on "Canada - Import, Distribution and Sale of Alcoholic Drinks by Canadian Provincial Marketing Agencies" also examined this issue:

"The Panel ... turned its attention to the relevance of Article XVII and in particular to the contention of the European Communities that the practices under examination contravened a national treatment obligation contained in paragraph 1 of that Article. The Panel noted that two previous panels had examined questions related to this paragraph .... The Panel considered, however, that it was not necessary to decide in this particular case whether the practices complained of were contrary to Article XVII because it had already found that they were inconsistent with Article XI".[22]

(5)   "having due regard to the other provisions of this Agreement"

It was agreed in discussions at Geneva in 1947 that this phrase "covers also differential customs treatment maintained consistently with the other provisions of the Charter".[23]

(6)   "commercial considerations"

(a)   Relationship of sub-paragraphs (b) and (c) to sub-paragraph (a)

The 1984 Panel Report on "Canada - Administration of the Foreign Investment Review Act" includes the following finding:

"The Panel takes the view that, through its reference to sub-paragraph (a), paragraph 1(c) of Article XVII of the General Agreement imposes on contracting parties the obligation to act in their relations with state-trading and other enterprises 'in a manner consistent with the general principles of non-discriminatory treatment prescribed in this Agreement for governmental measures affecting imports or exports by private traders'. This obligation is defined in sub-paragraph (b), which declares, *inter alia*, that these principles are understood to require the enterprises to make their purchases and sales solely in accordance with commercial considerations. The fact that sub-paragraph (b) does not establish a separate general obligation to allow enterprises to act in accordance with commercial considerations, but merely defines the obligations set out in the preceding sub-paragraph, is made clear through the introductory words 'The provisions of sub-paragraph (a) of the paragraph shall be understood to require ...'. For these reasons, the Panel considers that the commercial considerations criterion becomes relevant only after it has been determined that the governmental action at issue falls within the scope of the general principles of non-discriminatory treatment prescribed by the General Agreement".[24]

(b)   Charging of different prices

See the Interpretative Note to paragraph 1.

(c)   Tied loans

The London Report provides: "The view was generally held that a country receiving a loan would be free to take this loan into account as a 'commercial consideration' when purchasing its requirements abroad. The position of countries making such 'tied loans' was another question".[25]

---

[21]L/5504, adopted on 7 February 1984, 30S/140, 163, para. 5.16.
[22]L/6304, adopted on 22 March 1988, 35S/37, 90, para. 4.27 (citing the material above from the Panel Reports on "Belgian Family Allowances" and "Canada - Administration of the Foreign Investment Review Act").
[23]EPCT/160, p. 5; EPCT/183, p. 3.
[24]L/5504, adopted on 7 February 1984, 30S/140, 163, para. 5.16.
[25]London Report, p. 17, para. 1(a)(v).

See the Interpretative Note to paragraph 1(b).

(d) "customary business practice"

The report of a Sub-committee which considered the articles of the Charter on State trading during the Geneva meetings of the Preparatory Committee notes that "It was the understanding of the Sub-Committee that the expression 'customary business practice' was intended to cover business practices customary in the respective line of trade".[26]

(7) Paragraph 1(c): "No contracting party shall prevent any enterprise ... within its jurisdiction"

The 1984 Panel Report on "Canada - Administration of the Foreign Investment Review Act" includes the following treatment of a claim under this paragraph relating to undertakings concerning purchases of goods, submitted to the Canadian government by prospective foreign investors, which became legally binding on the investor if the investment were allowed:

"The United States requested the Panel to find that the purchase undertakings obliging investors to give less favourable treatment to imported products than to domestic products prevent the investors from acting solely in accordance with commercial considerations and that they therefore violate Canada's obligations under Article XVII:1(c).

"The Panel takes the view that, through its reference to sub-paragraph (a), paragraph 1(c) of Article XVII of the General Agreement imposes on contracting parties the obligation to act in their relations with state-trading and other enterprises 'in a manner consistent with the general principles of non-discriminatory treatment prescribed in this Agreement for governmental measures affecting imports or exports by private traders'. This obligation is defined in sub-paragraph (b), which declares, *inter alia*, that these principles are understood to require the enterprises to make their purchases and sales solely in accordance with commercial considerations. The fact that sub-paragraph (b) does not establish a separate general obligation to allow enterprises to act in accordance with commercial considerations, but merely defines the obligations set out in the preceding sub-paragraph, is made clear through the introductory words 'The provisions of sub-paragraph (a) of the paragraph shall be understood to require ...'. For these reasons, the Panel considers that the commercial considerations criterion becomes relevant only after it has been determined that the governmental action at issue falls within the scope of the general principles of non-discriminatory treatment prescribed by the General Agreement. The Panel saw great force in Canada's argument that only the most-favoured-nation and not the national treatment obligations fall within the scope of the general principles referred to in Article XVII:1(a). However, the Panel did not consider it necessary to decide in this particular case whether the general reference to the principles of non-discriminatory treatment referred to in Article XVII:1 also comprises the national treatment principle since it had already found the purchase undertakings at issue to be inconsistent with Article III:4 which implements the national treatment principle specifically in respect of purchase requirements.

"The United States requested the Panel to find that the undertakings which oblige investors to export specified quantities or proportions of their production - are inconsistent with Article XVII:1(c) because the export levels of companies subject to such undertakings cannot be assumed to be the result of a decision-making process based on commercial considerations.

"As explained in paragraph 5.16 above, Article XVII:1(b) does not establish a separate obligation to allow enterprises to act in accordance with commercial considerations but merely defines the obligation of the enterprises, set out in sub-paragraph (a) of Article XVII:1, to 'act in a manner consistent with the general principles of non-discriminatory treatment' prescribed in the General Agreement. Hence, before applying the commercial considerations criterion to the export undertakings, the Panel first had to determine whether Canada, in accepting investment proposals on the condition that the investor export a certain quantity or proportion of his production, acts inconsistently with any of the general principles of

---

[26] EPCT/160, p. 4.

non-discriminatory treatment prescribed in the General Agreement. The Panel found that there is no provision in the General Agreement which forbids requirements to sell goods in foreign markets in preference to the domestic market. In particular, the General Agreement does not impose on contracting parties the obligation to prevent enterprises from dumping. Therefore, when allowing foreign investments on the condition that the investors export a certain amount or proportion of their production, Canada does not, in the view of the Panel, act inconsistently with any of the principles of non-discriminatory treatment prescribed by the General Agreement for governmental measures affecting exports by private traders. Article XVII:1(c) is for these reasons not applicable to the export undertakings at issue".[27]

The 1988 Panel Report on "Japan - Trade in Semi-conductors" includes the following treatment of a claim under Article XVII:1(c):

"The Panel ... turned to the contention of the EEC that the measures by the Japanese Government were contrary to Article XVII:1(c), according to which "no contracting party shall prevent any enterprise under its jurisdiction from acting in accordance with the general principles of non-discriminatory treatment prescribed in [the General] Agreement". The Panel considered that, once a measure had been found to be inconsistent with a specific provision of the General Agreement, it was no longer meaningful to address the question of whether or not the measure was also contrary to principles underlying that Agreement and therefore the Panel, having already found the Japanese measures to be inconsistent with Article XI, did not consider it necessary to examine them in the light of Article XVII:1(c)".[28]

(8) *State trading enterprises in countries maintaining a complete monopoly of their import trade*

The US Draft Charter contained a separate Article 28 concerning expansion of trade by any Member establishing or maintaining a complete or substantially complete monopoly of its import trade. This Article envisaged the negotiation by each such Member of an arrangement providing for a minimum periodic value of imports from the other Members. This Article was kept with the same wording provisionally in the London and New York Draft Charters, and was deleted at Geneva. The Geneva Report states that the Preparatory Committee believed that the text of the revised Article 31 (requiring negotiations to limit or reduce protection afforded by import or export monopolies) would be sufficiently flexible to permit any appropriate negotiations with a Member which maintained a complete or substantially complete monopoly of its external trade, and that since no representative of such a country had attended the sessions of the Committee, the matter remained open for the Havana Conference.[29]

The Report of the Working Party on the "Accession of Poland" noted "that the foreign trade of Poland was conducted mainly by State enterprises and that the Foreign Trade Plan rather than the customs tariff was the effective instrument of Poland's commercial policy. The present customs tariff was applicable only to a part of imports effected by private persons for their personal use and it was in the nature of a purchase tax rather than a customs tariff". The Working Party agreed "that due consideration had to be given to these facts in drawing up the legal instruments relating to Poland's accession".[30] The Working Party further noted that "Poland would grant to each contracting party, in respect of imports into Poland and purchases by Polish agencies, treatment no less favourable than that accorded to any other country".[31] Paragraphs 5 through 7 and Annex A of the Protocol of Accession of Poland provide for annual consultations with the CONTRACTING PARTIES with a view to reaching agreement on Polish targets for imports from the territories of the contracting parties as a whole in the following year; for an annual review of trade in the preceding year between contracting parties and Poland; and for a

---

[27] L/5504, adopted on 7 February 1984, 30S/140, 163, paras. 5.15-5.18.

[28] L/6309, adopted on 4 May 1988, 35S/116, 159-160, para. 123.

[29] London Report, p. 18, New York Report p. 29, Geneva Report p. 29. See also Secretariat Note of 1988 on this issue in MTN.GNG/NG7/W/15/Add.1 p. 1-3. The USSR was appointed as a member of the Preparatory Committee for the ITO Charter by the ECOSOC Resolution which called the UN Conference on Trade and Employment, but according to the Geneva Report (p. 6) the USSR "indicated that it did not feel able to participate in the work of the Preparatory Committee as it had not found it possible to devote sufficient preliminary study to the important questions which were the subject of the Committee's discussion".

[30] L/2806, adopted on 26 June 1967, 15S/109, 110, para. 7.

[31] *Ibid.*, 15S/110, para. 9.

bilateral consultation mechanism.[32] Schedule LXV and the Polish import commitment were modified on 5 February 1971.[33] In December 1989, Poland announced its intention to request renegotiation of its terms of accession in view of the entry into force 1 January 1990 of laws establishing a market economy for which the customs tariff would be the effective instrument of commercial policy.[34] At the February 1990 Council meeting a Working Party was established to examine the request of the Government of Poland to renegotiate the terms of accession of Poland.[35]

The Report of the Working Party on the "Accession of Romania" notes that "Romania stressed that the Romanian producing units and foreign trade enterprises operated on international markets like similar enterprises in market-economy countries, in accordance with criteria of an exclusively commercial character. It was agreed that because of the absence of a customs tariff in Romania the main concession to be incorporated in its Schedule would be a firm intention of increasing imports from contracting parties at a rate not smaller than the growth of total Romanian imports provided for in its Five-Year Plans".[36] This commitment is included in Annex B of the Protocol of Accession of Romania, which also provides for biennial consultations, and for a bilateral consultation mechanism.[37] In 1991, Romania was granted a temporary waiver of its obligations under Article II in order to enable it to implement a new customs tariff in the context of measures for transition to a market economy, and pending renegotiation of its Schedule; Romania also requested renegotiation of its accession protocol in the light of, *inter alia*, the abolition of its former system of central planning.[38] At the February 1992 Council meeting a Working Party was established to examine the request of the Government of Romania to renegotiate the terms of accession of Romania.[39]

The Report of the Working Party on the "Sixth Review of Trade with Hungary under the Protocol of Accession" records, *inter alia*, the question of the Canadian representative why Hungary made no notifications under Article XVII and what it considered to be state trading and the observation that at the very least foreign trade enterprises under administrative supervision would qualify for notifications under Article XVII.[40] In response

> "the representative of Hungary said that the trade pattern was shaped by the competitive position of firms, that it was not decided or organized by the State and that it was not under any administrative supervision. Article XVII referred to state-owned enterprises or private enterprises having exclusive privileges in foreign trade matters; it referred to enterprises not to countries. At the preparatory phase of the Havana Charter negotiations, there had been proposals to draw up special provisions for countries with a complete monopoly of foreign trade, but these proposals died away and were not discussed in Havana. The GATT consequently did not contain any special provision for countries with complete monopoly of foreign trade; there was no such category as state-trading country in the GATT legal system and any existing legislation based on this notion was not in conformity with the GATT. The monopoly of foreign trade in Hungary or the form of ownership of production means had no relevance to Article XVII".[41]

3. Paragraph 2

Article 8 of the US Draft Charter (the most-favoured-nation clause) included within its scope "all matters relating to internal taxation or regulation referred to in Article 9" (the national treatment clause of the US Draft

---

[32] 15S/46, 49, 51-52. For Reviews under this Protocol see 16S/67; 17S/96; 18S/188; 18S/201; 19S/109; 20S/209; 21S/112; 22S/63; 24S/139. See also L/5396, C/W/401 and discussion at SR.38/1 p. 8-10, C/M/165, C/M/167. See also references to this Protocol under Article II.

[33] L/3416 (notification by Poland of intent to renegotiate); C/M/64, p. 17-18; L/3475, "Third Review under the Protocol of Accession", adopted on 2 February 1971, 18S/188, section C, "Renegotiation of Schedule LXV - Poland", 18S/198-200 (noting adoption 5 February 1971 of modification of Schedule LXV by postal ballot).

[34] SR.45/ST/11, L/6634, C/M/238 p. 10-13.

[35] C/M/239, p. 5. The Working Party has not yet presented its report.

[36] L/3557, adopted on 6 October 1971, 18S/94, 95, paras. 6-7.

[37] 18S/5, 7-8, 10. For reviews under this Protocol see 20S/217, 24S/149, 27S/166, 30S/194, 32S/85, 35S/337. See also references to this Protocol under Article II.

[38] L/6967, Decision of 4 December 1991, 38S/80.

[39] C/M/254 p. 5-6; see also L/6838 and Add.1, L/6981, SR.47/2 p. 15-16. The Working Party has not yet presented its report.

[40] L/5977, adopted on 22 May 1986, 33S/136, 147-148, para. 36.

[41] *Ibid.*, 33S/148, para. 37.

Charter, which included in turn "laws and regulations governing the procurement by governmental agencies of supplies for public use other than by or for the military establishment"). The last sentence of paragraph 1 of the proposed Article 8 provided: "The principle underlying this paragraph shall also extend to the awarding by Members of governmental contracts for public works, in respect of which each Member shall accord fair and equitable treatment to the commerce of the other Members." During the first session of the Preparatory Committee in London, it was agreed to change the most-favoured-nation clause, the national treatment clause and the provisions on state trading as follows.

"Under the revision recommended by the Preparatory Committee [the awarding of government public works contracts and the purchase of supplies for governmental use] are removed from the scope of the most-favoured-nation clause."[42]

"The Preparatory Committee is of the opinion that the awarding of public works contracts is more closely related to the question of the treatment of foreign nationals and corporations than to the treatment of the trade in goods. It is considered that Chapter V of the Charter should be confined to matters affecting trade and that questions relating to the treatment of nationals, etc., should be the subject of future agreements developed under the auspices of the International Trade Organization ...".[43]

"The Preparatory Committee considered the provision in Article 9 of the United States Draft Charter for national, as distinct from most-favoured-nation, treatment in respect of governmental purchases of supplies for governmental use. Such provision would require the elimination of the many 'buy-national' laws under which national governments are required to give preference to domestic products in purchasing their administrative supplies. As it appears to the Preparatory Committee that such a commitment would lead to exceptions almost as broad as the commitment itself, the Preparatory Committee has omitted this commitment."[44]

"Since paragraph 1 of Article 8 of the United States Draft Charter had been amended by deletion of the provision relating to governmental contracts, it was felt necessary to insert a new paragraph in Article 31 dealing with the subject. A distinction was made as between governmental purchases for resale, which are covered by this paragraph, and purchases for governmental use and not for resale. The discussion on this latter point was prompted by the consideration that in some countries purchases of industrial and other equipment of various types from abroad might well be effected through the medium of state enterprise and that, while it might be difficult in certain circumstances to observe the rule of 'commercial considerations' for such purchases, it was at least necessary to provide that the rule of 'fair and equitable treatment' should apply but that in applying it full regard should be given to all relevant circumstances."[45]

The 1952 Panel Report on "Belgian Family Allowances" notes: "As regards the exception contained in paragraph 2 of Article XVII, it would appear that it referred only to the principle set forth in paragraph 1 of that Article, i.e. the obligation to make purchases in accordance with commercial considerations and did not extend to matters dealt with in Article III."[46]

See also generally the 1979 Agreement on Government Procurement as amended.[47]

(1) "imports of products for immediate or ultimate consumption in governmental use and not otherwise for resale ..."

Concerning the definition of "governmental" and "resale", see the material collected under Article III:8(a).

---

[42]London Report, p. 9, Chapter III para. A.1((d)(i). See also discussion at EPCT/C.II/PV/13 p. 50-52.
[43]*Ibid.*, para. A.1(d)(ii).
[44]*Ibid.*, para. A.1.(d)(iv).
[45]London Report, p. 17, para. 1(a)(v).
[46]G/32, adopted on 7 November 1952, 1S/59, 60, para. 4.
[47]26S/33, as amended by Protocol of amendment done on 2 February 1987, which entered into force on 14 February 1988, 34S/12.

(2) "goods"

The US Draft Charter provisions regarding non-discriminatory administration of State trading enterprises applied to "purchases or sales of any product or service". It was considered during discussions at the London session of the Preparatory Committee that this article, in conformity with certain others in the Charter, should refer to goods only and not to services. This point is made clear in the interpretative note.[48]

(3) "fair and equitable treatment"

During discussions at London, the US delegate explained the original draft of this clause by saying:

"that most-favoured-nation treatment should also apply to the awarding of government contracts. But it could not be applied to government purchases with the same precision which was possible in the case of fiscal measures. That was why the phrase 'fair and equitable treatment' had been used in the Draft Charter".[49]

4. Paragraph 3

See the Interpretative Note, as well as paragraph 4 of Article II and its Interpretative Note. See also the discussion of the addition of paragraph 3 in the 1954-55 Review Session, below at page 486.

In the 1989 Panel Report on "United States - Restrictions on Imports of Sugar"

"The Panel ... examined the issue in the context of the provisions of the General Agreement related to Article II. It noted that negotiations on obstacles to trade created by the operation of state-trading enterprises may be conducted under Article XVII:3 and that a note to that provision provides that such negotiations

'may be directed towards the reduction of duties and other charges on imports and exports or towards the conclusion of *any other mutually satisfactory arrangement consistent with the provisions of this Agreement* (See paragraph 4 of Article II and the note to that paragraph).' (emphasis added).

"The negotiations foreseen in Article XVII:3 are thus not to result in arrangements inconsistent with the General Agreement, in particular not quantitative restrictions made effective through state-trading that are not justified by an exception to Article XI:1. The Panel saw no reason why a different principle should apply to quantitative restrictions made effective by other means".[50]

5. Paragraph 4

(1) "Contracting parties shall notify the CONTRACTING PARTIES"

During the 1954-55 Review Session, when it recommended the addition of paragraph 4 requiring contracting parties to provide the CONTRACTING PARTIES with information concerning trade by State enterprises, the Review Session Working Party on Other Barriers to Trade agreed that "a contracting party would not be expected to supply information which it is unable to obtain without amending its legislation existing at the time of the adoption of this amendment".[51]

The CONTRACTING PARTIES agreed that the first notifications under paragraph 4 should be submitted not later than 1 February 1958 and any new notifications, or information to bring prior notifications up to date, annually thereafter.[52] In 1958 the CONTRACTING PARTIES appointed a Panel to examine the notifications received

---

[48]London Report, p. 17, para. 1(a)(i).
[49]EPCT/C.II/25, p. 5. See also EPCT/C.II/PV/13, p. 50-51.
[50]L/6514, adopted on 22 June 1989, 36S/331, 342, para. 5.4.
[51]L/334 and Addendum, adopted on 3 March 1955, 3S/222, 228, para. 28.
[52]6S/23, para. (a).

from governments and to consider improvements in the procedure for notification. Paragraphs 8(c) and 20 to 23 of the 1960 Final Report of the Panel, reproduced above on page 473, discuss the scope of notification. That Report also drew up the questionnaire on state trading notifications under Article XVII:4(a) which is still in force.[53] The presently used procedures for notifications and reviews under Article XVII were adopted on 9 November 1962. Under these procedures, contracting parties have been invited to submit by the end of January 1963, and subsequently every third year, new and full responses to the questionnaire at 9S/184, and to notify changes to the basic notifications in the intervening years.[54]

The Committee III Report in 1962 on "Obstacles to Trade of Less-developed Countries" set out a "Supplementary Questionnaire on State-Trading Enterprises" in order to elaborate aspects of State trading operations relevant to the work of Committee III for the liberalization of trade barriers to exports of less-developed countries.[55]

Notification obligations under Article XVII were subsequently discussed in the Committee on Trade in Industrial Products in 1970 and 1971,[56] and in the Council in 1986.[57]

The Uruguay Round Understanding on the Interpretation of Article XVII of the GATT 1994 provides *inter alia* for improvements in notification under Article XVII:

> "Each Member shall conduct a review of its policy with regard to the submission of notifications on state trading enterprises ... . In carrying out such a review, each Member should have regard to the need to ensure the maximum transparency possible in its notifications so as to permit a clear appreciation of the manner of operation of the enterprises notified and the effect of their operations on international trade.
>
> "Notifications shall be made in accordance with the questionnaire on state trading adopted on 24 May 1960 ... it being understood that Members shall notify the enterprises referred to in paragraph 1 whether or not imports or exports have in fact taken place.
>
> "Any Member which has reason to believe that another Member has not adequately met its notification obligation may raise the matter with the Member concerned. If the matter is not satisfactorily resolved it may make a counter-notification to the Council for Trade in Goods, for consideration by the working party set up under paragraph 5, simultaneously informing the Member concerned."[58]

See also the notification requirements under the Resolution of 4 March 1955 on "Liquidation of Strategic Stocks".[59]

(2) "import mark-up"

See the Interpretative Note. A 1987 Note by the Secretariat on "Article XVII (State-trading Enterprises)" notes with regard to Article XVII:4(b) that this provision has been rarely used, and with regard to Article XVII:4(c) that this provision does not appear to have been used.[60]

---

[53] 9S/184.

[54] 11S/58. The most recent full notifications under this procedure can be found in the addenda to L/7161 of 11 January 1993 (updates in addenda to L/7374 of 11 January 1994 and L/7623 of 11 January 1995). A list of notifications received by the CONTRACTING PARTIES under the 1962 procedure up to 1987 can be found in Annex V of the Note by the Secretariat on Article XVII dated 11 August 1987, MTN.GNG/NG7/W/15. The CONTRACTING PARTIES to GATT 1947 decided in December 1994 that if a measure is subject to a notification obligation both under the WTO Agreement and the GATT 1947, the notification of such a measure to the WTO shall, unless otherwise indicated in the notification, be deemed to be also a notification of that measure under the GATT 1947 (L/7582).

[55] L/1768, adopted on 16 November 1962, 11S/176, 187.

[56] L/3496.

[57] L/5955, C/W/495, C/M/195 p. 24-25, C/M/196 p. 6-7, C/M/198 p. 11-12.

[58] Paras. 2-4.

[59] 3S/51.

[60] MTN.GNG/NG7/W/15 p. 10. For an instance of use of Article XVII:4(b) see C/M/205, p. 15-16; C/M/206, p. 15; L/5937/Add.2/Suppl.2.

B. Relationship between Article XVII and other GATT Provisions

The report of discussions at the London session of the Preparatory Committee notes that "It was agreed that when marketing boards buy or sell they would come under the provisions relating to State-trading; where they lay down regulations governing private trade their activities would be covered by the relevant articles of the Charter. It was understood that the term 'marketing boards' is confined to boards established by express governmental action".[61] See the second Note *Ad* paragraph 1 of Article XVII, as well as Article 30 of the Havana Charter.

1. Article II

See the discussion of Article II:4 above.

2. Article III

See the discussion of "non-discriminatory treatment" above at page 475.

The 1988 Panel Report on "Canada - Import, Distribution and Sale of Alcoholic Drinks by Canadian Provincial Marketing Agencies"

> "... examined the contention of the European Communities that the practices complained of were contrary to Article III. The Panel noted that Canada did not consider Article III to be relevant to this case, arguing that the Interpretative Note to Articles XI, XII, XIII, XIV and XVIII made it clear that provisions other than Article XVII applied to state-trading enterprises by specific reference only. The Panel considered that it was not necessary to decide in this particular case whether the practices complained of were contrary to Article III:4 because it had already found that they were inconsistent with Article XI. However, the Panel saw great force in the argument that Article III:4 was also applicable to state-trading enterprises at least when the monopoly of the importation and monopoly of the distribution in domestic markets were combined, as was the case of the provincial boards in Canada".[62]

The 1992 Panel Report on "Canada - Import, Distribution and Sale of Certain Alcoholic Drinks by Provincial Marketing Agencies" examined the practices of Canadian provincial liquor boards with regard to the internal transportation of beer. The Report notes in this connection:

> "The Panel ... turned to Canada's argument that its right to deliver imported beer to the points of sale was an inherent part of Canada's right to establish an import monopoly in accordance with Article XVII of the General Agreement which was not affected by its obligations under Article III:4. The Panel noted that the issue before it was not whether Canada had the right to create government monopolies for the importation, internal delivery and sale of beer. The Panel fully recognized that there was nothing in the General Agreement which prevented Canada from establishing import and sales monopolies that also had the sole right of internal delivery. The only issue before the Panel was whether Canada, having decided to establish a monopoly for the internal delivery of beer, might exempt domestic beer from that monopoly. The Panel noted that Article III:4 did not differentiate between measures affecting the internal transportation of imported products that were imposed by governmental monopolies and those that were imposed in the form of regulations governing private trade. Moreover, Articles II:4, XVII and the Note Ad Articles XI, XII, XIII, XIV and XVIII clearly indicated the drafters' intention not to allow contracting parties to frustrate the principles of the General Agreement governing measures affecting private trade by regulating trade through monopolies. Canada had the right to take, in respect of the privately delivered beer, the measures necessary to secure compliance with laws consistent with the General Agreement relating to the enforcement of monopolies. This right was specifically provided for in Article XX(d) of the General Agreement. The Panel recognized that a beer import monopoly that also enjoyed a sales monopoly might, in order properly to carry out its functions, also deliver beer but it did not for that purpose have to prohibit unconditionally the private delivery of imported beer while permitting that of domestic beer. For these reasons the Panel

---

[61] London Report, p. 17.
[62] L/6304, adopted on 22 March 1988, 35S/37, 90, para. 4.26.

found that Canada's right under the General Agreement to establish an import and sales monopoly for beer did not entail the right to discriminate against imported beer inconsistently with Article III:4 through regulations affecting its internal transportation".[63]

3. **Article XI**

See the Interpretative Note *Ad* Articles XI-XIV and XVIII.

The 1988 Panel Report on "Canada - Import, Distribution and Sale of Alcoholic Drinks by Canadian Provincial Marketing Agencies"

"... examined the contention of the European Communities that the application by provincial liquor boards of practices concerning listing/delisting requirements and the availability of points of sale which discriminate against imported alcoholic beverages was inconsistent with Canada's obligations under Articles III:4, XI or XVII of the General Agreement. ... The Panel observed that the Note to Articles XI, XII, XIII, XIV and XVIII provided that throughout these Articles 'the terms "import restrictions" and "export restrictions" include restrictions made effective through state-trading operations'. The Panel considered it significant that the Note referred to 'restrictions made effective through state-trading operations' and not to 'import restrictions'. It considered that this was a recognition of the fact that in the case of enterprises enjoying a monopoly of both importation and distribution in the domestic market, the distinction normally made in the General Agreement between restrictions affecting the importation of products and restrictions affecting imported products lost much of its significance since both types of restriction could be made effective through decision by the monopoly. The Panel considered that systematic discriminatory practices of the kind referred to should be considered as restrictions made effective through 'other measures' contrary to the provisions of Article XI:1".[64]

The 1988 Panel Report on "Japan - Restrictions on Imports of Certain Agricultural Products" examined arguments by Japan responding to a claim by the United States regarding import restrictions maintained through the operation of a state enterprise.

"The Panel noted the view of Japan that Article XI:1 did not apply to import restrictions made effective through an import monopoly. According to Japan, the drafters of the Havana Charter for an International Trade Organization intended to deal with the problem of quantitative trade limitations applied by import monopolies through a provision under which a monopoly of the importation of any product for which a concession had been negotiated would have 'to import and offer for sale such quantities of the product as will be sufficient to satisfy the full domestic demand for the imported product' (Article 31:5 of the Havana Charter). Japan contended that that provision had not been inserted into the General Agreement and that quantitative restrictions made effective through import monopolies could therefore not be considered to be covered by Article XI:1 of the General Agreement. ...

"The Panel examined this contention and noted the following: Article XI covers restrictions on the importation of any product, 'whether made effective through quotas, import ... licences *or other measures*' (emphasis added). The wording of this provision is comprehensive, thus comprising restrictions made effective through an import monopoly. This is confirmed by the note to Articles XI, XII, XIII, XIV and XVIII, according to which the term 'import restrictions' throughout these Articles covers restrictions made effective through state-trading operations. The basic purpose of this note is to extend to state-trading the rules of the General Agreement governing private trade and to ensure that the contracting parties cannot escape their obligations with respect to private trade by establishing state-trading operations. This purpose would be frustrated if import restrictions were considered to be consistent with Article XI:1 only because they were made effective through import monopolies. The note to Article II:4 of the General Agreement specifies that that provision 'will be applied in the light of the provisions of Article 31 of the Havana Charter'. The obligation of a monopoly importing a product for which a concession had been granted 'to import and offer for sale such quantities of the product as will be sufficient to satisfy the full domestic

---

[63]DS17/R, adopted on 18 February 1992, 39S/27, 79-80, para. 5.15.
[64]L/6304, adopted on 2 February 1988, 35S/37, 89, paras. 4.22, 4.24.

demand for the imported product' is thus part of the General Agreement. The Panel could therefore not follow the arguments of Japan based on the assumption that Article 31:5 of the Havana Charter was *not* included in the General Agreement. The Panel found for these reasons that the import restrictions applied by Japan fell under Article XI independent of whether they were made effective through quotas or through import monopoly operations".[65]

See also the material excerpted from the 1989 Panel Report on "Republic of Korea - Restrictions on Imports of Beef - Complaint by the United States" above at page 472 on whether the maintenance of a producer-controlled import monopoly is as such a "restriction' under Article XI.

See also the material under Article II:4, and the material on State trading under Article III and Article XI.

4. Articles XII and XVIII

The use of State trading to administer balance-of-payments restrictions has been noted in a number of instances: see, for instance, certain of the measures examined in the 1962 "Uruguayan Recourse to Article XXIII". The 1970 "full consultation procedures" for balance-of-payments restrictions include "State trading, or government monopoly, used as a measure to restrict imports for balance-of-payments reasons" among the measures to be covered in the Basic Document for a full consultation under Articles XII:4(b) or XVIII:12(b).[66]

5. Part IV

Article XXXVII:3 of the General Agreement provides:

"The developed contracting parties shall:

(a) make every effort, in cases where a government directly or indirectly determines the resale price of products wholly or mainly produced in the territories of less-developed contracting parties, to maintain trade margins at equitable levels ...".

C. EXCEPTIONS AND DEROGATIONS

See Article XVII:2 and accompanying text.

III. PREPARATORY WORK AND SUBSEQUENT MODIFICATIONS

Provisions corresponding to Article XVII appear in Article 29 of the Havana Charter; in the US-UK *Proposals* in Chapter III-E; in the US Draft Charter in Articles 26-27; in the London and New York Drafts in Article 31; and in the Geneva Draft in Article 30. Provisions on State trading appear in Articles 29-32 of the Havana Charter; in the US Draft Charter in Articles 26-28; in the London and New York Drafts in Articles 31-33; and in the Geneva Draft in Articles 30-31. Article XVII in the 30 October 1947 text of the General Agreement consisted *mutatis mutandis* of the provisions of Article 29 of the Geneva Draft Charter and its interpretative notes, and corresponded to the present paragraphs 1 and 2 of Article XVII. The other provisions on State trading in the Charter were not taken into the General Agreement at that time.

Concerning the drafting history on treatment in the Charter of State trading by countries maintaining a complete or substantially complete monopoly of their import trade, see above at page 478.

At Havana, paragraph 2 of the Geneva Draft Article 30 (corresponding to paragraph 2 of GATT Article XVII) was amended, (1) to conform the language to the wording of Article 18:8(a) (corresponding to Article III:8(a) of GATT) "to avoid difficulties of interpretation" and (2) to extend the "fair and equitable

---

[65] L/6253, adopted on 22 March 1988, 35S/163, 229, paras. 5.2.2.1-5.2.2.2.
[66] L/3388, 18S/48, 53, Annex II.

treatment" rule to also cover "the laws, regulations and requirements referred to in paragraph 8(a) of Article 18".[67] Also at Havana, the first two paragraphs of the Interpretative Note *Ad* paragraph 1 were transferred to the body of the Charter and became Article 30 on Marketing Organizations.[68] The third paragraph of that Note was amended at Havana "so as to include purchases as well as sales and to take account also of relevant factors other than supply and demand".[69] The Interpretative Note *Ad* paragraph 1(a) was also revised at Havana,[70] and the interpretative notes to paragraphs 1(b) and 2 were deleted and do not appear in the Havana Charter. These drafting changes were not among those which were incorporated into the General Agreement in 1948.

In the 1954-55 Review Session, proposals were made to incorporate all or part of the other Havana Charter provisions on State trading into the General Agreement. The Working Party on "Other Barriers to Trade" considered a proposal "designed to apply to protection afforded through state monopolies the same principle with respect to negotiations as those that have been recommended for negotiation of tariffs", and recommended addition of Article XVII:3 and the interpretative note thereto.[71] The Working Party also recommended the addition of Article XVII:4 and the note thereto, as a result of its consideration of "proposals designed to provide the CONTRACTING PARTIES with information concerning state monopolies conducted by individual contracting parties and for the submission of pertinent information upon request".[72] A proposal was made to add a new article to the General Agreement, similar to Article 32 of the Charter, requiring that a contracting party consult with interested contracting parties before liquidation of non-commercial stocks; it was decided instead that the CONTRACTING PARTIES adopt a resolution on this subject.[73] The amendments to Article XVII were effected through the Protocol Amending the Preamble and Parts II and III of the General Agreement, and entered into effect on 7 October 1957.

IV. RELEVANT DOCUMENTS

London

Discussion:	EPCT/C.II/36, 37;
	EPCT/C.II/PV/5, 6, 13
	EPCT/C.II/ST/PV/1, 2, 3 & 6
Reports:	EPCT/C.II/52, 53

New York

Discussion:	EPCT/C.6/23, 34, 105

Geneva

Discussion:	EPCT/EC/PV.2/22
	EPCT/A/SR.14, 15, 17, 18, 37
	EPCT/TAC/SR.11
	EPCT/TAC/PV/27, 28
Reports:	EPCT/135, 160, 180, 183, 186,
	212, 214/Add.1/Rev.1
	EPCT/W/313

Other:	EPCT/189, 196
	EPCT/W/62, 65, 69, 70, 187,
	191, 195, 197, 198, 239, 272,
	301, 318

Havana

Discussion:	E/CONF.2/C.3/SR.28
Reports:	E/CONF.2/C.3/43;
	E/CONF.2/C.6/45

Review Session

Discussion:	SR.9/41, 47
Reports:	W.9/122, 177, 213, 231;
	236/Add.1, L/334, 3S/222
Other:	L/189, L/272/Add.1, 273
	W.9/20/Add.1, 28, 70, 78, 99,
	122

---

[67] Havana Reports, p. 66, para. 73.
[68] *Ibid.*, p. 115, para. 18.
[69] *Ibid.*, p. 114, para. 13.
[70] *Ibid.*, p. 115, paras. 15, 17.
[71] L/334, Report of the Working Party adopted on 3 March 1955, 3S/222, 228.
[72] *Ibid.*
[73] *Ibid.*, 3S/230 para. 36-40; see "Liquidation of Strategic Stocks", Resolution of 4 March 1955, 3S/51.

ARTICLE XVIII

GOVERNMENTAL ASSISTANCE TO ECONOMIC DEVELOPMENT

I.	TEXT OF ARTICLE XVIII, RELEVANT INTERPRETATIVE NOTES AND UNDERSTANDING ON THE BALANCE-OF-PAYMENTS PROVISIONS OF THE GATT 1994		488
II.	INTERPRETATION AND APPLICATION OF ARTICLE XVIII		496
	A. SCOPE AND APPLICATION OF ARTICLE XVIII		496
	1. General issues		496
	2. Preamble: paragraphs 1-6		497
	(1) "the objectives of this Agreement"		497
	(2) "the utmost secrecy"		497
	(3) "low standards of living"; "early stages of development"		497
	(4) "particular industry"		498
	(5) "with a view to raising the general standard of living" (paragraphs 3, 7 and 13)		498
	(6) Paragraph 4(b)		499
	(7) Paragraph 5: consultations when measures of a contracting party cause a decline in export earnings of developing countries dependent on exports of a small number of primary commodities		499
	(8) Annual reviews of measures applied under Article XVIII:C and D		500
	3. Article XVIII:A		500
	(1) "to modify or withdraw a concession"		501
	(2) "such concession was initially negotiated"		501
	4. Article XVIII:B: Import measures for balance-of-payments reasons		501
	(1) Paragraphs 8 and 9		501
	(a) Disinvocations of Article XVIII:B since 1979		501
	(2) Paragraphs 10 and 11: application of balance-of-payments measures		501
	(3) Paragraph 12: consultations and review of balance-of-payments measures		504
	(a) General		504
	(b) Notification of balance-of-payments measures		504
	(c) "shall ... consult with the CONTRACTING PARTIES": procedures and timing for consultations under paragraph 12		505
	(d) "as to the nature of its balance of payments difficulties": scope of consultations under paragraph 12		507
	(e) "the CONTRACTING PARTIES shall review all restrictions applied under this Section"		507
	(f) Sub-paragraphs c(ii), (d) and (e)		508
	(4) Balance-of-payments measures other than quantitative restrictions		508
	5. Article XVIII:C		508
	(1) Invocation of Article XVIII:C		508
	(2) Paragraph 14: "The contracting party concerned shall notify"		509
	(3) Paragraph 16: "the contracting party concerned shall consult"		510
	(4) Paragraph 18: consultations concerning products subject to concessions		510
	(5) Paragraph 21: "it may suspend the application of such substantially equivalent concession or other obligation"		511
	(6) Relationship between Article XVIII:B and C		511
	6. Article XVIII:D		511
	B. RELATIONSHIP BETWEEN ARTICLE XVIII AND OTHER GATT PROVISIONS		511
	1. Article III		511
	2. Article XII		511
	3. Article XIV		512
	4. Article XXIII		512
	5. Article XXIV		512
III.	PREPARATORY WORK AND SUBSEQUENT MODIFICATIONS		512
IV.	RELEVANT DOCUMENTS		513

I. TEXT OF ARTICLE XVIII, RELEVANT INTERPRETATIVE NOTES AND UNDERSTANDING ON THE BALANCE-OF-PAYMENTS PROVISIONS OF GATT 1994

Article XVIII*

Governmental Assistance to Economic Development

1. The contracting parties recognize that the attainment of the objectives of this Agreement will be facilitated by the progressive development of their economies, particularly of those contracting parties the economies of which can only support low standards of living* and are in the early stages of development.*

2. The contracting parties recognize further that it may be necessary for those contracting parties, in order to implement programmes and policies of economic development designed to raise the general standard of living of their people, to take protective or other measures affecting imports, and that such measures are justified in so far as they facilitate the attainment of the objectives of this Agreement. They agree, therefore, that those contracting parties should enjoy additional facilities to enable them (*a*) to maintain sufficient flexibility in their tariff structure to be able to grant the tariff protection required for the establishment of a particular industry* and (*b*) to apply quantitative restrictions for balance of payments purposes in a manner which takes full account of the continued high level of demand for imports likely to be generated by their programmes of economic development.

3. The contracting parties recognize finally that, with those additional facilities which are provided for in Sections A and B of this Article, the provisions of this Agreement would normally be sufficient to enable contracting parties to meet the requirements of their economic development. They agree, however, that there may be circumstances where no measure consistent with those provisions is practicable to permit a contracting party in the process of economic development to grant the governmental assistance required to promote the establishment of particular industries* with a view to raising the general standard of living of its people. Special procedures are laid down in Sections C and D of this Article to deal with those cases.

4. (*a*) Consequently, a contracting party, the economy of which can only support low standards of living* and is in the early stages of development,* shall be free to deviate temporarily from the provisions of the other Articles of this Agreement, as provided in Sections A, B and C of this Article.

(*b*) A contracting party, the economy of which is in the process of development, but which does not come within the scope of sub-paragraph (*a*) above, may submit applications to the CONTRACTING PARTIES under Section D of this Article.

5. The contracting parties recognize that the export earnings of contracting parties, the economies of which are of the type described in paragraph 4 (*a*) and (*b*) above and which depend on exports of a small number of primary commodities, may be seriously reduced by a decline in the sale of such commodities. Accordingly, when the exports of primary commodities by such a contracting party are seriously affected by measures taken by another contracting party, it may have resort to the consultation provisions of Article XXII of this Agreement.

6. The CONTRACTING PARTIES shall review annually all measures applied pursuant to the provisions of Sections C and D of this Article.

Section A

7. (*a*) If a contracting party coming within the scope of paragraph 4 (*a*) of this Article considers it desirable, in order to promote the establishment of a particular industry* with a view to raising the general standard of living of its people, to modify or withdraw a concession included in the appropriate Schedule annexed to this Agreement, it shall notify the CONTRACTING PARTIES to this effect and enter into negotiations with any contracting party with which such concession was initially negotiated, and with any other contracting party determined by the CONTRACTING PARTIES to have a substantial interest therein. If agreement is reached between

such contracting parties concerned, they shall be free to modify or withdraw concessions under the appropriate Schedules to this Agreement in order to give effect to such agreement, including any compensatory adjustments involved.

(b) If agreement is not reached within sixty days after the notification provided for in sub-paragraph (a) above, the contracting party which proposes to modify or withdraw the concession may refer the matter to the CONTRACTING PARTIES which shall promptly examine it. If they find that the contracting party which proposes to modify or withdraw the concession has made every effort to reach an agreement and that the compensatory adjustment offered by it is adequate, that contracting party shall be free to modify or withdraw the concession if, at the same time, it gives effect to the compensatory adjustment. If the CONTRACTING PARTIES do not find that the compensation offered by a contracting party proposing to modify or withdraw the concession is adequate, but find that it has made every reasonable effort to offer adequate compensation, that contracting party shall be free to proceed with such modification or withdrawal. If such action is taken, any other contracting party referred to in sub-paragraph (a) above shall be free to modify or withdraw substantially equivalent concessions initially negotiated with the contracting party which has taken the action.*

Section B

8. The contracting parties recognize that contracting parties coming within the scope of paragraph 4 (a) of this Article tend, when they are in rapid process of development, to experience balance of payments difficulties arising mainly from efforts to expand their internal markets as well as from the instability in their terms of trade.

9. In order to safeguard its external financial position and to ensure a level of reserves adequate for the implementation of its programme of economic development, a contracting party coming within the scope of paragraph 4 (a) of this Article may, subject to the provisions of paragraphs 10 to 12, control the general level of its imports by restricting the quantity or value of merchandise permitted to be imported; *Provided* that the import restrictions instituted, maintained or intensified shall not exceed those necessary:

(a) to forestall the threat of, or to stop, a serious decline in its monetary reserves, or

(b) in the case of a contracting party with inadequate monetary reserves, to achieve a reasonable rate of increase in its reserves.

Due regard shall be paid in either case to any special factors which may be affecting the reserves of the contracting party or its need for reserves, including, where special external credits or other resources are available to it, the need to provide for the appropriate use of such credits or resources.

10. In applying these restrictions, the contracting party may determine their incidence on imports of different products or classes of products in such a way as to give priority to the importation of those products which are more essential in the light of its policy of economic development; *Provided* that the restrictions are so applied as to avoid unnecessary damage to the commercial or economic interests of any other contracting party and not to prevent unreasonably the importation of any description of goods in minimum commercial quantities the exclusion of which would impair regular channels of trade; and *Provided* further that the restrictions are not so applied as to prevent the importation of commercial samples or to prevent compliance with patent, trade mark, copyright or similar procedures.

11. In carrying out its domestic policies, the contracting party concerned shall pay due regard to the need for restoring equilibrium in its balance of payments on a sound and lasting basis and to the desirability of assuring an economic employment of productive resources. It shall progressively relax any restrictions applied under this Section as conditions improve, maintaining them only to the extent necessary under the terms of paragraph 9 of this Article and shall eliminate them when conditions no longer justify such maintenance; *Provided* that no contracting party shall be required to withdraw or modify restrictions on the ground that a change in its development policy would render unnecessary the restrictions which it is applying under this Section.*

12. (*a*) Any contracting party applying new restrictions or raising the general level of its existing restrictions by a substantial intensification of the measures applied under this Section, shall immediately after instituting or intensifying such restrictions (or, in circumstances in which prior consultation is practicable, before doing so) consult with the CONTRACTING PARTIES as to the nature of its balance of payments difficulties, alternative corrective measures which may be available, and the possible effect of the restrictions on the economies of other contracting parties.

(*b*) On a date to be determined by them* the CONTRACTING PARTIES shall review all restrictions still applied under this Section on that date. Beginning two years after that date, contracting parties applying restrictions under this Section shall enter into consultations of the type provided for in sub-paragraph (*a*) above with the CONTRACTING PARTIES at intervals of approximately, but not less than, two years according to a programme to be drawn up each year by the CONTRACTING PARTIES; *Provided* that no consultation under this sub-paragraph shall take place within two years after the conclusion of a consultation of a general nature under any other provision of this paragraph.

(*c*) (i) If, in the course of consultations with a contracting party under sub-paragraph (*a*) or (*b*) of this paragraph, the CONTRACTING PARTIES find that the restrictions are not consistent with the provisions of this Section or with those of Article XIII (subject to the provisions of Article XIV), they shall indicate the nature of the inconsistency and may advise that the restrictions be suitably modified.

(ii) If, however, as a result of the consultations, the CONTRACTING PARTIES determine that the restrictions are being applied in a manner involving an inconsistency of a serious nature with the provisions of this Section or with those of Article XIII (subject to the provisions of Article XIV) and that damage to the trade of any contracting party is caused or threatened thereby, they shall so inform the contracting party applying the restrictions and shall make appropriate recommendations for securing conformity with such provisions within a specified period. If such contracting party does not comply with these recommendations within the specified period, the CONTRACTING PARTIES may release any contracting party the trade of which is adversely affected by the restrictions from such obligations under this Agreement towards the contracting party applying the restrictions as they determine to be appropriate in the circumstances.

(*d*) The CONTRACTING PARTIES shall invite any contracting party which is applying restrictions under this Section to enter into consultations with them at the request of any contracting party which can establish a *prima facie* case that the restrictions are inconsistent with the provisions of this Section or with those of Article XIII (subject to the provisions of Article XIV) and that its trade is adversely affected thereby. However, no such invitation shall be issued unless the CONTRACTING PARTIES have ascertained that direct discussions between the contracting parties concerned have not been successful. If, as a result of the consultations with the CONTRACTING PARTIES no agreement is reached and they determine that the restrictions are being applied inconsistently with such provisions, and that damage to the trade of the contracting party initiating the procedure is caused or threatened thereby, they shall recommend the withdrawal or modification of the restrictions. If the restrictions are not withdrawn or modified within such time as the CONTRACTING PARTIES may prescribe, they may release the contracting party initiating the procedure from such obligations under this Agreement towards the contracting party applying the restrictions as they determine to be appropriate in the circumstances.

(*e*) If a contracting party against which action has been taken in accordance with the last sentence of sub-paragraph (*c*) (ii) or (*d*) of this paragraph, finds that the release of obligations authorized by the CONTRACTING PARTIES adversely affects the operation of its programme and policy of economic development, it shall be free, not later than sixty days after such action is taken, to give written notice to the Executive Secretary to the CONTRACTING PARTIES of its intention to withdraw from this Agreement and such withdrawal shall take effect on the sixtieth day following the day on which the notice is received by him.

(*f*) In proceeding under this paragraph, the CONTRACTING PARTIES shall have due regard to the factors referred to in paragraph 2 of this Article. Determinations under this paragraph shall be rendered expeditiously and, if possible, within sixty days of the initiation of the consultations.

Article XVIII - Governmental Assistance to Economic Development

Section C

13. If a contracting party coming within the scope of paragraph 4 (*a*) of this Article finds that governmental assistance is required to promote the establishment of a particular industry* with a view to raising the general standard of living of its people, but that no measure consistent with the other provisions of this Agreement is practicable to achieve that objective, it may have recourse to the provisions and procedures set out in this Section.*

14. The contracting party concerned shall notify the CONTRACTING PARTIES of the special difficulties which it meets in the achievement of the objective outlined in paragraph 13 of this Article and shall indicate the specific measure affecting imports which it proposes to introduce in order to remedy these difficulties. It shall not introduce that measure before the expiration of the time-limit laid down in paragraph 15 or 17, as the case may be, or if the measure affects imports of a product which is the subject of a concession included in the appropriate Schedule annexed to this Agreement, unless it has secured the concurrence of the CONTRACTING PARTIES in accordance with provisions of paragraph 18; *Provided* that, if the industry receiving assistance has already started production, the contracting party may, after informing the CONTRACTING PARTIES, take such measures as may be necessary to prevent, during that period, imports of the product or products concerned from increasing substantially above a normal level.*

15. If, within thirty days of the notification of the measure, the CONTRACTING PARTIES do not request the contracting party concerned to consult with them,* that contracting party shall be free to deviate from the relevant provisions of the other Articles of this Agreement to the extent necessary to apply the proposed measure.

16. If it is requested by the CONTRACTING PARTIES to do so,* the contracting party concerned shall consult with them as to the purpose of the proposed measure, as to alternative measures which may be available under this Agreement, and as to the possible effect of the measure proposed on the commercial and economic interests of other contracting parties. If, as a result of such consultation, the CONTRACTING PARTIES agree that there is no measure consistent with the other provisions of this Agreement which is practicable in order to achieve the objective outlined in paragraph 13 of this Article, and concur* in the proposed measure, the contracting party concerned shall be released from its obligations under the relevant provisions of the other Articles of this Agreement to the extent necessary to apply that measure.

17. If, within ninety days after the date of the notification of the proposed measure under paragraph 14 of this Article, the CONTRACTING PARTIES have not concurred in such measure, the contracting party concerned may introduce the measure proposed after informing the CONTRACTING PARTIES.

18. If the proposed measure affects a product which is the subject of a concession included in the appropriate Schedule annexed to this Agreement, the contracting party concerned shall enter into consultations with any other contracting party with which the concession was initially negotiated, and with any other contracting party determined by the CONTRACTING PARTIES to have a substantial interest therein. The CONTRACTING PARTIES shall concur* in the measure if they agree that there is no measure consistent with the other provisions of this Agreement which is practicable in order to achieve the objective set forth in paragraph 13 of this Article, and if they are satisfied:

   (*a*) that agreement has been reached with such other contracting parties as a result of the consultations referred to above, or

   (*b*) if no such agreement has been reached within sixty days after the notification provided for in paragraph 14 has been received by the CONTRACTING PARTIES, that the contracting party having recourse to this Section has made all reasonable efforts to reach an agreement and that the interests of other contracting parties are adequately safeguarded.*

The contracting party having recourse to this Section shall thereupon be released from its obligations under the relevant provisions of the other Articles of this Agreement to the extent necessary to permit it to apply the measure.

19. If a proposed measure of the type described in paragraph 13 of this Article concerns an industry the establishment of which has in the initial period been facilitated by incidental protection afforded by restrictions imposed by the contracting party concerned for balance of payments purposes under the relevant provisions of this Agreement, that contracting party may resort to the provisions and procedures of this Section; *Provided* that it shall not apply the proposed measure without the concurrence* of the CONTRACTING PARTIES.*

20. Nothing in the preceding paragraphs of this Section shall authorize any deviation from the provisions of Articles I, II and XIII of this Agreement. The provisos to paragraph 10 of this Article shall also be applicable to any restriction under this Section.

21. At any time while a measure is being applied under paragraph 17 of this Article any contracting party substantially affected by it may suspend the application to the trade of the contracting party having recourse to this Section of such substantially equivalent concessions or other obligations under this Agreement the suspension of which the CONTRACTING PARTIES do not disapprove;* *Provided* that sixty days' notice of such suspension is given to the CONTRACTING PARTIES not later than six months after the measure has been introduced or changed substantially to the detriment of the contracting party affected. Any such contracting party shall afford adequate opportunity for consultation in accordance with the provisions of Article XXII of this Agreement.

Section D

22. A contracting party coming within the scope of sub-paragraph 4 (*b*) of this Article desiring, in the interest of the development of its economy, to introduce a measure of the type described in paragraph 13 of this Article in respect of the establishment of a particular industry* may apply to the CONTRACTING PARTIES for approval of such measure. The CONTRACTING PARTIES shall promptly consult with such contracting party and shall, in making their decision, be guided by the considerations set out in paragraph 16. If the CONTRACTING PARTIES concur* in the proposed measure the contracting party concerned shall be released from its obligations under the relevant provisions of the other Articles of this Agreement to the extent necessary to permit it to apply the measure. If the proposed measure affects a product which is the subject of a concession included in the appropriate Schedule annexed to this Agreement, the provisions of paragraph 18 shall apply.*

23. Any measure applied under this Section shall comply with the provisions of paragraph 20 of this Article.

Interpretative Notes from Annex I

Ad Article XVIII

The CONTRACTING PARTIES and the contracting parties concerned shall preserve the utmost secrecy in respect of matters arising under this Article.

Paragraphs 1 and 4

1. When they consider whether the economy of a contracting party "can only support low standards of living", the CONTRACTING PARTIES shall take into consideration the normal position of that economy and shall not base their determination on exceptional circumstances such as those which may result from the temporary existence of exceptionally favourable conditions for the staple export product or products of such contracting party.

2. The phrase "in the early stages of development" is not meant to apply only to contracting parties which have just started their economic development, but also to contracting parties the economies of which are undergoing a process of industrialization to correct an excessive dependence on primary production.

Paragraphs 2, 3, 7, 13 and 22

The reference to the establishment of particular industries shall apply not only to the establishment of a new industry, but also to the establishment of a new branch of production in an existing industry and to the substantial transformation of an existing industry, and to the substantial expansion of an existing industry supplying a relatively small proportion of the domestic demand. It shall also cover the reconstruction of an industry destroyed or substantially damaged as a result of hostilities or natural disasters.

Paragraph 7 (b)

A modification or withdrawal, pursuant to paragraph 7 (*b*), by a contracting party, other than the applicant contracting party, referred to in paragraph 7 (*a*), shall be made within six months of the day on which the action is taken by the applicant contracting party, and shall become effective on the thirtieth day following the day on which such modification or withdrawal has been notified to the CONTRACTING PARTIES.

Paragraph 11

The second sentence in paragraph 11 shall not be interpreted to mean that a contracting party is required to relax or remove restrictions if such relaxation or removal would thereupon produce conditions justifying the intensification or institution, respectively, of restrictions under paragraph 9 of Article XVIII.

Paragraph 12 (b)

The date referred to in paragraph 12 (*b*) shall be the date determined by the CONTRACTING PARTIES in accordance with the provisions of paragraph 4 (*b*) of Article XII of this Agreement.

Paragraphs 13 and 14

It is recognized that, before deciding on the introduction of a measure and notifying the CONTRACTING PARTIES in accordance with paragraph 14, a contracting party may need a reasonable period of time to assess the competitive position of the industry concerned.

Paragraphs 15 and 16

It is understood that the CONTRACTING PARTIES shall invite a contracting party proposing to apply a measure under Section C to consult with them pursuant to paragraph 16 if they are requested to do so by a contracting party the trade of which would be appreciably affected by the measure in question.

Paragraphs 16, 18, 19 and 22

1. It is understood that the CONTRACTING PARTIES may concur in a proposed measure subject to specific conditions or limitations. If the measure as applied does not conform to the terms of the concurrence it will to that extent be deemed a measure in which the CONTRACTING PARTIES have not concurred. In cases in which the CONTRACTING PARTIES have concurred in a measure for a specified period, the contracting party concerned, if it finds that the maintenance of the measure for a further period of time is required to achieve the objective for which the measure was originally taken, may apply to the CONTRACTING PARTIES for an extension of that period in accordance with the provisions and procedures of Section C or D, as the case may be.

2. It is expected that the CONTRACTING PARTIES will, as a rule, refrain from concurring in a measure which is likely to cause serious prejudice to exports of a commodity on which the economy of a contracting party is largely dependent.

Paragraph 18 and 22

The phrase "that the interests of other contracting parties are adequately safeguarded" is meant to provide latitude sufficient to permit consideration in each case of the most appropriate method of safeguarding those interests. The appropriate method may, for instance, take the form of an additional concession to be applied by the contracting party having recourse to Section C or D during such time as the deviation from the other Articles of the Agreement would remain in force or of the temporary suspension by any other contracting party referred to in paragraph 18 of a concession substantially equivalent to the impairment due to the introduction of the measure in question. Such contracting party would have the right to safeguard its interests through such a temporary suspension of a concession; *Provided* that this right will not be exercised when, in the case of a measure imposed by a contracting party coming within the scope of paragraph 4 (*a*), the CONTRACTING PARTIES have determined that the extent of the compensatory concession proposed was adequate.

Paragraph 19

The provisions of paragraph 19 are intended to cover the cases where an industry has been in existence beyond the "reasonable period of time" referred to in the note to paragraphs 13 and 14, and should not be so construed as to deprive a contracting party coming within the scope of paragraph 4 (*a*) of Article XVIII, of its right to resort to the other provisions of Section C, including paragraph 17, with regard to a newly established industry even though it has benefited from incidental protection afforded by balance of payments import restrictions.

Paragraph 21

Any measure taken pursuant to the provisions of paragraph 21 shall be withdrawn forthwith if the action taken in accordance with paragraph 17 is withdrawn or if the CONTRACTING PARTIES concur in the measure proposed after the expiration of the ninety-day time limit specified in paragraph 17.

Ad Articles XI, XII, XIII, XIV and XVIII

Throughout Articles XI, XII, XIII, XIV and XVIII, the terms "import restrictions" or "export restrictions" include restrictions made effective through state-trading operations.

UNDERSTANDING ON THE BALANCE-OF-PAYMENTS PROVISIONS
OF THE GENERAL AGREEMENT ON TARIFFS AND TRADE 1994

Members,

Recognizing the provisions of Articles XII and XVIII:B of GATT 1994 and of the Declaration on Trade Measures Taken for Balance-of-Payments Purposes adopted on 28 November 1979 (BISD 26S/205-209, referred to in this Understanding as the "1979 Declaration") and in order to clarify such provisions[1];

Hereby *agree* as follows:

Application of Measures

1. Members confirm their commitment to announce publicly, as soon as possible, time-schedules for the removal of restrictive import measures taken for balance-of-payments purposes. It is understood that such time-schedules may be modified as appropriate to take into account changes in the balance-of-payments situation. Whenever a time-schedule is not publicly announced by a Member, that Member shall provide justification as to the reasons therefor.

2. Members confirm their commitment to give preference to those measures which have the least disruptive effect on trade. Such measures (referred to in this Understanding as "price-based measures") shall be understood to include import surcharges, import deposit requirements or other equivalent trade measures with an impact on the price of imported goods. It is understood that, notwithstanding the provisions of Article II, price-based measures taken for balance-of-payments purposes may be applied by a Member in excess of the duties inscribed in the Schedule of that Member. Furthermore, that Member shall indicate the amount by which the price-based measure exceeds the bound duty clearly and separately under the notification procedures of this Understanding.

3. Members shall seek to avoid the imposition of new quantitative restrictions for balance-of-payments purposes unless, because of a critical balance-of-payments situation, price-based measures cannot arrest a sharp deterioration in the external payments position. In those cases in which a Member applies quantitative restrictions, it shall provide justification as to the reasons why price-based measures are not an adequate instrument to deal with the balance-of-payments situation. A Member maintaining quantitative restrictions shall indicate in successive consultations the progress made in significantly reducing the incidence and restrictive effect of such measures. It is understood that not more than one type of restrictive import measure taken for balance-of-payments purposes may be applied on the same product.

4. Members confirm that restrictive import measures taken for balance-of-payments purposes may only be applied to control the general level of imports and may not exceed what is necessary to address the balance-of-payments situation. In order to minimize any incidental protective effects, a Member shall administer restrictions in a transparent manner. The authorities of the importing Member shall provide adequate justification as to the criteria used to determine which products are subject to restriction. As provided in paragraph 3 of Article XII and paragraph 10 of Article XVIII, Members may, in the case of certain essential products, exclude or limit the application of surcharges applied across the board or other measures applied for balance-of-payments purposes. The term 'essential products' shall be understood to mean products which meet basic consumption needs or which contribute to the Member's effort to improve its balance-of-payments situation, such as capital goods or inputs needed for production. In the administration of quantitative restrictions, a Member shall use discretionary licensing only when unavoidable and shall phase it out progressively. Appropriate justification shall be provided as to the criteria used to determine allowable import quantities or values.

Procedures for Balance-of-Payments Consultations

5. The Committee on Balance-of-Payments Restrictions (referred to in this Understanding as the "Committee") shall carry out consultations in order to review all restrictive import measures taken for balance-of-payments purposes. The membership of the Committee is open to all Members indicating their wish to serve on it. The Committee shall follow the procedures for consultations on balance-of-payments restrictions approved on 28 April 1970 (BISD 18S/48-53, referred to in this Understanding as "full consultation procedures"), subject to the provisions set out below.

6. A Member applying new restrictions or raising the general level of its existing restrictions by a substantial intensification of the measures shall enter into consultations with the Committee within four months of the adoption of such measures. The Member adopting such measures may request that a consultation be held under paragraph 4(a) of Article XII or paragraph 12(a) of Article XVIII as appropriate. If no such request has been made, the Chairman of the Committee shall invite the Member to hold such a consultation. Factors that may be

---

[1] Nothing in this Understanding is intended to modify the rights and obligations of Members under Articles XII or XVIII:B of GATT 1994. The provisions of Articles XXII and XXIII of GATT 1994 as elaborated and applied by the Dispute Settlement Understanding may be invoked with respect to any matters arising from the application of restrictive import measures taken for balance-of-payments purposes.

examined in the consultation would include, *inter alia*, the introduction of new types of restrictive measures for balance-of-payments purposes, or an increase in the level or product coverage of restrictions.

7. All restrictions applied for balance-of-payments purposes shall be subject to periodic review in the Committee under paragraph 4(b) of Article XII or under paragraph 12(b) of Article XVIII, subject to the possibility of altering the periodicity of consultations in agreement with the consulting Member or pursuant to any specific review procedure that may be recommended by the General Council.

8. Consultations may be held under the simplified procedures approved on 19 December 1972 (BISD 20S/47-49, referred to in this Understanding as "simplified consultation procedures") in the case of least-developed country Members or in the case of developing country Members which are pursuing liberalization efforts in conformity with the schedule presented to the Committee in previous consultations. Simplified consultation procedures may also be used when the Trade Policy Review of a developing country Member is scheduled for the same calendar year as the date fixed for the consultations. In such cases the decision as to whether full consultation procedures should be used will be made on the basis of the factors enumerated in paragraph 8 of the 1979 Declaration. Except in the case of least-developed country Members, no more than two successive consultations may be held under simplified consultation procedures.

Notification and Documentation

9. A Member shall notify to the General Council the introduction of or any changes in the application of restrictive import measures taken for balance-of-payments purposes, as well as any modifications in time-schedules for the removal of such measures as announced under paragraph 1. Significant changes shall be notified to the General Council prior to or not later than 30 days after their announcement. On a yearly basis, each Member shall make available to the Secretariat a consolidated notification, including all changes in laws, regulations, policy statements or public notices, for examination by Members. Notifications shall include full information, as far as possible, at the tariff-line level, on the type of measures applied, the criteria used for their administration, product coverage and trade flows affected.

10. At the request of any Member, notifications may be reviewed by the Committee. Such reviews would be limited to the clarification of specific issues raised by a notification or examination of whether a consultation under paragraph 4(a) of Article XII or paragraph 12(a) of Article XVIII is required. Members which have reasons to believe that a restrictive import measure applied by another Member was taken for balance-of-payments purposes may bring the matter to the attention of the Committee. The Chairman of the Committee shall request information on the measure and make it available to all Members. Without prejudice to the right of any member of the Committee to seek appropriate clarifications in the course of consultations, questions may be submitted in advance for consideration by the consulting Member.

11. The consulting Member shall prepare a Basic Document for the consultations which, in addition to any other information considered to be relevant, should include: *(a)* an overview of the balance-of-payments situation and prospects, including a consideration of the internal and external factors having a bearing on the balance-of-payments situation and the domestic policy measures taken in order to restore equilibrium on a sound and lasting basis; *(b)* a full description of the restrictions applied for balance-of-payments purposes, their legal basis and steps taken to reduce incidental protective effects; *(c)* measures taken since the last consultation to liberalize import restrictions, in the light of the conclusions of the Committee; *(d)* a plan for the elimination and progressive relaxation of remaining restrictions. References may be made, when relevant, to the information provided in other notifications or reports made to the WTO. Under simplified consultation procedures, the consulting Member shall submit a written statement containing essential information on the elements covered by the Basic Document.

12. The Secretariat shall, with a view to facilitating the consultations in the Committee, prepare a factual background paper dealing with the different aspects of the plan for consultations. In the case of developing country Members, the Secretariat document shall include relevant background and analytical material on the incidence of the external trading environment on the balance-of-payments situation and prospects of the consulting Member. The technical assistance services of the Secretariat shall, at the request of a developing country Member, assist in preparing the documentation for the consultations.

Conclusions of Balance-of-Payments Consultations

13. The Committee shall report on its consultations to the General Council. When full consultation procedures have been used, the report should indicate the Committee's conclusions on the different elements of the plan for consultations, as well as the facts and reasons on which they are based. The Committee shall endeavour to include in its conclusions proposals for recommendations aimed at promoting the implementation of Articles XII and XVIII:B, the 1979 Declaration and this Understanding. In those cases in which a time-schedule has been presented for the removal of restrictive measures taken for balance-of-payments purposes, the General Council may recommend that, in adhering to such a time-schedule, a Member shall be deemed to be in compliance with its GATT 1994 obligations. Whenever the General Council has made specific recommendations, the rights and obligations of Members shall be assessed in the light of such recommendations. In the absence of specific proposals for recommendations by the General Council, the Committee's conclusions should record the different views expressed in the Committee. When simplified consultation procedures have been used, the report shall include a summary of the main elements discussed in the Committee and a decision on whether full consultation procedures are required.

II. INTERPRETATION AND APPLICATION OF ARTICLE XVIII

A. Scope and Application of Article XVIII

1. General issues

The present text of Articles XII and XVIII was agreed in the 1954-55 Review Session, and entered into effect on 7 October 1957. The principal source concerning the drafting of Articles XII and XVIII:B, C and D is the Report of the Review Working Party on "Quantitative Restrictions".[2] Section XVIII:A was redrafted in the Review Working Party on Schedules and Customs Administration, together with Article XXVIII; the Report of that Working Party[3] is the principal source concerning its drafting.

Articles XII and XVIII:B have been amplified by detailed consultation procedures introduced in 1970, by "simplified" consultation procedures for developing countries introduced in 1972 and by provisions on the application of the Articles and consultation procedures laid down in the 1979 Declaration on Trade Measures Taken for Balance-of-Payments Purposes, which extend the GATT examination of the balance-of-payments provisions from quantitative restrictions alone to all trade measures taken for balance-of-payments purposes.

The Report of the Review Working Party on "Quantitative Restrictions" notes concerning the general orientation of Article XVIII as redrafted in 1955:

"... The general concept of the new Article is that economic development is consistent with the objectives of the General Agreement and that the raising of the general standard of living of the underdeveloped countries which should be the result of economic development will facilitate the attainment of the objectives of the Agreement. In that sense, the new text represents a new and more positive approach to the problem of economic development and to the ways and means of reconciling the requirements of economic development with the obligations undertaken under the General Agreement regarding the conduct of commercial policy.

"The recognition of this general concept led the Working Party to the conclusion that a suitable solution could be found in an application to the special circumstances of economic development of the principle underlying Article XIX, i.e. that when a country is faced by a conflict between a vital domestic interest and the interests of its exporters as secured by the provisions of the General Agreement, it should, in the last resort, be possible for the government of that country, without infringing its obligations under the General Agreement, to take such action as it considers to be necessary, on the condition that any other contracting party affected by such action would also be free to take such measures as may be necessary to restore the balance of benefits. It is clear that such a condition has an important restraining influence since, before taking action, the government concerned would have to weigh carefully the advantages and disadvantages of unilateral action. Moreover, the new Article contains a number of safeguards to ensure that the exercise of the right to deviate from an obligation under the Agreement would be strictly limited to cases where no other alternative measure consistent with the Agreement would be available, that the new provisions would be reserved exclusively to those under-developed countries which really need such facilities, and that the measures permitted under the Article should be directly related to the requirements of economic development and therefore would contribute in a positive manner to the growth of the country's economy as a whole. Finally, in the various sections of the Article, resort to unilateral action is only permitted after various requirements regarding consultation with the CONTRACTING PARTIES and, in certain cases, negotiation with individual governments have been complied with. Those safeguards are such that it may be reasonably expected that the number of cases in which action under Article XVIII would be taken without the concurrence of the CONTRACTING PARTIES or without agreement with the contracting parties affected would be reduced to a minimum".[4]

---

[2]L/332/Rev.1 and Addenda, adopted on 2, 4 and 5 March 1955, 3S/170.
[3]L/329, adopted on 26 February 1955, 3S/205, 215.
[4]L/332/Rev.1 and Addenda, adopted on 2, 4 and 5 March 1955, 3S/170, 179-180, paras. 35-36.

2. Preamble: paragraphs 1-6

The Report of the Review Working Party on "Quantitative Restrictions" notes that

> "The *Preamble* contains the recognition of the general principles governing the Article and attempts to define the special problems which economic development may raise for countries having a low standard of living. It also sets out the criteria by which the contracting parties would be considered to be entitled to the facilities of this Article."[5]

(1) "the objectives of this Agreement"

During the Review Session, when the present text of Article XVIII was drafted, it was also agreed to incorporate the amended text of the Preamble to the General Agreement into the General Agreement as a new Article I entitled "Objectives". However, this change did not enter into effect because the Protocol Amending Part I and Articles XXIX and XXX did not achieve the necessary unanimous approval and was abandoned. See also references to "objectives" in the Preamble, Articles XXXVI:1 and XXXVII:2(b)(iii), and the Note *Ad* Article XXXVI:1.

(2) "the utmost secrecy"

The Note *Ad* Article XVIII, which incorporates the former text of Article XVIII:2 before the Review Session, provides that "The CONTRACTING PARTIES and the contracting parties concerned shall preserve the utmost secrecy in respect of matters arising under this Article". See the discussion on secrecy in balance-of-payments consultations in the chapter on Article XII.

(3) "low standards of living"; "early stages of development"

The Report of the Review Working Party on "Quantitative Restrictions" notes that

> "... resort to Article XVIII would not be open to all contracting parties, but, apart from Section D, only to countries which are in the early stages of their development and whose economy can only support low standards of living. This limitation appears to be justified by the fact that it would be more difficult for countries having limited resources at their disposal and depending on primary production to rely exclusively on measures consistent with the General Agreement in order to solve the transitional problems which may arise from the implementation of programmes of economic development ...".[6]

See the Interpretative Notes to paragraphs 1 and 4. See also the 1949 "Questionnaire relating to statements in support of measures for which a release is sought under Article XVIII".[7]

In the 1957 Panel Report on "Applications by Ceylon," the "Panel on Article XVIII Applications" considered the eligibility of the applicant under paragraph 4(a) to resort to Section C of Article XVIII. See paragraph 4 of this report for the various criteria used by the panel (per capita gross national product; share of manufacturing, mining and construction in the gross national product).[8] The 1958 Report on "Consultations and Review Regarding Balance-of-Payments Restrictions" notes "the recommendation of the Chairman of the CONTRACTING PARTIES that it be placed on record that twelve of the contracting parties applying balance-of-payments import restrictions at present fulfil the requirements of Article XVIII:4 and that their restrictions be considered as being applied under Article XVIII:B rather than Article XII".[9]

---

[5] *Ibid.*, 3S/182, para. 41.
[6] *Ibid.*, 3S/180-181, para. 37.
[7] Adopted on 10 August 1949, II/63-65.
[8] L/751, adopted on 28 November 1957, 6S/112, 113, para. 4.
[9] L/931, adopted on 22 November 1958, 7S/90, 92, para. 8. The twelve contracting parties referred to were: Brazil, Chile, Ghana, Greece, India, Indonesia, Malaysia, Myanmar, Pakistan, Sri Lanka, Turkey and Uruguay.

In a few instances consultations have been conducted concerning balance-of-payments measures without reference to either Article XII or Article XVIII.[10] In another instance a contracting party has consulted concerning the same measures under Article XVIII:B and subsequently under Article XII.[11]

(4)   "particular industry"

See the Interpretative Note.

(5)   "with a view to raising the general standard of living" (paragraphs 3, 7 and 13)

The Report of the Review Working Party on "Quantitative Restrictions" notes that this phrase "has been used instead of the words 'in order to raise the general standard of living' which was contained in earlier drafts. The Working Party felt that this more flexible form of words would cover cases where the direct contribution which the establishment of a new industry was expected to make to the general standard of living of the country was not appreciable".[12]

The Decision on "Safeguard Action for Development Purposes" of 28 November 1979 provides as follows:

"1.   The CONTRACTING PARTIES recognize that the implementation by less-developed contracting parties of programmes and policies of economic development aimed at raising the standard of living of the people may involve in addition to the establishment of particular industries[13] the development of new or the modification or extension of existing production structures with a view to achieving fuller and more efficient use of resources in accordance with the priorities of their economic development. Accordingly, they agree that a less-developed contracting party may, to achieve these objectives, modify or withdraw concessions included in the appropriate schedules annexed to the General Agreement as provided for in Section A of Article XVIII or, where no measure consistent with the other provisions of the General Agreement is practicable to achieve these objectives, have recourse to Section C of Article XVIII, with the additional flexibility provided for below. In taking such action the less-developed contracting party concerned shall give due regard to the objectives of the General Agreement and to the need to avoid unnecessary damage to the trade of other contracting parties.

"2.   The CONTRACTING PARTIES recognize further that there may be unusual circumstances where delay in the application of measures which a less-developed contracting party wishes to introduce under Section A or Section C of Article XVIII may give rise to difficulties in the application of its programmes and policies of economic development for the aforesaid purposes. They agree, therefore, that in such circumstances, the less-developed contracting party concerned may deviate from the provisions of Section A and paragraphs 14, 15, 17 and 18 of Section C to the extent necessary for introducing the measures contemplated on a provisional basis immediately after notification.

"3.   It is understood that all other requirements of the preambular part of Article XVIII and of Sections A and C of that Article, as well as the Notes and Supplementary Provisions set out in Annex I under these Sections will continue to apply to the measures to which this Decision relates.

"4.   The CONTRACTING PARTIES shall review this Decision in the light of experience with its operation, with a view to determining whether it should be extended, modified or discontinued".[14]

---

[10]Israel (BOP/R/90, BOP/R/101, BOP/R/113, BOP/R/129, BOP/R/142, BOP/R/155, BOP/R/170, BOP/R/187, BOP/R/195, BOP/R/210); Portugal (BOP/R/62, BOP/R/93, BOP/R/106, BOP/R/111, BOP/R/118, BOP/R/125, BOP/R/134, BOP/R/145, BOP/R/152); South Africa (BOP/R/92, BOP/R/211).

[11]Greece (Consultations under Article XVIII:B in BOP/R/89, BOP/R/100, BOP/R/114, BOP/R/123; Article XVIII:B disinvoked, 1984; consultation under Article XII, BOP/R/160; Article XII disinvoked 1987).

[12]L/332/Rev.1 and Addenda, adopted on 2, 4 and 5 March 1955, 3S/170, 182-183, para. 42.

[13]Footnote 1 to the Decision provides: "As referred to in paragraphs 2, 3, 7, 13 and 22 of Article XVIII and in the Note to these paragraphs".

[14]L/4897, Decision of 28 November 1979, 26S/209.

(6) Paragraph 4(b)

The Report of the Review Working Party on "Quantitative Restrictions" notes that "The clause in sub-paragraph 4(b) reading 'whose economy is in the process of development' should not be construed as a legal limitation on the eligibility of countries to submit applications under Section D, but as a general indication of the type of economy whose need that Section is intended to meet".[15]

On 19 May 1965, Australia accepted the Protocol Introducing Part IV with a Declaration stating, *inter alia*, that Australia was "one of the contracting parties referred to in Article XVIII:4(b) of the General Agreement, the economy of which is in the course of industrial development and which is seeking to avoid an excessive dependence on a limited range of primary products for its export earnings but which is not a less-developed country".[16]

(7) Paragraph 5: consultations when measures of a contracting party cause a decline in export earnings of developing countries dependent on exports of a small number of primary commodities

During the 1954-55 Review Session, Pakistan proposed that when any developing country was affected by a decline in imports by a particular country of primary commodities exported by it, or by measures likely to lead to such a decline, the developing country be able to ask for consultations; the proposal stated that "where a grave threat has arisen or is likely to arise to the economy of an under-developed country consequent upon measures taken by the government or quasi-government organizations of another contracting party the former may be able, at the discretion of the CONTRACTING PARTIES, to invoke the procedure of multilateral consultations".[17] A sub-group of Review Working Party IV which studied the Pakistan proposal proposed the present text of Articles XVIII:5 and XXII:2.[18] The Report of Review Working Party I on "Quantitative Restrictions" notes that the insertion of paragraph 5 had been recommended "to refer specifically to the consultation procedure under Article XXII in cases of sudden falls in the sale of primary commodities".[19]

The Resolution on "Particular Difficulties Connected with Trade in Primary Commodities" adopted in the Eleventh Session in 1956 provided, *inter alia*, that the CONTRACTING PARTIES "*Resolve* ... that it would be appropriate for them to enter into consultations on problems arising out of the trade in primary commodities pursuant to the provisions of paragraph 2 of Article XXII and of paragraph 5 of Article XVIII ...".[20] The Report of the Working Party that drafted the Resolution, on "Particular Difficulties Connected with Trade in Primary Commodities", also noted the ruling made at the Tenth Session that the CONTRACTING PARTIES have the competence to deal, at the request of one or more contracting parties, with difficulties arising in connexion with international trade in primary commodities.[21] The Report provides that

"... In addition to this broad competence which would make it possible for any contracting party to submit to the CONTRACTING PARTIES any particular difficulties which it was experiencing in connexion with trade in primary commodities, and which difficulties were in its view such as to impede the attainment of the objectives of the General Agreement, there are specific provisions in the General Agreement which afford an opportunity for contracting parties to secure consideration of special problems arising in this field ... difficulties of this kind would be appropriate matters to bring forward under Article XXII, which, when the revised text comes into effect, will provide not only for bilateral consultations, but also for consultations with the CONTRACTING PARTIES as a whole. Finally, the revised text of paragraph 5 of Article XVIII makes particular reference to problems arising out of exports of primary commodities and for consultations regarding these problems in accordance with the provisions of Article XXII".[22]

---

[15] L/332/Rev.1 and Addenda, adopted on 2, 4 and 5 March 1955, 3S/170, 186, para. 54.
[16] Status of Legal Instruments, p. 2-14.2. See also statements of Australia, New Zealand and South Africa, 2SS/SR.4 and 5.
[17] W.9/134; see also L/291.
[18] W.9/180, "Report by Sub-Group C on the Pakistan Proposal Relating to the Off-take of Primary Commodities"; see also Spec/92/55 and the Report of the Working Party on "Organizational and Functional Questions", L/327, adopted on 28 February, 5 and 7 March 1955, 3S/231, 244, para. 42.
[19] L/332/Rev.1 and Addenda, adopted on 2, 4 and 5 March 1955, 3S/170, 182, para. 41.
[20] Resolution of 17 November 1956, 5S/26, 27, para. 3.
[21] See ruling at SR.10/19, p. 218.
[22] L/592/Rev.1, adopted on 17 November 1956, 5S/87, 88, para. 1.

The Report of the Working Party in the Fourteenth Session on " Impact of Commodity Problems on International Trade" further noted: "... The General Agreement offers facilities for bilateral and multilateral consultations of which governments may avail themselves when difficulties arise in international commodity trade. ... Contracting parties, whether importing or exporting countries, can avail themselves of the provisions of Article XXII of the General Agreement and initiate consultations under that Article when difficulties arise in connexion with their commodity trade".[23]

In 1981 Peru requested consultations with the United States under the Resolution of 4 March 1955 on the liquidation of strategic stocks and the provisions of Article XVIII:5 and Article XXII:1 of the General Agreement because of prejudice caused to the economy of Peru by the liquidation of United States strategic stocks of silver.[24]

See also Articles XXXVI:4 and XXXVII:2, and the material in this Index on Articles XXII:2 and XXV:1.

(8) Annual reviews of measures applied under Article XVIII:C and D

The Report of the Review Working Party on "Quantitative Restrictions" notes:

"Paragraph 6 of the preamble provides for an annual review of the deviations from the provisions of the Agreement. This review is intended to provide an opportunity for discussing the effects of the measures applied under Sections C and D, the progress made by the industries in question and the general operation of these Sections. It is agreed that the CONTRACTING PARTIES shall not withdraw their concurrence or modify the terms of a concurrence during the period of validity for which it has been given, or request the withdrawal or modification of a measure applied in full accordance with the terms of that concurrence".[25]

All measures applied pursuant to the provisions of Section C were reviewed annually.[26] The seventh and most recent review, conducted at the Twenty-fourth Session in November 1967, noted that Ceylon was no longer applying measures under Section C.[27] No contracting party has had recourse to Section D.

3. Article XVIII:A

The Report of the Review Working Party on "Schedules and Customs Administration" notes as follows concerning the drafting of Article XVIII:A at the Review Session:

"... Section A ... permits a contracting party, which comes within the definition in paragraph 4(a) ... to enter into negotiations for the modification of a concession, in order to promote the establishment of an industry, with the country with which it was initially negotiated and with other substantially interested countries. If agreement is not reached within sixty days the matter may be referred to the CONTRACTING PARTIES. If the CONTRACTING PARTIES find that the contracting party which initiated the negotiation has made every effort to reach an agreement and has offered an adequate compensatory adjustment they can allow the contracting party to modify or withdraw the concession.

"The Working Party recommends an addition to Section A to provide that the CONTRACTING PARTIES may allow the applicant contracting party to modify or withdraw concessions in cases where it is unable, for good reasons, to provide adequate compensation; the provision corresponds to that of Article XXVIII:4(d) including the right of other contracting parties to modify or withdraw substantially equivalent concessions initially negotiated with that contracting party".[28]

---

[23]L/1103, adopted on 20 November 1959, 8S/76, 84, para. 35.
[24]L/5264.
[25]L/332/Rev.1 and Addenda, adopted on 2, 4 and 5 March 1955, 3S/170, 182, para. 41.
[26]Reports of these annual reviews appear at 7S/71, 8S/97, 9S/101, 10S/106, 11S/158, 13S/65, 14S/127, and 15S/65.
[27]15S/65.
[28]L/329, adopted on 26 February 1955, 3S/205, 215, paras. 22-23. See also documents from the Review Session on the drafting of Article XVIII:A: reports in W.9/17, W.9/43, Sec/54/140, W.9/206, W.9/212+Corr.1; proposals in W.9/37, W.9/39, W.9/40, W.9/49.

As of March 1994, Section A of Article XVIII had been invoked nine times: by Benelux on behalf of Suriname (1958), Greece (1956, 1965), Indonesia (1983), Korea (1958), and Sri Lanka (twice in 1955 and once each in 1956 and 1957).

See also: the provisions of the Decision of 28 November 1979 on "Safeguard Action for Development Purposes" above at page 498; the Interpretative Notes to Section A; and the material under Article XXVIII:4.

(1) "to modify or withdraw a concession"

The Decisions of 19 November 1968 and 26 March 1980 on "Procedures for Modification and Rectification of Schedules of Tariff Concessions" include in their scope modifications resulting from action under Article XVIII.[29] The Guidelines adopted on 10 November 1980 on "Procedures for Negotiations under Article XXVIII" provide in paragraph 10 that "These procedures are in relevant parts also valid for renegotiations under Article XVIII, paragraph 7 ...".[30]

(2) "such concession was initially negotiated"

See Article XXVIII; see also the discussion of "floating initial negotiating rights" under Article XXVIII.

4. Article XVIII:B: Import measures for balance-of-payments reasons

(1) Paragraphs 8 and 9

The Report of the Review Working Party on "Quantitative Restrictions" notes that

"... Although all countries in balance-of-payments difficulties inevitably have a large number of problems in common and, therefore, the procedures relating to balance-of-payments restrictions are not fundamentally different, nevertheless the countries coming under Section B of Article XVIII face special additional problems which the provisions have been adjusted to meet. The Working Party has recognized that for such countries balance-of-payments difficulties will tend to be generated by development itself. In addition, paragraph 9, although modelled on paragraphs 1 and 2 of Article XII, recognizes that the reserve problem for these countries is one of the adequacy of the reserves in relation to their programme of economic development, that for this reason the word 'imminent' which occurs in paragraph 2(a) is inappropriate in this context, and that in order to safeguard their external position these countries may need over a period of time to control the general level of their imports in order to prevent that level from rising beyond the means available to pay for imports as the progress of development programmes creates new demands".[31]

(a) Disinvocations of Article XVIII:B since 1979

Contracting parties having disinvoked Article XVIII:B since 1979 are indicated in Table B following the chapter on Article XII. See also the Secretariat Note of 24 June 1988 on "Consultations Held in the Committee on Balance-of-Payments Restrictions under Articles XII and XVIII:B since 1975".[32]

---

[29]L/3131, 16S/16; L/4962, 27S/25, para. 1.
[30]C/113 and Corr.1, 27S/26, 28, para. 10.
[31]L/332/Rev.1 and Addenda, adopted on 2, 4 and 5 March 1955, 3S/170, 183, para. 44.
[32]MTN.GNG/NG7/W/46, para. 31.

(2) Paragraphs 10 and 11: application of balance-of-payments measures

The Report of the Review Working Party on "Quantitative Restrictions" notes that

> "Paragraphs 10 and 11 reproduce in substance the provisions of sub-paragraph 2(b) and of paragraph 3 of Article XII. These paragraphs have however been re-arranged and the thought contained in the first sentence of sub-paragraph 3(d) of Article XII has been omitted as it was already expressed in the first two paragraphs of Section B ...".[33]

See also the material in this volume on paragraphs 2(b) and 3 of Article XII.

The 1979 "Declaration on Trade Measures Taken for Balance-of-Payments Purposes" provides that:

> "The CONTRACTING PARTIES,
>
> "*Having regard* to the provisions of Articles XII and XVIII:B of the General Agreement; ...
>
> "*Reaffirming* that restrictive import measures taken for balance-of-payments purposes should not be taken for the purpose of protecting a particular industry or sector;
>
> "*Convinced* that the contracting parties should endeavour to avoid that restrictive import measures taken for balance-of-payments purposes stimulate new investments that would not be economically viable in the absence of the measures;
>
> "*Recognizing* that the less-developed contracting parties must take into account their individual development, financial and trade situation when implementing restrictive import measures taken for balance-of-payments purposes; ...
>
> "*Agree* as follows:
>
> "... The application of restrictive import measures taken for balance-of-payments purposes shall be subject to the following conditions in addition to those provided for in Articles XII, XIII, XV and XVIII without prejudice to other provisions of the General Agreement:
>
> "(a) In applying restrictive import measures contracting parties shall abide by the disciplines provided for in the GATT and give preference to the measure which has the least disruptive effect on trade[34];
>
> "(b) The simultaneous application of more than one type of trade measure for this purpose should be avoided;
>
> "(c) Whenever practicable, contracting parties shall publicly announce a time schedule for the removal of the measures.
>
> "The provisions of this paragraph are not intended to modify the substantive provisions of the General Agreement".[35]

In the three parallel Panel Reports in 1989 on "Republic of Korea - Restrictions on Imports of Beef" in response to complaints by Australia,[36] the United States,[37] and New Zealand,[38] the Panel, having decided that the

---

[33]*Ibid.*, 3S/183, para. 45.
[34]Footnote 1 to the Decision provides: "It is understood that the less-developed contracting parties must take into account their individual development, financial and trade situation when selecting the particular measure to be applied".
[35]L/4904, adopted on 28 November 1979, 26S/205, preamble and para. 1.
[36]L/6504, adopted on 7 November 1989, 36S/202.
[37]L/6503, adopted on 7 November 1989, 36S/268.
[38]L/6505, adopted on 7 November 1989, 36S/234.

consistency of restrictive measures with Article XVIII:B could be examined under Article XXIII, examined Korea's Article XVIII:B justification for its import restrictions on beef, which it was contended were not justified because it was alleged that Korea no longer had balance-of-payments problems.

"... The Panel noted that Korea had maintained import restrictions on beef on balance-of-payments grounds since 1967. The Panel noted the condition in paragraph 9 of Article XVIII that 'import restrictions instituted, maintained or intensified shall not exceed those necessary: (a) to forestall the threat of, or to stop, a serious decline in its monetary reserves, or (b) in the case of a contracting party with inadequate monetary reserves, to achieve a reasonable rate of increase in its reserves'. The Panel noted further that paragraph 11 required the progressive relaxation of such restrictions 'as conditions improve' and their elimination 'when conditions no longer justify such maintenance.'

"Article XV:2 of the General Agreement provided that '[i]n all cases in which the CONTRACTING PARTIES are called upon to consider or deal with problems concerning monetary reserves, balances of payments or foreign exchange arrangements, they shall consult fully with the International Monetary Fund.' The latest full consultation concerning Korea's balance-of-payments situation in the Balance-of-Payments Committee had taken place in November 1987, the report of which had been adopted by the CONTRACTING PARTIES in February 1988. The next full consultation was scheduled for June 1989. The Panel considered that it should take into account the conclusions reached by the Balance-of-Payments Committee in 1987.

"At the full consultation in the Balance-of-Payments Committee with Korea in November 1987, '[t]he prevailing view expressed in the Committee was that the current situation and outlook for the balance of payments was such that import restrictions could no longer be justified under Article XVIII:B'.[39] Moreover, the full Balance-of-Payments Committee had 'stressed the need to establish a clear timetable for the early, progressive removal of Korea's restrictive trade measures maintained for balance-of-payments purposes' and had expressed the expectation that 'Korea would be able in the meantime to establish a timetable for the phasing-out of balance-of-payments restrictions, and that Korea would consider alternative GATT justification for any remaining measures, thus obviating the need for such consultations'.[40]

"The Panel noted that all available information, including figures published by the Korean authorities and advice provided to it in February 1989 by the International Monetary Fund, had shown that the reserve holdings of Korea had increased in 1988, that Korea's balance-of-payments situation had continued to improve at a good pace since the November 1987 consultations, and that the current economic indicators of Korea were very favourable. According to information provided to the Panel by the International Monetary Fund, the Korean gross official reserves had increased by 9 billion dollars to 12 billion dollars (equivalent to three months of imports) by end 1988. The Panel concluded that in the light of the continued improvement of the Korean balance-of-payments situation, and having regard to the provisions of Article XVIII:11, there was a need for the prompt establishment of a timetable for the phasing-out of Korea's balance-of-payments restrictions on beef, as called for by the CONTRACTING PARTIES in adopting the 1987 Balance-of-Payments Committee report."[41]

The Panels each suggested that the CONTRACTING PARTIES recommend that:

"(a) Korea eliminate or otherwise bring into conformity with the provisions of the General Agreement the import measures on beef introduced in 1984/85 and amended in 1988; and,

"(b) Korea hold consultations with [Australia, New Zealand and the United States] and other interested contracting parties to work out a timetable for the removal of import restrictions on beef justified since 1967 by Korea for balance-of-payments reasons and report on the result of such consultations within a period of three months following the adoption of the Panel report by the Council".[42]

---

[39] Footnote 1 to this paragraph refers to BOP/R/171, paragraph 22.
[40] Footnote 2 to this paragraph refers to BOP/R/171, paragraph 23, and notes that the full text of the Balance-of-Payments Committee's conclusions is contained in Annex I to each of these Panel Reports.
[41] *Ibid.*, paras. 98-101, 120-123, and 114-117 respectively.
[42] *Ibid.*, paras. 109, 131 and 125 respectively.

See also paragraphs 2, 3 and 4 of the Understanding on the Balance-of-Payments Provisions of the GATT 1994.

(3) Paragraph 12: consultations and review of balance-of-payments measures

(a) General

The Report of the Review Working Party on "Quantitative Restrictions" notes that "it was also agreed to insert an additional provision in [sub-paragraph (f)] to the effect that when they are called upon to take any action under paragraph 12 the CONTRACTING PARTIES would take fully into account the special factors existing in the case of under-developed countries which have been described in the Preamble of the Article".[43]

(b) Notification of balance-of-payments measures

The "Procedures for dealing with new import restrictions applied for balance-of-payments reasons" adopted in 1960 provide that "any contracting party modifying its import restrictions is required to furnish detailed information promptly to the Executive Secretary, for circulation to the contracting parties". A footnote to this paragraph notes: "Under established procedures, contracting parties should furnish such information not only when they wish to initiate a consultation pursuant to Articles XII:4(a) or XVIII:12(a) but whenever any significant changes are made in their restrictive systems".[44]

The 1972 Decision on simplified procedures for balance-of-payments consultations under Article XVIII:12(b) (cited below *in extenso*) noted that "There are a number of developing contracting parties, mostly the newly independent countries, which maintain import restrictions. ... the adoption of the 'streamlined' procedures set forth in paragraph 3 above should contribute substantially to easing the way for all developing countries to define their position regarding their restrictions in relation to the GATT provisions. It is therefore proposed that, upon approval of the new procedures, the secretariat be instructed to enquire and discuss with each of these developing countries with a view to establishing a complete list of the contracting parties invoking Section B of Article XVIII of the Agreement".[45]

Paragraph 3 of the 1979 Declaration provides: "Contracting parties shall promptly notify to the GATT the introduction or intensification of all restrictive import measures taken for balance-of-payments purposes. Contracting parties which have reason to believe that a restrictive import measure applied by another contracting party was taken for balance-of-payments purposes may notify the measure to the GATT or may request the GATT secretariat to seek information on the measure and make it available to all contracting parties if appropriate".[46]

Paragraph 8 of the Understanding on the Balance-of-Payments Provisions of the GATT 1994 provides as follows:

"A Member applying new restrictions or raising the general level of its existing restrictions by a substantial intensification of the measures shall enter into consultations with the Committee within four months of the adoption of such measures. The Member adopting such measures may request that a consultation be held under paragraph 4(a) of Article XII or paragraph 12(a) of Article XVIII as appropriate. If no such request has been made, the Chairman of the Committee shall invite the Member to hold such a consultation. Factors that may be examined in the consultation would include, *inter alia*, the introduction of new types of restrictive measures for balance-of-payments purposes, or an increase in the level or product coverage of restrictions.

---

[43] L/332/Rev.1 and Addenda, adopted on 2, 4 and 5 March 1955, 3S/170, 184, para. 48.
[44] Procedures approved on 16 November 1960, 9S/18, para. 2.
[45] L/3772/Rev.1, approved by the Council on 19 December 1972, 20S/47, 49, para. 4.
[46] L/4904, adopted on 28 November 1979, 26S/205, 207, para. 3. See also discussion on this issue in CG.18/W/9/Rev. 1, 22 October 1976. Nigeria began consulting in the Committee on Balance-of-Payments Restrictions in 1984 following a "reverse notification" by another contracting party.

For instances of "reverse notification" of restrictions or requests to the Secretariat to seek information on restrictions maintained by another contracting party, see the 1987 Note by the Secretariat on "Articles XII, XIV, XV and XVIII"[47].

In 1965, procedures were adopted relating to import restrictions maintained by newly-independent countries; it was suggested to such countries that "even if they were not yet in a position to determine whether they wished to invoke the provisions of Article XVIII as justification for some or all restrictions in force, they might submit descriptive material relative to their entire import control system, without prejudice to the consistency of the measures maintained with their obligations under GATT".[48]

See also the material on notification under Article XII.

(c) "shall ... consult with the CONTRACTING PARTIES": procedures and timing for consultations under paragraph 12

The Report of the Review Working Party on "Quantitative Restrictions" notes that the main difference between the provisions of Article XVIII:12 and the corresponding provisions of Article XII:4 "relates to the periodicity of the consultations under sub-paragraph (b)" and further notes that "The remarks and agreed statements referring to consultations under Article XII and which are reproduced in paragraphs 6 to 11 of this report apply also to consultations under paragraph 12 of Article XVIII".[49]

The 1979 Declaration on "Trade Measures Taken for Balance-of-Payments Purposes"[50] states, with regard to examination of balance-of-payments measures in the Committee on Balance-of-Payments Restrictions, that "The Committee shall follow the procedures for consultations on balance-of-payments restrictions approved by the Council on 28 April 1970 (18S/48-53, hereinafter referred to as 'full consultations procedures') or the procedures for regular consultations on balance-of-payments restrictions with developing countries approved by the Council on 19 December 1972 (20S/47-49, hereinafter referred to as 'simplified consultation procedures') subject to the provisions set out below."[51]

The 1970 "full consultations procedures" referred to in the Declaration describe the arrangements and procedures originally agreed in 1958 for consultations under Article XII:4(b) and Articles XVIII:12(b) as revised in the Review Session, as they had evolved to 1970. The 1970 procedures deal with the contents of the consultations, the documentation for the consultations, the time schedule for the consultations, arrangements for consultation with the International Monetary Fund, the composition of the Committee on Balance-of-Payments Restrictions, and the reports to be prepared on the consultations. Attached to the 1970 procedures are a plan of discussion for balance-of-payments consultations, and a list of points to be covered in the basic document for the consultations.[52]

The "simplified consultation procedures" referred to in the Declaration provide:

"(a) each year, the secretariat establishes a schedule showing the contracting parties acting under Article XVIII:B which are required to consult under paragraph 12(b) that year;

"(b) each of these contracting parties should submit to the CONTRACTING PARTIES a concise written statement on the nature of the balance-of-payments difficulties, the system and methods of restriction (with particular reference to any discriminatory features and changes in past two years), the effects of the restrictions and prospects of liberalization;

---

[47] MTN.GNG/NG7/W/14, dated 11 August 1987, para. 36.
[48] 14S/161.
[49] L/332/Rev.1 and Addenda, adopted on 2, 4 and 5 March 1955, 3S/170, 183-84, para. 46.
[50] L/4904, adopted on 28 November 1979, 26S/205.
[51] 26S/207, para. 6.
[52] L/3388, presented to the Council on 28 April 1970, 18S/48.

"(c) the statements received will be circulated to all contracting parties and presented to the Committee on Balance-of-Payments Restrictions for prior consideration, so that the Committee may determine whether a full consultation is desirable. If it decides that such a consultation is not desirable, the Committee will recommend to the Council that the contracting party be deemed to have consulted with the CONTRACTING PARTIES and to have fulfilled its obligations under Article XVIII:12(b) for that year. Otherwise, the CONTRACTING PARTIES will consult the International Monetary Fund, and the Committee will follow the procedures applicable hitherto for a full consultation; and

"(d) arrangements will be made with the International Monetary Fund for the supply of balance-of-payments statistics for each country submitting a statement in accordance with paragraph (b) above".[53]

"It should be noted that this proposal relates only to the periodic consultations provided for in Article XVIII:12(b). Consultations under Article XVIII:12(a) will continue to follow the existing rules. Consultations with developed countries acting under Article XII will be held annually in the usual manner".[54]

Thus, the "full consultations procedures" agreed in 1970 apply to all consultations under Article XVIII:12(a); in certain cases the "simplified consultation procedures" agreed in 1972 apply to periodic consultations under Article XVIII:12(b).

The 1979 "Declaration on Trade Measures taken for Balance-of-Payments Purposes" provides that

"1. The procedures for examination stipulated in Articles XII and XVIII shall apply to all restrictive import measures taken for balance-of-payments purposes.

...

"8. In the case of consultations under Article XVIII:12(b) the Committee shall base its decision on the type of procedure on such factors as the following:

"(a) the time elapsed since the last full consultations;

"(b) the steps the consulting contracting party has taken in the light of conclusions reached on the occasion of previous consultations;

"(c) the changes in the overall level or nature of the trade measures taken for balance-of-payments purposes;

"(d) the changes in the balance-of-payments situation or prospects;

"(e) whether the balance-of-payments problems are structural or temporary in nature.

"9. A less-developed contracting party may at any time request full consultations".[55]

Paragraphs 7 and 8 of the the Understanding on the Balance-of-Payments Provisions of the GATT 1994 provide as follows:

"All restrictions applied for balance-of-payments purposes shall be subject to periodic review in the Committee under paragraph 4(b) of Article XII or under paragraph 12(b) of Article XVIII, subject to the possibility of altering the periodicity of consultations in agreement with the consulting Member or pursuant to any specific review procedure that may be recommended by the General Council.

---

[53] L/3772/Rev.1, approved by the Council on 19 December 1972, 20S/47, 48-49, para. 3.
[54] *Ibid.*, para. 4.
[55] L/4904, adopted on 28 November 1979, 26S/205, 206-208.

"Consultations may be held under the simplified procedures approved on 19 December 1972 (BISD 20S/47-49, referred to in this Understanding as 'simplified consultation procedures') in the case of least-developed country Members or in the case of developing country Members which are pursuing liberalization efforts in conformity with the schedule presented to the Committee in previous consultations. Simplified consultation procedures may also be used when the Trade Policy Review of a developing country Member is scheduled for the same calendar year as the date fixed for the consultations. In such cases the decision as to whether full consultation procedures should be used will be made on the basis of the factors enumerated in paragraph 8 of the 1979 Declaration. Except in the case of least-developed country Members, no more than two successive consultations may be held under simplified consultation procedures."

Further concerning balance-of-payments consultations, see Section II.C under Article XII.

(d) *"as to the nature of its balance of payments difficulties": scope of consultations under paragraph 12*

General scope: The 1979 "Declaration on Trade Measures taken for Balance-of-Payments Purposes" provides that "All restrictive import measures taken for balance-of-payments purposes shall be subject to consultation in the GATT Committee on Balance-of-Payments Restrictions ... "[56]

External factors adversely affecting the export trade of the contracting party applying restrictions: See the material in this Index under Article XII:4(e) and Section II.C under Article XII. The Report of the Review Working Party on "Quantitative Restrictions" notes that the Working Party agreed

"that ... the scope of consultations under paragraph 12 of Article XVIII was the same as that of consultations under Article XII and that the clarification contained in paragraph 4(e) of Article XII and in the related interpretative note would apply equally to consultations undertaken under Section B of Article XVIII".[57]

Prior consultations on balance-of-payments matters: In November 1984, proposals were made in the GATT Council by Chile regarding the use of prior consultations under Article XVIII:12 and XII:4 as a preventive mechanism aimed at avoiding import restrictions by countries suffering balance-of-payments difficulties, and focusing on obstacles to expansion of trade.[58] Following consultations on this question in the Balance-of-Payments Committee, a Report was made to the Council by the Chairman of the Committee in March 1985 in which it was recognized that, in view of the text and drafting history of Article XII:4(a) and XVIII:12(a) there was nothing to prevent a contracting party in balance of payments difficulties from holding prior consultations with the Committee under the normal procedures of these Articles.[59] Such consultations, which would be full consultations, would, *inter alia*, take due account of all factors, including external factors, affecting the consulting country's balance of payments.[60]

(e) *"the* CONTRACTING PARTIES *shall review all restrictions applied under this Section"*

The Interpretative Note to this provision indicates that the review of restrictions under Article XVIII:12(b) and the review to be conducted under Article XII:4(b) of restrictions under Article XII were intended to be initiated on the same date.[61] This review was carried out by the CONTRACTING PARTIES in 1958-59. Part I of the resulting document discusses the financial background of the restrictions and discriminations, recent changes in the use of restrictions and the then-current level of restrictions and discrimination in the use of restrictions. Part II contains separate notes describing the restrictions in force as at the end of 1958 or early in 1959, in the twenty-five contracting parties resorting to Article XII or Article XVIII:B at that time.[62] See also the material on Article XII:4(b) in this Index.

---

[56] *Ibid.*, 26S/207, para. 4.
[57] L/332/Rev.1 and Addenda, adopted on 2, 4 and 5 March 1955, 3S/170, 184, para. 49.
[58] C/M/183.
[59] C/M/186.
[60] C/132; 32S/46.
[61] L/332/Rev.1 and Addenda, adopted on 2, 4 and 5 March 1955, 3S/170, 184, para. 46.
[62] MGT(59)76, dated 30 July 1959; see also material on the background of this review at 6S/39-40, paras. 13-16.

(f)   Sub-paragraphs c(ii), (d) and (e)

The Report of the Review Working Party on "Quantitative Restrictions" notes concerning paragraph (e) that it was added "in order to allow a contracting party to withdraw from the General Agreement at shorter notice than is provided in Article XXXI" in the circumstances specified.[63]

In the three parallel Panel Reports on "Republic of Korea - Restrictions on Imports of Beef" in response to complaints by Australia,[64] the United States,[65] and New Zealand[66], the Panel examined whether the consistency of restrictive measures with Article XVIII:B could be examined within the framework of Article XXIII. "It was the view of the Panel that excluding the possibility of bringing a complaint under Article XXIII against measures for which there was claimed balance-of-payments cover would unnecessarily restrict the application of the General Agreement. This did not preclude, however, resort to special review procedures under Article XVIII:B. Indeed, either procedure, that of Article XVIII:12(d) or Article XXIII, could have been pursued by the parties in this case. But as far as the Panel was concerned, the parties had chosen to proceed under Article XXIII".[67] See further under Article XXIII.

(4)   Balance-of-payments measures other than quantitative restrictions

See the discussion of surcharges for balance-of-payments purposes under Article XII:1. Concerning waivers granted in connection with the imposition of surcharges, see under Article II and Article XXV.

The Committee on Legal and Institutional Framework, which prepared the text of Part IV, recommended an amendment to Section B of Article XVIII to permit a less-developed contracting party to use temporary import surcharges, in place of quantitative restrictions, to safeguard its balance of payments.[68] This Recommendation was referred to the Committee on Trade and Development which considered the question in an Ad Hoc Group on Legal Amendments during 1965/1966.[69]

The Report of the Balance-of-Payments Committee on its work during the years 1970-1974 discusses the treatment of balance-of-payments surcharges during that period.[70]

The 1979 "Declaration on Trade Measures taken for Balance-of-Payments Purposes" provides, *inter alia*: "The procedures for examination stipulated in Articles XII and XVIII shall apply to all restrictive import measures taken for balance-of-payments purposes. ... The provisions of this paragraph are not intended to modify the substantive provisions of the General Agreement".[71] However, paragraph 2 of the Understanding on the Balance-of-Payments Provisions of the GATT 1994 provides, *inter alia:* "It is understood that, notwithstanding the provisions of Article II, price-based measures taken for balance-of-payments purposes may be applied by a Member in excess of the duties inscribed in the Schedule of that Member."

5.   **Article XVIII:C**

(1)   Invocation of Article XVIII:C

Releases have been granted under Section C of Article XVIII to Cuba, Haiti, India and Sri Lanka.[72] Some other contracting parties, including Greece[73], Indonesia[74] and Malaysia[75] have notified certain import regulations

---

[63]L/332/Rev.1 and Addenda, adopted on 2, 4 and 5 March 1955, 3S/170, 184, para. 47.
[64]L/6504, adopted on 7 November 1989, 36S/202.
[65]L/6503, adopted on 7 November 1989, 36S/268.
[66]L/6505, adopted on 7 November 1989, 36S/234.
[67]*Ibid.*, 36S/227, para. 97; 36S/303, para. 119; and 36S/265, para. 113 respectively.
[68]L/2281, para.7 and Annex II; L/2297, para. 6.
[69]13S/76; 14S/141.
[70]L/4200.
[71]L/4904, adopted on 28 November 1979, 26S/205, 206, para. 1.
[72]See the list of such releases in the Index of the BISD, e.g. at 38S/141.
[73]L/3460.
[74]L/5452, L/5597.

taken for development purposes under Section C of Article XVIII. The measures applied pursuant to the provisions of Section C were reviewed annually. The last review was conducted at the Twenty-fourth Session in November 1967.[76]

The 1979 Decision on "Safeguard Action for Development Purposes" provides that "... there may be unusual circumstances where delay in the application of measures which a less-developed contracting party wishes to introduce under Section A or Section C of Article XVIII may give rise to difficulties in the application of its programmes and policies of economic development for the aforesaid purposes. ... in such circumstances, the less-developed contracting party concerned may deviate from the provisions of Section A and paragraphs 14, 15, 17 and 18 of Section C to the extent necessary for introducing the measures contemplated on a provisional basis immediately after notification".[77] See further at page 498 above.

The 1986 Report of the Group on "Quantitative Restrictions and other Non-Tariff Measures" provides that "The Group noted that some progress had been made in bringing existing quantitative restrictions into conformity with the General Agreement. ... However, it also noted that ... countries invoking ... Article XVIII:C had not followed the prescribed procedures".[78]

(2) Paragraph 14: "The contracting party concerned shall notify"

Before Article XVIII was re-drafted at the Review Session of 1954-55, Article XVIII permitted the institution or maintenance of certain measures but only on the condition that a contracting party "shall notify" the existing or proposed measures in question. The 1949 Report of the Working Party on "Notifications of Existing Measures and Procedural Questions" studied the question of notification under Article XVIII. The question was raised whether "existing legislation" covered by the derogation to Part II of the General Agreement in the Protocol of Provisional Application or accession protocols (see the chapter in this Index on provisional application) had to be notified or whether it could be retained even if not notified. In response, the Working Party concluded "that there is no obligation on the part of a contracting party to notify a measure permitted by sub-paragraph 1(b) of the Protocol of Provisional Application or sub-paragraph 1(a)(ii) of the Annecy Protocol".[79]

In the Interpretative Note to paragraphs 13 and 14 it is recognized "that, before deciding on the introduction of a measure and notifying the CONTRACTING PARTIES in accordance with paragraph 14, a contracting party may need a reasonable period of time to assess the competitive position of the industry concerned". With respect to this Interpretative Note and its reference to "a reasonable period of time", the Report of the Review Working Party on "Quantitative Restrictions" noted: "it is recognized that this period should normally not exceed two years".[80] See also the Note *Ad* paragraph 19 of Article XVIII.

A Questionnaire on "Information to accompany notifications under Section C, and applications under Section D, of Article XVIII" was approved on 15 October 1958 for the guidance of contracting parties.[81]

In 1958, a Panel on Article XVIII considered certain notifications by Ceylon of measures under Article XVIII:C. The Panel noted that the Ceylon Government had imposed temporary import controls on certain products in anticipation of the concurrence of the CONTRACTING PARTIES. "... The Panel recognized that these measures, which had not been notified to the CONTRACTING PARTIES before they were put into force, were of the type contemplated in the proviso to paragraph 14 of Article XVIII: it [expressed] the hope that if the need for similar temporary measures should arise in the future, the Ceylon Government would inform the CONTRACTING PARTIES before putting such measures into force."[82]

---

[75] C/W/448, p. 38.
[76] For reports on annual reviews, see: 7S/71, 8S/97, 9S/101, 10S/106, 11S/158, 13S/65, 14S/127, 15S/65.
[77] L/4897, Decision of 28 November 1979, 26S/209.
[78] L/6073, adopted on 26 November 1986, 33S/160, 169, para. 35.
[79] GATT/CP.3/60/Rev.1, approved on 10 August 1949, II/49, 62, para. 100.
[80] L/332/Rev.1 and Addenda, adopted on 2, 4 and 5 March 1955, 3S/170, 189, para. 65.
[81] L/888, 7S/85-88. It was understood that this questionnaire would replace the questionnaire approved in 1949 (II/63-65) for governments notifying measures under Article XVIII as it stood prior to the Review Session.
[82] L/932, "Notifications by Ceylon", adopted on 22 November 1958, L/932, 56S/75, 78, para. 8.

(3) Paragraph 16: "the contracting party concerned shall consult"

The Report of the Panel on Article XVIII Applications in 1957 concerning "Applications by Ceylon" notes, concerning the consultation provided for in Article XVIII:16:

"First, the Panel endeavoured, in the light of the provisions of paragraphs 1, 2 and 13 of Article XVIII, to see whether the objectives of each measure proposed was to assist the establishment of a particular industry as defined in the relevant Note to Annex [I], if such industry was established with a view to raising the general standard of living of the Ceylonese people and if the measure proposed was required to promote the establishment of that industry.

"As regards the first criterion, the Panel examined, in the light of the data submitted by the Ceylon delegation, whether there was already a domestic production of the articles covered by each Ceylonese application, or, if such a production existed, whether the programme involved a substantial transformation of an existing industry, or a substantial increase in production for an industry which satisfied at present only a small fraction of the domestic demand. As regards the second criterion, the Panel had at its disposal estimates prepared by the secretariat with respect to the added national income which the new production was likely to bring about. ...

"The Panel then considered with the Ceylon delegation the alternative measures which might be available under the Agreement, such as tariffs (or tariff quotas) and subsidies, and took into account the practical difficulties which reliance on these measures might create for the achievement of the objectives proposed by the Ceylon Government.

"Finally, as regards the possible effect of the measures on the commercial or economic interests of other contracting parties, the Panel had at its disposal estimates prepared by the secretariat concerning the probable effects of the measures not only on the imports of the products covered by the applications but also on imports of other products, such as raw materials, capital equipment and spare parts which would be required from the establishment or expansion of domestic production and consumer goods for which an increased demand should normally result from increased wages, salaries and profits".[83]

The 1959 Panel Report on "Notifications by Ceylon" recorded the following statements in its report:

"The Panel has been guided by its understanding that the provisions of Section C of Article XVIII are intended to be used only in special circumstances where no measure consistent with the other provisions of the General Agreement is practicable to permit a contracting party coming within the scope of Article XVIII:4(a) to achieve the purpose of promoting the establishment of a particular industry with a view to raising the general standard of living of its people. While the procedures of Section C of Article XVIII are explicitly intended to facilitate the general economic development of less-developed countries, their use must be limited to cases where the criteria set forth in that Article are fulfilled".[84]

"The Panel has noted that for a number of these notifications by Ceylon the exporting countries to be affected were often countries with a lower standard of living. It suggests that in granting future releases under Article XVIII the CONTRACTING PARTIES may wish to take account of the effects of the proposed measures not only on the economic development of the applicant country, but also on the economy of countries which may likewise be in the early stages of economic development and whose viability and solvency depended predominantly on exports".[85]

(4) Paragraph 18: consultations concerning products subject to concessions

The Report of the Panel on Article XVIII Applications in 1957 concerning "Applications by Ceylon" notes that "Whenever an application involved items the duties on which were bound under the GATT, the Panel

---

[83]L/751, adopted on 28 November 1957, 6S/112, 114-115, paras. 6-9.
[84]Part I of L/1113, adopted on 20 November 1959, 8S/90, 91, para. 5.
[85]*Ibid.*, 8S/92, para. 7.

considered whether the conditions laid down in paragraphs 13 to 16 were fulfilled, then invited the Ceylon delegation to enter into consultations with the parties concerned in accordance with paragraph 18 of Article XVIII ...".[86]

(5) Paragraph 21: "it may suspend the application of such substantially equivalent concession or other obligation"

See the Interpretative Note.

(6) Relationship between Article XVIII:B and C

In the Report of the Working Party on the "Accession of Tunisia" the representative of Tunisia pointed out that "as a provisional member, Tunisia had observed the provisions of Article XVIII:B of the General Agreement together with the appropriate procedures governing its application and would continue to do so in the future. He recalled, nevertheless, that Article XVIII:C of the General Agreement and the 1979 CONTRACTING PARTIES' Decision on Safeguard Action for Development Purposes recognized to developing countries the right to protect infant domestic industries ... A member recommended that Tunisia not invoke Article XVIII:B to justify protective measures taken for development purposes to establish or protect infant industries. Rather, Tunisia should adhere to the provisions of Article XVIII:C or XVIII:D, or other GATT provisions as appropriate, to justify protection for these reasons ...".[87]

6. Article XVIII:D

Section D of Article XVIII applies to those contracting parties within the scope of sub-paragraph 4(b). The Report of the Review Working Party on "Quantitative Restrictions" notes with regard to Section D of Article XVIII that "the scope of the Section and the procedural provisions of that Section are the same as for Section C, but all the measures without exception have to be concurred in by the CONTRACTING PARTIES before they can be introduced".[88] A Questionnaire on "Information to accompany notifications under Section C, and applications under Section D, of Article XVIII" was approved on 15 October 1958 for the guidance of contracting parties.[89]

Section D has not been invoked.

B. RELATIONSHIP BETWEEN ARTICLE XVIII AND OTHER GATT PROVISIONS

1. Article III

The Report of the Working Party on the "Accession of Costa Rica" includes a discussion of Costa Rica's selective consumption levy. Some members of the Working Party pointed out that "neither Part IV nor Article XVIII of the General Agreement authorized the discriminatory application of levies contrary to Article III".[90]

2. Article XII

See under Article XII and at page 497.

---

[86] L/751, adopted on 28 November 1957, 6S/112, 115, para. 10.
[87] L/6277, adopted on 12 December 1990, 37S/30, 36, para. 25.
[88] L/332/Rev.1 and Addenda, adopted on 2, 4 and 5 March 1955, 3S/170, 189, para. 64.
[89] L/888, 7S/85-88. It was understood that this questionnaire would replace the questionnaire approved in 1949 (II/63-65) for governments notifying measures under Article XVIII as it stood prior to the Review Session.
[90] L/6589, adopted on 7 November 1989, 36S/26, 33, para. 32.

3. Article XIV

The Report of the Review Working Party on "Quantitative Restrictions" noted that "Appropriate references to Section B of Article XVIII have been introduced in the text of Article XIV; through these insertions, the application of balance-of-payments restrictions by under-developed countries are governed by the provisions of Article XIV as regards deviations from the rule of non-discrimination".[91]

4. Article XXIII

See under Article XXIII for material on the relationship of that Article with Article XVIII:B and with Article XVIII:C and D.

5. Article XXIV

See references under Article XXIV to relationship with Article XVIII.

III. PREPARATORY WORK AND SUBSEQUENT MODIFICATIONS

Corresponding provisions in the Havana Charter are contained in Articles 13 and 14; in the London and New York Drafts, in Article 13; and in the Geneva Draft, in Articles 13 and 14.

The text of Article XVIII has been replaced twice. Firstly, at the Second Session in September 1948 it was decided to replace the original text of Article XVIII with provisions reflecting Articles 13 and 14 of the Havana Charter.[92] These amendments were effected by the Protocol Modifying Part II and Article XXVI of the GATT, which entered into effect on 14 December 1948. Secondly, as noted at page 496 above, the present text of Article XVIII was agreed at the Review Session in 1954-55, where the balance-of-payments articles of the General Agreement were extensively debated in the Review Working Party on Quantitative Restrictions. Concerning the Review, see the documents listed below and the Report of the Working Party, which contains a "description of the purpose and intent of the various amendments proposed, as well as agreed statements the purpose of which is to clarify the meaning of certain provisions, with a view to facilitating the interpretation of those provisions in the future".[93] At the same time, Article XVIII:A was redrafted in the Review Working Party on Schedules and Customs Administration.[94] The new text of Article XVIII, contained in the 1955 Protocol Amending the Preamble and Parts II and III of the GATT, entered into force on 7 October 1957.

---

[91] L/332/Rev.1 and Addenda, adopted on 2, 4 and 5 March 1955, 3S/170, 177, para. 27.
[92] See Report of the Working Party on "Modifications to the General Agreement", adopted on 1 and 2 September 1948, GATT/CP.2/22/Rev.1, II/39, 41, para. 14.
[93] L/332/Rev.1 and Addenda, adopted on 2, 4 and 5 March 1955, 3S/170 (passage cited is in paragraph 2, 3S/170).
[94] L/329, adopted on 26 February 1955, 3S/205, 215.

IV. RELEVANT DOCUMENTS

London

Discussion: EPCT/C.I and II/PV/4

Geneva

Discussion: EPCT/A/PV/22, 23, 26, 39;
EPCT/TAC/PV/11, 19, 22, 27
Reports: EPCT/135, 162, 165, 167, 197
Other: EPCT/W.313

Havana

Discussion: E/CONF.2/C.2/SR.13, 14, 15, 23, 26
Report: E/CONF.2/C.2/41 and Add.1
E/CONF.2/45/Rev.1, 51

CONTRACTING PARTIES

Discussion: GATT/CP.3/SR.39, 40, 43, 44
GATT/TN.2/SR.3, 4, 7, 8
Reports: GATT/CP.3/60/Rev.1, G/39

Review Session

Discussion: SR.9/14, 15, 16, 25, 26, 36, 37, 38, 40, 42, 45, 47
Reports: L/332/Rev.1+Adds., L/327, L/329
3S/179-189, 215, 244
W.9/101+Add.1, 126, 154, 180, 184/Rev.1, 189, 198, 206, 208, 212, 225, 233, 236/Add.2
Other: L/189+Add.1, 272, 277, 282
W.9/17, 18+Add.1, 22, 23, 31, 32, 35, 37, 39+Add.1, 40, 43, 49, 51, 52, 106, 115, 154, 175, 189/Add.1, 196, 210, 221, 226
Sec/50/54, 134/54, 145/54, 158/54
Spec/3/55, 8/55, 10/55, 14/55, 15/55, 17/55, 26/55, 34/55, 35/55, 133/55, 138/55, 139/55, 143/55, 154-156/55, 176/55

ARTICLE XIX

EMERGENCY ACTION ON IMPORTS OF PARTICULAR PRODUCTS

I. TEXT OF ARTICLE XIX 515

II. INTERPRETATION AND APPLICATION OF ARTICLE XIX 516
    A.   SCOPE AND APPLICATION OF ARTICLE XIX 516
        1.   Paragraphs 1 and 2 516
            (1)   "as a result of unforeseen developments" 517
            (2)   "being imported ... in such increased quantities" 518
            (3)   "cause or threaten serious injury to domestic producers ... of like or directly competitive products" ... 518
            (4)   "in respect of such product" 518
                (a)   Non-discriminatory invocation of Article XIX 519
                (b)   Price discrimination 521
            (5)   "to the extent and for such time as may be necessary" 521
                (a)   Extent of action under Article XIX 521
                (b)   Duration of action under Article XIX 522
            (6)   "to suspend the obligation in whole or in part or to withdraw or modify the concession": Nature of action under Article XIX 522
            (7)   Paragraph 1(b) 523
            (8)   "shall give notice in writing to the CONTRACTING PARTIES" 523
            (9)   "in critical circumstances" 524
        2.   Paragraph 3 524
            (1)   "If agreement among the interested contracting parties with respect to the action is not reached" 524
            (2)   "not later than ninety days after such action is taken" 525
            (3)   "to suspend ... the application ... of such substantially equivalent concessions" 526
            (4)   "to the trade of the contracting party taking such action" 527
            (5)   "upon the expiration of thirty days from the day on which written notice of such suspension is received by the CONTRACTING PARTIES" 528
            (6)   "the suspension of which the CONTRACTING PARTIES do not disapprove" 528
    B.   RELATIONSHIP BETWEEN ARTICLE XIX AND OTHER GATT PROVISIONS 529
        1.   Articles I and XIII 529
        2.   Article XVIII:A 529
        3.   Article XXIII 529
        4.   Article XXIV 529
        5.   Part IV 529
        6.   Article XIX actions and rectification and modification of schedules 529
    C.   EXCEPTIONS AND DEROGATIONS 530
        1.   Special safeguards provisions in certain protocols of accession 530
        2.   Arrangement Regarding International Trade in Textiles (MFA) 531
    D.   "VOLUNTARY EXPORT RESTRAINTS" AND GREY-AREA MEASURES 532
    E.   WORK UNDERTAKEN IN THE GATT ON SAFEGUARDS 534

III. PREPARATORY WORK AND SUBSEQUENT MODIFICATIONS 537

IV. RELEVANT DOCUMENTS 538

V. NOTIFICATIONS TO THE SECRETARIAT OF ACTIONS UNDER ARTICLE XIX 539

I. TEXT OF ARTICLE XIX

Article XIX

Emergency Action on Imports of Particular Products

1. (*a*) If, as a result of unforeseen developments and of the effect of the obligations incurred by a contracting party under this Agreement, including tariff concessions, any product is being imported into the territory of that contracting party in such increased quantities and under such conditions as to cause or threaten serious injury to domestic producers in that territory of like or directly competitive products, the contracting party

shall be free, in respect of such product, and to the extent and for such time as may be necessary to prevent or remedy such injury, to suspend the obligation in whole or in part or to withdraw or modify the concession.

(b) If any product, which is the subject of a concession with respect to a preference, is being imported into the territory of a contracting party in the circumstances set forth in sub-paragraph (a) of this paragraph, so as to cause or threaten serious injury to domestic producers of like or directly competitive products in the territory of a contracting party which receives or received such preference, the importing contracting party shall be free, if that other contracting party so requests, to suspend the relevant obligation in whole or in part or to withdraw or modify the concession in respect of the product, to the extent and for such time as may be necessary to prevent or remedy such injury.

2. Before any contracting party shall take action pursuant to the provisions of paragraph 1 of this Article, it shall give notice in writing to the CONTRACTING PARTIES as far in advance as may be practicable and shall afford the CONTRACTING PARTIES and those contracting parties having a substantial interest as exporters of the product concerned an opportunity to consult with it in respect of the proposed action. When such notice is given in relation to a concession with respect to a preference, the notice shall name the contracting party which has requested the action. In critical circumstances, where delay would cause damage which it would be difficult to repair, action under paragraph 1 of this Article may be taken provisionally without prior consultation, on the condition that consultation shall be effected immediately after taking such action.

3. (a) If agreement among the interested contracting parties with respect to the action is not reached, the contracting party which proposes to take or continue the action shall, nevertheless, be free to do so, and if such action is taken or continued, the affected contracting parties shall then be free, not later than ninety days after such action is taken, to suspend, upon the expiration of thirty days from the day on which written notice of such suspension is received by the CONTRACTING PARTIES, the application to the trade of the contracting party taking such action, or, in the case envisaged in paragraph 1 (b) of this Article, to the trade of the contracting party requesting such action, of such substantially equivalent concessions or other obligations under this Agreement the suspension of which the CONTRACTING PARTIES do not disapprove.

(b) Notwithstanding the provisions of sub-paragraph (a) of this paragraph, where action is taken under paragraph 2 of this Article without prior consultation and causes or threatens serious injury in the territory of a contracting party to the domestic producers of products affected by the action, that contracting party shall, where delay would cause damage difficult to repair, be free to suspend, upon the taking of the action and throughout the period of consultation, such concessions or other obligations as may be necessary to prevent or remedy the injury.

II. INTERPRETATION AND APPLICATION OF ARTICLE XIX

A. SCOPE AND APPLICATION OF ARTICLE XIX

1. Paragraphs 1 and 2

A Working Party in 1950-51 on "Withdrawal by the United States of a Tariff Concession under Article XIX of the General Agreement" examined the complaint of Czechoslovakia that the United States, in withdrawing a concession on women's fur felt hats and hat bodies, had failed to fulfil the requirements of Article XIX. The Report of the Working Party notes that

> "In attempting to appraise whether the requirements of Article XIX had been fulfilled, the Working Party examined separately each of the conditions which qualify the exercise of the right to suspend an obligation or to withdraw or modify a concession under that Article.

"Three sets of conditions have to be fulfilled:

"(a) There should be an abnormal development in the imports of the product in question in the sense that:

"(i) the product in question must be imported in increased quantities;

"(ii) the increased imports must be the result of unforeseen developments and of the effect of the tariff concession; and

"(iii) the imports must enter in such increased quantities and under such conditions as to cause or threaten serious injury to domestic producers of like or directly competitive products.

"(b) The suspension of an obligation or the withdrawal or modification of a concession must be limited to the extent and the time necessary to prevent or remedy the injury caused or threatened.

"(c) The contracting party taking action under Article XIX must give notice in writing to the CONTRACTING PARTIES before taking action. It must also give an opportunity to contracting parties substantially interested and to the CONTRACTING PARTIES to consult with it. As a rule consultation should take place before the action is taken, but in critical circumstances consultation may take place immediately after the measure is taken provisionally".[1]

Legislation of acceding governments implementing Article XIX ("safeguards legislation") has been a subject of examination in certain recent accession negotiations. In the reports of the accession working parties concerned, members of the accession working party generally have not deemed the absence of a serious injury requirement in such legislation, or the complete absence of such legislation, to be as such inconsistent with the General Agreement. The acceding governments have generally confirmed their intention to abide by the provisions of Article XIX in any instance of application of measures under Article XIX.[2]

(1) "as a result of unforeseen developments"

The members of the Working Party cited above on "Withdrawal by the United States of a Tariff Concession under Article XIX", except for the United States, agreed

"that the term 'unforeseen development' should be interpreted to mean developments occurring after the negotiation of the relevant tariff concession which it would not be reasonable to expect that the negotiators of the country making the concession could and should have foreseen at the time when the concession was negotiated".[3]

The same Working Party also agreed "that the fact that hat styles had changed did not constitute an 'unforeseen development' within the meaning of Article XIX"[4], but that the effects of the special circumstances of this case, "and particularly the degree to which the change in fashion affected the competitive situation, could not reasonably be expected to have been foreseen by the United States authorities in 1947, and that the condition of Article XIX that the increase in imports must be due to unforeseen developments and to the effect of the tariff concessions can therefore be considered to have been fulfilled".[5]

---

[1] GATT/CP/106, report adopted on 22 October 1951, GATT/CP.6/SR.19, Sales No. GATT/1951-3.
[2] See Working Party Reports on accessions of Bolivia, L/6542, adopted on 19 July 1989, 36S/9, 19-20, para. 29; Costa Rica, L/6589, adopted on 7 November 1989, 36S/26, 38-39, paras. 47, 49; El Salvador, L/6771, adopted on 12 December 1990, 37S/9, 22-23, paras. 40-41; Guatemala, L/6770, adopted on 6 February 1991, 38S/3, 12, paras. 33-34; Tunisia, L/6277, adopted on 12 December 1990, 37S/30, 38, para. 31.
[3] GATT/CP/106, report adopted on 22 October 1951, GATT/CP.6/SR.19, Sales No. GATT/1951-3, p. 10, para. 9.
[4] *Ibid.*, p. 12, para. 11.
[5] *Ibid.*, p. 13, para. 12.

(2) "being imported ... in such increased quantities"

In discussions concerning Article 40 of the Charter (the Article corresponding to Article XIX) during the Havana Conference, it was agreed to insert the word "relatively" between "such" and "increased", "so as to make it clear that Article 40 could apply in cases where imports had increased relatively to domestic production, even though there might not have been an absolute increase in imports as compared with a previous base period".[6] The Working Party on "Modifications to the General Agreement", which met directly after the Havana Conference, considered amendment of Article XIX to conform to this wording but decided not to do so, on the basis that "It was also the understanding of the Working Party that the phrase 'being imported ... in such increased quantities' in paragraph 1(a) of Article XIX was intended to cover cases where imports may have increased relatively, as made clear in Article 40, paragraph 1(a), of the Havana Charter".[7]

(3) "cause or threaten serious injury to domestic producers ... of like or directly competitive products"

The Working Party Report on "Report on the Withdrawal by the United States of a Tariff Concession under Article XIX" notes that "the statistics bearing on the relation between imports and domestic production up to mid-1950 show a large and rapidly increasing volume of imports, while at the same time domestic production decreased or remained stationary. On the whole, therefore, they constitute evidence of some weight in favour of the view that there was a threat of serious injury to the United States industry".[8] However, the Working Party also pointed out that

> "To sum up, the available data support the view that increased imports had caused or threatened some adverse effect to United States producers. Whether such a degree of adverse effect should be considered to amount to 'serious injury' is another question, on which the data cannot be said to point convincingly in either direction, and any view on which is essentially a matter of economic and social judgment involving a considerable subjective element. In this connection it may be observed that the Working Party naturally could not have the facilities available to the United States authorities for examining interested parties and independent witnesses from the United States hat-making areas, and for forming judgments on the basis of such examination. Further, it is perhaps inevitable that governments should on occasion lend greater weight to the difficulties or fears of their domestic producers than would any international body, and that they may feel it necessary on social grounds, e.g. because of lack of alternative employment in the localities concerned, to afford a high degree of protection to individual industries which in terms of cost of production are not economic. Moreover, the United States is not called upon to prove conclusively that the degree of injury caused or threatened in this case must be regarded as serious; since the question under consideration is whether or not they are in breach of Article XIX, they are entitled to the benefit of any reasonable doubt. No facts have been advanced which provide any convincing evidence that it would be unreasonable to regard the adverse effects on the domestic industry concerned as a result of increased imports as amounting to serious injury or a threat thereof; and the facts as a whole certainly tend to show that some degree of adverse effect has been caused or threatened. It must be concluded, therefore, that the Czechoslovak Delegation has failed to establish that no serious injury has been sustained or threatened".[9]

(4) "in respect of such product"

A Secretariat Note of 1978 on "Modalities of Application of Article XIX" notes that Article 29 of the US Draft Charter, on "Emergency Action on Imports of Particular Products" made no reference to the question whether it was intended to be applied on a most-favoured-nation basis or not. However, this Note indicates that an United States internal memorandum gave the following information regarding the historical background for the United States draft:

> "These relevant provisions (of Article XIX) follow closely in substance those in the first detailed escape clause, contained in Article XI of the 1942 trade agreement with Mexico ... At the time the United States

---

[6] Havana Reports, p. 83, para. 11.
[7] II/39, 43-44, para. 30.
[8] GATT/CP/106, report adopted on 22 October 1951, GATT/CP.6/SR.19, Sales No. GATT/1951-3, p. 21, para. 26.
[9] *Ibid.*, p. 22-23, para. 30.

was putting escape clauses comparable to Article XIX into bilateral trade agreements and was proposing the multilateral negotiation of comparable language it had no authority to take action under such a clause in other than a non-discriminatory manner and therefore must have contemplated its non-discriminatory use".[10]

The Report of the Havana Conference Sub-Committee D on Articles 40, 41 and 43 of the Charter makes the following comment concerning discussions at Havana:

"The Sub-Committee was unanimous in its understanding of this Article that action taken by Members under paragraphs 1(a), 1(b) and 3(b) - as distinct from paragraph 3(a) - should not involve any discrimination against the trade of any Member. As the Geneva text might leave room for doubts on this point, it was felt that this intention, as interpreted by the Sub-Committee, should be expressly stated in the Charter. The Sub-Committee decided therefore to recommend that this interpretation be embodied in a footnote attached to the Article and forming part of the Charter".[11]

Accordingly the Sub-Committee proposed the following Interpretative Note to Article 40, the Article corresponding to Article XIX of the General Agreement:

"It is understood that any suspension, withdrawal or modification under paragraphs 1(a), 1(b) and 3(b) must not discriminate against imports from any Member country".

In the discussion of the Report of Sub-Committee D in Committee III of the Havana Conference, the deletion of this footnote was requested on the basis that "the application of Article 40 would in many cases be discriminatory and the footnote might create a chain of withdrawals of concessions". In reply it was stated that "the intention of the Article was set forth in the footnote. Paragraph 3(a) offered counteraction against emergency actions; the phrase 'to the trade of the Member' showed a discriminatory characteristic not evident in the other paragraphs ... the general intent of Article 40 was to provide time to rectify possible miscalculations of a concession. Since concessions were negotiated on a non-discriminatory and most-favoured-nation basis, their withdrawal should also be on that basis ... The intent of the footnote was that any action, except that taken under paragraph 3(a), should be in conformity with the most-favoured-nation concept".[12] The footnote was further examined by a working party which added the phrase, "and that such action should avoid, to the fullest extent possible, injury to other supplying Member countries"[13]; this Note was included in the Charter. However, it was not among those Charter changes which were brought into the General Agreement in 1948.

(a) Non-discriminatory invocation of Article XIX

The "Report on the Accession of Japan" of the Ad-Hoc Committee on Agenda and Intersessional Business in 1953 mentioned the views of contracting parties that "emergency action under Article XIX would have to be non-discriminatory and would thus have to be applied to the trade of all contracting parties, including those which were in no way responsible for the circumstances requiring redress".[14] A suggestion to add an additional clause to Article XIX permitting a discriminatory application of safeguard measures in case of "serious disruption of trade conditions" was rejected.[15]

During the Review Session of 1954-55, Denmark, Norway and Sweden proposed to add a new paragraph at the end of Article XIX on the lines of the Charter Interpretative Note, concerning non-discriminatory invocation of Article XIX. The records indicate that as this proposal did not meet with the general approval of Sub-Group B of Working Party II, it was withdrawn. The Sub-Group considered both this and another Scandinavian proposal to be unnecessary.[16]

---

[10] L/4679, p. 1, para. 4.
[11] Havana Reports p. 82, para. 9.
[12] E.CONF.2/C.3/SR.32, p. 2-3.
[13] E/CONF.2/C.3/49; approval by Committee III without comment at E/CONF.2/C.3/SR.34, p. 7.
[14] L/76, adopted on 13 February 1953, p. 2, para. 6.
[15] *Ibid.*, para. 7.
[16] W.9/193, p. 13.

In an informal note of 26 May 1964 on the "Rationale for Dealing with Market Disruption through the Application of Article XIX", the Executive Secretary stated, *inter alia*:

> "There can be no serious question that the intention of the drafters of Article XIX was that action ... should be of a non-discriminatory character. This indeed is a logical counterpart of the provisions of Article I and Article XIII. This is also borne out by the legislative history and both practice and theory since the drafting of the Article. ... The fact, however, that it was necessary to record this understanding in the legislative proceedings also suggests, however, that the language itself is not conclusive".[17]

In the same Note, the Executive Secretary suggested:

> "as worthy of examination ... to place upon the existing provisions of Article XIX an interpretation which I think they can bear ... and which would in carefully defined circumstances entitle an importing country to protective measures which would be restricted in application to imports from a supplying country which were in fact creating the disruptive situation. It could be argued that the situation results from a combination of the increase of the particular exports in question from the particular source, and the obligation to refrain from discriminatory measures to remedy the situation. If so it would reasonably follow that the obligation regarding non-discrimination could be suspended within the existing language of Article XIX ...".[18]

This interpretation was, however, contested and did not meet with approval.[19]

A Secretariat Note of 1978 on "Modalities of Application of Article XIX" states: "In view of the fact that emergency actions under Article XIX are to be taken in respect of 'such product' and not in respect of individual contracting parties, the indication is that Article I applies."[20]

During the discussion in the Council in March 1978 concerning the EEC's invocation of Article XIX with respect to measures on imports into the United Kingdom of television sets from Korea, "a large number of representatives ... spoke on the matter and expressed the opinion that Article XIX did not provide for the discriminatory application of measures to limit potentially disruptive imports. They considered the measures in question to be clearly inconsistent with GATT provisions. Some delegations expressed serious concern about the use of Article XIX on a selective basis, in particular when this was done in a manner discriminating against a developing country".[21]

The 1980 Panel on "Norway - Restrictions on Imports of Certain Textile Products" examined an Article XIX action by Norway, which consisted of introduction of global quotas on nine textile items. Imports from the EEC and EFTA countries were not subject to these quotas, nor were imports from six developing textile exporting countries with which Norway had concluded bilateral arrangements. The size of the global quotas was calculated on the basis of average imports in 1974-76 from the countries included in the quotas; the quotas were allocated to importers but not allocated by supplier country. The Panel Report provides: "The Panel was of the view that the type of action chosen by Norway, i.e. the quantitative restrictions limiting the importation of the nine textile categories in question, as the form of emergency action under Article XIX was subject to the provisions of Article XIII which provides for non-discriminatory administration of quantitative restrictions. ... The Panel was of the view that to the extent that Norway had acted with effect to allocate import quotas for these products to six countries but had failed to allocate a share to Hong Kong, its Article XIX action was not consistent with Article XIII".[22]

---

[17] L/4679, Annex 2, p. 47-48.
[18] *Ibid.*
[19] L/4679, p. 7.
[20] L/4679, p. 11, para. 35.
[21] C/M/124 p. 19. The 1978 Secretariat Note on "Modalities of Application of Article XIX" states that "This case is the only one in the history of the GATT in which Article XIX action has unilaterally been taken on a discriminatory basis with regard to a single source of supply in a transparent manner." (L/4679 p. 14). The EEC action was revoked after conclusion of a voluntary export restraint arrangement as from 22 June 1979; C/M/134, L/4613/Add.1.
[22] L/4959, adopted on 18 June 1980, 27S/119, 125-126, paras. 14, 16. See further under Article XIII.

(b) Price discrimination

The 1978 Note by the GATT Secretariat on "Modalities of Application of Article XIX" notes that

"A number of actions of a quantitative and tariff-type nature have been linked to the price of the products concerned. In practice, such measures, although applied on a global basis, may have been selective in their application to one or a limited number of countries. In the current ten-year period, ten such instances have been notified, compared to eight during the preceding twenty years. Some of these measures took the form of special customs valuation methods levied for imports at lower prices during a short agricultural or horticultural season. In addition to these measures, there were a few cases in the earlier years where specific duties or surtaxes were replaced by ad valorem rates".[23]

In Council discussion of a 1977 Article XIX action by Finland imposing a surcharge on imports of tights below a basic price, the representative of Singapore noted that Article XIX referred to "any product" and stated that this action was aimed at low-cost suppliers in developing countries. The representative of Finland stated that the measure was fully in accordance with Article XIX.[24]

During discussion in the Committee on Trade and Development in March 1983 of a Canadian Article XIX action on leather footwear, which exempted footwear above a certain value, it was stated that "This price discrimination was not only contrary to the letter and spirit of Article XIX, but also established a dangerous precedent, and had an adverse effect on the export interests of developing countries. ... The representative of Canada stated that in the view of his authorities, the Article XIX action referred to ... was consistent with the relevant provisions of the General Agreement, and the price discrimination element in the action did not constitute a new precedent under the GATT". Several other contracting parties expressed concern at the price-discriminatory use of Article XIX and stated that they regarded a discrimination between suppliers, either geographically or on the basis of prices, as an infringement of GATT rules.[25] Canada's Article XIX action on imports of footwear was discussed again in the GATT Council meeting in March 1985. Concern was expressed at "Canada's application of price breaks in the context of this Article XIX action. Such devices could produce such a narrow and selective definition of source that the action could no longer be said to be truly non-discriminatory. This would appear to conflict with the fundamental principles of the General Agreement".[26]

(5) "to the extent and for such time as may be necessary"

(a) Extent of action under Article XIX

The 1951 Report of the Working Party on the "Withdrawal by the United States of a Tariff Concession under Article XIX" noted that

"the Czechoslovak representative questioned whether the substantial increase in rates of duty involved in the withdrawal were necessary to prevent or remedy the alleged injury and whether the re-establishment of prohibitive duties to enable an uneconomic industry to prolong its existence was consistent with the purposes of the General Agreement. The other members of the Working Party considered that it is impossible to determine in advance with any degree of precision the level of import duty necessary to enable the United States industry to compete with overseas suppliers in the current competitive conditions of the United States market, and that it would be desirable that the position be reviewed by the United States from time to time in the light of experience of the actual effect of the higher import duties now in force on the economic position of the United States industry".[27]

---

[23]L/4679, para. 45.
[24]C/M/119 p. 21-22.
[25]COM.TD/114, p. 10, paras. 41-43.
[26]C/M/186, p.5.
[27]GATT/CP/106, report adopted on 22 October 1951, GATT/CP.6/SR.19, Sales No. GATT/1951-3, p. 24-25, para. 34-35.

(b) Duration of action under Article XIX

At the 1946 London Preparatory Conference it was stated during the course of the discussion of Article 29, the draft Article corresponding to Article XIX, that "the Article provided only for a temporary relaxation of commitments, not for a permanent revision".[28] It was also stated that "the general purpose of Article 29 is to deal with an emergency situation. In general you would expect that it would be short-term, but it does not necessarily have to be under the terms of the Article".[29]

The 1951 Report of the Working Party on the "Withdrawal by the United States of a Tariff Concession under Article XIX" concluded that

> "action under Article XIX is essentially of an emergency character and should be of limited duration. A government taking action under that Article should keep the position under review and be prepared to reconsider the matter as soon as this action is no longer necessary to prevent or remedy a serious injury. In the case under review events which have occurred after it was decided to raise the duties would indicate that it would be desirable for the United States Government to follow the trends of consumption, production and imports in the following months with a view to restoring the concession on hat bodies in whole or in part if and as soon as it becomes clear that its continued complete withdrawal cannot reasonably be maintained to be permissible under Article XIX".[30]

It was also stated that Article XIX required that the original tariff concessions should be wholly or partially restored "if and as soon as the United States industry is in a position to compete with imported supplies without the support of the higher rates of import duty".[31]

The 1984 Report on "Safeguards" by the Chairman of the Council states, *inter alia*:

> "There is a convergence of views that safeguard actions are not intended to protect domestic producers for an unlimited period of time. Safeguard actions are emergency measures which should therefore be temporary by definition and progressively liberalized during the period of their application, unless they are maintained for such a short time as to make this impractical".[32]

(6) "to suspend the obligation in whole or in part or to withdraw or modify the concession": Nature of action under Article XIX

The Report of the Havana Conference Sub-Committee on Articles 40, 41 and 43 notes: "The question was raised whether, in taking action under paragraph 1 of Article 40 [which corresponded to GATT Article XIX], Members would be limited to the reimposition of measures which had been in effect prior to the entry into force of the Charter. It was agreed that the text as drafted does not limit the measures which Members might take".[33]

A 1987 Secretariat Note on "Drafting History of Article XIX and its Place in GATT" notes that tariff measures notified under Article XIX have included increases in specific duties, increases in ad valorem duties, surcharges, surtaxes, imposition of a minimum value for duty, increases in compound duties, compensatory taxes, tariff quotas, and imposition of surtaxes and charges on products imported below a minimum price. Non-tariff measures that have been notified include outright embargoes and bans on import licences, global quotas, discretionary licensing, import deposit schemes, import authorization and other import restrictions. A few actions have involved both tariff and non-tariff measures. During the period 1950-59, actions taken were predominantly tariff measures (80 percent). The next ten-year period saw a rise in the use of non-tariff measures (45 percent)

---

[28]EPCT/C.II/38, p.5.
[29]EPCT/C.II/QR/PV/5, p.77.
[30]GATT/CP/106, report adopted on 22 October 1951, GATT/CP.6/SR.19, Sales No. GATT/1951-3, p. 29-30, para. 50.
[31]*Ibid.*, p. 26 para. 38.
[32]MDF/4, 31S/136, 137, para. 7.
[33]Havana Reports, p. 83, para. 10.

and in the period 1970-79 non-tariff measures constituted the majority (70 percent) of all actions invoked. For the 1980-87 period the share of tariff and non-tariff measures was about equal.[34]

At the 1946 London Preparatory Conference, it was stated that "Language has been inserted in paragraph (1) … which makes it clear that members invoking the Article may withdraw or modify concessions in respect of preferences as well as concessions in respect of tariffs and obligations regarding quantitative restrictions, etc".[35] Individual schemes of preferences for developing countries have provided for certain safeguard mechanisms under which the preference-giving countries have reserved the right to withdraw preferences if they deem it necessary.[36]

(7) Paragraph 1(b)

The purpose of this paragraph was explained at the London Preparatory Conference as follows: "… this right of withdrawal or modification will extend to cases where a country's trade is injured by reason of the loss in whole or in part of a preference which it previously enjoyed in another market".[37]

(8) "shall give notice in writing to the CONTRACTING PARTIES"

The 1951 Report of the Working Party on the "Withdrawal by the United States of a Tariff Concession under Article XIX" examined also the conformity of the United States actions with the notice and consultation requirements of Article XIX, and noted, "In this connection the Working Party wishes to draw the attention of the CONTRACTING PARTIES to the desirability of delaying, as far as practicable, the release of any public announcement on any proposed action under Article XIX, as a premature disclosure to the public would make it difficult for the government proposing to take action to take fully into consideration the representations made by other contracting parties in the course of consultations".[38]

After a discussion on notification of Article XIX actions, including whether such actions could be notified by countries other than those taking them, at its April 1981 meeting the Committee on Safeguards agreed, *inter alia*, on the following conclusion:

"3. All actions taken under Article XIX, and to the extent possible, other actions which serve the same purpose will be notified to the CONTRACTING PARTIES. In addition, it will be open to contracting parties to bring up any matter in accordance with the Understanding Regarding Notification, Consultation, Dispute Settlement and Surveillance".[39]

Lists of Article XIX actions notified to the Secretariat appear in the following notes:

-- Factual Note on Safeguards prepared by the Secretariat in 1973.[40]

-- Study on "Emergency type actions in the widest sense" prepared by the Secretariat in 1975.[41]

-- Secretariat Note of 5 July 1978 on "Modalities of Application of Article XIX", including a table of Article XIX actions.[42]

-- Secretariat Note of 26 March 1982, including a revised and updated list of measures taken since 1978 and notified under Article XIX, as well as of "grey-area" measures.[43]

---

[34]MTN.GNG/NG9/W/7, dated 16 September 1987, p. 4.
[35]London Report, p. 10, para. 3(b)(i).
[36]COM.IND/W/88/Rev.1, Annex C.
[37]EPCT/C.II/PV/12, p. 12.
[38]GATT/CP/106, report adopted on 22 October 1951, GATT/CP.6/SR.19, Sales No. GATT/1951-3, para. 46.
[39]L/5151, paras. 20-28.
[40]COM.IND/W/88/Rev.1, dated 18 January 1973.
[41]MTN/SG/W/1.
[42]L/4679.
[43]Spec(82)18 and Rev.1-Rev.3 (through 22 May 1984).

-- Background Note by the Secretariat prepared in 1987 including an "Inventory of Article XIX Actions and other Measures which Appear to Serve the Same Purpose".[44]

A table of Article XIX actions notified to the Secretariat up to October 1993 appears at the end of this chapter.

(9) "in critical circumstances"

At the Havana Conference, it was decided to substitute the words "in circumstances of special urgency" for "in critical circumstances" as a clarifying change.[45] However, this was not among those Charter changes which were brought into the General Agreement in 1948.

In practice, the provision that in critical circumstances action may be taken provisionally without prior consultation has been applied in a large number of cases.[46]

2.   Paragraph 3

(1) "If agreement among the interested contracting parties with respect to the action is not reached"

With reference to import restrictions under Article XIX applied by Australia on motor vehicles and on footwear which had been in effect since 1974/75 (with some interruption in the application of the restrictions on motor vehicles), the European Communities, in 1982, notified the intention to suspend tariff concessions granted by the Community on selected imports from Australia "in accordance with the procedures of paragraph 3(a) of Article XIX".[47] Australia then requested that a meeting of the Council be convened within thirty days of the Communities' notification "in order to discharge the responsibility of the CONTRACTING PARTIES under paragraph 3(a) of Article XIX of the General Agreement".

In February 1982, Australia requested the Council to disapprove the proposed action (see at page 526 below). During the discussion on this matter the representative of the EEC stated that "The Community recognized Australia's right to invoke the provisions of Article XIX. At the same time, it considered that the entire procedure provided for under Article XIX should be followed, which included the offer of compensation. ... He pointed out that there was no requirement that there be a prior agreement between the parties in order for the affected party to take action under Article XIX. He said that the element of agreement concerned the compensation, and that if there were no agreement on this issue, the affected party was free to take retaliatory action as provided for in Article XIX, unless the CONTRACTING PARTIES disapproved".[48] The Australian representative agreed that "there was no need for a prior agreement for the type of action contemplated by the Community".[49]

The Report in 1984 by the Chairman of the Council to the Fortieth Session on "Safeguards" noted that:

"There is a convergence of views that contracting parties should retain the right given to them in the General Agreement to re-establish the balance of rights and obligations under the Agreement if this is significantly modified. At the same time, it is recognized that the right to retaliate can, in practice, be used more effectively by some contracting parties than others. There is furthermore a convergence of views that the threat of retaliation could have a deterrent effect against the application of safeguard actions; the possibility of retaliation could also promote agreement on compensation. There is, at the same time, a recognition that retaliatory action has trade disruptive effects. The conclusion that many participants draw is that, wherever possible, constructive settlements should be reached involving compensation rather than the retaliatory withdrawal of benefits ...".[50]

---

[44]MTN.GNG/NG9/W/2/Rev.1 and Corr.1.
[45]Havana Reports, p. 83, para. 13.
[46]C/111, p. 8.
[47]L/4526/Add.23, L/4099/Add.25; see also documents on Australian action on motor vehicles, L/4526, and on footwear, L/4099.
[48]C/M/155, p. 4, p. 5.
[49]C/M/155, p. 6.
[50]MDF/4, 31S/136, 137 para. 8.

A Secretariat Note on "Drafting History of Article XIX and its Place in GATT" states that, as of 1987, there had been 20 instances of agreement or offers of compensation, usually when the Article XIX action took the form of a tariff increase. There were 10 such cases during 1950-59, eight cases in 1960-69, one case in 1970-79 and one case in 1980-87. With the declining incidence of compensation, there had been an increasing incidence of invocation of Article XIX:3.[51]

(2)   "not later than ninety days after such action is taken"

The period provided in Article XIX:3 for notification of any proposed suspension of obligations or concessions was extended on several occasions by decisions of the CONTRACTING PARTIES, including certain cases from 1952 through 1964 which are listed in the accompanying table.[52]

More recently, the practice has evolved of extending the ninety-day period referred to in paragraph 3(a) of Article XIX through bilateral agreement between the contracting parties concerned with subsequent submission of a joint communication to the other contracting parties to the effect that they, for example, "have agreed that their reciprocal rights and obligations under the General Agreement will be maintained and for this purpose have agreed that the ninety-day period set forth in Article XIX:3(a) shall be considered to expire on"... [date fixed].[53] The texts of such communications are published in addenda to the basic documents on the respective safeguard measures referred to in the table at the end of this chapter.

In the February 1975 Council meeting

"the representative of the European Communities stated that, in connection with the recent Article XIX action on imports of certain footwear taken by Australia, the European Communities had asked for a prolongation by mutual agreement of the period of ninety days, referred to in paragraph 3(a) of Article XIX. There were several precedents for such a prolongation by mutual agreements between the parties. The Australian delegation, however, believed that a decision of this nature would have to be taken by the CONTRACTING PARTIES. He therefore asked whether any other contracting party was of the opinion that such a decision would come under the jurisdiction of the CONTRACTING PARTIES and whether such contracting party would have objections to such a decision. A number of representatives stated that they had never encountered any difficulty in reaching agreement with the other party for an extension of the period referred to in Article XIX:3(a) in order to continue consultations rather than having recourse to retaliation. ... The representative of the European Communities stated that ... it appeared to him that no objection had been voiced in the Council to the extension of the time limit for a reasonable period of time".[54]

In 1981, Australia raised again, but did not pursue, the procedural question of whether or not contracting parties to the GATT may agree bilaterally to extend the ninety-day period referred to in Article XIX or whether, since the General Agreement makes no provision for bilaterally agreed extensions of the ninety-day period, such an extension should be approved by the CONTRACTING PARTIES.[55]

By a communication dated 14 January 1984, the EC notified a proposed compensatory adjustment, to take effect on 1 March 1984, in response to a US Article XIX action on certain specialty steels. At the GATT Council meeting in February 1984 the United States representative requested the Council to extend the time limit under Article XIX:3(a) for an additional thirty days, stating that "more time should be allowed for the two parties to reconcile the major discrepancies and problems in the Community's calculations before the Community retaliated". The EC representative stated that the EC could not agree to the US request for a further extension. In response to a question regarding whether the Council would be competent to take the decision requested of it,

---

[51] MTN.GNG/NG9/W/7, dated 16 September 1987, p. 5.

[52] See, e.g., decision of 29 October 1952 "to extend by ninety days the period provided under Article XIX:3 for the Turkish Government to notify the CONTRACTING PARTIES of any suspension of equivalent obligations or concessions which it might propose", SR.7/11, p. 1, L/44/Add.1.

[53] See also L/7219/Add.3-5 (reference to "the time period set forth in Article XIX:3(a) within which [contracting party] must notify any intention to suspend substantially equivalent concessions").

[54] C/M/103.

[55] L/5026/Add.10, L/4099/Add.20; no subsequent Council discussion of this case.

Decisions by the CONTRACTING PARTIES extending time limits under Article XIX:3

Australia		
Motor mowers	Decision of 19 September 1960	L/1217/Add.1, 9S/267
Woollen piece goods	Decision of 31 August 1961	L/1546, 10S/270
	Decision of 16 November 1961	L/1638, 10S/270
Heat-resisting glassware	Decision of 6 July 1964	C/M/21
Germany		
Hard coal products	Decision of 17 November 1958	L/920, 7S/128
United States		
Bicycles	Decision of 17 October 1955	L/433, 4S/31
Clinical thermometers	Decision of 8 September 1958	L/803/Add.2
Cotton typewriter ribbon cloth	Decision of 18 November 1960	L/1397, 9S/267
Dried figs	Decision of 29 October 1952	G/39, 1S/107
	Decision of 8 November 1952	G/39, 1S/28
	Decision of 23 October 1953	2S/26
Lead and zinc	Decision of 22 November 1958	L/940
	Decision of 27 May 1959	L/1012, 8S/179
	Decision of 20 November 1959	L/1078, 8S/179
	Decision of 4 June 1960	L/1246, 9S/267
Linen towelling	Decision of 14 September 1956	5S/32
Safety pins	Decision of 4 April 1958	L/624/Add.2
Spring clothes pins	Decision of 24 April 1958	L/757/Add.1
Stainless steel table flatware	Decision of 18 February 1960	L/1076/Add.1, 9S/267

the Director-General said that "if the Community agreed to the US request for an extension of the date of entry into force of the retaliatory measures, this could be done. If the Community did not agree, its retaliatory measures could be put into place on 1 March unless the Council were to disapprove of them; but, in the absence of disapproval, the Council could not postpone the entry into force of the measures, because this was the Community's sovereign right".[56]

(3) "to suspend ... the application ... of such substantially equivalent concessions"

In the February 1982 Council discussion of proposed EEC measures under Article XIX:3 with respect to Australia,[57] the Australian representative stated that

"Australia did not dispute the right of a contracting party to take action, but it disputed the nature and the extent of this action and whether or not there existed a substantial equivalence".[58]

"... although a contracting party was entitled to re-establish the balance of concessions, it was not entitled to calculate retrospectively and to take retaliatory action on alleged trade losses over a subsequent period of years beyond the original ninety-day consultative period. ... In the case of motor vehicles, one single atypical year (1974) had been chosen as the base representative period, whereas the normal GATT practice was to use the three-year average, as the EEC had done in the case of footwear. Nonetheless, even when applying the EEC's method and statistical base, but using normal three-year base periods, imports of motor vehicles from the EEC in each year between 1975 and 1980 significantly exceeded the average levels achieved in the base periods. Also, the EEC's actual share of the Australian market in each of these years was higher than in either of the base periods. Thus, on the basis of either market shares or actual trade levels, the EEC had no basis on which to take retaliatory action.

---

[56]C/M/174, p. 11; notification under Article XIX:3, L/5524/Add.15.
[57]L/4099/Add.25, L/4526/Add.23; discussion at C/M/155 p. 1-11.
[58]C/M/155, p. 6.

"Turning to footwear, he said that Australia had similar conceptual and practical problems. In addition, although Australia's Article XIX action on footwear had ceased on 31 December 1981, the EEC sought to take retaliatory action which was totally open-ended. His delegation rejected the notion that the EEC could, at any time in the future, impose a discriminatory tariff on one or all of the items listed in [the EEC's notifications of proposed action], at any level of duty, despite the fact that its rights under Article XIX had expired, and when the Article XIX action taken by Australia itself had expired".[59]

The EEC representative responded that "in the case of motor vehicles, Australia had set up a quota restriction as well as a customs surcharge ... in order to ensure that 80 percent of the Australian market would be reserved for local production. This had resulted in considerable injury for European producers during the previous seven years ... Australia now had the intention of continuing this action on motor vehicles for another three years". He stated that Australia's offer of compensation had not been acceptable to the EEC because it "did not compensate for the seven years of injury experienced by it".[60]

Other contracting parties also expressed concern at the open-ended nature of the proposed EEC suspension of bindings. It was stated that, "since the damage calculated by the Community referred to a time period, countermeasures might also be expected to be limited in duration ... on the only previous occasion when the CONTRACTING PARTIES had decided not to disapprove a countermeasure - the 1952 case of Turkish countermeasures to US Article XIX action on dried figs - the Turkish action was to be effective only for the period in which the US continued to impose the increased duty on dried figs". The representative of the European Communities stated that "the suspension of concessions was temporary, since any EEC action would remain in force only for the time strictly necessary to compensate the damage".[61]

In March 1985, in response to a notification by the EC of proposed compensatory measures in response to a Canadian Article XIX action on imports of footwear[62], at the Council meeting the representative of Canada stated that "Canada did not question the right of a contracting party to suspend concessions pursuant to Article XIX:3(a) if a mutually satisfactory settlement could not be found. However, the contracting party was required to limit such suspensions to substantially equivalent concessions or other obligations. Canada considered that the Community's proposals did not meet that requirement, and it did not accept the basis for the level of the proposed suspensions, i.e. the Community's calculation of trade impairment in the area of Can.$58 million. Nor did Canada accept that a total embargo on the import of any product (as the Community proposed with respect to Canadian footwear products) could be justified as a suspension of substantially equivalent concessions or other obligations".[63]

The table of Article XIX actions following this chapter notes all known instances to date of action under Article XIX:3.

(4) "to the trade of the contracting party taking such action"

In the discussion of the report of Sub-Committee D in Committee III at the Havana Conference, it was stated with regard to paragraph 3(a) of Article 40, which corresponds to Article XIX:3(a) of the General Agreement:

"Paragraph 3(a) offered counteraction against emergency actions; the phrase 'to the trade of the Member' showed a discriminatory characteristic not evident in the other paragraphs".[64]

---

[59] C/M/155, p. 2-3.
[60] C/M/155, p. 4.
[61] C/M/155, p. 6, 7.
[62] L/5351/Add.22, proposing a one-year total import ban on Canadian footwear and one-year increases in duties applicable to imports of certain products from Canada.
[63] C/M/186, p. 4.
[64] E/CONF.2/C.3/SR.32, p. 3.

(5) "upon the expiration of thirty days from the day on which written notice of such suspension is received by the CONTRACTING PARTIES"

In past instances, these words have been understood to mean that the thirty days started counting on the date of receipt of the written notice in the GATT Secretariat. See, e.g., the notice of a 1952 action under Article XIX:3(a) by Belgium against the United States:

"As written notice of this suspension was received on the 22 April, the suspension became effective on 22 May 1952".[65]

In the February 1982 Council discussion noted above on the EC's Article XIX:3 action against Australia, the Chairman ruled that "Article XIX:3 indicated that a contracting party could not take retaliatory action before the expiry of thirty days or if it were disapproved by the Council. This did not mean that a contracting party was compelled to take such action at the end of the thirty-day period".[66]

(6) "the suspension of which the CONTRACTING PARTIES do not disapprove"

The CONTRACTING PARTIES have never "disapproved" of a countermeasure to a withdrawal pursuant to Article XIX:3(a). There is only one instance of the CONTRACTING PARTIES in session taking a formal decision *not* to disapprove proposed compensatory action, in the case of Turkish action under Article XIX:3(a) against the US in 1952.[67]

The notice of a 1952 action under Article XIX:3(a) by Belgium against the United States, referred to above, is phrased as follows:

"It was reported in GATT/AIR/14 of 23 April 1952 that the Government of Belgium had engaged in consultations with the Government of the United States, concerning the action of the latter in modifying the concession on hatters' fur in Part I of Schedule XX, and had announced its intention to suspend, under the provisions of Article XIX:3(a), the application of the following concession in the Schedule of Benelux to the trade of the United States: ... Since no request had been received from any contracting party to secure consideration of the proposed action, the proposed suspension of the concession on Item 312 in Schedule II, to the trade of the United States, is deemed to be a substantially equivalent concession, under the Agreement, the suspension of which the Contracting Parties do not disapprove, within the terms of paragraph 3(a) of Article XIX ...".[68]

The Report of the Review Session Working Party on "Quantitative Restrictions" noted, with respect to the phrase "the suspension of which the CONTRACTING PARTIES do not disapprove" that "it is clear, both from the text itself and from the practice followed so far by the CONTRACTING PARTIES, that the contracting party affected is not obliged to obtain prior approval from the CONTRACTING PARTIES and that the object of the phrase quoted is merely to indicate that the CONTRACTING PARTIES have a right to require adjustments in the action taken if they consider that the action goes beyond what is necessary to restore the balance of benefits".[69]

At the 7 February 1984 Council meeting in discussion of proposed EEC compensatory measures under Article XIX:3(a) with respect to a United States Article XIX action on certain specialty steels, the United States argued that the proposed EEC action was "excessive by the standards of Article XIX:3(a)". The EEC representative stated that if, after the date of implementation of the EEC's measures, "the United States considered that the Community's measures were excessive, then the CONTRACTING PARTIES would have the right, as stressed by a working party in 1955, 'to require adjustments in the action taken if they consider that the action goes beyond what is necessary to restore the balance of benefits'".[70] The US then submitted a request for a decision

---

[65]L/9.
[66]C/M/155, p. 10.
[67]Decision of 8 November 1952, L/57, 1S/28-30, SR.7/15.
[68]L/9.
[69]L/332/Rev.1 and Addenda, adopted on 2, 4 and 5 March 1955, 3S/170, 182, para. 39.
[70]C/M/174, p. 11-12.

disapproving the measures notified by the EEC.[71] At the 22 February 1984 Council meeting, the US representative stated that the EEC measures "would exceed the level which could be considered 'substantially equivalent' to the US action, and that therefore, the CONTRACTING PARTIES should disapprove of the Community's proposal unless it was modified to conform with the criteria of Article XIX. The United States had tried to ensure ... that its safeguard action was proportionate to the injury that the US industry had suffered. It was equally important for the integrity of the safeguard process that any retaliatory action did not exceed the effect of the measures; and the question of the quality of responsive measures to safeguard actions should be a matter of concern for the Council". The two parties agreed to continue consultations to find a satisfactory solution.[72]

B. RELATIONSHIP BETWEEN ARTICLE XIX AND OTHER GATT PROVISIONS

1. **Articles I and XIII**

See the discussion above beginning on page 519 concerning "Non-discriminatory invocation of Article XIX".

2. **Article XVIII:A**

The 1951 Working Party "Report on the Withdrawal of a Tariff Concession by the United States" noted, in relation to Article XVIII as it existed prior to its amendment in 1955:

"... it must be commented that any proposal to withdraw a tariff concession in order to promote the establishment or development of domestic production of a new or novel type of product in which overseas suppliers have opened up a new market is not permissible under Article XIX but should be dealt with under other provisions of the Agreement, such as Article XVIII. On the other hand, it may be permissible to have recourse to Article XIX if a new or novel type of imported product is replacing the customary domestic product to a degree which causes or threatens serious injury to domestic producers".[73]

3. **Article XXIII**

See under Article XXIII.

4. **Article XXIV**

See under Article XXIV.

5. **Part IV**

See under Part IV.

6. **Article XIX actions and rectification and modification of schedules**

The Report of the Working Party on "Preparation of the Second Protocol of Rectifications and Modifications and Legal Status of the Consolidated Schedules" noted:

"The question was raised in the Working Party of giving effect to withdrawals of concessions under Article XIX ... by means of including such withdrawals in protocols of rectifications and modifications. The Working Party considered that this would be an undesirable procedure since all withdrawals would thus be given an irrevocable character and eventual reinstatement of such concessions would be difficult".[74]

---

[71]L/5524/Add.21-22, L/5524/Add.22/Corr.1.
[72]C/M/175, p. 2-3; no further Council discussion.
[73]GATT/CP/106, report adopted on 22 October 1951, GATT/CP.6/SR.19, Sales No. GATT/1951-3, p. 21, para. 28.
[74]G/34, adopted on 8 November 1952, 1S/64, 65, para. 5.

The current Procedures for Modification and Rectification of Schedules of Tariff Concessions[75] do not provide for certification of changes in schedules resulting from Article XIX action.

C. EXCEPTIONS AND DEROGATIONS

1. Special safeguards provisions in certain protocols of accession

Certain protocols of accession contain special safeguards provisions for consultations and possible remedial action if any product is being imported "in such increased quantities or under such conditions as to cause or threaten serious injury ...". Paragraph 4 of the Protocol for the Accession of Poland provides as follows:

"(a) If any product is being imported into the territory of a contracting party from the territory of Poland in such increased quantities or under such conditions as to cause or threaten serious injury to domestic producers in the former territory of like or directly competitive products, the provisions of (b) to (e) of this paragraph shall apply.

"(b) The contracting party concerned may request Poland to enter into consultation with it. Any such request shall be notified to the CONTRACTING PARTIES. If, as a result of this consultation, Poland agrees that the situation referred to in (a) above exists, it shall limit exports or take such other action, which may include action with respect to the price at which the exports are sold, as will prevent or remedy the injury.

"(c) Should it not be possible to reach agreement between Poland and the contracting party concerned as a result of consultation under (b), the matter may be referred to the CONTRACTING PARTIES who shall promptly investigate the matter and who may make recommendations to Poland or to the contracting party which initially raised the matter.

"(d) If following action under (b) and (c) above, agreement is still not reached between Poland and the contracting party concerned, the contracting party shall be free to restrict imports from the territory of Poland of the product concerned to the extent and for such time as is necessary to prevent or remedy the injury. Poland shall then be free to deviate from its obligations to the contracting party in respect of substantially equivalent trade.

"(e) In critical circumstances, where delay would cause damage difficult to repair the contracting party affected may take action provisionally without prior consultation, on the condition that consultation shall be effected immediately after taking such action".[76]

Paragraph 5 of the Protocol for the Accession of Hungary and paragraph 4 of the Accession of Romania contain identical provisions as follows:

"(a) If any product is being imported, in the trade between [Hungary] and contracting parties, in such increased quantities or under such conditions as to cause or threaten serious injury to domestic producers of like or directly competitive products, the provisions of (b) to (e) of this paragraph shall apply.

"(b) [Hungary] or the contracting party concerned may request consultations. Any such request shall be notified to the CONTRACTING PARTIES. If, as a result of such consultations, it is agreed that the situation referred to in (a) above exists, exports shall be limited or such other action taken, which may include action, if possible, with respect to the price at which the exports are sold, as will prevent or remedy the injury.

"(c) Should it not be possible to reach agreement between the parties concerned as a result of consultation under (b), the matter may be referred to the CONTRACTING PARTIES who shall promptly investigate the matter and who make appropriate recommendations to [Hungary] or to the contracting party concerned.

---

[75] Adopted on 26 March 1980, 27S/25.
[76] 15S/46, 48-49, para. 4.

"(d) If, following action under (b) and (c) above, agreement is still not reached between the parties concerned, the contracting party concerned shall be free to restrict the imports of the products concerned to the extent and for such time as is necessary to prevent or remedy the injury. The other party shall then be free to deviate from its obligations to the contracting party concerned in respect of substantially equivalent trade.

"(e) In critical circumstances, where delay would cause damage difficult to repair, such preventive or remedial action may be taken provisionally without prior consultation, on the condition that consultation shall be effected immediately after taking such action".[77]

The Report of the Working Party on "Accession of Hungary" notes in this respect:

"Members of the Working Party considered it important to have in a protocol of accession a specific safeguard clause. Representatives of countries maintaining quantitative restrictions against Hungary's exports indicated in this connexion that the inclusion of such a safeguard clause would facilitate the removal of the restrictions [maintained inconsistently with Article XIII]. The representative of Hungary could agree to the inclusion of a safeguard clause, provided it operated on a reciprocal basis. He also stated that his acceptance of such a safeguard clause was in anticipation of the early elimination of quantitative restrictions maintained against imports from Hungary, inconsistently with Article XIII. Paragraph 5 of the draft Protocol has been prepared taking into account these views".[78]

2. Arrangement Regarding International Trade in Textiles (MFA)

The Arrangement Regarding International Trade in Textiles (MFA) of 20 December 1973[79] included special safeguard provisions but provided, in paragraph 6 of its Article 1, that "the provisions of this Arrangement shall not affect the rights and obligations of the participating countries under the GATT". The period of validity of the MFA was extended several times, most recently by the Protocol Maintaining in Force the Arrangement Regarding International Trade in Textiles of 9 December 1993, which provided that the Arrangement was to be maintained in force until 31 December 1994, at which time the MFA expired.[80] Trade in textiles and clothing is now governed by the Agreement on Textiles and Clothing in Annex 1A of the WTO Agreement. Article 1:6 of this Agreement provides: "Unless otherwise provided in this Agreement, its provisions shall not affect the rights and obligations of Members under the provisions of the WTO Agreement and the Multilateral Trade Agreements".

The question whether, in the light of Article 1:6, a party to the MFA could invoke GATT provisions for restrictive actions relating to textile products, was discussed in the Textiles Surveillance Body on several occasions.[81] Paragraphs 9, 23 and 26 respectively of the Conclusions of the Textiles Committee adopted on 14 December 1977, 22 December 1981 and 31 July 1986 which are confirmed in and attached to the 1977, 1981 and 1986 Protocols Extending the Arrangement Regarding International Trade in Textiles, provided, *inter alia*, "that in order to ensure the proper functioning of the MFA, all participants would refrain from taking measures on textiles covered by the MFA outside the provisions therein before exhausting all the relief measures provided in the MFA".[82] With regard to paragraph 23 of the Conclusions, the view was expressed "that, pursuant to Article 1:6 of the MFA, resort to any of the provisions of the GATT was fully consistent with the objectives of this paragraph".[83] The representative of Colombia, speaking on behalf of developing exporting countries, said "that the MFA, as extended by the new Protocol adopted by the Textiles Committee, constituted the multilaterally

---

[77]20S/3, 4-5 (Hungary); 18S/5, 7, para. 4 (Romania). Concerning the use of these safeguard clauses by contracting parties see the Working Party Report on "Trade with Hungary - Seventh Review under the Protocol of Accession", L/6535, adopted on 19 July 1989, 36S/416, 422 para. 38; also, the Working Party Report on "Trade with Romania - Sixth Review under the Protocol of Accession", L/6282, adopted on 2 February 1988, 35S/337, 344-345 paras. 25-26, 30-31, and L/6155; see also Working Party Report on "Accession of Greece to the European Communities", L/5453, adopted on 9 March 1983, 30S/168, 178-179 paras. 30 and 32.

[78]L/3889, adopted on 30 July 1973, 20S/34, 35 para. 9.

[79]TEX.NG/1, 21S/3; L/5276, 28S/3.

[80]L/7363 (text of Protocol); COM.TEX/76, Annex II (Decision by the Textiles Committee).

[81]24S/28, 44-48, paras. 60-70; COM.TEX/SB/210, 225, 255.

[82]L/4616, 24S/5, 7, para. 9; L/5276, 28S/3, 8, para. 23; L/6030, 33S/7, 14, para. 26.

[83]COM.TEX/W/127, para. 14.

agreed special framework governing international trade in textiles. It would therefore be the only legal basis for future bilateral agreements between exporting and importing participants".[84]

D. "Voluntary Export Restraints" and Grey-Area Measures

During the discussion in the Council in March 1978 concerning the EEC's invocation of Article XIX with respect to the imposition of import restrictions on monochrome television sets imported into the United Kingdom from Korea, the Korean representative stated that these restrictions were imposed in violation of the relevant provisions of the GATT, and "expressed concern that acquiescence on the part of the CONTRACTING PARTIES in this case might be utilized as a precedent for legitimizing selective import restrictions in the conduct of international trade". The Hong Kong delegation "emphasized that Article XIX was not susceptible of being invoked on a discriminatory basis. He referred to [discussions during the Havana Conference and in 1953, noted above at page 519 and following] ... The only derogation from this principle of non-discrimination was in the Textiles Arrangements, which would not have been necessary if Article XIX had been capable of being used in a selective manner. ... A large number of representatives also spoke on the matter and expressed the opinion that Article XIX did not provide for the discriminatory application of measures to limit potentially disruptive imports". It was also stated that "voluntary restraint agreements were often forced upon the weaker members of the GATT ... there was no provision in the General Agreement that provided a legal basis for discriminatory restraints, even when they were supported by an agreement of a voluntary nature".[85]

A Note by the Director-General on "Safeguards", which is annexed to the 1984 Report on "Safeguards" by the Chairman of the Council to the Fortieth Session of the CONTRACTING PARTIES, notes as follows:

> "Export restrictions are generally prohibited under Article XI unless covered by an exception. Measures limiting exports to certain contracting parties only are, in any case, contrary to the provisions of Article XIII (except in the exceptional situations laid down in Article XIV) which provides for the non-discriminatory application of such restrictions. It may be argued that this is a very legalistic way of looking at the matter and that 'voluntary export restraints' are not, in fact, export restrictions but import restrictions which are administered by the exporting country. They would, once again, only be in conformity with the General Agreement if they were justified under a particular exception to Article XI and administered in accordance with the provisions relating to the non-discriminatory administration of quantitative restrictions contained in Article XIII. In fact 'voluntary' export restraints are clearly contrary to the present rules of the General Agreement and are only 'outside the General Agreement' in the sense that governments have not brought them formally to the GATT for examination".[86]

Grey-area measures have been examined by panels under Article XXIII on a number of occasions. In 1980, the Panel on "EEC - Restrictions on Imports of Apples from Chile" examined a suspension by the EEC of imports of apples from Chile, after arrangements were reached with four other Southern Hemisphere suppliers for the restraint of their exports of apples to the EEC. In its findings,

> "The Panel examined the EEC measure in relation to Article XIII:1. The Panel found that the EEC suspension applied to imports from Chile was not a restriction similar to the voluntary restraint agreements negotiated with the other Southern Hemisphere suppliers on the basis primarily that:
>
> "(a) there was a difference in transparency between the two types of action;
>
> "(b) there was a difference in the administration of the restrictions, the one being an import restriction, the other an export restraint; and
>
> "(c) the import suspension was unilateral and mandatory while the other was voluntary and negotiated.

---

[84]*Ibid.*, para. 17.
[85]C/M/124, p. 18-20.
[86]MDF/4, p. 6, para. 11; MDF/4 appears at 31S/136 but the Annex is not reproduced.

"... Notwithstanding the Panel's conclusions regarding the lack of similarity of the restrictions with regard to Article XIII:1, and in light of XIII:5, the Panel proceeded to consider the EEC import suspension against Chile and the voluntary restraint agreements with other Southern Hemisphere exporters as 'quotas' for purposes of the Panel's examination of the EEC measure under XIII:2".[87]

In 1989, the Panel on "EEC - Restrictions on Imports of Dessert Apples - Complaint by Chile" examined a later suspension by the EEC of imports of apples from Chile. With regard to Article XIII:2 and :4, "...the Panel did not find any basis in the General Agreement for the EC taking into account as 'special factors' the restraint alleged to have been exercised in previous years by other suppliers".[88]

See also the 1988 Report of the Panel on "Japan - Trade in Semi-conductors", which examined, *inter alia*, a third-country market monitoring scheme established by Japan after the 1985 Arrangement with the United States concerning Trade in Semiconductors. In its findings,

"The Panel examined the parties' contentions in the light of Article XI:1. ... The Panel noted that this wording [of Article XI:1] was comprehensive: it applied to all measures instituted or maintained by a contracting party prohibiting or restricting the importation, exportation or sale for export of products other than measures that take the form of duties, taxes or other charges.

"The Panel noted that the CONTRACTING PARTIES had decided in a previous case that the import regulation allowing the import of a product in principle, but not below a minimum price level, constituted a restriction on importation within the meaning of Article XI:1 (BISD 25S/99). The Panel considered that the principle applied in that case to restrictions on imports of goods below certain prices was equally applicable to restrictions on exports below certain prices.

"The Panel then examined the contention of the Japanese Government that the measures complained of were not restrictions within the meaning of Article XI:1 because they were not legally binding or mandatory. In this respect the Panel noted that Article XI:1, unlike other provisions of the General Agreement, did not refer to laws or regulations but more broadly to measures. This wording indicated clearly that any measure instituted or maintained by a contracting party which restricted the exportation or sale for export of products was covered by this provision, irrespective of the legal status of the measure".[89]

"... The Panel concluded that the complex of measures constituted a coherent system restricting the sale for export of monitored semi-conductors at prices below company-specific costs to markets other than the United States, inconsistent with Article XI.1".[90]

With regard to the possibility of using dispute settlement proceedings under the General Agreement to enforce agreements between contracting parties providing for "voluntary export restraints", it may be noted that a Decision of the CONTRACTING PARTIES provides that "The determination of rights and obligations between governments arising under a bilateral agreement is not a matter within the competence of the CONTRACTING PARTIES". A footnote to this decision provides that "This Decision by its terms clearly refers only to the determination of the rights and obligations as between the parties to the bilateral agreement and arising from it.

---

[87]L/5047, adopted on 10 November 1980, 27S/98, 114, paras. 4.11-4.12. The Panel found the EEC measure to be inconsistent with paragraphs 1, 2(a), 2(d) and 3(b) first sentence of Article XIII; *ibid.*, para. 4.25.
[88]L/6491, adopted on 22 June 1989, 36S/93, 131 para. 12.24.
[89]L/6309, adopted on 4 May 1988, 35S/116, 153-154, paras. 104-106.
[90]*Ibid.*, 35S/158, para. 117.

It is, however, within the competence of the CONTRACTING PARTIES to determine whether action under such a bilateral agreement would or would not conflict with the provisions of the General Agreement".[91]

A series of lists of "grey-area measures" have been compiled by the Secretariat, most recently in 1987.[92]

E. WORK UNDERTAKEN IN THE GATT ON SAFEGUARDS

A Secretariat Note of 1987 on "Work Already Undertaken in the GATT on Safeguards" describes the history of discussions on safeguards as follows:

At the time that Japan's accession to the GATT was under discussion in February 1953, some contracting parties wished to retain the right to apply discriminatory quantitative restrictions on imports from Japan.[93] They suggested that an additional safeguard clause should be introduced into the General Agreement, arguing that a large number of Article XIX actions, which would have to be applied on a most-favoured-nation basis, might lead to a general raising of barriers to world trade. Other contracting parties felt that no additional safeguard clause was required. A suggestion was made that in order to avoid a higher general level of barriers to world trade, contracting parties might bring cases to the GATT under Article XXIII, paragraph 2, under which the CONTRACTING PARTIES could authorize the application of safeguard actions on a discriminatory basis. However, some delegations pointed out that there might be circumstances in which the procedures of Article XXIII would be too slow in operation to provide adequate safeguards, and they suggested that if the CONTRACTING PARTIES failed to reach a decision within thirty days, provisional safeguard measures might be taken pending a decision of the CONTRACTING PARTIES. In the end there was no agreement on the application of Article XXIII along these lines.

Japan became a contracting party in September 1955 without any new general safeguard clause being added to the General Agreement. Some contracting parties invoked Article XXXV on Japan's accession. In a number of cases, Japan negotiated bilateral trade agreements containing special safeguard clauses and then the countries concerned disinvoked Article XXXV. Some countries did not invoke Article XXXV but nevertheless continued to discriminate against Japan.[94]

At the November 1959 Session of the CONTRACTING PARTIES, some delegations stated that sharp increases in imports, over a brief period of time and in a narrow range of commodities, could have serious economic, political and social repercussions in the importing countries. The CONTRACTING PARTIES accordingly decided that the secretariat should prepare a factual study on the question of "market disruption".[95] The outcome of the study showed that a wide variety of products, chiefly textiles and clothing products, were subject to import restrictions applied by a number of countries to deal with market disruption.[96] In June 1960 a Working Party on "Avoidance of Market Disruption" was established. In November 1960, a Decision was adopted recognizing that

"(a) In a number of countries situations occur or threaten to occur which have been described as 'market disruption'.

"(b) These situations generally contain the following elements in combination:

---

[91]Decision of 9 August 1949, II/11 (relating to a matter raised by Cuba with reference to a Cuba-US agreement providing for trade preferences). See also L/1636 (Note of 1961 by the Executive Secretary stating that CONTRACTING PARTIES have jurisdiction to examine consistency of bilateral agreements with rights of third GATT contracting parties).

[92]Spec(82)18 dated 26 March 1982; Spec(82)18/Rev.3 dated 22 May 1984; L/6087, dated 28 November 1986; Secretariat Note on "Inventory of Article XIX Actions and Other Measures which Appear to Serve the Same Purpose", MTN.GNG/NG9/W/2/Rev.1, dated 17 August 1987, and Corr.1 dated 31 August 1987; Background Note by the Secretariat on "'Grey-Area' Measures" dated 16 September 1987, MTN.GNG/NG9/W/6. See also various reports under the Trade Policy Review Mechanism since 1989.

[93]L/76.

[94]See, e.g., L/1164, page 33.

[95]8S/22.

[96]L/1164.

"(i) a sharp and substantial increase or potential increase of imports of particular products from particular sources;

"(ii) these products are offered at prices which are substantially below those prevailing for similar goods of comparable quality in the market of the importing country;

"(iii) there is serious damage to domestic producers or threat thereof;

"(iv) the price differentials referred to in paragraph (ii) above do not arise from governmental intervention in the fixing or formation of prices or from dumping practices. ...

"(c) These situations have often led governments to take a variety of exceptional measures. In some cases importing countries have taken or maintained discriminatory measures either outside the framework of the General Agreement, or contrary to the provisions of the General Agreement. In some other cases exporting countries have tried to correct the situation by taking measures to limit or control the export of the products giving rise to the situation.

"(d) Such measures, taken unilaterally or through bilateral arrangement, may in some cases tend to cause difficulties in other markets and create problems for other contracting parties".[97]

The same Decision provided for a programme of work. This work did not lead to the elaboration of any generally applicable solutions, however,[98] but indirectly to the negotiation of a special safeguard clause relating to a single industrial sector - cotton textiles.

The Short-Term Arrangement Regarding International Trade in Cotton Textiles (STA)[99] came into force on 1 October 1961 for a twelve-month period pending a long-term solution. A year later, the STA was superseded by the Long-Term Arrangement Regarding International Trade in Cotton Textiles (LTA)[100] which came into force on 1 October 1962 for a five-year period and continued into force until 31 December 1973. The stated objectives of the LTA, as of the STA, were two-fold: to promote the economic progress of developing countries by providing larger opportunities for exchange earnings, while ensuring that cotton textiles trade developed in such a way as to avoid disruptive effects in individual markets. Later, the Arrangement Regarding International Trade in Textiles, commonly known as the Multifiber Arrangement or the MFA,[101] covering textile products of man-made fibre and wool as well as cotton, entered into force on 1 January 1974 for a period of four years. As noted above on page 531, the MFA was extended a number of times and finally expired at the end of 1994.

The Tokyo Declaration adopted in September 1973, which launched the Tokyo Round of multilateral trade negotiations, stated that these negotiations should aim, *inter alia*, to "include an examination of the adequacy of the multilateral safeguard system, considering particularly the modalities of application of Article XIX, with a view to furthering trade liberalization and preserving its results".[102] The Trade Negotiations Committee established a negotiating group on safeguards in February 1975 to carry out the task set out in the Ministerial mandate. However, in spite of intensive efforts made in the final stage of the Tokyo Round, and a narrowing of differences, it did not prove possible to reach agreement within the framework of the Round.[103]

In the "GATT Work Programme" agreed on 29 November 1979 to follow up on the Tokyo Round results, it was agreed that "Continued negotiations on safeguards constitute an essential element in the GATT Work Programme and should be carried out as a matter of urgency in accordance with the agreement reached in the

---

[97] 9S/26, 26-27, Decision of 19 November 1960 on "Avoidance of Market Disruption - Establishment of Committee"; see also L/1374, Report of the Working Party on "Avoidance of Market Disruption - Establishment of Committee", adopted on 19 November 1960, 9S/108.

[98] In May 1964, after two years of experience with the LTA and at the time when the Kennedy Round was under preparation, the Executive Secretary of GATT made some unofficial "preliminary suggestions" (see above, page 520) which were rejected and not pursued.

[99] 10S/18.

[100] 11S/25.

[101] 21S/3.

[102] MIN(73)1, Declaration of Ministers approved at Tokyo on 14 September 1973, 20S/19, 21, para. 3(d).

[103] Concerning negotiations on safeguards in the Tokyo Round, see further *The Tokyo Round of Multilateral Trade Negotiations: Report by the Director-General of GATT*, April 1979, p. 90-95, and the *Supplementary Report* of January 1980, p. 14-17.

Council on this matter".[104] The separate Decision on "Safeguards" of the same date provided that "The CONTRACTING PARTIES stress the need for an agreement on an improved multilateral safeguard system. The CONTRACTING PARTIES reaffirm their intention to continue to abide by the disciplines and obligations of Article XIX of the General Agreement. A Committee is established to continue discussions and negotiations … with the aim of elaborating supplementary rules and procedures regarding the application of Article XIX of the General Agreement, in order to provide greater uniformity and certainty in the implementation of its provisions".[105] At the same time it was decided to establish the Sub-Committee on Protective Measures of the Committee on Trade and Development.[106]

At its meeting in April 1981, the Committee on Safeguards adopted the following conclusions:

"(i) the provisions of Article XIX of the General Agreement continue to apply fully and at the present time the rules and procedures for their application remain unchanged;

"(ii) the CONTRACTING PARTIES will continue to keep the matter under examination and discussion and to this end the Committee on Safeguards will expedite its work;

"(iii) All actions taken under Article XIX, and to the extent possible, other actions which serve the same purpose will be notified to the CONTRACTING PARTIES. In addition, it will be open to contracting parties to bring up any matter in accordance with the Understanding Regarding Notification, Consultation, Dispute Settlement and Surveillance.[107]

In November 1982, the CONTRACTING PARTIES meeting at Ministerial level adopted a Ministerial Declaration, paragraph 7(vi) of which provided that "the contracting parties undertake, individually and jointly … to bring into effect expeditiously a comprehensive understanding on safeguards to be based on the principles of the General Agreement".[108] The Decision adopted on the same date on "Safeguards" provides:

"The CONTRACTING PARTIES decide:

"1. That, having regard to the objectives and disciplines of the General Agreement, there is need for an improved and more efficient safeguard system which provides for greater predictability and clarity and also greater security and equity for both importing and exporting countries, so as to preserve the results of trade liberalization and avoid the proliferation of restrictive measures; and

"2. That to this end, effect should be given to a comprehensive understanding to be based on the principles of the General Agreement which would contain, *inter alia*, the following elements:

"(i) Transparency;

"(ii) Coverage;

"(iii) Objective criteria for action including the concept of serious injury or threat thereof;

"(iv) Temporary nature, degressivity and structural adjustment;

"(v) Compensation and retaliation; and

"(vi) Notification, consultation, multilateral surveillance and dispute settlement with particular reference to the role and functions of the Safeguards Committee".

---

[104]L/4884/Add.1/Annex VI, adopted on 28 November 1979, 26S/219, 220, para. 2.
[105]L/4898, adopted on 29 November 1979, 26S/202.
[106]L/4899, Decision of 28 November 1979 on "Examination of Protective Measures Affecting Imports from Developing Countries"; concerning this Sub-Committee see the chapter on Part IV.
[107]L/5151.
[108]L/5424, Ministerial Declaration adopted on 29 November 1982, 29S/9, 12, para. 7(vi).

The Ministerial Declaration of 20 September 1986 launching the Uruguay Round provided that

> "A comprehensive agreement on safeguards is of particular importance to the strengthening of the GATT system and to progress in the Multilateral Trade Negotiations.
>
> "The agreement on safeguards:
>
> "-- shall be based on the basic principles of the General Agreement;
>
> "-- shall contain, *inter alia*, the following elements: transparency, coverage, objective criteria for action including the concept of serious injury or threat thereof, temporary nature, degressivity and structural adjustment, compensation and retaliation, notification, consultation, multilateral surveillance and dispute settlement; and
>
> "-- shall clarify and reinforce the disciplines of the General Agreement and should apply to all contracting parties".[109]

The WTO Agreement includes an Agreement on Safeguards, which includes provisions on conditions for application of safeguards measures ("those measures provided for in Article XIX of GATT 1994"), determination of serious injury or threat thereof, application of safeguard measures, provisional safeguard measures, duration and review of safeguard measures, level of concessions and other obligations, developing country WTO members, termination of pre-existing Article XIX measures, and prohibition and elimination of grey-area measures. The Agreement also provides for notification, consultation, dispute settlement and surveillance of measures in this area.

III. PREPARATORY WORK AND SUBSEQUENT MODIFICATIONS

The Havana Charter provision corresponding to Article XIX is Article 40; in the US Draft, Article 29; in the London and New York Drafts, Article 34; and in the Geneva Draft, Article 40. Concerning the antecedents of the "escape clause" in the US Draft Charter, see page 518 above.

Article XIX has been amended only once. In the Review Session of 1954-55, it was agreed to change the term "obligations or concessions" (paragraph 3(a) and (b)) to "concessions or other obligations".[110] This change was effected through the 1955 Protocol Amending the Preamble and Parts II and III, and came into force in October 1957. Various other amendments to Article XIX were proposed in the Review Session but rejected.[111]

---

[109] Min.Dec., section I.D, 33S/19, 24-25.
[110] W.9/236, Legal and Drafting Committee report on drafting changes to various Articles.
[111] See Statement of Recommendations submitted by Sub-Group B to Working Party II, W.9/193, p. 12-13.

IV. RELEVANT DOCUMENTS

London

Discussion:	EPCT/C.II/38
	EPCT/C.II/QR/PV/5

New York

Discussion:	EPCT/C.6/29+Corr.1-2, 34, 40
Reports:	EPCT/C.6/28/Rev.1, 97/Rev.1, 105
Other:	EPCT/C.6/W/8, 66, 87

Geneva

Discussion:	EPCT/A/SR.11, 12, 35
	EPCT/TAC/PV/28
Reports:	EPCT/135, 189, 196, 212, 214/Rev.1/Add.1
	EPCT/W/313
Other:	EPCT/W/272, 301

Havana

Discussion:	E/CONF.2/C.3/SR.17, 32, 35
	E/CONF.2/C.3/D/2, 4, 7-11, 13
Reports:	E/CONF.2/C.3/37, 49, 52
	E/CONF.2/C.3/D/W/12
Other:	E/CONF.2/C.3/D/1-7

CONTRACTING PARTIES

Report:	GATT/CP/106 (Published in November 1951: *Report on the Withdrawal by the United States of a Tariff Concession under Article XIX*, Sales No. GATT/1951-3.)

Review Session

Discussion:	SR.9/16, 25
Reports:	W.9/124, 193, W.9/236
Other:	L/273, 275, 277, 283
	W.9/21, 45,
	Spec/3/55, 4/55, 85/55, 94/55

V. NOTIFICATIONS TO THE SECRETARIAT OF ACTIONS UNDER ARTICLE XIX

(Situation as at 1 January 1995)

General notes:

(1) The only actions listed are those which have been notified under Article XIX. This table does not include other quantitative restrictions or "emergency actions" notified without reference to Article XIX.
(2) Product descriptions are abbreviated.
(3) Column on affected countries is based on claimed interest or on information on principal or substantial suppliers furnished by governments taking actions, and may therefore be incomplete. In some instances, these statistics indicate largest suppliers.

N°	Date introduced	Date terminated	Contracting party	Product	Measure taken	Affected countries, territories or customs unions, compensation, retaliation	References
1.	1.12.50	June 1956 XXVIII:4 reneg.	US	Women's fur felt hats and hat bodies	Value-bracketed ad valorem duties replaced by compound rates for products between certain prices	Austria, Czechoslovakia, France, Italy, UK. *Compensation* to France, Italy at Torquay. Czechoslovakia brought dispute under Article XXIII:2.	GATT/CP/83, GATT/CP/5/22, GATT/CP.5/SR.22 & 23; Panel report GATT/CP/106: adopted at GATT/CP.6/SR.19. SECRET/63/Add. 1-2
2.	9.2.52	14.9.58	US	Hatters' fur	Ad valorem duty replaced by compound rates subject to an ad valorem floor and ceiling	Argentina, Belgium, France; Benelux took *Article XIX:3* action 22.5.52	SECRET/CP/19 & Add.1, GATT/ CP/ 140 & Add.1, L/9, L/851 & Add.1
3.	30.8.52	1966 XXVIII:4 reneg. (nomencl. rev.)	US	Dried figs	Specific duty increased	Greece, Italy, Turkey. Turkey took *Art. XIX:3* action 23.2.53 (see BISD 1S/28). *Compensatory reductions* made by US to a number of countries in 1966.	AIR/23, L/14, L/40, L/44, L/57, L/72, L/83, L/145, L/147, L/161, L/284, L/2592, G/39, G/70, BISD 1S/28
4.	1.7.54	30.6.59	US	Alsike clover seed	Specific duty increased for imports above a fixed annual quota, which was increased 1 July 1955 and 2 July 1957	Canada, Belgium	AIR/47, L/216, L/662, L/1532 & Add.1
5.	3.55	Oct. 1955 XXVIII reneg.	Greece	Apples	Specific duty replaced by increased ad valorem duty plus 75% surtax	Canada, which was *compensated*	L/346 & Corr.1: unpublished Canadian letters dated 21.5.62, 6.5.63, 7.4.70.
6.	19.8.55	Jan 1961 XXVIII:4 reneg.	US	Bicycles	Duties per unit increased, as well as floors and ceilings with respect to ad valorem equivalents. On 12 December 1960, US Supreme Court invalidated the action on one out of four subitems in question.	Austria, Belgium, Netherlands, Germany, UK (all *compensated in 1956)*; France, Italy.	AIR/77, 79 & 214, L/433, 6/PSC, C/M/2, SECRET/ 136/Add.1-4
7.	26.7.56	1966 XXVIII:4 reneg. (nomencl. rev.)	US	Towelling of flax, hemp or ramie	Ad valorem duty increased	Belgium, Japan, Netherlands, United Kingdom. *Compensation* to Benelux, U.K. in June 1957. *Compensatory reductions* made by US to a number of countries in 1966.	AIR/90 & 92, L/548, L/573 & Add.1, L/2592

N°	Date introduced	Date terminated	Contracting party	Product	Measure taken	Affected countries, territories or customs unions, compensation, retaliation	References
8.§	3.10.56	June 1961 XXVIII:1 reneg.	Greece	Electric refrigerators	Ad valorem duty increased	United States, which was *compensated*	L/541, L/575, SECRET/131/ Add.7: letters (unpubl. 21.5.62 and 7.4.70)
9.	14.6.57	14.12.57	Canada	Strawberries	Minimum values for duty (increased specific duties)	United States	L/642
10.	9.11.57	Feb. 1961 XXVIII:4 reneg.	US	Spring clothespins	Specific duty increased.	Benelux, Denmark, Hong Kong, Sweden. *Compensation* to Denmark, Sweden, Benelux	L/757 & Add.1, L/758, SR.12/21, AIR/128 & 214, C/M/2, SECRET/ 136/Add. 5-7
11.	29.11.57	28.1.66	US	Safety-pins	Ad valorem duty increased.	Germany, Japan, United Kingdom. *Compensation* to Germany, UK in Jan. 1962.	AIR/105, L/624 & Add.1-2, AIR/125, L/1746, L/2565
12.	12.2.58	15.6.59	Canada	Frozen peas	Minimum values for duty (increased specific duties)	United States (only supplier)	AIR/124, L/1017
13.	27.2.58	15.5.58	Australia	Printed cotton textiles	Ban on import licences. Japan had agreed to reduce exports already covered by licenses and firm orders. Licences thus redundant could not be used to import from any other source, but might be used on other categories of goods from any country. Action modified 1 April 1958. Licences issued against other quotas but value of licences issued to any individual quota holder not to be in excess of his imports in same licensing period in 1957; also, of total value licensed, not more than 50 per cent to be imported prior to 30 June 1958.	Japan	L/797 & Add.1-2
14.	22.5.58	7.1.66	US	Clinical thermometers	Ad valorem rate increased.	Japan	L/803 & Add.1 & Corr. 1 and Add.2, AIR/138, L/2566
15.	4.9.58		Germany	Hard coal and hard coal products	Repeal of general licence from countries outside the ECSC. Further contracts subjected to individual licensing.	Norway, United Kingdom, United States; *compensation* was offered	L/855, L/920
16.	1.10.58	22.10.65 (ores + concentrates) 22.11.65 (metals)	US	Lead and zinc	Separate country-allocated quarterly quotas representing 80% of average competitive imports during 1953-1957.	Canada, Mexico, Peru for lead and zinc; Australia, South Africa, Yugoslavia (lead)	L/819, L/859, L/940, L/1078, L/2489, IC/SR.41

ARTICLE XIX - EMERGENCY ACTION ON IMPORTS OF PARTICULAR PRODUCTS

N°	Date introduced	Date terminated	Contracting party	Product	Measure taken	Affected countries, territories or customs unions, compensation, retaliation	References
17.	1.1.59	1.1.61 (XXVIII:1 re-neg. with effect from same date)	Austria	Porcelain	Specific duty increased	Czechoslovakia, Germany, which were both *compensated* prior to action	L/863 & Add.1, SECRET/120 & Add.1-3
18.	1.4.59	20.5.60 (new tariffs introduced)	Australia	Footwear	Import licensing issued to the extent of 100% of imports during financial year 1956-57. All footwear transferred from licensing categ. B (under which quotas were interchangeable among a wide variety of goods) to categ. A (under which quotas were related to particular goods), to reduce substantially only rate of import of casual footwear. Background was marked increase in licences issued for imports from Hong Kong and other sources after Japan agreed Dec. 1958 to export restraints on casual footwear. Action modified 1 August 1959 (for some items 100% of 1957-58 imports, for some items 75%, for another 50%).	Japan, Hong Kong	L/974 & Add.1-2
19.	1.11.59	11.10.67	US	Stainless steel flatware	Various compound duties replaced by increased ad valorem duties or compound duties depending on the article, for imports valued under certain price when imported in excess of a tariff quota. In 3.1958 President had decided that "a full evaluation of Japan's voluntary export limitation system was necessary because of the promise it held of relieving the situation ... In July 1959 after a supplemental investigation another report was submitted. It is on the basis of this entire investigation and history that the action ... is taken" (L/1076). On 7.1.66, quotas increased and over-quota rates reduced retroactive to 1.11.65.	Japan	L/791, L/1076 & Add.1, AIR/177, L/2543, L/2953 See also item 62.
20.	30.5.60	17.7.61 (new tariff introduced)	Australia	Motor mowers and engines	Global non-discriminatory licensing of engines for motor mowers at 25% of requirements; for other engines at 100% of requirements; for motor mowers at 100% of 1959 imports.	United Kingdom, United States	L/1217 & Add.1, AIR/204, L/1527
21.	22.9.60	11.10.67	US	Cotton typewriter ribbon cloth	Duties increased to various higher ad valorem rates.	Germany, Japan, United Kingdom. UK *compensated* January 1962.	L/1313, W.17/13, L/1746, L/2953

N°	Date introduced	Date terminated	Contracting party	Product	Measure taken	Affected countries, territories or customs unions, compensation, retaliation	References
22.	26.5.61	31.12.64 XXVIII:1 reneg.	Australia	Piece-goods and non-pile fabrics, woollen	Compound duties (piece-goods) and ad valorem duties (fabrics), replaced by higher temporary duties	Italy, United Kingdom, France, Germany, Japan, Benelux. EEC was *compensated*	L/1497, AIR/243, L/1546, L/1612, L/1638, L/2455, SECRET/156/Add.4
23.	14.12.61		Nigeria	Cement	Import licences prohibited, except for contracts concluded prior to 14.12.61.	Germany, Israel, United Kingdom	L/1781
24.	17.6.62	1.2.74 (concession partly restored 11.1.67, 1.5.72, 1.2.73)	US	Sheet glass (principally window glass)	Increased specific duties varying with type of glass	EEC; UK; Japan (*compensated* December 1962); Sweden (*compensated* December 1967). EEC took *Article XIX:3 action* 4.6.62; partly restored 1.6.67; fully restored 1.1.73	L/1509, & Add.1-3, L/1803, L/1951, L/1959, L/2743, L/2784, L/2953, L/2959, L/3316, L/3317, L/3664, L/4188
25.	17.6.62	1.1.73 (concession partly restored January 1972)	US	Wilton and velvet carpets	Ad valorem duty increased	EEC, Japan, Sweden. *Compensation* to UK and Japan December 1962. *Art. XIX:3 action* by EEC: see preceding item.	L/1530 & Add.13, L/1803, L/1951, L/1959, L/2953, L/3378, L/4188
26.	9.7.62	11.1.64 (New tariff introduced)	Australia	Timber	Non-discriminatory global quota licensing on basis of 25% of imports in the 2 year period ending 30.6.62. Firm orders at 8.7.62 licensed with debit where necessary against future quotas for the relevant timbers.	Canada, Brazil, British Borneo, Malaya, United States	L/1812 & Corr.1 & Add.1-2
27.	31.7.62	May 1967 XXVIII renegotiation (Kennedy Round)	Australia	Parts for refrigerating appliances	Additional specific duties for some parts, additional ad valorem duty for others, on top of bound ad valorem rate	United Kingdom, United States	L/1819, L/2791, SECRET/156/Add.7
28.	3.8.62	4.6.63	Australia	Antibiotics	Non-discriminatory quantitative licensing on an administrative basis. Licensing periods of 6 months. For certain antibiotics: 1 imported unit per each 9 locally-produced units purchased after 2.8.62. For others, licences issued at annual rate of 20% of 1961-62 imports.	France, United Kingdom, United States	L/1820 & Add.1
29.	12.10.62	May 1967 XXVIII renegotiation (Kennedy Round)	Australia	Forged steel flanges	Additional ad valorem duty	Germany	L/1863, L/2791, SECRET/156/Add.4

N°	Date introduced	Date terminated	Contracting party	Product	Measure taken	Affected countries, territories or customs unions, compensation, retaliation	References
30.	5.11.62	28.2.64 (new tariff introduced)	Rhodesia; from 1.1.64 Southern Rhodesia only	Cotton & rayon piecegoods	Import restrictions on products of a certain weight and valued under a certain f.o.b. price per sq.yd.		L/1898, L/2213
31.	27.2.63[1]	22.4.65 XXVIII renegotiation (Kennedy Round)	Australia	Linseed oils	Duty-free entrance and specific duties (depending on tariff item) replaced by increased duties	Argentina, India	L/1981, L/2455
32.	23.2.63 and 26.2.63	November 1966	Peru	Lead arsenate and valves, respectively	Specific duty introduced on duty-free lead arsenate; increased specific duty on valves		L/1979, L/1896
33.	24.2.64[2]	9.3.64	Austria	Chicken eggs	Suspension of liberalization		L/2148 + Add.1
34.	15.2.64	31.12.70	France	Foundry pig-iron	Introduction of specific duty, whenever higher than the ad valorem duty. Minimum protection reduced November 1966. Action was recommended by ECSC, but affected only France's and Italy's obligations. Disinvocation was made by EEC.	Benelux, Australia, Canada, Germany, Norway, Spain, Sweden, Finland, United Kingdom	L/2139, L/2183, L/2197, L/2531, L/2532, L/2536, L/2719, L/2731, L/3165, L/3170, L/3505
35.	15.2.64	31.12.70	Italy[7]	Foundry pig-iron	As above	Germany, Spain	L/2197, L/2536, L/2719, L/3505
36.	14.5.64	March 1968 XXVIII:4 renegotiation	Australia	Heat-resisting glassware of a minimum price	Specific duty introduced for imports valued over certain f.o.b. prices	France, United Kingdom, United States; EEC compensated	L/2220, C/M/21, AIR/529, C/M/33, Spec(67)6, L/2985
37.	10.12.64	1.1.82	Germany	Petroleum and shale oils etc.	Import licences introduced		L/2321 & Corr.1
38.	4.3.65	1.9.65	Australia	Copper, brass sheet and strip	Quantitative restrictions introduced during a period of temporary shortage of Australia-produced unwrought copper		L/2373, L/2474
39.	22.4.65[3]	31.5.71	Greece	Tyres	Specific duties replaced by higher ad valorem duties. Increase reduced in April 1966	United States, which was compensated in May 1971; Norway	L/2431 & Add.1, letter from Greece 13.1.75
40.	14.1.66	1.1.69	Australia	Polyethylene twine, cordage rope and cable	Quantitative restrictions introduced	Japan	SECRET/162, L/2961 & Add.1; see also item 48.

N°	Date introduced	Date terminated	Contracting party	Product	Measure taken	Affected countries, territories or customs unions, compensation, retaliation	References
41.	29.4.66	24.6.1982	Australia	Alloy steels	Additional specific duty, less 40% of f.o.b. price	Benelux, United States, Japan	SECRET/163, L/5343
42.	30.6.66	May 1980	Spain	Cheese	Individual licensing, and temporary ban on imports, followed 5.6.70 by agreement with EEC liberalizing certain items via regulating duties subject to threshold prices. Certain items required certificate (issued for some items by Spain; for others by exporting country but approved by Spain). For some items Spain opened global quota, distributed quarterly on basis of imports in 1963/64/65, the EEC counting as a whole. Regulating duties increased in March 1972, pending consultations with principal supplying countries concerning new threshold prices	EEC, Norway	L/2670, L/3407 & Add.1: See also item 105
43.	2.2.67	Date of termination unknown	Spain	Synthetic rubber	Tariff heading sub-divided into two; 15% provisional customs duty imposed on synthetic rubber based on polybutadiene.	United States (compensated 21.3.69), Canada (compensated 12.11.70) and EEC (compensated 4.3.70)	L/2820 & Add.14, L/3323 & Add.1, L/3375
44.	21.4.67	1.7.89	Australia	Used 4-wheel drive vehicles	Quantitative restrictions imposed	United States	L/2787 & Add.1, NTM Inventory
45.	14.11.67	1.1.68	Austria	Matches	Quantitative restrictions within the limits of a global quota open to all contracting parties		L/2920 & Add.1
46.	17.11.67	31.12.68	Canada	Turkeys	In view of threat of imports from US, special valuation levied for imports at distress prices to protect against being sold at less than cost	United States	L/2924 & Add.1
47.	19.12.67	1.9.72	Australia	Knitted coats and the like	Quantitative restrictions imposed	Japan, EEC	L/2957, L/3834
48.	4.1.68	1.1.69	Australia	Polypropylene twine, cordage and cable	Same as for item 40	Japan, United States	See item 40.
49.	17.3.68	30.12.71	France	Horsemeat	Quantitative restrictions imposed. Global quota initially opened from 1.4.68 to 31.8.68, distribution of which was based on 1967 imports	Argentina, Canada, Poland, Spain	L/3000, L/4182

ARTICLE XIX - EMERGENCY ACTION ON IMPORTS OF PARTICULAR PRODUCTS

N°	Date introduced	Date terminated	Contracting party	Product	Measure taken	Affected countries, territories or customs unions, compensation, retaliation	References
50.	15.7.68	1.3.69	Austria	Oilcakes	Specific duty imposed	Argentina; United States (which *proposed* Article XIX:3 action 12.12.68 (not implemented))	L/3046 & Add.1-4
51.	12.9.68	2.11.68	Canada	Potatoes	"Action" taken under Section 40-A-7(c) of Canadian Customs Act on imports entering Western Canada. (Reference to this Act was made in respect of item 46 when special valuation was introduced.)	United States, *compensated* through advanced implementation 1.10.68 of Kennedy Round reduction of duty on cranberries	L/3066 & Add.1
52.	30.10.68	31.12.68	Canada	Corn	Idem, for whole of Canada	United States	L/3097 & Add.1
53.	19.5.69	Partial termination Aug. 1969; date of complete termination unknown	Italy	Raw silk	Measure adopted at Community level. Notification stated, *inter alia*, that EEC Council decided in 1968 to support Italian efforts *inter alia* by reintroducing, over 1.1.70 to 31.12.76, existing Common External Tariff customs duty on raw silk and establishing EEC duty-free quota for raw silk equal to difference between demand for and production of raw silk within the EEC; and by applying same Common External Tariff duty on permanent basis from 1.1.76, if in 1976 Italian silkworm cocoon production made possible production of at least 1,000 tons/yr of raw silk. Partial removal in August 1969 concerned silk waste.		L/3231 & Add.1
54.	9.6.69	1.9.72	Australia	Knitted shirts	Quantitative restrictions introduced		L/3217, L/3834
55.	21.2.70	20.2.74	US	Pianos	Increased ad valorem duty	Japan, EEC	L/3314, L/3371 & Add.1, L/4005
56.	7.5.70	16.6.73	Canada	Motor gasoline	Resulting from conditions under which increasing quantities of motor gasoline had been entering the Ontario market, discretionary licensing introduced for imports into Canada (east of Province of Manitoba). Not envisaged that overall volume would be significantly affected.	United States	L/3400, L/3877

N°	Date introduced	Date terminated	Contracting party	Product	Measure taken	Affected countries, territories or customs unions, compensation, retaliation	References
57.	2.6.70	29.11.71	Canada	Men's and boys' woven fabric shirts	Surtax applied for imports from all countries except for products in transit on or before 2.6.70 and except for shirts subject to export restraint or equivalent intergovernmental arrangements. To limit restrictive impact and ensure equity, quantitative exemptions established for countries with recent substantial interest "consistent with that set out in Annex B of the [Cotton Textiles Arrangement]". Surtax was the lesser of either twice the amount by which Can$24 per dozen exceeded the f.o.b. price or Can$24.		L/3402, L/3613 & Add.1. See also items 60 and 82.
58.	1.1.71	21.3.71	Israel	Radio equipment	Increased ad valorem duty		L/3424 & Add.1
59.	21.5.71	21.7.71 and 18.8.71 (for frozen strawberries)	Canada	Fresh and preserved frozen strawberries	Surtax	United States, Mexico	L/3539 & Add.1-2
60.	30.11.71	31.12.78 (subsumed in action No. 82)	Canada	Men's and boys' shirts, woven or knitted	Global quotas with country reserves for imports under a certain price.	Hong Kong, Japan, Korea, Macao, Malaysia, Poland, Romania, Singapore, Trinidad and Tobago	L/3613 & Add.1, L/4143 & Add.1, L/4453/Add.4. See also items 57 and 82
61.	1.5.72	30.4.76 and 30.4.79	US	Ceramic tableware articles	Various increased compound duties for imports valued under or between certain prices depending on the article. Some high-value goods also included. Action terminated on 30 April 1976 for earthen and china steins and mugs and lowpriced earthen tableware, and on 30 April 1979 for certain high-priced earthen dinnerware or other tableware, and for certain low-priced and medium-priced china tableware.	Japan, EEC	L/3678, L/3700 & Add.1 & 2, L/4326, C/M/78. Replies to GATT/AIR/112
62.	1.4.73	31.12.73	EEC	Tape recorders	Import licences limited to a certain quantity; action taken by EEC but applied to Italy	Japan, Korea	L/3847, L/3892, L/3977, C/M/86, SR.29/1
63.	30.6.73	3.8.73	Canada	Fresh cherries	Surtax introduced	United States which was *compensated*	L/3887 & Add.1-6
64.	1.5.74	30.4.78	US	Ball bearings	Increased ad valorem or compound rates, depending on the item, if valued not over certain unit prices	Japan, Canada, EEC	L/3897, L/4016 & Add.1-3, C/M/95. Replies to GATT/ AIR/1128

Article XIX - Emergency Action on Imports of Particular Products

N°	Date introduced	Date terminated	Contracting party	Product	Measure taken	Affected countries, territories or customs unions, compensation, retaliation	References
65.	12.8.74	1.1.76	Canada	Cattle, beef, veal	Annual global quotas, based on 5-year average US imports. First quota for 12.8.-30.9.74, thereafter quarterly; administered so as to ensure that relative shares of each of Canada's main suppliers would bear a reasonable relationship to past patterns of trade, market trends and historical performances. Measure taken in context of a temporary beef stabilization programme. After 1.1.76 imports from Rhodesia continued to require an individual import licence.	United States. Holding that the action did not provide access for cattle and meat on an equitable basis and failing to reach agreement, *US suspended substantially equivalent concessions* 12.8.74-1.1.76 pursuant to Article XIX:3. Also affected: Australia, New Zealand	L/4072 & Add.1-5, L/4118 & Add.1. Replies to GATT/AIR/1128
66.	1.10.74	1.1.82 (Partial removal 22.11.77)	Australia	Certain footwear	Quantitative restrictions, to a level of 20% greater than imports in 1972/73. Quotas allocated to established importers without restriction as to source of supply. High-priced footwear exempted from import licensing on 22.11.77.	EEC, Japan, Korea, Malaysia, Spain, India, Hong Kong, Portugal; *retaliation proposed by EEC*	L/4099 & Add.1-26, C/M/103, 107, 113, C/M/155 item 1, C/M/156 item 2. See also items 73 and 89.
67.	1.2.75	8.12.76 (partial removal 30.3.75)	Australia	Motor vehicles	Global quotas; removed for light commercial vehicles 30.3.75.	EEC, Japan, United States	L/4149 & Add.1.9, C/M/103, 107, 113. See also item 85.
68.	1.1.75	5.3.76	Australia	Hot-rolled and cold-rolled sheets and plates of iron or steel	Global quotas	Japan, United States	L/4166 & Add.1-7, C/M/105, 107, 114
69.	1.3.75	27.4.88	Australia	Certain apparel	Additional duties in excess of a tariff quota	Canada, EEC, Egypt, Hong Kong, India, Japan, Pakistan, Romania, Sweden, Switzerland, United States	L/4162 & Add.1-3, C/M/103, 105, 114
70.	1.3.75	25.5.76	Australia	Ophthalmic frames, sunglass frames and sunglasses	Quotas allocated to importers without restriction as to source of supply. Each importer granted a licence for a 6-month period equal to no more than half his established quota. (Frames: limitation to 75% of 1973/74 imports; sunglasses to 85% of 1973/74 imports)	EEC, Japan	L/4169 & Add.1-6 & Corr.1, C/M/107, 113

N°	Date introdu-ced	Date terminated	Contracting party	Product	Measure taken	Affected countries, territories or customs unions, compensation, retaliation	References
71.	1.4.75	18.3.76	New Zealand	Woven polyester fabrics (extended coverage May 1975)	Import licences. Allocations for 1975-76 were 60% of 1973-74 import volume. Certain items remain under control after termination of the action. Licence allocation to be 100% of 1976-77 volume levels.	Japan, United States	L/4172 & Add.1-5
72.	1.1.76	31.8.78	Canada	Worsted spun acrylic yarns below a certain price	Global quota for products under a certain export price (determined in accordance with the Anti-Dumping Act). Permits already issued for Jan.-June 1976 delivery were honoured and included as part of quota; distribution of import permits was based on historical performance of importer over two years ending 31.3.76. 10% of quota allotted to importers without historical performance in this period. Gradually phased out as from 30 June 1978.	Japan, Korea	L/4344 & Add.1-2
73.	1.5.76	1.1.82 (Partial removal at 22.11.77)	Australia	Sand boots and shoes; parts of footwear	Included within scope of restrictions under item 66. Footwear already subject to licensing maintained at 140% of 1972-73 volume. Sand boots/shoes incorporated into non-leather footwear licensing category (quota for which was consequently increased). This additional quota allocated to individual importers after account taken of goods in bond and in transit as at 7.5.76; base period for this allocation widened to include imports 1.7.74-31.12.75, and quotas thus allocated could be used to import sand shoes/boots and other non-leather footwear (quota available for non-leather footwear could also be used for sand shoes/boots). Licensing controls on imports of parts for footwear restricted annual import value to 140% of 1973-74. Allocations to individual importers made on basis of 1973-74 imports after account taken of goods in bond and in transit. High-priced footwear exempted from import licensing on 22.11.77.	Sand boots and shoes: Korea. Parts: Germany, Italy, Portugal	L/4099/Add.3 and 6, Add. 16, Add.23. See also items 66 and 89.
74.	25.5.76[a]	31.12.78	Australia	Files and rasps	Quotas allocated to importers on the basis of import performance in 1974 and 1975 and without restriction as to source of supply	United States	L/4351 & Add.1-3. Letter (unpublished). See also item 92.

Article XIX - Emergency Action on Imports of Particular Products

N°	Date introduced	Date terminated	Contracting party	Product	Measure taken	Affected countries, territories or customs unions, compensation, retaliation	References
75.	14.6.76	13.2.80	United States	Specialty steel	Orderly marketing agreement (signed 11.6) with principal supplier (Japan) covering three years, plus three-year restraints on imports from other foreign suppliers. Quota system replaced by a transitional one, with progressively larger bi-monthly quotas, 12 June 1979	Japan, Argentina, Austria, Sweden, Canada, Finland, France, UK, Germany, Korea, Mexico, Spain, Norway	L/4314, L/4318, L/4368 & Add.1-57, C/M/112, 113, 114.
76.	1.7.76	27.4.88	Australia	Knitted and woven dresses	Additional specific duties for imports in excess of tariff quota, applied to import clearances after 1.7.76		L/4364/Add.1
77.	1.7.76	31.12.78	Canada	Work gloves	Three-year global quota for imports under a certain export price (determined in accordance with Anti-Dumping Act). Subquota for 100% cotton gloves (as opposed to leather gloves) based on actual imports during 1975. Quota divided quarterly. Permits distributed according to historical performance of importers 1.1.74-15.6.76. 10% allotted to importers with no or little historical performance	Hong Kong	L/4382 & Add.1
78.	7.7.76	23.12.76	Canada	Textured polyester filament yarn	Surtax for imports exported at less than a specified value, applied on m.f.n. basis among exporting countries. Surtax equal to difference between export price as defined in Anti-Dumping Act and values as specified for four different categories.	United States	L/4374 & Add.1-3
79.	10.8.76	9.8.79	Australia	Electrical chest freezers	Global import licensing, applying to all imports other than those under existing special trading arrangements provided for in New Zealand Australia Free Trade Agreement, which were "administered separately". Licences allocated on basis of importers' performance 1.7.74-30.6.76	EEC	L/4387 & Add.1; Letter, unpublished
80.	8.10.76	9.10.79	Canada	Double-knit fabrics	Global quota distributed among importers semi-annually based on their individual historical import performance. (Prior to action there were restraint arrangements with a number of countries renewed annually as from 1972.)	Japan, United States, Singapore, Hong Kong, Malaysia	L/4450 & Add.1-5, C/M/123

N°	Date introduced	Date terminated	Contracting party	Product	Measure taken	Affected countries, territories or customs unions, compensation, retaliation	References
81.	18.10.76	31.12.76	Canada	Beef and veal	General import permit replaced by individual permit control. Permits issued on basis of global quota allocated among supplying countries in accordance with their market shares in the base period (not specified)	New Zealand	L/4437 & Add.1, C/M/117
82.	29.11.76	31.12.78	Canada	A range of clothing items	Global quotas at 1975 levels, administered (other than for outerwear) on basis of importer's 1975 performance in each product category. Goods in transit on or before 29.11.76 exempted from quota. All existing quota and restraint arrangements were suspended by these measures. Outerwear imports limited to 2.3 million units from all sources	Austria, United States, Hong Kong, Korea	L/4453 & Add.1-4
83.	27.12.76	31.12.79	Finland	Women's panty hose	Surcharge equivalent to difference between a basic price and import price applied non-discriminatorily on all imports taking place under that price	Singapore, United Kingdom	L/4461 & Add.1-2, C/M/119
84.	28.6.77	30.6.81	US	Footwear	Agreement with Korea 21.6.77 in which Korea will carry out export restraints for a period up to 1.7.81 and be assisted in this by US import restrictions for certain items.	Korea	L/4477 & Add.1, L/4525 & Add.1, C/M/112, C/M/119 item 16, C/M/124
85.	12.7.77	1.1.85	Australia	Passenger motor vehicles	Global quotas	EEC, Japan; *retaliation proposed by EEC*	L/4526 & Add.1-25, C/M/ 123, C/M/155, item 1, C/M/156 item 2; see also item 67
86.	22.7.77	22.6.79	EEC	Portable TV sets from Korea	Annual quotas applying only to imports into United Kingdom. On 22 June 1979 a VER came into effect.	Korea, other suppliers: Japan and Singapore	L/4613 & Add.1, C/M/112, 124 and 134, SR.34/1

Article XIX - Emergency Action on Imports of Particular Products

N°	Date introduced	Date terminated	Contracting party	Product	Measure taken	Affected countries, territories or customs unions, compensation, retaliation	References
87.	23.9.77	8.11.79 (Partial removal 22.2.79)	Australia	Brandy	Temporary additional specific duties increasing the margin between customs and excise rates existing at the time of binding (1947). Tariff quotas applied at level equivalent to 40% of 1975/76 imports. A further temporary specific duty above the tariff quota. Tariff quotas allocated on basis of imports 1.9.76-31.8.77. (Identical measures applied to whisky imports.) Same basis used for quotas after 22.2.79. Cognac exempted from measures as from 22.2.79 (L/4569/Add.8).	EEC (France, Germany, Italy), Cyprus, Greece, Spain, Yugoslavia	L/4569 & Add.1-12
88.	10.11.77	9.5.79	Australia	Fixed resistors	Import licences; entitlements determined as one unit (after 10.5.78 two units) of import quota for each unit purchased or irrevocably committed for delivery from Australian production; irrevocable commitments as at 22.9.77 allowed entry on special licences valid for sixty days from 10.11.77. Goods in transit or in bond allowed entry on special licences if entered within 21 days of date of the announcement or arrival. Licences transferable between individual importers under certain circumstances.		L/4603 & Add.1
89.	22.11.77	1.1.82	Australia	Thongs, gumboots and sporting footwear (see items 66 and 73)	Thongs with value for duty below certain prices plus parts thereof, included within scope of existing quantitative restrictions (with value between certain prices quota is 100% of imports; for parts 100% of 1976/77 imports). Import licensing procedures for certain specialist sporting footwear and gumboots (because of administrative difficulties regarding definitions). Exemption of high-priced footwear from import licensing (removed on 1.9.80). "Threshold" price level to be adjusted each 6 months in accordance with movements in footwear component of Australian consumer price index.	EEC	L/4099/Add.4-26; See also items 66 and 73.

N°	Date introduced	Date terminated	Contracting party	Product	Measure taken	Affected countries, territories or customs unions, compensation, retaliation	References
90.	1.12.77	30.11.81 (partial removal July 1980)	Canada	Footwear, other than footwear of rubber or canvas	Global quota at levels corresponding to annual average 1974-76, administered by permits to importers having imported 1.9.76-31.8.77 at pro rata share calculated on performance during base period. Committee was to distribute small amount reserved to meet unforeseen circumstances. Removal of certain specialized footwear notified in July 1980. Global quota (total amount unchanged) extended up to 30.11.1981. Importers who had imported under the quota system were entitled to pro rata share of total quota based on performance during first two years of quota.	EEC, Brazil, US, Korea, Poland, Romania, Spain, United States; *retaliation proposed by EEC* (see Add.41)	L/4611 & Add.1-50, SR.34/1
91.	1.3.78	27.4.88	Australia	Wool worsted yarns	Global tariff quotas (additional specific duty). Base period for individual importer's quota entitlements will be the twelve month period ending 30 November 1977. Initial quota allocations for six month period beginning 1 March 1978 valid for twelve months.	EEC	L/4659 & Add.1-5
92.	29.3.78[5]	31.12.78	Australia	Round blunt chain-saw files	Included in action on files and rasps.		L/4351/Add.2 & 3; unpublished letter; See item 74.
93.	11.4.78	10.4.81	US	CB radio receivers	Increased ad valorem duty to be phased down in three decrements and phased out 10 April 1981. The items were also removed from GSP.	Japan, Korea	L/4634 & Add.1-2
94.	21.4.78	18.2.82	Australia	Double-edged safety razor blades	Quantitative restrictions for two years. In first year imports restricted to sixteen million, individual importer's quota allocations based on twelve-month period ended 31.12.77. Allocations for second year to be announced later.		L/4666 & Corr.1 & Add.1
95.	26.5.78	15.5.80	EEC	Preserved cultivated mushrooms (CCCN 20.02A)	Suspension of import licences. Not applied to third countries which could assure that their exports did not exceed a reasonable quantity. Measure amended several times 1978-79 and suspended after principal suppliers had given necessary assurances. From 16.5.80 surveillance introduced.		L/4678, L/4994, L/5105. See items 104 and 106.

ARTICLE XIX - EMERGENCY ACTION ON IMPORTS OF PARTICULAR PRODUCTS

N°	Date introduced	Date terminated	Contracting party	Product	Measure taken	Affected countries, territories or customs unions, compensation, retaliation	References
96.	1.7.78	30.4.80	Australia	Hot and cold rolled and galvanized sheets and plates of iron and steel	Global quota, allocated on basis of clearances during 1977.		L/4696 & Add.1
97.	17.11.78	Nov.1982	US	High-carbon ferro-chromium	Additional specific duty for products with customs value below a certain price.	South Africa, Rhodesia, Japan, Yugoslavia, Brazil (bound to Canada and Rhodesia)	L/4702 & Add.1-6 (Letter by US Delegation of 18 March 1982)
98.	1.1.79	30.6.84	Norway	Various textile items	Global import quotas calculated on average imports 1974-76 from countries included in the quotas. Nondiscriminatory allocation to importers according to 1976-77 shares. Six bilateral agreements in force from 1.1.78 for 4 to 5 years could not be suspended by unilateral action and were not included in quotas. EFTA and EEC imports also excluded. 1980 (half-year) quotas adjusted to "revised and more precise conversion factors and changes in market demand".	Hong Kong, United States; Hong Kong brought dispute under Article XXIII:2.	L/4671, L/4689, L/4692 & Add.1-19. L/4815, C/M/126-128, 134, 135, 139 and 141. Panel report L/4959, BISD 27S/119
99.	6.1.79	Jan. 1982	US	Lag screws or bolts	Increased ad valorem tariff for two items; for two other items ad valorem duties introduced in addition to an existing specific duty.	Japan, Canada, EEC	L/4742 & Add.1-27
100.	8.1.79	31.12.80	Iceland	Furniture, cupboards and cabinets, windows and doors	Import deposit (35% of invoice amount, blocked for ninety days). Deposit not required in case of amounts below IKr 20,000 per transaction.		L/4771
101.	23.2.79	23.2.84	US	Clothespins	Global quota for imports valued above a certain price. Separate quota allocation for three different price brackets. Allocations may be shifted from unfulfilled to filled categories.	Poland, Germany, Romania, Netherlands	L/4759 & Add.1-3
102.	17.1.80	17.1.84	US	Porcelain-on-steel cooking ware	Additional specific duty, to be phased down and out over four years, applied to all ware below a certain price.	Japan, Spain, Korea, Italy, France, (Mexico)	L/4889 & Add.1-15, Letter and memorandum concerning compensation from Spain (not published)

N°	Date introduced	Date terminated	Contracting party	Product	Measure taken	Affected countries, territories or customs unions, compensation, retaliation	References
103.	21.2.80 (retroactive to 1.1.80)	31.12.80	EEC (UK)	Yarn of synthetic fibres	Import authorization from third countries required up to maximum quantities set for polyester yarns and polyamide yarns. Exempted from measure: imports of about $65 million from third countries which enter EC under free-trade agreement or under agreement concerning trade in textiles.	US, Canada, Japan; *Compensation* to the US paid in the form of prior-to-schedule MTN tariff reductions on imports from US (Took place on 1.9.80 instead of 1.1.1981)	L/4942 & Add.1-6; Unpublished letters from EEC and US of 4.2.81
104.	15.4.80	31.12.84	EEC	Cultivated mushrooms in brine [CCCN 07.03E]	Import subject to production of an import document, issued to traditional importers on the basis of 1977-78 imports, within limits fixed periodically by the Commission. Provision made for licences to new suppliers.	Hong Kong, Spain	L/4994 & Add.1. See also items 95 and 106; see OJ L330/1 of 18.12.84
105.	7.5.80[6]	Dec. 1980 (Art. XIX action replaced by VERs)	Spain	Cheeses	Partial suspension of liberalization.	EEC, Austria, Finland	L/4978 & Add.1-2 See also item 42.
106.	16.5.80	31.12.80	EEC	Cultivated mushrooms originating in Hong Kong and Spain [CCCN 20.02A]	Licences refused until solution found to difficulties (after imports liberalized 16.5.80, EEC market was exposed to threat of serious injury as a result of licence applications for imports from these countries substantially in excess of traditional EEC imports from them).	Hong Kong, Spain	L/4994 & Add.1, L/5105, L/5207. See items 95 and 104.
107.	15.9.80[7]	1.4.82	Australia	Certain works trucks and stackers	Licensing limited to $3 million for all goods specified: $1 million for 1.4.-30.9.80 and $2 million for 1.10.80-31.3.81. Importers' quota entitlements based on performance in calendar year 1978, transferable between products and importers. Quotas applied to imports from all sources, but goods of Papua New Guinea origin (PATCRA goods) exempted.	EEC, Japan	L/5026/Rev.1 & Add.1:20
108.	1.11.80	1.11.83	US	Preserved mushrooms	Increased duties for three years	Canada	L/5027, L/5088 and Add. 1-16

N°	Date introduced	Date terminated	Contracting party	Product	Measure taken	Affected countries, territories or customs unions, compensation, retaliation	References
109.	1.12.81	30.11.88 (full termination); partial termination 30.11.85 (see Add.19 and 25)	Canada	Non-leather footwear	Global quotas	EEC, United States, LDCs (Korea); *retaliation proposed twice by EEC* (see Add. 8 and 21)	L/5263 & Add.1-36
110.	3.8.81	20.11.81	EEC (UK, Ireland)	Frozen cod fillets	Embargo for products below certain reference price	Canada	L/5193 & Add.1-4
111.	9.7.82	30.11.88 (full termination); partial termination 30.11.85 & 1.4.86 (see Add.20, 27, 30)	Canada	Leather footwear	Global quota; later exemption of higher priced footwear (see Add.9).	EEC, Brazil, Spain, US; *retaliation proposed twice by EEC* (see Add.3/Rev.1 and Add.22)	L/5351 & Add.1-39
112.	27.8.82	31.12.83	Australia	Hoop and strip of iron and steel	Tariff quota		L/5365 & Corr.1 & Add.1
113.	3.9.82	10.10.82	Switzerland	Dessert grapes, fresh	Increased tariff	EEC	L/5364, L/5371
114.	15.10.82	15.3.83	Canada	Yellow onions	Tariff surtax	US	L/5392 & Add.1-10
115.	13.10.82		EEC	Dried grapes	Compensatory tax	Australia, US	L/5399 & Add.1-50
116.	1.1.83	16.4.83 (replaced by VER)	EEC (France, UK)	Tableware and other articles ... of stoneware	Global quota	Korea: as from 16.4.83 Korea undertook to make exports of these products to France and UK subject to export licences and set quantitative limits for calendar years 1983-85 (see Commission Reg. No 873/83, OJ L 96/8, 15.4.83)	L/5447 & Add.1
117.	1.4.83	9.10.87	US	Heavyweight motorcycles	Increased duties	Japan	L/5493 & Add.1-17

N°	Date introduced	Date terminated	Contracting party	Product	Measure taken	Affected countries, territories or customs unions, compensation, retaliation	References
118.	20.7.83	30.9.89	US	Specialty steel	Additional tariffs and quotas	EEC, Brazil, Korea and others (*OMAs* concluded with Austria, Argentina, Canada, Japan, Poland, Spain, Sweden); *action under Article XIX:3(a) by Canada* concerning quota restriction (see Add.10 and 31) and *EEC* covering tariff and quota restriction (see Add.15, 50 + 74)	L/5524 & Add.1-128
119.	19.7.83	24.2.88	Australia	Certain filament lamps	Increased duties	Hungary, US, others	L/5526 & Add.1-18
120.	5.8.83	19.6.85	Australia	Non-electrical domestic refrigerators	Increased duties		L/5529 & Add.1-2
121.	20.4.84	31.12.86	EEC (France)	Certain electronic piezo-electric quartz watches with digital display	Global quotas (see Regulation (EEC) N° 1087 of 18.4.84)	Hong Kong, Japan, Korea, Macao, Taiwan	L/5645 & Add.1-16
122.	25.7.84	1.1.89	Chile	Sugar	Tariff surcharge		L/5672 & Add.1.4
123.	2.11.84		South Africa	Certain footwear	Increased duties; suspension of existing binding		L/5725, L/6318 (amendment of L/5725)
124.	27.11.84	1.1.89	Chile	Wheat	Additional specific duties		L/5861 & Add.1-5
125.	1.1.85	31.12.85	Canada	Fresh, chilled and frozen beef and veal	Global quota	Australia, EEC, New Zealand, Nicaragua; *retaliation proposed by EEC*	L/5767 & Add. 1-10, L/5785
126.	18.6.85	13.7.89 (replaced by No. 141)	EEC	Morello cherries (processed)	Charge on imports below a minimum price; see Regulation (EEC) N° 1626/85 of 14.6.85	Hungary	L/5841 & Add.1-3
127.	9.8.85		South Africa	Malic Acid	Increased duties; suspension of existing binding		L/5860
128.	28.9.85	1.1.89	Chile	Edible vegetable oils	Increased duties		L/5935 & Add.1-3
129.	17.1.86	21.9.91	EEC	Provisionally preserved raspberries	Charge on imports below a certain price; see Regulation (EEC) N° 67/86 of 15.1.86		L/5957
130.	19.4.86	1987 (date not supplied)	EEC	Sweet potatoes	Suspension of issue of import certificate; see Regulation (EEC) N° 1146/86 of 18.4.86		L/5988

Article XIX - Emergency Action on Imports of Particular Products

N°	Date introduced	Date terminated	Contracting party	Product	Measure taken	Affected countries, territories or customs unions, compensation, retaliation	References
131.	6.86		South Africa	Tall oil fatty acids; Certain pipettes, flasks etc.; Certain high carbon steel wire; Certain sparking plugs	Increased duties		L/6002
132.	2.6.86	14.11.86	Finland	Porous fiberboard impregnated with bitumen	Import surcharge		L/6026
133.	19.3.87	31.10.91	Austria	Broken rice	Quotas	EEC (Italy)	L/6144, L/6144/Add.1
134.	30.3.87	Terminated; date not supplied	EEC (Spain)	Certain steel products	Quotas; see Commission Recommendation N° 77/328/CECA of 15.4.77	Canada, Turkey	L/6179 & Add.1-6
135.	20.10.87	15.4.88	South Africa	Optical fibres and optical fibre bundles	Suspension of tariff bindings		L/6228 & Add.1
136.	12.87	31.10.88	EEC	Frozen squid	Suspension of imports at certain price levels	Canada	L/6271 & Add.1
137.	5.88	Terminated; date not supplied	EEC (Portugal)	Refrigerators and freezers	Quotas; See OJ C/116 of 3.5.88		L/6344
138.	13.7.89		EEC	Processed cherries	Charges on imports under certain conditions; See Regulation (EEC) N° 1989/89 of 4.7.89		L/6560 & Add.1-5
139.	19.3.90	4.94	Austria	Prepared fowls other than in containers of glass or airtight metal containers	Import quotas; initial restriction for last 6 months of 1991 extended to 30 June 1992 and then to 30 June 1993		L/6653 & Add.1-2
140.	1.1.91	25.9.91	EEC	Certain semi-processed red fruits	Charges on imports under certain conditions; see Regulation (EEC) N° 3797/90		L/6820 & Add.1
141.	1.1.91	30.4.92	EEC	Provisionally preserved cultivated mushrooms	Maximum import quantity allocated by means of import licences; see Regulation (EEC) N° 809/91		L/6821 & Add.1

N°	Date introduced	Date terminated	Contracting party	Product	Measure taken	Affected countries, territories or customs unions, compensation, retaliation	References
142.	1.9.91	4.94	Austria	Certain types of cement and certain preparations containing cement	Import quota; increased for period 1 Sept. 1991 - 31 Dec. 1992. Country-specific quotas of 300,000 tonnes in total for 11-month period starting 1 February 1993 for imports from Poland, Romania, Czech Republic and Slovak Republic; additional global quota of 100,000 tonnes introduced for twelve-month period starting 1 April 1993. Imports originating in EC or EFTA member States exempted.	Poland, Romania, Czech Republic and Slovak Republic	L/6899 & Add.1-8, Add.7/Suppl. 1; C/M/252
143.	18.9.91	31.12.91	Czech & Slovak Republic	Agricultural products: live bovine animals, beef, butter, potatoes, starches and inulin, rape or colza seeds and oil, margarine, glucose syrup, molasses, grape wine	Global import quotas	Waiver of Article II granted 4 December 1991 for renegotiation of Schedule X	L/6907, L/6968
144.	9.11.91	31.5.92	EEC	Atlantic salmon	Minimum import price	Norway, Canada, Chile	L/6977
145.	8.4.92	31.12.92	Hungary	Cement	Temporary surcharge		L/6996
146.	8.4.92	31.12.92	Hungary	Intra-ocular lenses	Import quota		L/6996
147.	15.11.92	11.93	Hungary	Certain paper products	One-year import quotas administered by license on first-come-first-served basis; quotas apply for imports from all sources except Finland and EC.		L/7123
148.	26.2.93	30.6.93	EEC	Whitefish (Cod, haddock, coalfish, hake, monkfish)	Minimum price for imports; extended on 13 March 1993 to cover Alaska pollack.		L/7194

N°	Date introdu-ced	Date terminated	Contracting party	Product	Measure taken	Affected countries, territories or customs unions, compensation, retaliation	References
149.	15.4.93	11.93	Austria	Certain types of fertilizers	Global import quotas of 30,000 tonnes for mixtures of ammonium nitrate with calcium carbonate or other inorganic non-fertilizing substances, 30,000 tonnes for fertilizers containing nitrogen, phosphorus and potassium, for 1-year period starting 15 April 1993; imports originating in EC or EFTA member States exempted.	Czech Republic, Romania, Slovak Republic	L/7204 & Add.1-4, L/7204/Suppl.1
150.	21.6.93	31.12.94	Canada	Boneless beef	Surtax of 25 percent of value for duty applied on boneless beef imports in excess of 48,014,000 kg; imports originating in US exempted.	Australia, New Zealand	L/7219 & Add. 1-18

NOTES:

. Date of notification to the secretariat.
. Date of L/ document.
. Date of notification.
. Date of communication.
. Date of communication.
. Date of notification.
. Date of notification. Backdated to quota year starting 1.4.80.

ARTICLE XX

GENERAL EXCEPTIONS

I. TEXT OF ARTICLE XX AND INTERPRETATIVE NOTE AD ARTICLE XX 562

II. INTERPRETATION AND APPLICATION OF ARTICLE XX 563
    A. SCOPE AND APPLICATION OF ARTICLE XX 563
        1. General 563
        2. Preamble of Article XX 563
            (1) "arbitrary or unjustifiable discrimination between countries where the same conditions prevail" 564
            (2) "disguised restriction on international trade" 565
        3. Paragraph (b) 565
            (1) "necessary to protect human, animal or plant life or health" 565
            (2) Publication, notification and consultations concerning measures taken under paragraph (b) 570
        4. Paragraph (c): "relating to the importation or exportation of gold and silver" 573
        5. Paragraph (d) 573
            (1) General 573
            (2) "necessary" 574
            (3) "to secure compliance" 578
            (4) "laws or regulations which are not inconsistent with the provisions of this Agreement" 580
            (5) "the enforcement of monopolies operated under paragraph 4 of Article II and Article XVII" 581
            (6) "protection of patents, trade marks and copyrights" 582
            (7) "the prevention of deceptive practices" 583
            (8) Preshipment inspection 583
        6. Paragraph (g): "relating to the conservation of exhaustible natural resources" 583
            (1) "relating to ... conservation" 583
            (2) "exhaustible natural resources" 585
            (3) "made effective in conjunction with restrictions on domestic production or consumption" 586
        7. Paragraph (h): "undertaken in pursuance of obligations under [a] commodity agreement" 587
        8. Paragraph (i) 591
        9. Paragraph (j) 592
            (1) "local short supply" 592
            (2) "The CONTRACTING PARTIES shall review the need for this sub-paragraph" 594
        10. Trade and environment 595
    B. RELATIONSHIP BETWEEN ARTICLE XX AND OTHER ARTICLES OF THE GENERAL AGREEMENT 595
        1. Article III 595
        2. Articles XXII and XXIII 595
        3. Article XXIV 596

III. PREPARATORY WORK AND SUBSEQUENT MODIFICATIONS 596

IV. RELEVANT DOCUMENTS 597

I. TEXT OF ARTICLE XX AND INTERPRETATIVE NOTE AD ARTICLE XX

Article XX

General Exceptions

Subject to the requirement that such measures are not applied in a manner which would constitute a means of arbitrary or unjustifiable discrimination between countries where the same conditions prevail, or a disguised restriction on international trade, nothing in this Agreement shall be construed to prevent the adoption or enforcement by any contracting party of measures:

(*a*) necessary to protect public morals;

(*b*) necessary to protect human, animal or plant life or health;

(*c*) relating to the importations or exportations of gold or silver;

(*d*) necessary to secure compliance with laws or regulations which are not inconsistent with the provisions of this Agreement, including those relating to customs enforcement, the enforcement of monopolies operated under paragraph 4 of Article II and Article XVII, the protection of patents, trade marks and copyrights, and the prevention of deceptive practices;

(*e*) relating to the products of prison labour;

(*f*) imposed for the protection of national treasures of artistic, historic or archaeological value;

(*g*) relating to the conservation of exhaustible natural resources if such measures are made effective in conjunction with restrictions on domestic production or consumption;

(*h*) undertaken in pursuance of obligations under any intergovernmental commodity agreement which conforms to criteria submitted to the CONTRACTING PARTIES and not disapproved by them or which is itself so submitted and not so disapproved;*

(*i*) involving restrictions on exports of domestic materials necessary to ensure essential quantities of such materials to a domestic processing industry during periods when the domestic price of such materials is held below the world price as part of a governmental stabilization plan; *Provided* that such restrictions shall not operate to increase the exports of or the protection afforded to such domestic industry, and shall not depart from the provisions of this Agreement relating to non-discrimination;

(*j*) essential to the acquisition or distribution of products in general or local short supply; *Provided* that any such measures shall be consistent with the principle that all contracting parties are entitled to an equitable share of the international supply of such products, and that any such measures, which are inconsistent with the other provisions of the Agreement shall be discontinued as soon as the conditions giving rise to them have ceased to exist. The CONTRACTING PARTIES shall review the need for this sub-paragraph not later than 30 June 1960.

Interpretative Note *Ad* Article XX from Annex I

Sub-paragraph (h)

The exception provided for in this sub-paragraph extends to any commodity agreement which conforms to the principles approved by the Economic and Social Council in its resolution 30 (IV) of 28 March 1947.

II. INTERPRETATION AND APPLICATION OF ARTICLE XX

A. SCOPE AND APPLICATION OF ARTICLE XX

1. General

The 1984 Panel Report on "Canada - Administration of the Foreign Investment Review Act" notes, with regard to the argument that certain measures fell within Article XX(d):

"Since Article XX(d) is an exception to the General Agreement it is up to Canada, as the party invoking the exception, to demonstrate that the purchase undertakings are necessary to secure compliance with the Foreign Investment Review Act".[1]

The 1989 Panel Report on "United States - Section 337 of the Tariff Act of 1930" found that "… it is up to the contracting party seeking to justify measures under Article XX(d) to demonstrate that those measures are 'necessary' within the meaning of that provision".[2]

The 1991 Panel Report on "United States - Restrictions on Imports of Tuna", which has not been adopted, includes the following finding regarding the presentation of arguments to a panel concerning both the positive prescriptions of the General Agreement and the exceptions in Article XX:

"The Panel noted that the United States had argued that its direct embargo under the MMPA could be justified under Article XX(b) or Article XX(g), and that Mexico had argued that a contracting party could not simultaneously argue that a measure is compatible with the general rules of the General Agreement and invoke Article XX for that measure. The Panel recalled that previous panels had established that Article XX is a limited and conditional exception from obligations under other provisions of the General Agreement, and not a positive rule establishing obligations in itself.[3] Therefore, the practice of panels has been to interpret Article XX narrowly, to place the burden on the party invoking Article XX to justify its invocation,[4] and not to examine Article XX exceptions unless invoked.[5] Nevertheless, the Panel considered that a party to a dispute could argue in the alternative that Article XX might apply, without this argument constituting *ipso facto* an admission that the measures in question would otherwise be inconsistent with the General Agreement. Indeed, the efficient operation of the dispute settlement process required that such arguments in the alternative be possible".[6]

2. Preamble of Article XX

The preamble was inserted into the exceptions article of the commercial policy chapter of the draft ITO Charter during the London session of the Preparatory Committee. At that time one delegation stated that "Indirect protection is an undesirable and dangerous phenomenon. … Many times the stipulations 'to protect animal or plant life or health' are misused for indirect protection. It is recommended to insert a clause which prohibits expressly [the use of] such measures [to] constitute an indirect protection …".[7] In discussions in the Technical Sub-committee of Committee II at London, the following proposal was made.

---

[1] L/5504, adopted on 7 February 1984, 30S/140, 64, para. 5.20.
[2] L/6439, adopted on 7 November 1989, 36S/345, 393, para. 5.27.
[3] The note to this sentence refers to the Panel Report on "United States - Section 337 of the Tariff Act of 1930", adopted on 7 November 1989, BISD 36S/345, 385, para. 5.9.
[4] The note to this sentence refers to the Panel Reports on "Canada - Administration of the Foreign Investment Review Act", adopted on 7 February 1984, 30S/140, 164, para. 5.20 and "United States - Section 337 of the Tariff Act of 1930", adopted on 7 November 1989, 36S/345, 393 para. 5.27.
[5] The note to this sentence refers to, e.g., the panel report on "EEC - Regulation of Parts and Components", adopted on 16 May 1990, L/6657, 37S/132, para. 5.11.
[6] DS21/R (unadopted), dated 3 September 1991, 39S/155, 197, para. 5.22.
[7] EPCT/C.II/32 (Note of the Netherlands and the Belgo-Luxembourg Economic Union, 30 October 1946).

"... it had been the practice in international agreements to include such exceptions as those laid down in Article 32 [XX], but only exceptions to provisions on import prohibitions and restrictions. The exceptions of Article 32 [XX] covered a far wider field.

"In order to prevent abuse of the exceptions of Article 32 ... the following sentence should be inserted as an introduction: 'The undertakings in Chapter IV of this Charter relating to import and export restrictions shall not be construed to prevent the adoption or enforcement by any Member of the following measures, provided that they are not applied in such a manner as to constitute a means of arbitrary discrimination between countries where the same conditions prevail, or a disguised restriction on international trade'."[8]

This suggestion was generally accepted subject to later review of its wording, particularly as to whether the scope of the Article should be limited to import and export restrictions.[9] See also Article XX(b) below.

(1) "arbitrary or unjustifiable discrimination between countries where the same conditions prevail"

In the 1982 Panel Report on "United States - Prohibition of Imports of Tuna and Tuna Products from Canada", the Panel examined a US prohibition on imports of tuna and tuna products from Canada, imposed 31 August 1979 following the seizure by Canadian authorities of US fishing vessels and fishermen in disputed waters.

"The Panel noted the preamble to Article XX. The United States' action of 31 August 1979 had been taken exclusively against imports of tuna and tuna products from Canada, but similar actions had been taken against imports from Costa Rica, Ecuador, Mexico and Peru and then for similar reasons. The Panel felt that the discrimination of Canada in this case might not necessarily have been arbitrary or unjustifiable. ..."[10]

The 1983 Panel Report on "United States - Imports of Certain Automotive Spring Assemblies" examined a ban on imports, under an "exclusion order" of the U.S. International Trade Commission, of certain automotive spring assemblies which the Commission had found under Section 337 of the Tariff Act of 1930 infringed United States patents. The Panel decided to first examine the applicability of Article XX(d).

"Looking first at the Preamble, the Panel interpreted the word 'measure' to mean the exclusion order issued by the United States International Trade Commission (ITC) under the provisions and procedures of Section 337 since, in the view of the Panel, it was the exclusion order which operated as the measure preventing the importation of the infringing product.

"The Panel noted that the exclusion order was directed against imports of certain automotive spring assemblies produced in violation of a valid United States patent from all foreign sources, and not just from Canada. It found, therefore, that the exclusion order was 'not applied in a manner which would constitute a means of arbitrary or unjustifiable discrimination against countries where the same conditions prevail'."[11]

The Panel Report was adopted "on the understanding that this shall not foreclose future examination of the use of Section 337 to deal with patent infringement cases from the point of view of consistency with Articles III and XX of the General Agreement".[12] Such examination took place during the panel proceedings on "United States - Section 337 of the Tariff Act of 1930".

---

[8]EPCT/C.II/50, p. 7.
[9]*Ibid.*, p. 9; EPCT/C.II/54/Rev.1, p. 36.
[10]L/5198, adopted on 22 February 1982, 29S/91, 108, para. 4.8.
[11]L/5333, adopted on 26 May 1983, 30S/107, 125, paras. 54-55.
[12]C/M/168, p. 10.

(2) "disguised restriction on international trade"

The 1982 Panel Report on "United States - Prohibition of Imports of Tuna and Tuna Products from Canada" notes that the Panel "felt that the United States' action should not be considered to be a disguised restriction on international trade, noting that the United States' prohibition of imports of tuna and tuna products from Canada had been taken as a trade measure and publicly announced as such".[13] In discussions on this report at the 22 February 1982 Council meeting, the representative of Canada noted that "Canada did not consider it sufficient for a trade measure to be publicly announced as such for it to be considered not to be a disguised restriction on international trade within the meaning of Article XX of the General Agreement".[14]

The 1983 Panel Report on "United States - Imports of Certain Automotive Spring Assemblies" also notes that

> "The Panel ... considered whether or not the exclusion order was 'applied in a manner which would constitute ... a disguised restriction on international trade'. The Panel noted that the Preamble of Article XX made it clear that it was the application of the measure and not the measure itself that needed to be examined. Notice of the exclusion order was published in the Federal Register and the order was enforced by the United States Customs at the border. The Panel also noted that the ITC proceedings in this particular case were directed against the importation of automotive spring assemblies produced in violation of a valid United States patent and that, before an exclusion order could be issued under Section 337, both the validity of a patent and its infringement by a foreign manufacturer had to be clearly established. Furthermore, the exclusion order would not prohibit the importation of automotive spring assemblies produced by any producer outside the United States who had a licence from Kuhlman Corporation (Kuhlman) to produce these goods. Consequently, the Panel found that the exclusion order had not been applied in a manner which constituted a disguised restriction on international trade".[15]

3. Paragraph (b)

(1) "necessary to protect human, animal or plant life or health"

During the Geneva session of the Preparatory Committee, in discussions concerning paragraph (b) and its relationship to the preamble of this article, it was agreed to delete the phrase (which had appeared in the New York draft of paragraph (b)) "if corresponding domestic safeguards under similar conditions exist in the importing country". The reasons for the proposed deletion were that this would be difficult to implement, and "as for the protection needed for exporting countries, to see that this is not abused ... that is afforded one by the headnote to the Article ...".[16] It was stated at that time that "in view of the misuses which have been made in the past of sanitary regulations, and of damages caused in this way to exporting countries, it would be regrettable if we were to renounce any clarification of the provisions of sub-paragraph (b). However, the discussion which was raised here shows clearly that this Committee is against any possibility of this provision being used as a measure of protection in disguise".[17]

The record of the discussions at the Havana Conference in the Third Committee on the corresponding provision in the Charter notes:

> "The Committee agreed that quarantine and other sanitary regulations are a subject to which the Organization should give careful attention with a view to preventing measures 'necessary to protect human, animal or plant life or health' from being applied in a manner which would constitute a means of arbitrary or unjustifiable discrimination or a disguised restriction on international trade and to advising Members how they can maintain such measures without causing such prejudice. In view of this, the Committee assumes that the Organization will establish a regular procedure with a view to investigating

---

[13] L/5198, adopted on 22 February 1982, 29S/91, 108, para. 4.8.
[14] C/M/155.
[15] L/5333, adopted on 26 May 1983, 30S/107, 125, para. 56.
[16] EPCT/A/PV/30, p. 11; see also *ibid*. p. 14-15.
[17] EPCT/A/PV/30, p. 13.

(in consultation, when it considers this advisable, with other intergovernmental specialized agencies of recognized scientific and technical competence, such as the FAO) any complaints that might be brought by a Member as to the use of the exception in sub-paragraph 1(a)(iii) of Article 45 [(b) of XX] in a manner inconsistent with the provisions of the preamble to that paragraph".[18]

In the 1987 Panel Report on "Japan - Customs Duties, Taxes and Labelling Practices on Imported Wines and Alcoholic Beverages", in discussing the claim of Japan that discriminatory or protective taxes on various alcoholic beverages could be justified as designed to meet the objective of taxation according to ability to pay, the Panel noted the scope provided to domestic tax systems under Article III; it also noted that "... The 'general exceptions' provided for in GATT Article XX might also justify internal tax differentiations among like or directly competitive products, for instance if 'necessary to protect human ... or plant life or health' (Article XX(b)). The Panel found, therefore, that the General Agreement reserved each contracting party a large degree of freedom to decide autonomously on the objectives, level, principles and methods of its internal taxation of goods".[19]

The 1990 Panel Report on "Thailand - Restrictions on Importation of and Internal Taxes on Cigarettes"[20] examined measures by Thailand prohibiting imports of cigarettes. The Panel found that these measures were inconsistent with Article XI. Thailand claimed that the restrictions were justified under Article XX(b) because measures which could only be effective if cigarette imports were prohibited had been adopted by the government to control smoking and because additives in United States cigarettes might make them more harmful than Thai cigarettes. The Panel heard from an expert of the World Health Organization (WHO).

"The Panel ... defined the issues which arose under [Article XX(b)]. In agreement with the parties to the dispute and the expert from the WHO, the Panel accepted that smoking constituted a serious risk to human health and that consequently measures designed to reduce the consumption of cigarettes fell within the scope of Article XX(b). The Panel noted that this provision clearly allowed contracting parties to give priority to human health over trade liberalization; however, for a measure to be covered by Article XX(b) it had to be 'necessary'.

"The Panel noted that a previous panel had discussed the meaning of the term 'necessary' in the context of Article XX(d), which provides an exemption for measures which are 'necessary to secure compliance with laws or regulations which are not inconsistent' with the provisions of the General Agreement. The panel had stated that

'a contracting party cannot justify a measure inconsistent with other GATT provisions as "necessary" in terms of Article XX(d) *if an alternative measure which it could reasonably be expected to employ and which is not inconsistent with other GATT provisions is available to it*. By the same token, in cases where a measure consistent with other GATT provisions is not reasonably available, a contracting party is bound to use, among the measures reasonably available to it, that which entails the least degree of inconsistency with other GATT provisions'.[21]

"The Panel could see no reason why under Article XX the meaning of the term 'necessary' under paragraph (d) should not be the same as in paragraph (b). In both paragraphs the same term was used and the same objective intended: to allow contracting parties to impose trade restrictive measures inconsistent with the General Agreement to pursue overriding public policy goals to the extent that such inconsistencies were unavoidable. The fact that paragraph (d) applies to inconsistencies resulting from the enforcement of GATT-consistent laws and regulations while paragraph (b) applies to those resulting from health-related policies therefore did not justify a different interpretation of the term 'necessary'.

---

[18]E/CONF.2/C.3/SR.35.
[19]L/6216, adopted on 10 November 1987, 34S/83, 124, para. 5.13.
[20]DS10/R, adopted on 7 November 1990, 37S/200.
[21]The note to this paragraph refers to the Panel Report on "United States - Section 337 of the Tariff Act of 1930", L/6439, adopted on 7 November 1989, paragraph 5.26.

"The Panel concluded from the above that the import restrictions imposed by Thailand could be considered to be 'necessary' in terms of Article XX(b) only if there were no alternative measure consistent with the General Agreement, or less inconsistent with it, which Thailand could reasonably be expected to employ to achieve its health policy objectives. The Panel noted that contracting parties may, in accordance with Article III:4 of the General Agreement, impose laws, regulations and requirements affecting the internal sale, offering for sale, purchase, transportation, distribution or use of imported products provided they do not thereby accord treatment to imported products less favourable than that accorded to 'like' products of national origin. The United States argued that Thailand could achieve its public health objectives through internal measures consistent with Article III:4 and that the inconsistency with Article XI:1 could therefore not be considered to be 'necessary' within the meaning of Article XX(b). The Panel proceeded to examine this issue in detail.

"The Panel noted that the principal health objectives advanced by Thailand to justify its import restrictions were to protect the public from harmful ingredients in imported cigarettes, and to reduce the consumption of cigarettes in Thailand. The measures could thus be seen as intended to ensure the quality and reduce the quantity of cigarettes sold in Thailand.

"The Panel then examined whether the Thai concerns about the *quality* of cigarettes consumed in Thailand could be met with measures consistent, or less inconsistent, with the General Agreement. It noted that other countries had introduced strict, non-discriminatory labelling and ingredient disclosure regulations which allowed governments to control, and the public to be informed of, the content of cigarettes. A non-discriminatory regulation implemented on a national treatment basis in accordance with Article III:4 requiring complete disclosure of ingredients, coupled with a ban on unhealthy substances, would be an alternative consistent with the General Agreement. The Panel considered that Thailand could reasonably be expected to take such measures to address the quality-related policy objectives it now pursues through an import ban on all cigarettes whatever their ingredients.

"The Panel then considered whether Thai concerns about the *quantity* of cigarettes consumed in Thailand could be met by measures reasonably available to it and consistent, or less inconsistent, with the General Agreement. The Panel first examined how Thailand might reduce the *demand* for cigarettes in a manner consistent with the General Agreement. The Panel noted the view expressed by the WHO that the demand for cigarettes, in particular the initial demand for cigarettes by the young, was influenced by cigarette advertisements and that bans on advertisement could therefore curb such demand. At the Forty-third World Health Assembly a resolution was approved stating that the WHO is:

> 'Encouraged by ... recent information demonstrating the effectiveness of tobacco control strategies, and in particular ... comprehensive legislative bans and other restrictive measures to effectively control the direct and the indirect advertising, promotion and sponsorship of tobacco'.[22]

"The resolution goes on to urge all member states of the WHO

> 'to consider including in their tobacco control strategies plans for legislation or other effective measures at the appropriate government level providing for: ...
>
>> (c) progressive restrictions and concerted actions to eliminate eventually all direct and indirect advertising, promotion and sponsorship concerning tobacco'

"A ban on the advertisement of cigarettes of both domestic and foreign origin would normally meet the requirements of Article III:4. It might be argued that such a general ban on all cigarette advertising would create unequal competitive opportunities between the existing Thai supplier of cigarettes and new, foreign suppliers and was therefore contrary to Article III:4.[23] Even if this argument

---

[22]The note to this paragraph refers to the Forty-third World Health Assembly, Fourteenth plenary meeting, Agenda Item 10, 17 May 1990 (A43/VR/14; WHA43.16).

[23]The note to this sentence provides: "On the requirement of equal competitive opportunities, see the Report of the panel on 'United States - Section 337 of the Tariff Act of 1930' (L/6439, paragraph 5.26, adopted on 7 November 1989)'".

were accepted, such an inconsistency would have to be regarded as unavoidable and therefore necessary within the meaning of Article XX(b) because additional advertising rights would risk stimulating demand for cigarettes. The Panel noted that Thailand had already implemented some non-discriminatory controls on demand, including information programmes, bans on direct and indirect advertising, warnings on cigarette packs, and bans on smoking in certain public places.

"The Panel then examined how Thailand might restrict the *supply* of cigarettes in a manner consistent with the General Agreement. The Panel noted that contracting parties may maintain governmental monopolies, such as the Thai Tobacco Monopoly, on the importation and domestic sale of products.[24] The Thai Government may use this monopoly to regulate the overall supply of cigarettes, their prices and their retail availability provided it thereby does not accord imported cigarettes less favourable treatment than domestic cigarettes or act inconsistently with any commitments assumed under its Schedule of Concessions.[25] As to the pricing of cigarettes, the Panel noted that the Forty-third World Health Assembly, in its resolution cited above, stated that it was:

'Encouraged by ... recent information demonstrating the effectiveness of tobacco control strategies, and in particular ... policies to achieve progressive increases in the real price of tobacco.'

"It accordingly urged all member states

'to consider including in their tobacco control strategies plans for ... progressive financial measures aimed at discouraging the use of tobacco'.[26]

"For these reasons the Panel could not accept the argument of Thailand that competition between imported and domestic cigarettes would necessarily lead to an increase in the total sales of cigarettes and that Thailand therefore had no option but to prohibit cigarette imports.

"The Panel then examined further the resolutions of the WHO on smoking which the WHO made available. It noted that the health measures recommended by the WHO in these resolutions were non-discriminatory and concerned all, not just imported, cigarettes. The Panel also examined the Report of the WHO Expert Committee on Smoking Control Strategies in Developing Countries. The Panel observed that a common consequence of import restrictions was the promotion of domestic production and the fostering of interests in the maintenance of that production and that the WHO Expert Committee had made the following recommendation relevant in this respect:

'Where tobacco is already a commercial crop every effort should be made to reduce its role in the national economy, and to investigate alternative uses of land and labour. The existence of a tobacco industry of any kind should not be permitted to interfere with the implementation of educational and other measures to control smoking'.[27]

"In sum, the Panel considered that there were various measures consistent with the General Agreement which were reasonably available to Thailand to control the quality and quantity of cigarettes smoked and which, taken together, could achieve the health policy goals that the Thai government pursues by restricting the importation of cigarettes inconsistently with Article XI:1. The Panel found therefore that Thailand's practice of permitting the sale of domestic cigarettes while not permitting the importation of foreign cigarettes was an inconsistency with the General Agreement not 'necessary' within the meaning of Article XX(b)".[28]

---

[24] The note to this sentence provides: "Cf. Articles III:4, XVII and XX(d)".

[25] The note to this sentence provides: "Cf. Articles III:2 and 4 and II:4".

[26] The note to this sentence refers to Forty-third World Health Assembly, Fourteenth plenary meeting, Agenda Item 10, 17 May 1990 (A43/VR/14; WHA43.16).

[27] The note to this sentence refers to 1982 Expert Committee on 'Smoking Control Strategies in Developing Countries', page 69; cited at page 16 in the WHO Submission to the Panel of 19 July 1990.

[28] DS10/R, adopted on 7 November 1990, 37S/200, 222-226, paras. 73-81.

In the November 1990 Council discussion preceding the adoption of this Panel Report, the representative of Thailand stated that "it was clear from the present Panel report that Thailand's cigarette régime was based on public health policy considerations. His Government intended to take all measures necessary to prevent an increase in tobacco consumption, and to reduce it if possible. Thailand took heart from the report that a set of GATT-consistent measures could be taken to control both the supply of and demand for cigarettes, as long as they were applied to both domestic and imported cigarettes on a national-treatment basis. He concluded by saying that as a contracting party, Thailand intended to abide by its GATT obligations. It had lifted its import ban, and its present laws and regulations were in accordance with the national-treatment principle. On the other hand, Thailand needed to ensure that it would not be forced to accept conditions imposed above and beyond its GATT obligations".[29]

In the 1991 Panel Report on "United States - Restrictions on Imports of Tuna", which has not been adopted, the Panel examined the provisions of the Marine Mammal Protection Act (MMPA) providing for a prohibition of imports of certain yellowfin tuna and yellowfin tuna products, and the import ban imposed under these provisions.

"The Panel noted that the United States considered the prohibition of imports of certain yellowfin tuna and certain yellowfin tuna products from Mexico, and the provisions of the MMPA on which this prohibition is based, to be justified by Article XX(b) because they served solely the purpose of protecting dolphin life and health and were 'necessary' within the meaning of that provision because, in respect of the protection of dolphin life and health outside its jurisdiction, there was no alternative measure reasonably available to the United States to achieve this objective. Mexico considered that Article XX(b) was not applicable to a measure imposed to protect the life or health of animals outside the jurisdiction of the contracting party taking it and that the import prohibition imposed by the United States was not necessary because alternative means consistent with the General Agreement were available to it to protect dolphin lives or health, namely international co-operation between the countries concerned.

"The Panel noted that the basic question raised by these arguments, namely whether Article XX(b) covers measures necessary to protect human, animal or plant life or health outside the jurisdiction of the contracting party taking the measure, is not clearly answered by the text of that provision. It refers to life and health protection generally without expressly limiting that protection to the jurisdiction of the contracting party concerned. The Panel therefore decided to analyze this issue in the light of the drafting history of Article XX(b), the purpose of this provision, and the consequences that the interpretations proposed by the parties would have for the operation of the General Agreement as a whole.

"The Panel noted that the proposal for Article XX(b) dated from the Draft Charter of the International Trade Organization (ITO) proposed by the United States, which stated in Article 32, 'Nothing in Chapter IV [on commercial policy] of this Charter shall be construed to prevent the adoption or enforcement by any Member of measures: ... (b) necessary to protect human, animal or plant life or health'. In the New York Draft of the ITO Charter, the preamble had been revised to read as it does at present, and exception (b) read: 'For the purpose of protecting human, animal or plant life or health, if corresponding domestic safeguards under similar conditions exist in the importing country'. This added proviso reflected concerns regarding the abuse of sanitary regulations by importing countries. Later, Commission A of the Second Session of the Preparatory Committee in Geneva agreed to drop this proviso as unnecessary.[30] Thus, the record indicates that the concerns of the drafters of Article XX(b) focused on the use of sanitary measures to safeguard life or health of humans, animals or plants within the jurisdiction of the importing country.

"The Panel further noted that Article XX(b) allows each contracting party to set its human, animal or plant life or health standards. The conditions set out in Article XX(b) which limit resort to this exception, namely that the measure taken must be 'necessary' and not 'constitute a means of arbitrary or

---

[29] C/M/246, 23 November 1990.
[30] The note to this sentence refers to EPCT/A/PV/30/7-15.

unjustifiable discrimination or a disguised restriction on international trade', refer to the trade measure requiring justification under Article XX(b), not however to the life or health standard chosen by the contracting party. The Panel recalled the finding of a previous panel that this paragraph of Article XX was intended to allow contracting parties to impose trade restrictive measures inconsistent with the General Agreement to pursue overriding public policy goals to the extent that such inconsistencies were unavoidable.[31] The Panel considered that if the broad interpretation of Article XX(b) suggested by the United States were accepted, each contracting party could unilaterally determine the life or health protection policies from which other contracting parties could not deviate without jeopardizing their rights under the General Agreement. The General Agreement would then no longer constitute a multilateral framework for trade among all contracting parties but would provide legal security only in respect of trade between a limited number of contracting parties with identical internal regulations.

"The Panel considered that the United States' measures, even if Article XX(b) were interpreted to permit extrajurisdictional protection of life and health, would not meet the requirement of necessity set out in that provision. The United States had not demonstrated to the Panel - as required of the party invoking an Article XX exception - that it had exhausted all options reasonably available to it to pursue its dolphin protection objectives through measures consistent with the General Agreement, in particular through the negotiation of international cooperative arrangements, which would seem to be desirable in view of the fact that dolphins roam the waters of many states and the high seas. Moreover, even assuming that an import prohibition were the only resort reasonably available to the United States, the particular measure chosen by the United States could in the Panel's view not be considered to be necessary within the meaning of Article XX(b). The United States linked the maximum incidental dolphin taking rate which Mexico had to meet during a particular period in order to be able to export tuna to the United States to the taking rate actually recorded for United States fishermen during the same period. Consequently, the Mexican authorities could not know whether, at a given point of time, their policies conformed to the United States' dolphin protection standards. The Panel considered that a limitation on trade based on such unpredictable conditions could not be regarded as necessary to protect the health or life of dolphins.

"On the basis of the above considerations, the Panel found that the United States' direct import prohibition imposed on certain yellowfin tuna and certain yellowfin tuna products of Mexico and the provisions of the MMPA under which it is imposed could not be justified under the exception in Article XX(b)."[32]

In this connection see also the unadopted 1994 Panel Report on "United States - Restrictions on Imports of Tuna".[33]

See also the "Streamlined Mechanism for Reconciling the Interests of Contracting Parties in the Event of Trade-Damaging Acts", discussed below, which provides, *inter alia*, that "A measure taken by an importing contracting party should not be any more severe, and should not remain in force any longer, than necessary to protect the human, animal or plant life or health involved, as provided in Article XX(b)".[34]

(2) Publication, notification and consultations concerning measures taken under paragraph (b)

The provisions of Article XXII in the 30 October 1947 text of the General Agreement (and the corresponding provisions in Article 41 of the Havana Charter) provided for consultations concerning "such representations as may be made by any other contracting party with respect to [various enumerated matters and] sanitary laws and regulations for the protection of human, animal or plant life or health, and generally all matters affecting the operation of this Agreement". The listing of specific matters in Article XXII was deleted as unnecessary during the 1954-55 Review Session; see Section III under Article XXII.

---

[31] The footnote to this sentence refers to the Panel Report on 'Thailand - Restrictions on Importation of and Internal Taxes on Cigarettes', adopted on 7 November 1990, 37S/200, 222-223, DS10/R, paras. 73-74.
[32] DS21/R (unadopted), dated 3 September 1991, 39S/155, 198-200, paras. 5.24-5.29.
[33] DS29/R, dated 16 June 1994, paras. 5.28-5.39.
[34] C/M/236, pp. 6-7; 36S/67.

During discussions in the Third Committee at the Havana Conference,

"The Committee agreed that quarantine and other sanitary regulations as well as other types of regulations must be published under Article 37 [X] and that the provisions for consultation in Article 41 [XXII] required Members to supply full information as to the reason for and operation of such regulations".[35]

According to the Interpretative Note *Ad* Article 41 of the Havana Charter

"The provisions for consultation require Members, subject to the exceptions specifically set forth in this Charter, to supply to other Members, upon request, such information as will enable a full and fair appraisal of the matters which are the subject of such consultation, including the operation of sanitary laws and regulations for the protection of human, animal or plant life or health, and other matters affecting the application of Chapter IV".

In 1969, the United Kingdom notified new measures imposed in the wake of the 1967/68 outbreak of foot-and-mouth disease in the United Kingdom, including a ban on certain meat imports and imposition of requirements regarding compliance with animal health requirements, hygiene and public health inspection with respect to imports of boneless beef from countries where foot-and-mouth disease is endemic. The measures were accompanied by a reduction of the duty on beef imports. The notification stated "It must be emphasized the new measures are being taken solely as a result of the need to maintain high standards of animal and public health in the United Kingdom. There is no question of attempting to provide protection for our domestic industry and we consider the new measures to be fully compatible with the GATT and with Article XX in particular".[36]

Following the nuclear accident at Chernobyl in the Soviet Union, the EEC in May 1986 suspended imports of live animals, fresh meat and certain other fresh foods from certain East European countries. In the May 1986 meeting of the Council, the representative of Hungary stated that the selection of countries within a 1000 kilometer radius of the accident was unjustified and arbitrary; the radiation level had risen throughout most of Europe since the accident, and certain countries outside that radius had experienced a greater level of radiation than some within it. Hungary also recalled the recommendation of the World Health Organization according to which there was no public health justification to ban imports from East European countries. He expressed Hungary's willingness to have its food products checked for radiation at the border by importing countries, and/or to certify freedom from radioactive contamination for each shipment. The representative of the EEC stressed that the measures were temporary and conservative, and stated that necessary data on radiation levels had not yet been received.[37] Austria notified the contracting parties of a temporary prohibition on imports of certain dairy, vegetable and fruit products originating in certain countries of Eastern and Southern Europe, following the Chernobyl accident; the prohibition was stated to be "in accordance with Article XX(b)".[38]

At the May 1989 Council meeting, Chile drew attention to the problem it had faced regarding the United States' suspension of imports of Chilean fruit on the basis of suspected food contamination. Chile suggested that the Chairman hold consultations with interested contracting parties to study ways of setting up machinery which, while protecting the rights of contracting parties, would minimize the damage caused by similar measures. The delegate of Chile stated that "The measures taken had ... involved hundreds of millions of dollars of fruit and vegetables which had had to be destroyed or re-exported, confiscated or prohibited from entry because two grapes had been found to contain toxic chemicals. This situation had led Chile to believe that contracting parties should have a permanent expeditious system to hold consultations speedily, to exchange information and to arrive jointly at decisions -- in short, a crisis management body ... to ensure that measures adopted would be in keeping with the dimension of the threat".[39] A number of

---

[35] E/CONF.2/C.3/SR.35, pp. 6-7.
[36] L/3251.
[37] C/M/198, p. 28-31.
[38] L/5998, 27 May 1986; removal of measures, Add.1, 11 June 1986.
[39] C/M/232, p. 24.

contracting parties supported this proposal, underlining the importance of the issues raised by Chile for food exporting countries. Others stated that governments had to be free to act expeditiously when human health was endangered, and could not be expected to consult extensively on the trade impact of their actions before responding to an urgent threat to human health.[40]

At its meeting on 11 October 1989, the Chairman read out an agreed text, which noted that "During the course of the consultations and in the light of comments made by delegations, there seems to have emerged a consensus amongst the participating delegations that the matter under discussion is of interest to all contracting parties. Another element which emerged during the informal consultations was that some delegations, despite their recognition that a genuine problem exists, are doubtful whether it will be possible for their respective authorities in capitals to agree on a formalized GATT structure to deal with the problem". The Council agreed to the Chairman's proposal that the Council take note of his recommendation, entitled "Streamlined Mechanism for Reconciling the Interests of Contracting Parties in the Event of Trade-Damaging Acts", that the following guidelines be used in the event of a trade-damaging act:

"1. A measure taken by an importing contracting party should not be any more severe, and should not remain in force any longer, than necessary to protect the human, animal or plant life or health involved, as provided in Article XX(b).

"2. The importing contracting party should notify the Director-General as quickly as possible. A notification by telephone should be followed immediately by a written communication from the importing contracting party, which would be circulated to contracting parties.

"3. The importing contracting party would be expected to agree to expeditious informal consultations with the principally concerned contracting party as soon as a trade-damaging act has occurred, with a view to reaching a common view about the dimension of the problem and the best way to deal with it effectively".[41]

In December 1989, at the Forty-fifth Session, Austria informed the CONTRACTING PARTIES that with effect from 1 December 1989, Austria had limited traffic of certain heavy trucks during night hours on certain Austrian transit roads; the representative of Austria stated that "This measure has become unavoidable due to the intolerable increase in heavy traffic on certain transit routes causing extreme noise and pollution seriously endangering the health of the adjacent Austrian population. This measure has been taken in accordance with Article XX(b) of the General Agreement". The measure applied to trucks of all nationalities, including Austrian trucks. Austria also noted that in retaliation Germany had decided to ban as of 1 January 1990 the circulation of 212,000 Austrian lorries during night hours in the entire territory of Germany. Consultations were held under Article XXII:1 regarding the German measure in spring 1990.[42]

In 1991, Peru drew the Council's attention to restrictions imposed on exports of Peru following the cholera epidemic in Peru, and sought application of these 1989 guidelines, referring to a World Health Assembly resolution calling on member States not to apply to countries affected by the cholera epidemic import restrictions not justifiable on public health grounds. Pursuant to the 1989 guidelines, the EEC notified a prohibition on imports from Peru of certain food products unless accompanied by a certificate of freedom from cholera, and Austria notified with reference to Article XX(b) a prohibition on imports of fishery products from Peru.[43] In October 1993, Austria notified two prohibitions on importation of certain live animals and animal products from specific countries or districts, imposed in line with Article XX(b) and in order to prevent the introduction of classical swine fever and of foot-and-mouth disease into Austria; the notification was without reference to the 1989 guidelines. In July and October 1994 Austria again notified such restrictions.[44]

---

[40]C/M/232, p. 23-29; see further C/M/231, C/M/234, C/M/235.
[41]C/M/236, pp. 6-7; 36S/67.
[42]SR.45/ST/22, DS14/1, C/M/241.
[43]C/M/248, 249, 250, 251; statement of Peru with relevant WHO press releases, Spec(91)12; communication from Peru, L/7038; EEC notification, L/6845 (notification of modification of measures in L/6845/Add.1); notification by Austria, L/6917.
[44]L/7302, L/7303 (1993); L/7503, L/7544 (1994).

A Secretariat Note of 1991 on "Trade and Environment" includes a list of quantitative restrictions for which Article XX(b) has been cited as a justification. The list was drawn from the Inventory of Quantitative Restrictions maintained by the Secretariat.[45]

4. Paragraph (c): "relating to the importation or exportation of gold and silver"

The Panel Report on "Canada - Measures Affecting the Sale of Gold Coins", which has not been adopted, examined a tax measure of the province of Ontario imposing a retail sales tax on gold coins and exempting from this tax Maple Leaf gold coins struck by the Canadian Mint. The Panel noted that while both the Maple Leaf and the Krugerrand were legal tender in their respective countries of origin, both were normally purchased as investment goods, and therefore considered that the Maple Leaf and Krugerrand gold coins were not only means of payment but also "products" within the meaning of Article III:2.[46]

5. Paragraph (d)

(1) General

The Working Party on "The Haitian Tobacco Monopoly" in 1955 examined whether the licensing of tobacco imports by the Tobacco Régie required a release under the provisions of Article XVIII:12: "... the representative of Haiti stated that the measure was necessary to secure compliance with the Law of 16 February 1948, which established the Tobacco Régie ... and that it was 'not applied in a manner which would constitute a means of arbitrary or unjustifiable discrimination between countries where the same conditions prevail, or a disguised restriction on international trade.' In the light of this statement the Working Party considered that Article [XX(d)] would be applicable to the measure if the basic regulations were not in conflict with any provision of the Agreement".[47]

The 1989 Panel Report on "United States - Section 337 of the Tariff Act of 1930" dealt with the claim by the European Economic Community that the special "Section 337" procedure for enforcing patent claims against imported products treated such products less favourably than the procedures applicable to patent claims involving products of domestic origin, contrary to Article III:4, and that this special procedure was not justified under Article XX(d) as "necessary" to enforce U.S. patent laws against imports.

> "The Panel noted that the parties to the dispute agreed that, for the purposes of Article XX(d), Section 337 can be considered as 'measures ... to secure compliance with' United States patent law ... and ... examined whether, in respect of the elements of Section 337 found to be inconsistent with Article III:4 of the General Agreement, the conditions specified in Article XX(d) to justify measures otherwise inconsistent with the GATT are met. These are:
>
> - that the 'laws or regulations' with which compliance is being secured are themselves 'not inconsistent' with the General Agreement;
>
> - that the measures are 'necessary to secure compliance' with those laws or regulations;
>
> - that the measures are 'not applied in a manner which would constitute a means of arbitrary or unjustifiable discrimination between countries where the same conditions prevail, or a disguised restriction on international trade'.
>
> "The Panel noted that each of these conditions must be met if an inconsistency with another GATT provision is to be justifiable under Article XX(d). A measure which does not meet any one of these

---

[45] L/6896, p. 93. Concerning the Inventory of Quantitative Restrictions, see under Article XI in this Index.
[46] L/5863 (unadopted), dated 17 September 1985, para. 51.
[47] L/454, adopted on 22 November 1955, 4S/38, 39, para. 6. Before the revision of Article XVIII in the Review Session, Article XVIII:12 provided for notification and concurrence with regard to certain measures affecting imports which were not otherwise permitted by the General Agreement. See also references to this report under Article III.

conditions, for example the condition that it must be 'necessary to secure compliance' with a law consistent with the GATT, cannot be justified under Article XX(d)".[48]

(2) "necessary"

The 1983 Panel Report on "United States - Imports of Certain Automotive Spring Assemblies" examined claims by Canada regarding an exclusion order issued by the U.S. International Trade Commission (ITC) under Section 337 of the Tariff Act of 1930, including arguments that "The exception under Article XX(d) did not justify trade restrictive measures taken pursuant to Section 337 on two grounds: (1) differential treatment of foreign products involving a separate adjudicating process was not 'necessary' to secure compliance with United States patent laws, and (2) the law with which compliance was sought (Section 337) was 'inconsistent with the provisions of this agreement', i.e. Article III of the GATT".[49] In its findings,

"The Panel considered whether the ITC action, in making the exclusion order, was 'necessary' in the sense of paragraph (d) of Article XX to secure compliance with United States patent law. In this connection the Panel examined whether a satisfactory and effective alternative existed under civil court procedures which would have provided the patent holder Kuhlman with a sufficiently effective remedy against the violation of its patent by foreign producers including the Canadian producer Wallbank Manufacturing Co. Ltd. ....

"... it was the view of the Panel that the only way in which, under existing United States law, Kuhlman's right to the exclusive use of its patent in the United States domestic market could be effectively protected against the importation of the infringing product would be to resort to the exclusion order procedure. For the above reasons, therefore, the Panel found that the exclusion order issued by the ITC under Section 337 of the United States Tariff Act of 1930 was 'necessary' in the sense of Article XX(d) to prevent the importation and sale of automotive spring assemblies infringing the patent, thus protecting the patent holder's rights and securing compliance with United States patent law."[50]

"The Panel did not ... exclude the strong possibility that there might be cases ... where a procedure before a United States court might provide the patent holder with an equally satisfactory and effective remedy against infringement of his patent rights. In such cases the use of an exclusion order under Section 337 might not be necessary in terms of Article XX(d) to secure compliance with laws and regulations (i.e. United States patent law) which were not inconsistent with the General Agreement."[51]

"... The Panel pointed out that its finding ... that the exclusion order issued by the ITC was 'necessary' within the meaning of Article XX(d) had been made on the basis of existing United States law. It carried no implication that the use of Section 337 was an entirely satisfactory means of dealing with patent based cases".[52]

In the Council discussion of the Panel Report, the representative of Canada stated "that the Panel qualified its conclusions by emphasizing that it was under existing United States law that Section 337 orders would often be necessary. This would seem to suggest that if a contracting party elects not to equip itself with effective enforcement procedures with respect to imports for its law of general application, then it is free to deny national treatment, even to the extent of having a discriminatory adjudicative process".[53] Some other contracting parties also expressed concern at the Panel conclusions.[54] The Panel Report was adopted "on the understanding that this shall not foreclose future examination of the use of Section 337 to deal with patent infringement cases from the point of view of consistency with Articles III and XX of the General Agreement".[55]

---

[48] L/6439, adopted on 7 November 1989, 36S/345, 392, paras. 5.22-5.23.
[49] L/5333, adopted on 26 May 1983, 30S/107, 120, para. 37.
[50] Ibid., 30S/126, paras. 58, 60.
[51] Ibid., 30S/127, para. 66.
[52] Ibid., 30S/128, para. 68.
[53] C/M/161, p. 11; C/W/396, para. 4.
[54] C/M/161, pp. 12-16.
[55] C/M/168, p. 10.

The 1984 Panel Report on "Canada - Administration of the Foreign Investment Review Act" examined the argument by Canada that, if the Panel were to find purchase undertakings entered into between foreign investors and the government of Canada to be inconsistent with Article III:4, these would fall under Article XX(d) because the purchase undertakings were "necessary to secure compliance" with the Foreign Investment Review Act.

"... On the basis of the explanations given by Canada the Panel could not ... conclude that the purchase undertakings that were found to be inconsistent with Article III:4 are necessary for the effective administration of the Act. The Panel is in particular not convinced that, in order to achieve the aims of the Act, investors submitting applications under the Act had to be bound to purchasing practices having the effect of giving preference to domestic products. It was not clear to the Panel why a detailed review of investment proposals without purchasing requirements would not be sufficient to enable the Canadian government to determine whether the proposed investments were or were likely to be of significant benefit to Canada within the meaning of Section 2 of the Foreign Investment Review Act."[56]

The 1989 Panel Report on "United States - Section 337 of the Tariff Act of 1930" contains the following passage:

"The Panel noted that the United States and the Community interpret the term 'necessary' differently. They differ as to whether it requires the use of the least trade-restrictive measure available. They also differ as to whether 'necessity' to use measures that accord less favourable treatment to imported products can be created by a contracting party's choice, in its national legislation, of enforcement measures against domestic products that would not be effective against imports ...

"It was clear to the Panel that a contracting party cannot justify a measure inconsistent with another GATT provision as 'necessary' in terms of Article XX(d) if an alternative measure which it could reasonably be expected to employ and which is not inconsistent with other GATT provisions is available to it. By the same token, in cases where a measure consistent with other GATT provisions is not reasonably available, a contracting party is bound to use, among the measures reasonably available to it, that which entails the least degree of inconsistency with other GATT provisions. The Panel wished to make it clear that this does not mean that a contracting party could be asked to change its substantive patent law or its desired level of enforcement of that law, provided that such law and such level of enforcement are the same for imported and domestically-produced products. However, it does mean that, if a contracting party could reasonably secure that level of enforcement in a manner that is not inconsistent with other GATT provisions, it would be required to do so.

"Bearing in mind the foregoing and that it is up to the contracting party seeking to justify measures under Article XX(d) to demonstrate that those measures are 'necessary' within the meaning of that provision, the Panel considered whether the inconsistencies that it had found with Article III:4 can be justified as 'necessary' in terms of Article XX(d). The Panel first examined the argument of the United States that the Panel should consider not whether the individual elements of Section 337 are 'necessary' but rather whether Section 337 as a system is 'necessary' for the enforcement of United States patent laws. ... The Panel did not accept this contention since it would permit contracting parties to introduce GATT inconsistencies that are not necessary simply by making them part of a scheme which contained elements that are necessary. In the view of the Panel, what has to be justified as 'necessary' under Article XX(d) is each of the inconsistencies with another GATT Article found to exist, i.e. in this case, whether the differences between Section 337 and federal district court procedures that result in less favourable treatment of imported products within the meaning of Article III:4, as outlined above ... are necessary".[57]

The Panel went on to discuss the necessity of certain aspects of Section 337 which it had found were inconsistent with Article III:4:

---

[56]L/5504, adopted on 7 February 1984, 30S/140, 164-165, para. 5.20.
[57]L/6439, adopted on 7 November 1989, 36S/345, 392-393, paras. 5.25-5.27.

"The United States suggested that Section 337 can be justified because, under United States law, it provides the only means of enforcement of United States patent rights against imports of products manufactured abroad by means of a process patented in the United States. ... The Panel considered that, even if it were accepted that a different scheme for imports alleged to infringe process patents is necessary, this could not in itself justify as 'necessary' in terms of Article XX(d) any of the specific inconsistencies with Article III:4 summarised in paragraph 5.20 above. In any event, the Panel did not consider that a different scheme for imports alleged to infringe process patents is necessary, since many countries grant to their civil courts jurisdiction over imports of products manufactured abroad under processes protected by patents of the importing country. The Panel noted that, in the 1988 Omnibus Trade and Competitiveness Act, the United States has in fact amended its law to this effect (see Annex II).

"The United States also suggested that certain features of Section 337 are necessary in order to permit Presidential review, which is in the interests of respondents ... The Panel did not believe that this provided an argument for necessity in terms of Article XX(d), since Presidential review is not necessary in order to secure compliance with United States patent legislation; it is not, of course, available in United States patent litigation involving challenged products of domestic origin.

"The United States suggested that Section 337 is needed because of difficulties with service of process on and enforcement of judgments against foreign manufacturers .... As regards service of process, the difference in procedures between Section 337 and federal district courts was not itself alleged to be inconsistent with any GATT provision; and the Panel did not see why any of the inconsistencies with Article III:4 are a necessary accompaniment of arrangements for effective service of process where imported products are concerned. However, as noted in paragraph 5.19 above, the Panel found the differences in procedures for the enforcement of judgments to be inconsistent with Article III:4 in that they provide for the possibility of *in rem* general exclusion orders against imported products when no equivalent remedy is available against products of United States origin; and that they provide for automatic customs enforcement of exclusion orders while the enforcement of a court injunction requires the initiation of proceedings by the successful party.

"The United States stressed the importance to its system of enforcement of *in rem* orders, and the Panel considered this question at some length. The Panel agreed with the United States that taking action against infringing products at the source, that is at the point of their production, would generally be more difficult in respect of imported products than in respect of products of national origin: imported products are produced outside the jurisdiction of national enforcement bodies and it is seldom feasible to secure enforcement of the rulings of a court of the country of importation by local courts in the country of production. *In personam* action against importers would not in all cases be an adequate substitute for action against the manufacturer, not only because importers might be very numerous and not easily brought into a single judicial proceeding, but also, and more importantly, because as soon as activities of known importers were stopped it would often be possible for a foreign manufacturer to find another importer. For these reasons the Panel believed that there could be an objective need in terms of Article XX(d) to apply limited *in rem* exclusion orders to imported products, although no equivalent remedy is applied against domestically-produced products.

"A limited *in rem* order applying to imported products can thus be justified, for the reasons presented in the previous paragraph, as the functional equivalent of an injunction enjoining named domestic manufacturers. However, these reasons do not justify as 'necessary' in terms of Article XX(d) the inconsistency with Article III:4 found in respect of general exclusion orders; this is that such orders apply to products produced by persons who have not been named as respondents in the litigation, while no equivalent measure applicable to non-parties is available where products of United States origin are concerned. The United States informed the Panel that the situations which under Section 337 could justify a general exclusion order against imported products are a widespread pattern of unauthorised use of the patented invention or process and a reason to infer that manufacturers other than respondents to the investigation might enter the United States market with infringing products. However, the Panel saw no reason why these situations could not also occur in respect of products produced in the United States. Nevertheless, the Panel did not rule out entirely that there could sometimes be objective reasons why general *in rem* exclusion orders might be 'necessary' in terms of Article XX(d) against imported products even though no equivalent measure was needed against products of United States origin. For example, in the case of imported products it might be considerably more difficult to identify the source of infringing products or to prevent circumvention of orders limited to the products of named persons, than in the case of products of United States origin. Of course, the United States could bring the provision of general exclusion orders into consistency with Article III:4 by providing for the application in like situations of equivalent measures against products of United States origin.

"As noted above, the Panel found an inconsistency with Article III:4 in the fact that Section 337 exclusion orders are automatically enforced by the Customs Service, whereas the enforcement of injunctions against products of United States origin requires the successful plaintiff to bring individual proceedings. However, in this case the Panel accepted the argument of necessity in terms of Article XX(d). A United States manufacturer which has been enjoined by a federal district court order can normally be expected to comply with that injunction, because it would know that failure to do so would incur the risk of serious penalties resulting from a contempt proceeding brought by the successful plaintiff. An injunction should therefore normally suffice to stop enjoined activity without the need for subsequent action to enforce it. As far as imported products are concerned, enforcement at the border by the customs administration of exclusion orders can be considered as a means necessary to render such orders effective.

"The Panel considered the argument of the United States that many of the procedural aspects of Section 337 reflect the need to provide expeditious prospective relief against infringing imports. ... The Panel understood this argument to be based on the notion that, in respect of infringing imports, there would be greater difficulty than in respect of infringing products of domestic origin in collecting awards of damages for past infringement, because foreign manufacturers are outside the jurisdiction of national courts and importers might have little by way of assets. In the Panel's view, given the issues at stake in typical patent suits, this argument could only provide a justification for rapid *preliminary* or conservatory action against imported products, combined with the necessary safeguards to protect the legitimate interests of importers in the event that the products prove not to be infringing. The tight time-limits for the *conclusion* of Section 337 proceedings, when no comparable time-limits apply in federal district court, and the other features of Section 337 inconsistent with Article III:4 that serve to facilitate the expeditious completion of Section 337 proceedings, such as the inadmissibility of counterclaims, cannot be justified as 'necessary' on this basis.

"The United States did not advance, nor was the Panel aware of, any other arguments that might justify as necessary any of the elements of Section 337 that had been found to be inconsistent with Article III:4 of the General Agreement. On the basis of the preceding review and analysis, the Panel *found* that the system of determining allegations of violation of United States patent rights under Section 337 of the United States Tariff Act cannot be justified as necessary within the meaning of Article XX(d) so as to permit an exception to the basic obligation contained in Article III:4 of the General Agreement. The Panel, however, repeats that, as indicated in paragraphs 5.32 and 5.33 above, some of the inconsistencies with Article III:4 of individual aspects of procedures under Section 337 could be justified under Article XX(d) in certain circumstances".[58]

The 1992 Panel Report on "United States - Measures Affecting Alcoholic and Malt Beverages" examined, *inter alia*, the invocation of Article XX(d) with respect to a discriminatory requirement that imported beer be distributed through in-state wholesalers:

"The Panel then recalled the United States alternative argument that the requirement that imported beer be distributed through in-state wholesalers, which requirement was not imposed in the case of beer from in-state breweries, was justified under Article XX(d) as a measure necessary to secure compliance with laws or regulations which were not inconsistent with the provisions of the General Agreement. ...

---

[58]*Ibid.*, 36S/393-396, paras. 5.28-5.35.

"… The Panel also noted the practice of the CONTRACTING PARTIES of interpreting these Article XX exceptions narrowly, placing the burden on the party invoking an exception to justify its use.

"The Panel recalled the position of the United States that there was no reasonable alternative to the existing regulatory scheme in the various states which required out-of-state and imported beer to be distributed to retailers via in-state wholesalers while allowing in-state beer to be shipped directly from producers to retailers. The United considered that the wholesaler was the only reasonable place for beer excise taxes to be collected for out-of-state and foreign products, but that there was no such necessity with respect to products from in-state producers that were, by definition, under the jurisdiction of the state. The Panel further recalled the position of Canada that the burden was on the United States to specify and demonstrate the consistency with the General Agreement of the laws for which it was trying to secure compliance and to show that there were no less trade restrictive measures available to secure compliance with them.

"The Panel was of the view that even if, as argued by the United States, the requirement to use wholesalers is considered as a 'measure to secure compliance' in terms of Article XX(d) and the respective state liquor laws are considered as 'laws … not inconsistent with the provisions of this Agreement' notwithstanding the above-mentioned Panel findings on inconsistency with Article III, the United States has not demonstrated that discriminatory requirements to use wholesalers are 'necessary' in terms of Article XX(d) to enforce the liquor tax laws. The Panel recalled a finding of an earlier panel 'that a contracting party cannot justify a measure inconsistent with another GATT provision as "necessary" in terms of Article XX(d) if an alternative measure which it could reasonably be expected to employ and which is not inconsistent with other GATT provisions is available to it'.[59] The Panel considered that the United States has not met its burden of showing that the specific inconsistency with Article III:4 of the discriminatory wholesaler requirements in the various states is the only reasonable measure available to secure enforcement of state excise tax laws. The fact that not all fifty states maintain discriminatory systems indicates to the Panel that alternative measures for enforcement of state excise tax laws do indeed exist".[60]

The same Panel also examined the United States' invocation of Article XX(d) with respect to a requirement in some states that alcoholic beverages transported into the state be transported by state-licensed common carriers while in-state producers could deliver their product in their own vehicles.

"The Panel was of the view that its considerations with respect to Article XX(d) in relation to the wholesaler requirement apply equally here. It was incumbent upon the United States to demonstrate that particular laws for which compliance is being sought are consistent with the General Agreement and that the inconsistency with Article III:4 of the discriminatory common carrier requirement for imported beer and wine is necessary to secure compliance with those laws. In the view of the Panel, the United States has not demonstrated that the common carrier requirement is the least trade restrictive enforcement measure available to the various states and that less restrictive measures, e.g. record-keeping requirements of retailers and importers, are not sufficient for tax administration purposes. In this regard, the Panel noted that not all fifty states of the United States maintain common carrier requirements. It thus appeared to the Panel that some states have found alternative, and possibly less trade restrictive, and GATT-consistent, ways of enforcing their tax laws. The Panel accordingly found that the United States has not met its burden of proof in respect of its claimed Article XX(d) justification for the common carrier requirement of the various states".[61]

(3) "to secure compliance"

In the Panel Report on "EEC - Regulation on Imports of Parts and Components" the Panel examined the consistency with the General Agreement of Article 13:10 of Council Regulation No. 2176/84 on anti-

---

[59]The footnote to this sentence in the panel report refers to the Report of the Panel on "United States - Section 337 of the Tariff Act of 1930, adopted on 7 November 1989, 36S/345, 392.
[60]DS23/R, adopted on 19 June 1992, 39S/206, 282-283, paras. 5.40-5.43.
[61]*Ibid.*, 39S/287-288, para. 5.52.

dumping. This provision was intended to prevent circumvention of anti-dumping duties on finished products through the importation of parts or materials for use in the assembly or production of like finished products within the EEC. Japan considered this provision to be inconsistent with the EEC's obligations under Articles I and II or III, and not justified by Article VI of the General Agreement. The EEC considered both the application of Article 13:10 and the Article itself to be justified by Article XX(d). "The Panel considered that the '*measure*' referred to in Article XX is the measure requiring justification under Article XX and that, therefore, the imposition of anti-circumvention duties inconsistent with Article III:2 is the 'measure' in the present case. It further considered that the '*laws or regulations*' to be examined under sub-paragraph (d) are the laws or regulations the contracting party invoking Article XX(d) claims to secure compliance with, in the present case the Council Regulations Nos. 2176/84 and 2423/88 (except for the anti-circumvention provision) and the individual Council regulations imposing definitive anti-dumping duties on finished products from Japan."[62]

"The Panel noted that, in order for a measure to be covered by Article XX(d), it must '*secure compliance with*' laws or regulations that are not inconsistent with the General Agreement. The Panel therefore proceeded to examine the question of whether the imposition of anti-circumvention duties inconsistent with Article III:2 is a measure 'to secure compliance with' the EEC's general anti-dumping regulations and the individual regulations imposing definitive anti-dumping duties. The essential argument of Japan on this point was that Article XX(d) permits contracting parties to take only measures to enforce the obligations provided for in the laws or regulations consistent with the General Agreement. The only part of the EEC's anti-dumping regulations that requires enforcement is the part establishing the obligation to pay anti-dumping duties. The anti-circumvention duties do not serve to secure the payment of these duties and can therefore in the view of Japan not be considered to be securing compliance with the EEC's anti-dumping regulations. The essential argument of the EEC was that the terms 'to secure compliance with' should be interpreted more broadly to cover not only the enforcement of laws and regulations *per se* but also the prevention of actions which have the effect of undermining the objectives of laws and regulations. In the view of the EEC, the anti-circumvention duties, being levied only in narrowly defined circumstances in which the objectives of the EEC's anti-dumping regulations are clearly being undermined, therefore secure compliance with these regulations within the meaning of Article XX(d).

"The Panel concluded from the above that the interpretative issue before it was: Does the qualification 'to secure compliance with laws or regulations' mean that the measure must prevent actions inconsistent with the obligations set out in laws or regulations, or does it support a more expansive interpretation according to which it would also cover a measure which prevents actions that are consistent with laws or regulations but undermine their objectives?

"The Panel first examined this interpretative issue in the light of the *text of Article XX(d)*. The Panel noted that this provision does not refer to objectives of laws or regulations but only to laws or regulations. This suggests that Article XX(d) merely covers measures to secure compliance with laws and regulations as such and not with their objectives. The examples of the laws and regulations indicated in Article XX(d), namely 'those relating to customs *enforcement*, the *enforcement* of monopolies ..., the *protection* of patents ... and the *prevention* of deceptive practices' (emphasis added) also suggest that Article XX(d) covers only measures designed to prevent actions that would be illegal under the laws or regulations. This conclusion is further supported by the fact that the provision corresponding to Article XX(d) in the 1946 Suggested Charter for an International Trade Organization used the terms 'to *induce* compliance with' while Article XX(d) of the General Agreement uses the stricter language 'to *secure* compliance with' (emphasis added).

"The Panel then examined the alternative interpretations in the light of the *purpose of Article XX(d)* and found the following. If the qualification 'to secure compliance with laws and regulations' is interpreted to mean 'to enforce obligations under laws and regulations', the main function of Article XX(d) would be to permit contracting parties to act inconsistently with the General Agreement

---

[62]L/6657, adopted on 16 May 1990, 37S/132, 194-195, para. 5.12.

whenever such inconsistency is necessary to ensure that the obligations which the contracting parties may impose consistently with the General Agreement under their laws or regulations are effectively enforced. If the qualification 'to secure compliance with laws and regulations' is interpreted to mean 'to ensure the attainment of the objectives of the laws and regulations', the function of Article XX(d) would be substantially broader. Whenever the objective of a law consistent with the General Agreement cannot be attained by enforcing the obligations under that law, the imposition of further obligations inconsistent with the General Agreement could then be justified under Article XX(d) on the grounds that this secures compliance with the objectives of that law. This cannot, in the view of the Panel, be the purpose of Article XX(d): each of the exceptions in the General Agreement - such as Articles VI, XII or XIX - recognizes the legitimacy of a policy objective but at the same time sets out conditions as to the obligations which may be imposed to secure the attainment of that objective. These conditions would no longer be effective if it were possible to justify under Article XX(d) the enforcement of obligations that may not be imposed consistently with these exceptions on the grounds that the objective recognized to be legitimate by the exception cannot be attained within the framework of the conditions set out in the exception.

"For the reasons indicated in the preceding paragraphs, the Panel found that Article XX(d) covers only measures related to the enforcement of obligations under laws or regulations consistent with the General Agreement. The Panel noted that the general anti-dumping Regulation of the EEC does not establish obligations that require enforcement; it merely establishes a legal framework for the authorities of the EEC. Only the individual regulations imposing definitive anti-dumping duties give rise to obligations that require enforcement, namely the obligation to pay a specified amount of anti-dumping duties. The Panel noted that the anti-circumvention duties do not serve to enforce the payment of anti-dumping duties. The Panel could, therefore, not establish that the anti-circumvention duties 'secure compliance with' obligations under the EEC's anti-dumping regulations. The Panel concluded for these reasons that the duties could not be justified under Article XX(d)".[63]

(4) "laws or regulations which are not inconsistent with the provisions of this Agreement"

In discussing a proposed amendment to the Havana Charter provision corresponding to Article XX(d), "designed to exempt measures against so-called 'social dumping' from the provisions of Chapter IV, the Sub-committee expressed the view that this objective was covered for short-term purposes by paragraph 1 of Article 40 [XIX] and for long-term purposes by Article 7 in combination with Articles 93, 94 [XXIII] and 95".[64]

The 1983 Panel Report on "United States - Imports of Certain Automotive Spring Assemblies" notes that the Panel "concluded that the laws and regulations which were not inconsistent with the General Agreement and with which compliance was to be secured were the patent laws of the United States, since the case in question was based on the allegation of an infringement of patent rights under United States patent law."[65]

The 1988 Panel Report on "Japan - Restrictions on Imports of Certain Agricultural Products" examined certain import quotas maintained by Japan. In response to the invocation of Article XX(d) by Japan in relation to import restrictions administered by an import monopoly, the Panel found that "Article XX(d) only exempts from the obligations under the General Agreement measures necessary to secure compliance with those laws and regulations 'which are not inconsistent with the provisions of [the General] Agreement'. Article XX(d) therefore does not permit contracting parties to operate monopolies inconsistently with the other provisions of the General Agreement. ... The Panel therefore found that the enforcement of laws and regulations providing for an import restriction made effective through an import monopoly inconsistent with Article XI:1 was not covered by Article XX(d)".[66]

---

[63]*Ibid.*, 37S/195-197, paras. 5.14-5.18.
[64]Havana Reports, p. 84, para. 19.
[65]L/5333, adopted on 26 May 1983, 30S/102, 125, para. 57.
[66]L/6253, adopted on 2 February 1988, 35S/163, 230, para. 5.2.2.3.

The 1991 Panel Report on "United States - Restrictions on Imports of Tuna", which has not been adopted, examined the "intermediary nations" embargo on imports of tuna under the US Marine Mammal Protection Act (MMPA), which required that the United States authorities implement a prohibition on imports of yellowfin tuna and yellowfin tuna products from "intermediary nations"; at the time of this panel proceeding the United States customs authorities refused entry to shipments of yellowfin tuna unless the importer declared that no yellowfin tuna or yellowfin tuna product in the shipment were harvested with purse-seine nets in the Eastern Tropical Pacific Ocean by vessels of Mexico. The Panel found that these measures and the provisions of the MMPA mandating them were inconsistent with Article XI:1.

"The Panel then proceeded to examine the consistency of the 'intermediary nations' embargo with Article XX(d), which the United States had invoked. ...

"The Panel noted that Article XX(d) requires that the 'laws or regulations' with which compliance is being secured be themselves 'not inconsistent' with the General Agreement. The Panel noted that the United States had argued that the 'intermediary nations' embargo was necessary to support the direct embargo because countries whose exports were subject to such an embargo should not be able to nullify the embargo's effect by exporting to the United States indirectly through third countries. The Panel found that, given its finding that the direct embargo was inconsistent with the General Agreement, the 'intermediary nations' embargo and the provisions of the MMPA under which it is imposed could not be justified under Article XX(d) as a measure to secure compliance with 'laws or regulations not inconsistent with the provisions of this Agreement'".[67]

In this connection, see also the unadopted Panel Report of 1994 on "United States - Taxes on Automobiles".[68]

(5) "the enforcement of monopolies operated under paragraph 4 of Article II and Article XVII"

The London Report on discussions in the Preparatory Committee notes that "There was general agreement that restrictions or prohibitions on private trade might be imposed in order to protect the position of state-trading enterprises operated under other articles ...".[69] Accordingly, the London and New York Charters included in Article 25:2 [XI:2] an exception to the general prohibition on quantitative restrictions, for import and export prohibitions or restrictions on private trade for the purpose of establishing a new, or maintaining an existing, monopoly of trade for a state-trading enterprise operating consistent with the Charter articles on state trading. During discussions at the Geneva session of the Preparatory Committee, it was agreed to delete this provision from the article on quantitative restrictions, and to add language clarifying that such measures would be covered by the commercial policy exceptions clause corresponding to the present GATT Article XX(d).[70] The proposal to make this change was explained as follows:

"... these examples given under sub-paragraph (g) [XX(d)] are, in fact, only examples ... if any law or regulation is consistent with Chapter V, then any measure which is necessary for the enforcement of that law is taken care of here. ... the sole reason for mentioning state trading monopolies specifically here was that, in the case of a monopoly, the enforcement of that monopoly depends upon a prohibition against private trade, and in order to make it perfectly clear to certain Delegates that that was permitted, state trading monopolies were inserted as one of the examples".[71]

It was also noted that "It is only if and when you have a monopoly that you need it protected by a restriction on imports. If by any chance you have a State-trading enterprise which is not a monopoly, it would no doubt simply go into the market and buy and sell alongside private traders, and there would be no occasion to have any restriction in that case at all".[72]

---

[67] DS21/R (unadopted), dated 3 September 1991, 39S/155, 202, paras. 5.39-5.40.
[68] DS31/R, dated 11 October 1994, para. 5.67.
[69] London Report, p. 12, para. III.C.1(i).
[70] See EPCT/W/208 (US proposal), EPCT/W/223 p. 8-9, discussion at EPCT/A/PV/21 p. 4-8,
[71] EPCT/A/PV/33 p. 12-13.
[72] EPCT/A/PV/33, p. 15.

In the 1988 Panel Report on "Japan - Restrictions on Imports of Certain Agricultural Products", in response to an argument by Japan concerning certain import restrictions administered through import monopolies:

> "The Panel further examined whether Article XX(d) of the General Agreement justified import restrictions made effective through import monopolies. The Panel noted that Article XX(d) permits measures necessary to the enforcement of monopolies. Article XX(d) therefore permits measures necessary to enforce the exclusive possession of the trade by the monopoly, such as measures limiting private imports that would undermine the control of the trade by the monopoly. However, Article XX(d) only exempts from the obligations under the General Agreement measures necessary to secure compliance with those laws and regulations 'which are not inconsistent with the provisions of [the General] Agreement'. Article XX(d) therefore does not permit contracting parties to operate monopolies inconsistently with the other provisions of the General Agreement. The General Agreement contains detailed rules designed to preclude protective and discriminatory practices by import monopolies (cf. in particular Article II:4, the note to Articles XI, XII, XIII, XIV and XVIII, and Article XVII). These rules would become meaningless if Article XX(d) were interpreted to exempt from the obligations under the General Agreement protective or discriminatory trading practices by such monopolies. The Panel therefore found that the enforcement of laws and regulations providing for an import restriction made effective through an import monopoly inconsistent with Article XI:1 was not covered by Article XX(d)".[73]

(6) "protection of patents, trade marks and copyrights"

Drafts for an "Agreement on Measures to Discourage the Importation of Counterfeit Goods" were circulated in 1979 and 1982.[74] The preamble of the revised draft noted, *inter alia*, "that the contracting parties are exercising their rights under Article XX of the General Agreement, *inter alia*, to adopt or enforce laws and regulations relating to the protection of trademarks". Following the Decision on Trade in Counterfeit Goods contained in the Ministerial Declaration of 29 November 1982,[75] the Director-General held consultations with the Director-General of the World Intellectual Property Organization (WIPO) on legal and institutional aspects involved in trade in counterfeit goods.[76] See also the 1985 Report of the Group of Experts on Trade in Counterfeit Goods.[77]

In the 1983 Panel Report on "United States - Imports of Certain Automotive Spring Assemblies", "The Panel noted that, as far as it had been able to ascertain, this was the first time a specific case of patent infringement involving Article XX(d) had been brought before the CONTRACTING PARTIES".[78] "The Panel noted that the GATT recognized, by the very existence of Article XX(d), the need to provide that certain measures taken by a contracting party to secure compliance with its national laws or regulations which otherwise would not be in conformity with the GATT obligations of that contracting party would, through the application of this provision under the conditions stipulated therein, be in conformity with the GATT provided that the national laws or regulations concerned were not inconsistent with the General Agreement. In this connection the Panel noted in particular that the protection of patents was one of the few areas of national laws and regulations expressly mentioned in Article XX(d)."[79]

In the Panel Report on "United States - Section 337 of the Tariff Act of 1930", "The Panel noted that in the dispute before it the 'laws or regulations' with which Section 337 secures compliance are the substantive patent laws of the United States and that the conformity of these laws with the General Agreement is not being challenged".[80] In relation to the criterion of "necessary" in terms of Article XX(d), "The Panel

---

[73]L/6253, adopted on 2 February 1988, 35S/163, 229-230, para. 5.2.2.3.
[74]L/4817, L/5382.
[75]L/5424, 29S/19.
[76]See the Report by the Director-General on these consultations in C/W/418.
[77]L/5878, dated 9 October 1985; see also background note by the Secretariat on "Trade in Counterfeit Goods", MDF/W/19, dated 10 January 1985.
[78]L/5333, adopted on 26 May 1983, 30S/107, 124, para. 51.
[79]*Ibid.*, 30S/124-125, para. 53.
[80]L/6439, adopted on 7 November 1989, 36S/345, 392, para. 5.24.

wished to make it clear that this does not mean that a contracting party could be asked to change its substantive patent law or its desired level of enforcement of that law, provided that such law and such level of enforcement are the same for imported and domestically-produced products. However, it does mean that if a contracting party could reasonably secure that level of enforcement in a manner that is not inconsistent with other GATT provisions, it would be required to do so".[81]

(7) *"the prevention of deceptive practices"*

It was agreed during discussions at the London sessions of the Preparatory Committee that the words "deceptive practices" were broad enough to cover cases of false marking of geographical origin.[82]

In 1987, during the Working Party on the Accession of Portugal and Spain to the EEC, in response to a question regarding an EEC regulation on the use of the term "sherry", the EEC stated that the regulation in question "constitutes a measure designed to prevent deceptive practices. It is therefore justified under Article XX(d) of the General Agreement".[83]

(8) *Preshipment inspection*

A 1989 Background Note by the Secretariat on "Preshipment Inspection"[84] discusses the application of Article XX(d) in this connection.

6. Paragraph (g): "relating to the conservation of exhaustible natural resources"

(1) *"relating to ... conservation"*

In the 1988 Panel Report on "Canada - Measures Affecting Exports of Unprocessed Herring and Salmon", the Panel examined the issue of whether export prohibitions of certain unprocessed salmon and unprocessed herring, conceded to be contrary to Article XI:1 of the General Agreement, were or were not justified by, *inter alia*, Article XX(g).

> "... The Panel noted that both parties agreed that Canada maintains a variety of measures for the conservation of salmon and herring stocks and imposes limitations on the harvesting of salmon and herring. The Panel agreed with the parties that salmon and herring stocks are 'exhaustible natural resources' and the harvest limitations are 'restrictions on domestic production' within the meaning of Article XX(g). Having reached this conclusion the Panel examined whether the export prohibitions on certain unprocessed salmon and unprocessed herring are 'relating to' the conservation of salmon and herring stocks ...
>
> "Article XX(g) does not state how the trade measures are to be related to the conservation and how they have to be conjoined with the production restrictions. This raises the question of whether *any* relationship with conservation and *any* conjunction with production restrictions are sufficient for a trade measure to fall under Article XX(g) or whether a *particular* relationship and conjunction are required. The Panel noted that the only previous case in which the CONTRACTING PARTIES took a decision on Article XX(g) was the case examined by the Panel on 'United States - Prohibition of Imports of Tuna and Tuna Products from Canada' but that that Panel had found that the party invoking Article XX(g) did not maintain restrictions on the production or consumption of tuna and thus had not been required to interpret the terms 'relating to' and 'in conjunction with'.[85] The Panel therefore decided to analyze the meaning of these terms in the light of the context in which Article XX(g) appears in the General Agreement and in the light of the purpose of that provision.

---

[81]*Ibid.*, 36S/393, para. 5.26.
[82]EPCT/C.II/50, p. 5, 9; EPCT/C.II/54/Rev.1, p. 37.
[83]L/5984/Add.2, p. 2.
[84]MTN.GNG/NG2/W/11/Add.1, 19 October 1989.
[85]The footnote to this sentence refers to 29S/91.

"The Panel noted that some of the subparagraphs of Article XX state that the measure must be 'necessary' or 'essential' to the achievement of the policy purpose set out in the provision (cf. subparagraphs (a), (b), d) and (j)) while subparagraph (g) refers only to measures 'relating to' the conservation of exhaustible natural resources. This suggests that Article XX(g) does not only cover measures that are necessary or essential for the conservation of exhaustible natural resources but a wider range of measures. However, as the preamble of Article XX indicates, the purpose of including Article XX(g) in the General Agreement was not to widen the scope for measures serving trade policy purposes but merely to ensure that the commitments under the General Agreement do not hinder the pursuit of policies aimed at the conservation of exhaustive natural resources. The Panel concluded for these reasons that, while a trade measure did not have to be necessary or essential to the conservation of an exhaustible natural resource, it had to be primarily aimed at the conservation of an exhaustible natural resource to be considered as 'relating to' conservation within the meaning of Article XX(g). The Panel, similarly, considered that the terms 'in conjunction with' in Article XX(g) had to be interpreted in a way that ensures that the scope of possible actions under that provision corresponds to the purpose for which it was included in the General Agreement. A trade measure could therefore in the view of the Panel only be considered to be made effective 'in conjunction with' production restrictions if it was primarily aimed at rendering effective these restrictions.

"Having reached these conclusions the Panel examined whether the export prohibitions on unprocessed salmon and unprocessed herring maintained by Canada were primarily aimed at the conservation of salmon and herring stocks and rendering effective the restrictions on the harvesting of salmon and herring. The Panel noted Canada's contention that the export prohibitions were not conservation measures *per se* but had an effect on conservation because they helped provide the statistical foundation for the harvesting restrictions and increase the benefits to the Canadian economy arising from the Salmonid Enhancement Program. The Panel carefully examined this contention and noted the following: Canada collects statistical data on many different species of fish, including certain salmon species, without imposing export prohibitions on them. Canada maintains statistics on all fish exports. If certain unprocessed salmon and unprocessed herring were exported, statistics on these exports would therefore be collected. The Salmonid Enhancement Program covers salmon species for which export prohibitions apply and other species not subject to export prohibitions. The export prohibitions do not limit access to salmon and herring supplies in general but only to certain salmon and herring supplies in unprocessed form. Canada limits purchases of these unprocessed fish only by foreign processors and consumers and not by domestic processors and consumers. In light of all these factors taken together, the Panel found that these prohibitions could not be deemed to be primarily aimed at the conservation of salmon and herring stocks and at rendering effective the restrictions on the harvesting of these fish. The Panel therefore concluded that the export prohibitions were not justified by Article XX(g)."[86]

In the 1991 Panel Report on "United States - Restrictions on Imports of Tuna", which has not been adopted, the Panel also examined whether the prohibition on imports of certain yellowfin tuna and certain yellowfin tuna products from Mexico and the provisions of the Marine Mammal Protection Act (MMPA) under which it was imposed could be justified under the exception in Article XX(g).

"... The Panel noted that the United States, in invoking Article XX(g) with respect to its direct import prohibition under the MMPA, had argued that the measures taken under the MMPA are measures primarily aimed at the conservation of dolphin, and that the import restrictions on certain tuna and tuna products under the MMPA are 'primarily aimed at rendering effective restrictions on domestic production or consumption' of dolphin. The Panel also noted that Mexico had argued that the United States measures were not justified under the exception in Article XX(g) because, *inter alia*, this provision could not be applied extrajurisdictionally.

"The Panel noted that Article XX(g) required that the measures relating to the conservation of exhaustible natural resources be taken 'in conjunction with restrictions on domestic production or

---

[86]L/6268, adopted on 22 March 1988, 35S/98, 113-115, paras. 4.4-4.7.

consumption'. A previous panel had found that a measure could only be considered to have been taken 'in conjunction with' production restrictions 'if it was primarily aimed at rendering effective these restrictions'.[87] A country can effectively control the production or consumption of an exhaustible natural resource only to the extent that the production or consumption is under its jurisdiction. This suggests that Article XX(g) was intended to permit contracting parties to take trade measures primarily aimed at rendering effective restrictions on production or consumption within their jurisdiction.

"The Panel further noted that Article XX(g) allows each contracting party to adopt its own conservation policies. The conditions set out in Article XX(g) which limit resort to this exception, namely that the measures taken must be related to the conservation of exhaustible natural resources, and that they not 'constitute a means of arbitrary or unjustifiable discrimination ... or a disguised restriction on international trade' refer to the trade measure requiring justification under Article XX(g), not however to the conservation policies adopted by the contracting party. The Panel considered that if the extrajurisdictional interpretation of Article XX(g) suggested by the United States were accepted, each contracting party could unilaterally determine the conservation policies from which other contracting parties could not deviate without jeopardizing their rights under the General Agreement. The considerations that led the Panel to reject an extrajurisdictional application of Article XX(b) therefore apply also to Article XX(g).

"The Panel did not consider that the United States measures, even if Article XX(g) could be applied extrajurisdictionally, would meet the conditions set out in that provision. A previous panel found that a measure could be considered as 'relating to the conservation of exhaustible natural resources' within the meaning of Article XX(g) only if it was primarily aimed at such conservation.[88] The Panel recalled that the United States linked the maximum incidental dolphin-taking rate which Mexico had to meet during a particular period in order to be able to export tuna to the United States to the taking rate actually recorded for United States fishermen during the same period. Consequently, the Mexican authorities could not know whether, at a given point of time, their conservation policies conformed to the United States conservation standards. The Panel considered that a limitation on trade based on such unpredictable conditions could not be regarded as being primarily aimed at the conservation of dolphins.

"On the basis of the above considerations, the Panel found that the United States direct import prohibition on certain yellowfin tuna and certain yellowfin tuna products of Mexico directly imported from Mexico, and the provisions of the MMPA under which it is imposed, could not be justified under Article XX(g)."[89]

In this connection, see also the unadopted Panel Report of 1994 on "United States - Restrictions on Imports of Tuna"[90] and the unadopted Panel Report of 1994 on "United States - Taxes on Automobiles".[91]

(2) "exhaustible natural resources"

The New York (Drafting Committee) Report notes in this context that "As it seemed to be generally agreed that electric power should not be classified as a commodity, two delegates did not find it necessary to reserve the right for their countries to prohibit the export of electric power".[92]

In the 1982 Panel Report on "United States - Prohibition of Imports of Tuna and Tuna Products from Canada", "The Panel ... noted that both parties considered tuna stocks, including albacore tuna, to be an exhaustible natural resource in need of conservation management"[93]: see the material from this report directly

---

[87]The footnote to this sentence refers to the Panel Report on "Canada - Measures Affecting Exports of Unprocessed Herring and Salmon", L/6268, adopted on 22 March 1988, 35S/98, 114, para. 4.6.
[88]The footnote to this sentence refers to the same Panel Report, same paragraph: 35S/98, 114, para. 4.6.
[89]DS21/R (unadopted), dated 3 September 1991, 39S/155, 200-201, paras. 5.30-5.34.
[90]DS29/R, dated 16 June 1994, paras. 5.11-5.17, 5.21-5.27.
[91]DS31/R, dated 11 October 1994, paras. 5.56, 5.59-5.66.
[92]New York Report, p. 31, general comments on Article 37; see also source at EPCT/C.6/89, p. 4.
[93]L/5198, adopted on 22 February 1982, 29S/91, 108, para. 4.9.

below. In the 1988 Panel Report on "Canada - Measures Affecting Exports of Unprocessed Herring and Salmon", the Panel "agreed with the parties that salmon and herring stocks are 'exhaustible natural resources'".[94]

In this connection, see also the unadopted Panel Report of 1994 on "United States - Restrictions on Imports of Tuna",[95] and the unadopted Panel Report of 1994 on "United States - Taxes on Automobiles".[96]

(3) "made effective in conjunction with restrictions on domestic production or consumption"

The US Draft Charter included an exception to the commercial policy chapter for "measures ... relating to the conservation of exhaustible natural resources if such measures are taken pursuant to international agreements or are made effective in conjunction with restrictions on domestic production and consumption" and a corresponding exception in the chapter on commodity agreements for "intergovernmental commodity agreements which appropriately relate to ... the conservation of reserves of exhaustible natural resources ... Provided that such agreements are not used to accomplish results inconsistent with the objectives of [the chapters on commodity agreements or restrictive business practices]".[97] During the London session of the Preparatory Committee, the proposal was made to drop the proviso regarding restrictions on domestic consumption citing the case of a country with deposits of manganese, "which is very ample for our present and prospective domestic consumption but which is not very ample if we allow free exports of it".[98] It was stated in response that "One of the ways in which export prohibitions could be used ... is for protective purposes. ... It is possible for a raw material producing country, which wishes to industrialize, to do so behind a protective arrangement which is extremely effective, and that is preventing anybody else getting the raw material to use in his already existing industries".[99] The proposal was not accepted.[100]

In the 1982 Panel Report on "United States - Prohibition of Imports of Tuna and Tuna Products from Canada" the Panel found that the import ban in question was inconsistent with Article XI:1 and not justified by Article XI:2(c), and examined the US argument that its measures were justified by Article XX(g).

"The Panel noted that the decision of the United States Government was based on Section 205 of the United States Fishery Conservation and Management Act of 1976. The Panel was informed that the purpose of the Fishery Conservation and Management Act of 1976 was to ensure that certain stocks of fish were properly conserved and managed, to support and encourage the implementation and enforcement of international fishery agreements for the conservation and management of highly migratory species, and to encourage the negotiation and implementation of such additional agreements as necessary. It furthermore noted that Section 205 of the Fishery Conservation and Management Act of 1976 contained provisions designed to discourage other countries from seeking to manage tuna unilaterally and from seizing United States fishing vessels which were fishing more than 12 miles off their coasts.

"The Panel also noted that the United States had applied limitations on the catch of some species of tuna (e.g. Pacific and Atlantic Yellowfin and Atlantic bluefin and bigeye), during the time the import prohibitions on tuna and tuna products from Canada had been in force. The Panel found, however, that even if an import restriction could, at least partly, have been necessary to the enforcement of measures taken to restrict the catches of certain tuna species, an import prohibition on all tuna and tuna products from Canada as applied by the United States from 31 August 1979 to 4 September 1980 would not sufficiently meet the requirements of Article XI:2, firstly because the measure applied to species for which the catch had not so far been restricted in the United States (such as albacore and skipjack) and

---

[94]L/6268, adopted on 22 March 1988, 35S/98, 113, para. 4.4.
[95]DS29/R, dated 16 June 1994, paras. 5.13-5.20.
[96]DS31/R, dated 11 October 1994, para. 5.57.
[97]US Draft Charter, Articles 32 and 49; see London Report pp. 60, 63.
[98]EPCT/C.II/QR/PV/1, p. 15 (proposal of Brazil).
[99]EPCT/C.II/QR/PV/1, p. 20-21.
[100]See discussion at EPCT/C.II/QR/PV/5, p. 77-82, report at EPCT/C.II/59, p. 5, para. 11.

secondly because it was maintained when restrictions on the catch were no longer maintained (e.g. Pacific yellowfin tuna in 1980). ...

"The Panel ... noted that both parties considered tuna stocks, including albacore tuna, to be an exhaustible natural resource in need of conservation management and that both parties were participating in international conventions aimed, *inter alia*, at a better conservation of such stocks. However, attention was drawn to the fact that Article XX(g) contained a qualification on measures relating to the conservation if they were to be justified under that Article, namely that such measures were made effective in conjunction with restrictions on domestic production or consumption.

"The Panel noted that the action taken by the United States applied to imports from Canada of all tuna and tuna products, and that the United States could at various times apply restrictions to species of tuna covered by the IATTC [Inter-American Tropical Tuna Commission] and the ICCAT [International Convention for the Conservation of Atlantic Tunas]. However, restrictions on domestic production (catch) had so far been applied only to Pacific yellowfin tuna, from July to December 1979 under the Tuna Convention Act (related to the IATTC) and to Atlantic yellowfin tuna, bluefin tuna and bigeye tuna under the Atlantic Tunas Convention Act (related to the ICCAT), and no restrictions had been applied to the catch or landings of any other species of tuna, such as for instance albacore.

"The Panel also noted that the United States representative had provided no evidence that domestic consumption of tuna and tuna products had been restricted in the United States.

"The Panel could therefore not accept it to be justified that the United States prohibition of imports of all tuna and tuna products from Canada as applied from 31 August 1979 to 4 September 1980, had been made effective in conjunction with restrictions on United States domestic production or consumption on all tuna and tuna products".[101]

In the 1988 Panel Report on "Canada - Measures Affecting Exports of Unprocessed Herring and Salmon",

"... The Panel noted that both parties agreed that Canada maintains a variety of measures for the conservation of salmon and herring stocks and imposes limitations on the harvesting of salmon and herring. The Panel agreed with the parties that ... the harvest limitations [are] 'restrictions on domestic production' within the meaning of Article XX(g)".[102]

A Secretariat Note of 1991 on "Trade and Environment" includes a list of quantitative restrictions for which Article XX(g) has been cited as a justification. The list was drawn from the Inventory of Quantitative Restrictions maintained by the Secretariat.[103]

7. **Paragraph (h): "undertaken in pursuance of obligations under [a] commodity agreement"**

In order for a measure to be covered by Article XX(h) and the Interpretative Note *Ad* Article XX(h), the intergovernmental agreement in question must: (a) conform to criteria submitted to the CONTRACTING PARTIES and not disapproved by them; (b) be itself submitted and not disapproved; or (c) conform to the principles approved by the Economic and Social Council in its Resolution 30(IV) of 28 March 1947.

The US Draft Charter provided for a chapter on commodity policy, and therefore its article on elimination of quantitative restrictions provided for an exception for "export or import quotas imposed under inter-governmental commodity agreements concluded in accordance with the provisions of Chapter VI." The London Report notes that "There was general agreement that ... import or export quotas imposed under inter-governmental commodity agreements concluded under the Charter might be used"[104] and accordingly the

---

[101]L/5198, adopted on 22 February 1982, 29S/91, 107-109, paras. 4.5-4.6, 4.9-4.12.
[102]L/6268, adopted on 22 March 1988, 35S/98, 113, para. 4.4.
[103]L/6896, p. 94. Concerning the Inventory of Quantitative Restrictions, see material at the end of the chapter on Article XI.
[104]London Report, p. 12, para. III.C.1(i).

London and New York Draft Charters provided for such an exception in Article 25:2 (corresponding to GATT Article XI:2). The London Report also notes that it was agreed that an exception from the general rule of non-discrimination in quantitative restrictions was necessary where "Some element of discrimination in import and export restrictions may be needed in order to carry out inter-governmental commodity agreements under the commodity policy provisions of the Charter …".[105]

The Preparatory Committee at its London session adopted a resolution noting that governments were already taking action on the lines proposed in the Charter chapter on commodity agreements, and requesting the United Nations to appoint an Interim Co-ordinating Committee for International Commodity Arrangements.[106] In response, the Economic and Social Council of the United Nations on 28 March 1947 adopted ECOSOC Resolution 30(IV), as follows:

"The Economic and Social Council,

"Noting that inter-governmental consultations are going forward actively with respect to certain internationally traded commodities, and

"Considering the significant measure of agreement regarding commodity problems and the co-ordination of commodity consultations already reached both in the First Session of the Preparatory Committee of the United Nations Conference on Trade and Employment, and in the Preparatory Commission on World Food Proposals of the Food and Agriculture Organisation of the United Nations:

"*Recommends* that, pending the establishment of the International Trade Organization, Members of the United Nations adopt as a general guide in inter-governmental consultation or action with respect to commodity problems the principles laid down in Chapter VII as a whole - i.e., the chapter on inter-governmental commodity arrangements of the draft Charter appended to the Report of the First Session of the Preparatory Committee of the United Nations Conference on Trade and Employment - although recognizing that discussion in future sessions of the Preparatory Committee of the United Nations Conference, as well as in the Conference itself, may result in modifications of the provisions relating to commodity arrangements, and

"*Requests* the Secretary-General to appoint an interim co-ordinating committee for international commodity arrangements to keep informed of and to facilitate by appropriate means such inter-governmental consultation or action with respect to commodity problems, the committee to consist of a chairman to represent the Preparatory Committee of the United Nations Conference on Trade and Employment, a person nominated by the Food and Agriculture Organization of the United Nations to be concerned in particular with agricultural primary commodities, and a person to be concerned in particular with non-agricultural primary commodities."[107]

During discussions at the Geneva session of the Preparatory Committee, it was agreed that the exception for measures under commodity agreements should be applicable to all provisions of the commercial policy chapter of the Charter. Accordingly, the article on general exceptions to the commercial policy chapter was amended to insert an exception for measures undertaken in pursuance of obligations under intergovernmental commodity agreements concluded in accordance with the Charter chapter on such agreements.[108] The rationale behind this change was stated as follows:

"… the implication is that the only exceptions to Chapter V which would be necessitated by the provisions of any possible commodity arrangement would be the use of quotas. We venture to doubt

---

[105]London Report, p. 14, para. III.C.3(d)(iv).
[106]London Report Annexure 9, p. 48.
[107]Text reprinted in *Review of International Commodity Arrangements*, ICCICA, Geneva, November 1947, p. 8-9. Subsequent ECOSOC Resolutions (110(VI), 296(XI), 373(XIII) and 462 (XV)) substituted first ICITO and later the CONTRACTING PARTIES to the General Agreement as the body to nominate the Chairman of ICCICA; the last of these provided for an additional member familiar with the problems of developing countries. See also G/17 and G/17/Add.1 on ICCICA activities 1947-1952.
[108]See EPCT/W/137 (proposal by U.K.), EPCT/W/208 (proposal by U.S.), EPCT/103 p. 47, EPCT/W/223 p. 4-5, EPCT/B/PV/5 p. 44-46, EPCT/A/PV/25 p. 32-34, EPCT/A/SR/30 p. 2, EPCT/A/PV/30 p. 4-6.

that and think that it would be wrong for the Charter to express the thought that the only way of dealing with the commodity problem is by a quota scheme. ... There is also the point that one can easily think of exceptions which might be needed under other Articles. I might mention one, and that is Article 31 [XVII] which is headed 'Non-discriminatory administration of state-trading enterprises'. Clearly, if the State were a party to a commodity arrangement and it were also a trader in that commodity, it would be bound to give precedence in its state-trading operations to the provisions of the commodity arrangement into which it had entered, and not so much to the considerations to which its attention is directed by Paragraph 1 of Article 31."[109]

Thus, in the General Agreement as concluded 30 October 1947, paragraph (h) (Article XX:I(h)) provided an exception for measures "undertaken in pursuance of obligations under intergovernmental commodity agreements, conforming to the principles approved by the Economic and Social Council of the United Nations in its Resolution of March 28, 1947, establishing an Interim Co-ordinating Committee for International Commodity Arrangements". The "principles" referred to in the ECOSOC Resolution are, as noted above, those of the Charter chapter on commodity agreements, which became in due course Chapter VI of the Havana Charter. Chapter VI of the Charter provided for intergovernmental commodity agreements with respect to "primary commodities", defined as "any product of farm, forest or fishery or any mineral, in its natural form or which has undergone such processing as is customarily required to prepare it for marketing in substantial volume in international trade".[110] Chapter VI also provided certain general principles and procedural requirements for agreements concluded thereunder.

Article XXIX:1 of the General Agreement provides that the contracting parties "undertake to observe to the fullest extent of their executive authority the general principles of Chapters I to VI inclusive ... of the Havana Charter". A proposal to give provisional effect to Chapter VI of the Havana Charter pending entry into force of the Charter was submitted to the Executive Committee of ICITO when it met at Annecy on 22 July 1949. A Working Party prepared a proposal which was not acted upon.[111]

During the Review Session of 1954-55, paragraph (h) was examined in the Review Working Party on Organizational and Functional Arrangements in the context of the question of the GATT's involvement in the area of commodity trade generally, and in the context of an ECOSOC Resolution of 5 August 1954 establishing the Advisory Commission on International Trade with some of the responsibilities formerly assigned to ICCICA.[112] Certain delegations sought insertion into the General Agreement of provisions on the lines of Chapter VI of the Charter.

In response, a separate Working Party on Commodity Problems was established and met during the Review Session to consider "specific proposals for principles and objectives to govern international action designed to overcome problems arising in the field of international trade in primary commodities and the form of an international agreement necessary to administer and apply those principles; ... the relationship between the parties to such an agreement with, on the one hand, the CONTRACTING PARTIES and, on the other hand, with any other international organizations exercising responsibilities in the field of international trade in primary commodities ...".[113] The Working Party drafted a Special Agreement on Commodity Arrangements containing "general principles governing provisions of all commodity arrangements" and setting out procedural and institutional provisions for dealing with commodity agreements. The draft Agreement contemplated the negotiation of agreements among governments, the implementing measures for which would possibly conflict with GATT obligations unless provision were made. It was envisaged that the GATT and the proposed Special Agreement would be linked by an amendment to Article XX:I(h).[114] Discussions

---

[109] EPCT/B/PV/5, p. 44-45. See also EPCT/A/PV/19 p. 13.

[110] This same definition was used for the (linked) Charter obligations with regard to export subsidies on primary commodities, and is utilized in the definition of "primary products" in paragraph 2 of the note *ad* Section B of Article XVI of the General Agreement (also referred to in the interpretative note to Article XXXVI:4). See the material in this Index on Article XVI and its drafting history.

[111] GATT/CP.3/72; see also ICITO/19, ICITO/20, ICITO/21, ICITO/22.

[112] L/189/Add.2.

[113] L/301; see 3S/238.

[114] See L/320, Interim Report of the Working Party, February 1955, including the annexed draft Special Agreement on Commodity Arrangements.

concerning this draft during the Review Session did not result in consensus, and the Working Party was held over to the Tenth Session.[115]

Meanwhile, in the context of the Review it had been agreed to amend Article XX. The Report of the Review Working Party on "Organizational and Functional Arrangements" notes as follows:

"The Working Party felt that, in view of the steps being taken to develop new principles relating to the conclusion of commodity agreements, Article XX:I(h) required amendment. Accordingly, the Working Party recommends the substitution for the existing sub-paragraph of the Article of a new text. The Working Party considered that Article XX:I(h) does not itself establish principles for the conclusion of commodity agreements, but stipulates conditions under which measures taken pursuant to commodity agreements may be excepted from the provisions of the General Agreement ...

"In order that the exception provided for in the present Article XX:I(h) might continue to apply to commodity agreements concluded or which may be concluded, in accordance with the principles approved by the Economic and Social Council in its Resolution of 28 March 1947, the Working Party recommends that an Interpretative Note be added to the amended Article."[116]

The interpretative note to Article XX(h) states: "The exception provided by this sub-paragraph extends to any commodity agreement which conforms to the principles approved by the Economic and Social Council in its Resolution 30(IV) of 28 March 1947."

At the Tenth Session in the fall of 1955, discussions on commodity issues continued. The Working Party on Commodity Problems submitted a final report which included the draft Special Agreement "with the recommendation of the Working Party that subject as far as possible to resolution of outstanding differences, it be accepted by them as embodying the criteria to which intergovernmental commodity arrangements should conform in order to benefit from the exception provided in the first part of paragraph (h) of Article XX of the General Agreement as revised at the Ninth Session. The Working Party assumes, that, if the CONTRACTING PARTIES find this Agreement satisfactory for that purpose, they will record their intention of recognizing formally when the revised GATT comes into effect that the Agreement has been considered under Article XX(h) and not disapproved."[117] However, due to differences of view concerning various issues, the Working Party report and its draft Agreement were not adopted, and the issue was deferred to the Eleventh Session.[118] At the Eleventh Session in the fall of 1956, it was recognized that it was unlikely that agreement could be reached on the lines of the draft Special Agreement. Instead, an alternative approach was adopted, embodied in the Resolution of the CONTRACTING PARTIES on "Particular Difficulties connected with Trade in Primary Commodities"[119] which focused on general multilateral review, problem-specific consultations and the possible convening of an intergovernmental meeting on a case-by-case basis. The Working Party Report on "Particular Difficulties connected with Trade in Primary Commodities" notes that

"The Working Party gave consideration to the question whether the Resolution should include a statement of objectives to be sought and principles to be applied in inter-governmental commodity arrangements. The view was widely held in the Working Party that such objectives and principles would need to take into account the circumstances of the particular commodity agreement under negotiation and should, therefore, be left to each negotiating conference subject, so far as the contracting parties are concerned, to any review by the CONTRACTING PARTIES in accordance with the relevant provisions of the General Agreement".[120]

---

[115]See discussion at SR.9/18, 19, 23, 27, 34, 38.
[116]L/327, adopted on 28 February, 5 and 7 March 1955, 3S/231, 239, paras. 20, 22.
[117]L/416, Final Report of the Working Party, October 1955, p. 2, para. 5. See also Tenth Session discussions, SR.10/13, 14, 19.
[118]See Chairman's statement on points of difference, SR.10/14 p. 158; decision to defer at SR.10/19, p. 219-220.
[119]5S/26; see L/592/Rev.1, Report of the Working Party on "Particular Difficulties Connected with Trade in Primary Commodities, adopted on 17 November 1956, 5S/87, para. 1. See Eleventh Session discussions at SR.11/2 and adoption of the Resolution at SR.11/18, as well as later reports on commodity problems at L/1103, adopted on 20 November 1959, 8S/76; and L/1656, adopted on 4 December 1961, 10S/83.
[120]L/592/Rev.1, adopted on 17 November 1956, 5S/87, 89, para. 7.

See also the material on consultations on commodity issues under Articles XVIII:5, XXII:2 and XXV:1. See also the unadopted Panel Report of 1994 on "EEC - Import Régime for Bananas".[121]

In response to arguments that commodity matters lay outside the competence of GATT, the CONTRACTING PARTIES ruled at the Tenth Session in 1955 that they were competent, pursuant to Article XXV:1, to deal with commodity problems.[122] This view was confirmed in subsequent reports on commodity trade problems.

Article XXXVIII:2(a), which was added to the General Agreement by the 1965 Part IV Protocol, provides that the CONTRACTING PARTIES "shall ... where appropriate, take action, including action through international arrangements, to provide improved and acceptable conditions of access to world markets for primary products of particular interest to less-developed contracting parties and to devise measures designed to stabilize and improve conditions of world markets in these products including measures designed to attain stable, equitable and remunerative prices for exports of such products". See also the corresponding provisions in Article XXXVI:4.

A Memorandum of Agreement on Basic Elements for the Negotiation of a World Grains Arrangement is attached to the Geneva (1967) Protocol to the General Agreement on Tariffs and Trade.[123] The International Grains Arrangement, consisting of a Wheat Trade Convention and a Food Aid Convention, was negotiated under the auspices of the International Wheat Council in cooperation between the FAO and UNCTAD in 1967, and has expired. The Arrangement Regarding Bovine Meat[124] and the International Dairy Arrangement[125] were negotiated during the Tokyo Round of multilateral trade negotiations.

A Secretariat Note of 1991 on "Trade and Environment" includes a list of quantitative restrictions for which Article XX(h) has been cited as a justification. The list was drawn from the Inventory of Quantitative Restrictions maintained by the Secretariat.[126]

No contracting party has ever submitted a complaint under Articles XXII or XXIII that a measure taken in pursuance of a commodity agreement was inconsistent with the General Agreement, and no commodity agreement has ever been formally submitted to the CONTRACTING PARTIES under Article XX(h).

8. Paragraph (i)

This paragraph was proposed by New Zealand at the Geneva session of the Preparatory Committee in 1947. New Zealand explained it as follows:

"The purpose of this amendment is to provide for the case of countries like New Zealand which maintain as a matter of permanent policy price stabilization schemes covering, generally, the whole range of their economy. Any country which, like New Zealand, stabilizes its general price levels is faced with the problem that the world price for certain commodities, particularly raw materials which it exports, will be substantially higher than the stabilized domestic price for the like commodity.

"The best way of explaining that is, I think, to give a practical example. In New Zealand the price of leather to domestic users such as, for instance, the footwear industry is sold at a price very much below the world level. Now, in the circumstances it becomes necessary to ensure, by means of export controls, that the local requirements of leather are satisfied - otherwise, if that is not done, there would be no leather for the local market or, alternatively, it would be necessary to let the local price of leather rise to the world level. We do not assume that it would be contemplated that the effect of the Charter would be to compel the abandonment of the price stabilization schemes, and therefore we have brought

---

[121] DS38/R, dated 11 February 1994, para. 166.
[122] SR.10/19, p. 218.
[123] 15S/18.
[124] 26S/84.
[125] 26S/91.
[126] L/6896, p. 95. Concerning the Inventory of Quantitative Restrictions, see under Article XI in this Index.

forward this amendment. It is true that it has been suggested that the same result can be achieved by the method of export taxes, but we, and I think other countries who have tried that method, have found it unsatisfactory and, indeed, impracticable, because the world price of primary commodities is subject to such wide variations that the rate of tax has to be varied too frequently".[127]

During the discussion of this proposal, it was "pointed out that the provision only applied in cases where a general scheme of internal price stabilization was in operation, and it could not be used to afford protection to national industry by a country which had no such plan".[128] The various concerns expressed at the danger of abuse in the utilization of this exception clause led to the addition of the proviso contained in the second part of paragraph (i).

The 1950 Report of the Working Party on "The Use of Quantitative Restrictions for Protective and Other Commercial Purposes"[129] examined, *inter alia*, the use of export restrictions on raw materials to promote a domestic fabricating industry.

"... The Working Party took note of the fact that since the exemption provided for in [Article XX(i)] referred to export restrictions associated with a governmental stabilization plan, and not to the plan itself, the various provisos listed in [Article XX(i)] were meant to apply only to the export restrictions and not to other aspects of such a plan.

"The Working Party concluded that the Agreement does not permit the imposition of restrictions upon the export of a raw material in order to protect or promote a domestic industry, whether by affording a price advantage to that industry for the purchase of its materials, or by reducing the supply of such materials available to foreign competitors, or by other means. However, it was agreed that the question of the objective of any given export restriction would have to be determined on the basis of the facts in each individual case.

"There was some discussion of certain cases in which, on the one hand, a country would be maintaining export restrictions on a raw material which had the effect of assisting a domestic industry processing that material, and on the other hand would be maintaining a prohibition or a severe restriction on imports of the finished product. There was general agreement that in such a case a contracting party, in considering whether the export restrictions were justified by [Article XX(i)], would have to give close examination to the question whether these export restrictions in fact operated to increase the protection afforded to the domestic industry".[130]

9. Paragraph (j)

(1) "local short supply"

The report on discussions in the London session of the Preparatory Committee notes that "The Preparatory Committee agreed that during a post-war transitional period it should be permissible to use [quantitative] restrictions to achieve the equitable distribution of products in short supply, the orderly maintenance of war-time price control by countries undergoing shortages as a result of the war, and the orderly liquidation of temporary surpluses of government-owned stocks and of industries, which were set up owing to the exigencies of war, but which it would be uneconomic to maintain in normal times. ... all these exceptions would be limited to a specified post-war transitional period, which might, however, be subject to some extension in particular cases".[131] These three situations were provided for in Article 25:2 of the London and New York Drafts of the Charter (corresponding to GATT Article XI:2).

---

[127] EPCT/A/PV.36, p. 22.
[128] EPCT/A/SR.40(2), p. 13.
[129] GATT/CP.4/33 (Sales No. GATT/1950-3).
[130] *Ibid.*, paras. 11-13.
[131] London Report, p. 11, para. III.C.1(b).

During the Geneva session of the Preparatory Committee, it was decided to move these three postwar temporary exceptions to Article 43 (general exceptions to the commercial policy chapter) as a new second part of Article 43. Measures of these three types were to be removed in principle not later than 1 January 1951; it was stated that "The effect of this would be to permit during the transitional period the use of differential internal taxes and mixing regulations as well as quantitative restrictions in order to distribute goods in short supply, to give effect to price controls based on shortages and to liquidate surplus stocks or uneconomic industries carried over from the war period".[132] Accordingly, Article XX in the 30 October 1947 text of the General Agreement included a Part II consisting of three paragraphs corresponding to the three situations noted above. Paragraph XX:II(a) provided for measures

> "essential to the acquisition or distribution of products in general or local short supply; *Provided* that any such measures shall be consistent with any multilateral arrangements directed to an equitable international distribution of such products or, in the absence of such arrangements, with the principle that all contracting parties are entitled to an equitable share of the international supply of such products".

It was stated during the course of the discussion at Geneva in 1947 that the phrase "general or local short supply" was "understood to include cases where a product, although in international short supply, was not necessarily in short supply in all markets throughout the world. It was not used in the sense that every country importing a commodity was in short supply otherwise it would not be importing it".[133]

Part II of Article XX further provided that "Measures instituted or maintained under part II of this Article which are inconsistent with the other provisions of this Agreement shall be removed as soon as the conditions giving rise to them have ceased, and in any event not later than January 1, 1951; *Provided* that this period may, with the concurrence of the CONTRACTING PARTIES, be extended in respect of the application of any particular measure to any particular product by any particular contracting party for such further periods as the CONTRACTING PARTIES may specify".

At the Fifth Session in 1950, it was decided to prolong the validity of all three paragraphs of Article XX:II until 1 January 1952, by a decision under Article XXV:5 waiving until that date the obligation of contracting parties instituting or maintaining measures under part II of Article XX to discontinue them or seek permission for their continuance.[134] Further such decisions extended this waiver until 1 January 1954[135] and 1 July 1955[136]. In the Review Session of 1954-55, it was agreed that the substance of paragraph (a) of Section II should be retained for the time being, subject to review not later than 30 June 1960, but that the remainder of paragraph XX:II should be deleted.[137] A Resolution on "Liquidation of Strategic Stocks" was also adopted.[138] The Report of the Review Working Party on "Other Barriers to Trade" notes in this connection:

> "In connexion with the proposed suppression of Section II of Article XX, one member of the Working Party made the point that the need for the exception in Section II(b) was not limited to shortages subsequent to the war, but might be needed in the event of a natural catastrophe. The Working Party considered, however, that other provisions of the Agreement were adequate to cover the application of restrictions when required by any natural catastrophe, and therefore did not consider it necessary to retain or amend the exception in Section II(b)".[139]

---

[132]Passage cited from EPCT/A/PV/30 p. 22; report at EPCT/W/245; discussion at EPCT/A/SR/30 p. 3-5, EPCT/A/PV/30 p. 21-27, EPCT/A/SR/33 p. 1-2, EPCT/A/PV/33 p. 2-7.
[133]EPCT/A/SR.40(2), p. 15.
[134]Decision of 30 November 1950 on Extension of Time-Limit in Article XX Part II, GATT/CP/94; see Report on "Amendment to the Last Paragraph of Part II of Article XX", GATT/CP.5/32, II/46, 48, paragraph 7.
[135]II/28.
[136]2S/27.
[137]L/334, and Addendum, adopted on 3 March 1955, 3S/222, 230, para. 41.
[138]Resolution of 4 March 1955, 3S/51. See also references to this Resolution under Articles X, XVII and XXII in this Index.
[139]L/334, and Addendum, adopted on 3 March 1955, 3S/222, 230-231, para. 42.

Section II(a) then became paragraph (j) of Article XX. This change was effected through the Protocol Amending the Preamble and Parts II and III of the General Agreement and entered into effect on 7 October 1957.

In 1949, Czechoslovakia complained that export restrictions applied by the United States discriminated against Czechoslovakia because the export licensing system favoured countries in the European Recovery Program (the OEEC area). The United States stated that these measures were consistent with Article XXI, and also stated that they were consistent with the short-supply exception in Article XX which required "that any controls exercised to promote the distribution of commodities in short supply shall be consistent with any multilateral arrangements directed to an equitable international distribution of such products".[140]

The 1950 Report of the Working Party on "The Use of Quantitative Restrictions for Protective and Other Commercial Purposes"[141] also examined the use of export restrictions for short-supply items under then-Article XX:II(a).

"... The Working Party discussed the proviso ... requiring the observation of the principle of equitable shares for all contracting parties in the distribution of the international supply of a product in local or general short supply, and noted that the word 'equitable' is used in Article XX:II(a) and not the word 'non-discriminatory' which is used in Article XIII.

"In respect of this type of restriction, general agreement existed on the following statements:

"(a) Apart from situations to which the provisions of Article XX:II(a) are applicable, the practice referred to is inconsistent with the provisions of the Agreement.

"(b) Although the requirement of Article XX:II(a) relates to the total international supply and not the supply of an individual contracting party, nevertheless if a contracting party divert an excessive share of its own supply to individual countries (which may or may not be contracting parties) this may well defeat the principle that all contracting parties are entitled to an equitable share of the international supply of such a product.

"(c) What would not be regarded as an equitable share if it were the result of a unilateral allotment by a contracting party could not appropriately be defended as equitable within the meaning of Article XX:II(a) simply because it had been the consequence of an agreement between two contracting parties.

"(d) The determination of what is 'equitable' to all the contracting parties in any given set of circumstances will depend upon the facts in those circumstances."[142]

(2) *"The CONTRACTING PARTIES shall review the need for this sub-paragraph"*

When the need for paragraph (j) was reviewed at the Sixteenth Session in 1960, the CONTRACTING PARTIES noted "that the contracting parties have resorted to the provisions of this sub-paragraph in a relatively limited number of cases and that it is generally recognized that it would be appropriate to retain such provisions to enable contracting parties to meet emergency situations which may arise in the future". It was decided to retain the paragraph and to review the matter again in 1965.[143] At the Twenty-second Session in 1965, the CONTRACTING PARTIES decided that paragraph (j) "should be retained for the time being" and to review the need for it again in 1970.[144] At the Twenty-sixth Session in 1970, the CONTRACTING PARTIES

---

[140]CP.3/38.
[141]GATT/CP.4/33 (Sales No. GATT/1950-3).
[142]*Ibid.*, paras. 8-9.
[143]9S/17.
[144]Decision of 15 March 1965, 13S/18.

adopted a recommendation of the Council that paragraph (j) be retained with no provision for further review.[145]

10. Trade and environment

See the discussion at the Council meetings of 6 February, 12 March and 8 October 1991, and in the minutes and working papers of the Group on Environmental Measures and International Trade and the Subcommittee on Trade and Environment of the Preparatory Committee for the WTO.[146]

B. RELATIONSHIP BETWEEN ARTICLE XX AND OTHER ARTICLES OF THE GENERAL AGREEMENT

1. Article III

The 1983 Panel Report on "United States - Imports of Certain Automotive Spring Assemblies" examined the consistency of Section 337 of the Tariff Act of 1930 and its application to the imports of certain spring assemblies from Canada with Articles III and XX(d). The Panel found Article XX(d) to apply and "considered that an examination of the United States action in the light of the other GATT provisions referred to … was not required".[147] This Panel Report was adopted subject to an understanding that its adoption "shall not foreclose future examination of the use of Section 337 to deal with patent infringement cases from the point of view of consistency with Articles III and XX of the General Agreement".[148]

The 1989 Panel on "United States - Section 337 of the Tariff Act of 1930" found, concerning the relation between Article III and Article XX(d):

> "The Panel noted that Article XX is entitled 'General Exceptions' and that the central phrase in the introductory clause reads: 'nothing in this Agreement shall be construed to prevent the adoption or enforcement … of measures …'. Article XX(d) thus provides for a limited and conditional exception from obligations under other provisions. The Panel therefore concluded that Article XX(d) applies only to measures inconsistent with another provision of the General Agreement, and that, consequently, the application of Section 337 has to be examined first in the light of Article III:4. If any inconsistencies with Article III:4 were found, the Panel would then examine whether they could be justified under Article XX(d)".[149]

The 1990 Panel on "Thailand - Restrictions on Importation of and Internal Taxes on Cigarettes" referred to the use of non-discriminatory measures consistent with Article III in interpreting the scope of "necessary" measures under Article XX(b); see page 566 above.

2. Articles XXII and XXIII

In discussions of the article on exceptions to the commercial policy chapter of the Charter in the London Session of the Preparatory Committee, it was stated in relation to Article 30 of the draft Charter [XXII and XXIII] that "one of the main objectives of Article 30 was to prevent evasion of the provisions of Chapter IV. If a Member country used the exceptions of sub-paragraph (b) [XX(b)] as a means of protection, Article 30 provided that another Member might make representations to the ITO and so obtain satisfaction. It

---

[145]Decision of 20 February 1970, L/3361, 17S/18; see L/3350.
[146]C/M/247, C/M/248, C/M/250, SR.49/2; TRE/1-14, TRE/W/1-21, and documents in PC/SCTE series. See also Decision of the CONTRACTING PARTIES on follow-up to the recommendations in the area of trade of the United Nations Conference on Environment and Development, SR.48/1, p. 12-16, 39S/330; debate on environmental labelling at C/M/260, p. 40-56; Secretariat Note on the UN Conference on Environment and Development held in Rio de Janeiro, Brazil, from 3 to 14 June 1992, L/6892/Add.3, 39S/303, and earlier notes on the UNCED Preparatory Committee at L/6892 and Add.1-2; Minutes of Council meeting on UNCED followup, C/M/269; and Report of the EMIT group at L/7402. The Secretariat has also issued to the public summaries of meetings of the EMIT and SCTE groups, in the TE document series.
[147]L/5333, adopted on 26 May 1983, 30S/107, 126, para. 61.
[148]C/M/168.
[149]L/6439, adopted on 7 November 1989, 36S/345, 385, para. 5.9.

was almost impossible to draft exceptions which could not be abused, if good faith was lacking. The League of Nations had adopted an Article on the lines of Article 30, precisely because they had been unable to formulate exceptions which would exclude all possibility of abuse".[150]

3. Article XXIV

In 1987, during the Working Party on the Accession of Portugal and Spain to the EEC, in response to a question regarding an EEC regulation permitting the use of the term "sherry" to describe certain liqueur wines of the United Kingdom, Ireland and Cyprus but not liqueur wines of South Africa, the EEC stated that the regulation in question "constitutes a measure designed to prevent deceptive practices. It is therefore justified under Article XX(d) of the General Agreement" and that the preferential treatment of certain products was "consistent with the GATT by virtue of Article XXIV, which permits customs unions to be formed in accordance with the needs of the integration process they plan to carry out".[151]

III. PREPARATORY WORK AND SUBSEQUENT MODIFICATIONS

Provisions corresponding to those in Article XX appear in the US Proposals in Chapter III-G; in the US Draft Charter in Article 32; in the London and New York Drafts, in Article 37; in the Geneva Draft in Article 43; and in the Havana Charter in Article 45. In each of these drafts these provisions were exceptions to the commercial policy provisions of the Charter. Separate policy-based exceptions were provided for the Charter chapters on commodity agreements and restrictive business practices.

The article on commercial policy exceptions originally included four national security provisions which were separated during the Geneva session of the preparatory committee and became exceptions to all obligations in the Charter; see Section III under Article XXI.

At Havana, an exception was added for measures "necessary to the enforcement of laws and regulations relating to public safety", which term, in the view of the drafters, included the legal concept of "public order" ("ordre public").[152] In addition, an exception was added for measures "taken in pursuance of any intergovernmental agreement which relates solely to the conservation of fisheries resources, migratory birds or wild animals", as a corollary to a similar provision added to Article 70, the exceptions provision in the chapter on commodity agreements.[153] The Working Party on "Modifications to the General Agreement", which met during the Second Session in September 1948 and considered which of the changes made at Havana should be brought into the text of the General Agreement, did not decide to take either of these changes into the General Agreement.

See above at pages 589 and 593 concerning the amendments to sub-paragraph (h) and Section II of Article XX agreed during the Review Session of 1954-55. These changes were effected through the Protocol Amending the Preamble and Parts II and III, which entered into force on 7 October 1957.

---

[150]EPCT/C.II/50, p. 6.
[151]L/5984/Add.2, p. 2.
[152]Havana Reports, p. 84, para. 18, referring to Charter Article 45:1(a)(ii); see also French text of same document (para. 18, p. 92).
[153]Havana Reports, p. 84-85, para. 21, referring to paragraph 1(a)(x) of Article 45 of the Charter.

IV. RELEVANT DOCUMENTS

London

Discussion:	EPCT/C.II/12, 32, 35
Discussion:	EPCT/C.II/QR/PV/1, 5
Report:	EPCT/C.II/54/Rev.1, 59

New York

Discussion:	EPCT/C.6/41

Geneva

Discussion:	EPCT/EC/SR.2/3, 5, 22
	EPCT/A/SR/19, 21, 25, 30, 32, 33, 36, 40(1), 40(2)
	EPCT/A/PV/22+Corr.1-5, 23+Corr.1-2, 26+Corr.1-3, 30
	EPCT/WP.1/SR/10,11
	EPCT/TAC/SR/11
	EPCT/TAC/PV/28
Reports:	EPCT/103+Corr.3, 135, 141, 142, 154+Corr.1-3, 180, 186, 189, 196, 212, 214/Add.1/Rev.1
Other:	EPCT/W/23, 24, 28+Corr.1, 44, 45, 46, 62, 98, 137, 145, 157/Rev.1, 194, 208, 212, 223, 227, 252/Rev.1, 260+Corr.1, 263, 264, 269, 272, 280, 281, 284, 293, 301, 313

Havana

Discussion:	E/CONF.2/C.3/SR.17, 32, 33, 35
Report:	E/CONF.2/C.3/37

Review Session

Discussion:	SR.9/17, 27, 47
Reports:	W.9/105, 122, 123, 177, 213, 231, 236/Add.1; L/334, L/327; 3S/230, 239
Other:	L/189+Add.2, L/261/Add.1, L/264/Add.1, L/273, L/274, L/275, L/276
	W.9/20/Add.1, 50, 78

ARTICLE XXI

SECURITY EXCEPTIONS

I. TEXT OF ARTICLE XXI 599

II. INTERPRETATION AND APPLICATION OF ARTICLE XXI 600
   A. SCOPE AND APPLICATION OF ARTICLE XXI 600
      1. Paragraphs (a) and (b): "it considers ... essential security interests" 600
      2. Paragraph (a): "furnish ... any information" 601
      3. Paragraph (b): "action" 602
         (1) "relating to fissionable materials or the materials from which they are derived" 602
         (2) "relating to the traffic in arms, ammunition and implements of war and to such traffic in other goods and materials as is carried on directly or indirectly for the purpose of supplying a military establishment" 602
         (3) "taken in time of war or other emergency in international relations" 602
      4. Paragraph (c): "any action in pursuance of its obligations under the United Nations Charter for the maintenance of international peace and security" 605
      5. Other invocations of Article XXI 605
      6. Procedures concerning notification of measures under Article XXI 605
   B. RELATIONSHIP BETWEEN ARTICLE XXI AND OTHER ARTICLES OF THE GENERAL AGREEMENT 606
      1. Articles I and XIII 606
      2. Article XXIII 606
   C. RELATIONSHIP BETWEEN ARTICLE XXI AND GENERAL INTERNATIONAL LAW 608

III. PREPARATORY WORK 608

IV. RELEVANT DOCUMENTS 610

I. TEXT OF ARTICLE XXI

Article XXI

Security Exceptions

Nothing in this Agreement shall be construed

(a) to require any contracting party to furnish any information the disclosure of which it considers contrary to its essential security interests; or

(b) to prevent any contracting party from taking any action which it considers necessary for the protection of its essential security interests

   (i) relating to fissionable materials or the materials from which they are derived;

   (ii) relating to the traffic in arms, ammunition and implements of war and to such traffic in other goods and materials as is carried on directly or indirectly for the purpose of supplying a military establishment;

   (iii) taken in time of war or other emergency in international relations; or

(c) to prevent any contracting party from taking any action in pursuance of its obligations under the United Nations Charter for the maintenance of international peace and security.

II. INTERPRETATION AND APPLICATION OF ARTICLE XXI

A. SCOPE AND APPLICATION OF ARTICLE XXI

1. Paragraphs (a) and (b): "it considers ... essential security interests"

During discussions in the Geneva session of the Preparatory Committee, in response to an inquiry as to the meaning of "essential security interests", it was stated by one of the drafters of the original Draft Charter that "We gave a good deal of thought to the question of the security exception which we thought should be included in the Charter. We recognized that there was a great danger of having too wide an exception and we could not put it into the Charter, simply by saying: 'by any Member of measures relating to a Member's security interests,' because that would permit anything under the sun. Therefore we thought it well to draft provisions which would take care of real security interests and, at the same time, so far as we could, to limit the exception so as to prevent the adoption of protection for maintaining industries under every conceivable circumstance. ... there must be some latitude here for security measures. It is really a question of balance. We have got to have some exceptions. We cannot make it too tight, because we cannot prohibit measures which are needed purely for security reasons. On the other hand, we cannot make it so broad that, under the guise of security, countries will put on measures which really have a commercial purpose". The Chairman of Commission A suggested in response that the spirit in which Members of the Organization would interpret these provisions was the only guarantee against abuses of this kind.[1]

During the discussion of the complaint of Czechoslovakia at the Third Session in 1949 (see page 602) it was stated, *inter alia*, that "every country must be the judge in the last resort on questions relating to its own security. On the other hand, every contracting party should be cautious not to take any step which might have the effect of undermining the General Agreement".[2]

In 1961, on the occasion of the accession of Portugal, Ghana stated that its boycott of Portuguese goods was justified under the provisions of Article XXI:(b)(iii), noting that

"... under this Article each contracting party was the sole judge of what was necessary in its essential security interest. There could therefore be no objection to Ghana regarding the boycott of goods as justified by security interests. It might be observed that a country's security interests might be threatened by a potential as well as an actual danger. The Ghanaian Government's view was that the situation in Angola was a constant threat to the peace of the African continent and that any action which, by bringing pressure to bear on the Portuguese Government, might lead to a lessening of this danger, was therefore justified in the essential security interests of Ghana".[3]

During the Council discussion in 1982 of trade restrictions applied for non-economic reasons by the EEC, its member States, Canada and Australia against imports from Argentina (see page 603), the representative of the EEC stated that "the EEC and its member States had taken certain measures on the basis of their inherent rights, of which Article XXI of the General Agreement was a reflection. The exercise of these rights constituted a general exception, and required neither notification, justification nor approval, a procedure confirmed by thirty-five years of implementation of the General Agreement. He said that in effect, this procedure showed that every contracting party was - in the last resort - the judge of its exercise of these rights". The representative of Canada stated that "Canada's sovereign action was to be seen as a political response to a political issue ... Canada was convinced that the situation which had necessitated the measures had to be satisfactorily resolved by appropriate action elsewhere, as the GATT had neither the competence nor the responsibility to deal with the political issue which had been raised. His delegation could not, therefore, accept the notion that there had been a violation of the General Agreement".[4] The representative of Australia "stated that the Australian measures were in conformity with the provisions of Article XXI:(c), which did not require notification or justification".[5] The representative

---

[1] EPCT/A/PV/33, p. 20-21 and Corr.3; see also EPCT/A/SR/33, p. 3.
[2] GATT/CP.3/SR.22, Corr. 1.
[3] SR.19/12, p. 196.
[4] C/M/157, p. 10.
[5] C/M/157, p. 11.

of the United States stated that "The General Agreement left to each contracting party the judgment as to what it considered to be necessary to protect its security interests. The CONTRACTING PARTIES had no power to question that judgement".[6]

The representative of Argentina noted that it had attempted to submit to GATT only the trade aspects of this case and stated "that in order to justify restrictive measures a contracting party invoking Article XXI would specifically be required to state reasons of national security ... there were no trade restrictions which could be applied without being notified, discussed and justified".[7]

Paragraph 7(iii) of the Ministerial Declaration adopted 29 November 1982 at the Thirty-eighth Session of the CONTRACTING PARTIES provides that "... the contracting parties undertake, individually and jointly: ... to abstain from taking restrictive trade measures, for reasons of a non-economic character, not consistent with the General Agreement".[8]

The question of whether and to what extent the CONTRACTING PARTIES can review the national security reasons for measures taken under Article XXI was discussed again in the GATT Council in May and July 1985 in relation to the US trade embargo against Nicaragua which had taken effect on 7 May 1985.[9] While a panel was established to examine the US measures, its terms of reference stated that "the Panel cannot examine or judge the validity or motivation for the invocation of Article XXI(b)(iii) by the United States".[10] In the Panel Report on "United States - Trade Measures affecting Nicaragua", which has not been adopted,

"... The Panel noted that, while both parties to the dispute agreed that the United States, by imposing the embargo, had acted contrary to certain trade-facilitating provisions of the General Agreement, they disagreed on the question of whether the non-observance of these provisions was justified by Article XXI(b)(iii) ...

"The Panel further noted that, in the view of Nicaragua, this provision should be interpreted in the light of the basic principles of international law and in harmony with the decisions of the United Nations and of the International Court of Justice and should therefore be regarded as merely providing contracting parties subjected to an aggression with the right of self-defence. The Panel also noted that, in the view of the United States, Article XXI applied to any action which the contracting party taking it considered necessary for the protection of its essential security interests and that the Panel, both by the terms of Article XXI and by its mandate, was precluded from examining the validity of the United States' invocation of Article XXI.

"The Panel did not consider the question of whether the terms of Article XXI precluded it from examining the validity of the United States' invocation of that Article as this examination was precluded by its mandate. It recalled that its terms of reference put strict limits on its activities because they stipulated that the Panel could not examine or judge the validity of or the motivation for the invocation of Article XXI:(b)(iii) by the United States ... The Panel concluded that, as it was not authorized to examine the justification for the United States' invocation of a general exception to the obligations under the General Agreement, it could find the United States neither to be complying with its obligations under the General Agreement nor to be failing to carry out its obligations under that Agreement".[11]

2. Paragraph (a): "furnish ... any information"

During the discussion at the Third Session of a Czechoslovak complaint concerning United States national security export controls, in response to a request by Czechoslovakia for information under Article XIII:3 on the export licensing system concerned, the US representative stated that while it would comply with a substantial part of the request, "Article XXI ... provides that a contracting party shall not be required to give information which

---

[6] C/M/159, p. 19; see also C/M/157, p. 8.
[7] C/M/157, p. 12; C/M/159, pp. 14-15.
[8] L/5424, adopted on 29 November 1982, 29S/9, 11.
[9] C/M/188, pp. 2-16; C/M/191, pp. 41-46.
[10] C/M/196 at p. 7.
[11] L/6053, dated 13 October 1986 (unadopted), paras. 5.1-5.3.

it considers contrary to its essential security interests. The United States does consider it contrary to its security interest - and to the security interest of other friendly countries - to reveal the names of the commodities that it considers to be most strategic".[12]

The "Decision Concerning Article XXI of the General Agreement" of 30 November 1982 (see page 605 below) provides *inter alia* that "Subject to the exception in Article XXI:*a*, contracting parties should be informed to the fullest extent possible of trade measures taken under Article XXI".[13]

3. Paragraph (b): "action"

(1) "relating to fissionable materials or the materials from which they are derived"

The records of the Geneva discussions of the Preparatory Committee indicate that the representative of Australia withdrew its reservation on the inclusion of a reference to "fissionable materials" in the light of a statement that the provisions of Article 35 [XXIII] would apply to Article XXI; see below at page 606.[14]

(2) "relating to the traffic in arms, ammunition and implements of war and to such traffic in other goods and materials as is carried on directly or indirectly for the purpose of supplying a military establishment"

During discussions in the Geneva session of the Preparatory Committee, in connection with a proposal to modify Article 37(g) [XX(g)] to permit export restrictions on raw materials for long-term defense purposes, the question was put whether the phrase "for the purpose of supplying a military establishment" would permit restrictions on the export of iron ore when it was believed that the ore would be used by ordinary smelting works and ultimately for military purposes by another country. It was stated in response that "if a Member exporting commodities is satisfied that the purpose of the transaction was to supply a military establishment, immediately or ultimately, this language would cover it".[15]

At the Third Session in 1949, Czechoslovakia requested a decision under Article XXIII as to whether the US had failed to carry out its obligations under Articles I and XIII, by reason of the 1948 US administration of its export licensing controls (both short-supply controls and new export controls instituted in 1948 discriminating between destination countries for security reasons). The US stated that its controls for security reasons applied to a narrow group of exports of goods which could be used for military purposes[16] and also stated that "the provisions of Article I would not require uniformity of formalities, as applied to different countries, in respect of restrictions imposed for security reasons".[17] It was also stated by one contracting party that "goods which were of a nature that could contribute to war potential" came within the exception of Article XXI.[18] The complaint was rejected by a roll-call vote of 17 to 1 with 3 abstentions.[19]

(3) "taken in time of war or other emergency in international relations"

The 1970 Working Party Report on "Accession of the United Arab Republic" notes that in response to concerns raised regarding the Arab League boycott against Israel and the secondary boycott against firms having relations with Israel, the representative of the UAR stated that "the history of the Arab boycott was beyond doubt related to the extraordinary circumstances to which the Middle East area had been exposed. The state of war which had long prevailed in that area necessitated the resorting to this system. ... In view of the political character of this issue, the United Arab Republic did not wish to discuss it within GATT. ... It would not be reasonable to ask that the United Arab Republic should do business with a firm that transferred all or part of its profits from sales to the United Arab Republic to an enemy country".[20] Several members of the working party supported the

---

[12]GATT/CP.3/38, p. 9.
[13]L/5426, 29S/23-24, para. 1.
[14]EPCT/A/PV/33, p. 29; see also EPCT/A/PV/33/Corr. 3.
[15]EPCT/A/PV/36, p. 19; see also proposal referred to at EPCT/W/264.
[16]GATT/CP.3/38; GATT/CP.3/SR.22, p. 8.
[17]GATT/CP.3/SR.22, p. 4-5.
[18]GATT/CP.3/SR.20, p. 3-4.
[19]GATT/CP.3/SR.22, p. 9; Decision of 8 June 1949 at II/28.
[20]L/3362, adopted on 27 February 1970, 17S/33, 39, para. 22.

views of the representative of the UAR that the background of the boycott measures was political and not commercial.[21]

In November 1975 Sweden introduced a global import quota system for certain footwear. The Swedish Government considered that the measure was taken in conformity with the spirit of Article XXI and stated, *inter alia*, that the "decrease in domestic production has become a critical threat to the emergency planning of Sweden's economic defence as an integral part of the country's security policy. This policy necessitates the maintenance of a minimum domestic production capacity in vital industries. Such a capacity is indispensable in order to secure the provision of essential products necessary to meet basic needs in case of war or other emergency in international relations".[22] In the discussion of this measure in the GATT Council, "Many representatives ... expressed doubts as to the justification of these measures under the General Agreement ... Many delegations reserved their rights under the GATT and took note of Sweden's offer to consult".[23] Sweden notified the termination of the quotas as far as leather and plastic shoes were concerned as of 1 July 1977.[24]

In April 1982, the EEC and its member states, Canada, and Australia suspended indefinitely imports into their territories of products of Argentina. In notifying these measures they stated that "they have taken certain measures in the light of the situation addressed in the Security Council Resolution 502 [the Falkland/Malvinas issue]; they have taken these measures on the basis of their inherent rights of which Article XXI of the General Agreement is a reflection".[25] Argentina took the position that, in addition to infringing the principles and objectives underlying the GATT, these measures were in violation of Articles I:1, II, XI:1, XIII, and Part IV. The legal aspects of these trade restrictions affecting Argentina were discussed extensively in the Council.[26] The measures were removed in June 1982. Argentina sought an interpretation of Article XXI; these efforts led to the inclusion of paragraph 7(iii) in the Ministerial Declaration of November 1982, which provides that "... the contracting parties undertake, individually and jointly: ... to abstain from taking restrictive trade measures, for reasons of a non-economic character, not consistent with the General Agreement"[27] and also led to the adoption of the text below at page 605.

On 7 May 1985 the US notified the contracting parties of an Executive Order prohibiting all imports of goods and services of Nicaraguan origin, all exports from the US of goods to or destined for Nicaragua (except those destined for the organized democratic resistance) and transactions relating thereto.[28] In Council discussions of this matter, Nicaragua stated that these measures contravened Articles I, II, V, XI, XIII and Part IV of the GATT, and that "this was not a matter of national security but one of coercion".[29] Nicaragua further stated that Article XXI could not be applied in an arbitrary fashion; there had to be some correspondence between the measures adopted and the situation giving rise to such adoption.[30] Nicaragua stated that the text of Article XXI made it clear that the CONTRACTING PARTIES were competent to judge whether a situation of "war or other emergency in international relations" existed and requested that a Panel be set up under Article XXIII:2 to examine the issue.[31] The United States stated that its actions had been taken for national security reasons and were covered by Article XXI:(b)(iii) of the GATT; and that this provision left it to each contracting party to judge what action it considered necessary for the protection of its essential security interest.[32] The terms of reference of the Panel precluded it from examining or judging the validity of the invocation of Article XXI(b)(iii) by the US. Concerning the Panel decision on this issue, see page 601 and the discussion of Article XXIII below. When the Council discussed the Panel Report, Nicaragua requested that the Council recommend removal of the embargo; authorize special support measures for Nicaragua so that countries wanting to do so could grant trade preferences aimed at re-establishing a balance in Nicaragua's pre-embargo global trade relations and at compensating

---

[21]*Ibid.*, 17S/40, para. 23.
[22]L/4250, p. 3.
[23]C/M/109, p. 8-9.
[24]L/4250/Add.1; L/4254, p. 17-18.
[25]L/5319/Rev.1.
[26]L/5317, L/5336; C/M/157, C/M/159.
[27]L/5424, adopted on 29 November 1982, 29S/9, 11.
[28]L/5803.
[29]C/M/188, p. 4.
[30]C/M/188, p. 16.
[31]L/5802; C/M/191, pp. 41-46.
[32]C/M/191, pp. 41,46.

Nicaragua for the damage caused by the embargo; and prepare an interpretative note on Article XXI. Consensus was not reached on any of these alternatives. The Panel Report has not been adopted. At the meeting of the Council on 3 April 1990 Nicaragua announced the lifting of the trade embargo. The representative of the US announced that the conditions which had necessitated action under Article XXI had ceased to exist, his country's national security emergency with respect to Nicaragua had been terminated, and all economic sanctions, including the trade embargo, had been lifted.[33]

In November 1991, the European Community notified the contracting parties that the EC and its member States had decided to adopt trade measures against Yugoslavia "on the grounds that the situation prevailing in Yugoslavia no longer permits the preferential treatment of this country to be upheld. Therefore, as from 11 November, imports from Yugoslavia into the Community are applied m.f.n. treatment ... These measures are taken by the European Community upon consideration of its essential security interests and based on GATT Article XXI."[34] The measures comprised suspension of trade concessions granted to the Socialist Federal Republic of Yugoslavia under its bilateral trade agreement with the EC; application of certain limitations (previously suspended) to textile imports from Yugoslavia; withdrawal of GSP benefits; suspension of similar concessions and GSP benefits for ECSC products; and action to denounce or suspend the application of the bilateral trade agreements between the EC and its member states and Yugoslavia. On 2 December the Community and its member states decided to apply selective measures in favour of "those parties which contribute to progress toward peace". Economic sanctions or withdrawal of preferential benefits from the Yugoslavia were also taken by Australia, Austria, Canada, Finland, Japan, New Zealand, Norway, Sweden, Switzerland, and the United States.

At the Forty-seventh Session in December 1991, Yugoslavia referred to the Decision of 1982 on notification of measures taken under Article XXI (see page 605 below) and reserved its GATT rights. In February 1992 Yugoslavia requested establishment of a panel under Article XXIII:2, stating that the measures taken by the EC were inconsistent with Articles I, XXI and the Enabling Clause; departed from the letter and intention of paragraph 7(iii) of the Ministerial Decision of November 1982; and impeded the attainment of the objectives of the General Agreement. Yugoslavia further stated:

> "The situation in Yugoslavia is a specific one and does not correspond to the notion and meaning of Article XXI(b) and (c). There is no decision or resolution of the relevant UN body to impose economic sanctions against Yugoslavia based on the reasoning embodied in the UN Charter....the 'positive compensatory measures' applied by the European Community to certain parts of Yugoslavia [are] contrary to the MFN treatment of 'products originating in or destined for the territories' - taken as a whole - 'of all contracting parties'".[35]

In March 1992, the Council agreed to establish a panel with the standard terms of reference unless, as provided in the Decision of 12 April 1989, the parties agreed otherwise within twenty days.[36] At the April 1992 Council meeting, in discussion of the notification of the transformation of the Socialist Federal Republic of Yugoslavia (SFRY) into the Federal Republic of Yugoslavia (FRY) consisting of the Republics of Serbia and Montenegro, the EC representative said that until the question of succession to Yugoslavia's contracting party status had been resolved, the Panel process which had been initiated between the former SFRY and the EC no longer had any foundation and could not proceed.[37] At the May 1992 Council meeting, in a discussion concerning the status of the FRY as a successor to the former SFRY as a contracting party, the Chairman stated that "In these circumstances, without prejudice to the question of who should succeed the former SFRY in the GATT, and until the Council returned to this issue, he proposed that the representative of the FRY should refrain from participating in the business of the Council". The Council so agreed.[38] At the June 1993 Council meeting this decision was modified taking into account United Nations General Assembly Resolution 47/1 to provide that the FRY could

---

[33] C/M/240, p. 31; L/6661.
[34] L/6948.
[35] DS27/2, dated 10 February 1992.
[36] C/M/255, p. 18.
[37] C/M/256, p. 32.
[38] C/M/257 p. 3 and Corr.1.

not continue automatically the contracting party status of the former SFRY and that it shall not participate in the work of the Council and its subsidiary bodies.[39]

4. Paragraph (c): "any action in pursuance of its obligations under the United Nations Charter for the maintenance of international peace and security"

India's 1994 background document for simplified balance-of-payments consultations notes that while almost all of India's trading partners received most-favoured-nation treatment in the issue of import licences, import licences were not issued for imports from countries facing UN mandated sanctions, at present Iraq, Fiji, Serbia and Montenegro".[40] Brazil's 1994 notification on import licensing notes that the import licensing system of Brazil applies for goods entering from or exported to any country except for those covered by UN embargoes.[41] The import licensing notification of Cyprus similarly notes that imports from certain countries are prohibited in accordance with United Nations resolutions.[42] The 1993 licencing notification of Norway notes that all imports from Iraq and Serbia/Montenegro are prohibited.[43]

5. Other invocations of Article XXI

The United States embargo on trade with Cuba, which was imposed by means of Proclamation 3447 by the President of the United States, dated 3 February 1962, was not formally raised in the CONTRACTING PARTIES but notified by Cuba in the inventory of non-tariff measures. The United States invoked Article XXI as justification for its action.[44]

6. Procedures concerning notification of measures under Article XXI

During the Council discussion in 1982 of trade measures for non-economic reasons taken against Argentina (see page 603), it was stated by the countries taking these measures that "Article XXI did not mention notification" and that many contracting parties had, in the past, invoked Article XXI without there having been any notification or challenge to the situation in GATT.[45] Argentina sought an interpretation of Article XXI. Informal consultations took place during the Thirty-eighth Session in November 1982 in connection with the adoption of the Council report to the CONTRACTING PARTIES, in so far as it related to these trade restrictions.[46] As a result, on 30 November 1982 the CONTRACTING PARTIES adopted the following "Decision Concerning Article XXI of the General Agreement":

> "*Considering* that the exceptions envisaged in Article XXI of the General Agreement constitute an important element for safeguarding the rights of contracting parties when they consider that reasons of security are involved;
>
> "*Noting* that recourse to Article XXI could constitute, in certain circumstances, an element of disruption and uncertainty for international trade and affect benefits accruing to contracting parties under the General Agreement;
>
> "*Recognizing* that in taking action in terms of the exceptions provided in Article XXI of the General Agreement, contracting parties should take into consideration the interests of third parties which may be affected;

---

[39] C/M/264, p. 3.
[40] L/5640/Add.7/Rev.6, 18 August 1994; see also BOP/321 of 24 October 1994.
[41] L/5640/Add.54.
[42] L/5640, 24 January 1994.
[43] L/5640/Add.2/Rev.4, 13 October 1993.
[44] COM.IND/6/Add.4, p. 53 (notification); MTN/3B/4, p. 559 (response citing binding resolution under Inter-American Treaty of Reciprocal Assistance). See also Council discussion May 1986 concerning US measures authorizing denial of sugar import quota to any failing to certify that it does not import sugar produced in Cuba for re-export to the US, stated by US to be a "procedural safeguard" against transshipment of sugar in violation of the embargo; C/M/198 p. 33, L/5980. See also statement by Cuba in L/7525.
[45] C/M/159, p. 18.
[46] See L/5414 (Council report); see also C/W/402, W.38/5, L/5426.

"That until such time as the CONTRACTING PARTIES may decide to make a formal interpretation of Article XXI it is appropriate to set procedural guidelines for its application;

The CONTRACTING PARTIES *decide* that:

"1. Subject to the exception in Article XXI:*a*, contracting parties should be informed to the fullest extent possible of trade measures taken under Article XXI.

"2. When action is taken under Article XXI, all contracting parties affected by such action retain their full rights under the General Agreement.

"3. The Council may be requested to give further consideration to this matter in due course".[47]

See the references to this Decision above in the case of EC measures on trade with Yugoslavia.

B. RELATIONSHIP BETWEEN ARTICLE XXI AND OTHER ARTICLES OF THE GENERAL AGREEMENT

1. Articles I and XIII

During the discussion at the Third Session of the complaint of Czechoslovakia that US export controls were administered inconsistently with Articles I and XIII (see page 602), the US representative stated that these restrictions were justified under Article XXI(b)(ii). In calling for a decision, the Chairman indicated that Article XXI "embodied exceptions to the general rule contained in Article I". In a Decision of 8 June 1949 under Article XXIII:2, the CONTRACTING PARTIES rejected the contention of the Czechoslovak delegation.[48]

2. Article XXIII

During discussions in Geneva in 1947 in connection with the removal of the provisions now contained in Article XXI and their relocation in a separate exception (Article 94) at the end of the Charter, the question was raised whether the dispute settlement provisions of Article 35 of the New York Draft [XXII/XXIII] would nevertheless apply. It was stated that "It is true that an action taken by a Member under Article 94 could not be challenged in the sense that it could not be claimed that a Member was violating the Charter; but if that action, even though not in conflict with the terms of Article 94, should affect another Member, I should think that that Member would have the right to seek redress of some kind under Article 35 as it now stands. In other words, there is no exception from the application of Article 35 to this or any other Article".[49] The addition of a note to clarify that the provisions of paragraph 2 of Article 35 [XXIII] applied to Article 94 was rejected as unnecessary.[50]

See the discussion above of the Czechoslovak complaint concerning export controls, in which the CONTRACTING PARTIES made a decision under Article XXIII:2 as to "whether the Government of the United States had failed to carry out its obligations under the Agreement through its administration of the issue of export licences".[51]

During the discussion of the trade restrictions affecting Argentina applied for non-economic reasons, the view was expressed "that the provisions of Article XXI were subject to those of Article XXIII:2". Argentina reserved its rights under Article XXIII in respect of any injury resulting from trade restrictions applied in the context of Article XXI.[52]

---

[47] L/5426, 29S/23.
[48] GATT/CP.3/SR.22, p. 9; II/28.
[49] EPCT/A/PV/33, p. 26-27.
[50] EPCT/A/PV/33 p. 27-29 and EPCT/A/PV/33/Corr.3.
[51] GATT/CP.3/SR.22, p. 9.
[52] C/M/157, p. 9; C/M/159, p. 14; C/M/165, p. 18.

Paragraph 2 of the "Decision Concerning Article XXI of the General Agreement" of 30 November 1982 stipulates that "... when action is taken under Article XXI, all contracting parties affected by such action retain their full rights under the General Agreement".[53]

The 1984 Panel Report on "United States - Imports of Sugar from Nicaragua" examined the action taken by the US government to reduce the share of the US sugar import quota allocated to Nicaragua and distribute the reduction in Nicaragua's allocation to El Salvador, Honduras and Costa Rica. The Panel Report notes that "The United States stated that it was neither invoking any exceptions under the provisions of the General Agreement nor intending to defend its actions in GATT terms ... the action of the United States did of course affect trade, but was not taken for trade policy reasons".[54]

"The Panel noted that the measures taken by the United States concerning sugar imports from Nicaragua were but one aspect of a more general problem. The Panel, in accordance with its terms of reference ... examined those measures solely in the light of the relevant GATT provisions, concerning itself only with the trade issue under dispute."[55]

"... The Panel ... concluded that the sugar quota allocated to Nicaragua for the fiscal year 1983/84 was inconsistent with the United States' obligations under Article XIII:2.

"The Panel noted that the United States had not invoked any of the exceptions provided for in the General Agreement permitting discriminatory quantitative restrictions contrary to Article XIII. The Panel therefore did not examine whether the reduction in Nicaragua's quota could be justified under any such provision."[56]

The follow-up on the Panel report was discussed in the Council meetings of May and July 1984. The United States said that it "had not obstructed Nicaragua's resort to GATT's dispute settlement process; it had stated explicitly the conditions under which the issue might be resolved; and it recognized that Nicaragua had certain rights under Article XXIII which it had reserved and could continue to exercise".[57] Nicaragua stated that it was aware of its rights under Article XXIII.

In July 1985, following a request by Nicaragua for the establishment of a panel to review certain US trade measures affecting Nicaragua, the right of a contracting party to invoke Article XXIII in cases involving Article XXI was discussed again in the GATT Council.[58] At its meetings in October 1985 and March 1986 respectively the Council established a panel with the following terms of reference to deal with the complaint by Nicaragua:

"To examine, in the light of the relevant GATT provisions, of the understanding reached at the Council on 10 October 1985 that the Panel cannot examine or judge the validity of or motivation for the invocation of Article XXI(b)(iii) by the United States, of the relevant provisions of the Understanding Regarding Notification, Consultation, Dispute Settlement and Surveillance (BISD 26S/211-218), and of the agreed Dispute Settlement Procedures contained in the 1982 Ministerial Declaration (BISD 29S/13-16), the measures taken by the United States on 7 May 1985 and their trade effects in order to establish to what extent benefits accruing to Nicaragua under the General Agreement have been nullified or impaired, and to make such findings as will assist the CONTRACTING PARTIES in further action in this matter".[59]

In the Panel Report on "United States - Trade Measures affecting Nicaragua", which has not been adopted, the Panel noted the different views of the parties regarding whether the United States' invocation of Article XXI(b)(iii) was proper, and concluded that this issue was not within its terms of reference; see above at page 601. With

---

[53] 29S/24.
[54] L/5607, adopted on 13 March 1984, 31S/67, 72, para. 3.10.
[55] Ibid., 31S/73, para. 4.1.
[56] Ibid., 31S/74, paras. 4.3-4.4.
[57] C/M/178, p. 27.
[58] C/M/191, pp.41-46.
[59] C/M/196, p. 7.

regard to Nicaragua's claim of non-violation nullification or impairment, the Panel "decided not to propose a ruling in this case on the basic question of whether actions under Article XXI could nullify or impair GATT benefits of the adversely affected contracting party".[60]

When the Panel's report was discussed by the Council in November 1986, the US representative stated that "Nullification or impairment when no GATT violation had been found was a delicate issue, linked to the concept of 'reasonable expectations'. It was not simply a question of trade damage, since no one doubted the existence of trade damage. Applying the concept of 'reasonable expectations' to a case of trade sanctions motivated by national security considerations would be particularly perilous, since at a broader level those security considerations would nevertheless enter into expectations ... the Panel had acted wisely in refraining from a decision that could create a precedent of much wider ramifications for the scope of GATT rights and obligations ...".[61] The representative of Nicaragua stated that her delegation could not support adoption of the report, *inter alia* because it could only be adopted once the Council was in a position to make recommendations.[62]

C. RELATIONSHIP BETWEEN ARTICLE XXI AND GENERAL INTERNATIONAL LAW

The 1986 Panel Report on "United States - Trade Measures Affecting Nicaragua", which has not been adopted, notes the different views of the parties to the dispute concerning the relationship between Article XXI and general international law including decisions of the United Nations and the International Court of Justice.[63]

In discussion at the Forty-seventh Session in December 1991 concerning trade measures for non-economic purposes against Yugoslavia, the representative of India stated that "India did not favour the use of trade measures for non-economic reasons. Such measures should only be taken within the framework of a decision by the United Nations Security Council. In the absence of such a decision or resolution, there was a serious risk that such measures might be unilateral or arbitrary and would undermine the multilateral trading system".[64]

III. PREPARATORY WORK

In the US Draft Charter, and London and New York Draft Charter texts, the Article on exceptions to the commercial policy chapter included the provisions of what is now GATT Article XXI (see Article 32, US draft; Article 37, London and New York drafts). Also in these drafts, the exceptions clause for the chapter on commodity agreements included provisions excepting arrangements relating to fissionable materials; to the traffic in arms, ammunition and implements of war and traffic in goods and materials for the purpose of supplying a military establishment; or in time of war or other emergency in international relations, to the protection of the essential security interests of a member (Article 49:2, US Draft; Article 59(2), London Draft; Article 59(c), New York Draft). At Geneva it was decided to take paragraphs (c), (d), (e) and (k) of Article 37 and place them in a separate Article.[65] It was agreed that this Article would be a general exception applicable to the entire Charter.[66] The corresponding security exception was also removed from the commodity chapter. The security exception provisions became Article 94 in Chapter VII of the Geneva draft Charter, which was virtually identical to the present text of Article XXI.

The text of Article 94 was extensively discussed at Havana in the Sixth Committee on Organization. Article 94 became Article 99 of the Charter on General Exceptions, of which paragraphs 1(a) and (b) were almost identical to those of Article XXI, the only differences being (i) an addition in the first line of paragraph (b) as follows: "to prevent any Member from taking, *either singly or with other States*, any action ...", and (ii) an addition to paragraph (b)(ii) as follows: "a military establishment *of any other country*". Article 99 also

---

[60]L/6053 (unadopted), dated 13 October 1986, paras. 5.4-5.11.
[61]C/M/204, p. 9.
[62]C/M/204, p. 17. See also communication from Nicaragua at C/W/506.
[63]L/6053, unadopted, dated 13 October 1986, para. 5.2.
[64]SR.47/3, p. 5.
[65]See proposal at EPCT/W/23, reports on discussions in Commission A (commercial policy) at EPCT/WP.1/SR/11, EPCT/103 p. 43, EPCT/A/PV/25 p. 38-42.
[66]EPCT/A/PV/25 p.39-42.

included a paragraph 1(c) exempting intergovernmental military supply agreements[67]; a paragraph 1(d) on trade relations between India and Pakistan (dealt with in the General Agreement by the provisions of Article XXIV:11); and a paragraph 2 providing that nothing in the Charter would override the provisions of peace treaties resulting from the Second World War or UN instruments creating trust territories or other special regimes.

However, "on examining several of the proposals submitted by delegations relating to action taken in connection with political matters or with the essential interests of Members, the Committee concluded that the provisions regarding such action should be made in connection with an article on 'Relations with the United Nations', since the question of the proper allocation of responsibility as between the Organization and the United Nations was involved".[68] Accordingly a new Article 86 of the Charter on "Relations with the United Nations" was drafted, including the former paragraph 1(c) of Article 94 [XXI:(c)].

Article 86 of the Charter dealt with various institutional questions such as the conclusion of a specialized agency agreement between the ITO and the UN. It also stated, in paragraphs 3 and 4, that:

"3. The Members recognize that the Organization should not attempt to take action which would involve passing judgement in any way on essentially political matters. Accordingly, and in order to avoid conflict of responsibility between the United Nations and the Organization with respect to such matters, any measure taken by a Member directly in connection with a political matter brought before the United Nations in accordance with the provisions of Chapters IV or VI of the United Nations Charter shall be deemed to fall within the scope of the United Nations, and shall not be subject to the provisions of this Charter.

"4. No action, taken by a Member in pursuance of its obligations under the United Nations Charter for the maintenance or restoration of international peace and security, shall be deemed to conflict with the provisions of this Charter".

The interpretative notes to paragraph 3 provided that:

"1. If any Member raises the question whether a measure is in fact taken directly in connection with a political matter brought before the United Nations in accordance with the provisions of Chapters IV or VI of the United Nations Charter, the responsibility for making a determination on the question shall rest with the Organization. If, however, political issues beyond the competence of the Organization are involved in making such a determination, the question shall be deemed to fall within the scope of the United Nations.

"2. If a Member which has no direct political concern in a matter brought before the United Nations considers that a measure taken directly in connection therewith and falling within the scope of paragraph 3 of Article 86 constitutes a nullification or impairment within the terms of paragraph 1 of Article 93, it shall seek redress only by recourse to the procedures set forth in Chapter VIII of this Charter".

The purpose of these provisions was explained by the Sixth Committee as follows:

"Paragraph 3 of Article [86], which like paragraph 4 is independent in its operation, is designed to deal with any measure which is directly in connection with a political matter brought before the United Nations in a manner which will avoid conflict of responsibility between the United Nations and the Organization with respect to political matters. The Committee agreed that this provision would cover measures maintained by a Member even though another Member had brought the particular matter before the United Nations, so long as the measure was taken directly in connection with the matter. It was also agreed that such a measure, as well as the political matter with which it was directly connected, should remain within the jurisdiction of the United Nations and not within that of the Organization. The Committee was of the opinion that the important thing was to maintain the jurisdiction of the United Nations over political matters and over economic measures of this sort taken directly in connection with such a political matter, and nothing in Article [86] could be held to prejudice the freedom of action of the United Nations to settle such

---

[67] See Havana Reports, p. 118, para. 32 and p. 145-147.
[68] Havana Reports, p. 153, para. (a).

matters and to take steps to deal with such economic measures in accordance with the provisions of the Charter of the United Nations if they see fit to do so.

"It was the view of the Committee that the word 'measure' in paragraph 3 of Article [86] refers only to a measure which is taken directly in connection with a political matter brought before the United Nations in accordance with Chapters IV and VI of the Charter of the United Nations and does not refer to any other measure".[69]

The Charter provisions in Articles 86 and 99 were not taken into the General Agreement. While Article XXIX:1 provides that "The contracting parties undertake to observe ... the general principles of Chapters I to VI inclusive and of Chapter IX of the Havana Charter", the Note *Ad* Article XXIX:1 provides that "Chapters VII and VIII ... have been excluded from paragraph 1 because they generally deal with the organization, functions and procedures of the International Trade Organization". In this connection, during the discussion at the Sixth Session of the CONTRACTING PARTIES of the US suspension of trade relations with Czechoslovakia it was stated with reference to Article 86, paragraph 3 of the Havana Charter that "although Chapter VII of the Charter was not specifically included by reference in Article XXIX of the Agreement, it had surely been the general intention that the principles of the Charter should be guiding ones for the CONTRACTING PARTIES".[70]

The present text of Article XXI dates from the 30 October 1948 Geneva Final Act. It has never been amended. Amendment of Article XXI was neither proposed nor discussed in the 1954-55 Review Session.

IV. RELEVANT DOCUMENTS

Geneva

Discussion:	EPCT/WP.1/SR/11
	EPCT/A/SR/25, 30, 33, 40(2)
	EPCT/A/PV/25, 30, 33, 40(2)
Reports:	EPCT/103
Other:	EPCT/W/23

See also London, New York and Geneva document references concerning Article XX.

Havana

Discussion:	E/CONF.2/C.5/SR.14
	E/CONF.2/C.6/SR.18, 19, 37
	and Add.1
Reports:	E/CONF.2/C.5/14
	E/CONF.2/C.6/45, 93, 104
Other:	E/CONF.2/C.6/12/Add.9
	E/CONF.2/C.6/W/48

---

[69]Havana Reports, p. 153-154, paras. (b)-(c).
[70]GATT/CP.6/SR.12, p. 4.

INDEX

The following index covers the body text of this book but not the Appendix tables or the text of they General Agreement itself. References to individual contracting parties have not been indexed except for disputes or material relating to legal determinations regarding application of the General Agreement.

Disputes have been indexed under the name of the contracting party to whose measures the dispute relates, except for the Uruguayan Recourse to Article XXIII, which has been indexed under Uruguay. The headings for cases do not exactly correspond to the official titles used in the Basic Instruments and Selected Documents series and in this book, but have been chosen as a quick reference to the country, measure and product involved. For the purposes of this subject index only, "disputes" include claims brought under Article XXIII:2, disputes that resulted in panel reports, and consultations under Article XXII:2. Separate tables of invocations of Article XXIII, and consultations under Articles XXII:1 and XXII:2 appear in the chapters on Article XXIII and XXII.

A

Acceptance of GATT 910-912, 916
    reservations on acceptance 910-912
    territorial scope 917, 918
Accession 1017-1027
    and participation in regional trade agreements 843
    by governments of non-self-governing territories 1017
    examination of legislation 517
    procedures 1018-1020
    provisional accession 1024
    relation to non-application of GATT 1037
    terms in accession protocols 1021
    voting on 1018, 1098
Accession protocols
    interpretation in dispute settlement 730
    standard provisions 48, 909, 913, 1021-1023, 1074
    withdrawal of provisional application 1012
Accession protocols, special provisions in 411
    application of MFN clause 48-49
        Argentina 48, Costa Rica 1023, Egypt 48, 1023, Germany 48, Hungary 48, 413, 530-531, 621, 1023, Japan 49, Philippines 1023, Poland 413, 478, 530, 621, 1023, Portugal 49, Romania 413, 479, 530, 621, 1023, Spain 49, Switzerland 1023, Thailand 1023, Uruguay 49; *see also under* names of particular contracting parties
Administration of trade measures: non-discriminatory administration 297, reasonableness 297, uniformity 297
Administrative guidance 315, 316, 339
Advertising material, importation of 280
Agreement on ASEAN Preferential Trading Arrangements 52, 57
Agreement on Government Procurement 46, 115, 191, 194, 480, 715, 752, 881, 918
Agreement on Implementation of Article VI 46, 228-230, 232, 233, 237, 238, 242, 243, 246, 248, 249, 252, 254, 714-716, 752, 918, 1066
    and dispute settlement 716
    coexistence with WTO Agreement 253-255
Agreement on Implementation of Article VII 238, 246, 263-265, 714, 748, 752, 915, 918
Agreement on Import Licensing Procedures 280, 349, 351, 407, 414, 714, 716, 918
Agreement on Interpretation and Application of Articles VI, XVI and XXIII 224, 228, 232, 237, 238, 242, 246, 249, 251-253, 452, 455, 456, 458-462, 464, 666, 698, 715, 716, 918
    and dispute settlement under Article XXIII 464, 698, 715, 716
    coexistence with WTO Agreement 253-255
Agreement on Technical Barriers to Trade 281, 291, 714, 715, 748, 752, 918
Agreement on the Importation of Educational, Scientific and Cultural Materials (Florence Agreement) 281
Agreement on the Organization for Trade Cooperation 758, 769, 1027, 1086, 1130-1131, 1133
Agreement on Trade in Civil Aircraft 115, 349, 714, 915
Agricultural product, definition 331
Agricultural trade, barriers to exports from developing countries 1040
ALADI 56
Amendments 7, 713, 1003-1009
    amendment protocols 1004
    amendments to Schedules of concessions 1005
    declarations on acceptance of amendment protocols 1040, 1068
    majority required for entry into effect 1004
    procedure for submission of amendments for acceptance 1003
    relationship between GATT and Tokyo Round agreements 713, 1008
    reservations on acceptance of 1007
    summary history 7, 1002
    to Article XXIV 843
Annecy Round 41, documents 18
Annexes to the General Agreement, legal status of 1029
Antarctica 919
Anti-dumping duties, *see also* Anti-dumping and countervailing duties, Anti-dumping and counter-vailing duty proceedings, Countervailing duties, Dumping, Injury
Anti-dumping 222-239, 247-252, 255
    basic price systems 231-233
    monitoring schemes 233
    Recommendation concerning "best information available" 253
    Recommendation on procedures for on-the-spot investigations 253
    Recommendation on time-limits for questionnaires 253
    Recommendation on transparency of anti-dumping procedures 253
    special problems of developing countries 229, 1066
    use of measures other than anti-dumping duties to offset dumping 237, 238
Anti-dumping - price comparisons 223-231, 240-241
    adjustments for differences affecting price comparability 230
    allowance for export tax rebates and duty drawback 240

burden of proof in establishing existence of dumping 231
constructed value 226-227
custom-built products 227
export price 223
hierarchy of criteria for determining normal value 225
like product determination 227-228
normal value in state-controlled economy countries 228
related parties (exporter's sales price) 224
transshipment of goods 224
use of average normal values 225-226
use of best information available 227

Anti-dumping and countervailing duties
consultations concerning 621
duration of validity 237
imposition in addition to bound duties, under Art. II 85-86, 231, 250
imposition on basis of injury to industry in third country 248
like product 227-228
most-favoured-nation treatment 46
retroactive effect 237

Anti-dumping and countervailing duty proceedings 231-237
and most-favoured-nation treatment 249-250
and price stabilization systems for primary commodities 248
application with respect to tenders 230, 242
collections of legislation 252
definition of material injury 241
determination of material injury 241
determination of material injury, definition of industry 245-247
determination of threat of material injury 242-243
initiation of investigations 233-236
material injury, causation of 244
narrow interpretation of Article VI as an exception 249-250
provisional measures 236

Appellations of origin 290, 583
Arab League
Arab League Convention preferences, authorization for, under Art. I:3 44
boycott of trade with Israel 602

Arbitration 768
determination of extent of nullification or impairment 700
rights concerning particular concessions 67, 811-812, 944, 947-949, 951, 955, 957-958

Argentina, trade sanctions against, by EEC, Canada and Australia 600-601, 603, 605-606
Arrangement Concerning Certain Dairy Products 619, 880
Arrangement Regarding Bovine Meat 591
Arrangement Regarding International Trade in Textiles 349, 531, 535, 717; *see also under* Multi-Fiber Arrangement
Article I, *see* Most-favoured-nation treatment, Preferences
Article II, *see* Concessions, Schedules, Duties and charges other than tariffs
Article III, *see* National treatment, taxes, regulation, mixing regulations
Article IV, *see* Films
Article V, *see* Transit
Article VI, *see* Anti-dumping, Countervailing duties, Injury
Article VII, *see* Customs valuation
Article VIII, *see* Customs administration, Customs formalities, Customs facilitation
Article IX, *see* Marking of products
Article X, *see* Administration of trade measures, Notification requirements, Publication
Article XI, *see* Quantitative restrictions, Supply-management import quotas
Articles XII, XVIII:B, *see* Balance-of-payments consultations; Balance-of-payments measures; Balance-of-payments provisions
Article XIII, *see* Quantitative restrictions - administration
Article XIV, *see* Quantitative restrictions, discrimination in
Article XV, *see* Financial system, International Monetary Fund
Article XVI, *see* Subsidies
Article XVII, *see* State trading
Article XVIII:C, Article XVIII:D, *see* Economic development, safeguard action
Article XIX, *see* Safeguards action
Article XX, *see* General exceptions
Article XXI, *see* Security exceptions
Article XXII, *see* Consultations
Article XXIII, *see* Dispute settlement or Nullification or impairment
Article XXIV:1-2, *see* Territorial application of GATT, Customs territory
Article XXIV:3, *see* Frontier traffic
Article XXIV:5-10, *see* Customs unions and free-trade areas
Article XXIV:12, *see* Regional and local governments and authorities
Article XXV, *see* Organization of GATT, Competence of the CONTRACTING PARTIES, Waivers of obligations
Article XXVI, *see* Acceptance of GATT, Definitive application of GATT, Entry into force of GATT, Deposit, Registration
Article XXVI:5(c), *see* Succession
Article XXVII, *see* Concessions, withholding or withdrawal of
Article XXVIII, *see* Concessions - renegotiation
Article XXVIII*bis*, *see* Trade negotiations
Article XXIX, *see* Havana Charter
Article XXX, *see* Amendments
Article XXXI, *see* Withdrawal from GATT
Article XXXII, *see* Contracting parties
Article XXXIII, *see* Accession to GATT
Article XXXIV, *see* Annexes to the General Agreement
Article XXXV, *see* Non-application of the General Agreement
Articles XXXVI, XXXVII, XXXVIII, *see* Trade and development, Part IV
ASEAN 52
ASEAN Common Effective Preferential Tariff Scheme (CEPT) 57
ATA Carnet for the Temporary Admission of Goods 281
Australia, acceptance of Part IV Protocol 1068
change in base date for margins of preference 43
territorial application of GATT 917, 1083
Australia, disputes brought against
countervailing duties on glacé cherries 744
subsidy on ammonium sulphate 36, 657-658, 664, 681
Authentic texts 913-915

B

Bahamas, de facto application of GATT 119
Balance-of-payments consultations 378-391, 504-508
conclusions and recommendations of Committee 391
consideration of external factors affecting balance of payments 367, 374, 389-390
consultation timing and references (table) 383, 395, 505
Council consideration of Committee reports 392
documentation for consultations 385-387
expanded consultations 389
IMF role in, *see also under* International Monetary

Fund 367, 385-388, 431
  matters discussed in 388-90
  obligation to consult 372, 383
  prior consultations on trade barriers and balance of payments 390, 507
  procedure if inconsistency with Article XII found 373
  procedures, general 361, 378-379, 496
  scope of; application to non-quantitative measures 379, 507
  secrecy of 387
  simplified consultation procedures 383-385, 504-506; relationship to full consultations 385
Balance-of-payments measures 501-508
  adjustment obligations 368
  administration of 369-371; *see also* Quantitative restrictions, administration of
  administration through State trading or government monopoly 485
  application of 502, 503
  by European Economic Community 361, 800, 836
  conditions for use, under Article XII 362, 367, under Article XVIII:B 501
  dispute settlement and 702-703
  in customs unions or free-trade areas 836-837
  measures other than quantitative restrictions - import deposits 364-365, 432-433
  measures other than quantitative restrictions - import surcharge 79, 363-366, 433, 508, 1046
  most-favoured-nation treatment and 29
  notification of introduction or intensification 302, 380-381, 504
  quantitative restrictions 366
  review conducted under Article XII:4(b) 373
  review conducted under Article XVIII:12(b) 507
  special review provisions, and relation to Article XXIII 508
  use of, to protect infant industries 511
Balance-of-payments measures, discrimination in 418-424
  1959 IMF Decision on elimination of discrimination 419
  equivalent in effect to discrimination permitted by IMF 420
  exception for measures under IMF "scarce currency" clause 422
  exception for territories with common quota in the Fund 421
  temporary, with consent of CONTRACTING PARTIES 421
Balance-of-payments provisions
  countries invoking Articles XII or XVIII (table) 395
  disinvocation of Article XII 368
  disinvocations of Articles XII or XVIII since 1979 (table) 395
  relationship between Articles XII and XVIII:B 378, 498, 501-502, 505, 507
  Review Session proposals on "scarce currency" 375
  Review Session revisions 361, 375, 418, 496
Bangkok Agreement 51, 56
Bangladesh, accession of 1025
Barcelona Convention and Statute on Freedom of Transit of 20 April 1921 214
Basic Instruments and Selected Documents (BISD) 8, 19
Basic price systems (see also Anti-dumping) 231-233
Belgium, disputes brought against
  discriminatory restrictions on dollar-area imports 689, 702
  income tax practices 459-462, 762, 1074
  levy on goods from countries without family allowance laws 31, 33, 47, 191, 197, 199, 201, 475-476, 480, 1076
Belgium, territorial application of GATT 917, 1083
Books, newspapers and periodicals, facilitation of trade in 281
BOP, *see* Balance-of-payments
Border enforcement of regulations 136-139, 201
  relationship between Article III and Article XI 201-204
Border tax adjustments 86, 136-139, 144-148
  and anti-dumping or countervailing duty proceedings 240
  and customs valuation 262
  destination principle 145, 448
  forward shifting of internal taxes 1044
  most-favoured-nation treatment and 31, 197
  multilateral consultations on 620
  notification of tax adjustment legislation 146, 302
  rebates of duties and taxes borne by the like product 241
  relation between rules on imports and rules on exports 448
  taxes eligible for adjustment 144-145
  treatment of exports of developing countries 1044, 1065
Border tax adjustments, *see also* Taxes
Brazil, disputes brought against
  countervailing duties on milk powder from the EEC 738
  internal tax discrimination 127, 128, 167, 204, 721, 1075, 1080
Brussels Tariff Nomenclature 112
Budget and financial operations of GATT 1088, 1114, 1122-1127
  application of UN financial and staff rules 1122
  arrears in payment 1127
  budget of ICITO 1122
  decisions on budget 1125
  scale of contributions to budget 1126
  Working Capital Fund 1127

C

Cambodia, change in base date for margins of preference 43, de facto application of GATT 119, GATT status of 1025
Canada, accession of Newfoundland 918
Canada, disputes brought against
  application of "value for duty" law to potato imports 86, 260, 747, 761
  countervailing duties on grain corn from US 244
  export restrictions on unprocessed herring and salmon 327, 583-587
  discriminatory provincial sales tax on gold coins 141, 152, 155, 199, 573, 728, 830-831, 833-834
  Foreign Investment Review Act 32, 124, 165, 167-168, 173-174, 189, 201, 475-477, 563, 575, 617, 643, 651, 657, 674, 704, 734, 750, 751, 758, 878, 997
  import quotas on eggs and egg products 341, 721
  import quotas on ice cream and yoghurt 329-331, 333, 336, 338, 342, 346, 750
  provincial liquor boards (1988) 88-89, 93, 178, 322, 476, 483-484, 691, 694, 726, 757, 831, 834, 836, 1077
  provincial liquor boards (1992) 94, 130, 132, 150, 152, 167-169, 177, 178, 181, 202. 322, 483, 694, 700, 726, 749, 757, 832, 834-836, 1079
  withdrawal of concessions on lead and zinc 71, 456, 740, 944-945, 948-949, 952
Cartagena Agreement (Andean Group) of 1988 57

CD-ROM publications 19
Certifications of changes to Schedules 112-115
Chairman's rulings 1097
Chernobyl nuclear accident, trade restrictions 571
"Chicken war" arbitration (1963) 944, 948
Chile, consultations with
    internal taxes on whisky and pisco 759
Chinese Taipei 437, 877, 1017, 1095
    observer status 1104
Cholera, trade restrictions 572
Citation style for footnotes 3
Code of Standard Practices for Documentary Requirements for the Importation of Goods 279
Committee of Participating Countries 51
Committee on Anti-Dumping Practices 229, 233, 242, 246, 253, 715-716, 1066
Committee on Balance-of-Payments Restrictions 378-392, 505, 1113-1114
    conclusions and recommendations of 391
    Council consideration of Committee reports 392
    election of Chairman 1113
    membership 379, role 390, terms of reference and activities 378, 1114
Committee on Budget, Finance and Administration 1113, 1125
    election of Chairman 1113
    establishment and terms of reference 1125
    membership 1114
Committee on Customs Valuation 259, 264, 714
Committee on Import Licensing 414
Committee on Subsidies and Countervailing Measures 240, 241, 246, 253, 445, 449, 451, 452, 458, 461, 725, 755, 757
Committee on Tariff Concessions 72, 96, 106-107, 110-111, 1113-1114
    election of Chairman 1113
    establishment and terms of reference 1114
Committee on Trade and Development 351, 1041-1050, 1064-1065, 1070, 1110-1111
    election of Chairman 1111
    mandate and activities 1045-1050, 1110
    reviews of the implementation of Part IV 1048
    Sub-Committee on Protective Measures 536, 1050, 1111
    Sub-Committee on Trade of Least-Developed Countries 1050, 1111
    work on amendment of GATT, 1965-66 508, 683, 764, 1046, 1065
Committee on Trade in Civil Aircraft 115
Commodity agreements
    and Part IV commitments 1055-1057, 1070; Article XX(h) exception for measures under 587-590;
    Havana Charter provisions on 587-590, 1057
    International Sugar Agreement 456
Commodity trade
    competence of the CONTRACTING PARTIES 878
    consultations on measures reducing developing country exports 499
    consultations on New Zealand marketing of butter in UK 877
    consultations on trade in dairy products 619
    consultations under Article XXII:2 618-619
    consultations under Article XXV:1 876-877
Compensation
    as alternative to removal of measure 676, 677, 686
    award of compensation for damage to trade 679, 680, 682, 683, 764
Competence of the CONTRACTING PARTIES
    commodity problems 878
    environmental issues and international trade 880
    government procurement 881
    investment 878
    liquidation of non-commercial stocks 879
    market disruption 879
    restrictive business practices 879
    services 881
    surplus disposal issues 879
    tax issues 880
Competition, conditions of
    national treatment 125, 156, 164, 169, 175, 177, 195
    non-violation nullification or impairment 666
Competitive opportunities, equality of 164-168
Competition policy, *see* Import monopoly, restrictive business practices, state trading
Competitive relationship, protection of
    national treatment 125, 128, 133, 140, 160, 161, 167, 202
    non-violation nullification or impairment 657, 658
Concessions 67-85, 88-93, 110-112; *see also* Schedules
    arbitration on scope 67
    by governments with monopoly of all import trade 73-74, 478-479
    change in tariff nomenclature 70, 112
    conditions or qualifications on 75-77
    conversion from specific to ad valorem duties 70-71
    dates applicable to 83-85
    description of, in schedules 110
    drafting history 73, 75, 77, 88
    export duties and taxes 73
    impairment by change in valuation or currency conversion rules 87
    import monopoly operation 88-90
    modification or withdrawal of 71
    modification, actions constituting 69-72
    non-tariff measure 74
    on subsidies 74, 463
    on supply-management import quotas under Article XI:2(c) 328
    operations of State trading enterprises 481, 486
    scope 67-68
    screen quotas 210
    tariff quotas 75
    tariff reclassification 72
    withholding or withdrawal of 115, 927-929, notification of 301, list of cases 929
Concessions - renegotiation 937-964
    and trade in new products 943
    arbitration concerning concession value or renegotiation rights 767, 944, 947-949, 951, 955, 957-958
    Article II waivers pending completion of schedule renegotiation 949
    as resolution of non-violation nullification or impairment 664, 712
    by developing countries, under Article XVIII:A 500, 957
    compensatory withdrawals of concessions 947-952
    conversion from specific to ad valorem duty rates 70-71, 944-945, 948-949, 954
    dispute settlement concerning 712
    drafting history 117, 810, 937-938, 940, 943, 947, 953, 963-964
    Harmonized System 106-110, 939-941, 949, 953, 961-962
    in context of Article XXIV:6 810-814, 842-843, 943-944, 948, 950-952, 957-959, 961, 963
    initial negotiating rights 938-940, 943, 947-950, 959,

963
    institution of a tariff quota 946
    non-tariff concessions 943
    principal supplying interest 937, 939-945, 956, 960, 964
    procedure 107, 810, 941-942, 955, 959-962
    renegotiation after an increase in value 945-946
    renegotiation in "special circumstances" under Article XXVIII:4 953-955
    reservation under Article XXVIII:5 of right to modify schedule 955-956
    submission of claims of interest 941, 962
    substantial supplying interest 930, 939-942, 944, 945, 947, 956, 959-960, 963
    sympathetic consideration procedure 953, 963-964
    time-limits for invocation of Article XXVIII:3 950-952
    timetable 938
Concessions, value of 943-949
Conciliation 766-767
Confidentiality of information
    balance-of-payments consultations 387
    balance-of-payments documentation submitted by IMF 388, 433
    exception to transparency requirements 297
    protection of confidential information in dispute settlement 752
Confidentiality of proceedings
    balance-of-payments consultations 387, 497
    renegotiations under Article XXVIII 956
Consensus 761, 1024, 1087, 1097-1099, 1108-1109
Consular fees 276, 284
Consultations 612-622
    Article XXII:1 consultations as basis for panel request 617, 673
    Article XXIII:1 consultations as basis for panel request 674
    Article XXXVII consultations as basis for panel request 674, 1065
    border tax adjustments 620
    claim of substantial trade interest 612, 613
    consultations under other provisions as basis for panel request 700
    definition of "measures", *see* Measures of a contracting party
    GATT provisions requiring 619
    implementation of Part IV 1065
    liquidation of strategic stocks 620
    measures reducing developing country commodity exports 499
    negotiating history of provisions on 621
    notification of requests for consultations under Article XXII:1 304, 616, 671
    Procedures under Article XXII 612-613, 706-707
    provided for under Protocols of Accession 621
    residual import restrictions 614
    restrictive business practices 621, 879
    sanitary laws and regulations 571
    scope of consultations under Article XXII 615-616
    under Article XXII:2 (table) 619
    under Article XXV:1 876, 877
    under Article XXXVII:2 1061, 1065
    Understanding Regarding Notification, Consultation, Dispute Settlement and Surveillance (1979) 614
Consultative Group of Eighteen (CG-18) 380, 385, 430, 432, 434, 1115, 1132
    establishment and terms of reference 1115
Contracting parties
    definition of 1013

CONTRACTING PARTIES 1094-1099, 1116-1117
    Chairman's powers at sessions 1096
    Chairman's rulings 1097
    decision-making 1097, 1098, on adoption of dispute settlement panel reports 761
    decisions by 1128
    election of officers 1095
    list of sessions, dates, documents issued 12-14
    meetings at Ministerial level 1096
    postal and telegraphic voting 1098
    regular sessions 1095
    relationship to bodies established under Tokyo Round Agreements 1099
    Rules of procedure 1094
    special sessions 1096
Convention on Privileges and Immunities of the Specialized Agencies 1130
Costa Rica
    accession protocol, phaseout of quantitative restrictions 349, 1023, phaseout of import surcharges, 1023
Cotton Textiles Committee 717
Council of Representatives 1100-1111
    agenda items, "other business" 1107
    agenda items, customs unions and free-trade areas 1106
    agenda items, dispute settlement 1106-1107
    agenda items, Trade Policy Review Mechanism 1106, Overview of Developments in the International Trading Environment 301
    convening of 1105
    decisionmaking, voting, consensus 1108
    discussions before adoption of agenda 1108
    establishment, functions, relationship with CONTRACTING PARTIES 1100-1101
    membership 1101
    observer status 1102-1104
    officers and subsidiary bodies 1104
    rules of procedure 1105
    ten-day rule for agenda 1100, 1105
    working parties 1111-1113
Counterfeit goods 582
Countertrade
    special tariff treatment granted for 34
Countervailing duties
    relationship between subsidy rules and countervailing duty rules 251
    use of measures other than, to offset subsidization 237, 238
    see also Anti-dumping and countervailing duties, Anti-dumping and countervailing duty proceedings, Injury, Subsidies
Critical circumstances
    and notice and consultation requirement for safeguards actions 524
Cuba, disputes brought against
    import restrictions on textiles 657
Cultural materials, see Agreement on the Importation of Educational, Scientific and Cultural Materials
Currency
    convertibility, as eliminating justification for discriminatory BOP measures 419
    devaluation and revaluation, and changes in bound specific duties 87
    see also under Financial system
Customs administration
    bonding requirements, interest charges and costs 87, 270-271
    penalty charges 282
    user fees for customs services 28, 31-32, 55, 87,

269-271, 273-274, 276, 284, 801, 821
Customs Convention on the ATA Carnet for the Temporary Admission of Goods 281
Customs Convention on the Temporary Importation of Packings 280
Customs Convention on the Temporary Importation of Professional Equipment 280
Customs Co-operation Council 97, 106, 264, 279, 280, 332; CCCN nomenclature 331
Customs facilitation
    importation of educational, scientific and cultural materials 281
    reduction of trade barriers to insecticides 281
Customs formalities
    administration of quantitative restrictions, exchange controls 280
    ATA Carnet for the temporary admission of goods 281
    balance-of-payments measures 281
    consular formalities 280, 284
    documentary requirements for the importation of goods 279
    import licensing 405
    importation of samples and advertising material 280
    pre-shipment inspection 281, 583
    quota administration 404
    rules of origin and certificates of origin 278
    temporary importation of packings 280
    temporary importation of professional equipment 281
Customs territory 794, 799, 917-918
    and membership in International Monetary Fund 422
    and sovereignty 422
    application of Articles XIII and XIV 422
    relationship to discriminatory BOP measures 422
Customs unions
    renegotiation of concessions under Article XXIV:6 810-814, 842-843, 943-944, 948, 950-952, 957-959, 961, 963
Customs unions, free-trade areas and interim agreements 796, 798-812, 814, 815, 817, 819-825, 827-829, 836-847
    action by CONTRACTING PARTIES under Article XXIV:7 816-819
    and historical preferences 42
    and negotiations on accession to GATT 843
    and Part IV 799, 800, 809, 826, 827, 843, 844
    application of Article XX exceptions 596, 823
    calculation of incidence of duties 800, 803-807
    communication of change in interim agreement plan and schedule 304
    definition of "substantially all the trade" 824-826
    dispute settlement concerning 706-708
    drafting history 798, 803, 805, 806, 808, 810, 816, 829, 845-847
    duties and charges other than tariffs 820, 821
    examination of agreements under Article XXIV 815, 841
    exclusion of agricultural sector 825, 826
    inclusion of non-contracting parties 798, 799, 829, 847
    involving State-controlled economy countries 821, 822
    non-reciprocal free-trade areas 799
    notification 304, 814, 816
    observer status in GATT 1102
    participation 798-799
    quantitative restrictions 645, 800-801, 822-823, 836-840
    relationship between paras. 4 and 5-9 of Article XXIV 796-798
    requirement for a "plan and schedule" 807, 808
    requirement not to increase protection 803-807
    reverse preferences, one-way free-trade areas 799, 800, 826, 843, 844
    rules of origin 802, 803, 827
    safeguards action by members 838-840
    transitional period for interim agreements 808-810
    treatment of "other regulations of commerce" 801, 820-823
Customs valuation 259-266
    actual value versus arbitrary or fictitious values 260
    Agreement on Implementation of Article VII 263-265
    change in rules as impairment of concession 87
    conversion rates of exchange 262
    methods of valuation 259
    most-favoured-nation treatment 30
    software 265
    stability and transparency of rules 263
    treatment of interest charges 265
    use of fixed values 261
Czech and Slovak Republic, restoration of GATT relations with United States 1037
Czech Republic
    accession to GATT 1026, 1027
    interim application of GATT to 1027
Czechoslovakia, reduction of bound specific duties and 1953 revaluation 87, suspension of obligations reciprocally with United States 1037

D

Date of this Agreement 909-910
    Article XXVI 909
    for currency conversion in customs valuation under Art. VII:4(b) 263
    for existing administrative review procedures under Art. X:3(c) 298
    for existing direct consignment requirements under Art. V:6 216
    for "other duties and charges" on bound items under Art. II:1(b) 83-85
    reference date for bound specific duties, under Art. II:6 83
De facto application of the General Agreement 921-923; de facto contracting parties' access to GATT dispute settlement 644
Debt, external
    and balance-of-payments consultations 389, 432
Decision on "Safeguard Action for Development Purposes" 498, 501, 509, 511
Decisions of the CONTRACTING PARTIES
    interpretation in dispute settlement 730
Declaration Giving Effect to the Provisions of Article XVI:4 457, list of contracting parties for which Declaration is in force 457, reservation on acceptance 457, 461
Declaration on Trade Measures taken for Balance-of-Payments Purposes (1979) 79, 362, 366, 371, 376, 378-381, 385-387, 389-391, 436, 496, 502, 504-508, 1063
Definitive application of GATT 6, 910-912, 916-917
Deposit of GATT instruments 916
Deposit/refund schemes 150
Deputy Directors-General, appointment of 1129
Developing countries
    status as developing country under Part IV 1041
    status as country qualifying under Article XVIII:4 378, 497-498
Development, *see* Economic development

Development measures 124
Dillon Round 41, documents 18
Diplomatic gifts and baggage, reciprocity in treatment 35
Direct consignment requirements, for preferential duty rates 75, 216, direct shipping requirements 75
Directly competitive or substitutable product 159-161
    drafting history of provisions on 206
Director-General 1128, 1129
    annual report to Council on issues affecting the trading system 301
    appointment 1129
    appointment of 1096, 1128
Discretionary legislation 134, 645, 733
    as prohibition or restriction under Article XI:1 315
    examination of safeguards legislation 517
    under Protocol of Provisional Application 1075-1080
Disequilibrium, general (Article XII:5) 375
Dispute settlement
    and anti-dumping or countervailing duty actions 700, 702
    arbitration 768
    Article XXIV:6 negotiations 707, 811, 841, 944, 948, 957-958
    balance-of-payments measures 702, 703
    complaints not actively pursued 675
    concerning measures implementing WTO Agreement 713
    drafting history 654, 668, 673, 700, 705, 768, 769
    exchange controls or exchange restrictions 704
    good offices, conciliation, mediation 766, 767
    issues dealt with by Council of Representatives 1106-1107
    macroeconomic imbalance 668, 669, 689
    measures to implement customs union or free-trade area 706-708, 840-842
    measures under textile arrangements 717, 718
    non-violation nullification or impairment 657-671
    nullification or impairment resulting from "any other situation" 668-671
    prima facie nullification or impairment 655-657
    referrals of disputes under other agreements 718
    relationship between "violation" and "non-violation" claims 667
    renegotiation of concessions under Article XXVIII 712, 941-942, 944-945, 957, 959
    safeguard actions 704
    trade restrictions applied for non-economic reasons 705, 706
    waivers of obligations 709-712
Dispute settlement - consultations
    consultation requests by more than one contracting party 671
    duty to consult 671-673
    notification of consultations 671
    prerequisite for referral under Article XXIII:2 672
    refusal to consult 672, 673
Dispute settlement - countermeasures
    authorization of countermeasures 692-700
    authorization of trade retaliation under Tokyo Round Agreements 698, 716
    countermeasures under general international law, and GATT 718
    decisions on authorization of suspension of concessions 695-700
    determination of extent of suspension of concessions 696-700, 949, 955
    determination that circumstances are "serious enough" 690-692
    non-MFN basis of suspension of concessions under Article XXIII:2 696
    proposals for suspension of concessions 692-700
Dispute settlement - decisions
    1966 Procedures 634, 638, 641-642, 674, 712, 728, 746, 763-766
    1979 Understanding 632-637, 641, 643, 649, 655-656, 661, 667, 672, 673, 675-677, 682, 685-688, 692, 711, 714, 716, 721-724, 727, 730, 735, 745-748, 752, 755, 758, 759, 763, 764, 766, 767, 958
    1982 Decision 636, 637, 643, 653, 676, 677, 685-688, 696, 724, 727, 746-748, 759, 761, 766, 767
    1984 Decision 637, 643, 724, 725, 732, 746
    1989 Improvements 638-643, 671, 673, 675, 685, 687, 688, 723-725, 727-730, 745-748, 752, 759, 760, 761, 763-768
Dispute settlement - implementation of results
    compensation as alternative to removal of measure 676, 686
    examination of implementation in subsequent dispute 834-835
    multilateral surveillance 686-689
    obligation to implement on MFN basis 685
    reasonable period of time for implementation 684, 685
    reconvening of panel to review implementation 684, 687-689, 692, 726
Dispute settlement - panel procedure
    applicability to disputes under Tokyo Round Agreements 714, 715
    Article XXII:1 consultations as basis for panel request 673, 674
    Article XXXVII consultations as basis for panel request 674, 1065
    change in panel membership 725
    change in subject matter of a proceeding 738-740
    choice between use of panel or working party 721
    claims in the alternative 667
    claims not raised by applicant contracting party 740-742
    complaints by two or more contracting parties on same measures 728
    confidential information, protection of 752
    confidentiality and privacy of proceedings 747
    defences not raised by the respondent contracting party 742, 743
    disputes involving developing contracting parties 763-766
    estoppel 731
    expert information 748
    general 745
    panel establishment 721-723
    panel formation by Director-General 725
    panel membership 723-725
    participation by third parties 752-754
    preliminary objections 734-740
    prerequisite of consultations 672
    presumptions and burden of proof 749
    Procedures under Article XXIII for developing countries (1966) 1046, 1065
    reconvening of panel or working party 689, 726
    request for establishment of panel 675
    requirement to notify bilateral settlements of disputes 745
    right of panel to seek information 748
    role of Secretariat 748
    Roster of non-governmental panelists 724, 725
    special terms of reference 728
    standard terms of reference 727
    time deadlines for panels 746, 747

time deadlines in urgent cases 747
treatment of dispute if mutually agreed solution reached 743-745
Dispute settlement - panel reports
adoption of panel reports subject to conditions 762
blocking of adoption 761
consideration and action on 759-763
dissenting opinions 755
legal nature of panel reports 758
precedential effect 755-759
Dispute settlement - participation by third parties 753, 754
claims not raised by applicant contracting party 740-742
defences not raised by the respondent contracting party 742, 743
Dispute settlement - recommendations and rulings 675-687
function of panels 676
objective 676, 677
panel report in event of mutually agreed solution 744, 745
recommendation of waiver 677
recommendations in "non-violation" cases 680-684
recommendations regarding "violation" complaints 677
recommendations with respect to measures found GATT-inconsistent 677, 679, 680
role of recommendations and of rulings 675
specific remedies 678-680
where no finding of violation or of non-violation nullification 684
Dispute settlement - scope
acts of private parties (see also Private/public distinction) 650
balance-of-payments measures 508
benefits "under the General Agreement" 653
change in subject matter of proceeding 738-740
definition of "matter" 675
discretionary legislation 645
enforcement of Uruguay Round standstill commitments 654
exchange controls or restrictions under IMF Articles 440
interpretation of Decisions of CONTRACTING PARTIES 730
interpretation of other multilateral agreements 732
linkage of complaints 675
matters not within GATT competence 643
measures as applied versus measures as such 733, 734
measures no longer in effect 649, 744
measures not yet in effect 648
measures under general exceptions 595, 704
measures under security exceptions 606-607
regulation of foreign direct investment 643
requests for rulings 653
rights under bilateral agreements 719-721
scope of panel terms of reference 730, 732-742
waivers of obligations 887
Dispute settlement - subjects
de facto contracting parties 644
disputes brought for non-self-governing territories 644
entities no longer having status as contracting parties 644
Dispute Settlement Understanding 643
Documents 8-19
Basic Instruments and Selected Documents 8, 11-12
derestriction rules 1116-1118, issuance and circulation 1116
drafting history documents, list of series 9-11
GATT documents, list of active series 14-16
how to obtain copies 19

lists and indexes 18-19
past negotiating rounds 18
Session documents 12-14
Status of Legal Instruments 8
Domestically-prohibited goods, notification of export 302
Drafting Committee Report (New York Report) 5
Dumping: exchange 222, freight 222, service 222, social 222, 580
use of measures to offset, other than anti-dumping duties 237, 238, 348
Duties 78, 82-83; *see also* Schedules
definitional relevance of policy purpose 83
distinction between duties and internal taxes 82-83
ordinary customs duties 78
relationship to internal taxes or charges 127, 198-201
Duties and charges other than tariffs 78, 80-82, 85
application of MFN exceptions for historical preferences 43
charges on transfer of payments 81
consular fees 276, 284
fees for services rendered 87, 99, 269; activities includable in "services" 273; ad valorem structure, 274; drafting history of provisions 284; limitation to cost of services rendered 271, 284
import deposit schemes 80-81
import surcharges 79
most-favoured-nation treatment and 28
pre-shipment inspection charges 277
protective effect 277, 278
reference date for binding under Art. II:1(b) and (c) 83-85
revenue duties and import taxes, 81, in customs unions or free-trade areas 820-821
statistical taxes 277
tariff reclassification and 72
Duty drawback
and anti-dumping or countervailing duty proceedings 240
and free-trade areas 806
Duty remission 240, 806
conditional on mixing of imports with domestic products 187

E

EC, consultations with
export refunds on malted barley 765
sugar export regime (Article XXIII:1, 1982) 671
EC, disputes brought against
anti-circumvention ("screwdriver") regulation 39, 82-83, 127, 134-135, 137, 148, 174, 198, 200, 578, 580, 645-647, 715, 733, 743
apples from Chile (1980) 100, 332, 338, 341, 344-346, 400, 402-403, 408, 410, 532, 650, 678, 755, 1061
apples from Chile (1989) 399, 401-402, 404, 407, 409, 533, 650, 652, 654, 679, 680, 682, 729, 731, 743, 750, 756, 832, 1042, 1056, 1062
apples from Chile (1993-94) 744, 747
apples from US (1989) 652, 679, 729, 731, 756
application of tariff quota on newsprint 69, 100, 402, 409, 722, 945-946, 957-958
Argentina panel request on Art. XXVIII rights on soyabeans/cakes 712
arbitration on "chicken war" unbindings on poultry (1963) 811, 944, 948
Article XXIV:6 negotiations between Canada and EC (1974) 670, 707, 712, 722, 723, 811, 841, 957
Article XXVIII rights of Canada on ordinary and quality

wheat 720, 768, 811, 947. 951
Community import régime for bananas (1994) 69, 71, 101, 319, 325, 399, 407, 591, 649, 708, 725, 754, 799, 819, 827, 829, 1044, 1058
countervailing charges on lemons 747
discriminatory derogation to requirement to "spin-chill" poultry 649, 744
export refunds on malted barley 765
export refunds on sugar - complaint by Australia 450, 454, 456, 654, 722, 728, 740
export refunds on sugar - complaint by Brazil 450, 455, 456, 722, 725, 728, 740, 1044, 1070
export restrictions on copper scrap 743
export subsidies on pasta products 452, 461, 725, 755
export subsidies on wheat flour 451, 452, 457
import quotas on Hong Kong products 318, 732, 734, 742
member states' import régimes for bananas (1993) 330, 331, 344, 347, 708, 725, 738, 747, 753, 754, 765, 766, 799, 819, 827, 829, 1044
minimum import price scheme, licenses, deposits (tomato paste) 34, 80, 87, 270-271, 277, 319, 321, 332, 334, 338, 341, 364, 752, 755
operation of beef and veal regime 655
purchasing requirement for animal-feed proteins 36, 80, 139, 160, 162, 167, 171, 186, 189, 199, 201, 678
subsidies on canned fruit and raisins 658-659, 663-665, 741
subsidies to processors & producers of oilseeds (followup 1992) 170, 660, 683-684, 688-689, 695-696, 700, 712, 726, 953, 958
subsidies to processors and producers of oilseeds (1990) 170, 194, 202, 317, 449, 464, 659-661, 664-666, 668, 683, 716, 733, 813-814
tariff treatment of citrus imports from Mediterranean countries 660-663, 707-708, 721-722, 728, 734-735, 753, 766, 799, 819, 829, 841-842, 844
tariff quota concession on "high-quality" beef 31, 75
trade measures against Yugoslavia 604, 644, 673
EC, representation 1109
Economic and Social Council (ECOSOC) 3,4,280, 689
Economic development
Article XVIII, general orientation of 496
measures for "raising the general standard of living" 498
status as country qualifying under Article XVIII:4 497
Economic development, safeguard action 508, 510, 511
annual reviews of actions under Article XVIII:C and D 500
Article XVIII:D 499, 511
consultations on measures proposed under Article XVIII:C 510
dispute settlement and measures authorized under Article XVIII:C 704
notification of measures proposed under Article XVIII:C 303, 509
notification of measures proposed under Article XVIII:D 303
Releases under Article XVIII:C 508
Economies in transition
trade policy training courses 1051
Editorial conventions used in this book 2
Effective rate of protection 68; *see also* Tariff escalation
Egypt: accession protocol reservation for development tax 101, 1023; participation in Arab League preferences under Article I:3 44, 48
Electricity 585
Embargoes, see also Quantitative restrictions 320

Employment
and balance-of-payments measures 372
Havana Charter provisions 372, 668
Enabling Clause (Decision of 28 Nov. 1979) 53, 55-59, 1068
and Article XXIV 58, 843, 844
and Generalized System of Preferences 53, 55-56
and least-developed developing countries 45, 47, 53, 55
and waivers of obligations 888
preferential arrangements notified under 56
scope 32, 54
Entry into force of General Agreement 923
Environmental measures, *see also* references to United States, disputes brought against, Marine Mammal Act import restrictions on tuna, and Superfund taxes on petroleum and imported chemicals
Environmental measures
competence of the CONTRACTING PARTIES 880
deposit charge on containers 150
labelling 595
Polluter-Pays Principle 147
taxes 147
trade and environment 595
truck transit restrictions 572
Equitable share of world export trade (Article XVI:3)
consideration of "special factors" 456
definition 453-455
market share of developing countries 1056
reference period for examining shares 456
Estoppel 731
European Coal and Steel Community (ECSC) 882
European Economic Community
use of balance-of-payments measures by 361
European Unit of Account (EUA) 827-828
Exceptional circumstances, waivers of obligations in 885
Exceptions, arguments in the alternative 751
Exceptions, burden of proof regarding 750-751
Article VI 23, 750
Article XI:2(c) 329-330, 750, 753
Article XX 563, 578, 750-751
Article XXIV:12 831
exceptions not raised by respondent in dispute settlement 742-743, 833
existing legislation clause in PPA 751, 1083
Exceptions, general (Article XX), *see* General exceptions
Exceptions, narrow interpretation of 750-751
Article VI 46, 249-250, 750
Article XI:2(c) 330, 750, 753
Article XX 563, 578, 750-751
Article XXIV:12 831-833
Exceptions, security, *see* Security exceptions
Exchange controls, Code of Standard Practices for Administration (1950) 280
Exchange rates, *see* Financial system
Existing legislation 911, 1072-1083
border application of existing AD/CVD legislation 101, 1073
burden of proof regarding 751, 1083
internal taxes and regulations imposed on non-MFN basis 48, 204, 1073
mandatory character 1075-1078, 1080
modification of 1080, 1081
notification of 1082
Export credit programmes 446
Export duties and taxes, concessions on 73
discussions on, in GATT 353
Understanding on export restrictions and charges 352
Export inflation insurance schemes 460, 462

Export restrictions
    and customs unions or free-trade areas 823
    discussions on, in GATT 352
    exception for shortages of food or essential products 326
    export prohibition on merino sheep (Australia) 326
    for price stabilization, under Article XX(i) 592
    for protective purposes 325, 592
    grading or marketing of commodities in international trade 326
    inventories of 353
    minimum quality standards for exports 326
    national security 601-602, 606
    permitted by provisional application of GATT 1076
    to control domestic price 326
    Understanding regarding export restrictions and charges 352
Export subsidies, *see* Subsidies, export
Export taxes 592

F

Films, cinematograph 209-211
    drafting history of provisions 206, 210-211
    screen quota concessions 210
    taxes on 197
Final Act, agreements to vary texts attached to Final Act 1007
Financial regulations 1088
Financial system, and trade measures 362, 366-367, 375, 429-440
    adjustment of specific duties 430
    Article XXIII and IMF exchange controls or restrictions 440
    difference between exchange measures and trade measures 430, 435, 436, 439-441
    discrimination on currency grounds (Article XIV) 420-422
    drafting history of provisions 429-431, 436, 437, 439, 441
    enforcement of permissible exchange controls 438
    exchange measures frustrating intent of GATT 435, 438
    exchange rate fluctuations 430
    exchange rate guarantee schemes 460
    exchange restrictions 436
    export inflation insurance schemes 460
    general disequilibrium (Article XII:5) 375
    IMF Articles scarce currency provisions 375, 422
    IMF standby arrangements and GATT 432
    multiple currency practices 439, 240, 271, 420, 447
    taxes on transfer of payments 149
    trade measures enforcing permissible exchange controls 436
    trade measures equivalent to exchange rate changes 436
Fish, customs rules for determination of origin 33,
    fisheries disputes 718, whales as fisheries product 331
Fissionable materials, and security exceptions 602, 608
    applicability of dispute settlement 705
Florence Convention, see Agreement on the Importation of Educational, Scientific and Cultural Materials
Food and Agriculture Organization 4, (FAO) 566, 588, 591
Foot-and-mouth disease 571
France, consultations with
    trade measures of 1968 619, 670
France, disputes brought against
    compensation tax on imports 42, 79
    export subsidies on wheat and wheat flour 446, 452, 453, 456, 617, 674
    import restrictions 317-318, 677, 693, 698, 761
    income tax practices 459-462, 762, 1074
    statistical fees, stamp tax on customs duties 78, 275, 277,
France, schedules remaining in force 119
France, territorial application of GATT 917, 1083
Frontier traffic 795
    definition 796
    drafting history 795
    intra-German trade 796
    Italy and Vatican City, San Marino 47, 796
Functioning of the GATT System (Decision of 1989) 301

G

Gabon, status of Schedule XLVII 119
GATT 1947 1090, 1091, 1093
GATT 1994 1089-1090
GATT publications 19
General exceptions 563-596, 750-751
    and customs unions or free-trade areas 596, 823
    and dispute settlement 595, 704, 750-751
    arbitrary or unjustifiable discrimination 564
    disguised restriction on international trade 565
General exceptions - conservation 583-586
    conservation of extrajurisdictional natural resources 584-585
    definition of "exhaustible natural resources" 585
    examination of whether measures "relate to conservation" 583-585
    restrictions on domestic production or consumption 586-587
General exceptions - enforcement 573-583
    drafting history 580, 581, 583
    enforcement of state-trading monopolies 581-582
    limitation to enforcement of GATT-consistent laws or regulations 573, 580, 581
    measures "necessary to secure compliance" 574-578
    measures to "secure compliance" 578-580
    necessity and use of least trade restrictive measure 575, 578
    necessity and use of measure least inconsistent with GATT 575-577, 757
    patent rights 582
General exceptions - gold and silver 573
General exceptions - human/animal/plant life or health 565-572
    and suspension of transit 217
    drafting history 565, 566, 569-571
    guidelines for notice and consultation (Streamlined Mechanism) 572
    measures "necessary" under Article XX(b) 566-568, 570
    notification and consultation concerning measures 570-572, 621
    protection of extrajurisdictional life or health 569-570
    tax differentiation 566
General exceptions - measures under commodity agreements 587-591
    drafting history 587-589
General exceptions - price stabilization 591, 592
    drafting history 591
General exceptions - short supply 592-594
    drafting history 592-594
    equitable share of international supply 594
Generalized System of Preferences (GSP), 710, 820, 1063,

1067
  1971 Decision 32, 49, 55-56, 58
  under Enabling Clause 53, 55-56
Geneva Final Act (of Second Session, ITO Preparatory
  Committee, 1947) 5
Geneva Report (ITO Preparatory Committee Second Session
  Report) 5
Germany, disputes brought against
  import duties on starch and potato flour 658, 661
  import treatment of sardines 658, 664, 665, 681
Germany
  enlargement of, 1990 918
Germany, special arrangements for intra-German trade 48,
  796
Global System of Trade Preferences Among Developing
  Countries (GSTP) 57
Gold and silver 500, 573, 620, 728
  gold coins as "product" 155, 830, 833
  liquidation of strategic stocks of silver 500
Good offices 764-767
  under 1966 Procedures 764-766
Goods en route, treatment in import quotas 407; see also
  under back-dated quotas
Government procurement 479-481, 881
  Agreement on Government Procurement 191
  charges on goods procured 198-199
  competence of the CONTRACTING PARTIES 881
  definition of 190-193
  drafting history of provisions 190, 193, 479, 480, 485
  exception from MFN and national treatment 47, 190-193
  procurement by sub-national units of government 191, 830
Grading or marketing of commodities
  butter marketing scheme (Australia) 326
  exception from ban on quantitative restrictions, Article XI:2(b) 326
Graduation 58
Grapes, scuppernong (vitis rotundifolia) 157, 161
Greece, disputes brought against
  special import taxes 127, 149, 440
Grey-area measures, see Voluntary export restraints
Group of Three 1048
GSTP 57
Gulf Cooperation Council Unified Economic Agreement 57

H

Haberler Report 1039
Harmonized Commodity Description and Coding System, see Harmonized System
Harmonized System 38, 70, 72, 84, 106-110, 887, 939-941, 949, 953, 961-962
  decision on floating initial negotiating rights 939-940
  implementation in schedules of future changes in HS nomenclature 108-110
  procedures for conversion of schedules to HS nomenclature 106
  Protocols of tariff concessions 107
  status of schedules 108
Havana Charter 3-6, 9-11, 41, 44
  Article 31 (import monopolies) 90-93, text 91-92
  article on relations with the United Nations 609
  Chinese and Russian translations 913, 1121
  commodity agreement chapter 587-590, 1057
  consultation provisions, commercial policy chapter 621
  dispute settlement provisions 700, 769
  drafting history, general account of 3-6

failure to enter into force 998
final provisions 924
full employment provisions 372, 668, 669
general exceptions 608
negotiating documents, list 9-11
provisions on commodity agreements 997
provisions on privileges and immunities 1121, 1129
provisions on subsidies 465
provisions on tariff negotiations 994
relation to GATT Schedules of concessions 1027
relations with United Nations 877, 1120
relationship with General Agreement 589, 610, 996-999
Spanish-language text 913, 1121
supersession of Part II of General Agreement 997, 999
text 6
Havana Reports (Committee reports, Havana Conference) 6
Headquarters agreement with Switzerland 1088
  see also Privileges and Immunities 1130
Health measures, WHO proposals for facilitation of trade in insecticides 281
Historical preferences (see also preferences, historical) 40-43, 60
Hungary, accession protocol
  anti-dumping provisions 228
  consultation and dispute provisions 621
  provisions on quantitative restrictions 413
  provisions on safeguards 530-531
  reservation to Article XV:6 1023

I

Implementation Conference 1089
Import deposit schemes
  for balance-of-payments reasons 364-365, 432, 433
  as duties and charges other than tariffs under Art. II:1(b) 80-81, 364-365
Import licensing
  administration of 405
  Agreement on Import Licensing Procedures 351, 407, 414
  discretionary, as quantitative restriction 319
  notification of import licensing procedures 302
Import monopoly
  as quantitative restriction in itself 472
  differential mark-ups by 93-96
  effect of Havana Charter Article 31 90-93
  effect of side-agreement on concession 89
  exception for enforcement of, under Article XX 581-582
  mark-ups, application of Article III:2 to 132
  reasonable margin of profit allowed 94
  under Article II:4 88-96
Import restrictions
  exception for enforcement of domestic supply management schemes 327-344
Import surcharges
  and Part IV 1042
  as duties and charges other than tariffs under Art. II:1(b) 79
  for balance-of-payments reasons 363-366, 433
India, special arrangements with Pakistan 829
Inflation, export inflation insurance schemes, as export subsidy 460
Initial negotiating rights 501, 940
  and non-violation nullification or impairment under Art. XXIII 665
  basis for determining existence of 110

floating initial negotiating rights 939-940, 993
listing of, in schedules 110-111, 938-939
Injury, material (Article VI)
    causation of 244
    definition of 241, 242
    definition of industry 245-247
    determination of 241, 242
    exclusion of "related" producers in determination of industry 246
    injury to industry in a third country 247
    material retardation of establishment of an industry 243
    provisions on primary commodity price stabilization systems 248
    relation to "serious prejudice" 450
    threat of material injury 242
Injury, serious (Article XIX) 518
Insecticides, facilitation of trade in 281
Insurance 881
    export inflation insurance schemes 460
Intellectual property rights
    and Article XX(d) exception 582
    enforcement, and national treatment 163-164, 166-170, 175
Interest charges and costs in connection with customs bonding regime 87
Inter-governmental organizations, relations with 1102, 1104, 1121, 1132
    consultations with, in dispute settlement 689
    International Monetary Fund 433-436, 438-439, 441
Interim Commission for the International Trade Organization (ICITO) 6, 1119-1125
    application of UN financial and staff regulations 1122
    budget 1125
    Executive Committee 1119
    Executive Secretary 1123, 1127-1128
    functions 1120
    list of documents issued 11
    membership 1119
    privileges and immunities 1130
    Rules of procedure 1122
    Secretariat 1122-1123
    termination and transfer of assets to WTO 1123-1125
Interim Co-ordinating Committee for International Commodity Arrangements (ICCICA) 588
Internal quantitative regulations (see mixing regulations) 183-189
Internal taxes, see Taxes:
    border tax adjustments 86, 136-139
International Bank for Reconstruction and Development 4
International Civil Aviation Organization (ICAO) 214
International Convention Relating to the Simplification of Customs Formalities 1923 279, 284, 309
International Convention to Facilitate the Importation of Commercial Samples and Advertising Material 33, 280, 718
International Court of Justice 601, 608, 718, 719, 769, 875, 1121
    request for advisory opinions from 719, 769
    review by 769
International Dairy Arrangement 591, 880
International Labour Organization 4
International law, general
    and dispute settlement under GATT 732
    and measures under Article XXI 608
    counter-measures under, and GATT 718
    treaty law 832
International Monetary Fund 4, 87, 98, 284, 375, 421, 689, 702, 1132

and consideration of financial matters in GATT 431, 433-434
and exchange dumping 222
approval of discrimination in exchange restrictions 420
Articles of Agreement 149, 303, 375, 419-420, 422, 704, 827
Articles of Agreement and export subsidies 458
Articles of Agreement provisions on par values 97, 262
countries sharing a common quota in 422
decision on elimination of discriminatory BOP measures 419
determination of 149
direct consultation with non-member contracting parties 438
enforcement of exchange controls permitted under IMF Articles 436, 438
institutional cooperation with the GATT 376, 433-434, 441
membership 422
multiple currency practice provisions in Articles of Agreement 440, 447
provisions applying to non-Members of the Fund 99
observer status in GATT 1102
relative roles of the Fund and the GATT 429, 441
role in balance-of-payments consultations 367, 385-388, 431, 441
scarce currency clause in Articles of Agreement 375, 422-423
International Sugar Agreement 455, 456, 740, 1045, 1055, 1070
Interpretation of GATT 758, 875-876
    and imposition of new obligations 758, 875
    Chairman's rulings 875
    effect of Havana Charter provisions 997
Interpretative notes, legal status of 1029
Intersessional Committee 1100
Investment, foreign direct, regulation 878
    and national treatment 124, 165-166, 173-174, 189
Ireland
    change in base date for margins of preference 43
Italy, MFN exception for customs regime with Vatican City, San Marino 47, 796
Italy, disputes brought against
    discriminatory purchase subsidies for agricultural machinery 124, 125, 162, 164, 167, 173, 175, 194, 657
    Italian restrictions affecting imports from Israel 620
    Italian restrictions affecting imports from US and others 620
    restrictions on imports from US and others 322

J

Jamaica, change in base dates for margins of preference 43
Jamaica, disputes brought against
    margins of preference 43, 677, 921, 1083
Japan
    accession to GATT 519, 534, 669, 910, 1024
    invocation of Article XXXV with respect to 1033-1034
    special status of certain islands 49
    territorial application of GATT 795, 917, 1083
Japan, disputes brought against
    import quotas on 12 agricultural items 90, 317, 323, 328-335, 337-339, 341, 346-348, 411, 484, 580, 582, 648, 652, 653, 685, 732, 750, 755, 758, 762
    import quotas on beef (Australia, New Zealand) 744
    import quotas on beef and citrus products (US) 744
    import quotas on leather (Canada, 1980) 728, 743, 744

import quotas on leather (India, 1979) 765
import quotas on leather (US, 1979) 649, 728, 743, 744
import quotas on leather (US, 1984) 316-318, 411, 655, 656, 657, 732, 741, 743, 747, 756
import quotas on leather footwear 756
import restrictions on tobacco from US 649, 743, 744
import restrictions on thrown silk 435, 649, 744
nullification or impairment of benefits of EC 654, 670
pricing and trading practices for copper in Japan 652, 748, 767
semiconductor trade arrangement with US 31, 238, 315, 321, 339, 478, 533, 648, 652, 655, 667, 742, 753
tariff on imports of spruce-pine-fir (SPF) dimension lumber 37, 67
taxes and labelling of imported wines and alcoholic beverages 140, 146, 150, 156, 160, 198, 290, 566, 617, 673, 759

K

Kennedy Round
documents 18
Korea, disputes brought against
anti-dumping duties on polyacetal resins from the United States 243, 244
import restrictions on beef 79, 82, 89-90, 323, 472, 502-503, 508, 672, 703, 728, 735, 740, 759

L

Labelling 595; *see also* Marking of products
Languages - authentic texts 913, Schedules 914
Languages, working 915-916
League of Nations 59, 278, 291, 331, 332, 927, 1014
Least developed developing countries, special treatment for 1058
Enabling Clause decision (1979) 32, 45, 47, 53, 55
Sub-Committee on Trade of Least-Developed Countries 1050
Legislation, mandatory versus discretionary 133-136, 733, 1075-1080
Liechtenstein, succession to contracting party status 795, 918
Like product (Article I) 35-39
Like product (Article III) 155-158, 171-172
definition of 155
determination in light of purpose of Article III 171
Like product (Article VI) 227, 228
definition 227
difference between French and English texts 227
Like product (Article XI:2(c)) 331
examples 332
imported in any form 334
Liquidation of non-commercial or strategic stocks 486, 500, 593, 620, 879, advance notification 303
Local governments and authorities, *see* Regional and local governments and authorities
Lomé Convention 889
London Report (ITO Preparatory Committee First Session Report) 4
Long-Term Arrangement Regarding International Trade in Cotton Textiles 535, 717

M

Madrid Agreement for the Repression of False or Deceptive Indications of Source on Goods 291
Malawi, change in base date for margins of preference 43
Margins of preference 40-43, 45; *see also* Preferences, historical
Market disruption 534, 669, 879
Marking duties 85
Marking of products
drafting history 289-291
marking with regard to characteristics other than origin 181, 289
marks of origin 288-291
notification of measures concerning marks of origin 288, 302
protected regional or geographical names 289
recommendations on marks of origin 288
truth in marking 289, 583
use of European language on labels as conveying European origin 290
Maximum price control measures 135, 197
Measures as applied versus measures as such 517
Measures no longer in effect 649, 744
Measures not actually applied 135, 136
Measures not yet in effect 133, 648
MERCOSUR 56, 58, 844
Modification and rectification of Schedules 112-115
Minimum price arrangements, dairy products 880
Minimum price requirements
as condition of domestic sale, and Article III 177
as condition of exportation or importation, and Article XI:1 321
Mixing regulations 183-189
and national treatment rules 189
application in time of shortages 187
border enforcement of 201
duty reduction conditional on mixing with domestic products 187
exception for those existing as of specified dates (Art. III:6) 187
modification of "grandfathered" mixing regulations 188
prohibition on allocation of amounts between sources of supply 189
protective effect 186
Modification or withdrawal of concessions, *see under* Concessions - renegotiation
Monetary matters, *see* Financial system
Monopoly, import, *see* Import monopoly
Montevideo Treaty (ALADI) 56
Most-favoured-nation (MFN) treatment 24-60
and administration of quantitative restrictions 410
and agreements other than GATT 45
and anti-dumping or countervailing duty proceedings 30, 32, 46, 55, 249-250
and charges other than tariffs 28, 32
and import surcharges 28
and internal taxes or regulations 30
and methods of levying duties or charges 30
and Part IV 1042
and unbound tariffs 28
and variable levies 29
application to individual cases and "balancing" 35
application to internal taxes and regulations 197
drafting history 30, 32, 35, 40, 42-44, 47-48, 59-60
government procurement 46-47
reciprocity and conditional MFN 30, 33, 35
relationship to "non-discriminatory treatment" in Article XVII:1 475
safeguards action (Article XIX) 518-521
tariff quotas 409

trade conducted at MFN and at other duty rates 30
Multi-Fiber Arrangement 349, 531, 535, 717
Multiple currency practices
   exchange taxes or fees 271
   and IMF Articles of Agreement 420, 447
   and internal taxes 149, 439
   and scope of Article III 149
   as dumping or subsidization 240
   as subsidies 447
   IMF Decision on 421

N

National treatment (Article III) 124-127, 129, 131-138, 140, 141, 144-148, 150, 152, 155-168, 170, 171, 172-184, 186-189, 191-195, 197-206; *see also* taxes, regulation, mixing regulations
   and Article XVIII 511
   and case-by-case application of legislation 173
   and foreign investment regulation 124, 165, 166, 173, 174, 189
   and marking of products 181
   and state trading monopolies 131-133
   and subsidies 124, 164, 165, 173, 194-196
   application of Protocol of Provisional Application 204
   drafting history of provisions 130, 131, 136, 141, 144, 148-150, 156, 159, 161, 162, 174, 177, 181, 183, 184, 187-191, 193, 194, 196, 197, 205, 206
   equality of competitive opportunities 164-168
   exception for certain existing internal taxes (Art. III:3) 161, 162
   exceptions to 204, 205
   formally identical requirements versus formally different requirements 168
   government procurement exception (Art. III:8(a)) 190-193
   limitation to measures on products 125
   purpose 125-127, 158, 171
   relationship to Article II 198-201
   relationship to "non-discriminatory treatment" in Article XVII:1 475
   relevance of policy purpose of internal measures 127
   relevance of tariff concessions 127
   relevance of trade effects 128, 129
   scope 124
   scope of regulations permitted under 125
   state trading and 475
   treatment of individual cases and "balancing" 169-171

Netherlands, disputes brought against
   income tax practices 459-462, 762, 1074
Netherlands, territorial application of GATT 917, 1083, Netherlands Antilles application of Schedule II, Part D 119
New Zealand, disputes brought against
   anti-dumping duties on power transformers from Finland 227, 242, 244, 245, 678, 701
New Zealand, renters' quota on films 210
Newfoundland 918, 929
Newly-independent States
   de facto application of General Agreement 921, 923
   succession to GATT 919-921
Non-application of the General Agreement 1031-1038
   and succession under Article XXVI:5(c) 1033
   and voting on accession 1033
   continuing invocations of Article XXXV (table) 1034
   drafting history of provisions 1037, 1038
   former invocations of Article XXXV (table) 1034-1036
   multilateral review of 1033
   preconditions for invocation of Article XXXV 1031, 1032
   suspension of obligations between US and Czechoslovakia, 1951-92 1037
Non-discriminatory treatment
   administration of quantitative restrictions 410
   mixing regulations (Art. III:7) 189
   quantitative restrictions and customs unions or free-trade areas 800, 801, 822, 823, 836-840
   under Article XVII:1, relationship to MFN and national treatment 475
Non-enforcement of measures in dispute 135-136
Non-governmental organizations (NGOs), relations with 1133
Non-reciprocity 987-988, 1057
   and renegotiations under Article XXVIII 1057
Non-self-governing territories
   accession to GATT 1017
   acceptance of GATT in respect of 917-918
   as developing contracting parties 1041
   change in sovereignty 929
   invocation of non-application clause on behalf of 1033
   negotiation of concessions on behalf of 927
   participation in customs unions or free-trade areas 799
   resort to dispute settlement on behalf of 644
Non-tariff measures
   Inventory of Non-Tariff Measures 302
Norway, disputes brought against
   import restrictions on apples and pears 728, 1073, 1077-1078, 1082-1083
   import restrictions on textiles from Hong Kong 400-401, 520, 704, 739, 740
   procurement of Trondheim toll collection equipment 679, 751
Notification in GATT, notification requirements
   adjustment of specific duties (Art. II:6) 301
   bilateral settlements of disputes 745
   border tax adjustments legislation 146, 302
   change in interim agreement plan and schedule (Art. XXIV:7(c)) 304
   changes in preferences for developing countries 305
   customs unions, free-trade areas, interim agreements 304, 814-816
   during transition to WTO 308-309
   exports of domestically-prohibited goods 302
   general 300
   implementation of Part IV 1048
   import licensing procedures 302
   improvement and streamlining of 300
   IMF non-members' trade and financial data 438
   introduction or intensification of BOP measures 302, 380-381, 504
   legislation "grandfathered" by provisional application of GATT 509
   liquidation of strategic stocks 303
   measures and policies affecting trade in agriculture 303
   measures concerning marks of origin 288, 302
   measures proposed under Art. XVIII:C or XVIII:D 303
   modification or withdrawal of concessions (Art. XVIII:A) 301
   modification or withdrawal of concessions (Art. XXVIII) 301
   non-tariff measures 302
   products imported or exported by State-trading enterprises 303, 481, 486
   quantitative restrictions 302
   reports when effect not being given to Art. XXXVII:1

commitments 304, 1048
  requests for consultations under Article XXII 304, 616
  requests for consultations under Article XXIII:1 304
  requests for establishment of a panel (Art. XXIII:2) 304
  safeguards actions under Art. XIX 304, 523
  schemes under Generalized System of Preferences 305
  subsidies 303, 449
  summary notes on 300
  trade and financial data of nonmembers of IMF (Art. XV:8) 303
  Understanding Regarding Notification, Consultation, Dispute Settlement and Surveillance (1979) 300
  withdrawal from GATT 304, 1011
Nullification or impairment - infringement of GATT obligations 655-657
  irrelevance of trade effects 655
  presumption of adverse impact on other contracting parties 655, 657
  prima facie nullification or impairment 655
  effect of renegotiations under Article XXIV:6 813-814
  reasonable expectations at time of negotiating the concession 813- 814
Nullification or impairment - non-violation 657-671
  definition 657, 659, 661-662, 665, 668
  introduction or increase of subsidy 658-660
  measures approved by the CONTRACTING PARTIES 662
  national security trade sanctions 706
  offsetting of transmission of world prices 659, 660
  procedural requirements for non-violation complaints 666-667
  reasonable expectation at time concession negotiated 657-665
  relevance of concessions 660-665, of date of concession 663-665, of initial negotiating rights 665
  relevance of statistics on trade flows 665
  renegotiation of Schedules and 664
  upsetting the competitive relationship 657-659, 663

O

Objectives of GATT 999
  Article XXXVI 1056
  in Article XVIII:1 497
  in dispute settlement 654, 689
  in Preamble 21
Observer status in GATT 1094-1095, 1100-1104, 1116
  international organizations 1104
  Tokyo Round Agreement Committees 1099
Occupied areas and territorial application of GATT 919, 925
Ordre public 596
Organization for Economic Co-operation and Development (OECD) 145
Organization for European Economic Co-operation (OEEC) 318, 350, 458, 594, observer status in GATT 1102
Organization for Trade Cooperation 434, 758, 769, 911, 1027, 1086, 1130, 1133,
Organization of GATT 1086-1133
  Council of Representatives 1100-1111
  Deputy Directors-General 1129
  Director-General 1128-1129
  Intersessional Committee 1100
  joint action by the CONTRACTING PARTIES 874-877, 1094-1097, 1116-1117
  observer status 1094-1095, 1100-1104, 1116
  political questions 877
  Secretariat 1127

trade negotiations and 1118
voting 881
Origin of products 32-33, 288
  appellations of origin 289, 583
  for purpose of application of Schedules 75
  in context of free-trade area agreements 802-803, 827
  in relation to most-favoured-nation treatment 32
  labelling of, and most-favoured-nation treatment 33
  notification of measures on marking of origin 288, 302
  recommendations regarding marking rules 288
  rules of origin, harmonization of (Art. VIII) 278
  special rules applying to fish 33
Ottoman Empire, preferences under Article I:3 44

P

Packings, temporary importation of 280
Pakistan, special arrangements with India 829
Palestine 1014, status of concessions made on behalf of 927-928
Panel reports
  examination of same measures as another panel report 755-757
Par value, reduction in, and adjustment of specific duties 97
Par values, basis for conversion exchange rate for customs valuation 262
Part IV
  and customs unions or free-trade areas 799, 800, 809, 826, 827, 843, 844
  consultations concerning implementation of Part IV 1048
  drafting history 1039-1040, 1042, 1051, 1061, 1096
  legal relationship with Parts I-III of GATT 1042
  Protocol 1040
Payments, see also Financial system, and trade measures 436
Payments, transfer of, charges on
  and discriminatory internal taxes 149
  as charges other than tariffs under Art. II:1(b) 81
  as frustration under Art. XV:4 of intent of Art. III 150
Perishable products
  supply-management import quotas (Article XI:2(c)(i)) 334
Philippines, accession protocol reservation for sales and excise taxes 205, 1023
Poland
  accession protocol, anti-dumping provisions 228
  accession protocol, consultation and dispute provisions 621
  accession protocol, import expansion commitment 73, 478
  accession protocol provisions on quantitative restrictions 413
  accession protocol, reservation to Article XV:6 1023
  accession protocol, safeguards provisions 530
Polluter-Pays Principle 147
Portugal, preferences with colonies 49, territorial application of GATT 795, 917, 1083
Preferences between developing countries (South-South) 1043, 1068
  1971 Protocol for Trade Negotiations among Developing Countries 50
  Agreement on ASEAN Preferential Trading Arrangements 52
  Bangkok Agreement (ESCAP) 51, 1043
  notified under Enabling Clause 56, 844
  Tripartite Agreement (India, Egypt, Yugoslavia) 53, 1043

Preferences for developing countries (Enabling Clause)
    53-59, 1042, 1067
  application of balance-of-payments measures 376, 1063
  notification of changes 305
Preferences, Generalized System of (GSP)
  and application of balance-of-payments surcharges 376
Preferences within former Ottoman Empire (Art. I:3) 44
  Arab League Convention preferences 44
Preferences, existing, authorized in accession protocols 48
Preferences, historical 40-43, 60
  and charges other than tariffs 43
  and customs territory 794
  and customs unions or free-trade areas 42, 828, 846
  base dates for determining margins of preference 43
  change in, due to tariff reclassification 42
  Concessions on preferential duty rate in Schedules 85
  direct consignment (shipping) requirements 75, 216
  margins of preference, binding against increase 41-42
  negotiating history of provisions 60
  negotiations for reduction in 40
  non-application to quantitative restrictions 40
  reinstatement 42
  UK quotas for meat under Article XIV:5(b) 423
Preparatory Committee for the World Trade Organization
    103, 1087-1089, 1093, 1123
Preparatory work, GATT and ITO, overview 3-11, 20
Pre-shipment inspection 264, 277, 281; see also Customs
    formalities
  and customs valuation 264
Price controls
  maximum 135, 177, 197
  minimum 177
Price discrimination and safeguards actions under Article
    XIX 521
Price stabilization schemes, operations under, as subsidies
    446, 452
Price stabilization schemes, export restrictions necessary
    for, under Article XX(i) 591
Primary product, for purposes of Article XVI:3 452
Principal supplier rule 938, 992-993
Privileges and immunities 1129-1130
  headquarters arrangements with Switzerland 1088, 1130
Products as such, regulations affecting 164, 175
Proposals for Expansion of World Trade and Employment
    (1945) 3
Protocols of accession (see accession protocols) 48
Protocols of amendment 1004
Protocol of Provisional Application
  reservations on acceptance of 911
Provincial governments and authorities, see Regional and
    local governments and authorities
Provincial liquor boards 94
Provisional application of GATT 6-8, 1072-1084
  existing legislation clause 1072-1082; see also Existing
      legislation
  and 1955 amendments to GATT 463
  and dispute settlement 730
  termination 8, 924, 1091
Public notice, requirements for
  advance notice of import restrictions under Article
      XI:2(c) 345
  advance notice of quota amount or value under Article
      XIII 407
Public order 596
Publication
  advance, of quota amount or value, under Articles X
      and XIII 407
  agreements affecting international trade policy 296

exception for confidential information 297
measures affecting trade 295-296
of measures affecting trade 294
quarantine and sanitary regulations 571
Publications, GATT and WTO 19
  microfiche 20
Punta del Este Declaration 654

Q

Quantitative restrictions 315-353; see also Import
    restrictions, Export restrictions, Supply-management
    import quotas
  as anti-dumping or anti-subsidy measure 238, 348
  back-dated quotas 407
  consultation procedures for residual restrictions 317,
      350, 614
  definition of 315
  discussions on, in GATT 350
  drafting history of provisions 321, 326-328, 331, 334,
      337, 340, 344, 345, 347, 348, 353, 354
  exception for import quota on animal feed (Art.
      XI:2(c)(iii) 345
  exception for import quotas to remove surplus (Art.
      XI:2(c)(ii)) 344, 345
  exception for regulations on grading or marketing of
      commodities 326
  export restrictions on raw materials to protect local
      processors 325
  for enforcement of domestic food supply management
      schemes 327-344
  import licensing 319
  import or export prohibitions 320
  import quotas 317
  import restrictions affecting developing countries 1048
  misuse of balance-of-payments exceptions for 324
  multilateral reviews conducted in 1950, 1958-59 350
  negotiations on concessions regarding 351
  non-discrimination requirement, absence of waivers of
      414
  notification of, 302, inventories of, 351
  producer-controlled import monopoly as 472
  relevance of trade effects of 316
  residual restrictions 317, 614
Quantitative restrictions - administration of 399
  administrative formalities as obstacle to quota utilization
      404
  Agreement on Import Licensing Procedures 407, 414
  allocation of quotas among supplying countries 401
  back-dated quotas 407
  Code of Standard Practices (1950) 280, 370, 405-406,
      408-409
  contract sanctity 280, 406
  customs unions or free-trade areas and 800-801, 822-
      823, 836-840
  non-discrimination requirement 399-401, 410, 519-520,
      606, 800-801, 822-823, 836-840
  non-equivalence of import quotas and voluntary export
      restraints 400
  public notice requirements as subsidiary claim 411
  tariff quotas 402
  treatment of "goods en route" 407
  use of "special factors" in allocating quotas 403
Quantitative restrictions - discrimination in 417-424
  historical quota preferences under Annex A 423
Quantitative restrictions, for balance-of-payments reasons
  removal 69

R

Reciprocity
  and developing countries 987, 988
  measurement of value of concessions 986
  reciprocity clauses, and most-favoured-nation treatment 33, 35
  reciprocity in treatment of diplomatic gifts and baggage 35
Reclassification, tariff 96
Reference period
  for allocation of quotas under Article XIII 402
  for Article XIX:3 526
  proportionality requirement under last paragraph of Article XI:2 346
Regional and local governments and authorities 130, 830-836
  application of national treatment rules to 130, 141, 191
  definition 836
  dispute settlement concerning measures 708-709
  drafting history 830-832
  government procurement of 191
  provisional application of GATT and measures of 835, 1079-1080
  purpose and scope of Article XXIV:12 830-833
  reasonable measures to be taken to ensure GATT observance by 141, 833-835
Regulation
  "affecting" internal sale, etc. of imported products 175, 176
  affecting "products as such" 164, 175
  bans on advertising 179, 180
  cost-based differential transportation charges 183
  derogation from alcohol prohibition laws for local wines 135, 178
  derogation from processing requirements for poultry 163
  differential postal rates 163
  discrimination in 30, 31
  exemption of local producers from distribution requirements 135
  formally identical versus formally different 168
  intellectual property rights enforcement 163, 164, 166-170, 175
  limitation on listing (offering for sale) of products 178, 179
  national treatment with respect to 162
  permissible 179-181
  preventing enterprises from following commercial considerations 477
  price controls 177, 178, 197
  procedures for enforcement of intellectual property rights 166
  product quality or quantity 179-181
  requirement for importers to purchase domestic products 162, 199
  requirement to display "we sell foreign eggs" sign 162
  requirement to sell imported beer and wine via local wholesalers 167, 178
  restrictions on access of imported beer to points of sale 167
  standardization of products 177
  subsidies for purchase of domestic products 162
  substantive vs. procedural 175
  transportation 181-183
Related parties, treatment in anti-dumping or countervailing duty proceedings 246
Reservations
  in accession protocols 1023
  on acceptance of amendments 1007
  reservations on acceptance - Protocol of Provisional Application 1084
  to Article XXVI 911
  to Declaration Giving Effect to the Provisions of Article XVI:4 457, 461
Residual restrictions 317
  Hard-core Waiver decision (1955) 317
  Procedures for notification and consultations 317, 350, 621, 1048
Restrictive business practices 650, 879
  consultations 621, 651
  dispute settlement concerning 650
Revenue duties, on products produced in developing countries 1064
Reverse compensation 812
Reverse preferences, *see* Customs unions and free-trade areas
Review Session (1954-55) 21, 31, 42, 60, 74, 81, 92, 93, 97, 117, 144, 184, 188, 194, 197, 206, 211, 224, 228, 247, 255, 288, 291, 368, 372, 375, 392, 402, 429, 433-435, 438-441, 445, 447, 449, 451-453, 457, 463, 467, 481, 486, 496-497, 499, 512, 519, 589, 618, 621, 636, 654, 669, 758, 829, 847, 890, 911, 923, 925, 930, 937, 940, 953- 954, 957, 964, 986, 994, 998-999, 1038, 1086, 1133
  amendments 7, 1002
  and Article XXIX:3 998
Romania, accession protocol
  anti-dumping provisions 228
  consultation and dispute provisions 621
  import expansion commitment 74, 479
  provisions on quantitative restrictions 413, 530
  reservation to Article XV:6 1023
Ruggiero, Mr. Renato
  Director-General to CONTRACTING PARTIES 1129
  Executive Secretary of ICITO 1120
Rules of origin
  for most-favoured-nation treatment, harmonization of 278
  for preferential treatment 279
  textile agreements 279
  see also Origin of products
Rulings, requests for 653

S

Safeguards action 516-532
  and Part IV obligations 1045
  and Schedules of concessions 529
  Article XIX actions, lists compiled by Secretariat 523
  Article XIX actions, table 539
  by members of a customs union or free-trade area 838-840
  dispute settlement and 704
  duration of 522
  examination of safeguards legislation 517
  nature of actions under Article XIX 522
  non-discriminatory application 39-40, 518-521, 1045
  notice and consultation requirements 523
  prerequisites 516, - increased imports 518, - serious injury 518, - unforeseen developments 517
  suspension of concessions in response to 524-529
  textiles, and MFA 531
  work undertaken in GATT on safeguards issues 534-537
Samples, importation of commercial 280
San Marino, MFN exception for customs regime with Italy

47, 796
Sanctions, *see* Trade restrictions applied for non-economic reasons
Sanitary and phytosanitary regulations 565
   consultations concerning 621
   foot-and-mouth disease 571
   notification 570, 572
   publication 571
   restrictions on exports of Peru following cholera epidemic 572
   trade restrictions after Chernobyl accident 571
   US suspension of imports of Chilean fruit 571
Scarce currency 375
Schedules 67-115; *see also* Concessions, Harmonized System
   amendment of, application of Article XXX 99
   as integral part of Part I of General Agreement 99
   authentic text of 110, 914
   certification 112-115, 961
   classification of new products 96
   classification of products in 96
   computer format for submission to Secretariat 109
   consolidated 105
   conversion methods for duty rates 67, 71
   description of concessions in 110
   drafting history 77, 116, 117
   effect of multilateral form of 103
   Harmonized System 110
   indication of date of concession (Art. II:1(b)) 84
   indication of initial negotiating rights (INRs) 110, 938-939
   list of Schedules of contracting parties 119
   loose-leaf 105, 106, 110, 111
   modification or rectification, procedures for 112-115, 962, 1005-1006
   negotiated on behalf of non-self-governing territories 927-928
   preferential 85
   rectification to reflect changes in national customs tariffs 111
   safeguards action under Article XIX and 529
   withholding or withdrawal of concessions 115
Screen quotas, for exhibition of foreign films, concessions on 210, 943
Secretariat 1122-1125, 1127-30
   and Tokyo Round agreements 1128
   pension arrangements 1123
   privileges and immunities 1130
   role in dispute settlement 748
Security exceptions 600-610; *see also* Trade restrictions applied for non-economic reasons
   and customs unions or free-trade areas 823
   and transit rights 217
   definition of "essential security interests" 600
   dispute settlement and 606-607, 705-706
   drafting history 600, 602, 606, 608-609
   fissionable materials 602
   non-disclosure of information for security reasons 601
   notification of measures taken under Article XXI 605
   relationship to general international law 608
Serious prejudice 450, 451; *see also under* Subsidies
   definition 450, relation to "injury" 450
Services 481, 881, dumping 222
Short-Term Arrangement Regarding International Trade in Cotton Textiles 535
Silver 500, 620
Slovak Republic, accession to GATT 1026-1027, interim application of GATT to 1027

Slovenia, accession of 1026
Smoking on GATT premises 1114
Sources of law 8
South Africa, change in base dates for margins of preference 43
South Pacific Regional Trade and Economic Cooperation Agreement (SPARTECA) 57
Southern Rhodesia, *see* Zimbabwe
Spain, disputes brought against
   prohibition of imports of codfish from Denmark 620
   restrictions on internal sale of soyabean oil 139, 156, 171, 186, 758, 762
   tariff treatment of unroasted coffee 28, 37, 67
Spain, preferences with certain territories 49, territorial application of GATT 795, 917, 1083
SPARTECA 57
Special and differential treatment for developing countries
   anti-dumping 229, 1065-1066
   application of balance-of-payments measures 376, 1063
   border tax adjustments 1065
   countervailing duties 1066
   dispute settlement 763-766
   in Tokyo Round agreements 45, 47, 229-230
   legal assistance in trade disputes 1051
   market access and export support for agricultural products 1040
   outward processing 34
   preference schemes 1067
   revenue duties 1065
   safeguards action 1064
   subsidies 1065, 1066
   technical cooperation and training 1050, 1051
   trade negotiations 987-988
   see also Enabling Clause
Special exchange agreements 437-438
   accepted by contracting parties 437
   exceptions and derogations from requirement to enter into 438
Specific duties
   adjustment after currency devaluation (Art. II:6) 97-99
   and European Unit of Account 827-828
   conversion to ad valorem duties 70, 944-945, 948-949, 952, 954
   notification of adjustment of 301
   reference date for Art. II:6 83
Stamp taxes 79
Standstill commitment, Uruguay Round
   enforcement in dispute settlement 654
State trading 92, 472-486
   and national treatment 131-133, 475
   Article XX exception for enforcement of state trading monopolies 581-582
   as means of administering quantitative restrictions 321, 582, administering BOP restrictions 485
   drafting history 473-478, 481, 485, 486
   in State-controlled economy countries 478
   marketing boards 473
   negotiations on operations of State trading enterprises 481, 486
   notification of import mark-up 482
   notification of products imported or exported by 303, 481, 486
   obligation to act in accordance with commercial considerations 475-476, 480
   of developing-country products 485, 1045
   right to establish or maintain State-trading enterprises 472
State-trading enterprise, definition of 473-475

State-controlled-economy countries
    anti-dumping and determination of normal values for 228
    participation in free-trade areas under Article XXIV 821-822
    Schedule concessions by 73
    State-trading enterprises in 478
Statistical taxes 78
Status of Legal Instruments 8, 19
Sub-national units of government, *see* Regional and local governments and authorities
Subsidies 445-467
    concessions in Schedules 74, 463
    consultations under Article XVI:1 451
    definition 239, 439, 446-448, 450
    drafting history of provisions 445, 447, 448, 450-453, 457, 465-467
    exception from national treatment rules, scope of 195-196
    effect on trade 448-450
    exemptions from internal taxes 447
    export credit programmes 446
    financed by non-governmental levy 446
    government contribution 446, 453
    multiple currency practices as 240, 439, 447
    national treatment and 124, 164-165, 173, 194-196
    notification of extent and nature of subsidization 303, 449
    operations under price stabilization schemes 446, 452
    price support systems 446
    reduced internal transport charges for exports 447
    relationship between subsidy rules and countervailing duty rules 3251,
    review under Article XVI:5 463
    serious prejudice to interests of another contracting party 450
    use of measures to offset, other than countervailing duties 237, 238
Subsidies - calculation of amount 458
    examination of evidence 239
    export remission or rebates of duties and taxes 240
    Guidelines on Amortization and Depreciation 240, 253
    Guidelines on Physical Incorporation 241, 253
Subsidies, export 457-462
    arm's-length pricing rule under Article XVI:4 460
    bi-level pricing of exported product 458-462
    contracting parties for which Article XVI:4 is in force 457
    Declaration Giving Effect to the Provisions of Article XVI:4 457
    deferral of corporate income tax on export sales 458-462
    developing countries 462
    export inflation insurance schemes 460, 462
    illustrative lists of export subsidies 457-460
    of developed countries competing with developing countries 1056
    primary product, definition of 452, 461
    standstill clause in Article XVI:4 457
    subsidization of primary product component of processed product 461
Succession
    and dispute settlement proceedings 644
    Czech Republic and Slovak Republic 1026-1027
    Czechoslovak Republic 1014
    Palestine 1014
    status of concessions with respect to successor State 927-928

Yugoslavia 644, 1014, 1094, 1102
Zimbabwe 1013
Succession to GATT contracting party status under Article XXVI:5(c) 919-921
Suggested Charter for an International Trade Organization, 1946 (US Draft Charter) 4
Supersession of General Agreement, *see* Havana Charter
Supply-management import quotas under Article XI:2(c) 327-344
    advance public notice requirement 345
    application in case of processed food products 334
    application to "like product" in any form 331
    concessions concerning 328
    elements and burden of proof regarding 329
    governmental measures to restrict supply 339
    limitation to "agricultural or fisheries product" 331
    perishability of the product 334
    proportionality requirement 346
    reference period for proportionality requirement 346
    relationship with other concessions 328-329
    requirement of restriction, not prohibition, of imports 330
    requirement that domestic scheme restrict supply 340
    requirement that import quota be "necessary" 337
    restriction only of processed form of the product 338
    seasonal import restrictions 337
    use of discretionary licensing 346
    use of miscellaneous "basket" quotas 346
    see also Quantitative restrictions
Surcharge, *see* Import surcharge
Surplus disposal 879
Suspension of concessions 677
Sweden, disputes brought against
    anti-dumping duties on nylon stockings 231, 232, 240, 249, 700, 750
Switzerland 374
    accession protocol, exception for certain import restrictions 349, 1023
    provisional accession to GATT 1024
    relations with Liechtenstein 795, 918
Sympathetic consideration, *see* Concessions - renegotiation

T

Tariffs, *see also* Schedules
    classification 38, 67-68, 96
    escalation 68
    nomenclature 70
    reclassification 72, 96
    replacement of quantitative restrictions by 69
    tariff protocols; form, effect and signature 104, procedure for finalizing 104
    tariff quotas 100; concessions concerning 75
    value-break tariffs and MFN 39
Tariff quotas 945-946
    and non-discrimination requirement under Article XIII 402
Taxes, *see also* Border tax adjustments
    allowance for export tax rebates in customs valuation 262, in dumping margin 240
    and most-favoured-nation treatment 31, 197
    arm's-length pricing rule under Article XVI:4 460
    border tax adjustments 144, 145, 147, 148
    credits against 195, 196
    discrimination 141, 142, 144-147, 149-152, 156-161
    excise 141, 144, 146-148, 150, 151, 161, 195, 196, 1065
    exemption from 475

imposed "directly or indirectly" 141, 146
imposed by local governments and authorities 130, 141
income or corporate profits 144
levied on duty-paid value of imports 152
national treatment 141, 142, 144-146, 148, 150, 152, 155-162
on films 197
on products produced in developing countries 1044, 1064
on transfer of payments 149
preferential internal 204
processing 48, 141, 204
   income or corporate profits 460
   reduction in, as subsidy 447
   relationship to import charges 198-201
sales 146
taxes occultes 146
turnover or cascade 145, 146, 150, 241
value-added tax 146
Technical cooperation services to developing countries 1050-1051
Television programmes, trade in 209
Territorial application of GATT 917-918
   areas under military occupation 919, 925
   drafting history 795, 845
Territorial claims 918, 1095
Textiles 657, 704, 717, 718, 739, 740, 765
   dispute settlement under Article XXIII 717, 718
   GSP treatment 56
Textiles Committee 717
Textiles Surveillance Body 717
Textiles Surveillance Body (TSB) 718
Thailand, accession protocol reservation for business and excise taxes 205, 1023
Thailand, disputes brought against
   Import restrictions and taxes on cigarettes 131, 134-135, 179, 333, 337, 566-570, 595, 646, 689, 730, 748, 1078
Technical Committee on Customs Valuation 264, 265
Tied loans 190, 194, 476
Tokyo Round documents 18, 19
Tokyo Round Agreements 915
   acceptance in respect of non-self-governing territories 918
   and dispute settlement under Article XXIIII 713-715
   authentic texts 915
   document derestriction practices 1118
   observer status in Committees 1099
   relationship to CONTRACTING PARTIES 1099
   relationship to GATT rights 713, 1008, 1099
   servicing by GATT Secretariat 1128
Torquay Round 18, 41, documents 18
Trade and development 1039-1051, 1053-1058, 1059-1068, 1070
   commitments of developed contracting parties 1061-1067
   commitments under Art. XXXVII:1 304
   commitments under Part IV 1055
   joint action 1055, 1070
   principles and objectives 1055
Trade and environment 595, 880, 1113
   Group on Environmental Measures and International Trade 1113
Trade Expansion and Economic Co-operation Agreement (India, Egypt, Yugoslavia) 52
Trade negotiations 986-994
   and historical preferences 40-41
   and preferences within regional trade agreements 843

binding of low tariffs 991
developing countries in 987, 988, 1057
drafting history 117, 986, 991, 994
formula tariff-cutting 939-940, 992-993
joint negotiations 993
measurement of value of concessions 986
negotiating procedures 990
non-tariff concessions 989
organization of 1118
principal supplier rule 938, 992, 993
procedures for negotiating rounds (list) 991
sponsorship of 986
tariff negotiations on request/offer basis 990, 1032
tariff protocols 104-105
Uruguay Round 1118
Trade Negotiations among Developing Countries, Protocol (1971) 50, 57
   application under Enabling Clause 51
Trade Negotiations Committee 1118
Trade Policy Review Mechanism 301, 305-308, 1106
Trade restrictions applied for non-economic reasons 600-605
   Arab League boycott of trade with Israel 602
   boycott of Portuguese goods by Ghana 600
   compliance with UN sanctions 605
   EC trade measures against Yugoslavia 604
   Ministerial Declaration 1982 601, 603
   notification of 604-606
   suspension by EEC, Canada, Australia of imports from Argentina 600-601, 603, 605-606, 705
   Swedish import quota on footwear 603
   US embargo on trade with Cuba 605
   US embargo on trade with Nicaragua 603, 604, 706
   US national security export controls 600-602, 606, 705
Trade sanctions, *see* Trade restrictions applied for non-economic reasons
Training courses, GATT 1051
Transfer of payments, charges for 81
Transit 213-217
   aircraft in transit 214
   charges on transit 216
   neighbouring countries 215
   trucking restrictions 215, 572
Transparency, *see* Notification requirements, Publication
Transportation
   delivery restrictions 181-183
   national treatment and 181-183
   reduced internal transport charges for exports as subsidies 447
Treaty Establishing the Southern Cone Common Market 56, *see also* MERCOSUR
Treaty functions of GATT
   depositary function for instruments 916
   registration of treaties 924
Treaty of Rome 361, 612, 645, 706, 796-797, 799-800, 805, 817, 818, 822-824, 827-828, 836, 840
Trieste, Free Territory of, trade with contiguous countries 796
Tripartite Agreement (India, Egypt, Yugoslavia) 53
Turkey, disputes brought against
   discriminatory reduction in tariffs and application of Art. XXIV 620, 842
   export bonus and import tax scheme 439, 447

U

Unilateral measures 692
United Kingdom, disputes brought against

British Steel loyalty rebate for buyers not using imported steel 620
exemptions of domestic "utility goods" from purchase tax 152
discriminatory quotas on imports from "dollar area" countries 744, 752, 1043
import quotas on cotton textiles from Israel 717, 744
United Kingdom, territorial application of GATT 917, 1083
United Nations 601, 604, 605, 608, 609, 877, 914, 924, 1054, 1095, 1120-1123, 1130-1132
application of UN financial and staff rules 1122
decisions on international status of certain territories 919
Economic and Social Council 1131-1132
financial and staff regulations, and ICITO 1122
guidance on political questions 877, 1095, 1131
Joint Staff Pension Fund 1123
laissez-passer 1130
observer status in GATT 1095, 1102
relations with 609, 877, 1120, 1130-1132
specialized agency status 1120, 1130-1132
United Nations Treaty Series 916, 924
United Nations Conference on Trade and Development (UNCTAD) 49, 279, 591, 1050, 1069
United Nations Educational, Scientific and Cultural Organization (UNESCO) 281
United States
restoration of GATT relations with Czech and Slovak Republic 1037
suspension of GATT obligations reciprocally with Czechoslovakia 1037
territorial application of GATT 917, 1083
United States, consultations with
liquidation of strategic stocks of silver 620
suspension of customs liquidation by the US 619
United States, disputes brought against
anti-dumping duties on cement from Mexico 233, 234
anti-dumping duties on salmon from Norway 236, 674-675, 737-738
Article XIX action on fur felt hats and hat bodies 516-518, 521-523, 704
charges and miximng requirement for cigarette tobacco 142-144, 149, 152-155, 158-159, 184-187, 190, 196-197, 283, 647, 671, 729, 730, 742, 749
collection of countervailing duties on certain footwear imports from Brazil 757
conversion of duties on Vitamin B12 67, 71, 682, 720
countervailing duties on pork from Canada 240, 249, 251, 678, 750
countervailing duty proceedings on wine and grape products 46, 246, 247, 249, 251, 648
customs user fee 28, 31-32, 55, 87, 99, 101, 268-269, 271, 273-274, 278, 282-284, 730, 741, 758
discriminatory import restriction on sugar from Nicaragua 100, 404, 414, 607, 705, 734, 743
duty increase on certain products of Brazil under Section 301 723, 765
EC panel request on US retaliation for EEC hormone directive 672
embargo of trade with Nicaragua 601, 603, 607-608, 666, 672, 684, 706
export subsidy on tobacco 620, 1044, 1056, 1066, 1068
Hawaii requirement to display "we sell foreign eggs" sign 162, 181
import ban on certain automotive spring assemblies 564-565, 574, 580, 582, 595, 756, 762
import embargo on Canadian tuna and tuna products (1982) 330, 564-565, 585-587, 649, 650, 655, 679, 719, 744
import fees and restrictions on sugar under Section 22 waiver 77, 317, 661, 662, 667, 684, 686, 689, 710, 712, 742, 763, 886, 1077
import quota on sugar under Headnote to Schedule XX 76, 317, 481, 674, 735, 741
import restrictions on certain sugar-containing products (1985) 694
import restrictions on dairy products 684, 690, 692-693, 695-697, 699
import restrictions on woolen suits from Brazil 765
income tax practices (DISC) 458, 460, 462, 688, 721, 761, 762
manufacturing clause of copyright law 320, 691, 694, 741, 1074, 1077, 1080, 1082
Marine Mammal Protection Act import restrictions on tuna (1991) 33, 125, 137, 164, 175, 203, 288, 320, 563, 569-570, 581, 584-585, 646, 647, 745, 751, 760
Marine Mammal Protection Act import restrictions on tuna (1994) 139, 164, 204, 570, 585, 586, 647, 725, 729, 733, 739, 760
measures affecting beer, wine and cider 126-127, 129-130, 133, 135, 140, 142, 150, 157, 161, 167, 171, 177-178, 182, 195, 203, 577-578, 747, 751, 832, 835-836, 1079-1080, 1083
measures affecting export of magnesium from Canada 745
measures affecting imports of softwood lumber from Canada 234-236, 239, 678, 702, 731-732
MFN application of countervailing duty law (Brazilian footwear) 30, 32, 35, 39, 55, 250, 464, 679, 715, 730, 734, 736, 742, 757, 823
MFN application of countervailing duty law (Indian fasteners) 30, 46, 649, 715, 744
national security export restrictions 410, 414, 600-602, 606, 705
procurement of a sonar mapping system 191
Section 337 of the Tariff Act of 1930 125-126, 166, 168-169, 175-176, 180, 563, 566-567, 573, 575-577, 582, 595, 733, 735, 739, 745, 750, 751, 757, 762
Superfund taxes on petroleum and imported chemicals 125-126, 128, 133-135, 141, 147, 150, 155, 167, 176, 201, 645, 648, 656, 657, 694, 698, 699, 728, 733, 765, 949
taxes on automobiles 127, 139, 144, 155, 159, 164, 171, 175, 177, 581, 585, 586
Uranium, *see* Fissionable materials
Uruguay, disputes brought by
Uruguayan recourse to Article XXIII 29, 72, 316, 369, 653, 655, 666, 670, 672, 674, 675, 677, 681, 687, 690, 691, 697, 702, 710, 711, 725, 730, 738, 739, 749, 761, 1082
Uruguay Round 1118
document series 17-19
standstill commitment, enforcement of 654
US Draft Charter 4

V

Variable levies
and customs unions or free-trade areas 800
and most-favoured-nation treatment 29
and non-discrimination obligations under Article XIII 410
imposition on bound items 29, 72
non-violation nullification or impairment 660
Vatican City, MFN exception for customs regime with Italy 47, 796

Venezuela, Art. III:3 exception for certain internal taxes existing in 1947 161
Vienna Convention on the Law of Treaties 832
Voluntary export restraints 532-534
   and dispute settlement 533
   non-equivalence to import quota 532
Voting 1097-1098, 1109
   accession to GATT 1097-1098
   decision-making on adoption of dispute settlement panel reports 761
   in Council of Representatives 1109
   postal and telegraphic voting 1098
   postponement of vote at Session to permit postal voting 1098
   procedures 1097
   roll-call votes 1097
   secret ballot 1097
   voting majority 829
   waivers of obligations 1097-1098, 1109

W

Waivers of obligations 882-889
   absence of waivers of Art. XIII non-discrimination requirement 414
   and non-violation nullification or impairment of concessions 661
   Article II waivers pending completion of schedule renegotiation 102, 949
   Article XI 414
   Article XVI 464
   as recommended outcome of GATT dispute 677
   dispute settlement and 709-712, 887
   effect 886
   exceptional circumstances required 885
   extension or expansion of 887
   notification of request for 304
   procedures for decision on 883, 1097-1098, 1101, 1109
   scope of waiver power 882, 883
   termination 888
Whales, status as fisheries product 331
Withdrawal from GATT 508, 1011-1012
   notification of 304, list 1011
   withdrawal of provisional application 1084
Working Capital Fund 1127
Working parties in GATT 1111-1112
   establishment and procedures 1111
   termination and reconvening of 1112
World Bank, *see* International Bank for Reconstruction and Development
World Customs Organization, see Customs Co-operation Council
World Health Organization (WHO) 281, 566-568, 571, 689, 748
World Intellectual Property Organization (WIPO) 582
World Trade Organization 8, 924, 1047, 1086-1093, 1124-1125
   budget 1126
   coexistence with GATT 1947 8, 59, 103, 308-309, 713, 924, 1047-1048, 1088-1093, 1113-1115, 1123-1126
   depositary functions 1124
   Preparatory Committee for 8, documents 16

XYZ

Yugoslavia, EC trade measures against 604, 644, 673; Council participation 1102, participation in Uruguay Round 1118, status as a contracting party 877, 1014, 1094

Zambia, change in base dates for margins of preference 43
Zimbabwe, change in base dates for margins of preference 43, contracting party status of 1013